# Man of a Million Fragments: The True Story of Clay Shaw

*by*

Donald H. Carpenter

Copyright ©2014 by Donald H. Carpenter, LLC. All rights reserved. This book is protected under the copyright laws of the United States of America. No part of this book may be reproduced or transmitted in any form or by any means, electronic or mechanical, including photocopying, recording, or by any information storage and retrieval system without the written permission of the author, except where permitted by law.

Published in 2014 by Donald H. Carpenter LLC.

ISBN 9780692226414 (pbk.)
ISBN 9781301028757 (eBook)

## Donald H. Carpenter LLC
P.O. Box 111538
Nashville, TN 37222-1538
www.donaldhcarpenter.com

### Publisher's Cataloging-in-Publication

Carpenter, Donald H.
    Man of a Million Fragments: The True Story of Clay Shaw / Donald H. Carpenter.
        p. cm.
    Includes bibliographical references.
    ISBN  9780692226414  (softcover edition)
1. Shaw, Clay (1913-1974). 2. Louisiana—Politics and government—20th century. I. Title.
E748.L71 C41  2014

Cover art by Charles Hooper.

# Man of a Million Fragments: The True Story of Clay Shaw

*by*

Donald H. Carpenter

# Contents

Introduction . . . . . . . . . . . . . . . . . . . . . . . . . . . . . . . . . . . . . . . . . . . . . . i

## PART I

1 · The Early Years . . . . . . . . . . . . . . . . . . . . . . . . . . . . . . . . . . . . . . . 1

2 · World War II . . . . . . . . . . . . . . . . . . . . . . . . . . . . . . . . . . . . . . . . 14

3 · The Opening of International House . . . . . . . . . . . . . . . . . . . . . 29

4 · Promotion Continues for the International Trade Mart . . . . . . . . 41

5 · The Trade Mart Opens . . . . . . . . . . . . . . . . . . . . . . . . . . . . . . . 48

## PART II

6 · The Caribbean and South America . . . . . . . . . . . . . . . . . . . . . . 61

7 · 906 Esplanade . . . . . . . . . . . . . . . . . . . . . . . . . . . . . . . . . . . . . 75

8 · A Return to South America . . . . . . . . . . . . . . . . . . . . . . . . . . . 85

9 · A Letter to the CIA . . . . . . . . . . . . . . . . . . . . . . . . . . . . . . . . . 93

10 · A Break From the Mart . . . . . . . . . . . . . . . . . . . . . . . . . . . . . 103

11 · The Louisiana Purchase 150th Anniversary Celebration . . . . . . . . 117

12 · The Mart at its Peak . . . . . . . . . . . . . . . . . . . . . . . . . . . . . . . 135

13 · A Trip to Mexico . . . . . . . . . . . . . . . . . . . . . . . . . . . . . . . . . . 148

14 · Shaw Manages International House (Part 1) . . . . . . . . . . . . . . . 159

15 · Shaw Returns to Cuba . . . . . . . . . . . . . . . . . . . . . . . . . . . . . . 174

16 · An Architect is Selected . . . . . . . . . . . . . . . . . . . . . . . . . . . . . 184

17 · An Encounter at the Airport . . . . . . . . . . . . . . . . . . . . . . . . . . 195

18 · The Election of John F. Kennedy .................. 207

19 · The Number Two Man at the CIA Comes to Town. ............ 222

20 · A Critical Point for the Mart ..................... 232

21 · A "Mysterious" Trip, and a Tragedy in Dallas .............. 240

22 · The Mart Hits New Lows as a New Building Begins to Rise. ....... 256

23 · Clay Shaw Retires ........................... 265

## PART III

24 · The Beginning of the Jim Garrison Investigation ............ 279

25 · An Arrest in the Kennedy Assassination ............... 291

26 · Appeals and Delays on the Way to Trial. ............... 405

27 · A Verdict, and Another Arrest ..................... 426

## PART IV

28 · Turning the Tables: A Lawsuit is Filed ................ 453

29 · A Key Court Decision, and a Job Offer ................ 458

30 · Free at Last? A Cruise on the Mediterranean. ............. 471

31 · The Beginning of the End ...................... 483

32 · The End? Not Just Yet ......................... 494

33 · A Plaque on a Building ........................ 508

Aftermath ................................. 515

Acknowledgments. ............................ 520

Endnotes ................................. 527

# Man of a Million Fragments: The True Story of Clay Shaw

*by*

Donald H. Carpenter

# Introduction

The assassination of President Kennedy in Dallas, Texas on November 22, 1963, was the most shocking and memorable public event of most peoples' lives. Like the bombing of Pearl Harbor, the event which began World War II for the United States, or the events of 9/11, most people could, years later, remember where they were when they first heard the news.

Lee Harvey Oswald was arrested the same day. A loner-type who had defected to Russia in 1959, married, and then returned to the United States in 1962, he was in the process of trying either to get back to the Soviet Union, or to get to Cuba, at the time of Kennedy's assassination. Two days later, on Sunday, November 24, 1963, as Oswald was being moved from one location to another, a local nightclub owner named Jack Ruby shot and killed him. Ruby, a character with connections both to the local police and to underworld figures, was perhaps not quite as mysterious as Oswald, but his motive for shooting Oswald was murky. Ruby was tried and convicted of shooting Oswald, and died three years later.

Oswald was born in New Orleans, had lived there at certain points in his life, and most importantly, had lived there from April until September 1963, approximately two months before the assassination of President Kennedy. After Oswald's arrest, the FBI was interested in, among other things, activities Oswald had engaged in while residing in New Orleans. He had tried to join an anti-Castro Cuban group, pretending to be in sympathy with them, and had wound up fighting with some of its members in a public spat. He also had handed out pro-Castro leaflets on street corners in New Orleans, including outside the International Trade Mart building at the corner of Camp and Common streets. That institution was managed at the time, and had been essentially since its beginnings in the mid-1940s, by a person named Clay Lavergne Shaw, a somewhat prominent New Orleans citizen known for his participation in numerous civic affairs, for his leadership of the Trade Mart itself, and to a lesser degree, for being a homosexual of refined tastes.

Immediately after the assassination, two leads developed out of New Orleans that the FBI investigated and quickly dismissed. In one of them, a sometime private investigator and heavy drinker named Jack Martin reported to the local district attorney's office that a person he knew by the name of David Ferrie, an offbeat pilot who wore cheap wigs (his real hair had fallen out years before) and who allegedly liked hanging around with young boys whom he taught to fly, had known Oswald in an outfit called the Civil Air Patrol some years before, and that Ferrie was going to fly Oswald to safety after the assassination. The Secret Service and the FBI checked Ferrie out, and interviewed Martin, in which conversation Martin supposedly admitted that he had made the allegations while intoxicated, and that he didn't have any firsthand knowledge that Ferrie had actually known Oswald, or was going to be any kind of getaway pilot for the assassination.

In the second prong of stories arising out of New Orleans, a colorful, rotund, local attorney named Dean Andrews claimed that while he was hospitalized under sedation during the day following the assassination, he received a telephone call from a sometime client he identified by the name of "Clay Bertrand," who asked him to go to Dallas and represent Oswald on the criminal charges related to President Kennedy's assassination. When interviewed by the FBI, Andrews maintained that Oswald had consulted with him during the previous summer about matters dealing with his discharge from the Marines, and about his wife's immigration issues. Andrews was uncertain in his physical description of "Clay Bertrand," and ultimately admitted that he might have dreamed the whole episode about receiving the telephone call from him. Later, the Warren Commission sent a young attorney, Wesley Liebeler, to New Orleans to interview Andrews, among others. As a result of that interview, a lengthy transcript was produced, wherein Andrews wandered all over the map in his description of his past dealings with Oswald, and his descriptions of "Clay Bertrand." The FBI made an attempt to find "Clay Bertrand" in New Orleans, but was unsuccessful. The second strand of the New Orleans stories was ultimately dismissed by authorities as being unverifiable, and as having little to do with the actual assassination.

During the years that followed, from 1964 until late 1966, a healthy skepticism developed among the general public about the official conclusion that Oswald had committed the assassination, and had committed it alone. This skepticism was fueled by the combination of Oswald's mysterious background, including his having defected to the Soviet Union and then returned with a spouse (something that was very rare indeed), the fact that Ruby shot Oswald two days after the assassination, silencing the alleged killer forever, along with Ruby's own mysterious friendships, the fact that most government records related to the assassination, such as FBI, CIA and Secret Service records, were all sealed for seventy-five years in accordance with normal Federal rules for government records, and the fact that the Warren Commission, which investigated the assassination for President Lyndon Johnson and the Federal government, produced a comprehensive report that was sometimes incomplete, and sometimes incorrect. Additionally, a growing body of books, and articles in newspapers and magazines, made the case for a wider conspiracy involving others besides Oswald; some versions had it that Oswald had nothing to do with the actual assassination. By the end of 1966, the skepticism about the official conclusions related to the assassination had reached a crescendo, and a majority of the American public did not believe what the government was telling them.

It was in that atmosphere that the district attorney of New Orleans, Jim Garrison, began his own investigation into the Kennedy assassination. By October 1966, he was informally questioning attorney Dean Andrews about the identity of the mysterious "Clay Bertrand." Soon he began to focus on members of the anti-Castro Cuban community in New Orleans, some of whom had encountered Oswald during 1963. Garrison also picked up on Jack Martin's old identification of David Ferrie as having known Oswald, and as having possibly been a getaway pilot for Oswald immediately after the assassination.

Garrison's main focus during the first several months of his investigation was related most closely to David Ferrie and the anti-Castro Cuban community. Ferrie was brought in for questioning, as were some of the Cubans, and most of the activity in Garrison's office and among his investigators seemed to be concentrated in that direction. Ferrie denied ever knowing Oswald, or having any connection to the assassination, as he had done in 1963. He immediately, as he also had in 1963, pointed the finger at Jack Martin as the person who had started investigators looking in his direction, accusing Martin of having a certain jealousy toward him that manifested itself in such accusations.

Regarding the anti-Castro Cuban community, Garrison had gotten hold of a left-wing theory that Oswald, rather than being a communist, as the official conclusions had stated, was in reality an anti-communist posing as a communist, and had worked in some way with members of the anti-Castro Cuban community to effect Kennedy's assassination. The anti-Castro Cubans that Garrison's office interviewed all denied that, and immediately rejected Garrison's theory of such a conspiracy in the assassination.

Regarding "Clay Bertrand," Garrison had identified him, at least in his own mind, as his fellow New Orleanian, Clay Shaw, former Managing Director of the International Trade Mart. Garrison and Shaw knew each other slightly. Both had been active in civic affairs over the years, Garrison at one time working as an attorney for long-time Mayor de Lesseps "Chep" Morrison's office, and Shaw dealing with Morrison on a regular basis from the mid-

1940s until the early 1960s. They also had both been present at a speech President Kennedy gave in New Orleans in May of 1962, where he dedicated the Nashville Avenue Wharf.

Dean Andrews had stated that "Clay Bertrand" had called him on past occasions to represent "gay kids" who had gotten into trouble with the law. Although Andrews never identified "Bertrand" as being Clay Shaw, Garrison knew that Shaw was gay, and that he was a prominent member of that community in the French Quarter (also referred to with some frequency by its old French name of "Vieux Carré") section of New Orleans. Accordingly, by the end of November 1966, Garrison had concluded that Shaw was "Bertrand," but that his involvement in the actual assassination, if any, was relatively minor and indirect. Shaw was asked to come in for questioning just before Christmas 1966, but the focus was still on David Ferrie and the anti-Castro Cuban community.

Garrison's investigation rocked along in secret for several months, although word leaked out to various individuals in New Orleans. Television reporter Sam DePino may have been the first newsman to learn of an investigation into the Kennedy assassination by Garrison's office, although DePino did not know much about it at the time; his superiors would not let him pursue the story more actively in the early stages. In an attempt to find out if the FBI knew any details, DePino advised the FBI of Garrison's investigation during the first week of November 1966; he formed the impression that the FBI may have already known of it. Sometime later, Aaron Kohn, Managing Director of the Metropolitan Crime Commission, a non-profit organization devoted to fighting corruption among public officials, as well as vice activities in the city, also learned of the investigation. Kohn had been a reluctant supporter of Garrison as district attorney during Garrison's first term from 1962 to 1966. However, he had broken with Garrison during the fall of 1966 over activities in Garrison's office that he regarded as corrupt, and by the time he learned of Garrison's Kennedy assassination investigation, he was a firm opponent of Garrison.

Kohn and some of the anti-Castro Cubans advised the FBI of Garrison's investigation. Maintaining the official position that Oswald had committed the assassination and committed it alone, the FBI was always on the alert for any new information that might arise related to the assassination, particularly any information that might contradict its official conclusion. Accordingly, the FBI was very interested in Garrison's investigation, even if Garrison had no intention of asking for its cooperation, and the FBI had no intention of volunteering it.

Garrison's investigation broke in the news with a story in the local afternoon newspaper on February 17, 1967. Although David Ferrie was not identified in the story, he contacted one of the story's authors and volunteered that Garrison was investigating him, while firmly denying the accusations that had been laid at his doorstep. The printing of the story brought a swarm of out-of-town news reporters to New Orleans, anxious for any new information about the assassination. In a bizarre twist, five days later, on February 22, 1967, David Ferrie's nude body was found at his residence. If Ferrie had been Garrison's main suspect, that suspect was now dead, and many, including some of the members of Garrison's own staff, thought the investigation would quietly die away as well.

But it didn't. Seemingly without missing a beat, the investigation refocused on Clay Shaw, and a potential witness emerged who could supposedly tie Shaw, Ferrie, and Oswald together. Accordingly, on March 1, 1967, Shaw was unexpectedly arrested, astounding all of those who had known him for years, and throwing his life into instant disarray. After his arrest, theories about the Kennedy assassination, and who was involved, reached a new intensity of theorizing and speculation, and for the next several years New Orleans would be the center of most of that focus. After numerous delays in the trial date, and appeals by Shaw's attorneys, the trial was finally held in early 1969. Other indictments and hearings would cause the criminal aspect of the case to persist until the early 1970s, and a civil suit filed by Shaw against his accusers would drag on until 1978, some four years after his death.

The Garrison investigation, as it came to be known, shone a light on a number of individuals, including Clay Shaw and David Ferrie, and others, who had never been publicly discussed related to the assassination of President Kennedy. Once the story of the investigation broke in the newspapers, and in the national media, it brought forth numerous additional individuals, many of whom volunteered information about things they had supposedly witnessed, or had heard through another party, or general information about the background of Shaw, Ferrie, or other publicly identified objects of Garrison's investigation. Many of those who came forward were residents, or former residents, of the French Quarter, the rectangular area near the river in New Orleans that has attracted many interesting people, and many tourists, over the years. Some of those who came forward were convicts, serving time in Federal or state prison, who volunteered information based upon what they had read or heard in the media. Many others came forward, with varying degrees of credibility, either innocently volunteering information they had heard, or in some cases manufacturing outright information that they thought the prosecution (or the defense) would want to hear. The newspapers in New Orleans and elsewhere were filled with daily stories about such individuals, who emerged for brief moments of time, then disappeared, with no one ever again questioning them in any detail about their stories in order to obtain an indication of their credibility. Some of those individuals lived long lives, and died within the last few years. Others barely survived Garrison's investigation, with some meeting violent deaths.

Who was Clay Shaw? It was a question asked by many people the day he was arrested and in the days and weeks that followed. Many ask it even to this day. A discreet, seemingly mysterious man, a homosexual who was widely respected in his local community by people of all stripes, a person who ran an organization called the International Trade Mart, which people in New Orleans knew well, but which to those outside the city also seemed somewhat mysterious, and a person with alleged connections to the Central Intelligence Agency (CIA).

Shaw's alleged CIA connections were reported (somewhat inaccurately) shortly after his arrest, but never documented, and never brought up by the prosecution during his trial. Shaw himself publicly denied ever having had any connection with the CIA. In December 1973, some eight months before he died, an independent news service, quoting a co-author of an upcoming book about the CIA, reported that Shaw had been involved with the agency. By that time, his criminal case was over, and the media had lost interest, so no one bothered to ask Shaw directly about the report. Besides, his mother had just passed away, and shortly thereafter he suffered a brain seizure. By the time he recovered to some degree from the seizure, he had been diagnosed with cancer, and died several months later.

By the time of Shaw's death in 1974, the criminal case against him had been thoroughly discredited. Congressional investigations into the CIA and the Kennedy assassination during the mid-1970s looked into Shaw peripherally, but drew no conclusions that he had any involvement. By 1983, when the local New Orleans newspaper ran, on the 20th anniversary of President Kennedy's assassination, an article about the discredited Garrison investigation that resulted in the indictment and prosecution of Shaw, almost all of Garrison's aides were critical of the very investigation in which they had participated, and even Garrison admitted that he probably should have shut the investigation down after Ferrie's death.

However, things change, and attitudes change along with them. Garrison, who had earlier written both a non-fiction book about the assassination (which did not mention Shaw's case to any degree) and a novel, published in 1988 his own version of the case against Clay Shaw for the first time. In it, he resurrected the case as presented at trial, as if he believed it with a religious fervor. Hollywood soon came calling, in the form of director Oliver Stone, and in December 1991, the movie *JFK* was released to great popularity. The movie, heavily based upon Garrison's book, presented the view that Shaw was closely involved in the assassination, even if his exact role was murky.

Although the movie was controversial, its conclusion that Shaw was involved in the assassination was accepted by many viewers, and revived a waning interest in the Kennedy assassination. Congress decided to empanel a special board, the Assassination Records Review Board, to review and declassify, much earlier than otherwise would have happened, most of the records held by governmental agencies such as the CIA, FBI, Secret Service, Department of State, and others. The Board also had authority to collect private records, and in so doing collected Clay Shaw's personal papers, Jim Garrison's records of the case, and the records of the defense team kept by Shaw's long-time personal attorney, Edward Wegmann. Since those records were opened or collected during the 1990s, many researchers have poured through them, backward and forward, trying to connect the dots related to any particular theory of the assassination, but especially one that might connect Shaw, Ferrie, or other characters unearthed by the Jim Garrison investigation, with the assassination.

But, again, who was Clay Shaw in this convoluted and changing scenario? The CIA memos that were released related to Shaw indicated that he had been a source for the agency from late 1948 into 1956. One or two memos indicated that he may have even volunteered to do some "work" for them, such as attend a trade show for the agency, or send out some inquiries under his name for its benefit. Almost all memos issued after his arrest in 1967, however, were consistent with the idea that he had been a source of information, and nothing more, during the years already mentioned. However, one memo mentioned his connection with an internal CIA program called QKENCHANT, which generated new speculation that his role was deeper than merely being an information source, a role the details of which supposedly have never been fully revealed.

And what was the International Trade Mart, exactly? The easy answer was that it was an organization designed to help promote international trade between New Orleans businesses and the rest of the world, specifically Latin America. But, what were the details of its founding, its day-to-day operation? What was Shaw's exact role in this business? Did he use the organization as a cover to become involved as a CIA source?

Did Shaw know Oswald or David Ferrie? Even after Shaw's acquittal, many people thought that he had known Ferrie, and that Ferrie had known Oswald. Even if Shaw himself was not directly connected with the assassination, his relationships left much to question.

What about other aspects of Shaw's life? He had written or co-written several plays in his youth, or in young adulthood, and he had lived in New York City for seven years, from the beginning of 1936 to near the end of 1942, when he went into the Army. His Army service was somewhat of a mystery, too, with some saying that he had been an employee of the Office of Strategic Services (OSS) during the war.

Had he ever been married? If not, who were his significant companions over the years, or did he have one or more in particular? What about the whips and chains supposedly seized from his residence the night of his arrest? Were they, in fact, an old Mardi Gras costume, or did they indicate an interest on his part in sadistic and masochistic activities?

This book, then, tells the story of Clay Shaw's life from its very beginnings until his death. In addition to being a biography of Shaw, though, it is also the story of the International Trade Mart, and to a lesser degree, its sister organization International House, which were parts of a multi-pronged, city-wide international trade movement in New Orleans during the 1940s and forward, perhaps peaking during the 1950s. It is also a retelling of the Jim Garrison investigation, and how it related directly to Shaw, and to a certain degree, an examination of the credibility of many, though perhaps not all, of the individuals who generated publicity during that investigation in one form or another. The story touches on many topics of the era, including the city of New Orleans itself, the Cold War, racial segregation in the old South, and homosexuality, for which the city of New Orleans, and the French Quarter in particular, provided a relatively friendly environment.

The details of Shaw's life are reconstructed from numerous interviews of individuals who knew him, worked for him, socialized with him, or of individuals who had some connection with the Garrison investigation, such as several prosecutors who worked in Garrison's office. The reconstruction of Shaw's life is also based upon the many documents that have been collected or released over the years, particularly during the 1990s. Those include not only thousands of governmental documents, but those contained in other collections as well, such as the collections related to the International Trade Mart and International House. Barring the release of some new governmental information or the discovery of some significant private collection, I believe this is the most complete story of Shaw's life that can be told.

# PART I

# 1 · The Early Years

Clay Shaw was born on March 17, 1913, in Kentwood, Louisiana, a small town located approximately ninety miles north-northwest of New Orleans. His father, Glaris Lenora Shaw, was also born in Kentwood, in 1887, and married Alice Herrington, a native of Monticello, Mississippi.[1]

Shaw's father joined the Army in 1908 at age twenty, and served a three-year term in, among other places, the Philippine Islands.[2] After leaving the Army in February 1911, Glaris Shaw began an apprenticeship in saw filing, and worked for a lumber company in the Kentwood area until 1916. For the next two years, he worked as a mill superintendent in a small town in Colorado; his wife and young Clay lived there with him. Years later, Clay Shaw would partly attribute his lack of the stereotypical Southern accent to the time he spent in Colorado as a child.

In January 1918, Glaris entered the Army again, this time to serve in World War I, and was discharged in October 1919.[3] By this time, the family had moved to 3607 Banks Street in New Orleans, where Clay Shaw, known in those early years as Lavergne (or "Vern") Shaw, attended Crossman Grammar School. Except for an almost seven-year period in New York City from early 1936 to late 1942, and his Army service from November 1942 to January 1946, Clay Shaw lived in New Orleans the remainder of his life.

After the war, Clay's father worked as a draftsman/engineer at J. De Tarnowsky Company,[4] as well as at a variety of other jobs during the 1920s, including for the Louisiana Box and Lumber Company from 1920 to 1923, taking training with the Veterans Bureau from 1923 to 1926, and working with the Railway Audit and Inspection Company from 1927 to 1930. By 1926, the family had moved to 3519 Baudin,[5] and soon thereafter to 325 South St. Patrick Street, and Glaris Shaw was now working again as a "saw filer," probably while training with the Veterans Bureau.[6] In 1930, he joined the Bureau of Prohibition, a division of the Department of the Treasury.[7] It is possible that Glaris Shaw may have worked two jobs during some periods because, as is shown in 1929, his occupation is listed in the city directory as a "checker" for the United Fruit Company.[8] Clay Shaw's mother, Alice, worked off and on as a schoolteacher, taking time off to raise her son, but returning to teaching in the depths of the Great Depression.

Clay Shaw graduated from Warren Easton High School in New Orleans in 1928, at the age of fifteen. At the time, the school was an all-boys high school, all white, with a mostly male faculty.

The 1927 edition of the *Eastonite*, the annual for Warren Easton High School, showed a photo of a thirteen-year-old Shaw looking somewhat fat in the face, with a crop of thick, dark hair standing higher than normal, serving as quite a contrast to the tall, lean Shaw with prematurely graying hair who would emerge less than two decades later. One of the members of the senior class that year was Harnett Kane, who became a somewhat prominent New Orleans writer soon thereafter, known for books about the Huey Long era and other Louisiana matters.[9]

Shaw's high school yearbook photo, taken around age 13 (Courtesy: New Orleans Public Library)

Shaw's graduation year of 1928 saw him in a class with Herman Stuart Cottman, sometimes known as "Bunny." Cottman and Shaw would co-write several plays together during the late 1920s and the first half of the 1930s, but would drift apart during Shaw's time in New York City in the late 1930s. *The Eagle*, a publication of the graduating class of the school included in the annual that year, commented that Cottman was known about the school for his excellent dramatic work during his stay there.[10] Leon Hubert was also a senior in 1928. Hubert later served as district attorney of Orleans Parish, and as an attorney for the Warren Commission following President Kennedy's assassination.

Herman Stuart Cottman. Shaw's co-author on early plays, yearbook photo, taken around age 15 (Courtesy: New Orleans Public Library)

There was no individual photograph of Clay Shaw in the 1928 high school annual, but there was a photo of Shaw and Cottman together as part of the Dramatic Society. Shaw again had a stunning head of dark hair standing somewhat high on his head, not unlike the main character of Henry in the film *Eraserhead*, while Cottman was very neat and conservative in dress.[11] The biographical paragraph of Shaw said that he had come to Warren Easton in 1925, and that as of graduation had not yet decided what occupation he intended to follow. Out of an almost all-male faculty, Shaw selected Miss Jessie Tharp, the drama teacher, as his favorite teacher. His hobby was acting, and he had been one of the more prominent members of the Dramatic Society. Listed as one of Shaw's favorite sayings, under the hobby designation, was: "I ain't proud!"[12]

As part of the 1928 annual, the seniors published the *Turkey Buzzard*, a satirical "future newspaper" that was supposed to have been written on June 1, 1948, some twenty years later. It purported to show what each graduate would be doing at that time. Several of the articles in the publication were about students murdering people, or doing other horrific deeds, in the future. The role assigned for "LeVergne" (the spelling of Shaw's middle name by others varied throughout his life) Shaw was as a columnist giving "Advice to the Lovelorn." The setup was that individuals would write advice columnist LeVergne Shaw with various problems, addressing him as "Aunt LeVergne" or "Madame LeVergne," and that Shaw would answer them, much like Dear Abby or Ann Landers might have done at a later date.

One of the letters was from a married woman who noticed that whenever her husband returned late at night, he always had a pair of silk stockings in his pocket, and wanted to know what to do. Shaw answered that if the husband was getting home late at night, if the woman sent him her address, he would come over early in the evening and talk with her about the case. Another letter was from a "boy" of forty-nine, very much in love with a woman of twenty-three. The woman didn't have enough money for the two of them to get married, but wanted to move away, get married, and keep it a secret until she had enough money to support them both. Shaw advised the man to wait until the woman was financially able to support them both before marrying her. Still another letter was from a man who said that his girl had moved out of the country to live; he wondered why she wouldn't write to him. Shaw advised him not to waste his young life on irresponsible women, saying that if the woman cared for him, she would at least write to him. "Don't throw away your life," he advised.[13]

Another part of the annual had a comic newspaper listing the graduates as different characters; Shaw was listed as "Maggie." He also received, as LeVergne Shaw, what was intended to be the humorous award of Favorite Actress.[14]

Around the age of fifteen, about the time of his graduation in the spring of 1928, Shaw became involved in Le Petit Theatre du Vieux Carré, an up-and-coming local theater known locally as simply Le Petit Theatre. One of his first notices, or possibly his very first notice, appeared in a workshop performance of *The Rising of the Moon*, by Lady Gregory. Shaw appeared under the name La Vergne Shaw, playing the role of Patrolman X, on May 8 and 9, 1928.[15]

Perhaps because of his size, Shaw appeared several times in the role of a policeman in various productions, as in *Michael and Mary*, by A.A. Milne, in May 1932. He also appeared as a policeman in *Once in a Lifetime*, by Moss Hart and George S. Kaufman.[16] Shaw often appeared in minor parts of the plays, or participated in non-acting parts, particularly under the Properties section.[17]

Future attorney Eberhard Deutsch also acted in the mid-1920s;[18] Deutsch would later become a prominent lawyer in New Orleans, employing future District Attorney Jim Garrison for a time. His firm would later represent Garrison personally, as well as Garrison's office of district attorney, including during many junctures of Garrison's prosecution of Shaw, and with regard to Shaw's civil suit against Garrison.

The artist William Spratling, who in a few years would move permanently to Taxco, Mexico, to begin a long career in the silver jewelry industry there, played bit parts at the theater in the last few years of the 1920s.[19] If he and Shaw crossed paths at that time, however, Shaw did not consider it an official meeting of any sort, because when he met Spratling in 1955 on a trip to Mexico, he would describe it as if it was the first meeting between the two.

Some individuals whom Shaw encountered during his time with Le Petit Theatre in the late 1920s and early 1930s recalled him, or remained close friends with him, for decades. Among those was Muriel Bultman, daughter of a prominent funeral home owner in New Orleans. Born to a wealthy family, Muriel Bultman spent time at boarding schools in Europe in the 1920s and 1930s, and received a degree from the University of Alabama, somewhat uncommon for a female in those days. She later married briefly, then opened her own shop as a talent agent, interacting with people in the theater, opera, and movies in both New York and Hollywood. In March 1931, she worked as a volunteer, along with Shaw (listed as Levergne Shaw), on several plays at Le Petit Theatre, including *The Apple Cart* and *The Poor Nut*. She worked as a volunteer for *Hedda Gabler*, by Henrik Ibsen, in April-May 1931. She also worked with Shaw (working as Lavergne Shaw), under the Properties section of different plays, in January and February 1932.[20]

Another person whom Shaw met during his activity with the theater was Mary Moore Sanborn. Sanborn's credits include appearances in *The Joy of Living*, by Herman Sudermann (April 1926), *Dear Brutus* by J.M. Barrie, the author of *Peter Pan* (June 1926), and *A La Creole*, by Flo Field (March 1927). In February 1928, Sanborn appeared in *Anna Christie* by Eugene O'Neill, and in February and March 1929 in *The Women Have Their Way*, by Serafin and Joaquin A. Quintero. In March 1930, she appeared in *The Silver Cord* by Sidney Howard, in the lead role of Mrs. Phelps.[21] Sidney Howard would later become a famous screenwriter, drawing the lone credit for the screenplay for the movie *Gone with the Wind*, although many others worked on it.

In an interview more than seventy years later, Mary Moore Sanborn's daughter, Marymor Cravens, told the author that some in the Le Petit Theatre circle thought that Shaw might have been a person of mixed black and white descent, a rumor about Shaw which would follow him his entire life, and would emerge more fully after his arrest in 1967. Mrs. Cravens said that it had not mattered to her mother whether he was or not, but others had noted that Shaw never brought his family around to watch him perform, or to attend any of the plays he had written, and people sometimes speculated about his background.[22]

Mary Moore Sanborn, though very friendly with Shaw over the period of at least a decade, still either was unaware of his homosexuality, or held the duality of views that people in New Orleans often held about homosexuals, placing them into either respectable categories, or groups that referenced fear or repulsion. In a letter to another daughter at boarding school in Europe, Sanborn mentioned how "everyone's nerves were on edge" about the amount of homosexuality going on at boarding schools. She added, regarding the subject of homosexuality, "That's a new one for you."[23]

Another person Shaw might have met during his early Le Petit Theatre days was the writer Flo Field, who in 1927 had a satirical hit play, *A La Creole*. Mary Moore Sanborn had appeared in the play. Flo Field and Shaw would be good friends in later years.

Herman Stuart Cottman, Shaw's co-author on four plays, and two years older, appeared as early as October 1926 in *The Swan*, written by Ferenc Molnar. Cottman appeared to have the more prominent acting roles, appearing in *Caesar and Cleopatra*, by George Bernard Shaw, in April 1928.[24] He also appeared, in September 1929, in a workshop production of *Fennel*, by Jerome K. Jerome.

Another regular performer in that era was Howard F. Bogner, who appeared in quite a few plays, often playing major parts, in the late 1920s and early 1930s. Years later, in the mid-1960s, he would become Muriel Bultman's second husband for a brief period of time, before they divorced around the time of Shaw's trial. The artist Boyd Cruise, later known for his paintings and his sponsorship by the prominent businessman L. Kemper Williams, did some work at Le Petit Theatre during the late 1920s and early 1930s as well.[25]

The most successful collaboration of Shaw, using the name Le Vergne Shaw, and Cottman, using the name H. Stuart Cottman, was the one-act play *Submerged*, published in 1929, about men trapped at the bottom of the ocean in a submarine. The play was written as part of a one-act-play tournament sponsored by the Alumni Association of the New Orleans School of Speech and Dramatic Art. A newspaper article published around the time of the play's early performances in New Orleans, probably 1929 or 1930, contained an interesting quote from the authors: "We knew better than to put any girls in our play." The article stressed that the play was geared primarily for boys.[26]

*Submerged* was directed by Jessie Tharp, Shaw's drama teacher in high school. For many years Tharp was one of the most prominent personalities at Le Petit Theatre, acting in many plays, and directing many along the way as well; she would also star in Shaw's play, *Memorial*, at the end of 1948.

Louis Fischer designed the production of *Submerged*. A lifelong friend of Shaw from his Le Petit Theatre days, she was born in Mobile, Alabama, and became an important part of the great French Quarter scene of the 1920s through the 1960s. Many who passed through the artistic and social scenes in the French Quarter knew her, and she accumulated a diverse group of artists, gays, and other French Quarter dwellers around her. She knew Gloria Vanderbilt well, in addition to an array of famous literary figures and actors. Fischer was known almost as much for her physical unattractiveness as for her social skills, and seemed remarkably undisturbed by it. Grace Charbonnet recalled attending a party in the 1940s at which Fischer was present; she came up behind Fischer while she was surrounded by a large group. Fischer turned around, spotted Charbonnet, and proclaimed, "Well, here we have the most beautiful woman in New Orleans, and the ugliest one, together!"[27]

In May and June 1929, Shaw appeared in a bit part as a soldier in *The Queen's Husband* by Robert Emmet Sherwood. For that part, Shaw used the name of Clay La Vergne Shaw.[28] During the 1930s, Sherwood, a popular playwright and later screenwriter for the movies, would, act as an advisor to President Franklin Roosevelt.

In 1929, at the age of sixteen, Shaw began work as a clerk at Western Union Telegraph Company.[29] In 1930, he was an operator for Western Union, and his father is shown in the city directory as a clerk at an unspecified company, probably United Fruit.[30]

Shaw's boss at Western Union was John C. "J.C." Jackson, the district manager. Shaw would work with Jackson for almost six years, before transferring to New York City with Western Union at the beginning of 1936. After Shaw returned to New Orleans in 1946 to work with the newly created International Trade Mart, he would occasionally work with Jackson on issues related to telegrams and their processing. Jackson followed Shaw's career with some pride.

Gordon Jackson, Jackson's grandson, recalls that his father, also named Gordon, and his father's brother, Robert, were Shaw's contemporaries, and knew him well during that 1929 to 1935 period; Robert Jackson graduated in the same high school class as Shaw. Robert Jackson was an intellectual who studied with John Dewey and Margaret Mead at Columbia University while getting a doctorate in educational psychology, and who also had a clinical practice on the side. He and his wife, Sylvia, a thorough-going liberal, accepted Shaw as a fellow intellectual and devotee of high culture.[31]

Gordon Jackson recalls that Shaw's sexual orientation wasn't really a secret to any of the family members, and not an issue in their dealings with him. He recalls his father telling him that Shaw once surprised him "when Shaw tried to hold hands with him in the back seat of a car on a drunken evening."[32] The advance was rebuffed, but no harm was done to the friendship, or to Shaw's relationship with the family.

Shaw appeared at Le Petit Theatre in the workshop production of *A Knight at an Inn*, by Lord Dunsany, as a merchant sailor. Herman Cottman appeared in that same workshop as A.E. Scott-Fortesque.[33] Cottman also appeared in a workshop production of *Grey Feather*, playing the role of Clayton, a yacht steward, on August 1, 1930.[34]

The next play authored by Shaw and Cottman, *A Message From Khufu*, was published in 1931. A tale of the raiding of an ancient Egyptian tomb, with deadly consequences, it was the duo's most successful play after *Submerged*.

Those two early plays Shaw co-wrote with Cottman were generated as part of a nationwide student drama contest sponsored by a publisher, Row, Peterson and Company, of Evanston, Illinois. Claude Merton Wise, a University of Wisconsin speech and drama professor, was involved with the publisher in selecting the plays. The authors of the plays would receive up to a fifty percent royalty on production of the plays, and a five percent royalty on book sales of the plays.[35]

By the time *Submerged* and *A Message from Khufu* were published, Wise had moved from Wisconsin to the Speech and Drama Department at Louisiana State University in Baton Rouge, Louisiana. The two plays received attention, to some degree, throughout the country, with performances in small theater productions in all parts of the United States. *Submerged* was more popular, but *A Message from Khufu* was also performed regularly throughout the 1930s and 1940s. Shaw would draw royalties from the plays, in modest amounts, into the 1970s.[36]

In 1930, the royalties for *Submerged* were $343.30, with 652 copies sold. In 1931, 1,033 copies of *Submerged* were sold, generating royalties of $679.57, its most successful year of book sales, and probably of performances as well. That year, 223 copies of *A Message from Khufu* were sold, generating royalties of $39.42.[37]

During 1932, the most severe year of the Great Depression, all authors of plays in the series accepted a ten percent reduction in royalties as a percentage of sales. That year, *Submerged* sold 606 copies, yielding royalties of $37.56, while *A Message from Khufu* sold 194 copies, generating royalties of $14.84. Royalty income from stage productions was severely reduced during the 1930s, as many theaters cut ticket prices to keep patrons attending their productions.

There were more than forty different titles in the Row, Peterson and Company collection, which generated royalties to authors spread across the United States. Claude Wise received a yearly notice of the royalties paid to authors; *Submerged* continued to sell 500 to 800 copies per year throughout the 1930s and into the early 1940s. Sales of *A Message from Khufu* continued to climb throughout the 1930s, peaking in 1938 with sales of 394 copies and royalties of $27.30. Sales and royalties declined after the early 1940s, although they sporadically rose and fell over the next thirty years.[38]

Some Internet references indicate that a British film called *Men Without Women* was made from Shaw and Cottman's play, *Submerged*. However, that film appears to have been generated from a different source.

Shaw appeared as the Emperor Nero in a workshop production of *The Emperor Discourses*, by Claude Derbes, on August 11, 1931, under the name C.L. Shaw.[39] As can be seen, Shaw experimented with a variety of names related to his acting and playwriting in the late 1920s through the mid-1930s. He was still not yet known as Clay Shaw to most people at this point; most of his family and friends called him "Vern."

By 1931, the Shaw family had moved to 4907 Willow Street. Glaris was listed in the city directory as a salesman (although he had already begun his tenure with the U.S. Treasury Department), and Clay Shaw was listed as Laverne (no "g") Shaw, no doubt reflecting the name he had begun using in the Le Petit Theatre.[40]

Sometime in 1931, Shaw took an additional job as secretary to L.S. "Mac" McClaren at International Harvester Company. McClaren, a recent law graduate who had been unable to find enough legal work to earn a living during the depths of the Great Depression, had transferred with the company from Memphis to New Orleans to head up the credit and collection division for southern Mississippi and southern Louisiana.[41]

That job would only last a short period, as Shaw continued with Western Union, but his friendship with McClaren would last four decades. McClaren eventually moved to McComb, Mississippi, where he served as district attorney, and in the Mississippi state legislature. Shaw would later see him periodically while speaking at Rotary or Kiwanis Club events in the McComb area. McClaren, having been a prosecutor, and having known Shaw personally, followed closely the events of Shaw's arrest and prosecution, and was supportive throughout that period.

In 1932, Glaris Shaw is listed in the city directory as an "agent," with the family living at 1527 North Broad Street.[42] Shaw's father first served as an agent in the Prohibition Service of the U.S. Department of the Treasury; after Prohibition ended, he became an employee of the Alcohol Tax Division of the Treasury.

In May 1934, Shaw was in the cast of *A Lady with Five Husbands*. In January 1935, he served as Assistant to the Director in *Night over Taos*.[43] In June 1935, Shaw and Cottman's three-act play, *The Cuckoo's Nest*, was performed at a summer workshop of the theater. Jessie Tharp directed, and the program mentioned that Shaw and Cottman's earlier plays, *Submerged* and *A Message from Khufu*, had won local tournaments for playwriting.[44] Louis Fischer was involved as the stage designer for the play.

Another person Shaw encountered in Le Petit Theatre, during the mid-1930s, was Kay Lucas. Lucas would later marry a doctor, William Leake, and suffer through an abusive marriage, during which her twin children were killed by a passing vehicle. She was hospitalized for mental problems, and eventually divorced in Florida. Later, she acted on stage in New York, and performed for U.S. troops in Europe.

The question of whether Shaw ever had a heterosexual relationship, particularly a sexual one, or at least an attempt at one, came up fairly often in interviews with those who knew him. Kay Lucas possibly hinted at one in a letter that she wrote to Shaw years later, a month or so after his arrest in March of 1967. After hearing of his arrest in the news, Lucas, now remarried, sent him a couple of telegrams, and then a lengthy letter, from her residence in the state of Washington, offering her support. In the letter, she identified herself more fully, referencing their friendship from years before, and asked, "Do you recall a long, long night on 727(?) St. Anne when we tried the 'NOBLE EXPERIMENT?'"[45] The address could have referred to St. Ann Street in the French Quarter in New Orleans; Shaw lived at 727 St. Ann Street briefly in 1942 (He also lived at 627 St. Ann Street immediately upon returning to New Orleans after World War II). The letter also referenced knowing Shaw during his New York City days after leaving New Orleans.

Lucas also wrote to Shaw two years later, not long after after he was acquitted on March 1, 1969, offering her congratulations, and said, "In a strange way (I'm sure unknown to you) you've been a person who has had a profound influence on me and my life, and my memories of you are always with joy and laughter.....from chess games, concerts...shared troubles, and honest affection...& 727 St. Anne."[46] There is no indication Shaw responded directly to her letters or telegrams, other than with the same form letter with which he responded to the enormous volume of correspondence he received after his arrest. Apparently, the two had been out of touch for many years, and Shaw had not seen Lucas since the early 1940s, prior to his entering military service for World War II.

The family does not appear at all in the 1933 city directory, and no directory was published for 1934, although clearly they were living in New Orleans; Glaris Shaw's Treasury records indicate that he was an agent in New Orleans during that period. By 1935, Glaris Shaw is shown as an investigator for the U.S. Internal Revenue Service (as part of the Department of the Treasury), and the family was living at 8422 Panola. Clay Shaw was listed as C. LaVergne Shaw, and was employed as a salesman at Western Union.[47] With Clay Shaw's move to New York City at the end of 1935, and his father and mother's move to Shreveport as a job transfer, the family disappears from the New Orleans city directories. In September 1935, due to a transfer with the Department of the Treasury, Shaw's father moved to the Casa de Fresa Hotel in Hammond, Louisiana, where he stayed until January 1936, before moving to the residence at 455 Egan Street in Shreveport, Louisiana, where he and Shaw's mother would live until the early 1950s.[48]

Shaw's father would generally serve with some distinction as a member of the Alcohol Tax Division until his retirement in mid-1953. However, in the spring of 1953, just months before his retirement, the Treasury Department investigated Glaris Shaw for a series of incidents that occurred from December 1945 to June 1947, when he made large purchases of whiskey from two liquor companies for members (judges) of the Federal District Court in his territory, at the request of those members. Shaw's father explained to the internal Treasury officials that it was a means of "maintaining a cordial and close working relationship with the member of the court." Shaw was warned that such purchases could be portrayed as a conflict of interest, and might place him and his department in an embarrassing position; he was advised to refrain from such activity in the future.[49]

In November 1935, shortly before his departure from New Orleans to work in New York City for almost seven years, Clay Shaw, in perhaps his last involvement with Le Petit Theatre during that era, served as scenic assistant on *Elizabeth the Queen*. In early 1936, he transferred to New York City with Western Union. He apparently saw an opportunity to combine the corporate career ladder with the possibility of turning his early playwriting skills into an even larger success. One of the individuals with whom Shaw interacted at Western Union in New York City was Keith Bruce Mitchell, who was Director of Sales. It is unclear if Shaw knew Mitchell before leaving New Orleans, but by 1935 Shaw was in the sales department there. Mitchell, who was gay, became a lifelong friend of Shaw, and later served as Vice President of International Relations with Western Union, often testifying before Congressional committees in the 1950s and 1960s.

Not long after arriving in New York City, Shaw met Judson O'Donnell. His friend, Muriel Bultman, who was also working in New York City, introduced the two of them. Shaw and O'Donnell would share an apartment for a time in New York City, until O'Donnell moved to the West Coast and Shaw went off to World War II. It is unclear if the two had a physical relationship, but in later years they would leave money to each other in their wills, and the two would each often direct young men going between New Orleans and southern California, where O'Donnell settled, to look up his close friend for insight into the local scene.

O'Donnell also co-wrote a play called *What Big Ears?*, which opened and closed very quickly in 1942. O'Donnell's co-author was Jo Eisinger, the future screenwriter, who was part of Shaw and O'Donnell's group in New York City at the time. O'Donnell would move to California in the 1940s, register as a Republican, and work as a script reader for a studio. As an interesting aside, in 1951, while living next door to actress Barbara Payton, O'Donnell would witness a fist fight between actor Franchot Tone and Payton's boyfriend, Tom Neal, over the affection of the beautiful actress. O'Donnell was quoted in several newspaper articles about the brawl, which was big news in Hollywood at the time.

Another of Shaw's friends from this era was the writer Lyle Saxon, a former newspaper reporter who wrote several best-selling books about various aspects of Louisiana, and New Orleans in particular. Saxon wrote *Fabulous New Orleans*, a book portraying New Orleans against the background of Mardi Gras, and *Gumbo Ya-Ya*, a collection of folk tales from Louisiana. Saxon, during the mid-to-late 1930s, worked for the writer's portion of the Works Progress Administration (WPA). Like Shaw, Saxon was gay. He also served as a mentor to many young writers in the French Quarter during the 1920s and 1930s.

Shortly after arriving in New York City, Shaw wrote Saxon a letter from his new address at 45 West 12th Street in Manhattan. Shaw described the approximately 100-year-old house he had found, which was occupied by "an incredibly aged female named Miss Perkins. Like everything in the house, she rates as an early American antique..." Shaw had the top floor, which held a large bedroom and bath; the downstairs had a large library filled with books that would allow Shaw to "cultivate my mind a little now..."[50] Interestingly, in light of his later gregariousness, Shaw commented, with regard to him not knowing anyone yet in New York City, that, "I suppose I'm a very perverse sort of egg but you don't know how pleased it makes me to walk down the streets and realize I know practically nobody among these teeming millions... Such an almost giddy feeling of freedom, no ties, no obligations, etc...." Shaw said that he was "caught up in the hustle and bustle of the metropolis and having the time of my life."[51]

Shaw commented that he was sorry he had not seen Saxon during a visit he made to Shreveport before going to New York City, but he indicated he had met "Little Clive" one night, and that Clive spent the evening "regaling me with various experiences he has had in all parts of the country. Really, he makes Kraft-Ebbing read like a Sunday school tract . . . what a boy . . ." Shaw closed the letter by saying that there was "much I should like to tell you, but the Postal regulations being the things they are I'm afraid I shall have to wait for a personal interview."[52]

Shaw's reference to "Little Clive" and the Krafft-Ebing report were interesting early indicators of Shaw's familiarity and comfort with sexual practices, at least to a theoretical extent. The Krafft-Ebing report was a set of case studies dealing with what was considered sexual perversity in Europe during the 1880s. Among other things, the book coined the term "masochism." Although its author, an Austro-German sexologist and psychiatrist, wrote the book in such a way and with a title that was intended to discourage lay readers, the book was highly popular with them anyway, and went through many printings and translations. Many individuals, including some who were gay, used the book as a "how to" manual. In the author's interviews with various individuals in preparation of this book, several of them mentioned the Krafft-Ebing report as having been useful to them during their young sexual years.

Also shortly after arriving in New York City in 1936, Shaw met writer William March, who had some New Orleans connections as well. Years later, Shaw would share his memories of March, whom he also knew later in New Orleans, with March's biographer, English author Roy S. Simmonds. He recalled some of March's eccentricities, his method of writing, his parties with large quantities of cold martinis, and his ideas for what eventually became March's most famous work, *The Bad Seed*. Another Shaw friend from the New York days, Marion Seidenbach, her husband, Shaw and March formed a social group that saw each other numerous times during Shaw's almost seven-year period there.[53]

*The Cuckoo's Nest*, the full-length play co-authored by Shaw and Herman S. Cottman, was published in 1936, although it had been performed in New Orleans the year before. The story, a farce about a very eccentric family who take up residence in a strangely deserted boarding house in New York City, was not as successful as the first two, shorter plays.

Mary Moore Sanborn wrote to her daughter, Cynthia, in Europe in August 1936, concerning the publication of *The Cuckoo's Nest*, "Did I ever tell you that the boys, Shaw and Bunny [Herman Stuart Cottman], sold our play to the same publisher who has bought their other two [*Submerged* and *A Message From Khufu*]? I understand he is plugging it quite hard in his new catalog. This is *The Cuckoo's Nest*. You remember that it was my idea, title, and roughly sketched plot, and they wrote it while I was in England? I'm to get 20% of what it brings in royalties. This will never be anything to brag about, but may in time bring me $50 or $60 a year. The publishers have made around $8,000 out of *Submerged*. Bunny and I are now embarked on a one-actor for the same market, to be called (so far) *Light*."[54]

Marymor Cravens, Mary Moore Sanborn's daughter, recalled that Shaw had dinner with her and her mother in New York City in the late 1930s, when she was attending a boarding school in Peekskill, New York, and he was living in the city. She lost touch with Shaw after the 1930s, although she may have seen him once or twice on business to New Orleans, until his arrest and trial toward the end of his life.[55]

During his time in New York, Shaw often saw Robert Jackson and his wife, Sylvia, who were by now living in the New York City area. Sylvia's brother, Ken Williams, was in the advertising and public relations industry, and later restored properties in various places, including one in Puerto Rico. Ken Williams was gay, and knew Shaw in that social circle as well.

Many writers have tried to place Shaw, politically, in the right-wing conservative camp, but Gordon Jackson, J. C. Jackson's grandson, is skeptical of that, based upon Shaw's longtime friendship with his uncle Robert and his wife Sylvia. If Shaw were a conservative, "he wouldn't have garnered such gushing affection from Sylvia, who was an in-your-face liberal and something of a political correctness cop." Jackson added that, "Robert was less political, more intellectual, and I suspect that Shaw, like him, saw politics as being a bunch of lies on the mere surface of things and not terribly interesting."[56]

On March 21, 1938, Shaw and his co-author, Herman Stuart Cottman, signed a contract with The Dramatic Publishing Company to publish their play, STOKERS, which the two had initially copyrighted in 1932. Perhaps their least-known play, it concerned a political radical, perhaps a Communist, among a ship's crew, who tries to persuade his fellow crew members to blow up the ship for political reasons. In the end, the radical admits his true motive is personal revenge rather than ideology. The contract gave the publisher the rights to publish the play, and to be the agent for the play. It allowed the publisher to change the title if necessary, but the authors held the copyright. Royalties from amateur stage productions, radio, and television would be split 50/50 between the authors and the publisher. Professional stage productions and motion picture royalties would be split, with 10 percent going to the publisher and 90 percent going to the authors. For copies of the play sold as a book, the publisher would keep 95 percent of the royalties, with 5 percent going to the authors. The two authors would split their own royalties 50/50. In the contract, Shaw used the name of LeVergne Shaw, a variation of the pen name he had used in his Le Petit Theatre days. Four individuals witnessed the signing of the contract, including Shaw's friend Judson O'Donnell, and Joe Eisinger.[57] Eisinger would go on to become a prolific screenwriter for the motion picture industry, sometimes using his own name, sometimes using pseudonyms, and often being paid well for uncredited script-doctoring work.

Professor Michael Snyder, presently at Oklahoma City Community College, has made the most in-depth survey of Shaw's plays. He commented that, "Clay Shaw's early plays tell us about the man: his desires, his psychology, and his politics". He found indications of homo-eroticism in all four of the plays co-authored with Cottman. In the three one-act plays, *Submerged*, *A Message from Khufu*, and *Stokers*, the action centers on "half dressed men trapped in enclosed spaces: a wrecked submarine, an Egyptian tomb, and a steam-powered yacht's boiler room, respectively." In the three-act play, *The Cuckoo's Nest*, a handsome youth comes between a husband and his wife, not in the standard way by having an affair with the wife, but rather by criticizing her, and actually getting into a physical fight with her, to the husband's delight. Afterwards, the husband invites the youth into his business, using some "phallic, homoerotic" humor.[58]

Professor Snyder also found what he thought was evidence of Shaw's anti-Communism in at least one of the plays, and a sort of anti-colonialism in another. In his most dramatic conclusion, he found that *Submerged* contained symbolism where the commander of the submarine wished to sacrifice himself for the good of the entire vessel, symbolism possibly related to the sacrifice of a future commander-in-chief, John F. Kennedy, "for the good of the body politic." Professor Snyder concluded that Shaw's often professed "liberalism" was, in fact, a pretense, and that he was, in fact, an establishment, anti-Communist conservative.[59] As the reader will find, the author parts company with Professor Snyder on that conclusion (other than the anti-Communism and anti-colonialism aspects).

In September 1938, Shaw (now as Clay Shaw) took over the unpaid position as business manager of the Actor's Repertory Company in New York City. The small company, formed in 1935, was an experimental acting group which had recently undergone a reorganization, and was down to only eleven members. Director Worthington Miner had left stage direction and gone into the new field of television. Now, the actors paid their own expenses while appearing in other shows, and Shaw and his friend, Judson O'Donnell, produced some of the productions at the Vanderbilt Theater. One of the main productions during Shaw's tenure there was of veteran actress Cecilia Loftus in her "Impressions and Impersonations," as the British actress impersonated entertainers such as Ethel Barrymore and Fanny Brice, or read selections from various plays of the day.

By the summer of 1938, Shaw was living at 334 East 53rd Street, using the name C. LaVergne Shaw. It appears he made the switch to Clay shortly thereafter, for in the 1939 telephone directory he is listed as Clay Shaw, and shown at 112 West 11th Street. It is possible that the permanent switch to Clay had to do with his employment in the business world of New York City, first with Western Union, then with the Lee Keedick agency, which managed prominent public speakers, where he would be employed by 1939.

**Shaw in approximately late 1930s (Courtesy: National Archives)**

Some biographical summaries say that Shaw attended some classes at Columbia University while living in New York City. However, Columbia University has no record of such attendance.[60] It is possible that Shaw attended some informal class held at the university that was not part of its official curriculum. At his trial in 1969, Shaw testified that his formal education ended with high school, and that he did not attend college.

Before working for Lee Keedick, Shaw made a major stab at becoming more involved in the theater. A newspaper article that appeared on January 25, 1939, in the *The New Orleans Item*, written by New Orleans writer and Shaw friend Harnett Kane, dealt with Shaw at the midway point during his time in New York. The article mentioned Shaw's status as the unpaid business manager of the Actors Repertory Theater, and compared Shaw with Orson Welles, who had already achieved great success with his *The War of the Worlds* radio broadcast (but was still two years away from directing the motion picture, *Citizen Kane*), saying that Shaw was often mistaken for him, and even combed his hair like him. The somewhat glowing article mentioned that Shaw's theater group was offering three veterans of the theater–Alison Skipworth, Cissie (Cecilia) Loftus, and Walter Hampton–in *The Rivals*. It added that group had earlier put on *The Cradle Will Rock*, also with Loftus. Kane wrote that the theater had "done it all in less than six months," and commented that New Orleans had given Shaw to New York City.[61]

The article, entitled "Lavergne Shaw, Ex-Little Theatre Actor, Broadway's New 'Boy Wonder'" [Le Petit Theatre was often referred to as the "Little Theater"], went on to say that Shaw had recently quit his "well paying" job at Western Union, because he wanted to try his hand on the professional stage. Shaw indicated that he was "simply fed up" with office work, and wanted to try whatever he could find in the theater. Shaw recalled regularly attending plays, fifteen years before, in the St. Charles theater district of New Orleans, indicating that he had rarely missed a show there. When he had started at Warren Easton High School, his interest in actual participation accelerated. From that point on, he worked, in one way or another, in practically every production that went on at the school. [62]

Regarding Shaw's acting abilities, Kane recalled Shaw, during their school days together, as being somewhat of a "ham," an assessment with which Shaw did not disagree. "I don't believe I could ever act worth a darn," Shaw said in the article. "Whatever ability I have in the theater lies I realize now in another direction." The article discussed Shaw's early plays, co-written with Herman Stuart Cottman, particularly *Submerged*, which it said had been performed more than 2,000 times to date. [63]

The article indicated that Shaw had transferred to New York with Western Union, becoming a district manager of the Times Square area from 40th Street to 50th Street in New York City, the heart of the theater district. Shaw rekindled his simmering interest in theater by attending first night productions, and meeting people in show business. In 1938, Shaw asked Western Union if he could take three months off to think about changing careers, but a few weeks after doing so, he gave them a month's notice and left the company. According to the article, Shaw had served as business manager for a short period at Chapel Playhouse of Connecticut, before coming back to New York and becoming the business manager of Actors' Repertory Theater. Shaw shared an office with the playwright, Judson O'Donnell. [64]

There is little or no evidence of activity for Actors Repertory Theater after 1939, however, indicating it failed to survive the 1930s. Judson O'Donnell would soon be sent to the West Coast to represent William A. Brady in the production there of *Outward Bound*. O'Donnell wrote to Muriel Francis around that time, mentioning the type of work he was doing, and discussing different plays, mostly from a business standpoint. Francis was also living in Hollywood at that time. [65]

Sometime in 1939, Shaw began working for the Lee Keedick agency. Lee Keedick had started his agency in New York City in 1907, representing at least two polar explorers, including Sir Ernest Shackleton and Roald Amundsen, on their speaking tours. He later represented numerous celebrities, including actors, historians, and authors such as Sir Arthur Conan Doyle, H.G. Wells, G.K. Chesterton, Edna St. Vincent Millay, Thornton Wilder, and Maurice Evans. [66] Shaw would work for the lecture bureau, with one known interruption, up until the time of his entry into World War II in November 1942. At the time of Shaw's employment with the Lee Keedick agency, if not before, he surpassed his father in annual salary [67] and would never earn less again, except during the years he served in the Army in World War II.

During his time at the Lee Keedick agency, Shaw managed tours for, among others, Secretary of Labor Frances Perkins, Admiral Harry Yarnell, William Beebe, a scientist, the British poet laureate John Masefield, the British journalist and author Sir Phillip Gibbs, and the British historian Phillip Guedalla. [68]

It has generally been assumed that once Shaw moved to live to New York City in 1936, he did not return to New Orleans to live until immediately after the war in January 1946. However, in the spring of 1942, he was actually living again in New Orleans, working for Louisiana Shipyards, Inc., an organization for which both Theodore Brent and Rudolf Hecht, the two most important figures behind the future International Trade Mart, would serve as Vice-Presidents. Shaw shows his address in March 1942 at 727 St. Ann Street (the site of the "long long night...when we tried the 'NOBLE EXPERIMENT'" to which Kay Lucas Dart would later refer). [69]

During this time, Shaw exchanged a series of letters with Norman Cousins, editor of *Saturday Review of Literature*, whose lectures were managed by the Lee Keedick agency. Shaw indicated to Cousins, who was coming to New Orleans to give a lecture, that "my limited apartment space precludes my offering you bed," but "I can offer you board, for I've found a very decent cook who is quite good at preparing such New Orleans delicacies as crawfish bisque and gumbo and I am anxious that you sample her wares." Shaw urged that Cousins stay over for a day or so, saying that he would find it "a fascinating place and it will be looking its best at the time of your visit what with the azaleas, camellias, wisteria and other local flora with which the town abounds."[70]

Shaw indicates that he was presently "working hard building ships—we launch our first one tomorrow and after that they should come from the ways about one a week. New Orleans is simply being ringed with all sorts of naval and military installations. There is our shipyard and one now building by a local character named Andrew Jackson Higgins, who promises to turn out 200 ships in a year by assembly line methods and bids fair to become the Henry Ford of the ocean ways." Shaw added that, "The government is building a $12 million embarkation base which will house 25,000 men during the period between their arrival here and their being shipped out to the four corners of the earth. Add to all this eight or ten miscellaneous plane plants, bomber bases, and other war industries and we seem to be rapidly becoming number one bomb target of the country."[71] The industrialist Andrew Jackson Higgins's company manufactured a variety of watercraft instrumental in the U.S. military's efforts during World War II.

The company Louisiana Shipyards, Inc. had been formed in 1941 by a group of prominent citizens looking to capitalize on the pre-war goal of the Roosevelt administration to beef up American shipbuilding. The company built a shipyard, and partnered with the American Ship Building Company of Cleveland, which organized Delta Ship Building Company, Inc. as a separate entity to build the ships. Shaw apparently had taken a leave of absence from the Lee Keedick agency to return to New Orleans and work for the company, perhaps in an effort to do his part in the war without actually serving in the military. However, by November 1942 he would enter the Army.

Shaw apparently asked Cousins, who would play an important role during the war with literary activities, to find some way for Shaw to assist in that regard. Early efforts by Cousins were apparently unsuccessful, but on October 28, 1942, he wrote to Shaw at the Lee Keedick agency address at 475 Fifth Avenue in New York City, offering Shaw the job of Publicity Director of the 1943 Victory Book Campaign, which Cousins would head. Cousins hoped that Shaw could obtain a leave of absence in order to serve in the position; Shaw's services would be required from November 5, 1942 to March 5, 1943.[72] However, by that time, Shaw was about to enter actual military service, and his response, if any, to Cousins's letter has apparently not survived.

Shaw's work with Brent and Hecht, during a period so close to his entering military service before the war, perhaps helps to explain how and why he would be offered the position of managing the relatively new International Trade Mart immediately after his exit from military service in January 1946. Apparently, both Brent and Hecht were impressed by the work he did in 1942, whatever that consisted of, and thought of him as the man who could run such an important new civic organization after the war.

# 2 · World War II

Since Shaw's arrest in 1967, there has been much speculation about his activities during the war. Many believe that he served with military intelligence in the Army, or even with the Office of Strategic Services (OSS), the wartime predecessor to the CIA. What follows is the most complete account of Shaw's wartime activities that can be pieced together from official documents, and from interviews with some of those who served with him. Military records from the World War II era, especially concerning an individual who was not a leading figure, are notoriously sketchy and fragmented, but through it all a relatively clear and convincing picture emerges.

In 1942, after almost seven years in New York City, Shaw was drafted into World War II. Shaw's military record was destroyed in 1973, along with those of numerous others who served during that time period, in a notorious fire at a Federal records depository in St. Louis, Missouri. However, a fairly complete copy survives, because Shaw's criminal defense attorneys obtained it after his arrest in March 1967, when questions about his service arose.

Shaw's Report of Physical Exam and Induction is dated October 16, 1942. It shows his occupation as "Booking Manager of Lecture Bureau," at a salary of $250 per month, or $3,000 per year (some records indicate his salary at this time to have been $3,900/year). It describes his work as managing and arranging lecture tours for celebrities. The report indicates that he was born in Kentwood, Louisiana, and had been employed for two years at the lecture bureau. It also shows that Shaw had filed a registrant's affidavit for the draft on July 22, 1941.[73]

Shaw was inducted November 6, 1942, at Fort Dix, New Jersey. He quickly became part of the Medical Corps and was sent to Camp Pickett, Virginia. Some accounts indicate that he may have been placed in the Medical Corps because of his homosexuality, the theory being that the Army shoveled homosexuals in that direction, but there is no meaningful evidence of that.

On December 1, 1942, while at Camp Pickett, he suffered an injury to his back while practicing carrying patients, for which he was given a thirty-minute heat treatment. Though seemingly trivial at first glance, Shaw's back would continue to trouble him. He developed a slight limp from it which, years later, would be used as one of the identifying points against him by one of the witnesses at his trial. Also at Camp Pickett, on March 1, 1943, Shaw undertook a second physical examination, this time related to entrance to Officer Candidate School (OCS). The report gives his height as 74-1/2 inches (6'2-1/2", at least an inch and a half shorter than his normal estimated height of 6'4" or 6'5"), and a weight of 184 pounds. His chest X-ray was normal.[74]

By mid-April 1943, he was at Camp Barkley, Texas, attending Officer Candidate School. The records show that he had an injury classified as "myositis, acute, lumbo-sacral," and possible arthritis.[75] Shaw awakened on April 15, 1943 with a slight pain in his lower back. Two days later, while practicing "hasty entrenchment" and "creeping and crawling," the pain became more severe. On April 19, the pain worsened in his lower back, and he developed numbness in his left leg. He went to the infirmary, where he was referred to the orthopedic clinic. The complaint report said that Shaw drank occasionally, smoked one pack of cigarettes per day, and had no history of cancer, diabetes, or tuberculosis, that he had undergone the usual childhood diseases, and had undulant fever in 1940 in Houston, Texas.[76]

As a result of his injury, he was unable to flex his spine or straighten his leg. A report on May 4 dealt with the sciatica in his left leg. It indicated that he had no left ankle jerk, and had hypoesthesia in the upper outer third of his left thigh, and about the left external malleolus. The report indicated that he suffered pain on pressure along the course of the left sciatic nerve, and under the sciatic notch, and that he appeared to have sciatic neuralgia, and a possibility of prolapsed intervertebral disc. The report recommended a spinal puncture with spinal aerogram, and studies of protein content of fluid.[77] Shaw was back to light duties for two weeks beginning May 12, 1943.

Shaw began active service as an officer August 4, 1943,[78] assigned to the 127th General Hospital Unit. This unit was activated on January 15, 1943 at Camp Claiborne, near Alexandria, Louisiana, and would last until it was inactivated on October 13, 1945. However, Shaw did not see this unit to its completion, as he would depart in early 1944 for another assignment.[79]

The 127th General Hospital Unit was associated with a hospital at the University of Texas, and the unit's initial publication was entitled *127th General Hospital Texas Longhorns*. The first edition of that publication appeared on February 10, 1943. It was published monthly until August 1943, when the unit was alerted for overseas movement; there were eight issues during that period. Publication resumed on V-E Day with Volume II, Number 1, in Nancy, France, where it was published through the final edition on September 5, 1945.[80]

During the existence of the 127th General Hospital Unit, one of the members kept a diary, intervals of which have survived. A diary entry for August 7, 1943, at Camp Claiborne, indicated that Second Lieutenant Shaw was assigned to the unit, joining it from Camp Barkley, Texas. An entry on August 10, 1943 indicated that Second Lieutenant Shaw had been assigned as "Assistant Det. Comdr." and that final preparations were completed for leaving the present station at Camp Claiborne.[81] Shortly thereafter, the unit moved out of Camp Claiborne, Louisiana with 700 individuals packed on a hot train.[82] The train trip from Louisiana to Camp Shanks, New York lasted four days and three nights and was very uncomfortable, with some cars having only gas-lighted coaches. It arrived in Camp Shanks, New York, near the New Jersey border, on August 15, 1943.[83] The troops were stationed near New York City throughout mid-August, from August 19, 1943 to August 22, 1943.[84]

The original plan was for the unit to go overseas immediately from Camp Shanks, but a last-minute change had them go to Fort Devens, Massachusetts.[85] On August 28, 1943, the unit moved through Albany, New York to its new destination, near the town of Ayer, Massachusetts, thirty miles northeast of Boston. The notes for the first interval of the unit diary end on September 4, 1943.[86]

The unit spent six weeks at Fort Devens.[87] On October 7, 1943, in Boston, the unit boarded the *Mauretania*, which carried four separate General Hospital units to England. Five nurses from the American Red Cross boarded along with the units. The ship sailed the following day, October 8, and docked at Liverpool on October 17. Trains carrying the members of the units left Liverpool on October 17 for Taunton, Somerset, in southwest England. There, the units were transported seven miles away to Sandhill Park (sometimes termed "Sand Hill Park"), near the village of Bishop's Lydeard, which was the unit's home until May of 1944.[88]

Upon arrival in England, the 127th General Hospital Unit was made part of the Services of Supply (SOS), which was involved in the European Theater of Operations for the United States Army (ETOUSA). The 127th General Hospital, a 1,000-bed general hospital with no direct admissions except in emergency, was opened at Sandhill Park on November 5, 1943. The roster of officers included, under Administration, Clay L. Shaw, Second Lieutenant, ASN0-2047494, MAC Branch, Asst. Det. Comdr. (Duty), under Major Morgan B. Aynesworth.[89]

The unit's operations at Sandhill Park, one mile from Bishop's Lydeard, were very closely regulated by the Southern Base Section of the Services of Supply. The mail was censored, and there was a lot of Army red tape, numerous inspections, and court martials. However, the general schedule was not rushed at that time, months prior to the D-Day invasion, and there was plenty of opportunity for relaxation, visiting London, and even taking trips to Scotland. Many of the personnel also visited nearby castles and other sites, such as the Cathedral at Wells, Exeter, Plymouth, and Bristol.[90]

One of the individuals Shaw met shortly after his arrival in England was Alison Marks, a social worker with the Red Cross assigned to the 127th General Hospital Unit. Marks counseled patients who had been injured in battle, or were otherwise hospitalized. She quickly became friends with Shaw, and even had a romantic interest in him, although he failed to reciprocate.[91]

One night Marks, who was a bird lover of sorts, dragged Shaw out into the cold from the Officers' Club to hear a nightingale at Bishop's Lydeard, the small village nearby. Years later, after Shaw was arrested, Marks wrote to him and recalled that incident. She also remembered it more than thirty years later, in 1999, when the author interviewed her from her retirement home in Massachusetts. Marks, five years older than Shaw, died in 2008, shortly before she would have turned 100 years old.

Marks was like many women interested in Shaw at one time or another; they either never married or had very short, unhappy marriages. When the author contacted Marks in August 1999, it turned out that she had saved letters Shaw had written to her during World War II, after they had become separated, with Shaw moving to a different unit and then going on to France, and Marks remaining in England. She had even saved the original envelopes in which the letters were mailed.

Another person who knew Shaw in the 127th General Hospital Unit was Jack Holman, who later became a Catholic priest. Years later, Holman recalled:

"We had a 1st Lt. warrant officer by the name of Clay Shaw who later figured in the Kennedy Assassination investigations. He was, I learned, a socialite from New Orleans and went to trial during the investigations. I had several contacts with him. He was required to check all the buildings including the barracks every day to see that things were in order. I was on night duty a lot and would wake up in my bunk to find him inspecting our quarters. At first it made me uncomfortable but as I got to know him, didn't think much about it until he showed up when I was in the showers. Our latrines and showers were all open without privacy shields. Always pleasant, a good conversationalist always asked about my family, how things were going, if I liked my work, etc, etc. I thought he might be "queer" (gay) but he never made a pass. When we were on board the Mauritania coming to England, he spent more time with the enlisted men than he did with the Officers which we thought was great. He would sometimes sit with us in the crowded big salon or ball room. No chairs. Once he asked me to sing for the guys. I am ham enough that I jumped at the chance. He seemed to like the light classical. The guys wanted popular songs like "Paper Doll" and "Moonlight Becomes You", "Don't sit under the Apple Tree". They would often join in. He wanted to hear "Donkey Serenade", and Gershwin tunes. Of course, there were the usual songs like "Mareseatdoats" "Elmer's Tune", songs of that era."[92]

The diary portions for the 127th General Hospital Unit resume on January 1, 1944 in England. An entry on January 3, 1944 indicated that Lieutenant Shaw dispatched to "DS St. Hilda-College at Oxford, Oxon." An entry dated January 6, 1944 shared that Lieutenant Shaw was sent to this same location once again. An entry on January 20, 1944 indicated that Lieutenant Shaw "dy to leave of absence for six days." There were no entries to the diary after January 21, 1944.[93]

It is unclear exactly what Shaw did at the college, although it probably had to do with a public relations event (or training for such) related to the U.S. Army's efforts in Southern England. The present-day archivist at St. Hilda's said that college carried on normally during the war, with no military presence. She suggested that perhaps Shaw went instead to St. Hugh's, another college at Oxford often confused with St. Hilda's, which during the war had been requisitioned as a military hospital for head injuries. The archivist at St. Hugh's indicated that important work with penicillin was done there during the war, but that no records have survived referencing visits by Shaw.

The leather-bound history of the 127th General Hospital Unit, published some years after the war, contains a paragraph in the Briefing section of the book that states, "Clay Shaw, who was associated with the 127th General Hospital for a short time, is manager of the International Trade Mart in New Orleans, La."94

Following Shaw's departure from the unit, personnel in the 127th General Hospital Unit continued their duties, tending to the sick and injured from the battles in Sicily. By the spring of 1944, everyone knew the invasion of France was imminent. Soldiers in the hospital were told to return to their units, and there were a number of German air raids. On May 4-6, 1944, the 127th General Hospital Unit left Sandhill Park and spread across the war zone. Officers and enlisted men went to Salisbury Plains in South Central England, where it was very cold even through May. Most of the men, including many officers, lived on grass-floored tents, but ate in heated mess halls. Camp Fargo, as it was known, was located on moors, ten miles north of the town of Salisbury. The open moors, thirty miles north of Southampton, were used for training for the eventual invasion of France. The eleven weeks there were used to toughen the troops; the training consisted of calisthenics and marches, gas recognition, and aircraft recognition. The 127th General Hospital Unit crossed to Normandy on July 31, 1944, almost two months after the D-Day invasion.95

Long before that, however, Shaw had departed the unit for a more challenging role, including a promotion. On February 21, 1944, Second Lieutenant Shaw was transferred from the 127th General Hospital Unit to D/S Headquarters of the Southern Base Section of the Services of Supply, serving first with the Public Relations section, and then joining the staff of Brigadier General Charles O. Thrasher.96 Southern Base Section of the Services of Supply was located first in the basement of Wilton House. It then moved to Fugglestone Camp in Nissen huts, four miles west of Salisbury, Wiltshire, near Wilton Village. Among the men in Southern Base Section were 15,000 "colored" troops.97

Shortly after arriving at Headquarters of Southern Base Section, Shaw wrote his friend Alison Marks back at the hospital. Opening the letter with, "Alison my dear," Shaw indicated that he was settling into the chaotic nature of the new job, which involved showing visiting dignitaries around. He said that he also would be taking over the Speakers' Bureau for the base, and was charged with arranging for American officers to address British groups, and giving a number of speeches himself. Shaw mentioned that he was sharing a Nissen hut with Lieutenant Gordon Berger, and that the two had made it homey, with carpet on the floor and reading lamps over the bed. Shaw indicated to Marks that he would miss their pleasant evenings of port, coffee, gin and coke, and conversation together. Shaw thanked her for her patience in listening to his "monologues," and indicated that he would look forward to seeing her soon.98

Although he had left the medical arena by this time, in a Roster of Officers issued in Spring 1944, Shaw was listed as a First Lieutenant MAC in the Administrative section, still assigned to the 127th General Hospital Unit.99 He wrote Marks again around this time, on April 2, 1944, indicating that, "I begin this letter with penitence and with metaphorical sackcloth on my body and ashes on my head," apologizing for his tardiness in writing. Shaw indicated that two weeks before, he had been taken from the Public Relations office and brought into General Thrasher's office, where he became the general's aide. Shaw described the busy nature of the place during what was essentially the lead-up to the D-Day invasion of June 1944, but without specifying precisely what was happening. He said that, "Sometimes I heave a gentle, nostalgic sigh for the placid days of the hospital when I had nine jobs which I could handle with comparative ease instead of one which keeps my shoulder to the wheel and my nose to the grindstone until all hours of the day and night."[100]

Shaw thanked Marks for her good wishes on his birthday and said that, "Personally, I wish it were my last...and I should just quit having them were it not for the fact that my hoary head (which this new job will undoubtedly make hoarier) would belie such action. As I make my progression under the arches of the thirties I keep feeling that I have managed to do very little, somehow, so far. But I suppose in considering that I have lived through two wars and a major depression just surviving is something."[101]

Shaw indicated that he was homesick. "If the Russians keep going at their present rate maybe we all will go back sooner than I would have at one time thought possible. We must plan to have a big celebration when we finally set foot again on the sacred soil of Manhattan."[102]

According to General Order #10, issued by Headquarters, Services of Supply, ETOUSA (European Theater of Operations, United States Army), Colonel Charles Thrasher of the General Staff Corps was assigned as Commanding Officer of Southern Base Section on July 20, 1942, the same day Southern Base Section was organized at Fugglestone Camp at Wilton, Wiltshire, England.[103] Shaw would often, in later years, point to the eventual General Thrasher as a major influence on his life, especially in terms of organizational and managerial skill.

Charles O. Thrasher was born on a farm near Paxton, Illinois. His family later moved to Indiana for a while, but he graduated from high school in Gilman, Illinois in 1906. He attended the University of Illinois, then joined his father's gain-brokerage business in 1910. In 1916, he went to Officer's Training Corps at Fort Sheridan in Illinois. He served in France during World War I at General Depots of Divisional and Army Dumps. In October 1919, he was commissioned as a Major in the Reserve Corps. In 1920, he returned to the Army as quartermaster at Wilbur Wright Field in Dayton, Ohio, where he stayed until 1925. He then went to Baltimore, also as a quartermaster, and in 1928 to teaching at a quartermaster school in Philadelphia. From 1929 to 1930, he was enrolled at the Army Industrial College in Washington, D.C., where he helped develop a Quartermaster equipment and storage system. From July 1933 to July 1936, he was at Fort Shafter in Hawaii, then in San Francisco until June 1940, still with the Quartermaster Corps. Thrasher was promoted to Lieutenant Colonel in August 1939, when he worked on research into clothing for U.S. Army personnel. In June 1940, he was part of a planning division responsible for the supply of quartermaster equipment to the West Coast and Alaska, related to the mobilization of industry on a wartime basis, and for surveys of productivity, men, and materials. He developed plans for the enlargement of the Port of Seattle Quartermaster Depot, and Port of Embarkation. In October 1940, he was the Seattle commanding officer of the Depot and Port of Embarkation, as a sub-command of the Port of San Francisco under Major General John C.H. Lee. Thrasher was promoted to full Colonel on February 1, 1942. In May 1942, he went with General Lee to Great Britain to help establish the Services of Supply in the European Theater. Thrasher, at the time of World War II, was married with two sons and two daughters. One of his sons, Lieutenant Charles O. Thrasher, Jr., also served in the U.S. Army during World War II.[104]

Thrasher, being the consummate career man, was always attuned to details affecting Army morale and public relations. As Shaw was arriving with the 127th General Hospital Unit to be attached to Southern Base Section in November 1943, General Thrasher sent a letter to all Services of Supply units in the Southern Base Section regarding officers who would be speaking about the Allied relationships to audiences in England. Thrasher specified that they must be good speakers, tactful, and able to relate well to a British audience. He added that they must have a good personality, and a belief in U.S.-British economic cooperation after the war was over.[105] It is likely that those very qualities soon brought Shaw to his attention.

A member of Thrasher's staff, Captain Edward H. Weitzen of the Quartermaster Corps, soon became a friend of Shaw.[106] Weitzen later worked for or ran several businesses, and died in the early 1990s.

Shaw shared a tent with Gordon Berger when he first transferred to Headquarters of Southern Base Section. A roster of officers at Headquarters Command of Southern Base Section as of January 31, 1944, showed First Lieutenant Gordon J. Berger as part of the Signal Corps. Berger, who spent almost all of his life in or around Montreal, Quebec, Canada, was a United States citizen who crossed the border and volunteered at Plattsburgh, New York, shortly after the war began. Berger would know Shaw through the remainder of the war, and would visit him in New Orleans in 1957.

Gordon Berger brought Shaw over to his team on the public relations staff under newly promoted General Thrasher. Years later, Berger wrote that, "Clay was another gem. Handsome, eloquent, and brilliant, he was at home with anyone. As a representative of the foremost lecture bureau in the United States, his job had been to sell and manage prominent people...He exuded diplomacy and charm on demand at any level. Before I kidnapped him, he had been an adjutant for a field hospital and he was delighted at the chance to be involved in an area much more suited to his talents."[107]

One of Shaw's first assignments at Southern Base was to coordinate with Gordon Berger on escorting Walter White, President of the National Association for the Advancement of Colored People (NAACP), who was on a fact-finding mission and would be submitting a report directly to President Roosevelt. The purpose of the report was to evaluate the treatment accorded to black soldiers in the European Theater of Operations. White had requested that his visit not be accompanied by the usual band of top Army brass that accompanied an important official; he wanted to see firsthand, and without interference, how black troops were being treated. However, Colonel Jock Lawrence, Berger's immediate boss, recommended to General Thrasher that Berger, the more rough-cut and unassuming soldier, accompany White rather than Shaw, since Shaw was very sophisticated in manner, and came from the South.[108] Shortly thereafter, however, General Thrasher took Shaw to be a member of his own staff as his aide-de-camp. Shaw moved into the house occupied by the general and another top aide.[109]

When Shaw joined the Headquarters unit, Southern Base Section was in Nissen huts in a field in Southern England. A transcript of a radio broadcast on the Mutual Broadcasting System as of March 7, 1944, had reporter John Thompson in London describing General Thrasher's office in his Nissen hut. The broadcast by Thompson was a very detailed report on the Services of Supply, and Thrasher's responsibilities.[110]

The Training and Security Division was discontinued on April 5, 1944. Gordon Berger was made Chief of the Public Relations Section of the General Staff at Headquarters, and staff members of that division were also made part of Public Relations.[111] It was in that manner that Shaw and Gordon Berger both more directly joined General Thrasher's Headquarters staff.

A roster of officers dated March 27, 1944 shows Shaw as being on the Commanding General staff as Aide-de-Camp to General Thrasher.[112] However, it was not until April 18, 1944 that General Order number 52, signed by Thrasher, officially appointed Shaw, who had by then been promoted to First Lieutenant, as Aide-de-Camp.[113]

Beginning in at least early 1944, Southern Base Section had begun to receive administrative orders dealing with Operation Overlord, better known to most as the D-Day invasion of Continental Europe, which took place on June 6, 1944. Administrative Order #7, for example, requested that Southern Base Section "assist troops with embarkation to achieve maximum efficiency."[114]

On May 29, 1944, Shaw wrote to Alison Marks again, commenting that his busy schedule was continuing, that he rarely left the office until late evening, "and am so tired I simply fall into my virginal couch and sleep a deep and dreamless sleep 'til I leap from my bed to take up the fray anew each morning." Shaw closed the letter by saying that, "The weather today has been like summer back home, filling me with vague nostalgia for the beach at Lake Pontchartrain or Laguna on your own Cape Cod. How tired I am of this war and how I want to go home."[115]

On June 13, shortly after the D-Day invasion, Shaw wrote Marks again, indicating that, "I have, for so long, spent my days and nights in doing things that I can't talk about (for military—not moral reasons) that my letters are becoming the veriest weather reports. For the past two months I have been so security conscious that my letters have been naught but sound and fury, signifying nothing. Now that D-day is here I don't know how much of the ban has been lifted so I suppose I shall have to continue saying nothing as elaborately and in as many different ways as I can think of."[116]

Shaw continued that, "Now that D-day has at last come I find that there is no very pertinent comment one can make about it. The whole thing is so tremendous and the stakes so high that one is at a loss for words—a rare condition for me as you know. I do hope that this is the final act of what must certainly be the bloodiest and maddest episode of mankind's sanguinary and insane history. How I yearn for it all to be over and how well I understood the Psalmist when he sang, 'How beautiful upon the mountains are the feet of the messengers of peace!' In spite of your pretense that you will return to a civilian life of dullness and no validity, I don't believe a word of it. I hope to see you in the years to come and show you that the ways of peace can be quite a lot more pleasant (though sometimes quite as destructive) as the ways of war."[117]

Commenting further on his nonstop busy days, Shaw said, "I've really led a celibate life. However that can go on for just so long. Even now, I begin to feel my ears growing more pointed, my flanks shaggier, and yesterday in looking in the mirror I noticed a suggestion of vine leaves twined among my greying curls."[118]

After commenting that he hadn't had a day off for eight weeks, and that he normally worked until ten every night, Shaw indicated that he didn't know what would happen to him but that he wouldn't be surprised if the two of them met again on the Continent.[119] As it turned out, Shaw would soon go to France, but Marks would remain behind in England, and the two would not see each other again until the late 1960s.

With D-Day now past and operations soon moving to the Continent, General Thrasher realized that the ending months and years of World War II, however long it would last, were important to the careers of all military men, and he sometimes felt it necessary to jog those who served under him to avoid the cutting of corners and to maintain discipline. In a series of notes on August 2, 1944 to his men, Thrasher went into a detailed discussion of maintaining discipline and correcting personal weaknesses. He urged the men to relearn how to salute properly, and to take care of basic details that would make an impression upon superiors, and upon the English allies. The memo was generally a very tough talk, reminding his officers to set an example and not rest on their laurels.[120]

On September 1, 1944, Southern Base Section of Supply in England ceased its operations and became Southern District, UK Base of the Services of Supply. Southern Base Section had completed its mission of supplying the invading troops in connection with Operation Overlord.[121]

Once Southern Base Section ended, its personnel were originally supposed to have become Channel Base Section, as part of a Continental Communication Zone Section staged at Fontainebleau, near Paris, but its mission was quickly changed to that of Oise Section, centered in Rheims, France.[122] Oise Section was formed on September 15, 1944, as part of the Continental Communication Zone Section, which operated under General Dwight Eisenhower's Supreme Allied Headquarters Command. Many of the personnel who had been in Southern Base Section, including General Thrasher, Gordon Berger, and Shaw, were assigned to Oise Section.[123]

The men who made up Oise Section had been stationed at Wilton, Wiltshire, England after the D-Day invasion. The first section moved from Wilton, embarking at Portland south of Weymouth, England, on September 14, 1944, landing on September 16, 1944 at Omaha Beach, France, where the D-Day invaders had landed more than three months earlier. The section learned upon landing that it was to be known as Headquarters, Oise Section, Communication Zone, European Theater of Operations of the United States Army ]ETOUSA].[124]

The section proceeded to Rheims (sometimes spelled "Reims), France, which had been liberated on August 29. General Charles Thrasher moved into headquarters at Rheims first, along with a set of WACs and civilian women.[125] General Thrasher, along with the WACs and the civilian women employees, entered Rheims on September 17, 1944. Others from the initial group arrived in Rheims on September 18 and September 19, 1944.

Oise Section, commanded by Thrasher, with Shaw as his personal aide, was a complex organization. "Oise" was a department of French government in north central France, and the Oise Section covered a territory of northern France, Belgium, and Luxembourg. It was one of seven sections of the Communications Zone, commanded by General John C.H. Lee (sometimes sardonically referred to by his admirers as "Jesus Christ Himself" Lee), a favorite of General Eisenhower for his dependable performance. All sections coordinated their separate missions in order to assure maximum cooperation. Oise Section was to relieve the Advance Section as it moved east of the Seine River towards Germany. Oise Section expanded as the armies advanced, tripling in size during the period January 1945 through March 24, 1945. Almost one quarter of France was eventually under Oise Section.[126] Supreme Headquarters, Allied Expeditionary Force (SHAEF) with General Eisenhower in command, Oise Section, and the Assembly Area command were all in Rheims, France from the fall of 1944 through the end of the war in Europe.[127] As of V-E Day in May 1945, Oise Section had 5,104 officers, 153 warrant officers, 2,415 nurses, and 63,739 enlisted men and enlisted women combined.[128]

The Section supplied the media with written material and photos, and used a magnetic wire recorder to interview personnel for release to radio stations. Seven hundred to 1,000 stories per month were released, and photographers were used as well, to highlight the activities of the Section.[129] Duncan Hazlewood, a sketch artist in the unit, made drawings for the Oise Historical Section.[130]

On November 15, 1944, a Jewish synagogue was opened at Rheims, representing an important step in reversing the former Nazi presence. Shortly thereafter, on Thanksgiving Day 1944, General Thrasher presented the American flag to the Archbishop at Rheims Cathedral.[131]

The Finance Section of the Services of Supply moved from Southern Base Section initially to Channel Base Section, near Paris, and then to Oise Section, where it remained permanently for the remainder of the war. An Information and Education Office was formed on December 20, 1944, which was attached to Special Service in Information Services until March 7, 1945, then with G-3 until May 2, 1945, then a Special Staff Section by General Order as part of the new Oise Intermediate Section. The Information and Education Office distributed maps, United States Armed Forces Information (USAFI) materials, booklets and other materials, including fact sheets. USAFI was relatively unknown for a while, but was later publicized by the unit; it gave off-duty classes and educated the troops.[132]

Special Services was responsible for troops' recreation and entertainment, including movies and music. The Army Exchange Service sold cigarettes, soft drinks, and other goods. The unit occasionally encountered shortages of various goods.[133]

The Claims Divisions handled traffic accidents, procurement, looting and depredation, theft, property damage, and other claims against the United States government arising from the activities of its personnel and equipment.[134] The Military Labor Service provided administration and supervision over German POW units, Italian service units, and Mobile civilian labor units.[135]

Engineers were needed to construct buildings, roads, railroads, light plants, and bridges, among other things. For instance, a hospital and printing plant were both built in the area with the brainpower and muscle of the Americans stationed there. Some of the less sophisticated tasks employed the use of POWs, local civilians, and alien labor, to free Army personnel for more important duties.[136]

Since Oise was an intermediate section, many supplies and personnel passed through its territory. Canals were used to help transportation. The canals had to be surveyed and rehabilitated, as they were essentially useless in the form discovered by the United States Army. Supplies and personnel were stored at Rheims to relieve the transportation system. Barges arrived on February 23, 1945 for use on the canals.[137]

Railroads were used extensively for transportation as well. In a surviving memo of a staff conference on December 9, 1944, General Thrasher stressed, as he had before, the seriousness of railroad cars backed up at Oise. Thrasher issued a directive cautioning about proper leading of the men after a train wreck in December 1944, caused by debris falling off one of the cars. Mail and clothing had been pilfered from some of the railroad cars, and Rheims was plagued by rail congestion during the period January to March 1945. Meetings were held with representatives from the Section Transportation Office about congestion in the area.[138]

During this period of time, Congressman Overton Brooks, who represented the district in north Louisiana that included the City of Shreveport, visited with Shaw at Rheims. He wrote a letter to Shaw's parents on December 28, 1944, indicating that Shaw had asked him to tell them that their son was doing well.[139]

**Shaw with Congressman Overton Brooks at Oise Section mess hall, probably late 1944 or early 1945 (Courtesy: National Archives)**

Shaw in France, probably 1944 or 1945. Shaw is second from right on front row; Gordon Berger is third from left on front row (Source unknown)

Brigadier General Charles O. Thrasher, around 1944 (Courtesy: National Archives)

General Thrasher, as commanding general of Oise Section, was given responsibility for maintaining and defending the crossing of the Meuse River, and for protection of installations against counterattack, an operation known as "Thrasher-Force," with a forward command point at Charleville. The 101st Airborne Division passed through in late December 1944, as part of the defense of the Ardennes Forrest, also known as the Battle of the Bulge.[140]

During the period of the Battle of the Bulge, General Thrasher issued a command discussing German soldiers operating in U.S. Army uniforms. The memo said that the German soldiers were reconnaissance agents and radio operators reconnoitering bridges and roads leading to the Meuse River. The soldiers carried small vials of sulfuric acid to escape arrest. Thrasher ordered that if any of his soldiers encountered any American soldiers in the area, they were to question them about such subjects as the World Series, the capital of their home state, and the "American way of life," in order to determine if they were really American soldiers. The memo added that the German soldiers were using American vehicles, but carrying German radios.[141]

There were continuing shipping and logistical problems encountered by Oise Section, including those involving fuel, food, freezes, and floods. By February 1945, the supply depots were adequate, but were dependent upon transportation availability. The personnel supply that could have helped to keep cargo moving forward was strained due to those taken for infantry training and non-military labor companies, which had to have military personnel.[142]

On April 2, 1945, Oise Section became Oise Intermediate Section, which was divided into three districts, including Marne, Luxembourg, and Lorraine; Luxembourg was inactivated on May 12, 1945, and became part of Marne.[143] It continued its basic functions, however, until the V-E Day, when its focus would change somewhat.

One morning at breakfast, General Thrasher informed Berger and Shaw that the war was over. That evening, he was going to a party given by the Chimay family, who owned the residence where Thrasher and his staff had been living. He also accepted an invitation on behalf of Berger and Shaw for them to attend a party in celebration of the victory given at the residence used by Kay Summersby, General Eisenhower's driver.[144] Summersby, after initially writing an ordinary account of her experiences during the war, expanded on those memories with a memoir during the 1970s that maintained that she and Eisenhower had a romantic, but non-sexual, affair during the war.

On May 8, 1945, General Lee sent a letter to General Thrasher, which read as follows. "On this day of victory, I send to you and each soldier in the Oise Intermediate Section my heartfelt congratulations on a job well done. The mission your command has accomplished in receiving our forces and supplies, and then hastening their movement to the areas where they were needed and on time have been superb. To you and your command, who have carried on in the past, many times under arduous conditions, thus making possible this victory, goes my grateful appreciation."[145]

Shortly after the war in Europe ended, Shaw was replaced as aide-de-camp and given various assignments to wind down his service. James Brugger, who served with Shaw on General Thrasher's staff from May until November 1945 and would himself serve as aide-de-camp to Thrasher, recalled that "Clay had been the aide (not immediately before me) and had been with the General through the period of most intense activity for the supply and logistical services under the General's command during the build-up of the U.S. military force in England in preparation for the invasion of the Continent. Those were the 'glory days' of the Thrasher command and (as deduced by one who came along later) Clay's contributions to the effort resulted in his promotion to the position of Secretary to the General Staff, with the rank of Major, and made him one of the General's most trusted advisors, not in strategic or tactical matters but rather in questions of administration and in relations with other levels of command, with our allies, and with local communities and governments."[146]

Brugger added that, "Clay's well-cultivated military bearing, courtly manner, and fluency of speech all served to make him an impressive figure in any group. They certainly contributed to his effectiveness in dealing as the General's vicar with the heads of the individual services and staff sections most of whom were lieutenant colonels or full colonels."[147]

By May 26, 1945, Shaw was at the Signal Corps Photographic Center at Long Island City, New York. A report there shows that he was inflicted with cellulitis, and confined to the quarters for those with that condition. On May 29, he was reported with "abscess open," but was back on duty by May 30.

James Brugger said that Shaw's assignment at the Signal Corp Photograph Center, "had to do with a film about the 'Red Ball Express,' the system improvised by the Ordinance Unit in Oise Base Section to keep General Patton's tanks supplied with fuel as they raced across Europe faster than the original logistical plan had envisioned. I don't know how much Clay may have had to do with the shooting of the film, but he was sent to New York to have a hand in its final editing (and, presumably, to assure that Oise Base Section's part in the heroic supply achievement was suitably recognized). He had just returned from that assignment when I became a member of the General's household so I heard only snatches about it, including some good natured kidding about his travel and lodging expenses. He mentioned staying at the Beaux Arts Hotel, indicating he had known it from when he had worked for an agency booking lectures and other talent."[148]

Like most of Shaw's Army colleagues, including Gordon Berger, Brugger did not know Shaw was a homosexual. "He didn't talk about sexual conquests in the way that was common in the barracks and, to a lesser extent, at tables where officers dined; but there were none of the niceties of mannerism, posture, or speech that usually went along with what we called 'fairies' or 'fags' (you can see how outmoded I am in such matters). Women were attracted to Clay, including attractive members of the local aristocracy but it was never apparent that he was in pursuit of opportunity. Was that a sign? Not to a puritan boy like me."[149]

Brugger commented that following Shaw in the position of being the General's aide was a tough assignment. "In the interest of full disclosure, it shouldn't surprise you that during the six months or so I was serving as General Thrasher's aide, I felt an occasional twinge of resentment at the comparisons that were made between Clay's performance in that role and mine. He was the 'golden boy.' I was 'nice try, but no cigar.' It was a fair enough judgment, but it didn't help me deal with an assignment for which I wasn't prepared and probably wasn't very well suited and in which I was most of the time miserable."[150]

Rheims, France, is situated in the champagne-making area of the country. During the war, Shaw became friends with local members of the champagne aristocracy, a number of whom would remember him more than twenty years later when he was arrested. The most notable was Princess Jacqueline du Chimay, whose family members were owners of a local champagne business; they also owned the house where General Thrasher and his immediate staff lived. James Brugger recalled that, during his time on Thrasher's staff, "We had the Prince and Princess to dinner at least once I can remember and they were on the guest list for any social events we held—usually informal gatherings, perhaps with a little non-competitive croquet."[151]

After V-E Day, Oise Intermediate Section increased its activities with planning and operations in connection with readjustment and redeployment, moving men and materials backwards from the front across France, to be shipped back across the Atlantic Ocean.[152] Personnel, equipment, and freed POWs now moved in the opposite direction, westward across France to the Atlantic Ocean.

Immediately preceding V-E Day, as well as afterwards, Oise Intermediate Section helped with thousands of displaced persons from Germany, as well as Recovered Military Personnel (returning prisoners of war). Enormous camps were set up to accommodate them, and to take care of the medically ill. Approximately 150,000 displaced persons, and approximately 100,000 returning personnel, were handled for periods of two days to three weeks. Existing camps were well located to handle the needs of those returning individuals.[153]

After V-E Day, Oise Intermediate Section continued to supply Allied troops in Germany, and also the thousands of troops who poured into the Assembly Area Command (a separate and distinct headquarters under Communications Zone, established at Oise one month before V-E Day to process redeployed troops) for return to the United States or to the Pacific Theater. Approximately 300,000 enemy prisoners of war were held in or near Rheims, France at the peak. More than half of them were used as laborers.[154]

Oise Intermediate Section also processed equipment to the United States, to the Pacific Theater, or within the European Theater, and built camps for the Assembly Area Command. On September 22, 1945, Oise Intermediate Section assumed command of Assembly Area Command, and all of its personnel were consolidated into Oise Intermediate Section.[155]

General Thrasher commanded Oise Intermediate Section until his successor, Brigadier General T.S. Bresnahan, took over on November 4, 1945, in preparation for Oise Section Headquarters assuming new duties as Headquarters for the Western Base Section in Paris on January 15, 1946.[156]

After D-Day, Nancy, France was the location of the 127th General Hospital, and it was part of Oise Intermediate Section. However, Shaw never saw his friend Alison Marks again after their separation in early 1944, and indeed would not hear from her again until 1967, shortly after his arrest.

Many of the documents related to the day-to-day operations of Oise Section, Oise Intermediate Section, and even Southern Base Section of the Services of Supply, have disappeared over the years. Many were destroyed even before the end of the war. A Secret Register of Headquarters Base, related to Communication Zone, ETOUSA, contained a list of many entries that were indicated as being "Destroyed by Fire." It indicates they were destroyed by Corporal Logan T. Sullivan of the 377th Engineering G.S. Regiment, and witnessed by Captain Harlan H. Hugg. A small minority of those documents were Oise Section documents, including notes relating to command and staff conferences, engineering operational orders, administrative orders, and "Intel notes." Most of them appear to have been destroyed by late summer 1945.[157]

In a letter dated July 1, 1945 to General Dwight D. Eisenhower, Lieutenant General J.C.H. Lee recommended various individuals for promotion. Among them was General Charles O. Thrasher, whom Lee recommended be promoted from Brigadier General to Major General.[158] Two months earlier, in May 1945, General Lee had worked up a list of reasons Thrasher should be promoted. He noted that Thrasher had become a Brigadier General on February 22, 1944, and had served as Commanding General of the Southern Base Section of Supply, helping supply the invasion of June 1944 for the landing on the European continent. He also noted Thrasher's help from the Oise Intermediate Section in supplying the troops in defense of the Ardennes Breakthrough (later known as the Battle of the Bulge). Lee indicated that those two major functions alone justified Thrasher's promotion to Major General.[159]

After the war in Europe was over, Lee, as one of his many functions, oversaw the handling of claims against the United States government in France and other countries. In a memo to General Thrasher in mid-August 1945, Lee discussed the nature of claims in Switzerland against the United States arising from erroneous bombing of Swiss towns, activities of U.S. military internees in Switzerland since 1942, and U.S. military personnel on leave in Switzerland. Personnel attached to the Oise Intermediate Section were detached to Switzerland to assess the claims.[160] It is unclear if Shaw was among them, although he would later indicate that he had been to Basle (sometimes spelled as "Basel"), Switzerland "many times."

While some accounts of Shaw's life have him serving as Chief of Staff under General Thrasher, such a promotion, if it happened, must have occurred at the very end of his military service, after he had been promoted to the rank of Major. During the years 1944 and 1945, rosters of officers and various administrative orders show others as Chief of Staff to Thrasher, with Shaw serving as Aide-de-Camp. The latest available roster of officers, undated but probably issued during the early fall of 1945, shows Shaw with the rank of Major, serving as Secretary of the General Staff, with three Colonels separating him from General Thrasher, with one of the Colonels serving as Chief of Staff.[161] General Thrasher left Oise Intermediate Section in the fall of 1945, as did Shaw, so perhaps Shaw occupied the position for a very brief period before the two men went different paths.

At least one Kennedy assassination conspiracy theorist has unearthed an episode, or perhaps would-be episode, that allegedly occurred under General Thrasher's command while Shaw was on his staff. The episode specifically concerns Thrasher rather than Shaw, but as one could have viewed the account as possibly coloring Shaw's own reputation, we discuss it here.

On October 22, 1945, five and a half months after V-E Day, Major William H. Haight, of the Infantry I and E Section, Headquarters, Oise Intermediate Section, Theater Service Forces of European Theater, gave a sworn statement saying that General Thrasher had made certain statements about turning German POWs over to the French that Haight thought merited an official investigation. Apparently, the way Thrasher had phrased his remarks indicated to Major Haight that the prisoners of war might possibly be subject to abuse, or at least abusive conditions, presumably by either French forces or the French population. He indicated that Thrasher had made the remarks at a conference in the Cordeliers Building in Rheims, on or about the first or second Saturday morning of 1945, approximately nine and a half months earlier.[162]

On November 5, 1945, General Walter Bedell Smith, who was Chief of Staff to General Eisenhower at the time, and who would later be one of the early directors of the Central Intelligence Agency, sent a memo to General John C.H. Lee; he attached Major Haight's sworn statement. Smith's memo mentioned a telephone conversation that had taken place that same day between General Eisenhower and General Lee, and Smith asked Lee to let him know the results of the investigation into the POW issue. Smith mentioned he was doing his own investigation at the same time.[163]

On November 12, 1945, Major General Carter B. Magruder, Chief of Staff, Headquarters, Theater Service Forces, sent a memo to General Smith, referring to Major Haight's sworn statement about the remarks allegedly made by Thrasher about the turnover of German POWs to the French. Magruder said that Colonel Stubblebine, Thrasher's Chief of Staff at the time, had said that he was not present at the meeting where Thrasher allegedly made such remarks, but that it would have contradicted Thrasher's usual policies. Magruder added that Thrasher was back in the United States until the end of November, and that Haight's sworn statement had been sent to the Inspector General for investigation.[164]

As late as December 23, 1945, General Magruder's memo was still being passed around top officials of the General Staff Corps under Eisenhower.[165] However, records of such an investigation into General Thrasher have apparently not survived, and there appears to be no evidence he was ever disciplined for his actions, or that his actions were even determined to be improper.

After Shaw's death in 1974, it developed that he had been a contact for the Central Intelligence Agency from 1948 to 1956; rumors of it had circulated even before his death. Some have also maintained that Shaw served with the Office of Strategic Services (OSS), the predecessor to the CIA during World War II. However, there is nothing in Shaw's military personnel records, or any surviving military files, that indicates such was the case. Indeed, in 2008, the government released personnel files related to what it maintained to be all personnel who had served with OSS during the years 1942 through 1945; Shaw's name was not among them.

Shaw was recommended for separation on November 15, 1945, while at Fort Monmouth, New Jersey. He was officially released in mid-January 1946. Now that the war was over, he needed a job. Like so many others whose lives had been disrupted, he essentially had to begin his career over. Fortunately, a good opportunity was beckoning him back to New Orleans, one that would change his life, his reputation, and his fortunes.

# 3 · The Opening of International House

The original idea to form the International Trade Mart in New Orleans, with which Shaw became so uniquely identified from 1946 through the remainder of his life, along with its sister organization, International House, and the Free Trade Zone, had originated in 1940.[166] In the spring of that year, plans were made for a Pan-American Fiesta to be held in New Orleans during 1942 and 1943. Nelson Rockefeller, then Coordinator of Inter-American Affairs in the Roosevelt administration, was an early supporter of the idea, and he also endorsed the idea of a Pan-American Center to be built and established in New Orleans. On August 15, 1940, a meeting was held in the Hunt Room at the St. Charles Hotel in New Orleans, related to the fiesta. The fiesta was to begin on October 12, 1942, and was expected to run for approximately a full year; the general idea was to celebrate the 450$^{th}$ anniversary of Columbus's "discovery" of America in 1492. Charles Nutter, a wire service newsman who had been in New Orleans for approximately eighteen months at the time, and who would later become Shaw's counterpart at International House, was an active participant in the meeting.[167] The fiesta was postponed due to the outbreak of World War II, but the idea of holding it after the war persisted.

The intention of the event was part of a city-wide effort to make New Orleans more of an "international" city, building on the diverse history of the city, with its Spanish and French influences, its relative proximity to Latin America, its successful port (the second-busiest in the nation after New York City, with large imports of coffee, bananas, and other goods from Latin America and Africa), and the consulates of foreign countries already located there. The individuals behind the effort were generally prominent businessmen in the manufacturing and shipping industries whose businesses, not surprisingly, would tend to benefit through increased trade with foreign countries. Although the planning had begun seriously during the administration of Mayor Robert Maestri, who served two terms as mayor, by 1946 many, perhaps most, of the businessmen behind the concept were supporting the new "reform" candidate, deLesseps "Chep" Morrison, who would be elected that year and serve, generally with great popular support, until 1961. Historians have debated how much actual reform took place during Morrison's tenure, but he at least cultivated the image of bringing change. Morrison pushed the idea of New Orleans as a gateway to Latin America as one of the major themes of his administration.

International House got going first, with pre-opening promotional activity beginning during 1944. Prior to former newsman Charles Nutter's arrival as permanent Managing Director of International House in early 1946, that position was held by J. Stanton Robbins. Robbins had been an associate of Nelson Rockefeller, and knew many important individuals in Washington, D.C. Among those was a young State Department employee named Alger Hiss. In late February 1945, Robbins had written to Hiss, addressing the letter to "Dear Alger," saying that he had wanted to see him before Robbins came to New Orleans to run International House, but had not been able to; Robbins hoped that Hiss and his wife Priscilla would come to visit him soon. He enclosed a booklet about International House, and said that, "Hilda and Judy are with me now and the big girls will come down in June.[168]

In mid-May, Robbins received a letter from Hiss. Opening the letter with "Dear Stan,"

Hiss wrote that he had found Robbins' letter of more than two months before after he returned from his Yalta trip; he indicated that he had been "near pneumonia" after returning from that trip, and had failed to respond. Hiss enclosed a list of delegates to the United Nations Conference of International Organization, which was ongoing at the time and would continue into June. Hiss, who wrote the letter on stationery of that organization, gave his best wishes to Robbins and his wife.[169]

Robbins wrote Hiss again at the end of June 1945, passing on comments he had heard from the Minister of Economy for Guatemala. The Minister indicated that Alger Hiss had been a major contributor to the success of the recent conference, held in San Francisco, as its Secretary-General.[170]

Meanwhile, in early July 1945, Mario Bermúdez, who would become a very influential and important figure in the international movement in New Orleans, but who was then only at the beginning of his long career, wrote to Robbins, indicating that he had noticed that interest for the planned International House among the local foreign consular corps was waning. Bermúdez recommended a Latin Department, and a Foreign Language Institute. He also indicated that perhaps the name should be changed from "International House," saying that those words tended to imply a dormitory in the Spanish-speaking world.[171]

In a typed history of the International Trade Mart and International House written in about 1977, it was mentioned that Corinne "Lindy" Boggs, wife of long-time Congressman Hale Boggs, and a congresswoman herself for more than two decades after his death, had coined the slogan, "Dedicated to world peace, trade, and understanding," that was ultimately used by International House. That history also mentioned that J. Stanton Robbins had left International House at the end of 1945 to return as a tourist bureau manager in the east.[172] Charles Nutter immediately replaced Robbins as Managing Director.

Theodore Brent and Rudolf Hecht were the two most important figures related to the International Trade Mart ("the Mart") during the first ten years of its existence. Brent was President of Mississippi Shipping Company, and had a long history in the shipping and railroad industries. Brent was gay, and served as somewhat of a mentor to young gay men in the business world, including both Clay Shaw and J.B. Dauenhauer, Shaw's main assistant at the Mart for the entire time Shaw was employed there.

Rudolf Hecht had been active in banking circles in New York earlier in the century, and in New Orleans from the 1920s forward, with Hibernia National Bank. Like Brent, he was a high official with Mississippi Shipping Company, which operated ships under the name Delta Line, and which transported coffee, bananas, and other goods, and passengers between New Orleans, South America, and Africa. While generally a respected businessman, Hecht had somewhat of a checkered reputation in New Orleans. Many New Orleanians had lost money with Hecht's bank during the Great Depression, and hard feelings remained among some. The FBI had investigated Hecht related to accusations of perjury connected to his banking activities, but a U.S. Attorney in New Orleans had recommended that the investigation end because the statute of limitations period had passed. It was even rumored that, some years earlier, a car in which Hecht was being driven had been involved in an accident one night, as a result of which a black man was killed; Hecht had, supposedly, somehow avoided an investigation.

A third man heavily involved in the founding of the Mart was Herbert Schwartz, an executive with Maison Blanche, a prominent local department store. Schwartz, however, moved to New York City within a few years and no longer played an active role during its penultimate years.

A wide variety of New Orleans businessmen formed the complete Board of Directors and financial supporters of the Mart. These included leaders of banks, insurance companies, shipping companies, export/import firms, and other manufacturing and commercial entities who were interested in the growth of New Orleans commerce. One prominent person was Seymour Weiss, President of the Roosevelt hotel, at the time arguably the most well-known hotel in New Orleans. Ralph Nicholson, publisher of *The New Orleans Item* newspaper, also claimed a spot on the Board.

The initial Executive Committee of the Board of Directors of the International Trade Mart consisted of Theodore Brent, President; Herbert Schwartz, Vice-President; R.K. Longino, Vice-President; C. Earle Colomb, Vice-President; Rudolf S. Hecht, Chairman of the Executive Committee; and Kenneth C. Barranger, Secretary-Treasurer.

Interestingly, Edgar Stern, a prominent New Orleans lawyer and businessman, declined initially to be on the Board of Directors. The Stern family owned, among other things, WDSU-TV and radio; WDSU-TV Channel 6 was the first television station in New Orleans, beginning operations in the mid-1940s. Stern's wife, Edith, was an heir to the Sears Roebuck fortune; in later years, after Edgar Stern's death, she and Clay Shaw would become friends. She would lend great support to him, financial and otherwise, during his more trying times.

C. Earle Colomb served on the Board of Directors as a representative from an organization called the Young Men's Business Club of New Orleans. The club, which was originally organized in 1919, had enjoyed a resurgence of activity during the period in which the Mart was beginning to promote itself; many of its members were in their thirties and forties.

C.G. Staubitz, manager of the Sears Roebuck store in New Orleans before the war, was hired as the General Manager of the Mart on a temporary basis during the preliminary period—before Shaw's arrival back in New Orleans in early 1946.[173] It is unclear if Brent and Shaw had any communication about the proposed Mart during the war, although it seems likely; Staubitz's departure seemed to coincide neatly with Shaw's arrival back in New Orleans.

A preliminary memorandum on the proposal for the International Trade Mart, probably prepared by Theodore Brent in 1945, indicated that the purpose of the Mart was to increase trade through the Port of New Orleans. It noted that other cities already had similar ideas in the works. "The Mart should be a non-profit organization," the memo said. Profits would come into the city, and its businesses, through increased shipments through the Port of New Orleans. As a non-profit, the Mart would operate free of Federal income taxes, and a measure was in the state legislature to exempt it from real estate taxes as well. The extremely large and successful Chicago Merchandise Mart had been studied as an example of how the Mart should be run, and how goods should be displayed. The building to be purchased should be modernized, and tenants should be sought out very carefully. The general manager would need to be a very versatile employee who could handle all phases of the business, from leasing space to dealing with tenants to promoting the Mart in the larger community.[174]

The unnamed writer indicated that, although the institution would be modeled on the Chicago Merchandise Mart, it would be a pilot plan in a much smaller building. The activities of the Mart would have to be coordinated with International House and other city organizations. While the Mart would be non-profit in nature, the worth of the organization would be demonstrated by showing itself capable of being a "medium of sales" to relevant business if it was to survive.[175]

Potential competitors for the Mart included the cities of Dallas, which was proposing a Merchandise Mart in early 1945, San Francisco, which proposed a Western Merchandise Mart, Highpoint, North Carolina with its Furniture Mart, and Miami, Florida with its proposal for a Pan American Exposition Merchandise Mart.

Mississippi Shipping Company was one of the largest initial subscribers for bonds related to financing the International Trade Mart. It subscribed to $50,000 worth, as did the New Orleans Public Service, Inc., the major local utility.

The minutes of a meeting of the Board of Directors of the Mart in early March 1948 noted that it had been twenty-eight months since operations began, which would place the official beginning of activity in approximately the fall of 1945.[176] Mart Realty Company was formed in October 1945 to purchase the building that would eventually be used to house the International Trade Mart.[177] A press release from November 14, 1945 announced the purchase of the Baldwin Building by Mart Realty Company, and said the building would be converted to an international merchandising center known as the International Merchandising Mart. The release went on to say that Charles G. Staubitz was acting as Manager while preliminary work was underway. Later, a version of that memo would bear a handwritten note that said, "Major Shaw 4th Floor" at the top of the page; Charles G. Staubitz's name would be crossed out, and that of Clay Shaw handwritten in.[178]

The Baldwin Building, built around 1895, was purchased from Baldwin Realty in November 1945 for $195,000.[179] The building had originally been built for the Baldwin Company, for use as a wholesale mill supply business.[180] It had five ancient elevators, very little heating or plumbing, and required extensive renovation, the cost of which was estimated at more than $500,000, with numerous alternatives available for construction.[181] Operating income, assuming 90% occupancy, was estimated at $283,000 in initial budgets, and operating expenses were estimated at $176,000.[182] The resale of the building, soon thereafter, by Mart Realty Company to the actual International Trade Mart Corporation would be priced to cover all the expenses related to the original purchase of the building, with no profit or loss to shareholders of Mart Realty Company.[183]

The general plan for the five-floor building was to have firms that handled general merchandise on the first floor, paying the highest rents, firms doing import-export work on the second floor, firms handling household furniture and furnishings on the third floor, and apparel companies on the fourth floor, with the fifth floor for firms selling miscellaneous items such as drugs, cosmetics, stationery, jewelry, and novelties, paying the lowest rent. Foreign trade bureaus and tourist offices would also be accepted as tenants. However, there were to be no professional firms with attorneys, accountants, architects, or doctors. The preference was to have manufacturing companies that either exported from, or imported to, the United States. The emphasis was on Latin American trade, but countries from all areas of the world were solicited, including Europe and the Far East.[184]

In January 1946, the Mart took out temporary space at 607 Gravier Street in the nearby International Building, the building that would eventually house International House when it opened in the fall of 1946. The Mart rented two offices in the building jointly with Greater New Orleans, Inc., a civic group that promoted growth in the metropolitan area. The rent for the space was $95.84 per month.

Shaw was discharged from the Army in mid-January, 1946. Several days later, Theodore Brent wrote a letter to the Executive Committee of the International Trade Mart announcing that he had hired "Major Clay L. Shaw." He noted that Shaw had just spent two years with the headquarters staff in Britain and France as an aide to General Thrasher in mounting the invasion on D-Day, and in the Department of Supply with headquarters at Rheims, France. Brent mentioned that he had known Shaw for fifteen years, which would put the date of their meeting at approximately 1930 or 1931. He said that Shaw was born and raised in New Orleans (a misstatement that may have been deliberate to give Shaw more local credibility, and has been repeated often over time), and had done publicity and promotional work in New York. Brent went on to say that he knew Shaw's "facility of mind," and had determined to make use of it. He said he had asked Shaw to study the report of the architect-engineers, and Brent's memo concerning the needs and opportunity for the Mart, and that he had asked Shaw to prepare a "line of attack," step by step. Shaw was hired month-to-month, with no guarantee. He was to find, and deal with, potential tenant prospects, and to sell space in the Mart—"a task for which he is admirably suited." Brent went on to assure the board that he personally underwrote the intelligence and vigor of Shaw's effort.[185]

Shaw's first day of work at the Mart was January 21, 1946.[186]. He soon settled into an apartment at 627 St. Ann Street in the French Quarter.[187]

**Shaw with image of International Trade Mart, around 1946 (Courtesy: National Archives)**

**Charles Nutter, Shaw's business counterpart, Managing Director of sister organization International House (International Trade Mart Collection, Louisiana Research Collection, Tulane University)**

The "line of attack" prepared by Shaw, probably with Brent's close supervision, indicated that selling the Mart was in many ways like any other sales job. One needed to decide; (1) What are we selling?, (2) To whom do we sell it?, and (3) What is the best way to do it? It recommended producing a simple brochure, and a cover letter, describing the Mart's purposes, and targeting manufacturers in the New Orleans area who wanted overseas business, manufacturers located outside of New Orleans who wanted overseas business, and manufacturers who wanted to sell in the southern United States, The cover letter should stress the non-profit, civic-minded nature of the project.[188]

From the beginning of his tenure at the Mart, Shaw's duties appeared to cover the management of the entire operation, from finding tenants for the offices, receiving visiting dignitaries, making speeches, writing articles, and generally publicizing the Mart in every way possible, while working within budgetary constraints. The early letters signed by Shaw, in February and March 1946, showed no title for him, but by May, he was signing letters as the Sales Manager. As the building moved closer to opening in 1948, he acquired the title of Managing Director for which he would be best known.

The Mart began to hire lower-level administrative employees right away to help with the massive mailings and lease promotions. Shaw advised the Mart's attorney in February 1946 that it was employing Miss Goldie N. Moore as secretary, at a salary of $150 per month.[189] Moore had lived in St. Louis for several years, and had returned to New Orleans shortly after the war. She was the sister of Irma Lagan, who was Theodore Brent's personal secretary, and Shaw hired Moore on Brent's recommendation.[190] The two sisters had a front-row seat on what is generally considered to be one of the most exciting periods in New Orleans history, certainly on the civic and commercial side of things. Goldie Moore is normally identified as Shaw's secretary, and indeed she occupied that position for more than fifteen years. However, Shaw's personal secretary for the first four years was Mary Catanese, hired around the same time as Moore. During those first four years, Moore functioned more as secretary to Shaw's assistant, J.B. Dauenhauer.

J.B. Dauenhauer, the Assistant Managing Director, handled the accounting of the finances of the Mart, payroll preparation, and general administrative tasks related to everyday problems with tenants. He rarely participated in the numerous social events, such as cocktail parties and receptions for local and foreign groups or individuals. Shaw enjoyed a good working relationship with Dauenhauer for almost twenty years; Dauenhauer was very supportive of Shaw, and respected him as the boss. An early memo indicates that a reporter from *The New Orleans Item* had called wanting pictures of Dauenhauer for an article about him assisting Shaw. Dauenhauer ran the request by Shaw, to make sure there was no problem with it.[191]

According to Andrew Moore, who was a cousin of both Goldie Moore and Irma Lagan, and who interned at the Trade Mart during the summers of 1954 and 1955, Theodore Brent "was well known and active in the business and civic communities but his social life was a complete cipher." Brent never married, and lived with J.B. Dauenhauer, and Dauenhauer's friend, Edgar Lee, in Brent's house on Broadway Street, near the Mississippi River. Over the years, Brent acquired a reputation as being a sort of "Queen Bee" of the New Orleans gay community. He saw to it that his "protégés," including Shaw, J.B. Dauenhauer, and Edgar Lee, were placed in good jobs. For his part, Lee ran a ship's passenger store for the Delta Line ships owned by Mississippi Shipping Company.[192]

Moore recalled that Goldie Moore "always admired and absolutely revered" Shaw. "She tolerated no suggestions about his alleged homosexuality," even long after she knew the rumors to be true.[193] Goldie Moore's refusal to hear about Shaw's sexual orientation mirrored the attitude of many women who knew Shaw over the years. Shaw would occasionally escort quite a number of women on dates, and many either never suspected, or at the very least, quickly dismissed the idea of his homosexuality, even for years after his death.

While some believed years later that they had always known Shaw and Dauenhauer were gay, others who worked at the Mart at the time insist they did not know. Richard Doskey, a student intern during 1949 and 1950, indicated that he did not think it was generally known around the Mart, and that he only learned in 1967, after Shaw's arrest, when there was speculation about the issue in the media and in talk around the city. Doskey said that he never knew that Brent was gay.[194]

Like any organization, the Mart had successes and failures among its early employees. For example, J.B. Dauenhauer remained with the Mart through all of the Shaw years, as did Goldie Moore. Mary Catanese, Shaw's primary secretary for the first four years, also did an excellent job, as did some of the building and maintenance personnel hired later, after the building was finally ready for opening. However, John (Jerry) H. Curtis, who was hired as a sales representative in July 1946, was more of a mixed picture. Curtis, who was let go in the fall of 1947, was originally hired on terms where he would get 2.77% of each three-year lease he closed. He was advanced $75, had to pay his own expenses, and his one-month contract was extended as necessary. He did a mediocre job in securing signed leases, and often wrote Shaw very detailed letters outlining his activities, while producing less than spectacular results. He generally covered the Midwest, including the all-important Chicago area.[195]

The first Mississippi Valley Foreign Trade Conference was held in March 1946. This annual conference (the name would change slightly over the years) would be held in New Orleans throughout Shaw's tenure as Managing Director. The purpose was to bring together all of the players in the international trade arena in New Orleans and the Mississippi Valley area—representatives of shipping companies, manufacturing companies who exported or imported goods, and political and organizational proponents of low tariffs and free trade. Shaw quickly became Secretary to the organization, and served in that capacity for many years.

In March 1946, Shaw summarized to Brent the progress thus far. The Mart had contacted approximately 1,800 firms in New Orleans, seeking the names of customers and suppliers of those firms as potential tenants. It had received 375 individual names, and sent letters to them. In April, the Mart, using other sources, would begin mailing to approximately 12,000 customers and 2,500 suppliers; Shaw estimated that the Mart would probably sell space to one percent of those, after hard work. He proposed to try to attract key firms within an industry, each of whom would then need to staff the space with a "man" who could supervise staff, write strong sales letters, close leases, supervise accounting procedures, and deal with the public. The parent company would need a sales manager and a supporting unit in the home office.[196]

The early promotional letters signed by Clay Shaw in the spring of 1946 indicated that rental rates for the Mart would range from $4.00 to $5.65 per square foot, and that the Mart would be ready as early as June 1947. The letters stressed the non-profit nature of the undertaking, saying that a large portion of the rent in excess of the operational costs would go to advertising to promote the building, and the businesses within. Fifty percent of the lease payments would be used to embellish the premises, up to five percent of the total lease.

Some of the early letters to Shaw in the job address him as "Major Shaw." Shaw continued to use "Major" for his name in some correspondence, and in making hotel and other travel reservations, during at least the first two years after his return in January 1946. Like many returning servicemen, he found that the title perhaps could give one an edge in obtaining hotel rooms, or airline seats or train seats, when facilities were crowded.

The letters indicated that the Mart would consolidate information on Latin America and give it to tenants in a convenient form, possibly a newsletter. Some of the letters in mid-1946 mentioned new airline service from New Orleans to Venezuela via Havana, and to Mexico City. It was mentioned that approximately 100,000 Latins (the term was commonly used for Latinos at that time) were expected to visit New Orleans in 1946 (and presumably thereafter), and that many of them could be expected to visit the International Trade Mart once it opened. It was stressed that "ITM was in no sense an exhibition, exposition, or fair," but was more of a permanent mart used to display goods that could be purchased on site from the various businesses.

*TIME* magazine published a story in early 1946 about the efforts on the part of the City of New Orleans to establish close connections with Latin America. The article contained a profile of the new mayor, deLesseps "Chep" Morrison, then only thirty-four years old, noting that while he did not know Spanish at that time, he intended to learn it.

As early as March 1946, Shaw began to work hard at generating publicity for the Mart—speaking at civic clubs such as Lions Clubs, Rotary Clubs, Kiwanis Clubs, and other organizations in various cities around the Mississippi Valley region, including Chicago, St. Louis, Kansas City, and Memphis, and in New York City. He almost always made a good impression on his listeners, and news of the new institution in New Orleans, whose long-term existence was then still very uncertain, slowly began to spread. With the demand for his time growing, Shaw brought on several sales representatives, including Jerry Curtis and C. Alden Baker, to help him spread the message of the Mart, particularly in the Chicago area.

In giving speeches to local civic organizations and trade organizations in various cities throughout the South and Midwest, Shaw's talks often centered around the topic "New Orleans: The International City." He often received follow-up letters that praised him as having given one of the finest speeches to those organizations in recent memory. Shaw almost always spoke extemporaneously, and it is rare to find a written copy of one of his speeches. Although he often spoke on the same general mix of topics, he was particularly adept at tailoring that mix of topics to the audience before him.

The speaking commitments required a great deal of travel. In later years, Shaw was known as being reluctant to fly; he preferred to take trains, or occasionally drive, although he did not particularly care for driving, either. However, in an early letter to J.B. Dauenhauer, written during a stay in New York City, he commented, "Am flying to Chicago Monday. No more trains!"[197] And, despite the fear, he did fly at least occasionally late in his life. In approximately May 1974, he flew to North Carolina to visit old friends after he knew his health was declining, and the end was near.

Various news media, including *The New York Times*, *TIME*, *The Christian Science Monitor*, and various import/export and business sector publications, ran stories either about International House, the International Trade Mart, or the general effort in New Orleans to promote trade, especially with Latin America. The publication of the Federal Reserve Board of Atlanta also ran a lengthy article, which the Mart reprinted and distributed heavily.

In a sign of the times, in response to its mass promotional mailings, the Mart received a reply from the Post Office in St. Paul, Minnesota, advising it to use the zones of a city in its mailings. The letter stated, "The zone system of addressing mail has come to stay." The zone system divided major cities into separate zones, each with its own number, the inclusion of which on a mailing address would supposedly speed the letter to its destination; it was a predecessor to the zip code system, which would begin to replace it within twenty years.

Although the specific field was new to him, Shaw very quickly settled into the mission of the Mart. In April 1946, he wrote a letter to U.S. Senator Allen Ellender (D-LA), supporting a line of credit to Great Britain and deriding the "lunatic fringe" and "isolationists" who opposed it. He called for liquidation of the "sterling bloc" to restore free and full foreign trade. Shaw indicated that he was for breaking down all trade barriers, and discussed how poor people were in Great Britain at the time, noting that he had been there within the past six months. [198]

On the domestic side, the Mart marketed itself primarily to thirty-one states comprising the Mississippi Valley region, essentially the southern U.S., the Midwest, and some states bordering those regions. Around May 1946, Shaw began a three-month trip through that region to promote the Mart to prospective tenants.[199] Shaw also agreed to be listed as a speaker with several speakers' bureaus,[200] and he attended various conventions of sales executives and marketing managers.

In June 1946, Shaw received an invitation to address the Southern Men's Apparel Club. Sometime later, he received an invitation from the club's president for him and "Mrs. Shaw" to attend a dance at the Roosevelt hotel. Shaw replied that he would be out of town on that night. That set a pattern of sorts that Shaw would follow through the years, of often declining to attend a couples' function, especially if it was specifically noted in the invitation, generally using the excuse that he would be absent from the city, or otherwise occupied, on that date.

Meanwhile, International House was moving along as planned. It had moved into its ten-story building at 607 Gravier Street on June 14, 1945, with the official opening planned for the fall of 1946. Other tenants occupied parts of the building, but International House, with its restaurant, meetings rooms, foreign language translators, and general social atmosphere for visiting businessmen and foreign representatives, quickly established itself as a somewhat unique institution in the city, and perhaps the country as well.

In August 1946, Shaw received an invitation from Mario Bermúdez to speak later that month to a group of Latin American students at International House. Bermúdez, the director of the Latin American Department of International House at the time, was an important figure in Shaw's life during the 1940s, 1950s and 1960s. A Colombian immigrant, he came to the United States during the early 1940s to study hotel management, and quickly moved into international relations in one form or another, first for International House, and later as the Director of International Relations for the City of New Orleans. The Department of International Relations was part of the government of the City of New Orleans. However, one-half of its expenses were paid out of the budget for International House, and one-half by the City of New Orleans. Once the Mart building opened in 1948, its office moved there; the Mart's contribution to its operation was free office space. The Director of International Relations at the time of International House's opening was Raphael J. Urruela, who would resign in 1948 after a scandal; Bermúdez then took his place. For three decades, the charismatic, hard-working Bermúdez would be an important figure in New Orleans' link to the Latin American countries, and to Europe as well, especially Spain. He traveled often to foreign countries, much more so than Shaw did, and he accompanied Shaw on several important trips, including two lengthy trips to the Caribbean and South America in 1949 and 1951, promoting the International Trade Mart and the City of New Orleans.

Bermúdez later would also serve as an important figure in the Cordell Hall Foundation, which operated an exchange program for teachers between the United States and Latin America. He also helped numerous Latin American immigrants become established in New Orleans, and a rather lively permanent community developed, at least partially from those efforts. Many individuals whom the author interviewed who had known Bermúdez expressed their strong belief that he was a bisexual (some claimed to have known it firsthand). As such, he overlapped neatly between the business community and the gay community, something relatively few acquaintances of Clay Shaw did in his compartmentalized life.

Towards the end of August 1946, Shaw noted in a letter to a potential tenant that the reconstruction of the building was beginning in the fall, and that total signed leases represented approximately fifty percent occupancy. A press release toward the end of September 1946 announced that leases totaling a third of a million dollars had been signed for the ITM. It also mentioned that Shaw had just returned from a month's trip to New York City, conferring with industrial and business groups there. The press release referred to the remodeling of the Baldwin Building at Camp and Common Streets, and indicated that the cornerstone laying was planned for International Week in New Orleans, November 14-19, 1946.

Individuals who wrote letters of inquiry about rental space or jobs during that era often referred to their race or religion in the letters, a sign that at least some employers in the area (and in that era) weighed such factors in offering employment. As an example, a letter to New Orleans Public Service, Inc., the main local utility, asking about office space at the Mart, indicated that the writer was a white, unmarried Gentile. Other letters noted that the writer was Catholic, for example; New Orleans has always had a very heavy Catholic population.

During 1946, Shaw first met "Chep" Morrison, who had been elected to the first of four terms as mayor of New Orleans early that year. Shaw's early letters are written to "Mr. Morrison," but very soon he began to address Morrison as "Chep." Morrison had been part of a citywide reform ticket, supported by many of the same businessmen who supported International House and the International Trade Mart. He ousted two-term Mayor Robert Maestri, and promptly joined a unified effort to promote Latin American trade, and to closely tie New Orleans, commercially and culturally, to Latin America.

Shaw also established a regular connection with the Export/Import clinic at the Memphis International Center. W.R. Herstein, President of the organization, and Bess Noble, an employee with the United States Department of Commerce in Memphis, were key participants.

Another important development for New Orleans during 1946 was the opening of Moisant Airport, at that time one of the largest airports in the world. The airport was located about fifteen miles from downtown New Orleans, and greatly expanded facilities beyond what the previous main airport had provided.

With the opening of the new international airport, Brent had urged Shaw to take steps to get an airline terminal in the Mart.[201] Shaw made attempts to interest all the major airlines, including Pan Am, Eastern, Delta, National, Mid-Continent, American, and Chicago and Southern Air Lines. His idea was to have a passenger terminal on the first floor of the Mart, possibly with several or all airlines participating, utilizing trucks to take baggage to the airport, and limousines to transport passengers.[202] In his offer to American Airlines, he noted that most space was intended for manufacturing firms, but that New Orleans needed an air passenger terminal downtown, possibly on one of the lower floors of the Trade Mart.[203]

The New Orleans Foreign Trade Zone charter was granted in September 1946. The authorization to apply for the charter had been given to the Louisiana legislature in 1934, and application had been made to the Foreign Trade Zone's board in 1942. The establishment of a Foreign Trade Zone in New Orleans would allow imported goods to be shipped through the Port of New Orleans on the way to another foreign destination duty-free, and provide an important incentive for ships to use the port.

By the fall, the decision to go forward with the Mart was still uncertain. In September 1946, Shaw wrote to salesman Jerry Curtis that the building was 40% leased; the Board of Directors had hoped that it would be 60% leased by October. However, Shaw thought the Board would go ahead with the project, restore the building, and open the Mart. He praised Curtis for the job he had done, and indicated that if things did not work out, no blame would be placed on him.[204]

By this time, Brent often sought out Shaw's opinion on a variety of things not directly connected with the Mart. In October 1946, Shaw sent a memo to Brent, giving his recommendations for classical music to be played on ships at sea owned by Mississippi Shipping Company, and operated as Delta Line. Interestingly, Shaw noted that he had listed no vocal music because he "knows very little about it and cares less."[205]

Meanwhile, the Mart's sister organization, International House, opened in mid-October 1946. It offered hospitality, a club, meeting rooms, translators, clerical assistance, and a restaurant, all of which was available both for foreign and domestic business visitors. The Thomas F. Cunningham Library, consisting of books and magazines dealing with foreign affairs and international trade-related issues, was located here as well.

New Orleans held an International Week during November 1946 to celebrate the new international thrust of the city, and the formal dedication of International House. Sam Jones, who had served a term as governor of Louisiana during the early 1940s, was the keynote speaker at that dedication. The celebration also gave publicity to the International Trade Mart, which was then in the very early stages of building restoration. It was a hectic, event-packed week that had been planned and promoted for many months, the outgrowth of years of ambition.

As evidence of its importance, Congressman Hale Boggs was a speaker at the ceremony for the Mart. A sign was erected on the Mart building, which was by then undergoing restoration. Twenty-one flags of the various American republics (North, Central, and South America) were displayed, and a bronze plaque was placed on the third floor commemorating the inauguration of construction. A band was hired, and traffic was blocked off. Theodore Brent introduced Boggs, and the United Nations theme was played.[206] After the festivities had passed, Shaw expressed to Jerry Curtis his great relief that it was finally over.[207]

Mark J. Trazivuk, a native of Czechoslovakia who was involved with international shipping interests for much of his life, was appointed Latin American Director of the Mart around this time. During 1945, Trazivuk had consulted with Rudolf Hecht about the proposed International Trade Mart. He knew international trade culture to some degree, and he had earlier worked on a proposed Niagara Falls fair. He had surveyed the national scene for competition, and had proposed some possible names for the new Mart, including Mississippi International Mart, and Southern American International Mart. Trazivuk traveled to Havana, Cuba, in late October 1946 to do promotional work for the Mart, and after his return in late November, he wrote a report to Shaw that detailed his four weeks of marketing effort for the Mart.[208] He also wrote a letter to the *Times-Picayune* about his trip, commenting, among other things, on aviation safety there, and how skilled Cuban pilots were. Trazivuk originally had wanted the job of Managing Director, but the directors decided Shaw was more suitable for that post.[209]

In November 1946, Shaw wrote to *Architectural Forum* magazine, suggesting it publish an article about the building and the organization. He noted that the idea behind the Mart was of a civic-sponsored, non-profit, streamlined trading center, which could house 300 to 400 lines of U.S. manufacturing, and Latin American buyers could find the goods they needed on display.[210] American buyers could also find goods from Latin American in this same location.

Although the cocktail bar in the Mart later became a fixture of New Orleans business social occasions, it was not decided to have a bar in the Mart until sometime after promotional and leasing activity began. T.J. Bradshaw of International House proposed having the bar on the first floor of the Mart, after he initially understood that no airline would be putting a terminal there. Shaw advised Brent that the Mart should consider the idea, if the first floor did not sell out to merchandise-related firms. Brent's position was that a snack bar was needed, but he still wanted to consider whether a real bar was necessary.[211]

As the Mart completed its first full year of promotion, and planning for its eventual opening, many in New Orleans sought to get in on the renovation of the building, and the start-up of operations. Shaw's old friend Muriel Bultman Francis wrote to her parents discussing the idea of having her brother Fritz participate in the interior design of the building. She suggested that her parents call Shaw and arrange a meeting between him and Fritz; she said that she would drop Shaw a note as well. She noted how "personal friendship" and influence played a large part in decisions concerning public projects such as the Mart, and suggested her parents talk to architect Rathbone DeBuys and the engineering firm of Godat and Heft, along with "Shaw's boss," whose name she could not recall. She said the "home town boy" was the angle they should be pushing for her brother.[212]

Although the Mart was able to close many leases, and the general progress was a forward one, as 1946 ended it became obvious that the original planned opening date of mid-1947 was not going to be achieved. Letters written in late 1946 noted that the opening of the Mart was now set for October 1947, even though the Mart was more than fifty percent leased by the end of 1946.

As 1946 came to a close, Shaw could take pride in the fact that the Mart was moving toward restoration and that it was approximately half-leased. Construction had finally begun by the end of the year. He took the opportunity to relax in the warm New Orleans weather, laying out on his balcony and sunbathing during the period shortly before Christmas. He penned a note of thanks to Jerry Curtis for the fruitcake Curtis had sent him.[213]

After having been in New York City since 1935, in New Orleans only briefly, and then in the Army for more than three years, Shaw was able to re-connect with many of his old acquaintances from the Le Petit Theatre days. One of those was Louis Fischer, the stage designer and bookstore owner who held regular gatherings of French Quarter residents, artists, and other assorted characters; some thought of Fischer as the "Gertrude Stein of New Orleans." Among others, Shaw met Terry Flettrich, a cute, Russian-born woman who would soon become one of New Orleans first television personalities. He also met Chris Blake, who would become a longtime New Orleans chef, playwright and restaurateur.

Sometime during 1946, Shaw met Arthur Jefferson "Jeff" Biddison, who would become a close friend for the rest of his life. Some stories have Shaw meeting Biddison in Lafitte's Blacksmith Shop, a prominent bar in the French Quarter that catered to both gay and straight clientele. Biddison supposedly was a rough-cut Oklahoma boy who wore cowboy boots, and whose father, Valjean Biddison, had been a judge back in Oklahoma who had presided over some of the judicial proceedings which followed the 1921 race riots in Tulsa. It was said that New Orleans had "opened his eyes" to a free-wheeling sexual lifestyle for which he had yearned, but had never experienced before.

Biddison and Shaw soon roomed together, and would be essentially a couple for the next half-decade. During this era, both Shaw and Biddison would often escort young women on dates to social functions. Sometimes they would take turns escorting the same woman; if Shaw were out of town, Biddison would do the honors. But their true interests lay elsewhere.

# 4 · Promotion Continues for the International Trade Mart

The second Mississippi Valley Trade Conference was held in January 1947, in New Orleans, and Shaw was an active participant, speaking or moderating panel discussions. He was also active in welcoming out-of-town participants, and was on his way to becoming a familiar figure in Mississippi Valley trade circles for the next nineteen years.

In early 1947, he is shown living at 1014 Royal Street, and his occupation is listed as manager at the International Trade Mart.[214] On January 14, 1947, Shaw filled out an application for some type of unidentified service or product, most likely a life insurance policy. On the application, he gave the value of his estate as $5,000.[215] That estate value would grow considerably over the next twenty years, although there is some debate about exactly how much Shaw's net worth was at the time of his arrest.

Also in January 1947, Shaw made a claim for compensation due to his back injury during physical training during the war. The claim listed his birth date as March 17, 1915, rather than 1913, his height as 6'4", and his weight at 200 pounds. The claim indicated that his service had begun at Fort Dix, New Jersey, on November 6, 1942, and he had continued as an enlisted man until August 3, 1943, when he received his officer's commission as a second lieutenant at Camp Barkley, Texas. He served as an officer of increasing rank until his discharge at Fort Monmouth, New Jersey, as part of the General Staff Corps (Demobilization) on January 15, 1946. In his claim, he attributed the nature of his injury as a crushed spinal cartridge inflicted in March 1943.[216] Shaw's claim was ultimately denied by the Army.

Although the leadership of the Mart was anxious to have a building full of tenants as soon as possible, it rejected some that did not fit the initial standard. For example, businesses that were not willing to have a sales representative present in their spaces at all times were rejected. It was the intention of the Mart leadership that a visitor should be able actually to purchase the goods on site, rather than having to order them from a distant location. Additionally, a certain number of spaces were held in the hopes that foreign consulates, foreign tourist associations, and foreign trade groups, primarily from Latin American and European countries, could be accommodated if they decided to lease at a date closer to the opening of the Mart.

Cecil Shilstone was an early investor in the Mart. In a letter in late February, Shaw acknowledged receipt of the money Shilstone had sent for purchase of bonds.[217] Almost exactly twenty years later, Shilstone would be one of three major private contributors to New Orleans District Attorney Jim Garrison's investigation into the Kennedy assassination, which would result in Shaw's arrest on conspiracy charges.

Some Mart backers feared confusion among the general public about the various roles of the Mart, International House and other international facilities in New Orleans. In late February 1947, Shaw wrote to Herman Deutsch, a prominent columnist for the *Item*, the afternoon newspaper, asking him to write either a column or an editorial delineating the various organizations for the general public's information; Shaw mentioned that local businessman Clem Bernard had mentioned to him recently that he had talked to Deutsch about the same issue.[218]

**Shaw at front door of International Trade Mart, probably pre-opening, 1946-48
(International Trade Mart Collection, Louisiana Research Collection, Tulane University)**

Although the Mart used form letters to market itself to prospective tenants, individual inquiries were usually answered in an individualized fashion. It was evident that Shaw took the task very seriously, attempting to answer even the most arcane and unusual questions about international trade, the purpose of the Mart, and the reasons why a prospective tenant should lease space in the Mart.

Whenever the Mart would receive a letter inquiring about specific products, including raw materials or finished goods, or information about, for example, a specific Latin American country, it generally would refer the inquiry to the World Trade Development Department at its sister organization, International House. This was partly because International House was already open and functioning, whereas the Mart was in the early stages of building restoration, but also partly because of a delineation in function between the two organizations. That distinction was not always clear, however, and in later years the lack of clarity would lead to a lengthy, and somewhat heated, conflict between the two organizations. Although the founders of International House overlapped with the founders of International Trade Mart, each organization had its own set of directors, bondholders, and members, and over time the two groups would begin to grow apart.

As remodeling progressed on the building, the Mart Realty Company was dissolved and the International Trade Mart continued its pre-opening activities. Bank accounts were opened in its name, and Shaw was trusted enough to be given signature authority, along with Theodore Brent, Herbert Schwartz, and Kenneth Barranger, the Mart's attorney.

In March 1947, Shaw received a letter from Clarence E. Becker, in response to one of the Mart's promotional letters. Becker was with the Gulfport Shipping Company in Gulfport, Mississippi, but had apparently been stationed at the Pentagon during the war. He commented that the last time he had seen Shaw was in Becker's office at the Pentagon, when Shaw was back on one of his trips from overseas.[219] Some newspaper articles around the time of the opening of the International Trade Mart indicated that Shaw had come back to Washington from France after the war in Europe ended, in order to assist in the writing and editing of a film for the Army. That portion of his resume was omitted in almost every account of his background during the years to follow, although it appears in at least one early resume that may have been distributed.

Another reference to Shaw's returning to the United States, and Washington in particular, is in Gordon Berger's self-published account of their days in Southern Base Section and Oise Section during World War II. As mentioned earlier, James Brugger, who served with Shaw and Berger, recalled that the purpose of Shaw's trip was to participate in a film about the Red Ball Express, the system of truck convoys used by the Allies to supply eastward movement troops in Europe after D-Day.

While Shaw had started his post as Sales Manager in early 1946 at a salary of $7,000, he was given the position of General Manager and Assistant Secretary to the Board of Directors for the period from April 1, 1947 to April 1, 1948. His new salary was $10,000 per year. It was a very decent salary for those days, almost three times what his salary had been with Lee Keedick in late 1942, and would partially account, along with his forward-thinking real estate investments in the French Quarter, for Shaw's dramatic increase in wealth during the next two decades.

Theodore Brent continued to advise Shaw, although he seemed to give him somewhat of a free hand in directing the Mart's daily progress. There is no direct evidence that Shaw and Brent were ever involved physically, although Brent was known to make not-so-subtle advances to eligible young men who dropped by the Trade Mart to see Shaw and J.B. Dauenhauer. One such prospect told the author that Brent had a method of sitting beside a young man, dropping his hand down to the person's leg and making a covert gesture beneath the table. Shaw and Dauenhauer sometimes felt it necessary to warn unsuspecting young men about the potential advances of the fatherly figure they referred to as "Ole Miss," a play on words referencing Brent's role with Mississippi Shipping Company.

The determination of the Mart founders, especially Theodore Brent, to hold bondholder pledges very seriously was illustrated by an incident in May 1947. Victor H. Elsas passed away after committing to buy $2,000 worth of bonds in the Mart. When Shaw wrote to Jason Elsas, Victor's son, seeking to confirm the commitment, the family at first refused to do so, indicating that Victor Elsas had passed away. Shaw showed the response to Brent, and suggested that perhaps the Mart should abandon that avenue. Brent questioned that strategy, saying that he did not understand why the Elsas family could not purchase the bonds, as the family had "plenty of money." Shaw persevered, writing Jason Elsas and asking him to honor the commitment.[220] Jason Elsas first answered that the estate of Victor Elsas would honor the commitment, but shortly thereafter Victor Elsas's widow, Bertha, engaged the family attorney, Monte Lemann, of the prestigious firm of Monroe and Lemann, to intervene. Lemann conferred with Herbert Schwartz, one of the Mart's three main founders, who advised that there would be no criticism of the family if it did not honor the commitment to purchase the bonds. Lemann then wrote to Bertha Elsas, urging her to forget about the bond purchase commitment, copying Shaw on the letter,[221] and that seemed to be the end of the matter. As a sidelight to the whole affair, Shaw advised Jason Elsas on May 20th that the bond issue had not yet been oversubscribed, and that it still needed bond subscribers to finance the Mart. However, in a letter to J.F. Odenheimer, President of the Lane Cotton Mills Company, on May 7, 1947, Shaw said that the bond issue of $550,000 had been oversubscribed, with pledges of $610,000.[222]

Shaw established good relations with the New Orleans media, and indeed with most of the media personnel he dealt with. WDSU-TV had been offered space in the Mart when the television station first opened, but the station owners and management decided to open their own building. The main newspapers in New Orleans, the *Times-Picayune*, the *Item*, and the *States*, as well as various radio outlets, were marketed by Shaw for publicity related to the continuing progress of the Mart.

By mid-1947, promotional letters from the Mart began to indicate that the opening was projected for early to mid-1948. Approximately two-thirds of the space had been leased by mid-1947, but there were still units of from 300 to 1,000 square feet available. Some of the letters indicated that increases in building and labor costs during the early period of restoration had necessitated increased financing, and thus delayed construction.

Kenneth Barranger handled the legal work for the Mart. During 1946, the first full year of pre-opening activity, he earned a fee of $150 per month. Beginning in January 1, 1948, he received $100 per month, as much of the legal work related to the start-up had disappeared. He also generated additional fees related to specific tasks during the period 1945 through 1948, including, for example, an invoice in August 1947 that included $5,000 of legal fees and $1,451.90 in expenses. Legal fees were charged to the building until August 1948, then were charged to operating income and netted against revenues. Barranger handled incorporation issues, legislation issues, and tax issues, and also handled employee issues dealing with garnishment of wages or termination. He would serve as the Mart's counsel until his resignation in 1962, shortly after fellow attorney Lloyd Cobb became President.

In 1947, Shaw met with representatives of the Chicago Merchandise Mart to inquire about early promotional material and methods used for that venture. The Mart had largely used the Chicago Merchandise Mart, partly owned by Joseph P. Kennedy, father of President Kennedy, as an inspiration for its own project.

Shaw began to be one of the points of contact for many people interested in promoting the state of Louisiana. For example, in August 1947, he received a letter from Caye A. Nelson, Industrial Agent for the state government. The letter noted the approaching opening of the Mart, and it also mentioned the upcoming 150th anniversary of the Louisiana Purchase between the U.S. and France, which would occur in 1953. Nelson noted that Louisiana should start early on a project to celebrate the anniversary, as St. Louis had beaten New Orleans to the punch on the 100th anniversary in 1903.[223]

The architect of the building restoration was Rathbone DeBuys, and the engineering firm was Godat and Heft. Godat, Heft and DeBuys had inspected the old Baldwin building in June 1945, as part of the initial exploration of whether the building could be turned into the Mart. Over the next three years, until the opening of the Mart, there were the usual disputes and disagreements related to change orders, delays in construction, costs, and interior design. Shaw wrote to Godat related to changes in tenant layouts, indicating that such changes should not delay completion, that the Mart should be charged a fair and reasonable rate for such new construction, and should receive a fair credit for deleted walls.[224] Although Shaw could be particular about costs, he allowed Godat to travel to Nashville marble quarries to inspect a particular type of marble there.[225]

There were ego issues with which to contend throughout this process. For example, the prominent architect, Rathbone DeBuys, complained that his name had been left out of a news release announcing the start of remodeling.[226] There is no record that Shaw responded in writing to the complaint.

Other issues cropped up periodically. Shaw noted to Godat and Heft that the City architect had classified the building as a collection of stores rather than as an office building. That could have affected zoning issues, and city regulation issues, and Shaw said that he hoped that could be changed.[227]

Although the Mart sought to establish relations with foreign countries, particularly

Latin America, it was decided early on that local consular offices would not be allowed space in the building, but that instead space should be limited to firms and entities with a more commercial bent. Shaw found it necessary to reiterate this point in a letter to the Consul General of Argentina, in a letter prior to the opening of the Mart.[228] The policy, however, was later revised, in the interest of getting more foreign tenants into the building.

The original leases had called for occupancy on October 1, 1947, but with the delays in construction, money had to be refunded to tenants who canceled because the building was not ready. Leases could be sold by a canceling tenant to another prospective tenant. The first mortgage money to finance operations could not be touched until sufficient three-year non-cancelable leases were in place. Although the original plan was to sign only five-year initial leases at the stated highest rental rates, both the lease term and the price per square foot were softened in order to obtain enough tenants to access that financing.

In a memo to Brent in early October 1947, Shaw discussed the status of the Mart, writing, "I feel it wise to get our domestic lease situation well in hand and to sign up firm leases well over the $600,000 figure which is the break-even point before we begin any serious and sustained effort to bring Latin American tenants into the building."[229]

Shaw continued his speaking engagements throughout 1947, speaking in places such as Columbus, Ohio, Columbus, Georgia, Brookhaven, Mississippi, and Memphis, Tennessee, and in front of organizations such as the Fort Worth Export/Import Club, Columbus, Ohio Advertising Club, Memphis Rotary Club, and Brookhaven, Mississippi Lions Club. The topics included "Foreign Trade and the International Trade Mart" and "Economic Interdependence between the United States and Latin America."

Salesman Jerry Curtis was dismissed in the fall of 1947, primarily because his efforts had produced few actual leases.[230] After his termination, Curtis wrote a letter to Shaw, thanking him for his courteous treatment during and after Curtis's employment. That set another pattern in Clay Shaw's life—remaining on good terms with most people, even under somewhat adversarial conditions. It was rare for someone to have personal animosity toward Clay Shaw, and that lack of animosity helped to form a bedrock of support for him during more troubling times. Sometime after Curtis left, it was learned that he had passed a bad personal check to a hotel in Milwaukee while working for the Mart,[231] and had wound up serving a prison term.

The Mart employed several Latinos to help secure leases from firms and organizations in Latin America and the Caribbean. Its representative in Mexico, Victor Ortiz Campillo, submitted his reports in Spanish, which would then have to be translated. Rafael "Rae" Ordorica, another representative, had a business, Hemisphere Promotion Company, located in La Paz, Bolivia. From 1947 to 1949, he worked for a $12,000 annual salary, plus expenses, to represent a combination of organizations, including the Mart, the City of New Orleans, International House, and the Port of New Orleans throughout Latin America.

Such cooperation among the organizations was typical during that era. The alignment between major business interests, the city and the port gave New Orleans a unified front that would last for a number of years.

The Mart used other representatives to market it in Latin America as well, including a J.W. Ormond, whose name appears, then quickly disappears, from the records.[232] After Mark Trazivuk's efforts in Cuba, the Mart utilized the services of New Orleanian Pierre Villere in an attempt to obtain leases from Cuban entities. Shaw traveled to Cuba himself in 1947, as part of that effort to interest Cuban businessmen and trade organizations to take space in the Mart.[233]

Shaw's early biographical fact sheets distributed by the Mart indicate that he was born in New Orleans, but this is contradicted by other evidence that he was born in Kentwood, Louisiana, and moved to New Orleans at the age of five. Most versions of his biography mention him living in New York City from late 1935 or early 1936, and going directly into the Army for World War II in late 1942, returning to New Orleans in January 1946.

Some more detailed biographies circulated by the Mart during this time refer to Shaw as a native of New Orleans; other versions said that he was born in Kentwood, Louisiana. Some of the biographies indicated that he was born on Saint Patrick's Day, March 17, 1913. The ones that indicated that he was born in Kentwood, Louisiana, often indicated that he had moved to New Orleans at age five. Some of the biographies mentioned his time in New York City during the 1930s and early 1940s. Generally, the official version was what follows below, and it offers an interesting look into how some of the earlier details of his life were catalogued at this later point.

He had worked as a claims agent for Western Union Company, first in New Orleans, then in New York City in the midtown region, managing approximately forty branch offices. He left Western Union in 1937 to do freelance publicity and public relations work, then moved to the Lee Keedick agency, handling such speakers as Frances Perkins, Secretary of Labor under President Franklin Roosevelt, Harold Ickes, Franklin P. Adams, the actor Maurice Evans, William Beebe, Admiral Harry Yarnell, and Sir Phillip Gibbs. The biographies often quote Shaw as saying that, "I got awfully tired of celebrities."

Shaw then served under General Charles Thrasher in the Army during World War II, as part of a large supply unit that directed supplies to troops for the D-Day invasion in June 1944, and later supplied advancing troops in Belgium, Luxembourg, and Northern France, including those in the First, Third, and Ninth Armies. The bios say that Shaw received a Bronze Star for his part in moving the $82^{nd}$ and $101^{st}$ Airborne Divisions into combat in record time at the time of the German breakthrough in Ardennes. When General Thrasher's staff formed a secondary position in the face of the German attack along the Meuse River, Shaw was then awarded the Croix de Guerre by the French government, and the Legion of Merit by the U.S. Army. Most of the later biographical summaries issued by the Mart condensed the information about his Army service to a minimum.

The issue of the particular medals awarded to Clay Shaw during his World War II military service has never been completely clarified. Some biographies have him being awarded the World War II Victory Medal, the Legion of Merit, the Croix du Guerre and the Bronze Star. The only official summary of Shaw's military record available today shows only the World War II Victory Medal, awarded to many soldiers of that era. It is possible he received the Croix du Guerre from the French government as a result of being in his position as a chief aide to General Charles Thrasher, who was importantly positioned at Rheims, France, in close proximity to President Eisenhower's command headquarters. The author has found no independent verification that Shaw received the Bronze Star, which would arguably be the highest medal listed among the ones normally associated with his name.

The biographies went on to state that Shaw then decided to make his residence in New Orleans, and that he had to sell the space in the Mart with nothing but floor plans and architects' drawings to show to potential tenants. Shaw was sometimes quoted as saying that selling the actor Maurice Evans reading Shakespeare at $2,000 per night was easy by comparison to selling space for the entire Mart building. Some of the early biographies mentioned that, when speaking of New Orleans being in competition with other cities for business through the port, Shaw would say that when he visited other port cities, he was often made to feel like a combination "Fifth Columnist and Trojan Horse." As an example of such treatment, one of the early versions of his biography mentioned that, in a recent appearance on radio in New York, he was introduced by host Tex McCrary as "an enemy within our gates."

While he was working during the start-up period for the Mart, Shaw completed his play, *Memorial,* which would have a short run in New Orleans at the end of 1948. Shaw never got the desire to be a playwright out of his blood, although by 1950 he had abandoned such activities in any meaningful sense for at least the following decade.

The Mart used the local Bauerlein Advertising Agency as its main outside source for promotions and public relations. The firm helped to design brochures, printed some of the Mart's promotional materials, and assisted with publicity in trade publications, newspapers, direct mail campaigns, and export journals. The firm was awarded a budget of $25,000 for the period from December 1, 1947 through April 30, 1948.

Even before the Mart had opened, the potential competition from other cities was looming. In December 1947, Hecht wrote to Shaw about Miami's efforts to build a 21-story building for Latin American Trade. In a response to Hecht, Shaw dismissed the idea, saying that Miami had little to offer besides an airline passenger terminal.[234] As 1947 ended, the Mart opening may have been somewhat behind schedule, but there was comfort that surely 1948 would see the results of the hard work and planning of the past two years.

# 5 · The Trade Mart Opens

The first half of 1948 saw ongoing marketing efforts, as Shaw continued to speak around the Southeast and Midwest. There were also meetings with contractors and subcontractors to discuss the continuing restoration issues. The Mart insisted on a certain uniformity of design among the tenant spaces. Some of the rooms at the new Mart were painted in powder blue and bright yellow shades, while others were painted in oyster white. The leadership at the Mart continued to hold firm in its decision not to lease space to certain types of businesses. Rudolf Hecht reiterated this in a letter to Colonial Trust Company, a financial company.[235]

Meanwhile, International House continued in a coordinated effort with the City of New Orleans regarding various functions to promote the city. For example, in January 1948, James G. Aldige, Jr., with Public Relations for the City of New Orleans, wrote to Shaw about the press headquarters, located at International House, that had been set up related to Mardi Gras festivities.[236]

Another sales representative employed by the Mart during its pre-opening period was John B. Erskine in the Chicago area. His employment agreement was drafted in early March 1948.[237] After a couple months of relatively little activity, Shaw wrote advising him to make personal calls, and to not rely solely on direct mail, commenting that some contacts sign immediately, whereas others take six to eight months.[238] Shaw further advised that the Mart firmly insisted on at least three-year leases, as Erskine had inquired about tenants who wanted a shorter term.[239] The agreement with Erskine was canceled by mid-1948, after little success.[240] In April 1949, Erskine wrote inquiring whether any of the tenants currently in the Mart had been signed by him; he had apparently reviewed a list of tenants and recognized some of the names as companies upon which he had supposedly called.[241]

The Mart also made use of businessmen traveling to Latin America to help spread information about the organization. One such person was Robert H. Brown of Illinois Central Railway, who traveled to Central America in 1948, carrying a letter from Theodore Brent establishing him as an unofficial representative of the Mart.

Although the Mart had initially planned, as International House did, to require dues for members, the Board of Directors reversed that decision in March 1948, prior to the opening, because of the difficulty of enforcing such a requirement.

In late March 1948, Shaw wrote a long memo to Brent related to the Mart's opening, with his suggestions about how to make it a lively, functional, successful operation. He suggested hiring a Public Relations Director, using direct mail to continue reaching prospective tenants, and customers of those tenants, bringing businessmen from other cities to New Orleans, gathering tenants' stories and suggestions into Mart literature, and holding model exhibits and seasonal shows.[242]

During April 1948, there was an uprising in Mario Bermúdez's country of Colombia, which began after the assassination of a presidential candidate and included riots in Bogotá. The chaos spread throughout the country, and claimed almost 200,000 lives. The CIA, newly formed in the United States, was rumored to have some involvement in the activity. A newspaper column published on April 21, 1948 by noted writer Walter Lippman discussed the issue of what the CIA knew or did not know; Lippman gave his view that the role of an intelligence agency like the CIA was to analyze information, most of which was not secret, rather than to engage in covert activities. It was an issue that would come up time and again in the CIA's history.

At the same time that Colombia was in turmoil, the third Mississippi Valley World Trade Conference was held at the Roosevelt hotel in New Orleans. Shaw again participated in moderating or speaking at panel discussions, and used the conference as an opportunity to continue to promote the upcoming opening of the Mart.

An article in the *Wall Street Journal* in late April 1948 discussed New Orleans's continuing efforts to attract international trade through its port. The article discussed the Mart, described as a five-story windowless structure, and it indicated that Belgium had already taken offices in the building. The piece also discussed International House, its unique ten-story building, and its World Trade Development Department, which coordinated efforts to induce companies to export and import goods through New Orleans.[243]

As of May 1948, Shaw was continuing with his standard collection of speaking topics throughout most major cities in the Mississippi Valley region. When requests were made for an advance transcript of his speech, Shaw politely advised that he always spoke extemporaneously, but he sometimes provided a statement that gave the essential points of his speech. Those points usually included discussions of the soon-to-be opened International Trade Mart, International House and its activities, airlines' hubs and routes that impacted New Orleans, the proposed Tidewater Channel that would link New Orleans directly with the Gulf of Mexico without ships having to traverse the entire length of the Mississippi River south of New Orleans, and the Free Trade Zone at the Port of New Orleans, which allowed goods to be shipped to, and stored or displayed in, the city, then sold to customers in the inland United States without them having to pay import duties.

In May 1948, Roy Bartlett, an employee of the Roosevelt hotel, wrote to Shaw suggesting that Theodore Brent should be honored for his general civic-mindedness, a service that Bartlett felt had gone unrecognized.[244] Indeed, Brent is little remembered since his death in 1953, although at one time he was one of the most important business leaders in the city.

Interest in the Mart, which had been high even in the 1945-46 period when it had first been publicized, continued among some of the newspaper and magazine writers who anticipated its 1948 opening. Charles T. Taylor, senior economist with the Federal Reserve Bank in Atlanta, had written an article in 1946 about the idea for the International Trade Mart in its infancy. Late in 1948, he inquired how things were going since the Mart had opened.[245] Shaw answered that the article Taylor had written for one of the Federal Reserve Board publications had been useful in promoting the Mart, which had distributed thousands of copies of the article during the previous two years.

Shaw was by now in regular contact with officials representing, in some fashion, almost every Latin American country. In May 1948, the Consul General of Bolivia invited Shaw to a meeting at International House to discuss the possibility of New Orleans businessmen attending an international fair in La Paz, Bolivia.

On May 31, the Mart received its official street address—124 Camp Street. The total cost to restore the building had exceeded $1,000,000, with an additional amount in excess of $100,000 for the architect/engineering fees.

Shortly before the opening of the Mart, Shaw opened a charge account for the Mart at Antoine's Restaurant in New Orleans.[246] At the time, Antoine's was probably the most famous restaurant associated with New Orleans. The income and prominence that his job at the Mart gave to Shaw allowed him to regularly patronize, not only Antoine's, but later Brennan's and other fine restaurants through New Orleans, a practice that he would continue for the rest of his life.

Shaw was continuing to handle various problems, and their related details, as the opening approached. In mid-June, he wrote to architect Rathbone DeBuys, referring to a recent meeting and conversations they had had about mismatched marble in the passageway between the vestibule and the elevator lobby. Shaw indicated that he had tried to avoid "just this situation," and that, "Speaking as representative of the owner," it was his position that the marble quarry had assumed that the Mart had been pressured for time and would be forced to accept the mismatched marble. Shaw said that, "Recriminations at this stage can serve no useful purpose," but it was "a wretched situation caused by serious failure of supervision." Shaw closed by saying that he understood the job would be properly completed by July 1, "to spare the owner embarrassment on opening day."[247]

As the Mart approached its opening date, some of Shaw's letters took a more urgent tone with potential tenants, advising them of a lower percentage of remaining space than he sometimes advised the Board of Directors. He also found it necessary to emphasize that the Mart would have no sales staff of its own to help sell goods, but that the individual merchant would need to have staff on hand, so that potential customers could purchase the goods at the Mart. Goods were not to be simply put on display to be ordered from a remote location.

**Front view of International Trade Mart (International Trade Mart Collection, Louisiana Research Collection, Tulane University)**

As New Orleans prepared to bask in the glory of the Mart's long-awaited opening, one of the more unfortunate dilemmas of the era was captured in a letter from Dorothy M. Blackman of Columbus, Ohio, to Mayor Chep Morrison. In the letter, she complained about the racial segregation in streetcar seating that she had witnessed during her June 1948 visit. Morrison replied diplomatically but without apology, indicating that the laws of the State of Louisiana required such a system. Morrison later ran several times for governor of Louisiana, and during his last run in 1963, he campaigned on a civil rights platform.

On June 30, 1948, NBC broadcast a story about the opening of the Mart. Famed newscaster John Cameron Swayze, NBC's first television news anchor, mentioned that he had interviewed Clay Shaw, who had indicated to him that seventy cents out of every dollar of New Orleans' income came, directly or indirectly, through the Port of New Orleans.[248] Swayze would anchor the evening news at NBC until the mid-1950s, when Chet Huntley and David Brinkley took over. Swayze was perhaps more famous for a set of commercials for Timex watches that he made over a period of two decades.

The Mart opened on July 1, 1948, although the official grand opening took place some months afterward. The Mart building was open to visitors from 9:00 a.m. to 5:00 p.m., Monday to Friday, and 9:00 a.m. to noon on Saturday. The Mart was approximately 75% leased as of the date of opening. Even though the official opening of the Mart was months away, local media all highlighted the unofficial opening in July 1948. Each major New Orleans newspaper ran a special insert section, with detailed stories about all aspects of the Mart, Shaw, and the key men behind the project. Articles about the Mart's opening also appeared in many newspapers and magazines nationwide, including the *New York Herald Tribune* and in *Newsweek* magazine. The building opened with features that were somewhat modern at the time. In addition to the elaborate air conditioning system, the Mart was outfitted with a brand new sprinkler system.

Many of the local foreign consuls participated in the opening of the Mart. The flags of various countries were raised on the roof of the Mart, and would continue to fly there from that point forward.

In the midst of the opening of International Trade Mart in 1948, Raymond Moley, a former member of President Franklin Roosevelt's "Brain Trust," and a liberal turned conservative, wrote a column that discussed both the Mart and International House, and the goals of both organizations. The column mentioned the oppressiveness of the Huey Long regime in Louisiana some years before, and how the Long family had made a comeback with the recent election of Huey's brother Earl Long as governor. Moley also discussed activity in New Orleans during the war to promote international trade, and to begin the Mart and International House, and the reform regime under Chep Morrison, who had been elected in 1946.

Upon the opening of the Mart, it hired a Public Relations Director, John Leonard. Among his immediate functions was to begin a newsletter for tenants. The newsletter contained information about events at the building, tenant requests, questions about building policies, information related to exporters and importers with goods to sell, and to requests by mail or phone about specific types of goods or services. The newsletters, which appeared weekly when first launched, were mostly put together from either news clippings, or from letters from readers of the newsletter, some of whom were tenants, but others of whom had an international connection and received the newsletter courtesy of the Mart.

Local and out-of-town groups began to visit the Mart immediately after it opened, and Shaw, Leonard or J.B. Dauenhauer would show them around the building, and explain the purpose behind the organization. Many of the groups were high-schoolers from various parts of Louisiana, making a day trip to New Orleans. Others were from further away, such as the visiting group of students from the University of Notre Dame. Shaw had been advised of their visit by Greater New Orleans, Inc., a prominent civic organization, and had written them a letter offering to give a tour.

By mid-1948, Shaw was still living at 1014 Royal Street.[249] With his relatively large salary and position of authority, he was soon able to begin investing in real property, and living in more prominent space.

Shaw attended a press party for Chicago and Southern Airlines, given at International House to commemorate the inaugural flight from New Orleans to Venezuela.[250] He also addressed a group of visiting Latin American students, at the invitation of Mario Bermúdez, who at that time still signed himself as the Director of the Latin American Department of International House.[251]

Among the early tenants of the Mart was a company called Latin American Reports. The weekly reports were edited by William G. Gaudet, a former State Department employee who had an interest in Latin America. Much later, Gaudet's name would surface in several connections with the Kennedy assassination, and with Shaw's possible involvement in it. Gaudet was developed as a CIA connection in the late 1940s, and periodically provided the CIA with information gathered about specific countries in Latin America. He was reimbursed for his costs, but was not paid any additional compensation for his services. He was never employed by the agency, nor did he ever have a hand in covert operations.

Meanwhile, Shaw continued to speak around the Southeast and Midwest, and attend international trade-related conferences in other cities. He attended the Mid-Continent World Trade Council in Cedar Rapids, Iowa, and the Export-Import Conference in Memphis, Tennessee. He also spoke to the Joseph A. Maybin Import-Export Institute, a New Orleans training facility that had opened after World War II for students and businessmen interested in the subject of international trade.

The Mart received an interesting inquiry in July 1948: a letter from local businessman Louis Boasberg, written to Shaw, about South American buyers for pinball machines.[252] In June 1971, Boasberg was arrested, along with New Orleans District Attorney Jim Garrison, on fraud and racketeering charges related to kickbacks from pinball machine operators to the district attorney.

A local stenographer, Helen Dietrich, proposed putting a stenographic service in the Mart; she later decided against doing so, because of cost, and because she didn't have the right person to staff it.[253] More than twenty years later, as a court reporter, Helen Dietrich would secure the job of providing major portions of the official transcript for Clay Shaw's trial on conspiracy charges related to the assassination of President Kennedy.

In addition to promoting the Mart through speeches in other states, Shaw constantly spoke before local groups, and at conventions held in New Orleans, as well. Examples of those included speeches to the New Orleans Credit Men's Association, the National Sanitary Supply Association regional meeting, the first New Orleans Area Sales Conference, and to the Women's Committee of New Orleans Public Service, Inc.

Although one of the main purposes of the Mart was to reach out to foreign nations, especially those in Latin America, early on it was noted how difficult it was to interest foreign merchants and foreign government agencies in taking out space.[254] This set a pattern that would prevail over the years; most of the space was taken by individual American businesses of varying sizes. For whatever reason, foreign governments, while always on a friendly basis with the Mart, seemed to prefer space in other buildings in New Orleans. Sometimes, they were able to get more favorable rental rates, and they also could be positioned closer to U.S. government agencies located in other buildings.

Some of the tenants who had leased space in the Mart upon its opening had already fallen behind in payments by the fall of that year. Knowing that the Mart had more demand for space than supply, Shaw was firm in dealing with tenants who fell behind, immediately sending them telegrams threatening suit for nonpayment.

Since 1946, Shaw had formed close working associations with Charles Nutter, Managing Director at International House, effectively Shaw's counterpart at that organization, and Richard B. Swenson, Public Relations Director with the Board of Commissioners of the Port of New Orleans. Years later, after Shaw's arrest, both men would give behind-the-scenes accounts of their knowledge of Shaw to a representative of *LIFE* magazine, Holland McCombs, who led an effort within the magazine to head off further cooperation with Jim Garrison's probe into the Kennedy assassination.

Shaw also participated directly in International House activities. In the fall of 1948, Shaw was appointed to the Information Committee of International House.[255] He also attended an International House reception for visiting Miami, Florida businessmen, and was invited to serve on the Steering Committee of the World Trade Development Committee of the organization.

Since taking his initial position with the Trade Mart in early 1946, Shaw's speeches and other promotional activities had made him a popular civic figure locally. In August 1948, he was asked to serve as a judge at the Miss New Orleans contest held at Ponchartrain Beach. The winner was Barbara Jean "Bobby Jean" Floyd, whom Shaw had a direct hand in choosing. Six months later, while on a trip to South America, the publicity-minded Miss Floyd would marry a pilot, George Cauthen, in Colombia, and engage in a series of highly public incidents, including fights, whether real or faked, with her new husband, and the marriage would be annulled during 1949. The spectacle would reach its zenith while Shaw was on his own lengthy trip to South America during the spring of 1949, and indirectly cause a bump in his own celebrity status on the trip.

By this time, most people referred to Shaw simply as Clay Shaw. However, he still received an occasional letter addressed to Lavergne Shaw. One such letter was from W.M. Russell, Industrial Manager of the Lincoln County Chamber of Commerce in Brookhaven, Mississippi, who had been referred by Robert Lee Jones, a relative of Shaw in that area.

Rudolf Hecht, perhaps the most influential person in the organization after Theodore Brent, was a frequent world traveler. Hecht dictated detailed accounts of many of his trips, and had them distributed to friends, employees and other businessmen. One such trip was the one he made to Africa and Europe in 1948. Many of his trips, including that one, lasted for several weeks, or even much longer, and he often visited a dozen or more countries on such trips. In an admiring letter after reading one of his narratives, Shaw indicated that he lived "vicariously" through Hecht's own travels.

Shaw's efforts on behalf of the Mart brought him into contact with various prominent individuals and public figures, some while they were in office, and some before they were in office. One such person was Jennings Randolph, who, prior to Shaw meeting him, had been a congressman from West Virginia for several terms; in the late 1950s, he would be elected to the United States Senate from West Virginia, and serve for almost thirty years. Shaw met with him in Randolph's capacity as assistant to the President, Capitol Airlines of Washington, D.C., as part of Shaw's effort to secure an airline terminal in the Mart.[256]

The Mart had eventually decided to place a cocktail lounge in the building. It was set up as a concession leased out to an operator, rather than being run by the Mart management, as was the building.[257] The lounge provided a convenient meeting place for after-work get-togethers among the international trade community members, and for casual visitors to the Mart.

As Shaw had worked in public relations prior to and during the war, he naturally made the best use of those connections in promoting the Trade Mart during its pre-opening phase. One of the persons with whom he dealt was Bill Edgar, Jr., of the American Cable and Radio Corporation. Shaw had run into him at a convention not long after the opening of the Mart, and in a follow-up letter Edgar referenced, "Wilton, Southern Base, and the rest," referring to their time spent working together in southern England prior to the D-Day invasion.[258]

A 1948 invitation to "Mr. and Mrs. Clay Shaw" for a black-tie dinner at Antoine's Restaurant, sponsored by the New Orleans Association of Commerce for the American Businessmen's Club of Amsterdam, was sent to Shaw, but he declined due a previous engagement.[259] The Philippine consulate invited "Shaw and Mrs. Shaw" to a reception for the birthday of the Philippine presidency. Shaw extended best wishes to His Excellency, but declined due to a "week's absence" from the city.[260]

In November 1948, Shaw addressed the Pontalba Study Group, a civic group of thirty women in New Orleans. In January 1949, the group would hold its regular meeting at the Mart.[261] Civic groups were beginning to use the Mart for meetings and other activities, as they had International House's building for almost two years.

There was no cessation of the promotion for the Mart leading up to the official grand opening. Shaw attended the National Foreign Trade Council Convention in New York City during the second week of November 1948, visiting with his friend, K. Bruce Mitchell, the Western Union senior official[262] The convention, related to the foreign trade industry, was a well-attended one that Shaw would attend annually for many years.

Prior to the grand opening of the Mart, Shaw had worked with numerous writers for newspapers, magazines, and in-house corporate publications, related to the festivities. Among them was Stanton P. Nickerson, who worked for the in-house publication of Ethyl Corporation. Nickerson apparently knew Shaw on a more purely social level as well; in a letter to Shaw, Nickerson said, "Give my best to Jeff."[263] Later, in February 1949, Nickerson mentioned his upcoming visit for Mardi Gras, and suggested he could use "the extra bed at 'Chateau Shaw-Biddison'."[264]

The official grand opening of the Mart was held in November 1948, during another International Week celebration. The local media, including radio, television, and the several newspapers, once again all gave the Mart, along with the city's other international outreach efforts, great publicity. The official dedication for the Mart was held November 29 and 30, 1948. Theodore Brent issued invitations to elected officials around the country, including Representative Emmanuel Celler of Brooklyn.

**Another view of International Trade Mart (International Trade Mart Collection, Louisiana Research Collection, Tulane University)**

During the International Week celebration, the city decided that the Mart could not decorate Canal Street in celebration of its opening, due to a Shrine Circus in process at the time. However, two blocks of Camp Street were lit with floodlights for three nights. A platform for speaking was erected, and the Fair Grounds Race Track had entertainment during the week. Governor Earl K. Long was asked to attend the official opening.[265]

Newspaper ads, with pictures of the Mart, appeared in newspapers in Chicago, Kansas City, St. Louis, and Cincinnati, among others. The large display ads highlighted the building, a windowless concrete structure with an unusual shape, positioned at the corner of Camp and Common streets, with glass brick corridors, and plate glass display windows from which the various goods for sale could be viewed by potential customers, a figurative "street of merchandise."

After the grand opening, The Mart began to hold periodic meetings with tenants, with Shaw and public relations man John Leonard in attendance. The first meeting was held in December 1948, where the idea of a one to two percent rebate on purchases from tenant businesses by visitors to the Mart was discussed. The idea was that a merchant would send a rebate for goods purchased to the Mart management, which would then forward the rebate to the buyer of the goods, in an amount up to and including a customer's roundtrip airfare to New Orleans, and $20 per day for expenses incurred, up to five days.

At the end of 1948, after approximately six months of actual operations, the Mart awarded all employees one week's salary as a bonus.[266] That pattern would generally continue during all of the prosperous years.

**Shaw at ease, around 1948 (International Trade Mart Collection, Louisiana Research Collection, Tulane University)**

Le Petit Theatre's production of Shaw's three-act play, *Memorial* took place every evening from December 13 to 21, 1948, with a matinee on December 19. Shaw wrote the play under the name of Allen White, which were the maiden names of his two grandmothers. The play was directed by Monroe Lippman, a drama professor at Tulane University; Jessie Tharp, Shaw's drama teacher in high school, and herself a long-time director of plays at the theater, played the lead role of a domineering mother. Ethel Crumb Brett, a friendly rival of Louis Fischer for stage design in New Orleans, was the set and costume designer for the play.[267] At his trial, Shaw would testify that the pseudonym Allen White that he used as the author of *Memorial* was the only time he had ever used another name to identify himself, although he had used slight variations of his real first and middle names to identify himself as the co-author of his earlier plays, and in stage roles.

*Memorial* dealt with a wealthy widow, a rich and powerful woman who dominated a small mill town in South Carolina. She idealizes her son, who had been killed during World War II, in an over-the-top fashion, determined to do anything to keep her memory of him alive. When a sergeant from her son's unit comes to visit, tension begins to rise as he is attracted to the son's widow, while the elderly mother pursues her plans to erect a statue in her son's honor. As the play progresses, details emerge that put a very unflattering picture on her son's life, including, in the penultimate scene, a revelation by the sergeant from his unit that Phillip had died in a cowardly way, not as a hero. The play ends with the domineering mother painfully absorbing the truth that has been revealed about her son.[268]

A short article in the *Item* at the time of the production indicated that Jacob Wilk, a producer for Warner Brothers Studios, was interested in the play as a possible movie production.[269] The play had been submitted to Warner Brothers by its director, Monroe Lippman; May Ross reviewed the play for assistant producer Jacob Wilk. Ross found that, "Although this play offers good writing and poignant situations, it is again the story of a fanatically possessive mother. It seems to me that this theme is shop-worn by this time. Also, the denouement is no surprise. By now, we have come to expect that the dead 'hero' will be revealed as a coward. One who failed in his crucial hour because he could not make his own decisions."[270] Probably as a result of Ross's summary of the play's action, and her critical analytical comments, Warner Brothers chose not to make the play into a film.

Professor Michael Snyder, who has analyzed all of Shaw's plays, found *Memorial* "interesting" in that it confirmed his position that Shaw took a very "skeptical attitude toward Communism," revealing the person in the play closest to having "Communist" sympathies to actually be motivated more by personal, rather than ideological, motives. Shaw dealt with the issue of homosexuality "as the result of (s)mothering and the lack of paternal influence" on the son, which Snyder said was a "common theme in the 1950s—the threat of what was called 'Momism'" and attributing this as a primary cause of homosexuality.[271]

Snyder found that *Memorial* "fits pretty well in with the others [Shaw plays] in theme and writing style." The play used the idea of "the necessity of violent sacrifice of a 'rogue' individual for the good of the body politic," reinforcing Professor Snyder's conspiracy view that Shaw might have been involved, however indirectly, in the assassination of President Kennedy.[272] Snyder concluded, "I don't think it's a great play. Shaw lacks subtlety—his writing and dialogue can be corny and melodramatic, and the idea of making the woman the symbol of all that is evil and oppressive, which Shaw does, would seem fairly misogynist to today's audiences, but is fascinating" nevertheless.[273]

Around December 1948, several important events happened related to Shaw and the Mart. First, a Czechoslovakian trade exhibit leased space in the Mart for the one-year period from April 1949 to April 1950. That exhibit would be one of the more controversial episodes in International Trade Mart history, and it also led to Shaw's initial contact with the Central Intelligence Agency, and the Federal Bureau of Investigation, on or before December 27, 1948.[274] The communication with the CIA began an almost eight-year period during which Shaw would meet with local CIA officials and discuss his observations related to issues that arose in the international trade community. Of particular interest to the CIA was the initial, very lengthy trip Shaw made to the Caribbean, Central America, and northern South America from March to May 1949, and a later trip to southern South America in January and February 1951. The CIA would provide Shaw with a list of questions and topics, and on his return he would present his observations to the agency officials. That eight-year relationship, which apparently ended permanently in 1956, would publicly be revealed initially, in distorted fashion, in the last year of Shaw's life. Further details would not become available until after Shaw's death, and the relationship remains controversial to this day.

Shaw also was interviewed by the FBI during the course of the Czech exhibit presence in the Mart. Richard Doskey, who served as one of the first student interns at the Mart, during the 1949 to 1950 period, recalls two FBI agents calling on Shaw one day. The agents showed their credentials to Doskey, and he sent them in to see Shaw, but he never learned the gist of the conversation.[275] It is possible the FBI agents were continuing to monitor the situation of the Czechoslovakian exhibit at the Mart during the period from April 1949 to

April 1950. However, because of Shaw's homosexuality, and that of J.B. Dauenhauer, the FBI would never utilize Shaw as a source, to the extent the CIA did, after the issue of the Czech exhibit was resolved in 1950.

# PART II

# 6 · The Caribbean and South America

In early 1949, Shaw was bedridden for ten days due to an illness,[276] but by mid-January he was back to Mart activities full-time. He was still flying regularly at this time. In late January, he spoke before the World Trade Institute at the University of Omaha, then was supposed to fly to Wichita, Kansas, to appear before the Chamber of Commerce Foreign Trade Committee. However, he was unable to get to Wichita because of ice on the airfield, and no trains were available after he arrived in Kansas City late at night.

By 1949, Shaw was living at 537 Barracks Street, and is shown in the city directory as the General Manager of the Mart.[277] He was still living with Jeff Biddison, and they had become a very social couple, hosting parties and dinners for small groups. A medical school graduate doing his intern work in New Orleans recalls getting an invitation to a party, which soon turned into a weekend "in bed." Shaw was not among the participants, but Biddison very much was.

It is unclear what Shaw and Biddison understood the ground rules of their relationship to be. One man told the author of taking a trip to Shreveport with Biddison, during which the two had sexual relations. The man was a friend of Shaw as well, and as a courtesy, he made Shaw aware of the incident. Shaw thanked him for informing him about it, but had no obvious reaction to the news.

Signs of potential tension between International House and the Mart, always present since their beginnings, soon flared up again. In early January 1949, Charles Nutter wrote to Hecht, expressing concern about duplication of effort between the Mart and International House. Nutter felt that everything at the Mart, except the actual management and operation of the building, should be centralized in International House, using its setup to deal with various aspects of international trade.[278]

With the Mart mostly full, Shaw, Hecht and Brent occasionally still debated whether to allow particular tenants into the Mart. In January 1949, a small argument occurred over the Harrison Line of Steamers, a shipping interest, and its desire to take 1,000 square feet of office space in the building. At the time, the Mart was holding space for foreign governmental or business organizations or, secondarily, for those merchants who sold goods that could be placed in a display window.

**Shaw with unidentified woman (International Trade Mart Collection, Louisiana Research Collection, Tulane University)**

The tenant's newsletter of January 12, 1949, noted that Willard E. Robertson, President of Southern Steel Craft, was in New York City attending the National Boat Show. Southern Steel Craft occupied third floor space in the Mart at the time.[279] In 1967, Robertson, then the Volkswagen distributor in the New Orleans area, among other interests, was one of the three businessmen who privately helped to finance the investigation by District Attorney Jim Garrison into the assassination of President Kennedy.

John Leonard, the Public Relations Director, announced at a tenants' meeting that approximately one thousand visitors per day were now coming into the Mart. There were the usual problems associated with office buildings, such as pilfering of purses and other items left unattended on or around office desks. Consideration was given to allowing tenants to hire a plainclothes detective to guard the premises against such crime. Problems with tenants were arising as well; some workers would prop emergency exit doors open for easier ingress and egress, rather than use the building's main entrance, creating another security issue.

Shaw began to advise tenants, outside consultants, news organizations and potential lessees about a several-month trip to the Caribbean, Central America and South America to promote the Mart, and to seek potential tenants from those areas. At a tenants' meeting in late February 1949, Shaw more officially announced his upcoming trip, which he said would last approximately three months. Mario Bermúdez would accompany Shaw on the lengthy trip, representing the City of New Orleans and International House. Shaw requested that tenants provide the names of contacts in Latin America with whom he should visit, and offered to do whatever he could to promote their individual businesses. John Leonard followed up that meeting with a memo to tenants in early March, indicating that Shaw's departure would be March 10.[280]

In preparation for this initial trip to Latin America, Shaw took Spanish lessons from Albert LeMón. LeMón, a native of Colombia, had lived in New Orleans for approximately four years, and worked at Maison Blanche Department Store. As a result of those initial lessons, Shaw became proficient enough to be understood on his trip, at least with basic phrases.[281] Years later, LeMón's son told the author that, while Shaw had a natural inclination for the proper phrasing and intonation of Spanish, and adapted more quickly than some students, he never gained real fluency in using the language.[282]

Although the current focus of New Orleans's efforts was primarily to attract trade to and from Latin America through its port, the country that had the greatest amount of trade with New Orleans at the time was Belgium. Belgium was the first country to open a consular office in the Mart; Charles Leonard was the Consul General of Belgium in New Orleans. In its efforts to obtain tenants with an international flavor, the Mart had reversed its earlier position on accepting consular offices as tenants. Shaw had met Leonard well before the opening of the Mart; an invitation from Leonard to Shaw in the spring of 1947 invited Shaw to visit with Leonard after hours at the Belgian consular office, then located on St. Charles Avenue, for a "stag cocktail."[283]

The Mart held space open in hopes of getting twelve to fifteen countries to have some type of official representation in the building, and it was decided to continue to hold those spaces until the end of 1949. An important part of the purpose of Shaw's trip to the Caribbean, Central and South America was to induce those special types of tenants to take out space.[284] As of June 1949, the countries of Argentina, Belgium, Guatemala, Czechoslovakia, Nicaragua, Panama, and El Salvador had arranged to have space in the building in some official form.[285]

Vigorous attempts were made to get other countries to place an exhibit in the Mart, including Brazil. Shaw wrote to Brazilian officials, indicating that he planned to visit Rio de Janeiro in late May 1949,[286] although that trip wound up being delayed until 1951. The Mart corresponded with various Brazilian officials in an effort to get a Brazilian trade group into the Mart. Brazil held an international industrial and commercial exposition, similar in focus to the Mart, around that same time. It also tried to establish a Permanent Industrial Exposition at the old Hotel Quitandinha on a mountaintop twenty-five miles from Rio de Janeiro; Theodore Brent advised Shaw against the Mart participating in that, saying that the Quitandinha was in a beautiful location, but too remote from Rio; he feared someone was trying to get rid of a "white elephant." Among other countries, Shaw showed a group of travel agents from Havana, Cuba through the Mart, in an attempt to induce some agreement with that country.

The Mart continued its tough stance with delinquent tenants. By early 1949, enough tenants had fallen in arrears that Shaw felt it necessary to send those more than ninety days late a notice that the locks on their doors would be changed, and/or legal action taken, if the accounts were not made current in a timely fashion.[287]

By now, the Mart was receiving regular inquiries related to specific, sometimes exotic, products. Sometimes International House, open and functioning before the Mart, forwarded such inquiries along. The types of products being sought included everything from Swiss watches to specific types of fertilizer, or seeds, or specific types of craft items, jewelry, or agricultural products. One request, in early 1949, passed along by G.E. Roper, Jr., Assistant Director of World Trade Development Department at International House, related to a new seasoning called "MSG" (monosodium glutamate). Roper advised Shaw it could be obtained from a Chicago firm.[288]

Shaw sometimes displayed his sly, deadpan humor in answering inquiries. One man wrote from a South American country, asking about an ingredient for his cookie-making business; the ingredient was for making the wafers harden to a certain consistency. With tongue firmly in cheek, Shaw replied that he was unfamiliar with the product, and regretted that he could not help the man with "the hardness of your wafer."

Both the U.S. State Department and the U.S. Commerce Department showed an interest in the Mart, and International House, from the very earliest stages. Several of the founders of both organizations, including Brent and Hecht, had close ties with congressmen, senators, and other national government officials. The State Department and Commerce Department offices in New Orleans frequently coordinated with the Mart and International House related to diplomatic events, such as visiting dignitaries and heads of state.

Occasionally, the Mart would receive a request for foreign stamps from interested persons who assumed the nature of the Mart's clientele would generate them.[289] After several such requests, Mart personnel knew to hold aside such stamps to send along to satisfy customers seeking this specific collectible.

The Latin American trip had initially been planned for 1947, but was postponed due to the general delay in the overall progress of restoring the building and opening the Mart. It finally occurred from approximately March 10, 1949 through May 20, 1949. As Shaw was about to begin the trip, Public Relations Director John Leonard gave him a letter of introduction to Thomas R. Curran with the United Press Association in Buenos Aires, Argentina. In a separate letter to Curran, Leonard indicated that he had liked his job with the Mart since he began in October 1948. He praised Shaw to Curran, and asked Curran to send greetings to all of his former friends in the newspaper business;[290] Leonard had once worked for Joseph L. Jones with United Press Association in Panama.

A CIA memo dated February 18, 1949, and authored by Lyman B. Kirkpatrick, who years later would be the CIA's Inspector General who investigated the agency's failed Bay of Pigs Invasion, discussed Shaw's upcoming first trip to the Caribbean, Central and South America on behalf of the Mart. The memo says that Shaw would be briefed before he left, and Kirkpatrick attached a list of questions and requirements, placed in order for each South American country, indicating the information needed from Shaw after he returned from his trip. The memo phrased it as requirements for a "manager of a trade mart," as if the

CIA thought of Shaw's work in a somewhat generic fashion, such as the manager of a trade fair of the sort that exhibited throughout Europe.[291]

While on the trip, Shaw's main communications went primarily through J.B. Dauenhauer or Mary Catanese. Shaw wrote somewhat regular accounts of the trip from major stops along the way, beginning in the Caribbean.[292] In an early letter to Mary Catanese, Shaw thanked her for her birthday card on his thirty-sixth birthday, which took place on March 17, 1949. He noted that he was doing okay with his Spanish after a week in Cuba; via the same letter, he gave J.B. Dauenhauer a general report on the visit in Cuba.[293]

Shaw visited Haiti early in the trip. He sent another letter back to Mary Catanese, this time to be translated into French at International House and then sent to the Haitian officials he had just met, acknowledging the visits and thanking them for meeting with him.

At the same time Shaw was on his trip, flying to each country, Theodore Brent was traveling by ship to Africa and southern South America. Originally, he and Shaw were to have coordinated their travels, and met in Brazil. J.B. Dauenhauer, who lived with Brent along with Dauenhauer's companion, Edgar Lee, kept Brent and Shaw apprised of developments within their circle of friends.[294]

Shaw and Mario Bermúdez, already somewhat close, became even better friends as a result of the lengthy trip to Latin America. The April 1949 issue of the *New Orleans Port Record* magazine shows a cartoon of Shaw and Bermúdez by the artist Algird Kuraitic with the caption, "We could make such beautiful music together," (meaning New Orleans and Latin America). The accompanying article mentioned that a Latin American Tourist Bureau had been proposed for the Mart, and a photo showed Shaw and Bermúdez in the Dominican Republic during an early stage of the trip.

The length of the trip, and the foreign environment, apparently weighed on Shaw. Some of his letters to Dauenhauer have terseness in tone that rarely appears in his correspondence over the years. It likely was difficult for him to be away from the home front while various crises were developing. In one letter, written from Barranguilla, Colombia, Shaw instructed Dauenhauer to tell interior decorator Alma Rawlinson that he would "wring her neck" unless the office décor was completed when he returned; he was tired of her "fooling around."

Alma Rawlinson had been selected as the interior decorator the Mart recommended to tenants for the design of their spaces. Her name was given to new tenants and vice versa, in the hope that tenants would coordinate their own interior décor with that of the Mart. Later, the Mart paid one-half of Rawlinson's travel expenses to Chicago to market tenants at the Merchandise Mart there, in hopes that she could also interest them in taking space at the International Trade Mart. For any who eventually leased space, she would be given one month's rent as a commission. The Mart gave her a letter of introduction to present her credentials to the management at the Merchandise Mart.[295] Rawlinson eventually met with Joseph Kennedy, one of the owners of the Merchandise Mart, and the father of then-Congressman and future President Kennedy.[296]

In another letter, written from Panama, Shaw instructed Dauenhauer to hold firm on tenants wanting to cancel leases, and he also indicated that he did not want Frank Dane and "his promotional schemes" in the building. "Frank Dane" was an alias used by an independent promoter named Charles Chicarelli, who had an idea for a Mid-Century Exposition in New Orleans that apparently never went anywhere, although he attempted to interest numerous businessmen in the project. Shaw was always skeptical of the venture, which Dane was actively promoting in 1949. Later, during the summer, Shaw wrote to the Consul General of the Netherlands in New Orleans, dismissing Dane's proposed Mid-Century International Exposition to be held September to October 1950. Shaw said that Dane had explained it to him months before, and that it had sounded nebulous and tentative.[297]

In early April 1949, J.B. Dauenhauer wrote to Herbert Schwartz, Rudolf Hecht, and Kenneth Barranger, summarizing comments in a letter from Shaw related to his trip to South America, written from Barranquilla, Colombia. Shaw indicated there had been constant activity, meetings, and dinners, going from nine o'clock in the morning until the wee hours of the night. Shaw noted that it would be nice to eat one meal by himself, and said that his Spanish was improving to the point where he could make his simplest needs known, and that the Latins were killing them with kindness.[298] The International Trade Mart records contain a photo of Shaw at a coffee plantation in Colombia during the lengthy trip.

While in Colombia, the humorous antics related to the current Miss New Orleans, "Bobby Jean" Floyd, whom Shaw had helped select while a judge during the contest the previous year, hit their crest, creating a minor scandal that was widely covered by the newspapers in Latin America. Shaw told Dauenhauer that he was apologizing to everyone in Colombia for his choice.[299]

In mid-April, Shaw indicated to Dauenhauer that he had recommended to Rudolf Hecht that he continue on to southern South America. The trip was definitely to cover the Caribbean, northern South America, and Central America, but whether to proceed on to Chile, Argentina, and Brazil had been left open. Shaw said that he loathed more travel, but was willing to do it for the good of the Mart, which was getting a lot of attention from the trip. He also indicated again his weariness of the numerous ongoing official gatherings he had to attend.[300]

Hecht responded to Shaw's suggestion, sharing that he and the Executive Committee had decided that Shaw's party should stick to the original itinerary, and not go on to southern South America.[301] Shaw responded from Quito, Ecuador, that he had spoken to Brent, who was now in Rio de Janeiro, and they had agreed that at Lima, Peru, Shaw and Bermúdez would turn north and work their way back through Central America.[302]

The fourth Mississippi Valley World Trade Conference was held April 21-22, 1949, at the Roosevelt hotel. While the event was again successful in attendance and publicity, Shaw missed the conference, which occurred during his trip.

The most serious issue to erupt while Shaw was gone was the controversy over the Czechoslovakian exhibit at the Trade Mart, which began its lease at the end of April 1949; the leasing of space had earlier served as the means for Shaw's first contact with the CIA and FBI. Protests were organized from local groups over having such an exhibit, due to the recent takeover by a Communist government in Czechoslovakia, one of the many pivotal events that demonstrated an escalation of the Cold War.

Some of the protests had been organized by the Young Men's Business Club, which had been so cooperative with the Mart during its formation and opening ceremonies. The officials of the Young Men's Business Club, including Ivor Trapolin, Clem Bernard, and William Guste, were very much against it. Guste, who was the chairman of the Committee on the Czech Exhibit formed by the group, would be elected in 1972 as Louisiana's attorney general, and serve for several terms. In a letter to J.B. Dauenhauer from San Jose, Costa Rica, Shaw lashed out at Trapolin, saying he was infuriated by his "stupidity" and that of YMBC, saying that, "His ancestors burned witches in Salem and sat as inquisitorial judges in Spain." Shaw indicated that he wanted to address the Young Men's Business Club, and the Knights of Columbus, another group involved in the protest and led by Ivor Trapolin's brother, F. Winter Trapolin, when he returned to town, if the issue was still alive.[303] The New Orleans Lions' Club also passed a resolution against the exhibit, as did the Saint Matthew Holy Name Society. Dauenhauer replied that Brent and Lloyd Cobb, then a rising young lawyer in the city, and member of the Mart's executive board, had met with Trapolin and Clem Bernard about the Czech situation. The two YMBC leaders promised not to make statements to the newspapers without notifying the Mart leaders in advance.[304] Brent had returned from South America in early May to help deal with the situation, and was able to dampen the initial controversy relatively quickly.[305]

Shaw, Brent, and Hecht were strongly for the idea of including the Czech participation throughout the time the exhibit was in the Mart, and Shaw recommended renewing the lease as the expiration date approached in the spring of 1950.[306] Shaw advised Brent that the Mart should simply remain silent as the renewal date approached.[307]

Brent continually took a very active role in trying to defuse the matter. He sought advice from State Department officials, and from Clarke Salmon, a top official with Bauerlein Advertising, the Mart's outside public relations consultant. He also met with representatives of the protesting groups and tried to explain the Mart's position.

The basic issue was whether an exhibit associated with a Communist government should be allowed to lease space in the Mart. The Mart's position was that it was seeking to facilitate peaceful trade with other countries, no matter what type of government they had, and that goods for sale in New Orleans from the Soviet Union were already available. There was even a suggestion that the exhibit had been arranged by the government that preceded the Communist one in Czechoslovakia, and so the officials who would maintain the Czech exhibit were not Communist officials at all (according to FBI files released years later, however, representatives for the exhibit did have Communist ties). However, the entire issue became moot at the end of April 1950, when the Czech government made no effort to renew the lease after a year in the building.

John Leonard, the Public Relations Director, wrote to Shaw in Panama in early May, asking how Shaw liked his "old stomping ground." Leonard, who had been stationed in Panama when he had been a news correspondent years before, recommended that Shaw see Bill Arango while he was there, and also that Shaw try the famous Pergola Bar at the Hotel Tivoli. Leonard discussed the matter of the Czech exhibit, which he said had been relegated to the back pages of the local newspapers by that time, with "no editorials in papers, no letters printed." Leonard mentioned that Al Johnson had just been assigned by the *Item* to cover the Mart, and suggested the local Foreign Policy Association as a possible networking group.[308]

By the time Shaw arrived in Central America during the second week of May, he was worn out, and somewhat irritated, by the length and stress of the entire trip. He indicated to Dauenhauer that he would be back on May 25th—"Thank God!"[309] From Tegucigalpa, Honduras, he wrote that he was tired, and that he never wanted to see "a Rotarian, a government official, a cocktail, or a canapé." Although Shaw and Bermúdez visited most of the Central and northern South American countries, they did not go to Mexico, nor did they visit Bolivia in South America, as it was engaged in a revolution at that time.

In mid-May, while Shaw was on the return leg of the trip, J.B. Dauenhauer sent him a letter in Honduras indicating that a Board of Directors meeting was set for May 26 to discuss raising money to pay off some of the contractors used in the remodeling of the Mart building, and to pay off the upgrading of the air conditioning system. Dauenhauer cautioned Shaw that Theodore Brent had asked him "at least ten times" to remind Shaw about the board meeting, and urged Shaw that he had "better ride a broom in if you miss the plane."[310]

Dauenhauer further reiterated that local activists Ivor Trapolin and Clem Bernard of the Young Men's Business Club had promised Mart officials they would make no statements to the press about their opposition to the Czech exhibit that had just opened in the Mart without advising them in advance. Dauenhauer indicated that a "Brooklyn Jew" named Kahn would run the Czech exhibit.[311] Harry Kahn was the subject of a decades-long FBI investigation that tracked his activities with the Communist party.

Shaw's total expenses for the trip were approximately $1,675. However, he secured two leases in Venezuela early in the trip that more than paid for those expenses.[312]

Upon arriving back in New Orleans, Shaw immediately applied for renewal of his passport, which had originally been issued in May 1947.[313] He indicated to the passport authorities that he was going to be taking another trip to South America, this time to Peru, Chile, Argentina, Uruguay, Brazil, and Mexico. The stated purpose of that trip, similar to the one just ended, would be to work out methods with Latin American businessmen for promoting the sale of products through the Mart.[314] However, that second South American trip would not take place until early 1951.

Shaw did not leave his life as a playwright behind when he left the country. Shaw's full-length play, *Memorial*, had run for a week at Le Petit Theatre in New Orleans during December 1948. The local newspapers had run articles about it, and there were even rumors of a movie deal in the works. Shaw must have discussed it with businessmen he encountered during his Central and South American trip.[315] He had written to a Rene Grau D shortly after his return in May. Rene Grau D replied from Bogota, Colombia (he was an employee of Philips Colombiana), asking Shaw about the play, and whether it had "reached Broadway yet."[316] By that time, however, interest in the play apparently had subsided, and Shaw did not address the issue in his reply ten days later.[317] Apparently, the play was only performed during its initial run.

After his Latin American trip, Shaw continued his diplomatic efforts, writing to many of the governmental officials he had met in Central and South America, and the Caribbean, thanking them for their hospitality, and expressing hope that they would take out space in the Mart. He also wrote to the newly-elected president of Costa Rica, congratulating him on the success of his government, following the takeover by a civilian government from a military government.[318] Shaw also continued his numerous speaking engagements, appearing before the Chamber of Commerce in McComb, Mississippi, and before the Export/Import Club in Fort Worth, Texas, where he talked about his trip.

Shaw also immediately resumed his heavy local business social schedule. He attended a party given by the Consular Corp of New Orleans honoring A.E. Hegewisch, one of the founders of International House. He also made an appearance at a cocktail party at the home of the Consul General of Cuba. Shaw had visited Havana, Cuba in March 1947, as part of his pre-opening promotional activities, and had stopped there again on his recent trip.

Around this time, Theodore Brent advised the Board of Directors that the total cost of the Mart, including repairing deficiencies in the air conditioning system that were discovered upon opening, had exceeded budget by approximately $50,000, out of a total cost of more than $1,185,000. Brent reported that, as of mid-1949, the Mart was ninety percent leased.[319]

Shaw continued to send marketing letters to prospective tenants in an attempt to fill the remaining space. He indicated to potential tenants that the Esso Road News had run a story on the Mart in its *Motoring Magazine*, distributed to 12 million people, and targeted toward drivers crisscrossing the country on business and pleasure trips.[320] Esso was the former name of Exxon Corporation in the United States; the name is still used at gas stations in many parts of the world.

For the six months that ended June 30, 1949, the Mart had total revenue of $133,426, with total operating expenses of $101,865. Some of the main operating expenses were travel of $3,157, and entertainment of $3,686. However, interest over and above normal operating expenses was hefty at $26,617. Net income after all expenses was $5,248, and the Mart's Board of Directors was pleased about the progress during the first full six months of operations following the official opening ceremonies. Shaw began searching for a CPA firm to audit the books twice yearly.[321]

Beginning July 1, 1949, International House offered beginning, intermediate, and advanced Spanish lessons at twelve dollars per month, six dollars for International House members. The language program had been part of the original plan for the institution, but it had taken a few years to put a staff in place.

In 1949, the Executive Committee of the Board of Directors consisted of Brent, Hecht, Lloyd Cobb, William Zetzmann, Seymour Weiss, Lester Alexander, and Sam V. Massimini. William Zetzmann would become President of the Trade Mart upon the death of Theodore Brent in mid-1953; Lloyd Cobb would succeed Zetzmann as President upon Zetzmann's death in 1962. Seymour Weiss, as described previously, was one of the owners of the Roosevelt hotel.

In addition to Czechoslovakia, and seemingly undeterred by possible criticism, the Mart tried to interest other Communist countries. Poland inquired about the progress of the Mart in a series of letters from 1947 through 1949. In one letter to Shaw, Professor Henryk Drozdowski mentioned the character of Scarlett in *Gone with the Wind*, which he described as a popular novel in Poland. In July 1949, the Mart tried to interest Yugoslavia, also under Communist domination, to take a space in the Mart. Responding to a request by the Yugoslavian Embassy for information, Shaw pointed out that Czechoslovakia had its exhibit, and he named other countries that also had taken out space.[322] However, neither Poland nor Yugoslavia, by now both firmly under Communist regimes, ever took space in the Mart.

In August 1949, looking for other approaches to fill the remaining vacancies, the Mart continued to relax its rule on three-year leases (Czechoslovakia had already taken out a one-year lease), offering favored potential tenants a one-year lease instead.[323] It was an effort both to fill the building to capacity, and to induce the desired types of tenants into the building.

By mid-1949, the relationship with John Leonard, the Mart's first full-time Public Relations Director, had deteriorated. He was terminated effective July 30, 1949, and deductions were made from his final check for charges owed to the restaurant at International House, and to the cocktail lounge at the International Trade Mart. He also was accused of having incurred personal expenses at Arnaud's Restaurant and Brennan's Restaurant, and having those personal charges invoiced to the Mart. Leonard had been hired the previous October for a ninety-day trial period, kept on after the period expired, but then had been notified in May 1949 that his position would be eliminated.[324] He had been hired at a salary of $500 per month.

After his termination, Leonard complained to the Louisiana Department of Labor about deductions made from his final check.[325] The Mart responded quickly, listing the debts Leonard supposedly owed, and also alleged that Leonard had borrowed money from the Mart's petty cash fund.[326] In an effort to resolve the matter, Shaw wrote to Leonard offering to return the amounts deducted from the final paycheck, and to pay Leonard's original moving expenses, which had been contingent upon him staying for a longer duration.[327] That effectively ended the episode.

The Mart produced a buyer's directory for September 1949, showing a list of tenants. While Belgium was the only country which had placed its local consulate in the Mart by this time, Argentina, Czechoslovakia, Guatemala, Honduras, Nicaragua, and Panama also had some type of exhibit in the building.

Officials of the Mart pushed the idea of a commemorative stamp showing the International Trade Mart. Shaw worked on the project with Clem Bernard, the aforementioned representative of the Young Men's Business Club, who owned his own printing business. They enlisted the support of Congressman Hale Boggs, who introduced a bill authorizing the stamp in Congress; Theodore Brent contacted several congressmen as well. Eventually, however, the idea was dropped after opposition from the Post Office, which argued the Mart, as of that time, had little historical significance to commemorate.

In the second half of 1949, Shaw hired Glenn E. Weekley to replace John Leonard as Public Relations Director. Weekley had worked at small newspapers in Pennsylvania from

1935 to 1940, had helped with public relations with the Army Air Force from 1940 to 1945, and had worked for Baton Rouge newspapers from 1945 to 1947. By August 1949, he had turned thirty-one years old and had just received his Master of Arts degree from the Brazilian Institute at Vanderbilt University, and knew both Spanish and Portuguese.[328]

Shaw wrote to Weekley in early September, care of J.D. Hood in Jena, Louisiana, indicating that he was being offered the job on a trial basis.[329] The work would be for the Mart, but Weekley also would be an assistant to Vaughn Bryant at International House. Weekley responded to Shaw in mid-September from his address at Vanderbilt University, confirming that he would start on October 1, 1949.[330]

Weekley would stay in the position for several years, a tenure that saw the Mart grow to full occupancy of its building, and otherwise develop the successful early years of its existence. Weekley helped to solidify the Mart's presence with several in-house publications, and established good relations with tenants through regular dialogue. Among his projects was a tenant questionnaire that gathered data on the volume of the tenants' businesses that had been generated by their presence in the Mart.[331]

Responding to the survey, one tenant commented that the Mart had too many ticket agencies, shipping companies, and plain offices, but not enough goods for sale to consumers. The complaint had a ring of truth to it, as the Mart did not succeed in attracting the number of manufacturing concerns, particularly from foreign countries, for which it had planned. The Mississippi Shipping Company had a purser's office in the building; Shaw's friend and lover at the time, Jeff Biddison, worked in that office for a while. The Office of International Relations for the City of New Orleans was located in the Mart as well, staffed by Mario Bermúdez and Carmen Anguis.

City and local civic officials now could count on Shaw to serve regularly on committees devoted to one purpose or another. In July, Shaw was appointed to the Reception and Entertainment Committee for the visit of the Minister of Foreign Affairs of Colombia. In August, he served on the Ecuadorian Disaster Relief Committee after an earthquake hit that country.

And, of course, Shaw's public speaking continued. Mario Bermúdez again invited Shaw to address a group of visiting Latin American students, a custom that would continue for several years. At the time, Bermúdez used International House stationery for his position as Director of International Relations for the City of New Orleans.[332]

**Shaw with group of visiting students (International Trade Mart Collection, Louisiana Research Collection, Tulane University)**

Shaw also spoke to an increasing number of local groups, including Le Petit Salon, on "Latin America and New Orleans,"[333] and to the Needlework Guild. He spoke to the Rotary Club in Kentwood, Louisiana in September 1949,[334] and to the Kiwanis Club in Alexandria, Louisiana, in north-central Louisiana.[335] For the latter speech, he flew from New Orleans to Alexandria, Louisiana, some 250 miles away by road. Nonstop air service had made a lengthy rail or automobile trip from New Orleans to northern Louisiana into an approximately one-hour trip.

The artist Philip Steegman, of London, exhibited his paintings at the Mart during the year; he was noted for, among other things, a 1931 portrait of the writer Somerset Maugham. In the course of his life, Shaw came into contact with many writers and artists. Among them was Frances Parkinson Keyes, who lived in the French Quarter. He had especially admired her use of photos in her recent picture book, *This is Louisiana*, which came out in 1949.[336] Shaw would later work with Keyes regarding her possible participation in the celebration of the 150th anniversary celebration of the Louisiana Purchase in 1953.

In September 1949, Rudolf Hecht took another lengthy trip, this time through the South Pacific, and on to Asia and the Middle East, and then back through Europe. He sent Shaw several letters relating his experiences on the trip. In one letter written from Perth, Australia, he gave Shaw his impressions of New Zealand. He commented that he had gone from Auckland, New Zealand to Sydney, Australia by flying boat, covering 1,400 miles in eight hours.[337] In another letter, written from Hong Kong, Hecht gave his impressions of Australia.[338] Throughout other, often lengthy letters from this around-the-world trip, Hecht gave detailed descriptions of Indonesia, Singapore, Manila, Hong Kong, Bangkok, India, and Damascus, before flying on to Brussels, Belgium on his way back to the United States. Interestingly, one country that Hecht, who was Jewish, did not visit on that trip was the newly formed nation of Israel, perhaps because of the volatile situation there.

The Mart contained a theater where groups could meet, and also where films were shown from time to time. One example of this outreach occurred when J.B. Dauenhauer scheduled a meeting for a French club that wanted to use the theater.[339] In September, Shaw arranged a tour for "ladies" of the Fine Arts Club of New Orleans for April 1950; he also showed them the film, "New Orleans, the International City."[340] The film had been made in a joint effort with the city government, International Trade Mart, International House, and other civic organizations, emphasizing the efforts of New Orleans to generate international trade and cooperation.

In late September, Shaw wrote to Max Finlay, of the Wood Grange Metal Stamping Company in London, England, saying that Joseph M. Rault, Jr. had recently been in to see him, and had asked him to write Finlay about finding a distributor in the United States.[341] In early 1967, Rault would be one of three businessmen who, as the quickly-formed Truth and Consequences organization, would privately finance Orleans Parish District Attorney Jim Garrison's investigation into the assassination of President Kennedy, which ultimately led to Shaw's arrest and trial.

As the end of September approached, the Mart was approximately ninety-three percent leased. Shaw and the Executive Committee of the Board of Directors held out hope that more foreign government offices—consuls, trade associations, or foreign businesses—would lease the remaining space.

Appearing on radio, and later television, became somewhat of a regular event for Shaw. Sometimes he appeared in order to promote something specific to the Mart, but he also participated on panels related to general trade and foreign affairs issues, or simply in a broadcast during which, for example, a radio station used the Mart lobby as a location for an individual day's broadcast.

Shaw's trip to southern South America and Mexico, countries he had missed on his first trip, was originally scheduled to begin October 11, 1949, with him returning shortly before Christmas.[342] However, the trip was again postponed until a later date, because of conflicts in scheduling.

The tenants' newsletter kept everyone informed of public activities and travels on behalf of the Mart and the city's international efforts, whether done by Shaw or other representatives. The edition of October 12, 1949, discussed the upcoming goodwill trip to the Yucatan Peninsula of Mexico to take place November 13-20, an eight-day trip sponsored by International House that would take the participants to Mérida, Progreso, Campeche, Chichén Itzá, Uxmal, and Champotón.[343] Shaw did not accompany the group on that trip.

The newsletter that was published two weeks later indicated that Shaw was in New York City on a series of business conferences, and would return on November 2nd.[344] As he had a year earlier, Shaw attended the National Foreign Trade Council Convention at the Waldorf-Astoria in New York City. Shaw attended that convention for well over a decade as part of his ongoing promotional efforts.

Theodore Brent was a benefactor of the Crippled Children's Hospital, the organizing committee for which was located in the International Trade Mart building during the years 1949-50. Shaw served as publicity director of Crippled Children's Hospital, Inc. during that same period, and the first meeting for the proposed hospital was held in mid-October 1949 in Shaw's office.[345]

By late 1949, the Mart and International House were beginning to receive international men of prominence on a regular basis. Shaw announced to tenants that Harold Wilson of the Board of Trade of Great Britain would be speaking at International House.[346] Wilson later would serve as Prime Minister of Great Britain during the 1960s and 1970s, but at the time he was still an emerging young politician. The Consul General of India in New York City, the Honorable Ramji Ram Saksena, made a New Orleans visit during the first week of December, and toured the Mart and International House, among other sites.

By now Shaw was known as something of an authority on international trade, even though he had very little direct training in the area. In late 1949, Charles Taylor with the Federal Reserve Bank of Atlanta, who had written an article about the Trade Mart project in its early stages in 1946, asked for Shaw's input about the effects of the devaluation of foreign currencies on the sales of products of tenants in the Mart.[347]

Occasionally, the Mart would give small Christmas gifts to important businessmen and public officials around the city or the country who could help the Mart in some way. In the early years, the gift was often a twelve-month subscription to *Latin American Reports*, which was published by Mart tenant William G. Gaudet.

During 1949, the issue arose of whether New Orleans should seek to hold the Inter-American Association of Broadcasters Convention, which had typically been held outside of the United States. Shaw favored the idea, as did Charles Nutter of International House, who invited the group in a letter to the organization, located in Havana, Cuba. However, Dave McGuire, Public Relations Director for the City of New Orleans, raised the race issue, and considered it inadvisable to hold the convention in New Orleans. The race issue would rear its head numerous times during the 1940s, 1950s and 1960s with regard to international visitors who were persons of color, and how to handle them. The natural inclination of those groups seeking to promote international trade, such as the International Trade Mart, International House, and to a less-focused degree, the Port of New Orleans and the City of New Orleans, was to make their invitations to participate all-inclusive, to the extent that was possible. However, the natural tension that arose in accommodating black visitors in the segregated South, even those who were heads of foreign countries, could not be totally discounted.

Soon after its formation had been known to the general public, and continuing over the years, the Mart received letters from graduating college students, or from others seeking jobs in the international trade field.[348] However, other than an occasional student intern, or a Public Relations Director, the Mart never filled any post above the level of secretary, mainly because its primary function was as a building to house tenants with an international interest. Shaw, the Public Relations Director, and members of the Executive Committee of the Board of Directors were the primary forces in generating publicity for the Mart, and promoting the occupancy of the building. The Mart was looked upon as one part of a larger, somewhat unified effort that included International House, the City of New Orleans Department of International Relations, and other civic groups such as the Greater New Orleans Chamber of Commerce, and the Port of New Orleans, in promoting international trade. It had no real need for a large staff, or for employees with highly specialized skills.

Occasionally, Shaw gave out conflicting information regarding Mart policies, depending upon the person or institution requesting the information. For example, he told Georgia Marble Company that the Mart did not have credit information on tenants, nor did it evaluate the service quality of tenants.[349] However, in a letter to the Kinnear Manufacturing Company, Shaw advised that Mr. Julio A. Salas of Colón, Panama, was a good credit risk, that he knew him very well.[350]

In spite of some slowly emerging differences, the Mart continued to work closely with the City of New Orleans, International House, the Port of New Orleans, the Chamber of Commerce, and many other civic organizations on a regular basis. Among the coordinated activities used by the international trade community to entertain visiting businessmen and diplomats was a trip on the Good Neighbor boat, owned by the Dock Board, which was used to transport sightseers and partiers up and down the Mississippi River from New Orleans.

In December 1949, Shaw sent a letter of introduction for William Gaudet, publisher of *Latin American Reports*, for Gaudet's use in meeting with Lieutenant Colonel Alfredo Tejada with the purchasing department of the Ministry of War in Lima, Peru.[351] Gaudet was beginning a trip through South America, and he later wrote to Shaw from there, giving his best holiday wishes to Shaw, J.B. Dauenhauer, and Theodore Brent. Gaudet mentioned that he had caught food poisoning on his way from Lima, Peru to Santiago, Chile, and that he was working his way to Uruguay to catch a steamer home.[352] Shaw had requested that Gaudet obtain a letter of recommendation praising the International Trade Mart from the Ministry of War in Peru.

The annual report for 1949, the first full year of operations, showed rental income of $270,787, with total operating expenses totaling $253,246, resulting in a nice first-year profit that pleased almost everyone. Of the operating expenses, salaries totaled $71,529. The Mart was 90.5% occupied for the full year, and 600 lines of merchandise were on display in the various tenant spaces. Beyond the management and administrative staff, most of the employees were maids, porters, elevator operators, and building maintenance personnel, many of whom would soon be unionized.

What sort of private life did Shaw live in the late 1940s and into the early part of the 1950s? Almost twenty years later, after his arrest on March 1, 1967, *LIFE* magazine writer Holland McCombs (McCombs had been a writer for *Fortune* magazine at the time of the opening of International House and the Mart, and knew Shaw and others involved in the international trade movement in New Orleans) and three others who knew Shaw in the buttoned-down straight world weighed in on the subject, in an attempt to dissuade *LIFE* magazine from wholeheartedly joining and supporting District Attorney Jim Garrison's investigation into the Kennedy assassination, and taking an anti-Shaw slant in its coverage. Besides McCombs, the other contributors were Charles Nutter, Shaw's long-time counterpart as former Managing Director of International House, Richard Swenson, former Director of Public Relations at the Board of Commissioners of the Port of New Orleans, and William McFadden Duffy, former Public Relations Director at International House.

In early 1946, Nutter was busy getting International House going when Theodore Brent called him to say that he was sending over a young man to start work for the Mart.

(McCombs commented that "Brent was a lover of handsome young men and always had them around him.") Shaw showed up, wearing his Major's uniform from World War II, because his military clothes were the only working clothes he had immediately following the war. Nutter recalled that the uniform was much too small, that the sleeves ended about six inches above Shaw's wrists.

After commenting to McCombs on the excellent job Shaw had done in getting the Mart going, attending many cocktail parties, banquets, and receptions, Nutter shared that Shaw "was always the genteel, witty, gracious and entertaining gentleman…Yes, we knew about his life in the gay world. Though many who knew and worked with him did not know that he was queer at all and many did not know it until this thing [the Garrison investigation] broke. But he had a lot of those boys and young men around. Had lots of them working around the Trade Mart. Single men. Rarely hired any young married men—and he never dated girls—would drive around in that open car with those blonde kids with their long hair waving in the wind."[353]

Regarding Shaw's politics, Nutter said that, "I suppose he was a liberal Democrat. I was a Republican then but could never get an argument out of him. He was not much interested in politics. He worked for Kennedy a bit. But he was interested in cultural pursuits, preserving the French Quarter and that gay world they talk about."[354]

Richard Swenson recalled that Shaw "has been indifferent to the ramifications of politics, to religion, and to most things except his amazing running of that complicated Trade Mart, cultural and intellectual pursuits—and the boys. My wife had an attractive sister in New Orleans and we tried and tried to get Clay to join us as a date for her. But he always had a plausible and polite way of getting out of such things—nothing ever upset his poise, and he had a multitude of problems at the Trade Mart."[355]

Swenson went on to say that Shaw "associated with queer guys. You have to ring a bell to get in the outside gate of his house. Then there's a second gate. Gwen and I surprised him and I'm afraid by calling on him unannounced. He was in disarray. There was a bottle of champagne on the table and there was a young fellow walking around upstairs. Finally Clay called him down and introduced us. We left him alone down there (French Quarter) after that."[356]

William McFadden Duffy added that, "Clay was never political minded…Clay was always the poised, gracious urbane gentleman. He was always entertaining dignitaries from all over. Clay would come in looking spectacular, but always kind, genteel and had a way of turning fine compliments that pleased the ladies. He'd have a couple of drinks, visit around and quietly fade away. His political views were so quiet, few knew them. Over the 14 years I attended many meetings with him and never heard him mention politics. He was interested in plays, books, paintings, the gay world and running the Trade Mart and he organized it so smoothly."[357]

Holland McCombs declared that he had known Shaw since 1947, "and for ten years I did not know he was a deviate. When I learned about it (somewhat like the Swensons) I was sorry for him, but the fact did not interfere with our long-time friendship…He was always gracious, genteel, kind and generous of his time and efforts in behalf of others…He was spectacularly handsome, impeccably mannered, elegantly dressed…His feminine friends found him a great and witty and entertaining companion. The gals fairly drooled over him… I remember once when Clay strolled into a big and brilliant cocktail party, a candid beauty of a girl said, 'Clay Shaw is the most expensive looking man I ever saw'."[358]

McCombs added that Shaw was "a man who lived two distinct and separate lives. Like some others of his time and place—one above Canal Street and the other below…In the big business world of the uptown side he was an appreciated and distinguished member of society. But when he left the Trade Mart in the later afternoon and crossed over into the shadows of the narrow streets of downtown, he entered into his gay world that attracted many denizens of many shades of shadowy lives. Clay knew them and played with them in the bedrooms of the Quarter."[359]

# 7 · 906 Esplanade

In the year 1950, the Mart's progress continued unabated. In a letter to a prospective tenant, Shaw commented that the Mart idea was not a new one—in fact, he said, the idea of a marketplace is one of the oldest in human history, bringing buyers and sellers together. He also noted that the Mart currently had only twelve un-leased spaces.[360]

Shaw was well known to the local media by this time. In January, he accepted an invitation to the dedication of radio station WMRY, and spoke a few sentences on the air during the ceremony.[361] He also was invited to the opening of new administrative and studio facilities for WDSU-TV, in April 1950.[362] Shaw had come to know many writers of national magazines, local radio and early television personalities, and numerous local and national newspapers reporters.

Shaw's proposed second trip to South America, this time to the southernmost countries located there, was moving closer to being a reality. In a memo to Hecht in early January 1950, Shaw attached an itinerary for himself and Mario Bermúdez,[363] showing a planned visit to Chile, Argentina and Brazil soon thereafter.[364] However, the trip was again postponed due to conflicts in scheduling.

In January 1950, Chep Morrison won re-election to a second term as mayor of New Orleans. Shaw wrote congratulating him on his "sweeping victory," going on to say, "It is the City of New Orleans and its people who should be congratulated."

Morrison could always count on Shaw to participate in a publicized event, or on a civic committee. In the same month as his campaign victory, he asked Shaw to participate in the dedication ceremony for an overpass at Elysian Fields and Florida Avenue.[365] In April, he invited Shaw to serve as a member of the General Citizens' Committee for the inauguration of the newly-elected commission council.[366] Earlier, during Morrison's absence, acting Mayor Bernard J. McCloskey had invited Shaw to serve as a member of the Arrangements Committee for the visit of the Spanish ship "Juan Sebastion De Elcano."[367]

The citywide effort to make New Orleans an international city continued on many fronts. In early 1950, as part of ongoing efforts to interact with Latin America, civic officials in New Orleans formed an International Tourist Bureau to funnel tourists through New Orleans to Central and South America.[368]

The Mart, under Glenn Weekley's direction in public relations, produced several new pieces of promotional material during this time. One was a brochure designed around the questions: Who, What, Where and How? The Who were people such as buyers and sellers, the What was the International Trade Mart, the Where was the Mississippi River, and the How was the Gulf of Mexico. Another brochure told the general history of the Mart to that time.

The Mart by now had begun to market directly to buyers for department stores. A buyers' newsletter, published on a monthly basis, included articles about goods and customers at the Mart. Some of the newsletters carried columns written by Shaw, which emphasized the non-profit nature of the Mart, the lack of a profit motive, and the emphasis on spending all income above expenses on publicity for the Mart and its tenants. In a sign of the times, several of the headlined articles for the newsletter featured titles such as, "Jap Toys Continue Moving on Market" and "Jap Textiles Move Into U.S. Markets."[369] The buyers' newsletter was sent monthly to approximately 3,000 department stores around the country. The Mart also conducted a survey among those buyers to determine the types of goods they would like to see marketed in the tenants' display windows.

At Board of Directors' meetings in early 1950, Shaw's annual salary was increased from $10,000 to $12,000; the Executive Committee had approved the increase in October 1949. Discussion at these board meetings around this time concentrated on the problems the Mart had encountered becoming a success, including; 1) that the countries of Latin America had substantially used up the dollars accumulated during World War II, and 2) that it was difficult to change cultural buying habits—people were used to going to department stores for consumer goods rather than patronizing an institution like the Mart.

The Mart now had 108 tenants, although there had been considerable turnover; 249 total leases had been executed since the beginning of leasing activity. The turnover was impacted largely because small import-export firms sprang up continuously, then often went bankrupt quickly. The annual report for 1949, which Shaw wrote, emphasized that foreign trade needed to be freed from tariffs, regulations, and currency controls before international trade could be a complete success.

WWL Radio broadcast a live program from the lobby of the Mart on a weekly basis during this period. It would often open with the following: "This is John Kent speaking to you from the busiest corner in New Orleans—it's the main lobby of the famed International Trade Mart." The announcer would often give a brief description of the Mart's purpose and history.

A transcript of one program, broadcast by Kent on February 14, 1950, shows a general discussion of the proposed International Mississippi Valley World Trade Fair that was slated to take place in 1953, the year of the Louisiana Purchase sesquicentennial; Shaw, Lloyd Cobb, and Mayor Joseph Darst of St. Louis, Missouri were on the program. The plan was that the fair would open in St. Louis, then move to New Orleans in conjunction with the Louisiana Purchase celebration there. Shaw moderated the discussion, which also included Paul J. Neff, President of Missouri Pacific Lines.[370]

In February 1950, Shaw wrote to Cecil London with *Time* magazine's advertising department in St. Louis, complimenting him on his upcoming move to San Francisco; Shaw advised that San Francisco was a much nicer city than St. Louis.[371] Years later, after describing why he liked to live in New Orleans, Shaw commented that if he did not live in New Orleans, he would probably live in San Francisco.

The same month, Shaw wrote to Brent, indicating his support for Federal subsidies to the U.S. Merchant Marine. He indicated that the U.S. must match support that foreign governments gave to their shipping lines, and he recommended that a long-term public relations campaign be mounted, using Congress and the Maritime Commission to generate support for the funding.[372]

The tenants' newsletter kept everyone informed, not only of products for sale, either for import or export, but also of the arrival of new tenants in the building. The newsletter for February 22, 1950, announced that the Louisiana wing of the Civil Air Patrol was now located in the Mart.[373] The Civil Air Patrol was an organization that catered to individuals interested in flying. Lee Harvey Oswald, as a teenager, was a member during the mid-1950s, as was David W. Ferrie, a person closely connected with District Attorney Jim Garrison's investigation into the Kennedy assassination in 1966-67; various young men, many of them minors, were involved in the organization, under the tutelage of veteran pilots.

Also in early 1950, the continuing problems with the Czechoslovakian exhibit were discussed at meetings. It was agreed that the exhibit would be allowed to stay, if no evidence of subversive activities was discovered. Clem Bernard of the Young Men's Business Club spoke against allowing the exhibit to stay; in March 1950, Bernard asked the Mart to hold off renewal of the lease for the exhibit until an upcoming YMBC meeting.[374] Shaw spoke in favor of the exhibit, mentioning that he had purchased a towel in New Orleans recently that indicated it had been manufactured in the Soviet Union. It was finally decided that the Mart would cancel the lease if Czechoslovakia broke relations with the United States, apparently a possibility at the time. Shaw wrote a memo to Hecht discussing the controversy; Shaw indicated that he had never led anyone with the Young Men's Business Club to believe that the exhibit's lease would not be extended as long as the rent was being paid, and the space was used solely for commercial purposes.[375]

Also in March, Herbert Schwartz, one of the original founders of the Trade Mart, who had moved to New York City with his company, resigned from the Board of Directors. Lloyd Cobb accepted an invitation to remain on the Executive Committee of the Board of Directors of the Mart. David Stern, now publisher of the *Item*, was also elected to the Board of Directors.

Shaw spoke at the Rotary Club of Shreveport in early March 1950 on "New Orleans: The International City." John Wray Young, an activist in the Rotary Club there, was present for Shaw's speech.[376] Young and his wife, Margaret Mary Young, acted as a team to produce and design plays at the Shreveport Little Theater from the early 1930s until the early 1970s. Shaw became good friends with them and their children over the years; in 1967, their daughter Jill would be importantly around Shaw at the time of his arrest and during the following months.

The Mart hosted an art exhibit by Colombian artist Marcel Gómez. Gómez was a painter who also worked as a translator at International House, translating documents for both International House and the Mart. Gómez, a native of the Cartagena, Colombia area, was gay, and possibly was related to the wife of Mario Bermúdez. Bermúdez had brought Gómez to New Orleans in the late 1940s in an attempt to assuage a restless period in Gómez's life. Later, after Shaw's arrest in March 1967, a rumor would arise that Gómez was involved sexually with both Garrison and Shaw, and that jealousy over the matter was at least part of the reason for Shaw's arrest and prosecution by Garrison.

The rumor enjoyed some circulation in the New Orleans area during 1967, and one of the national tabloid newspapers mentioned it in a 1969 article, although Gómez's name was not mentioned directly. Richard Townley, an investigative reporter with WDSU-TV Channel 6 at the time, heard of the rumor and checked it out, but was unable to verify it to his satisfaction.[377] By the time of Shaw's arrest in 1967, Gómez had returned to Colombia.

By 1950, Mardi Gras was revving up to its biggest level since World War II. In response to a letter the previous week from a friend, Allen Knolle, who was working in Washington State and had written that he was homesick for Mardi Gras, Shaw told him to start planning for Carnival in 1951.[378] By April 1950, Shaw had purchased a new home at the corner of Esplanade and Dauphine Streets. Allen Knolle wrote to him again, this time from Olympia, Washington, "In Seattle, I have heard that you are the proud owner of a beautiful new home."[379] Shaw responded, "I do indeed have a fine new house with two enormous mortgages to match...See you next Carnival."[380]

Ted Lala, who popped up periodically at odd moments in various promotional events in Hollywood and New York over the years, also knew Shaw. In March 1950, he wrote to Shaw recommending Joseph Zachariah as a personal representative, courier, or contact man, who could possibly do some work for the Mart; Zachariah was heading to Paris at the time, and had planned a stop in New Orleans. In closing, Lala wrote, "I trust things in your domain are progressing, and that life in the deep south continues to be interesting."[381]

Potential competition to the Mart continued to appear. A $20 million World Trade Mart was planned for Manhattan; the project supposedly would be larger than the Chicago Merchandise Mart. Miami was also making a major push on the foreign trade issue. It sent a representative, Victor Bennett, Chairman of the Department of Marketing at the University of Miami, to explore the International Trade Mart, in preparation for a possible $50 million foreign trade center in Miami. As he usually did when discussing a potential competitor organization in another city, Shaw dismissed it by saying that such talk had been going on for several years, and that he would "believe it when I saw it."[382] Shaw had earlier visited Bennett at the University of Miami, and had given a speech to the Sales Executive Club there,[383] earning him once more the by-now familiar accolade that he was "by far the best speaker we have had at our club."[384] Throughout his career, Shaw was always gracious in entertaining potential competitors who wanted to tour the Mart, or in speaking to their groups if requested.

The issue of potential competition from other cities in the international trade arena prompted Shaw to inquire of attorney Kenneth Barranger about whether other cities could use the term "International Trade Mart." This was an indicator of a constant realization that New Orleans had been first on the scene with its new Mart, but that the edge might not last very long.

Shaw's work ethic, and flexible schedule outside of normal working hours, allowed him to be active in various organizations and committees. He was a member of the Policy and Project Committee of the Central Liaison Committee of the New Orleans Trading Area, an organization established to implement cooperation and collaboration between organizations and individuals in New Orleans for the purpose of developing commerce and industry in the area. He also accepted an invitation to serve on the Arrangements Committee for the visit of the president of Chile.[385] In addition, he was involved in a campaign for a commemorative postage stamp dealing with the first colony in Louisiana Territory.[386]

In the spring of 1950, Hecht reported to the Board of Directors on the lack of response among many members regarding attendance and service on committees.[387] This was an early indicator of the growing difference between International Trade Mart and International House. International House, with its restaurant and meeting rooms, and membership structure, generally inspired more participation among its directors and supporters than did the Mart, whose primary purpose was to rent spaces to tenants, but which did not have the prevailing social environment present at International House.

Controversial promoter Frank Dane's reputation had followed him around. In April 1950, J. B. Dauenhauer advised Shaw that Portuguese officials exhibiting at the Trade Mart after the recent fair in Chicago had commented that Dane had been in Chicago promoting his Mid-Century Exposition, but that the Portuguese officials had heard unfavorable things about him.[388]

As far as Dauenhauer himself was concerned, he continued to avoid social events related to the Mart, preferring to work behind the scenes, do his job, and go home. In May, he asked Goldie Moore to respond to the Citizen's Committee to honor the Prime Minister of Pakistan at the Roosevelt hotel, so that he would not be asked to attend the function on May 23rd; Shaw was in Washington, D.C. at the time.[389]

The Mart continued to seek tenants related to foreign trade activity. In response to an inquiry from a trade organization in Finland, which was interested in moving its exhibit from Chicago to New Orleans, Shaw advised its representative that New Orleans was no hotter in the summer than Chicago or New York City, surely a stretching of the truth. He also advised that New Orleans was a city of "650,000 people with 200,000 Negroes,"[390] and that there was a great market for Finnish goods in the Mid-Continent area of the United States.[391]

The Mart also attempted to interest Sweden in taking a space in some form in the Mart. As Sweden was not known as a large current or prospective trading partner of the United States at the time, the effort was an example of the Mart's efforts to try to get as many international tenants as possible into the building and think beyond the country's traditional economic partnerships, even if the final result was somewhat minimal.

Japan, rebounding from its devastating defeat in World War II, lost no time in pursuing international trade connections. Almost immediately after the war, representatives from Japan were crisscrossing the United States in search of business markets. Even though its primary purpose had been to facilitate trade to and from Latin America, and to perhaps a lesser extent with Europe, the Mart very early on sought Japan as a tenant in some form in the Mart. Japan had been a large trader with the United States well before World War II, and much cotton had been shipped to Japan through New Orleans prior to the war. Approximately $600 million of imports and exports to and from Latin America had passed through the Port of New Orleans in 1949, Shaw told the Ministry of International Trade and Industry for Japan.[392] Shaw also used Belgium's record of trade through New Orleans as an example of potential growth for Japan, since large amounts of imports from Belgium entered through the Port of New Orleans.[393] Shaw met with Japanese trade representatives at the Foreign Trade Fair in Chicago in August 1950, pushing the idea of Japanese representation in the Mart; he had earlier met with Japanese trade representatives in New York City. The efforts to gain Japanese representation in the Mart were not limited to Shaw; Theodore Brent actually wrote to General Douglas MacArthur, then still ruling Japan in his post-war role as Supreme Commander of the Allied Powers, requesting that Japan establish some type of agency in the Mart.[394]

Shaw served as a committee member on the Third Inter-American Congress of Municipalities, held in May 1950 in New Orleans.[395] He also served on the Executive Committee of the Industry Army Conference of 1950, an effort to develop better relations between American industry and the U.S. Army in the New Orleans area.[396] Earlier in the year, he served with Rudolf Hecht on the formation of the International Art Association.[397]

Shaw's friends, John Wray Young and Margaret Mary Young, continued to keep in touch. In May 1950, Geneva Palmer wrote to Shaw, advising him that Margaret Young had referred her to Shaw for a possible job as a hairdresser on a steamship line; she noted that the Youngs were opening a new production of *The Heiress* at the Shreveport Little Theater that week.[398]

In May 1950, Shaw visited Washington, D.C., causing him to turn down an invitation to attend a Propeller Club dinner in honor of Hale Boggs in New Orleans;[399] a letter from Glenn Weekley indicated that Shaw would return to New Orleans in two weeks.[400] Shaw and Mario Bermúdez sometimes visited various officials in Washington, including State Department officials and officials of foreign embassies in the United States, in preparation for their trips to Latin America or Europe. On other trips to Washington, Shaw would sometimes meet with IRS officials regarding tax issues related to the business structure of the Mart.

Tana Losada, with *Norte Magazine*, one of many publications at the time geared toward a mainly Latin American audience, solicited an ad from the Mart, and passed along to Shaw greetings from his long-time friend, Muriel Bultman Francis, who was running her talent agency in New York City. Losada mentioned that she had stayed at the Bultman's home in New Orleans recently, but that Shaw had been traveling up north at the time.[401]

In mid-1950, Mary Catanese, Shaw's secretary for the first four years, married and became Mary Craft. She left the Mart's employment and moved to Brooklyn, New York. A year later, the American Machine and Foundry Company sought a reference for her from Shaw.[402] Shaw responded that she had been an "extremely able employee, intelligent, courteous, tactful and capable of assuming responsibility."

Shaw continued to answer inquiries regarding oddball products. In late June 1950, he answered such a request from Managua, Nicaragua, this one for reproductions of animals other than horses (lions, elephants, swans) for use with merry-go-rounds.[403] The Mart answered many letters about specialized foreign products, and where they could be obtained. Such products included evaporated milk, cellophane, bamboo and ratan products, tallow fat, gum resin, tung oil and tung seeds, cacao beans, rubber bands, and cane fishing poles.

The Mart building initially had problems with its air conditioning system, but generally found that the system gave the building a cutting-edge atmosphere during the late 1940s and early 1950s. Air conditioning rapidly was becoming more widely used in the South, and was a great factor in increased productivity in extremely hot, humid regions such as New Orleans. J.M. Guillory, Manager of the Industrial and Commercial Division of New Orleans Public Service, Inc., wrote Shaw, advising him that even in severe winters, businesses in New Orleans might need to run air conditioning on warm, humid days. He indicated that the Mart's special electric rate was exceptionally low, and designed for air conditioning use all year long.[404]

As of July 1950, Shaw was still flying when time was of the essence. An expense statement captured his flight from New York City back to New Orleans. However, that same month he drove from New Orleans to Miami, Florida.[405]

The newsletter for August 9, 1950 reported that Shaw was attending the first International Trade Fair in Chicago, from August 3-10, 1950.[406] The Mart took out an exhibit at the fair, also known as the First United States International Trade Mart (a temporary rather than permanent exhibition). Shaw continued to suffer from the back injury that had plagued him since he first sustained it during basic military training in 1943. During the International Trade Fair in Chicago, he experienced a new round of pain.[407]

Shaw dealt not only directly with Mayor Chep Morrison; he also worked with various assistants of Morrison. One of those was W. Ray Scheuring, Executive Assistant to the mayor.[408] In a bizarre chain of events, Scheuring was killed in early 1961 during an altercation with an off-duty policeman on the Greater New Orleans Bridge leading to the West Bank of the Mississippi River. The man was the brother of New Orleans police officer Aloysius Habighorst. Habighorst's brother was represented at trial by Irvin Dymond, who later served as Shaw's lead attorney during his criminal trials. Officer Habighorst was the booking officer when Clay Shaw was arrested, and later testified that Shaw had freely admitted that he used the name "Clay Bertrand" as an alias, an important factor in the case against Shaw. The story emerged about a year after Shaw's arrest, and approximately a year before his trial; some have speculated that the story originated out of Officer Habighorst's hard feelings toward Irvin Dymond, who Habighorst felt did not do an adequate job defending his brother against the charges of killing Scheuring. Habighorst's testimony was never heard by the jury, as Shaw's attorney had not been present when Habighorst supposedly asked him about use of the "Clay Bertrand" alias, and because other police officials testified in contradiction to Habighorst about how booking procedures were carried out.

Shaw's abilities to communicate on the radio had not gone unnoticed among the New Orleans community. He received a request from the Jesuit House of Studies Building Fund, asking that he do a radio spot supporting the organization, whose purpose was to house a seminary to educate Jesuit priests.[409] Shaw responded that, "Although I am not a Catholic, I think such a project is a very good thing."[410] However, Shaw told the organization that the Mart's policy prohibited him from doing the spot.

By 1950, John Leonard had become City Editor of the *Southwest Citizen*, in Lake Charles, Louisiana. He wrote to Shaw requesting information from the American Chamber of Commerce in Paris.[411] Apparently, Shaw's effort to smooth over Leonard's dismissal had minimized any lasting hard feelings.

One of Shaw's many contacts among newsmen in New Orleans was Clayton Fritchey, editor of the *Item*.[412] Clayton Fritchey later moved to Washington, D.C. and served in various positions of public service in the Department of Defense. He also was an official with the Democratic National Committee, and served as Press Secretary to Adlai E. Stevenson in his presidential campaigns of 1952 and 1956.

In spite of its sweeping activities on behalf of international trade, the Mart decided during 1950 not to participate in hosting the United Nations Economic and Security Council; Theodore Brent advised Shaw that the Executive Committee had met and decided against it.[413] It was too large, too long of an event, and too costly to hold, Brent said. Shaw had initially recommended it, if the financing could be obtained. At one point, he had even tried to lean on Brent to have the Mississippi Shipping Company, of which Brent was President and Hecht was also a top officer, finance the major portion of the conference. However, Brent told him that it was important for such things to have broad-based support within the international trade community, saying, "We [Mississippi Shipping Company] will do our part. You can count on it. But others must do their part as well."

George Haverstick was a person who knew Shaw during this era, in both the gay community and the business community. Haverstick worked for the Port of New Orleans, and later for the Free Trade Zone. He also rented space at one of Shaw's residences. Haverstick was a somewhat unusual individual, known for holding his breath when he became angered or perplexed about something.[414] He was in New Orleans until the early 1960s, when he moved to San Diego, where he became a lawyer and city administrator.

In March 1950, Shaw had sold his residence at 537 Barracks Street to the famed French Quarter realtor Maybart Frost Morrison Blackshear, also known as "Frosty" Blackshear. Frosty Blackshear was an aunt of Lindy Boggs, wife of long-time Congressman Hale Boggs, who later served as Majority Leader of the House of Representatives, and also served on the Warren Commission after President Kennedy's assassination. After Hale Boggs' death from a plane crash in Alaska in 1972, Lindy Boggs then ran for Congress and served until 1997. Frosty Blackshear had been married twice at the time she began dealing with Clay Shaw on various real estate transactions. A lively personality, she was known for buying and selling properties throughout the French Quarter.

Shaw sold the property to Blackshear for $15,000, which netted him more than $7,500 after the payment of all loans, and considering his original down payment of $1,500. It was an early example of how Shaw increased his wealth over the years, in addition to his handsome salary. He would buy a rundown residence, live in it even while it was being remodeled or restored, then sell it once it was in a much better state of repair than when he had purchased it. He was able to deduct many of his ordinary expenses along the way, this easing the tax burden as well. After twenty years of such activity, in addition to earning a high salary, living relatively frugally, and enjoying the naturally upward pricing momentum of French Quarter property, he arrived in 1967, the year of his arrest, at his highest level of personal wealth.

After selling his residence, Shaw then purchased a set of properties at the corner of Dauphine Street and Esplanade Avenue. The set of properties consisted of 906 Esplanade, a four-story brick main building, along with a three-story set of slave quarters and a two-story carriage house, both of which fronted Dauphine Street. The carriage house at 1313 Dauphine Street served at Shaw's residence at the time of his arrest in March 1967, when it was famously raided by authorities. Shaw had originally planned to renovate the carriage house first, but changed course and decided instead to work on 906 Esplanade.[415] He estimated it would cost approximately $3,000 to complete the initial repairs and remodeling.

Shaw purchased the entire property for $42,500, and by late August 1950 had spent approximately $5,000 for improvements.[416] The property had nine units, eight occupied by tenants, and one by Shaw. The majority of it was financed by a commercial loan institution, but a significant amount was financed privately by businessman Carl Naihaus.[417] Shaw lived in the fourth floor of the building at 906 Esplanade during a portion of his ownership.

Shaw used Edward F. Wegmann, an attorney with the firm of Dart, Guidry and Price, as his civil attorney for real estate transactions. Edward Wegmann would remain Shaw's civil attorney throughout the rest of Shaw's life, and would play a very active role in Shaw's criminal defense, beginning seventeen years later, offering extremely important support during the darkest hours of Shaw's life. Wegmann and Shaw had dealt with each other on opposite sides as well; in January 1950, Wegmann had written to Shaw, indicating that he was representing Camille J. Alleman, a visitor who had slipped and fallen in the Mart.[418]

Immediately, Shaw and Wegmann began to run into various issues with the new property. First, they had to deal with the Office of Housing Expeditors, a governmental body left over from the war that dealt with rent control issues. Regarding the property at 906 Esplanade and its subsidiary properties, the main issue was the amount of rent that could be set for each apartment unit in the buildings. Rents were still somewhat tightly controlled, and could not be raised without official permission. However, the issue was complicated by the improvements that Shaw had done to the some of the units, and Wegmann attempted to argue that they were, in effect, new units that should be freed from rent control. When the Office of Housing Expeditors tried to impose maximum rental prices on some of the units, Wegmann complained that their comparisons were of dissimilar units in other locations.

Shaw and Wegmann also had issues in dealing with the Vieux Carré Commission. That body regulated buildings, both commercial and residential, in the French Quarter, and could rule on everything from architectural design to exterior upgrades. Shaw and Wegmann dealt with the commission regarding replacing wooden balconies at 906 Esplanade, as well as installing a new plate glass window and completing visible plumbing work. Shaw would continue to deal, intermittently, with the Vieux Carré Commission as he bought and sold various properties throughout the 1950s and 1960s.

Although Shaw was normally the epitome of diplomacy in dealing with different types of individuals across the board, he had some of the most trouble with neighbors near the 906 Esplanade properties. In July 1950, he responded to a letter from Mrs. Alma L. Hascall, a neighbor at 1309 Dauphine, who had complained about the noise from parties held at Shaw's property, and about a young blonde tenant, unidentified, who paraded around in scanty clothing. She complained that parties were being held until 2:00 or 3:00 in the morning, with loud music being played, that some of the tenants were wearing daring French bathing costumes, and that the blonde tenant had been involved in a rape and robbery case at 906 Esplanade just before Shaw purchased the property. She also protested that she was not a "Negro," as Shaw's blonde tenant had remarked, and furthermore she maintained that attorney Felix J. Puig, who lived at 1310 Dauphine Street, agreed with all of her comments. In an uncharacteristically scathing letter of response, Shaw was totally unsympathetic to her complaints. He did allow that she should let him know if any noise disturbed her, but maintained that he could not control what his tenants wore, and that he did not care what the race of the people were who lived at 1309 Dauphine Street, that all citizens of the United States had the same rights. Years later, after another such dispute, this time with a tenant, June Rolfe, Shaw would make an enemy, one who would later be a reporter who attended his trial, very unsympathetically, in 1969. In the case of Alma Hascall, however, she passed away in February 1967, less than a month before Shaw's legal troubles began.

**Shaw preoccupied with his thoughts, late 1940s or early 1950s (International Trade Mart Collection, Louisiana Research Collection, Tulane University)**

The Mart had begun to publish a Spanish-language newsletter called *Noticias Comerciales*, distributed throughout Latin America, as part of its overall thrust to appeal to businesses in those countries. After some criticism over the accuracy of the Spanish used in the publication, Shaw requested that Mario Bermúdez review all translations from English into Spanish for use in the newsletter.[419]

Shaw continued his busy speaking schedule, talking before the Lakeshore Lions Club in Baton Rouge, the Cooperative Club at the Roosevelt hotel in New Orleans, the Morgan City, Louisiana, Rotary Club, the Shreveport, Louisiana Rotary Club, and before the Ruth McEnery Stuart clan at the home of Mrs. Alexander Hyman in New Orleans. He also spoke to the chapter meeting of Epsilon Sigma Fraternity at the St. Charles Hotel,[420] and addressed the local chapter of Delta Kappa Gamma society of women educators.[421]

Shaw still attended to some of the smallest details involved in running the Mart. In September 1950, he wrote to J. Gibson Kerr, a member of the Scottish Council, apologizing that no one had been at the Mart to help him on a recent visit; Kerr had apparently complained that no receptionist was available, and that no one else bothered to help him when he stopped by.[422]

Shaw's family continued to refer to him as "Vern," as they had known him since childhood.[423] His cousin, Peggy Day, sometimes wrote to him in care of the Trade Mart, advising of her recent activities. Shaw's activities in New Orleans had long been separate from that of his family, almost a necessity considering his personal life. His parents lived far away in Shreveport, at least a six-hour drive, and most of his other close relatives were scattered from Baton Rouge to various parts of Mississippi, a minimum of an hour away. None lived in New Orleans for any length of time.

The Mart maintained a detailed scrapbook of its ongoing activities, and also kept a list of publications that had published articles about it in some form. As of 1950, that list totaled approximately fifteen pages of different publications. A majority of the publications were in the United States, but a large number were also in Latin America.

The tenants' bulletin for November 10, 1950, signed by Shaw, was devoted entirely to the issue of terrorism in Puerto Rico. Earlier in 1950, Puerto Rican independence activists had attempted to assassinate President Harry Truman in Washington, D.C., in an incident in which a Secret Service agent and one of the terrorists were killed.

Shaw invited his old New York friend Ken Williams, at that time Sales Manager for Madain Thomas Creations, to attend Mardi Gras in early 1951.[424] Shaw had known Williams through Robert Jackson, son of Shaw's old boss J.C. Jackson at Western Union in New Orleans, and had met with him again on a trip in October 1950.

After the Mart opened, and in the years that followed, its advertising budget became relatively lean. It preferred to use its own internal publications and direct mail as methods of reaching people, rather than placing display advertisements in publications. In December 1950, Shaw advised George Kein, with the advertising department of *The New York Times*, that the Mart declined to place an ad in the international edition of that influential publication.[425] Shaw similarly decided against advertising in publications related specifically to Latin America, including *Vision* and *Norte Magazine*, which pursued him for a number of years.

One of Shaw's many functions with the Mart was as building manager. As such, in 1949 he had joined the New Orleans chapter of the Building Owners and Managers Association, and had given a talk before the group at the Roosevelt hotel regarding the history of the International Trade Mart and its various activities.[426]. Although he usually delegated the task of attending the group's meetings to J.B. Dauenhauer, he was present for a December 1950 meeting related to civil defense, which dealt at least partly with a potential atomic bomb attack.

Shaw's old friend from New York City theater days, Judson O'Donnell, had relocated in the 1940s to Hollywood, California, where he was dependent on Shaw for some assistance. In December 1950, Shaw wrote him, advising O'Donnell to, "Please wire me present status of home. I have notice of foreclosure. Is sale going through? Regards."[427] Shaw signed the telegram "Lavergne."

Shaw also continued to communicate with another old social friend from New York City, Marion Seidenbach. Shaw had lived near Seidenbach and her husband Carl during the hectic days in New York City. In December 1950, he wired her a greeting of, "Happy birthday, Darling."[428]

Officials from other cities with an eye to competing with New Orleans regarding the international trade concept sought the help of Mart officials in designing their own organization. In August 1950, at the International Trade Fair in Chicago, Shaw met with Leland Cutler of the San Francisco World Trade Center Authority; Cutler had met Shaw on a visit to New Orleans the previous May. In December, Shaw wrote to Cutler, advising him of some of the features of the International Trade Mart, mentioning that there were no windows in the building, and that space on the first floor, and near elevators, garnered higher rent than other locations. Shaw commented that he hoped to be in San Francisco by the summer of 1951, and would visit with Cutler at that time.[429]

The newsletter dated December 20, 1950 indicated that Miss Maria Imelda Paprotna, owner of the European Import-Export Company, had opened the business the previous Friday in Suite 132 of the Mart. The entry went on to say that Paprotna, who was staying at the Hotel New Orleans, would go to Europe later in the month to check up on merchandise to be imported for sale in the shop. Among those attending the opening of Paprotna's business were Mayor Chep Morrison and the Consul General of Germany.[430]

The idea for a proposed chocolate (cocoa) processing facility had been in Theodore Brent's mind for some time, and somehow this new tenant became involved in the potential project. In a lengthy letter to soon-to-be Mart tenant Paprotna in September 1950, Shaw outlined Brent's thinking about it. Shaw asked for the reaction from her "principals" in Germany, and said that New Orleans investors were currently interested in the project. He asked that she send someone over from Germany to talk to the local investors.[431]

In November 1950, Shaw wrote to her again, this time mentioning the earlier efforts to establish a cocoa-related manufacturing plant in New Orleans through a Chicago company. He said that the efforts had fallen apart, and elaborated that the current investors did not want to establish a candy manufacturing company, but rather a cocoa-processing facility.[432] The idea of the cocoa facility would linger for several years.

At the end of 1950, the Mart awarded all of its employees one week's additional salary as a bonus, continuing the tradition begun in 1948.[433] The second full year of operations had been at least as successful as the first, with the promise of many more to come.

# 8 · A Return to South America

The annual report for 1950 showed rental income of $264,257, and normal operating expenses of $199,931, both down slightly from 1949. Interest expense over and above normal operating expenses was $44,757, yielding a net income of $21,229, up from $17,774 in 1949. Based upon a survey of tenants, it was estimated that approximately $50 million in goods had been sold through the Mart. European governments were becoming more interested in trade with the Mid-Continent area of the United States; Belgium, Netherlands, France, Italy, and Germany had private trade exhibits at the Mart. Colombia and Cuba also had displays. It was noted that thirty-six original leases would expire in July 1951, and estimated that ten to twelve of those tenants would leave the building. However, the increased use of the Mart as an actual trading center, as planned, was noted as well, along with the fact that several new publications meant to increase the public's awareness were being produced by the Mart.[434]

The actual occupancy of the building decreased slightly during 1950, to 88%, from its peak of above 90% in 1949. The constant turnover among tenants was a problem, but the Mart was also continuing to hold spaces for the potential of additional foreign exhibits.[435] The Mart made an arrangement with another broker/agent, Albert Serkes of New York, to try to fill the remaining spaces; the Mart was willing to pay him ten percent of the value of any leases arranged by him.

Maria Paprotna had a friend in Germany, Karl Haller, Jr., and she went to visit him in early January 1951. Shortly after she arrived, she sent a telegram to the Mart, indicating that she had had discussions with manufacturers in Germany, and that the Haller family company was interested in investing in the proposed cocoa-processing facility. She indicated that Karl Haller, Jr., who was in his thirties, would be the company's representative, and could come to New Orleans in approximately two months to discuss the project.[436]

Shaw continued to handle many routine inquiries made to the Mart. Among the letters he received in January 1951 was one from W.J. Sheridan, Vice President of Aurora Specialty Company of East Aurora, New York, which sold boxed paper products.[437] Later in the year, Shaw replied to an inquiry about rubber monkeys made in occupied Japan.[438] In answer to many of those inquiries, Shaw simply advised the writer of possible avenues for finding the offbeat product.

As a resident of the French Quarter for several years now, Shaw was very active in French Quarter activities. In January 1951, he received a letter announcing his appointment as one of the vice presidents of the Vieux Carré Committee. The letter was signed by Joseph W. Rault. Rault was a lawyer, and at the time President of the Chamber of Commerce. Over the years, he was also active with International House, serving as President during the second half of the 1950s. He was the father of Joseph W. Rault, Jr., who in 1967 would be one of the three main founders of Truth and Consequences, Inc., an organization formed to provide private financial support for Jim Garrison's investigation into the assassination of President Kennedy.

In the tenants' bulletin for January 4, 1951, Shaw announced that he was leaving on January 9 on his much-delayed trip to southern South America. The trip would cover Chile, Brazil, Argentina, and Uruguay, and possibly other countries, if time allowed; it would not include a return through Mexico.[439]

This trip to southern South America, long planned and repeatedly delayed, was finally put together somewhat hurriedly, and perhaps without as much enthusiasm as his earlier trip to the Caribbean, Central America and northern South America in 1949. After all, the Mart was mostly full at the time of this trip; the only hope was that one of the southern South American countries would eventually take space in the Mart. Only a relatively small amount of material has survived related to that trip; some details were captured in a few letters Shaw wrote after he returned.

In late January 1951, Shaw wrote to Brent and Hecht from Sao Paulo, Brazil, reporting on his visits to Chile, Argentina, Paraguay, and Uruguay. He mentioned that former Mart sales representative Rae Ordorica had been expelled from Bolivia, after being in Argentina for some time. Shaw also discussed a proposal to meet with famed Argentine First Lady Eva Perón, in an attempt to get Argentina to take out space in the Mart, a proposal that had been discouraged by other Argentineans in the government.[440]

Mario Bermúdez also accompanied Shaw on this trip, and together they met Vicente Manzorro, with the Ministry of Education in Buenos Aires, Argentina. Shaw and Bermúdez discussed having a potential exhibit of Manzorro's kindergarten children's paintings sometime during the next year at the Mart.[441]

**Shaw with Mario Bermúdez (left) prior to departure on international trip, probably early 1950s (International Trade Mart Collection, Louisiana Research Collection, Tulane University)**

Shaw took the time to remember his co-workers back home during his travels. During his time in South America, Shaw purchased various gifts of jewelry, including an aquamarine and four amethysts, for the women in the Mart office. Determined to make sure his money was not spent for naught, he followed up with the merchant in late April about the progress of those purchases.[442]

The Mart's weekly newsletters to tenants continued to report on important news within the Mart framework. The edition for February 14, 1951, reported on Shaw's return from his five-week trip to South America, noting that he had seen Chile, Argentina, and Brazil.[443]

One of Shaw's young friends was Stan Picher, who lived in Chicago during the 1950s, and later in San Francisco. Shaw had invited him to Mardi Gras, but at the time of the event in 1951, Shaw was in South America. Picher came anyway, so J.B. Dauenhauer made reservations for him at the Roosevelt hotel.[444] Picher was a friend of Chicago art dealer Joseph W. Faulkner; together they had the Main Street Book Store there. Joseph Faulkner would become somewhat well-known later in the 1950s for helping to expose a sensational art forgery fraud involving Elmyr de Hory, one of the most successful forgers of all times.

Picher was not the only friend of Shaw whose travel plans for Mardi Gras were brought into question that year. Ken Williams, Shaw's friend from his New York City days, wrote inquiring about the status of Mardi Gras, which had been affected by the outbreak of the Korean War. J.B. Dauenhauer wired Williams that Shaw was in South America at the time, but that Mardi Gras was being held on a limited basis, although all major parades had been canceled.[445]

Shaw may have missed the Mardi Gras celebration that year because of the trip, but was back at his desk by mid-February. In a letter to the Minister of Exterior Relations in Brazil, Shaw thanked him for showing Shaw around Rio de Janeiro, and he described the drive to Petropolis outside of the city as one of the most "marvelous" experiences of his life.[446]

It proved somewhat difficult for Maria Paprotna's friend Karl Haller to gain admittance to the United States. Being a German citizen, he ran into post-war scrutiny. In a letter to Theodore Brent in February, J.L. Barnicle, Traffic Representative of the Mississippi Shipping Company in Washington, D.C., indicated that the American consul in Germany had turned applications for admittance into the United States from German citizens over to military authorities, and to the newly-formed Central Intelligence Agency, to be checked and re-checked prior to admittance.[447]

Meanwhile, Theodore Brent continued to show an active and alert mind in dealing with all sorts of issues related to international trade in New Orleans. During the late 1940s and early 1950s, he often weighed in on the St. Lawrence Seaway that was being proposed along the U.S.-Canadian border, and which would allow vessels to travel from the Atlantic Ocean to the Great Lakes along the border between U.S. and Canada. The seaway was seen by some in the New Orleans area as potentially competitive with a proposed Intercoastal Canal that would provide a more direct shipping route from New Orleans to the Gulf of Mexico than down the Mississippi River. In February 1951, Brent wrote to A.B. Paterson, President of New Orleans Public Service, Inc., expressing support for the St. Lawrence Seaway. Brent shared that he had never participated in the opposition to the Seaway, and that New Orleans businessmen needed to stop opposing it, in order that support could be generated for the proposed Intercoastal Canal. Brent said the opposition to the St. Lawrence Seaway was only making enemies who might otherwise support the Louisiana project.[448] In March 1951, Brent wrote to Senator Allen Ellender, Louisiana's senior senator, analyzing the pros and cons of the St. Lawrence Seaway proposal.[449] He also wrote to Representative Henry D. Larcade, Jr., pushing the idea of the seaway south of New Orleans along the tidewater channel from New Orleans to the Gulf of Mexico.[450]

**Shaw with Theodore Brent (center) (International Trade Mart Collection, Louisiana Research Collection, Tulane University)**

Shortly after the trip to southern South America, Shaw went to Colombia on a brief business trip with Mario Bermúdez. Overall, he made at least three trips to Colombia, more than to any other South American country. The fact that Bermúdez was from Colombia contributed to the additional closeness of that country with New Orleans' efforts to increase international connections, compared to the remaining Central American, Caribbean and South American countries.

Shaw's travels abroad with other New Orleanians were noted by the Department of State on various occasions. In February 1951, while on the trip to southern South America with Bermúdez, the State Department office in Montevideo, Uruguay, indicated that Shaw and Bermúdez had stopped by to visit. The conversation centered on the Port of New Orleans, and the types of courses related to international relations offered by Louisiana universities. The State Department representative indicated that the two visitors left "an excellent impression."[451]

Shaw had visited the American Embassy in Buenos Aires, Argentina on his trip in the early part of the year, and the Department of State contacted him later to ask his opinion of the United States Information Service (USIS),[452] a Federal government agency devoted to promoting the United States' national interest in foreign countries.

It is interesting to note that as of 1951, Shaw had not yet been on a single promotional trip to Europe for the Mart. However, Charles Nutter, in a letter to Rudolf Hecht, noted that International House had an upcoming mission trip to Europe, and that Shaw had told him the month before that he wanted to go on the trip in order to thank the various Western European governments who had placed exhibits in the Mart. Nutter noted Shaw's efforts in Washington, D.C. along with Mario Bermúdez and Richard Swenson of the Port of New Orleans, conferring with European ambassadors and trade commissioners.[453] The Department of State in Washington, D.C. indicated that a New Orleans delegation that included Shaw, Swenson, and Bermúdez, had visited its office regarding an upcoming International House trip to Europe in September 1951. The memo reported that the group was very "public relations conscious." Shaw, who was the spokesman for the group, requested that appropriate personnel in diplomatic missions abroad be alerted to assist the visiting group on their trip. Bermúdez was going ahead two weeks earlier than the rest of the group to help arrange meetings.[454] The European trip was subsequently delayed until 1952.

The main investors interested in the prospective cocoa-processing facility were Theodore Brent, Rudolf Hecht, Lloyd Cobb, and Pendleton Lehde, another prominent figure in the New Orleans international business community. In a letter to Hecht in March 1951, Brent reiterated his long-standing desire to have a cocoa-processing plant in New Orleans; he indicated that an earlier effort to establish one with the Warfield Company of Chicago had ended because of that company's financial misfortunes.[455]

The Sixth Mississippi Valley World Trade Conference was held at the Roosevelt hotel in New Orleans during April 1951. The Mart also participated in the Eighth Annual Import/Export Clinic in Memphis, Tennessee in October 1951.

The newsletter of April 11, 1951, noted the arrival of Dr. Albert Serkes, a foreign trade consultant in New York City. The article mentioned that Serkes had been one of New Orleans' most enthusiastic boosters for many years.[456] Serkes' role was to help to find tenants to fill the remaining spaces in the Mart, although the results of his efforts were mixed.

In early May 1951, Shaw heard from Richard de Ayala, who was one of the owners of a champagne company in Rheims, France. When Shaw had served in Rheims under General Thrasher from the fall of 1944 into the fall of 1945, he had made friends among the prominent families in that area, many connected to the champagne industry. Ayala mentioned that "Renee has asked me about you many times, but I didn't have your address." He went on to say that he recalled Shaw leaving the Oise Section quite early, shortly after his arrival at SHAEF. Ayala noted that he also had served with the U.S. Army in the Oise Section, but wound up with the Western Base Section in Paris until the end of the war. He mentioned that Jean Seydoux, another champagne industry member from the Rheims area, shared that he had seen Shaw recently during a trip to the U.S.[457] In his reply two weeks later, Shaw addressed Ayala as "Dear Bunny," and said it was good to hear from him after all of these years, and to know that he was back in business and doing well. Shaw indicated that when he had gotten out of the Army in early 1946, he had come to New Orleans for a visit, and had been asked to take over the operation of the Mart. Shaw indicated that he had lost touch with most people from the war, but that Ed Weitzen, who also had served directly under General Thrasher, was now assistant to the president of the Bulova Watch Company in New York City. Shaw indicated that General Thrasher had become president of a large furniture distributing company in Kansas City, Missouri, but that he had recently retired, and was living the "Life of Riley," and passed on Thrasher's address to Ayala. Shaw said that he personally knew a liquor distributor in Shreveport, Louisiana, and would tell him about Ayala's products. Shaw asked Ayala to remember him to Renee, and to the Chimays when Ayala saw them. Shaw ended by saying that he hoped to find some good excuse to come to France and renew his pleasant relationship with the friends he had met in Rheims.[458]

During 1951, the Mart hired a college student named John J. Kelleher, giving him the position of Trade Analyst. Although the Mart designated his position as Trade Analyst, he really was more of an intern who assisted with correspondence, showed visitors around the Mart if Shaw or J.B. Dauenhauer were not available, and performed otherwise routine tasks under Shaw's or Dauenhauer's direction on a part-time basis. Most of the young men hired as Trade Analysts over the years were either college students, or young male members of the Latino community that gravitated around International House and the Mart.

Dauenhauer and his companion, Edgar Lee, Jr., took a European trip during May and June 1951. Shaw sent a letter of introduction to Sir Harold Boulton in New York City, asking for his assistance with Dauenhauer's and Lee's hotel stays in Great Britain.[459] Dauenhauer and Lee traveled through New York City, where they met with a member of the German consulate who presented them with two applications for admission into Germany. The itinerary for the entire trip included London, Brussels, the Hague, Amsterdam, Hamburg, Berlin, Geneva, Rome, and Paris. In a letter to Dauenhauer from the German consulate in New York City, Richard A. Fiessler enclosed the applications along with some instructions, and said,

"Best wishes for speedy recovery for Mr. Shaw," referring to a leg injury Shaw had recently suffered.[460]

In May 1951, Shaw wrote to Antonio Cirera, consul of Spain in New Orleans, mentioning that he had been and was still sick, but would be back to work the following week.[461] In June, Shaw wrote to Frank Runyan, the president of the Merchandise Mart in San Francisco, indicating that his possible trip to San Francisco was uncertain; his leg was still troubling him, and he might have to go in the hospital for ten days to fix the problem. Runyan and his wife had been in New Orleans recently, and had invited Shaw to San Francisco.[462] Shaw had injured his leg seriously as he was completing the remodeling of a portion of his property at 906 Esplanade Avenue. As a result of not being able to walk up several flights of stairs, he allowed another tenant to take the penthouse for a period, instead of occupying it himself.[463]

Glenn Weekley took an active role in suggesting ideas to promote the international trade effort; he proposed forming a committee to advise foreign trade commissions on the types of products that would sell in the Mid-Continent area.[464] Shaw approved the idea, and the committee was formed by June 1951.[465]

Also in June, a group of New Orleans businessmen, including several representatives from International House, made a trip to Venezuela on a trade mission, but Shaw was not among them.[466] After making a trip to Colombia in November 1951, Shaw would never again return to South America. His earlier travels there were primarily an effort to fill up the building, and he had generally succeeded in that regard, his next few years of traveling tended to reflect an increased emphasis on Europe.

In late June, Shaw wrote to Rudolf Hecht, who was traveling in Europe at the time, discussing the proposed cocoa plant in further detail. He indicated that Maria Paprotna had mentioned that Karl Haller was interested in establishing the plant, and would like to meet with investors.[467] Two weeks later, Hecht wrote to Shaw from Europe indicating that he had met with Karl Haller, Jr. and had discovered that Haller's interest in the proposed factory was a personal one, and that the Haller family company was not directly interested in the investment. He also indicated that he had learned that Maria Paprotna was engaged to marry Haller.[468]

Hale Boggs, the congressman from New Orleans, announced himself as a candidate for governor of Louisiana in the 1951 election; Boggs thought highly enough of Shaw that he sought his thoughts and suggestions regarding the upcoming gubernatorial campaign.[469] Earlier in his life, Boggs had been law partners with Chep Morrison and his half-brother, Jacob Morrison. Together, Boggs and Morrison were extremely important political figures in the New Orleans area from the mid-1940s through the 1960s. Boggs and Morrison each ran for governor of Louisiana, Morrison three times unsuccessfully. Boggs went on to lose the 1951 gubernatorial election.

Among other officials, Shaw dealt with the local representatives of the U.S. Department of Commerce in New Orleans on a regular basis. In August 1951, Harold C. Jackson and Paul L. Vogel wrote, thanking him for helping to entertain the French Optical Mission that had recently visited the city.[470]

The Guatemalan exhibit moved out of the International Trade Mart, showing the difficulty that the Mart had even in keeping basic international tenants from its targeted Latin American market.[471] Sometimes the lack of interest in space in the Mart on the part of international trade associations and governmental departments was purely a matter of budget, but it was also partly due to the fact that the Mart, for all its uniqueness, was simply a building, competing for tenants on price and location with many other buildings.

The relatively new United Nations was still somewhat popular in the United States in those days, and Chep Morrison appointed Shaw as a vice president of the committee to celebrate United Nations Day, in the fall of each year, for several years during the 1950s.

Shaw immediately warmed to the assignment, speaking to the New Orleans Business and Professional Women's Club about the role of the United Nations in the world.[472]

In November 1951, Shaw traveled again to Colombia to be a judge in the Miss Colombia contest. Shaw had been appointed to the jury in August by Rafael Escallón Villa, the mayor of Cartagena, and the contest took place during the city's Independence Day.[473] Shaw was instructed to fly to the city of Barranquilla, near Cartagena, and to bring a black tuxedo and one or two costumes.[474]

The event was noteworthy because Shaw delivered a speech of some length in Spanish to the crowd. He wrote the speech in English, then had it translated prior to his departure. In the speech, he acknowledged his own lack of confidence with the Spanish language, and he noted that citizens of North America were "very stupid" with languages, and that he was no exception. Any mistakes he made in the speech, he said, were ones "of the lips," and "not of the heart."

In the speech, he told the audience that the task before him was like picking "the most beautiful flower" in the garden. He echoed that sentiment in a post-trip letter to the mayor, where he commented that picking Miss Colombia was a pleasant task, but that it had been very difficult to choose among all the lovely contestants; the eventual winner was Senorita Leonor Navia Orejuela.[475]

The November 1951 trip to Colombia was also noteworthy in that it was Shaw's last trip to South America, although in later years it was generally thought that he had traveled often to that continent. Many also came to think that Shaw was fluent in Spanish, but the events of this trip, and other evidence, show otherwise. It is highly unlikely that his knowledge of Spanish increased dramatically after travel to that area became less of a priority. It is true that he made trips in the later 1950s to Mexico, Cuba, and Puerto Rico, and took some vacations to Mexico in the 1960s, but there is little evidence that he mastered Spanish to any large degree beyond the level he had reached by the end of 1951.

In December 1951, following Shaw's visit to Colombia, he received a letter from Bonifacio Velez, who had been in the audience at the beauty contest. In the letter, Velez confirmed the closing of the Colombian exhibit in the Trade Mart, and explained that he was writing the letter to Shaw in Spanish, because Shaw had spoken very elegantly in Spanish at the beauty contest. However, the letter was translated into English for Shaw's reading.[476] Shaw had written to Velez in English in November, because his Spanish was "lamentable." The purpose of that letter had been to try to salvage the Colombian exhibit in the Mart.[477]

After the initial years of reaching out to Latin America, the Mart and International House were now thinking in terms of seeking more European business. Shaw commented in a letter in November 1951 that the proposed trade mission to Europe, originally scheduled for September 1951, had been canceled due to conflicts in the schedules of the various participants, but had been rescheduled for the spring of 1952.

Theodore Brent and Rudolf Hecht continued their efforts to make the proposed cocoa facility a reality. Since cocoa was an important product available for shipping from Africa, having a processing plant in New Orleans would fit in neatly with Brent and Hecht's overall business interests. However, Maria Imelda Paprotna had begun to default on commitments from her own business to customers and to foreign governments, and soon letters began to arrive at the Mart concerning attempts to locate her without success. Because of her connection to the cocoa project, Shaw generally defended her in replies, indicating that she had gone to Germany to get married to Haller, and that she had been delayed in returning due to difficulties with her visa, but that she should give proper attention to customer complaints as soon as she returned.[478]

New Orleans in the 1950s was known more as a business city than a tourist city, although tourism was strong as well. The administrations of Mayor Chep Morrison concentrated on bringing new business to the area. A big score in 1951 was the opening of the Kaiser Aluminum plant, owned by industrial giant Henry Kaiser, which opened in Chalmette, near New Orleans. Shaw was invited to the opening of the plant.[479]

The Mart had kept track of the number of people visiting the building since it opened. In 1951, more than 117,000 people visited the building. Many were visiting to meet with the numerous business people within, but many were groups of students and other parties interested in touring the building as an attraction.

Shaw's parents continued to live in Shreveport, Louisiana during 1951. In January 1952, Shaw traveled on a goodwill trip to Kansas City with other New Orleans businessmen, at the invitation of the International Trade Club of Greater Kansas City. On his way back to New Orleans, Shaw broke his train trip at Shreveport, in order to visit his parents and some friends in the Shreveport area.[480]

The annual report for the year 1951 indicated that total rental revenue was $265,619, up slightly from 1950. The Mart was rented at 88% capacity over the entire year. Most original three-year leases had expired, but a majority of them had been renewed. Operating expenses totaled $203,424, with interest expense over and above that of $43,004, leaving operating income of $21,235, flat compared to the year before, but still a success in terms of the expectations of the Mart's founders. The report commented that the U.S. government had been re-arming its military services after World War II, spending dollars overseas for raw material, and spreading the purchases over several years to avoid shortages in consumer goods—that had helped to increase international trade to some degree. During 1951, the Mart had held several sample shows in the building, separate from the individual tenant displays, showcasing a variety of goods. Also, the Mart continued its radio show on WWL Radio, providing news about the happenings of the Mart and its tenants.[481]

# 9 · A Letter to the CIA

The population of New Orleans at the beginning of 1952 was 586,400. A report on the city's economy for 1951 said that fourteen out of sixteen business indicators hit new records that year, including retail sales volume, bank deposits, and wholesale sales.[482]

By 1952, Shaw was still living at 906 Esplanade, and shown as the Managing Director of the Mart in the city directory.[483] However, Jeff Biddison and Shaw had parted ways. One friend of Shaw recalls him telling his friend Louis Fischer about the news; Shaw was somewhat emotional, on the verge of tears. The two, however, would eventually evolve into being good friends, and business associates in real estate, after Biddison had worked at several types of jobs during the middle 1950s. "They were lovers and it changed over time to each had their own boys and so on like that," according to Dr. Martin Palmer, a mutual friend. "But they were very fast friends."[484]

Hale Boggs continued to work closely with the City of New Orleans from his seat in the U.S. House of Representatives. He wrote Shaw, indicating that he was sponsoring a House resolution endorsing and recognizing the International Trade Fair in New Orleans, and the Inter-American Cultural and Trade Center.[485] The international trade field in the United States had suffered somewhat during the Korean War (the Chicago International Trade Fair was canceled due to "world conditions;"[486]) and the resolution was intended to boost the visibility and draw of such business.

Shaw had planned to visit the Yucatan Peninsula in Mexico as part of a New Orleans trade delegation in early 1952, including a group from International House, but had to cancel due to a conflict in his schedule. Glenn Weekley, the Mart's Public Relations Director, was active in the delegation, which made the trip in February.

Shaw continued his activities in helping the investors with the proposed cocoa facility. In mid-January 1952, he traveled to the Henry Grady Hotel in Atlanta to survey local candy manufacturers regarding their openness to the factory.[487] He also prepared a slick-cover memorandum report under his name, entitled "A Proposed Chocolate Processing Plant," distributed to potential investors, financiers, and other interested parties.

In late January, he wrote to Mario Bermúdez, who was in Mexico City at the time, indicating that he hoped Bermúdez's scholarship program was coming along well. Shaw also related that the Colombian exhibition was closing, an indicator of the somewhat uneven performance of the Mart in reaching its goals.[488]

During 1952, the Mart continued to receive its usual series of inquiries for interesting and offbeat products. For example, a handwritten letter from Billy Murphy of Houston, Texas inquired about an Egyptian herb, which grew along the Nile River, that he could use to regain his strength.[489]

The Joseph A. Maybin Import/Export Institute had closed by this time, and students had been transferred to the S.J. Peters School.[490] However, after 1952, there would be no institution in the city specifically devoted to training students in the import/export field, other than the major universities. The GI Bill had run its course, causing many specialty institutions of that sort to disappear.

In February, Glenn Weekley corresponded with Dr. Jutta Schaller, a trade consultant with the West German government. Dr. Schaller had written from Munich, Germany explaining that the publication *Wer Liefert* was an East German-sponsored publication operating in West Germany.[491] Weekley had come across the publication, and told Schaller that he had brought the publication to Shaw's attention, and that Shaw had passed it on to "our Counter Intelligence Service."[492]

In one of his few, if not his only, written communication directly to the Central Intelligence Agency, Shaw wrote to his contact, Hunter Leake II, at the CIA's office in the old Masonic Temple building. The letter discussed the East German publication *Wer Liefert*, and enclosed the letter from Dr. Schaller discussing an East German entity that was trying to become involved in international trade circles. Shaw referenced an earlier conversation he had with Leake about the same subject, and the substance of that conversation is captured in one of the CIA reports concerning Shaw which has survived over the years. The letter was not addressed to the Central Intelligence Agency, but simply to Hunter Leake II at the address on St. Charles Avenue.[493] The address is where the CIA and other Federal governmental agencies, including the Department of State in New Orleans, were located at the time.

In late February 1952, an unidentified author sent a lengthy letter to Daniel Rudsten with the mayor's office in Boston, Massachusetts. The letter discussed Boston's efforts to develop an International Trade Mart similar to that of New Orleans. The writer said that he had conferred with Shaw and other staff members at the Mart, and had discovered that the separate nature of the Mart and International House had been "accidental to some degree." The writer made the following points: 1) wives of consular officials had no place of their own to meet, at either the Mart or International House; 2) there was no storage space in the Mart, other than the tenants' offices; and 3) there was no place for airport passengers waiting to disembark to the New Orleans main airport in suburban Kenner; the writer indicated the Mart should have been designed as a transportation terminal as well as a trade mart.[494]

Shaw continued his many civic duties during 1952. He accepted the co-chairmanship of the import committee of the Export Managers' Club.[495] He also served as publicity chairman for the local Italian Flood Relief Committee. The committee had been formed in late 1951 by some of the city's prominent Italian-American residents, and was chaired by George Piazza; it was a city-wide effort. As part of his duties, Shaw sent announcements to be used as radio spots to raise funds for the relief effort. According to a February 1952 press release, donations totaled $31,147 in cash, with an estimated $4,936 in donations of medicine, clothing and food.[496] In 1967, George Piazza's son, also named George, who had become a young lawyer by that time, emerged in the Jim Garrison investigation as a somewhat close acquaintance of David Ferrie, and as the lawyer representing Ferrie's longtime friend James Lewallen in Lewallen's dealings with Garrison's office. However, Piazza was killed in an airliner crash at the end of March 1967, less than one month after Shaw's arrest.

Part of the purpose of the Mart, International House, the Free Trade Zone, and the other efforts of New Orleans to attract international trade was, of course, to increase the business done by local merchants, whether or not they were directly involved in international trade. Owners of many different types of businesses saw a clear benefit from the focus on international trade, both because of the goods that would flow through New Orleans, and because of the number of visitors such an effort would bring. Consequently, Brent and Hecht kept pressure on board members to be active participants in Mart duties. In a March 1952 letter to Brent, Seymour Weiss, President and Managing Director of the Roosevelt hotel and himself a prominent man, indicated he would be out of town and would miss the upcoming nominating committee meeting, which would nominate a new set of members of the Board of Directors. Weiss wrote that he hoped his absence would not be construed as lack of interest.[497]

At a Board of Directors meeting in late March 1952, it was discussed that Shaw was going to Europe during April to attend half a dozen business fairs; in Milan, Lyon, Basle, London, Brussels, and Paris. It would be Shaw's first visit to Europe since he had served in the Army in England and France during the period from 1943 to 1945. Theodore Brent told the board that the Mart was doing well, and that it now must broaden its activities, the main reason for Shaw's trip. Shaw discussed a new project—a "New Orleans Import Special Train"—to visit large cities in the Mississippi Valley region, a program which was still in its infancy, with no costs yet incurred. There was also discussion of a trip Shaw and Mart attorney Kenneth Barranger had made to Washington, D.C. in the fall of 1951, in an effort to obtain an IRS ruling that, as a non-profit entity, the Mart was tax-exempt. It was a ruling that had to be renewed each year, and no decision had been handed down at the time of the board meeting.[498]

The Mississippi Valley World Trade Conference again held its annual meeting in New Orleans in 1952. The Conference invited General George Marshall to speak, but he was on vacation in Mexico at the time, was committed to three speeches in New England when he returned, and could not attend the conference.[499]

The European trip by New Orleans businessmen occurred from April 5 to June 3, 1952. Shaw went to Washington first, then on to New York City and Europe. His total expenses during that trip were $1,793.19. Unlike the earlier promotional trips Shaw and Bermúdez had taken to Latin America, the European trip consisted of a much larger group.

Shaw had been in Europe during World War II, of course, but primarily in England and France. He wrote to J.B. Dauenhauer from Italy in mid-April, saying, "Rome was all you said it was—details on my return—will write again from Switzerland."[500] Dauenhauer responded to Shaw about a week later saying that Irma Lagan, Brent's secretary, had received a cable from Brent, who was off on another ocean voyage. He also indicated that Maria Paprotna Haller wanted to drop her business's current space in the Mart and add another; Dauenhauer asked if that was acceptable to Shaw and Brent. In a postscript, Dauenhauer noted that two letters marked "personal" had arrived for Shaw, one of which was from Judson O'Donnell, and that he was sending them to Shaw in Brussels.[501]

The Mart published a new tenant directory in 1952, which listed the personnel of all tenants. Jeff Biddison was noted still to be employed by Delta Line, although he would leave for another job later that year. Marcel Gomez and Mario Bermúdez were with the Department of International Relations for the City of New Orleans, and as of May 1952, they were joined by a young woman from New York—Beryl Donnath. The April 1952 issue of *The Breeze*, an in-house newsletter of International House, noted that Donnath would be the new secretary for the Department of International Relations of International House; Donnath was currently packing her things in New York City for the move to New Orleans. The article also mentioned that Donnath had intended originally to visit New Orleans only for a few days, but that she had found the job and decided to stay.[502] After Shaw's arrest in 1967, he would use Beryl Donnath for assistance in typing portions of a diary he kept for at least eight months following the arrest.

Also in the tenant directory, Shaw's friend George Haverstick was shown as working for the Standard Oil Company, or Esso, as it was known in those days. Clay J. Calhoun with the Heartland Trading Company was also a tenant; he later was reportedly investigated by District Attorney Jim Garrison's office, at least briefly, as possibly being the mysterious "Clay Bertrand," the shadowy character whose name surfaced after the Kennedy assassination.

In June 1952, Shaw wrote to Charles Empson at the Embassy of Great Britain in Washington, D.C., expressing his desire for British goods to be represented in the Trade Mart. Shaw noted that he would be in Washington in November, and hoped to see Empson then, adding that Charles Arning, the British consul in New Orleans, had been into the Mart to see him about the matter a day or two before.[503]

John J. Kelleher, who had been the first trade analyst hired at the Mart, was looking for a permanent job as of mid-1952. Rather than being hired by the Mart, however, which had no openings, he used his connections of working for Shaw to further his search. Shaw composed a letter of introduction indicating that Kelleher was a graduate student at Tulane, completing his thesis on foreign trade, and was seeking employment in that field; Shaw wrote to both the Mississippi Shipping Company and Alcoa Steamship Company on behalf of Kelleher.[504] Upon Kelleher's departure, the Mart hired a new trade analyst, Manuel O. Delgado, Jr. for the position.

The Mart always pushed an uncompromising view of foreign trade, supporting free trade free of tariffs. In a letter dated July 1, 1952 to Robert H. Johnson, the president of American Exporter in New York City, Shaw mentioned his recent two-month trip to Europe. He criticized protective tariffs, and discussed the "buy American" concept popular at the time, indicating that those who believed in free trade should bring their message to the "unconverted."[505]

At a Board of Directors' meeting in July 1952, it was decided to re-subscribe to *Latin American Reports*, the publication published by William Gaudet, even though the cost had increased. Theodore Brent thought the publication useful, and although New York City interests wanted it to re-locate there, Brent wanted it to remain in New Orleans. Shaw reported on his recent trip to Europe, mentioning that tariffs were still a big problem. He also noted that the Russians were using the Marshall Plan in a propagandistic way, saying that it was the U.S.'s way of dumping overproduction of goods on an impoverished Europe. On the positive side, Shaw commented that European trade was increasing due to the creation of the international atmosphere in New Orleans. He noted that the Mart was now 98% rented, with only two spaces available for rental, and that seventy percent of the tenants were involved in international trade in some way.[506]

After his trip to Europe in April and May 1952, Shaw followed up with the normal letters to various individuals he had met in the commercial and governmental worlds of the countries he visited. He also wrote to Rudolf Hecht, mentioning the Detroit delegation that had been in Europe at the same time, and also representatives of the proposed San Francisco World Trade Center, which had yet to be developed. He commented that the New Orleans delegation to Europe the following year needed to be a very large one, to offset the efforts of other cities.[507]

Additionally, he sent a letter to one of his hostesses, Mrs. J.F. Vreden-Van Den Brine, thanking her for showing him around the canals of Amsterdam, and for a "delightful" luncheon she had hosted. He mentioned a proposed return trip in June 1953, with an even larger New Orleans delegation. In the letter, he also discussed "cultured" Europeans and Americans, saying, "There are some individuals who share a common awareness of the things that make life valuable and worthwhile, and when they meet, they recognize what they have in common instantly."[508]

The Mart continued to work closely with many other New Orleans institutions, although there were natural territorial and political elements that sometimes made even those institutions competitive with the Mart. The Board of Commissioners of the Port of New Orleans was one such group. In a letter to E.H. Lockenberg, General Manager of the Board of Commissioners, Theodore Brent designated Shaw as the Mart's representative for a project regarding re-surveying the Port, and drawing a new large scaled, detailed map. Around the same time, the Board of Commissioners proposed producing a film about the Port of New Orleans, and requested that the Mart, along with other civic groups, pay a portion of the expenses.

In some of his correspondence with the Board of Commissioners of the Port, Shaw also related the sensitivity Mart officials felt over potential new competition. In a letter to Richard Swensen, the Board of Commissioner's Public Relations Director, Shaw commented about the recently received annual statistics report from the Port of Houston, Texas, and commented, "Anything Houston can do, we can do better."[509] In a letter to Lewis Bourgeois, Director of Commerce for the Board of Commissioners, Shaw discussed Dallas's proposed

International Trade Mart, saying that he did not believe Dallas was a very auspicious spot for an international center of trade, but that "competition is the life of trade, and imitation is the sincerest form of flattery."[510] In another letter to Bourgeois in December, Shaw, responding to recent comments by Bourgeois about the number of nations represented in the Mart, wrote that ten countries maintained commercial offices in the Mart, but that "well over" twenty nations' goods were on display and for sale there.[511]

The Mart was noted for its display of flags from various countries on top of the building. As of mid-1952, approximately sixty flags had flown on the top of the building at one time or another during the previous year, in varying group combinations[512]

The Board of Commissioners of the Port tracked by category the largest groups of items that passed through the Port of New Orleans, which the Mart then often used as part of its own promotion. By far the two largest products were coffee and bananas, but the Port also tracked vehicles and other large ticket items as well.

Theodore Brent, then approaching eighty, continued to serve as President of the Mart; audited financial statements were addressed to him by Peat, Marwick, the Mart's outside accounting firm. Kenneth Barranger, the Mart's attorney, advised the auditors that, as of 1952, no lawsuits were pending for or against the institution, and there were no fixed obligations for legal services rendered.[513]

By mid-1952, Maria Paprotna and Karl Haller were married. Paprotna's business in the Mart had begun to run into financial difficulties, and she was late paying the rent. In a memo to Shaw in mid-June 1952, Hecht discussed Karl Haller's continuing visa problems, and indicated that "your friend" Mrs. Haller had called him twice recently. Hecht indicated she had begun to get into her monetary problems, and noted the rental issue, but Hecht had told her to discuss it with Shaw first.[514]

The cocoa project had not gotten far off the drawing board. It had been mainly Brent's idea; Hecht was also very interested, however. In a letter to Shaw in late June, Hecht indicated that he was willing to put up at least $5,000, and possibly as much as $7,500, if it was necessary to make the project a success.[515]

In August 1952, Shaw consulted with Glenn Weekley, who was still serving as Public Relations Director, regarding a proposal to emphasize exports more, as special programs during the first few years had mainly emphasized imports.[516] By now, Weekley had been at the job approximately three years, and had been an important force in what could be looked back upon as the Mart's most successful period. He had been largely responsible for beginning and/or implementing several publications of the Mart, including: 1) the newsletter that dealt with issues of interest about trade and/or the Mart on a weekly basis, 2) the buyers' newsletter, produced on a monthly basis to department stores and gift store buyers, 3) a commercial digest, sent monthly to business writers at newspapers and magazines, and 4) *Noticias Comerciales*, a quarterly publication in Spanish distributed to importers and department store proprietors in Latin America.[517]

The number of people visiting the Mart continued to be strong in 1952, at approximately 15,000 to 20,000 per month. The initial interest among the general public had leveled off somewhat, but the Mart continued to be visited by school groups and delegations of businessmen from various cities and towns. One new attraction, which had started the previous year, was an international sample show in the lobby. Various wares from overseas were exhibited, including china, glass, small house wares, jewelry, toys, decorative accessories, and handicrafts.

Shaw continued his regular speaking schedule, talking with groups such as the Pascagoula, Mississippi Rotary Club, the Southern Regional Conference of the National Office Management Association, held at the Jung Hotel in New Orleans, the Southern Regional Student Nurse Recruit Conference, also held in New Orleans, the New Orleans Credit Men's Association, the Piggly Wiggly Convention Luncheon, held at the Roosevelt hotel, the Rotary Club of New Orleans, the New Orleans Pilot Club, the Export Manager's Club at International House, the New Orleans Lions Club, and the New Orleans Secretaries Association. As that schedule shows, Shaw had cut back even on his regular domestic travel to promote the Mart through more local speaking efforts. With the building close to being as fully occupied as possible, there was less point in incurring the expenses that more extensive travel would require.

The Mart had long been interested in having Japan as a tenant, because of its importance as a major exporter, but it also began to pursue Thailand and other Asian countries, in an effort to broaden its reputation as an international center of sorts, even if the results steered away from its original goal of primarily courting Latin American countries. The number of foreign countries who had an actual presence in the Mart was disappointing, but with a full building, at least the institution was profitable.

A proposal had been made to run an "Import Special" train from New Orleans to the major cities along the Kansas City Southern Railway Line. The proposal called for four or five railroad cars to be converted and decorated in New Orleans, for the purpose of carrying and promoting merchandise to those major cities. Illinois Central Railway would provide the cars, and the City of New Orleans and its various civic organizations would pay the expenses; local trade officials would ride along with the merchandise and help promote New Orleans. However, the idea was eventually dropped for lack of interest.

Although almost no one thought so at the time, the Mart arguably was close to reaching its peak of operations during the year 1952, at least for many years to come. Occupancy was close to 100%. However, the only way the institution could expand was to build a new building, or buy a larger one, and the newness had worn off to a large degree. That, combined with the increasing competition, or proposed competition, from other cities, and even from other institutions within New Orleans, all contributed to a sort of plateau effect upon the Mart.

Some were concerned about the effects of popularity and success, of course. The idea of the Mart being a sort of experiment that could be enlarged if the idea was successful had been there from the beginning, but it became a possible reality once the Mart approached full occupancy in the early 1950s. In early August 1952, Theodore Brent, now less than a year from the end of his life, wrote Shaw a long letter, detailing the need for both the Mart and International House to have more space; the idea was that the Mart needed either to keep growing, or it would founder. Shaw responded, saying that it might not be necessary for the two institutions to own their own buildings; he envisioned a nine-story building that would hold both organizations, and be able to offer tenants the space they needed.[518] Brent also wrote to Rudolf Hecht, who was traveling in Europe, disclosing that Brent, Charles Nutter, and Shaw had, back in mid-July, talked by conference call with local realtor Harry Latter about using Asher Lowich, of Lowich Brothers in Waco, Texas, to help secure additional space; Lowich had discussed a rent-to-own option with them earlier in 1952, and had also been in to see Nutter about that possibility. Brent told Hecht that he used to feel that both the Mart and International House should have their own buildings, calling it a "hereditary feeling," and saying the reasoning behind it was "so we couldn't be put out in the cold on a bad winter's day." However, Brent said that he now felt that leased premises were a possibility.[519] Hecht responded from Paris, saying he opposed the Mart renting a building. Hecht said that he had asked Harry Latter to pursue selling the existing building, and indicated that he would like to see the Mart and International House occupy the same building.[520]

Brent continued to contribute ideas to both the Mart and International House in various areas. In a memo to Richard Jones, then-President of International House, Brent commented that the food quality at International House's restaurant was keeping people away. He noted that Seymour Weiss had earlier recommended getting an executive chef for the restaurant, and Brent believed that the organization might be able to afford one at that point.[521]

Shaw met trade show icon Helen Brett, who staged large exhibitions in major cities across the U.S. for many years, on August 28, 1952.[522] Brett began her organization, still in existence today, in 1946. The New Orleans Gift Show, staged by Brett, was held from September 28 through October 2, 1952. Brett had called upon Shaw in an attempt to convince Mart tenants to participate in the show, held at the Roosevelt hotel. Some tenants chose to participate in the show, with mixed results.

Shaw spoke to Rotary Clubs in Tallulah, Louisiana, Paterson, Louisiana, and in Monroe, Louisiana, on a swing to the northern part of the state in October 1952. After his trip, he received a letter from M.F. Rice, with Gulf Refining Company, thanking him for the speech to the Monroe Rotary Club; Rice said that most members thought it was one of the finest addresses they had heard that year.[523]

The spirit of the Mart's mission sometimes filled even the administrative employees below Shaw and Dauenhauer. In October 1952, Goldie Moore, on a vacation to San Francisco with friends, toured the Western Merchandise Mart in that city.[524] Moore, hired at a very early stage in the Mart's development, would remain an employee within the Mart's framework until the 1980s.

Interest in the cocoa-processing project continued throughout 1952. In a letter to Karl Haller in mid-October, Rudolf Hecht drove home the point that New Orleans businessmen interested in the project wanted at least 51% control of the eventual investment and operation.[525] Cocoa was primarily an African and South American product, and Delta Line already had ships traveling to and from both of those continents. Bringing cocoa in through the Port of New Orleans to be processed would complement the already existing set of operations.

In a memo in October to Brent and Hecht, Shaw indicated that the Mart was attracting more of the type of tenants originally envisioned, but that there were not enough import-related firms; the international-type tenants were mostly export-related firms, and foreign trade commissions. He commented that even local import firms in New Orleans showed a lack of interest in Mart-related foreign goods, and that other cities, such as Dallas, were actively competing for foreign goods.[526] As mentioned earlier, however, Shaw had been recommending that the Mart emphasize exports more in its displays, literature and festivals, probably because the mix of tenants had developed that way.

The Mart was also still interested in airlines as tenants. One of the parties interested in taking space in the Mart at this time was KLM Airlines, whose representative, George L. Boggs, knew Shaw and communicated with him on a somewhat regular basis. The opening of that office was intended for the fall of 1952, but was delayed due to internal company agendas.

Shaw continued to see his old friends, Louis Fischer and her husband Lawrence. In October 1952, Shaw sent Lawrence Fischer some Egyptian stamps of which the Mart had come into possession, saying, "See you soon."[527]

In November 1952, Shaw again attended the National Foreign Trade Council Convention in New York City, as he had for several years at this point, and would continue to do for most years during his tenure. He attempted to stay at the Waldorf Astoria, where the conference was held, but the hotel was booked solid.[528]

Shaw's traveling and speaking schedule had gradually been supplemented more by special events at home. He attended cocktails for German and Swedish dignitaries, a dinner for the Secretary of the Republic of Liberia, a reception for the Ambassador of Denmark to the United States, a reception for officers of a visiting Argentine naval ship, a reception for the Ambassador of Japan to the US, and a luncheon for the Minister of Interior and Public Health of Saudi Arabia. Among other special events that year was a trip in June 1952 on the Mississippi Shipping Company's (Delta Line's) *Del Sud* ship from New Orleans to Houston, carrying New Orleans businessmen on a regional trade mission trip. Shaw also was invited to various general New Orleans civic events, such as the dedication of a city health center, at the invitation of the mayor's office.[529]

Shaw also assisted the local U.S. State Department office with a group of visiting NATO journalists.[530] One member of the group, a British writer, later wrote an article for a British magazine, asking why Great Britain had no exhibit in the Mart. Noting the article, Shaw wrote Michael Buzon of the State Department that, "The bread that we cast upon the waters on that occasion is already being returned to us toasted and well buttered."[531]

Shaw could not make every event, obviously, and he had to decline, for instance, two events put on by the United Fruit Company. One was the formal opening of the company's new banana terminal in December 1952.[532] The other was a reception for Latin American journalists at the New Orleans Country Club, an event partially sponsored by International House.[533] Shaw also declined an invitation from Governor Robert F. Kennon to attend the Southern Governors' Conference in November 1952, as he would be attending the annual National Foreign Trade Council Convention in New York City at the time.[534]

The Mart's service employees, such as elevator operators, porters, and maintenance personnel, were now unionized. In addition to the normal labor/management conflicts, wages were still subject, to some extent, to wage and price controls left over from World War II. Sometimes, the Wage Stabilization Board would uphold new wage rates that had been agreed upon by the Mart.[535]

Assistant Manager J.B. Dauenhauer handled most of the direct employee relations with the service employees. The workers had attempted to organize during 1949, but the Mart had appealed the union categorization which affected such an organization. However, in December 1949, the National Labor Relations Board had dismissed the Mart's appeal, and an election for unionization had been held in 1950. The Mart already paid rates that were at or close to the union rate for the Building Service Employees' International Union, so the changes that took place, at least in that capacity, were minimal.

Perhaps demonstrating why the workers had felt compelled to want to organize, Dauenhauer was known for taking a tough stand with the hourly employees. In a memo in December 1952, he wrote James B. Mitchell, referring to a garnishment of wages order Dauenhauer had recently received. He told Mitchell to either pay the debt immediately, or be fired as of the following Monday.[536]

Harold C. Jackson and Paul L. Vogel, with the New Orleans office of the U.S. Department of Commerce, wrote to Shaw, thanking him for the Mart's courtesies shown to visitors from the Peru Department of Finance.[537] Shaw would deal with those representatives regularly, and Paul Vogel would later join International House World Trade Development Department during the latter part of the 1950s.

Shaw continued to reach out to the media in efforts to publicize the Mart. In December 1952, he exchanged letters with Worldwide Broadcasting System regarding a radio series to be broadcast from the Mart. Shaw had earlier talked with Leo G. Morrell, during the National Foreign Trade Council Convention in New York City, about the proposal.[538]

Also in December 1952, Shaw made a $25 payment to Hibernia National Bank to be applied to a loan in the name of Lloyd Mercadel. Mercadel was an African American whom Shaw used for odd jobs on restoration projects at his French Quarter properties over many years. And, in the same month, Shaw helped to host a Christmas party for a group of visiting Cornell University students who were touring the South. Shaw won thanks and praise from group leader Gerhard Voss for arranging the party so well.[539]

The Mart's effort to induce countries from Latin America to have representation in the building seemed to have peaked by the early 1950s. One of the problems was that many of the Latin American countries had economies that were not terribly diverse at the time, at least as far as the export-import trade was concerned. Panama, for instance, imported many goods, but exported mostly bananas, which were controlled by the United Fruit Company, which had offices elsewhere in New Orleans. Additionally, some Latin American countries found that taking out space in the Mart had not served any useful purpose. In mid-December 1952, the Commercial Attaché of Honduras wrote Shaw, declining an offer of space in the building; he said that Honduras had had space there before for some time, without any satisfactory results.[540] Shaw had tried to meet in late 1952 with the Commercial Counselor of the Embassy of Nicaragua in Washington, D.C., but had to cut his trip short due to illness.[541]

In late 1952, Shaw wrote to Leland W. Cutler with the San Francisco World Trade Center Authority. Shaw congratulated Cutler on the good news that the project in San Francisco was underway, although clearly he must have had mixed feelings about the new potential competition. Shaw mentioned that another six-week trip to South America was planned for mid-February 1953, that the Mart was 98% rented, and that the backers were now thinking about a larger building.[542] Shaw's planned trip to South America, according to the itinerary, would have covered the period from February 18, 1953 through March 9, 1953, and would have included the countries of Panama, Peru, Chile, Argentina, Uruguay, Brazil, Venezuela, and Cuba. However, the trip was eventually canceled.

The income statement for 1952 showed the best year to date for the Mart. Revenues were $287,984, and total expenses, including interest expense, were $254,012, leaving a surplus of income over expenses of $33,973, the best result thus far.[543]

In late 1952, New Orleans was preparing to celebrate the 150th, or sesquicentennial, anniversary of the Louisiana Purchase by the U.S. from France in 1803. An association had been formed to promote the event, and to create a series of happenings during the year 1953 that would culminate in a major celebration in October of that year. A local motion picture theater man, E.V. Richards, Jr., was selected as Chairman of the Louisiana Purchase 150th Anniversary Association. The association had an interim Managing Director, General Raymond Hufft, while the idea continued to germinate during the year 1952, but Hufft had made it clear that he would only work up until the start of fundraising, when he would be ready to turn over responsibilities to someone else. That someone turned out to be Clay Shaw, who officially accepted the Managing Director position in February 1953. Shaw's selection had to do with the Mart being now almost completely filled, with no room for expansion until plans to build or buy a new building could be realized; Shaw's talents for organization and carrying out a plan had been widely recognized around the city. With the Mart's building full, and with no new building in the works, and Shaw's planned trip to South America in early 1953 having been canceled, possibly because of both the expense and lack of urgency, Shaw now had the time to dedicate to this important position.

Shaw's active social life continued at its normal pace as well. Don Schueler, a young college graduate from New York City, had recently moved to New Orleans. One day, he was walking along the street with Walter Perseveaux, a local French Quarter "high camp" entertainer, when Shaw pulled up in his convertible. He invited the two of them to a party, where Schueler spoke with Shaw at some length for the first time. Schueler recalled, in particular, Shaw's poise and "mellifluous voice," and noted immediately that Shaw had certain features that other people might associate with having "Negro blood" or "a touch of the tar brush." Schueler had no negative reactions, however, and learned from that first interaction with Shaw that he was a successful businessman, and was also gay, and that the fact that he was gay was known to "everyone that mattered," and yet that had not stopped his progress in the business world.

Schueler also recalled Shaw's important work at the time of restoring French Quarter buildings. When Schueler first moved to New Orleans, he recalled that many of the balconies had missing slats, and there were rats crossing some of the streets, even during the daytime. Schueler recalled that the New Orleans gay world of that era was much looser and "more fun" than what he had experienced in New York City; there were more gay bars concentrated in a smaller area, they were easier to find, and some of them had a mixture of all types of "civilized, educated, artistic people" from around the city.[544]

Many of the New Orleans gay bars of the era drew mixed crowds, and the homosexual activity was often diverse. Married men dabbled in it, and some gay men married, often working out an arrangement, even if unspoken, with their straight partner. Some Catholic priests frequented gay bars, employing a Clintonesque definition of celibacy. There were men who tried it for a while, then gravitated away from it; others came to it relatively late in life.

# 10 · A Break From the Mart

The year 1953 was significant for the Mart in several ways. Entering the year, the Mart was essentially 100% occupied. Even if the mix of tenants was less international in focus than originally planned, and even if the Mart had not attracted as many exhibits from foreign governments as its founders wanted, there was little that could be done about it. The space was filled, with no immediate prospects for expansion, and it would be impossible to turn down tenants from that point forward simply because they were not the ideal type; maintaining the profitability of the institution was most important. Even though it was a non-profit institution, it was still important for the revenues generated by rentals to exceed expenses, in order for the project to be a success.

Secondly, Shaw took most of the year off from his duties as Managing Director of the Mart to serve in the aforementioned position with the 150$^{th}$ anniversary celebration of the Louisiana Purchase, which would not conclude its activities until October 1953. The Mart Board of Directors decided early on that it could spare Shaw, important though he had been from its beginning through 1952, because the essential work of building the Mart's occupancy, and promoting it around the country and the world, had been completed, at least until a new, larger building could be found or built.

Third, in mid-1953, Glenn Weekley left his position as the Mart's Public Relations Director, and was ultimately replaced by David Baldwin. Baldwin, whose ancestors at one time had owned the Baldwin Building that ultimately became the Mart, was a former newspaper reporter from New Orleans who had recently served with the Central Intelligence Agency in India. He had been a covert operative there, and had been fired by the CIA for becoming romantically, or at least physically, involved with a woman, Lillian Baxter; during the relationship, certain classified information was divulged. As a result of his termination, Baldwin returned to New Orleans, and began work with Bauerlein Advertising Agency, where he was placed in a position dealing with publicity related to the 150$^{th}$ anniversary celebration of the Louisiana Purchase. He shortly thereafter joined the official association celebrating the anniversary as its Public Relations Director, and worked there with Shaw, in his capacity as Managing Director, during most of 1953. When Shaw returned to the Mart in October 1953, Baldwin came with him as the Mart's Public Relations Director, replacing Glenn Weekley.

The annual report for 1952 indicated that the Mart had been 95.28% occupied for the entire year. The total accumulated surplus, the excess of revenues over expenses from the beginning of operations through the end of 1952, was $78,820. European imports were increasing, as were exports, through the Port of New Orleans. During 1952, the Mart had held the second International Sample Show in its lobby, with 800 lines of merchandise representing forty states and twenty foreign countries. Approximately 66% of tenants had displays of salable merchandise, while the remainder used their rental space as offices. It was still hoped that the Mart could attract more sellers of merchandise rather than service firms and pure office tenants, and that suitable replacements could be found as leases expired.[545]

A memo in mid-January from Shaw directed Mart employee Audrey Copping to process a check for $585 to pay for a cabin on the *Del Sud*, Mississippi Shipping Company's passenger ship, from Rio de Janiero to New Orleans, for his return trip from the journey to South America that was soon canceled.[546] Shaw's planned trip in February 1953 was part of a group accompanying Mayor Chep Morrison,[547] and would have originated with a flight from New Orleans to Montevideo, Uruguay.[548] By early February, however, the trip had been canceled, and Shaw soon accepted the post of Managing Director for the Louisiana Purchase Sesquicentennial. A letter from Shaw to Gwen Swenson, the wife of Richard Swenson, indicated that Shaw was not going to South America, so he could sit for her at the Swenson's home while the family was away from New Orleans.[549]

In early February 1953, Rudolf Hecht chaired a Board of Directors meeting. He indicated that the Mart did not need to do much promotional activity, as it was close to being 100% occupied. He noted Shaw's appointment as Managing Director of the Louisiana Purchase 150th Anniversary Association, which needed Shaw for the rest of the year. Hecht had cabled Theodore Brent, who was traveling aboard ship in the southern hemisphere, that General Raymond Hufft had resigned, and that Shaw would be taking over his duties; Brent had cabled his agreement. Hecht noted that, with the Mart fully occupied, Shaw would not need to travel and make speeches as much as he had done during the first seven years, that he had a capable assistant in J.B. Dauenhauer, and that the Louisiana Purchase celebration also would promote international trade to some extent. During Shaw's leave throughout most of 1953, half of his salary would be paid by the Mart, and half by the Louisiana Purchase celebration; Shaw would begin his new duties as soon as possible.[550]

The 1953 International Sample Show, held at the Mart, featured furniture from Mexico and Italy, glassware from France and Germany, ceramics from Belgium and the Netherlands, embroidered slippers and delicate saris from India, rattanware from the Philippines; approximately 300 fine lines of imported merchandise in all.[551] A preview of the sample show was held during Mardi Gras, and the official show was held the following week. Tom Richards, a designer often recommended by the Mart to its tenants, designed the overall setup of the show. He had helped with an exhibit for the country of India held in the Mart several years earlier, and he also would help design another Indian exhibit held there in August 1953. The sample show was held in approximately 2,500 square feet scattered throughout the building, and was sponsored jointly by the Mart and the Free Trade Zone of the Port of New Orleans.

The Mart received some correspondence, during February and April 1953, from Dr. Jutta Schaller of the German-American Trade Promotion Company in Munich, Germany. The letters were regarding shipping samples of beer to the Mart for the third International Sample Fair. The previous year, Dr. Schaller had been the subject of CIA memos regarding some information that she had given to Shaw, who had then passed it on to Hunter Leake, his contact at the New Orleans CIA office.[552]

Mart officials clearly recognized the need for more space; at a meeting of the Contributors and Debenture Holders in March 1953, the issue was frankly discussed at length. A committee was looking into the matter, but it was cost-prohibitive to add even one additional floor, and somewhat impractical to sell the building, as it had been designed specifically for the Mart. It was further decided that, given the uncertainties, it was not in the Mart's best interest to call its bonds in early.[553]

Although occasionally in his speaking career Shaw provided a written text of a speech in advance, he usually strongly resisted such requests. In March, Mayor Chep Morrison wrote to individuals scheduled to speak before the Louisiana Municipal Association Convention, requesting speeches in advance from all participants.[554] Shaw replied in a handwritten note to Dave McGuire, Publicity Director for the City of New Orleans, saying that he always spoke extemporaneously, and asked if a prepared address was really essential.[555] It appears that his off-the-cuff style worked, as Shaw's speeches continued to earn him the usual praise. After a speech to the New Orleans Secretaries Association in April 1953, its president, Josephine M. O'Meallie, wrote, "I feel sure that by now you must realize we are all fans of Clay Shaw!"[556]

Shaw continued to regularly participate in events organized by the mayor's office. In April, Chep Morrison invited Shaw to be at the head table for a luncheon for the National Editorial Association, held at the Jung Hotel.[557]

Although he did not particularly like to drive a car, Shaw owned an automobile for most of his adult life, and occasionally drove it even on long-distance trips. After an invitation to speak to the Mississippi Retail Hardware Association Convention, held at the Buena Vista Hotel in Biloxi, Mississippi in April 1953, Shaw mentioned in his confirmation letter that he might drive over to the meeting from New Orleans the morning of the speech.[558]

By 1953, questions had arisen about Karl Haller, the prospective investor in the proposed cocoa-processing facility. It had become evident that there were legitimate concerns about how serious Haller's intent was, and also about his ability to participate in the financing of the project. In a memo to Hecht in mid-April, Shaw discussed the issue of having 51% local control, and questioned whether Hecht should meet with Haller again in Germany.[559] Apparently, Hecht decided to bring the matter to an end. In late April, Hecht wrote to Haller, mentioning that Brent had become seriously ill, and had not been at his desk since December 1952. Hecht further indicated that since Brent had been the main advocate of the project, he thought the matter should be considered permanently closed.[560]

In mid-May 1953, Shaw received a letter from his friend, Ella Brennan, written on Brennan's Restaurant stationery. Brennan's had opened shortly after Shaw's return to New Orleans after the war, and soon became a serious competitor to other, older, upscale restaurants in the city. Brennan indicated how much she appreciated all of the business Shaw had brought to the restaurant, and she speculated that he must know their menu by heart. She told him about some wild game and fish items that were not on the menu, including pheasant, partridge, grouse, Dover sole, and frog legs, and including "your favorite, Poulet Perigord." She said that many of those items had been imported by air, and that any of them could be prepared for Shaw with advance notice. She closed by indicating that, "We want to stress what a pleasure it is to serve you and make things just the way you want it whether dining alone or with others."[561]

The Mart was still trying to interest the British government in opening a trade exhibit, but having very little luck. WDSU-TV owner Edgar B. Stern, Jr. wrote to Shaw that one British Board of Trade official had said that, in the United States, "People do not buy, but have to be sold." Stern went on to say that the British Board of Trade was not convinced of the usefulness of having an office in the Mart.[562]

At this stage of operations, in an effort to keep the building completely occupied amidst growing competition from other buildings in the area, the Mart was readily accepting one-year leases, with a one-year renewal option, quite a change from its initial stated requirement of five-year leases back in 1946.[563] However, the Mart still did not accept any tenants who made retail sales of common over-the-counter goods, possibly because owner of retail stores in New Orleans were among the Mart's supporters and bondholders.[564]

In late May 1953, Shaw spoke before the Greater New Orleans Council of Civic Club Presidents about his ongoing parallel role with the Louisiana Purchase 150th Anniversary Association, which is covered in detail in the next chapter. The ultimate celebration was scheduled to be held during the last two weeks of October, when the weather was best in New Orleans, and would include games, pageants, and parades. It also would include visits by President Eisenhower and the president of France, although not at the same time, and would be capped by a re-enactment of the signing of the original Louisiana Purchase agreement by representatives of the United States and France. Shaw indicated that much publicity had already been obtained in *Reader's Digest, Colliers*, and the *Saturday Evening Post*.

In many speeches during his tenure with the Louisiana Purchase 150th Anniversary Association, Shaw combined promoting both the celebration and the Mart. He spoke before the Southeastern Regional Conference of Delta Kappa Gamma Society, the Research Club of

New Orleans, and the Hammond Rotary Club, visiting Latin American students at International House (again at the invitation of Mario Bermúdez), the Boswell Club at La Louisiane Restaurant, Alcee Fortier Senior High School, as part of its Constitution Day program, the New Orleans Secretaries Association at La Louisiane Restaurant, and at Metairie Country Day High School. Shaw also was the commencement speaker at graduation ceremonies at Francis T. Nicholls High School on St. Claude Avenue.

Glenn Weekley submitted his resignation letter as Director of Public Relations June 1, 1953. It was friendly to the Mart; he regretted having to leave, but indicated that he had gotten a more lucrative offer from Kaiser Aluminum Company, which had recently built its large plant in Chalmette, Louisiana, near New Orleans.[565] Weekley's shoes would be difficult to fill, as his professional efforts on behalf of the Mart had been expanding at a continuing pace; he had recently written and produced a booklet entitled *Building Imports Through ITM*, and had begun writing a weekly column for *The New Orleans Item Industrial Weekly*.

Manuel Delgado, the student Trade Analyst, took over some of Glenn Weekley's duties, then Jorge "George" Navarro began as an interim Public Relations Director in July 1953.[566] An Argentinian who spoke several languages, Navarro left in the fall to return to Argentina. After Navarro's departure, David Baldwin joined the Mart, returning with Shaw in October from the Louisiana Purchase 150th Anniversary Association. Baldwin soon began to write the newspaper columns about happenings at the Mart, and in the international trade community in general, that Glenn Weekley had previously written.

Another major event during 1953 was the death of Theodore Brent in early June. Brent had been a "rags-to-riches" success story in the railroad, shipping and international trade fields. He had started in 1896 as a stenographer for the Fort Scott and Memphis Railroad in Kansas City, Missouri, and then worked his way up in the railroad industry, before entering the shipping industry and moving to New Orleans in the early part of the 20th century. Brent was not only a mentor for Shaw in both his personal life and in his business career, he was also widely respected throughout the New Orleans business community, and with his death, the Mart lost a large portion of its guiding force.

Brent, already ill, had journeyed on a lengthy ocean voyage in February 1953, but a month later was incapacitated due to illness.[567] He died at his home at 401 Broadway Street in New Orleans. Funeral services were held at the House of Bultman, the most prominent funeral home in the city, which two decades later would hold funeral services for Clay Shaw. The funeral home was owned by the family of Muriel Bultman, later known as Muriel Francis, a longtime acquaintance of Shaw, and a noted participant in various civic, artistic and charitable causes. Shaw was a pallbearer at Brent's funeral.

Various civic associations around New Orleans passed resolutions honoring Theodore Brent after his death. A resolution by the Foreign Commerce Committee of the Chamber of Commerce noted that Brent was a "staunch and fearless advocate of what he believed right and proper in all things, and constantly fought to protect the rights of the individual against government encroachment in matters affecting international trade and commerce." A resolution by the New Orleans Traffic and Transportation Bureau similarly noted Brent's prominence in the fields of maritime commerce and international trade. A resolution by the entire Chamber of Commerce expressed similar thoughts. In August 1953, a plaque was placed in International House in Brent's honor; the plaque mentioned his association with Delta Lines, the International Trade Mart, International House, Mississippi Valley Association, the Crippled Children's Hospital, the Federal Barge Lines, and the Traffic and Transportation Bureau.

A New Orleans newspaper clipping dated June 13, 1953, said that the bulk of Brent's estate had been left to the Alton Ochsner Medical Foundation. His will, dated February 11, 1953, set forth that Brent had never been married, and indicated that he had left $100,000 to the St. Charles Avenue Presbyterian Church in memory of his mother, Mary, his stepmother, Alice, and his sister, Fanny. He also left $13,000 to his secretary, Irma Mae Lagan, $3,000 to his former secretary, Miss C.R. Quinn, and $5,000 each to three cousins. Additionally, $5,000 was provided to his mother's grandniece, $2,000 to his housekeeper, Mamie Murphy, and $1,000 each to servants Gussie Johnson and her husband, Ernest Johnson. Brent also left individual gifts of $10,000 each to Edgar Lee, Jr. and to Harry B. Leche. He gave $5,000 each to Stanley M. Lecour and to J.B. Dauenhauer, $3,000 to L.M. Westbrook, and $2,000 each to Clay Shaw and Mrs. Belle Loper. Each of the New Orleans individuals to whom Brent left specific gifts was designated as "my friend."[568]

Brent's estate was represented by the powerful New Orleans firm of Monroe and Lemann. J. Blanc Monroe had founded the law firm around 1910; his father, Frank Adair Monroe, had been Chief Justice of the Louisiana Supreme Court. Monroe, who would die in April 1960, was also legal counsel to Ochsner Clinic, and was on the Board of Directors of the Mississippi Shipping Company (which operated Delta Line).[569] He was known for representing various interests of the State of Louisiana during the first half of the Twentieth Century, including administering or fighting damage claims related to the Great Flood of 1927. The Monroe and Lemann firm allegedly had ties to the CIA in New Orleans, beginning with the agency's founding in the late 1940s.

The residue of Brent's estate, after the individual gifts, was valued at $1,603,817, and was left to Ochsner Foundation. Brent had been the second member of the board of trustees of Ochsner Foundation when it was founded in the mid-1940s, and had initially contributed $100,000 to it for the construction of a hospital building; he had also arranged for the purchase of land for the hospital from Illinois Central Railroad. In 1952, he had announced that he planned to donate $400,000 to the hospital fund, if the amount was matched by other donors. J. Blanc Monroe, the attorney for both Brent and Ochsner Clinic, had been instrumental in getting Brent initially interested in Ochsner's work, and in Brent leaving his estate to the Ochsner Foundation.[570]

Brent's promise to donate $400,000 to the Foundation in 1952 resulted in his donation of the assets of Coast Transportation Company, apparently owned by him, which included a seagoing tugboat called the Titan, which was leased to a barge line. He valued the total contribution to the Foundation at $400,000, but the tugboat was involved in several collisions, which resulted in lawsuits against the Foundation. The tugboat was ultimately sold by the Foundation in January 1954 for $175,000.[571]

In July 1953, the Board of Directors of the Mart selected William Zetzmann, President of Zetz Bottling Company, and a leading participant in the formation of both International House and the International Trade Mart, as the new President of the Mart. July 7, 1953, was the fifth anniversary of the actual opening of the Mart, and Shaw presented the Board of Directors with an informal five-year report. He discussed the growth of the Mart, and the recent failed idea to have a New Orleans Import Special train, which had been canceled due to lack of interest; the Import Special train also would have conflicted with a promotional train trip planned by the Louisiana Purchase celebration. During the meeting, the board also approved the purchase of a cooling tower, and work to repair cracks in exterior walls. Resolutions from around the city honoring Brent were read into the minutes of the Board of Directors meeting.[572]

During 1953, due to Shaw's absence, J.B. Dauenhauer ran more of the day-to-day activities of the Mart than in any previous year. He advised tenants that the Mart would be closed June 10, 1953, in memory of Theodore Brent.[573] Another memo later that month advised tenants not to use emergency exit doors for normal exiting, and not to prop doors open, as drunks had been found sleeping in the stairwells, and other undesirable characters could enter the building without notice.[574]

Dauenhauer continued his policy of threatening to fire employees who had their wages garnished. Two that met his wrath during 1953 were James S. Mitchell, who was having his wages garnished for the third or fourth time, and Stella Dent. Dauenhauer advised them both to pay up, or be fired.

Dauenhauer used his position not only with those who crossed him, but on behalf of his intimates as well. Dauenhauer's companion, Edgar Lee, Jr., used him as a credit reference occasionally. Dauenhauer and Lee had met in the early 1930s. Edgar Lee owned Shops at Sea, a concession on the Mississippi Shipping Company passenger liners; Theodore Brent had undoubtedly given him that opportunity.[575]

Dauenhauer worked closely with Hollis Bridges, the building superintendent, in managing the various hourly employees. Dauenhauer would often instruct Bridges to allow after-hours access to Hardy Williams, a photographer the Mart often used or recommended during this period to take photos of various tenants' exhibits.

The Mart building was open to visitors on weekdays and at least part of the day on Saturdays, and during 1953 more than 216,000 visitors came into the Mart. Of those, approximately 211,000 were individuals, and approximately 5,750 visited in groups. However, on holidays and Sundays, the building was monitored by a guard service, and was closed to visitors. Employees and tenants had to register with the guard service upon entering and exiting the building. On Mardi Gras day each year, visitors were allowed into the building, as many used the cocktail lounge there during the holiday. However, masks were not allowed to be worn above the first floor of the building, nor were visitors allowed above the first floor during off-hours.

The successful cocktail lounge at the Mart was owned and operated by an independent outside entity. Gross revenues totaled between $4,000 and $5,000 per month during the early 1950s, and the Mart took approximately two percent of that total as its share.

The Helen Brett Trade Show, billed as a "Buyer's Mardi Gras," was held in August 1953 at the Roosevelt Hotel. It was not well attended, although some Mart tenants participated. Brett would continue to hold an annual show in New Orleans for many years.

The local media continued to cover the Mart, demonstrating its ongoing importance to New Orleans. In August 1953, WDSU-TV conducted interviews with various Mart exhibitors on the "Our House" television show.[576]

Shaw continued to serve with various organizations and committees, even as he managed the Louisiana Purchase celebration. One was the National Defense Transportation Association, a group of transportation industry owners and representatives, and governmental people. It was a way of staying connected with local people involved in shipping industries.

Although most of the speeches Shaw gave during 1953 were on behalf of the Louisiana Purchase celebration, he also gave at least his usual quota on behalf of the Mart during the months before and after assuming his position with the Louisiana Purchase Association. In January, he spoke to the Pontalba Study Club at the home of Mrs. George Renaudin, and to a class at Loyola University on "Economic History of the American People." In October, he spoke to the New Orleans Business and Professional Women's Club, for National Business Women's Week, at International House, and he was the principal speaker at the American Public Works Association Convention, held at the Roosevelt hotel in New Orleans. In November, he spoke to "Les Quarante Ecolieres" at the home of Mrs. Charles H. Gillen, to military personnel at the New Orleans Port of Embarkation, and to the Alexandria, Louisiana, Rotary Club. In December, he spoke to the Southwest Region of the Association of International Relations Clubs, at the YMCA on Gravier Street.

Mary Ellen Moore, one of the secretaries, had left the Mart in late 1952. In December 1953, in a letter to the new Mart President, William Zetzmann, Shaw listed all of the current administrative employees, which included Audrey Copping, Josephine Pennestri, Mrs. Owen Grace, Goldie Moore, J.B. Dauenhauer, David Baldwin, and Louis Vargas.[577]

Many of the employees of businesses with offices in the Mart would remain loyal to Shaw years later during his legal troubles. Dorothy M. Nix was an employee with the Roosevelt Travel Service; she would correspond with Shaw over the years, and remain supportive long after getting married and leaving New Orleans.

Changes in personnel were taking place outside of the Mart as well. Richard Swenson, the public relations man for the Board of Commissioners of the Port of New Orleans, left the area around this time to take a job with the Virginia State Ports Authority in Norfolk, Virginia. Swenson would keep in touch with Shaw over the years, and would emerge as one of his defenders after Shaw's arrest in 1967. Shaw's friend George Haverstick joined the Dock Board Public Relations office in July 1953.[578]

V. Gordon Isaacson was the New Orleans representative for Colonial Trust Company in 1953. He later went to work for the World Trade Development Committee of International House, and even for the Mart after Shaw retired.

Helen Gladstone, who would later give tours of historic areas of New Orleans, applied for a job with the Mart during 1953. She had lived in New York, and supposedly had worked for a national security organization writing propaganda letters for publications and newspapers, and making speeches for different causes. Although she came to know Clay Shaw somewhat well through French Quarter activities, she was never hired by the Mart.

William Kent Taliaferro, Jr., wrote to J.B. Dauenhauer looking for a summer job in office work. He had graduated in early June from Tulane University, with an English degree and a minor in French. However, the Mart had no need for a new full-time employee at the time. In a few years, coincidentally, Shaw would befriend a different William Taliaferro, who ran a maintenance-on-call service that Shaw used to perform repairs and service on his real estate properties.

As of 1953, James Bezou was Secretary of the Consul General of Belgium in New Orleans. Sixteen years later, in the summer of 1969, in one of the more explosive developments in the aftermath of Clay Shaw's trial, District Attorney Jim Garrison was quietly accused of fondling one of Bezou's sons at the New Orleans Athletic Club. The incident was never prosecuted, but word of it has hung over Garrison's reputation to the present day, and has helped give rise to, or feed already existing, speculation that Shaw and Garrison might have had some sexual connection that led to Garrison's seemingly obsessive pursuit of Shaw through the courts.

Houston was coming on strong as a competitor to New Orleans in 1953, in both population size and international trade. A letter to Charles Nutter, from Loyal Phillips, publisher of the *St. Petersburg Independent*, included an enclosed article from his newspaper that maintained Houston was now the second largest port in the United States, after New York City, replacing New Orleans in that position.[579]

Mayor Chep Morrison responded with humor as the competition between Houston and New Orleans grew. He mailed the clipping of an article comparing the population of the two cities to the mayor of Houston, and commented that there was no way Houston had more people than New Orleans, even if one counted all the cows in Houston as people.

It was around this time that Shaw assisted his parents in purchasing a home in Hammond, Louisiana, approximately sixty miles from New Orleans, and located in Tangipahoe Parish, about thirty-five miles from Shaw's birthplace of Kentwood.

Although busy with his duties with the Louisiana Purchase celebration, Shaw still handled numerous individual tasks related to the Mart. In September, he wrote letters to prospective employers on behalf of Manuel O. Delgado, who had been a trade analyst at the Mart during the year. Delgado was a graduate student at Tulane, and Shaw gave him a supportive reference.[580]

The new trade analyst who replaced Delgado was Louis C. Vargas. Vargas was a student at Tulane, studying economics and foreign trade; he worked half a day each day at the Mart. He was born in New Orleans; his father was Panamanian, and his mother American. The Mart and International House each took one student per year, using them to run down inquiries for information from tenants, and answer letters of inquiry from the public about products. The pay was $25 per week for working from 1:00 p.m. to 5:00 p.m. each day.[581]

Mario Bermúdez's Office of International Relations for the City of New Orleans, located in the Mart, had been handling the translation and typing of international letters, even ones in English with only occasional Spanish words. However, in September 1953, International House acquired a typewriter with accent marks and other Spanish characters, and began typing those letters for the Trade Mart; there were usually no more than seven such letters in any one week.[582]

As of September 1953, nine nations had commercial representation in the Mart. Those included Belgium, Canada, Cuba, France, West Germany, Italy, Japan, the Netherlands, and the Philippines.[583] The list clearly shows the influence of Western Europe and Japan in international trade following World War II, and the weakening influence of Latin America in New Orleans. By this time, Cuba was the only Latin American country that maintained official space in the Mart.[584]

The Young Men's Business Club continued to have a representative on the Mart's Board of Directors. Once the Czechoslovakian Trade Exhibit issue had passed, the two organizations worked well together during the early 1950s. In October 1953, Bernard K. Oppenheim was selected as the club's representative on the Mart's board.

In early October, Shaw received a letter from the writer Frances Parkinson Keyes. Keyes had recently purchased Beauregard House in the French Quarter, and was now a part of the fabric of the district. She enclosed a copy of the manuscript "Little Old New Orleans" for Shaw's review in editing and correcting. It was her contribution to a "Book of Knowledge" collection, slated for publication shortly. In response to a request by Shaw, she indicated that she would be willing to entertain the Greek royal family, or other celebrities, on their upcoming visits to New Orleans, but she made it clear that she was doing so for Shaw personally, and not for any committee that might be looking after such visitors.[585] Shaw responded at the end of the month, stating that he was just ending his duties with the Louisiana Purchase Sesquicentennial and that he had read her manuscript. Shaw mentioned that he had recently received a note from Reverend Miller Cragon, an Episcopalian clergyman in England, who let Shaw know he had been to a party with Keyes, her friend Deanie, Scoop Kennedy, and *Item* columnist Herman Deutsch. Shaw said that, as for his own leisure activities, he had "been lying in the sun in Biloxi," after his Louisiana Purchase celebration duties, and was now "fit and fine." He said he was looking forward to seeing Keyes and Deanie in December, and he hoped that they would both accept "the long delayed dinner in my patio."[586]

With the Mart at peak occupancy, there was rarely a need for Shaw to speak out of town. In late October, Shaw wrote to the Chamber of Commerce in Augusta, Georgia saying that he could only attend if the Chamber paid his expenses. Otherwise, he would have to wait for other speaking engagements in the area.[587] In previous years, Shaw had generally found a way to travel to make a speech, often by combining several speeches in the same general area, or on the same train route.

In October 1953, the *Saturday Evening Post* ran a prominent article about International House, the Mart's sister organization. It indicated that the institution provided bilingual babysitters, and dance partners for visiting businessmen. An accompanying photo showed a crowd of men and women in the lobby, among which almost everyone looked age sixty or older. The article further indicated that the institution had an annual budget of $250,000, and that the revenues came from 2,300 dues paying members, and from office rentals.[588]

International House published a weekly bulletin entitled *Trade Winds*. The issue for November 18, 1953 included a mention that Lloyd A. Ray had visited International House, bringing as his guest the U.S. Ambassador to Guatemala. Lloyd Ray was an employee of the

CIA's office in New Orleans from the late 1940s through the 1960s; he managed the office after the retirement of the original manager, William Burke, in the early 1960s.[589] Around the time of Ray's visit to International House, the CIA was actively involved in the operation that ultimately overthrew the government of Guatemala and installed a new government. The operation is one of the most famous (or infamous, depending on one's political view) in the CIA's history.

In early November 1953, Shaw assisted N.A. Russell, the regional manager of Western Union Telegraph Company, in hosting Western Union's International Department Sales Conference in New Orleans.[590] Shaw's old friend, K. Bruce Mitchell, a vice president of Western Union in New York City, attended, as did J. C. Jackson, District Manager for Western Union in New Orleans, who originally had hired Shaw with the company in the late 1920s.[591] Shaw visited with Mitchell again shortly thereafter[592] when he made his customary attendance at the New York Foreign Trade Council Convention, staying at the Beverly Hotel.[593]

The 40th Annual National Foreign Trade Council Convention was held in mid-November 1953 at the Waldorf Astoria Hotel and Shaw was again in attendance. Besides promoting the Mart, attending the convention served the additional purpose of allowing Shaw to visit social friends he had made in New York City during the time he lived there in the 1930s, and on prior business trips.

Shaw would often invite acquaintances and old friends from other parts of the country to visit New Orleans, with the promise of showing them around town. In November, Shaw wrote Irving S. Preston, President of TransAmerican Construction Company of Smithtown, Long Island, suggesting that he bring his wife, Alice, down for a visit. Shaw ended the letter by remarking that it "would be nice to see you after so many years."[594]

Shaw regularly hosted out-of-town visitors for lunch or dinner, even if they were not coming to New Orleans specifically to tour the Mart. In late 1953, he hosted Gwen Randolph for dinner. Randolph was fashion editor of *Today's Woman* magazine, which promoted itself as "the magazine Young Wives Live By."[595]

Shaw's Christmas card list at the end of 1953 contained the names of General Charles Thrasher, L. Arnold Weissberger, a New York lawyer long noted for representing writers and others artists, Francis Parkinson Keyes, the noted New Orleans historical novelist, Shaw's friends Stan Picher and Joseph Faulkner of the Main Street Book Store in Chicago, Val Dufour, a Louisiana native who later became a television actor, especially in soap operas, Carl Cramer, a New Orleans sculptor who designed a bust of Theodore Brent after his death, K. Bruce Mitchell, Shaw's old friend and Western Union Vice President in New York City, Mr. and Mrs. Cecil Foster of Muskegon, Michigan, John Hanlen of Philadelphia, Phillip Carey Jones of Los Angeles, California, the Episcopalian minister Miller Cragon, at that time living in Canterbury, England, the actress Kay Francis, Patrick O'Rourke, then living in Phoenix, Arizona, Mr. and Mrs. Lee Keedick of New York City, and Mr. and Mrs. Thomas N. Brahney of New Orleans. Many of these individuals either had played key roles in Shaw's life, or would as time went by.

Of those on the list, several notably surfaced after Shaw's arrest, all in very different ways. For example, Thomas Brahney presided over a bail hearing the night of Shaw's arrest, releasing Shaw on $10,000 bond. Joseph Faulkner, who ran a well-known art gallery in Chicago and who in the late 1950s had exposed a large fraud involving counterfeit paintings, would write to various Federal public officials, including the U.S. attorney general, in Shaw's defense, within days of Shaw's arrest. Cecil Foster would write Shaw a series of cautiously worded, but seemingly nervous, almost anxious, letters, hinting at some past history between the two. One of Foster's nieces by marriage told the author that Foster was gay, or at least had participated in gay activities in the past, but had eventually married and settled down. Whether true about Foster or not, a number of young men who passed through New

Orleans during that period dabbled, so to speak, in gay life before moving on to marriages of one sort or another. Some of the marriages were the traditional kind, but others were arrangements, whether one-sided or through mutual agreement, whereby the husband could quietly continue his alternative sexual lifestyle.

At a meeting in December 1953, the Executive Committee of the Mart approved a group disability plan for Mart employees. It was decided that the issue of medical and surgical insurance, and a retirement plan, would be explored during 1954. Under the group disability plan, a maximum of $5,000 in annual salary would be subject to the coverage.[596]

The Mart continued to receive its share of interesting letters of inquiry. In December, Shaw responded to one concerning shipping of oysters to New Orleans, advising the writer that the city was well supplied with oysters from beds near the city.[597]

The Mart continued to seek out large corporate tenants, including Ingalls Shipbuilding Corporation of Pascagoula, Mississippi, one of the largest companies of its type in the world. However, as of 1953, the company was still deciding whether it needed space in the Mart.[598]

Meanwhile, International House, which also rented space in its building to selected tenants, lost a large one at the end of 1953. Federal Barge Lines, which had become privately owned, canceled its lease on the upper three floors of the International House building; the empty space totaled 13,000 square feet.[599]

Beginning in 1953, if one looks closely enough, one could see a change in the tone of responses from representatives of the Mart to members of the general public inquiring about products, services, foreign countries and policies. Prior to mid-1953, either Shaw or, beginning in 1949, Glenn Weekley, had usually given very detailed responses to all inquiries, except those considered totally frivolous or designated for the "Nutcase file." However, with Shaw's absence beginning in February 1953, to manage the Louisiana Purchase 150th Anniversary Association, and with Glenn Weekley's departure in the middle of that year, the duties of answering those letters fell increasingly to J.B. Dauenhauer and, later in the year, upon the beginning of his employment with the Mart, to David Baldwin, whom Shaw brought over from the Louisiana Purchase celebration. In the earlier years, one could sense the pride Shaw took in answering even some of the smallest inquiries in great detail, attempting to help the inquirer toward whatever goal he or she had, and one could sense a similar attitude on Glenn Weekley's part. However, Dauenhauer and Baldwin usually issued much more cryptic responses, and often one could sense their disinterest, and even irritation, at having to answer some of the letters. That change during 1953 would never be totally reversed. It was possible that the peak of Shaw's own interest occurred prior to 1953 as well, due mainly to the challenge of getting the Mart going, bringing the building up to as close to 100% occupancy as possible, and then looking for a new goal to tackle. For the next twelve years of Shaw's tenure, although there would be many more highly publicized events, and the Mart would still generate much attention in New Orleans, and to a lesser degree around the country, it remained first in a sort of holding pattern, then in a steeply declining pattern, never to completely regain the initial enthusiasm once held among its founders.

The Mart employees, however, continued to receive their annual bonus at the end of 1953. And why not? After all, the building was completely occupied, the Mart was at the peak of its local fame and influence, and the general business community knew little or nothing of the plateau the institution had reached.

Sometime in the early to mid-1950s, perhaps in 1953, Shaw met William Formyduval, a quite handsome, somewhat happy-go-lucky, bisexual man from Whiteville, North Carolina. Kenneth Reynolds, a French Quarter artist originally from England, recalls that he and his companion at the time, David Hart, met Formyduval at Ponchartrain Beach and invited him to their residence. Shortly thereafter, the two introduced him to Shaw, beginning a two-decade long friendship that ended with Shaw's death.

Many members of the Formyduval family, including some who spell the last name

Formy-Duval, live in and around the Whiteville area. After an inquiry by the author to one of the family members, Mike Formy-Duval, who has done some genealogical work on the family, described William Formyduval to the author, in 2000, in the following way:

"Our timing is quite ironic. I did a book (more along the lines of a genealogical book) on the Formy-Duvals back in 1995 and am working on an updated version to perhaps publish another one next year. Of all the family members that I came across, William Henry (Bill to some folks) Formy-Duval was one of the most unusual characters that I encountered. I wanted to learn more about him myself and have found all this to be quite interesting. He was a very unusual and talented man. William Henry was born in 1925 and died of cancer in Whiteville, NC in 1980. He lived to only be 55 years old. Actually he died in the VA Hospital in Fayetteville, NC (about 60 miles from Whiteville but buried in Whiteville)...

"William Henry was very nice looking as a young man and was extremely talented. Unfortunately he became an alcoholic (not the type that hurts people or got into serious trouble) and never could get his talents quite focused .Everyone in our area really liked him immensely. He served in the army in WWII. After his mother and father died, his Aunt Mae (Formy-Duval) Hobson sort of took him in and was quite protective (and influential) of him. Mae had a Hotel in Whiteville and was sort of wealthy (not rich by any means but had more money than most in this area) and kept William Henry (or tried to) on a short leash. He never worked but he could do all kinds of artistic things.

"My mom and dad remember him quite well and I remember him too but I never knew him personally back then when I was in high school. I just remember him walking around town. He always wore flip flops in the summer, fall & spring and those gray hushpuppy shoes in the winter. My dad used to wait on him at the Whiteville Post Office back in the 60's and 70's.

"William Henry would 'run away' during his drinking periods & binges and catch a bus and go to New Orleans. Somehow along the way he met Clay Shaw. I know Shaw was gay and I am not positive about William Henry but would guess that he probably was bi-sexual. I know he had all the women chasing him around these parts so I am not positive about his sexual preference. These women would all be in their 70's today and I would rather not divulge any names as it might tend to get me in trouble with one or two of the local "little old ladies" that are now grandmothers down here. I have heard some really good tales about these women chasing him though. He would have one coming in the front door and one going out the back door (so to speak) so he had some great sexual exploits I've heard.

"Anyway back to Clay Shaw......

"I don't know how they met but probably through some mutual friend and it may have been at a party or perhaps the health club that Shaw frequented. As I stated earlier William Henry would get drunk and run down there to N O and after a period of time Aunt Mae would send someone down there to "fetch" him usually after his money ran out. Several times she sent Jimmy [his brother]. Clay Shaw came up to Whiteville and visited William Henry and met Mae. Somehow he got her interested in going down there to N O and they would take some of the older homes in the French Quarter and fix them up and sell them. I know for a fact that William Henry would design the layouts and supervise the work and Aunt Mae and maybe Shaw would provide the money.

"One of the houses was the 'Audubon' House on [505] Dauphine Street. I know that Shaw and William Henry corresponded some back and forth over the years as I once saw a short letter that had Clay Shaw's signature. This was after the Garrison persecution. Clay was telling him to hang on to his signature, that it might be worth something one day and if he (W-H) was down on his luck he could sell it, that he would have enough to buy some 'hominy and grits with red-eye gravy.' He was saying all this jokingly of course to a certain extent.

"Everyone and I mean everyone that I have talked to and that met the man (Shaw) really liked him. No one (and I mean no one from this area) knows anything about Clay Shaw and the Kennedy Assassination so there is no story for you on that particular subject (not from here or anywhere else that I know of). Clay Shaw was well liked and well respected by everyone that I have talked with and not one soul believes he ever had anything to do with Ruby/Oswald and President Kennedy's death. I want you to know that I am quite sure of this so that there is no misunderstanding or mis-communication. I personally think Clay Shaw got a 'raw deal' and until someone proves otherwise will continue to believe this. Jim Garrison in my opinion ruined the man for his own personal gain. Clay Shaw went broke and was ruined financially (from what I've heard) trying to defend himself because of Jim Garrison. Of course, I will tell you I am not an authority (as you probably are) on this subject. But it is my personal opinion that William Henry never knew anything about this and I think that Clay Shaw didn't either.

"Shaw referred to William Henry as Wilmry (William & Henry being shortened & combined to Wilmry) in his communiqués. His pet name for William Henry I suppose. William Henry had a habit of stealing stuff from hotels. He liked to take door handles like the glass type in the older hotels and he would take serving trays and things like this. He once ran off to the Seychelles (I hope I have spelled this correctly) [Islands] and lived there (off the coast of Africa) for a year or two. I have heard the story that he wrote his Aunt Mae asking for money ($600.00) to come home on and when she sent it to him, he stayed another year (he had to have the money to show he had a visible means of support or they would oust him off).

"He would do paintings on seashells and sell them to make spending money which he probably bought booze with. Jimmy had shown him an article or picture of these islands and he just decided he would go there so he hopped a freighter and went down. I have seen his passport and saw where he entered there and maybe he went to Mexico a couple of times. I saw a letter where some young lady was down there in Mexico and told him to "come on down" and he would tear off and go just to party and drink with them. He was a fun person to be around and I guess people just liked him and liked for him to party with them. He could tell great stories and could really entertain the people around him. He was a real charmer. I know that he was funny but his folks (brother, sister and Aunt Mae) didn't think his charades were funny back then although they can laugh about it now. Jimmy didn't like to have to go bring him back but when Aunt Mae told him, he would have to do it.

"I will tell you one interesting story to give you a better perspective of William Henry. A story that I was recently told that came from Jimmy Formy Duval and his sister Nancy. Aunt Mae gave Jimmy the money to fly down to N O to bring William Henry back to Whiteville. Jimmy didn't want to go but did as he was told (you didn't balk when Mae told you to do something, she was a tough old bird. He got down there and got William Henry out of jail. I think he had been arrested for public drunkenness. Jimmy finally got him out of jail then William Henry refused to leave his dog down there and balked on Jimmy. Finally William Henry said he had an idea. He found a cane and sunglasses and put a leash on his dog and pretended he was blind. Jimmy was somewhat skeptical but went along with it, anything to get him to come on home. They got on the plane to come back and the flight attendants bought the charade and even moved he and Jimmy up into the first class section so they would be more comfortable and have room for his mongrel. Jimmy said that everything was going fine until about half way back after Bill had a couple of drinks, he asked the flight attendant for a magazine to read!! Jimmy said he thought that the crew was going to throw them all off the plane, dog and all...

"I had thought that William Henry...had never married, but I did find out that he once married a Louise Clairmont form San Antonio, Tx. I don't know how long it lasted but they did not have children and it ended shortly as best I can tell. I am told she was very artistic too and did some family portraits of a couple of the family members and was well liked. I don't know whatever happened to her and there is no contact from her with any of the family members now so I don't even know if she is still living or has passed away."[600]

William Formyduval's presence among Clay Shaw's New Orleans friends met with a mixed reaction over the years. Many thought he was an interesting and unique character, often fun to be around, but others were repelled by his excessive drinking. Women liked him; one of Shaw's young women friends maintained that she and Shaw freely "shared" the bisexual Formyduval. Others described the relationship as being one where Formyduval was "kept" by Shaw, and some say that Formyduval was sometimes a participant in sado-masochistic activities, even without Shaw being present. Formyduval could certainly contribute more than his share to party and sexual situations, but being basically unemployed and free to party and drink all during the day, he sometimes was very intoxicated before the others at a gathering got started.

**Members of the "Formyduval family" of Whiteville, North Carolina on the occasion of Mae Hobson's second marriage on December 16, 1949. Left-right are Ruth Moore (Glass), John B. Glass, Sarah Hill Moore, Shaw's friend William Henry Formyduval, Mae Hobson, Frank Hobson, Marietta Moore, Henry Johnson (Photo courtesy of Ruth Glass)**

Shaw's friend Gaines Kincaid, who had lived in New Orleans during the very early 1950s before moving to New York City, recalls Shaw and Formyduval visiting New York City once, and the three of them planned to see *Visit to a Small Planet*, a play by Gore Vidal. Kincaid remembers Formyduval becoming thoroughly intoxicated before the three of them were to leave for the play, so Shaw simply left him behind in the hotel room, sound asleep.[601]

After meeting Formyduval, Shaw would often vacation in the Whiteville, North Carolina area. He and Formyduval, and other members of the family, would venture down to Myrtle Beach and spend much of their time there. When Shaw was arrested years later, members of the family, and immediate friends of the family, who had met him over the years, were unanimous in their support for him, although the matriarch, Mae Hobson, expressed some uncertainty to at least one person. In May of 1974, when Shaw knew he had cancer and was dying, he made a final pilgrimage to Whiteville to visit with the family and community which had formed such an important part of his life.

Most of the surviving members of the Formyduval family were reluctant to speculate on the nature of Formyduval's exact relationship with Shaw. Shaw and Formyduval fell away from each other in the mid-1960s, before Shaw was arrested. The two kept in touch with each other, though, directly or indirectly, for the rest of Shaw's life. Shaw left Formyduval a cash bequest in his will.

At least one person thought that Formyduval's alcoholism masked, or perhaps led to, a darker side. "I have no idea what WH and Clay fell out about, it could have been anything. I certainly have no doubt that WH would steal to support his alcoholism. WH was not a stable person; he believed he was the person he was in his mind. He was a charmer, a liar, a thief, a manipulator and an alcoholic."

Clay Shaw's life had many coincidences and unusual factors, especially when one considers the nature of the criminal charges against him during his last decade of his life. Regarding William Henry Formyduval, there is just such a coincidence: Formyduval's mother's name was Marguerite, the same as Lee Harvey Oswald's mother.

By 1953, Shaw had moved into 1313 Dauphine Street, the carriage house to the set of properties he had purchased earlier at 906 Esplanade; 1313 Dauphine was now a separate residence. He continued the carefully compartmentalized life he had been leading. One person who lived in the old slave quarters adjacent to Shaw's residence recalls his own lover being summoned down one night for what may have been a suicide attempt at the residence; the windows and doors were all wide open, and Shaw had left the premises. More than fifty years later, memories of the exact details of the incident are understandably hazy.

# 11 · The Louisiana Purchase 150th Anniversary Celebration

During 1953, New Orleans celebrated the 150th anniversary of the Louisiana Purchase. The penultimate event of the Louisiana Purchase celebration was a visit by President Eisenhower in October 1953. Originally scheduled for October 31, 1953, the entire final week of activities, and the main ceremony, had to be moved up two full weeks to October 17 in order to accommodate a sudden change in Eisenhower's schedule. Shortly before that event, the prominent TV personality Ed Sullivan visited New Orleans as part of the celebration, and was given a buffet luncheon and reception in his honor at the Roosevelt hotel.[602]

In the years leading up to 1953, prominent citizens in New Orleans had begun to prepare for a large celebration of the 150th Anniversary, or sesquicentennial, of the Louisiana Purchase of 1803, whereby the newly formed United States of America purchased approximately one-third of its continental territory from France in one fell swoop. It was felt by some that fifty years earlier, in 1903, St. Louis had beaten New Orleans to the punch in celebrating the 100th anniversary of the Purchase, and prominent New Orleanians were determined that it not happen again.

Informal planning for the celebration had begun as early as the late 1940s. Attorney Lloyd Cobb communicated in 1949 with Joseph M. Darst, the mayor of St. Louis, about a possible joint celebration between the two cities. However, there were those in New Orleans who wanted it to have the main celebration, as St. Louis had held it fifty years earlier.

Around 1950, an idea had been floated to have a small trade fair in New Orleans during 1953, following a larger World Trade Fair in St. Louis earlier in 1953. The idea never took root, however, and was instead transformed into the 150th anniversary celebration of the Louisiana Purchase, to take place primarily in New Orleans. International House and the New Orleans Chamber of Commerce both formed committees to promote the proposed idea.

Accordingly, in 1952, a Louisiana Purchase Sesquicentennial Commission was formed to explore the idea of the celebration, and how best to implement it. In late March of that year, William Zetzmann called a meeting to begin the process. The original meeting was held on April 1, 1952, for the purpose of deciding whether New Orleans should take on the task of having such a large celebration. Among the attendees at that meeting were Zetzmann, Lloyd Cobb, Seymour Weiss, and Joseph Rault.[603]

Zetzmann served as President of the commission, which was in effect a predecessor organization to the body that ultimately carried out the celebration, known as the Louisiana Purchase 150th Anniversary Association. However, Zetzmann became ill during the summer of 1952 and needed to step aside, and local officials soon convinced local theater owner E.V. Richards to take over the effort.[604] Richards, who knew many important Hollywood figures, including heads of the various studios, and director Cecil B. De Mille, could use his influence in the motion picture industry in order to promote the celebration.[605]

Charles Nutter, Shaw's counterpart as Managing Director of International House, soon joined the Board of Directors. Nutter had been an early advocate of New Orleans being the primary city to celebrate the sesquicentennial. He had sent a memo to Rudolf Hecht on February 24, 1947, proposing an exhibition in New Orleans in 1953 to coincide with the

150th anniversary, and had written an account of the actual Louisiana Purchase, entitled *America's Best Buy*.

At around the same time, the board decided to hire General Raymond Hufft as Managing Director for the introductory phase of the Association, and Hufft took over that position on August 1, 1952. The first Board of Directors meeting of the Association was held October 20, where the purpose of the newly created organization was more specifically discussed. The Association was a Louisiana state creation, but it received assistance from the Federal government, state government, local New Orleans government, and from private contributions. The total initial budget, which would cover the entire period of activity, from August 1, 1952 through December 31, 1953, was $500,000. Most of the expenditures were to go to salaries, advertising, billboards, brochures, traveling expenses, and special events, such as a pageant and other celebrations in October 1953.[606]

General Hufft served as Managing Director of the Louisiana Purchase 150th Anniversary Association during the organizational phase that took place through the end of 1952. However, Hufft advised the Board of Directors of the Association up front that he was only interested in occupying the position until major fundraising began, that he did not want to be directly involved in fundraising efforts. Accordingly, Hufft submitted a resignation letter to E.V. Richards at the end of January 1953, reminding Richards of his earlier conditions.[607] Shaw would soon take his place.

In one of the many unusual "connections," however tenuous the link, that seemed to follow Clay Shaw around, an interesting item pops up in the collection of records from the Association. It is a letter from General Hufft, during the period before Shaw took over, to Colonel Edwin A. Walker, U.S. Army, in San Francisco; the letter was dated October 10, 1952. In it, Hufft talked of old times, his retirement from the Army, and the possible promotion of Walker.[608] Walker would later become a general, and would then be removed from active duty in the early 1960s because of controversial activities at his post in Germany. In April 1963, Lee Harvey Oswald shot through the window of Walker's home in Dallas, Texas in an attempt to kill him, less than eight months before the assassination of President Kennedy.

At a meeting of the Board of Directors of the Louisiana Purchase 150th Anniversary Association on February 2, 1953, a discussion was held about choosing a successor to General Hufft. Before the meeting, Rudolf Hecht had indicated that Shaw might be interested in the position, if he could be given a leave of absence from the Mart. Shaw, who had joined the Board of Directors of the Association in late 1952, had already attended a December 22 meeting of the Executive Committee of the board.[609] Hecht had spoken to Theodore Brent, who also supported the idea. Shaw, who was also present at the February meeting, accepted the offer. He was hired at the annual salary of $13,000, the same that he was making at the Mart. It was agreed that no publicity would be given to the change until the idea had been approved by the Mart's complete Board of Directors.

Shaw was loaned from the Mart, but the Mart continued to pay half of his salary during his absence; the loan of Shaw, together with the partial payments of his salary, constituted the Mart's contribution as a civic institution to the celebration. Other civic organizations and businesses around the city generally made monetary contributions. The office used by the Association was at 609 International Building, the building that housed International House; International House donated the space as its contribution to the celebration.

Monk Simons, an executive with D.H. Holmes Company in New Orleans, and a former football hero who had played on the Tulane University team that appeared in the very first Sugar Bowl game, during which Tulane defeated Temple 20-14, had a practice over the years of sending newspaper clippings to locally prominent officials about their activities. Simons wrote Shaw a letter of congratulations upon his taking over as Managing Director of the Association. As he normally did, Simons enclosed a clipping announcing Shaw's new job.[610] Simons had earlier written E.V. Richards, congratulating him for being selected

Chairman of the Louisiana Purchase 150th Anniversary Association, and had also enclosed a newspaper clipping of that announcement.[611]

Richards was perhaps the most prominent New Orleanian in charge of the Association, directing Shaw's daily activity. Streuby Drumm with New Orleans Public Service, Inc. (NOPSI), a large local utility, and another prominent local citizen, also was active in the Association. Although an attempt had been made to get prominent local Sears Roebuck heiress Edith Stern to serve the Association, she responded that she had never received an official invitation, and would be too busy to serve during 1953.[612]

David Baldwin, who had returned to New Orleans in 1952 after his employment with the Central Intelligence Agency in India had been terminated, began work at Bauerlein Advertising Agency, and was soon working on the account related to the Louisiana Purchase 150th Anniversary Association. At the end of September 1952, David Baldwin generated a six-point memo to General Raymond Hufft, outlining the beginning of the publicity campaign for the celebration.[613] After about six months on the account, Baldwin joined the Association itself as Director of Public Relations, at a maximum salary of $7,500, and worked under Shaw for the final eight-month period of activity. Scott Wilson, who owned his own public relations firm located in the St. Charles Hotel, also had offered his services to the Association.[614] However, Shaw informed Wilson that the Association had decided to have its own Public Relations Director as a salaried employee, and indicated that Baldwin was starting with the Association on February 25, 1953. As mentioned previously, after the end of the celebration in late October 1953, Shaw would bring Baldwin back with him to the Mart as Public Relations Director, replacing Glenn Weekley, who had left in June to join Kaiser Aluminum.

Clint Bolton, who also worked with Bauerlein's, Inc., was part of the team promoting the sesquicentennial celebration. Bolton was a New Orleans writer and advertising man who later would be mentioned in a number of the memos generated by the Jim Garrison investigation, as someone who might have been involved around the edges of right-wing activity in New Orleans.

Barbara Corbin was the main secretarial employee of the Association. Denis Barry, an accountant who had worked as Streuby Drumm's assistant at NOPSI, also was hired. Mayor Chep Morrison had recommended Barry to E.V. Richards as someone who could handle accounting and auditing functions. Richards referred Barry's name to Wallace Davis, who was in charge of the overall accounting for the Association, and to Kenneth Barranger, who acted as the Association's attorney.[615] Barry would later become an attorney, and would share office space and expenses with Jim Garrison in the late 1950s, before Garrison first ran for district attorney. After Garrison took office as district attorney in 1962, Barry served as assistant district attorney under Garrison during part of Garrison's first term of office.

Among the other employees of the Association was Phyllis B. Wellford, who worked as a receptionist/typist, Theone B. Maher (Denis Barry's sister), who was employed as secretary to David Baldwin, and Marcella Billups, who worked for the two-month period of September and October 1953, when the activity was most intense. As he had done with his Trade Mart employees, Shaw gave departing employees who needed it a letter of recommendation at the end of the Association's existence.

Men who held prominent positions within the city's administrative structure lent their talents to planning the celebration. Richard Swenson, at the time still Public Relations Director of the Board of Commissioners of the Port of New Orleans, was Chairman of the Transportation Committee. Admiral Whitaker F. Riggs, Jr., representing the Chamber of Commerce, was Chairman of the Banquet Committee.

There was a concerted effort to keep the decisions in the hands of those who knew the city best. John A. Reilly, a Chicago resident, had sought the position of executive assistant/office manager eventually awarded to Shaw.[616] However, General Raymond Hufft advised him that the board of the Association wanted "a New Orleans man" in the position.[617]

When Shaw took over in mid-February 1953, he was deluged with offers for different types of services related to the celebration. James Aldige, Jr., who ran a public relations firm, wrote offering to help.[618] Shaw replied that he had just been selected for the new position, had not gotten his "feet wet yet,"[619] and suggested Aldige let two weeks pass before discussing his ideas. Stanley J. Reyes wrote Shaw, offering his services as a producer-director concerning a potential film about the Louisiana Purchase.[620] Shaw replied that he was still settling in, but suggested they talk further down the line.[621]

Shaw also heard from Elmo Avet, a New Orleans interior designer, who offered to discuss his ideas about the celebration with Shaw.[622] Shaw replied a few days later, agreeing to let Avet to drop by his office. Shaw told Avet that he was working from 8:00 a.m. to 6:30 or 7:00 p.m. most days, and that all ideas for the celebration were welcomed.[623]

Shortly after taking over, Shaw spoke to a meeting of French Quarter merchants and residents about the planned eight-month long celebration effort. Bob Cahlman of the Gallery Circle Theater was also present at that meeting; Cahlman would later play a role in explaining Shaw's presence in a set of photographs that surfaced after his arrest, which some thought showed Shaw and accused fellow conspirator David Ferrie, whom Shaw had denied knowing, together in some of the same photos.

Shaw began communicating with New Orleans-area personalities about the project. In late February, he wrote writer Harnett Kane, thanking him for sending the Association a Louisiana Purchase edition of *Queen New Orleans: City by the River*, Kane's history and travel guide to the city published in 1949. Shaw added, "hope we can have lunch together soon."[624]

Shaw also wrote to Norman Cousins, editor of *Saturday Review*, discussing the possibility of having a special edition of the magazine about the Louisiana Purchase. Shaw described the planned celebration in general terms, and noted that he regretted having missed Cousins' recent lecture in New Orleans.[625]

At the Board of Directors meeting on March 9, 1953, it was discussed that the Association itself had a minimum budget of $250,000, of which $90,000 had already been raised. A resolution was passed that asked the City of New Orleans to finance $100,000 in promotional expenses.[626] The estimated budget for the administrative office for 1953 was slightly more than $40,000, of which $29,500 was for salaries.[627]

A brochure explaining the Louisiana Purchase was printed and was mailed to all interested inquirers. A kit of materials that could be used to promote the celebration had also been developed, and was distributed to interested civic organizations around the entire country.

The Post Office agreed to use the Association's die hubs in order that letters could be stamped with the Louisiana Purchase notice.[628] The die hubs were sent to the Post Offices of the four largest cities in Louisiana. Natchitoches, in north Louisiana, the oldest settlement in the Louisiana Purchase, requested that the Association provide it with die hubs as well, but Shaw responded that the city would have to purchase its own set.[629]

Additionally, a bill was introduced by Congressman Hale Boggs in the U.S. House of Representatives to produce a commemorative fifty-cent piece memorializing the celebration; the bill easily passed the U.S. House of Representatives, but became bogged down in the U.S. Senate. The Association delayed plans for distribution of the coins until a more certain outcome could be determined. The Association also ordered 10,000 seals commemorating the Louisiana Purchase. The design chosen was in the same style that had been used for a celebratory seal for the Community Bank of Humboldt, South Dakota.[630]

Shaw was soon busily involved in raising money for the celebration. He wrote to H. LeFevre of Avondale Marine Ways, Inc. thanking him for a $1,000 contribution. Shaw indicated that he believed the celebration would do a great deal, nationally and internationally, to focus attention on New Orleans as the key city in the Mississippi River Valley, and that it would repay, to the businesses supporting it, many times the contributions made to support it.[631]

As part of the fundraising effort, Shaw reached out to numerous businesses asking for donations. One on which he particularly leaned was Brennan's Restaurant, owned at the time by Owen Brennan. Shaw had become a regular patron upon the restaurant's opening, and had become friends with Owen and his sister, Ella. Shaw sometimes asked for contributions by referencing such ongoing relationships. In a letter to Owen Brennan, Shaw noted that other restaurants had contributed, and said, "I want to talk to you and Roy Alciatoire about a Gourmet's Week which I outlined to Ella the other night, which would take place in November."[632] Roy Alciatoire was one of the owners of Antoine's Restaurant, one of the premier restaurants in New Orleans, and indeed across the nation, at that time.

An emerging local politician with whom Shaw worked regarding the celebration was Victor H. Schiro, who would later serve two terms as mayor of New Orleans.[633] Shaw wrote to Schiro, who at the time was a member of the New Orleans Commission Council, asking that the Council approve a substantial contribution to the Louisiana Purchase Commission; Shaw pointed out that the State of Louisiana had already approved $100,000 for the celebration.[634] In April, Schiro agreed to appear in an upcoming Louisiana Purchase-related skit, playing the role of Napoleon for two nights.

The early activities of the Association demonstrated that its leaders were interested in reaching a wide demographic in promoting the upcoming celebration. Their efforts included sponsoring a Louisiana Purchase Essay Contest, in which 63,000 New Orleans school children participated.[635] Pitney Bowes accepted a design of a Louisiana Purchase symbol for its metered mail.[636] And, among the major media outlets targeted for publicity were *Time*, *Colliers*, *Newsweek*, and *Reader's Digest*.

In May, Shaw agreed to speak to the Mississippi Retail Hardware Association Convention at the Buena Vista Hotel on the Gulf Coast, indicating that he would either go to the Gulf coast for the weekend before the speech, or drive over from New Orleans that morning.[637] That same month, he spoke to the New Orleans Secretaries Association at La Louisiane restaurant; the topic was, appropriately enough, "The Louisiana Purchase."[638] Shaw also spoke at the Alcee Fortier Senior High School in New Orleans. Afterwards, participant E.P. Devron wrote to David Baldwin that "Mr. Shaw's presence and talk was the high point of our Constitution Day Program."[639]

Another promotional device used by the Association was a restaurant table mat that displayed a map of the Louisiana Purchase, along with a brief history of the Purchase. The Association ordered samples of the mat in mid-1953 from Aatell and Jones, Inc.; Shaw commented to A.J. Jacquot, Jr. of that company that the mat was "an attractive piece of work."[640] Upon receiving the samples, however, it was noticed immediately that the placemats contained an error. In the printed details, it said that the territories that comprised the Louisiana Purchase had been purchased for $25 per acre, when the rate had been for $25 per square mile. The placemats were later corrected to show that the territory was purchased for four cents per acre.[641]

In a letter to Mr. Jacquot pointing out the placemat error, David Baldwin briefly discussed a central point of controversy regarding the Louisiana Purchase: Did the territories purchased from France comprise all or parts of thirteen future states or seventeen future states?[642] Earlier, it had been decided to seek the services of a historian/researcher for assistance in solidifying the Association's position that there were portions of seventeen eventual states, rather than thirteen, carved out of the Louisiana Purchase territory.[643]

Clarke Salmon, Sr., an executive at Bauerlein's, early on urged the creation of a handbook giving suggestions to newspaper editors for talking up the event.[644] Salmon also was involved in some of the original discussions about the seventeen-state theory, which competed with other theories that promoted smaller numbers of states as being more accurate. In a letter to Salmon, Baldwin discussed the controversy, saying that, in the theory that said that seventeen states, or at least portions of them, had been created from the original territory, portions of Mississippi, Alabama, Texas, and New Mexico were included. The opposing theories said that some or all of those areas either had not been part of the purchase, or had joined the union at a later date.[645]

The Library of Congress's position was that fifteen states had been involved in the original Louisiana Purchase. Of the grand total of seventeen states at issue in the controversy, seven states were wholly within the purchase area, four states were largely within it, two were partly in and partly out of the territory, two merely had corners within the area, and two states, Texas and New Mexico had been renounced by the United States as part of the purchase agreement, and were only acquired later.[646]

Robert Tallant, a New Orleans writer of historical novels, some dealing with voodoo or other aspects of Louisiana history, also disputed the notion that seventeen states had made up the original Louisiana Purchase territory. In a letter to E.V. Richards, Tallant said that only thirteen states had been part of the Territory. He said that, for example, no part of Texas had been included in the purchase. Tallant also indicated that St. Louis had previously celebrated 1804, instead of 1803, as the year of purchase, because the Purchase area had been divided into Louisiana, and an area north of there, and that the division had taken place in 1804.[647] Richards responded by acknowledging that perhaps thirteen states were all that had made up the official Louisiana Purchase territory, but said that it was good for the publicity of the celebration to keep the issue alive; he said that Clarke Salmon, Charles Nutter, and local attorney John Minor Wisdom all agreed with him. However, Richards indicated he would think about the issue and get back to Tallant on the subject.[648] The Association, however, stuck with its original position.

Of all of the seventeen states that the Association maintained had been formed, in whole or in part, from the Louisiana Purchase territory, New Mexico was the most debatable of all. George H. Gardiner of the Chamber of Commerce in New Orleans passed on to Shaw a clipping which took a humorous tone about the controversy related to New Mexico.[649] Someone in New Mexico had proposed sending some soil to Louisiana for the celebration, although many in New Mexico disputed that it had been formed from the territory that comprised the Louisiana Purchase. Shaw replied that he would fan the flames of the controversy by sending the clipping (which had appeared in the *San Diego Union* newspaper) to Tulane University for a rebuttal supporting the idea that a portion of New Mexico had indeed been part of the original purchase.[650]

A suggestion was made by Streuby Drumm to tie in the Louisiana Purchase celebration with a convention of the American Municipal Association, to be held in late November and early December. However, Shaw advised Drumm that the Louisiana Purchase celebration would close up shop no later than October 31, 1953, and that no tie-in would be possible, unless the mayor specifically requested it.[651]

Arthur J. Chapital, Sr., President of the New Orleans branch of the National Association for the Advancement of Colored People (NAACP), wrote to E.V. Richards, wanting to know what part "Negroes" would play in the sesquicentennial celebration. He hoped that only the "honorable historical facts" would be portrayed, without references to "disgraceful" slave practices. He added that he believed that such unfortunate sections of history should be minimized, as the United States was looked upon as an emblem of true democracy, and that any display of slavery would only serve to humiliate fifteen million loyal black citizens of the United States, whose ancestors had been "pawns in a vicious system."[652]

Dr. G.A. Ackal, President of the Louisiana Sugar Cane Festival and Fair Association in New Iberia, Louisiana, communicated regularly with the Association. He had asked that New Iberia be given individual recognition at the celebration. David Baldwin responded, thanking Ackal for the publicity he had given to the celebration in the *Daily Iberian* newspaper, but said that New Iberia could not be honored individually, that only large cities were being recognized in that manner, with the exception of Natchitoches, Louisiana as the oldest settlement in Louisiana.[653] Dr. Ackal later invited Shaw to be present at the coronation of Queen Sugar XII, the winner of the festival pageant, on September 26, 1953, in New Iberia. However, Shaw advised him that he could not attend, as he was not planning to leave New Orleans until after the celebration was over, but that he hoped Dr Ackal could join them at the celebration for presidential ceremonies in October.[654] Shaw later wrote again to Dr. Ackal, congratulating him on the "bang-up job" Ackal had done handling the coronation of Queen Sugar.[655]

The celebration had its occasional critics as operations moved into full swing. Marie Bezou wrote a letter to the editor of the *New Orleans States*, making specific critical comments for the large scale celebration, and copied Shaw on the letter.[656] Shaw wrote a handwritten note to David Baldwin on the letter, asking, "Do you think we should answer her?" He eventually answered her directly, saying that he would bring her suggestions to the attention of the Executive Committee.[657]

As with any large civic venture, it was necessary to raise large amounts of money, and gain the participation of numerous institutions. Conversely, individuals and institutions sought to benefit from the celebration as well. For example, the American Legion solicited the Association to advertise on buses attending the American Legion National Convention. However, Shaw responded that the Louisiana Purchase celebration could not afford to spend such advertising money, as it was having trouble raising enough to pay for things for which it had already contracted.[658]

James F. Bezou, who was with the Belgium consulate in New Orleans, wrote on behalf of "Athenee Louisiannais," a group of white Creoles in the city, offering to entertain the French delegation while it was in New Orleans. Shaw acknowledged his letter, and offered to meet and talk over the offer.[659]

The Louisiana Purchase 150th Anniversary Association rode the wave of national publicity that occurred naturally regarding the event. Various publications around the country ran articles recounting the monumental transaction, and the Association requested permission to reprint many articles and send them to inquirers, saving it much of the expense of generating its own publicity. Historian Bernard de Voto wrote an article for *Colliers*, a prominent magazine during that era. David Baldwin enclosed the article to R.T. Andrews, and thanked him for alerting General Raymond Hufft that de Voto would also be doing an article about the sesquicentennial for *Ford Times*[660]

*Nation's Business* magazine promised to devote a cover to the Louisiana Purchase.[661] Meanwhile, it was decided to use video footage of Mardi Gras festivities to "sell" the Louisiana Purchase celebration to "New Yorkers" interested in attending or contributing.[662]

Governmental units and organizations in other states followed the Association's progress during the year, and some of them requested information about the methods being used to promote the celebration. Theodore Lafair, in charge of the Atlantic City, New Jersey, Centennial and Diamond Jubilee of Light Association, wrote to Shaw discussing Atlantic City's upcoming seventy-fifth anniversary celebration in 1954.[663] He requested copies of all promotional materials, souvenir programs, and other information that would be useful to him in planning the celebration. Shaw responded with a full kit of materials, and offered to answer any questions Lafair might have.[664]

The interest in this heralded anniversary garnered interest well beyond U.S. borders. Inquiries came from all over the world for information related to the Louisiana Purchase. For example, Mrs. W.H. Dawson wrote from Australia, saying she had heard about the celebration from the United States Information Service in Australia;[665] Shaw sent her a map and other promotional materials.[666]

During 1952, it had been decided to seek publicity through both major presidential campaign organizations in rallies held in the New Orleans area.[667] The plan was to have the president of the United States, whoever it turned out to be, present at the final ceremony in October 1953, as part of the re-enactment of the signing of the original agreement that had formalized the Louisiana Purchase. The presidential race between Dwight Eisenhower and Adlai Stevenson was a tight one, with the outcome far from certain, so plans had to be crafted to include both possible leaders. In early October 1952, David Baldwin wrote to Clayton Fritchey, who had been editor of the *Item* when Baldwin had been a reporter there in the late 1940s. Fritchey, who worked in the newspaper business and in various government and political functions throughout his career, was at the time working for the Stevenson for President campaign headquarters in Springfield, Illinois. Baldwin provided suggested remarks about the Louisiana Purchase to Fritchey for inclusion in a speech Adlai Stevenson would give in New Orleans on October 10, 1952.[668] In late 1952, after the election, Baldwin showed the bipartisan spirit of the Association by suggesting to Raymond Hufft that the Association solicit a mention of the Sesquicentennial in newly-elected President Eisenhower's inaugural speech.[669]

The problem of raising money was always part of the Sesquicentennial process. At a meeting of the Board of Directors of the Association in late May 1953, it was discussed that approximately $140,000 of contributions had been received, with slightly more than $24,000 outstanding in pledges. The cash balance was approximately $61,500 at the time, but at least $80,000 more needed to be raised in order to meet the minimum budget that had been prepared in February. Two-thirds of the total budgeted amount had been raised, and a significant portion expended, but the big events and celebrations were still to come. Magazines and newspapers in Louisiana and around the country had given much free publicity to the Association, and the celebration, but the constant need to raise money in order to make the events as successful as possible hung over the Association throughout the process.[670]

Shaw wrote to Joseph Montgomery, of the United Fruit Company, requesting a contribution to the celebration. In the solicitation letter, Shaw commented that it was a "God-given opportunity to dramatize all over the world the point that you and I and all of us have been preaching these last seven years…namely, that New Orleans is the key city and port of the entire Valley region."[671]

Offers of products and services continued to come in to the Association, which helped to offset some of the financial worries. Charles H. Blake, an out-of-town musician, wrote to Isidore Newman, Co-Chairman of the Association, offering to provide musical services for the celebration.[672] Shaw replied for Newman two weeks later, saying that the Association's first preference was to use someone locally, but that if Blake would send more information on what he could do for the celebration, he would be considered.[673]

Mortimer Frankel wrote directly to Governor Robert Kennon in March, offering his services writing and producing radio programs for the celebration.[674] Kennon forwarded the letter to E.V. Richards, who passed it on to Shaw. Frankel wrote to Shaw in late March, elaborating on his offer to coordinate national radio coverage;[675] Shaw replied, mentioning budgetary concerns, and sent the standard kit dealing with the planned celebration. In a letter in mid-April, Shaw wrote Frankel again, noting that other states were forming commissions, and that the celebrations would be coordinated nationwide by the various commissions.[676] In his reply to a later Frankel letter, Shaw reiterated his concerns about the budget.[677]

In promoting the celebration, the Association did not shy away from emphasizing the historical and political importance of the event. In some letters to inquirers, Shaw mentioned that the development of the huge territory from a colonial wilderness had been an accomplishment of free enterprise, self-reliance, and pioneering spirit, and was third in importance only to the Declaration of Independence and the Constitution.[678]

In a letter to Shaw, Beverly Brown, who had her own television, radio, stage and screen service company in New Orleans, noted the increasing influence of television among the general public.[679] That represented quite a change in the ten years since Shaw had begun with the Mart, when radio and print dominated, and television had been a foreseeable, but not yet so important, method of mass communication. With this advice in mind, the Association used television for some events. One hour of a beauty pageant related to the celebration was broadcast to 70,000 television screens in the New Orleans area; the Association paid Brinkerhoff Agency $24.76 for the leasing of a wire from Southern Bell that allowed them to televise the event,[680] and the actual air time was donated by the local television station. In addition, CBS Television planned to feature the Louisiana Purchase on its *You Are There* program.[681]

The event was promoted to teachers and students in the nation's public schools. Ads were placed in *Teachers* magazine, and in *4-H* magazine. The book *Stars in Their Eyes*, about the men involved in the Louisiana Purchase, was commissioned by the Association to be written by author Clayton Rand, a friend of William Zetzmann. The association purchased $5,000 worth of copies of the book, which was printed by Dixie Press in Gulfport, Mississippi, and distributed by them to appropriate outlets.

Russ McFarland with the National Press Club in Washington, D.C., wrote Shaw, asking him if any additional help would be needed to publicize the celebration.[682] Shaw replied, saying no additional help would be needed, but asked McFarland to visit with him if he got down for the celebration.[683]

The city officials behind the celebration had decided that the primary purpose was to celebrate the event with a spectacular show that would benefit the city through national publicity, rather than to attract large numbers of visitors to New Orleans for the celebration itself. An unsigned memo to Shaw in August discussed the possibility that some of the promotional literature was being geared toward visitors, and mentioned that, "We are not interested in attracting tourists" to the events themselves.[684] A proposal had been made to produce counter cards commemorating the celebration, to be sent to hotels and tourist associations. However, another unsigned memo to Shaw reiterated that the Association was not interesting in attracting tourists, and that "perhaps we are going too far afield."[685] Along similar lines, P.J. Rinderle, of the Chamber of Commerce for New Orleans, advised that the Chamber would not include information about the celebration in a film it had produced promoting New Orleans, but would merely make a very general mention of the original Louisiana Purchase in the film.[686]

One of Shaw's appeals for funds went to J.M. Engster of Walgreens, the drugstore chain. Shaw noted the publicity that had already been generated for New Orleans, and the subsequent number of visitors to New Orleans, resulting in additional business.[687] That appeal, of course, somewhat contradicted the Association's internal goal of not attracting tourists for the actual celebrations.

Another appeal for contributions was to Longino and Collins, Inc., a sausage manufacturer; the company declined to make a contribution. A graphic on the company's letterhead stationery showed a manufacturing plant with a tall smokestack, and the slogan: "The South's Most Sanitary Meat Food Plant."[688]

In a letter to Earle Newton, Editor of *American Heritage* magazine, David Baldwin suggested that the publication run a piece dealing with the conflicting views of the number of states created by the Louisiana Purchase.[689] Shaw also was involved in the potential *American Heritage* article, writing to an old New York acquaintance, Carl Carmer, an historical writer living at Irvington-On-Hudson, New York. Shaw opined that although it had been years since they had met, from pictures he had seen, the years were treating Carmer kindly. Shaw said that he hoped that Carmer would get down to New Orleans for the celebration.[690] When Carmer replied, sending his wife Betty's best wishes,[691] Shaw responded that the summer weather was "fierce" in New Orleans, and suggested that Carmer not venture down until fall.[692]

The article in *American Heritage* magazine was eventually published. The Association had the choice of paying for four-color prints of two paintings that would be included along with the text of the article, but Shaw rejected that expense.

The Association, and its celebration of the event, drew a fair number of employment applications. Frances Bryson Moore, who had spent fifteen years as a reporter and publicity director, recommended her niece for employment. Many of the applicants came by reference from Bee Robertson's employment service. Lola Anderson, who had a Master's degree from the University of Missouri, was one of the applicants. Maud Ellen Farrar, a New Orleans woman who was educated, well-traveled, and spoke several languages, also applied for a position.

Even in the early to mid-1950s, applicants for employment in New Orleans often listed their religion as standard information, if they were Catholic, and some noted their language skills, particularly in either Spanish or French. Some applicants, both male and female, noted if they did not have any children, which fact apparently gave the employer the impression that the prospective employee could work longer and more flexible hours.

One interesting person with whom Shaw crossed paths during 1953 was Edward L. Bernays. Bernays, who died in 1995 at age 103, was a nephew of Sigmund Freud, and an influential figure in 20$^{th}$ century public relations, crowd psychology, and as an advisor to governments and corporations. He allegedly was an advisor to the United Fruit Company in its activities that led to the overthrow of the elected government in Guatemala by the CIA in 1954. Bernays had written Shaw, discussing a possible commercial tie-in with the Eisenhower visit in October. However, Shaw declined such an arrangement, instead sending Bernays the standard kit of promotional materials.[693] Bernays replied to Shaw that, "I understand the situation and do indeed appreciate your cooperation in this matter."[694]

The Association sometimes had a less than enthusiastic relationship with organizations in other locations that wished to participate in the celebration. Generally, the officials behind the New Orleans affair sought the cooperation of institutions in other parts of Louisiana, and across the country, only to the extent that it would benefit the New Orleans celebration. Many localities had their own celebrations, and the Association generally avoided direct tie-ins with those celebrations. Monita Goldsby wrote to E.V. Richards, mentioning the proposed celebration in Baton Rouge, and inquiring how she could coordinate with the New Orleans activities.[695] Richards scrawled on the letter, "Shaw—send her something." Richards further indicated to Shaw that other locations should be encouraged to have their own celebrations independently of the New Orleans celebration, and that the Association could only offer advice to those independent celebrations. Shaw enclosed the standard promotional literature with his reply.

Local organizations in Louisiana inquired frequently about holding their own celebrations. Mrs. Camille Cazedessus wrote Shaw, also asking about a Baton Rouge celebration; she was with the Women's Auxiliary of Our Lady of the Lake Hospital there. Shaw advised her that local celebrations were up to the individual organizations rather than the Association.[696] Ms. Cazdussus's son, Camille, Jr. would later become nationally known as a promoter of collectibles related to author Edgar Rice Burroughs, who wrote the Tarzan novels and science fiction stories.

Shaw cooperated with state officials to the extent needed to make the celebration a success. Dave Pearce, the long-time Louisiana Commissioner of Agriculture, asked Shaw to a meeting at the state capitol in Baton Rouge in June, for the purpose of fusing together the resources of state agencies and festival groups in support of the main Louisiana Purchase observation in New Orleans.[697] However, when Richard Walker, with the Louisiana Department of Commerce and Industry, suggested to E.V. Richards that the Association should get state agencies more involved with the celebration, Richards passed the letter on to Shaw with a note that, "A political bandwagon, either City or State, will not parade here if we keep faith."[698]

Along with inquiries about the proposed commemorative fifty-cent piece, public inquiries about other types of memorabilia came into the Association. One asked about a commemorative stamp from the Post Office; Shaw replied that the Post Office would issue such a stamp only in the St. Louis area, because there were no large organized philatelic activities in New Orleans.[699] Phyllis Wellford advised another inquirer that there would be no commemorative deck of playing cards made as part of the celebration.[700] The Association also fielded inquiries dealing with films that might be available discussing the Louisiana Purchase, and those seeking pictures of Louisiana's governors from 1803 to 1953. Others wondered about flags that commemorated the Louisiana Purchase.

Samuel Burr, Jr., Chairman of the Department of Education at American University, and a relative of Aaron Burr, wrote for information about the celebration. David Baldwin answered the letter with some interest, picking up on the last name, and discussing Burr being made an honorary member of the Society of the Louisiana Purchase.

The ultimate celebration in October would include the first ever public meeting of Rex and the King of Comus other than on Mardi Gras day. David Baldwin explained the normal Mardi Gras tradition to an inquirer at General Foods Corporation, perhaps not entirely accurately; in the same letter, Baldwin also suggested using Calumet baking powder to make a 150-foot tall cake related to the event.[701]

Baldwin's more spectacular and humorous suggestions were often rejected by Shaw and Richards, or by others. At an early meeting, Baldwin had suggested staging a fight on board a barge in the Mississippi River, with everyone participating dressed in period costumes.[702] Another of Baldwin's ideas was to have City Park in New Orleans create a "Living Map," using trees and plants from the seventeen states that made up the Purchase territory; Baldwin noted that City Park already had a Living Clock.[703] The Board of Commissioners at City Park responded to Baldwin that his idea for the "Living Map" had been referred to the Grounds Committee.[704]

In addition to his sometimes far-out suggestions, David Baldwin often ended his memos with a comment that perhaps reflected, in a humorous way, his former CIA training. At the end of a memo he sent to Shaw regarding an article Clint Bolton was writing, he suggested, "Please chew and swallow after reading."[705]

Individual relatives of Thomas Jefferson, and other prominent individuals connected with the original Louisiana Purchase, contacted the Association during the year, either offering to help, or requesting to participate in the official ceremonies. James Louis Randolph Kean, a descendant of Jefferson, planned to attend the series of final ceremonies; the mayor of Baton Rouge was to introduce him to the crowd.[706]

There was some talk of bringing in a reproduction of the ship *Santa Maria*, which was the largest of the three ships used by Columbus in his voyage across the Atlantic Ocean in 1492. However, the Association rejected that idea, perhaps fearing it would detract from the U.S.-French nature of the original event.[707]

The Bienville Statue Subcommittee was part of the New Orleans Committee of the Association. Some of the members included Richard Foster, the Bezou Brothers (James and Henry), H.A. Sawyer, and Joseph M. Rault. The subcommittee worked to commission a statue of Jean-Baptiste Le Moyne de Bienville, the "Father of New Orleans," a multi-term governor of French Louisiana who had a major role in founding New Orleans in 1718.

Another writer with whom Shaw communicated was the New Orleans writer Frances Parkinson Keyes. He sent a copy of Harnett Kane's book, *Queen New Orleans*, to publisher Julian Messner, and suggested that it bind some of Keyes's books as part of the celebration.[708] In April, Keyes advised Shaw that Julian Messner would issue a small printing of a boxed set of two of her Louisiana-related novels. She mentioned her current trip to Europe, and the possible use of the Beauregard House for part of the Louisiana Purchase celebration. She added that she had been struggling after two months of illness, that she was going to Washington soon, and would take a rain check on Shaw's recent dinner invitation.[709] Shaw replied that he was looking forward to Keyes's upcoming book on Saint Theresa of Avalon, indicating that Theresa was a "favorite" of his because she had combined "a thoroughly sensible and practical life with a rich interior one." Shaw added that he would let Keyes know if the Association needed her back earlier than planned for participation in the festivities.[710]

However, by early September, Keyes advised Shaw that she was in London, after being in France, and that she could not be in New Orleans by October 17, 1953, which she now understood was the new date of the main celebration events. She added that "Deanie joins me in wishing you kind regards."[711] Shaw replied, confirming that Eisenhower would visit two weeks earlier than originally expected. He mentioned Herman Deutsch's *Item* columns from London, saying he assumed that Keyes had seen Deutsch during her visit.[712]

Shaw communicated with E.I. Dupont de Nemours and Company, asking for a copy of its book celebrating the company's 150th anniversary;[713] the company agreed on the use of those materials. Harold Brayman responded for the company, asking that Shaw gives his best regards to Charles Nutter, indicating that he and Nutter both used to be Washington correspondents for their respective media services.[714]

Contributions for the celebration, which had begun coming in as early as the spring of 1952, totaled $197,424 by the end of September 1953. Expenses through that date were $126,152. However, the largest block of expenditures would occur in October, with the visit of President Eisenhower and the re-signing of the Louisiana Purchase agreement, and the two-week concentration of festivities leading up to it.

In the midst of Shaw's ten-month tenure as Managing Director of the Association, he had to decline an invitation from Ray Cantrell of the Jung Hotel for a get-together with a group in the hotel's Cotillion Lounge; Shaw advised that he was speaking to the Southern Pine Association on behalf of the celebration.[715] Shaw's personal promotional appearances on behalf of the celebration were constant and varied. For instance, in the midst of his eight-month tenure, Shaw served as Master of Ceremonies at a program honoring the U.S. Marine Company that was dedicated to the Louisiana Purchase celebration.[716]

Charles Nutter had advised Shaw in the spring of 1953 that prominent television show host Ed Sullivan had devoted ten to fifteen minutes of his weekly show to the Ohio Sesquicentennial, so Shaw wrote to Louis Clay of the Clay-Dutton Company, asking if Clay could suggest that Sullivan promote the Louisiana Purchase Sesquicentennial on his show as well.[717] In a letter to Tom Dutton of Clay-Dutton a month later, Shaw acknowldged that Ed Sullivan would mention the celebration on the Sunday night before the Eisenhower visit in October.[718] A letter from Shaw in mid-July to Chris Cross, of Kenyan and Eckhardt, Inc., mentioned that Sullivan would be in New Orleans on October 28, 1953.[719] The date was selected before the Association knew of Eisenhower's change of plans, which would cause the entire set of final festivities to be moved forward two weeks, from October 31st to October 17th.

There had always been some uncertainty as to the exact date of President Eisenhower's availability, and the final celebration depended upon his attendance. After all, the culmination of the celebration would be two weeks of parades, pageantry, and fireworks around the time of President Eisenhower's assumed visit in October.[720] As of mid-August, no programs for the final series of events had been printed yet, as the Association was still waiting upon Eisenhower's representatives to firm up the date.[721] By late August, however, it became known that Eisenhower's visit had been moved up by two weeks, causing the two-week period of festivities that would cap the celebration to be hurriedly moved forward in its entirety.

Accordingly, the main celebrations would take place from October 4 through October 17, 1953, capped by Eisenhower's visit on October 17. Ten performances of the Sesquirama, a play commemorating the Louisiana Purchase, would be performed, along with a symphonic cavalcade of American greatness during the preceding 150 years. There also would be fireworks displays, square dancing on Canal Street, a military parade and the parades of Rex and Comus (for the first time ever other than on Mardi Gras day).[722]

The Sesquirama was a gigantic pageant, with approximately 1,000 people in the cast, depicting the purchase and growth of the Louisiana territory. The October 10th performance honored the city of Natchitoches. Shaw advised Mrs. C. Vernon Cloutier, a member of the cast from Natchitoches, that the Association could not pay her way to New Orleans, as the act that created it stated that members of the cast would serve without salary or expense.[723]

Another idea had been to have the Tulane-Army football game to be televised on October 31, 1953, with mention of the Sesquicentennial activities.[724] That idea was abandoned for good, however, once the date of President Eisenhower's visit was moved up two weeks, as all of the festivities would be well over before Halloween.

The Association was still getting inquiries about the commemorative fifty-cent piece. However, Shaw advised the Chamber of Commerce that there would be no such commemorative coin, as the bill authorizing it had failed to pass the U.S. Senate.[725]

Carl Cramer, who would design the busts of both Theodore Brent and Rudolf Hecht after their deaths, solicited the job of creating a bust of Eisenhower, for a proposed fee of $800. He requested to observe Eisenhower personally for a brief period before he designed the bust.[726] The Association, however, chose not to commission such a bust as part of the celebration.

Shaw was often complimented after his speeches promoting the Louisiana Purchase celebration. Harlean James of the American Planning and Civic Association wrote, saying he had heard Shaw's speech at International House, and requesting a copy of it. He indicated that Shaw's speech had made the audience feel as if they were present at the actual Louisiana Purchase negotiations.[727] Shaw replied, as he always did, that he had no text of the speech, but rather that he had, as always, spoken extemporaneously; he instead enclosed a copy of Charles Nutter's brochure, *America's Best Buy*, about the original Louisiana Purchase.[728]

An acquaintance of Shaw, Lillian Meyer, suggested a friend of hers as someone who could perform music for the celebration. However, Shaw, after indicating that he was "glad to hear from you again," wrote that there would be no musical activity at the celebration, and that the Association would not need her friend's services. He concluded the letter by saying that he hoped things were going well for her, and that she had gotten her affairs in New York straightened out, and he inquired when she was coming back to New Orleans.[729]

Despite his decline of such musical offerings, Shaw encouraged John J. Morrissey of the Tulane University band to write a Louisiana Purchase march that would be used during the final festivities.[730] Morrissey indicated he would write the march around October 1; Shaw urged him to donate any proceeds from the march to the Association.[731]

Horace Renegar of Xavier College, a predominantly black college in New Orleans, wrote a memo to the Association, raising the possibility of having a "Negro-white" joint musical effort, perhaps Beethoven's Ninth Symphony, performed by the New Orleans Symphony and the Xavier Chorus. Renegar felt that would counter Communist claims of racial intolerance in the South.[732]

The Lutheran Layman's League inquired if it could have a float in the parade that would be part of final festivities. Shaw replied that the parade was a Carnival parade only, meaning that only Mardi Gras-related floats would be allowed.[733]

David Baldwin suggested that the celebration tie in with United Nations Day, which also would be in October. In a letter to Glen Douthit, with the Public Relations Department of the City of New Orleans, Baldwin mentioned that Shaw and Mario Bermúdez had recently returned from Washington, where thirty-two ambassadors had pledged to be present in October during the celebration.[734]

As part of the effort to ensure black participation, even if limited, in the celebration, Shaw exchanged information with John E. Rousseau of the *Pittsburgh Courier*, at the time one of the most widely circulated and prestigious black newspapers in the country. The material exchanged dealt with consumer tastes and statistics and demographics among the black population; New Orleans' "Negro" population at the time was estimated to be 29% of the total population.[735]

More early ideas for the celebration included concentrating on major historic personalities connected with the Louisiana Purchase, such as Thomas Jefferson, Robert Livingston, and James Monroe.[736] Another idea was to have all railway freight cars entering and leaving New Orleans have the slogan "150$^{th}$ Anniversary Purchase-America's Best Buy" emblazoned on the sides.[737]

It was intended to have all of the governors from all of the states created from the Louisiana Purchase Territory, and from the original thirteen colonies, thirty governors in all, to attend the final festivities. However, almost all governors declined the invitation, citing schedule conflicts.

Despite these thorough efforts, not everyone was pleased with the almost year-long celebration. Even before the two weeks of penultimate festivities had begun, Marshall McClelland, in an article for *FORWARD*, a publication of the Junior Chamber of Commerce in New Orleans, called the Louisiana Purchase observance the "biggest flop of 1953." He added that advertising agencies had reaped the major benefit of the celebration.

The Association printed detailed maps of the Louisiana Purchase for those who needed them to promote or study the event. The maps were very popular with teachers and students, and the demand for the maps increased dramatically as the celebration neared its zenith. In response to one letter, after festivities were over, inquiring why Louisiana Purchase maps had been mailed out late, David Baldwin replied to Georgia C. Rawson of State Teachers Magazines, Inc. that the hectic schedule during the two weeks ending October 17 was to blame; the Association had received 25,000 to 30,000 requests for maps during October.[738]

As late as early December, Shaw wrote several times to various teachers' magazines, advising that the Association was now shut down completely, and that all requests for maps received prior to November 15, 1953 had been filled. He indicated that he would see to it that maps were sent to each of the publications, which could then fill any outstanding requests from their readers if they wished.[739]

As with any organization that generates great publicity, the Association got its share of crank mail. In a memo to E.V. Richards, Shaw sarcastically referred to a Mr. Teunnison in Washington, D.C. Shaw indicated that he had sent a letter April 1 giving Teunnison the "politest brushoff" he could think of. Shaw added that he had known Teunnison by mail for several years, and that Teunnison had been "advising" Shaw how to run the International Trade Mart during that period.[740]

E.V. Richards invited famed Hollywood director Cecil B. DeMille to be Master of Ceremonies during President Eisenhower's visit in October. In a letter to Richards responding to the invitation, DeMille referred to his production of *The Ten Commandments*, which was then close to starting production.[741] DeMille had been officially invited by the governor of Louisiana and the mayor of New Orleans, and he and his wife were to be in New Orleans on October 17, 1953. Additionally, DeMille cut three radio recordings, using his distinctive voice in support of the celebration.[742]

Many types of persons participated in the celebration in their own way, not always with the enthusiastic support of the Association. Miss Amy Boudreau of New Orleans exhibited her poems at the celebration. Afterwards, she wrote Shaw requesting a certificate of appreciation on the work she had done on behalf of the celebration.[743] In a handwritten note on memo paper, Shaw penciled to Barbara Corbin, "Send her a Blankety blank certificate."

Shaw was asked to serve as one of 100 people on an honorary reception committee at a civic dinner celebrating the 20th anniversary of the first Sugar Bowl football game; Lester Lautenschlaeger, Chairman of the Sugar Bowl Appreciate Committee, issued the invitation. The event would take place October 9 and 10, 1953, a week before the major planned festivities. [744]

Shaw communicated during the celebration with his old boss, J. C. Jackson of Western Union; he had hired Shaw as a telegraph operator in the late 1920s. Shaw asked Jackson to obtain the cable code "LAPURCHASE" for use on communications.[745] Jackson recommended Shaw to speak to a group of Western Union employees in Alexandria, Louisiana.[746] Shaw suggested the two have lunch one day soon, and indicated that he was anxious to hear news of Robert and Sylvia, Jackson's son and daughter-in-law in the New York City area.[747]

Shaw wrote to W. J. Gosen, who was the Louisiana delegate to the Calaveras County Frog Jumping Contest in California. Shaw asked him to invite all the delegates at the contest to the Louisiana Purchase celebration, and added, "Best wishes to Frog Jubilee and May the Best Frog Win."[748]

One of the objectives of the celebration was to convince ambassadors from numerous foreign countries to attend the main celebration in October. In August, Shaw and Mario Bermúdez called on a number of those ambassadors at their embassies in Washington, D.C. Afterward, Shaw corresponded with them to confirm their ability to attend the main function. The ambassadors represented countries such as Saudi Arabia (whose ambassador gave Shaw a watch as a gift), Belgium, Germany, Luxembourg, Great Britain, Sweden, Turkey, Guatemala, Dominican Republic, Austria, Portugal, India, Israel, Pakistan, and the Netherlands. As of mid-September, ambassadors from thirty-four countries were planning to attend the final ceremony. Among the ambassadors who immediately indicated they could not attend were those representing Cuba, Denmark, Australia, and Sweden.

The Association worked with the U.S. Department of State in insuring that proper protocol was followed in dealing with the various countries that would be involved in the celebration. Abba Eban of Israel, who at the time was Vice-President of the United Nations General Assembly, and who had been an active figure in the Zionist movement, accepted the invitation to attend. However, Dag Hammarksjold of Sweden, who at the time was the Secretary-General of the United Nations, could not attend the celebration. Many of the ambassadors came in a motorcade from Washington to New Orleans. The ambassadors were given a sightseeing trip, which included not only New Orleans, but nearby plantations as well, and a reception at Middlegate Gardens, the country home of Rudolf Hecht in Pass Christian, Mississippi, which contained elaborate Japanese gardens and statuary.

Shaw arranged for press and photographic coverage of the ambassadors, giving newspaper editors a form letter with the general guidelines for covering the visits. David Baldwin coordinated the activities of members of the print, radio and television press who were attending the celebration, gathering information from them in order to issue their credentials.

Shaw, Bermúdez, and others continued to work on the ambassadors, trying to elicit acceptances from as many as possible. As of October, ambassadors from forty-nine countries had been invited; ten had definitely declined to attend. Some ambassadors who initially accepted, such as those from South Africa, Saudi Arabia, and India, had changes of plans and ultimately could not attend.

The Chamber of Commerce wrote to Shaw, requesting information on the prominent out-of-town persons who were scheduled to visit New Orleans to attend the celebration. At the time, the Chamber of Commerce used the slogan "America's Most Interesting City," and also proclaimed that New Orleans was the "Heart of America's New Commercial Frontier," on its stationary[749]

Individual prominent New Orleans citizens acted as hosts for the ambassadors and other personnel of countries who attended the celebration. Edgar Stern acted as host for Israel, Joseph Rault for France, Lloyd Cobb for Panama, Neville Levy for the Philippines, and Rudolf Hecht for Argentina.

One somewhat notable person with whom Shaw dealt near, and after, the end of the Association was Antony L. Geyelin, a businessman in Philadelphia. Geyelin was a descendant of Pierre Clement de Laussat, a French politician who had served as governor of Louisiana during the period when Napoleon decided to sell the Louisiana Territory to the United States. As such, Laussat was responsible for transferring the colony to the United States. Geyelin had corresponded with Association officials throughout 1953 with suggestions about the celebration, and how he might be involved. He also corresponded directly with President Eisenhower's representatives, and with Congressman Hale Boggs, about his participation in the celebration. He and his wife came to New Orleans and were present for the final festivities. In mid-1954, long after the festivities were over, Geyelin brought to Hale Boggs's attention the fact that his wife's hotel room for the period shortly after the celebration had not been reimbursed by the Association. Although the matter came up while Shaw was on a trade mission to Europe during the period April through June 1954, Boggs brought it to Shaw's attention upon his return. Shaw replied to Mrs. Geyelin that Mr. Geyelin had agreed to be responsible for his wife's hotel room at the Jung Hotel, and that Mr. Geyelin should have brought the matter to the attention of the Association while it was functioning, if he wished to be reimbursed for the expense. Shaw indicated the Association was now completely shut down, that the records had been sent to the State Auditor, and that he would be unable to help them with the reimbursement.[750]

Shaw had to deal with many special requests for tickets to the main events. One person from whom Shaw received requests concerning the October festivities was Dr. Nicholas J. Chetta, who was Coroner of Orleans Parish. Chetta had asked for six invitations to the final celebrations held in Jackson Square,[751] and Shaw was able to accommodate Chetta's party.[752] Years later, shortly before Shaw's arrest, Dr. Chetta would perform the autopsy on David Ferrie. He also would testify at Shaw's preliminary hearing several weeks later, after Shaw's arrest, regarding his activities in the administration of sodium pentothal to main prosecution witness Perry Russo, and regarding hypnotism of Russo.

On October 17, 1953, President Eisenhower arrived at Moisant Airport in New Orleans at approximately nine o'clock in the morning, and was met by Governor Robert F. Kennon, Mayor Chep Morrison, E.V. Richards, and John Minor Wisdom. He arrived in downtown New Orleans to lead a parade down to Jackson Square, to a reviewing stand that had been set up there. After the Rex and Comus parades were completed, E.V. Richards presented the mayor of New Orleans and the governor of Louisiana. Richards then presented Cecil B. deMille, who acted as Master of Ceremonies. DeMille narrated the historical re-enactment of the transfer in 1803 of the Louisiana Territory from France to the United States. The re-enactment of the signing of the Louisiana Purchase then took place, with the president and the Ambassador of France participating. Richards presented the Ambassador of France, H.E. Henri Bonnet, and then President Eisenhower, who delivered a short address on "World Trade," which was broadcast on more than twenty television stations. The entire final ceremony lasted approximately two hours. Richards presented both the president and the Ambassador of France with tokens of appreciation on behalf of the people of New Orleans and the State of Louisiana. With the ceremonies completed, the president returned to the airport.[753]

Rathbone DeBuys, who had been the architect responsible for designing the extensive remodeling effort of the International Trade Mart building from 1946 to 1948, wrote to Shaw saying, "Permit me to congratulate Your Majesty on a job well done–the Sesquicentennial. You certainly made something out of nothing–except a Great Date. It must be wonderful to have at your command the innumerable Ambassadors and other High-Ups—in addition to the President. Perhaps you will now decide in which Country you will run for President, having such a powerful acquaintance throughout the world. Of course I saw most of it on television with all the comforts of a big chair, and it was really impressive."[754] Shaw replied a few days later, saying, "Many thanks for your nice letter. In any celebration of the scope and magnitude of this one, the credit must be shared by many hands. However, I know I speak for everybody who participated in saying that your kind remarks are appreciated. Thanks again for taking time to write, and I hope to see you soon."[755]

After the end of the celebration, the Association continued to receive many letters. Most dealt with request for brochures, maps, or other information related either to the Louisiana Purchase, or to the celebration. Others dealt with invoices from vendors that needed to be routed to the right person or organization. Shaw answered most, if not all, of the letters received after the Association shut down.

In late October, after the Association had wound down its major activities, Shaw cut an agreement with former employees Marcella Billups, Theone Maher, and Phyllis Wellford, to mail the remaining approximately 15,000 Louisiana Purchase maps that had been requested. Shaw agreed that the Association would pay the three women a total of $450; the dollar amount was to be adjusted based upon the final total quantity of maps mailed. The mailing was to be done from an apartment at 834 Chartres Street, and would take approximately three to four weeks, as time allowed.[756] E.V. Richards and Shaw soon wrote to the employees, noting the generally positive comments about the events, and announcing that two weeks' salary would be given to each of them as a bonus.[757]

In early November, E.V. Richards wrote to Shaw saying, "I am just coming out of the 'daze'." He mentioned the closing down of the celebration, suggested they needed to put together a memory book with photos and other material, and advised Shaw that, "In closing let me again thank you for what President Eisenhower himself told me was a very high level affair."[758]

**Shaw, probably in early 1950s (International Trade Mart Collection, Louisiana Research Collection, Tulane University)**

In late November, Mayor Chep Morrison wrote to Shaw, indicating that the City of New Orleans would present plaques to the officers and several key committee members of the Louisiana Purchase 150th Anniversary Association; Shaw was to receive a plaque as well. The presentation would take place on December 1, 1953.

The bill to produce a commemorative half-dollar coin observing the Louisiana Purchase Sesquicentennial eventually passed the Senate, but too late for the celebration, effectively rendering the issue moot. President Eisenhower vetoed the bill in early 1954, finally ending the matter.[759]

An income statement for the period from April 1, 1953 through December 31, 1953, showed contributions of $213,149 with expenditures of $209,571. Salaries were more than $31,000, publicity expenses exceeded $25,000, and display advertising approached $25,000. The expenses of the pageant alone were almost $41,000, and expenses associated with the visits of President Eisenhower and representatives of France exceeded $20,000.

In December 1953, after the celebration and the related clean-up of operations had ended, E.V. Richards and Shaw wrote again to the employees of the Association, indicating the success of the entire operation. The letters noted that the advance of the visit by President Eisenhower by two weeks had put everyone under great pressure, but that the employees had performed admirably. The letter reiterated that all employees would receive two weeks' salary as a bonus, and added, "Thanks and good luck until the Bicentennial [of the Louisiana Purchase] in 2003."[760]

Throughout his long career, Shaw was generally hailed by all for his organizational skills, his charm, and his good judgment in dealing with people. In a rare occurrence of an exception to that, Shaw would be chastised by Elizabeth B. Keane, secretary to E.V. Richards, for failing to invite a Mr. and Mrs. H.K. Oliphant to an unveiling of a Louisiana Purchase mural in April 1955, long after the Association had disbanded; Oliphant had been Richards's "confidential man" for years. Ms. Keane put the blame squarely on Shaw, in a letter to him after the event, indicating that she had heard Richards telling Shaw to use his own judgment about whom to invite, and that the Oliphants had been hurt by Shaw's neglect.[761] Actually, Shaw had sent Oliphant an invitation, but it had only arrived at the last minute, leaving Oliphant unable to attend the event.[762] It was a rare putdown for someone generally recognized as a master of good manners and skillful handling of people.

# 12 · The Mart at its Peak

The Mart's annual report for 1953 showed total rental income of $285,006, other income of $3,931, operating expenses other than interest totaling $219,295, and interest expense totaling $39,833, for a surplus of $29,149, all in all a very successful year. The net worth of the organization rose from $75,310, at the end of 1952, to $104,459 at the end of 1953. The major operating expenses were salaries and wages of $89,262, advertising of $28,636, depreciation of $41,886, utilities of $12,490, entertainment expenses of $2,788, and traveling expenses of $485. This was the Mart at its peak, fully occupied, with a minimum of traveling expenses, but still promoting itself actively through advertising as it looked to the future. The annual report for 1953 also reiterated that the International Trade Mart originally had been a pilot program, using a somewhat smaller building in order to test its potential success. That building was now too small to serve its original purpose. Eleven foreign countries were now represented officially in the Mart, including Great Britain and Switzerland. Trade between the East and West blocs had the potential to expand, although the Mart had to be careful in how it positioned itself regarding that issue. Additionally, the newness had worn off, and the Mart had to do different things in order to generate publicity for itself.[763]

By 1954, the Executive Committee of the Mart's Board of Directors was actively seeking to sell the building and begin the process of either buying a larger building, or building a completely new building, in order to enable further expansion. A tentative plan developed to sell the existing building, and lease it back from the new owners. This effectively began a twelve-year period during which the Mart struggled to implement that seemingly simple plan, a period that was marked by several grand announcements along with accompanying setbacks.

By 1954, Shaw was living at 1313 Dauphine Street, the original carriage house of the property at 906 Esplanade.[764] He would use that property periodically for the next fifteen years, even as he bought and sold, and lived in, other properties on nearby French Quarter streets.

New technological innovations continued to come onto the market. In February 1954, Shaw accepted an invitation to attend the showing of "Electronic Without Attendant" elevatoring put on by the Otis Elevator Company.[765] However, in response to an inquiry about telephone answering machines, Shaw responded that no one in New Orleans handled that type of equipment.[766]

In mid-February 1954, Shaw received a form requesting a recommendation on Raymond I. Broussard for an insurance bond. Shaw did not complete the form, but instead answered that he had not seen much of Broussard for several years. He mentioned that he had known him fairly well several years before, and knew that he was now married, with an "excellent reputation." Shaw said that he felt certain that the company's trust "would not be misplaced" in granting him a bond, but cautioned that he did not have enough later data on Broussard to complete the form.[767]

Among the members of the Board of Directors of the Mart that year was Theodore H. Lyons, Chairman of the Board of I.L. Lyons and Company, a wholesale drugstore products company, and David Stern, publisher of the *Item*. Alex Rallston, Jr. was selected as the Young Men's Business Club representative to the Mart for 1954.

The major bondholders of the Mart during 1954 were the Mississippi Shipping Company with $100,000, the Board of Commissioners of the Port of New Orleans with $32,000, the United Fruit Company with $26,000, New Orleans Public Service, Inc. (NOPSI) with $103,000, and the Waterman Steamship Company with $25,000.

At a meeting of the Contributors and Debenture Holders of the Mart in April 1954, it was mentioned that seventy-three of Theodore Brent's friends had contributed to his memorial. Shaw also reported on his activities with the Louisiana Purchase 150th Anniversary Association, announcing that half of his salary for 1953 had been paid by that organization. David Stern made a motion that the Mart take a stand against trade with Russia, and with Communist satellite countries, but he withdrew it after some discussion.[768]

From the progression in other aspects of how the Mart viewed Communist governments, it may be imagined that such a motion as the one offered by Stern would be seen favorably by his associates. In the early years of the Mart, particularly from the startup years of 1946 through 1948, but even including the first few full operating years, Mart officials had taken a relatively friendly view of the Communist Bloc countries. However, with the Korean War, and the Cold War intensifying during the early 1950s, Mart officials had begun to refer inquiries from the general public regarding Communist countries to the embassies of those countries, in somewhat truncated responses.

At an Executive Committee meeting in June 1954, attendees discussed a $2,000 Mart-sponsored scholarship contribution to the Cordell Hull Foundation, a newly formed organization dedicated to the memory of the late Secretary of State, who had served during the Roosevelt administration. The Foundation was dedicated to the exchange of teachers between the United States and Latin America. A discussion also was held about how to handle visits to the Mart by groups of children under high school age. Some groups had been disorderly, and tenants had objected to their behavior. David Baldwin, the new Public Relations Director, had objected to showing such groups around the Mart, and had banned their visits for a short period of time. In a memo to Shaw in late March, Baldwin indicated that, in his opinion, such children were not interested in foreign trade, and that they engaged in "gum-chewing, hair-pulling, elbow-jabbing, and so on," which disturbed the tenants in the building.[769] His efforts did not last long, however, as the ban was opposed by certain employees at International House, primarily Charles Nutter and William McFadden Duffy.

Duffy, Baldwin's counterpart as Public Relations Director at International House, complained to Charles Nutter about Baldwin's new rule. Duffy said that the Mart and International House were both civic-oriented institutions, and that they should accommodate all school groups in a display of public spirit. To do otherwise, Duffy argued, would be to discourage interest in the two institutions.[770] In a memo in early June, Baldwin indicated that the policy had been reversed, and that all school children were now allowed to take tours of the Mart.[771]

Baldwin had personality clashes with several of the individuals around the Mart and International House, and particularly disliked Nutter. In 1961, shortly after Charles Nutter had resigned as Managing Director of International House, Baldwin's friend Jesse Core, who had replaced Baldwin as Director of Public Relations, wrote to Baldwin, then with the Public Relations Department of the American Medical Association in Chicago, suggesting that he apply for Nutter's job. Baldwin wrote back, sarcastically suggesting that Core should apply for it himself. In the letter, Baldwin opined that Nutter had "little charm," and Baldwin further projected a general disparagement toward his time as part of the Mart/International House community.[772]

Another person who found Nutter difficult to work with was E.O. Jewell, the former General Manager of the Port of New Orleans. Jewell, sixty-four years old as of 1954, had since moved to the Port of Norfolk, Virginia. He would return to New Orleans soon to work at International House under Nutter, in a somewhat contentious relationship, perhaps due both to Nutter's cantankerous personality and to Jewell's failure to fully accept Nutter's authority.

At the same meeting at which the open-door policy toward children was discussed, $250 was approved as the Mart's contribution toward the entertainment during Ethiopian President Haile Selassie's upcoming visit to New Orleans. More mundane matters, such as a new set of Mart postcards deemed unsatisfactory by Shaw because of a pinkish tint to them, also were discussed. On a more ominous note, Shaw mentioned that Houston, Texas was now bringing much more merchandise through its port than was New Orleans.[773]

The word soon got out about a potential new Mart building, and very quickly interest was aroused among local architects. In a letter to the relatively new Mart President, William Zetzmann, Sam V. Massimini, a member of the Board of Directors, asked that consideration for the design be given to Herbert Benson, a close friend.[774]

The year 1954 also was important because it marked the beginning of Shaw's involvement with the Foreign Policy Association of New Orleans. The organization had been founded in 1944, but had become dormant in recent years and now was being re-activated. Anne O. Busby was Acting Director of the newly revived organization, which was affiliated with a national Foreign Policy Association, located in New York City. During this time, the New Orleans chapter often dealt with Charles Bushong, the national organization's Southern Regional Director.[775]

A letter to Shaw, from Rear Admiral K.D. Ringall (U.S. Navy, Retired), indicated that Shaw had been elected Program Chairman in his absence, replacing Dean Cole. Ringall commented that the position was the most important committee job in the Association; Shaw would have the responsibility of selecting speakers for each meeting.[776] Shaw, who had officially become a new member as of February 28, 1954, confirmed his appointment in a letter to William T. Walshe, President of the organization.[777]

The Foreign Policy Association's main speaker during 1954 was Perle Mesta, an important Washington, D.C. socialite during the 1950s, who had served as the U.S. Ambassador to Luxemburg from 1949 to 1953. Shaw wrote to her in early September, acknowledging her acceptance.[778]

In preparing for Mesta's visit, Shaw dealt with Jim Leslie, then with the Bauerlein Agency, which the Mart was still using for advertising and public relation services. In a letter to Leslie in early October regarding the speech, Shaw instructed him to deliver a publicity layout to printer Alfred Moran. Moran later would be noteworthy as one of only a handful of prominent New Orleanians who expressed negative sentiments toward Clay Shaw, after Shaw's arrest in 1967. Moran also was an associate of the Central Intelligence Agency, having a much more involved role than did Clay Shaw, although the two men probably never knew of each other's involvement. Moran, among other things, fronted for a business the agency ran.

Perle Mesta spoke to the Foreign Policy Association meeting on October 20, 1954. In a letter to Glen Douthit, Director of Public Relations for the City of New Orleans, Shaw mentioned that he had arranged with Marcel Gomez to have Mario Bermúdez's "black hearse" made available for transporting the speaker.[779]

While some of the individuals with whom Shaw interacted in the organization were familiar faces from the International Trade Mart and International House, some were new. Among those was Eberhard P. Deutsch, a prominent New Orleans attorney, and brother of New Orleans newspaper columnist Herman Deutsch. Deutsch was a member of the Board of Directors of the group, but he was also the main partner of Deutsch, Kerrigan, and Stiles, a blue-chip New Orleans law firm, a firm for which Jim Garrison worked for a time prior to being elected as district attorney. Over the years, Deutsch, Kerrigan, and Stiles would represent both Jim Garrison individually and the office of the district attorney in many situations during Garrison's tenure, including several sets of litigation concerned with Shaw's criminal troubles, and with Shaw's subsequent civil suit against Jim Garrison.

Another attorney with whom Shaw interacted on the Foreign Policy Association was John Minor Wisdom, who was very prominent in Republican party circles during the 1950s. Shaw also had dealt with Wisdom the previous year during the Louisiana Purchase 150th Anniversary celebration. Wisdom would later serve as a judge on the Fifth U.S. Circuit Court of Appeals, located in New Orleans, and become well known for his decisions upholding earlier key Supreme Court rulings in civil rights cases involving school desegregation, for which he would be loathed by many whites in the South, and loved by many African Americans of the era. However, he also would rule on several important issues related to Shaw's prosecution and civil suits. Among the most important of those rulings were ones which required Judge Herbert Christenberry, the U.S. Federal District Judge in New Orleans, to hold a lengthy hearing that ultimately resulted in a permanent injunction against further prosecution of Shaw, and an appellate decision upholding that ruling the following year.

The Foreign Policy Association operated on a fiscal year that ran from mid-year to mid-year. During the first year of renewed operations, the budget, which Shaw participated in preparing, called for a $4,200 salary for the Executive Director and $2,500 for speakers throughout the year.[780]

In his role as Program Chairman, Shaw dealt with some of his contacts in the public speaking sector. He renewed contact with Robert Keedick, son of Lee Keedick of the Lee Keedick agency in New York City. Shaw had worked for that organization from 1939 until late 1942, when he was drafted into the Army. The Lee Keedick agency billed itself as "manager of the world's most celebrated lecturers," and the organization sponsored many speaking tours over the years. Robert Keedick had contacted Shaw at the suggestion of Anne Busby, who had informed Keedick that Shaw was Program Director.[781] Shaw responded, indicating that he was surprised to see Robert Keedick's name back on the letterhead, and expressed kind regards to Keedick's father, and to "Miss Schenk," referring to Elizabeth Schenk, a long-time employee of the agency. In a later letter to Keedick, Shaw mentioned mutual acquaintances such as Adelaide Stedman, John C. Caldwell, and Mrs. Raymond Clapper.[782]

Another organization with which Shaw dealt that placed speakers for different organizations and events was the Columbia Lecture Bureau. Tom Richards was Southern representative for Geiser and Boomer, an affiliated agency, and he pressed upon Shaw to use him, saying, "Clay, you know I can use the business."[783] Among the speakers Richards pushed for was Hanson W. Baldwin, who was *The New York Times* military correspondent for many years.[784] Shaw recommended Richards's agency, and the speaking engagement of Hanson W. Baldwin, to Charles Bushong of the National Foreign Policy Association,[785] and Baldwin subsequently spoke at the meeting of February 4, 1955, for a fee of $500.

Shaw sought other prominent speakers during that first year. One was the actor Douglas Fairbanks, for the March 1955 meeting; Fairbanks was unable to commit to that date.[786]

Another potential speaker was the Shah of Iran, who was newly installed as leader after a joint CIA/British-sponsored coup that had recently overthrown the previous government. Shaw had received a letter from the Shah's representative, indicating that the Shah was going to be visiting New Orleans on his tour of the United States.[787] Shaw responded, inviting the Shah to speak before the Foreign Policy Association of New Orleans. He pointed out Louisiana's oil production, saying, "You would find here a most sympathetic and interested audience for your address."[788] However, the Shah apparently never spoke before the group.

Another speaker sponsored by the Foreign Policy Association that year was Chester Bowles, who recently had served as the United States Ambassador to India and Nepal. Shaw had to sandwich his appearance in between the scheduled dates for performances of two musical organizations in New Orleans, so that potential attendees would not be caught between conflicting events. Nevertheless, Mrs. L. Kemper Williams, wife of an important New Orleans businessman and benefactor of various non-profit organizations, complained about the date of the meeting, giving Shaw an opportunity to use his own diplomatic skills in averting a small crisis.[789]

As Program Chairman, Shaw had to use his judgment regarding the types of speakers who would bring out a large audience. Rudolf Hecht had suggested a Mr. Rodriguez, the governor of Pangasinan Province in the Philippines, but Shaw resisted, putting it wryly to Hecht, "We wouldn't get a corporal's guard" as turnout for his appearance.[790]

Rudolf Hecht himself appeared as a speaker at the second meeting of the 1954-55 year of the Foreign Policy Association, discussing his 8,500-mile, four-week trip through Russia. Earlier in 1954, a delegation of New Orleans businessmen, including Shaw, had journeyed again to Europe, promoting the city and its international trade institutions; Hecht left the party in Hamburg, Germany to go on to Russia. In a letter from Europe, Shaw reported to William Zetzmann that Hecht had been "happy as a child on Christmas morning" when he parted with the group.[791] Hecht had taken a large quantity of motion pictures on his trip, and he showed those to the meeting, while narrating his experiences and answering questions about the trip. After the event, Shaw commented to Foreign Policy Association members that Russia had cut itself off in the 20th century, that "Leningrad, Kiev, and Odessa might as well have been on the other side of the world," and that Churchill had been right in describing Russia as "a riddle wrapped in a mystery inside of an enigma."[792]

The Mississippi Valley World Trade Conference was again held in New Orleans. The Mart sponsored 25% of the cost of the official cocktail parties at the event, up to a maximum of $400. However, Shaw was in Europe at the time and missed the event.

Great Britain, wanting goodwill among the New Orleans business community, finally placed an office in the Mart in April 1954, after many years of effort by the Mart's representatives to entice them into the building. Edgar Stern had made a serious effort on the Mart's behalf to secure the country as a tenant.

The aforementioned 1954 trip to Europe that Shaw took with Hecht and other New Orleans businessmen was the last trip to Europe for him as a representative of the Mart, and one of only two he took there during his entire tenure as Managing Director. As Shaw prepared for his two-month trip, he wrote to one of his old friends from his time living in Rheims, France during World War II. Shaw mentioned that he was leaving the next day on a six-country tour, winding up in Paris. He said that he would be going to Rheims to see the caves there, and hoped to see his friend during his visit.[793]

He also advised his old New York friend, Marion Seidenbach, of his trip, while thanking her for remembering his recent birthday. Shaw commented to Seidenbach that, "Birthdays are melancholy occasions brightened by being remembered by people one is fond of." Shaw indicated that he might go to Spain alone for two weeks after the business portion of the European trip, where he would be traveling with forty or more people. He said that Seidenbach's tales of her own travels there had made him feel that Spain was a place that had "something to tell me." He added that he planned to return to New York City on the Liberté around the end of May, and hoped to see her then. Shaw remarked that, "Life now is pleasant, quiet, placid, and not too exciting," saying that occasional trips to New York, Europe, and South America "make it not too bad." He acknowledged that, "Sometimes I do miss the hectic life we used to lead in the big city, but really don't know that I would want to do so again." Shaw closed by saying that he hoped to see Seidenbach "over a cup of tea or eggs Benedict at the Stork Club," that he hoped her business was going well, that her husband, Carl, was not working too hard, and added that he hoped "you have settled your inheritance and are now rolling in wealth."[794]

In his letter to Zetzmann, written from Brussels, Belgium, toward the end of the trip, Shaw said that the trip generally had been a good one, generating the right kind of publicity for New Orleans at a relatively low cost. He predicted that trade with Europe would grow in spite of various tariff issues between the two regions. He eventually decided to bypass Spain on the trip.[795]

After the European trip was over, the President of International House wrote to Zetzmann, thanking him for sending Shaw on what had been part of the 18th Trade and Travel Mission of International House; he mentioned Shaw's excellent speeches before various groups.[796] Despite glowing reviews such as this one, Shaw made far fewer international trips than did several employees associated with International House, such as Charles Nutter and Mario Bermúdez. In fact, after this trip, he would make few international trips in the course of his official Mart duties.

Although the Mississippi Shipping Company had been heavily involved in the formation of the Trade Mart, particularly with Theodore Brent and Rudolf Hecht as two of the founding fathers, the company maintained an independence from the Mart's operations. Harry X. Kelly, the President of the Mississippi Shipping Company, declined in 1954 to be on the Board of Directors of the Mart.

Clem Bernard, who had been the Young Men's Business Club's representative to the Mart during the controversy over the Czechoslovakian exhibit in 1949 and 1950, had become ill by this time and was resting, on doctor's orders.[797] Meanwhile, John H. Curtis, also known as Jerry Curtis, who had worked as one of the original leasing agents for the Mart during 1946, had had a turn of bad luck. James Barr of the Better Business Bureau of New Orleans, reported to Shaw the revelation that Curtis had been a deserter from the Army, that he had been apprehended by the FBI, and was now serving three to four years in prison for misrepresentation in the sale of vending machines.[798] Shaw replied that, "It's a pity, because he was a good salesman," and could do better than a life of crime. "I guess there is no changing some people."[799]

The Better Business Bureau also got involved with activities that were occurring within the walls of the Mart. The official policy of the Mart was that its tenants were not supposed to sell goods at retail. However, the Mart received complaints from local merchants, and from the local Better Business Bureau, that some of the tenants were doing just that. William Zetzmann responded that it was impossible to police the practice completely.[800]

Efforts to honor the memory of Theodore Brent continued in 1954. A Sculptor Committee headed by William Zetzmann and Rudolf Hecht, with Shaw as a member, worked with sculptor Carl Cramer to create a bust of Brent that was then placed in the International Trade Mart lobby on March 30, 1954. The law firm of Monroe and Lemann, led by prominent attorney J. Blanc Monroe, contributed to the Brent memorial. Cramer had earlier written to Zetzmann proposing the bust of Brent. The agreement with Cramer had been finalized at the end of 1953, with the committee agreeing to pay him $500 to produce the bust.[801]

**William Zetzmann (left) and Rudolf Hecht (right) with bust of Theodore Brent**
(International Trade Mart Collection, Louisiana Research Collection, Tulane University)

Brent had been a member of St. Charles Avenue Presbyterian Church. The Reverend John Samuel Land of the church indicated that Brent had united with the church in May of 1937, and had become a trustee in April 1943. Land described him as a faithful worshiper, always in his pew, and noted that Brent had bequeathed $100,000 to the church in memory of his mother, stepmother and sister.

Ochsner Medical Foundation announced the opening of a new convalescent pavilion-guest house called Brent House, named after the late shipping magnate. A sealed copper box containing various contents was inserted in the cornerstone of the structure; the Mart included a copy of the original survey for the founding of the Mart, and a photo of the completed Mart building.[802]

A letter from Albert W. Sherer, a Chicago businessman, to Charles I. Denechaud, a Mart board member, indicated that Sherer had known Brent well as a close friend during the early period of Brent's life; Sherer had known Brent's mother, father and sister well. Prior to moving to New Orleans, Brent had lived in Chicago and St. Louis, where he and Sherer had been constant companions, and Sherer recalled a time in which they traveled out West together while working for the St. Louis and San Francisco Railroad.[803]

The Mart continued to receive numerous letters of inquiry about various products. In response to an inquiry about mercury and lead, Shaw mentioned that mercury mines in Spain had been nationalized by the government, and suggested the inquirer submit his request to Minas de Almaden, S.A., in Madrid.[804] Other letters inquired about frozen custard machines, and about machinery for spices.

In the absence of Theodore Brent, and even with the elevation of William Zetzmann as the new Mart President, Shaw interacted even more with Rudolf Hecht, who had always operated somewhat behind the scenes, without ever assuming the presidency either of the

Mart or International House. In a letter to Hecht in early June, Shaw discussed several issues, including how a proposed sale of the building to the State of Louisiana had fallen through; the State needed 200,000 square feet, much more than the Mart building would provide. Shaw also discussed his recent European trip, saying he thought it had been worthwhile for the relationships established, at small cost. He mentioned Hecht's recent trip to Russia, adding, "The Russians have the capacity to plunge the world into a war, which I think would completely destroy the kind of life that we know." Shaw mentioned that he was still trying to sell the Mart as an institution, but that it was difficult to do with such limited space.[805]

In a memo to Hecht in mid-July, Shaw enclosed a recent pamphlet that he had seen dealing with East-West bloc trade. He commented that the pamphlet "seems to me to examine this vital problem with the absence of the usual heat, and with more than the usual light."[806]

In another memo to Hecht a few days later, Shaw attached a proposed ad for the sale of the building. The ad noted that the building had 75,000 rentable square feet, with annual rental revenue of $300,000. Shaw mentioned that the listed selling price of the building would yield a 17% return for the Mart.[807] Shaw had persistently made his feelings known about the need for a larger building to enhance the Mart's reputation, and even to satisfy his own need for a challenge. After reviewing the results of operations for the Mart for the first six months of 1954, Rudolf Hecht wrote to Shaw that the results looked satisfactory, and that he hoped a solution for Shaw's problem could be found, so that he could go on to "bigger things".[808]

Although the proposed cocoa facility never got off the ground, the Mart was still helping Karl Haller with his visa as late as mid-1954, long after the cocoa project had been abandoned. The Mart had always treated Maria Paprotna Haller somewhat gingerly in her delinquent status as a tenant, and possibly the efforts to obtain a visa for her husband were related to that effort. In June 1954, Shaw wrote to the United States Immigration Service, requesting that Karl Haller, Jr. of Stuttgart, Germany, have his visa extended for another six months. Shaw gave as the reason that Haller was there to organize a "chocolate plant," and that the Mart would guarantee that he would not become a "public charge."[809]

Shaw continued his usual participation on various boards and committees. He accepted an appointment to the Executive Committee of Greater New Orleans, Inc.,[810] and an appointment to serve on the World Trade Development Committee of International House.[811] Shaw also accepted, immediately after returning from his two-month trip to Europe, a position on the Board of Directors of The Lighthouse for the Blind.[812] General Raymond Hufft appointed Shaw to the "54" Club Committee of the New Orleans Athletic Club.[813]

J.B. Dauenhauer maintained the daily activities of bookkeeping, and supervising the hourly employees. In several notices to the new building superintendent, William Sheppard, Dauenhauer cautioned him about slack supervision of maids and porters, saying he was getting complaints about doors being left open, radios playing, breakages, and pilfering.

The Mart was still receiving inquiries from news writers around the country, although at a much slower pace than several years earlier. Shaw responded to a letter from John Kobler with the *Saturday Evening Post* requesting information about the Mart.[814] Kobler would later write a major biography of the gangster Al Capone.

The National Research Bureau, Inc. of Chicago wrote to Shaw, requesting a copy of his speech, "What Foreign Trade Means to Sales Executives," given recently to national sales executives in New York City.[815] Shaw replied in his usual manner that he always spoke from informal notes, adding that at some future meeting, a stenographer may catch "the pearls of wisdom" as they "drip" from his lips; he had always felt a written speech detracted from "spontaneity."[816]

Shaw was a member of the New Orleans Association of Building Owners and Managers, although he usually sent J.B. Dauenhauer in his place to the meetings. At the annual meeting of the organization in 1954, the "Keep Christ in Christmas" movement was discussed; buildings managers were told to design their holiday decorations around a cross, nativity scene, or a star.[817]

Fred Greschner, who had been the building superintendent at the Mart for the first three years, relied upon Shaw for a job recommendation. Shaw wrote to George F. Johnson, Director of Physical Plant at Tulane University, giving his confidence and support to Greschner.[818]

International visitors continued to pass through New Orleans, emphasizing the city's importance as a trade center. Shaw attended a dinner for Haile Selassie I, emperor of Ethiopia,[819] and a cocktail party and dinner for the ambassador for Liberia to the United States, which was held aboard the Delta Line's *Del Mar* ship.[820] However, Shaw declined an invitation to a July 4, 1954 celebration of Philippine Independence Day, indicating that he was going to visit his family that weekend.[821]

A major event of sorts during 1954, more related to the logistics of it than to the publicity, was the visit to New Orleans of President William Tubman of the country of Liberia in northwest Africa. Tubman served as the country's president from 1944 until 1971, when he died. The visit of a black African president to a Southern city, even one as unique as New Orleans, was a touchy matter during the 1950s. The visit was carefully planned, with a minimum of public exposure. Tubman's party was to arrive on a Sunday, with a departure early on Monday morning. The Liberian flag was to be raised from early Sunday morning until Sunday afternoon, then lowered. The City of New Orleans had compiled a list of local "Negroes" who should be invited to meet President Tubman. Shaw served as Vice-Chairman of the reception committee for the event; that committee also included Mayor Chep Morrison. The party arrived by ship at the dock on Esplanade Avenue, where waiting cars took them immediately to predominantly black Xavier University, where President Tubman was awarded a degree, then directly to the Roosevelt hotel for the party's brief stay. David Baldwin and George Haverstick of the Dock Board were on "car assignment," assisting with the transportation of various members of Tubman's party.

Shaw had a more specific assignment for David Baldwin than transportation, however—one that perhaps recalled for Baldwin his CIA days; Shaw set it out in a somewhat elaborate memo. Baldwin was to go to the Roosevelt hotel, pre-register all guests in Tubman's party, then label all room keys carefully and get them to the appropriate member of the reception committee, who would then quickly escort the guests to the appropriate rooms; the 12th floor was reserved for the Liberian party.[822] As black U.S. citizens were not allowed to stay at the Roosevelt hotel in those days, it was necessary to have an absolute minimum of interaction between Tubman's party and the white guests. The event went off as planned, and afterward Shaw wrote to Seymour Weiss of the Roosevelt hotel, thanking him for his help during the visit. Shaw said he recognized the risks and difficulties related to visits of that kind, but that New Orleans must strive to trade with all peoples.[823]

There was bad news for the Port of New Orleans during 1954. Statistics for June year-to-date showed that the number of vessels coming through was down approximately 5% from 1953, and import tons were down 18 to 20%; export tons were up slightly. By product, bags of coffee were up slightly, but stems of bananas were down seven to eight percent.

As 1954 progressed, it became obvious that even if the Mart was able to sell its building, it would be a while before it would be able to move into a new, larger facility. Space for buildings was limited in downtown New Orleans, and a possible merger with International House, and financing for the project, would need to be firmed up. In an article about the Mart in *Southern Banker*, a magazine published in Atlanta, Georgia, text referring to a move to a larger building was removed shortly before publication, because of the extremely tentative nature of that prospect.

Shaw's connections from his New York days continued to pay off. He received a letter from George Herz with Scandinavian Airlines in New York. Herz had been the assistant of Danton Walker, a gossip columnist, and an associate of Shaw's when he had lived in New York City. Herz's letter asked if Shaw could meet with visiting important personages with the airline from Europe, and asked for Shaw to contact him on his next visit to New York City for dinner or drinks.[824] Shaw agreed to met with the airline's representatives if possible, and added that he had not seen Danton Walker in several years, but still exchanged Christmas cards with him.

Shaw had his normal quota of speeches during 1954, although as with 1953, most of them were delivered in Louisiana, a change from his pattern during the Mart's early years of widespread promotion. He spoke to the Gentilly Women's Club, the Greater Gentilly Civic Council Installation Dinner, the Loyola University Business Alumni, the Houma, Louisiana Rotary Club, the Couples Club of New Orleans, the South Central Regional Clearinghouse Association in Thibodaux, Louisiana, the Thibodaux Rotary Club, the Quote Club of New Orleans, the Young Men's Business Club, the Women's Traffic and Transportation Club, the Metairie, Louisiana Rotary Club, the Eunice, Louisiana Rotary Club, the Orleans Club, the Junior League of New Orleans, and at Amite (Louisiana) High School on Career Day. The most common topic of his speeches during 1954 was the subject of "World Trade Today."

The Mart was now marketing itself not only to Latin America and Europe, but to the South Pacific as well. In a letter to W. Marion, of the Chamber of Manufactures of New South Wales, Sydney, Australia, Shaw mentioned the coordinated effort of the Mart, International House, the Chamber of Commerce, the Free Trade Zone, and other institutions in trying to open up markets in the Southern portion of the United States to exporters from other ports around the world. He noted that prior to World War II, most imported goods had entered the United States through New York City for consumption in the Northeast.[825]

Other cities in far-flung places continued to be interested in the international trade issue. In response to an inquiry, Shaw sent information about the history of the Mart to parties interested in a merchandise mart in Winnipeg, Manitoba.[826]

Shaw also spoke to the Industrial Development Conference in Baton Rouge regarding foreign trade,[827] in one of the few instances in which a Shaw speech was reduced to written words. The conference was held at Louisiana State University, and Shaw told a famous story about speaking using notes pinned to his clothing for hints about topics. Shaw's criminal defense attorney, Irvin Dymond, would use the same device in a speech he gave in Chicago after Shaw's criminal trial in 1969. The conference was sponsored by the Louisiana Department of Commerce and Industry, with participation by, among others, Ethyl Corporation.

Shaw accepted an appointment by Mayor Morrison to the Citizens' Committee for Testimonial Luncheon to honor Rear Admiral T.G.W. Settle.[828] Shaw's years-old friendship with Morrison, along with the good rapport he shared with Congressman Hale Boggs, were good examples of the consistently good impression Shaw made over the years on important public figures. He always seemed to know how to work best with them, giving his important and relevant input to solving a particular problem or situation, without seeming to directly challenge them, such that the person always felt that Shaw was a person in whose dependability and performance there was "no question."

In maintaining these relationships, Shaw kept up the policy of communicating with Louisiana's elected representatives regarding issues important to the Mart. In one such letter to U.S. Senator Russell Long, commenting on a recent speech Long had given about foreign trade, Shaw set out in very general terms the Mart's position on free trade.[829] Shaw also, at the urging of Congressman Overton Brooks of north Louisiana, sent a $100 contribution on behalf of the Mart to, and signed the Mart up as a member of, the National Rivers and Harbors Congress, which worked for flood control and navigation issues.[830]

While David Baldwin and J.B. Dauenhauer were quite curt in their replies to members of the general public seeking information, Shaw continued his normal helpful manner, while answering a smaller number of inquiries than in the past. He sent literature related to the international trade issue and specific products to Charles L. Luedtke of the Economic Intelligence Service, Inc. in Washington, D.C..[831] In response to an inquiry about having New Orleans' street criers represented at the 20th Annual National Folk Festival, Shaw wrote to Sarah Gertrude Knott of the *St. Louis Globe Democrat*, referring her to the New Orleans Recreational Department, and indicating that the subject was outside of his field of expertise; Shaw had worked with her as part of the Louisiana Purchase 150th Anniversary celebration.[832] Shaw also gave a detailed, thoughtful response to an engineer seeking to move to the West Indies to work.[833]

The Mart was continuing to watch its advertising budget, and target publicity only in directions it thought could help. In June 1954, Shaw declined for the Mart to participate in advertising in *Esquire's* October edition about New Orleans, citing budgetary reasons.[834]

Shaw continued to be a favorite among various New Orleans women whom he encountered, either while making speeches or while serving on committees of one type or another. In a memo to Shaw from Anne O. Busby of the Foreign Policy Association of New Orleans, she wrote that Mrs. Hamilton Polk Jones had called and said to tell Shaw "HELLO" three times.[835]

Representatives of foreign countries regularly showed their appreciation for Shaw as well. Eikichi Araki, Japan's Ambassador to the United States, wrote Shaw thanking him for his goodwill and assistance with Japan's recent exhibit in the Mart.[836]

Local institutions still could be counted on to seek out Shaw's cooperation for specific tasks. Raymond A. Nix, a professor at John McDonough High School, contacted Shaw seeking his cooperation in taping a five minute message on "My Definition and Description of Democratic Leadership."[837]

Despite his performance with the Central Intelligence Agency that had resulted in his termination, David Baldwin continued to be friends with Thomas B. Lemann, one of the attorneys in the law firm of Monroe and Lemann, which was rumored to have handled some of the CIA's legal affairs in New Orleans. In one letter to Lemann, Baldwin addressed him as "My dear Lemann."[838] Lemann was the father of writer Nicholas Lemann; Baldwin was married to Lemann's stepsister.

The name of another Baldwin friend, Jesse Core, appears in Mart records beginning in early 1954. Baldwin and Core had been friends as newspaper reporters in New Orleans in the late 1940s, and had served together in India in the early 1950s, Baldwin with the CIA, and Core on a temporary assignment with the United States Information Agency (USIA). Core was now in Dallas, working for an industry trade journal, and several telegrams capture Baldwin's plans to visit him in February 1954.[839]

One immediate effect of David Baldwin's service as Public Relations Director was that the tenants' newsletter had diminished in size and importance by early 1954. Baldwin, however, continued a newspaper column, one that had been started by Glenn Weekley, for a special weekly edition of the *Item*, which dealt with the same issues that had been covered in the newsletter. Shaw sometimes wrote a memo to Baldwin, passing along an item that could potentially be used in both the newsletter and in Baldwin's column.[840]

The United States Supreme Court decision ordering Southern schools to desegregate, along with the generally tense racial environment in the South, was often a deciding factor of organizations planning to hold conventions there. In 1954, the Inter-American Press Association was considering holding a convention in New Orleans, but some of its board members had great concerns about racial discrimination in the city. The board's vote to hold the convention in New Orleans was 13-10, and Mario Bermúdez was invaluable in helping to overcome opposition to New Orleans. The decision came only after much discussion about whether "Negroes" would attend the convention, and if so, how many.[841] Some members of the organization referred to an earlier incident in New Orleans, when a delegate from Haiti had been refused admittance to a hotel, and had returned home to his country. Major hotels in the city had agreed to cooperate in handling black attendees, as they had in the past for foreign black dignitaries. Roland Huson, publisher of a newspaper in rural Zachary, Louisiana, made a presentation for New Orleans to the board meeting in Rio de Janeiro, Brazil. Huson requested assurance from the City of New Orleans that there would be no discrimination against attendees, and Mayor Morrison wired such assurance to the gathering.

The Minister of Commerce and Industry in Jerusalem, Tamar Woolf, visited with Shaw in the Mart during the fall of 1954. Shaw responded to a letter she wrote to him upon her return, indicating that he had not known that Israel had so many products for sale. He added that he hoped to make it to Israel one day, but he did not know when that would be.[842]

Shaw was still attending to many small details, particularly those that affected the image of the Mart. After receiving a set of postcards displaying the Mart building, Shaw found them unsatisfactory, but the vendor, Tichnor Brothers, refused to yield and demanded payment. Shaw wrote to Mart attorney Kenneth Barranger, noting that on the postcards, the building was pinkish in color, the sidewalk in front of it was yellow, and the grey corners were "a sickly purple." Shaw said this was "not expected by me," as the finished product differed markedly from a proof he had reviewed, and "why have a proof if it doesn't match the finished product?" Shaw commented that if Barranger agreed the Mart owed the money to the printer, Shaw said, "We will pay but we do not intend to use," and went on to say that, "If I were Tichnor Brothers, my face would be as pink as the building at the idea of releasing such a grotesque job to the public."[843]

One of the Mart's early tenants, Halliburton Oil Well Cementing Company, moved out in November 1954, after a little over five years as a tenant in Unit 438. The organization decided it needed more space, and the Mart, being approximately 100 percent occupied, could no longer fulfill its needs.[844]

Henri Gomez was a young acquaintance of Mario Bermúdez; he also was friends with Jeff Biddison and Shaw. In November 1954, he wrote to Shaw, inquiring if Shaw would be attending the National Foreign Trade Council Convention in New York City that year. Gomez at the time was with New York University Department of Marketing. He asked Shaw to give Mario Bermúdez his best wishes, and to look him up in New York City, indicating that perhaps he could have Shaw over for dinner.[845]

Shaw indeed again attended the National Foreign Trade Council Convention, held at the Waldorf Astoria Hotel. He booked his own room at the Beverly Hotel at 50th Street and Lexington, requesting a well-furnished suite high up in the building, noting that he had to do some entertaining during the event.

On December 1, after returning from New York City, Shaw wrote to John Wray Young, answering Young's letter that had arrived during his absence. Shaw mentioned that he had had a pleasant week in New York City, but that there was little he wanted to see in the theater at that time. He said that he enjoyed *The Rainmaker*, and had fun at a Mae West show in the Latin Quarter. Shaw indicated that he had seen *Can Can*, a popular musical going on at the time, but he nominated it "for worst show in history." He added that it was "good that dedicated souls like you exist to provide good theater outside of NYC." Shaw indicated that he had reserved two tickets for the Sugar Bowl football game for Young's son, Jock, and asked him to give their daughter, Jill, his best wishes.[846]

At the end of 1954, the Board of Directors of the Mart held a meeting at the boardroom of the Mississippi Shipping Company; the meeting was held there to avoid publicity. The purpose was to consider a concrete proposal to buy the existing Mart building. The offer was made by Louis Cooper, Benjamin Kaufman, and Nathan Jacobs, New York City investors. The proposal was to buy the building for $1,500,000, subject to a first mortgage of $453,000, and a second mortgage of $657,000. Four hundred thousand dollars was to be paid directly to the Mart—$200,000 immediately, and the remaining $200,000 with a note payable ninety days after the International Trade Mart organization left the building. The proposal was that the International Trade Mart could occupy the building for two years after the sale, at a cost of $100,000 per year, renewable for up to five years.

Rudolf Hecht mentioned his hope that the Mart and International House could be combined in a new building. Mayor Morrison had agreed to lease a plot of land at the corner of Poydras Street and Loyola Street, for one dollar per year for 99 years, for a new building. It was estimated that a new building might cost approximately $4,000,000 to $5,000,000. The Mart might still be contingently liable to the original debenture holders for $657,000 even after the sale of its building, which could impact future borrowing. The Mississippi Shipping Company was still one of the largest bondholders. Some attendees also raised concerns about the growth of Miami, Florida, and its efforts there to start an Inter-American project, and about getting bondholders to release the Mart from liability before any large amount of debt was incurred.[847]

The countries officially represented in the Mart as of the end of 1954 included Belgium, Great Britain, Canada, Cuba, France, Germany, Italy, Japan, the Netherlands, Philippine Republic, Puerto Rico, and Switzerland.[848] The Mart was, as Shaw put it, "bursting at the seams." It was obvious that the organization would soon need a larger building, Shaw told a reporter for a local newspaper article. An accompanying photo of Shaw showed him looking classically mature, with a fair amount of grey hair, but with a handsome, rugged face.[849]

As 1954 drew to a close, Mart officials were generally happy about another good year. Income totaled $290,370, expenses before interest were $242,917, interest expense was $38,330, yielding a net income of $9,123, down somewhat from 1953 levels. Among the expenses, salaries were $105,069, advertising was $36,386, depreciation was $43,294, and utilities were $13,086.[850] While the Mart was experiencing the benefit of revenue from being more or less fully occupied, it also was facing a plateau of that revenue, due to lack of additional space and competition from other buildings in the area, along with expenses that were increasing due to inflationary pressures. Without a new, larger building, it would be impossible for the Mart to move forward, and even difficult to prevent it from regressing.

# 13 · A Trip to Mexico

By 1955, Shaw was solidly identified as "Mr. International Trade Mart." In an article the previous year in *This Week in New Orleans*, a small local magazine, the writer discussed the "famous and unique" International Trade Mart, which he said owed much of its success to the "skill, good taste, and administrative ability" of "quiet, dignified, and very capable Clay Shaw," who had guided its progress from the very beginning.

In January 1955, Shaw appeared on *Dateline*, a New Orleans TV program on WDSU-TV, Channel 6. It was moderated by Bill Monroe, at that time a local New Orleans television newsman, later the moderator on NBC's *Meet the Press* program. The topic of the discussion was, "Is it in the economic interest of greater New Orleans to encourage trade with foreign countries?" Shaw and Cyril R.C. Laan gave the pro side, with Gilbert J. Durbin and Lamont Rolanda giving the con side.[851]

At a meeting of the Board of Directors, along with certain bondholders, in early January 1955, it was discussed that International House had looked into upgrading its own building, and found that it would have to spend $400,000 to $500,000 to do so; the new building would be known as International Center. One of the proposals being floated was that the Mart and International House would continue to operate separately, but share a building.[852]

Shaw spoke at a meeting of the Young Men's Business Club, seeking the organization's support for financing of a proposed new building for the Mart. In a memo to Rudolf Hecht shortly after the meeting, Shaw indicated that most members seemed to support the idea until a young attorney named William Guste opposed it, saying it would set a precedent. However, Shaw indicated that he believed the Mart could still count on the Young Men's Business Club for support.[853] Guste had also been involved, a few years earlier, in the Czechoslovakian exhibit controversy.

In February, Shaw wrote to Hecht, mentioning the New Orleans Civic Center location as a possibility for the new building.[854] It would be one of several locations seriously considered over the next decade.

Foreign visitors continued to pour into New Orleans. From late February into early March, the Inter-American Investment Conference was held in New Orleans, bringing in many Latin American leaders; Rudolf Hecht was the co-chairman along with Edgar R. Baker, Managing Director of Time-Life International. Shaw acted as host for some international visitors during the conference. Afterward, he received a handwritten letter from M. Ayub, former permanent Undersecretary of the Treasury in Pakistan, thanking him for taking so much time to show Ayub and his wife the Mart and the French Quarter; Ayub hoped that he could welcome Shaw to Pakistan sometime.[855]

During the Inter-American Investment Conference, Hecht hosted the members attending the conference at a reception and luncheon held at Middlegate Gardens in Pass Christian, Mississippi, the summer home of Hecht and his wife, built to perpetuate memories of their earlier travels to Japan. The gardens were furnished with Japanese statuary, and are now called Middlegate Japanese Gardens; the Hechts often entertained visitors there. The gardens were open to the public until 1969, when Hurricane Camille did severe damage to them.

Cecilia Grace, a Mart employee at the time, was loaned for use at the Inter-American

Investment Conference.⁸⁵⁶ Shaw indicated to Hecht that David Baldwin, still Public Relations Director at that time, and his secretary also could be used, but that neither spoke Spanish, while Grace did, making her more useful for the conference.⁸⁵⁷

Mart officials were still deciding if, and how much, it would contribute to various civic events on a case-by-case basis. For the Inter-American Investment Conference, the Mart had initially pledged to give $500, but when the conference fell short on contributions, it upped its contribution to $1,000, and allowed for more if the conference could not meet its budget.⁸⁵⁸

David Baldwin announced his intention to leave the Mart early in 1955. Shaw advised Hecht in early February that Baldwin would be leaving on March 1 to take a job as Publicity Director with I.L. Lyons and Company, the New Orleans wholesale drugstore supply company.⁸⁵⁹

Baldwin had always seemed out of place at the Mart. Clearly caught between the loss of a job with the CIA and trying to find his proper station in life, he was impatient with basic Mart duties, and had personality conflicts with some of the International House personnel. As he neared the end of his tenure at the Mart, Baldwin appeared even less interested in the job. After having been out sick for a few days, he dictated a memo to Shaw in mid-February, indicating that he had a facial condition that looked "like bird shot had hit it." He asked if Shaw had reached any conclusion on his replacement, adding that he could train whoever it was on Monday when he returned; he shared that he would be back to the office on that date, even if he had "to wear the pillowcase of a Klansman."⁸⁶⁰

On the eve of his departure from the job, Baldwin received a letter from a group in Alabama wanting to take a tour of the Mart. He scribbled a note to his secretary, Josephine Pennestri, on the letter, saying, "Jo: not my baby anymore. Please handle. DGB"⁸⁶¹

Baldwin had his share of foul-ups during his tenure at the Mart. For example, in January 1955, Shaw brought his attention to a restaurant bill Baldwin had incurred with Jack Crawford and Art Whitcomb of VISION Magazine. The restaurant tab was for $135.50, a rather large sum for the mid-1950s. Baldwin agreed to pay the charge himself.⁸⁶²

The annual report for 1954, prepared by William Zetzmann, President of the Mart, emphasized that in 1954 the Mart had embarked on an elaborate advertising plan, which cost approximately $20,000, for the purpose of benefiting its tenants. One of the original selling points of the Mart had been that any surplus of income over expenses, of which the Mart had almost $30,000 for 1953, would be used to the benefit of tenants. The ads had been placed in publications around the South. Zetzmann also emphasized the expenses related to Shaw's participation in the trade mission that had visited Italy, France, Switzerland, Germany, the Netherlands, Belgium and England in the spring of 1954.⁸⁶³

At a special Executive Committee meeting in mid-March 1955, the issue of the tenant Maria Paprotna Haller and her business, European Import-Export Company, finally came to a head. The business had been behind on rental payments for some time, but the Mart had babied Haller for several years because of the interest in her support for the now-abandoned cocoa-processing facility. Haller and her husband, Karl, had visited Zetzmann at his office, acknowledging that her business was behind on rent, but promising to pay; Lloyd Cobb had represented her. The Mart had first lien on her property, and all indebtedness was satisfied through the seizure of the assets from her company. However, Kenneth Barranger, the Mart's attorney, advised that she must leave the Mart, so that its interests could be protected; many customers had written regarding merchandise ordered from her business, but not received. Additionally, the Italian Trade Commission wanted the space. Rudolf Hecht sympathized with her trying to get back on her feet; he had been the one who had initially "discovered" her and her husband as potential partners in the cocoa venture. Seymour Weiss said that he had private reasons for not participating in the discussion. The Executive Committee declined her request to remain as a tenant. In other moves, more related to cost cutting, the Committee decided not to send Shaw on a trade mission to the Far East, not to contribute to the upcoming Spring Fiesta, and not to send a representative to an upcoming Toronto fair.[864]

At a meeting of the Contributors and Debenture Holders at the end of March, Rudolf Hecht explained that the initial proposed site for a new Mart building by the New Orleans Civic Center had been rejected, but that a nearby site was possible. He acknowledged that the outcome of the whole matter was uncertain, and that it was difficult to say more at that time.[865]

April brought the passing of Herbert Schwartz, one of the original founders of the Mart. At the time of the Mart's founding, Schwartz had been with Maison Blanche Department Store in New Orleans. He had moved to New York City later in the 1940s, and had little to do with the Mart afterwards.[866]

At a Board of Directors meeting in mid-April, it was reported that an estimated 80 to 85% of current tenants would move with the Mart to a new building when it opened, if such a move happened within a reasonable period of time. Before that could happen, though, the Mart would need to sell its building, and if it was to combine with International House, that organization would need to sell its building as well.[867]

In April 1955, John Wray and Margaret Mary Young celebrated their twenty-fifth year of productions at the Shreveport Little Theater. Shaw sent a telegram giving his apologies that he could not be with them that evening, but commented on "your inspiring demonstration of what a community theater can be," and said that he would "look forward to the 50th at which I promise to be present."[868]

In May 1955, the International Motor Exhibition was held in New Orleans, sponsored by the Board of Commissioners of the Port of New Orleans. Shaw was on the committee to organize the exhibition, which was held at the Roosevelt hotel.

At an Executive Committee meeting at approximately the same time, it was announced that the sale of the building was expected to go through on May 12, 1955. The funds from the sale of the building would be invested in U.S. Treasury securities. The Mart would pay all real estate taxes, insurance and maintenance costs during its lease tenure with the new owners; that tenure was for twenty-seven months, renewable for up to five years.[869]

On May 12, the Mart building was indeed sold for $1,500,000, to five men from New York City. According to the terms of the sale, the Mart could remain a tenant in the building for up to seven years, but most thought it unlikely that it would stay there that length of time. The Mart needed a new building, at least 200,000 square feet, and as soon as it vacated the premises, the old Mart building would become a regular office building.[870]

The relationship between the Mart and International House, although beginning a long move in a more contentious direction, was still close during 1955. Charles Nutter offered some of that continuity in relationship, as he still was Managing Director of International House, although he had purchased the small *Rogers Daily News*, in Rogers, Arkansas. Nutter bought the newspaper for his son to operate; it was his intention to continue to serve International House. For his part, Shaw served on a civic committee that held a luncheon to celebrate ten years of International House operations; for his efforts, he received another letter of thanks from Mayor Chep Morrison.[871]

Richard Jones, President of International House at the time, re-appointed Shaw to the World Trade Development Committee of International House.[872] Jones also met with Shaw concerning an international food fair to be held in New Orleans during March or April of 1956.[873]

In other signs of cooperation, William McFadden Duffy, Director of Public Relations for International House during the 1950s, offered to help the Mart with its publicity efforts until someone could be found to replace David Baldwin.[874] Rudolf Hecht, who always straddled the fence between both organizations, spoke before the U.S. House Ways and Means

Committee with a seven-page statement on international trade agreements.[875]

Jesse Core was appointed Public Relations Director effective June 1, 1955. Core, who at the time lived in Dallas, Texas, had served in the U.S. Department of State in India with the United States Information Agency (USIA), and had traveled in Europe, North Africa and the Near East. He formerly had been on the staff of the *Item*, with United Press International (UPI), and with the *Cotton Trade Journal*.

Shaw received several resumes for the opening of Public Relations Director. Shaw advised applicant Wright McKenzie of Atlanta, Georgia, that he wanted the new Public Relations Director to speak fluent Spanish. He acknowledged that David Baldwin had not, but that it would have been much better if he had known the language.[876] Shaw advised applicant Henry Hurt Keith in late April that he wanted someone from the New Orleans area for the job; Shaw also mentioned that he might not fill the job for some time. Keith had been recommended by north Louisiana Congressman Overton Brooks.[877] However, in a letter earlier in April, Shaw advised Dr. Werner Seldis, who had written on behalf of applicant Edgar Baer, that he had already hired someone, as things had been piling up due to the position being unfilled for two months.[878]

Another person who applied was Warren Hampton, then in Havana, Cuba.[879] Shaw replied that he remembered him from a 1947 visit to New Orleans to seek counseling. Warren Hampton's name later comes up in FBI memos dealing with Mario Bermúdez and Marcel Gomez, in the aftermath of Shaw's arrest in 1967.

Despite the earnest interest from these other men, it was apparent that Jesse Core always had the inside track. Core was friends with the recently departed David Baldwin, and knew in advance that Baldwin would be leaving the position. A letter in January 1955 from travel agent Logan Perkins had advised Shaw that Ovid Williams (Bill) Pierce (author of *The Plantation*) had recommended Core for any job for which he was applying.[880]

The correspondence directly between Shaw and Core further illustrates the longstanding intention for the position. In early March 1955, Jesse Core had written to Shaw, while he was under consideration for the job. Core indicated that he wanted the job very badly, and he recounted in a long, somewhat humorous letter his knowledge of languages. He said that he wanted to learn Spanish, but did not yet sound as if he knew much. He also mentioned, jokingly, that he liked to nap after lunch, and mentioned, in a more serious vein, the possibility of taking the Mart job on a trial basis, in order that Shaw and other officials could see that he could do the work properly.[881] Shaw responded in mid-March, mentioning Core's lengthy letter, indicating that he was waiting on plans for the proposed new building, and that he would handle publicity himself until he received them. Shaw also emphasized his preference that whoever filled the position should be fluent in Spanish, but he assured Core that he was under serious consideration.[882] Core wrote another letter to Shaw in late March, this time in Spanish, indicating that he was going to master the language before he took the position in the summer.[883] In mid-May, Shaw wrote to Core, confirming a recent telephone conversation they had, when Shaw had offered Core the position. The terms were that it would be on a three-month trial basis, at a salary of $500 per month; Core would start on June 1.[884]

In mid-year 1955, the Mart put out a special report under William Zetzmann's name, but obviously prepared with heavy participation from Shaw, and perhaps even written by him. The report discussed both the historical progress of the Mart, and intentions of its owners moving forward. It reported on the recent sale of the Mart building, and on a planned new structure that would be completed at some point in the future. It noted that the Mart had opened in 1948 with 64.7% occupancy, and was now at 96.3% occupancy; a deficit of ($9,497) at opening was now an accumulated operating surplus of $113,582. The building, which at 75,000 rentable square feet was now too small for the Mart's importance and capabilities, had been sold for $1,500,000, then leased back at $100,000 per year. The change in financial structure had created a surplus of $1,500 from operations for the first month of the new arrangement. A search was then very much underway for a new site on which to construct a new building that would house both the Mart and International House. The report mentioned that the new Civic Center site had been rejected by the City Planning Commission, because of aesthetic issues. A constitutional amendment to exempt the Mart and International House from taxation was being proposed, but voters statewide had yet to approve such an amendment. The Mart had a $484,000 total surplus after the sale of the building, and payment of existing loans.

The report briefly noted Shaw's leadership in the operations of the Mart; it also discussed that David Baldwin had left in March 1955 as Public Relations Director, and had been replaced by Jesse Core, a newspaperman from Dallas who had traveled and worked in many areas. The report further lamented that many types of merchandise relevant to international trade were not yet represented in the Mart, that the mixture could be improved. It also noted Shaw's recent speech on Maritime Day, May 24, at the San Diego Propeller Club.[885]

Richard Swenson, formerly with the Port of New Orleans, had by now left Norfolk, Virginia, and had become Port Director in Gulfport, Mississippi.[886] Shaw asked him to come over to New Orleans and have lunch one day, and gave his best to Swenson's family.

Clem Bernard, long active with the Young Men's Business Club, had printed some of the bonds for the original Mart bond issuance years before. In May 1955, he wrote to Shaw, indicating his interest in printing some or all of the bonds that would be used to finance the proposed new building.[887]

The newly activated Foreign Policy Association of New Orleans was going strong again. Shaw remained as Program Chairman for another year. Gilbert Mellin was hired on a part-time basis as Executive Director.[888] Mellin had a Ph.D. from University of Pittsburgh; his dissertation in the early 1950s had been on the history of the Mississippi Shipping Company. James Leslie, the advertising man, was now Publicity Chairman of the group.

In his role, Shaw continued to interact with national speaking bureaus to obtain speakers at events. He wrote to Grace Sims Peat of Distinguished Personalities regarding securing Randolph Churchill as a speaker.[889] He also continued to correspond with Robert Keedick of the Lee Keedick agency, always expressing his best wishes for the family, Elizabeth Schenk, and the office force at his old employer.[890]

Mayor Chep Morrison wrote to New York Governor Averell Harriman and former President Harry Truman, attempting to convince them to speak before the group. Shaw also enlisted the help of John Minor Wisdom to prevail upon perennial presidential contender Harold Stassen to make a visit,[891] and Shaw wrote directly to Stassen inviting him.[892]

Averell Harriman, New York Governor and possible 1956 presidential contender, spoke before the group in early December 1955. After the speech, Shaw wrote to Clayton Fritchey, former editor of the *Item*, now active in national Democratic Party circles, that there seemed to be a tremendous disinterest locally regarding Harriman as a candidate for president. Shaw indicated that New Orleanians seemed to view him as a radical, because of his wealth and his somewhat lenient attitude toward Russia, and that his calm demeanor did not inspire excitement or interest. Harriman spoke in reasonable, measured tones, Shaw said, and if he wanted to be president, he needed some advice on advertising and inspiring large numbers of people. People are swayed through mass media, Shaw indicated, and Harriman did not perform well in that environment. Even so, Shaw indicated that he was proud the group had secured him to speak before them.[893]

The group managed to attract a mixture of interesting personalities of the era. For example, another speaker during that fiscal year was the famous journalist Dorothy Thompson, who spoke in January 1956. Thompson was famous for, among other things, covering Nazi Germany during its early days, becoming one of the first American journalists expelled from the country, and for covering Israel shortly after its founding, becoming an early critic of the new nation.

Shaw's speeches during 1955 included presentations in January to the Vicksburg, Mississippi Chamber of Commerce, where Shaw donated his $100 honorarium to the Foster Parents for War Children, in February to the Sertoma Club meeting at the Monteleone hotel, and in March to the Junior League of New Orleans, and the Orleans Club. He spoke to the School of Banking of the South at Louisiana State University in June, where he received "more favorable comments on your speech than any other" at the school.[894] In July he spoke to the Beta Sigma Phi State Convention of Young Businesswomen. In September, he spoke to the Executives' Club of Louisiana. In October, he spoke before Women of the Motion Picture Industry, Ladies of Les Quarante Ecobin, and to the sophomore class of Business Administration at Tulane University. As had been the norm in recent years the topic of most of his speeches was "World Trade Today."

Shaw was declining more and more of the invitations to speak in out-of-the-way locations that held limited appeal beyond the opportunity to meet with one small group. In April 1955, for instance, he turned down an invitation to speak to the Mena, Arkansas Chamber of Commerce, indicating that he would be traveling in the eastern United States during most of April.[895]

Regarding special events, he began the year by accepting an invitation from Edgar Stern to meet Mrs. Franklin D. Roosevelt, who was serving as Chairwoman of the Board of Governors of the American Association for the United Nations. A few days later, he accepted an invitation to be the guest of Percival Stern, of Interstate Electric Company, at a dinner of businessmen to discuss the Junior Achievement Program. Later in January, Shaw was the main speaker before a special seminar on international affairs sponsored by the Foreign Policy Association of New Orleans.

In the spring, he accepted an invitation to attend a reception to celebrate the 25th anniversary of H.E. Generalissimo Rafael L. Trujillo's election as president of the Dominican Republic. In May, he accepted an invitation by Charles Arning, the British consul in New Orleans, to a cocktail party on June 9, 1955 celebrating the birthday of Queen Elizabeth II.[896] Although the Queen's actual birthday was April 21, it was officially celebrated on June 9 that year.

In early September, Shaw declined an invitation from Dr. G.A. Ackal to the Louisiana Sugar Cane Festival. Shaw had met Dr. Ackal in 1953 during the Louisiana Purchase anniversary celebration. The festival was to be held September 23 to 25 in New Iberia, Louisiana, several hours from New Orleans at the time, but Shaw replied that he was trying to get a new building "on the way," and that kept his "nose to the grindstone."[897] However, he did find time in September to attend the Cordell Hall Foundation Dinner at the end of the month; the principal speaker was Governor Frank Clement of Tennessee. According to the bylaws of the Cordell Hull Foundation, the current governor of Tennessee, Hull's home state, served as President of the organization.

The number and types of goods imported into the U.S. had increased during the first ten years of the Mart's operation. A Shaw letter in early 1955, in response to an inquiry, commented that there were now 600 lines of goods from forty-eight states and twenty-five countries represented in the Mart, and that twelve countries now had some type of trade office in the building.[898]

From July 1 through 10, 1955, Shaw made his first extended visit to Mexico, a ten-day trip sponsored by International House. Several International House representatives accompanied him on the trip, along with some leading businessmen; the group primarily visited Mexico City, Cuernavaca, and Taxco. Shaw had crossed briefly into Mexico from California while making a speech in San Diego earlier in the year,[899] but this was his first time to venture into the main part of the country. An acquaintance in Mexico City had sent Shaw an article earlier in the year about the city of San Luis Potosi; Shaw had responded that he hoped to make it there someday.[900]

The Mart had never been able to induce Mexico to place its consul in the building, but at the time of Shaw's trip there, his hopes were higher. He wrote to Fernando Gonzalez de la Roza, local consul of Mexico, indicating that he hoped Mexico would join the existing twelve countries that had consular or trade offices in the Mart.[901]

The group was able to meet with the president of Mexico, who usually declined to meet with foreign delegations. Mexico was still primarily an agricultural economy, dependent upon the U.S. for both imports and exports; being cordial to a group who could aid in these efforts was beneficial. Shaw prepared a ten-page report about the trip for the Board of Directors upon his return.[902]

While in Taxco, Mexico, the traveling group called on William Spratling, the New Orleans artist and writer who had pioneered the silver jewelry business in Taxco, and Natalie Vivian Scott, a former New Orleans resident who had a colorful career as a Red Cross nurse, newspaperwoman, playwright, and social worker. Scott, during the 1920s, had associated in New Orleans with an eclectic band of artists, including William Faulkner, Lyle Saxon, Sherwood Anderson, and Spratling. After the visit by the New Orleans contingent, Scott wrote to *Item* columnist Herman B. Deutsch, brother of attorney Eberhard Deutsch, who would represent Jim Garrison's office so fiercely during the 1960s and 1970s. She commented that, among the delegation was the "President of the International Trade Mart [meaning Shaw]" with "the bookish name," whose last name she knew was "either Shaw or Zetzmann." She went on to comment that more Taxco residents spoke English than members of the U.S. delegation spoke Spanish, and commented about how the group had gone "down the hill to Bill Spratling's."[903] Scott's comment about "the bookish name" for Shaw probably referred to the days when she had known him in the late 1920s and/or early 1930s as part of the Le Petit Theatre crowd under the name of Le Vergne Shaw, which he had used in that environment.

Upon his return to New Orleans, Shaw wrote to William Spratling in Taxco, indicating that he had enjoyed the visit to Spratling's home, and that it was "nice to finally meet you." Shaw remarked that, "You have become a legend here in New Orleans," and invited Spratling to come to New Orleans where they could do further "dining, wining, and talking." Shaw summed up his visit by saying that, "The glimpse I had of your present life in Taxco makes me dissatisfied with the nose to the grindstone, shoulder to the wheel realities of my life here. However, once you get into these duties it is hard to get away. Having the strength to do so is, I suppose, what makes one a legend."[904]

Shaw also wrote to Natalie Scott after his return, in response to Scott's letter to him, which had mentioned her old friends Charles and Eleanor Nutter. In discussing the delegation's visit, Shaw said, "I agree that the members of our delegation were, by and large, free from that annoying spirit of superiority which the insecurity of most Americans makes them adopt when traveling abroad." Shaw indicated that he had every intention of revisiting Taxco for a long period.[905]

The Mart continued to receive its usual share of inquiries about foreign products. In a letter to Jorge Alayeto of Havana, Cuba, J.B. Dauenhauer discussed how few Cuban cigars were sold in New Orleans at that time, due to tariff issues; firms would import the tobacco and make the cigars in the United States.[906] Other inquiries concerned French-made dolls and imported sea shells. The number of such inquiries, however, appeared to be diminishing, compared to the earlier years of operation.

In response to an inquiry from the St. Louis Convention and Publicity Bureau, Shaw estimated that tenants at the Mart were doing about $100,000,000 in gross sales per year, and that the Mart was drawing approximately 240,000 visitors annually, although he did not know how many came to New Orleans specifically for that purpose.[907]

Beginning with the Korean War, and the escalation of the Cold War climate, the Mart had taken on a less friendly attitude toward Communist nations. Aside from Communist nations, however, the Mart generally took a neutral view of governments, however weak or solid their democratic leanings. In a letter to Allen G. Brookes of the Embassy of the Union of South Africa in Washington, D.C., after a recent visit, Shaw said that he hoped "business or pleasure will bring you back to us."[908]

Rudolf Hecht left on a ninety-day trip around the world after the sale of the Mart building to the New York City investors. He and Shaw exchanged several letters during the trip, primarily about the aftermath of the sale. In one letter, Shaw indicated that the Mart building would remain valued at $100,000 for property tax purposes, as long as the Mart paid the taxes, even though it was no longer the owner of the building, but rather a tenant.[909]

Shaw continued to generate newspaper coverage with some regularity. A letter from Andres Horcasitas congratulated Shaw on his "always right activities and good publicity," adding "un fuerte abrazo" from "your old friend," and enclosing a newspaper clipping about a recent exhibit of Philippine goods at the Mart, which showed a picture of Shaw with a male and female representative of the Philippine exhibit.[910]

The evolution of technology continued its march in every facet of American life in the mid-1950s, and the Mart was affected just like any other organization. The Mart had always used elevator operators in the building, but a letter to J.B. Dauenhauer from Elevator Consulting Engineers enclosed a booklet entitled, "The Growth of Automatic Elevators."[911]

The Mart was still examining each potential method of promoting itself, and deciding up or down on each opportunity for outreach. For instance, it cut its membership contribution to the National Rivers and Harbors Conference from $100 to $25 during 1955. On the other hand, in an effort to increase visibility, Shaw wrote to the New Orleans Hotel Association, asking that its members place a small card advertising the Mart under the glass in the bureau of each hotel room; Shaw indicated that foreign trade commissioners in the Mart had requested that service. However, the Association replied that glass covered bureaus were no longer used.[912]

Magazines geared toward marketing in Latin America continued to pursue the Mart for advertising. *VISION*, and its Atlanta-based representative, John F. "Jack" Crawford, visited with Shaw regularly during the 1950s. In a 1955 letter, Crawford indicated that he was "intrigued with plans" for the new Mart.[913] Mart officials had never been very enamored with *VISION*, however, or the audience it reached.

J.B. Dauenhauer continued to take a hard line with employees whose wages were garnished. He fired Mary Nicholas, a maid, for that reason; she filed for unemployment, but was denied. Dauenhauer also issued regular warnings to tenants. A memo in February advised about a "confidence man" slipping into the building, posing as a telephone repairman.[914]

The Mart continued to feel the growing competition from other cities; San Francisco's World Trade Center project was proceeding. Leland W. Cutler, chairman of the organization, advised Shaw that contractors were currently bidding for the building construction.[915]

These new projects would have willing participants at the ready. For one, the Japanese were continuing to make major efforts to increase their exports around the world, particularly with the United States. However, as William Zetzmann noted to the Japanese consul in New Orleans, U.S. exports to Japan in 1955 were approximately 2.5 times imports from Japan to the U.S.[916]

The office administrative employees for the Mart during 1955 were Goldie Moore, Audrey Copping, Cecilia Grace, Josephine Pennestri, and Mimi Alba. The Trade Mart had a new student intern as Trade Analyst as well—Leopoldo Herrera, also known as "Polo."

Another name that comes up during 1955 was Aurelie Alost, a tall, dark haired, willowy young woman who worked at the time for the Italian State Tourist Office, which had recently become a tenant in the Mart. In March 1967, a few days after Shaw's arrest, a source would report indirect information to the FBI that Alost had made statements to the effect that David Ferrie, one of the alleged conspirators in a plot to assassinate President Kennedy, had in years past come by to visit Shaw at his office in the Mart, this at a time when the major issue of whether Shaw and Ferrie had ever known each other was first emerging into public discussion.

A local reporter covering business matters during the year was Iris Turner of the *New Orleans States*. Later known as Iris Kelso, she covered a variety of political, commercial and social topics in the New Orleans area, both in her news stories and her columns, and dealt with Shaw at times.

Some of the Mart tenants had begun using Jean Seidenberg, a local photographer. Seidenberg would later take several striking photos of Clay Shaw, particularly for use in Latin American publications.

In July 1955, David Baldwin, now gone from the Mart, wrote to Prince Youssuf Mirza in Calcutta, India, copying Jesse Core on the letter; Core and Baldwin had served together in India several years before. Baldwin had known the prince during the time he had worked there with the CIA. However, in his letter, Baldwin indicated that he had been working with the *Louisville Courier Journal* while he was in India during the years 1950 to 1952.[917]

The fate of Maria Paprotna's business, European Export-Import Company, ended unpleasantly, even after the business was evicted from the Mart. In a letter to a customer of the business inquiring as to its fate in mid-August 1955, Shaw replied that in March 1955, the sheriff had seized the business's inventory and sold it at auction. Shaw indicated that John Paprotna, a relative of Maria, owned a gift shop in New Orleans, and might be able to assist the inquirer.[918]

Many important foreign personalities passed through New Orleans, and visited either the Mart, or International House, or both, during the 1950s. Among the business cards to be found in the collection of papers for the organizations is that of Jacques R. Chirac, future president of France from 1995 to 2007.

During 1955, Shaw and International House Public Relations Director William McFadden Duffy volunteered to attend the Czechoslovak Engineering Exhibition at Brno, Czechoslovakia as observers for the CIA, provided expenses were paid by the Agency. Shaw indicated that he thought he could arrange to attend the exhibition without members of the Board of Directors of the Mart knowing that he was traveling there on behalf of the CIA.[919] The CIA eventually deemed that Shaw's and Duffy's services in that regard were not necessary. This is one of at least two known examples in which Shaw seemed to stop merely being a passive source for the agency, and volunteered to take positive action in a particular area. However, even interviews conducted with Shaw after his lengthy international trips were based, in part, upon Shaw's observations in response to particular questions and topics provided to him in advance by the CIA.

*Latin American Reports*, the newsletter put together by former State Department employee William Gaudet, was undergoing a transformation. In a letter to Shaw in late August, Gaudet confidentially advised Shaw of a proposed new magazine to replace the newsletter. Gaudet requested that Shaw write a letter to the editor, giving Shaw's opinion of the new magazine. Gaudet said he did not really care if the letter was unfavorable; he merely wanted enough response to print a section related to it.[920]

Gaudet's idea was that the magazine would emphasize the more pleasant and profitable side of Latin America, instead of concentrating on revolution and bloodshed, as his regular newsletter sometimes did; a press release put out by Gaudet just two months earlier had discussed the overthrow of Juan Peron in Argentina.[921] Gaudet provided Shaw with a sample copy of the magazine, hoping the Mart would advertise there.[922]

The Mart was still the center of much interest by various business organizations around the country. In August 1955, John Lynn of the American Farm Bureau Federation wrote to

Shaw, commenting on his recent trip to New Orleans. He said the Mart had been one of the highlights of his recent tour, but noted that there were no agricultural commodities on display in the building.[923] Shaw replied, saying, "I have given a great deal of thought to your recent letter," but noted that agricultural commodities, such as grain or cotton, did not lend themselves to the setup at the International Trade Mart. He also noted that bananas and coffee imports had their own separate marketing system, and therefore presumably did not need the Mart's help as much.[924]

Even with the decline of the Mart's momentum, a variety of publications continued to run articles on it, and on International House. As an example, in September 1955, *South* magazine ran an article on both institutions.

Shaw attended the Houston International Trade Exposition in September 1955, staying at the Shamrock-Hilton Hotel. He also attended the Texas State Fair in Dallas in October 1955, representing the Trade Mart with an exhibit; Jesse Core attended along with him. One of the people Shaw and Core interacted with that year was Egil E. Krough, President of the Washington State International Trade Fair; his son, also named Egil Krogh, would later be head of the Special Investigation Unit in the Nixon White House, also known as the "Plumbers."

Having had a Dallas connection for some time, Jesse Core naturally promoted Shaw's profile to members of the Dallas media. In one such letter in early October 1955, Core wrote that "Shaw is a lecturer and world traveler, a writer of distinction, and a very knowledgeable person in terms of world trade."[925] Core also wrote to Decherd Turner, editor of the *Literary Supplement* of the *Dallas Times-Herald*, mentioning that Shaw had reviewed a book called *Trade Barriers* the previous summer for the *Dallas Morning News*.[926]

The idea of a new building was always on Shaw's mind during this time. In mid-October, he wrote to Rudolf Hecht, responding to a proposal for an Industrial Museum in New Orleans. Shaw indicated that, "My personal desire is to make our new building as big a basket as possible and put all possible eggs into it."[927]

As had happened for several years, Shaw was appointed by Mayor Chep Morrison as one of the officials on the committee to celebrate United Nations Appreciation Day in October 1955; it was the U.N.'s tenth anniversary year. Afterwards, Morrison congratulated Shaw on his usual excellent job with that celebration.[928] Shaw also received a letter from May L. Fleury, President of Westside Business and Professional Women's Group, thanking him for his inspiring address before it regarding the United Nations.[929]

In November, Gordon E. Brown, with General Electric Company, invited Shaw to attend a closed-circuit TV announcement of "one of the most important GE developments in recent years."[930] Shaw had to decline an invitation to a reception for the King of Belgium, saying he had to be in New York City for the National Foreign Trade Council Convention in mid-month.[931] After his return, he helped to organize and preside over an Appreciation Day Luncheon for Louisiana's Congressional delegation on December 1, 1955; Hale Boggs responded with a letter thanking Shaw for his efforts.[932]

Shaw and the Mart also participated in a World Trade Day clinic in Memphis in November 1955. A New Orleans group of trade consuls took a trip to Oak Ridge, Tennessee to inspect the atomic installation there, prior to going to Memphis. The World Trade Day clinic, sponsored by the Advertising Club of Memphis, brought nine foreign trade commissioners to Memphis to participate. Shaw's long-time acquaintance, Bess Noble, with the U.S. Department of Commerce in Memphis, invited Shaw to be one of the main speakers at the event. Afterward, she wrote to him, indicating that she was glad she had asked him to speak instead of her top boss, the U.S. Secretary of Commerce, adding, "You said just the right thing and just enough."[933]

When in New York for the National Foreign Trade Council Convention, Shaw often visited old friends he had known during the 1930s, and some of his New Orleans friends who lived there as well. In November 1955, Muriel Bultman Francis wrote from New York to her father in New Orleans, indicating that Shaw and Joe St. Cyr, co-owner of the London Shop in New Orleans, had stopped over for drinks on a Sunday afternoon.[934]

In December 1955, Monk Simons, the executive with D.H. Holmes department store and fromer Tulane University football player, sent a letter to Shaw, along with a clipping reporting a recent Shaw speech about the potential expansion of International House and the International Trade Mart.[935] Earlier in the year, Simons had sent Shaw a clipping about the same subject, and Shaw had replied that "We are without a home," but had seven years to resolve the problem.[936]

At a Board of Directors meeting in December 1955, it was noted that Miami's large new center, to be built in a reclaimed swamp, was moving forward. Meanwhile, the Mart was still considering where to put its new building; management was still hoping for a site near the new New Orleans Civic Center.[937]

William Zetzmann reported to the Board on the same day about the various activities of the Mart during the year. Shaw had gone to Mexico, Houston, and Dallas, representing the Mart on trade missions and fairs, and he had also helped organize Memphis World Trade Day. The Mart had spent $2,000 to sponsor scholarships for Latin American Students through the Cordell Hall Foundation. Ominously, Zetzmann continued to spotlight potential competition from other cities—Miami's new Inter-American Center, and the efforts by Houston, San Francisco, and Mobile, Alabama.[938]

# 14 · Shaw Manages International House (Part 1)

The Mart's sister organization, International House, while generally successful, had its own issues. At a meeting of the Policy Committee of International House in early January 1956, Charles Nutter gave a presentation wherein he summed up the organization's activity to date, as well as its shortcomings. He said that International House had lost ground from its original goals, that it was trying to sell too many different ideas, and that other organizations were doing essentially the same things. He suggested a ten-year plan of operation, along with a celebration of the centennial of the Civil War in 1961, to help the city generate publicity. He pointed to rapid industrialization up and down the Mississippi River as a promising development. Nutter also sought immediate clarification of his authority over staff members, discussed the need for a pension plan for International House employees, and requested a substantial increase in his salary. Nutter indicated that a pension plan had been promised to him when he had started, and William Zetzmann backed him up on that point, as well as on the issue of Nutter's authority over staff employees.[939] After the meeting, Rudolf Hecht wrote a letter to International House President Richard Jones, objecting that the minutes of the meeting did not include all remarks which had been made at the meeting, including Nutter's remark that, "We had stumbled into unauthorized activities," or Nutter's remark that he could save the organization $50,000 if he was allowed to reorganize it using his ideas.[940]

In early 1956, Jesse Core, still in his first year as Public Relations Director with the Mart, wrote to Dr. Wirt Williams, a Mississippi-born writer then teaching at Los Angeles State College in California, indicating that their mutual friend David Baldwin was now writing speeches for the governor of Pennsylvania at a "good salary."[941] Core, being married with a child, could not always attend the after-hours events in which the Mart participated. In February, he wrote a note to Shaw regarding the upcoming farewell dinner for the Consul General of Ecuador, being held at the Roosevelt hotel. Core indicated that he could not afford to pay the ticket price, the babysitter, and parking fees, and preferred not to go alone to the banquet.[942]

By this time, Core was answering most letters of inquiry received at the Mart. More and more letters from the general public were requests for information about foreign countries from students in elementary or high schools around the country.

Meanwhile, Shaw had moved to the property at 505 Dauphine Street, the old John J. Audubon home.[943] Several separate properties came together, with a swimming pool in the middle. Shaw would later have the reputation of having installed the first swimming pool in the French Quarter, and he would often tell the story that, in order to get around regulations laid down by the Vieux Carré Commission, he had to call the swimming pool a "fish pond." Some have disputed that Shaw could claim the first swimming pool in the Quarter, but there is no doubting that the one he had was extremely popular with both local and out-of-town visitors.

In mid-January, William Zetzmann wrote to George Dinwiddie of New Orleans Public Service, Inc., asking Dinwiddie to study the possibility of a pension plan for Mart employees, noting that Mart officials had been thinking along those lines recently.[944] Shaw pushed for such a plan throughout his entire tenure at the Mart, but would eventually retire without such benefits.

Rudolf Hecht died of heart failure on January 18, 1956. It was a sudden death, catching most by surprise. Hecht had been a tremendous force in the New Orleans business world for several decades and, with his passing, the Mart and International House lost a second important founding father, after Theodore Brent's passing in 1953. Although many businessmen were responsible for the early activity of the two organizations, it is arguable that Brent and Hecht were the two most important. It was the end of an era of sorts. The executive offices of the Mart were closed on January 19, 1956, in honor of Hecht. That same day, Carl Cramer, the sculptor who had created the bust of Theodore Brent, wrote to William Zetzmann, offering to create a fitting tribute to Hecht.[945]

During 1955, Shaw had written to Hecht, discussing Congressman Daniel Flood's bill to provide $100,000,000 for international trade centers. Shaw, suggesting the Mart should get behind it, indicated that the proposal would provide 15,000 jobs to the "deserving and faithful" in the international trade field.[946] In early January, Hecht had followed up in a memo to Shaw about the issues Shaw had raised, and about trade issues in general.[947] However, Hecht died shortly thereafter.

In February 1956, Shaw wrote to Charles Logan, the Mart's labor negotiator, saying that as a result of the new minimum wage law, which would raise hourly rates from 75 cents to $1.00 per hour effective March 1, 1956, hours for hourly employees were being cut from 40 to 35 per week. Shaw noted that even with the cut in hours, the total annual increase in hourly payroll would be about $2,000. He warned that any more mandated raises would cause the Mart to use outside building maintenance services in the future.[948]

The Mart continued to deal regularly with such labor issues related to its hourly employees. An inspection by the U.S. Department of Labor for the period from January 26, 1953 through April 30, 1954 had found that hourly employees were not being paid overtime for hours in excess of forty hours per week, and that no accurate record of hours for the chief building engineer had been kept, aside from those for his regular eight-hour shift. The Department further found that during that period, there had been a total underpayment of approximately $2,400 to ten employees. Shaw had advised the Department of Labor's representative that the Board of Directors had decided not to make restitution of back wages related to that underpayment. However, the Department of Labor advised that the Mart could be held liable for back wages, plus an equal amount in damages.[949]

In February 1956, the Policy Committee of International House recommended that Shaw be designated as Director of the World Trade Development Department. With the Mart fully occupied, and in somewhat of a holding pattern while the search for a new building continued, Shaw was looking for projects to occupy himself, and the leaders of the two organizations were similarly looking for ways to keep him busy. Shaw was to take the additional assignment without a salary increase for 1956, although his salary was to be reappraised during the year, based upon general economic conditions.

Bess Noble, of the U.S. Department of Commerce in Memphis, Tennessee, continued to be active in the annual Mississippi Valley World Trade Conference. In February 1956, she wrote Shaw, suggesting speakers for various panels at the upcoming conference.[950]

While the Mississippi Valley World Trade Conference had originally been part of the overall international trade picture in New Orleans from the mid-1940s into the 1950s, it had never attracted much interest from Latin American companies and representatives. Toward the end of 1956, Shaw wrote to Paul Klemens, Assistant Sales and Export Manager of Columbia Machine, Inc. in Vancouver, Washington, explaining the conference; Klemens had written Shaw inquiring about attending it. Shaw advised that it attracted five hundred to six hundred people each year, but said that only a few were from Latin America. He advised that it was not worthwhile to attend in order to meet potential Latin American customers, as most of the attendees were from the Mississippi Valley area. However, Shaw thought that some of them might be helpful to Klemens's company.[951]

In March 1956, Jesse Core, continuing to work his Dallas connections, wrote again to Decherd Turner, editor of the Literary Supplement of the *Dallas Times-Herald*, indicating that Shaw would like to review a copy of *World Without Barriers*, by Emanuel R. Posnack, for the newspaper.[952] Posnack, a patent lawyer and inventor, had written the book to argue against barriers to the free flow of people, goods, and cultural exchange across national borders.

The Mart continued to receive exotic and often bizarre product information. In a memo in March 1956, Jesse Core discussed some recent product news sent to the Mart, "For live camels, zebra and tiger skins, ostrich feathers and ivory pieces from Africa, write to Box 599, Khartoum, Sudan."[953]

In early April, Jesse Core wrote to David Baldwin, giving him a rundown of recent happenings in New Orleans. Baldwin was now handling public relations for the governor of Pennsylvania, and living in the capital city of Harrisburg. Core discussed recent hunting trips he had taken, and mentioned that several prominent New Orleanians had passed away unexpectedly, including Owen Brennan, owner of Brennan's Restaurant, Rudolf Hecht, and Tom Caplinger, owner of the famed mixed gay-and-straight bar Lafitte's Blacksmith Shop (later Cafe Lafitte's in Exile). Core also discussed what he called local "red hunts," noting that Bob Barnes, an employee of the Chamber of Commerce, had been fired by the Chamber for associating with James Dombrowski, who headed the Southern Conference Education Fund (SCEF), an organization that worked to end segregation and the disenfranchisement of African Americans in the South. Dombrowski, a Methodist minister, was regarded as a radical, even a Communist, in many circles in the South. He would be the subject of a famous court case that partly involved District Attorney Jim Garrison; Shaw's attorneys would, a decade later, cite the precedent from that case in seeking to halt prosecution of Shaw. Jesse Core added that Herman Liveright, Program Director for WDSU-TV, had been dismissed from the station after refusing to answer questions regarding his possible Communist affiliations before the U.S. Senate Internal Security Subcommittee.[954]

Core took time off during the summer to go to Texas for "intelligence training" with the Air Force Reserve.[955] After he wrote to Shaw from the training center, Shaw replied the following week, "Learn all you can about counterespionage, you never know when it might come in handy."[956]

Shaw reviewed the activities of the World Trade Development Department, and submitted a report to the Board of Directors of International House in late April. He concluded that the Department did not need a full-time director, but was in capable hands with George L. Sawicki, Assistant Director at the time. A subcommittee of the Board of Directors of International House, however, responded to Shaw's report, disagreeing with his conclusion.

Over the years, Shaw served on many boards and committees, regarding a wide range of special projects, for which he put in many extra hours of work. In April 1956, after being invited to serve on the reception committee for National Maritime Day by Harry X. Kelly, President of the Mississippi Shipping Company, an invitation which assured Shaw that he would be a member in name only, without any special duties to take up his time, Shaw replied that he was "always glad to accept any appointment which has no duties."[957]

At a meeting of the Executive Committee of the Board of Directors in late May, it was discussed that the Mart would give the Cordell Hull Foundation only $1,000 that year, instead of the requested $2,000. Shaw pointed out that the Mart now had rental expense since the sale of the building.[958]

Locally prominent companies continued to ask for the Mart's assistance on individual tax and political issues. For example, in June, E.D. Wingfield, Vice-President of Freeport Sulphur Company, wrote to Shaw regarding a proposed tripling of the severance task on sulfur, asking that the Mart get in touch with U.S. Senators who might have some influence over the proposal.[959]

The Mart continued to re-evaluate all expenses in the wake of its plateau in revenues. It laid off its newest "trade analyst," Leopoldo Herrera, in early 1956, due to a general staff reduction; Shaw provided him with a letter of recommendation.[960] In July, Jesse Core advised an inquirer that the newsletter that for years had been sent out by the Mart to various outside parties had been discontinued in May, due to the pressure of other business; he indicated the Mart was planning another issue sometime in the future.[961] Shaw had earlier commented, in response to an inquiry, that the newsletter to outside parties had not been issued in February "due to circumstances beyond our control," but that it would resume on a bi-monthly basis in March.[962] In response to another inquiry regarding sample fairs held in the Mart, Shaw replied that they had been discontinued due to the amount of traffic through the building, but that they might be resumed with a newer, larger building when it materialized.[963]

Being a public institution, with most of its directors, and its top employee, involved in numerous civic affairs, the Mart sometimes became a target of politicians running for office and seeking endorsements. One such person was Oliver P. Schulingkamp, who was running for traffic judge in mid-1956. Schulingkamp had sent Zetzmann a letter seeking his support. Shaw gave his advice to Zetzmann in a handwritten note on the letter, saying, "I think we should steer clear of politics." Zetzmann responded in his own handwritten note, saying, "I have already forgotten about this."[964]

Shaw went along with other New Orleans businessmen on a mid-continent tour that stopped in Kansas City, Omaha, St. Louis and Minneapolis. Jimmy Fitzmorris, then a New Orleans city councilman, and later a candidate for governor, went on the trip as well.

Shaw declined another invitation to attend the annual Louisiana Sugar Cane Festival in New Iberia, Louisiana that year, indicating that he was out of state on the dates of the festival; [965] Shaw had periodically declined such invitations. Surprisingly, though, he also had to decline a dinner at Brennan's with Lucille Ball and Desi Arnez, hosted by Mayor Chep Morrison.[966]

Shaw was part of the group of city officials who hosted the Ambassador to the United States from Denmark in May of 1956. The Ambassador wrote to Shaw, thanking him for his hospitality, and mentioning recordings of music by Miss LaVergne Smith, a New Orleans singer, that Shaw had given him, indicating that he would not only play them, but would consider her for an engagement in Denmark.[967]

Shaw met with officials from the International Cooperation Administration in Washington, D.C., regarding a marketing conference and study tour the administration was conducting of various cities. Back in New Orleans in June, he appeared on "French Quarter Forum," a program on WTPS-Radio.[968]

Among other special events, he also was invited to a reception in honor of Governor and Mrs. Frank T. Clement of Tennessee, held on January 1, 1957. The event was hosted by Mr. and Mrs. Mario Bermúdez. Bermúdez knew Clement well from his involvement with the Cordell Hull Foundation.

Shaw gave his full quota of speeches during 1956. In January, he appeared at the Biloxi, Mississippi Rotary Club. The visit was arranged by Warren Jackson, an insurance agent who had had a hand in the large mural at the Louisiana Purchase celebration. In March, he spoke before the Junior League of New Orleans, the student body of the College of Business Administration at Loyola University, the Crowley, Louisiana Chamber of Commerce, and the Moss Point, Mississippi Rotary Club. In April, he spoke before the Slidell, Louisiana Kiwanis Club. In May he found himself at the Hammond, Louisiana Kiwanis Club, the Third District Kiwanis Club of New Orleans at Johnny's Restaurant on Rampart Street, and he gave the commencement address at Gulf Park College in Gulfport, Mississippi.

Shaw declined an invitation in May to the American Society for Metals Dinner Dance.

The official inviting him had encouraged Shaw to bring his wife, advising that she would find it "most enjoyable."

In July, he spoke at the Grace Church Couples Club, and in September to the New Orleans Junior Chamber of Commerce, the Rotary Club of Hammond, Louisiana, and to the closing banquet of the Business and Professional Women's Club at Napoleon Patio at Broussard's Restaurant; Camilla Mays Frank was the chairman of that group.

In October, Shaw spoke to the Rotary Club in Jackson, Mississippi, before 175 high school students at a Junior United Nations function held at International House, and to the Memphis Public Affairs Forum on "Foreign Problems of the Next Administration;" Shaw stayed at the old Peabody Hotel in Memphis on the latter trip.

In November, Shaw was at the Lafayette (Louisiana) Sales Executive Club, at the Houma, Louisiana Woman's Club, and at the Midwest International House Luncheon in Cincinnati, Ohio. Also in November, he declined an invitation to speak to the Faculty Club at Nicholls State College in Thibodaux, Louisiana in February 1957, indicating that he would be on a trip elsewhere at that time, but could speak later in 1957. The same month, he also met with the City Park Women's Club at City Park Casino in New Orleans.

Shaw was still in touch with his Shreveport friends John Wray and Margaret Mary Young. In preparation for a Shaw trip to Shreveport, John Wray Young wrote to him, asking for a photo and biographical information. He also asked Shaw to "please stay with us," indicating Shaw's continuing closeness to the family, a closeness that would quietly manifest itself after his arrest.

The local broadcaster John Kent continued his show entitled "News from the International Trade Mart." A transcript of that program from the mid-1950s mentioned that "Shaw, who once managed a lecture bureau, is a speaker in demand himself," with over 500 speeches in ten years promoting the Mart.

The Helen Brett Trade Show was now an annual fixture in New Orleans. It was held again at the Roosevelt hotel in July; the Mart had a suite there promoting itself, and mentioned the event in its newsletter, which still appeared occasionally.

At a meeting of the Board of Directors in early July, the proposed merger of International House and the Mart was discussed. It was noted that the Pan American Life Insurance Company had taken the position that it would not release the Mart from contingent liability on the first mortgage, even though the new owners of the building had primary liability.[969]

Charles Nutter, Shaw's counterpart at International House, had been summoned to Washington to serve on a Congressional committee assignment, at the urging of Congressman Hale Boggs. The Mart agreed to allow Shaw to assume the duties of Managing Director for International House, while still handling his normal Mart responsibilities, for the remaining months of 1956. His salary was to be increased to $18,000 per year, with International House paying half of that salary for the duration of his dual management duties.[970] In the midst of his new duties with International House, Shaw stepped back from being Program Chairman of the Foreign Policy Association of New Orleans.

At a joint meeting of the Executive Committees of International House and International Trade Mart a week later, it was formally agreed that fifty percent of Shaw's salary would be paid by each organization, and that it would be temporarily raised to Charles Nutter's level while Shaw held the position at both institutions. It also was discussed that a proposed Basin Street property could be acquired for $1 per year from the City of New Orleans; the Basin Street property was the newest potential location for a new building that would combine both organizations. The Mart needed 150,000 square feet, and International House 50,000 square feet; an additional amount was needed for potential expansion.[971]

One of the objections to placing the new International Trade Mart building on the Basin Street site, also known as the "neutral strip," was that it would destroy the view there, and that it would create a traffic hazard. That view was expressed by Leonard Huber, of the

Louisiana Landmarks Society, in a letter to Shaw. Huber also suggested that the Mart and International House should buy property adjoining the old City Hall building, and have the city deed the present City Hall building to them to use for International House. Huber offered that a high rise "Trade Center" building could be built on the adjacent property.[972]

At another joint meeting of the Executive Committees of both organizations a week later, Shaw reported on a cook with ten years of experience at International House's restaurant who was out sick. He inquired as to the general policy for handling lengthy employee illnesses, indicating that he opposed a general sick leave policy, because it might be abused; he instead proposed that each situation should be left to the discretion of the Managing Director. He also discussed the potential new building site on Basin Street; some members did not like that location. An active participant in the discussion was Joseph Rault, Sr., who would serve as President of International House the following year.[973]

In mid-July 1956, Charles Nutter wrote to Richard G. Jones of the Jackson Brewing Company, the current President of International House, about the current state of the organization. Nutter said that International House had neglected Europe, to some extent, since its founding, although European countries had supported the Mart more than Latin American countries. Nutter suggested that Shaw be appointed as European Director to open a European office of International House (such an office had been promised in 1947); Nutter said his suggestion should be implemented in the next two to three months. He indicated that Shaw could stay in Europe for a year or so, then come home to direct activities in New Orleans for a while.[974] There were several versions of Nutter's letter to Jones; another of them mentioned the position of European Director, but did not mention Shaw specifically for that position.

The existence of International Trade Mart-type operations in other countries also came to the Mart's attention. At mid-year 1956, J.B. Dauenhauer received a letter from Enrique A. Mantello of Basle, Switzerland, indicating that an organization called Permindex was to be opened in 1958 in Basle, with 300,000 square feet of space; Mantello had visited New Orleans not long before.[975] Shaw replied to the letter, saying that he had been in Basle many times, and indicated his interest in the progress of the proposed new organization.[976]

Shaw continued his policy of writing positive letters of recommendation for anyone who had met his expectations while working at the Mart. He gave one to Manuel Delgado, recommending him highly.[977] Earlier, he had given a letter to Marcel Gomez, recommending him without reservation as well.[978]

J.B. Dauenhauer continued to deal with employee problems below the administrative level. He fired yet another employee, Antoine M. Bolliole, Jr., for having his wages garnished. Such dealings with employees were a product of the times as much as with Dauenhauer's personality, and could not be carried on so easily today, especially with such an image-conscious institution as the Mart.

Mimi Alba had left the Mart by this time to begin schooling to become an airline stewardess. She wrote to the employees at the Mart, indicating that she had to go to gym class, and that she would be thin when finished. The general training school was for eight weeks, then if placed with an airline, she would have additional training with that particular carrier.

The trade mission visit to Mexico the year before had apparently born fruit. In mid-1956, the Mexican government put on a two-month exhibition in the Mart, in collaboration with the American Foreign Power Company.[979]

After the sale of the Mart building, the Mart and International House sought a state constitutional amendment that would exempt all trade organizations with assets of not less than $250,000 from all state and city taxation. Based upon that description, the amendment would only have applied to International House and the International Trade Mart.

Shaw did not take an international trip on behalf of the Mart during 1956. Early in the year, he wrote to Ted Sexton of Sexton Funeral Chapel in Leavenworth, Kansas, thanking him for an illustrated map of the proposed Kansas City trade mission, which would include New Orleans businessmen; Shaw indicated that he hoped Sexton and his wife would be on the next International House "junket, whenever that is."[980] In April, he wrote to Franklin Lane, General Secretary of the American Chamber of Commerce in Italy, saying that it was "high time for another trade mission to Europe," and that he hoped to be on it.[981]

Shaw received a form from Lee S. Thomas, with the Department of Commerce in New Orleans, to be completed in order to become a member of a U.S. trade mission to an international trade fair later in the year.[982] Shaw did not make the trip, however.

Shaw continued to answer a number of routine inquiries. In one, he reiterated the requirement that a tenant that sold physical products must have a sales representative present in the space.[983] In another letter, Shaw stated that everything on display in the space must be for sale immediately to a buyer, not simply available for order.[984] Although the Mart had relaxed some policies over the years, those two, which had been in place initially, were still in effect, at least selectively.

Shaw also still responded to inquiries about individual products, such as zippers manufactured in other countries.[985] In response to an inquiry about the "drug market" in Central and South America, Shaw responded with a question, "Do you wish to sell drugs to the Latin American market, or do you wish to import drugs from there?"[986]

To the extent that other Mart employees besides Shaw participated in outside activities at the Mart's expense, such activities generally were related to promoting the Mart, or at least something to do with the international trade field. Goldie Moore, for some years now the Mart's main secretary, served as Vice President of the International Relations Committee of the local Altrusa Club, a women's civic organization.[987] However, she declined an invitation to be a member of Executive Secretaries, Inc., saying that she and Shaw had discussed the matter, and had decided that her time was too limited.[988]

During this time, the Mart was sometimes asked to become involved in projects in which it really had no interest. Robert S. Smith had been Western Manager for *TIME-International*, and had lived in New Orleans in the early to mid-1950s. He then moved to New York City to find better opportunities, but he continued to stay in touch with people in the international community, and local media in New Orleans. In March 1956, he wrote Tommy Griffin, a popular columnist for the *Item*, telling him about a new venture: a proposed American Museum of Immigration.[989] He also later wrote a letter to Jill Jackson, a local radio personality, bringing the matter to her attention;[990] Smith copied the letters to Shaw.

Shaw replied to Smith, who was then living at Number 10 West Ninth Street, an area in which Shaw had lived during part of his time in New York City. Two friends of Shaw's, Priscilla Peck and Marty Mann, currently lived in the same building; Shaw commented that he loved that region of New York City above all others. He also mentioned the new swimming pool at his residence on Dauphine Street, and remarked how wonderful it was to have it open for use.[991]

Two weeks later, Shaw again wrote to Smith, saying how pleased he was at the connections Smith had made in the movement to begin the museum. Shaw commented that the museum was a great idea, and that he might even part with ten of his own dollars in support of it.[992]

Smith was trying to find New Orleans officials who would sign on to be members of a local committee there that would promote the proposed museum. In a letter in mid-May, Shaw told Smith that he had tried to persuade William Zetzmann to serve as the local chairman, but that Zetzmann was too busy with his roles with the Mart, and to a lesser extent with International House; Shaw also mentioned that Zetzmann's health was not good. Shaw recommended that Smith get in touch with William Helis, the son of a shipping magnate of the same name, saying that the younger Helis was "young, rich and energetic."[993]

In late May, Shaw wrote to Smith again, advising that he was leaving the next day for a two-week vacation at Crescent Beach in South Carolina, no doubt visiting the Formyduval family. Shaw mentioned that Mildred Cardenas, who had been Bob Huart's secretary, was now working with the Protocol Division of the United Nations, and staying with Alicia Cordozo Velez, in New York City; Shaw thought Smith might like to have a drink with her to promote the proposed museum. Shaw concluded the letter by saying he was off to Brennan's Restaurant to help them dedicate a new building, with a television broadcast at noon that day.[994]

Smith kept the correspondence going; in mid-June, he wrote Shaw that he had seen Richard and Gwen Swensen in New York City the week before.[995] The idea for the proposed museum continued to limp along. In late September, Smith asked if Shaw could arrange a meeting with William Helis, and also with the Superintendent of Schools in New Orleans, in order to promote the idea. He still had not filled the position of Chairman of the committee to promote the museum in New Orleans, and continued to inquire if William Zetzmann, or New Orleans businessman C.C. Walther, would at least join the committee. In the same letter, Smith mentioned Shaw having two jobs now, referring to Shaw's dual role at the Mart and International House during Nutter's absence.[996]

The attempt to interest Shaw and other Mart and International House officials in the proposed museum apparently tapered away in the fall of that year. Smith wrote to Shaw again in October, noting that he was "sorry we couldn't have spent a more leisurely time *en famille* without the pressure of our respective jobs," and indicated that they could do that in New York City when Shaw visited there the next time.[997]

Membership in International House was desired as much for the social nature of the institution as for its international trade goals, and few wanted to give up its privileges. Once he had moved out of New Orleans to Norfolk, Virginia, Richard Swenson, formerly Public Relations Director with the Board of Commissioners of the Port of New Orleans, had been dropped from the Board of Directors of International House. Beginning in late 1955, however, Swenson, now with the Port of Gulfport, Mississippi, wrote letters to Rudolf Hecht,[998] International House President Richard Jones,[999] and to William Zetzmann,[1000] objecting to his exclusion.

During the 1950s, Shaw was regularly involved in assisting with some civic causes unrelated to the Mart's general sphere of activity. For example, at the end of May 1956, Shaw wrote to Al Alice of the General Gas Corporation, asking for a contribution to New Orleans's symphony orchestra.[1001] He was also, of course, involved with local theaters at various points in his life, and generally served on boards related to various activities whenever the Mart directors thought his participation was worthwhile.

The Mart's efforts to interest Latin American countries to become tenants in some fashion had never been a consistent success. In another sign that the Mart's original mission had faltered to some degree, Shaw was still trying to interest Argentina in placing an office of some type in the Mart. He wrote to Rudolph Frigerio in Washington, D.C., asking when Argentina could join Belgium, Great Britain, Canada, Japan, Cuba, France, Germany, Italy, the Netherlands, the Philippine Republic, Puerto Rico, and Switzerland, in having some type of trade promotion center in the building.[1002]

With the good record that Shaw had built up during the years when Theodore Brent and Rudolf Hecht effectively supervised his performance, he had gained a great deal of autonomy in his job performance. He took care of most details related to the Mart for William Zetzmann, and Zetzmann gave him a free hand. However, in perhaps an ominous note, board member Lloyd Cobb wrote to Shaw in August 1956, after reviewing Shaw's purchases at Brennan's and other local restaurants. Cobb indicated that Shaw's personal account should be segregated from the International Trade Mart account at such establishments. Prior to that, all of Shaw's restaurant charges, personal and business, had been combined into one statement in Shaw's name, and presumably separated later. Cobb copied the letter to Zetzmann.[1003]

Shaw had encountered Albert D. Meltz, Vice President with Rachlin and Company in Newark, New Jersey, when the Mart had sold its building to the New York investors in 1955. Meltz was now contracted to sell the International House building, in case the two organizations decided to merge. For that, it would be necessary for Meltz to obtain a Louisiana real estate broker's license. Meltz wrote to Shaw, indicating that he had completed the application for the license, but that the regulations appeared to require that he should also take an exam; he asked if that requirement could be waived by the governor, or by someone else in authority.[1004] Shaw replied that he actually might have to take the exam, and explained that local favorite Chep Morrison, who had been running for governor in the recent election against Earl Long, Huey Long's younger brother seeking a second full term, had been defeated, and that the Mart's influence would expire as soon as current Governor Robert Kennon was out of office.[1005]

The number of visitors coming into the Mart building was at or near an all-time high in 1956. During most months, the count exceeded 20,000 guests, and sometimes even 23,000. The institution's reputation with the general public was still very high, even as its operational performance and its reputation within the international community were arguably declining.

Scott Wilson, who owned his own public relations agency, Wilson and Associates, headquartered at the St. Charles Hotel, announced that he had opened a Washington, D.C. office. Barbara Corbin, who had worked as the main secretary under Shaw for the Louisiana Purchase 150th Anniversary Association, would be working in that office.[1006]

During 1956, Jesse Core attended the 1956 State Fair of Texas, occupying a booth promoting the Mart in the International Section of the fair. Shaw apparently did not attend the event that year.

Shaw guest-wrote the "Lagniappe" column of June 29, 1956; the column, normally written for the *Item* by Tommy Griffin, covered a wide variety of local and national subjects. Shaw's guest column for that day covered subjects such as the supply of coffee to troops during the Korean War, the best route from New Orleans to South America, and Japan's role in imports through the Port of New Orleans.[1007]

The Mart's efforts to get into a new building, and to merge with International House, became the subject of competition among the local news media outlets. In late October 1956, Bill Monroe, News Director of WDSU-TV, wrote to Shaw complaining that WDSU had not been given an even break about news related to the Mart's plans for the then-proposed Basin Street property, and expressing frustration that the local newspapers had gotten the story before his television station.[1008]

The Mississippi Valley World Trade Council was organized in 1956 to give continuity to the Mississippi Valley World Trade Conference, which had been held every year since the mid-1940s. The Council was formed under the direction of the Export Managers' Club in New Orleans, with cooperation from the Mart, International House, the Port of New Orleans, the Chamber of Commerce, and the New Orleans Board of Trade. After ten years of a St. Louis group managing the Mississippi Valley World Trade Conference, the Council was formed to take over the conference and related activities. Shaw was still Secretary to the group, which held meetings in the Executive Offices of the Mart, and the Articles of Incorporation, dated August 28, 1956, show Shaw's home address at the time of 505 Dauphine Street.[1009] There were 45 members on the Council, and the initial meeting for the formation was held on April 10, 1956, at the Roosevelt hotel, although an earlier, more informal meeting had been held at the Mart on February 16, 1956.

Shaw would soon sell his property at 505 Dauphine Street, the old John J. Audubon home, to a Mrs. Artelle Trelford of Houston, Texas. Mrs. Trelford was very wealthy, and paid Shaw a good price for the property. Shaw held the mortgage himself; Trelford was to pay over a number of years, and a balance existed even at Shaw's death. The sales price and the interest income, however, helped Shaw's position significantly, and put him on the road to financial independence.

The racial integration issue going on in New Orleans during the 1950s often affected, to some degree, events considered by International House and the Mart. In a discussion of the issue in mid-April 1956, Charles Nutter wrote to Michael Buzon, Jr. of the International Educational Exchange Service with the United States Department of State. Nutter said that New Orleans was not in a position to properly entertain and handle visitors who were "persons of color," due to the reaction against the "forces of moderation" because of the Supreme Court decision on integration of public schools. Nutter opined that it would serve no useful purpose to bring such visitors to New Orleans, and that it would be impossible to handle them with the proper courtesy and respect due them, and their impressions of the city would be unfavorable.[1010]

The racial divide in New Orleans continued in full force, as it did throughout the South, for many years. Fifteen years later, the Mart and International House were still struggling with the issue. In September 1970, after Shaw's departure, Basil Rusovich, then an important member of the Mart's Board of Directors, indicated in a memo that the policy regarding having "colored people" as guests in the then relatively new Mart building's bar or main dining room was that it was not to be encouraged, but that such individuals would be allowed in with a member if it was "IMPORTANT" to the member's business.[1011]

A new World Trade Center opened in San Francisco during 1956. Charles Nutter spoke at the opening celebration, along with Mayor Chep Morrison. The Center in San Francisco would grow in importance over the years. On November 22, 1963, the day of President Kennedy's assassination, Shaw would be touring the Center in preparation for a speech to its members when news of what had just taken place in Dallas first reached him.

In the mid-1950s, there was much continuing discussion about how New Orleans was losing international business to other cities. In a letter to George Chaplin, then editor of the *Item*, Paul M. White, Jr., in declining to renew his membership in International House, commented that New Orleans' problems in that regard stemmed from the following areas: 1) its airport facilities were outdated; 2) there were either no air connections to Latin America from New Orleans, or bad connections that involved transfers; 3) Miami was actively soliciting business from Latin America, in direct competition with New Orleans; 4) the Florida newspapers gave better news coverage to international trade and development than did the Louisiana newspapers; and 5) New Orleans banks were apathetic about Latin American business accounts. White criticized International House and Shaw, who was then acting as Managing Director during Charles Nutter's absence, saying that the institution was not doing a good enough job in promoting international business; he also criticized the expensive Trade Mission trips to Europe sponsored by the organization.[1012] Chaplin forwarded the letter to Shaw for his review.

By this time, local businessmen trusted Shaw to the extent that he could be a sounding board for possible new ideas, and to discuss changes in the business community. In September, Robert R. Barkerding, local head of the South American Division of Texas Transport and Terminal Company, wrote to Shaw that there were a "lot of interesting things going on" and "hope we can get together one of these days for a little loose conversation."[1013]

In the fall, Shaw received a letter from Hale Boggs, thanking him for his help during the Democratic congressional primary during the summer. Boggs noted that he had Republican opposition in the upcoming general election, and indicated that a vote for a Republican was a vote against the South's continuance of power and influence in the nation's capital.[1014] At the time, the Republican Party was almost non-existent in Louisiana.

Shaw appeared on the *Today* show on NBC in October 1956, along with Mayor Chep

Morrison. His appearance generated some correspondence from old friends, such as Bess Noble with the Department of Commerce in Memphis. She commented that her good friend, Helen Davis, said that Shaw "looked just as handsome on TV as he does in person, so suave and cordial."[1015] He also received a letter from E.O. Jewell, who formerly had been with the Board of Commissions of the Port of New Orleans, then briefly with International House, but who had since moved to Toledo, Ohio, to work for the Port there.[1016] A photo of Shaw in the *Times-Picayune* of October 18, 1956, showed a clean-cut, striking image, with his hair very gray at age forty-three.

Also in October, Shaw's friend Judson O'Donnell from California stopped into New Orleans, and he and Shaw executed wills, witnessed by employees at the Mart. Goldie Moore was a witness, as was at least one intern working for the Mart during that period. O'Donnell had met Shaw through Muriel Bultman Francis in New York City during the 1930s, and the two had lived together. The two had both worked in a small theater group in the late 1930s, but neither had ultimately achieved much success in that field. In O'Donnell's will, he left Shaw everything.[1017] He identified himself as having been born March 16, 1911, in Minneapolis, Minnesota, and indicated that he was widowed, and had been in California since 1940. Although Shaw's will from that year has apparently not survived, Shaw may have left everything to O'Donnell in that early version. In 1975, a year or so after Shaw's death, O'Donnell still seemed under the impression that Shaw had left him his entire estate. However, Shaw's final will left O'Donnell only the income from the note that secured the Spanish Stables property at 716 Governor Nicholls Street, not an insignificant bequest.

At a special joint meeting of the Boards of Directors of International House and International Trade Mart at the end of October, Lloyd Cobb presented a report of the joint Building Committee of the two organizations; that committee had been formed to explore a potential new building site that would combine both organizations. It was concluded that the only workable site was the Old Terminal Station site on Basin and Canal Streets. Development in the city had been moving away from the river, and toward the Basin Street location. Lloyd Cobb displayed a model of a potential new building set, and indicated he had made a study of the Basin Street location on his own. Cobb envisioned tropical and botanical gardens among the buildings, and said that the organizations should make them "unique, awe-inspiring and glamorous." The attendees at the meeting all seemed in agreement to proceed with the Basin Street property. Chep Morrison was also in attendance, and gave the city's position on cooperation with the two organizations. As a side matter, it was reiterated that Miami, San Francisco and New York City were all now actively competing with New Orleans in the international trade arena.[1018]

In 1956, the CIA was concerned about shipments of mercury from Spain and Italy to the Soviet bloc. Apparently, CIA employee Hunter Leake approached Shaw, who was still not only Managing Director of the Mart, but also Acting Director of International House in Charles Nutter's absence, about receiving information on mercury shipments from Spain and Italy. Shaw offered to inquire about such shipments by using World Trade Development Department letterhead to write to companies in Spain and Italy about their stocks of mercury.[1019] However, the CIA eventually determined it did not need Shaw's services related to the question of mercury shipments.

Shaw's service to the Central Intelligence Agency as a source of information seemed to have ended in 1956. Although anything is possible, all records released thus far indicate that there was no further contact after that year. The official reason given, years later, was that Shaw had become so absorbed in his real estate properties in the French Quarter that he had eased back on international traveling. Shaw's travels to South America and Europe had essentially ended. He made a trip to Cuba in 1957, and another to Puerto Rico in 1958, to assist that commonwealth in establishing an international trade center, and he would later visit Mexico, England, France, and Spain after his retirement. However, his international traveling days in the service of the Mart, which had begun, to any large degree, in March 1949, were essentially over after July 1955. According to the CIA's official records, Shaw's information generated eight reports from late 1948 through 1956. Only six of those reports had survived as of his arrest in March 1967, however.

**Shaw with unidentified businessmen, probably late 1950s (International Trade Mart Collection, Louisiana Research Collection, Tulane University)**

Toward the end of November, Shaw again attended the National Foreign Trade Council Convention in New York City; it was his tenth attendance at that conference in as many years. Jesse Core sent information about Shaw's history to New York newspapers prior to the conference.

A Cuban Panorama was held at the Mart from November 23 to November 24, 1956. The promotion came less than two-and-a-half years before the overthrow of the Cuban government by Fidel Castro in January 1959.

Many small business publications found reason to mention Shaw in their in-house publications. One such publication was *The Grapevine*, a publication of Southern Bell Telephone Company; Shaw was mentioned in an article toward the end of the year.[1020]

Over the years since its opening, the Mart periodically had flag-raising ceremonies on top of the building to celebrate important days for particular countries, such as a birthday of a monarch, the celebration of independence for a particular country, or the birth of a country. During 1956, flag-raising ceremonies to celebrate individual nations' important national days continued to be carried out regularly; in July, Shaw asked Vic Malandro, manager of the cocktail lounge located in the Mart, to provide two bottles of champagne for such an upcoming event.[1021] The Mart files contain photos of a 1956 Philippine flag raising ceremony, with Shaw notably present throughout. However, as the end of 1956 approached, in another sign of cost cutting, it was decided to terminate such ceremonies beginning January 1, 1957, pending a reconsideration of that change at a later date. The decision was not without controversy, however, and in a later memo to Shaw, Jesse Core suggested raising individual country flags on each country's national holiday.[1022]

The newsletter, *Latin American Reports*, ceased operations at the end of 1956. The magazine that replaced it had begun publication earlier in the year. In November, Shaw wrote to William Gaudet about a change in office space for *Latin American Reports*.[1023] One of the employees for Gaudet at *Latin American Reports* was Dinty Warmington-Whiting, who worked as an editor.[1024] Whiting, who had earlier worked for the Department of State's Foreign Service, graduated from Tulane Law School in 1956, and soon moved to Florida to practice law. He would become involved in several fraud schemes during the 1960s, and spent several years in prison.

In mid-December 1956, Jesse Core wrote to Shaw, giving a list of the local news media personalities to whom bottles of whisky should be sent; the Mart made such annual gifts to promote good relations with the press. Among the local television stations, only certain employees at WDSU-TV Channel 6 were named, including on-air personalities Mel Leavitt and Terry Flettrich.[1025]

In late 1956, Shaw heard again from his old French friend, Richard de Ayala of Rheims, France, who ran his family's champagne company. Ayala noted that it had been many years since he had heard from Shaw, although he knew that Jean Seydoux, another representative of the champagne industry from Rheims, had seen Shaw a year or so before on a trip to New Orleans. Ayala asked Shaw, "Should you meet any members of the old Oise Section, convey my best wishes."[1026] Shaw replied early in 1957, addressing Ayala as "Dear Bunny," and indicating that he would place a note mentioning Ayala champagne in the Mart's newsletter. Shaw indicated that he had seen General Charles Thrasher on a trip to Kansas City, Missouri, several weeks before, and that they had "fought the European war over again." Shaw noted that he hoped to be in Europe in the spring, and would try to get to Rheims at that time.[1027]

Tom Maupin, one of the founders of Maupintour, which designed luxury tours to distant parts of the world, had written to Shaw in May of 1956 about proposed trips to Russia.[1028] That was before the Hungarian revolution in the fall of 1956, which blunted interest in traveling to Russia. H. (Hank) Neil Mecasky, Jr., who was partners with Maupin in the travel agency, wrote Shaw again to say that, "Tom and I have decided to go to Hawaii for three weeks," and asked Shaw about joining them there.[1029] Maupin and Mecasky both lived in Lawrence, Kansas, where Maupintour was located.

By the end of 1956, at the age of forty-three, Shaw had reached a nice plateau in his life. He was head of a prominent civic organization, and was quite visible in the news, but not overly so, respected around town in the business community and in the gay community, and very active socially. As he always had, Shaw would accompany various women in need of an escort to certain social functions. Some of these were society women of New Orleans, but others were single women, for instance in the local Latino community that associated with the Mart and International House, or ones whom he knew simply had no significant other to accompany them somewhere. New Orleans attracted many single women who made their way there from small towns and rural areas around the South, looking to establish a career that would give them a certain independence, in a city that would provide them with many social and entertainment options. Most of them worked in clerical and secretarial jobs, but they jealously guarded their independence; many of them either never married, or had unhappy short marriages. Some were just passing through New Orleans, for various reasons. Shaw lent his arm, and little more, to such women in need of a date. There was even a term for a gay man like him: a "walker."

On the gay side of things, which was Shaw's only sexual side, he probably was more active than ever, at least as far as his work life and travel allowed. He had probably never had an exclusive sexual arrangement with any partner, at least for any length of time, and he and Jeff Biddison had broken up several years before. His relatively new friend, William

Formyduval, came and went for varying periods of time, and Shaw had ample opportunity to seek varied types of relationships.

It is by no means certain that Shaw had any kind of sea change in his outlook on sexual activity, or the practices in which he engaged, since his early adulthood, but his growing affluence and stature in the community probably gave him more opportunity than ever for meeting younger partners, spending money on them, and engaging in various activities he had practiced before. It is easy to speculate that with the passing of Theodore Brent and Rudolf Hecht, the two most important founding members of the Mart, who had given Shaw a free hand but looked over his shoulder constantly, that perhaps Shaw was now free to be a little less careful with his private activities. Also, the long period of time from approximately 1954 until the new Mart building would be completed after Shaw's retirement in October 1965, brought Shaw's traveling down to a more manageable state. With rare exceptions, there was no international travel after 1955, the only major trip being the month-long trip to Puerto Rico in early 1958. There were no more lengthy business jaunts to Europe or South America, and Shaw was immersed in the more humdrum activity of managing a fully-occupied building that badly needed to expand, but had no concrete plan or location to do so.

When Shaw was arrested in March 1967, the district attorney's men who searched his residence found whips, pieces of leather, and a dark hood and gown. The list of items seized was published in the local newspapers, and there was an ominous sound to it that soon had New Orleans buzzing. Many thought it was much ado about nothing. Shaw would indicate that the items seized were part of Mardi Gras costumes he had used for several years before his arrest. Even to this day, there are debates, both inside and outside the gay community, about whether Shaw engaged in sadism and masochism role-playing, as was whispered about at the time.

An incident that occurred during the author's research illustrates this conflict of opinion regarding Shaw's sexual proclivities. While at dinner one night with two men who had been friends for more half a century, both of whom had known Shaw very well, the author broached the subject of the alleged S&M. One of the men quickly dismissed it, saying he didn't think Shaw had ever engaged in it. He had not even finished his answer, however, when the other man turned to him and nodded, indicating that yes, Shaw had indeed been involved in those activities. Some of the people who knew Shaw have found it embarrassing to talk about the subject; others have dismissed it as embarrassing to the gay community, a type of disparaging talk reflecting that straight people assumed all gay people engaged in such things. Still others, however, have wished that there could have been a more frank discussion of the subject, even at the time of Shaw's arrest—at least partly to make the point that there was no natural connection between such activity and an actual violent crime like, for instance, the assassination of President Kennedy.

Along with Shaw's S&M, a legend arose over the years that Shaw only had one nipple. That unusual allegation was captured in a memo that resulted from District Attorney Jim Garrison's investigation of Shaw, and was based at least partly upon what one or more acquaintances of Shaw told the officials. The author was skeptical of this at first, but over a period of years of interviewing individuals who had known Shaw intimately, a number volunteered, without any prompting, that Shaw indeed had a missing nipple. None of the individuals knew exactly why the nipple was missing, or how it had been removed. One man commented that it looked as if it had not been surgically removed in a safe manner, leading one to speculate that perhaps it had been torn off during an S&M session.

Indeed, several individuals related that in their physical involvement with Shaw, he showed a more than casual interest in having his nipples subjected to what many would find extremely painful attention. Several of the individuals were asked to bite Shaw's nipples as hard as they could, and seemingly no amount of pressure was too much for him.

Some of the individuals who were asked, unexpectedly, to participate in Shaw's requests were repelled by them. Nipple-biting or pinching was one thing. However, others were asked to do things that many might find as or more bizarre. For example, Shaw asked some individuals to beat him severely with a belt or a whip. He asked others to defecate or urinate on him. The man who gave the most detailed account of his sadomasochistic experiences with Shaw was, when the author met him, a mild-mannered man in his mid-80s. The man had been married and divorced as a young man, but had gradually realized his homosexuality, and was visiting New Orleans once when he stopped in at Pat O'Brien's, the famous bar in the French Quarter. Shaw was there as well, as he often was; it was a favorite place of his for meeting out-of-towners. Shaw and the man struck up a conversation, and within half an hour, the man was over at Shaw's apartment, ready for a sexual encounter. Quickly, the episode turned in a sadomasochistic direction, as Shaw asked the man to beat him with great force. Later, Shaw would ask the man to relieve himself on him, while Shaw lay in a shallow area of his swimming pool. More than half a century later, the man chuckled with amusement when he recalled how ironic it was that Shaw had expected him to be a "sadist."

Despite his reservations about participating in such activities, the man and Shaw became somewhat good friends, as far as sexual play was concerned, and over a period of time he was able to witness Shaw acting the role of sadist as well. Another young man would sometimes come to see Shaw when the first man was there, a person the first man described as the most extreme masochist he had ever seen. Shaw would adopt an authoritarian military bearing, and order the young man about with severe domineering tones of voice, forbidding him to enter or leave a room without permission, and directing him to subject himself to tremendous amounts of pain. Shaw would sometimes beat him until it seemed he could take no more. He would burn the young man with cigarettes, and subject him to many of the same procedures that Shaw himself had undergone. Once, the second young man showed up at the first man's doorstep, by himself, needing a room for the night to recover after a session with Shaw. The first man helped him to remove his clothing, and settled him into a bed for the night, as he obviously could not go to his parents' home, where he lived, in such condition. The young man was beaten "black and blue," and the first man could have believed he wouldn't even survive the night, had he not witnessed such an aftermath before.

It should be noted that, however bizarre such practices seem to many, perhaps most, they are generally completely voluntary activities on the part of all participants. There is certainly no indication that Shaw ever forced anyone to do something they didn't want to do in such an intimate situation. Such practices occur to some degree in the heterosexual community as well, and there are both male and female providers of such services, who offer them for monetary compensation, in every major city in the country.

Writer Gore Vidal knew Shaw during this period. "Shaw's party world was built around visiting celebrities—Somehow I came into his orbit."[1030] Vidal said that he met Shaw "a number of times in the 1950s when he was living with a strung out Marine and giving parties for visiting firemen like myself—highly correct parties, let me quickly say—I knew nothing of his alleged S/M side."[1031]

Don Schueler recalls attending a small party at Shaw's residence along with Vidal and Shaw's friend William Formyduval. At one point, Formyduval passed out from drinking, next to Vidal, and Vidal reacted, "Well, Clay, why don't you just put a bell jar over him and preserve him the way he is?" Schueler also recalls Shaw intervening in a political argument between Schueler and Vidal by saying, "All I believe in is beauty and ecstasy." Schueler remembered Shaw years later for that remark, placing him in the category of an un-fanatical person only mildly interested in politics or political theory—"a hedonist in a nice sort of way," "a sensualist."[1032]

# 15 · Shaw Returns to Cuba

The new year began with Shaw taking a short trip to Havana, Cuba.[1033] Meanwhile, the Mart was arguably beginning its most frustrating period of seeking both a new building and a possible merger with International House, a campaign that ultimately would not end well.

With his recent experience at actually managing International House, in addition to the issue of making a joint effort to obtain a new building and possibly combine the two organizations, Shaw continued to attend the Executive Committee meetings there. At one such meeting in early January 1957, it was discussed that Henry Kaiser, of the Kaiser Aluminum Company, had proposed an aluminum roof for the new combined building that would house the Mart and International House. A discussion was held of a recent trade mission to Europe; the mission would have included Russia in its itinerary, but with the recent suppression of a democratic movement in Hungary by the Russians, Russia was eliminated, causing many expected participants to drop out of the trip entirely.[1034]

William Zetzmann commented that he had never seen two people work more harmoniously together than Shaw and Charles Nutter.[1035] Shaw had moved seamlessly into the management position at International House during Nutter's absence, then turned it back to Nutter months later as if he had never left.

At an International House Executive Committee meeting in late January, the news of the death of S.V. (Sam) Massimini of Gulf Engineering Company was noted. Discussion was held of a new Theodore Brent Award, which would be given annually to recognize leaders in Latin America who had rendered service in social, economic, cultural, political or educational fields. Opposition to the proposed building site at Canal and Basin Streets was also discussed. Export managers had opposed the plan, which called for the building to be built on stilts, for several blocks in length, over the neutral ground near those two streets. Many felt that design would detract from the image of the two institutions, and by extension the international trade community in general.[1036] Perhaps most significantly, the New Orleans City Planning Commission opposed the newly proposed Basin Street location for a new Mart building, as it had opposed the Civic Center site two years earlier. Much of the opposition had to do with the issue of competition among buildings for upscale tenants; a brand new building housing the two esteemed civic organizations could be a formidable competitor.

Joseph Rault, Sr., President of International House that year, advised the Boards of Directors of both organizations that considerable public opposition had also developed to the use of the Basin Street site, and that various options for a new site were being discussed.[1037] At a meeting of the Mart's Contributors and Debenture Holders in mid-March, it was mentioned that the Mart was even considering buying back its building and simply adding floors.[1038]

At the same time, another proposed location at the foot of Canal Street at Eads Plaza also was getting some negative attention. A group of local attorneys indicated that no building could ever be built upon that spot, due to prior legal agreements.[1039] The possibility of finding an agreeable location seemed dim.

William Zetzmann's annual report for 1956 announced that the Mart had been 98.4% occupied that year.[1040] That good news, however, was somewhat overshadowed by the continuing pressure on rental rates and increased operating expenses, which kept a limit on net income.

Shaw still met with visiting groups at the Mart. In February, he received a handwritten letter from Jimmie Fitzpatrick, from the small town of Jonesboro, Louisiana, and State Vice President of the Louisiana Association of Future Farmers of America. The letter thanked Shaw for meeting with the group, and said that, "Of all the men we met in New Orleans, you were the one who was most admired and talked of—not one officer who did not talk of your fine manner, tact and poise."[1041]

Now that Shaw was back to Mart duties alone, instead of managing International House as well, his salary had reverted to its original level. However, in mid-March he received a $3,000 annual raise.[1042]

It was more necessary than ever for the Mart to expand its size, as its direct competition was growing steadily. Shaw advised Zetzmann that a letter had recently been sent to all tenants, soliciting them for a new eight-story International Center in Mobile, Alabama. Shaw commented that this was "further evidence that our leadership is being challenged seriously, and that we must extend our facilities to maintain our pre-eminent position."[1043]

Zetzmann, in a report to the Board of Directors in mid-March, summed up the long process of trying to get into a larger building. He pointed out how Rudolf Hecht had died before the City of New Orleans could buy the land that would serve as a location for the new building, and that International House had opposed the Basin Street location. On a more positive note, he indicated that a surplus of income over expenses of $25,000 was expected for the full year 1957.[1044]

At an Executive Committee meeting shortly before Zetzmann issued his report, another potential site for the new building was discussed. The location was at the corner of Perdido and Carondelet Streets, and could be optioned for $10,000. However, Lloyd Cobb vigorously opposed the site, partly because the word "perdido" meant "lost" in Spanish, and partly because the area around that site was "blighted." Cobb was also opposed to how the commitment by International House to build a new building, and join together, had been obtained, so he voted against the measure proposing the site.[1045]

A week later, a meeting of the full Board of Directors of the Mart was held, and it was discussed that it was necessary to extend the Mart's lease on its current building through October 10, 1959, as the original lease agreement with the new owners was expiring. The Mart was willing to put up $5,000 for a one-year option on the purchase of property for a new location, if a suitable property could be found. Board member Durel Black mentioned a complex he was building at the foot of Canal Street. He indicated that it would have a cultural center, a music shell, and possibly an auditorium and art museum. He encouraged both organizations to move there, if they could agree on it.[1046]

At a joint meeting of the Executive Committees of both organizations in early April, it was discussed frankly that there had been no real progress on a new building. Officials at the Mart were the main proponents of finding or building a new building, and combining with International House; resistance to that from the International House side had begun relatively early. Since its opening, members of International House had become used to its location, particularly patrons at its restaurant, which was highly regarded by many in the business community. International House could be financed by revenues from its restaurant and other social activities, and had less of a direct need for expansion. The idea of combining with the Mart, and moving to a new location away from the Central Business District, was not appealing to many International House members. The resistance was heightened by the fact that although the organizations had begun with more or less joint leadership, over time International House had developed its own set of members, some of whom had very little interest in the work of the International Trade Mart. Still, International House was very interested in at least remodeling its building, and many members there were still open to the idea of a merger.

Meanwhile, the Mart continued its cooperation on various civic events. The Associated

Press Managing Editors' Association was to meet in New Orleans in November of 1957, for the first time since 1937.[1047] Shaw replied to local editor George Healy that the Mart would do its share of entertainment for the gathering.[1048]

Shaw purchased a property at 923 Burgundy Street on April 1, 1957 for $34,009, and subsequently sold it on April 1, 1960 for $38,000. Shaw's actual profit on the sale of individual properties was sometimes relatively small, but he was often able to deduct many types of expenses against such profit. Rental property operations were not as tightly monitored by the taxing authorities in those days as they became in the 1980s, and owners had wider latitude in writing off various kinds of costs against revenues. Another factor was that Shaw usually lived in the properties as he refurbished them, so that his own living expenses were, at least to a degree, captured in the total costs of owning the property.

In 1957, an issue that would come up in some of the memos generated during Jim Garrison's investigation into President Kennedy's assassination, a decade later, had its beginnings. An article in the *Times-Picayune* of April 2, 1957, discussed a new venture by the Freeport Sulphur Company: a new nickel and cobalt processing plant in Braithwaite, Louisiana. The new venture would involve shipping ore from Moa Bay, Cuba to the Braithwaite facility, where it would be turned into liquid sulphur, which then would be transported back to the Moa Bay facility concentrating plant. Production was to begin in the summer of 1959, and the venture would mean that Louisiana would be the largest nickel producing state in the country, and its cobalt output would be the largest in the Western Hemisphere. The plant would increase nickel production in the United States fourfold, and cobalt production would double.

The mines in Moa Bay were on Cuba's northeast coast; the initial processing would take place at the plant there. Cuban American Nickel Company, a subsidiary of Freeport Sulphur Company, would operate the refinery. It was estimated that the company could sell seventy percent of the product to private consumers, and also could contract to sell large amounts to the United States government. Freeport Sulphur Company, at the time, was the second largest sulphur producer in the country. Canada, at the time, produced about 80% of the free-world's nickel.

Charles Nutter wrote to E.D. Wingfield, Vice President of Freeport Sulphur, congratulating him on the new plant; Nutter mentioned that the project had been discussed at an Executive Committee meeting at International House, and the committee had decided it would like to hold a dinner and reception for company officials gathered in the area for the project.[1049] The project was ultimately aborted, however, by the takeover of Cuba's government by Fidel Castro in January 1959, and the company's plans never came to fruition.

During Jim Garrison's investigation, a man by the name of James Plaine told investigators that Shaw was a part-owner in the nickel mine, creating a side issue that some writers mention to this day, often linking Shaw to earlier alleged hijinks of the Freeport Sulphur Company. However, there is no evidence that Shaw had anything to do with any aspect of the project, including the nickel mine. Certainly, no evidence of ownership appears in his financial or tax records.

In mid-April 1957, the *Times-Picayune* reported that seven cartoonists were going to be demonstrating their talents at the Roosevelt hotel. Among the artists were Al Capp, who produced the *Li'l Abner* comic strip, and Walt Kelly, who produced the *Pogo* strip. Jesse Core asked Shaw if he wanted to attend the gathering, and Shaw jotted a handwritten note on the article that he would attend if he was in town.[1050]

In April 1957, Joseph M. Rault sent a letter to William Zetzmann discussing the possible merger between International House and the Mart. One of the suggestions was that Charles Nutter could remain as Managing Director of the combined organization, and that Shaw could serve as head of a revitalized World Trade Development Committee; Rault suggested that $25,000 to $50,000 in payroll expenses could be saved by a merger.[1051]

At an Executive Committee meeting of the two organizations in mid-June, Joseph Rault opposed any kind of deal for a site that did not include a two-year option during which both parties could make their final decisions. William Zetzmann, on the other hand, said that insisting on a two-year option would make any such deal impossible for any site currently available. The question then arose as to whether the Mart would move forward on its own with a particular site, if the decision was one that had to be made immediately. Rault indicated that International House may not go along with any such deal, if the Mart acted in a unilateral fashion.[1052]

At another joint Executive Committee meeting a few days later, the lack of progress on the new building was discussed. A two-year option was needed to study any site thoroughly, and to work out the funding for a new building. However, International House did not want to agree to a merger without first agreeing to a particular site. Sites were available at the time, but any deal for them would have to be done immediately. Lloyd Cobb indicated that the potential merger of the two organizations was at a standstill.[1053]

International House was having its own revenue problems at the time, although not as critical as those at the Mart. Bar and restaurant business was down somewhat in late 1956 and early 1957, due to a general economic downturn, which may have contributed to some of its resistance to moving forward with the expansion.

In the midst of the efforts to combine the two organizations and find a new building, the Mart business continued in a relatively normal fashion during these fully occupied years. Shaw responded to Pierre Clemenceau, consul of Haiti in New Orleans, mentioning their recent lunch to discuss an office in the Mart to promote Haitian tourism, noting that the Italian Tourist Bureau had been in the Mart for about two years at that point, and discussing the size and possible cost of an office for Haiti.[1054]

Shaw also found time to meet with visiting businessmen. In June 1957, he met with a group that included Peter Simpson Stovall, Vice-President of Hollandale Seed and Delinting of Hollandale, Mississippi. Stovall followed up with a letter, thanking Shaw for his courtesy during that visit, and regretting that Shaw had been unable to join him for lunch.[1055]

Shaw still responded to his share of routine inquiries to the Mart. One involved a brief reply to men in Wisconsin who had inquired about starting a veterinary practice in Venezuela.[1056] In another response, Shaw explained to an inquirer that the International Trade Mart was rather like the Chicago Merchandise Mart, except that it was much smaller, and dedicated primarily to export-import commodities.[1057] Still another inquiry involved the exportation of wet salted Louisiana alligator skins.[1058]

Another inquiry Shaw received had to do with the potential for foreign beer sales in the United States; the writer was General Manager of a large Latin America brewer, Cerveceria y Malteria Paysandu of Uruguay. Shaw replied that there was to date only a small market for imported beers in the United States. Most of those were European beers in limited quantities, and among Latin American beers, only Carta Blanca, made in Monterrey, Mexico, had penetrated the southern United States.[1059]

While Shaw continued to reply to a number of inquiries, and while he usually provided the most helpful response of the entire staff at the Mart, even some of his helpful attitude had worn off as the years progressed, as shown in his response to a letter from Richard R. Daniels of the School of Public Health at the University of California. Daniels had written complaining of the treatment he and his wife had received in the German exhibit, in the Cozart shop in the Mart, and by the receptionist in the lobby. Shaw replied that he had spoken with the receptionist about the matter, but said that the two other entities were tenants of the Mart, and that not much could be done about Daniels's complaint.[1060]

During the first half of 1957, Shaw's cousin Clay Atkins became involved in a theft from his employer, Texan Publishing Company in Bellaire, Texas. The theft resulted from Atkins authorizing additional payroll to himself that had not been approved by the owners of the business. In order for Atkins to avoid prosecution, Shaw reimbursed the amount at issue in early July 1957.[1061]

Clay Atkins was married to Tulip Atkins. The two would eventually divorce, and Tulip Atkins would, to some degree, pursue Shaw romantically; while friendly to her, Shaw obviously did not reciprocate fully. Tulip Atkins sometimes came to visit Shaw in New Orleans with Shaw's mother, Alice. She would receive an individual bequest from him in his will.

Shaw was still on the Board of Directors of the Foreign Policy Association of New Orleans, but Robert D. Hess was the new Program Chairman. Shaw served on the program committee, along with prominent attorneys Eberhard Deutsch and John Minor Wisdom.[1062] In this capacity, Shaw continued to deal with familiar names; he spoke before the Kaffeeklatsch Committee, at the initiation of Mrs. Hamilton Polk Jones, in late August.[1063] He also maintained his interaction with Robert Keedick of the Lee Keedick agency in New York, Shaw's old employer from 1939 to 1942. The Lee Keedick stationary indicated that 1957 was the 50th anniversary of the agency.[1064] Shaw advised Keedick that he was no longer Program Chairman, but indicated that he had been delighted to learn that Dr. Catherine Gavin, the noted British historical novelist, would lecture for Keedick's agency.[1065]

John F. (Jack) Crawford, formerly with *VISION* magazine in Atlanta, was now with *The New Yorker* in Atlanta. He wrote Shaw, seeking membership lists of the New Orleans Country Club, and the Metairie (Louisiana) Country Club, saying he had been told the lists were very good for seeking business.[1066] Shaw replied that he knew a few people who moved in those "exalted circles," but that the lists were unobtainable, that security for those organizations was "only slightly less elaborate" than for the British Crown Jewels in the Tower of London.[1067]

Shaw's friend Miller Cragon, the Episcopalian clergyman, visited New Orleans in June 1957. He called for Shaw when Shaw was out, and Shaw responded with a telegram to him in care of Dr. Hugh English, asking if Cragon could come for dinner on Thursday at 716 St. Phillips Street; Shaw advised Cragon that he could bring English along as well.[1068]

Marcel Gomez was still working under Mario Bermúdez with the Department of International Relations for the City of New Orleans; he sometimes showed groups around the Mart as well. In July, Norwood Jatho, Sr. with the U.S. Department of Labor wrote to Shaw, complimenting Gomez for taking trainees in his department around the Mart and International House. He said that, "When you call on Mr. Gomez, he makes you feel like you were doing him a favor to ask a favor of him."[1069]

Lloyd Cobb invited Shaw to attend a visiting group of Brazilian cattlemen and ranchers at his Marydale Farm in St. Francisville, Louisiana, indicating that "Mireille and I would be delighted if you could join us."[1070] Shaw accepted the initiation, and would visit Cobb's farm occasionally over the next few years. At his trial in 1969, Shaw's visits to the farm would become an issue related to a supposed sighting of Shaw in the small town of Clinton, Louisiana, to the east of St. Francisville.

Shaw gave a variety of speeches during 1957. Early in the year, he addressed the Rotary Club of Columbia, Mississippi, and later in the month, he spoke in Havana, Cuba.[1071] In February, he addressed the Unitarian Church Adult Forum Committee, the Ladies Town Club of New Orleans, and the Sales Division of Western Union Telegraph Company in New Orleans. In March, he spoke to the Century Club of Coral Gables, Florida, to the Junior League of New Orleans, and to the Arkansas Basin Development Association in Tulsa, Oklahoma, where his speech received front-page coverage in the *Tulsa Tribune*.

In one instance of a speaking engagement that came with some controversy, Shaw addressed the Young Men's Business Association in Little Rock, Arkansas. Some members of the audience differed with him on the tariff issue, and about international trade in general; some of the railroad industry representatives in the audience did not care for Shaw's praise of river traffic as a means of moving goods.

In April, Shaw spoke to the Altrusa Club of New Orleans. In May, he spoke to the freshman and sophomore classes of the School of Business at Tulane University, and at the Rotary Club of Lake Charles, Louisiana, where he enjoyed a tour of the Port and a local rock crushing plant. In June, he spoke to the Claiborne Couples Club, and in July he spoke to the Orleans Club on "The Crisis in World Trade."

October was a busy month, with speaking engagements to the student body of Benjamin Franklin High School, and to the Institute of Oriental Relations. Also in October, he was invited to speak at a National Advisory Council dinner by Reginald C. Reindorp, Director of the Institute of Latin American Studies at Mississippi Southern College in Hattiesburg, Mississippi.[1072] He also spoke to the Optimist Club of New Orleans.

He gave a speech on "The Crisis in International Trade" in late October to a luncheon at the accounting firm of Peat, Marwick. After the speech, H.J. Williams, who had invited Shaw to give the talk, wrote to William Zetzmann that Shaw's performance had been highly complimented by members of the group, and that it was the "outstanding event of the meeting."[1073]

Also during October, Shaw spoke to a very large group at the National Convention of the American Institute of Certified Public Accountants (AICPA). Alvin H. Jennings, President of the group, wrote thanking Shaw for his speech and saying, "Your talk was one of the highlights of the meeting."[1074] Shaw also received a letter from Merle S. Wick of the New York Stock Exchange, who referenced this same speech and enclosed a book about the Exchange.[1075] The event, held in New Orleans, was the 70th annual meeting of the group.

In mid-November, Shaw spoke to the Durham Sales Executives Club in Durham, North Carolina, on "What Foreign Trade Means to the Executive," at the Hope Valley Country Club. Shaw had gone to Greensboro, North Carolina, and a friend had then driven him on to Durham. After he returned to New Orleans, he received a letter from J. Frank Jarman, President of the group, indicating that many people had been complimentary of Shaw for his speech. Jarman added that, "You are a wonderful and genial person."[1076] Shaw replied later in the month, thanking Jarman for his kind comments, and for Jarman's enclosure of cartons of cigarettes made in Durham, North Carolina, such as the Coupon, Picayune, Home Run, and One Eleven brands. Shaw said the cigarettes brought back memories of his adolescence, when he used to sneak into the wash shed to try one or the other brand in his efforts to become a cigarette smoker. He added that the next time he was in Durham he would smoke a brand "made in your lovely city—probably Pall Malls."[1077]

Shaw continued to interact with a variety of local and national businessmen and media figures. In April, E. Newton Wray, President of KTBS-TV in Shreveport, Louisiana, wrote to Shaw about the new television Channel 12 in New Orleans, and asked to meet with Shaw to discuss the new operation.[1078] Shaw also wrote a letter of introduction on behalf of Paul Martin, the husband of Shaw's friend Ella Brennan, of Brennan's restaurant, to the Minister of National Economy in Mexico, Gilbert Loyo; the letter described Martin as an "outstanding businessman in New Orleans."[1079]

Shaw heard from Monte Lemann of the Monroe and Lemann law firm, who asked about foreign firms that might be interested in donating to a fund for International Legal Studies.[1080] Shaw suggested several possibilities, listing both tenants of the Mart and some outside of the Mart structure, including shipping companies and coffee importers.[1081]

William N. Owen, Jr. of the *Journal of Commerce* in New York City spoke to Shaw about a proposed international edition of the magazine. He followed up with a letter, indicating that he would see Shaw in New York City in December upon Owen's return from Europe, and that Shaw could reach him in London during the next three months.[1082]

Some potential tenants that the Mart had sought years earlier were finally taking space. George Boggs, with KLM Airlines, wrote to J.B. Dauenhauer from Paris, indicating that he had finally received approval to take office space in the Mart, and that he would sign the lease upon his return to the United States.[1083]

Shaw continued to market foreign governments as potential tenants. He wrote to H.R.P. Katzenberg, Undersecretary of the Department of Commerce and Industry for Pretoria of the Union of South Africa, suggesting that the government open a trade promotion office in the Mart.[1084]

Shaw still interacted regularly with his friend and former tenant, George Haverstick, now with the Free Trade Zone of the Board of Commissioners of the Port of New Orleans. Haverstick passed along a letter to him from Acme Carriers, Inc., referencing a recent luncheon that Shaw and Haverstick had with its representatives. Haverstick wrote his own note to Shaw on the letter, "Clay—Many thanks for your company at lunch with these prospects— Let's hope that all that glitters is gold."[1085]

Clem Bernard, owner of the Clem I. Bernard Company, a printing concern he had begun some years earlier, passed away suddenly in November 1957; his son, Frank Bernard, took over the business.[1086] Clem Bernard had been active years before in the controversy over the Czechoslovakia exhibit at the Mart, while he had been the Young Men's Business Club's representative to the Mart.

J.B. Dauenhauer continued his strict policies with regard to hourly personnel. In a memo to building superintendent Hollis Bridges, he indicated that if maids were discovered eating in offices, they should be fired on the spot.[1087]

The Mart still felt the tension of labor relations with its hourly employees. After a union demand for higher wages toward the end of the year, the Executive Committee decided to hire Gulf Janitorial, Inc. to clean the building, and to lay off its own cleaning-related employees.[1088]

Over the years, Dauenhauer had tended to shy away from attending Mart-related events, preferring to keep a low profile. However, he accepted an invitation to a reception preview of an exhibit entitled "Contemporary Japan" at the Roosevelt hotel. Dauenhauer's note to Goldie Moore, written on the invitation, said, "Please call and accept for me and Edgar."[1089]

Japan held its major exhibit in the Mart in 1957, and in other cities, such as San Francisco and Denver. The show promoted Japan's various consumer products, which were quickly becoming a fixture in the American landscape, and shared information about aspects of Japanese culture not seen before by most Americans. The exhibit drew a lot of publicity, and was considered a success, and an indication of Japan's growing importance in the field of international commerce.

Officials at the Mart were cold, however, to the idea of holding an exhibit for the Soviet Union. Robert Brown of Delta Motor Line had written to Shaw in June, asking Shaw to visit with him about having a temporary exhibit for the Communist powerhouse. Brown indicated that one was going to be held at the Centennial Exposition in Oklahoma City for six weeks, and that the exhibit would pass through New Orleans on its way back to the Soviet Union.[1090] Shaw replied that he would discuss it with the Executive Committee, but feared it might generate unfavorable publicity. He added that since the Hungarian revolt the year before, anti-Russian feelings had been increasing, and he worried that public reaction might be unfavorable.

Maintaining the close relationship that often existed between the Mart and other local civic organizations, Shaw had a hand in helping to elect the up-and-coming William G. Helis, Jr., as President of Greater New Orleans, Inc. The group was responsible for promoting all types of business development in the city. Helis, whose name would appear years later in an unconventional FBI memo related to Shaw following Shaw's arrest, wrote a letter thanking Shaw for his efforts.[1091]

Meanwhile, problems were developing for a long-standing political friend of Shaw, Chep Morrison, the mayor of New Orleans who served almost four complete terms from 1946 until 1961. Although he had been elected as a reform candidate in 1946, pledging to clean up corruption that had flourished under the ten-year administration of Mayor Robert Maestri, his immediate predecessor, Morrison's administrations never completely escaped the banner of corruption themselves. During the 1950s, this situation reached somewhat of a fever pitch in New Orleans, and continued for several years and through several different episodes. In 1957, Morrison went on television to discuss the "police situation," and the battle against graft and corruption that he had framed for his administrations. The morning after his speech, he sent a copy of it to Shaw (and presumably to others, as well).[1092] The Young Men's Business Club passed a resolution on the current police scandals, opposing the mayor on several points.

Several years earlier, in the midst of another episode of the police scandals, Morrison had been forced to accept outside assistance, in the form of a former FBI agent named Guy Banister, who was made an assistant police chief. The earlier police scandals also had brought to town a man by the name of Aaron Kohn, who helped to investigate the 1953-54 round of corruption charges, and soon thereafter formed an organization known as the Metropolitan Crime Commission. Banister and Kohn later would be important figures in New Orleans-oriented theories and episodes related to the Kennedy assassination, although they played vastly different roles.

The Mart had often received inquiries over the years from individuals interested in entering the import-export business. Shaw usually gave very general advice on the subject, although sometimes he worked up a fairly lengthy letter in response. In 1957, in answer to one such inquiry about the import business generally, and in particular about Mellinger Company, which gave a course on exports and imports, Shaw responded that one should have some background information on a business before entering it; he deferred judgment on the Mellinger Course, although he indicated that the company had been in business for quite a while, and should be able to provide references from successful customers.[1093] As with many other types of inquiries during that period, Shaw's response was perhaps more to the point, and less full of helpful details, than it would have been in the early years of operation.

An emerging figure during these years was Captain J.W. Clark, who worked for the Mississippi Shipping Company (Delta Line). In 1957, he also was head of the local Propeller Club. During the 1960s, he would be President of the Mississippi Shipping Company, and during the 1970s, some years after Shaw's departure, he would serve as President of the International Trade Mart as well.

Ross J. Pritchard, director of the Program of International Studies at Southwestern at Memphis (now Rhodes College), wrote Shaw, indicating he would be at the Biloxi, Mississippi Southern Regional Session of the American Assembly, and would like to see both the International Trade Mart and International House.[1094] A scholarship in Theodore Brent's name now exists at Rhodes College, showing a lasting connection between an important influence in the Mart's beginning and this educational institution.

The number of people entering the building, whether for commercial or educational reasons, or just out of curiosity or as tourists, increased again in 1957. During most months, the number of visitors exceeded 20,000, and in May more than 26,000 people visited the Mart. Even though the Mart had reached its peak in occupancy levels, rental rates, and overall income in excess of expenses some years before, in a sense it was just reaching its zenith as a New Orleans institution in the mind of the public.

Thomas (Tommy) Griffin, who wrote the "Lagniappe" column for the *Item*, sometimes allowed guest columnists to substitute for him when he was on vacation. Griffin, a supporter of Shaw's progress at the Mart, had allowed Shaw to write a guest column the year before. In July 1957, Charles Nutter, Shaw's counterpart at International House, took his turn in writing a guest column for Griffin.[1095]

International House, meanwhile, was hitting its peak in the mid-to-late 1950s as well.

As mentioned earlier, however, unlike the Mart, it was not totally dependent upon building expansion for an increase in revenues and profit. During the ten months that ended October 31, 1957, total income, including specifically the portion related to income from dues-paying members, was up from 1956. The restaurant also was once again doing well, as the recession had ended earlier in the year. Gross restaurant sales were approximately $257,000, gross rental income was approximately $118,000, and gross dues income was approximately $210,000. At an Executive Committee meeting of International House at the time, it was noted that the building was more than 100% occupied; even the attic was rented.[1096]

The individual members of International House often had little connection with the Mart. Although joint meetings of the Boards of Directors and the Executive Committees of the two organizations had been held to discuss the possibilities of combining into a new building, and moving to a new location, at Executive Committee meetings of International House directors only, often no official discussion was held of the potential merger or move.

With the departure of George Sawicki as Assistant Director of the World Trade Development Department at International House, Shaw was once again loaned to International House to head that department. However, the Mart continued to pay Shaw's full salary.[1097] In fact, William Zetzmann had already advised Joseph Rault, President of International House, that the Mart's Executive Committee preferred that International House not pay any of Shaw's salary to head the department.[1098] Apparently, the growing division between the two organizations over the issues of combining, and moving into a new location, had caused some Mart Executive Committee members to worry about whether Shaw would have divided loyalties if he drew his salary from both organizations.

The question of selecting an architect to design a new building was certain to be a politically sensitive matter. In a letter to the Board of Directors in early September, Zetzmann indicated that a secret ballot had picked two firms to be architects for the new building. Both of those firms were members of the organizations: Benson and Riehl, and Goldstein, Parham and Labouisse.[1099] Rathbone DeBuys, architect for the original Mart building, said that engaging in a competition among architects for the new building would be counterproductive, as it would cause a lot of hard feelings. DeBuys said the Mart should draw an architect by lot. He said that his firm was too small to complete the project, but that he would be willing to serve as a consultant in picking an architect.[1100]

Separate from the issues between the two organizations, the international trade movement in New Orleans was at a plateau, to some degree. This was due partly to competition from other cities, but also to domestic issues, such as the growing tension related to the civil rights movement; that tension would flower more fully during the 1960s. However, things were still happening on the international front. For instance, Roland von Kurnatowski, editor of *Inter-American Information Services* in New Orleans, had recently announced an English-Spanish magazine for New Orleans.[1101]

Although the Mart was fully occupied, a number of rental spaces in the building had always been occupied by what could be termed "sister organizations." For example, the City of New Orleans Department of International Relations had always had an office there. The local Export Manager's Club, and the Mississippi Valley World Trade Council, both had spaces in the Mart. Although originally those spaces had been taken in an attempt to support the Mart during its period of initial operations, with the building fully occupied, such tenants now potentially kept other tenants, including some the Mart specifically would have been interested in securing, from taking out space in the building.

The Mart was looking for ways to spread its expenses to other organizations in order to remain profitable, even if it meant changing its original position. In September 1957, an internal memo declared that Shaw would serve International House as Director of the World Trade Development Department, but now it was noted that International House would pay half of his salary during that tenure.[1102]

The Mart continued to treat Shaw as a prime asset of the institution, dependent to some degree on his reputation. An undated press release about Shaw, clearly in the 1956-57 era, gave an abbreviated biography and indicated, "As a close student of international monetary systems, trade patterns, and tariff restrictions, he has been widely quoted by newspapers, trade journals, and popular magazines."[1103]

The Mart continued to be a place for foreign exhibitions. "Vision of Chile," sponsored by the government of Chile, was held at the Mart for sixty days during the fall of 1957. Chile never became a tenant of the Mart, however.

Shaw helped to sponsor a United Fund drive, collecting money for various charities. In a letter at the end of November, he thanked Aurelie Alost of the Italian Tourist Commission for her efforts on the drive.[1104]

Shaw was again appointed by Mayor Chep Morrison to serve on the United Nations Day Honorary Committee.[1105] When the day arrived, Shaw spoke at the Lawless Memorial Chapel at Dillard University, a historically black college in New Orleans.[1106]

In late October 1957, Shaw advised E. Davis McCutcheon, a Board member who worked for D.H. Holmes Company, that the Mart had taken an option on ground at Carondelet and Perdido streets. Shaw indicated that most of the Board had been in favor of proceeding with that location, but some members doubted the Mart's ability to finance the new building.[1107]

At the end of October, Jesse Core wrote to his friend, Dinty Warmington-Whiting, in Geneva, Florida. Core asked how Whiting's law practice was going, and mentioned a luncheon the two had the year before with Elena Lyons.[1108] Originally from Mexico, Elena Lyons was married to a member of the I.L. Lyons wholesale drugstore supply company family. She was involved in various activities around New Orleans, and Shaw became friendly with her and her daughters. A strikingly attractive woman with a vivacious personality, she was a favorite of any man who encountered her. Jesse Core wrote to Richard Cross of WDSU-TV, mentioning his idea for a Spanish language television show, to be hosted by Lyons; Core indicated that Lyons spoke both English and Spanish perfectly.[1109]

In early November, Core informed Shaw that Robert Kent of the Voice of America wanted to tape an interview with Shaw for November 13th; Core indicated that Walter Hoover of the Chamber of Commerce was involved in the project as well.[1110] Core also communicated with Jill Jackson of WWL-TV regarding the debut of a new local show on that channel.[1111]

At an Executive Committee meeting of International House in mid-December, a major topic of conversation was that Mario Bermúdez had recently suffered a mild heart attack, and would be in the hospital for two weeks, followed by a two-month recovery period, and then a gradual return to work. A pension plan was approved for George Sawicki, who had recently retired from the World Trade Development Department. However, no discussion of a new building was reflected in the minutes.[1112]

As 1957 came to a close, William Zetzmann indicated to employees that they would again be receiving a bonus check in the envelope with their salary check, equal to 2% of salary for each person.[1113] Shaw's total compensation for 1957 was $17,375 (his annual salary had been raised to $18,000 about three months into the year), plus a bonus of $347.50. J.B. Dauenhauer, Shaw's assistant director, had a salary of $7,000 per year. Jesse Core, the Public Relations Director, also had a $7,000 salary. Goldie Moore, the main secretary of the organization, was paid a salary of $4,200 per year; everyone else in the executive offices was paid much less. Audrey Copping, an employee since the 1940s, was no longer employed at the Mart, having left at the end of April.[1114]

# 16 · An Architect is Selected

The 13th Annual Mississippi Valley World Trade Conference was held in late January 1958, with the usual participation by the Mart and other trade-related civic groups in the New Orleans area. The conference featured Senator Albert Gore of Tennessee, father of the future vice president under President Clinton, as a luncheon speaker.[1115]

In a report to members of the Executive Committee in February, William Zetzmann said that he hoped to announce plans for the new building around the time of the 10th anniversary celebration of the Mart later in the year. During 1957, the Mart had been 99% occupied, and had grossed approximately $297,000 in rental income, with a surplus of income over expenses of approximately $15,000—well below Zetzmann's original estimate of $25,000, but still respectable.[1116]

At a meeting of the Executive Committee in mid-March, it was discussed that Southern Pacific Railroad had offered two squares of land near where Canal Street, Poydras Street, and Tchoupitoulas Streets bordered. The Mart would have a two-year option to purchase the two squares of land for approximately $240,000. The option for the first year would cost $5,000, and the option for the second year would cost $7,500. If the building was constructed there, a spur railroad track would go to the location to bring in heavy exhibits.[1117]

Shaw was, as usual, busy juggling various commitments and invitations. He had to decline an invitation from Congressman Hale Boggs and his wife to a Mardi Gras party in Washington, because his schedule would not allow it.[1118]

In February 1958, the name of Dr. Mary S. Sherman, an orthopedic surgeon murdered in 1964, around whose death conspiracy theories have formed, including some connecting it with the assassination of President Kennedy, appeared on a membership list for the Foreign Policy Association of New Orleans. Her address was shown as 3101 St. Charles Avenue, the same address where her horribly burned body was found more than six years later. Although Shaw had cut back on his activities in the Foreign Policy Association, it is likely that he knew Dr. Sherman. After Shaw's arrest, District Attorney Jim Garrison would make an effort to find a connection between Shaw and Dr. Sherman's murder, although he never publicly made such an allegation.

By early 1958, the tenant *Latin American Reports* was behind on its rent, and had been for some time. In a letter to William Gaudet, Shaw advised that the magazine owed the Mart almost $1,600, and that a substantial payment would have to be made, or the business would have to vacate the premises; Shaw indicated that the Mart had cooperated as much as possible during the past seven years.[1119] By early May, however, Shaw had worked out an arrangement whereby the magazine was moved to another office, and the Mart had taken out an ad in the publication. The Mart netted the cost of the ad against rent owed to it by *Latin American Reports*.[1120]

In late February 1958, Shaw left for San Juan, Puerto Rico. He spent approximately one month there, helping the Puerto Rican government with plans to develop a Caribbean Trade Mart. He had written to the Puerto Rican representatives in early February, indicating that he would arrive on February 20 and stay approximately one month, possibly renting an apartment while there. Among other things, Shaw assisted in conducting a study/survey about the proposed project.[1121]

As had been the case with prior lengthy trips, Goldie Moore and J.B. Dauenhauer kept

Shaw apprised of events back in New Orleans.[1122] In early March, Dauenhauer wrote to Shaw, mentioning that William Horton had told him that all painting on a residential building Shaw was restoring should be completed soon. Dauenhauer mentioned that "Bill" Formyduval had made a change to Shaw's original plan, and Dauenhauer understood that Edward Wegmann, Shaw's attorney, would write him about it. He also mentioned that Shaw had received an envelope marked "personal" from Melo Maranto.[1123]

A week or so later, Dauenhauer again wrote to Shaw, indicating that "Carol, Edgar, and I went to the house but could not get in, left a card for one of the Negroes to have Horton call me." Dauenhauer went on to say that Edgar had received a letter from Formyduval saying he was coming to New Orleans, and indicated that Formyduval had called "Carol" and Joe "last Sunday," asking them to have Horton call Formyduval in North Carolina. Dauenhauer said that the painting at the house was now completed, and that only the tiles in the kitchen were left to be done. He closed by saying that he was "Sorry you have been too busy to enjoy the weather in Puerto Rico."[1124] The "Carol" and "Joe" referred to Carroll Glynn and Joe St. Cyr, two close friends of Shaw at the time. The two operated The London Shoppe in the French Quarter.

In mid-March 1958, Leon S. Felde wrote to Shaw in San Juan, Puerto Rico, care of Dr. Leo Suslow of the Economic Development Administration there. Felde said that, "I hate to trouble your rest in Puerto Rico," and enclosed some information related to airplane specifications.[1125]

Shaw had flown to San Juan from New Orleans, but he changed his plans and returned to New Orleans on a Waterman Steamship boat, sailing on March 19 and arriving March 24.[1126] After his visit, Shaw prepared a somewhat detailed report related to the feasibility of the Caribbean Trade Mart. He made the visit and prepared the report under a contract with the Puerto Rican government, and received compensation for his services.[1127]

It was the first visit Shaw had made to Puerto Rico in approximately five years. and upon his return, he wrote to Doña Felicia Rincon de Gauthier, City Manager of San Juan, Puerto Rico, indicating that he had noticed many changes in San Juan since his earlier visit.[1128] The trip would be Shaw's last out of the continental United States on behalf of the Mart.

At a meeting of the full Board of Directors in late March, it was noted that, according to the terms of the sale of the building several years earlier. the Mart could remain in the building for a total period of seven years and three months from the date of the original sale, a period that would end in the early 1960s. Lloyd Cobb mentioned that he wanted to relieve International House of any obligation it had toward the Mart in seeking a new building, so that the Mart could decide on the merits of the location around Canal Street and Poydras Street without having to worry about internal International House attitudes.[1129]

In a report to the Board of Directors in late March, William Zetzmann commented on the current state of the Mart, and its results of operations for 1957. Although the Mart had been 99% occupied during 1957, the rental rates had been set ten years before, when the Mart had first opened, and had not increased since that time. Zetzmann said it was not advisable to raise them at the current time, as the Mart was in a somewhat "precarious" position. The main problem was still the need for a larger building to accommodate tenants' needs for larger spaces within the building. He said that Mart officials were looking at an area near the river, where the Southern Pacific Railroad was willing to sell two squares of ground for approximately $240,000. He also noted Shaw's speeches and other activities during the previous year, and the success of the large Japanese exhibit that had been held at the Mart.[1130]

Local and visiting businessmen still considered the Mart worthy of their attention. In April, Shaw was invited by George J. Young, District Sales Manager of Braniff Airways, to have lunch in May with Charles Beard, the president of the airline.[1131]

Around this time, the Mart closed the door on yet another proposed location. In late April, William Zetzmann wrote to Benson and Riehl, Architects in New Orleans, indicating that the proposed site at Carondelet and Perdido streets, which had been considered for a while, was not feasible, and was no longer under consideration.[1132]

Shaw accepted an invitation from Mayor Morrison to be a member of the Honorary Citizens' Committee for the Inauguration of the Mayor and City Council.[1133] May 5, 1958 marked the beginning of Morrison's fourth term as mayor of New Orleans.

In May, Shaw hosted the governor of Oregon, Robert D. Holmes, and his wife, giving them a tour of both International House and the Mart.[1134] Earlier in the month, Shaw had addressed the World Trade Committee of the Jacksonville Chamber of Commerce, in a meeting the group held at the Mart.

At this point, Shaw's travels to Central and South America in the late 1940s and early 1950s must have seemed somewhat of a distant memory to him. In April, he received a letter from Manfred H. Askowitz of Barranquilla, Colombia, who recalled a night in Cartagena years before, when Shaw had been on a trip through Colombia with Mario Bermúdez. Askowitz remembered the rooftop garden of the hotel, with guitars strumming, and palm leaves rustling; Shaw had just finished writing either a novel or a play (Askowitz could not recall which). Askowitz was now looking for work in the U.S. and asked for Shaw's help.[1135] As was typical with such inquiries, Shaw was noncommittal, merely remarking that he did not get to South America as often as he would like.

Still, the Mart kept a toehold in South American activities. The same month, both Shaw and Zetzmann sent telegrams to Alberto Lleras Camargo, upon Camargo assuming the Presidency of Colombia. Shaw indicated his congratulations, and commented that Camargo's ascension marked "a turning point in your country."[1136]

After several years of discussing a new building, and having its plans frustrated by one turn of events or another, and after dangling the project before local architects, Mart officials decided to seek opinions from architects in other parts of the United States. Edward Durell Stone was, at the time, one of the most prominent architects in the country. A native of Arkansas, he was politically well connected through his friendship, since childhood, with U.S. Senator J. William Fulbright, Chairman of the powerful Senate Foreign Relations Committee. Partly through Fulbright's connections, as well as through his own talents, Stone received commissions to design many different governmental buildings and commercial projects. He designed, or participated in designing, Radio City Music Hall in Rockefeller Center in New York City, the Museum of Modern Art in New York City, the Stanford Medical Center in Palo Alto, California, the North Carolina State Legislative building, the Florida State Capitol, and the Museum of Anthropology in Xalapa, Veracruz, Mexico. More recently, he had designed the U.S. Pavilion at Expo 58, a World's Fair held in Brussels, Belgium in 1957.

The exact origins of the relationship between architect Edward Durell Stone, and what eventually became the new Mart building, are somewhat hazy. Years later, in a letter to the *Times-Picayune* in 1986, Jesse Core recalled that Muriel Bultman Francis, who was then operating her own business in New York City, had known Stone firsthand, and had called Shaw during the stalemate over building the new Mart in the mid-1950s, in hopes of pushing the project forward. Shaw and Lloyd Cobb then met with Stone, and the project began to move forward, albeit at a very slow pace, over the next decade.[1137]

In June 1958, William Zetzmann wrote to Paul Hoots, assistant to the President of New Orleans Public Service, Inc., mentioning the new Building Committee related to the proposed new Mart building; Lloyd Cobb would be the Chairman of the committee.[1138] It would be an early step on the long road to finally implementing the plan for a new, larger building.

At a combined Executive Committee and Building Committee meeting in June, Shaw advised the committees that Stone's fee was not to exceed $10,000, if his building plans were not approved.[1139] In mid-September, Stone wrote to Zetzmann, sending his agreement for services related to the proposed building. Stone noted that he had had dinner recently with Lloyd Cobb and Shaw to discuss details, and that it had been decided that a local architect would be found to assist him. The agreement called for a retainer fee of $5,000. Stone's services would be $1,200 per week, which would include two assistants. The monthly cost of technical employees' salaries, plus 200% overhead, would be paid as the project went along.

At a combined meeting of the Executive Committee and the Building Committee of the Mart in late June, an offer of two additional squares of land by the City of New Orleans was discussed; the two squares connected to the existing Dock Board building. It was proposed that those squares could be transferred to the Mart, and that the railroad tracks on that land could then be relocated. It was also discussed that Shaw had recently been in New York City to discuss the building project with the "noted architect" Edward Durell Stone. The Chicago architect Mies van der Rohe also was said to be interested in the project.[1140]

Some time after the arrival of Jesse Core as Public Relations Director, the Mart had begun to use Jean Seidenberg as a photographer. Seidenberg had known David Baldwin, who introduced him to Core. In a letter to Asher B. Shaw of Fiesta del Pacifico, Shaw noted that Seidenberg was a local artist who worked with Mardi Gras balls, and suggested that he could design clown heads for the Fiesta, similar to the work he did for Mardi Gras.[1141]

Shaw had recently served as one of three judges used to select guides for the Brussels World's Fair (Expo) at a contest held in Baton Rouge. Curt Siegelin, Executive Director of the Louisiana Department of Commerce and Industry, wrote thanking Shaw for being a judge at the event, and indicated that Governor Earl Long also thanked Shaw for his efforts.[1142]

Meanwhile, International House officials were still struggling with the same issues of joining with the Mart and moving to a new building. Many members wanted to maintain facilities in the current building, and at an Executive Committee meeting of the organization in November 1958, the discussions went back and forth between the two points of view. It was finally decided to poll the members of the organization, in a non-binding opinion survey.[1143] Beryl Donnath, who worked for Mario Bermúdez at the Department of International Relations, took notes for many of the meetings of the Executive Committee and the Board of Directors of International House during this period, including the documentation of this evaluation.

Many members of International House were still concerned about the dining facilities being moved to a location outside of the Central Business District, where people knew the location and were comfortable with it.[1144] International House continued to struggle with the conflict between its original purpose of promoting international trade, and the popularity of the social activities that had developed around its restaurant and meeting rooms. At a meeting in early August, Mario Bermúdez had warned that New Orleans was quickly losing ground to Miami and Houston on Latin American relations, particularly with Central America. He noted that Miami now had many more direct flights to Central America than did New Orleans.[1145]

International House had long struggled to clarify the purpose of its World Trade Development Department, and to find someone to manage it. The organization asked Shaw to analyze the department and report to the Board of Directors; Shaw had continued to serve as a member of the committee for that department while it was in a state of transition between managers. At a meeting in July, Shaw proposed that the next four meetings of World Trade Development Department officials be devoted to the specific topics of 1) the mission of the Department; 2) the specific programs and projects of the Department; 3) whether the current name accurately reflected the mission; and 4) the staffing of the Department. Shaw, who planned to go to Mexico during the next month, indicated he would be glad to continue working for the World Trade Development Department when he returned.[1146] By November, however, Paul L. Vogel had become the new director of the World Trade Development Department.[1147]

WDSU-TV Channel 6 announced that it was introducing editorial comment into its news programs.[1148] Shaw wrote to Robert D. Swezey, Executive Vice President of the station, saying that he had long felt editorial content should be a function of radio and television news, just as it was with other mass media, such as newspapers and magazines. He added that a "clear-cut, hard hitting" editorial policy could serve the community well.[1149]

The Mart still maintained its policy of requiring that all items on display be for sale on site. In a letter to the Charles Lessing Company in St. Louis, Shaw indicated that there was no point in filling a building with materials "which could only be looked at through a glass window".[1150]

A controversial tie to the past reappeared in 1958. The United States Mercantile Company, Inc. wrote to Shaw asking for a reference on Harry Kahn, who had managed the Czechoslovakian exhibit in the Mart from April 1949 through April 1950.[1151] Shaw replied that the tenant, under Kahn's management, had met its obligations, and had been well-managed. Kahn's activities were still being monitored by the FBI during the late 1950s.

Shaw remained in connection with Carl and Marion Seidenbach in New York City, his old friends from his years there during the late 1930s and early 1940s. He wrote to Marion Seidenbach, wishing her, "Happy Birthday, Darling," and indicated that he planned to be in New York City around December 19, and hoped to see them both at that time. He signed the telegram "Love, Clay."[1152]

Shaw heard again from his old friend, Holland McCombs. McCombs, who was now with *TIME* magazine, indicated he might be back in New Orleans one day soon.[1153] McCombs saw Shaw only irregularly over the years after the opening of the Mart in 1948, but apparently Shaw made a very favorable impression, as he did with many others, as McCombs would rise to Shaw's defense nearly a decade later, at a crucial time in Shaw's post-arrest ordeal.

Antonio (Tony) de Grassi, formerly with *TIME* in the Southeast, was now Pacific Advertising Director of *TIME*, living in Tokyo, Japan. He wrote Shaw, saying, "Hope this finds you busy and settled in a house," or "have you decided to become a nomad?" The references were to Shaw's by now regular habit of living in a property he had purchased, repairing and remodeling it, and then moving on to a different property. De Grassi added that, "I've been thinking of giving you a ring—reversing the charges, of course."[1154]

During International Week, the Mart sought out films about foreign countries for showings to school children in the New Orleans area. Approximately twenty countries assigned films to the Mart. Shaw served as Chairman of the Education Committee for the International Week celebration,[1155] working with, among others, Aurelie Alost, an employee of the Italian Tourist Commission office in the Mart, for films dealing with Italy.[1156]

On his 1955 trip to Mexico with other trade officials, Shaw had met William Spratling, the resident of Taxco, Mexico, who had lived in New Orleans during the 1920s, and who had been friends with writer William Faulkner at that time. In the early 1930s, Spratling had moved to Taxco, and had helped to start a silver jewelry industry there. After meeting him, Shaw had induced him to participate in a trade fair, which involved shipping some of Spratling's silver jewelry to a local shop owner named Marc Antony. For Spratling's visit to New Orleans for the fair, Shaw made reservations for him at the St. Charles Hotel.[1157] The seemingly simple transaction would turn into a several-year minor nightmare for Shaw and Spratling, as they attempted to straighten out the declared valuations for the jewelry with the U.S. Customs Service, in a process that would last into the early 1960s.

In mid-year, Shaw received a letter from Arthur Q. Davis announcing the opening of Orleans Gallery in the French Quarter.[1158] At Shaw's trial in 1969, Davis would be a defense witness for Shaw, related to the issue of whether Shaw had signed a visitor's log at the

Eastern Airlines VIP Lounge at the New Orleans airport, using the mysterious name "Clay Bertrand."

In June, Shaw addressed the Southern School of Banking in Baton Rouge, causing him to miss a banquet in honor of actor James Whitmore, held at the Wild Catter Room at the Roosevelt hotel.[1159] Also in June, Shaw attended a ceremony honoring Hale Boggs with the International Order of Merit, for steering the Reciprocal Trade Bill through the U.S. House of Representatives.[1160] In a telegram of congratulations to Boggs for his efforts, Shaw commented that, "Men of goodwill throughout the world owe you a vote of thanks."[1161]

Jesse Core, as Public Relations Director, also regularly made speeches, and sometimes substituted for Shaw, when Shaw was unavailable. In May, when Shaw was in New York City, Core took his place before the Couples' Club of St. Paul's Episcopal Church, speaking on a panel entitled "World Trade Today." Core specifically addressed the topic, "New Orleans International Trade Mart—10 Successful Years."

Shaw's own speaking schedule was as active as ever. In January, he addressed the New Orleans Chapter of the American Marketing Association, using the topic, "Marketing America's Imports." In March, he addressed the provisional members of the Junior League in a gathering at the Mart, and the Mothers' Club of St. Martin in Metairie, Louisiana. In April, he addressed the Gentilly Rotary Club. In June, in addition to his address before the Southern School of Banking at Louisiana State University in Baton Rouge, Shaw spoke to a convention of Mississippi Exchange Clubs. In July, he spoke to the Executives' Club of Louisiana. In September, he spoke to the Rotary Club of Thibodaux, Louisiana, before the Metairie Women's Club, the Fifth Assembly of the Junior United Nations in a gathering at International House, and before the Optimist Club of New Orleans at the Roosevelt hotel.

Also in September, Shaw spoke to the National Sales Executives Club at the Bayou Desiard Country Club in Monroe, Louisiana. After the speech, George Moses of Gay's Clothing Store in Monroe sent Shaw a pair of slacks in appreciation for the speech, indicating it was one of the best speeches the group had ever heard. Moses requested a copy of the speech, but as usual, Shaw indicated that he had not reduced his thoughts to writing, saying he might do so eventually.[1162]

In October, he spoke at St. Mary's Dominican College; after his speech, Mrs. W.P. (Alma) Deichmann, Program Chairman, said that her own career was assured after Shaw's dynamic speech, but she wondered if she would ever find "another Clay Shaw" for future speeches. Later in the month, he spoke before the Memphis World Trade Club. His old friend Bess Noble, who had arranged the speech, wrote to him afterwards that she was sorry she had been unable to attend, but that she understood Shaw's speech before the group had been the best of all. As usual, Shaw stayed at the old Peabody Hotel in Memphis during the visit.

In November, he spoke at a Boss's Night Banquet of the American Business Women's Association at Commander's Palace Restaurant. In early December, he spoke before the American Association of University Women at its chapter in Hammond, Louisiana. Later in the month, he addressed a group at the Louisiana Beer Wholesalers' Association at the Roosevelt hotel; when accepting that speech, Shaw had indicated that he appreciated the invitation, but noted that his knowledge of the beer business was very limited. Also in December, he addressed the American Society of Refrigerating Engineers, and the American Society of Heating and Air Conditioning Engineers, speaking to the topic, "The Crisis in World Trade—Russia Challenges the West."

Jack Crawford, who had been with *VISION*, the Latin American-oriented magazine, in Atlanta, was now with Blanchard-Nichols-Osborn, an advertising agency, also in Atlanta. Shaw wrote to him, summing up recent problems in the Middle East, comparing the situation there to two rug makers commenting on the prices of rugs at Macy's; Shaw opined that as long as any man's labor anywhere could be bought for $100 per year, no private property was safe anywhere.[1163]

The Mart had finally discontinued its newsletter completely. In its place, it had substituted *The Marketeer*, a more elaborate publication with photos of products sold at the Mart.[1164]

Shaw communicated during 1958 with Clarence K. Streit of Federal Union, Inc. The group, later called the Association to Unite the Democracies, was an organization, founded by Streit, which advocated the political integration of the democracies of Western Europe and other English-speaking countries of that time, including the United States, Canada, Australia, South Africa and New Zealand. In a letter to Shaw in October, Streit recalled Shaw's interest in Streit's "minority views" on Charles de Gaulle, and indicated that Shaw had gotten some play for them in the *Item*.[1165] Earlier in the year, Streit had communicated with other New Orleanians, including attorney Monte Lemann.[1166] A list of Federal Union supporters in New Orleans included Dr. Mary S. Sherman, the orthopedic surgeon.

Jesse Core continued his normal practice of distinguishing between Communist countries and other countries, in response to inquiries from the public. In response to letters in January requesting information about Hungary and Czechoslovakia, Core replied that Hungary, and later Czechoslovakia, "is a Communist slave state beyond our customary area of communications."[1167]

The Mart received its usual number of inquiries of various types during 1958. Shaw responded to M. Kimoto of Kobe, Japan, indicating that there were no importers of pearls in the New Orleans area, although there were some in the Gulf Coast region.[1168] He responded to Carlos A. San Roman, General Manager of Hotel Saxon in Mexico City, giving the history of the Mart, and indicating that only San Francisco currently had a comparable organization.[1169] He also responded to an inquirer seeking pisco, from either Chile or Peru, to use in making pisco sours; Shaw indicated that he had brought back a gallon of pisco for his own use several years before, but that it had gone very quickly, and he had never found a drop of it since.[1170] For his part, J.B. Dauenhauer responded to an inquiry about Japanese rubber boots.[1171]

The number of visitors entering the Mart dropped off noticeably in 1958. In no month was the total number of visitors in excess of 20,000, and most months it ranged between 15,000 and 18,000. After years of being somewhat of a tourist attraction as well as a commercial center, the newness had begun to wear off with the general public.

Shaw assisted Pendleton Lehde, who was attempting to travel to Eastern Europe, with his travel requirements. Lehde was a member of the Board of Directors of both the Mart and International House, and was a past President of the Foreign Policy Association of New Orleans. Shaw wrote to the United States Information Agency (USIA), recommending Lehde for the Agency's People-to-People Program.[1172] Shaw also wrote a letter to the Hungarian Embassy, recommending a visa for Lehde,[1173] and William Zetzmann wrote a letter on Lehde's behalf as well, recommending Lehde be approved for travel to the Eastern Bloc.

The Mart continued to contribute to various functions and organizations, as it had in the past. For instance, in July, William Zetzmann advised Harold Roberts, Finance Chairman of International Week, that the Mart would contribute $2,500 to the celebration in the fall.[1174]

In the second half of 1958, Mart officials were attempting to move forward on the new building. At a meeting of the Building and Executive Committees in late July, the engineering firm of Godat and Heft discussed relocating the railroad tracks on the two squares of land that would be provided by the City of New Orleans.[1175]

At another meeting of the two committees a week later, William Zetzmann introduced architect Edward Durell Stone. Stone's building fee would be 7% to 7.5% percent of the total contract amount. The building, which originally had been estimated at $4,000,000, was now at approximately $7,000.000. Stone would get a minimum fee of three times the drafting cost, not to exceed $10,000, even if the building never materialized. Preliminary costs were estimated at $1,200 per week, and could be stopped at any time. A local architect would be picked by the Board of Directors to work with Stone.[1176]

A draft program for the new International Trade Mart building, authored with heavy input from Lloyd Cobb, envisioned a new building so monumental, so unique, and so distinctive that it would symbolize New Orleans in the same way that the Statue of Liberty symbolized New York, that Sugarloaf Mountain symbolized Rio de Janeiro, and that the Golden Gate Bridge symbolized San Francisco. The draft discussed each of four main elements: 1) Exhibition Hall, 2) Office Block, 3) Garage, and 4) Landscaped Plaza. The exhibition hall would be on the ground floor, with approximately 60,000 square feet of space. The draft was revised to include a restaurant bar on the top floor, similar to the "Top of the Mark" at the Mark Hopkins International Hotel in San Francisco, with an observation platform on the roof. The landscaped plaza would be twenty-four feet up, and the office complex would begin at the landscaped plaza. The draft also envisioned a total tenant population of approximately 1,400, with approximately 1,500 daily visitors.[1177]

As the idea of a possible new Mart building spread among those associated with the organization, a sense of excitement gripped not only top Mart officials, but some of the employees as well. Goldie Moore, Shaw's long-time secretary, had come across a promotional folder entitled, "Trends in the Office." The folder showed a scene in an office at First National Bank in Colorado Springs, Colorado. Moore had inscribed a note next to the photo, and dated it April 7, 1958; the note said, "Showed to Clay—told him this was kind of desk I wanted in New Trade Mart. He told me to keep same and said quote, 'I promise you that's the kind of desk I'll get you.' unquote." The comment was initialed, "GM."[1178]

In approximately June 1958, Shaw was visited by Enrico Mantello, Vice President of Permindex of Basle, Switzerland. The organization was planning to open a major trade building in Rome, Italy to be called Centro Mondiale Commerciale. Mantello indicated that Ferencz Nagy, the last non-Communist Prime Minister of Hungary, was to be president of the new organization. Shaw had come to the organization's attention because of his "unique" experience with "permanent fairs," and because of the similarities between Centro Mondiale Commerciale and the International Trade Mart in New Orleans. On July 26, 1958, Mantello wrote Shaw, asking him to serve on the Board of Directors for the new organization.[1179] Shaw ran the idea by William Zetzmann, President of the Mart, who thought it would be worthwhile, but suggested that the Mart check out the people behind it, to make sure their reputations were good. Shaw asked Ettore Scampiccio of the Italian Trade Commission, which had offices in the Mart, to use his contacts in Italy to determine their credibility and standing. On August 7, 1958, Scampiccio wrote, indicating that the organization's supporters seemed to be of good reputation,[1180] and Shaw accepted a membership on the Board of Directors.[1181]

In early August, in a telegram to Enrico Mantello, Shaw officially accepted membership on the Board of Directors.[1182] Shaw's name was placed on the list of members of the board, and that listing generated several letters of inquiry during the next year. One inquirer, Sue Cardozo, wrote to Shaw about a possible job helping him with the new organization. However, Shaw replied that, although he served on the Board of Directors, he actually knew very little about the organization.[1183] An old friend from earlier years, Ann Wolf Carnahan, wrote to Shaw on April 14, 1959, asking for information about the organization; she indicated that she hoped Shaw was "well—happy—rich."[1184] Shaw replied May 5, indicating that he would be in New York City the following week and could meet her for drinks. He remarked that he was well enough, and reasonably happy, but that riches had "eluded my grasp." He gave his standard answer: that he knew little about the group, but had merely accepted the invitation to serve on its Board of Directors.[1185] In letters to Fred McDermott in September and October 1960, Shaw indicated he was not familiar with the day-to-day operations of the Rome operation, indicating that he had merely lent his name to the Board of Directors.[1186]

That was essentially Shaw's total involvement with Permindex and Centro Mondiale Commerciale. He never attended any of the board meetings. In letters to its officials, Shaw indicated that he was unable to attend the board meetings of July 5, 1960 and March 16, 1961, held in Rome, due to other commitments in New Orleans.[1187]

A few days after Shaw's arrest on March 1, 1967, an Italian newspaper, *Paesa Sera*, broke a story indicating that Shaw, through an organization called Permindex, which ran an institution in Rome called Centro Mondiale Commerciale, was connected to the Central Intelligence Agency. The 1967 story, apparently inspired by Communist suggestions, made its way to New Orleans, and the issue of Shaw's involvement with the Permindex and Centro Mondiale Commericale organizations came to light. Accordingly, his attorneys asked that Shaw have personnel at the Mart check through past files in order to reconstruct his contacts with Permindex from beginning to end. Ironically, the *Paesa Sera* article mentioned nothing of Shaw's actual CIA connection, as a source for its Domestic Contact Division from 1948 to 1956.

In August, Shaw received an invitation from Mayor Chep Morrison to attend the Final Parade and Review at Camp Leroy Johnson.[1188] Morrison, at that time, was a Brigadier General in the U.S. Army Reserve, and conducted the reserve training at the camp. Shaw was among various individuals Morrison invited annually to the event. Morrison also invited Shaw, as he had in past years, to be a member of the Honorary Committee for the Celebration of United Nations Day.[1189]

Shaw had already cut back some of his participation in the Foreign Policy Association of New Orleans, but in 1958 he continued to scale back even further. He wrote to Ruth Anne (Mrs. Stephen) Lichtblaw, declining committee membership on the "Great Decisions–1959" Committee of the Association; Shaw cited as his reason that the new Mart building was going to occupy all of his time.[1190] He also wrote to Gilbert Mellin, the current President of the Association, declining an invitation to serve on the Television Committee of the group.[1191] Shaw had earlier inquired of William Zetzmann whether the Mart should cut off donations to the Foreign Policy Association of New Orleans, in view of the tighter financial situation that had developed.[1192]

A controversy had arisen about the "Great Decisions" program. Herman Deutsch, the moderator, had been replaced by Findley Raymond, whom some suspected of being a Communist sympathizer. Alice Hunt, a local resident, went as far as writing to FBI Director J. Edgar Hoover personally, advising him of the change, and pointing a finger at Raymond; she enclosed a list of the participants on the previous year's panel discussions, which included Shaw.[1193] Although Hoover responded amicably to her letter, which made no direct mention of Shaw, the FBI took no action.

Nevertheless, Shaw continued to follow, and be apprised of, the activities of the Foreign Policy Association of New Orleans. In August, Gilbert Mellin advised him of the previous night's "Great Decisions of 1959" program on WYES-TV, and commented on the effectiveness of the program.[1194]

In September 1958, George Haverstick wrote to Shaw, outlining a plan for a sub-zone of the Foreign Trade Zone, which might be placed in the proposed new Mart building. At the time, Haverstick was Superintendent of Foreign Trade Zone No. 2, which was part of the Port of New Orleans. Haverstick indicated that the sub-zone would need to have a separate entrance and exit, with one customs guard on duty, and that it could use a portion of a floor already in use if the entrances and exits were all grouped together.[1195]

The same month, Shaw announced that George Sawicki, who had been employed with International House for several years, would be the representative for the Mart in London, England. The letter indicated that Sawicki would give periodic and special reports related to his activities there.[1196]

Also in September, Shaw gave a reference for Alberto LeMón. LeMón had taught Shaw

Spanish during the late 1940s, prior to Shaw's travels to Latin America. Shaw had known him both in business as well as personally, and also knew his brothers Augosto and Orlando. The memo indicated that the brothers wanted to bring another brother, Alfredo LeMoń, into the country. Shaw said that he would employ Alfredo once he came to the U.S., although the memo does not indicate the particular capacity in which he would be employed.[1197]

A column by Herman Deutsch in the *States-Item* newspaper (the *Item* had merged with another newspaper, the *States*) mentioned Shaw and Jesse Core introducing William Spratling to Councilman Victor Schiro, who later served two terms as mayor of New Orleans. According to the column, Spratling, after being introduced, had asked Schiro, "And where are you from?"[1198] Spratling had been away from New Orleans for well over two decades at that point, and seemingly had long since lost touch with happenings and personalities in the city.

The Mart was gearing up for its 10th anniversary celebration in the fall of 1958, and officials were deciding whom to invite to the celebration. In a memo to Shaw, Mario Bermúdez suggested that invitees should have the rank of "ambassador or nothing," except that commercial ministers from those countries that had space in the Mart would be acceptable as well.[1199]

A luncheon was held in mid-October to celebrate the anniversary. All prominent local city officials and businessmen in the international trade community were invited. The luncheon was held at the Roosevelt hotel, and Edward Durell Stone was introduced to the crowd as the architect who had been selected to design the new International Trade Mart building.

In early October, William Zetzmann sent a letter to Richard Freeman, President of International House that year. Zetzmann enclosed two pro forma statements of operations—one assuming an additional 75,000 feet, and the other assuming an additional 30,000 feet of space. In the proposal, both organizations would be in the new building, but would continue to function separately. Zetzmann realized that the accessibility of International House's restaurant was very important, and suggested that a restaurant high up, and overlooking the river, could overcome objections from members to a change in location.[1200] At a joint meeting of the Building and Executive Committees of the Mart shortly thereafter, it was discussed that public hearings might be necessary regarding the land swap with the City of New Orleans, and discussions were held concerning how to approach International House about making a definite decision to join forces with the Mart in moving to the new location.[1201]

In mid-October 1958, Jesse Core wrote to the famed writer William Faulkner, mentioning that William Spratling had been in the Mart's offices the previous weekend. Core indicated that Spratling had tried to call Faulkner from the Mart offices, but had been unable to reach him. Core said that Spratling had been interviewed during his visit by Albert Goldstein for the *Times-Picayune*, and that Spratling might be back in New Orleans by the end of October. Core indicated that Spratling's recent visit was only his second one to New Orleans in the past thirty years.[1202] He followed that up with a letter to Spratling at the end of October, mentioning the letter to Faulkner. Core also mentioned the idea of a large silver jewelry exposition in the Mart, and said he hoped that Spratling would be able to return soon.[1203]

In October 1958, Shaw wrote to Congressman Hale Boggs, proposing that the new Mart building be built with materials from various foreign countries. He suggested the project could be financed using counterpart funds generated by the U.S. foreign aid program, and held by the U.S. government. Shaw understood the proposal would need to secure U.S. governmental approval, as well as that of each individual affected nation as well. He indicated that State Department officials with whom he had spoken had said the idea would not work, because some of the foreign aid funds had already been spent, and that other countries, such as Japan, had no counterpart funds.[1204] Shaw would resurrect the idea in the mid-1960s, when construction of the new Mart building was finally underway.

Shaw continued to work on convincing potential tenants to fill the limited space available in the existing building. In November, he wrote to the Arab Information Center in New York City, indicating that he had recently been reading *Arab News and Views*, and had wondered if the organization might want to open a center in the Mart.[1205]

Shaw had begun to work with the new television station WYES-TV, as he had with WDSU-TV in prior years. In November, Shaw agreed to moderate a television panel dealing with free trade, which would appear in early December.[1206] Earlier in the year, Shaw had appeared on a local television show about the United Nations, and on another local show hosted by newspaper columnist Herman Deutsch.[1207]

In a letter to Charles Nutter in late November, Shaw recommended Orlando Garcia and Robert Gardner of Real Airlines to be members of International House; Shaw and J.B. Dauenhauer had sponsored the two men.[1208] In a letter to Richard Freeman in mid-December, Shaw noted the 15th anniversary of International House.[1209] In other news, Hazel H. Fort, the long-time librarian at International House, passed away during this same season.

The Building and Executive Committees of the Mart met again in late November. Discussions were held about how the agreement with Edward Durell Stone was personal to him, and would terminate upon his death. Shaw reported on the status of the swap of land, saying that it rested with the City Planning Commission. The plan was to have an eighty-foot setup left between the site for the new Mart building and the Dock Board building. Shaw indicated that the Mart should try to get Stone started on the preliminary drawings in December, because it would need the drawing from Stone in order to discuss financing with a bank or another financial institution. He said that Stone needed a signed contract, some definite details about the plot of land, and the requirements for the building. The budget for the new building was now approximately $8.5 million.[1210]

In December 1958, Shaw heard from his old friend Muriel Bultman Francis. Shaw was getting ready to take a year-end vacation to New York City, and Francis was working there in her capacity as head of Muriel Francis Associates, a publicity and public relations agency at 116 East 65th Street. Opening the letter with "Dear Clay," she went on to say that, "We made a reservation for you at the Waldorf for a single room and bath" for the period December 19 through December 23, 1958.[1211]

# 17 · An Encounter at the Airport

Shaw was part of many successful civic efforts in New Orleans over the years, but one effort that failed was an early attempt to bring a statue of Joan of Arc to New Orleans during the late 1950s. Several such statues were available for placement, and in the fall of 1958, the Citizens' Committee for a Joan of Arc Statue was formed; Mayor Chep Morrison asked Shaw to serve on the committee.[1212] C.C. Walther of Walther Brothers Company, Inc. was Chairman of the committee. A city-wide effort was made to have school children in New Orleans raise money to finance the purchase and placement of the statue. Opposition arose almost immediately to the idea of school children helping in such a manner, and the possibility loomed of a conflict with Latin American governments who wanted to place statues in New Orleans representing their own culture and history.[1213] Morrison had sounded Shaw out about the feasibility of the project almost as soon as it got underway, but by January 1959 the project was abandoned.

In early January 1959, Shaw received a letter from Jack Crawford, formerly of *VISION*, now with the advertising arm of *New Yorker*, enclosing a *New Yorker* article about Edward Durell Stone. Shaw thanked him for the article, and indicated that he would get it into the hands of approximately 500 business and civic leaders in New Orleans, adding that it should answer the question, "Why did you go out of New Orleans for an architect?"[1214]

*VISION* magazine carried its own article in January about Edward Durell Stone and his assignment to design the new International Trade Mart building. The article discussed Stone's designs, indicating that he quite often used grill architecture in his projects.[1215]

The issue of the *Wall Street Journal* for January 8, 1959, featured a front-page article about International House and Mario Bermúdez. The article was a straightforward one that placed a favorable slant on Bermúdez and the organization, and its dealings with Latin America and other countries.[1216]

In January, Shaw agreed to open the Mart payroll records to Southern Bell, the local telephone company, which was taking a survey of wage levels in the area.[1217] The Mart was still thought of as a premier institution in the city, even as it struggled with longer-term problems.

By 1959, the company that owned the *Times-Picayune*, New Orleans's morning newspaper, had purchased the *States-Item*, the afternoon newspaper, creating in effect one main set of newspapers, under one owner, for the New Orleans area. To many observers, this was the beginning of an effective monopoly of opinion in the New Orleans area that would affect how the citizenry viewed certain issues from that point forward. Irvin M. Orner had been the president of the *Item*. After the purchase, Orner attempted to resign from the Board of Directors of the Mart in late 1958, because of the demise of the independent *Item* and his own position there.[1218] William Zetzmann had written to Orner, refusing to accept the resignation, and indicating that he still needed Orner to serve on the Board of Directors, that the organization itself needed him.[1219] By early March 1959, however, Irvin Orner had moved to St. Petersburg, Florida to be General Manager of the *St. Petersburg Independent*.[1220]

At an Executive Committee meeting of International House in early February 1959, Charles Nutter reported that International House had approximately an $8,000 surplus of income over expenses during 1958. He summarized that the relationship of total income to total expenses over the years had ranged from a $25,000 annual surplus to a $16,000 annual deficit. However, he indicated that there had only been three deficits in the history of the organization through 1958. Nutter estimated that operations during 1959 would generate approximately $328,000 of gross income, and an estimated deficit of approximately $500.[1221]

One of Shaw's young friends during the 1950s was Val Dufour, a New Orleans-area man who became an actor, and lived in New York and Hollywood. During his career, he acted in a variety of westerns and other types of television shows, and wound up being primarily in soap operas. In early 1959, Shaw sent Dufour a telegram indicating he had booked some hotel rooms during Mardi Gras at the Senator Hotel for friends of Dufour. Shaw noted Dufour's absence and said, "We'll miss you. Best, Clay," also indicating that Dufour's friends should send a $60 check immediately to hold the rooms.[1222]

A memo from J.B. Dauenhauer, just prior to Mardi Gras day, reiterated the usual rules for the day. The building would be open, as would the bar. No one who was wearing a Mardi Gras costume or mask would be allowed above the first floor.[1223] A memo later in the month, also from Dauenhauer, indicated that only organizations with permission to solicit were allowed into the building. There were only two such organizations—Disabled American Veterans and Little Sisters of the Poor.[1224]

Shaw sent a telegram on March 16th to J. C. Jackson, his old boss at Western Union in New Orleans. "Happy Birthday," Shaw wrote. "May the luck of the Irish be with you." Shaw signed the telegram "Lavergne," a name he now used only with very old friends and family members.[1225]

In mid-March, William Zetzmann released a report on the Mart's 1958 operations to the Board of Directors. In it, he called 1959 the "Year of Decision." He indicated that the Mart should buy the land it needed at the very end of 1959, paying a small amount of prorated tax. In 1960, the Mart would be reclassified as a non-profit owner, paying no further tax as a result. Lloyd Cobb had found that the title to the Dock Board land was held by the City of New Orleans, which would positively affect the outcome of plans for the new building, if the Mart could convince the City to transfer the land to it. Meanwhile, plans for International House to join with the Mart were held open while International House conducted a survey of its members. In 1958, the Mart had produced a surplus of approximately $9,000 of income over expenses for the full year, even though the 10th Anniversary celebration, and the Mart's greater participation in International Week, had cost it significant additional expenses, compared with 1957. The occupancy rate for the full year was 96.6%, down somewhat from 1957. Tenants were reluctant to take space, or renew space, knowing that in two years they might have to move to a new building. Certain tenants, such as lawyers, doctors, and insurance agents, could not be taken in, but Zetzmann commented that the Mart might have to consider altering that policy. The Mart had never raised rents since the time it had opened, but on the positive side, 1958 had been more successful than 1955, when the building had been sold to new owners, and plans had first been announced for a new building. Zetzmann noted that the Mart still had a good public image in New Orleans, and around the nation, and that Edward Durell Stone gave a certain credibility to the proposed new building; Stone was a favorite of the U.S. Department of State, and had been portrayed well in the *New Yorker* article. Additionally, *Architectural Forum* had commented favorably on Stone's design of the U.S. Pavilion at the Brussels World's Fair. Zetzmann also noted that the 1958 Mississippi Valley World Trade Conference had been very successful, and that almost 202,000 people had visited the Mart during the year.[1226]

A "Lagniappe" column by Tommy Griffin in the *States-Item* of March 20, 1959, noted the recent Irish flag-raising at the Mart, in honor of St. Patrick's Day, and that the holiday coincided with Shaw's birthday: March 17th. The column also mentioned Ella Brennan Martin, owner of Brennan's restaurant, and noted the three green candles for past, present and future. The column went on to say there were sixty flags on the building, which were raised at 7:00 a.m. and lowered at 5:00 p.m. The first raising had been on July 7, 1948, in an informal ceremony shortly after the building opened, but before the grand opening in the fall of 1948.[1227]

The Mart and its directors were scrutinizing all expenditures at this point, in an effort to keep the organization with an annual surplus. At a meeting of the Contributors and Debenture Holders in mid-March, Shaw commented that the flags for display atop the building were re-purchased every nine months, for approximately $600.[1228]

There was suddenly a general atmosphere of good feeling within the Mart organization, with the alliance with Stone and the seemingly imminent plans for a new building. At a meeting of the Board of Directors later in March, Zetzmann indicated that the new building would be the greatest thing that ever happened to New Orleans, that it would bring more people than ever before to the city. Edward Durell Stone had commented that no other place had anything comparable to offer.[1229]

With Stone involved with designing the new building, Shaw's trips to New York City increased somewhat. He made at least three trips there during the first half of 1959, always staying at the Waldorf Astoria hotel. William Zetzmann accompanied Shaw on his trip in mid-July. Stone brought his wife, Maria, on a trip to New Orleans in the spring. Afterwards, she wrote Shaw thanking him for his kindness during their visit.[1230]

A premier showing of Stone's drawings of his plans for the new building was held on March 30, 1959 in New Orleans. The event, held at the Roosevelt hotel, was by invitation only.

Muriel Bultman Francis had participated, from the beginning, in the wooing and entertaining of Stone. In late March 1959, she wrote to Shaw and Jesse Core, indicating that she had talked to Maria Stone, who had said that "they would like Daddy to throw them a party" in New Orleans.[1231]

In late April, Shaw heard again from Muriel Bultman Francis, who indicated that she and her father, Fred Bultman, were going to Mexico City, the first visit there for her. She shared that she would be back in New Orleans on May 11, and in New York City later in the week.[1232] Shaw responded in early May, saying that he hoped she and her father were enjoying the trip and that he would be in New York May 11 through the 15, where he hoped to see her.[1233]

The competition from organizations in other parts of the country continued to heat up in 1959. In April, the Ninth Annual Pan American Commission Tour left from Tampa on a goodwill tour of Latin America. Also, representatives from Trade Marts in San Diego and Jacksonville came to New Orleans to visit the Mart and International House.

At a meeting of the Building and Executive Committees in early April, Zetzmann and Cobb said that it was time to approach International House again about their intentions. Cobb read aloud a letter to International House, requesting that its leaders advise the Mart of its position; a draft copy would be sent to George Dinwiddie, the new President of International House.[1234] Dinwiddie made suggested changes to the letter, which Zetzmann then incorporated before the letter was distributed to International House members.[1235]

The Press Club of New Orleans had begun operations on October 1, 1957. A new club space opened on April 18, 1959, at 508 Camp Street, across from the *Times-Picayune*. Shaw was a paid member of the club. Before selecting the new space, the Press Club had looked at space in the Mart, but did not want to invest in improvements if the Mart was going to be moving to a new building in the near future.[1236] Among the new slate of officers for the Press Club in 1959 were Bill Reed, a prominent television newsman with WWL-TV, Ed Planer with WDSU-TV, and Herman Kohlman, with the *Times-Picayune*. Kohlman would later become an attorney, join the offices of New Orleans District Attorney Jim Garrison, and become involved with the initial detainment of David Ferrie immediately after the assassination of President Kennedy in November 1963. That initial interest in Ferrie would help to begin a several-year chain of events leading to Shaw's arrest.

In early May 1959, Albert Terkuhle of Curtis and Davis, Architects and Engineers in New York City, copied Shaw on a letter he had sent to Nils Lundberg of Brooks-Harvey and Company in New York City. The letter indicated that Terkuhle had spoken to Shaw recently relative to a discussion he and Lundberg had the previous week. Remarking that "Walter and I enjoyed being with you and Frank last week," Terkuhle indicated that Shaw would be in New York City the following week, and that he had suggested to Shaw that he call Lundberg, so the two of them could get together.[1237]

In early May 1959, Jesse Core wrote to Shaw, who was in New York City at the time, indicating that he was going to try to get Shaw an appearance on the Sunday night television show "What's My Line?" Core also mentioned that Anna Schwartz had been in the Mart lounge, commenting that she had heard Hugh Downs interview Edward Durell Stone about the new Mart building on the "Monitor" program the previous Saturday; Core noted that Downs was also the announcer for *The Tonight Show* with Jack Paar.[1238]

Also in May, Shaw received a letter from John R. Campbell, a mural designer. The letter was addressed to Shaw at his residence at 927 Burgundy Street in the French Quarter, and referenced an earlier visit that Campbell and Jerry O'Leary had with Shaw at his home. Campbell indicated that he was "much impressed with your beautiful home and exquisite patio," with its swimming pool. Campbell indicated that it was a perfect setting for a painting, and commented on the nice paintings Shaw had on the walls in his home.[1239]

In June, Shaw wrote a letter to all current tenants of the Mart, in which he discussed preliminary floor plans for the new Mart building. The ground floor plan called for a bank, drug store, cigar stand, soft drink machines, and sandwich dispensers. Floors 2 through 10 would be available for large blocks of rental space, while floors 11 through 17 would be available for smaller rental spaces; Floors 2, 11, 16, and 17 were also open for entire floor rentals by one tenant. Rental rates per square foot would be $4.25 for 5,000 square feet or more, and $4.50 for smaller spaces. Corner spaces giving two viewpoints would be available for $4.75 per square foot. Shaw noted that the rates represented a moderate increase of 12% over rental rates set thirteen years before when the original Mart building was being marketed to potential tenants. Shaw further indicated that leases should be ready to sign within ninety days.[1240]

With the prospects for a new building far from certain, the Mart was now entertaining the idea of short-term tenants for the growing empty space in the current building. In a letter to Victor H. Baker, Trade Delegate of Austria, who had inquired about temporary space during International Week, Shaw indicated that a decorator should cost $750 to $1,000 for the three small spaces requested, and that "two capable girls could be obtained for $75/week each."[1241]

Shaw wrote to a prospective tenant that the Mart had some 700 lines of merchandise, from every state and from 24 foreign countries. The two-page letter was somewhat longer than most during this era, and harkened back to the pre-opening days of the Mart, when Shaw was trying to make a good impression on each potential new tenant. The Mart had not had that challenge during much of the 1950s, but with plans for a new building, which was mentioned in the letter, Shaw's old entrepreneurial attitude had returned.[1242]

Shaw replied to an inquiry from Guy L. Smith, indicating that the Mart was not a membership organization, but rather a permanent trade fair.[1243] In so doing, Shaw, perhaps carelessly, had utilized some of the very same terminology ("trade fair") that he had tried so studiously to avoid in promoting the Mart in the mid-1940s, prior to its opening.

Robert D. Hess became President of the Foreign Policy Association of New Orleans in 1959, replacing Gilbert Mellin. The organization had begun to have its share of controversy. W. Findley Raymond resigned after a recent WYES-TV program on the United Nations, which had generated some opposition because of what some interpreted as a pro-Communist slant among some of the participants. Raymond, appearing afterwards on Herman Deutsch's television program "Speak Your Piece," said he thought he had been made a scapegoat after the program aired; he also objected to the requirement that directors and committee chairmen of the Foreign Policy Association have a certain social standing.

George Dinwiddie, President of International House that year, wrote a letter to International House members, discussing the history of plans for the new International Trade Mart building, and how those plans had changed over the years. However, the Executive Committee of International House had voted to remodel its own building, rather than to join forces with the Mart and move into the new building.[1244] By October, the members of International House also had voted to stay in the current building and remodel it. Architects had quickly begun to work on the drawings for the remodeling, for which $300,000 had been budgeted.[1245]

In order to make its decision, International House had commissioned Belden Associates to conduct a research poll of the members. In a report issued in mid-July, Belden said that approximately 55% of the members favored remaining in the current building, while approximately 44% favored moving and joining together with the Mart in one organization.

Shaw still dealt somewhat regularly with members of the U.S. Departments of State and of Commerce in New Orleans. Edward A. Leland, Jr. was still the representative of the Department of Commerce, as he had been for some years. Michael Buzan, Jr., the representative of the Department of State in New Orleans, moved on to Washington in early 1959, in preparation for an assignment overseas; James M.E. O'Grady took Buzan's place.[1246]

Luis (Louis) Vargas, who had been a Trade Analyst with the Mart while a student in the early 1950s, sent Shaw a postcard from Panama showing the Panama Hilton hotel. Vargas indicated he had been in South America, which was "fabulous," and that he was looking forward to seeing Central America. He still referred to Shaw as "Mr. Shaw."[1247]

Shaw continued to entertain out-of-town visitors on a regular basis. Gerard de Vos, a Lake Charles businessman, thanked Shaw for showing him around on a Saturday, on his first visit ever to New Orleans. Frank E. Stanton, of the Long Beach Amusement Company in Long Beach, California, mentioned the Bloody Mary's he and Shaw had drunk on his visit to New Orleans.[1248] Sid and Eleni Epstein of Washington, D.C. thanked Shaw for treating them to lunch at Brennan's restaurant.[1249] Warren T. Lindquist, Executive Vice President of Downtown-Lower Manhattan Association, Inc., wrote Shaw thanking him for his recent visit to New Orleans; David Rockefeller was listed on the letterhead of the organization.[1250]

Holland McCombs, who had been a writer for *Fortune* magazine at the time of the opening of the Mart, was now working for Texas Instruments Company, which had been looking for a publications manager. McCombs wrote to Shaw occasionally, indicating that he hoped to get down to New Orleans soon for a visit.[1251]

There were the usual number of special events during 1959 that attracted Shaw's attention, or required his participation. In late winter, he received a group of U.S. State Department employees who were visiting New Orleans. After the visit, Shaw wrote to Robert M. Tuttle of the Foreign Service Institute of the Department of State. Shaw indicated that he had been impressed by the high level of confidence among members of the group, and that, "It is comforting to realize that such men as you and your colleagues will not only represent us abroad, but will more and more come to make decisions vital to the peace and prosperity of the United States—in fact of the Western world."[1252]

Mario Bermúdez and Shaw continued to work together on various events. Bermúdez invited Shaw to be a member of the welcoming committee at the airport for a visit by King Hussein of Jordan.[1253]

In May, Shaw was invited by the local Pepsi-Cola Bottling Company to a Press-Radio-TV cocktail party to meet Mrs. Alfred N. Steele, wife of the president of Pepsi-Cola.[1254] Mrs. Steele happened to be the actress Joan Crawford. The event was held at the Roosevelt hotel, but Shaw was unable to attend.[1255]

Shaw continued to push for new international representation in the Mart. Spain had never had an office in the building, but in a letter to the Spanish Office of Exterior Economy, Shaw noted that Belgium, Italy, England, Germany, and Switzerland all maintained offices in the Mart, and suggested that Spain should have one as well.[1256]

In spite of reservations among Mart officials about dealing with Communist governments, Shaw pursued the possible tenancy of the Polish government. In a letter to Stanislaw Zawadski, with the office of the Polish Commercial Councilor in New York City, Shaw said, "It is my firm conviction that such a [Polish Trade Center] in the International Trade Mart would do a great deal to open the markets of the southern United States to Polish goods."[1257]

Most of Shaw's speeches continued to be to organizations in the New Orleans area, unless he happened to be out of town for other reasons. In January, he addressed the Round Table Club of New Orleans, and the Newcomers' Club Luncheon at the Monteleone hotel. In March, he spoke to the West Bank Rotary Club Luncheon, and participated in a WYES-TV panel on international issues, a panel where all the other panelists were professors at colleges. In April, he spoke to the Junior League of New Orleans, the Recess Club of New Orleans, and the Executives' Club of New Orleans, the last of which noted in a promotional brochure for Shaw's speech that the new Mart building would open in 1961.

In May, he spoke to the Rotary Club of Metairie, Louisiana, to the New Orleans Credit Men's Association, to the Propeller Club Essay Contest Luncheon, to the Members' Council of the New Orleans Chamber of Commerce, and to the Ladies' Luncheon of the National Sales Executive Convention. In June, he spoke to the Garden District Library, and to the English Speaking Union. In July, he spoke to the Lions Club of New Orleans, and in August he spoke to the Variety Luncheon of Paramount Gulf Theatres.

In September, he spoke to the Rotary Club of Poplarville, Mississippi. In a letter afterward to Shaw, S.L. Richardson, the club's Secretary, noted that Louisiana was getting rid of a governor, "as you rightly should," referring to a growing frustration with the recent antics of current Governor Earl K. Long, whose term expired soon.[1258] Shaw also spoke that month to the Rotary Club of Hammond, Louisiana.

October was a busy month, with Shaw speaking to the Pontalba Study Club, to the Evangelical Church at South Claibourne and Jefferson, and to the Metairie Park Country Day School student body. He also moderated a panel about the United Nations at the United Nations Day Luncheon at the Monteleone hotel, and he moderated another television panel for WYES-TV.

In November, keeping up the pace, Shaw spoke to the Gentilly Rotary Club, to the Young Men's Business Club Commerce and Industries Bureau, to the Third District Kiwanis Club, to the Women's Society of Christian Service Group, to the Temple Sinai Sisterhood, and to the Altrusa Club of New Orleans at a Roosevelt hotel luncheon.

In December, he spoke to the Camp Street Improvement Association, to the Kiwanis Club of Mid-City at Lenfants Restaurant, and to the Downtown Kiwanis Club of New Orleans. Shaw declined several invitations to speak in late December 1959 and early January 1960, indicating that he would be out of town from December 15, 1959 to January 15, 1960.

In one of the more unusual invitations he received that year, Shaw was asked to attend the opening of Stemmons Freeway in Dallas on December 4th. The invitation was issued to Shaw by Horace Ainsworth, an official with the Dallas Trade Mart. However, Shaw advised he could not attend the opening.[1259] The Stemmons Freeway was the route used by the limousine carrying President Kennedy, his wife, and other occupants to exit the Dealey Plaza area in Dallas immediately after the shooting of the president on November 22, 1963. Had the assassination not happened, the freeway would have been used to transport the president's party to the Dallas Trade Mart after passing through Dealey Plaza.

The number of visitors to the Mart declined more steeply during 1959. The average now ranged from 13,000 to 18,000 per month, down from a peak of 20,000 to 25,000 only two years earlier.

Shaw continued to be involved in the more complicated inquiries received from the public. In response to someone complaining about a fee charged by Maher and Company, a tenant in the Mart building, Shaw advised the inquirer to get his facts straight before writing letters threatening drastic action. He went on to tell the writer not to initiate any more letters directly to his attention, as he had no knowledge or interest in the transaction at issue.[1260]

In response to a letter from a teacher in tiny Branch, Louisiana, whose pupils wanted to know why little Spanish boys in their reading book referred to money as "the little dogs," Shaw inquired of Marcel Gomez about the issue. It turned out that five-cent and ten-cent coins in Spain were called "perras chicas" (little dogs) and "perras gordas" (big dogs), respectively. The reason for this was that on one side of the coins was a lion which could be mistaken for a dog. Shaw advised that a "big dog" was worth approximately two cents or less in U.S. money at the time.[1261]

Barbara Makanowitzky, Research Editor of the Council for International Progress in Management in New York City, wrote to Shaw, inquiring whether the Mart had a program for the exchange of individuals with other countries. Shaw replied that there was no such program, except as it related to the Cordell Hull Foundation, which exchanged teachers between the United States and Latin America.[1262]

Shaw purchased a property at 927 Burgundy Street on June 1, 1959 for $37,872.21. He lived at the property for a while, then rented it out in the early 1960s, before selling it on October 1, 1963 for $42,500.

Shaw had sold his property at 505 Dauphine, several years before, to Mrs. Artelle Trelford. Shaw's prior loan for the property was now secured at the bank by the note from Mrs. Trelford to Shaw, who financed the purchase himself. He received a monthly payment of $447 from Mrs. Trelford, and paid the bank $389 per month.[1263]

Back at the office, Jerry E. Ryan, a fifth-year architecture student at the University of Virginia, wrote to Shaw, indicating that he was doing a project on the Mart; his father had been in to see Shaw recently. Shaw recommended that Ryan visit the Mart and see it for himself.[1264]

The Mart and International House employed various individuals of Latin American origin throughout their existence. Due to the connection with Mario Bermúdez, many were from Colombia, or had Colombian family roots. Carmen Martinez worked for International House during 1959, translating documents from Spanish into English, and vice versa. Carmen and her sister, Elena, were from Colombia, and both worked within the international trade community during the 1950s and 1960s. They also, for a number of years, ran a boarding house for international visitors to New Orleans. Both of them lived into their nineties, before passing away in the first decade of this century. Cecilia Grace, a Mart employee since the mid-1950s was still working there in 1959, holding down the front desk.

By the late 1950s, with the Mart's future somewhat uncertain, Jesse Core faced the possibility of having to find a new job. A curriculum vitae of Core's from that era showed David Baldwin, Core's predecessor as the Mart's Public Relations Director, as a reference. At the time, Baldwin was employed with the Department of Public Relations of the American Medical Association in Chicago.

In early August, Jesse Core wrote to columnist Tommy Griffin, informing him that David Baldwin's great-grandfather had built the Baldwin Building, which housed the Mart. Core explained how the Baldwin Building had been refurbished from 1946 to 1948, in order to become the Mart.[1265] Baldwin's family prominence helped to explain his connections around New Orleans, enabling him to land there in between jobs away from the city.

Shaw and Jesse Core still dealt regularly with various local media personalities. One was Ruth Barnett, who wrote the "Blue Book" column for a local newspaper. In one letter to Core, Barnett mentioned her "good friend Clay Shaw."[1266] In a letter to Tommy Griffin, who wrote the "Lagniappe" column for the *States-Item*, Core mentioned that Elena Monastario Lyons had appeared on television recently, practicing her "TV technique;" Core said she was "New Orleans's answer to Zsa Zsa."[1267]

Shaw wrote to U.S. Senator J. William Fulbright, mentioning that he had seen a newspaper column by George Sokolsky that had dealt with a recent Fulbright speech about the economic warfare between the Soviet Union and the western democracies. Shaw said that unless the Western democracies could get together economically, the Soviet system would grow stronger. Shaw also reminded Fulbright that, several years before, he had shown him around the Mart. Shaw now enclosed a photograph and descriptive material of the planned new Mart building "designed by your fellow Arkansan, Edward Durell Stone."[1268]

Shaw re-purchased the property at 1313 Dauphine Street on August 1, 1959, becoming its sole owner, and rented it until he made it his personal residence in the early 1960s.[1269] Because that was where he lived at the time of his arrest, it would become the residence most closely associated with him to the general public.

At a Board of Directors meeting in late August, it was discussed that two squares of ground were to be purchased from the Southern Pacific Railroad Company for $239,000, and that a similar amount of land would be acquired from the Dock Board, that the Mart would buy the Dock Board building, demolish it, and acquire whatever rights the City of New Orleans had in the land and buildings.[1270] A new leasing agent hired to sell leases for the planned new Mart building, Edmund Christy, was to have a six-month period of employment. He would draw a salary of $750 per month, and could collect up to $10,000 if all went well. However, he would collect nothing if the entire deal to construct the building fell through.[1271]

Although it had been Shaw's intention to provide the employees of the Mart with more benefits as the years progressed, that became impossible to do with the flattening financial situation. In August 1959, in response to an inquiry from a medical social worker asking about an employee who had developed tuberculosis, J.B. Dauenhauer responded that the Mart had no hospitalization insurance on its employees, only straight life insurance.[1272]

Monk Simons, with D.H. Holmes, wrote to Shaw, enclosing a newspaper photo of Shaw giving a parting gift to Ernest Theiler, Consul General and Trade Commissioner for the Swiss Consulate in New Orleans, who was departing the city.[1273] A photograph of Shaw with Theiler showed Shaw looking somewhat old at age forty-six, with essentially grayish white hair all over, and a somewhat fierce and leathery face.[1274]

At a meeting of the Executive, Finance, and Building Committees of the Mart in early September, it was discussed that $12,000,000 was now budgeted for the new building. Edward Durell Stone would work with Collins, Tuttle and Company to help facilitate the financing and construction. The Mart would have six months to obtain leases with terms of not less than fifteen years totaling $900,000, and leases with terms of not less than five years totaling $400,000.[1275]

Moisant International Airport in Kenner, Louisiana, outside of New Orleans was remodeled and upgraded during 1959, with its grand reopening set for the fall of that year. During this same time, a young teenager from Germany, Hermann Bockelmann, came to the U.S. via a ship, arriving in New Orleans on November 7, 1959. Also on board was a young man named Robinson, about twenty-seven years old, son of a rancher, who had been studying at the University of Munich. Bockelmann was to fly to Dallas from New Orleans, to meet up with a relative who lived there, but Robinson volunteered to show Bockelmann around New Orleans. Bockelmann stayed at the DeSoto hotel for a few days, before eventually preparing to leave on an evening flight to Dallas.

While seated in the airport, waiting on his plane, a tall, distinguished-looking man passed him by several times, then finally stopped to make conversation. The man made a very good initial impression, and Bockelmann assumed he was a prominent local official of some sort. The man, whom Bockelmann thought resembled the actor Jeff Chandler, turned out to be Clay Shaw. Shaw soon took Bockelmann to the airport bar and bought him several martinis; the two sat at a table in the bar and talked about Europe and America. When Bockelmann asked Shaw about American girls, he thought that Shaw seemed to be evasive on the subject. Bockelmann initially declined an offer to go eat with Shaw, but Shaw persuaded him, and the two went to a restaurant in the airport. They sat on a sofa at a table, and Bockelmann noted that Shaw sat next to him on the sofa, rather than across from him. After a while, Bockelmann felt Shaw's right hand moving along his left leg. Bockelmann protested against Shaw's actions, and Shaw became somewhat disappointed at Bockelmann's defensiveness. Bockelmann later said that in declining Shaw's invitations, he did not make any disparaging remarks about homosexuality, as he did not know American customs on the subject, and did not want to insult Shaw. However, he made it clear to Shaw that he was not gay himself.

After the two of them had eaten, Shaw insisted Bockelmann go with him for a ride in his new 1959 Ford Thunderbird, which he was anxious to show off. Bockelmann declined, and after a short discussion, Shaw seemed to give up on the subject. The two had exchanged addresses early on in their discussion, and Shaw had given Bockelmann his business card. Shaw said that he was waiting on relatives to arrive by plane, but he tried again to persuade Bockelmann to stay over and spend the night at his French Quarter home; Bockelmann declined that invitation as well. Bockelmann never heard from Shaw again.[1276]

Almost eight years later, approximately six months after Clay Shaw's arrest, William Wood, a former CIA employee and reformed alcoholic who was working for New Orleans District Attorney Jim Garrison in his Kennedy assassination investigation, under the alias of Bill Boxley, found Bockelmann's address in Shaw's address book, and went to Dallas to interview him, among others listed there. Bockelmann had gone on from New Orleans to Dallas the night he met Shaw, and in the eight years since had lived in Virginia for a while, and then had moved back to Dallas. Ironically, Boxley, noting that Bockelmann's name had a Germanic origin, initially thought that Bockelmann would be connected with a former CIA operation in Germany, and regarded Bockelmann with suspicion during the interview. Bockelmann took a very defensive posture, disliking Wood/Boxley's attitude, making him cooperative but still cool throughout.

Years later, the author interviewed Bockelmann, who confirmed the essential elements of the story, indicating that Shaw had, indeed, tried to pick him up in the New Orleans airport in 1959. Bockelmann said that he had been a young blonde-haired kid, and that given Shaw's orientation, perhaps it was a natural thing that occurred. He said he bore Shaw no grudge for it, and never thought that Shaw was guilty of the crimes Garrison charged him with years later.[1277]

Shaw always maintained good relations with the United States Navy, and its personnel stationed in New Orleans. In September, Rear Admiral W.G. Schindler, U.S. Navy, Commander of the Eighth Naval District wrote to Shaw, indicating that he had "enjoyed our stimulating association," and was grateful for the cooperation and support Shaw had given him during his time in New Orleans.[1278]

In mid-September 1959, Shaw wrote Zetzmann regarding a request from the Cordell Hull Foundation for the Mart to fund a $1,000 scholarship for a Latin American exchange student. Shaw wrote, "In view of the heavy obligations we are assuming, I think we should pass this up for the year."[1279] It was an important indication of the growing financial pressures on the Mart that it would even consider withholding a contribution to a foundation so closely allied with International House; the development also may have reflected the growing tension between the two organizations over the apparently failed attempts at a merger.

After years of being absent from the Mart, Colombia took space again in September. There were now fifteen foreign establishments of one sort or another, either governmental or commercial, in the Mart.

In the fall of 1959, local businessman Harold Roberts, a member of the Mart Board of Directors, wrote to Shaw, asking him to note points in defense of the Mart against the charges that it was a taxpayer-subsidized building. At the time, the Mart was trying to pass a state constitutional amendment, which had been written in such a way as to give the Mart and International House alone a large tax break. Shaw responded by pointing out that some things were best done by the public sector, mentioning the Post Office, telephone and telegraph companies, and ports. He reminded Roberts that excess profits generated by the Mart's operation were devoted to promotion of the Port of New Orleans through the tenants in the building; he commented that the proposed new larger Mart building would be continuing something the original Mart building had done for years on a smaller scale.[1280]

Shaw served on the Steering Committee of International Week for 1959. Early in the year, there had been a discussion among civic leaders about whether International Week should be continued, perhaps another sign of the weakening of interest in international issues among New Orleanians; most leaders, however, still believed that it should be held annually.

A bulletin from Shaw to tenants on October 1 announced that the Mart was opening a rental office for the new building. Edmund Christy would be the rental agent handling the new leases. Shaw urged tenants to choose space in the new building early, in order to get the best choice.[1281]

Shaw purchased the home at 908 Esplanade Street in October 1959; he would sell it in the spring of 1962. That residence was the other half of a twin set of properties, the first half of which, 906 Esplanade, Shaw had owned in the early 1950s. The property at 906 Esplanade had been a set of buildings that included the slave quarters and carriage house on Dauphine Street, with which he became more famously identified at the time of his arrest. The building at 906 Esplanade would figure prominently in Shaw's 1969 trial, when witness Charles Spiesel, after a dramatic onsite visit by the entire group of official courtroom participants, testified that it was most likely the location where he had heard Shaw and David Ferrie discussing the assassination of President Kennedy in 1963.

At a meeting of the Executive Committee of International House in mid-October, Charles Nutter mentioned that a group of men from New York City had visited twice in early October, meeting with Nutter and Shaw, wanting more information about the operations of the Mart and International House, in preparation for building a World Trade Center in lower Manhattan. The project would ultimately become the famous twin-tower complex destroyed on September 11, 2001.[1282]

At a meeting of the Building and Executive Committees in mid-October, Edmund Christy's employment situation was further discussed. It was reiterated that he was employed at a salary of $750 per month, and would receive a bonus if he was able to negotiate 65% of the potential leases, and if all plans to construct the new building went forward as planned. A discussion was held about contributions to various functions around the city; it was decided that the Mart would contribute $1,000 to the Cordell Hull Foundation, even though its student nominee the previous year had not accepted a scholarship. The contribution to International Week was trimmed to $500, and no contribution was made for United Nations Day, which was held during International Week that year. Pendleton Lehde mentioned that Maxim's restaurant in France might be interested in becoming the restaurant at the top of the new Mart building.[1283]

William Zetzmann wrote to Edmund Christy, setting out the terms of Christy's employment. Zetzmann indicated that Christy would get $750 per month, plus $50,000, to be paid at $10,000 per year, if the leasing goals were achieved by March 7, 1960. Those goals included $900,000 in future annual rental income from fifteen-year leases, and $400,000 in future annual rental income from five-year leases.[1284]

Lloyd Cobb had helped to draw up the agreement with Christy. Cobb's law firm was called Cobb and Wright, and at the time listed Herbert W. Christenberry, Jr. on the letterhead. Christenberry was the son of U.S. District Judge Herbert W. Christenberry, who in 1971 issued a permanent injunction against Shaw being further prosecuted by the New Orleans district attorney's office for any alleged offenses related to the Kennedy assassination.

International House continued its own operations independently of the Mart. Its trade missions to foreign countries, always a prime activity of the organization, continued in full force, with even more grandiose plans. In a letter to members in late October, George Dinwiddie mentioned an upcoming 23-day trip behind the Iron Curtain. The trip was scheduled to begin in April 1960, and would include stops in Moscow, Prague, and Budapest.[1285]

On October 27, 1959, Shaw appeared on a panel show that aired on WYES-TV during International Week. The panel discussed "Political, Education and Economic Problems of Hemispheric Solidarity," and included four Tulane University faculty members, and a Vice-President of Whitney Bank, in addition to Shaw.[1286] Shaw often found himself as the person with the least formal education on a panel, holding his own against fellow panelists with advanced degrees.

The local television newsletter *Off-Camera* carried an article in mid-November 1959 about Jack Sawyer, a young director at WVUE-TV; Sawyer directed various local shows, including "Bozo the Clown."[1287] Sawyer became a companion of Shaw's old friend, Jeff Biddison, and knew Shaw well during the 1960s and early 1970s. Sawyer would be largely responsible for preserving Clay Shaw's personal papers throughout the 1980s and early 1990s after Biddison's death in 1981; he eventually turned those papers over to the National Archives for permanent preservation and use by researchers.

Charles Leonard, consul of Belgium in New Orleans, retired in November; he had been in the position since the 1940s. Leonard decided to stay in the New Orleans area, soon taking a position with the Foreign Policy Association of New Orleans.

Also in November, Shaw received a letter from William Phillips of New York City, which discussed Phillips's sketches related to the new Mart building; the sketches called for bronze male and female figures. Phillips suggested that, "Perhaps you and Tom Dawson can come up to the studio the next time you visit NYC—by then I may have a study ready of something a good deal more frivolous."[1288] Shaw responded in early 1960 that he hoped to be in New York City in early February, and that he would give Phillips a call so that they could get together for a drink.

Tom Dawson, Shaw's companion mentioned in Phillips' letter, was an interior and artistic designer who worked for J. Walter Thompson advertising agency in New York City before moving to Los Angeles. A friend of writer James Leo Herlihy, Dawson was instrumental in bringing Shaw and Herlihy together in New York in October 1967, almost eight months after Shaw's arrest.[1289] Herlihy would invite friend and fellow author James Kirkwood to the gathering; Kirkwood would proceed to cover Shaw's case from that point forward, and go on to write the definitive book about Clay Shaw's 1969 trial.

At the end of November 1959, Shaw wrote to Kit Mueller, with *Architectural Forum* magazine, enclosing some before-and-after photos of his Vieux Carré properties. Shaw mentioned that, ten years earlier, the French Quarter had largely become a slum, and that it was now in a peculiar transitional state, where one saw "magnificently restored $100,000 homes cheek by jowl with crumbling negro tenements." Shaw said that "striptease joints and noisy bars may bracket a beautifully restored apartment building whose units rent for $200 to $300 per month." Shaw suggested that the magazine should do a general article on the restoration of the Vieux Carré that had taken place in recent years.[1290]

In December, Lloyd Cobb suggested that Shaw send a brochure on the new Mart to Clinton W. Murchison in Dallas, Texas.[1291] An oil man, Murchison was involved in various controversial political endeavors during the last century.

At a meeting of the full Board of Directors in mid-December, William Zetzmann indicated that the Mart was not yet ready to break ground on January 2nd, as had been planned. Shaw discussed the general progress of the new building, mentioning that the Mart was still negotiating with the Dock Board, and that an appraisal of the Dock Board property would be needed. He indicated that Edmund Christy had been working hard on acquiring the leases, and that 70% of the potential leases were committed, at least verbally. Christy reported that small tenants would move from the current Mart building to the new one, assuming the large tenants chose to do so as well. Standard Fruit Company was key to the deal, and it was important to sign it as a tenant. It also was noted that Lykes Shipping Company might not ultimately choose to be a tenant, but Shaw indicated the Mart had never counted on them to do so.

The garage had not yet been designed, but it was estimated that it would need a capacity of 600 cars. Lloyd Cobb said that the Mart should take possession now of the property, in order to be exempt from taxes from that point forward. Groundbreaking for the new property was now set to coincide with the holding of the Mississippi Valley World Trade Conference later in January 1960.[1292]

# 18 · The Election of John F. Kennedy

In early January 1960, Shaw wrote to Albert D. Meltz, who had been the broker on the sale of the Mart building during the mid-1950s. In the letter, Shaw discussed the restaurant that the Mart hoped to have in its new building, and indicated that he was to be in New York City in early February, where perhaps they could discuss the ideas further.[1293]

International House had 2,347 members as of January 11, 1960. The organization's members had decided not to join with the Mart in a single location, preferring to keep the familiar location in the Central Business District. The rift between the two organizations, always there, was growing wider, and would not be resolved for many years.

The high hopes for the new building that had grown over the past year now were diminishing rather quickly. At a meeting of the Building and Executive Committees in late January, Shaw advised that the Mart could not make the $900,000 in lease commitments required for financing. Standard Fruit Company, which would be the largest tenant, had not yet gotten out of its current lease at the YMCA building.[1294]

In January 1960, Shaw appeared on two half-hour television programs, both with the theme "Opportunities New Orleans." The two programs were held in conjunction with the Mississippi Valley World Trade Conference, held January 24-27. One of the programs was on WYES-TV, Channel 8, and the other was held on WWL-TV, Channel 4. Shaw coordinated his appearances with R.E. Stackpole, of the Foreign Commerce Committee of the Chamber of Commerce, and with Edwin A. Leland, Jr., of the World Trade Week Committee of the Chamber of Commerce.[1295]

Also in January, Shaw was at the head table for a dinner at the Export Managers Club, where Charles P. Taft, son of former President William Howard Taft and brother of former senator Robert A. Taft of Ohio, was presented. Shaw also attended a small informal dinner for Stanley Marcus of the Neimann-Marcus Company of Dallas in the later part of the month. The event was held at the Ponchartrain Hotel, and Shaw invited the Consul General of Japan to attend the function with him.[1296]

Representative Hale Boggs was the principal speaker at the 15th Annual Mississippi Valley World Trade Conference.[1297] Shaw and other Mart officials participated fully in the conference, in spite of the lingering uncertainty over the progress of the new building; the best outward face was put on all continuing activities, to the extent possible.

On February 2, 1960, a serious incident, with somewhat humorous overtones, occurred involving Mario Bermúdez. When he landed at the New Orleans airport after a flight from El Salvador, where he had attended the Pan-American Motorcade, Bermúdez was searched at the airport by agents of the United States Customs Service. Apparently, an anonymous caller had reported that Bermúdez was smuggling emeralds from Colombia into the United States. Additionally, a caller, presumably the same individual, was calling important officials around New Orleans, informing them that Bermúdez had been detained by the Customs Service, which prompted calls to International House officials and to City of New Orleans officials. After Bermúdez had been released, Mayor Chep Morrison soon responded with a letter to T.H. Lyons, Collector of Customs, complaining about the matter, saying he had received calls from individuals wanting more information about the incident. Morrison asked for a Federal investigation, and a letter stating that Bermúdez had nothing in his luggage that was improper.[1298] Charles Nutter also wrote to Lyons, asking if there was any case pending against Bermúdez as a result of the actions taken by the Customs Service. Nutter asked who had lodged the complaint, and indicated that people were phoning him in response to anonymous telephone calls they received; Nutter speculated it was the same person who had reported Bermúdez to the Customs Service.[1299]

Bermúdez wrote a letter to Colonel Provosty Dayries, Superintendent of Police in New Orleans, about the incident. He explained that on January 18, 1960, a representative of TACA Airlines had told him that a person named Luis Garcia had recently been in Guatemala, purporting to be Louisiana Governor-elect Jimmy Davis's representative in Central America, and requesting invitations for Governor Davis to visit Latin America. Bermúdez said that he had been informed on January 28, 1960 that Garcia had visited Mario Zirian, Director of the National Tourist Board in Guatemala, where he also told Zirian that he was Governor Davis's representative. Bermúdez said that Garcia had also denounced Mayor Morrison's political and private life, indicating that while the police covered up for Morrison, the public knew the truth about him; Garcia indicated that Morrison's Catholicism had cost him the governorship of Louisiana. According to Bermúdez, Garcia denounced the consul of Guatemala in New Orleans to the president of that country, accusing the consul of being a drunkard who fell asleep at public functions. Bermúdez noted that Governor Davis had indicated he had never heard of Garcia before, and that Garcia was not his representative. Bermúdez described how he had been searched at the airport and asked about narcotics, indicating that he had been "stripped to the bone." Bermúdez explained that Garcia had approached him for a job seven or eight years before, and had been turned down.[1300] The incident is also mentioned in FBI files dealing with Bermúdez, although the FBI was not involved directly in the actual incident.

At a meeting of the World Trade Development Committee of International House in February, Shaw announced that Permindex was opening its World Trade Center in Rome, Italy. He suggested that perhaps a Mississippi Valley area exhibition could be set up there.[1301]

When the Contributors and Debenture Holders convened in early March, William Zetzmann reported on the results of operations for 1959, and responded to criticism regarding the delay in the new building. Zetzmann indicated it was a difficult project to finance, and that there was not enough equity in the organization to find that financing easily. The Mart had purchased the land from Southern Pacific Railway in December 1959, and expected soon to demolish the building that was on the property. Zetzmann further indicated that Shaw and Pendleton Lehde were negotiating for the restaurant tenant and the garage tenant who would manage those two facilities.

Revenue for 1959 had totaled approximately $298,000, but expenses slightly exceeded revenues for the first time since the Mart's opening in 1948. The building had been 96% occupied for the full year, but rental rates had remained the same while expenses were still rising steadily, and the Mart had incurred almost $6,000 in expenses related to the new building. About 75% of the new building had been leased, and the Mart was trying to sell fairs, shows, and expositions for the new building. Zetzmann also noted that other cities had opened trade centers in recent years, and he commented on the new World Trade Center in Rome, Italy, operated by Permindex, with one million square feet of space.[1302]

In mid-March 1960, Jesse Core wrote to Paul Green of the Dallas Council on World Affairs indicating that Shaw was going to speak to the Export-Import Club in Dallas on May 11, 1960.[1303] Shaw still occasionally ventured out of town to make a speech, but maintained the policy of doing so usually only if he was going to be in the same area for another event.

In March, Shaw was invited to hear revisionist historian Charles Callan Tansill speak on "A Foreign Policy for Today." Shaw was invited to the event by Robert D. Hess, in his capacity as Acting Chairman of the Members Council of the Chamber of Commerce.[1304] The event was held at the Roosevelt hotel, which was somewhat of an ironic twist, since Tansill was a severe critic of President Franklin Roosevelt's foreign policy with regard to American entry into World War II.

Shaw also received an invitation to attend two luncheons to discuss tourist attraction creation, possibly with an idea to investing in new enterprises. The invitation was issued by Robert E. Wall, who indicated that he, Bryan Bell and Paul Martin, husband of Ella Brennan, also would be attending the event.[1305]

Still in March, Charles Nutter and Shaw were both honored by the Belgian Consul General with the Knight of the Order of the Crown award.[1306] Former Belgian consul Charles Leonard had proposed the award on behalf of his long-time comrades, with whom he had worked since 1946.[1307]

The Permindex project, Centro Mondiale Commerciale in Rome, was still on the radar as far as the Mart's interest, although the connection between the two had always been distant. Shaw wrote to Dr. Dov Biegen of World Trade International, Inc., indicating that he was trying to get a group of Mississippi Valley industrialists to have a permanent display with Permindex; Shaw said that he wanted the display to be portable enough to be moved to other fairs around the world. He asked Biegen to send rates and other information about the cost of exhibiting with Permindex. Shaw noted that he would be in New York City in April, and was looking forward to meeting with Biegen to discuss ways that the Mart and Permindex could cooperate. He ended by asking that Biegen send current information about developments with Permindex as they happened.[1308]

Ken Lott of Mobile, Alabama, requested that Shaw speak at the School of Banking of the South, held in Baton Rouge, Louisiana. After reading Lott's invitation, Shaw wrote Lott that he was "appalled" to find that he was expected to make a one and a half hour speech on "International Banking." Shaw said that he doubted that anyone, especially himself, could be interesting for that long of a period of time. However, he indicated he would do his best to fulfill the requirements.[1309]

At an Executive Committee meeting of International House in late March, it was mentioned that William McFadden Duffy, Publicity Director for International House, was resigning to go into business for himself in international public relations.[1310] Duffy had been with International House for more than a decade.

As the end of the month neared, the Mart had obtained only $600,000 in firm lease commitments, not enough to guarantee financing.[1311] Collins Tuttle was still interested in financing the main tower of the building, leaving the remainder of the new project to be financed with revenue bonds. Under such a proposal, the City of New Orleans would own the auditorium, but lease it to the Mart.[1312]

In early April, Shaw wrote a letter of recommendation for Richard Doskey, who had interned for the Mart during the late 1940s. Shaw indicated that he had known Doskey for ten years, and spoke well of his work for the Mart as a young man.[1313]

Shaw received a form letter from Cecil M. Shilstone, seeking Mart support for the Louisiana Council for the Vieux Carré; Shilstone was acting in his capacity as temporary chairman of that organization.[1314] Just seven years later, Shilstone would be one of the three businessmen who provided private financing for District Attorney Jim Garrison's investigation into the Kennedy assassination.

At a Board of Directors meeting of International House in mid-April, the upcoming visit of French President Charles de Gaulle in late April, and International House's cooperative efforts in that regard, was discussed.[1315] It was an event many in New Orleans would remember for years, as the city put its heart and soul into the celebration. In mid-April, Jesse Core wrote to Buckingham O. Marryat of American Airlines, referring to de Gaulle's visit on April 29; Core indicated that Mayor Chep Morrison had put Shaw in charge of the main evening dinner of the event.[1316] Shaw also served as chairman of a large civic reception for de Gaulle,[1317] but had to decline attendance at a ceremony honoring de Gaulle at the Council chamber at City Hall, due to other commitments.

Shaw also helped to arrange a dinner for a visiting Polish delegation, held at Brennan's restaurant, although he was unable to attend due to illness.[1318] After the dinner, James O'Grady, with the Department of State in New Orleans, wrote thanking him, saying that the dinner "showed very much the Shaw touch."[1319]

At a joint meeting of the Building and Executive Committees, it was discussed that revenue bonds would require a state constitutional amendment for authorization. The Mart had been asked to contribute $500 for the visit by French President Charles de Gaulle; a city-wide effort was underway planning the de Gaulle visit. The Mart was already running a deficit due to the new building costs, but it still contributed the $500 for the de Gaulle visit. Shaw indicated that Edward Durell Stone might have to be "pushed" in order to get the cost data necessary to obtain financing of the project, and he indicated that another person may have to be put on the job.[1320]

Countries continued to use the Mart for events publicizing their history, culture, and products for sale. British Week was held in the Mart April 25 to 30, 1960. Japan Week was held May 22 to 28, 1960.

**Shaw during a British exhibition at the Mart (International Trade Mart Collection, Louisiana Research Collection, Tulane University)**

In May, Shaw accepted an invitation to the dedication of a plaque to Frances Parkinson Keyes, the New Orleans writer. The dedication was held at Beauregard House, Keyes's home on Chartres Street. Also in May, Shaw declined an invitation to speak at the opening of a Saab automotive dealership in mid-June in Jacksonville, Florida, due to a conflict in New York City. Shaw was scheduled to speak in Jacksonville the day before, but would have to travel to New York City immediately afterwards.[1321]

In a letter to the Brazilian Government Trade Bureau in May, Shaw indicated his desire to have the Bureau place an office in the Mart.[1322] In a letter to Dorothy E. Ausfahl of

Belden Associates in Dallas, Texas, Shaw indicated that thirteen countries now had offices of one sort or another in the Mart: Belgium, Colombia, Cuba, Canada, France, Germany, Italy, Great Britain, Japan, Philippine Republic, Guatemala, Puerto Rico, and Switzerland.[1323] After twelve full years of operation, only four countries from Latin America and the Caribbean were represented in the Mart. Only one of those countries, Colombia, was in South America; major countries such as Argentina, Brazil, Chile, Peru, and Venezuela were not represented at all. Meanwhile, Europe had six countries represented in the Mart, and Asia had two. While this could be looked upon as a general success, it was surely a diversion of the Mart's original purpose to encourage trade and good relations with Latin America.

Many of the same prominent businessmen who had been with the Mart at the beginning were still active, keeping the Mart apprised of happenings in their own businesses. In May, Seymour Weiss of the Roosevelt hotel advised William Zetzmann that he had to miss a Mart-related meeting because the Teamsters Union had called elections for employees at the hotel; Weiss indicated that no hotel in the country currently had a contract with the Teamsters.[1324]

Shaw was on jury duty during the meeting of the Board of Directors in late May; Lloyd Cobb presided at the meeting. The most important item to be discussed was that the City would only issue $4,500,000 in revenue bonds for the new Mart building project, and the rest would have to be obtained through private loans.[1325]

In early June 1960, Shaw declined an invitation from the Young Republican Federation of Louisiana to meet with visiting delegates of the North Atlantic Treaty Organization (NATO). His decline was due to a previous commitment, but Shaw added, "I appreciate you remembering me."[1326]

Except for trips to New York City, Shaw was mostly in New Orleans during this period, participating in as many or more special events as he ever had. It was a way of being the Mart's representative, keeping the Mart visible during the long period of uncertainty.

On June 11, 1960, Shaw's residence was burglarized. Two wrist watches and a candelabra were stolen.[1327] Off in McComb, Mississippi, attorney L.S. McClaren, Shaw's former boss at International Harvester in the early 1930s, would read about the incident in the newspaper. Years later, the burglary also would make it into Jim Garrison's files about Shaw's history, although no particular significance was attached to it.

At a Board of Directors meeting of International House in mid-June, Charles Nutter told of his recent trip to the Soviet Union. Nutter had lived in the Soviet Union in the period of 1936-37,[1328] as a foreign correspondent from the United States, and had actually received a personal letter from Joseph Stalin while there, in response to an inquiry about Stalin's health.

For the fiscal year that ended June 30, 1960, the Port of New Orleans set all-time records on grain shipments, banana imports, custom collections, and general cargo imports.[1329] It was somewhat ironic that while the city was at, or close to, its peak performance as a business city and in population, two of the leading institutions representing the international trade community there were at odds, past their own zenith, and in the case of the Mart, in serious decline, hanging on to an optimistic rescue plan that might never come to pass.

Shaw and Edmund Christy went to New York City in mid-summer to explore financing, and the possibility of using another architect. A certain frustration had set in on all sides as the building failed to materialize. One firm, Taylor Company, indicated it could build the project for $13,000,000.[1330]

Shaw met with E.E. Schnellbacher of the U.S. Department of Commerce in Washington, who was in New Orleans to speak. This meeting, which was joined by Edwin A. Leland, Jr., was done at the invitation of Edward F. Sporl, Chairman of the World Trade Development Committee of International House, in an effort to maintain good relations between the major New Orleans organizations and officials in the nation's capital.

In September, Shaw accepted an invitation from Olaf C. Lambert, General Manager of the new Royal Orleans Hotel, inviting him to a cocktail reception to preview the hotel;[1331] the hotel opened October 8, 1960 at the corner of Royal and St. Louis Streets. At the end of the month, James J. Coleman, a prominent local businessman, invited Shaw to a luncheon at the Roosevelt hotel, to discuss future development of the New Orleans East area.[1332]

In October, Shaw received an invitation from Mayor Chep Morrison, requesting his attendance at a meeting to discuss the new Mart building, and other topics of interest to the community.[1333] Also in October, Mr. and Mrs. Eberhard P. Deutsch invited Shaw to a reception honoring the Austrian Ambassador to the United States.[1334]

In November, Shaw received another invitation from Chep Morrison, this time to a special meeting in the mayor's office to discuss the local school situation with community leaders.[1335] The issue of desegregation of local schools was very much in the news at the time, only six years after the historic *Brown v. Board of Education* ruling by the U.S. Supreme Court.

Aurelie Alost, of the Italian State Tourist Office in the Mart, wrote Shaw thanking him for the courtesy he had shown to an out-of-town guest of her office not long before, which included dinner at the new Royal Orleans Hotel restaurant. "My personal thanks for your warm hospitality," she wrote, signing the letter, "Aurelie."[1336] A few short years later, Alost's name would find its way into an FBI memo, wherein she was quoted, indirectly, as having said that David Ferrie and Shaw knew each other well, that Ferrie had even visited Shaw in his office at the Mart. However, she never officially reported having any such knowledge to any law enforcement authorities.

Marcel Gomez was still working from the Department of International Relations office in the Mart. He often assisted with translation of letters, and with coordinating efforts for visiting foreign dignitaries.[1337] Most who knew Gomez have doubted, or denied knowledge of, any physical relationship between him and Shaw. However, vague rumors arose after Shaw's arrest about such a relationship, one that might have even involved Jim Garrison.

Shaw corresponded in the fall with William Spratling in Taxco, Mexico. He advised that Mabel Simmons, a travel writer with the *Times-Picayune*, would be in Taxco soon, and asked if Spratling could make her feel at home. Shaw also indicated that a copy of Spratling's book, *More Human than Divine*, had not yet arrived on Simmons's desk, and that Spratling should alert his publisher.[1338]

While the new building seemed to be progressing somewhat, the completion date was being pushed further into the future. In response to an inquiry about the showing of German goods at the Mart, Shaw advised the inquirer that the new building should be ready in October 1962. He indicated that it would have an enormous exhibition hall, and that it would hold a number of international shows on a regular basis.[1339]

In the middle of the year, Shaw heard from George Sawicki, who had worked for a number of years with International House, but who had since retired and moved to London, England. In a letter to him, referring to the fact that Sawicki recently had a leg amputated, Shaw wrote that he was glad to know that the "loss of a limb has not quenched your inexhaustible optimism and good humor." Shaw sent a picture of Edward Durell Stone's design of the new building, along with some descriptive material. Noting that Sawicki was restoring his new home in England, Shaw mentioned that he had by now restored ten such locations, and had never failed to get pleasure from it.[1340]

Sawicki replied a few days later, indicating that he had not realized that Shaw had restored so many properties in the Vieux Carré. Sawicki commented that, although he had heard a lot about Shaw's exquisite taste in remodeling homes, he had never seen any of them.[1341] In a follow-up letter in mid-July, Sawicki commented on the picture and description of the new Mart building. He indicated that perhaps it would rejuvenate the "slummy port area" and Canal Street from Royal Street towards the river. Sawicki indicated that Shaw had done an outstanding job with the new building project, which he realized required an immense amount of work.[1342]

Estimates of the number of properties Shaw restored over the years have varied. Some he may have simply purchased, made some modest improvements to, then resold in a better market. Others were properties with multiple structures on them, which over time he turned into new street addresses where none had existed before. Often he made considerable changes to the existing house and grounds.

Shaw's speaking schedule continued at the same busy pace as during 1959. He began the year by speaking in mid-January to a dinner meeting of Kemper Insurance employees at the Roosevelt hotel. In February, he spoke at Phillips High School in Birmingham, Alabama. As a result of that speech he received an inquiry from a Sam Shaw in Birmingham, asking about the "L" that began Shaw's middle name. Shaw replied that the L stood for "Lavergne," which had been the name of a close family friend.[1343]

In addition to the speech at the high school in Birmingham, Shaw made two other speeches as part of a trip to attend the Birmingham Festival of Arts. He spoke at the Rotary Club there, and also to a meeting of civic workers. In a letter to William Zetzmann, Mary Rich, Festival Chairman, said that Shaw also made a "superb" television appearance in Birmingham. Shaw had to leave before the main ball, but he was able to meet not only with Rich and her husband, Paul, but also with a W.R. Lathrop. Shaw had met with Mary Rich and Lathrop on their visit to New Orleans in October 1959, which led to him being issued the invitation to participate in the festival events.[1344]

Shaw also spoke in February before the Louisiana Bottlers Association at the Monteleone hotel, and before the Southern Conference of Building Owners and Managers at the Roosevelt hotel. In March, Shaw gave two brief talks in honor of Port of New Orleans Day at the New Orleans Public Library Auditorium in the Civic Center. He also spoke before the City Park Women's Club at Delgado Art Museum, and before the Junior League Provisional Group at the Council Chamber at City Hall.

In April, Shaw spoke before the Kiwanis Club of Lee Circle, at Delmonico's restaurant. In May, Shaw spoke to the Dallas (Texas) Export-Import Club, held in the Downtown Club in the Texas Bank and Trust Commerce Building. He was invited by his old friend, Bess Noble with the U.S. Department of Commerce in Memphis, Tennessee, to speak before the Memphis World Trade Club. However, Shaw indicated that he had been called for jury duty during the relevant time, and that he had to stay in New Orleans for several weeks, as his service had already been postponed three times, and the judge had said that he would "serve this time or go to jail," and the key would be thrown away.[1345]

In June, Shaw spoke at a Joint Civic Luncheon marking the opening of the Jacksonville International Trade Mart. One of the members of the Jacksonville Mart offered to fly Shaw to Jacksonville, but he indicated he preferred to drive, and stay in Fort Walton Beach, Florida along the way.[1346] After his speech, Shaw wrote to the institution with some additional thoughts. He indicated that 70% of local business generated in New Orleans was attributable to the Port of New Orleans. He hedged the figure by saying that the estimate was at least fifteen years old, that the exact method of calculating it had been lost to the "mists of history," and that it may have been modified by industries that had moved in in the meantime, but he noted that some of those very industries had moved to New Orleans because of the Port.[1347]

In August, Shaw spoke before the Crescent City Stamp Club, at the Sheraton-Charles Hotel. He also spoke before the Export Expansion Committee, at the King Edward Hotel in Jackson, Mississippi, on the topic of "The Crisis in International Trade."

In September, Shaw spoke before the New Orleans Junior Chamber of Commerce in the Marine Room at L'Enfant's restaurant, on the topic of "The New International Trade Mart." In October, he spoke before the Exchange Club of New Orleans at the Sheraton-

Charles Hotel, and before the Exchange Club of Metairie, Louisiana, at the House of Lee, a Chinese restaurant in that nearby city. Also in October, Shaw participated in a panel discussion of the Baton Rouge Export Clinic at the Capitol House hotel there; the event was sponsored by the U.S. Department of Commerce, and Shaw again worked with Edwin Leland. Before the event, Shaw and Leland discussed planting certain questions in the audience, which might lead into interesting topics during the question-and-answer period.

In mid-November, Shaw gave two speeches on the same day at the Royal Orleans Hotel. One was before the Association of Power Transmission Machinery Manufacturers, and the other to the Multiple V-Belt Drive and Mechanical Power Transmission Association. Also in November, he spoke before the Propeller Club of Nicholls State College in Thibodaux, Louisiana. In December, Shaw spoke to the International Trade Bureau Luncheon of the Young Men's Business Club at the Roosevelt hotel.

By 1960, Shaw was again active in the Foreign Policy Association of New Orleans, having resumed his former position as Program Chairman. The group had somewhat of an active year, with several important events. The National Foreign Policy Association, with whom the Foreign Policy Association of New Orleans was affiliated, was accused in mid-year of having pro-Soviet leanings. The accusations were made by Father Richard Ginder, a conservative political columnist and Catholic priest who, in the late 1960s, fell into disrepute after police searching his home found photographs of young boys performing homosexual acts, and diaries written by Ginder discussing his own same-sex acts; Ginder served four years in prison.[1348] As a result of Ginder's accusations, however, which were made in a few newspaper columns, the Foreign Policy Association of New Orleans developed somewhat of a split among its membership. Some members proposed changing the name of the New Orleans group, but Shaw was against the name change, feeling that the overall charges were unsubstantiated.[1349] Dr. Alton Ochsner offered to resign from the National Foreign Policy Association until it could either clear its name, or the New Orleans group could change its name to distance itself from the national organization. Ochsner, a prominent surgeon active in conservative national and international causes, was very sensitive to the charge of being favorable toward Communism. Ochsner apparently indicated a concern about being able to travel overseas while affiliated with the National Foreign Policy Association while such charges were lingering, but Shaw indicated that passports were generally awarded on the merits of a particular mission overseas, not because of the groups one belonged to; Shaw further suggested that a letter be written to government officials or agencies, including the attorney general of the United States, and the Federal Bureau of Investigation, explaining the specific positions of the New Orleans Foreign Policy Association.[1350] Ultimately, the Foreign Policy Association of New Orleans decided to sever connections with the national organization.

Monk Simons continued his policy of sending Shaw newspaper clippings related to Shaw's activities. In July, he sent a clipping that included a photograph of Shaw with a Brazilian newsman, and an image of the proposed new Mart building.[1351]

George Chaplin, former editor of the *Item*, now editor of *The Honolulu Advertiser* in Hawaii, wrote to Shaw about a Hawaii delegation visiting New Orleans. A handwritten note at the bottom of the letter indicated that "Esta joins in a fond Aloha—we enjoyed having Glen with us," referring to a visit by Glen Douthit, Director of Public Relations for the City of New Orleans.[1352]

The Mart's mix of permanent employees was the same throughout 1960. A list of the employees shown on the Blue Cross insurance plan in December 1960 included Hollis Bridges, Jesse R. Core, III, J.B. Dauenhauer, J.P. LaFever, Darlyn Mercadal, Goldie M. Moore, Clay L. Shaw, and Shelby L. Spuhler. Darlyn Mercadal had been with the Mart three years as of 1960; Shelby Spuhler had begun work there in the mid-1950s. Employees with one to five years of service received one paid week of vacation per year.

At an Executive Committee meeting of International House in mid-July, special mention was made of the ongoing and long-time efforts of Mario Bermúdez, and his "very capable" assistant, Marcel Gomez.[1353] Perhaps as much as any single individual since the mid-1940s, Bermúdez had advanced the image of New Orleans as an international city. He brought a somewhat unique set of talents to his duties, and if those unique talents sometimes carried over into his personal life, no one seemed to mind terribly, and some may have even benefitted from it.

Throughout 1960, the Board of Directors and Executive Committee meetings at International House were filled with discussions about the ongoing remodeling efforts. Generally, the remodeling was considered a great success, and it helped to rejuvenate International House at a time when the Mart was very much in a state of flux. The two organizations had continued to grow apart, and there was a growing frustration on the part of some Mart officials that International House had avoided an opportunity to merge which might not appear again.

Shaw's old friend and former boss, L.S. "Mac" McClaren, was still in touch. McClaren, now in the Mississippi State Senate, was looking for a Rotary Club speaker for the August 31 meeting in McComb, Mississippi, and requested that Shaw perform that task. McClaren noted that the recent burglary at Shaw's residence had made the news, and that it had been reported how Shaw had slept through the incident.[1354]

Shaw also received a midsummer telegram from William Spratling in Taxco, Mexico. The Customs Department had alerted Spratling to some discrepancies related to the samples he had sent to the International Fair held in the Mart two years before. Spratling noted that he was copying the local jeweler, Mark Antony, on the news, and said it was the first problem he had had with Customs in thirty years of shipping jewelry to the U.S.[1355]

Shaw received a letter from Leopoldo "Polo" Herrera, who had worked for the Mart as a student intern, or Trade Analyst, half a decade before. Herrera was now District Sales Manager with Real Airlines of Brazil in San Francisco.[1356]

The number of visitors coming into the building declined again during 1960. The total number ranged between 13,000 and 17,000 each month, with the largest monthly number being 17,004, in December 1960.

Shaw wrote to the Commercial Attaché at the Embassy of Portugal in Washington, seeking Portugal's representation in the Mart. As he typically did, Shaw named the countries that currently had representation in the Mart; there were fourteen at the moment.[1357] Interestingly, one of the countries supposedly represented was Cuba, almost a year and a half after Fidel Castro's revolution of early January 1959. The Cuban consulate had been kept open by some anti-Castro Cubans, one of Shaw's few contacts with that element, whose numbers would swiftly grow in New Orleans during the early 1960s. The Mart had agreed to let the old consulate keep its office, although it soon began to fall behind on its rent.

Tim Pasma of Power Advertising wrote to Shaw, asking for information on railroads in South America to which he might sell rubber shock absorbers. Pasma had been with Olin Chamberlin of Port Publishing Company in New Orleans years before, and recalled to Shaw the "good old days" there with fond memories.[1358]

Shaw received a letter from Vaughn Bryant, who had been with International House in its early years, and was now the Director of International Relations with the Port of Houston. Bryant indicated that he was just back from a recent trip to England; he recalled how Shaw had liked England during his stay there during the war, and said that he could now easily see why Shaw felt that way about the country.[1359]

The New Orleans Chamber of Commerce passed on to Shaw an inquiry from Miss Joan S. Pokross at Harvard University Business School, who was inquiring about some of the commercial institutions in New Orleans, including the Mart. Shaw responded to her inquiry, giving some of the Mart's history.[1360]

Local leaders and businessmen continued to interact with Shaw regularly. Whitaker F. Riggs, Jr., Executive Vice President of the Chamber of Commerce in New Orleans, wrote to Shaw, asking his opinion of efforts to put a theater at the newly-remodeled New Orleans airport, in order to show promotional films about New Orleans. Shaw replied that the idea was worth studying, if the number of people sufficiently interested was already present.[1361]

Robert D. Hess, who had begun to interact more with Shaw in a number of areas, wrote admiringly of Shaw's natural speaking abilities. In a letter regarding a public meeting that had occurred the night before, Hess wrote to Shaw, "I tip my hat to a master of impromptu speech before an audience. You handled questions beautifully last night, as I have seen you do in the past."[1362]

Jack Crawford, the former *VISION* representative, now with *The New Yorker*, sent Shaw a volume of stories that had been originally published in the magazine. Shaw replied, expressing his appreciation, indicating that he read a story or two from the volume every night.[1363]

J.B. Dauenhauer still was occupied handling routine inquiries. In response to one, he indicated that there were no plans currently to resume the Mart's newsletter. In the letter, he did not mention *The Marketeer*, which was a short-lived, more expanded publication intended to replace the newsletter.[1364] In response to another inquiry, this time regarding "Maspan," crushed almond mix used in making pastries, Dauenhauer referred the inquirer to Lawrence Fischer of Charles Dennery, Inc. in Metairie; Fischer was the husband of Louis Fischer, noted for her artistic and social gatherings conducted from her apartment in the Pontalba apartment building.[1365]

Vendors of various sorts tried to get in on the new Mart building, as they had with the original building before it opened. In July, Mayor Chep Morrison passed along to Shaw a letter from Morey L. Sear, an agent with the Home Title Insurance Company in New Orleans. Morrison wrote a note across the letter saying, "To Clay Shaw: Morey Sear wants the Title Insurance for ITM site. Can we give it to his company? Chep."[1366]

The proposed new Mart building attracted interest in real estate circles across the country. In a letter to realtor Trammel Crow in Dallas, Texas, Shaw enclosed a brochure about the building, upon the request of Mart board member Pendleton Lehde.[1367]

News of the new Mart building spread throughout the international news community as well during the late 1950s and early 1960s. Among those expressing interest was Kay Ray, who was with *The News*, an English language newspaper in Mexico City. Ray corresponded with Jesse Core throughout 1960 in the hopes of getting a job at the new Mart when it opened. Core informed her, though, that he could not predict when the new building eventually would be built.

An article by Lucius Beebe in the July 1960 issue of *House and Home*, a South Louisiana home and garden magazine, discussed the history of some of the properties Shaw had owned to date; Shaw had been mentioned more peripherally in an earlier edition of the magazine that same year. The stories mentioned that in 1950, he had bought a six-room home for $9,500, made improvements of $150, and sold it a few years later for $15,000. That was undoubtedly the home at 906 Esplanade, which would later become the object of witness Charles Spiesel's testimony at Shaw's trial in 1969. That same house re-sold in 1960 for $30,000. Another example was where Shaw had bought four homes on a rectangular site for $22,000, designed private gardens for each, installed a common patio and swimming pool, and had sold them later for a total of $122,000. They were the four homes that made up the old John J. Audubon property at 505 Dauphine, and adjoining properties, purchased by Artelle Trelford in a deal that essentially set Shaw financially, at least until his legal troubles. Shaw was quoted in the article as saying that in the French Quarter, "People spend up to $75,000 to restore mansions next door to Negro-occupied slums." He added that, "The French Quarter is unique. You can disregard most of the rules for realty investment." Shaw also discussed Brennan's restaurant, and the contribution it had made to dining in New Orleans. Author Beebe wrote that Shaw was the "administrative genius of the town's flourishing" International Trade Mart, and "a native whom many regard as successor to the title of 'Mr. New Orleans' accorded the late writer Lyle Saxon." [1368] [1369]

In mid-August 1960, Jesse Core wrote to General Charles Cabell, Deputy Director of the Central Intelligence Agency, about speaking before the Foreign Policy Association of New Orleans, now no longer affiliated with the national Foreign Policy Association. Core enclosed a brochure about the Mart, and indicated that the completion date for the new building would be September 1962. Core wrote that, "When you come to New Orleans to address the Foreign Policy Association, we expect that construction will be underway."[1370]

In 1960, Core was head of the Press Relations Committee of the Foreign Policy Association of New Orleans. Core, at the time, was married to Lucy Ruggles, daughter of the publisher of the *Dallas Morning News*. As such, Core had access to prominent people in Dallas, including the mayor of the city, Earle Cabell. Cabell's brother was General Charles P. Cabell, Deputy Director of the Central Intelligence Agency and second in position only to famed CIA Director Allen Dulles. General Cabell had been making speeches around the country concerning foreign policy issues, and Core suggested to Shaw that perhaps Cabell could be persuaded to speak before the Foreign Policy Association of New Orleans. Shaw wrote to Cabell himself, indicating that he had heard through Core that Cabell had consented to address the group, which Shaw assured him was not affiliated with any national organization, an indirect reference to the recent controversy at the national Foreign Policy Association; Shaw mentioned that he understood that Cabell wished to speak only after the November 1960 presidential election.[1371]

In one of the many ironic touches surrounding Shaw's life, Shaw would introduce Cabell to the audience when he gave his speech in New Orleans in May 1961. The fact that Earle Cabell was mayor of Dallas at the time of President Kennedy's assassination, and his brother Charles was a prominent CIA employee who would essentially be fired by Kennedy in January 1962, months after the ill-fated Bay of Pigs Invasion in April 1961, have provided fertile ground for conspiracy theorists over the years. Shaw's brief association with Charles Cabell through his speech to the Foreign Policy Association of New Orleans has compounded the issue.

International House had moved ahead with its planned remodeling, clearly signaling that it would not join forces officially with the Mart, and would not be moving to the new Mart building, whenever it was completed. The September 1960 Bulletin of the Export Managers Club, the *Foreign Trader*, mentioned that the remodeled International House would be dedicated on November 29, 1960, with governors of all states invited to the ceremony.[1372]

In September 1960, Shaw wrote to Edward J. Steimel of the Public Affairs Research Council, in Baton Rouge, commenting on Steimel's analysis of the proposed bond amendment to finance the new Mart building.[1373] The Public Affairs Research Council was a state watchdog group that analyzed legislation and other proposals in the public interest, mainly from a business perspective. The Mart's favorable tax treatment, and the bond amendment to fund the Mart building, had caught the organization's eye. Steimel would, during the 1970s, be active in the efforts to pass a right-to-work law in Louisiana, after several highly publicized incidents of labor-related violence.

Also in September, Shaw wrote to Wylie F.L. Tuttle of Collins, Tuttle and Company in New York City, upon whom the Mart was relying at the time for financing of the new building. Shaw indicated that he was just back from a week of vacation, and that he expected the bond amendment to be approved by voters in the November 8th election.[1374]

In late September, Frances Goetz, of Delta Publishing Company, wrote to Shaw asking him to contribute a one-page feature story to appear in the publication *New Orleans Guide to Fun*.[1375] Over the years, Shaw had become one of the public figures to which media could dependably go for a cooperative contribution to various programs and publications concerning local commerce or culture.

In a letter to International House members, Captain Neville Levy, the current President, indicated that the remodeling effort that had begun in 1959, and had cost approximately $300,000, was nearing completion.[1376] Shortly after International House had been remodeled, Joseph Merrick Jones of Tulane University wrote to Levy, congratulating him on the completion of the renovation; Jones said the plans had been "superbly conceived."[1377]

Chep Morrison, who by 1960 had been mayor for fourteen years, actively supported the Mart's efforts to get into a new building. In a letter to Morrison in mid-October, Shaw praised Morrison's recent talk to a group about the new Mart building. However, Shaw indicated that Morrison was largely "preaching to converts," and that the task before all supporters of the Mart was to "carry the message to the infidel."[1378]

Representatives from the new World Trade Center in Rome, Italy, also known as Centro Mondiale Commerciale, kept the Mart apprised of happenings at its facility. A letter from its Publicity Department in October enclosed a copy of the Special Directory of Sporting Goods Exhibition held from August 22 through October 22, 1960. The letter was addressed to no one in particular at the Mart.[1379]

In late October, Morrison wrote to William Zetzmann, indicating that Zachary Strate, operator of the Fountainbleau Motel, had called Morrison recently and said that he knew someone who could finance all or part of the new Mart building. A note by Shaw, written onto the letter, indicated that he had called Strate recently, and Strate had indicated that he would call Shaw the next time his friend was in town.[1380] Strate would be convicted in a few years, along with Teamsters Union President Jimmy Hoffa, as part of a probe into that organization's activities. Strate, in 1967, would insert himself into New Orleans District Attorney Jim Garrison's investigation into the Kennedy assassination, in an attempt to bargain for his freedom from those earlier criminal convictions.

I.W. "Pat" Patterson, with the Louisiana Department of Commerce and Industry, wrote asking Shaw to serve on the Foreign Trade Export-Import subcommittee of the department. The purpose of the subcommittee was to originate programs and activities to induce businesses to relocate to Louisiana. Shaw attended a meeting of the group in Baton Rouge at the State Capitol Building.[1381]

In a report to the Board of Directors in late October, William Zetzmann indicated that the Mart's efforts to lease the new building had again been unsuccessful. It had been unable to generate enough leases in advance to obtain the necessary financing for its bonds, and had had to ask the City to issue bonds. The Dock Board had offered to finance the project with bonds; Houston and San Francisco were both in the process of building international centers with financing by their own Dock Boards.[1382] At a meeting of the Board of Directors the same day, the offer of Dock Board financing was discussed at great length. If the Dock Board would not provide financing, then it would be necessary to pass the new Constitutional Amendment 39, which would allow for other means of financing. Lloyd Cobb pointed out that International House and the Mart, when they were built in the 1940s, had been created because members of the business community felt that the Dock Board was not doing its duty properly at the time. He recounted the history of the relationship between the two institutions and the Dock Board, indicating that such financing had been turned down by the Dock Board three years earlier, but that recently it had changed its position. Cobb indicated the local community was "falling down on the job," and mentioned recent *Times-Picayune* editorials against Amendment 39, which created "special privileges" for the new Mart building project.[1383]

Shaw's friend, George Haverstick, was still in the New Orleans area. In November, there was an announcement that Moreland H. Hogan had purchased Lane Warehouse on Tchoupitoulas Street, and had appointed Haverstick to develop the property, in cooperation with local realtors.

Also in November, Shaw appeared on the "Sell Louisiana" program on WWL-TV. William Zetzmann wrote Shaw soon afterwards, complimenting him on his appearance.[1384]

Shaw spoke at an event at the Roosevelt hotel in November. Walter Hoover with the local Chamber of Commerce and Don Driscoll, President of Harlequin Productions in Los Angeles, California, were in the audience. In early December, Driscoll wrote to Shaw, asking if he would narrate a film sponsored by the New Orleans Chamber of Commerce, entitled "A View from the Quarter."[1385]

The New Orleans writer, Harnett Kane, spoke at the December meeting of the Foreign Policy Association of New Orleans. Shaw was still the key man involved in procuring speakers for the group. Charles Leonard, formerly the consul of Belgium in New Orleans, was now the Executive Director of the group.[1386] In a small typed note on the group's stationery, Leonard wrote to Shaw saying that, "If you have a top man in mind whom you know personally, it might be opportune to drop him a line with the idea that he might speak for us."[1387]

Mayor Morrison invited Shaw to another Executive Committee meeting of his administration, held at Morrison's office at the end of the year. The invitation mentioned various economic losses that New Orleans had sustained during 1960. It also mentioned a 1% sales tax that was burdening economic growth.[1388] A "Year-End Report to Citizens of New Orleans" by Morrison discussed the beginnings of forced integration in the New Orleans area, with four "Negro girls" entering into all-white schools after eight years of litigation.[1389]

In an Executive Committee meeting of International House in mid-December, President-elect Kennedy's recent election was noted, and it was discussed that he was considering the creation of a Latin American chair in his new Cabinet. A movement was underway in New Orleans to get Mayor Chep Morrison the job.[1390]

When Shaw was arrested in 1967 for allegedly playing a role in Kennedy's assassination, a number of individuals recalled Shaw saying good things about Kennedy, even recalling him verbally supporting Kennedy in the extremely close race against Vice President Richard Nixon. It is unlikely, however, that Shaw played any active role in Kennedy's campaign, even locally in New Orleans. Shaw was a relatively highly-paid employee of a very public institution, and his keeping the job depended to a great extent on not making any enemies among the powerful, wealthy businessmen behind the Mart. Taking sides in an election would have been just the way to alienate a number of Mart supporters for no good reason. And there was no real need to campaign for Kennedy in heavily Catholic New Orleans; Kennedy received one of his highest statewide percentages of votes against Nixon in Louisiana, and beat Nixon even more decisively in New Orleans.

Although Shaw had political views, he was simply not that political in an overt sense. He was friendly with Mayor Morrison, for instance, but it is likely that he would have been very cooperative with anyone in the mayor's office, as indeed he soon would be with Victor Schiro, who took over as mayor after Morrison departed for Washington. It was the same for governors or any public officials; Shaw was friendly and cooperative with all of them, for the benefit of the Mart.

The very political writer Gore Vidal described Shaw, in a lengthy interview in the June 1969 issue of *Playboy* magazine, as a "charming apolitical man" who, in Vidal's view, could have had nothing to do with Kennedy's death. Vidal reiterated that view in a 2007 conversation with the author, after a Vidal talk at Vanderbilt University; Shaw was not really interested in politics, Vidal said, only "parties."

Shaw was renting out his property at 1313 Dauphine Street during 1960. A statement from prominent French Quarter realtor "Frosty" Blackshear indicated that rental income for December 1960 was $160; after subtracting her 6% commission, total net rental income was $150.40.[1391]

By the end of 1960, the Mart was feeling the financial strain from its declining operations even more severely. In mid-December, Shaw wrote to Mario Bermúdez, responding to a request for the Mart to contribute another scholarship to the Cordell Hull foundation. Shaw indicated that "the present state of finances makes me feel that we will probably not be able to go along on this at present."[1392]

While Shaw had settled, years earlier, into a comfortable situation regarding his private life, even with its promiscuity and somewhat daring sexual experimentation, the opinion of New Orleanians about homosexuality was quite divided during the era of the mid-20th century. On the one hand, an upscale, or upwardly mobile, gay man like Shaw was tolerated, even accepted to a large degree, as long as he was able to keep his activities under wraps, away from anyone who wished not to know about it. On the other hand, "street trade," homosexuals who attempted to pick up individuals on the streets of the French Quarter, were seen as a nuisance that might interfere with tourism, and might be objectionable in other ways as well. During the 1950s, Mayor Chep Morrison had formed the Mayor's Special Citizens' Committee for the Vieux Carré, chaired for a time by his half-brother, Jacob Morrison. The committee was concerned mostly with vice crime, such as gambling and prostitution, but also with the issue of homosexuals cruising the French Quarter. Edgar Stern, Jr., the son of Edith Stern, and owner of WDSU-TV Channel 6, was on the commission, as was Owen Brennan, the owner of Brennan's restaurant until his death in 1955. The group gathered information related to laws and ordinances governing homosexuals in other cities around the country, and reviewed input from Chambers of Commerce in Boston, Chicago, Philadelphia, Cleveland, and other cities.[1393] Interestingly, some of those cities did not have statutes regulating sodomy, even sodomy between members of the same sex, only statutes regulating prostitution and loitering.

The Superintendent of Police in New Orleans at the time indicated to the committee that the French Quarter attracted many homosexuals, including lesbians. He said that most were gainfully employed, had family and income, and were not engaged in "crime for profit." He indicated, however, that they sometimes congregated together, resulting in complaints from other members of the public.[1394] Typical of such "nuisances" was a newspaper report of Mary M. D'Amico, who was arrested on February 20, 1959, for wearing men's clothing, including men's shoes, socks, shirt, pants, and sporting a man's haircut, and a "large male type ring" on the ring finger of her right hand.

Some in the straight community were terribly naïve about such activities, while others were tolerant but perhaps a bit distant on the subject. Natalie Scott, the former New Orleans resident now living in Taxco, Mexico, was typical of how some women in that era, especially women who were somewhat used to the idea, looked upon such relationships. Writing to a friend back in New Orleans from Taxco, Mexico, where two males from New Orleans were living together near her, Scott referred to them as "a pair."[1395]

The Special Citizens Investigating Committee, an independent committee formed to investigate police corruption in the mid-1950s, and managed by Aaron Kohn, who later would become Managing Director of the New Orleans Metropolitan Crime Commission, also looked into vice activities, including those involving homosexuality. A letter to the editor of the *Times-Picayune* in March 1954, collected in the committee's files, openly complained about the "rash of indecencies" during the recent Mardi Gras, attributing it to French Quarter establishments "which harbor and sell services of female impersonators." The letter went on to say, "They have become bolder by the day," due to the "apathy" of the mayor, the city council, the police and newspapers. The writer ended by asking why citizens of New Orleans should tolerate such "fugitives from Los Angeles with attending degradation to our city?"[1396]

Going back several more years to a letter dated June 1951 to Joseph L. Scheuering, Superintendent of Police, Richard R. Foster, then Chairman of the Mayor's Special Citizens Committee for the Vieux Carré, listed homosexual bars that catered to one sex or the other, including Dixie's Bar of Music, The Chez When, Starlet Lounge, Tony Becino's, Lafitte's

Blacksmith Shop, Nikki's Bar, and the Cinderella Club. Foster indicated that, "Leading criminologists and psychologists state that every sexual deviate is a potential murderer and the more of this type we drive out of New Orleans, the better New Orleans will be."[1397]

The issue of homosexuality cut across many strange lines. Right-wing groups like the American Nazi Party and the Ku Klux Klan were sometimes ridiculed for having homosexual members, or for being among organizations that attracted "perverts." In the 1960s, Murray Martin, leader of a Klan faction in Louisiana, responded to such a charge by saying that he was trying to eliminate any "undesirables" from his group. He said that the group had no "sex-perverts or homosexuals," and he defied anyone to find them there.[1398] The American Nazi Party leasder George Lincoln Rockwell also battled accusations about his group being a magnet for homosexuals.

Another example of this phenomenon was reflected in 1965 when Ed Butler, founder of the New Orleans-based anti-Communist group Information Council of the Americas (INCA), passed on to Dr. Alton Ochsner, a board member of the organization, an article from *The Washington Post* edition of February 19, 1965. The article dealt with an attempt to smear then-U.S. Senator Thomas Kuchel of California on a gay morals charge. Four individuals had tried to blackmail Kuchel, by alleging that he had been involved in a homosexual incident in February 1950, in Los Angeles, which had never come to light before. Butler commented to Ochsner in a note related to the article that such a smear tactic was sometimes used to discredit individuals, and could be very damaging to an organization.[1399]

In those days, many conservative, or "right-wing," political organizations, such as INCA, unless they were explicitly religiously-based, were friendlier, or at least not unfriendly, to homosexuality in general. Many members of conservative organizations were gay, although not openly so, and the fight against gay rights was simply not on the agenda for most such groups.

In closing, it is interesting to note that even many of Shaw's close friends had conflicting feelings about homosexuality. In August 1945, Muriel Bultman Francis had written from New York to her parents, discussing her recent weekend at Fire Island. She described the location as "overrun with rather queer characters," and added, "I kept thinking that this was one place where a good bomb would do a lot of good."[1400]

# 19 · The Number Two Man at the CIA Comes to Town

The year 1961 began with the continuing uncertainty related to the new building that had spilled over from 1960 and the preceding years. At a meeting of the Board of Directors in January, it was noted that the Mart's net worth was approximately $500,000. The Dock Board had agreed to cooperate in financing the new building with a bond issue, if a survey it was taking of the available rental and exhibition space in the area supported the idea. The Mart was cutting back on contributions to various civic causes, basically slashing those expenditures in half. The major problem the Mart faced in its current building was that tenants wanted longer leases than the Mart could give them, given its uncertain situation, and some were looking elsewhere. With no new building immediately on the horizon, the Mart was unable to offer them any short-term alternative. Additionally, the Cuban situation, the revolution that had occurred in 1959 and had escalated during 1960 in disrupting businesses operating on the island, had caused some losses to the Mart, indirectly, through its tenants' businesses.[1401]

In January 1961, Jack Harris of Norman, Oklahoma wrote to Shaw applying for the Cordell Hull Foundation Scholarship provided by the Mart. Harris had been a student at LSU, but was living in New Orleans at the time.[1402] Mario Bermúdez had been active since the beginning in the Cordell Hull Foundation, and would be throughout the next two decades, matching exchange teachers in the U.S. and Latin America. During his Kennedy assassination investigation, Jim Garrison would occasionally invoke the Cordell Hull Foundation as a mysterious, perhaps sinister, organization, without ever directly involving it in the investigation itself, and without making any specific allegations against it.

An article appeared in the *Wall Street Journal* on February 6, 1961, entitled "More Americans Move to Old Neighborhoods, Restore Antique Houses." Shaw was mentioned in a small portion of the article that dealt with the necessity of the new owners to ensure that changes they made conformed to historical design rules, regulations, or laws. Shaw indicated that at one residence, most probably the set of properties at 505 Dauphine and adjoining, which used to be the old John J. Audubon home, in order to install a swimming pool, he had to make it look like a fish pond, with statuary, and a rectangular-shape edge with old brick coping.[1403]

Shaw appeared on a panel involving the topic "Locating Overseas Markets" at the Monteleone hotel. The conference was sponsored by the U.S. Department of Commerce.

In February, J.B. Dauenhauer and Shaw both wrote letters of recommendation for Shelby Spuhler. Spuhler had been a "clerk-typist-office boy" from August 1956 through February 1961, but had been let go due to the Mart's financial situation.[1404]

At a meeting of the Executive Committee in mid-February, Shaw advised that it might be necessary to reduce the total budget for the new building to $10,000,000, down from a high of $13,000,000, to cut four floors from the height of the building, and to have someone else finance the plaza that would surround the building. He noted that no version of the building could be ready before 1963, the way things stood, and that the Mart would need to renegotiate the lease on its current building, and keep its assessment for property tax purposes at $100,000.[1405]

International House was offered the possibility of switching its building's electrical power from direct current (DC) to alternate current (AC), at a cost of $10,000. Although the New Orleans Public Service Company, Inc. (NOPSI) indicated that it would pay half of the cost, International House decided not to go through with the change.[1406]

The President of International House during 1960-61 was Captain Neville Levy, the President of Equitable Equipment Company. Levy was born in New Orleans in 1892, had graduated from Tulane University in 1913, and founded Equitable Equipment Company in 1921. He served in the U.S. Navy in both World War I and World War II. Equitable Equipment Company had approximately 1,000 employees in 1961.[1407]

At a meeting of Mart bondholders in mid-March, it was noted that the current building had only achieved 86% occupancy during 1960, a new low, and the organization had incurred a $17,000 loss for the year. The loss had mostly been due to a drop in rental income, as tenants left to find larger spaces in a more certain environment. However, some of the drop in income had come about because the Mart had cashed Treasury bonds in order to purchase some of the land that would be required for the new building. The Treasury bonds had been purchased in the mid-1950s, after the sale of the original building to outside investors. With the sale of the bonds, the Mart had given up the continuing interest income from them.[1408]

On the same day, William Zetzmann reported to the Annual Meeting of the Mart. He reiterated that the original plan for the Mart had been a pilot program, in a relatively small building, that would be replaced by a larger building if the plan worked, which it had. The larger building would have exhibition space, as was planned for the new building. However, the new building had failed to generate adequate long-term leases in order to obtain financing, and the cost of redoing Eads Plaza, the surrounding area that would be an important part of the exterior of the new building, and the failure to get long-term commitments for the exhibit hall, due to a failure of private financing, had caused the project to come to a standstill. The Mart had then turned to the Dock Board in hopes of financing the project with municipal bonds. Zetzmann noted that the Dock Board had contributed $10,000 to a study of exhibition space in the area, in order to determine if it would move forward with the financing. Additionally, developments in San Francisco, Houston, and New York City had closed the gap between New Orleans and its competitors. Amendment 39, which would have given the Mart special privileges that would have allowed it to go forward with the new building, had been defeated by Louisiana voters in the 1960 election.[1409]

An atmosphere of gloom settled over the Mart executives. At a meeting of the Board of Directors later in March, Zetzmann said that the failure to build the new building would set New Orleans back a hundred years.[1410]

In March, Shaw wrote to Paul Spargnapani, whose father was the Swiss consul in New Orleans, indicating that Spargnapani could use him as a reference. Shaw wrote Spargnapani in care of Nicholas Vartzikos in Washington, D.C., mentioning Carl Sprick in the letter.[1411] In a letter to Shaw, Spargnapani mentioned a recent death in Shaw's family, and suggested that the new Mart building might possibly be financed through Equitable, a life insurance company.

The recent death in Shaw's family was probably the one referred to in a telegram by William Zetzmann to Shaw at McKneely Funeral Home in Kentwood, Louisiana. In the telegram, Zetzmann indicated, "We wish to extend our deepest sympathy to you and your family in your hour of loss."[1412]

Shaw continued to be sought after for opinions regarding international trade. In late March 1961, he received a letter from Senator Jacob K. Javits of New York, asking him for comments on a proposed National Import Policy Act. Javits had been referred to Shaw by Gilbert Vorhoff of Hemisphere International Corporation.[1413]

Shaw's old friend L.S. McClaren wrote, asking him for assistance in arranging a tour of the Mart, and the New Orleans area, for the Home Demonstration Club of Pike County,

Mississippi, McClaren's home county. In April, Shaw wrote to McClaren confirming that he would be glad to arrange the tour.[1414]

Also in April, Shaw gave a letter of recommendation to "Miss Josephine Pennestri," who had applied to work for the government. Pennestri had worked for the Mart from May 1953 through January 1959.[1415]

In early May, Shaw wrote to Wylie Tuttle, President of Collins, Tuttle, indicating that, "The Trade Mart, I hope, is not dead but sleeping," and noting the continuing difficulty the Mart was having with the financing of the new building.[1416]

The Mississippi Valley World Trade Conference was held in early May at the Roosevelt hotel. The Mart continued to participate, as it always had done, even with the cloud of uncertainty hanging over its head. Gilbert M. Mellin was Program Chairman for the conference.

The long-delayed speech by General Charles Cabell, Deputy Director of the Central Intelligence Agency under Allen Dulles, to the Foreign Policy Association of New Orleans, finally took place on May 9, 1961. In early January 1961, Jesse Core had written again to Cabell at the agency, reminding him that the election was now over, and that the group needed a date for his speech. Core noted Cabell's recent speech before the Dallas Council on World Affairs, as reported in the *Dallas Morning News*, and indicated that the article had created much interest in New Orleans.[1417]

In late February, Walter Elder of the CIA wrote to Charles Leonard, Executive Director of the Foreign Policy Association of New Orleans, indicating that Cabell would speak on May 9, 1961. Elder asked Leonard to advise him of the arrangements, including audience size, time and place of the speech, and other relevant details; Elder indicated that Cabell would pay his own travel expenses.[1418] In late March, Jesse Core wrote to Elder, confirming the date of Cabell's speech, and requesting Elder to send a photograph and a biography of the General.[1419]

Charles Leonard provided Shaw a biographical sketch of General Cabell, who was at the time in the United States Air Force, and inquired if Shaw would be at the dinner preceding Cabell's talk. The biographical sketch indicated that Cabell was born on October 11, 1903, and that he had become Deputy Director of the CIA on April 23, 1953.[1420]

A press release, listing Shaw as Program Chairman and Jesse Core as Press Relations Chairman, stated that Shaw would introduce Cabell to the group. It also noted that Earle Cabell, General Cabell's brother, was now the mayor of Dallas, Texas. The speech would be at 8:30 p.m. at the Sheraton Charles Hotel. Jesse Core passed on a photo of Cabell to Shaw with a note saying, "I explained to Cabell's people that you will be in control of situation and can turn off questions with a too-short-time explanation."

A short meeting was held at 8:00 p.m., before Cabell's speech, to elect officers and directors, and to change the name of the group officially to the Foreign Relations Association of New Orleans.[1421] The name change was directly related to the controversy about the National Foreign Policy Association, and the alleged Communist influence in that organization. At the meeting before Cabell's speech, Shaw was elected Treasurer of the group for one year.[1422]

A Blue Card allowing two guests for admission to Cabell's speech was issued to pre-approved attendees. Several of the employees of the local CIA office in New Orleans attended Cabell's speech that night, which was on the topic of "Communist Science" (some references have it as "Communism and Science"). Additionally, Cabell's tenuous connection with Jesse Core was further illuminated according to information the CIA kept in its files: Cabell's grandfather and Jesse Core's grandfather had both served in the Civil War, although it is unclear from the information whether they served together, or merely at the same time.[1423]

After Cabell's speech, an article in the *States-Item* the next day commented that the CIA had received much of the blame for the failure of the recent Cuban invasion in April.[1424]

Tommy Griffin's "Lagniappe" column in the newspaper said that the Cabell speech had drawn the largest crowd in the history of the Foreign Policy Association of New Orleans, more than four hundred people, and that the Association had to waive the question-and-answer phase, because the CIA was keeping quiet on current affairs.[1425] Jesse Core wrote to Cabell after the event, but a notation on the letter indicates that it was never mailed. In the letter, Core thanked Cabell for his speech, and shared that he had tried to shield Cabell from questions, but that media questions were inevitable. Core dryly noted how reporter Stella Martin's lead article in a local newspaper had attempted to explain Cabell's own explanation of the CIA's traditional silence regarding events. Core thanked Cabell for his reference to Core in his speech, and mentioned that his uncle was a good friend of Cabell's brother, Dallas Mayor Earle Cabell.[1426]

International House continued to run the Cordell Hull Foundation, the managing of which it had taken over in 1955. It charged the Foundation a token cost of $1 per year; the governor of Tennessee continued to serve as Chairman of the Board of Trustees.[1427]

The big news for International House at the time, however, and the related setback that went with it, was the resignation of Charles Nutter as Managing Director on April 20, 1961. At an Executive Committee meeting in mid-May, Nutter's resignation was reviewed extensively. Board members Maurice Barr and Joseph Rault had discussed the situation with Nutter, but he said the resignation was irrevocable. He also requested a pension, but no pension rights had been accrued for him. Nutter also wanted pay for vacation time that he had not taken, and the two men had offered him one month's pay instead. Lloyd Cobb indicated his position as being in favor of accepting Nutter's resignation, but opposing the payment of any severance pay. The prominent surgeon Dr. Alton Ochsner chaired the meeting that dealt with this sensitive issue.[1428]

At another meeting of the Executive Committee of International House at the end of May, the issue of Nutter's separation request was still alive. Nutter had written a letter the week before, asking that the issue of his pension rights and vacation payments be reopened for discussion.[1429] The issue would linger for some time.

A notice in the New Orleans newspapers at the end of May indicated that Nutter was going to work for the Hallmark Foundation in Kansas City, Missouri as an executive officer. Nutter had started with International House at the end of 1945, before its official opening, and shortly before Shaw began as his counterpart at the Mart. He had been as active as Shaw in many different ways in civic affairs for the city of New Orleans, and in the international trade arena. He actually had taken far more international trips than Shaw from 1946 through 1960; that was mainly due to the difference in purpose between the two organizations.

A press release from International House in mid-June indicated that Nutter's resignation had become official on June 1, and that Shaw had been appointed Acting Managing Director of International House. Shaw had served in the same position for six months during 1956, when Nutter had gone to Europe as secretary to Hale Boggs's Committee on Foreign Trade Policy.[1430]

At the time of his resignation, Charles Nutter made $21,000 in annual salary.[1431] In a letter to Kenneth Barranger, International House's attorney, Nutter said that when he had been hired in the mid-1940s, Rudolf Hecht had promised to give Nutter credit for his years of newspaper experience toward a pension down the line.[1432] Nutter still owed International House some money related to advances on expenses, and that topic was a matter of discussion along with the pension issue.[1433]

While the pension issue was ongoing, a memo was unearthed, or generated, detailing a meeting on January 5, 1956. The meeting had been called to discuss the fact that Nutter and E.O. Jewell, a subordinate of Nutter's at International House, were not getting along. Apparently, other issues were discussed at that meeting as well, such as Nutter's salary, and his desire to have a pension plan. William Zetzmann and Richard Jones, who both attended the meeting, indicated that Rudolf Hecht had become livid upon learning that Nutter had purchased a local newspaper in Minden, Louisiana, which had subsequently failed, causing Nutter some financial difficulty. According to the later recollections of Zetzmann and Jones, Hecht went into a rage about Nutter, and would have fired him had he not passed away shortly thereafter. Both men said that Hecht opposed increasing Nutter's salary at the time, and the idea of a pension plan as well.[1434]

Some months later, in mid-November 1961, Nutter's old friend, Richard Swenson, who had been Public Relations Director with the Port of New Orleans in the early 1950s, wrote a letter to Lawrence Molony, a Board member of International House, supporting Nutter's version of the pension issue.[1435] Molony responded two days later, indicating that the pension matter had been considered, and was now closed.[1436]

After Shaw's appointment as Acting Managing Director of International House, he received a congratulatory letter from Congressman Hale Boggs. Shaw replied, thanking Boggs for his "flattering remarks" and saying that, "You looked fine on Huntley-Brinkley last night, but can you really read 5,000 words per minute?"[1437]

Shaw also received a congratulatory letter from New Orleans writer Harnett Kane. Kane mentioned his upcoming article on the Murchison family of Dallas, Texas.[1438] Shaw responded, saying that he hoped the piece on the Murchisons turned out well, and commented that they seemed to be a "fascinating family."[1439]

The Mart continued to receive inquiries related to its newsletter. In response to one such inquiry, Shaw replied that the Mart had discontinued the newsletter, and had no magazine to replace it. He indicated that the Mart intended to bring out a magazine in the future, but specific plans were uncertain at the time.[1440] The continuing questions related to the progress of the proposed new building had led the Mart to evaluate any such discretionary expenditures with more scrutiny than ever.

Shaw had tried to interest *The New York Times* in publishing a story about the Mart's new building efforts. However, Arnold H. Lubasch with the newspaper said that he could not proceed with the story until he had some new information regarding the progress.[1441] Shaw replied that he was just returning from vacation, but that he hoped that a forthcoming survey of rental and exhibition space, due at the end of June, would provide the needed info to prompt a new article in the newspaper.[1442]

Shaw also tried to interest *The New Yorker* in preparing an article about the new building. In a letter to Robert R. (Bob) Eckardt of *The New Yorker*, Shaw thanked him for sending a recent article in *Travel Weekly* magazine, and suggested that the story of the new Mart building should be written up in his publication.[1443]

Mayor Chep Morrison wrote Shaw, asking for a contribution to a campaign for changes in the charter to the New Orleans city government.[1444] By mid-year, Morrison would be appointed by President Kennedy to be the U.S. representative to the Organization of American States (OAS), which worked for common interests among the nations of North, Central, and South America, and the Caribbean.

Shaw served on the Central Area Committee, which was concerned with the Central Business District area of New Orleans, both in terms of rental space and general business conditions. Shaw periodically reported to the group on the progress of the new Mart building, such as it was.

Over the years, the Mart had received many requests for foreign stamps received on incoming mail. The Mart had generally been cooperative in trying to reply to such requests, but in a letter to such an inquirer in mid-1961, Goldie Moore replied that, although the Mart still received many such requests, the number of foreign stamps had decreased substantially, due to the increased use of postal meters.[1445]

One of the tenants of the Mart during 1961 was the Free Voice of Latin America, which broadcast a signal from New Orleans to Mexico, Central and South America. The Secretary-Treasurer of the group was William R. Klein, brother of Burton Klein, who would later be one of the defense attorneys who represented some of the minor figures charged during Jim Garrison's investigation into the Kennedy assassination. The Executive Director of the group was Ed Butler, who later would be active in Information Council of the Americas (INCA), an anti-Communist foreign policy-oriented group that had strong support from Dr. Alton Ochsner. Free Voice of Latin America had fallen behind on rent to the Mart in early 1961,[1446] but Butler thanked Shaw for his patience with the group, saying that the organization had great promise.[1447]

The film *View from the Quarter*, produced by the Greater New Orleans Chamber of Commerce, for which Shaw had done the narration, was completed and shown to interested parties during the summer of 1961.[1448] It was another example of the work that Shaw, and numerous others in the city, did as a matter of course on an ongoing basis to help the city emphasize its culture and history.

Shaw received a letter in August from B. Pederson of Pederson Portraits in Lake Charles, Louisiana, who had been with the engineering firm of Godat and Heft during the 1940s; Godat and Heft had been involved with the remodeling of the original Mart building from 1946 to 1948. Pederson had kept a set of fifty Kodachrome slides showing the construction of the original Mart building in various stages of completion, beginning with the original Baldwin building before remodeling had begun. He offered to sell the slides to the Mart for $100,[1449] but Shaw replied that the Mart had no use for them.[1450]

Shaw continued his full array of activities during 1961. In January, Marcel Gomez reminded him of a round table discussion he was participating in on WYES-TV; Henry Holland and Captain J.W. Clark also participated.[1451] In late January, Harry M. England invited Shaw to meet Herbert L. Barnet and Joan Crawford Steele of the Pepsi-Cola Company on February 1 at the Roosevelt hotel; Joan Crawford Steele was the famous actress, who was now married to the president of the Pepsi-Cola Company. Shaw had found it necessary to pass on an earlier invitation to meet Crawford, but this time he accepted.[1452]

In early May, Shaw participated with Edwin A. Leland, Jr., of the U.S. Department of Commerce, in a live television panel show on WYES-TV. Leland was chairman of the World Trade Week Committee, and the show was devoted to that celebration. Gilbert Mellin and J.H. Boyd, Manager of Foreign Trade Zone #2, were also on the television panel.[1453]

In early July, Shaw accepted an invitation by the soon-to-be-opened Playboy Club in New Orleans to meet the club's "bunnies" at the New Orleans Press Club location. The club, an outgrowth of *Playboy* magazine, opened in New Orleans at 725 Iberville Street in mid-October 1961; it was the third Playboy Club to open, after those in Chicago and Miami.

Also in July, Chep Morrison resigned, after serving more than fifteen years as mayor, in order to accept President Kennedy's appointment as the U.S. representative for the Organization of American States (OAS). A formal testimonial dinner was organized, with Captain Neville Levy as chairman; Shaw was invited to the dinner.[1454] In a telegram to William Zetzmann in mid-July, indicating that the president of Pakistan was visiting New Orleans, Morrison noted that his swearing-in ceremony in Washington was set for Monday afternoon, July 17, 1961.[1455]

Morrison's ceremony was noteworthy because Shaw attended, staying at the Sheraton Hotel in Washington.[1456] During the event, Shaw met President Kennedy for the first, and probably only, time. It would be an ironic twist of fate to be accused, less than six years later, of conspiring to murder the man he had met so briefly. Also present at the swearing-in was the new mayor, Victor Schiro, H.T. (Monte) Shalett, President of the New Orleans Aviation Board, U.S. Senators Allen Ellender and Russell Long, and U.S. Congressmen F. Edward Hebert and Otto Passman of Louisiana.

During July, Shaw also served as Master of Ceremonies for a ribbon cutting related to the opening of a Buyer's Market at the Mart. Although the Mart was struggling to keep the public's general interest going, it made every effort to see that its traditional activities continued as always.

In September, Shaw received an invitation from Cecil M. Shilstone to attend a luncheon for Captain Thomas Dumont of the United States Navy.[1457] Also that month, the new mayor, Victor Schiro, appointed Shaw to a NASA-New Orleans Coordinating Committee breakfast. Shaw would receive a police escort to NASA's nearby Michoud Assembly facility, where he took a plant tour.[1458] Several of the characters later involved in Jim Garrison's investigation into the Kennedy assassination either worked at the Michoud facility at the time of the investigation, or had worked there in prior years.

In October, Shaw accepted an invitation to attend an "Autographing Party" for Thomas Kuntz Griffin at Absinthe House; the invitation was issued by the Basement Book Shop on Zimple Street.[1459] In early December, Shaw declined an invitation from Edith Stern to attend a party later in the month, saying he would be out of town. He also declined an invitation to a reception for the Assistant Commandant of the U.S. Coast Guard, saying he had to be in Washington, D.C. in mid-December to testify before a Congressional committee. He also declined an invitation to a party in late December put on by WYES-TV, saying he would be out of town. In mid-December, Dr. Alton Ochsner wrote Shaw about a new organization called the Information Council of the Americas, also to be known as INCA; Ochsner was president of the new organization; the Right Reverend Monsignor Henry C. Bezou was also on the board.[1460] Bezou was the brother of James Bezou, who would be the Chancellor of the Belgium consulate in New Orleans during the 1960s. Consequently, Henry C. Bezou was the uncle of a young man whom, in 1969, District Attorney Jim Garrison would be accused of molesting in an incident at the New Orleans Athletic Club.

Also in December, Shaw received a letter from Horace Renegar, Assistant to the President of Tulane University. Renegar, referencing a previous conversation, asked Shaw about a possible visit by President Kennedy to New Orleans.[1461]

The long-smoldering matter of the dispute between the U.S. Customs Department and William Spratling came to a head in 1961. Spratling had, several years earlier, shipped jewelry samples in Shaw's name to New Orleans, to be sold at discounts at an international fair. The dispute generally was over the amount declared for customs purposes, and U.S. Customs had seized the merchandise because of the allegedly incorrect declaration of prices. In mid-1960, Shaw had written to Spratling, indicating that the Customs Collector was a Board member of the Mart who could straighten the matter out, although it might result in a $200 fine. Shaw had acted as Spratling's agent to settle the matter, and in September 1960 had sent a petition explaining the entire matter to the Customs Department. The original fine imposed by the Customs Department was $4,000. Shaw advised Spratling of the petition, adding that he hoped that Spratling could come to New Orleans for a visit soon, at a time when he would not have to worry about the incident. Meanwhile, Marc Antony of Maher and Company Jewelers sent a letter to Customs denying any responsibility, saying that he had only purchased the goods for the International Week fair. Spratling was concerned about fines, saying that his business was doing badly enough without incurring any extra expenses. He said that he had tried, over thirty years of working in the silver jewelry industry in Taxco, Mexico, always to pay the proper Customs duties. During the fall of 1960, nothing was really resolved, as negotiations continued between Marc Antony, Spratling, Shaw and the Customs Department. Shaw indicated along the way that he was "hungry" to visit Mexico again, and Spratling communicated his hope that Shaw would make the trip.

In April 1961, Shaw wrote to Customs Collector T.H. Lyons, the Mart Board member, explaining the background of the situation. Shaw said that the Mart had no knowledge of the true value of the goods; Spratling had sent them to be displayed at Marc Antony's retail shop, 331 Gallery. Zetzmann also sent a letter in April, vouching for the same facts. In August 1961, Lyons said that Shaw's civil liability for the incident was $50 plus a payment due of $262.60; he indicated that Spratling, and Maher and Company, owed the difference between the reduced fine of $762.60 and the amount paid by Shaw. In mid-October, Shaw wrote to Spratling, indicating that the amounts had to be paid by November 1, and indicating that he had visions of himself languishing in the Federal prison in Atlanta, Georgia. In a telegram to Spratling on November 2, Shaw advised that, "Collector pressing for payment of duty. Deadline yesterday. Please advise."[1462] Shortly thereafter, Spratling sent along a payment from his Black Tulip Galleries. Shaw indicated that, "This has been a miserable experience," and, "I find myself thinking wistfully, from time to time, how pleasant it must be to lead the even tenor of one's way in Taxco." In a letter to Spratling in mid-November, Goldie Moore indicated that Shaw was in the hospital for his annual checkup until the following week, but that, according to a letter from the Department of the Treasury dated November 17, 1961, the matter had been settled for a payment by the Mart of $762.60, a permanent reduction from the initial fine of $4,000.

Shaw's speaking schedule also continued normally throughout 1961. In January, he addressed the Vieux Carré Chapter of the Daughters of the American Revolution on the topic, "The New Trade Mart." In February, he addressed the Women's Auxiliary of the New Orleans Dental Association. That same month, Shaw spoke before the Memphis World Trade Seminar, held at the Peabody Hotel. The speech, which gave him the opportunity to reconnect with his old friend Bess Noble,[1463] was written up in Memphis's *Commercial Appeal* newspaper; the article indicated that Shaw had encouraged trade with Communist satellite countries.

In March, Shaw spoke to the Hotel Greeters of America, who were meeting at the Roosevelt hotel. In April, he spoke at a luncheon in Chicago for the Community of Interests Travel Mission to Chicago. He spoke at a luncheon of the National Association of Secretaries of State at International House the following month. In June, he spoke at the Boss's Day luncheon of the Women's Traffic and Transportation Club of New Orleans.

In September, Shaw spoke before the New Orleans Junior Chamber of Commerce. In October, he spoke before the Daughters of the American Revolution in Amite, Louisiana. He had been invited to the latter by Dorothy (Mrs. Wade) Garnier, who also invited Shaw and his mother out to the Garnier home, Fairview Farm.[1464] The topic of Shaw's speech was "Three Worlds—Ours, Theirs, and the Uncommitted."

Also in October, Shaw spoke before the Memphis Advertising Club. Bess Noble was unable to make the meeting, as she was speaking at the Rotary Club of Paris, Tennessee on the same day; based upon reports she heard of the Memphis meeting, she gave her usual liberal praise of Shaw as a speaker, in a letter to him.[1465] In November, Shaw spoke before the Society of World Relations about his travels, the general state of world affairs, and international trade; he had been invited to the meeting by Harnett Kane.[1466]

Shaw continued to advise inquirers that buyers could physically examine goods and purchase them at the Mart. He reiterated that the Mart was not a fair or an exhibition, but the reason he gave during this period was that it simply had no space for such events.[1467]

Other cities and states were continuing to inquire into the Mart's history and experience, with an eye to beginning their own international trade network. Shaw advised Governor Robert Holmes of Oregon that combined revenues for the Mart and International House were approximately $1,000,000 in 1961, with combined expenses totaling about the same. Shaw recommended operating the international trade environment in a general manner that encouraged trade all over the world, rather than organizing a regional center emphasizing trade with, for example, the Far East or Scandinavia.[1468]

Mississippi Southern College, later known as the University of Southern Mississippi, located in Hattiesburg, Mississippi, recently had begun its own institute dealing with Latin American relations. The institute worked with the Mart and International House, and Shaw participated in some of its programs. He critiqued the first monthly newsletter, bringing several mistakes to the attention of Ray Curtis, Acting Director of the institute. In a reply, Curtis indicated that the mistakes had been the result of getting the newsletter together too hurriedly, and quoted Franz Kafka as saying, "All human error is impatience."[1469]

Mayor Victor Schiro, who had recently taken over from Chep Morrison, complimented Shaw on his role as a member of the NASA-New Orleans Coordinating Committee during the recent Michoud Bidders Conference. Schiro mentioned that Dr. Wernher von Braun, a high official of NASA, and his associates, "were most expressive of their appreciation for your committee's work."[1470]

Cecilia Grace, who had worked for the Mart from 1951 to 1961, was now living in California and asking for a reference. Grace, who was born in Colombia, had worked as a receptionist and had directly assisted Shaw, David Baldwin, and Jesse Core, among others. She lost her job in 1961, due to a staff reduction caused by the general financial predicament of the Mart.

Shaw was probably grateful to have the challenge of running the Mart's currently more successful, sister organization, given the wheel-spinning situation in which the Mart found itself. During his reign as Acting Managing Director of International House, Shaw took care of even small details. In a note to Bob Best, who supervised the food and beverage operation, Shaw instructed him to get some brandy snifters, saying, "Many people (including me) don't like brandy in a small pony glass."[1471]

The second half of 1961 brought somewhat ominous news. At an Executive Committee meeting in mid-August, it was discussed that the Mart needed to borrow $10,000 to continue operations. Rental income was down even more, and expenses were up, due to Edward Durell Stone's fees, and because of the rental office, with a staffer, which had been initiated in an attempt to secure leases for the new building. It was decided that one staffer needed to be cut from the payroll, in order that the Mart could remain profitable, and that no publicity or promotional services should be incurred. The bleakest forecast was that the Mart would need to liquidate if the new building project was not successful in moving forward. One prospective date for liquidation would be when the current lease with the owners of the building expired in August 1962.[1472]

Shaw appeared on WWL Radio on two panels in mid-August. He was among four panelists discussing the topic "Latin American Profile."[1473]

Bess Noble wrote to Shaw in September, indicating that she had read an interesting article about the Mart in *"The Foreign Trader."* She said she was proud of Shaw and his accomplishments, and had not known before of his "fine war record" described in the article.[1474]

Maurice Barr, a Board member at International House, wrote to Shaw in mid-October, saying he wanted to discuss the propriety of letting "ladies" dine there during daytime hours. He understood that Saturdays for luncheons and special occasions were okay for female diners, but had reservations about allowing them during general business hours.[1475]

Jimmy Fitzmorris was seeking election as a Councilman at Large in the early part of 1962, and he requested a contribution from Shaw.[1476] During the 1970s, Fitzmorris would serve as lieutenant governor, and would also seek the office of governor, unsuccessfully, at the end of the 1970s.

In mid-October, Shaw assisted with the Permanent International Association of Navigation Congresses Banquet. Afterwards, Major General Charles G. Holle, U.S. Army (Retired), Secretary General of the XXth International Navigation Congress in Baltimore, Maryland, wrote thanking Shaw for his help with the dinner. Holle added a handwritten note saying, "Clay—I send my warmest personal regards and recall our association when I was" in New Orleans.[1477]

Mart officials continued to work with Dock Board officials during the fall of 1961. At an Executive Committee meeting in late October, it was mentioned that the Mart was waiting on the Dock Board to respond to its recently completed study of rental and exhibition space in the area of the new building. It also was noted that the land needed to be purchased soon from Southern Pacific Railroad, and that the Mart needed to borrow $10,000 immediately in order to move forward.[1478]

Glenn Stotz, who had worked as a trade analyst/intern at the Mart in the mid-1950s, was living in Baton Rouge in 1961; he had graduated from Tulane during the 1950s. In November, he wrote to J.B. Dauenhauer seeking employment, but the Mart had no openings at the time.[1479]

John W. Goemans, with the U.S. Department of State in Honolulu, Hawaii, wrote Shaw in November, indicating that he had enjoyed meeting him recently, and having Jesse Core show him around the Mart. Goemans indicated that he had passed on Shaw's greetings to George Chaplin, formerly with the *Item*.[1480]

At an Executive Committee meeting in mid-December, it was proposed that the Dock Board finance the proposed exhibition building and garage for the new Mart complex, and that the Mart finance the main high-rise building. Under that proposal, the Dock Board would lease two floors of the new tower building, at $140,000 for each floor, and it would also lease the exhibit hall and the garage to the Mart for its operations.[1481]

In December, while Shaw was still acting as Managing Director of International House after Charles Nutter's resignation, he testified before a Joint Economic Subcommittee of Congress. Invited by Hale Boggs, Shaw gave a four-page presentation which had been approved by the International House Executive Committee, members of which had critiqued the paper.[1482]

A possible indication of Shaw's eventual early death from lung cancer in 1974 came as early as the latter part of 1961. During those years, Federal income tax returns had a form on which one reported sick pay exclusions, and explained the reasons for the absences from work for a salaried employee. For 1961, Shaw reported that he had been hospitalized, from December 19 through December 22, for a diagnostic procedure involving a lesion of the left lung.[1483] On his 1962 income tax return, he would also report a diagnostic procedure, involving a suspected lung lesion, performed August 24 to 29, 1962.[1484] On his 1963 income tax return, he would report having the same procedure performed on April 13 through 17, 1963.[1485]

# 20 · A Critical Point for the Mart

In response to a January 1962 inquiry, Shaw replied that the current Mart building, the original home of the International Trade Mart, had been owned by Tra-Mar, Inc. of New York City since 1955.[1486] Ever since the Mart had sold its building to the investors from New York, it had leased the entire building and then subleased the individual spaces to tenants. This meant the Mart collected rent from tenants, as it had always done, and paid a fixed rental amount to the new owners. That arrangement had continued in every lease extension over the years.

The year 1962 was one of both continuity and change. The continuity consisted primarily of the expected normal day-to-day operations at the Mart, with the uncertainty of the new building, and even the Mart's actual existence, hanging over its head. The change resulted from the death of William Zetzmann, who had taken over as the second President of the Mart in 1953, after Theodore Brent's passing. Zetzmann served for almost nine years as President, and presided over the long, frustrating period of attempts to expand the Mart, to merge with International House, and, in general, to build upon the great progress that had been made during the years 1946 through 1953.

Shaw continued at his normal speechmaking pace during 1962. In January, he spoke to the membership of the New Orleans Athletic Club. In early May, he gave the banquet address at the University of Mississippi First Alumni Seminar; Governor Ross Barnett and William Winter, a future lieutenant governor and governor of Mississippi, were both present, and each either called Shaw or sent him a letter afterwards, congratulating him on the speech. After the speech, Shaw also received a letter from Frank M. Patty of Union Planters Bank in Memphis, Tennessee. Patty, a graduate of Ole Miss who had attended Shaw's banquet speech, apologized for an unnamed heckler in the crowd during the speech, explaining that the person was a retired Army Brigadier General and a member of the John Birch Society. Patty noted that, as both the heckler and General Edwin Walker demonstrated, "Professional soldiers, as a rule, are not qualified to determine a nation's foreign policy."[1487] Shaw responded that he had been heckled by others far more expert than that particular individual, and graciously added that the heckler had a right to his views, but agreed that on balance, "Professional military people are not the ideal shapers of the nation's foreign policy."

During the year, Shaw also gave speeches to the typical array of groups to whom he had spoken for many years, including the Junior League, Junior Chamber of Commerce, Rotary Club, Young Men's Business Club, and the CPA Wives Club.

International House had a total net worth of $129,328 at the end of 1961. The building rental operations of International House had generated revenues of $138,281, and had incurred expenses of $109,097, for a net of income over expenses of $29,184. Restaurant and bar revenues totaled $313,365, with a cost of sales of $142,235, yielding gross profit of $171,130; after all operating expenses, the restaurant and bar combined had net income of $7,456. International House had a different economic structure than the Mart, which had mainly one source of income: rental payments. International House, by contrast, had several major sources of revenue, and different types of expenses. For example, in 1961, it collected dues income of $274,350. It also incurred trade promotion expenses of $333,934, related to the various trade missions it sponsored to foreign countries, and generated $11,873 in revenue from its language classes. After all income and expenses of its various segments were taken into account, International House had total net income during 1961, over and above all expenses, of $3,480. Clearly, in 1961 the two organizations had continued to diverge, with International House meeting all of its expenses, while the Mart struggled to do so in the face of declining occupancy, static rental rates, and increased expenses, due both to inflation and to the efforts to begin a new building project.

In January 1962, Shaw wrote to Zetzmann and Pendleton Lehde, setting out the points of agreement that had been reached with the Dock Board on January 9, 1962. The Dock Board would acquire the Mart's two squares of land, and the Mart would buy the Dock Board's existing building, including the garage. The Dock Board would then build the new exhibition hall and the new garage facility, and lease those to the Mart, with only incurred interest payments due on the bonds for the first five years. The Mart would have ninety days to work out the financing of the main tower structure. The Dock Board would lease two floors in the tower building for fifteen years, at an annual rental of $140,000.[1488]

On January 16, 1962, Shaw addressed the Brown Derby Club at the New Orleans Athletic Club. The participants and members all wore brown derbies, and the photographs of that event show Shaw wearing one as well, looking rather old at age forty-eight, if still very distinguished. His hair was almost completely white, and his face more rugged than ever.

Shaw purchased the multi-unit Spanish Stables at 716 Governor Nicholls Street in mid-February 1962. He restored the units and turned it into a prime piece of property, which would sell in November 1964 for, at the time, the highest price an individual residential property had ever fetched in the French Quarter.

Meanwhile, tensions had developed between Jesse Core and Mario Bermúdez. Bermúdez wrote a note to Shaw in mid-February 1962, concerning officers from the Organization of American States (OAS) visiting New Orleans, and the rooftop flag raising ceremony at the Mart scheduled for their visit. Core wrote a note on the memo that said, "Bermúdez no longer asks. He just schedules. He's had his eyes on our little rooftop ceremony for years."[1489]

In February 1962, Josephine Lefevre, a Mart employee since 1959 who worked primarily for Jesse Core, married Jeff Hug, and the Mart gave them a gift on the occasion of their wedding.[1490] In 1967, both Jeff and Josephine Hug would be summoned before the Orleans Parish Grand Jury investigating the Kennedy assassination under the lead of District Attorney Jim Garrison.

Shaw had managed International House, in addition to managing the Mart, during the last half of 1961, and into 1962. In the spring of 1962, International House hired Paul A. Fabry to be the Managing Director, as a permanent replacement for Charles Nutter. Fabry was a Hungarian immigrant, highly educated, and had served in the Hungarian legislature prior to immigrating to the United States. At the time he was hired by International House, he worked for the E. I. du Pont de Nemours and Company in Wilmington, Delaware. In a letter to Shaw in late March, Fabry referred to their brief meeting at International House in February. Fabry indicated that he would like to get Shaw's advice and guidance during his first few days in New Orleans, and that he would be "most appreciative if you could set aside some time to give a candid review of International House operations." Fabry went on to say that he had recently seen Ferenc Nagy in Washington. Nagy, an old friend of Fabry and a former Prime Minister of Hungary, was one of the officials behind Permindex. Nagy had told Fabry about his connections with Shaw through Centro Mondiale Commerciale in Rome, Italy, and had relayed his best wishes to Shaw through Fabry. Fabry said that he hoped to establish a pleasant and fruitful relationship with Shaw, and trusted that he could come to Shaw frequently for information.[1491]

**Mardi Gras: Left to right are unidentified woman, Shaw, Willian Henry Formyduval (as Yul Brynner) (Photo courtesy of Ruth Ghass)**

In March, Shaw received a letter from Rodolphe Huart of the National Bank of Toledo; Huart, who had known Shaw during the 1950s, said, "By now, I imagine you must own at least 25 percent of the French Quarter."[1492] Shaw replied that he had just bought another building in the French Quarter, but that every time he bought one, he had to sell one. Shaw indicated that he felt a little like the Red Queen in *Alice in Wonderland*, saying, "In this country, you have to run twice as fast just to stay in the same place."[1493]

In the early months of 1962, Zetzmann was unable to attend Board of Directors meetings, or Executive Committee meetings, of Mart officials. His report for 1961 was presented to the Annual Meeting of the Mart in early March, by another Board member, Captain Stevens, who advised the gathering that Zetzmann was out due to illness. Stevens noted that in January 1962, the Dock Board, the City of New Orleans, and the Mart had spelled out the responsibilities of each institution for the new building. It was noted that several large buildings had come onto the market in the downtown area in the previous year, which added additional pressure to the task of obtaining financing and approval for the project.[1494]

At an Executive Committee meeting ten days later, Zetzmann was still the President. There was a long discussion of financing, the question of obtaining a sufficient amount of leases, possible bond issues, and the general prospects for the new building. Shaw indicated that the Mart was badly in need of new international flags for the roof, but that replacement would be deferred during the period of uncertainty.[1495]

Zetzmann died April 13, 1962, at age sixty-eight. A press release was issued two days later by Lloyd Cobb, which traced some of Zetzmann's history with the Mart, and his efforts to make the new building a reality. It indicated that Edward Durell Stone had been retained in August 1958, and that his design had been unveiled in March 1959. The plan now was for a building seventeen to twenty-two stories tall, backed by an auditorium with an 800-car garage, and 300,000 square feet of exhibition space.[1496]

By April 1962, the Mart had cut back on many of its normal civic contributions. Shaw advised the New Orleans Traffic and Transportation Board that the Mart could not afford to make a contribution that year, as it was borrowing money simply to operate.[1497]

In April, Shaw appeared on the program "Great Decisions: United Nations" on WYES-TV.[1498] Also in April, Shaw received a letter from Mayor Victor Schiro, asking him to serve on an advisory committee related to business conditions in New Orleans, on the second Thursday of each month.[1499] Shaw also served on the Inaugural Committee for Mayor Schiro, who had been elected to his first full term, at the invitation of Dr. Alton Ochsner.

At a meeting of the Board of Directors at the end of April, Lloyd Cobb was selected as the third President of the Mart. Cobb said he looked upon his presidency as a two-year job at most. He indicated that the Mart was now losing $20,000 to $30,000 per year; occupancy had fallen to 75%. Cobb said that the Dock Board was going to move ahead with the exhibition and convention facility; the Mart would lease it and operate it. He said that the height of the building would depend on the number of leases signed before financing was approved and construction began. He further noted that Edmund Christy, the leasing agent, had been let go due to the lengthy delay in moving forward, and that the obtaining of leases was now Shaw's responsibility. Board member James Coleman asked for those present who had any doubts or misgivings about the building project, or the future of the Mart, to state them candidly. Cobb indicated that Board members who were not active should be dropped the next year, as he wanted an active group to push the new building forward.[1500]

Congressman Hale Boggs wrote to Shaw on April 30, 1962, about the protocol for President Kennedy's upcoming visit related to dedicating the Nashville Avenue Wharf.[1501] Shaw had invited Label A. Katz of B'Nai B'Rith, the Jewish organization, to the ceremony. Katz wrote Shaw, thanking him for the invitation, and commented that Shaw's courtesy in that regard was "most characteristic" of him.[1502] Others wrote Shaw for tickets to Kennedy's speech, including Lawrence H. Stevens, Executive Vice President of Stone-Stevens, Inc., who was asking for tickets for Dr. G. Avery Lee, of St. Charles Avenue Baptist Church; Stevens indicated that William Zetzmann would have appreciated it if Shaw could obtain tickets for Lee.[1503]

President Kennedy appeared in New Orleans in May 1962 to dedicate the Nashville Avenue Wharf. The visit had been in the works for some time. In late 1961, Shaw's friend Bess Noble had written from Memphis, telling Shaw of her recent "delightful" trip to Puerto Rico, indicating that she felt "ten years younger." She also said that she had met Shaw's "friend," the mayor of San Juan, and that she was "quite a person"; Shaw had worked with the mayor during his 1958 trip to help Puerto Rico establish an International Center.[1504] Shaw responded to Noble in early January, indicating that President Kennedy might come to New Orleans in February.[1505]

The actual visit by Kennedy was on May 4, 1962; Shaw was on the reception committee for the president. Although Shaw had met Kennedy briefly the previous summer, he did not meet the president during this visit. In a letter following the event, Congressman Hale Boggs wrote to Shaw that he was sorry that everyone involved had not gotten the opportunity to meet Kennedy. Boggs indicated that Kennedy's time had been limited, and that "he appreciated you being there, and I did, too."[1506] During Kennedy's dedication of the Nashville Avenue Wharf, he gave an award to International House, and to the Port of New Orleans, but apparently not to the Mart.

The visit by President Kennedy would become important when Shaw was arrested in 1967. The main witness against Shaw, Perry Russo, testified that he had seen Shaw on three occasions, one of them being at Kennedy's appearance to dedicate the Nashville Avenue

Wharf. Russo testified that he saw Shaw in the crowd of people watching the president, and that Shaw, wearing what Russo termed "tight pants," had not been paying attention to Kennedy's speech, but rather had been looking around the crowd.

On May 7, 1962, just after Kennedy's visit, Jim Garrison was sworn in as district attorney, as he recently had been elected to his first term of office. Garrison had run for three other offices during the 1950s, but had failed to win. Now, with strong and stunning televised appearances and an effective performance in a televised debate, and despite a minimum of prominent supporters or contributions, he had pulled off a long-shot campaign. He entered office having done it on his own, owing no one for his success.[1507]

**District Attorney Jim Garrison (far left) being sworn in, 1962 (Photo courtesy of Denis Barry)**

Garrison's election several months earlier had garnered national attention, and Garrison and one of his chief assistants had been invited by former mayor Chep Morrison to visit Washington, stay at his Georgetown home there, and meet President Kennedy. Congressman Hale Boggs had arranged for a breakfast with the president and the Louisiana congressional delegation, including another New Orleans area congressman, F. Edward Hebert, and U.S. Senator Allen Ellender. Garrison and his assistant spent a night on the town in Washington the evening before the breakfast. The next morning, Chep Morrison arose early and went on to work without awakening the two men, who proceeded to oversleep and miss the breakfast entirely.[1508]

In May, Shaw received an invitation from the Playwrights Showcase Theater to attend the first performance of *The Umbilical Cord*, a three-act play by the well-known New Orleans playwright and prose writer, Christopher Blake; Shaw was unable to attend the performance. Also in May, Shaw appeared as the moderator on a panel at the 17th Annual Mississippi Valley World Trade Conference. The same month, Shaw appeared on a panel on WYES-TV that included Gilbert Mellin, and Edwin Leland of the Department of State in New Orleans.

The mayor of San Juan, Puerto Rico, with whom Shaw had worked during his 1958 trip, came through New Orleans in May, and a luncheon was held in her honor at Brennan's restaurant.[1509] As a female, the mayor's status was somewhat unusual for the 1950s..

As of the end of May, Shaw was quoting a rental rate of $4 a square foot for a fifteen-year lease in the new building. That compared with initial quotes of up to $5.65 per square foot for a five-year lease in the original building during 1946, although those earlier quoted rates had to be modified significantly, both in rate per square foot, and in length of contract. Shaw indicated that the current plans were for the building to be ready by October 1, 1964.[1510]

Shaw was still active in the Foreign Relations Association (formerly the Foreign Policy

Association) of New Orleans. In late May, he was re-elected to the Board of Directors for a three-year term.[1511] James Bezou, with the consulate of Belgium in New Orleans, had been selected as Program Chairman of the group, succeeding Shaw in that position.[1512]

Shaw's main regularly recurring consumption expenses during this era were alcohol, cigarettes, laundry, meals at restaurants, and flowers. Shaw often purchased flowers for many of his women friends, including Edith Stern, Artelle Trelford, who was purchasing a property from him on an installment note, Mario Bermúdez's wife, Paul Fabry's wife, the realtor "Frosty" Blackshear, his old friend Marion Seidenbach in New York City, Elena Lyons, and Louis Fischer.

In early June 1962, Shaw wrote to Chep Morrison, now the U.S. representative to the Organization of American States (OAS), saying, "You may not be aware of the acute situation in which International Trade Mart now finds itself. If the new Mart is to be completed by October 1964, we must keep alive the present organization. Daily the 225 Baronne Street Building raids us. Naturally, 225 Baronne wants our tenants and wants to prevent the new Mart from going up. (The builders even copied Edward Stone's Mart design in order to confuse the public image.) But we must do more than merely offset tenant losses: We must show new life, initiate new activities, demonstrate special usefulness, re-establish our identity as a unique and vital institution." Shaw went on to ask Morrison to help establish a Latin American Tourist Bureau, with help from Latin American countries, and offered Morrison a personal office in the current Mart building.[1513] In a follow-up letter two weeks later to Winston Lill, assistant to Morrison at the State Department, Shaw asked for Morrison to respond to the offer of a New Orleans office in the Mart. Shaw emphasized the point he had made earlier, saying that the Mart "needs adrenaline like now."[1514]

In addition to the proposal for a Latin American Tourist Bureau, an idea also had originated for a proposed Latin Trade Mart in New Orleans. Mario Bermúdez was in the loop on that proposal, and forwarded various sets of correspondence to Shaw during 1962 and 1963.

At an Executive Committee meeting in mid-June, the upcoming expiration of the Mart's lease, in mid-August, was discussed. The City of New Orleans had obligated itself to buy the two squares of land behind the two squares already owned by the Mart, which had been purchased from the railroad company. If the proposed bond issue was to pass, the project would go ahead. In the meantime, the Mart would have to renegotiate a lease with the owners of its original building, one that would continue until the new building could be completed, two or more years down the line. The Central Area Committee of the city had wanted a larger exhibition hall, but the project would have needed more land than was available to hold such a facility. The new terms of the lease with the City were that the rent for the two squares of land would drop from $100,000 to $80,000, and that any rental income from over and above 80% occupancy would be split 50/50 with the City.[1515]

In late June 1962, the Mexican consul in New Orleans wrote to Shaw, noting President Kennedy's "forthcoming visit to Mexico." The Mexican consul also noted the upcoming July 4th celebration in the United States, which would be the 186th anniversary of independence from Great Britain.[1516] Shaw responded in early July, after Kennedy's visit to Mexico, noting that, "It would seem that President Kennedy's visit to Mexico was a considerable success, and I am sure that he and your president can, in a cooperative spirit, solve the problems which confront our two countries."[1517]

In 1962, the Press Club of New Orleans was located in Room 108 of the Mart. Over the years since 1946, Shaw had established excellent relations with various members of the press corps, which would aid him to some extent following his arrest in 1967. The club's location in the Mart allowed Shaw to cement some of those friendships over a period of time.

The City of Houston, Texas had grown considerably during the 1950s, and now was breathing down New Orleans's neck, as far as activity through their respective ports was concerned. In a letter to an inquirer in early August, Shaw indicated that New Orleans, to that point, had always exceeded Houston in dollar volume of shipments, but that Houston sometimes surpassed New Orleans in gross tonnage, because Houston handled more bulk commodities. He indicated, however, that in 1961 New Orleans had still surpassed Houston in both dollars and tonnage.[1518]

As the Mart struggled to move forward with the new building, with occupancy declining and the overall performance generating a loss rather than a profit, Mart officials seriously considered whether to close the entire institution. The Executive Committee had made a decision earlier in the year to cease operations, but now had changed its position. At a meeting of the full Board of Directors on August 1, 1962, it was discussed whether the Mart should suspend operations August 12, 1962, when the current lease expired. The bond issue that would enable them to move forward with financing had passed, and the owners of the current building had come down to New Orleans from New York to renegotiate a new lease, on generous terms. The Mart was now losing $20,000 to $30,000 per year, based on the current occupancy, and the rent had been reduced by the building owners from $100,000 to $80,000 per year. Both the British and the Canadian local consuls in New Orleans had moved out, but supposedly both would return to the new, larger building. The lease extension with the old building would be for two years; the Mart executive offices would occupy 5,000 square feet in the old Mart. The Mart was even then working to establish an import-export exchange on the ground floor.

Lloyd Cobb said that it would be impossible to get a new tower built without an exhibition/convention facility, and that bonds for such a facility had already been sold. The current plan was for an expressway to run underneath this new design. He noted that there was much competition from other buildings that were progressing with similar ideas, which would only get worse as time went by. Rents had never been raised to tenants since the opening of the Mart in 1948, but they were now in line with rates charged by other buildings. The assessment of the property value had been raised initially to $500,000, and then cut back to $100,000. Finally, on an unrelated note, Cobb noted that Kenneth Barranger, the long-time Mart attorney who had been with the institution since its founding, had resigned, less than six months after Cobb became President, and had been replaced by James J. Coleman.[1519]

Obviously, it was a key point in time in the long struggle to expand the Mart operations and attempt to rise to new heights. Ultimately, the decision was made to go forward, and over the next year, important elements, such as financing and the combination of architectural talent needed to make the building a reality, fell into place.

In September, Shaw received a letter from Richard M. Boesen of a law firm in Lima, Peru; he was passing through New Orleans and had stopped to see Ray Forrester, Dean of the Tulane Law School, who had lived in the same apartment building with him when they had both been young lawyers in Chicago many years before. He commented that the road of life had taken them far from Chicago, and in quite different directions.[1520] Shaw had, in the past, been scheduled to appear with Forrester on local television panels related to various trade and political issues.

By the fall of 1962, Paul Fabry was well established at International House, just as the long simmering tensions between the organization and the Mart were getting close to the boiling point over the issues of the new building, and joining together into one organization. In a letter to Shaw at the end of October, Fabry said, "I am sure that our joint efforts for peaceful co-existence will set an example to politicians and businessmen in our naughty town."[1521]

In October, Shaw received a handwritten letter, on International Trade Mart stationery, from Delphine Roberts, representing Guy Banister Associates, Inc. The letter began with, "Dear Mr. Shaw," and proceeded to ask Shaw for a list of the Board of Directors of the Mart and then directed him to send that list to "Mr. Guy Banister Associates, Inc." at 531

Lafayette Street in New Orleans. The letter was signed, "Guy Banister nee D. Roberts."[1522] Shaw replied the next day, opening the letter with "Gentlemen," saying, "In reply to your recent request, you will find a list of our directors on the reverse side of this letter."[1523]

Guy Banister is a name that comes up in any discussion related to Jim Garrison's investigation into President Kennedy's assassination. A former FBI agent who had come to New Orleans during the mid-1950s to serve as a top police official as part of efforts to clean up corruption, Banister had been fired from the force in the later 1950s after an incident in a bar where he allegedly pulled out a pistol and threatened someone. He then went into private detective work, opening his own agency, and became involved in various right-wing activities, including both segregationist and anti-Castro Cuban efforts. One of his associates was David Ferrie, who became a chief target of Garrison in late 1966. Banister helped Ferrie with his defense against charges in the early 1960s, in nearby Jefferson Parish, that he had improper contact with an underage boy, charges that resulted in Ferrie being dismissed from Eastern Airlines; Banister also assisted Ferrie in his attempt to regain his job with the airline. Banister died in 1964, well before Jim Garrison began his investigation into Kennedy's death. Many have speculated that some of the supposed sightings of Shaw with David Ferrie could have been Guy Banister instead; the two men were both tall, with predominantly gray hair.

In October, Shaw became a charter member of a new organization called the International Movement for Atlantic Union, paying $10 in annual dues. A letter from Clarence Streit welcomed Shaw to the new organization.[1524] Streit had been involved in various organizations since the 1930s that aimed to strengthen the ties between the democracies of Western Europe and the English-speaking countries spread around the world, such as the United States, Canada, Australia, New Zealand, and South Africa.

In November, Shaw received a letter from George Chaplin, former editor of the *Item*, and for several years editor of *The Honolulu Advertiser*. The letter mentioned two of Chaplin's Hawaiian friends, both civic leaders, who would be visiting New Orleans soon. Chaplin went on to say that he didn't know "the chap" who had succeeded Charles Nutter with International House, and that he had been out of touch with Mario Bermúdez, but asked Shaw if he could put the two men in touch with someone at International House. Chaplin indicated that his wife passed on her greetings, and asked when Shaw was coming to Hawaii to visit. In a postscript to the letter, Chaplin added, "I gather Jim Garrison keeps things hopping—as any good D.A. should."[1525] The reference was to the newly-elected district attorney, elected as a reform candidate who pledged to clean up the district attorney's office, and to work full-time in the job.

In mid-December 1962, Shaw wrote to Chep Morrison with the latest news of the Mart building project. Shaw acknowledged that much of the enthusiasm and momentum for the Mart had been generated during Morrison's long administration. Shaw went on to note his "best wishes for a Merry Christmas and for a New Year that will bring you whatever you want most—a permanent solution of the Cuban problem, for example."[1526] As the U.S's OAS ambassador, Morrison was struggling constantly with the situation in Cuba.

# 21 · A "Mysterious" Trip, and a Tragedy in Dallas

On January 1, 1963, for his service to the international community, Shaw received the Chevalier du Merité Commercial award, a yellow-ribboned gold medal, from the French consul in New Orleans. It was an award the French government gave to a New Orleanian every New Year's Day, at a party given for the French community in New Orleans. The local newspaper carried an article detailing the ceremony, which was held at the home of French envoy Robert Picquet. The article mentioned that, after World War II, Shaw had received the French Croix de Guerre award for his service in Rheims, France after the D-Day Invasion. At the ceremony, Picquet told Shaw that, "Men of your quality are few. They are a credit to their country as well as to the people around them."

Not long after the ceremony, Shaw received a letter from Chep Morrison, which indicated Morrison's "congratulations on your receiving the Chevalier du Merité Commercial from the French government—They couldn't have chosen a more deserving person than you for this high honor. You are doing a splendid job, Clay, and I am quite proud of you. Keep up the good work!"[1527]

Though no longer mayor, Morrison continued to communicate somewhat regularly with Shaw. In March 1963, Shaw received a postcard from Morrison, who was visiting Oxford, England, to give a presentation. Morrison inquired about the progress of the new Mart tower building.[1528] Sometime in 1963, he sent Shaw an undated postcard of a scene in Mexico City, although the card was postmarked from Chicago.

During the late 1950s and early 1960s, Shaw had settled into a comfortable existence. He had gradually increased his net worth through the combination of his salary at the Mart, and the buying and selling of properties in the French Quarter.

During the 1950s, he had met Marilyn Tate, a New York woman married to a retired military officer. Tate entered the French Quarter real estate market, and soon established a major presence there. By the early 1960s, both Jeff Biddison and Shaw bought and sold properties through Tate's agency, and worked as agents there as well. In 1963, for example, Shaw had commissions of $997.50 from working through Tate's agency.

Shaw also continued to receive some royalties on two of the early plays he had co-written. In 1963, he received royalties of $117.62 for *Submerged,* and $5.49 for *A Message from Khufu.*

Lloyd Cobb's desire to have an active Board of Directors was ongoing in early 1963. Shaw had discussed the idea with William Zetzmann, Jr., who submitted a list of local men 35 to 41 years of age with income in excess of $20,000 per year.[1529] Cobb also had, the previous year, asked Jesse Core to put together a list of men as possible members of the Board of Directors; Core responded with a list that included Wallace Davis, Jr., Gilbert A. Vorhoff, Peter A.Q. Van Denburgh, Poche Waguespack, Jr., Richard L. Hinderman, Phillip M. Walmsley, Jerry K. Nicholson, James G. Aldige, Jr., and Leon Godchaux.[1530]

On January 12, 1963, Lloyd Cobb wrote to Lawrence A. Molony, the current President of International House, indicating that he was resigning from International House because of the failure of the two organizations to find a common cause.[1531] Molony replied to Cobb two weeks later, trying to give International House's side of the matter.[1532] Cobb's reply on

January 31st discussed the history of the long disagreement between the two organizations, going back into the middle 1950s and continuing to the present. He indicated that the Mart had been formed to help carry out the objectives of International House, but that the two organizations had grown apart, due to a different focus.[1533] In the midst of the exchange of those letters, Shaw also resigned from the Board of Directors of International House.[1534]

In January, Shaw appeared as a panelist on WWL-TV on the thirteenth and last telecast of a series of programs dealing with the topic "International Aspects of Human Relations." Shaw appeared on the show along with Gilbert Mellin, Leonard Oppenheim, Professor of Law at Tulane University (who took the place of Ray Forrester, Dean of the College of Law at Tulane), and Leo Zinser, Chairman of the Department of Speech at Loyola University, who was the moderator of the panel.[1535] It should be noted that Shaw, who had no college education, often participated over the years on such panel discussions, where every other member either had a doctorate in an academic subject, or a law degree. It was common for Shaw to interact with men who had a much higher level of formal education than he did, yet most would have agreed that he held his own with seeming ease.

Shaw purchased a property at 1445 Pauger Street, in the Marigny District, on February 1, 1963, for $20,297.60. He sold it on August 2, 1963, for $26,000, to Leonard and Terry Flettrich. Leonard Flettrich later would paint an enigmatic portrait of Shaw during his time of anguish after his arrest. Terry Flettrich was a local TV news personality and midday talk show host, one of the first on-air television personalities in New Orleans. The couple remained strong supporters of Shaw throughout his arrest and trial.

Shaw generally sold most or all of the properties he had owned, beginning in the 1940s, at a nice profit. Also, he generally either lived in the residences while he was improving them, or in other cases rented them out to others, where he was able to write off almost all operating expenses during the time he owned them, effectively lessening his own personal expenditures. Therefore, he was able to take a step up in net worth with each change of properties.

During this period of financial uncertainty, the Mart bent the usual rules to allow short-term tenants. During Buyer's Week in New Orleans, February 2 through February 7, 1963, the Mart made twenty spaces available at $50 per exhibitor, a far cry from its original purpose of seeking only five-year leases, at up to $5.65 per square foot, during the mid-1940s.

Shaw often contributed to local charities he deemed worthy. On February 19, 1963, Francis Doyle, of the Cultural Attractions Fund, wrote Shaw, thanking him for his pledge of support to the fund.[1536] He attended various types of cultural events, including opera, the symphony, and plays at neighborhood theaters. He often escorted women friends of varying status, but it was not unknown for him to bring along young male companions, even introducing them publicly to the mayor on occasion.

Although not traveling as frequently as he once had, Shaw was still communicating with old friends in New York and elsewhere. In March 1963, he heard from K. Bruce Mitchell, his old co-worker at Western Union in New York City. Shaw answered Mitchell in April, thanking him for the birthday greeting.[1537]

Shaw received a letter in early April 1963 from Southern Baptist Hospital, regarding his upcoming admission later that month. Shaw was in the hospital for his annual scan for a lung lesion, a ritual that had been ongoing for at least several years.[1538] It is possible that Shaw's concern about his lungs may have developed out of his association with Dr. Alton Ochsner, New Orleans's famed surgeon, who took over as President of International House as Shaw finished his interim stretch there in early 1962. Ochsner had become known, after World War II, as one of the leading opponents of smoking, having determined what he believed was a connection between smoking and lung cancer. It was a lonely battle for many years, as a number of doctors smoked in that era, but the connection was eventually accepted within the medical community.

On April 18, 1963, Mrs. Brett Howard of Ivon Obolonsky Publishers sent Shaw a copy of a new book, by local writer Herman Deutsch, concerning the assassination of Huey Long.[1539] Long had been assassinated in 1935, and Deutsch's book re-examined the case in some detail.

By the end of 1962, if not before, tensions had begun to develop between Paul Fabry, the new Managing Director at International House, and Mario Bermúdez. Since the late 1940s, the arrangement for Bermúdez's Department of International Relations had been as follows: the cost of his salary and expenses had been borne equally by the City of New Orleans and International House, with the Mart providing free office space as its contribution to the cause. In early 1963, probably under Fabry's prodding, Bermúdez and his staff were made to move out of the Mart, and into an office in International House.[1540] In a letter to Lloyd Cobb, Lawrence Molony, President of International House at that time, indicated that Bermúdez's office had been moved so that Fabry could better supervise and direct the activities of that department.[1541] Concern also had been voiced about the manner in which Bermúdez and his office were identified in news articles; some International House Board members found it confusing to see Bermúdez sometimes identified as being with International House, and at other times being with either the Mart or the City of New Orleans.[1542]

With his fierce good looks, imposing presence, and impeccable manners and speaking skills, Shaw continued to be a favorite with women. In correspondence during the spring of 1963, Marge Henderson of Ideas, Inc. in Memphis, Tennessee, invited him to a formal dedication of the new Memphis Metropolitan Airport, and also to speak at the Memphis Import-Export Clinic,[1543] as he had done many times before. Shaw replied, indicating that he had been approached for speaking at a local gathering that featured hula dancers, and that he was leaning toward accepting that instead, as he had spoken "too often in Memphis." Henderson replied that the two of them had "lots of gossip" to catch up on, and that she intended to "steal him away" from all the dignitaries who would want to follow him about, and that the two of them could find a "quiet corner" where they could talk. Shaw responded that he had been in the hospital for his annual checkup, but said that if the hula dancers in New Orleans did not keep him away from Memphis, then pile driving for the new building in June would ensure that he stayed in New Orleans.[1544] Marge Henderson would use Shaw as a reference when she was changing jobs. Shaw indicated that he had observed her in public relations in Memphis, Tennessee, over a five-year period, and that he thought she was "most capable" in that position.

D.H. Holmes Company had expressed an interest in operating the restaurant that would be at the top of the new Mart building. In mid-April, Board member E. Davis McCutcheon had written Shaw asking about the status of the new building.[1545] In September, McCutcheon wrote again, asking about the progress, and inquiring if D.H. Holmes would be able to operate the restaurant.[1546]

The Mart continued to host individual exhibits of various types. One such event, held beginning in late April and continuing to mid-May, was an exhibition of approximately ninety metaphysical paintings on canvas by Spanish artist Pedro Garcia-Lema, the "philosopher who paints." Letters were sent to schools and groups to promote the event.

In early May 1963, Shaw received a photograph of him taken at Willard E. Robertson's "Salutes the Gridiron" party. Shaw wrote to John Cieutat, Advertising Manager, International Auto Sales and Service in New Orleans, thanking him for the photo.[1547] Robertson, who owned the local Volkswagen dealership, would later become one of the three main private financial backers of Jim Garrison's investigation into President Kennedy's assassination.

The Mart had cut back seriously on all forms of advertising. In May 1963, a German industrial publication wrote Shaw, seeking advertising from the Mart. Shaw declined, but advised that the new building would probably be open in mid-1965; he indicated that the architect was still working on the plans.[1548]

Shaw received notices of many types of public events. On May 9, 1963, Mrs. Edwin Blum of the Women's Guild of the New Orleans Opera House Association wrote, advising Shaw of a project to convert the Wildlife and Fisheries building on Royal Street to an opera house.[1549] On August 12, 1963, Shaw received an invitation from theater manager Earl Kroepor to attend an opening of Federico Fellini's film *8-1/2*, opening on August 15; Shaw had to decline the invitation.

At a meeting of the Executive Committee in mid-May, Lloyd Cobb announced that the Mart had lost more than $40,000 during 1962, its worst performance ever, and that the Mart would do without a publicity department while the construction of the new building was ongoing.[1550] Jesse Core, who had been Public Relations Director for the Mart since 1955, would soon leave the Mart's payroll and open his own public relations firm, although he operated from an office in the Mart, and continued to handle the Mart's public relations work as an outside contractor.

A news clipping indicated that Mario Bermúdez would resign May 1, 1963 as Director of International Relations for International House. The article indicated that Bermúdez would remain with the City of New Orleans and the International Trade Mart, but that International House had withdrawn from its original agreement with the City of New Orleans whereby it had financed one-half of Bermúdez's salary and expenses.[1551]

In late May 1963, International House President Lawrence Molony wrote to Dr. Alton Ochsner, explaining that Bermúdez would not work under Paul Fabry.[1552] Shortly thereafter, arrangements were made whereby International House would cease to fund Bermúdez's department, while the Mart began to contribute funding as well as office space, in conjunction with the City of New Orleans.

Two years before, when Shaw had served as interim Managing Director at International House prior to Fabry's arrival, he had written a report detailing the activities of International House, and making suggestions for improvement. Although Shaw indicated that certain areas needed improvement, he described the Department of International Relations under Bermúdez in some detail without making any such suggestions.[1553] However, in a somewhat lengthy memo concerning Mario Bermúdez and the Department of International Relations, probably composed mainly by Paul Fabry in early 1963, the writer indicated that Bermúdez had employees conduct his personal business, including banking, payment of bills, and affairs with tenants at his personally-owned real estate properties. The memo indicated that Bermúdez did not report directly to Fabry, and that none of his projects came to fruition. It discussed how most of his activity was in Latin America, and that Bermúdez came and went as he pleased. His arrangements with the Organization of American States (OAS) and the Inter-American Municipal League had International House paying for Bermúdez's "junkets." The memo went on to say that Bermúdez might have been keeping travel agency commissions on numerous International House trade missions that had been made over the years.

Alberto Fowler was considered by International House for Bermúdez's job. Fowler had been a participant in the Bay of Pigs Invasion of Cuba in 1961, and had been captured by the Cuban government during that operation. He was freed the next year as part of a mass prisoner exchange for food and medicine provided by the United States government. A telegram from Paul Fabry in mid-May 1963, however, asked Fowler to postpone his visit for a planned interview, as a decision on filling that position was not imminent at the time.[1554] A new International Relations Committee of International House soon was formed due to the dissolution of the old Department of International Relations that had been run by Bermúdez since the 1940s. Mario Bermúdez eventually would leave city government as well, and Fowler would replace him as Director of International Relations for the City of New Orleans.

Instead of Fowler, William Richard Martin took Bermúdez's place at International

House. According to Martin's biography distributed by International House, he was born in the Dominican Republic, and had lived most of his life either there, or in Haiti. Martin graduated from Louisiana State University, and from Tulane University Law School. In 1967, after Jim Garrison's investigation of the Kennedy assassination had broken into the news, Martin would become an employee of Garrison's office for a time, and assist with the investigation. He also was a source of information for the New Orleans office of the Central Intelligence Agency during the 1960s, because of his international connections.

At a special meeting of the Executive Committee in early June, Lloyd Cobb indicated that the meeting had been called to consider a contribution to the new committee that had recently been formed, to be run by Mario Bermúdez. Cobb's recommendation was that the Mart fund it with a $10,000 contribution; he said that Bermúdez had been appointed for one year, with that appointment to be reviewed annually. Basil Rusovich, a member of the Committee, said that the the committee under Bermúdez should focus more on Europe, rather than on Latin America.[1555]

Shaw's restoration of homes, which had been written up in several magazines during the 1950s and 1960s, were still of interest to publications. In June 1963, William Hague, of *House & Garden* magazine, wrote to him regarding obtaining before-and-after photos of Shaw's residence at 1313 Dauphine Street.[1556]

In mid-year, as the idea for the new Mart tower building continued to take shape, Shaw began to deal with new issues related to the building. In July, he wrote to Vincent Furno, with Edward Durell Stone's firm, discussing the possibility of eliminating parking at the exhibition hall, and having the Mart building absorb that parking; he also discussed selling heating and cooling to the exhibition hall, with the Mart providing the equipment.[1557] In September, Stone wrote to Shaw, discussing the possible encroachment of the exhibition hall onto the plaza area, an open area next to the tower building.[1558]

Shaw wrote to George Chaplin, indicating that he could not make a firm commitment on traveling to Hawaii for a previously discussed period.[1559] The effort to build the new building was finally picking up speed, and Shaw would be fully occupied with it for the next two and a half years, until his retirement.

Shaw continued his speaking schedule during 1963, mostly in the New Orleans area. A major exception was his two-week trip to California and Oregon in November, which placed him in San Francisco on the day of President Kennedy's assassination. He generally spoke on the topics of "International Trade Today," "Selling Around the World," "Three Worlds," "Three Worlds—Ours—Theirs—and the Uncommitted," and "Crisis in International Trade." Among the familiar types of groups Shaw spoke before were the Junior Chamber of Commerce, the Kenner Rotary Club, the Kiwanis Club, the Southeastern Louisiana College Newman Club, and the Junior League.

In March, he spoke before the Junior League Provisional Course, held from March 18 through May 11, 1963. Another speaker during that course was New Orleans District Attorney Jim Garrison. Shaw spoke on March 28, 1963, and Garrison spoke on April 3, 1963. They were only two among many speakers the event had over the two-month period.

On June 12, 1963, Shaw spoke at Spring Hill College in Mobile, Alabama. Spring Hill College bills itself as Alabama's oldest institution of higher learning. It was the first Catholic college in the Southeast, the third oldest Jesuit college and the fifth oldest Catholic college in the United States, being founded in 1830.[1560] That same year, on July 27, another speaker at Spring Hill College was Lee Harvey Oswald, a young ex-Marine who had defected to the Soviet Union, then returned to the United States a few years later. Oswald's cousin, who attended the college, had helped to arrange for Oswald to speak there about his experiences in the Soviet Union from 1959 to 1962.

As the summer progressed, Shaw began to limit his speeches, even ones relatively far into the future, as he became more active with the progress of the new building. In September, he wrote to the Daughters of the American Revolution in Amite, Louisiana, informing them that he expected to be out of the country during March, April and May of 1964, and declining their invitation for that time.[1561]

Richard Swenson, who had been with the public relations department of the Port of New Orleans in the early 1950s, was now with the Port in Freeport, Texas. He wrote Shaw, indicating that he had just purchased a home there, and updating Shaw on news of his family.[1562]

At a meeting of the Board of Directors in early August, Cobb said that the bonds for financing construction would be delivered in two to three days, by Blyth and Company. The Mart had signed a $12,840,000 contract with Bloomfield Building Industries in December 1962. The railroad tracks that crossed the Mart's property where the building would be constructed were going to be removed and relocated. Cobb indicated that bona fide leases totaling annual revenue of $1,425,000 had been required to be delivered to Blyth and Company by October 8, 1963 for the project to continue, and that those leases were now in place within the ninety-day framework required of the Mart; that work had been accomplished primarily, he said, by Shaw and personnel employed with Bloomfield Building Industries. Cobb indicated that the exchange of property with the Dock Board also had been completed, and that demolition of the Dock Board building was to begin immediately. Once everything was cleared away, the Mart would be reimbursed $418,000 for the new wing of the building. The Mart would have assets between $450,000 and $500,000, and 50% interest in a thirty-three-story building for twenty years, then 75% interest in the building for the next thirty-six years. He said that the construction process was actually not as important as making the building a living, vital, alive organization to promote world trade and peace and understanding, and to bring prosperity to the city. The Mart would be tax-exempt on income, property, and ad-valorum taxes. The entire project would eventually revert to the City after fifty-six years.

Cobb's comment that the necessary leases had been signed seems to contradict testimony that he and Shaw would give at Shaw's trial in 1969, whereby both men testified that Shaw was so busy selling the leases as late as September 1963 that he could not have been away from New Orleans in order to take a trip to Clinton, Louisiana, although several witnesses testified they had seen him in that city in the company of Lee Harvey Oswald and/or David Ferrie. However, it is likely that selling of the remaining leases was ongoing, even after the minimum threshold had been reached, and that other activities related to the new tower building kept Shaw busy during that fall.

Among other activities during the year, Shaw was invited to participate in a campaign to save the famous streetcars of New Orleans. He received an invitation from John Kamas to a meeting at the home of Ola Holcomb at 934 Royal Street. The letter indicated that, "It's not too late" to save the cars from extinction.[1563]

A variety of other events occupied Shaw's time as well. In July, Shaw had to decline an invitation from WWL-TV to a luncheon honoring Walter Cronkite, in celebration of the opening of the CBS News Southern Bureau in New Orleans, due to a previous engagement.[1564] Miguel Bermúdez, son of Mario Bermúdez, was married on October 26, 1963. The day before, Donald Kendall with the Pepsi-Cola Company came to New Orleans, bringing with him once again the actress Joan Crawford on behalf of Pepsi. In October, Shaw accepted an invitation from Mrs. Edgar B. "Edith" Stern to a dinner at Antoine's restaurant. Shaw addressed the letter, "Dear Mrs. Stern," and added, "Thanks for remembering me."[1565]

It was announced to the Board of Directors that leases of one to five years for tenants of the new building were now acceptable to the financial backers, rather than the fifteen-year requirement that earlier had been set forth as a prerequisite for financing. That was a large breakthrough in terms of being able to fill the building and move the construction forward. It was also announced that the International Relations Committee under Mario Bermúdez was contracted to be in the Mart building for the next fifty-six years, in a deal worked out with the City of New Orleans. There had been tremendous opposition to the new building from the Central Area Committee, because of the tax benefits enjoyed by the Mart, but that issue had recently been resolved. The total cost of the new building now was expected to be approximately $35,000,000, and as of September 1963, approximately sixty percent of the building had been leased. Among other things, a service now was being explored through which helicopters could land directly on the new building. Lloyd Cobb said that he hoped the building could be the starting point to make New Orleans again one of the financial capitals of the Western Hemisphere.[1566]

On August 8, 1963, Shaw wrote to William Spratling in Taxco, Mexico, indicating that his longtime friend Jeff Biddison would be visiting that area, and asking Spratling to assist him with lodging and activities in the area.[1567] Shaw had not yet made it back to see Spratling, but Mexico would be one of the first places he visited upon retirement.

Shaw's assistance continued to be sought out by various individuals in New Orleans who appreciated his knowledge and his standing among the city's leadership. On August 12, 1963, Frank Hemenway of Hemenway Furniture Company sought Shaw's help in being named as a consultant on the Dock Board project involving the new Mart building.[1568]

At a meeting of the Executive Committee in mid-August, Lloyd Cobb said that the Mart was to take the entire 29th floor of the tower building, and one wing of the 30th floor, for its executive offices and clerical space; it would have a two-story room for a reception area. He indicated that the Traffic and Transportation Bureau would be in the building eventually, as would the New Orleans Tourist and Convention Commission; they both would use part of the Mart's executive office space. Cobb reminded the group that Jesse Core was leaving to go into business for himself, but that he was interested in retaining the Mart's account for public relations. Core's salary with the Mart was currently $10,000 per year, and Cobb recommended that the Mart retain him as an outside contractor at $500 per month, and allow him use vacant space, of which the current building had more than enough at the time. Cobb suggested that the Mart also could hire additional public relations firms, if necessary.[1569]

Shaw's old friend John Wray Young wrote to Shaw that he would be passing through New Orleans in August 1963. Young's letter mentioned his daughter, Jill, who was living in New Orleans at that time.[1570] Shaw and Jill Young would form a bond that would come into play in a unique way soon after Shaw's arrest

In August, Shaw received a letter from Hal Ross Yockey of the Ross Agency, a public relations firm. The letter, which opened "Dear Clay," indicated that Bill Stuckey had joined the public relations staff at the Ross Agency. Yockey stated that the Ross Agency was now entering its fourth year of service, and enclosed an article that gave a biography of Stuckey.[1571] Stuckey is notable because on August 17, 1963, he conducted a radio interview with Lee Harvey Oswald on a program called "Latin Listening Post;" the interview was conducted after Oswald's arrest for a street clash with anti-Castro Cuban exiles in New Orleans.

Hal Ross Yockey's son, known as Ross Yockey, became a reporter for the *States-Item*. In 1967, he would be one of two reporters for that newspaper who was considered notably favorable to Jim Garrison in the coverage of Garrison's investigation into the Kennedy assassination. Some of the articles that Yockey wrote helped to propel public interest in the investigation, particularly in the New Orleans area, to new heights. Yockey also wrote one or more articles about the case, under a pseudonym, for a local magazine. He eventually would be removed from the story by the newspaper's editor, because his relationship with Garrison was deemed to be too supportive.

On September 9, 1963, Shaw accepted an invitation from Alfred Moran to a cocktail reception Moran was holding at his home for ambassadors to the Organization of American States.[1572] Moran later would emerge as a potential witness during the criminal case against Shaw, when it was learned Moran had visited the Eastern Airlines VIP Room at the New Orleans airport on December 14, 1966, the day someone supposedly wrote the mysterious name "Clay Bertrand" in the guest register.

On September 3, 1963, Shaw wrote to Ruben M. Gaxiola, Consul General of Mexico, accepting an invitation to a reception to commemorate the Anniversary of Independence of Mexico, to be held on Sunday, September 15, 1963.[1573] The following day, September 16, would be open on Shaw's calendar, and years later, after his arrest, prosecutors would attempt to establish that date as the one when Shaw allegedly attended a party with Lee Harvey Oswald and David Ferrie, and discussed the assassination of President Kennedy. The date, however, conflicted with other statements of the prosecution's main witness, Perry Russo.

In September 1963, Shaw gave a letter of recommendation to Andrew Given Tobias Moore, II for admission to the bar in Delaware. Moore, already a member of the bar in Louisiana, had worked as an office clerk and temporary summer help at the Mart during the summers of 1954 and 1955. Prior to December 1956, he had been known as Emmett Assenheimer.[1574] He was a cousin of both Goldie Moore, Shaw's longtime secretary, and Irma Lagan, who had been Theodore Brent's secretary.

By early September 1963, Shaw had begun to arrange a two-week vacation for November. The trip, entirely by train, would be to Los Angeles, California, then up to San Francisco, and then across to Chicago, Illinois, where he would spend the Thanksgiving holidays with old friends Patrick and Edna O'Rourke. Shaw had had earlier contact with a group of men from the Portland, Oregon area who were planning a regional international trade conference, and he soon accepted a speaking engagement there that would take place during the course of his vacation trip. He also accepted another speaking engagement in Portland—a combined meeting of the Kiwanis and Rotary Club. Separately, Mario Bermúdez had met a man named J. Monroe Sullivan, who managed the San Francisco World Trade Center. Bermúdez suggested to Sullivan that he contact Shaw about giving a speech at the Trade Center there about the history of the Mart in New Orleans, and the new Mart complex; the speech would essentially be similar to those to be given later in Portland, Oregon.

Most of the individuals with whom Shaw had any kind of official meeting on this November 1963 trip had some history of meeting or corresponding with him months before. William R. Wells, Vice President of First National Bank of Oregon, had come through New Orleans in early May with a group which toured International House and the Mart. Shaw had shown the group around, and afterwards Wells wrote thanking Shaw for his courtesy towards the visitors.[1575] Wells then invited Shaw to speak at the 5th Annual Columbia Basin Export-Import Conference at the Benson Hotel in Portland, Oregon, to be held on November 25 and 26, 1963; Shaw was to be the noon luncheon speaker on November 26. Wells suggested that Shaw discuss the European market, but also urge people to think of the potential for the Columbia Basin World Trade Center in Portland during his talk. Wells confirmed that the conference would reimburse Shaw for his actual expenses.[1576] Goldie Moore sent Shaw's biography and photograph to the Portland Chamber of Commerce in mid-September, noting his participation in the Export-Import Conference.[1577] Shaw's photograph, and an article about his upcoming speech, appeared in the October 1963 edition of *Harbor News*, a Portland shipping industry publication.[1578] A brochure to publicize the conference was published, also showing Shaw's photograph and describing his career.[1579] David B. Porter, Assistant Public Relations Director with the Portland Public Docks, forwarded the *Harbor News* article to Goldie Moore the week before Shaw's speech.[1580] Shaw booked the cost of the train ticket for his entire trip to the Columbia Basin Export-Import Conference.

William Wells inquired of Shaw if he would be sending a prepared speech for distribution to attendees at the conference. As he usually did, Shaw responded that he had no prepared speech, but rather would speak from "rough notes," for maximum spontaneity.[1581]

Before getting to Portland, Oregon, Shaw would also meet with international trade representatives in Los Angeles and San Francisco. One of the directors of the Los Angeles

World Trade Center was Theodore A. Bruinsma, who had been present at the groundbreaking for the new Mart tower in October. Fred B. Vanderhurst, another director of the Los Angeles World Trade Center, had corresponded with Shaw in mid-1963. Shaw, responding to Vanderhurst's letter of inquiry about the Mart,[1582] had sent information on the history and financing of the institution.[1583] Once Shaw learned he would be in California during November, he wrote to Bruinsma, indicating that he would be in Los Angeles "around November 22, 1963," and that perhaps they could get together for a drink.[1584]

In early October, Lloyd Cobb sent a telegram to numerous individuals, both in and out of the New Orleans area, inviting them to a ceremony on October 16, 1963, marking the commencement of construction of the Mart's new tower building at Number 2 Canal Street.[1585] Various black and white photos of the event survive, with Shaw, Lloyd Cobb, Mayor Victor Schiro, and numerous others in suits and ties on a podium speaking to a crowd of people. Lloyd Cobb gave the main speech, indicating what the building would mean to a future New Orleans. J. Ronald Hanover of Cross Country Development Corporation, the leasing agent for the new building, was unable to attend, but offered Shaw best wishes on the groundbreaking ceremonies, and asked him to extend thanks to Goldie Moore, Darlyn Mercadal, Carmen Martinez, Jesse Core, and J.B. Dauenhauer for their assistance while Hanover had been in New Orleans recently.[1586]

A newspaper clipping on October 17, 1963 detailed the start of the new Mart, with Lloyd Cobb taking a sledgehammer to the old Dock Board building. The article mentioned that the Mart had sold the old building some years before and leased it from the new owners, and that International House had decided not to participate in the new building project. The article further indicated that the Mart had struggled in a building too small for its needs for years, and that approximately nineteen months before, in early 1962, the Mart had approached the brink of liquidation.

**Shaw with Lloyd Cobb (in helmet) at beginning of construction of new International Trade Mart, probably 1963 (International Trade Mart Collection, Louisiana Research Collection, Tulane University)**

Shaw received a letter from W.J. (Bill) Ford, Jr. of Strachan Shipping Company in Mobile, Alabama. Ford congratulated Shaw on the start of construction for the new Mart tower, saying that it had been a long and tough battle.[1587] Shaw replied that the erection of the tower would do a great deal to change the thinking of New Orleans, and change the sort of "drifting attitude" which had marked the city for the last decade.[1588]

With the new Mart tower underway, and Shaw's retirement approximately two years away, someone prepared a "Proposed Organizational and Operational Plan for The New International Trade Mart." The manuscript does not indicate who wrote it, but it called for a "more international" Managing Director, at a salary of $40,000 to $50,000 per year; it also suggested several distinct operating departments under the Managing Director. The manuscript, which was fifty-two pages in length, indicated that the new Managing Director could be a former Cabinet head, a former governor, or possibly a well-known military leader.[1589]

Shaw responded to various invitations for local events scheduled to occur during the period he would be on the West Coast by informing the requestors that he would be out of New Orleans from November 15 through December 1, 1963. On October 24, 1963, for example, Shaw wrote to John Oulliber, with the New Orleans chapter of the National Conference of Christians and Jews, declining an invitation to a dinner honoring prominent businessman C.C. "Bud" Walther, indicating his trip would prevent him from attending.[1590]

In late October, Shaw wrote to Edward Durell Stone, thanking him for Stone's gift of champagne in honor of the recent groundbreaking for the new Mart tower. Shaw recalled the struggle over several years to get the project going, and said that Mart officials were grateful for Stone's perseverance and patience over the past five years. Shaw wrote that Mart leaders "know we can count on your carrying out Lloyd's original request to create a building that will be unique, beautiful, and awe-inspiring."[1591]

In late October 1963, Shaw wrote to Martha Ann Samuel, who had inquired about the specific buildings he had restored. The list he generated included 537 Barracks Street, 906 Esplanade Avenue, 1313 Dauphine Street, 505-07-09-11-13-15 Dauphine Street (five buildings), 618 Dumaine Street, 923 Burgundy Street, 927 Burgundy Street, 908 Esplanade Avenue, and 716-24 Governor Nicholls Street.[1592]

The date eventually chosen for Shaw to speak at the World Trade Center in San Francisco would be Friday, November 22, 1963. Shaw had met and corresponded with assorted representatives from San Francisco as far back as the early 1950s, as they had attempted, with varying degrees of success, to begin a World Trade Center there; this speech was to be, to an extent, the continuation of existing relationships. Shaw confirmed his speech date in a letter to Monroe Sullivan a few days before he departed by train from New Orleans.[1593] Shortly before he left, Shaw received a telegram from Sullivan, indicating that a room had been reserved at the St. Francis Hotel for Shaw's arrival in San Francisco at 8:00 a.m. on Thursday, November 21.[1594]

In addition to the business socializing that Shaw did on the trip, he also visited with social friends in Los Angeles and San Francisco. The night before the assassination, he spent the evening and part of the night with James Dondson. Dondson had met Shaw in 1959, while on a trip to New Orleans during the Mardi Gras festivities; Dondson had been steered in Shaw's direction by Shaw's old friend Judson O'Donnell, and he had stayed at Shaw's residence during that trip. Dondson eventually would move into ownership of gay bars in San Francisco, and elsewhere, including some that catered to the "leather" trade, and he was familiar with the sadism and masochism scene. In an interview with the author years later, Dondson acknowledged that he knew Shaw had participated in S&M role-playing, but said that he had never actually joined in those activities with Shaw.[1595]

Accounts differ as to where Shaw was when he first heard the news of Kennedy's assassination on Friday, November 22, 1963. J. Monroe Sullivan, with the World Trade Center in San Francisco, recalled, immediately after Shaw's arrest, that he had been taking Shaw on a tour of the Center when the news arrived. Kennedy was shot at approximately 12:30 p.m. in Dallas, which would have been 10:30 a.m. in San Francisco. By the time the news was flashed to most people it was at least a half hour later, which would have made it 11:00 a.m. in San Francisco, near the time of Shaw's expected speech to the gathering. Some FBI memos have very indirect information to the effect that James Dondson and Shaw were together at the time Shaw heard the news; it is possible that both accounts are partially correct. Dondson recalled to the author that after the assassination had occurred, Shaw did not feel up to his usual partying and nightclubbing, preferring instead to spend a quiet evening. [1596]

Shaw continued on to Portland, Oregon a few days later. Some accounts have it that Shaw's speech before one or more of the Portland gatherings was canceled. A newspaper account from that era has Shaw showing up for his speech, not having been informed that it had been canceled due to the assassination.

After a couple of days in Portland, he moved on to Chicago by train to spend the Thanksgiving holidays with Patrick O'Rourke and his wife, Edna. It is unclear exactly how Shaw knew Patrick and Edna O'Rourke. Patrick O'Rourke was bisexual, and had lived in California during the 1950s; it is possible Shaw knew him through Judson O'Donnell. O'Rourke appeared on Shaw's 1953 Christmas card list as being in Phoenix, Arizona; he later would become an advertising salesman in the Chicago area. Edna O'Rourke had previously been Edna Anhalt, and had, along with her husband at the time, Edward Anhalt, written several award-winning screenplays, including one for the movie *Panic in the Streets*, which was filmed in New Orleans and released in 1950. Shaw's old co-author on early plays, Herman Stuart Cottman, appeared in a small role in the movie, which was directed by Elia Kazan.

Following President Kennedy's assassination on November 22, attention quickly focused on Lee Harvey Oswald's past. It was an odd one to say the least. There were very few individuals who had defected to the Soviet Union, married a Russian woman, and then, seemingly with relative ease, returned to the United States. Additionally, Oswald, who was born in New Orleans and had lived there at different junctures in his life, was in the city during a crucial period from April 1963 through September 1963, when he had attracted considerable attention for the aforementioned street altercation he had had with some anti-Castro Cubans.

After the assassination, several things happened in New Orleans in quick succession that would have a lasting effect on conspiracy theories related to the assassination, and play an important role in Jim Garrison's investigation into the assassination, which would begin in late 1966. One of the individuals involved was Jack Martin, a private detective type who also is generally described as an alcoholic by those who knew him at that time. According to Martin's FBI file, in 1939 he had applied to work for Naval Intelligence, and over the years had applied to police departments in Santa Monica, California, Hawthorne, California, and Memphis, Tennessee.[1597] Based upon some of his correspondence as late as 1967, he seemed to be on a first-name basis with Congressman Hale Boggs[1598] and U.S. Senator Russell Long.[1599]

Many legends circulated about Martin during the 1960s. In 1967, several months after the Clay Shaw arrest, Assistant District Attorney Andrew Sciambra reported to Jim Garrison that Martin's grandfather, named James Martin, was a member of the Bonnie and Clyde gang. James Martin had turned against the gang, and his body had later been found cut in half.[1600] Martin himself had been arrested for murder during the 1950s, after allegedly performing a botched abortion on a woman, who then died as a result; he was not prosecuted for the crime, however.

Guy Banister, the ex-FBI man and New Orleans police official who now ran a private detective agency, entered the picture through an incident that some credit for partly beginning a very long chain of events. The night of the assassination, Banister supposedly beat Jack Martin, who worked in Banister's office at the time, with a pistol. A police report dated November 25, 1963, summarized Martin's version of the beating. According to Martin, it was over some long-distance calls he had made on Banister's office telephone; Banister's secretary, Delphine Roberts, witnessed the beating. Although the beating has sometimes been described as "severe," Martin did not press charges for the beating, which resulted in three small lacerations on his forehead, and one on the rear of his head.

The report mentioned nothing about David Ferrie, Lee Harvey Oswald, or the Kennedy assassination in any respect.[1601] However, the incident has been transformed, in some conspiracy accounts, from an issue over telephone calls made from the office telephone to one where Martin had stolen or peeked into some of Banister's private files dealing with various activities in, for example, the anti-Castro Cuban movement. That story may have originated with a memorandum that Assistant District Attorney Andrew Sciambra, who would be a key participant in the case against Shaw, wrote to Garrison on October 28, 1968. The memo indicated that a source had told Sciambra that New Orleans area FBI agent Regis Kennedy, one of the agents who investigated the New Orleans aspects of the Kennedy assassination in 1963, had said that Guy Banister pistol-whipped Jack Martin because Martin had stolen some of Banister's "CIA files," and that Banister had been working with a CIA agent named Logan, who was assigned to local anti-Castro Cuban activist Sergio Arcacha Smith. Therefore, the information was not even firsthand from FBI agent Regis Kennedy, but merely Sciambra's source telling him that Kennedy had said that.[1602] Regis Kennedy, who would testify both before a grand jury in 1967, and at Shaw's trial in 1969, was never asked by prosecutors about the incident where Banister supposedly pistol-whipped Martin.

Regardless of the reason for the beating, over the weekend after the assassination Martin reached out to Herman Kohlman, the former newspaperman who was now with the district attorney's office. Martin indicated that a person known to both him and Banister, David Ferrie, might have been involved in the assassination. Ferrie was a local pilot known for his continuing associations with under-aged males (and others who were barely of legal age) whom he taught to fly, and with whom he socialized in a variety of questionable ways. Ferrie supposedly had a disease called alopecia, and had no hair on his head or body. He wore crude reddish wigs and fake eyebrows in an attempt to maintain a relatively normal appearance.

David Ferrie had been arrested more than two years earlier for corruption of a minor related to alleged improper sexual activity; he had been fired from his pilot's job at Eastern Airlines after the arrest. Later, he would be accused of attempting to bribe an assistant district attorney in the office of Richard Dowling, Jim Garrison's predecessor in office. Garrison and Dowling would discuss the issue in February 1962 during a televised debate, when Dowling was running for re-election, and Garrison was conducting an ultimately winning campaign to defeat him.[1603]

There were other strange stories about Ferrie as well. William Gurvich, another private security man who later worked within Jim Garrison's investigation into Kennedy's assassination, described visiting Ferrie's apartment once in 1957 and finding that Ferrie had cages filled with white mice, which he supposedly used in an attempt to develop a cure for cancer.[1604] At the time of the assassination, Ferrie worked as an investigator for G. Wray Gill, local attorney for New Orleans area Mafia leader Carlos Marcello, helping in Marcello's attempts to avoid deportation to another country. A few years before, Marcello had supposedly been scooped up and flown to Guatemala in a deportation effort ordered by Attorney General Robert Kennedy; legend had it that Ferrie had gone to Guatemala and flown Marcello back into the United States. It should be noted that both components of that account are disputed by some.

Martin told the district attorney's investigators that Ferrie had known Lee Harvey Oswald during the 1950s as part of the Civil Air Patrol they both belonged to, and that Ferrie, who had left on a trip to Texas the afternoon of the assassination, might have been involved as a "getaway pilot" for the assassins. The FBI and Secret Service soon questioned Ferrie and then released him. His Texas trip had been to southern Texas, hundreds of miles away from Dallas, and had only begun, by automobile, well after the assassination had taken place and Oswald had been detained. Before the Secret Service agents departed from their interview, however, Ferrie told them he suspected Martin of being the person who had fingered him to authorities. The Secret Service decided it needed to question Martin, who advised them that he had developed a case of "telephonitis" after drinking, and had made some calls with unprovable assertions about Ferrie. While the story seemed thoroughly discredited, Jim Garrison would return to it three years later in launching his investigation, with Martin still as a main source.

Another New Orleans man who emerged after the assassination was roly-poly, jive-talking attorney Dean Andrews. Andrews is often described as someone who could easily fit within one of the stories of New York writer Damon Runyon, and a brief reading of Runyon's short stories confirms that impression. However, Aaron Kohn, Managing Director of the New Orleans Metropolitan Crime Commission, had a more specific first impression of Andrews, which he described in a 1960 internal report. "Andrews is a short, fat, swarthy individual, glib, fast talking and gives more of the impression of a thug than of an attorney. He gives the superficial impression of being extremely candid and outspoken. He was dressed in a suit that was badly in need of cleaning and pressing, wore a shirt open at the neck which was somewhat dirty and made a highly unprofessional appearance." Andrews was accompanied on that meeting by an insurance agent named William Carraway, whom Kohn described as "in his 30s, was blonde, has very bad skin and appeared to be more at home in a bar room than in an insurance office."[1605]

Additionally, the FBI reported in 1967 that Dean Andrews, who almost always wore sunglasses, whether outside or inside and regardless of the time of day, had in 1954 applied for a job with the Immigration and Naturalization Service. According to background reports conducted at the time, people who knew Andrews described him as "poorly adjusted," "not well balanced," "unstable," and a "big talker," who had a habit of "stretching the truth."[1606]

Andrews claimed that, the day after the assassination, a Saturday, while he was a patient in a local hospital, he had received a call from a mysterious client, whom he identified as a "Clay Bertrand," asking him to represent Oswald. Andrews later notified the FBI, who came to interview him the following week. Andrews gave several conflicting descriptions of "Bertrand," and at times said that he had never even seen him, that he was simply "a voice on the phone" who referred clients to him, especially homosexual youths who had been busted for pandering, solicitation, or other sexual-related crimes. Andrews maintained also that Oswald had consulted with him during the summer of 1963, but could produce no records of Oswald or Bertrand ever being clients, nor did any of his office personnel recall such details. Within a few days, Andrews told the FBI that he may have dreamed up the whole episode of receiving the call from "Bertrand," but he resurrected the story when a Warren Commission lawyer came to interview him in mid-1964. That lengthy interview, which was widely read as the official account of Andrews's story of receiving the call, fails to give the full context of his numerous contradictions about the mysterious "Clay Bertrand," including his early description to the FBI that Bertrand was around twenty-two years of age and had blonde hair, nor does it detail the FBI's failure to find any trace of such a person, or Oswald, in Andrews's office records or in the memories of his office personnel.

Despite Andrews's flip-flopping, the FBI had searched for the mysterious "Clay Bertrand," without success. Three years later, when Jim Garrison began his investigation, one of the questions he returned to was: Who was this mysterious person who had tried to find legal representation for Oswald? Andrews had not indicated that "Clay Bertrand" had been involved in the actual assassination. Still, who was he?

Partly because Andrews had said that Oswald had come into his office with some "gay Mexicanos," the question arose very quickly after the assassination of whether Oswald was a homosexual, or had engaged in homosexual activity. Arthur Kaplan, a writer for the *Saturday Evening Post*, called Aaron Kohn of the New Orleans Metropolitan Crime Commission on November 25, 1963 to ask about various Oswald rumors, including whether or not Oswald and Ruby had some connection prior to the assassination, whether Oswald had ever been to Ruby's night club, and, most bluntly, if Oswald and Ruby were homosexuals.[1607]

Of course, with Andrews's contradictory accounts of whether he had even received such a phone call, and what "Clay Bertrand" looked like, and with Andrews's solid reputation as a serial exaggerator, if not an outright liar, one could easily have simply dismissed his story as not worth pursuing further. Or—one could have chosen to believe there was something there, which is what Jim Garrison did. If no one named "Clay Bertrand" could be located, was there anyone named Clay who associated with homosexuals and "Mexicanos," or even anyone from Latin America? Well, there was Clay Shaw.

One of the FBI's informants in New Orleans immediately after the assassination was Betty Parent, who would later become an informant for Jim Garrison's office. In an interview with local FBI agent Regis Kennedy in 1963, Parent told Kennedy she knew "numerous sex deviates" in the French Quarter, but knew of no one named "Clay Bertrand."[1608] She said that she knew a Clay Gould, who lived at 935 Dauphine Street, less than four blocks away from Clay Shaw at 1313 Dauphine Street. Interestingly, Parent did not mention Clay Shaw to the FBI, although by her description he would clearly have fallen in the "sex deviate" category, and he lived in the French Quarter.

Interestingly, by the time Shaw was arrested on March 1, 1967, the name of "Clay Bertrand" had morphed into "Clem Bertrand," based upon the assertions of the major witness against Shaw, Perry Raymond Russo, whose assertions emerged under hypnosis and/or sodium pentothal sessions administered at the direction of the district attorney's office. How Dean Andrews's "Clay Bertrand" could have become Perry Russo's "Clem Bertrand" has never been explained, although vagueness about such things did not exactly hurt the prosecution's case in the public mind; close enough was good enough.

Interestingly, Marguerite Oswald, Lee Harvey Oswald's mother, may have communicated with a "Clem" shortly after the assassination. Joseph Cooper, a Baton Rouge resident, told Assistant District Attorney Andrew Sciambra in 1968 that Marguerite Oswald had told him that she had called New Orleans attorney Clem Sehrt shortly after the assassination, asking him to help her son; Marguerite Oswald knew Sehrt from having lived in New Orleans earlier. Sehrt supposedly had said that he no longer practiced law.[1609] Ironically, Clem Sehrt would turn up years later as one of the defense attorneys representing one of the parties sued by Clay Shaw in a civil suit for damages related to his arrest.

Other characters who popped up to investigators in 1963 also appeared years later during Garrison's investigation. One of the many individuals who contacted the FBI after the assassination was Cedric Younger von Rolleston, also known as Arthur Dean Swift; his information in 1963 did not mention Shaw at all. Von Rolleston and his wife would, in 1967, contact District Attorney Jim Garrison's office with a totally different story, swearing that they had seen Shaw and Lee Harvey Oswald at the Bentley Hotel in Alexandria, Louisiana in 1963, and actually would be listed as potential witnesses in early prosecution court filings for the case, before eventually meeting with Shaw and his attorneys and withdrawing the story. The FBI memo in 1963 indicates that von Rolleston had corresponded with the Ambassador from the Soviet Union to the United States in 1952, from his residence in Swainsboro, Georgia. The FBI's agent in Savannah, Georgia, near Swainsboro, indicated that employers and acquaintances of von Rolleston considered him as a "neurotic" and as a "victim of a persecution complex."[1610]

Conspiracy theory thinking began almost on the day of the assassination, and stepped up considerably after Jack Ruby shot Oswald. As early as November 27, 1963, Cuban President Fidel Castro gave a speech at Havana University. He said that the issue of Oswald being a pro-Castro activist might have been an attempt to mislead public opinion, and he also questioned aspects of the entry and exit wounds to Kennedy's body, and whether shots had come from the front as well as from the rear of Kennedy's automobile. The CIA, monitoring the speech, concluded that Castro could have gotten all of the information in his speech from newspaper accounts.[1611]

In Europe, conspiracy theories also abounded. The Soviet Union helped to keep them going, maintaining that it was a conspiracy of right-wing elements in the United States. Many in Western Europe also thought it was a right-wing conspiracy to topple Kennedy. Others thought it was a Mafia/underworld type of conspiracy, because of connections Kennedy's father and family had with organized crime throughout the first half of the 20th century, and because of efforts by Attorney General Robert Kennedy to rein in organized crime. Some theorists believed that Oswald was not the assassin at all, and such thinking increased after attorney Mark Lane wrote a lengthy article, which appeared on December 13, 1963, questioning whether Oswald had actually been involved. Unlike some other theories, the idea of a Communist conspiracy pushing Oswald to commit the assassination was not taken seriously by mainstream media in Europe. In another twist, the Soviet Union maintained a familiar way of thinking in its regime, by alleging that "Trotskyite" literature had been found in Oswald's room.

One low-profile theory was that the assassination was racially motivated, because of Kennedy's stance on civil rights; that theory was more prominent in newly independent African countries. The thinking in some Arab countries was that there had been a Jewish conspiracy, because of Jack Ruby's involvement in the case. Others thought that elements of the United States government were involved in the assassination.

The momentum would pick up in the years following 1963, especially when the Warren Commission report failed to adequately clear up many aspects of the assassination, and important governmental records were sealed for the statutory requirement of seventy-five years. Accordingly, in late 1966, when Jim Garrison picked up the assassination investigation, the ground was very fertile for public support of his efforts.

Shaw returned to New Orleans, from his November trip to the West Coast and Chicago, only to find a letter waiting for him from Ruben M. Gaxiola, Consul General of Mexico in New Orleans. Gaxiola expressed his condolences and sorrow over the assassination of President Kennedy, and indicated that Mexican President Adolfo Lopez Mateos had proclaimed three days of national morning in Mexico.[1612] Shaw replied in mid-December, saying, "I have just returned from a long trip to find your kind and thoughtful letter of November 26. Believe me your expresses of condolence are most kind and very much appreciated. I feel as I am sure you do, that the tragic death of our President is a loss not only to the citizens of the United States but to men of good will everywhere in the world. Thanks again for writing."[1613]

After his return in early December, Shaw corresponded with all of the major personalities with whom he had dealt related to his speeches during the trip. On December 4, he wrote to William R. Wells, indicating that he was back home in New Orleans. Shaw said that he hoped his talk had done some good for the organization, and requested that Wells return a blown-up photograph of the Mart.[1614] Shortly after his arrival home, Shaw received a letter from Marion C. Kretsinger, Executive Secretary of the Rotary Club of Portland, thanking Shaw for his speech there on November 26, 1963.[1615] This evidence that Shaw gave at least some type of talk to both groups in Portland partly contradicts newspaper accounts to the contrary.

Shaw was invited to attend the meeting of the New Orleans Chamber of Commerce on December 11 by Joseph W. Simon, Jr., Executive Vice-President of the group. Along with Shaw, other invitees included Paul Fabry of International House and Aaron Kohn, Managing Director of the Metropolitan Crime Commission.[1616] Kohn later would play a very important role on Shaw's behalf during his involvement in Jim Garrison's investigation into the Kennedy assassination. After an initial period of support for Jim Garrison's work as district attorney, Kohn turned against Garrison in 1966, and served as a critical foil to Garrison throughout the remainder of the controversial district attorney's twelve years in office.

In mid-December, Shaw wrote to Fred Vanderhurst, saying he appreciated Vanderhurst's hospitality during his visit, and indicating that he had "enjoyed drinks with you and

Ted."[1617] He wrote the same day to J. Monroe Sullivan, thanking him for his hospitality as well.[1618] In none of the letters to individuals on the West Coast did Shaw mention the Kennedy assassination.

By late 1963, Shaw had re-evaluated certain ongoing commitments. In a letter to M.J. Gruber with Building Owners and Managers Association (BOMA), J.B. Dauenhauer indicated that Shaw had decided not to renew his membership for the fiscal year ending September 30, 1964.[1619]

At the end of 1963, employees of the Mart, as shown on its hospitalization plan, included Clay Shaw, J.B. Dauenhauer, Darlyn Mercadal, Hollis Bridges, and Goldie Moore. Delores V. Neely had been employed with the Mart during 1963, but she had left during the fall.

As 1963 drew to a close, Shaw received a letter from Eberhard P. Deutsch offering holiday greetings.[1620] Only a few short years away, Deutsch's firm would be actively involved in representing Jim Garrison's office on various appeals related to Shaw's criminal case. Shaw also ended the year by sending holiday greetings to various Board members of the Mart, including Seymour Weiss, Managing Director and President of the Roosevelt hotel.[1621]

One of the individuals Shaw had visited during his California trip in November was his second cousin, once removed, Faye Hogan, who grew up near his parents when they lived in Shreveport, Louisiana. Hogan left Louisiana after college and moved to California, becoming a minister. Years later, she recalled her early knowledge of Shaw prior to his visit:

"I was very young, early elementary school years in Shreveport, La. though I can't remember when I first heard about him (my family and his mother called him 'Vergne' or 'Verne'). My mother went to visit his mother often and I went outside to play while they talked or played cards. I remember that his father was a Federal Agent with what we today call the ATF but then I just heard a "G. Man" and he was never at home when we went to visit.

"...I just knew that he was 'Aunt Alice's' and 'Uncle Glaris's' grown son who lived in NEW YORK CITY! And had been an aide to a 'very important general' in WWII. And was writing a script for a play! It all sounded so glamorous. I really didn't meet him until I was much older and I can't remember when or where. I do remember sitting in awe the few times he came home to see his mother and he was very close to her. Never knew about his relationship with his father. His location and occupations were always known to my mother and father so they told me when he came to live in New Orleans and I drove by his house in the Quarter once when I was in collage but never visited him there.

"In 1961 I think it was, I had moved to Los Angeles. Clay came to L.A. on business, stayed at a hotel on Wilshire Blvd. (the Biltmore) and I picked him up there. I can still see him 'making his entrance' down the grand stairs into the lobby. Even in my later years, I thought he was most glamorous! We went to dinner and talked of nothing important that I remember. A second time, this time in 1963, I think only a day or so before the assassination but it could have been a day or two after, Clay came again to L.A. and stayed with a friend in West Hollywood. I picked him up there, we went to dinner at a small place on Sunset Blvd. He looked like a different person...

"...As long as I knew about Clay I knew about him being gay. His mother knew but I don't know when he told her. It made no difference to her. She adored him and was proud of everything he did. I assume his father knew but I can't say for sure. When I first heard about him being gay I really don't think it mattered to me. Too young to really understand. Later, as an adult, it really didn't matter to me one way or the other...

"...I remember him as polished, sophisticated, and with 'movie star' quality but also aloof when he wanted to be...a loner when he chose to be, and I would say very conflicted about his own identity..."[1622]

# 22 · The Mart Hits New Lows as a New Building Begins to Rise

The progress of the new Mart tower and complex was followed by many individuals in the international trade arena. In January 1964, Don Nay, with the Port of San Diego, wrote asking Shaw for information about the Mart.[1623] Shaw responded, indicating that the new building would have an exhibit hall in which international trade fairs would be held.[1624] Ironically, years before, during the period from 1946 to 1948, when the original Mart was being promoted to prospective tenants, the promotional mailings had emphasized that the Mart was not a trade fair, but more of a permanent exhibition. The plan now was that the new Mart would combine both international tenants with permanent office space and temporary fairs, as indeed the original Mart had eventually.

By 1964, Shaw was living again at 1313 Dauphine Street.[1625] He would remain there through his arrest and trial, and sell the property in the summer of 1969.

**1313 Dauphine Street in New Orleans, the small white structure: Shaw's residence during much of the 1960s and at the time of his arrest (Source unknown)**

In mid-January 1964, Shaw met with Pension and Group Consultants regarding a proposed pension plan for the employees of the Mart. The consulting firm indicated that it would submit a preliminary study within ten days.[1626] Shaw had hoped to put a pension plan for employees into place for some time, but the Mart's bad financial situation had effectively prevented any new benefits from being implemented.

In mid-January, Shaw received a letter from Paul Fabry, asking him to send him a list of people interested in International House's planned trip around the world.[1627] International House was continuing its long history of trade mission trips, with more ambitious and lengthier trips to more exotic lands. Shaw continued on good relations with Fabry, even as the two major institutions were still, in a sense, estranged from each other.

Mart employees were still answering routine inquiries almost as if it was 1948, the year of the original opening. In a letter to one inquirer, Shaw responded to a request for a speaker for an AM-FM clock radio.[1628] The same month, J.B. Dauenhauer responded to a letter passed on to the Mart from the New Orleans Chamber of Commerce. In his response, Dauenhauer indicated, as he had for years using form language, that, "ITM is a million and a half dollar streamlined, air-conditioned trading center," with "sales offices located in the Mart," and informed the inquirer that, "Merchandise can be examined and purchased on premises."[1629]

Behind the scenes, however, and away from the public eye, the Mart was struggling with how to proceed until the new building could be completed. At an Executive Committee meeting in early January, consideration was given to moving out of the current building when the lease expired on August 11, 1964. The idea would be to move out completely, halt major operations, and begin again with new tenants when the new building opened, hopefully in 1965. However, it was pointed out that rents still contributed a profit, which could offset promotional costs during the next year and a half to two years. It also was noted that it was unwise to turn current tenants over to another landlord until the completion of the new building. After consideration of all those aspects, the Executive Committee agreed that the Mart would stay in its current building for another year.[1630]

The Mart continued to seek out businessmen to participate in the organization. In early February, Willard E. Robertson, who owned the Volkswagen franchise in the New Orleans area, accepted a nomination to the Board of Directors.[1631]

At an Executive Committee meeting in mid-February, the progress of the building was discussed. The most notable item at the time was the removal of railroad tracks from the land obtained by the Mart, and their relocation to a nearby, but offsite, location.[1632] At another Executive Committee meeting in late February, it was noted that William Gaudet, publisher of *Latin American Reports*, had produced a 200-page report for the upcoming 1964 World's Fair in New York City. It was decided that the Mart would contribute $800 in cash and/or rental credits to Gaudet's organization. The Mart had long supported Gaudet in a general sense with his publishing efforts, and with patience in collecting rent from his business.[1633]

Meanwhile, work was continuing toward the new Mart building. In early March, Lloyd Cobb sent a telegram to eighty-two individuals issuing an invitation to the driving of the first foundation pile for the new Mart tower, which would take place on March 10, 1964.[1634]

In mid-March, Lloyd Cobb wrote to Harry Bloomfield of Bloomfield Building Industries in Memphis, which was constructing the new Mart tower. Cobb discussed that $15,000 of Shaw's annual salary would be charged to the project for Shaw's services in procuring materials (doors, hardware, onyx, chandeliers, aluminum louvers, and other items) from foreign governments. Cobb said that the Mart would guarantee that Shaw would at least save the project his salary amount, and that the arrangement would terminate either with Shaw's employment, or the completion of the project.[1635] It was a way of shifting part of Shaw's salary from ongoing operations to the building project, which was and had taken up much of his time for at least several years.

At a meeting of the full Board of Directors in late March, Cobb told the gathering that the target date for completion of the new building was now October 1, 1965. He indicated that a ceremony would be held in the fall of that year to commemorate the completion of the project.[1636] Whether coincidental or not, Shaw soon would pick that same date to retire from the Mart, at age fifty-two.

In April, Shaw appeared on a Focus program dealing with international issues, at Tulane University. Also on the panel was Leonard Oppenheim of Tulane Law School. The program, held on April 16, was shown on WWL-TV on April 19 and on WYES-TV on April 23.[1637]

At an Executive Committee meeting in late April, Shaw indicated that WWOM-TV, Channel 26, a local UHF station, was going to be starting up in the city, and that it would broadcast tenant activities at the Mart from 2:00 to 5:00 p.m. daily. The group also held a lengthy discussion of the restaurant and bar facilities that would be located in the new building.[1638]

In late April 1964, Shaw entertained Charles H. Liner, Jr., Executive Director of the Allied Arts Council of Metropolitan Mobile. Afterwards, Liner wrote that he appreciated the drinks "at your abode," and that "Tommy and I enjoyed the booze and chatter immensely."[1639] Liner occasionally directed young men visiting New Orleans from Mobile to Shaw for advice and assistance in seeing the city, or for lodging. One young man, although straight in orientation, became good friends with Shaw. Shaw would set him up on dates with eligible single females, and would sometimes invite him to respectable gay get-togethers as well. When the man made it clear to Shaw that he was not interested in gay sexual activity, Shaw accepted the limitations, and advised him to let Shaw know if he ever changed his mind.

In early May, Shaw received a letter from Siegfried B. Christensen of Christensen and Christensen, Attorneys at Law. He was running for judge, and indicated his qualifications in the letter. Among the associates of his firm were Harry Connick, who would later be a U.S. Attorney involved in Shaw's 1969 trial, and who would oust District Attorney Jim Garrison in 1973, in his second attempt to do so. Another associate was William Wessel, who would become Connick's chief assistant district attorney upon Connick assuming the office in 1974.[1640]

New Orleans, always somewhat of a magnet for tourists, was beginning to broaden its tourist appeal. A letter to Lloyd Cobb in May announced the opening of the Historical Wax Museum, with Isador Lazarus as Managing Director.[1641]

Shaw had picked up the pace somewhat on buying and selling of property in the French Quarter. He purchased one property in April 1964 for $19,582.40, and sold it in mid-September 1964 for $25,000. In May 1964, he purchased another property for $38,700,[1642] and sold it in September 1964 for approximately $50,000.[1643]

A brief Executive Committee meeting took place on May 21, 1964, during which a discussion was held of a possible rapprochement between the Mart and International House.[1644] In a memo addressed to the Executive Committee, Shaw indicated that a scheduled meeting for May 26th had been canceled due to the funeral of Chep Morrison.[1645] The former mayor and ambassador to the Organization of American States had perished, along with his small child, in a plane crash in Mexico. He recently had been defeated in a hotly contested gubernatorial race, the third time he had fallen short in his effort to be governor of Louisiana.

In late May, Shaw received a letter from Barbara Corbin, who had been his main secretary during the year he managed the Louisiana Purchase sesquicentennial celebration. She was now with Checci and Company in Washington, D.C. Corbin indicated that she had been in Chicago the previous week, and had spoken to David Baldwin and his wife, "Tite;" she indicated that Baldwin was on his way to a Democratic fundraiser in Washington. Corbin asked Shaw to give her best to Goldie Moore and other friends in New Orleans.[1646]

At an Executive Committee meeting in late May, there was a lengthy discussion of Shaw's salary; an informal discussion of the topic had been held in February. The salary, currently at $21,000, was officially raised to $30,000, with the new building project paying half, or $15,000 annually, retroactive from February 1, 1964 through occupancy of the new tower, expected to be on October 1, 1965. The increase was partly to account for the additional time, effort, and ideas that Shaw was contributing to the construction and planning of the new building complex. Shaw would be paid partially for managing the existing building, and partially for his services in procuring, as gifts from foreign governments, items to be integrated into the new building—doors, hardware, marble, onyx, chandeliers, and aluminum louvers. Board member Kemper Williams commented on Shaw's contributions to the Mart in the past, and noted his potential for contributions to Mart operations in the future. A discussion was also held of the possibility of each country in the world contributing its best piece of art for display in the tower; the idea of getting many countries to contribute to the new Mart had been ongoing for several years. A further discussion also was held about restaurant and bar facilities in the new building.[1647] After the meeting, Shaw requested from J.B. Dauenhauer a check for the difference in his salary from February 1, 1964 through May 27, 1964.[1648]

In early June 1964, Shaw wrote to Edward Durell Stone, discussing a proposed delegation to Spain to thank President Francisco Franco for his gift of a Spanish Plaza to be installed around the new Mart tower. Shaw proposed that the delegation would include Mayor Victor Schiro, Lloyd Cobb, and Stone. Shaw mentioned that the construction on the new building was going well, and that it was "thrilling" to see, after five years of waiting.[1649]

The Mart had discussed purchasing an additional two squares of land from Southern Pacific Railroad. At an Executive Committee meeting in early June, it was mentioned that the purchase price of those two additional squares would be $260,000, with $13,000 to be paid in cash; it was noted that a developer now wanted to construct an international hotel on that land.[1650]

In June, Shaw received a letter from Sales and Marketing Executives-International in New York City, asking for an update on his speaking activities.[1651] In perhaps what was an indication of his plans for the not-too-distant future, Shaw did not respond to the invitation.

An idea had been formulated to obtain Spanish and French government cooperation in building two plazas around the new Mart building. At an Executive Committee meeting in late June, it was formally decided that architect Edward Durell Stone, Lloyd Cobb, and Mayor Victor Schiro would go to Madrid and Paris to meet with General Franco and President de Gaulle to discuss the plazas; Mario Bermúdez would go on ahead to prepare the meeting. A further discussion was also held of the new ultra high frequency (UHF) television station, Channel 26, to be lodged in the new Mart building.[1652]

Shaw's speaking schedule during 1964, his next to last year at the Mart, went on as normal; most of the speeches were in the New Orleans area, as they had been for many years. In January, he spoke before the Propeller Club at the Roosevelt hotel, before the Round Table Club, a group interested in arts, sciences, and economic trends and developments, and before the International Trade Bureau of the Young Men's Business Club at Maylie's Restaurant.

In March, Shaw spoke before the historic Mobile (Alabama) Preservation Society, before the Junior League of New Orleans, and before the Rotary Club of Thibodaux, Louisiana. In April, he spoke before the Cosmopolitan International Club, which met in the Rose Room at Kolb's Restaurant in New Orleans. He also spoke that month before the Greater Gentilly Kiwanis Club at Siebenkittel's restaurant.

In May, Shaw ventured to Cedar Rapids, Iowa, to speak before the Foreign Trade Bureau of the local Chamber of Commerce, at an event entitled "New Orleans Night;" Shaw spoke about the new Mart building, still estimated to be completed by October 1965. In June, Shaw spoke before the Exchange Club of New Orleans at the Sheraton Charles Hotel, before the Churchmen's Brotherhood in Shaw's office at the Mart, and before the Metairie Rotary Club at Scalfoni's restaurant.

In July, Shaw spoke before the Kiwanis Club of Morgan City, Louisiana at the Hub Club Restaurant, and before the Picayune, Mississippi Rotary Club. Shaw had been invited to the latter event by Charles Nutter, who was then living in Picayune, Mississippi, and publishing the *Picayune Item*.[1653]

In August, Shaw spoke before the Sertoma International Club meeting at the Monteleone hotel, where he presented a slide show about the new Mart building. In September, he spoke before the Ladies' Auxiliary of the Home Builders Association at Brennan's restaurant, and before the Coffee Forum group of the Foreign Relations Association.

With all of the activities related to the new building that had occupied his time for the past several years, Shaw was no longer as active in the Foreign Relations Association as he had been during the 1950s and very early 1960s. However, he was still listed on the stationery as a member of the Board of Directors; another Board member during late 1964 was Alfred J. Moran.[1654] Moran and Shaw would have even more in common; they both had associations with the CIA, although in different capacities, and Moran was a longtime personal friend of its New Orleans employee, Hunter Leake, who had been Shaw's contact at the local office.

Shaw also spoke before the International Mission Conference, and the American Landmarks Association, both in Mobile, Alabama. Before those trips, Shaw received a letter from Chuck Liner of the Allied Arts Council of Metropolitan Mobile, saying, "Dear Clay, if you have not already made plans, you can stay with me in Mobile for the American Landmarks meeting."[1655]

In October, he spoke before the Kiwanis Club of Moisant at the Hilton Airport hotel. In November, Shaw spoke before the Tenth Annual Institute of the Mississippi State University and Mississippi Marketing Council, held in Jackson, Mississippi; his topic was "Marketing on an International Scope." He completed the year with a speech before the Rotary Club of Gentilly at the Vista Shores Country Club in New Orleans.

As the year entered its second half, the Mart's financial situation grew more problematic. At an Executive Committee meeting in early July, Shaw discussed the dilemma, revealing that the Mart was now losing $5,000 per month, and that there was no way to correct the situation except through more rental revenue, which was almost impossible. Tenants simply refused to renew leases, and prospective tenants refused to enter into new ones, at the current building, knowing that the Mart would be moving its operations to the new tower in the relatively near future. Shaw also indicated that International House had again declined the Mart's offer to join with them in the new building.[1656]

In early July, Shaw received a letter from Paul Fabry of International House, thanking him for referring George P. Dorsey as a possible member of the organization. In spite of the tensions between the Mart and International House, which were at their highest level, Shaw persisted in attempting to maintain a bridge between the two organizations. On the letter inviting Dorsey to be a member, Fabry handwrote a note to Shaw saying, "Many thanks, Clay—hope to see you soon."[1657]

In July, Shaw received a letter from Camilla Mays Frank of the Louisiana Society of the Daughters of the American Revolution. The organization wanted to present Lloyd Cobb with a framed copy of the Preamble to the Constitution in honor of Constitution Week; the event would be held at the Mart.[1658] Shaw had worked with Frank during the Louisiana Purchase celebration in 1953, and during various celebrations of the United Nations during the 1950s.

In late July, Shaw heard from C. Dewey Crowder, Jr., President of the City of Mobile Historic Development Commission. Crowder indicated that it had been nice to visit with Shaw recently, and shared that their mutual friend Charles Liner was currently traveling in Spain. Crowder commented that he hoped Shaw could bring Mario Bermúdez to Mobile, and that it had been nice to visit with the "Proprieter" of the Mart.[1659]

Shaw continued to hear from other individuals who had worked for him years before, speaking to his status and his ability to create lasting professional relationships. For instance, in early August, he received a letter from Glenn Weekley, who had been Public Relations Director at the Mart during the late 1940s and early 1950s. Weekley had left the Mart to work for Kaiser Aluminum, but by 1964 was Executive Vice President of the Home

Building Association of Greater New Orleans, Inc.[1660]

Shaw received a letter from Willard Robertson, thanking him for sending a flower arrangement in honor of the dedication ceremony at the formal opening of Robertson's Volkswagen Distributorship facilities.[1661] Shaw had attended the dedication ceremony on July 28, 1964, held at 4200 Michoud Boulevard.[1662]

At an Executive Committee meeting in mid-August, the group declined to seek a Polish exhibit in the new Mart, or to give free space to the Leadership Group for the Study of the Economic Opportunity Act. Lloyd Cobb mentioned that he had asked Shaw to put together an organization plan for the new Mart, and Shaw had completed it. Cobb said he disagreed with many of Shaw's opinions contained in the plan, but had wanted to give Shaw a chance to put his ideas into the revitalized Mart.[1663] It was a possible indication that Shaw's future, and that of the Mart, might not be on the same track.

In August, International House carried out its 50th Trade Mission trip, this one to Europe and Asia. Shaw had gone on very few of those trips over the years, a fact which emphasized the difference in the amount of international travel engaged in by Charles Nutter, and later Paul Fabry, as opposed to Shaw's own business travels.

At an Executive Committee meeting toward the end of August, Jesse Core's temporary arrangement in a public relations subcontracting capacity was discussed. Lloyd Cobb wanted to consider changing it, or at least making Core more specifically aware that it was not a permanent arrangement. The Board decided to continue with the current nature of the relationship for another year, until 1965, then on a month-to-month basis.[1664]

Mart officials continued to be on the list of invitations to socially relevant events. In addition to the Volkswagen ceremony mentioned earlier, several Mart representatives received an invitation to "A Working-Press" preview of the South's "Newest, Most Intimate Cocktail Lounge," located at Toulouse and Burgundy streets.

After the Cuban revolution in 1959, the consulate of Cuba in New Orleans had remained open for a time, with its offices in the Mart building. However, it had long ceased to have any official connection with the established government of Cuba under Fidel Castro. Mart officials had agreed to allow the consulate office to remain even though it was behind on rental payments, probably due primarily to its "unofficial" status at the time. Some correspondence from Mrs. Amparo Rocha, the consul of Cuba in New Orleans, indicated she did not want any correspondence sent to her indicating delinquency, as she was concerned about her credit reputation; she instead would come into the Mart office and deal with the matter of delinquent office rent in person.

Shaw worked with many individuals regarding the construction of the new Mart building, including those with the architect's offices, the construction company, and numerous designing companies. One of those individuals was Thomas Zung, an assistant to chief architect Edward Durell Stone. Zung corresponded with Shaw during the years after the Mart building was completed, including sending Shaw a postcard from Paris during 1966, after Shaw had retired, while Zung and his wife were on a trip to Europe. It should be noted here, though, the company that actually constructed the new Mart building was Bloomfield Building Industries of Memphis, Tennessee. It also operated Cross Country Development Corporation as the leasing agent for the new building. Dr. Henry Sender, a Tennessee architect enagaged by Bloomfield, had an important hand in the final building design as well.

One of the individuals whom Shaw knew during this period was George Dureau, a French Quarter artist and personality. Over the years after Shaw's death, Dureau would sometimes tell a story of visiting Shaw in the hospital during 1974, when Shaw was dying, saying that Shaw speculated that Jim Garrison had been correct in his theory of how the CIA, or some other secret governmental entity, would have used a person like Oswald in a secret mission. Dureau also told a story about Shaw offering to get him a passport in one day, for a potential trip to Spain in the early 1960s. Some have put the two stories together, and concluded that Dureau was saying that Shaw had given a "deathbed confession," and that the fact that he could have gotten Dureau a passport in one day indicated the influence Shaw had at the time within the Federal government. However, Dureau told the author, in an interview years later, that he certainly did not attribute any importance to whatever Shaw had told him while he was sick in the hospital during his last days. He said that Shaw was merely speculating, and Dureau did not take it as having any real connection to the assassination.[1665] Regarding the ability to get a passport in one day, the FBI inquired about that in 1964, during its investigation of how Oswald had obtained a passport so quickly in 1963. George F. Maddocks of the Department of State responded to the inquiry by saying that in the summer of 1963, it normally took no more than one business day to issue a passport, even a routine one.[1666]

At an Executive Committee meeting in mid-September, the matter of the new UHF television station, Channel 26, was discussed; the station was supposed to be situated in the new Mart tower building. Shaw also indicated that he was negotiating for materials to be supplied by foreign governments that would be used in the construction and décor of the new building.[1667]

When the Committee next met in early October, Lloyd Cobb indicated that the Inter-American Municipal League, which represented municipal governments in the United States and Latin America, might move its headquarters to New Orleans; if it did, the Mart would give it one free office. Mario Bermúdez was active in the organization. Cobb also shared that the new building was now behind schedule due to bad weather, but that the contractors believed it still would be finished by October 1, 1965.[1668]

Shaw sold the Spanish Stables property at 716 Governor Nicholls in October 1964. A pool was installed there on October 20, 1964, and would be a major source of entertainment for those who had access to it. At the time of the sale, the Spanish Stables sold for more than any residential property ever had in the French Quarter. Realtor "Frosty" Blackshear represented the purchasers who bought Spanish Stables from Shaw, the Tri-E Corporation. The owners of Tri-E were Dr. E.C. Cohen, Mr. Edwin Tannenbaum, and Mr. Edward Delery; the term "Tri-E" was taken from the first initial of the three men. The company was organized on September 22, 1964, shortly before the men purchased the property from Shaw.

In late October, Shaw received a letter from David M. Kleck, who owned his own advertising and public relations firm. Opening the letter, "Dear Clay," Kleck gave Shaw "many thanks" for his help in some matter then under consideration. Kleck went on to say that, "Your kindness brought back memories of the many times you helped us over difficult spots with the American and Foreign agony." Kleck concluded that, "Cynthia sends her best and appreciates you thinking of her."[1669]

At an Executive Committee meeting at the end of October, a discussion was held of the Dock Board's demand that the Mart guarantee the bonds for the exhibition facility. The Mart was in no position to do that at the moment, Cobb indicated, because it would require borrowing the money with few assets to place in collateral.[1670]

The precarious nature of finances at the Mart hit home again during 1964. In mid-November, Shaw received a telegram from Nathaniel Jacobs, one of the owners of the building, who lived in New York City; Jacobs indicated that his company had not yet received the Mart's rental payment.[1671] Shaw responded by telephone that a check would be sent the following week.

In mid-November 1964, Paul Fabry invited Shaw along on the 1965 European Mission trip planned by International House.[1672] However, because of the Mart's financial situation, the general status of the new building in progress, and the continuing tense relations with International House, Shaw did not make the trip.

Among the people with whom Shaw socialized during this period were the former playwright Flo Field, and her son, Sydney Field. Flo Field was one of those who, while tolerating

Shaw and appreciating his company, apparently had mixed feelings about homosexuals, as many did during that era. In a letter to her son, Sydney, on August 15, 1964, Flo commented on a recent *LIFE* magazine article about homosexuals in America, saying that there was now "so much being written on homos," but noting that the article gave "no explanation of them, however."[1673]

Flo Field apparently also took some exception to Shaw's friend, William Formyduval. In a letter to her son on November 28, 1964, she mentioned that Shaw had taken her home the night before after a get-together, and that, "'Your anathema' has long since gone back to S.C. where 'Aunt May' so evidently holds the reins." She went on to say that, "We had a delish dinner and the old fashion restored my soul and body. Clay had my typewriter fixed for me for $11," and "gave me a bunch of paperbacks, one by John Dicks Carr."[1674] A few months later, in early February 1965, Field would write to her son again, indicating that, "Clay is having a supper party tomorrow (Sunday) night—will call for me—Your anathema is back and there. I think he is mad as a 'March hare' as the saying is." Field also commented how Shaw had sold the Spanish Stables property recently, and that she was "quite sick and tired" of the ruining of the French Quarter, with motels on Chartres Street. "Why let it break your heart endlessly?" she asked.[1675]

In mid-December, Shaw agreed to participate in the selection of the United States participant in the World Sugar Cane Kingdom Festival, to be held the following year in Cali, Colombia. However, he did not make the trip, choosing to go to Mexico for a long vacation in October, after his retirement.

Another property owned by Shaw during this period was at 714 Toulouse Street. He purchased it from Mr. and Mrs. L. Kemper Williams in December 1964. L. Kemper Williams was a prominent New Orleanian, whose family had major interests in insurance and timber. Shaw sold the property in early 1966.

In mid-December, Shaw went to New York City to meet with Edward Durell Stone regarding various aspects of the new tower.[1676] Shaw had often combined a business trip to New York City around the holidays with a week or more of vacation in Manhattan.

At an Executive Committee meeting during the second week of December, Cobb reported on the recent trip to Spain that he had taken with other city officials. He indicated that Mario Bermúdez had opened the doors to Spanish officials, and had gotten Spain to join in the Inter-American Municipal League, with the group now being located in New Orleans. A discussion also was held on contributions of art from various countries, and whether Communist organizations should be allowed to donate such art; it was decided that the Mart would defer the matter to the U.S. Department of State. The Mart had been invited by International House to participate in its 53rd Promotion and Travel Mission, which would be visiting several Iron Curtain countries. Shaw, who had canceled his International House membership when Lloyd Cobb had broken relations between the Mart and International House, had rejoined the group, indicating that relations were at least slightly better now. Cobb reported that the new building was going up at approximately one floor per week. A discussion was held of the possible rental of space to the law firm of Deutsch, Kerrigan, and Stiles, and the firm of Terriberry, Rault, Young, and Carroll.[1677] Although the Mart normally did not rent to professional firms, Cobb pointed out that those firms represented steamship lines. It was an ironic twist, this late in Shaw's career, that the Mart would consider giving space to two law firms, one of whom would represent New Orleans District Attorney Jim Garrison in various matters, both personally and professionally, and the other included Joseph Rault, as Joseph Rault, Jr. would, in just over two years, be one of the three major private contributors to Garrison's Kennedy assassination investigation that eventually led to the arrest of Shaw.

Shaw's effort to obtain contributions of products made in various countries for use in the construction and decoration of the new Mart tower building met with mixed success.

Earlier in 1964, Shaw had written to the consul of Mexico in New Orleans suggesting that Mexico donate onyx to be used in elevator lobbies and lobbies on upper floors. Shaw wrote, "I have long been an admirer of Mexican onyx, and I think the beauty and utility of this material is not yet enough appreciated in this country."[1678] The consul of Mexico referred the letter to his national government in Mexico City. Shaw also wrote to the Belgian consul, suggesting that the Belgian carpet industry donate carpet for use in the building, but the consulate declined that request. In mid-1965, Shaw would write to the consul of the Netherlands in New Orleans, making a similar request about carpet, but it also was declined. In December 1964, he reached out to the consul of Japan in New Orleans, suggesting that Japan donate distinctive door locks for the new building.[1679]

An income statement for the full year 1964 indicated that the Mart had rental income of $177,669, and total income of $179,687, both new lows. Total expenses were $240,467, yielding a net loss of ($56,489), the worst year of financial performance in its history. Rent expense was $80,000, salaries were $66,095, advertising was $24,443, janitorial services were $19,739, utilities were $13,550, and entertaining expense was $2,401. Depreciation was minimal at $303, and travel also minimal at $160. Interest income was $9,706.[1680] The story was the same—salaries and other operating expenses had been rising steadily over the years, and rental income and occupancy percentages had fallen.

# 23 · Clay Shaw Retires

The year 1965 opened with the new tower building and its associated buildings well underway, and a major surprise in store. At an Executive Committee meeting on January 7, 1965, Cobb indicated that Shaw was anxious to retire as soon as possible. It is apparent from the notes to previous meetings that the topic had come up before, although no mention of it appears in Mart records until this particular Executive Committee meeting. Cobb indicated that Shaw was to make a list of qualifications needed for the job of Managing Director, which would be discussed at the next meeting.[1681]

It would be a fair question to ask: Why would Shaw retire so early? He was only fifty-one years old at the time of initially indicating his intentions to resign, and by the time he actually retired he would be only fifty-two, quite young for a man to retire, before the days of Internet billionaires in their twenties. There were many possible reasons for the retirement, some grounded in fact and others mere speculation.

The three men who had been the most important backers of the Mart, Theodore Brent, Rudolf Hecht, and William Zetzmann, under whom Shaw had served for the first sixteen years of his employment, had passed on. Lloyd Cobb, while active as well in both the Mart and International House during that entire time, perhaps also brought a change in vision that differed somewhat from what Shaw was used to. Some have told the author during the course of research that they thought Cobb was one of the reasons Shaw might have retired, but could cite no hard proof for such an assertion. Cobb was regarded by many as a forceful personality, used to getting his way, and using whatever means needed to secure it, and it is possible his management style rubbed Shaw the wrong way at a time when Shaw might have been sensitive to criticism for the Mart's declining performance. However, he did work under Cobb for approximately three and a half years, while seeing a very difficult project through to near-completion, before stepping aside. And Cobb would be very supportive in arranging a farewell luncheon for Shaw. There is little or no evidence that Shaw did not do his absolute best to carry out Cobb's wishes, as he had those of Zetzmann, Hecht, and Brent.

Another factor that bears on Shaw's decision was that his long years of investing in real properties had paid off handsomely. He had begun investing at a time when the French Quarter was beginning to be rejuvenated. Property values increased steadily from the 1940s through the 1960s, and Shaw had lived relatively frugally, considering his level of salaried and investment income, while building up his equity in the various properties he owned. Thus, by the mid-1960s, he was somewhat comfortable financially. Shaw was not a millionaire, particularly in 1960s dollars, but he had a net worth of at least several hundred thousand dollars.

It is also likely that Shaw was simply tired of running the Mart, which essentially had boiled down to managing a building, much as if he had been the manager of any other large commercial building in the city. The international flavor of it had worn off after the first ten years, to some degree, and it had been a matter of pure survival for the past half-decade. With retirement, Shaw could enjoy the money he had built up, live the way he wanted without as many restrictions, and not have the burden of a full-time job, and the numerous extracurricular activities that went along with the job and took many hours out of his leisure time.

Paul Fabry, who took over from Shaw at International House in 1962, remembers

Shaw describing his "pedestrian" duties at the "barely functioning ITM." Once, when Fabry asked what the purpose of the Mart was, Shaw told Fabry that, "The organization has only one purpose, and that is to give a certain Clay Shaw a good legitimate income," an assertion that Shaw repeated at times to Fabry.[1682]

Was Shaw's homosexuality a factor at all in either forcing his retirement or in causing him to resign voluntarily? It is unclear that it was a major factor, but there are some who told the author that, for example, Shaw might have been put in permanent charge of International House after Charles Nutter's departure, had some members of the organization not been unenthusiastic about having a gay person as the top employee there. It might have been an ideal move for Shaw; the Mart was declining, in danger of being closed permanently, and International House was still active and thriving to a degree, and the international travel was much greater, which would perhaps have given Shaw an opportunity to do the type of traveling he had thought would be a more consistent part of the Mart job. Such theories are also speculation; there is nothing in the Mart or International House paperwork that has survived that suggested any such concern. On the contrary, Shaw was given high marks, at least verbally within Board of Directors meetings of both organizations, for the joint management he provided for the Mart and International House during the two multi-month periods that he managed both organizations.

By early 1965, Shaw was no longer on the Board of Directors of the Foreign Relations Association. Slowly, methodically, he was winding down activities which had sustained him for almost twenty years, as he prepared for an early retirement.

With the projected opening date for the new tower still set for October 1, 1965, the Mart produced a five-page "History of the International Trade Mart" reporting on the organization's first almost twenty years of operation. Interestingly, the report made only a brief mention of Shaw.[1683]

In early February, Beryl Donnath was added to the Mart's payroll, as part of an agreement whereby the Mart would pay for secretarial service for Mario Bermúdez's activities for one year. The same month, Shaw met for a talk with Gary A. Bolding, a graduate student at Louisiana State University in Baton Rouge, who was writing a thesis on foreign trade.[1684] Years later, Bolding recalled Shaw coming across to him "as a man of considerable pride and probably a fair amount of ego," and "a little guarded in manner."[1685] If Shaw was restless in his job at the time, or pessimistic about the future of the Mart, he didn't indicate it in any way to Bolding.[1686]

Later in February, Shaw's father had surgery at Ochsner Hospital in New Orleans;[1687] Dr. Alton Ochsner personally supervised the surgery, and checked in regularly with Shaw's family. Shaw later sent Ochsner two crates of strawberries grown in the Hammond, Louisiana area, in gratitude for Ochsner's services.[1688]

During this time, Shaw paid some of the ongoing expenses for his parents, who had been living in Hammond, Louisiana since the early 1950s. In February 1965, he made a car insurance payment for a 1962 Rambler registered at 511 South Walnut Street in Hammond, the home where his parents lived.

Most of Shaw's trips during the early 1960s were by train, as they had been during the 1950s. He sometimes took pleasure trips to Los Angeles, San Francisco, Chicago, or New York City this way, using two travel agencies in the Mart to schedule his trips. By mid-1965, Shaw still had the 1959 Thunderbird he had purchased new, and he used it for trips to the Gulf Coast and around New Orleans.

As Shaw neared retirement, he had become somewhat known around New Orleans for his chess playing. Opinions differed on how well he could play the game, but his book purchases during the early 1960s show the occasional reading material about chess. Among the couples he played with during this time were Paul and Luly Fabry, and Robert Morgan and his wife, Jacqueline, a student at LSU Medical School.

Shaw was so thoroughly identified with the International Trade Mart, and during certain years with International House, that often invoices and statements related to his personal expenses, or expenses related to properties he owned, were sent to him at his business addresses. After his retirement, it would be necessary for the Mart to forward mail to him for some period of time.

Shaw had sold the property at 505 Dauphine Street, with the swimming pool, back during the 1950s to Mrs. Artelle Kirk Trelford, who paid Shaw for it on an installment note. Similarly, Shaw had sold the Spanish Stables property at 716 Governor Nicholls Street to the corporation called Tri-E, Inc. He also sold 908 Esplanade Avenue to Mrs. Rose Joseph Mood using the same method. Shaw often chose such installments to finance a sale, collecting the payments at a much better interest rate than he could have obtained on a certificate of deposit over a period of years.

During this last year of Shaw's work life, events concerning the Kennedy assassination were taking place, events he probably noted only peripherally, it at all. Even if he had noticed them with any degree of interest, he could not have foreseen the chain of events that would ensnare him two years later.

Over the years since President Kennedy's assassination, much has been made of the fact that the records of the Warren Commission, and other governmental agencies involved in the investigation, were sealed for seventy-five years, only to be opened in the year 2039. However, those limitations were coded into regulations of the National Archives existing at that time. As early as February 1965, Acting Attorney General Nicholas Katzenbach, acting on instructions from President Johnson, wrote to various governmental agencies, asking if exceptions could be made to this waiting period.[1689] Of course, critics would point out that records of the Warren Commission were only a portion of the governmental records at issue, and that additional records of such organizations as the FBI, the CIA, Department of State, and others were relevant to knowing the entire picture of the assassination.

While the controversy over Kennedy's assassination continues today, the conspiracy theories surrounding his death already were developing in these years immediately after the event. The Warren Commission had produced its official report of the investigation into the assassination during the fall of 1964. But, a growing body of skeptical articles began to appear, casting doubt on the officials conclusion that Oswald, and Oswald alone, had committed the assassination. Books also picked apart what the authors saw as errors, large and small, in the Commission's report, which sometimes seemed to discount its own exhibits contained in the twenty-six volumes that accompanied the report.

At an Executive Committee meeting in late February, the issue of Mario Bermúdez's recent resignation from the City was discussed. Bermúdez resigned effective May 1, 1965 after many years as the Director of International Relations for the City.[1690] He would become a top official with the Inter-American Municipal League, which represented city and regional governments throughout North, Central, and South America, and the Caribbean, and which had recently located its headquarters in New Orleans. Alberto Fowler would take Bermúdez's place as Director of International Relations for the City of New Orleans.

In mid-March, the Executive Committee discussed the exclusive club that the new Mart building would contain. One idea was that it be named the Plimsoll Club, after Samuel Plimsoll, and would be open to prominent New Orleanians and out-of-town personalities. Samuel Plimsoll was a 19th century British politician and shipping industry veteran, known for having contributed to the safety of oceangoing vehicles. At the same meeting, it was noted that the U.S. State Department did not object to Shaw asking the Soviet Union and Eastern European countries to donate art for display at the new Mart building.[1691]

At the Annual Meeting of Contributors and Debenture Members in mid-March, Lloyd Cobb indicated that a new floor for the building was going up every five working days; the project was now at the twenty-first floor of a projected total of thirty-three floors. Cobb said he still expected to move tenants in by October 1, 1965, and that the leases currently signed accounted for approximately seventy percent of the total rentable space.[1692]

The following week, Willard E. Robertson accepted a reappointment to the Board of Directors at the Mart.[1693] Robertson, the local Volkswagen distributor and President of International Auto Sales and Service, Inc., had become more active in local civic affairs during the early 1960s. That activity would soon take a much more serious turn.

Meanwhile, Shaw wrote to Robertson regarding Robertson's speaking at the upcoming 20th Annual Mississippi Valley World Trade Conference. Beginning his letter, "Dear Willard," Shaw went on to say that he was "delighted you can serve as panelist on our import session." Shaw indicated that he would need a photo and biographical data on Robertson; the topic of Robertson's speech would be "Marketing Foreign Made Goods at Home."[1694]

In March, Shaw declined an invitation to the opening of the Adonais Shop. The invitation had come from Shaw's friend, Roland Dobson, to whom Shaw offered "Best wishes in your new venture."[1695]

In a letter dated April 1, 1965, Shaw wrote an official resignation from the Mart to Lloyd Cobb. In it, he confirmed the several conversations they had had on the subject, and said that his resignation would be effective October 1, 1965. Shaw said that the new building would be ready by then, which would create a proper point for someone new to take over. He indicated that it had been "inspiring to work under your leadership into bringing this great dream about" and added "that under your leadership, I have had some part in bringing this shining vision into actuality will always be a source of the greatest pride to me."[1696]

At an Executive Committee meeting in early April, the name of the club to be installed in the new Mart building was again discussed at some length. Committee member Basil Rusovich argued against the name Plimsoll Club, suggesting instead Magellan Club.[1697]

Later that same month, Cobb again reminded the committee that Shaw had tendered his resignation, effective October 1, 1965, just a little over four months away. He recommended that a committee of three should be appointed, consisting of Lawrence Merrigan, Captain J.W. Clark, and Cobb himself. He proposed that three potential candidates to replace Shaw should be selected. One of the members questioned Shaw about whether he would be willing to stay on if he was given a raise; Shaw indicated that money was not a problem, but said that under the setup of operations in the new building it would be best to have a Managing Director who was internationally known.[1698]

As Shaw looked forward to retirement, he could look back on a distinguished career with the Mart. The entire operation, however, so filled with enthusiasm by all participants in the early years of the mid-to-late 1940s, seemed to have peaked during 1952 and 1953 in both occupancy of the building, and surplus of income over expenses. The middle 1950s formed the plateau of the endeavor, which was still successful on both counts, although the building had never attracted the level of international tenants its founders had hoped. By 1960, however, the Mart was beginning to have net losses, meaning that expenses exceeded income. Those losses increased through the remaining five years of Shaw's tenure, and would not reverse themselves until the Mart occupied the new building and began a rejuvenated operation.

Many have raised the question of how Shaw accumulated his wealth by the time he retired in October 1965. A very large ledger in his personal papers covering the years 1951 to 1965 indicates that Shaw's equity, primarily from the purchase and resale of various properties in the French Quarter, grew from a relatively small amount in 1951 to a balance of more than $102,000 by the end of 1965; the amount generally increased every year during that period. For example, the ledger shows that Shaw's equity was $14,368 at the beginning of 1951, and had risen to $30,164 by the end of 1953. The ending balance for 1956 was almost $33,000; for 1957, more than $44,000; for 1958, more than $59,000. By the end of 1961, it had grown to almost $70,000 and by the end of 1964, well over $89,000, before reaching more than $102,000 by the end of 1965.[1699] The ledger wasn't the only measure of Shaw's wealth; he also had money in certificates of deposit, and in loans where he financed the purchases of several of his most expensive buildings, and received regular principal-and-interest payments from the purchasers.

Someone clearly had taught Shaw the value of investment and accumulation of capital for material well-being. Directly or indirectly, it could have been Theodore Brent, or Rudolf Hecht, or any number of successful businessmen with whom Shaw had been associated since the early 1930s. He was an intelligent, observant person who probably learned as he went. He also lived relatively inexpensively, often living in older, less-than-spectacular homes while he was remodeling or restoring them, and he kept his automobiles for a number of years. Many of his travel expenses were paid for by the Mart, certainly those to the more exotic places, so he often was able to combine business travel with a certain amount of pleasure.

The ledger also shows the appearance of Mae Hobson, William Formyduval's matriarchal aunt from the town of Whiteville, North Carolina, who invested with Shaw in several properties, including the one at 1313 Dauphine Street, during the 1950s. That property was entered into the ledger on March 7, 1955, showing a value of $800 for the land and $5,532 for the building. Shaw had originally purchased the property at 1313 Dauphine Street along with the property at 906 Esplanade Avenue as a block purchase; it had become a separate address in the 1950s.

In late April, Shaw declined an invitation from author Frances Parkinson Keyes to see the Beauregard House furniture and memorabilia; he indicated he would be out of town on that date.[1700] Even in some of his social obligations, he was pulling back, as he began to concentrate on what he would do after his retirement.

The Mart had verbally agreed to continue occupancy of the old building until February 1, 1966.[1701] It was thought that would allow for a reasonable period of time in order to completely move into the new tower once it was completed.

One of the last major exhibitions done at the Mart prior to Shaw's retirement was "Mexico Week in New Orleans," held during the week of April 22-29, 1965; a plaque was presented to the Mart by Mexican President Miguel Aleman. Joseph N. Rault, Jr. was director of the event; in less than two years, Rault would be helping to finance New Orleans District Attorney Jim Garrison's investigation that led to the indictment and prosecution of Shaw.

At a meeting of the Executive Committee in early June, the name of the exclusive club at the new Mart was again discussed. Shaw proposed the name Galleon Club, indicating that a Plimsoll Club had recently been formed in Norfolk, Virginia. However, in the end, the name of Plimsoll Club was selected.[1702]

A week later, committee member Frank Normann asked if a group had been formed to find a replacement for Shaw. He was informed that it had, but had met only once.[1703]

Shaw continued to handle even the smallest details during the months leading up to his retirement. In early June, he answered a routine letter from an inquirer who had asked about some type of key chains, and where they could be obtained.[1704]

Other items of discussion at the Executive Committee meetings during the first half of the year included how to integrate the Spanish Plaza and the building of potential Plaza shops into the whole design of the new Mart.[1705] The Spanish Plaza would be a long-delayed, although important, item in the new Mart's overall design; it would not arrive in New Orleans from Spain until the late 1970s.

At a Board of Directors meeting in late June, the idea of the Plimsoll Club was discussed before the full Board. Plimsoll's history was further explained as a member of the British Parliament during the 19th century, who had worked to improve safety conditions of seafaring men. It was indicated that the club would be a separate and distinct corporation from the Mart.[1706]

Compared to the years 1946 through 1964, 1965 had much less activity for Shaw regarding speeches or special events. For one thing, his year only lasted nine months, until his retirement on October 1, 1965. Additionally, he was very involved with the continuing progress on the new Mart tower, as it approached completion.

In April, Shaw spoke before the Junior League of New Orleans Provisional Group, and before the Altrusa Club of Hattiesburg, Mississippi, on Pan American Day. He also spoke in Hattiesburg before the Mississippi Chemical Corporation.

In early May, Shaw spoke before the Vocational Guidance Conference at Louisiana State University of New Orleans. The event was sponsored by the Kiwanis Club of Greater Gentilly. A few days later, he spoke at a conference at the Graduate Business School at Louisiana State University in Baton Rouge. In advance of his visit to Baton Rouge, J. Taylor Rooks of the law firm of Kolb and Rooks wrote Shaw to note that he had read Shaw would be at LSU; Rooks reminded Shaw that he had seen him "on the coast" the previous July 4th, and invited Shaw to come by his home on Highland Road for a drink.[1707]

Also in May, Shaw spoke before the Morgan Edwards Chapter of Louisiana Colonialists in Amite, Louisiana, about French Quarter restoration, a topic upon which, by this stage of his life, he had considerable knowledge. Shaw was invited to the event by Dorothy "Mrs. Wade" Garnier; Shaw's mother was invited to attend as well. The two were invited to lunch at the Garnier's country home, Fairview Farms. Shaw followed up the visit with a letter to Mrs. Garnier, indicating that he was glad to have seen her over the weekend and looked forward to seeing her in New Orleans "with or without your friend from Columbia."[1708] Shaw received a letter after his speech from Mrs. Connor Sanders Davis, who wrote that many at the event thought Shaw was the best speaker the group ever had, echoing a sentiment Shaw had heard throughout his speaking career. Mrs. Davis added that she was glad Shaw's father could be there along with his mother.[1709] In a reply to Mrs. Davis, Shaw invited her to come to New Orleans to see what was, as far as he knew, the only Gallier Carriage House in existence.[1710]

In June, Shaw spoke before the School of Banking of the South in Baton Rouge. It was an appearance he had made for a number of years, and for which he was paid a speaking fee, usually $75. That was somewhat unusual in Shaw's speaking career, as he had given most speeches for no fee, in order to promote the Mart. Shaw dealt with Ken Lott of Mobile, Alabama, one of the principal organizers of the conference.

By mid-1965, hard feelings still existed between International House officials and Lloyd Cobb. In a letter to T. Sterling Dunn, current President of International House, Cobb objected to not being notified of meetings of Past Presidents of International House; he indicated he wanted to retain those privileges.[1711] Cobb had served as President of International House in the early 1950s.

As the middle portion of the year passed, Shaw began to wind down his activities. He had received a letter from *VISION* magazine, asking if he was interested in attending a World Economic Conference of the 100 largest companies in the world in the field of international trade.[1712] He declined, as by this time he was attending no more major events out of town.

In another area, Shaw had prepared a letter to all members of the Executive Committee concerning a potential retirement plan for the remaining employees. Shaw always had intended to put into place such a plan, but had never succeeded in doing so before the Mart ran into difficult economic circumstances in the late 1950s. Shaw had the current plan prepared more than one year earlier, but the board had not acted on it. Shaw would not be included in the plan he proposed; it only would affect the remaining employees, including J.B. Dauenhauer, Goldie Moore, Hollis Bridges, Darlyn Mercadal, David McMillan, a porter, and Elvira East, a maid.[1713]

In July 1965, the Greater New Orleans Amateur Radio Club approached Shaw about taking out approximately 600 square feet in the new Mart tower. John J. Uhl, who was the leader of the group, sought a free five-year lease, and indicated that the group would install first-class radio equipment which could reach Central and South America from New Orleans. The matter was discussed during Executive Committee meetings in mid-July and mid-August. Shaw wrote to Building Manager Hollis Bridges, directing him to allow members of the group to meet at the Mart in early September.

In early August, Shaw wrote to Tom Zung, one of Edward Durell Stone's assistants, care of the American Express office in Rome, Italy, where Zung was vacationing with his wife, Carol. Shaw indicated that he had just returned from a short vacation to South Carolina, no doubt to socialize at the beach with one or more members of the Formyduval family, and asked Zung to give him a call when he returned in September. Shaw indicated that he hoped the couple was "having the time of your lives," and asked if Zung had decided to form his own business, or if he would stay with Stone's firm.[1714]

Shaw wrote to Michael Mora, formerly with International House, and now with the Norfolk, Virginia Port Authority. He mentioned his vacation, indicating that he had been "getting some sun" on the South Carolina beaches.[1715] Shaw also wrote to Jack Sawyer, Jeff Biddison's friend at WVUE-TV, about having a filmed ballet about the new Mart. Shaw suggested that it could be put together using film taken while the Mart was under construction, then shown one week before the new building was to open.[1716]

At a meeting of the Executive Committee on September 9, a discussion was held about Shaw's successor. None had been selected, but ambassador Charles Burrows was the leading candidate; he was fifty-two years old. The salary the Mart was offering was $30,000, equivalent to what Shaw was earning at the time.[1717]

In mid-September, Hurricane Betsy swept through southeastern Louisiana, heading northward through New Orleans and other residential areas. The storm was one of the most powerful ever to make landfall in the United States, and caused major economic damage and loss of life. Shortly after Hurricane Betsy hit, Shaw wrote to Argyll Campbell of Congressman Hale Boggs's office, in reference to a Louisiana Night held at the National Press Club in Washington, D.C.. Shaw indicated that his personal real estate properties had not been touched by the hurricane, but that the new Mart structure had sustained considerable damage. However, Shaw estimated that the damage would delay completion by no more than sixty to ninety days.[1718]

Just before his retirement, Shaw wrote a letter of recommendation for Hollis Bridges, Building Superintendent and Chief Engineer at the Mart for the past eighteen years.[1719] He also wrote a letter of recommendation for Darlyn Mercadal, who had worked as a secretary at the Mart for eight years.[1720]

In mid-September, just two weeks before his retirement, Shaw received a letter from Bess Noble, with the U.S. Department of Commerce in Memphis. Noble said she had just read, with surprise, about Shaw's retirement, in *Foreign Trader* magazine. She talked about her great admiration for him, saying that he was one of her favorite people, and mentioned her own retirement plans; after forty years of working, she intended to travel to the Smoky Mountains, and to stay with a friend who owned a ranch near San Luis Potosí, Mexico.[1721] Shaw responded quickly, commenting that the recent Hurricane Betsy had been the worst storm he had seen, and noting that it had done approximately $250,000 damage to the new Mart tower, which meant a delay of two months in opening. Shaw thanked her for the nice comments in her letter, and indicated that now that he was about to retire, he was like the man who had given up smoking, and then tried to persuade his friends to follow suit. He recommended that she quit working, and enjoy the Smoky Mountains, San Luis Potosí, "and all points North, South, East, and West." Shaw opined that "one owed something to one's self, as the French say."[1722]

An Executive Committee meeting was held on September 23, 1965, shortly after Hurricane Betsy; it would be the last such meeting Shaw would attend. Mart officials were working on an informal lease for the current building, in order that it could continue occupancy there until at least February 1, 1966, due to the damage caused by Betsy; the possibility existed that it may need to remain there until April or May of 1966. Shaw candidly discussed his mixed emotions about leaving, and talked about the support he had received over the years from numerous Board members. He commented that the public did not fully realize how much time and effort Executive Committee members gave, without compensation, to the Mart. He indicated that he hoped his long-time staff could stay on, and that he wished he could have pushed a pension plan through before he retired. He said that he knew he had received much publicity and attention during his years at the Mart, but said the project was really the result of the efforts of many individuals, including those staff members. Seymour Weiss of the Roosevelt hotel, an original Mart Board member, commented on knowing Shaw for many years, and indicated that he regretted Shaw's decision to retire; he would be difficult to replace.[1723]

At the end of September 1965, Shaw had a four-day stay in the hospital. Some have wondered whether health issues had been a factor in his retirement. It is difficult to say with certainty, but the lung scans he had been having since the early 1960s seem to indicate that perhaps he had been pre-emptively monitoring his health, even as he maintained essentially the same lifestyle.

A retirement luncheon for Shaw had been planned, with invitations sent to many prominent individuals. As the luncheon neared, Louisiana Governor John McKeithen wrote to the Officers and Directors of the Mart, indicating that he could not attend, due to his schedule.[1724] Louisiana Attorney General Jack Gremillion also could not make the luncheon, but he wrote Shaw a letter, congratulating him on his career, and the manner in which he had fulfilled his duties.[1725] Less than a year and a half later, Gremillion would resist attempts to involve him in efforts to stop Jim Garrison's prosecution of Shaw.

Another person who was unable to make the luncheon was Seymour Weiss of the Roosevelt hotal.[1726] Weiss still may have had hurt feelings from the failure to invite him to sign the official plaque for use in the lobby of the new building. Other prominent supporters of the Mart had been asked to sign the plaque, and in mid-July Weiss had protested in writing to Lloyd Cobb about being neglected in that regard. In the letter, while praising Cobb for the dedication of the new Mart complex, Weiss pointed to his long record of efforts in support of the Mart from the very beginning, and indicated he had been hurt by the omission.[1727]

In a memo to Lloyd Cobb on September 29, 1965, Beryl Donnath reported that there had been ninety-five acceptances to the luncheon honoring Shaw, and forty-one "No" replies. Donnath indicated that Alberto Fowler was handling all arrangements for the luncheon.[1728]

The luncheon to honor Shaw upon retirement was held at the Royal Orleans Hotel on September 30, 1965. Beryl Donnath's memo to Lloyd Cobb the previous day had set out the program for the event.[1729] The invocation was given by Monsignor Henri Bezou. One of the major speeches was given by Lloyd Cobb, who indicated that although Shaw had planned to resign as soon as the new building became a reality, because of the delays in the building, Shaw had decided not to remain until its completion. A copy of Lloyd Cobb's remarks, in rough form, showed that Cobb discussed Shaw's history with the Mart, and the dismal picture of the Mart in the early 1960s, particularly in 1962, with its general loss of prestige, low occupancy of the building, and heavy financial losses. Cobb commented upon Shaw's heavy workload during the last three and a half years, as the Mart sought to begin and complete the new building, and called Shaw's life "a noteworthy contribution to the City of New Orleans." In a curious remark, he indicated that Shaw was leaving voluntarily; some might have wondered why it was necessary to mention it. Cobb also discussed the new building complex, now scheduled to be completed the following year, rather than by October 1, 1965, due at least partly to the delays caused by Hurricane Betsy.[1730]

A list of invitees to Shaw's retirement luncheon included a selection of individuals around the international trade field in New Orleans, officials with the City of New Orleans, and important personalities associated either with the new building or with Mart operations. For example, J.B. Dauenhauer was present, along with Jesse Core, and Glen Douthit, Public Relations Director for the City of New Orleans. Also invited were Paul Fabry of International House, Harry Bloomfield of Bloomfield Building Industries of Memphis, Tennessee, and George Talbott and John Hunley of Cross Country Development Corporation, the leasing agent for the new building.

The *Times-Picayune* ran an article about the luncheon held in Shaw's honor. Shaw was awarded the International Order of Merit Medal, the highest honor the City of New Orleans could bestow. Mayor Victor Schiro could not attend, so City Councilman Joseph V. DiRosa attended in his place and awarded the medal to Shaw. Edward Durell Stone, the lead architect of the new Mart tower building, also attended the luncheon, and called Shaw "one of the greatest, if not the greatest, client I ever had."[1731]

As a small tribute to Shaw, sometime near the time of his retirement, Goldie Moore had penciled onto one copy of the numerous brief biographies of Shaw that floated around the Mart files, "To cinch it for your clients, in the words of his secretary of 18 long years, she hasn't killed or quit him yet, and believes he's second to none." Moore, who had served Shaw from virtually the beginning of his employment in early 1946, and had been his primary secretary beginning in 1950, after the departure of Mary Catanese, would continue to work for more than eighteen additional years. She retired on February 1, 1984, after working there for thirty-eight years, and was given formal recognition of her service at a meeting of the Board of Directors on February 21, 1984. Moore would serve the Mart with pride throughout her career. In an article in *ITM News*, an in-house publication, in June 1978, it was noted that Moore had saved the original Mart plaque, which had been placed on the outside of the Baldwin Building during the Mart's operation there, when the building had been torn down.[1732]

On October 4, several days after his retirement, Shaw wrote to Dr. Ettore Scampicchio, the Italian Trade Commissioner, whose office was in the Mart, thanking him and his staff for "the touching ceremony last Friday." Shaw also thanked him for the marble fawn given to him by the group, and said that it was already installed in his garden. Shaw mentioned that he was soon leaving for an extended vacation to Mexico.[1733] The same day, Shaw wrote to Odette Reising, one of his tenants at 906 Esplanade when Shaw had owned it during the early 1950s, who had congratulated him on retirement, saying that he had a recent letter from a mutual acquaintance, and that, "We must get together and reminisce about the old days at 906."[1734]

Shaw also wrote to Larry Barry, who had lived in New Orleans during the 1950s, but was now Port Director at Natchez, Mississippi. Shaw indicated that, "The 18 years have slipped away quickly, although there are days when I think it has been a long, long road. I have done what I set out to do," but Shaw wrote that he did not "want to continue running the building."[1735]

Shaw corresponded with James Coleman, who had served as the Mart's attorney for the past three years, thanking him for a pen and pencil set Coleman had sent him. Shaw said he hoped to do a lot of writing in his retirement, and said that it had been an inspiration to him to work with dedicated civic leaders such as Coleman.[1736]

Shaw began to break certain ties almost immediately. He resigned from the New Orleans Athletic Club, noting that his activities during the next year or two would involve travel outside of New Orleans for much of the time.[1737]

Shaw sent a letter to the Hotel Majestic in Mexico City, indicating he would arrive there soon for a week's stay, part of a long-planned Mexican vacation.[1738] Shaw also wrote to Dr. B.N. Addis concerning ongoing restoration of the property at 714 Toulouse Street; Shaw indicated that he would be in North Carolina for three weeks beginning on the following Wednesday.[1739] In mid-October, Shaw took a driving trip to Whiteville, North Carolina, to visit the Formyduval family.

In late October, the Mart received a letter from the Young Men's Business Club of Greater New Orleans asking for payment of Shaw's annual dues. J.B. Dauenhauer answered the letter, informing the group that Shaw was no longer with the Mart, and requesting that Shaw's membership in the group be canceled, at Shaw's request.[1740]

By November 1965, Shaw was on his extended trip to Mexico, spending time in Mexico City, Taxco, Acupulco, and other cities, before catching a freighter on the Gulf Coast of Mexico back to New Orleans. In response to an inquiry that apparently had been addressed to Shaw, J.B. Dauenhauer indicated that Shaw was on vacation in Mexico, and would return around Christmastime; the letter did not give an indication that Shaw had retired.[1741] On November 25, Shaw sent a telegram to Jeff Biddison, indicating that he would be at the Acapulco Hilton until November 30, and would then move to the Hotel Montejo in Merida.[1742]

On November 29 in New Orleans, Charles Earl Daniels, a 23-year-old African-American painter Shaw had known since 1959, was arrested for exposing himself to a young girl waiting for a school bus. Daniels was wearing a sweater, but no clothing covering the lower half of his body. According to the police report, he "played with himself" until the school bus came along. Someone took down the license plate number of his car, and police determined that it was still registered to Clay Shaw. Shaw was contacted in Mexico by Jeff Biddison, and he said that he had sold the car to Daniels on November 1, approximately one month prior. In investigating Daniels's background, police found that he had been arrested for a similar act before, and was on probation. Daniels admitted to police he had exposed himself to others at least sixty or seventy times in his life; he also indicated that he had been discharged from the Army in 1964 for similar acts.[1743] Less than a year and a half later, the incident would draw the attention of Jim Garrison's investigators, and Daniels would be sought for questioning by both sides in the criminal case.

In early December, the Mart held an Executive Committee meeting, the first without Shaw. A long discussion was held about the nature of the Plimsoll Club, including which members of the community should be invited to join.[1744]

Toward the end of December, Shaw sent Muriel Bultman Francis a Christmas card while on his trip to Mexico. He said that he had been busy "poking around" the country, and that he was now on a Dutch freighter working its way up the Gulf Coast to New Orleans. Shaw indicated that he would be back on December 29, and commented that, "You would have loved this trip."[1745]

In 1965, Shaw had been paid a salary of $30,000, his largest ever, although because he retired at the end of September, he only reported $22,500 on his income tax return for the year. He also reported other income of $10,581 in 1965, the result of a netting of different categories of income and loss, of which the main item was interest income of $12,251, most of which came from the notes he held related to past sales of his properties.[1746]

The Mart tower building eventually would begin accepting tenants in early 1966, and have its grand opening during 1967. However, the Spanish Plaza portion of the new Mart building was not dedicated until April 12, 1978, as it took a number of years for the pieces that comprised the Plaza to arrive in New Orleans.[1747] Although there would be a great deal of publicity concerning the opening of the new Mart building, and the new location and expanded space did, in fact, rejuvenate the Mart for the next fifteen years or so, there was a disappointment among some architects about the quality of the design. In an article in *New Orleans Business* for the week of August 18-24, 1986, local architect Chuck Sanders of Perez Corporation was quoted as praising the New Orleans skyline in general, but describing the World Trade Center building, as it was known then, as "drab" and "clumsy looking," in effect just "standing out there by itself." Sanders went on to say that, given its prime location, "It should have been spectacular. And it wasn't."[1748]

In the years following Shaw's arrest, trial, and death, a number of individuals have commented that Shaw was the person mostly responsible for the design and construction of the Mart tower. Because of that, it may have seemed puzzling to a visitor to the tower that Shaw's name could be found nowhere on the plaques in the lobby of the building, which honored past officers of the International Trade Mart. Some may have wondered if his arrest was the cause; certainly employees with the Mart in later years were advised to downplay Shaw's association with the Mart. Former Public Relations Director Jesse Core even told the author that Lloyd Cobb had negative feelings toward Shaw, and was very likely the reason Shaw was not mentioned.[1749] More likely, the reason was that, while Shaw was the most visible face to the general public, and to his fellow employees the leader of the organization, in fact he was an employee hired by the Board of Directors of the Mart, many of whom were very wealthy prominent citizens of New Orleans, to carry out what they saw as policies initiated by them.

# PART III

# 24 · The Beginning of the Jim Garrison Investigation

On January 10, 1966, Shaw wrote to Clara Huge, Membership Secretary at International House, canceling his membership. Shaw indicated that he would be out of the country a great deal during the next two years.[1750] It was a significant step, considering his long involvement with the organization, and the local prestige attached to membership.

In early February 1966, Erik Nielsen, U.S. Sales Director with VISION, Inc. in New York City, wrote to the Mart indicating that he had recently learned "with great regret" about Shaw's retirement, and adding that, to him, Shaw had always been "Mr. International Trade Mart."[1751]

In a letter to an existing tenant in early March 1966, Lloyd Cobb shared that the first tenant had moved into the new Mart tower building. He advised the tenant to whom he was writing that its lease in the old building would terminate on July 31, 1966, and that the tenant should contact George Talbott of Cross Country Development Corporation to negotiate a lease for the new tower building.[1752]

At an Executive Committee meeting around this same time, Cobb announced that the aforementioned first tenant, de Laureal and Associates, Engineers, had moved into the new tower on February 28, 1966. Cobb said that leases of approximately sixty percent of the available space had been signed, with another ten to fifteen percent in negotiations. He announced that the Plimsoll Club was to open on August 1, 1966, with the revolving top-floor lounge opening about the same time.[1753]

The Mart continued to receive inquiries about Shaw for some time after his retirement. After such an inquiry from Carmen Anguis, Goldie Moore wrote that Shaw had retired in October, and that he had spent three months immediately thereafter in Mexico, returning after Christmas, and was now in California. She indicated that Mario Bermúdez, who had been Carmen Anguis's boss in past years, was still at the Mart building, and that Beryl Donnath was again working for him.[1754] Carmen Anguis had worked for Bermúdez back when Charles Nutter had been at International House; she was now in New York City, but was moving to Caracas, Venezuela soon. Anguis said that she had noticed changes in New Orleans on a recent return visit, particularly in the New Orleans skyline, with the new Mart tower going up.

In 1966, Shaw was listed in the city directory as being retired.[1755] He took a train trip to Charlotte, North Carolina in March 1966, probably related to another visit to the Formyduval family. Shaw's friend, and sometimes lover, William Formyduval, had gone to live in the Seychelle Islands, off the coast of Africa, earlier in the decade, but was probably back by early 1966. Shaw's records indicate that he paid for at least a portion of Formyduval's transportation to the islands, via Nairobi and Mombasa, Kenya.[1756] During his stay in the Seychelle Islands, Formyduval sent Shaw a postcard with a picture of Government House and Possession Store.[1757] For whatever reasons, perhaps Formyduval's drinking, and his inability to fit in well with Shaw's more sophisticated friends in New Orleans, the two had drifted apart, and would never regain the closeness they had for the better part of a decade.

By late March 1966, Shaw had gone to San Francisco to visit friends there,[1758] staying at the Mark Hopkins Hotel, which housed the famous top floor lounge called "Top of the

Mark." While there, Shaw received a letter from his longtime attorney Edward Wegmann, advising that Wegmann had missed a deadline for filing court papers related to some money Shaw was owed, thus missing the opportunity to take legal action; Wegmann apologized for the inaction, and promised Shaw it would not happen again.[1759]

Soon after returning, Shaw had a "chest consultation" with Dr. Leslie Guidry and Dr. Warren Coleman. Although there is no evidence that he had yet been diagnosed with any major ailment, the idea was clearly on his mind, and had been for some years.

At an Executive Committee meeting at the end of March, Cobb announced that he had taken over Shaw's membership in the Press Club of New Orleans; he indicated that Shaw's membership in the Foreign Relations Association of New Orleans had been discontinued, and would not be renewed. Gordon Isaacson, formerly with the National Bank of Commerce, had been hired as Executive Assistant to Cobb at $1,000 per month. Cobb also mentioned that John J. Uhl of the Greater New Orleans Amateur Radio Club still wanted to install a radio unit in the new Mart tower building after it opened.[1760]

J.B. Dauenhauer had continued with the Mart as well after Shaw's retirement, although as part of the leasing arm of the new building. In an Executive Committee meeting on May 26, 1966, Lloyd Cobb called Dauenhauer into the room to explain a recent bomb threat that had been received by telephone on the old Mart building; the threat turned out to be a false alarm.[1761]

In mid-June 1966, Goldie Moore wrote to the National Bank of Commerce, reminding them to send Shaw's bank statements and other notices to him at 900 Royal Street.[1762] The address was that of the Marilyn Tate Realty Company, where Jeff Biddison now managed some of Shaw's financial affairs.

In the summer of 1966, Shaw took a freighter to Europe. During his absence from New Orleans, he rented his residence at 1313 Dauphine Street to Mr. and Mrs. A. Rosado, the stepfather and mother of Alberto Fowler, the current Director of International Relations for the City of New Orleans. The Rosados, at the time, were living in Estorial, Portugal, but visiting family in New Orleans. Marilyn Tate's realty firm helped arrange the rental, and managed it during Shaw's absence. Jeff Biddison, now a major agent at the firm, handled the day-to-day details, as well as looking after Shaw's personal business during his absence. Shaw had advised friends to write to him care of Biddison, and when he returned he simply executed a postal forwarding order from Biddison's address back to his residence at 1313 Dauphine Street.

On June 22, 1966, Shaw purchased a one-way passage on the *S.S. Marageo* from New Orleans to Barcelona, Spain.[1763] In Spain, he met the widow of Alejandro Casona, a Spanish poet and playwright who had written a play Shaw was interested in introducing to an American audience. Earlier in 1966, Mario Bermúdez had corresponded with the widow, apparently with the intention of setting up a meeting between her and Shaw when Shaw and Bermúdez were in Spain together.[1764] The play, entitled *Los Árboles Mueren de Pie*, or *The Trees Die Standing*, first appeared in 1949 in Buenos Aires, Argentina. Once in Spain, Bermúdez, who was familiar with the play and knew the playwright's family, introduced Shaw to Casona's widow. Apparently, the negotiations were at least partly successful, because in the fall of 1966, upon his return to the United States, Shaw had Beryl Donnath, Bermúdez's secretary, set up a folder dealing with the subject.[1765]

It is unclear exactly how the play was translated into English before Shaw submitted it to an agent for possible production. It is doubtful that he did the translation entirely by himself, as legend has had it. More likely, he used one of the Latino members of the community around the Mart and International House to assist him with selecting appropriate English dialogue. The play is not well known in the U.S., being more popular in Europe years before Shaw took up the translation. Professor Michael Snyder has speculated that perhaps Shaw saw translating the play successfully, even with some help, as a way of jump-starting his literary reputation in retirement.[1766]

During his stay in Madrid, Shaw stayed at the Hotel Torre de Madrid, in Spain's capitol city. Six days after Shaw's arrest on March 1, 1967, a Spanish newspaper ran an article by writer Joaquin Amado about Shaw's trip to Spain during the summer of 1966. It said that he had arrived by ship in Barcelona, then traveled by train to Madrid, where on July 13, 1966, he leased apartment number 4 on the 21st floor of the Torre de Madrid through July 31, 1966, when he went to London. The article indicates that on July 29, Shaw was at a cocktail party for Mario Bermúdez in Madrid, where they ate dinner at an Italian restaurant, and partied until early in the morning. The story related how Shaw played chess and spoke fluent Spanish, according to a young man who attended the party. Shaw was in Spain to obtain an agreement for the translation and staging of the play *The Trees Die Standing* by Spanish author Alejandro Casona. Shaw presented the translation that had been prepared to Casona's widow, but the authorization to adapt the play had not been granted at the time, due to changes made in the English version. Everyone who met Shaw during his trip, the article said, had agreed that Shaw was an attractive person, and very flattering. The article went on to say that the wife of an unnamed "collaborator" of Shaw in New Orleans was in Madrid at the time. Shaw was not politically minded, according to the article, but he was widely respected, and had made a great fortune in real estate. Shaw sometimes went to a cocktail lounge in the Conde de Ziguena Street during his visit. According to the writer, Shaw had said that he would sell out in New Orleans, and move to an apartment in Madrid.[1767]

After leaving Spain, Shaw visited with friends in France and England. During that summer of 1966, David Sogge, a young American just out of high school and planning to start at Harvard University in the fall, was in Europe on vacation. He was hitchhiking on the outskirts of Paris, hoping to make it to London shortly, when along came a ride going all the way to London. The middle-aged man, whose name was Will Spencer, offered David Sogge a room for the night at his London apartment, and Sogge accepted before eventually finding his own accommodations. A few days after staying with Spencer, Spencer phoned Sogge and asked if he'd like to join him and a friend for a play that evening. Sogge accepted the offer; the friend turned out to be Clay Shaw.[1768]

Years later, Sogge remembered Shaw being a very large man, a theater buff who seemed to have seen many of the plays staged in London that summer. The play the three of them went to see that night was *Wait Until Dark*, starring Honor Blackman, soon made into a successful movie starring Audrey Hepburn. Sogge recalls Shaw, during their conversations, reciting lines from *The Tempest* and *The Importance of Being Earnest*. His knowledge of the theater seemed extensive, and Sogge remembers Shaw rattling off the names of several public figures as if he were personal friends of theirs, including Tennessee Williams, the poet Thom Gunn, Lucius Beebe, and Edward Durell Stone; Shaw also referred to William Faulkner as "Bill Faulkner."[1769]

In early 1967, shortly before Shaw was arrested, Sogge began thinking about his need for a summer job in a few months, and wrote to several contacts of his, including Shaw. Shaw wrote back a "friendly but subtly discouraging letter along the lines of 'Well, maybe I could suggest someone in the New Orleans telephone department who might need low-wage help in putting out new telephone books...'" Sogge found other employment in Cambridge, Massachusetts, where he was attending Harvard. Shortly thereafter, Sogge read of Shaw's arrest in the newspapers and was stunned by it, as practically everyone who had met Shaw was. Sogge would point to the Shaw prosecution, which he followed inconsistently, along with the much larger issue of the Vietnam War, as being among the episodes that helped to destroy some of his early political illusions. [1770]

A letter dated August 12, 1966 from Jeff Biddison to Shaw indicated that he had forwarded some mail to Shaw in Madrid, Spain. Biddison shared that a play with which he was involved at a local theater was a success, and that it was going to run through Labor Day weekend. Biddison said his workload was "staggering," and he spoke of buying a home on Royal Street in the name of his friend Jack Sawyer. He closed by indicating that he would call Shaw when Shaw arrived at their mutual friend George Gaston Johnston's place in New York City, on Shaw's way back from Europe. Apparently, Shaw was seeing Edith Stern along the way as well, perhaps in New York City, because Biddison closed by saying, "Give everyone my best - Edith, too!"[1771]

As of late August 1966, the office employees of the Mart consisted of Gerald Matherne, a twenty-year-old intern, Beryl Donnath, Goldie Moore, and Darlyn Mercadal. V. Gordon Isaacson, who had been active in banking circles during the 1950s, was also employed during 1966 to assist Lloyd Cobb with general matters after Shaw's departure. Beryl Donnath, also known as Leah Donnath, had moved into the Mart's employ as a result of Mario Bermúdez leaving the city's Department of International Affairs, and joining the Inter-American Municipal League. J.B. Dauenhauer had gone off the Mart's direct payroll, and onto that of Cross Country Leasing Association, which was designed to obtain and process leases for tenants in the new Mart building.

In mid-October 1966, Lloyd Cobb wrote to Louis Wall, Jr. of Gibson, Louisiana, commenting that the new building was in its last stages of completion. He advised Wall to wait until mid-January before bringing the Commerce Club of Nicholls State College to visit the new Mart building.[1772]

In the fall of 1966, Shaw took another train trip to North Carolina to see members of the Formyduval family. After that, he went to Jacksonville, Florida, for a stay at the beach before returning to New Orleans.

*Latin American Reports*, the magazine published by William Gaudet, continued its occupancy of the Mart after Shaw's departure. Although the magazine's operation had struggled with making its rental payments over a number of years, it continued to publish, perhaps because it still generated some support in the international trade community in New Orleans through advertisements and gift subscriptions. George V. Talbott, a leasing agent for the new Mart, reported to Lloyd Cobb on a proposed lease with the publication for 897 square feet in the new Mart tower, at $348 per month.[1773]

Shaw's father passed away in late November 1966, not long after Shaw returned from Europe. Among those who sent letters of sympathy was Delores, a member of Cecil Foster's family in Muskegon, Michigan.[1774] The funeral was conducted in Hammond, Louisiana, by Carroll Thomas, owner of Thomas Funeral home there. Thomas would soon become the source for information contained in one of the more perplexing memos generated as a result of Shaw's arrest in early 1967.

While Shaw was enjoying his first full year of leisure, other things were happening in New Orleans that involved District Attorney Jim Garrison. Garrison had now been district attorney of Orleans Parish since 1962. In his first term, he had become involved in a bitter dispute with a group of local judges, and the ensuing litigation had gone all the way to the U.S. Supreme Court, which resolved the dispute in Garrison's favor. He also had embarked on a "cleanup" of the Bourbon Street area, cracking down on prostitution, "B-girls" who defrauded strip-joint customers out of money, and other con activities that were going on in the French Quarter. Some cynically derided Garrison's campaign as all show and few results, but it appeared to be popular with the general public, and even caught the attention of the national media.

In 1965, Garrison ran for re-election, and won a hard-fought campaign. One of the candidates was Malcolm O'Hara, who would soon become a judge hearing some of the cases brought by Garrison's office, including, at least initially, the one against Clay Shaw. During the campaign, Garrison's medical records from his Army service were leaked to the press; they showed that Garrison had undergone psychiatric treatment during the 1950s, and had to leave the military reserves, although he was permitted to rejoin later. The records would surface again during the Clay Shaw case, but they had by that time arguably lost their impact locally.

**District Attorney Jim Garrison and family, probably mid-1960s (Victor Schiro Papers, Louisiana Research Collection, Tulane University)**

Aaron Kohn, Managing Director of the Metropolitan Crime Commission, an organization which monitored alleged instances of corruption among public officials in the New Orleans area, had followed Jim Garrison's career since the mid-1950s, shortly after Kohn arrived in New Orleans. One of his reports from December 9, 1971 recalled how he recently had seen Severn Darden, the district attorney from 1950 to 1954. Darden told him how Mayor Chep Morrison had repeatedly interfered with Darden's efforts to prosecute Morrison's allies. Darden said that Morrison had called him around 1952 and asked that Jim Garrison be appointed as an assistant district attorney; Garrison had been a precinct captain in Morrison's 1950 race for re-election as mayor of New Orleans.[1775] Like Shaw, Garrison had some friends in high places, sometimes the very same friends.

Several other reports in the Metropolitan Crime Commission files deal with a secret meeting Garrison, then Assistant District Attorney, had on August 25, 1957, with Mayor Chep Morrison and Marc Antony, foreman of the Grand Jury at the time. Morrison was then under investigation, along with Police Superintendent Provosty A. Dayries, for malfeasance in office. The various reports hinted that Garrison and Morrison had worked out a deal at the time, so that Morrison could avoid being indicted.[1776]

Kohn had been a former FBI employee before coming to New Orleans, and the Metropolitan Crime Commission cultivated confidential informants, much as FBI agents did. Accordingly, many of the memos of the organization were based upon information provided by such informants, who were not identified by name. One such memo dated March 29, 1967 indicated that Garrison had attended parties held in the late 1950s by a Texas millionaire named Frank Carruth, who had an apartment in the French Quarter. The informant said that they were "wild drinking parties" with plenty of naked women.[1777]

Aaron Kohn also had dealt extensively with Robert Kennedy, the president's brother. In the late 1950s, when Robert Kennedy had been counsel to a U.S. Senate subcommittee, headed by Senator John McClellan of Arkansas, which investigated organized crime in the United States, Aaron Kohn had kept Kennedy informed on various aspects of Louisiana corruption. In March 1959, Kohn wrote a lengthy memo to Kennedy dealing with Carlos Marcello, the Mafia chieftain in the New Orleans area, setting Marcello's life out in as complete an account as had been put together to that time.[1778] A few days later, Kohn wrote to Kennedy again, discussing the term "Mafia," and giving its origins and meaning.[1779]

A lengthy report dated March 10, 1958 perhaps pointed to some future actions by Garrison. One of Kohn's confidential informants indicated that on the night of March 8, 1958, Garrison, then Assistant District Attorney, had come into the Mardi Gras Lounge at 1:00 a.m. on March 6, dressed in his Louisiana National Guard uniform. According to the informant, Garrison was half-drunk, and talking loud and boastfully. Garrison said that he was the best and most convincing trial lawyer in the district attorney's office, that he could "make the jury cry." Garrison said he was going to "play his cards right" and be a "big man" in New Orleans before he was through. Garrison alluded to the meeting he had had with Chep Morrison back in 1957, and said that he had later testified truthfully before the Grand Jury, and that he had warned Morrison he was making a big mistake. Garrison then went on to tell the informant that he was interested in young "pussy," and asked the informant to send prospects to him, even if they were as young as sixteen years of age. Garrison said that he would fix cases in the district attorney's office, but not for money, only for influence, to become a "big man." When the informant asked Garrison about how to get a permit to carry a concealed weapon, Garrison told the man not to worry about a permit, simply to "just go ahead and carry it." Garrison said that, "I'll *nolle prosse* it" if the man ever got charged with carrying a concealed weapon without a license. Garrison ended the conversation by saying, "Now for Christ's sake, don't go up and tell all this to [Aaron] Kohn."[1780]

Strangely, though, in spite of such "red flags," Kohn had welcomed Garrison's initial election as district attorney in 1962, perhaps because Garrison's predecessor in office, Richard Dowling, had been perceived as even more corrupt. Kohn had even sent Garrison a congratulatory note after his election.[1781] In March 1963, Kohn submitted a personal contribution to a voluntary fund for the purpose of covering investigative expenses of the district attorney's office.[1782]

According to Kohn's own writings, a rumor about Garrison being involved with a nineteen-year-old girl at the Louisiana legislature in Baton Rouge in 1962 increased his negative perception of Garrison.[1783] However, in a letter dated July 2, 1962, Garrison agreed to allow Kohn to inspect any file in his office.[1784]

Kohn had long kept a file on Garrison, as he had on many public officials in New Orleans. In a report dated May 31, 1962, Kohn commented that Robert G. Haik, who had gone to law school with Garrison, had told Kohn that Garrison was "lazy," and could not make it in private practice, so working as a public official in the district attorney's office had saved him financially. Haik said that Garrison was easily diverted in pursuit of women, and that Garrison always ended the day at the Playboy Club, or some other "girlie spot." Haik related that Garrison thought the public did not mind those things about elected officials, and that he ultimately wanted to be a judge, perhaps a Federal judge.[1785]

The Metropolitan Crime Commission was concerned primarily with corruption among public officials, much of which was generated by so-called "victimless crimes," such as gambling and prostitution. Some thought the organization was less concerned with ordinary violent crime than it should have been, and overly concerned with voluntary types of activity that were labeled as crimes. In a report from March 1963, Kohn commented about a conversation he had recently had with Mayor Victor Schiro. Schiro had been concerned about the number of arrests for "abnormal" sex crimes. Kohn mentioned a project at Tulane University examining that very problem, and said that he was going to submit a paper on the topic.[1786]

In the early years, Garrison appeared to cater to Kohn's desire to stamp out such sex crimes. In a letter dated February 1, 1964, Garrison told Kohn that no one should be allowed to plea bargain to a lesser offense when charged with a "crime against nature," regardless of the person's background.[1787] Kohn responded a few days later, referencing his and Garrison's participation in a panel at LSU Medical School Psychiatry Association. Kohn mentioned the practice of some district attorneys' offices to accept simple battery pleas from persons arrested for alleged homosexual offenses; Kohn said he supported treatment for the offender.[1788] In a letter at the end of that month, Garrison gave Kohn a summary of his office activity, and mentioned the rigorous enforcement of crimes against nature, especially where children were concerned.[1789]

Kohn had his own critics from early on in his tenure in New Orleans. In a circular called *Civic Review*, published in 1963, Hubert J. Badeaux, who often appears as a source of information for authors inquiring about individuals allegedly connected with the Kennedy assassination, or some other New Orleans angle, decried the "Mafia-like tactics" of Garrison, his investigator Pershing Gervais, and the Metropolitan Crime Commission; Garrison passed the circular on to Kohn with a humorous letter.[1790]

By September 1964, Kohn had noted some turmoil within Garrison's office, leading to the resignation of his assistant Frank Klein, and predicted that the Metropolitan Crime Commission and Garrison were headed for a conflict.[1791] Klein could be volatile himself, though, and would soon rejoin Garrison's staff before resigning for good around the time of Clay Shaw's arrest.

That same month, Kohn interviewed Raymond Comstock, a former investigator for Garrison's office from May 1962 to May 1964. Comstock described the shifting alliances that took place between the district attorney's office and bonding companies, arrestees, and other parties, and talked about the amount of secrecy that went on in the office. Comstock also was critical of the way Garrison's chief investigator, Pershing Gervais, ran the investigative side of things.[1792]

Kohn closely followed Garrison's re-election campaign in 1965, during which one of Garrison's opponents, Malcolm O'Hara, first released records related to Garrison's psychiatric problems while in the Army, and his subsequent resignation. Kohn commented on a debate between the candidates for district attorney, noting "lies" told by Garrison, and saying that Garrison had a capacity for "pathological lying" that paralleled the late Chep Morrison.[1793]

As late as August 26, 1966, Garrison still was communicating in a friendly manner with Aaron Kohn. A letter on that date discussed the loan sharking problem in the area, and the recent documentary on NBC, reported by Walter Sheridan, in which Kohn had appeared discussing corruption in Louisiana; Garrison thanked Kohn for his support.[1794] However, by November 27, 1966, things had changed between the two men. Garrison sent a memo to his staff directing that no mail from the Metropolitan Crime Commission was to be accepted by the district attorney's office, and instructing his employees to return any such mail.[1795]

By the end of 1966, Garrison also had written to E.C. Upton, Jr., President of the Metropolitan Crime Commission, indicating that his staff would now return, unopened, any mail the organization sent to his office.[1796] Aaron Kohn, however, continued to have his sources in and around the district attorney's office, who kept up with goings-on there. Jesse Core, who had worked as Director of Public Relations under Shaw at the Mart from 1955 to 1963, recently had been working as a publicist for Jim Garrison. In late 1966, Core told Kohn that he had asked Garrison to find someone else to handle public relations for him, because Garrison's private and public life were starting to catch up with him.[1797] Core, who had helped managed publicity for Garrison's campaigns for district attorney in 1961 and 1965, had earlier mentioned to Kohn about regular poker games Garrison attended at the New Orleans Press Club, Garrison's hypersensitivity to criticism, and his jealousy.[1798]

Jim Garrison's military record shows that he was in the Army from June 23, 1942 until March 1, 1946. He was awarded various medals: Air Medal, American Defense Service Medal, American Campaign Medal, European Theatre Campaign Medal with two battle stars, and World War II Victory Medal. While overseas, Garrison was stationed at Shrivenham American University in England.[1799]

Jim Garrison also had aspirations to be a writer. As early as July 1952, he had submitted a mystery story, entitled *Foot Note to Murder*, to the A.L. Fierst literary agency.[1800]

Like Shaw, Garrison was generally regarded as handsome in his own way, and also like Shaw, he stood well over six feet tall, even besting Shaw by a couple of inches. Jesse Core referred to them as the "tallest men in town." He was considered to be well-read, and had a dry sense of humor that he often used to deflect criticism. Over the course of his career, he was well-known for slipping out of a tight corner just when it seemed he was through.

What became known generally as the Jim Garrison investigation into the Kennedy assassination, an investigation that would soon ensnare Clay Shaw, began during the fall of 1966. Most believed that Garrison and Shaw, while aware of each other on the citywide scene, were not especially close, but that there had been no bitterness or cross relations between the two. By the end of the case, many would wonder about their past relationship. Because of their above-average height, and other distinguishing characteristics, they were easily two of the most recognizable men in New Orleans, and by the time all was said and done, their images were familiar to anyone who followed daily news around the nation.

There has always been speculation about exactly when Garrison's investigation into the Kennedy assassination officially began. David Chandler, the *LIFE* magazine reporter who also had written for the *States-Item*, said the starting date of the investigation was November 25, 1966, when Garrison had a meeting with his staff and issued instructions about how to proceed. However, Chandler said that Garrison had been talking to attorney Dean Andrews about the issue of who the mysterious "Clay Bertrand" was as early as October 1966. Chandler said that Shaw's name had come up relatively early as possibly being "Clay Bertrand."[1801]

The general story today is that the re-investigation of the New Orleans aspects of the Kennedy assassination began for Jim Garrison after learning that Senator Russell Long had some doubts about the conclusions of the Warren Commission, one being that Oswald had acted alone. Garrison may have had doubts of his own, however, even before learning about those of Long, and while on a flight with Long from New Orleans to New York City, he had a conversation with him about those doubts. He recalled back to the unusual person, David Ferrie, who had been interviewed by representatives of his office shortly after the assassination.

As the investigation began informally, Garrison had discussions with Jack Martin, who had fingered Ferrie in 1963 as being associated with Oswald, and possibly flying a getaway plane from the assassination in Dallas. Garrison also followed up with attorney Dean Andrews, known to practically everyone in the legal community in New Orleans.

The FBI was aware of Garrison's investigation almost from the start. In early November 1966, newsman Sam DePino of WVUE-TV, discussing another matter with the FBI, advised that he knew of Garrison's efforts as well. DePino, possibly the first in the news media to be aware of it, had heard about it from an aide to Congressman Hale Boggs. DePino's suggestion to break the story on the air was shot down by the station's news director, who wanted more confirmation of the substance of the investigation. Others would inform the FBI about the investigation as time passed, and well before the public would know about it.

The aforementioned reporter, David Chandler, had separately begun investigating possible connections between David Ferrie and the Mafia as of November 1966. When he learned that Garrison was investigating connections between Ferrie, anti-Castro Cubans in New Orleans, and the assassination, he tried to steer Garrison toward a theory of Mafia involvement in the assassination, but was unsuccessful.[1802]

David Chandler became involved in the case in another way as well. David Ferrie had been arrested in 1961 on a charge related to improper sexual relations with a minor, in nearby Jefferson Parish. The case had eventually been dropped, but Ferrie had then been charged with bribery, this time in Orleans Parish. He was never prosecuted on that charge, however, and that case lay dormant until Garrison's Kennedy assassination investigation in 1966, when it popped up around the edges of that case. Chandler was apparently familiar with the bribery accusation, and began asking questions about it as part of a general inquiry into corruption in Garrison's office. Assistant District Attorney Charles Ward took Chandler's inquiries quite seriously, and soon attempted to haul Chandler before a grand jury, where he would have to make the accusations under oath.

LIFE magazine already had run stories raising questions about the official conclusions of the Warren Commission concerning the assassination, riding a wave that had emerged in 1966. *The New York Times* was beginning to explore the issue as well, behind the scenes. In addition, various authors had written books or prominent articles raising questions, and there was a growing feeling nationwide that the determination that Oswald had committed the assassination, and had done so alone, had been formed too hastily. There were simply too many unanswered questions, and a number of the answers that had been given were themselves being questioned anew.

In that atmosphere, LIFE sent one of its reporters, Richard Billings, to New Orleans to see what Garrison had. Garrison quickly agreed to share information with LIFE, in exchange for coverage of his investigation, and Billings would have an inside track on the early stages of the investigation.

Most of the early work concerning Garrison's investigation of the assassination, which was labeled the "Smith case" inside of Garrison's office, concentrated on David Ferrie and the anti-Castro Cuban community in New Orleans. Jimmy Johnson, a former associate of Ferrie's, re-established contact with him at Garrison's office's request, and became a source of information for the investigation about Ferrie's current activities.[1803] For the investigation, David Ferrie was given the nickname "Blackstone," Oswald was given the name "Patsy," and Guy Banister was given the nickname "Barney."

Eric Michael Crouchet, with whom Ferrie had been accused of having sexual relations in 1961 while Crouchet was still a minor, was interviewed, but found to be uncooperative. Also somewhat uncooperative was Sam Newman, who owned the building at the corner of Camp and Lafayette streets, where Guy Banister, former FBI agent and former assistant police chief in New Orleans during the 1950s, and later a private investigator, had his office; one portion of the building had its address stamped on a few of the leaflets handed out by Oswald, supposedly on behalf of the Fair Play for Cuba Committee, during his time in New Orleans in the summer of 1963.[1804] Although many writers have assumed that one could have entered Banister's office at 531 Lafayette Street by the address stamped on Oswald's leaflets, 544 Camp Street, in fact there was no entry, despite the two addresses occupying the same physical building.

In internal discussions about who the mysterious "Clay Bertrand" might be, several individuals with the name of Clay were kicked around, and it was decided, at least to Jim Garrison's satisfaction, that Clay Shaw was in fact the most logical choice. Once that conclusion had been drawn, there is little or no evidence that the question was ever revisited for any type of alternative explanation, such as that another person might fit the bill more accurately, or that, based upon his history of lying, exaggeration, and low self-esteem, attorney Dean Andrews had simply manufactured the story in order to insert himself into a very public situation.

Andrews was apparently highly amused, if not delighted, to again be a center of attention, and he began a months-long cat-and-mouse game with Garrison and his investigators. Andrews never would quite admit that Shaw was "Bertrand," but he never would rule it completely out, either. And as they had been years before, many of his statements were contradictory to one another.

On December 6, 1966, Lorraine G. Le Bouef, Jim Garrison's secretary, wrote to the U.S. Government Printing Office, expressing an interest in the district attorney's office purchasing a complete set of the Warren Report, including all twenty-six volumes of exhibits; she asked that the Printing Office invoice the district attorney's office for the set of books.[1805] The Printing Office informed Garrison's office that payment would need to be received first, so on January 3, 1967, Jim Garrison ordered the entire *Assassination of John F. Kennedy— Hearings Before the President's Commission*, at a price of $76.[1806] The letter mistakenly bore the date of January 3, 1966, so some have assumed over the years that Garrison actually began his investigation in early 1966, rather than toward the end of the year. In a memo to Assistant District Attorneys James Alcock, John Volz, Andrew Sciambra, Alvin Oser, and investigator Lou Ivon on January 16, 1967, Garrison announced, "We have received our copies of the Warren Commission Report."[1807]

Assistant District Attorney John Volz interviewed David Ferrie on December 15, 1966, in the district attorney's office. As he had when interviewed in 1963, Ferrie said that to his knowledge, he had never known Oswald, even if both of them had supposedly been in the Civil Air Patrol at the same time; he re-attributed his whole involvement as a possible suspect in the Kennedy assassination to Jack Martin. Ferrie claimed that Martin was a "psychopath," and was also jealous of Ferrie, because Ferrie worked as an investigator for attorney G. Wray Gill, for whom Martin was also interested in working. Ferrie said that he had ordered Martin out of Gill's office at one time, and Martin had never forgiven him. When Ferrie and Volz were discussing a story by Martin that Ferrie had been in Cuba in 1963, Ferrie commented that, "Martin somehow gets to be near the bride at every wedding and the corpse at every funeral," alluding to Martin's habit of inserting himself in prominent situations. Ferrie said that he was willing to submit to a polygraph examination or a sodium pentothal test. He was not asked about Clay Shaw during the meeting with Volz.[1808]

John Volz later would become a Federal prosecutor, and would be involved in such newsworthy prosecutions as those involving Louisiana Governor Edwin Edwards in 1986, and the BRILAB prosecution of famed New Orleans mobster Carlos Marcello in the early 1980s. Curiously, Marcello also pops up frequently in alternative Kennedy assassination conspiracy theories involving the Mafia.

Garrison became disappointed with Volz's failure to find new leads, or evidence based upon existing leads, and Volz was ultimately removed from the case. He did not participate in the prosecution of Clay Shaw, although he had returned to the case by January 1971, long after Shaw's trial and just after lead prosecutor James Alcock resigned to become a judge, to handle the district attorney's perjury case against Shaw during a lengthy hearing before Federal judge Herbert Christenberry, held to determine whether further prosecution against Shaw should be permanently halted.

After being subpoenaed by Garrison's office, Ferrie immediately advised the FBI of the subpoena.[1809] An FBI memo a week later reported on Ferrie's interview, saying that he had been questioned about his whereabouts on November 22, 1963. The FBI determined to find out more about the incident, why Ferrie was questioned, and what the entire inquiry was about.[1810]

On December 20, 1966, Aaron Kohn of the New Orleans Metropolitan Crime Commission also informed the FBI of Garrison's investigation, which he said was based upon information obtained from Jack Martin. Jack Martin would call the FBI on January 13, 1967, to report on the investigation.[1811]

By mid-December 1966, Shaw was back selling property for Marilyn Tate's real estate agency, following a year of fairly steady travel. In mid-December, he sold a residence at 5234-36 Pitt Street in New Orleans, for a price of $32,000, to a Robert Morrill.[1812] Around the same time, Shaw had received a note from the National Bank of Commerce, indicating that Charles E. Daniels, the African-American man to whom Shaw had sold his 1959 Thunderbird, and who had been arrested the month before for indecent exposure while driving Shaw's former car, had fallen behind on the car loan Shaw had co-signed for him.[1813]

Partly as a result of the "Clay Bertrand" angle, Shaw was asked to come in to the district attorney's office for questioning on December 23, 1966. Assistant District Attorney Andrew Sciambra, a brand new hire, conducted the interview, although Jim Garrison made an appearance at the end, and spoke with Shaw briefly. Shaw indicated that he was retired, and was primarily now a playwright, working with two local theaters—Le Petit Theatre and Gallery Circle Theater. Shaw said that aside from writing plays and doing theater work, he also was translating a play from Spanish to English.

Shaw was asked if he had ever met Oswald, particularly during an incident in August 1963, when Oswald had passed out pro-Cuban leaflets in front of the International Trade Mart building. Shaw indicated that he had not known Oswald, but recalled that Oswald had asked his assistant, J.B. Dauenhauer, for permission to pass out the leaflets, and that Dauenhauer had turned him down. He suggested that Sciambra ask J.B. Dauenhauer for more information about that encounter.

Shaw also was questioned about the presence of the old pre-Castro Cuban consulate in the Mart, which supposedly had drawn Oswald to the building in the first place. The consulate, which had been in the Mart for some time before Castro took power in Cuba, had remained in the building for several years after the Cuban revolution, under the direction of anti-Castro Cubans. The consulate had fallen behind on its rental payments, and eventually had to be evicted. Regarding the anti-Castro Cuban situation in New Orleans generally, Shaw indicated that he had known someone who placed Cuban refugees to the U.S. who were escaping the Castro regime, but that he did not directly know anyone in the anti-Castro Cuban liberation movement.

Shaw acknowledged to Sciambra that his memory might be incorrect on some points. In one instance, he said he had been on his way to San Francisco at the time of the assassination; it later emerged that he was actually already in San Francisco at the time. He indicated that he did not know Dean Andrews, and asked Sciambra what Andrews did for a living.

Although Shaw was asked to come in for questioning, he was not the main focus of the investigation at the time. David Ferrie seemed to fit that role, but Shaw was not asked if he knew Ferrie. Although Shaw would later recall that it was mentioned to him, during the interview, that Oswald had supposedly known someone named "Clay Bertrand" while living in New Orleans during 1963, it is unclear that he was asked if he had ever used the name. None of the memos generated by the district attorney's office during December 1966 or January 1967 mention Shaw at all, and it was not until late February 1967 that a memo summarizing the results of Shaw's interview on December 23, 1966 was even generated by Andrews Sciambra.[1814]

A young man named Layton Martens also was questioned on December 23, 1966. Martens had known both Shaw and Ferrie, but he was not asked directly about Shaw in the December interview. He said he had met Ferrie in the Civil Air Patrol in 1958, and in the interview he was asked about Cuban contacts, and Ferrie's alleged homosexuality. Martens said that he had heard that Ferrie knew Oswald through the Civil Air Patrol, but he did not know that firsthand. Martens said he never knew Oswald himself. [1815]

Martens rode to the district attorney's office along with Shaw; both had been picked up at their respective residences by Detective Lester Otillio. Shaw immediately wondered what the connection between him and Martens might be; Shaw knew Martens primarily through a mutual friend, Dr. Thomas Rafferty, a local psychiatrist who was also gay.

Martens, a good-looking college student, moved in both the gay and straight worlds, a not uncommon phenomenon. He would later marry, and it is murky as to whether he ever engaged in gay sexual activity, or simply accompanied older men to functions as a sort of "arm charm." While he had met Ferrie in the Civil Air Patrol, he first came to know Shaw during Mardi Gras festivities in 1965. He always maintained that he had disassociated himself from Ferrie by the time he met Shaw, and that to his knowledge, the two men did not know each other.

Around the same time, Pershing Gervais, Garrison's lead investigator at the time, called Agent Regis Kennedy of the FBI. Kennedy had been one of many FBI agents in the New Orleans area investigating Kennedy's assassination in 1963. Gervais told Kennedy that he was not involved in Garrison's Kennedy assassination investigation, and said that Garrison was trying to "hatch an egg." Gervais added that, "You know what happens when an egg does not hatch. There is a big smell." [1816] Shortly after the first of the year, Gervais also advised Aaron Kohn that he was not involved in Garrison's investigation.[1817] Gervais would soon leave Garrison's office.

Pershing Gervais was an example of how many previous writers about the Garrison-Shaw case have handled the subject politically. Gervais was, by all accounts, a corrupt, intimidating investigator, noted for fixing cases, and for accepting payoffs from both bonding companies and defendants. Yet, because he was critical of Garrison's Kennedy assassination investigation, some books taking the anti-Garrison position have quoted him as if he was a reliable witness. Gervais eventually would be targeted by the Federal government because of his corruption, and the Federal government would then lean on Gervais to set up Garrison on corruption charges, which would lead to Garrison's own 1971 arrest on racketeering charges, and his two trials during the next two years.

Meanwhile, Shaw knew little or nothing about all of this, except whatever he picked up from his own interview. He was leading the life of retirement he had planned, a life of writing without financial worries, nice meals, and freewheeling socializing without the burden of awaking early the next morning. During late 1965, and throughout the first nine months of 1966, Shaw traveled a great deal, and it was his first year without a regular salary. Accordingly, he drew down some from the personal monetary equity he had accumulated over a twenty-year period. His equity in his properties at the end of 1966 was $90,205. He also showed an approximately $50,000 balance of cash available to him.[1818]

# 25 · An Arrest in the Kennedy Assassination

Garrison's investigation began to pick up steam as 1967 began. A memo dated January 7, 1967 handed out assignments to Assistant District Attorneys James Alcock, John Volz, Richard Burnes, and Frank Klein, investigators Louis Ivon and William Gurvich, and to Alberto Fowler, and "Sam Spade." The memo was entitled "Smith" Case Memo, and the author was not indicated. The memo assigned different tasks to each of the persons named as receiving the memo; none of those tasks mentioned Shaw.[1819]

William Gurvich was a prominent local private detective who, along with his brothers, ran a security firm that did work for various governmental institutions, primarily the Port of New Orleans. He had joined the investigation at Garrison's urging, and would work on it until June 1967, when he "defected" in a spectacular fashion.

Alberto Fowler was born in New Orleans, and had worked in Cuba during the 1950s at his family's sugar business. Fowler initially had supported Castro's efforts at overthrowing the Batista government. After Castro took power, however, Fowler, like many others, became disillusioned with Castro's regime, and participated in the Bay of Pigs Invasion in April 1961. Fowler was captured during the invasion, and held in Cuba with many other prisoners until his release back to the United States almost two years later, a release effectuated by money paid to the Cuban government by the U.S. government. He lived in Florida for a while, then relocated to New Orleans to take on the position of Director of International Relations for the City of New Orleans after Mario Bermúdez resigned in the mid-1960s.

Fowler had mixed emotions about Kennedy and the Central Intelligence Agency, but thought Garrison might be on to something; Garrison used him mainly for information about individuals in the anti-Castro Cuba movement in New Orleans.[1820] Like many other individuals in the Latino community, Fowler had dealt somewhat regularly with Shaw, during Shaw's last couple of years at the Mart, while Fowler was Director of International Relations. In the summer of 1966, when Shaw had been on a three-month trip to Europe, he rented his place at 1313 Dauphine Street to Fowler's mother and her husband during their stay in New Orleans.

Garrison's office eventually would employ several researchers of college age, none of whom had any particular investigative experience, as investigators for his office. Among those were Jody Duek and Gary Sanders, who sometimes worked as a team roaming the French Quarter, and surrounding areas, in search of potential leads to interview. Two others were young Californians Steven Burton and Steven Jaffe, who had been interested in an alternative explanation of the assassination even before Garrison began his investigation; the two were used to run down leads on the West Coast.

Attorneys with some special knowledge were brought onto the staff as well. For example, Robert E. Lee, who had known David Ferrie some years before he became a lawyer, as an employee for Eastern Airlines, was hired, as was William R. Martin, former Director of International Relations at International House during the mid-1960s.

Raymond Beck, an investigator for Garrison, advised the FBI that he was not involved in the assassination investigation, but that longtime Garrison investigator Pershing Gervais was. However, Gervais told the FBI that this was not true, and said that he did not know what Garrison was trying to prove with it. Gervais indicated that he had spoken with David Ferrie only once, when Ferrie had tried to see Garrison.[1821]

Early on in the investigation, the issue of paying informants was discussed. Charles Ward, who eventually would disassociate himself from the investigation, and who would resign two years later to run against Garrison for district attorney, indicated that paying of informants was permissible, for both confidential and overt informers, if the information they gave could be verified.

Meanwhile, a year or so after Shaw's departure, Lloyd Cobb was having some difficulty retaining employees at the Mart. Rather than hire a new Managing Director, Cobb had, to a great extent, taken on the task of managing the Mart himself. Most of the important correspondence during the first few years after Shaw's retirement bore Cobb's signature. In mid-January 1967, Cobb composed a memo to the Executive Committee explaining that V. Gordon Isaacson, who had been assisting Cobb, had left after a disagreement over his duties. Cobb told the Board to expect the "normal" amount of fallout as a result of Isaacson's departure.[1822] In mid-July, employee Lisa B. Matkin would depart after leaving Cobb a resignation letter, indicating that she had expected to be used as a bilingual secretary. She said that she left Cobb the letter because she did not want an "unpleasant meeting," although her reasons, referring to "prevailing circumstances" at the Mart, were vague.[1823]

Meanwhile Shaw was continuing with his project of translating the play *The Trees Die Standing* into English, and attempting to market it. Shaw wrote to literary agent Tom Korman of the firm of Korman and Larner, asking if Casona's play was a marketable project, and indicating that he was inquiring about gaining the rights to it.[1824]

Also in mid-January, Mart Board member Seymour Weiss of the Roosevelt hotel advised the FBI that he had learned of Garrison's investigation. Weiss said the matter involved a suspected Cuban plot to assassinate Kennedy, and that he feared a Garrison press conference about the matter could damage the FBI, by showing that it had failed to uncover all elements behind the assassination. Weiss said that Garrison had four investigators assigned to the investigation.[1825]

The role of Andrew Sciambra, the assistant district attorney hired during the fall of 1966, just before the investigation cranked up, increased dramatically from the initial phase of the investigation to the end of February 1967, just before Shaw's arrest. Early on, Sciambra had shown a great deal of enthusiasm for Garrison's investigation, in contrast to several of Garrison's more experienced assistants, and made sure that he evolved into a key player.

In early 1967, Sciambra reported to Garrison about Miguel Torres, who knew some of the anti-Castro Cubans in New Orleans. Sciambra revealed the various bars frequented by Torres, also known as "Mike Silva."[1826] In early February, Torres, a convict then serving at the Louisiana State Penitentiary at Angola, Louisiana, was interviewed by investigators Lynn Loisel and Charles Jonau at the prison. Torres was not asked about Shaw in that interview.[1827] Later, however, after Shaw's arrest, he would be pressured to say that he had seen Oswald and Shaw together. He resisted the pressure, and soon thereafter appeared on an NBC News special broadcast critical of Garrison's investigation.

Jack Martin advised the FBI that he was an informant for Garrison's office, and said that Garrison would pay him $20 per visit for information.[1828] Martin would be used by Garrison throughout 1967 as a source of information, and also as an investigative tool, whereby Martin would call individuals and tape their conversations, and report the information back to Garrison's office. Lloyd Ray and Hunter Leake, both with the New Orleans CIA office, advised the FBI in early February that Martin had called the office on January 23, 1967 and asked them to call Garrison investigator Lou Ivon. The men declined to do so.[1829]

As 1966 turned into 1967, and January turned to February, Garrison's investigators occasionally asked individuals they interviewed whether they knew Shaw, and showed them his photo, among many others. However, the main focus was still on David Ferrie and the anti-Castro Cubans. As late as February 10, 1967, Jim Garrison wrote a five-page memo related to the "Smith Case," which dealt with various characters involved in the investigation.

Shaw was mentioned only as the International Trade Mart manager, and as a person who spoke Spanish, had ties with the Latin community, and lived a few blocks off of Esplanade Avenue on Dauphine Street.[1830]

Ferrie's residence was watched by Garrison's men; his activities were monitored. A memo dated February 9, 1967, from investigator Lou Ivon to Garrison, describes how Ivon and Assistant District Attorney James Alcock, who would eventually be the lead prosecutor at Clay Shaw's trial two years later, sat outside of Ferrie's place beginning at 8:20 in the evening; Ivon reported that Ferrie went to sleep at 12:07 a.m.[1831]

Garrison's investigators interviewed numerous acquaintances of David Ferrie, and as the interviews progressed, only Layton Martens and James Lewallen indicated that they knew both Shaw and Ferrie (Soon, Gordon Novel, one of the most colorful characters in the entire saga, who also knew both Shaw and Ferrie, separately, would enter the picture). However, both said they had met Shaw and Ferrie separately, and that, to their knowledge, the two men did not know each other. Long-time Ferrie friend Melvin Coffey was interviewed in Florida by John Volz and James Alcock; Coffey had gone with Ferrie and Alvin Beauboeuf on the driving trip to Texas shortly after the assassination. Coffey told the men he had known Ferrie since 1954, but that he did not know Shaw.[1832]

It seems to have been Andrew Sciambra who pushed hardest for the idea that Shaw and Ferrie did, in fact, know each other. Sciambra was one of the investigators who asked around in the gay community in the French Quarter about the individuals Garrison suspected of being involved in the assassination, and by February Sciambra was actively involved in interviewing Ferrie and individuals around the International Trade Mart. Sciambra also had been a part of the original interview with Shaw on December 23, 1966, so perhaps his focus on the possible connection began with that collection of tasks. On February 10, 1967, Sciambra interviewed J.B. Dauenhauer, Shaw's long-time Assistant Manager at the Mart. Dauenhauer described how Oswald had been told to move after distributing the leaflets in front of the Mart in 1963, but had refused to do so. Dauenhauer emphasized that he had very little to do with social functions at the Mart over the years, leaving those activities almost entirely to Shaw.[1833]

Carlos Bringuier, one of the anti-Castro Cubans who had tangled with Oswald on the streets of New Orleans in August 1963, and who had debated Oswald on Bill Stuckey's radio program shortly thereafter, was interviewed by Garrison and James Alcock on February 14, 1967; Bringuier had also come in for questioning in January 1967, when he had been questioned by John Volz and Alcock. As Bringuier later would relate to Aaron Kohn of the Metropolitan Crime Commission, Garrison's theory at the time was that Oswald was really an anti-Communist who had been brought to New Orleans by ultra-right conservatives, including William Reily of the Reily Coffee Company, where Oswald had worked for a time in 1963, and William Monteleone, one of the owners of the Monteleone hotel. However, Bringuier said, Garrison had not mentioned CIA involvement in the assassination during the February interview. After interviewing him, the two sent Bringuier to William Gurvich's New Orleans Patrol Service agency on Poydras Street, where Bringuier took a polygraph test. Bringuier said that after the meeting, he sent a letter to J. Edgar Hoover, asking for the FBI to investigate Garrison because of what Bringuier considered Garrison's bizarre ideas about the assassination. Bringuier also told Kohn that David Ferrie had come to him in December 1966 and said that Garrison was conducting an investigation, and that newsman Sam DePino had also told him about it in December.[1834]

The combination of Ferrie's own lifestyle and the pressure of Garrison's investigation of him were apparently taking their toll. By mid-February, investigators in Garrison's office were hearing that Ferrie was saying that he was sick, and would soon die. Other reports asserted that Ferrie was saying he would kill himself.[1835]

The media was rapidly becoming aware that Garrison's office was investigating the assassination. One of the most important of those would be Richard Townley, an investigative reporter for WDSU-TV Channel 6 in New Orleans. In an unpublished manuscript written after his involvement in the case was over, Townley said that he knew about the investigation a month or so before it became public knowledge on February 17, 1967. He had heard a rumor that Garrison was "up to something," and in late January had been told by another reporter that Garrison was indeed investigating the assassination. A member of the WDSU-TV Channel 6 news staff had been told by First Assistant District Attorney Charles Ward that an investigation was going on, but Ward had sworn the staff member to secrecy because he didn't believe the investigation would produce anything, and he was afraid that an early disclosure of it would "make us look like a bunch of asses."[1836]

Townley had a meeting scheduled with Ward about a different topic on February 15, two days before the investigation was made public by the local newspaper. When Townley mentioned the investigation into the assassination, Ward immediately pleaded, "I don't have anything to do with that." Townley was there to see Ward about a report he was doing on the loan sharking business in New Orleans, and Ward called in Sergeant Freddie Williams, a police detective who had headed up the district attorney's "rackets squad," but who had been removed from the investigating staff recently, to brief Townley on the loan sharking issue.

Williams proposed that Townley meet him at a bar the next day to discuss the loan sharking situation. It turned out that Williams was somewhat bitter at Garrison, because he felt he had been given a raw deal with his dismissal. Williams, who had been with Garrison for some years, filled Townley in on certain areas of Jim Garrison's actions, personal life, and background that, Townley theorized, might have accounted for Garrison launching the Kennedy assassination investigation. There was a growing disenchantment with Garrison among some important figures in New Orleans and statewide; he had become alienated to some degree from former supporters, and he had, not long before, engaged in the lengthy, acrimonious legal battle with a band of powerful local judges.

Williams informed Townley that the *States-Item* was going to break the story in a day or so, but neither man was that excited about it. Townley felt that "with Garrison's history, and the instability of the various people known to be involved in his probe, the thing would turn out to be a flop. In what turned out to be a case of monumental indifference, I shrugged off his [Williams's] tip with an 'I don't want to dignify that nonsense' attitude. After all I had the opinion of his [Garrison's] chief assistant that there was nothing to it, plus Garrison's history of shooting from the hip. I also had been unimpressed by the quality of the criticism leveled at the Warren Report and had adopted a rather hard-nosed 'show me' attitude."[1837]

On February 17, 1967, the afternoon newspaper broke the story of Garrison's investigation; a trio of newspaper reporters had heard the same rumors, and had begun to look into expenditures made by Garrison's office. One of the reporters who broke the original story for the *States-Item* was Rosemary James, who later would become a television reporter, columnist, and a familiar figure around New Orleans. She showed the story to Garrison before it ran, and Garrison refused to comment. Although James would be sharply critical of Garrison over the years for his prosecution of Shaw, she and Garrison remained professionally cordial to some degree.

James faced the usual forms of discrimination of that time, due to being one of the early female figures in a male-dominated news culture, and had to fight for all of her major breakthroughs in news reporting. As late as May 1973, after she had interviewed Jim Garrison on the eve of his own Federal trial on racketeering charges, Aaron Kohn received a call from E. Eric "Rick" Gisleson, the U.S. Attorney with the Organized Crime Strike Force. Gisleson expressed concern about the "reporter-whore" Rosemary James taping interviews with Garrison just before the trial.[1838]

Although no one was named in the story as a suspect, once the story broke, David Ferrie advised the FBI that he had contacted reporter David Snyder, one of the three reporters who co-wrote the story, at the suggestion of Pershing Gervais, Garrison's now former investigator. Snyder interviewed Ferrie, found his appearance weird but his intelligence intact, and ran a story telling Ferrie's side of the story. Ferrie maintained his innocence regarding the assassination.

On February 18, Andrew Sciambra and Lou Ivon interviewed David Ferrie at his residence. Sciambra had known Ferrie some years earlier, when he had worked at the small Lakefront Airport in New Orleans, and Ferrie had been a pilot there. Ferrie said that he had recently been sick and weak, and unable to keep food down. He said that he was suffering from encephalitis, had had no rest due to the media attention since the case broke in the newspapers, and that he was worried that he would be arrested. Ferrie said the media in general were "bastards," although individual reporters were okay. Ferrie suspected that Garrison's men were bringing Miguel Torres from an Angola prison to frame him because, he said, convicts would do most anything to get out of prison. Ferrie reiterated that Jack Martin had started the rumors that led to the investigation, and said that Garrison's "no comment" had stirred "more shit than an hour's speech." Ferrie said that some people, both local and national, were trying to destroy Garrison over the investigation. He hinted that Frank Klein, one of Garrison's former assistant district attorneys who had recently resigned, was among the local individuals, and that FBI Director J. Edgar Hoover was among the national ones. Ferrie said he did not care one way or the other, that "all cops are bastards," and that he had no use for any of them. He told Sciambra that he was still a "starry-eyed kid right out of law school," who still believed the inscriptions on the courthouse walls. Ferrie told Sciambra that he would one day see that it was "a stinking world," and that things Ferrie had told him when they worked together at the airport were true.

At one point during the interview, Sciambra asked Ferrie, "Dave, who shot the President?" Ferrie went into a lengthy explanation of muscle groups and skin layers, attempting to refute the single bullet theory of Kennedy's assassination. Sciambra asked if Ferrie had stayed with Clay Shaw during a trip Ferrie had made to Hammond, Louisiana, in November 1963, after the assassination but before Ferrie had been brought in for questioning, to which Ferrie responded, "Who's Clay Shaw?" When Sciambra mentioned the name, "Clay Bertrand," Ferrie asked, "Who's Clay Bertrand?" Sciambra told Ferrie that Dean Andrews had said the two men were the same, and Ferrie responded that Dean Andrews might tell them "anything," adding, "You know how Dean Andrews is."[1839]

On February 19, 1967, Assistant District Attorney James Alcock and Lou Ivon interviewed James Lewallen, who had been a close friend of David Ferrie for many years; Lewallen's attorney, George Piazza, was present. Lewallen, who currently worked for a division of Boeing, the aircraft company, now lived with his mother. He said that he had met Ferrie in early 1948, and had come to New Orleans in May of 1953, by way of Tulsa, Oklahoma. In 1958, he moved to 1309 Dauphine Street, next door to Clay Shaw. He said that Shaw was neighborly, and he saw him a few times until he moved away in December 1959. In 1960, he moved back to 1309 Dauphine, and lived there until the spring of 1964, during which time he occasionally went to Shaw's residence for a drink. He said that he had never seen Shaw with Ferrie, and never heard either man mention the other. Lewallen said that he had introduced an acquaintance of his, Dante Marochini, to Ferrie, and thought that he also had introduced him to Shaw (Marochini would later deny that he had ever met Shaw[1840]). Lewallen said that in the summer of 1963, he had introduced his boss at National Car Rental, where Lewallen was then working, to Shaw at the Mart, for the purpose of establishing a telephone outlet there for National Car Rental. Lewallen said that he had not seen Ferrie for at least six months, possibly a year, prior to the interview; the two had fallen out over a dispute about Ferrie flying a plane that Lewallen partially owned, without Lewallen's permission.[1841]

Perry Russo, who would soon emerge out of nowhere as the main witness in Garrison's probe, later would testify that Lee Harvey Oswald, wearing a beard, had roomed with Ferrie during September 1963. Many who knew Ferrie thought that if Russo had seen anyone, it must have been James Lewallen instead of Oswald. After Shaw's trial was over, chief criminal defense attorney Irvin Dymond would tell author James Kirkwood that he could not get Lewallen to "tell the truth," about whether he had been Ferrie's roommate at the time, that Lewallen, who by then was married and had a good job, simply did not want to become involved in the criminal case.[1842]

Jim Garrison then held a press conference, indicating that he had re-opened the investigation because it had not been completed; there were still unanswered questions. Garrison promised that there would be "arrests of individuals following our investigation," and that "in time to come there will be charges, and there will be convictions based on the charges." Garrison did not give any details, or names of suspects; he more or less simply acknowledged the investigation.

Word had spread quickly of Ferrie's arrest years before for alleged homosexual activity with a juvenile. Asked at a news conference on February 20 if homosexuality was an issue in the planning of the assassination, Garrison would not comment.[1843] However, he soon began telling at least some reporters, privately, as merely one of his theories about the case, that the assassination had been a homosexual "thrill-killing," in the manner of the Leopold-Loeb case in 1920s Chicago.

Garrison had not objected beforehand to the *States-Item* running the story of his investigation; he even had been told about it in advance, and asked for comment. However, once the investigation broke in the press, Garrison blamed the news media for jumping the gun in reporting about it, maintaining that it could impact the investigation's progress. Soon thereafter, three New Orleans businessmen—Joseph Rault, Jr., Cecil Shilstone, and Willard Robertson—formed an organization called Truth and Consequences, in order to help Garrison finance the investigation confidentially (*States-Item* reporter David Snyder had played a part in uncovering the investigation, prior to publication of the article that broke the story, by reviewing publicly available information about expenses incurred by the district attorney's staff for, among other things, travel to Texas and Florida). The private financing of a criminal investigation, a highly unusual move, would loom as an important issue years down the line for Shaw's defense team, both on appeals of the criminal case, and in a subsequent civil lawsuit.

Also on February 20, James Alcock interviewed Ampala Rocha, who was the Cuban consul in New Orleans during the late 1950s and very early 1960s. She said that she did not like Shaw that much, because after Castro had taken power in Cuba, he had attempted to collect back rental payments from the consulate instead of simply terminating the lease and allowing the consulate to leave. She said she never saw Shaw after early 1960.[1844] Some writers have tried to connect Shaw more closely with the anti-Castro Cuban movement, but the documentation that has survived shows that most, if not all, of the Cuban members of the anti-Castro movement in New Orleans did not know Shaw, except perhaps through the newspapers. Shaw and Alberto Fowler, for instance, only met after the assassination.

Aaron Kohn continued to pass around information about Garrison's investigation, either to newsmen with a critical bent, or to the FBI. In February 1967, after the story broke but before Shaw's arrest, Kohn was one of at least three individuals (the others were private investigator Joe Oster, who also had an ear to ground about the case, and local character Gordon Novel) who passed on to the FBI that Clay Shaw and "Clay Bertrand" were the same person. Therefore, in his haste to be critical of Garrison's investigation, Kohn sometimes passed along incorrect or unsubstantiated information, to curry favor with whoever was receiving the information.

On February 22, 1967, just five days after the story had broken, David Ferrie was found dead in his residence. Most reporters who had swarmed into New Orleans following the initial story of the investigation had quickly departed after Garrison's press conference. However, some reporters stuck around to speak with Ferrie, and one maintained that he had been with Ferrie until the wee hours of the morning the day his body was found.

Ferrie's death, so unexpected, brought the reporters who had departed, and then some, back to New Orleans; it also heightened interest in the probe, both locally and nationally. Even the Cuban Press Agency requested information about Ferrie, including how he was connected to the case, and whether his death was a suicide or murder.[1845] The Cuban government, like the Soviet government, had followed all developments in the Kennedy assassination case over the years, partly in their own self-interest, as some had suspected a Communist motivation behind the assassination.

Garrison called Ferrie "one of history's most important individuals," and maintained that his office had decided to arrest Ferrie before hearing of his death. He also said that Ferrie's death was a suspicious suicide; two vague letters were found in Ferrie's residence that could have been interpreted as such. However, the Orleans Parish Coroner soon concluded that Ferrie had died from an aneurysm, and that no foul play had been involved. Nicholas Chetta, the coroner, told the FBI that Jim Garrison had wanted the cause of death to be shown as "suicide." Chetta also advised the FBI that one of the notes Ferrie left behind was not really a suicide note, but rather a rambling attack on various figures.[1846]

Gordon Novel, who had called the FBI after the story broke to tell them about Ferrie being involved in a 1961 burglary of a bunker at a Schlumberger Company site near Houma, Louisiana, notified the FBI on February 23 that Garrison had contacted him recently seeking his help in the probe. Novel said that Garrison thought that Clay Shaw and "Clay Bertrand" were the same person, and wanted to know from Novel if Ferrie and Shaw knew each other.[1847] Shaw had known Gordon Novel several years before, because Novel had approached Shaw on several occasions in the past related to promotions with which he was involved.[1848] Novel had also known Ferrie.

Novel, only thirty at the time, had a history of various promotional efforts. He had been involved in the 1964 New York World's Fair, in auto racing, and night clubs. He had been featured in the newspapers on several occasions over the previous decade, including once when he had launched a helium balloon over the city that attracted considerable attention. Over the years he would claim to be involved in a number of famous cases, including the John DeLorean drug case in the 1980s and the Michael Jackson molestation case in 2005. Novel was colorful, knew a lot of important people, and seemed to be at the center of everything; the Garrison case was certainly no exception.

Senator Russell Long, who had discussed the case with Garrison the previous fall, began to discuss publicly his own views shortly after Ferrie's death. He said he had privately questioned the Warren Report since it had been released, and that he had indeed shared his concerns at length with Garrison in October 1966 on the plane trip. Long said he had called for reopening the investigation in November, and that he had encouraged Garrison to launch his probe.[1849] Long said, "The issue of whether there was a conspiracy related to President Kennedy's assassination originating in New Orleans was something the FBI should have investigated in 1963. And in fact the FBI did investigate it. Whether they uncovered everything there was to uncover is a different question." Long's statements in support of Garrison's probe generated mostly favorable comments from his constituents.

One of the individuals from whom Russell Long soon heard was Jack Martin, one of Garrison's main informants in the probe, particularly related to information regarding David Ferrie. Martin wrote Long several letters during the winter and spring of 1967. In one letter, he complained about the statement he supposedly had given to the Secret Service in November 1963, when Secret Service agents had confronted him and Martin admitted he had telephoned various individuals around New Orleans with inflammatory statements about Ferrie's possible involvement in the assassination. According to the memo generated by the Secret Service at the time, Martin had acknowledged that he suffered from "telephonitis," and had made the calls while intoxicated. In a letter to Long in April 1967, Martin said that he had never seen the statement the two Secret Service agents generated after their interview with him in 1963. He said the agents had used the term "telephonitis," and maintained that he had never intended his comments to be in an official statement. Martin said that on December 5, 1966, Garrison had sent a car for him, which brought him to Garrison's office, where the two had discussed Ferrie.[1850] Martin eventually went so far as to call one of the Secret Service agents in 1967, and record the conversation, where he tried to deny that he had ever said the things that were in the 1963 memo. The Secret Service agent wound up hanging up on Martin.

Shortly after Shaw's arrest, Senator Long also gave a brief statement in support of Garrison's investigation to *LIFE* magazine. He appeared on the CBS Sunday morning interview show *Face the Nation* on May 14, 1967, where he discussed his October 1966 talk with Garrison. Long said that he doubted Oswald was a good shot, or had a very good rifle. He suggested that Garrison should cooperate with the FBI, which he acknowledged Garrison had been slow to do, and that the FBI should also cooperate with Garrison.[1851]

In an interview with Murphy Martin of ABC News on February 24, 1967, Garrison said that no arrests would be made within the next three weeks, but that the assassination had been solved, that he knew all parties involved, and that it had been planned in New Orleans.[1852] It was a statement that would haunt him throughout his probe, and indeed for the rest of his life.

Eighty miles away in Baton Rouge, a young insurance salesman named Perry Raymond Russo soon emerged in the media. Russo had watched the developments involving Ferrie with growing interest. In an interview he held with New Orleans television newsman James Kemp on February 24, 1967, Russo said that, as November 1963 had approached, David Ferrie had specifically referred to President Kennedy and said, "We will get him and it won't be long." Ferrie also had made some remarks to the effect that he could fly the shooter to another country. Russo told Kemp that he never heard of Oswald before the assassination occurred, and that Ferrie had never mentioned being involved in any type of Cuban group, whether related to Cuban exiles or otherwise. Russo mentioned Ferrie's roommate, though not by name, saying that he had not been interested in politics. Russo said that he had mailed a letter to Garrison on Thursday, February 23, 1967, the day before the interview, telling Garrison the same things that he was telling Kemp in the interview. Russo said that the first time he had spoken publicly about Ferrie's conduct and comments was that day, February 24, 1967.[1853] Russo also gave interviews with other newsmen, including Bill Bankston of the main Baton Rouge newspaper, and Al Crouch with WBRZ-TV Channel 2 in Baton Rouge, and told essentially the same story.

Russo's letter to Garrison has never surfaced, not even at Shaw's trial two years later. However, Russo never contradicted his original story that, in the letter, he had said that he had known David Ferrie, and that Ferrie had made statements about killing Kennedy. He did not claim, in the letter, to have known or seen Oswald, or Clay Shaw, or to know of a plot by specific individuals to kill Kennedy, aside from Ferrie's vague statements.

It is unclear if Garrison's office received Russo's letter, or indeed if Russo actually sent it. However, reports of Russo coming forward to the press sparked immediate interest in Garrison's office, and the next day, Saturday, February 25, 1967, Andrew Sciambra was dispatched to Baton Rouge to interview Russo. The results of this interview are controversial, both because of additional things Russo supposedly said, which are reflected in the memo Sciambra would produce about the interview, and because of things Russo apparently did not say, and which are not reflected in the memo, but to which he would soon testify, under oath, at a preliminary hearing after Shaw was arrested. The discrepancies between what witnesses who appeared at Shaw's trial told Garrison's assistants and investigators, as reflected in contemporaneous memos, and what those witnesses later testified to at trial, is sometimes staggering; Russo is the outstanding example of that phenomenon.

Russo told Sciambra that he had seen Clay Shaw twice, once talking to David Ferrie at a service station owned by Ferrie, and later in the crowd at the Nashville Avenue Wharf, when it had been dedicated by President Kennedy in May 1962. Russo placed the sighting of Shaw at the service station as taking place before the assassination. However, Ferrie only owned the business after the assassination, so Russo would correct that issue at trial. Also, when shown photos of Oswald, Russo suggested that he looked like a roommate of Ferrie to whom Russo had been introduced in 1963.

Key assertions that would form the heart of the charges soon filed against Shaw, and to which Russo would soon testify at the preliminary hearing, were nowhere to be found in Sciambra's memo. Specifically, there is no mention of a "party" in September 1963, where Shaw, Ferrie, and Oswald sat around and discussed the future assassination while Russo sat listening; there was no mention of Shaw knowing Oswald at all. Also, there was no mention of Russo knowing Shaw under the name of "Clem Bertrand," as he would tesiify, or under the name of "Clay Bertrand."

The main focus on Shaw seemed to have crystallized during the last week of February, particularly after Ferrie had died and Perry Russo had emerged. For example, on February 25, 1967, the same day that Perry Russo was being interviewed by Andrew Sciambra in Baton Rouge, Louisiana, Lou Ivon, one of Jim Garrison's main investigators, wrote a memo to Garrison regarding the general subject of "Clay Bertrand." Ivon, a tough, no-nonsense, skeptical type of investigator, had been given the task of searching the French Quarter for anyone who might have known the mysterious "Bertrand." In the memo, Ivon wrote that of all of his sources in the French Quarter, none had ever known anyone who used the name of "Clay Bertrand." One source, "Bubbie" Pettingill, told Ivon that attorney Dean Andrews had told him that "Clay Bertrand" never existed. Ivon went on to say that if the name "Clay Bertrand" had been used widely in the French Quarter, his sources surely would have known about it. Jim Garrison pinned a note on the memo saying that a confidential informant with the initials "M.L." had been advised by Dean Andrews's assistant, Prentiss Davis, that "Bertrand" apparently did not exist, and that Andrews had never made any effort to locate him, as Davis would have known it if he had. [1854] Such definitive conclusions would soon change.

Years later, the author interviewed Lou Ivon and asked him directly about the contents of that memo. Ivon did not disavow the memo, but maintained that Andrew Sciambra had investigated on his own, and had made the connection between the name "Clay Bertrand" and Clay Shaw.[1855]

Congressman Hale Boggs told the FBI in late February that he did not think Garrison had any case. The FBI recommended that Boggs ask Garrison to turn over to the FBI any evidence he had related to the assassination, although it is unclear whether Boggs ever did so. Boggs also told the FBI that he considered Garrison to be a "mental case," and that he was worried that Garrison was making New Orleans the "laughing stock of the world."[1856] That was before Shaw's arrest on March 1, 1967; Boggs surely thought much less of Garrison's investigation after that point. Having known and worked with Shaw for more than twenty years, and having never expressed anything but a high opinion of him, Shaw's arrest must have been the clincher for Boggs. However, Boggs chose not to criticize Garrison publicly, or to get involved in the publicity surrounding Garrison's investigation during the entire multi-year unfolding of the story. Boggs, who had been a member of the Warren Commission in 1964, was probably anxious to avoid the heated controversy that swirled around Garrison's actions.

On February 27, Aaron Kohn encountered Frank Klein, who had again resigned not long before as Garrison's assistant district attorney, and Garrison investigator D'Alton Williams. Klein told Kohn that Garrison was the only one who knew the entire Kennedy assassination case, and that others only knew the parts assigned to them. He further said that all experienced prosecutors were assigned to the case, leaving only new assistants to deal with ongoing court cases, which had angered some judges.[1857] Later, whenever someone who had worked inside the investigation would criticize it, Garrison would respond that that person simply had not known the entire case, only a portion, implying that their impression of the case was therefore distorted.

Klein must have been unaware of the growing importance of Andrew Sciambra's involvement in the case. Sciambra was literally the newest attorney on Garrison's staff when the investigation began, and he would soon emerge as a key figure in gathering much of the "evidence" used against Shaw, even as most of the more experienced attorneys fell away from the case.

On the same day as the Kohn and Klein meeting, Perry Russo was in New Orleans, his home city, having come down from Baton Rouge to talk more at length with Garrison's men. Garrison's office decided to administer sodium pemtothal to Russo at a local hospital. After the session, Andrew Sciambra produced another memo, wherein he described what Russo supposedly said during questioning while under the influence of the drugs. For the first time, Russo indicated that Shaw had been introduced to him by Ferrie, at Ferrie's residence, as "Clay Bertrand," and that Ferrie, Shaw, and Ferrie's roommate (whom Russo now said looked similar to Oswald) had been together, and had discussed the upcoming assassination of President Kennedy.

That evening, Sciambra and Russo dined with Garrison and Richard Billings, the *LIFE* magazine reporter working with Garrison's office. According to Billings, when Sciambra mentioned that Russo had said that he had once met a tall white-haired man named "Bertrand" at Ferrie's residence, Russo insisted that he did not recall knowing anyone named "Bertrand."

On February 28, 1967, New Orleanian Albert Labiche advised the FBI that he had been named foreman of a grand jury Garrison was empanelling to hear witnesses related to the investigation. Labiche told the FBI that he had named mostly American Legion members, and acquaintances of his, as the other members of the grand jury, and that he would protect the FBI's name from any embarrassment related to their earlier involvement in the investigation into Kennedy's assassination.[1858] While the Kennedy assassination case was more or less officially closed in the FBI's records, the agency was sensitive to any suggestion that it had not investigated all possible angles prior to closing it.

The same day, Shaw was at home, entertaining a visitor, when two young men rang the doorbell and asked him if he was interested in buying insurance. It was a ruse; one of the men was Perry Russo, accompanied by someone from Garrison's office. The purpose of the visit was to give Russo a chance to see Shaw in person, for the purpose of identifying him.

At the time of Shaw's arrest, Charles Ward was Garrison's top deputy; Ward had indicated early on that he didn't think much of the investigation and, after Shaw's arrest, had told Garrison that he did not want to be involved in the prosecution of Shaw. Ward did participate in some angles of the investigation, though, even after Shaw's arrest; his name appears on memos related to the investigation at least as late as summer 1967. He also participated in some of the decision-making as the trial date first approached in Fall 1967.

On the eve of Shaw's arrest, activities at the International Trade Mart continued with plans for the official opening of the new building. During the period after Shaw left the Mart, the organization had been somewhat sensitive to publicity while the new tower building was being readied for completion. At the end of February 1967, George Healy, editor of the local newspaper, wrote asking if the Mart wanted coverage of its upcoming annual meeting; Healy indicated that a photographer and reporter had been put out of the 1966 meeting.[1859] In response, Board member Asahel Cooper, Jr. said that no coverage of the actual meeting was desired, but that the Mart would be issuing a press release afterwards.[1860]

After years of getting to the point of opening, the Mart directors were concerned about making the proper first impression. One issue of concern was that the Mart not be perceived as simply another office building, as had happened during the last decade in the old building. In a letter to Lloyd Cobb shortly after Shaw's departure, Captain J.W. Clark had emphasized his agreement that the Mart should have permanent displays of products of all nations, with particular emphasis on Latin American products.[1861]

By the time of his arrest, Shaw was at the pinnacle of his life. He was financially secure and retired, basically doing what he wanted. He had projects he wanted to complete and places he wanted to go, and he had the means to do so. He was accepted, in spite of his by now well-known homosexuality, by citizens of New Orleans from the highest levels of society down.

The issue of homosexuality, however, was still extremely controversial, and homosexuals lived in fear of arrest, social ostracization, loss of employment, or extreme embarrassment. Homosexuality was still considered a psychiatric illness, and the literature about it, including in popular media, tended to discuss it as an illness from which one could be "cured."

No meaningful expansion of gay rights took place in the United States until the 1970s. The 1960s could be considered the last very dark decade before the liberating years of the 1970s kicked in and lasted until the beginning of the AIDS epidemic in the early to mid-1980s.

However, the veil began to lift slightly during the 1960s, and the issue of homosexuality, primarily male homosexuality (lesbians were almost totally absent from any public discussion of the issue), began to be discussed more in the media. A San Francisco television station had produced a documentary on the subject, *The Rejected*, which aired in 1961. *The New York Times* ran an article on December 17, 1963, entitled, "Growth of Overt Homosexuality in City Provokes Wide Concern." The lengthy *Times* article quoted the police commissioner of New York City as saying, "Homosexuality is another one of many problems confronting law enforcement in this city. However, the underlying factors in homosexuality are not criminal but rather medical and sociological in nature."[1862]

*LIFE* magazine would weigh in with an article not long thereafter, and eventually *LOOK* magazine also would run one. Most of the articles around this time focused on certain stereotypes dealing with homosexuality, which caused many in the gay community much consternation. The articles tended to focus on either stereotypical "sissy" gays, or those who patronized "leather bars" dressed in dark leather outfits, and participated in sadomasochistic-like activities or imagery. Gays who fit into neither one of those stereotypes were usually not mentioned at all, or only in passing.

Ironically, the week of Shaw's arrest, on March 7, 1967, CBS ran an hour-long documentary, *The Homosexuals*. The report was hosted by Mike Wallace, and ran without commercials, supposedly because no advertiser would sponsor the program. The program made an attempt to be even-handed, although it is much criticized today for dabbling in stereotypes as well. Years later, when discussing the program, Mike Wallace recalled an incident that capsulized many peoples' duality of feelings toward homosexuality, whereby they tolerated it in theory, as long as they didn't know too much about the details of it. Wallace shared that producer Fred Friendly, who was overseeing the documentary, came to him after watching the initial editing of the film, and commented that Wallace had not included anything about what homosexuals actually "do." Wallace replied, "You mean what they do to each other?" After explaining some of those details to Friendly, the legendary CBS producer agreed that such things should be left out of the program.

One could argue that the various media articles about homosexuality were, for the most part, well-meaning attempts to portray the subject in non-inflammatory language, and to allow the viewers to digest something about this rarely discussed and controversial topic for the first time. However, there were still many openly hostile attitudes about the issue. As late as January 17, 1971, almost four years after Shaw's arrest, Merle Miller wrote an article in *The New York Times Magazine*, entitled "What It Means to be a Homosexual." In it, Miller candidly discussed his own homosexuality, and some of the harsh negativity expressed toward it.[1863] Most notable was his quote from writer Joseph Epstein, who had written in an article several months before in *Harper's Magazine*: "...however wide the public tolerance for it, it is no more acceptable privately than it ever was...private acceptance of homosexuality, in my experience, is not to be found, even among the liberal-minded, sophisticated, and liberated people...Nobody says, or at least I have never heard anyone say, 'Some of my best friends are homosexuals.' People do say—I say—'fag' and 'queer' without hesitation—and these words, no matter who is uttering them, are put-down words, in intent every bit as vicious as 'kike' or 'nigger.'" [1864] Epstein went on to state, "...If I had the power to do so, I would wish homosexuality off the face of the earth. I would do so because I think that it brings infinitely more pain than pleasure to those who are forced to live with it." [1865]

In a milder vein, but still getting the point across, film and stage director Mike Nichols told *Playboy* in June 1966 what many otherwise good liberals felt—that he was "getting a little sick of hearing about" homosexuality after the recent set of articles. "It used to be 'the love that dare not speak its name,' and now it won't shut up!"[1866]

After Shaw's arrest on March 1, 1967, he began to keep a diary of his daily activities and observations. The exact date he started this practice is uncertain, although it appears to have been in early April 1967. At that time, he went back and filled in the events that had occurred since his initial questioning by the district attorney's office on December 23, 1966. Apparently, he either had kept some daily notes and references beginning immediately after his arrest, or he reconstructed those early post-arrest days totally from memory. In any case, he quickly brought the diary up to date, and then continued it in more official form.

Shaw typed portions of the diary, and dictated other portions of it. For typing services, he utilized Beryl Donnath, the long-time secretary to Mario Bermúdez, and Dottie D'Amico. D'Amico was the sister of Marge Odair, who worked with Shaw and Biddison at Marilyn Tate's real estate agency. Odair and D'Amico had, some years before, been part of the Odair Sisters (which also included Sally Odair, later Sally Galjour), a singing group that appeared on WWL Radio's "Dawnbusters" program during the 1940s and 1950s. The program was one of the last efforts of "Big Radio" to compete with television, before television completely solidified its superiority.[1867]

The main purpose of the diary was to keep a log of Shaw's activities during his period under suspicion, until the outcome of the case, in hopes that he could sell the rights to his story to a publisher, a television network, or a motion picture studio. In fact, beginning in April 1967, a woman named Wilma Francis, a local casting agent with long ties to Hollywood, began working with Shaw and his defense attorney, Edward Wegmann, with the intention of selling the story in order to help pay Shaw's legal defense costs. Peter Dassinger, a local agent in New Orleans, also assisted in the project. Francis traveled to Hollywood during the late spring and summer of 1967 in her marketing efforts. At one time, the motion picture director Mervyn LeRoy, who had directed such movies as *I'm a Fugitive from a Chain Gang* and *Mister Roberts*, was at least somewhat interested in the project.

There are at least several versions of Shaw's diary, in different forms. Some of them are cryptic day-to-day references without any linking language, while other entries have the same reference points, but are longer and fill in the gaps of Shaw's brief thoughts. There are also several versions of a written narrative, where Shaw attempted to turn the fragmentary diary references into a more complete manuscript. The manuscript versions mostly go for a relatively short period of time, while the more cryptic diary references extend into mid-October 1967, around the time of an important court hearing that resulted in a postponement of Shaw's initial trial date, and marked the beginning of a Shaw trip to New York City for the remainder of the month. The diaries were then apparently discontinued, or else the portions that continued after mid-October 1967 have been lost.[1868]

On the October 1967 trip to New York City, Shaw met the writer James Kirkwood, who later would cover Shaw's trial from January to March 1969, and write a lengthy book about it, *American Grotesque*. In May 1968, however, Kirkwood came to New Orleans and interviewed Shaw and other participants on the defense side of the case, in preparation for an article that appeared in *Esquire* magazine in November 1968. In the *Esquire* article, Kirkwood quotes Shaw as saying that he was still keeping the daily diary (as of May 1968), but no versions that extend to such a time have surfaced.[1869]

In the diaries and narratives, Shaw reveals, to a somewhat surprising degree, what is going on in his mind and in his personal life, including, indirectly, his struggles with certain aspects of his lifestyle. He notes his daily activities, and names various individuals who associated with him during those critical months, although he sometimes mentions only their initials. He also comments on the numerous developments in the case that occurred, seemingly in an unending stream, throughout March, April, May, and June of 1967 and, to a lesser degree, throughout the summer and into the fall of that year.

In one of the narratives, Shaw recounted how he was initially questioned on December 23, 1966 in the district attorney's office. He had been picked up by Detective Lester Otillio and brought to the office at Tulane and Broad streets. Riding in the car with him was his young friend, Layton Martens, who had been picked up separately by Otillio. Martens was important because he turned out to be one of at least three individuals who admitted to knowing both Shaw and David Ferrie. Although Martens freely admitted knowing both men, he always said that he knew them separately, at different periods of time, and that to his knowledge, they did not know each other.

Shaw indicated in his narrative that he had been questioned primarily about the Cuban consulate that had been located in the Mart building. He said that Cuban refugees had occasionally been sent to him for help in getting jobs, but that he had been unable to help those individuals.

Layton Martens dropped by Shaw's residence later that afternoon and mentioned that the district attorney's men had questioned him about his knowledge of Lee Harvey Oswald in the Civil Air Patrol, to which Martens also had belonged; Martens had indicated he did not know anything about Oswald having been in the organization. Martens was also questioned about David Ferrie, and whether he had known Oswald. Shaw said it was during this conversation with Martens that he learned for the first time that Martens had known Ferrie, a person Shaw indicated was unknown to him at the time.

Shaw had gone to Hammond, Louisiana for part of the weekend of February 25 and 26, 1967, to visit his mother. Shaw's parents had lived there since the early 1950s, but his father had passed away the previous November. When he returned on Saturday, he found that his maid had left a note indicating that a Walter Sheridan had called for him. During the weekend, he sent out letters to owners of French Quarter "doubles" for real estate listings with the Marilyn Tate Agency, with whom Shaw had now been associated for several years. When Shaw had not returned Sheridan's call by Sunday evening, Sheridan called again, and identified himself as a reporter for NBC News. He asked Shaw if he could come to see him, and when Shaw asked when, Sheridan said immediately. Sheridan came to Shaw's residence, and the two discussed the issue of whether Shaw was the mysterious "Clay Bertrand" figure. Sheridan and Shaw discussed the differing descriptions of "Bertrand" that had been offered by Dean Andrews to the Warren Commission, and Shaw pointed out that neither one fit him. However, Sheridan told Shaw that Andrews had recently given a new description of Bertrand that did match him. Shaw denied to Sheridan that he had ever used an alias, and told him that, based solely on his being a public figure in the city, it would be difficult for him to assume a false identity.[1870][1871]

Two days later, on the afternoon of Tuesday, February 28, 1967, Shaw was entertaining a visiting friend. Shortly after the friend's arrival, he insisted that Shaw go upstairs and look out the window at a car that seemed to contain "detectives," as those outside were described by Shaw's visitor. Shaw was able to see four men sitting in a car on the curb outside of his residence, and they appeared to him as if they might indeed be law enforcement officials. A short time later, the doorbell rang, and when Shaw answered it, a young man was standing outside; he questioned Shaw about whether he needed insurance. Shaw answered that he was fully insured, and that he had company at the moment, so it would be impossible to talk. The young man asked if he could come back at another time; Shaw indicated that he would be open to that, but reiterated that he was already fully insured. [1872][1873] Shaw did not think anything more about the incident until a preliminary hearing held two weeks after his arrest, when Perry Russo testified that he was the young man who had come by that day, for purposes of seeing Shaw in person and verifying his identification.

Around midday on March 1, Shaw heard on the radio that a subpoena had been issued for him, so he called the district attorney's office, which confirmed that announcement. The power to subpoena an individual for such an interview had only been given to the office of the district attorney in January 1967. When Shaw returned to his home, he found Detective Lester Otillio, who had driven Shaw to the office back in December 1966, waiting to transport him once more for questioning. Otillio, in a memo to Louis Ivon, said that when he had arrived at Shaw's place, Sheriff's deputies were in the patio area waiting to serve the subpoena, and that Ronald Kabel, a maintenance man for Shaw, was also there. A crew from WDSU-TV Channel 6, having learned of the subpoena, was filming the premises. After a long period of waiting at the district attorney's office, Shaw was questioned for some period of time by Andrew Sciambra and investigator Louis Ivon. He never saw Jim Garrison that day, even though Garrison was present in the office and was the one who ultimately ordered Shaw's arrest.[1874][1875]

Shaw was asked if he had ever known either David Ferrie or Lee Harvey Oswald. He was shown pictures of various young men, whom he later speculated were "Ferrie's boys," whom Ferrie had known either in the Civil Air Patrol, or for sexual purposes, or both. After Shaw had denied knowing Ferrie or Oswald, or having any knowledge of a conspiracy to assassinate Kennedy, Sciambra indicated that the district attorney's office had witnesses who would testify to the contrary. Sciambra requested that Shaw take a sodium pentothal (or "truth serum") test (rather than a lie detector test, as is commonly indicated); if he didn't, Shaw would be arrested. Shaw refused to do so and, at that point, asked to call an attorney for assistance. The questioning stopped there, and Shaw attempted to reach his long-time civil attorney, Edward Wegmann. Upon learning Wegmann was out of town, Shaw tried to contact Wegmann's brother, William, who worked for a separate firm. William "Billy" Wegmann also was unavailable, but Salvatore "Sal" Panzeca of the same firm was able to come to Shaw's assistance.

The entire process of arresting, booking and releasing Shaw took several hours, during which, unbeknownst to him, his residence was searched by authorities, and various materials and personal items were confiscated. During the search, an acquaintance of Shaw, a former pilot named Owen Mitchell "Mitch" Wright, having heard of the arrest and the ongoing search, appeared upon the scene, making inquiries about it. When a local photographer, Irby Aucoin, tried to snap his picture, Wright became upset and was arrested in a resulting altercation. While Shaw was being booked near the fingerprint room, he saw Wright, who had been brought there after his own arrest. By that time, Edward Wegmann had arrived and joined in efforts to secure Shaw's release.

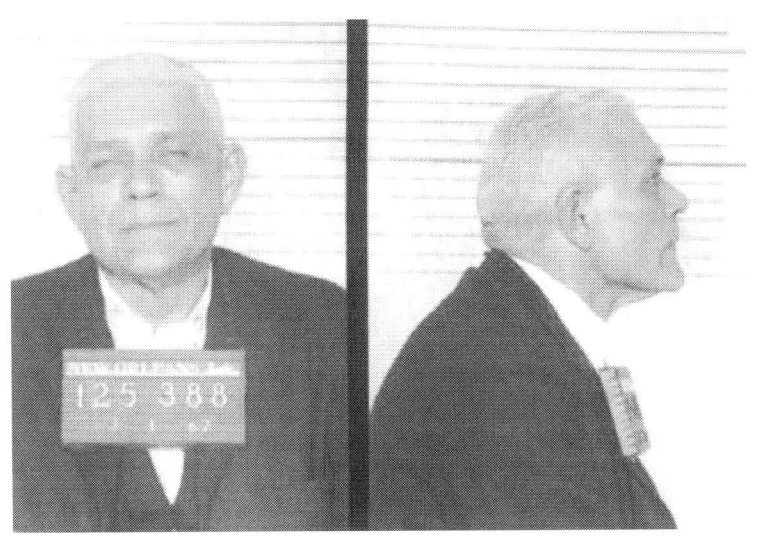

Clay Shaw's booking photo, evening of March 1, 1967 (Source unknown)

Meanwhile, Garrison's investigator, William Gurvich, read a statement announcing Shaw's arrest to anxious reporters; Gurvich would later maintain that Garrison had written the statement, and had offered a naïve Gurvich the opportunity to read it. Jim Garrison soon stepped out of his office and faced the waiting crowd. Asked if Shaw could be bonded out, Garrison calmly said, "If he wants to, yeah." A dramatic moment occurred when someone asked if Shaw had confessed to the crime; Garrison seemed somewhat stunned by the question, and paused noticeably before answering quietly, "No."

Shaw attended a bail hearing before Judge Thomas Brahney, Jr. and was released around nine o'clock that night, after posting a bond of $10,000. Wegmann and Shaw then went to a small bar on Gravier Street to discuss the shocking turn of events. After having a few drinks, they went to Wegmann's office to continue their discussion. It was during those conversations that Shaw apparently acknowledged his homosexuality to Wegmann. Shaw later would reflect how unusual it seemed that, having known Wegmann for approximately twenty years, it was the first time the two had ever discussed the subject. The exact details of the conversation are unknown, but surely Shaw expressed some fear that his personal life could be used against him in a criminal case. At the end of the evening, Shaw was taken to the home of Marilyn Tate, where his longtime friend Jeff Biddison was waiting, along with another acquaintance named Joe Mizell. After telling Tate, Biddison, and Mizell the story of what had happened to him that afternoon and evening, he went around the corner and spent the night at Biddison's home. The whole matter would be cleared up shortly, he thought.[1876]

Jim Garrison's office ultimately used three methods to charge Shaw with conspiracy in the assassination of President Kennedy. First, the district attorney's office had the power to charge an individual without going to a grand jury or using a preliminary hearing, and that was the method used the night of Shaw's arrest. However, prosecutors also would soon use both the grand jury and preliminary hearing as venues to charge Shaw with his alleged crime. The preliminary hearing would soon be scheduled for March 14-17, just two weeks after Shaw's arrest.

A preliminary hearing was normally requested by the criminal defense team, in order to learn more about the prosecution's case, and there was much speculation about Jim Garrison's motive in requesting such a hearing, since he had already officially charged Shaw with the crime. Some observers concluded that by using a preliminary hearing, open to the public, Garrison was generating publicity for himself, and also shielding himself from any future lawsuits by Shaw related to an improper arrest. However, the hearing was scheduled, and it was decided that a three-judge panel would hear Garrison's presentation and rule upon it, adding a possible new level of authority for the prosecution of Shaw, if the panel were to bind Shaw over for trial.

The day of Shaw's arrest, Wednesday March 1, 1967, James Lewallen also was questioned again. Lewallen was another person, besides Layton Martens and Gordon Novel, who had known both Shaw and David Ferrie. Like Martens, Lewallen maintained that, to his knowledge, Shaw and Ferrie did not know each other, although in Lewallen's case, he had known Ferrie both before and after the period during which he had known Shaw. Lewallen had lived next door to Shaw in the late 1950s and early 1960s.

On March 4, 1967, Lewallen took two polygraph tests with examiner Roy Jacobs. Jacobs performed most or all of the polygraph tests for Garrison's office related to the Kennedy assassination investigation at this stage; he had been trained at the noted Keeler Polygraph Training Institute in Chicago. Later, Garrison would complain that Jacobs always found the persons he examined to be deceptive, including many Garrison had hoped to use as witnesses in the trial. During the two tests, Lewallen indicated deception on several questions. For example, when asked if his friend Dante Marochini had known Shaw, Lewallen had said: "No." Lewallen explained his deception by saying that he had advised Marochini to see Shaw about a job, but he was not certain that Marochini ever did so, and therefore did not know firsthand if he knew Shaw or not. On another question, he was asked if he had been to Shaw's residence more than twice, and also was asked if he had spoken to Shaw since 1964. Lewallen had replied "No" to both questions, and had shown deception. Lewallen explained that he and a friend, William Munson, had thought of going into business together and, thinking Shaw might be of help with the venture, had called him, but had never heard back from him. Lewallen also showed deception when asked if Ferrie had talked about killing Kennedy. He had answered "No," and he had no explanation for the showing of deception. Lewallen had also shown deception when asked if he had ever seen Guy Banister in Ferrie's apartment. He had answered "No," but could not explain the showing of deception. Interestingly, on one particular question, Lewallen showed no deception: when he was asked if Ferrie and Shaw had known each other, he had answered "No." When asked if Ferrie had a roommate in September 1963, Lewallen explained that Ferrie had a roommate named Tommy, but he did not know the person's last name. Lewallen even discussed his sexual history with the polygraph examiner, indicating that he had first had sex with Ferrie in Cleveland years before, and that he had had sexual relations with Shaw on two different occasions. Overall, the examiner Jacobs concluded that Lewallen had substantially told the truth on his tests and interrogations taken as a whole.[1877]

Many thought that the person whom Perry Russo said was Ferrie's roommate in 1963, identified by Russo as Lee Harvey Oswald, was actually James Lewallen. However, Lewallen would never testify at any court hearing related to Shaw's arrest. The prosecution did not call him, because he was unhelpful to their case of proving that Shaw and Ferrie knew each other, but the defense could not count on him to be reliable under the prosecution's pressure. In an interview with author James Kirkwood in the spring of 1969, after Shaw's trial, Irvin Dymond said that that it would have been dangerous to have called him.[1878]

An FBI memo the day after Shaw's arrest captured Leonard Gurvich, brother of Garrison investigator William Gurvich, saying that during the execution of the search warrant on Shaw's residence the night of Wednesday, March 1, 1967, investigators had found hooks in the ceiling, with smudges of fingerprints visible near the hooks on the wooden beams high above the floor. Investigators also found ropes with a black gown attached suspended from the ceiling hooks, and a cat-of-nine-tails lying nearby.[1879] Such reports would become lore in New Orleans that has lasted to the present day, as rumors of Shaw's sadomasochistic role-playing competed with explanations mentioning his various colorful Mardi Gras costumes over the years in explaining such phenomenon.

Another FBI memo quoted a confidential informant as saying that news cameraman Irby Aucoin had told him that Dr. Charles B. Moore of Ochsner Hospital had been told by Aurelie Alost that David Ferrie had entrée into Shaw's office at any time.[1880] Alost had been with the Italian Tourist Commission in the Mart from the mid-1950s into the 1960s, but by 1967 was with the Heart Fund at Ochsner Clinic. Alost would never come forward to authorities with that information, however, and has resisted all efforts for comment over the years.

The FBI also summarized what they knew about Shaw in a memo the day after his arrest. The memo mentioned that the FBI had known about Shaw's homosexuality as early as 1954, and that in 1964 a confidential informant for the Houston office had advised that he had had sexual relations of a sadomasochistic nature with Shaw, and had described Shaw as "brilliant" and "powerful."[1881] The FBI's informant in 1964 was Albert E. Carr, a resident of eastern Texas who had come to the FBI's attention during a multi-state investigation into interstate transportation of stolen property; memos mentioning Albert E. Carr stretched from FBI offices in San Antonio to New Orleans. The FBI had known about Shaw's homosexuality in 1954 as a result of a proposed FBI project to monitor the trash of the German consulate in New Orleans, using personnel from the International Trade Mart to assist in that effort. The FBI had quickly determined that Shaw, and Assistant Managing Director J.B. Dauenhauer, were both homosexuals, and quickly abandoned the project, at least partly for that reason. Such information about Shaw, and the FBI's continuous monitoring of Jim Garrison's investigation, would for years reach all the way up to J. Edgar Hoover, and on to President Lyndon Johnson until his term ended in January 1969.

Also on the day after Shaw's arrest, J.B. Dauenhauer called Edward Wegmann and said that he had been subpoenaed by the district attorney's office. Wegmann arranged for the noted New Orleans criminal defense attorney Irvin Dymond to represent Dauenhauer during the interview.[1882] Dauenhauer answered questions about the history of the Mart, and at the end of his meeting with the district attorney's representatives, Dymond told newsmen that Dauenhauer had no knowledge of any conspiracy related to Kennedy's assassination, "if one existed."

Owen M. Wright, the former airline pilot who had been arrested the night of Shaw's arrest after becoming involved in a scuffle with a news cameraman outside of Shaw's residence, called FBI headquarters the day after he was arrested. He said that men had come to his former home on Barracks Street looking for him, and he wondered if they were FBI agents.[1883] He had earlier called the FBI after midnight, while intoxicated, to report Shaw's arrest as well as his own, and threatened to go to someone in Washington if something was not done about it.

Dean Andrews was interviewed by Garrison's office on March 2, 1967, the day after Shaw's arrest. Garrison had been speaking privately with Andrews since October 1966, but had not succeeded in getting Andrews to make a firm identification of Shaw as the mysterious "Clay Bertrand." Andrews described how when he was in law school, he had lived at the Pontalba Apartments, and that he had often gone to the Rendezvous Lounge, which he described as a "swinging place." Andrews said that he first heard the name "Clay Bertrand" around 1956 or 1957, and that Bertrand had a deep voice, and was intelligent and educated. Andrews said that he possibly first met Bertrand at Dixie's Bar of Music, and that he may have seen him at the corner of Dauphine Street and Esplanade Avenue. Shaw was known to patronize Dixie's Bar of Music, a well-known gay bar in the French Quarter patronized by straights as well, and he also lived near the corner of Dauphine and Esplanade. However, Andrews struggled in the memo to actually describe "Clay Bertrand," or to say how many times he had seen him.[1884] It is possible that this memo, vague as it was while still containing a few specifics, was part of a deal Garrison and Andrews supposedly had worked out, whereby Andrews would not identify Shaw as "Bertrand," but would also not firmly deny it

Shaw held a press conference the day after his arrest, in attorney Edward Wegmann's office. Shaw read a prepared statement wherein he denied ever knowing either Lee Harvey Oswald (he called him "Harvey Lee Oswald") or David Ferrie. Shaw said that he was "shocked and dismayed by these fantastic charges," which he said had no basis "in fact or in law," and said that he looked forward to clearing his name. When asked about a statement that United States Attorney General Ramsey Clark had made earlier in the day, to the effect that the FBI had investigated Shaw at the time of Kennedy's assassination and had cleared him, Shaw said that he had not been aware that he had ever been investigated. Shaw also denied ever knowing Dean Andrews.

Also during the day on March 2, 1967, W. Robert Morgan, a law student and friend of Shaw, reached Shaw at Wegmann's office; Morgan had been frantically trying to locate Shaw upon hearing of his arrest. The night before, on March 1, 1967, at 11:25 p.m., only hours after Shaw's arrest, Morgan had sent a telegram that said, "Clay—I can't express my shock and sympathy with mere words—my entire resources are available to you—loyally, W. Robert Morgan."[1885]

Morgan picked Shaw up at Wegmann's office, and the two men went to Morgan's residence in the Carol Apartments on St. Charles Avenue. Morgan asked Shaw to stay overnight, but Shaw declined, on Wegmann's advice. Shaw had known Morgan for several years prior to his arrest. Morgan's wife, Jacqueline, had been a medical student in New Orleans, graduating in the mid-1960s, and the three of them had sometimes played chess together. At the time of Shaw's arrest, Jacqueline Morgan was practicing medicine in the small town of Pleasant Hill, Louisiana, south of Shreveport in north Louisiana, while Robert Morgan attended law school in New Orleans. Shaw indicated that he was fonder of Jacqueline than he had been of Robert; he felt that, over time, Morgan had seemed to imitate him, and had redone the interior of his apartment to match Shaw's residence. Shaw understood that Morgan had means to make any such changes he desired; he supposedly had made a lot of money in an oil well supply business with his father-in-law in Shreveport, before moving to New Orleans and entering law school.[1886]

Morgan, apparently known for somewhat boastful behavior, indicated that he would put up $50,000 for Shaw's defense. During the next few days, Morgan invited himself to get-togethers for friends of Shaw held by realtor Marilyn Tate, bringing along a friend, attorney Edna Sakir. Morgan gave at least two interviews with major media outlets, including ABC News, and Shaw quickly began to suspect that Morgan was interested more in publicity than he was in Shaw's criminal defense. Several of Shaw's other friends, including Marilyn Tate, disliked Morgan immediately. Shortly thereafter, Morgan brought Shaw a $5,000 check as a contribution to the defense. Within a day or so, however, Morgan called Shaw asking him not to deposit it, saying that it had been written on the wrong bank account. No additional money was forthcoming from Morgan from that point on, and he quickly dropped away from the scene.

Mario Bermúdez, then representing the Cordell Hull Foundation, was traveling with former Tennessee governor Frank Clement. The two of them called Jeff Biddison to find out the details of Shaw's arrest, and Clement even went so far as to offer to represent Shaw if he needed an attorney. Shaw's friend Judson O'Donnell called as well, offering verbal support.

Two days after Shaw's arrest, a New Orleans source on "homosexual matters" told the FBI that, late in 1961, he had been approached by a group of homosexuals to act as counsel for a newly formed group in New Orleans, which would provide money for legal assistance to homosexuals in legal trouble. He said that the group was known as the "Clay Bertrand Society." He also said that "Clay Bertrand" was used as the name by uptown homosexuals to rent an apartment on Chartres Street to receive pornography, and that Shaw and local attorney Doug Jones had used it for that purpose. The memo did not identify the source, but it said that he was an attorney who was not officially connected with the group he was advising.[1887]

On March 3, 1967, Shaw noted that Dante Marochini had been subpoenaed by Garrison's office. Shaw recalled that he had been asked about Marochini, whom he did not know, by Garrison's men two days earlier.[1888] Marochini, a friend of James Lewallen who had also known David Ferrie, disappeared relatively quickly from the scene, and played no part in court hearings related to Shaw's arrest.

The same day, Shaw and Wegmann conferred with Vic Bernard of Bauerlein Advertising about the public relations aspect of his arrest.[1889] Shaw had worked with Bauerlein off and on during his years at the Mart, and also during the year he managed the Louisiana Purchase Sesquicentennial celebration. The public relations aspect of the case was always on the minds of Shaw and his attorneys from the day of his arrest, as Garrison was generating daily publicity across all major news outlets, local and national, with his public pronouncements.

Shaw soon began to ask, "Why me?" Then he would consider, "Why not me?" He wondered about the randomness of his predicament, and compared his experience to that of Chuck Walton, a San Francisco area friend, who had passed away with lung cancer close to the day that Shaw was arrested.[1890] Walton was an acquaintance of John Iacometti, who had lived in New Orleans and worked in the Mart building years before, but who now lived in San Francisco as well. Shaw also took the time to reflect on who his real friends were. He commented on his friend of twenty years, Jeff Biddison, saying that Biddison felt what Shaw felt more completely than anyone else, and was a person he could trust completely.[1891]

Shaw's diaries and narratives indicate that he was drinking in the mornings after his arrest. Many have commented that Shaw's ordeal caused him to drink heavier than he had before the arrest, and there is some anecdotal evidence that this was true during the first few months. However, many who had known Shaw prior to his arrest recalled him drinking often at lunch, and during the day when he didn't have to work, a custom not unusual in the New Orleans of that era. On March 11, 1967, Shaw noted in his diary that he had decided that he would have no hard liquor before noon each day.[1892]

Local character Gordon Novel continued to be involved around the edges of the investigation. Novel originally had been put in touch with Garrison, prior to Shaw's arrest, by Willard Robertson, a Garrison supporter both politically and financially. Robertson thought Garrison could use Novel's services in the electronics business to guard against eavesdropping on Garrison's office by the FBI or other government agencies, a concern of Garrison, who had chosen not to share information with such agencies. However, Novel immediately reported his talks with Garrison to the FBI office in New Orleans, and those conversations are captured in contemporaneous memos during late February 1967. In an interview that Novel and his friend, Rancier Ehlinger, had with Garrison's representatives in early March, Novel said that he had known Shaw since 1959, and had known Ferrie as well, but had never heard Ferrie mention Shaw. The exact details of Novel's break with Garrison remain cloudy, but apparently Novel refused to cooperate in incriminating Shaw, and began to feel pressure from Garrison's office. Novel had been involved, along with some others, in a break-in in 1961 at a bunker in Houma, Louisiana, owned by Schlumberger Corporation; the bunker had contained dynamite and other equipment used in oil exploration. Over the years, a story would evolve that the bunker contained weapons that were to be shipped to Cuba to be used in the Bay of Pigs Invasion. However, the police report describing the break-in is dated August 22, 1961, approximately four months after the Bay of Pigs Invasion.[1893]

Josephine Hug, who had worked at the Mart under Shaw for a number of years, also was interviewed by investigators. Apparently Hug, while out with her husband at a social gathering shortly after Shaw's arrest, had said that she had seen David Ferrie visit Shaw in his office. Someone had reported that to the district attorney's office, and Hug was brought in for questioning. After initially confirming to investigators that she had seen Ferrie and Shaw together, Hug later would retract those statements in an appearance before the grand jury, indicating that she had made a mistake in identification.

Some of the people summoned to Garrison's office were chosen because they lived, or had lived, close to Shaw. Garrison had a theory about "propinquity," whereby he thought he could show relationships that pertained to the assassination by how closely a person lived or traveled near another person already under suspicion. Some of the individuals associated with Garrison's office recalled Garrison telling them that, while the Warren Commisson and the FBI had interviewed thousands of people, he would solve the assassination "with an Esso roadmap and two or three city directories." The reference to an Esso roadmap related to another technique used by Garrison, that of studying routes between two cities, say Miami and Los Angeles, and noting how closely some supposedly relevant person who traveled that route had come to Dallas or New Orleans, thereby establishing a connection with either Shaw, Oswald, Ferrie, or perhaps Jack Ruby.

Tom Bethell, a Britisher who joined Garrison's staff at the end of 1966, conducted months of research at the National Archives in Washington on behalf of Garrison's office, reviewing governmental records related to the assassination, before returning to New Orleans in the summer of 1967. Bethell also kept a detailed diary of much of his time in Garrison's office, which captured his slowly growing skepticism about the case against Shaw, and the entire investigation.

Shortly after Shaw's arrest, an article appeared in an Italian newspaper, *Paesa Sera*, linking him to the Central Intelligence Agency. The Italian newspaper article mentioned Shaw's earlier connection with Centro Mondiale Commerciale in Rome, and indicated that the CIA was behind the organizations, and that, therefore, Shaw must be affiliated with the CIA as well. It was an ironic twist because, although Shaw had never had any active part in Centro Mondiale Commerciale, or the Permindex group behind it, he had, separately, been a contact with the local CIA office in New Orleans from 1948 to 1956. Also, the CIA had indeed gained the cooperation of individuals within the organization to some extent, intending to use it as a source of information about Communist activity in Europe, although that operation had nothing to do with Shaw's earlier CIA connection.

There had already been rumblings, prior to Garrison's investigation, about some employees of the Central Intelligence Agency bearing a grudge against President Kennedy for his failure to support the Bay of Pigs Invasion adequately in April 1961, particularly while the invasion was ongoing. Accordingly, there had already been rumors of possible rogue CIA agents being involved in the assassination; some suggested the agency officially had a role. Garrison pyramided the article from *Paesa Sera*, on top of the earlier CIA-involvement rumors, and by May the main headlines of the *States-Item* were screaming about possible Central Intelligence Agency participation in Kennedy's murder.

Years after the case was over, Jim Garrison would sometimes say that Clay Shaw had once been an employee of the Mississippi Shipping Company, with connections to the CIA through that company. Conspiracy writers have picked that up, and placed it in their accounts of the case. It is true that Theodore Brent, the first President of the International Trade Mart, was also the President of Mississippi Shipping Company, and that he hired Shaw as Managing Director of the Mart. It is also true that Shaw and Brent had known each other for approximately fifteen years prior to Shaw being hired by the Mart, and that Shaw had worked for a brief period in 1942 at the cooperative venture Louisiana Shipyards, Inc., in which both Brent and Rudolf Hecht were involved. Furthermore, some of Shaw's friends, such as Jeff Biddison and John Iacometti, worked in minor non-shipping positions for the company for brief periods after World War II. However, there is no record that Shaw ever was an employee of the Mississippi Shipping Company. The rumor appears to have originated with a memo dated August 9, 1967, from Lorraine LeBouef, Garrison's secretary at the time of Shaw's arrest. She told Garrison in the memo that she had learned that, fifteen years before, which would make it approximately in 1952, Shaw was an executive with either the Mississippi Shipping Company, or with Lykes Brothers, another shipping company located in downtown New Orleans.[1894] At the time, however, Shaw's only employer was the Mart. Shaw's actual CIA connection appears to have developed as a result of the Czech Trade Exhibit taking space in the Mart in late 1948, and the FBI and the CIA seeking information about the personnel there, and the nature of the exhibit.

Edward Wegmann, who had been Shaw's civil attorney for almost twenty years, but who had little criminal law experience, knew that Shaw would need a top-notch criminal attorney. Initially, Shaw was represented in court hearings by Guy Johnson, one of William Wegmann's law partners. However, it was quickly decided that if J.B. Dauenhauer did not need the services of Irvin Dymond after the initial meeting with the district attorney's representatives, Wegmann would attempt to enlist Dymond's services for Shaw. Dymond agreed to represent Shaw, and began as his attorney on March 9, 1967, a few days before the preliminary hearing was to begin.

Dymond already had a somewhat legendary reputation around New Orleans, and as soon as he became Shaw's chief defense counsel, local observers knew that Garrison would be in for a fight. A gruff, deep-voiced ex-boxer, Dymond combined a deep knowledge of the fine points of criminal law with a surface layer of old-fashioned respectability and a great talent for effective courtroom acting. He represented prominent defendants and wealthy individuals, but he also represented those around the edges. Back in 1953, a report by Aaron Kohn mentioned that while attorney Wray Gill, for whom David Ferrie later worked as a private investigator, represented New Orleans Mafia chieftain Carlos Marcello's "boys" and "whorehouses," Irvin Dymond represented the "really big houses."[1895] Among his other interests, Dymond raised fighting roosters at his farm across Lake Ponchartrain from New Orleans.

At the time of the hiring of Irvin Dymond, Shaw and Wegmann had discussed whether Shaw really needed a criminal defense attorney who was prominent on a national scale, such as Percy Foreman of Houston, or F. Lee Bailey, then a young Boston attorney who had gained prominence in several major criminal defense trials that had taken place in 1966 and early 1967. Garrison's actions had resulted in such media frenzy, and some wondered if Dymond could cope with that aspect of the defense. As effective as everyone agreed Dymond could be in the courtroom and behind the scenes, there would be some doubters among Shaw's supporters all the way though his trial, those who thought that Dymond was simply out of his league in this unique case.

On March 9, barely a week after his arrest, Edith Stern informed Shaw that she, Muriel Bultman Francis Bogner (Muriel Francis was married to Howard Bogner during the mid-1960s), and Mr. and Mrs. Moise Dennery had held a meeting the night before to discuss helping Shaw with his defense. That group had decided that it would be best to get the American Civil Liberties Union (ACLU) involved, that it would be better to help Shaw indirectly through that group than to contribute money directly to him and publicly organize his defense.[1896] That same day, however, Muriel Bultman Francis Bogner took it upon herself to send Edward Wegmann, through the family business, a check for $1,000 to be used in Shaw's defense.[1897]

Edith Stern's reluctance to get publicly involved, or directly involved, in Shaw's criminal defense led to Irvin Dymond, years later, contributing a wry anecdote about the situation. He said that, after an approach by the defense team to Mrs. Stern, she informed them that she could only contribute actual funds to the defense if a way could be found to make the donations tax-deductible.[1898]

At an Executive Committee meeting of the Mart the same day, Lloyd Cobb noted that J.B. Dauenhauer recently had been interrogated by Garrison's office, as had Goldie Moore.

Cobb said the district attorney had announced he would also question Carmen Martinez, who had worked as a clerk at the Mart for about a year, and Darlyn Mercadal. Cobb also reported that the district attorney's office had requested permission to examine the books and records of the Mart, and Cobb indicated he was making all of those available without subpoena, with inspection of those records to begin immediately after the meeting; the Executive Committee then formally approved Cobb's decision.[1899]

Shortly after his first meeting with Shaw, Irvin Dymond wrote to investigator Ralph Sneed. He referred to Clayton Blackshear, one of three waiters at the Steak Pit restaurant, and described him as being five feet ten inches tall, and 175 to 180 pounds. Dymond said he needed a photo of Blackshear as soon as possible, that he needed photo coverage of Ferrie's residence, and asked Sneed to check the arrest records of "Clay Bertrand", Clayton Blackshear, Patrick Layton Martens, William Dalzell, William Formyduval, Clay L. Shaw, and Clay Lavergne Shaw.[1900] Clayton Bleackshear was one of several names Shaw and his attorneys quickly came up with as someone who might be the mysterious "Clay Bertrand."

Approximately ten days after his arrest, Shaw telephoned a local taxi company requesting that a cab be sent to his residence; the cab driver turned out to be Marty Cocita. It was the beginning of a relationship that would last through the remainder of Shaw's life. Cocita sympathized with Shaw's plight, and taxied him around New Orleans from then on, sometimes at reduced cost. Although a legend of sorts developed that he transported Shaw at no charge, Shaw did make periodic payments to him, by both cash and check. However, the relationship hit a temporary bump a few weeks after Shaw began using Cocita. During a ride one evening, the two got into a conversation about the civil rights movement, then perhaps reaching its hottest point in Louisiana. When Shaw expressed sympathy for the civil rights movement in general, Cocita seemed to disapprove, and he failed to appear for several evenings; Shaw feared that he had angered him. However, when Cocita eventually reappeared, he denied that was the case, and said that he respected Shaw's position on the issue. Over the next seven and a half years, Shaw would attend family gatherings at Cocita's home, meet the entire family, and even attend the wedding of one of Cocita's children. When the writer James Kirkwood arrived in New Orleans initially to prepare his *Esquire* article about Shaw's plight, Shaw introduced him to Cocita, and when Kirkwood later covered Shaw's criminal trial, he also visited the Cocitas' home on occasion.

It had quickly emerged that the charges against Shaw were based upon the statement of a mystery witness who could testify that Shaw knew both Lee Harvey Oswald and David Ferrie, and that the three men had participated in a conspiracy to assassinate Kennedy. The identity of the mystery witness was a matter of great speculation between the date of Shaw's arrest and the beginning of the preliminary hearing on March 14, 1967. Shaw's defense team only would learn when the preliminary hearing began, but word did leak out to others. On March 10, 1967, John James Overstreet, Jr. wrote to Garrison, saying that he had attended a luncheon the day before, and had overheard that Perry Russo, an Equitable Life Assurance Company employee, would testify that Ferrie, Shaw, Oswald, and others had met on August 12, 1963, and planned or discussed the assassination. Overstreet said that he understood that Russo had only known Shaw as "Bertrand," and was surprised to see his picture on television and in the newspapers.[1901] As with many anecdotes passed around during Shaw's long journey through arrest and trial, there was some truth to the story, but with a dose of fiction as well. Russo had indeed identified Shaw, as "Bertrand," being present at the conspiracy party with Ferrie and Oswald, but he had not recognized Shaw's image in the media between 1963 and his first contact with Garrison's office. In fact, elaborate steps had been taken to be able to connect what he knew with Shaw.

An interesting perspective on Garrison's investigation was provided to the FBI at the time of Shaw's arrest by Robert Northshield, then Executive Producer of the *Huntley-Brinkley Report*, NBC's evening news show. Northshield indicated that the Garrison theory was "poppycock," that NBC News believed the story was "hogwash," and would track down all facets to fully report on them. Northshield reported, only partially accurately, that Garrison charged there had been a meeting with Shaw, Layton Martens (Northshield thought his name was "Martin Layton"), Ferrie, and an R. Richard Davis, and that the assassination had been planned by anti-Castro Cubans; he said that Garrison's office believed that Oswald had not been present at the meeting. Northshield mentioned a laundry truck as being part of the theory, and said that "Martin Layton" had been the trigger man.[1902] An internal FBI note attached to the memo indicated that Garrison had "hoodlum connections," and that he was known for shaking down homosexuals. The note further indicated that Garrison had recently bought a $70,000 home, and $25,000 worth of furniture, information provided by Metropolitan Crime Commission Managing Director Aaron Kohn.[1903]

As the preliminary hearing for Shaw approached in mid-March 1967, Northshield told the FBI that Perry Russo was the secret informant listed in Shaw's arrest papers. He indicated that at the preliminary hearing Shaw was to be portrayed as a "sadist" and "masochist" who made the plans for the assassination because he wanted to destroy the "world's most handsome man."[1904]

Some reporters, including James Phelan with the *Saturday Evening Post*, and Richard Billings with *LIFE* magazine, had by this time heard Garrison privately link the assassination to a ring of homosexuals, comparing it to the Leopold-Loeb murder case in Chicago in the 1920s—a "thrill killing" of sorts. Other reports reflected in FBI memos have Garrison attempting to connect Shaw with Walter Jenkins, Lyndon Johnson's former personal aide who was busted for homosexual activity in a Washington, D.C. restroom in 1964. Indeed, material about Jenkins's arrest could be found in Garrison's files years later.[1905]

Garrison would have many theories about the Kennedy assassination over the months that followed, with the mix of involved causes and individuals changing as time progressed. He soon abandoned the homosexual angle altogether in favor of the rogue CIA theory and would, more or less, stick with it for the remainder of his life.

After his arrest, Shaw immediately began to receive what became a flood of letters and telegrams from friends and acquaintances around the country, and even the world. Shaw had met many individuals in his almost fifty-four years, including many in the commercial, gay, and theater worlds. Many of the people who wrote had not seen him or heard from him in many years, some in as long as thirty years, but they remembered their brief interactions with him very fondly.

The day after his arrest, L.S. McClaren, for whom Shaw had worked in the early 1930s at International Harvester, wrote from McComb, Mississippi that, "A fellow never knows how many real friends he has until faced with an ordeal affecting one's life." McClaren said that he had held Shaw in the highest esteem since Shaw had worked for him almost forty years before.[1906]

Thomas H. Weil, who owned Weil Brothers Rare Prints in Miami Beach, Florida, wrote from Minneapolis on March 2, 1967 that he had "just read the incredible news." Weil continued that, "Having known you many years and heard you express your political and social beliefs," the "absurdity of the charges leaves me in a state of shock." Weil added that, "I am one of many who is asking: What can I do to help Clay at this horrible moment in his life?"[1907]

David Baldwin, who had worked as Public Relations Director at the Mart from late 1953 until early 1955, was now working for a division of the American Medical Association in Chicago. He wrote on March 2, 1967, saying that, "Garrison happens to be married to my Godchild and first cousin." He felt that the latest actions established "beyond argument his [Garrison's] psychopathic tendencies." Baldwin suggested that Shaw document his case for false arrest.[1908]

Don Schueler, a local college professor and Shaw friend since the early 1950s, responded to the arrest with a telegram on March 2, indicating his complete confidence in Shaw's innocence, and telling him to "write a book about it."[1909] Schueler's half-joking comment about Shaw doing a book, coming the day after his arrest, must have seemed bittersweet to Shaw, but it was an indication of how difficult many who knew him found it to believe the story of his arrest—or that it would not be resolved favorably in a few days, due to the discovery that it was based upon some misunderstanding.

George Haverstick, who known Shaw since the late 1940s, and had later worked for both the Board of Commissioners of the Port of New Orleans and the Free Trade Zone, was now living in San Diego, California. He wrote Shaw on March 3, saying that he wished he could be with Shaw to let him know that he cared greatly about him. He recalled that he had known Shaw for the past eighteen or nineteen years, and "you are the man I admire most. If I have a hero, he is you." Haverstick indicated that he had started law school the semester before, and had become very interested in civil liberties. He recommended that Shaw look into hiring some attorneys who were associated with the American Civil Liberties Union (ACLU), stating that Shaw needed to make a clear showing of his right to freedom, privacy, and expression without state interference. Haverstick closed by saying, "I care greatly, and I'm cheering for you."[1910]

Marcel Gomez wrote from Cartagena, Colombia; he had worked as a translator and office assistant to Mario Bermúdez during the 1950s and early 1960s, but had moved back to Colombia. He said that he had "read about you being detained," and that "none of your friends believe it possible." He thanked Shaw for his many kindnesses during the years Gomez had worked at the Mart, and said that his mother wished Shaw the best of luck. He closed the letter by using a phrase Shaw himself sometimes used with people, "Chin up, Boss." [1911]

Shaw's friend Tom Dawson sent a telegram from Los Angeles on March 3, indicating that he was "appalled and furious over this bizarre witch hunt." Dawson indicated that he supported Shaw unwaveringly, and asked Shaw to let him know if he could do anything in support.[1912] Shaw received a card from Pat O'Brien, owner of the famous nightclub in New Orleans, of which Shaw had long been a regular patron, saying, "Let me affirm my faith in you."[1913]

Among others responding early after Shaw's arrest was Martin Palmer, Shaw's doctor in New Orleans,[1914] The doctor had known Shaw since the 1950s, when he had come to New Orleans for his medical internship. He had become a social friend of Shaw, and knew a number of prominent individuals in the city. Some accounts have indicated that Dr. Palmer was also David Ferrie's doctor, but in an interview with the author, Dr. Palmer was adamant that he had never met Ferrie.[1915] There was also communication from another longtime friend, Don Doody,[1916] writing from Miami. Realtor "Frosty" Blackshear, aunt of Congressman Hale Boggs's wife, Lindy, sent a telegram indicating that she was "indignant" at Shaw's treatment, and had complete faith that he would "walk with his head high."[1917] Sculptress Claire Evangelista Morrison wrote a very poetic letter, indicating her admiration for Shaw, and mentioning how his example had helped her over the years.[1918]

Gordon Berger wrote from Montreal, Canada by telegram on March 3, 1967. Berger had served with Shaw during World War II, on the public relations staff of General Charles Thrasher. He mentioned with a sardonic tone that the "comic strips" were "now appearing on the front page," referring to the story of Shaw's arrest. Berger added that, "As one who shared room and board" with Shaw, he was "ready to attest to your charm with intelligent choice of food, suave manner with the ladies." Berger ended by saying that the whole story was "absurd," and asked Shaw dryly, "Have you lost your sense of public relations?"[1919]

Charles Bushong, former head of the national Foreign Policy Association, and now Assistant Director of the School of Continuing Education in New York City, wrote that he was "shocked at the charges." Bushong said that although "it has been some years since I have seen you...I will be pleased to be a character witness."[1920]

Reverend Miller M. Cragon wrote on March 3, 1967 from New York City, saying that, "You are very much in my thoughts and prayers," and "my concern is genuine." Cragon said he looked forward to a time, when the trouble was over, "to a pleasant evening of conversation such as we enjoyed so many years ago."[1921]

An interesting telegram came on March 3, 1967 from Joseph W. Faulkner, the noted art dealer and bookstore owner in Chicago. Faulkner, during the 1950s, had been instrumental in exposing the notorious art forger Emile de Hory, who had defrauded numerous collectors around the world. Faulkner now sent Shaw a copy of a telegram he had sent to President Lyndon Johnson, Senator Robert Kennedy, Attorney General Ramsey Clark, and Chief Justice Earl Warren of the U.S. Supreme Court, who had headed the Warren Commission, which investigated and reported on Kennedy's assassination in 1964. Faulkner's telegram stated that, "I have known Clay Shaw twenty years as a Southerner of considerable civic stature," that Shaw had "admired late President to point of worship," and that "the Federal Government has a duty to expose Garrison as neo-McCarthy psychopath."[1922]

Alison Marks, who had served with Shaw as a Red Cross volunteer assigned to the 127th General Hospital unit in late 1943 and early 1944 in England, watched the publicity from her home in Massachusetts; she had not seen Shaw since early 1944. She opened a letter to him by saying that, "I have often thought of you and wondered: Where, what, how," but she said that she was "always sure that you were at the top somewhere." Marks commented that the allegations "must be a frame-up," and that she hoped "you are not vulnerable." She said that Kennedy's death was "most unacceptable to me," and that she was "glad to read you admired him, too." Marks said that she hoped Shaw remembered her, and recalled how she had once "dragged you out in the cold to hear a nightingale at Bishop's Lydeard" in southern England during their brief time together.[1923]

The actor Phillip Carey Jones wrote from Los Angeles on March 3, saying that he was "filled with indignation." Jones said that, "I know your liberal convictions and lack of violence in your character," and while he conceded that the "Warren Commission might have been bamboozled by" the CIA, FBI, and Dallas police in placing blame on Oswald alone, he had no doubt Shaw was not involved. "My heart is with you," he said, and "I wish there was something tangible I could do."[1924]

David Sogge wrote from Cambridge, Massachusetts, where he was now in his first year at Harvard University. Sogge had met Shaw by chance during the summer of 1966, in London, England. He wrote on March 3 that he was "disturbed to learn of the allegations" against Shaw, saying that, "I abhor the filthy slander thrown at you," "a man I met only briefly" who "impressed me with unimpeachable character and a gentle manner." Sogge thanked Shaw for his December letter giving job prospects in the New Orleans area, but said that he had a job lined up for the summer in Cambridge, Massachusetts.[1925]

Shaw's old friend from years before, Cecil E. Foster, of Muskegon, Michigan, sent a telegram on March 3, 1967 that said, "Heartfelt sympathies—thoughts and prayers with you." It was signed simply "C."[1926] Foster would continue the correspondence throughout the two years between Shaw's arrest and trial; some of his letters hinted at deeply suppressed sentiments for Shaw that he felt uncomfortable putting down on paper. Foster had by this time been married for many years, living away from contact with Shaw, but he obviously still felt a strong, emotional connection.

Shaw's old friend Bess Noble, formerly with the U.S. Department of Commerce in Memphis, wrote, "Your friends in Memphis were stunned and distressed to learn of the fantastic charges," and they "have complete confidence in your integrity."[1927]

A letter with no date, and no envelope that has survived, came from "Bill," probably Frank William Mehrten, a Shaw friend in the gay community who had worked for McGraw-Hill Company in Chicago, and later lived in San Francisco. He sent Shaw a letter thanking him for cocktails recently in New Orleans, saying that, "Friends are behind you all the way," and that "Garrison is an ass." Mehrten said that, "I have often heard you speak well of the late President."[1928] Several of Shaw's friends recollected, in their correspondence to him, how Shaw had spoken well of President Kennedy.

Among the most interesting communications Shaw received after his arrest were telegrams during the first week, and a letter dated April 24, from a woman named Kay Lucas Leake Dart; Shaw had known her as Kay Lucas during his days at Le Petit Theatre in the 1930s. After an initial enigmatic late-night telegram on March 2, Dart sent two more five days later. One of them said, "If a pawn can help, I am she." The other one mentioned her "34 years of love and devotion," indicating that she had met Shaw in 1933.[1929] In the April letter, she said that she hoped to revive what she said had been a friendship between Shaw and her that had ended in the early 1940s. She now lived in Washington State, and had been married for sixteen years to John Dart, a psychologist some years younger. She recalled knowing Shaw in New York City as well.[1930]

The novelist James M. Cain, author of such novels as *Double Indemnity*, *Mildred Pierce*, and *The Postman Always Rings Twice*, wrote from his home in Hyattsville, Maryland "to express confidence" in Shaw. Cain said that, "I applaud your dignified manner" in the face of the "preposterous charge." Cain reminded Shaw that he was a writer, and had been introduced to Shaw by New Orleans international trade figure Reeder Spedden; the three had met over lunch. Cain said that Shaw had given him more background about New Orleans "than I've had in years of laborious reading."[1931]

Shaw received a card from his old friend Marion Seidenbach in New York City. She caught Shaw up on their mutual friends, and wrote that a reporter named Jerry Springer had called her to ask for an interview about her knowledge of Shaw.[1932]

Sarah Hill Moore of Fayetteville, North Carolina, a member of the general circle of the Formyduval clan in Whiteville, North Carolina, wrote Shaw on March 6, saying that it was "like a nightmare," and "something that can't be real." She volunteered her suspicion that Garrison "must be mentally ill," and suggested Shaw give a detailed response after his acquittal. She said it "made me furious" to see "Garrison's minions" taking five boxes of Shaw's books and papers from his residence.[1933]

One or two letters were negative, but these instances were from people who did not actually know him. One such note was from Mary Lou Baxter Hunter of Battle Creek, Michigan, sent on March 3, 1967. She said that she had seen Shaw on television, and that he was "older than his years." She warned him that if he talked, "he would be a dead duck." She said that she thought the assassination was a plot hatched in Cuba and that "Garrison has guts and isn't afraid of your gang." She added that, "God have mercy on your soul if you have one," and, "We are sorry that you let yourself get involved." She said that nineteen people had died since the assassination, and that Oswald had not fired the fatal shot.[1934]

Frank W. Manning, chief investigator for Louisiana Attorney General Jack Gremillion, reported to the FBI, shortly after Shaw's arrest, his concerns about the Garrison investigation. He said that he had investigated Garrison several years before, when Garrison was involved in the controversy with judges in New Orleans, and had found that Garrison was a "psychopath" who must have publicity or he would go into "fits of moodiness or depression." Manning said that Garrison had been involved in shakedowns of "sex deviates," and "may be one himself." Manning said that Garrison had earlier charged several hundred "deviates," and had dropped the charges after receiving payments from the accused. Manning also identified former chief Garrison investigator Pershing Gervais as a homosexual, an allegation others would make over the years as well.[1935] Manning's information should be viewed skeptically, however, as oftentimes people flung accusations at Garrison in a political attempt to fight whatever investigation in which Garrison happened to be involved at that time.

An example of the rumors that swirled around Garrison's alleged homosexuality was detailed in an FBI memo in mid-March, which said that a source had informed the Bureau that Shaw's defense team had hired the Pinkerton Detective Agency to expose Garrison, and his involvement with a fourteen-year-old boy, six months earlier. The FBI's informant had heard it from Irma E. Fasnacht, sister of Yvonne "Dixie" Fasnacht, owner of Dixie's Bar of Music, a prominent gay bar in the French Quarter, and an acquaintance of Shaw.[1936] Although that particular accusation did not go anywhere, two and a half years later a similar accusation against Garrison, again involving supposed relations with a boy of similar age, would gain traction in the New Orleans area, over a singular incident that supposedly happened at the New Orleans Athletic Club.

Reporter Merriman Smith of United Press International wrote to the FBI a few days after Shaw's arrest, indicating that Garrison had told him that some "high-status fags" had been involved at the lower echelons of the Kennedy assassination. Smith went on to describe such characters as Jack Martin and others, and commented upon how "dirty" the whole case was, and the number of "nuts" who were involved in it.[1937]

Garrison's office continued to work the gay underworld after Shaw's arrest, in search of potential cooperative witnesses. Bill McKenzie, a reputed homosexual and co-owner of the Finale Bar, told the FBI on March 7 that Garrison's office had approached him to cooperate with them in the investigation, offering to allow him to have female impersonators as entertainers in his bar if he did.[1938]

Thomas Compton, who had known Ferrie since 1954, and in whose dorm room in Hammond, Louisiana, Ferrie had stayed when he first returned from the Texas trip after the assassination, was soon interviewed by Garrison's investigators. Compton said that he did not know Shaw, and that Ferrie had never mentioned Shaw.[1939]

Over the years, there has been some speculation that Shaw had a criminal record in New York, possibly the result of an arrest related to homosexual activity. However, the district attorney's office ran an FBI fingerprint check on Shaw, which disclosed no prior arrests, either in the New Orleans jurisdiction, or in other parts of the country. In a memo to Louis Ivon, investigator Cliency Navarre reported that he could not even find any traffic violations on Clay Shaw, or on "Clay Bertrand" or "Clem Bertrand."[1940]

Around the time of Shaw's arrest, Charles Ward, Garrison's main assistant, received information from New York reporter Bob Greene tracing Shaw's background, at least partially from news clippings, for the period from 1946 to January 1967. Greene wrote that in New York City, Shaw had been in charge of forty Western Union offices, and then had gone into freelance advertising and public relations. Shaw had made trips to Cuba in 1949 and 1957, and in 1956 he also had managed International House when its Managing Director, Charles Nutter, had worked on the House Ways and Means Committee under Congressman Hale Boggs. The memo said that Shaw had testified in front of Congress about trade policy in 1956. The only time Shaw's name appeared on a police blotter was on June 11, 1960, when his residence at 927 Burgundy Street had been burglarized, while Shaw was sleeping; a wallet, $50 in cash, two $125 wrist watches, and a silver set valued at $625, were taken. The silver set was found discarded next door. Officer Frederick Soule, who in 1971 would be indicted along with Jim Garrison on kickback charges by a Federal grand jury, investigated the burglary. The memo went on to say that Shaw had lived at 1313 Dauphine Street continuously for approximately seven years, and that the residence had one large room downstairs, except for a small kitchen and a brick wall, with oriental rugs over gleaming cork floors.

The report contained an extra piece of information, which was that in 1946, Shaw's assistant at the Mart, J.B. Dauenhauer, had been arrested for homosexual acts with a man named Heinz, and that Theodore Brent, President of both the Mart and Mississippi Shipping Company, had bonded him out. According to the memo, Dauenhauer had pleaded guilty, and received a suspended sentence.[1941] Some conspiracy theory accounts of Shaw's case would later contain the anecdote about J.B. Dauenhauer, and compare Brent's role as a wealthy homosexual bonding out the younger homosexual in trouble with the figure of the mysterious "Clay Bertrand" during the 1960s, who also allegedly bonded out younger homosexuals who had been arrested. The writers made a clear link from Brent to Shaw, as if Shaw had stepped into Brent's important role.

Several key developments happened between Shaw's arrest on March 1 and the beginning of the preliminary hearing on March 14. For one thing, Shaw's arrest brought an immediate response in Washington, D.C. from Attorney General Ramsey Clark, and in New Orleans, where Shaw adamantly denied any type of involvement with the Kennedy assassination. Clark, almost impulsively, made a statement that Shaw had been investigated right after Kennedy's assassination, and no connection to the crime had been found. Such a statement from a high public official, of course, raised the question in many minds as to why Shaw had been investigated at all at the time. The day after Clark's statement, newspapers in New York and Washington quoted an unnamed Justice Department source as saying that Shaw and "Clay Bertrand" were the "same guy." The statements, which would be retracted three months later, caused many to suspect that Garrison might indeed be on to something.

On March 11, 1967, Shaw received a call from Donald Organ, an attorney who had worked with the district attorney's office until about two weeks before Shaw's arrest. He had called Shaw offering his services, and saying that he knew the inside of the case from his work in Garrison's office. Two years before, he had represented Garrison when the district attorney was in the midst of his battle with the judges on the local circuit.[1942]

Another significant development that occurred between Shaw's arrest and the preliminary hearing was his meeting with a Catholic priest, Father Edward Sheridan, the weekend before the hearing began. Shaw, who was not a Catholic, sought out the meeting after his arrest at the suggestion of his friend in Shreveport, Margaret Mary Young. Young and her husband, John Wray Young, had managed the Shreveport Little Theatre since the early 1930s, and were prominently known among small theater groups across the United States. The Youngs' daughter, Jill Young, lived in the French Quarter at the time of Shaw's arrest, and associated with him regularly during the months immediately afterward, attending plays, eating out, and visiting at Shaw's place. Father Sheridan had been positioned in New Orleans in earlier years, but was now in northern Mississippi. Shaw met secretly with Sheridan on Saturday, March 11, three days before the preliminary hearing began; Jill Young played a key role in bringing the two men together. In an interview with James Kirkwood, undated but probably conducted in May 1968 during Kirkwood's visit to New Orleans related to his *Esquire* article, Sheridan indicated that he had never known of Shaw during his period in New Orleans. He said that Shaw had told him both good and bad things about himself, and had discussed the great mental strain that the arrest was causing him. Sheridan said that he recommended that Shaw use a rosary, and press it during times of great stress for comfort. Sheridan expressed no particular point of view on Shaw's guilt or innocence, although he clearly was sympathetic to Shaw.

Jill Young would move away from New Orleans during 1967; by the fall, she would be back in her native Shreveport. During the spring of 1968, she married Brian Latell, who was, or shortly would become, a CIA employee, and worked on the agency's Cuba desk for many years. From 1990 to 1994, he was Director of the Center for the Study of Intelligence, a CIA division. A component of that division was the CIA's Historical Review Group, which had responsibility during the 1990s for declassifying internal documents related to the Kennedy assassination in cooperation with the government-created Assassination Records Review Board (ARRB). While nothing has appeared to indicate any sinister connection revolving around that turn of events, it is nonetheless one of numerous unusual connections that followed Clay Shaw around through his life, and for years after his death.

In mid-March, Myron Shaw, a French Quarter resident, told the FBI that Shaw was innocent of the charges against him, but that he was "queer for beatings," and that he had beaten Shaw on a number of occasions at his request.[1943] It is noteworthy that, as the investigation proceeded after Shaw's arrest, many of those called in for questioning were either gay individuals, or those who worked around gays and had some knowledge of their community in the French Quarter, or around David Ferrie's generally separate group. Almost no prominent members of the business community, many of whom had known and worked with Shaw for twenty years, were questioned by Garrison's office.

Carroll S. Thomas, a funeral home owner in Hammond, Louisiana, was being questioned by FBI agents about William Bryant Faust, a young man who was applying for employment with the FBI. Thomas, a former employer and family friend of Faust, also had conducted the funeral of Shaw's father in November 1966, only several months before. While the FBI agent was questioning Thomas about Faust's background, Thomas volunteered that he initially had thought the FBI had contacted him about another matter: the arrest of Shaw. Thomas said that he was a close personal friend of Shaw, and that he had met David Ferrie through Shaw.[1944] Thomas went on to volunteer that he did not think Shaw was involved in the assassination, and that Shaw was politically conservative. Over the years, the memo related to Carroll Thomas has generated much curiosity among those Kennedy assassination researchers concerned with Jim Garrison's investigation of Shaw. Thomas clearly knew Shaw, and as a prominent citizen of the local community, would not have been inclined to make up a story of Shaw introducing him to Ferrie. However, he never reported the information to Garrison's office over the next two years before Shaw's trial, and neither did the FBI. Nor did Thomas report the information after Shaw's first trial, when Garrison re-indicted Shaw on perjury charges, one of which was related to Shaw denying that he had known David Ferrie. Thomas died in 1970, and apparently that information with him. It is possible he was mistaken about Ferrie being the person introduced by Shaw, and it is also possible that, knowing Shaw as well as he did, he communicated with Shaw sometime after mid-March 1967, and before Shaw's trial, and Shaw was able to convince him that the person he introduced to Thomas was not David Ferrie. That is mere speculation, however, and the item is one of the more intriguing among all leads linking Shaw to Ferrie.

Carroll Thomas's observation of Shaw as a political conservative also conflicts with many who describe Shaw as either generally politically liberal (in terms of what that label meant at the middle of the last century, when civil rights for African Americans, the size of the Federal and state governments and their role in the economy, and U.S. dealings with the Communist Bloc nations were the main issues of the day), or as generally apolitical.

As the preliminary hearing loomed, Edward Wegmann regrouped regarding some of the developments. James Dondson, the young man who had actually spent the night before the assassination with Shaw, had recently called Wegmann. He told Wegmann he had tried to reach Shaw after hearing of the arrest, then had tried to reach Jeff Biddison. Dondson had been in Las Vegas recently, staying at the Sands hotel under the name James Nealy. He had been sent there by *LIFE* magazine, under the authority of reporter/photographer Lawrence Schiller, to meet with Jim Garrison, who was on a relaxation trip to Vegas following the uproar over Shaw's arrest. Schiller had worked on a study of homosexuals that *LIFE* magazine had conducted some time before, and had contacts in the gay community in San Francisco and other cities. Schiller wanted to photograph Shaw and Dondson together, since Dondson had been with Shaw shortly before the assassination; Wegmann refused to allow that photograph.[1945]

Lawrence Schiller, who later would write a variety of true-crime books, and produce television movies, was known at the time for contributing some of the more offbeat information about the Kennedy assassination. He told the FBI that he had information to the effect that Lee Harvey Oswald and his wife, Marina, had each engaged in homosexual relations with Michael Paine and his wife, Ruth, with whom the Oswalds had been close associates while in Dallas. He also indicated that his sources had told him that Clay Shaw and "Clay Bertrand" were indeed the same man. In perhaps his most bizarre claim, Schiller advised the FBI that his study of the homosexual world had led him to learn that each city's gay community had a code word to let others know when a gay member was in trouble; in New Orleans the code was "Clay Bertrand." There is no indication that the FBI gave any credence to those statements. Schiller was regarded as a wild card even by some of his fellow *LIFE* employees.

Wegmann also made a note to check out Tyrone Tooley, whom Shaw had known for two or three years prior to his arrest, through the psychiatrist Dr. Thomas Rafferty. Tooley was twenty-four years old, and had been charged with theft sometime before; Shaw had supposedly appeared as a character witness at his trial. Tooley was under treatment by Rafferty, and Shaw had written references for him to a bank in Brooklyn, New York, in the summer of 1966.[1946]

Clearly, Wegmann was venturing into some new territory with Shaw. Although he had represented Shaw since the late 1940s, they had never discussed Shaw's homosexuality and private life until Shaw's arrest. Accordingly, Wegmann was taking precautions to confirm that he was getting the full story from Shaw about his past activities, including anything that could have associated him with some of the figures involved in Garrison's probe.

The preliminary hearing began on Tuesday, March 14, 1967. Shaw noted in his diary that he had made a point of not drinking before going to court. "No Smoking" signs were noticeably present in the courtroom, but they did not apply to lawyers or to the accused. Shaw's chain smoking was noted even by the media at the time, this during an age when probably as great a percentage of the American population smoked as at any time before or since. The presiding judge of the three-judge panel that heard the evidence at the preliminary hearing was Judge Benjamin Bagert, with whom Shaw had gone to high school during the 1920s.

Perry Russo soon emerged as the main witness against Shaw. Russo seemed familiar to Shaw, but he couldn't place him. When Russo described going to Shaw's residence to see him in person on February 28, however, Shaw immediately remembered the young man who had appeared on his doorstep, offering to sell Shaw insurance. Throughout Shaw's long legal ordeal, which would stretch on until June 1978, some four years after his death, Russo was the only person to testify under oath that Shaw both knew Ferrie and Oswald, and discussed assassinating Kennedy in their presence.

As the preliminary hearing unfolded, it developed that Russo had undergone both the sodium pentothal (so-called "truth serum") test, and three sessions of hypnosis, all under the supervision of the district attorney's office. Russo had come to the district attorney's office's attention on February 25, 1967, after Ferrie's death on February 22. Russo's initial story to a Baton Rouge newspaper, and to reporters from several television stations in either Baton Rouge or New Orleans, was that he had once known David Ferrie, and that he had written a letter to Garrison's office explaining that, and offering to help. In the various interviews that he did before Garrison's office contacted him, Russo indicated that he had never known Oswald, and had never known the name until the time of Kennedy's assassination. He mentioned nothing about Shaw in any of the interviews. Those omissions and contradictions with his later testimony under oath would weaken Russo's credibility considerably, beginning almost immediately after the conclusion of the preliminary hearing. The letter Russo says he wrote to the district attorney's office a day or so after Ferrie's death has never surfaced. Shaw's criminal defense team requested that it be produced during Shaw's trial two years later, in February 1969, but at the time James Alcock, the assistant district attorney who tried most of the case against Shaw, indicated to the Court that the letter could not be found, and that he had not found anyone in the office who had ever seen it.

Transcripts exist for Russo's first and third hypnosis sessions. Russo had become highly agitated during the second hypnosis session, conducted midway between Shaw's arrest and the preliminary hearing, and no transcript or memo had been made of it.[1947] Russo later told writer James Phelan that during the second session, he had broken down and come out of a trance, after rambling at length.[1948]

During Russo's testimony, it became clear that he had some psychiatric problems in his background, and it occurred to Shaw that perhaps his former tenant Dr. Harold Lief, who was then with the Department of Psychiatry at Tulane Medical School, might be useful in evaluating Russo and his testimony, and determining why he might give false testimony.[1949] Dr. Lief was supportive of Shaw, and very critical of Garrison, at the time of the case.

Early on, Shaw's attorney Irvin Dymond highlighted an important contradiction in the case. Perry Russo had testified at length about being present at the conspiracy party where Shaw, David Ferrie, and Lee Harvey Oswald had supposedly discussed killing Kennedy. Oswald and Ferrie were both dead by now, and Shaw stood accused of being part of the conspiracy. Dymond asked what part Russo was to have played in the conspiracy, to which Russo replied: no part at all. To many, it seemed odd that the conspirators to a plot to assassinate the president would allow an outsider to overhear the conversation, and just as odd that Russo seemed to be under no suspicion at all from the prosecutor's office.

Two medical doctors, Nicholas Chetta and Esmond Fatter, also were important witnesses at the preliminary hearing. Dr. Chetta was the Orleans Parish Coroner who had performed the autopsy on David Ferrie a few weeks earlier, and had supervised the sodium pentothal session on Perry Russo. Dr. Fatter had performed the three hypnosis sessions on Russo between the time of Shaw's arrest and the beginning of the preliminary hearing. Dr. James Wall and Dr. Richard Zepernick had also both been present at Russo's sodium pentothal session, but neither was ever called as a witness, and both later avoided, as best they could, any contact with Shaw's defense attorneys.

Another witness was a young African-American man named Vernon Bundy. Bundy, then being held in the Orleans Parish jail on pending charges of his own, testified on the last day of the hearing, March 17, 1967. Bundy said that in 1963, he had seen Shaw out at the lakefront at Lake Ponchartrain, on the north side of the city, where Shaw engaged in a conversation with Lee Harvey Oswald. Bundy, a convicted drug user, had come to the attention of the district attorney's office after the preliminary hearing had begun several days earlier.

One story soon emerged about why Vernon Bundy decided to cooperate with Garrison's office. While under arrest, he had been placed in a cell with two burglary suspects, Albert Terrell Franklin and Carl Taddeus Alexis, whom Bundy's testimony could have cleared and kept from going to prison some time back. The two suspects were extremely angry with Bundy, and threatened him with physical harm because Bundy had refused to alibi them. Accordingly, Bundy cooperated with Garrison's investigator on whatever story they needed to hear, in order to get away from these two men.

Frances Bryson Moore, the New Orleans representative for *House and Garden* guides, and a former reporter for the *Item*, who had written an article about Shaw's restorations of various properties several years before, wrote to him on March 17, before the decision at the preliminary hearing to indict him. Moore said that she was "outraged" at the attempt to connect him to a "spectacular crime," and that she wanted Shaw to know how she felt before the official decision whether to indict him was handed down.[1950]

Shaw did not testify at the preliminary hearing, and the defense presented no witnesses. On Friday, March 17, 1967, after all testimony had ended, the three-judge panel overseeing the hearing deliberated for a time before agreeing that Shaw should be bound over for trial. Ironically, the preliminary hearing ended on Shaw's 54th birthday. Shaw received many birthday cards in honor of the occasion; his friend, realtor Marilyn Tate, said, "Wish we could celebrate under other conditions."[1951]

The most dramatic moment of the entire hearing had come when Perry Russo, on direct examination, had been asked to step down from the stand and place his hand over the man he said he had seen and heard discussing the proposed assassination with Ferrie and Oswald. Russo walked over to Clay Shaw and placed his hand over his head, ending his direct testimony on a tense, dramatic note.

The same day the hearing ended, Shaw sold his property at 714 Toulouse Street for $18,000, in order that he could make a down payment to his attorneys to provide for his defense. He also gave power of attorney to Edward Wegmann, so that Wegmann could transact business directly in Shaw's name.[1952]

Dymond began to hear from various parties around the country offering advice on the case, especially after the preliminary hearing. He received a telegram from Sol Dann, a former attorney for Jack Ruby, who suggested questioning Russo about his involvement with narcotics, as a user, buyer, or seller.[1953] He also heard from Arthur Locke King, an 85-year-old attorney from Georgetown, South Carolina; King warned against the dangers of mob psychology with a case so public, and advised that he had, years before, represented Edward D. Bingham, who had been accused of murdering his whole family. King had dealt with adverse news coverage and mass publicity in that case, and offered to confer with Dymond on the matter.[1954]

A few days before the preliminary hearing, a story had appeared in the local newspapers indicating that a woman in Omaha, Nebraska, Sandra Moffett McMaines, had disappeared along with her husband, just before she was supposed to meet with representatives from the district attorney's office. Garrison's investigators had traveled to Omaha on March 8, 1967, to interview McMaines and her husband, Harold, who initially had agreed to go back to New Orleans with the detectives, but had changed their minds after consulting with an attorney. The investigators, Kent Simms and Charles Jonau, called Assistant District Attorney Charles Ward the next day and consulted with him about the matter.[1955] The McMaines eventually decided not to go to New Orleans, and instead crossed the border into Iowa, which had no extradition agreement with Louisiana.

At the preliminary hearing a few days later, Perry Russo testified that one of the persons present with him at the party at Ferrie's apartment on the night of the alleged conspiracy discussion was Sandra Moffett, as McMaines was known at the time. Moffett, who had been Russo's girlfriend at one time, denied that she had been with Russo at a party at Ferrie's place in 1963, saying that she had only met Ferrie in 1965. Russo would reverse his testimony at Shaw's trial in February 1969, saying that Moffett had not been present at the party, although he privately clung to the belief that she had been there.

An article that appeared in the *Omaha World-Herald* newspaper on March 24, 1967, detailed Sandra Moffett and her past relationship with Perry Russo, from Moffett's perspective. Moffett, whose real first name was Lillian, had first met Russo while walking down Bourbon Street in 1962; she had gone by the name of Sandra in New Orleans. She got pregnant, supposedly by Russo, around the beginning of 1963; she said that Russo had become angry, and had told her to "get rid of it." She went to Texas, married a man named "Frank," left him after ten days, then moved back to New Orleans and moved in with "Jimmy," a friend of Russo. She said that she did not see Russo for approximately a full year after her release from the maternity ward on September 4, 1963; the baby was born on August 30, 1963. She said that, after re-connecting with Russo, she attended parties with him over the next couple of years. She attended a party in 1965 at a large home near Lake Ponchartrain with Russo, where political issues were discussed. She recalled that Russo referred to himself as a "leader" of young boys, and that he had once attempted suicide. She said that when Russo had testified at the preliminary hearing the week before that she had been at the party where Oswald, Ferrie, and Shaw had supposedly discussed assassinating Kennedy, Russo probably had assumed she would stand by his story. She said she had met her current husband in New Orleans in 1966, when she was on "skid row," and the two of them had then moved to Omaha. Harold McMaines said that Sandra had not fled from New Orleans to avoid trouble, as some had maintained, but had intended to move anyway.[1956]

Garrison's investigator Kent Simms checked on the child born to Sandra Moffett on August 30, 1963, of whom she maintained Russo was the father. Moffett's parents, who lived in Mobile, Alabama, had adopted the child, and had used the name of Sandra Ervin as the mother, naming as the father a (presumably non-existent) James R. Ervin.[1957]

Another person whom Russo had identified as being at the conspiracy party was his good friend, Niles "Lefty" Peterson. However, Peterson, who still lived in New Orleans, firmly denied that he had ever seen Clay Shaw, or heard talk of a conspiracy to assassinate Kennedy, although he acknowledged that he could have attended a gathering at David Ferrie's residence around the same time in 1963.

Even before the preliminary hearing was over on March 17, Garrison's case against Shaw began to show some serious cracks in the foundation. The beginnings of it had to do with a reporter named James Phelan, who several years before had written a favorable article toward Jim Garrison and his efforts as district attorney to clean up certain unsavory elements in the French Quarter, primarily B-drinking and the associated scams that go along with it. When news of Shaw's arrest broke, Phelan traveled to New Orleans in an attempt to gain an interview with Garrison. Garrison, besieged by media from all corners, sent word to Phelan that he was going to Las Vegas, to get away from the furor in New Orleans, and urged Phelan to join him out there. Phelan did, and while there meeting with Garrison, more than a week before the preliminary hearing was to begin, the two discussed Garrison's theory of the case. Phelan could make little sense of Garrison's overall theory involving Ferrie, Cubans, and Shaw, so in order to persuade him, Garrison gave him the memo his assistant district attorney, Andrew Sciambra, had written up, describing his first interview with Perry Russo on February 25, 1967, in Baton Rouge. He also gave Phelan a transcript of one of the hypnosis sessions conducted on Perry Russo by Dr. Esmond Fatter.

Reading the two documents later that night, Phelan was struck by the differences in the stories told in the two documents. Most notably, in the original interview with Russo by Sciambra in Baton Rouge, Russo had not mentioned the party attended by Ferrie, Oswald, and Shaw, where the assassination of Kennedy was discussed, about which he would soon testify at length at the preliminary hearing; he also did not indicate that he knew Shaw by the last name of "Bertrand." Although in the document Russo did seem to indicate that Ferrie and Shaw knew each other, he did not say anything about Shaw and Oswald knowing each other. Under hypnosis, on the other hand, Russo had supposedly identified Shaw by the name of "Bertrand," and also had related the story of the conspiracy party, with Ferrie, Shaw, and Oswald all present.

Phelan made copies of the documents, and returned the originals to Garrison. He then waited and attended the preliminary hearing in New Orleans from March 14-17, and was "stunned" to hear Russo testify about the conspiracy meeting involving Shaw, Oswald and Ferrie, and to hear Russo identify Shaw as "Clem Bertrand."

Phelan sought a meeting with Garrison immediately after Russo testified at the preliminary hearing, even going to Garrison's home at night to meet with him. He brought to Garrison's attention the discrepancies between Russo's testimony, the details related by Russo while under hypnosis, and the memo summarizing Russo's initial meeting with Andrew Sciambra. Garrison summoned Sciambra to his home, where Sciambra and Phelan engaged in a heated argument over what Russo had said and when. Phelan pointed out that, in the memo of the original meeting in Baton Rouge, Russo was described as having said that he had seen Shaw twice—once at the Nashville Avenue Wharf in 1962, where Shaw and Russo had both attended a speech by President Kennedy, then visiting New Orleans, and once at a service station owned by David Ferrie. The essence of the memo was that Russo said that he had seen Shaw twice, described the two occasions clearly, and the memo seemed consistent within itself regarding that issue. There was no mention in the initial memo of the party where Russo said that he had heard Shaw, Ferrie, and Oswald discussing the assassination, which would have been the third instance where he had supposedly seen Shaw, according to his sworn testimony at the preliminary hearing.

Phelan challenged Garrison to allow him to question Russo about the discrepancies between his testimony and the memo of the initial meeting with Sciambra, and the meeting broke up with everyone in a bad mood, and Phelan now on unfriendly terms with Garrison's assistants, if not with Garrison himself. Phelan went on to write an article about the initial phase of the investigation for the *Saturday Evening Post*. The article touched on Russo's discrepancies, but did not go into the full detail of them. Phelan eventually would testify at Shaw's trial about his discovery of the discrepancies between Russo's initial sworn testimony, and what Russo supposedly told Sciambra in their initial meeting in Baton Rouge on February 25, 1967.

Although Russo had initially placed the sighting of Shaw at Ferrie's service station as having occurred before the assassination, he later changed that detail to where it had occurred after the assassination. He had no choice; Garrison's investigators learned that Ferrie had owned his Gulf Oil Company service station on Veterans Highway from January 9, 1964 to November 30, 1964.[1958]

New Yorker George Gaston Johnston wrote to Jeff Biddison indicating that he understood Biddison might be having some additional expenses and could use some financial help, and enclosed a check for $1,000.[1959] It is likely that Johnston was intending the check for Shaw's defense, considering that the contribution came within such close proximity to Shaw's arrest, and the major newspaper headlines surrounding it. Johnston, a native of Arkansas and a graduate of Dartmouth College, was a New York businessman who owned a company called Johnston's No-Roach, a manufacturer of pesticide products. He soon established a scholarship in his name at Lyon College in Arkansas. Biddison had worked for Johnston during the 1950s as a salesman, and the two had remained as close friends. Johnston, who was also gay, would move to Brazil in the early 1970s; in the 1980s, Johnston was murdered there by his lover.

The playwright and chef Chris Blake wrote on March 18, saying Shaw was "the kindest person to me when I returned to New Orleans" after the war. Blake said his prayers were with Shaw, and enclosed his *Charlie Ration Cookbook*, intended for armed services personnel in Vietnam, which Blake termed a "million seller" that had attracted attention to his earlier writings.[1960]

Garrison's office looked at Blake as well, thinking he might be involved in the case in some way. A memo generated by investigator Kent Simms noted that Blake might have been the last person to be seen with Dr. Mary Sherman, the orthopedic surgeon who had been murdered in 1964, and that there may be a connection between Blake and Shaw. The article indicated that Blake was the "same type" as Shaw, meaning that he was a well-known member of the gay community involved in the arts and French Quarter activity. The memo also noted that Blake, who was currently writing a book of recipes to be sent to Vietnam for use by troops there, a project sponsored by the heirs to the Tabasco hot sauce company, was sending newspaper columns about recipes to Vietnam and "giving them ridiculous titles." The information about Blake had been given to Simms by a Mrs. Vizaid, who also mentioned that another homosexual named Paul Moss might be of use to Garrison's office.[1961]

Alison Marks wrote again from Massachusetts on March 18, saying that she was "outraged" by the "nightmare abomination" that was going on. "What in God's name motivates the DA?" she asked. She signed the letter, "Your ancienne friend and admirer."[1962]

A few weeks after his arrest, Shaw began a correspondence with Mrs. Edwin S. "Frances" Anderson of Amite, Louisiana. Frances Anderson's husband was a contractor who built roads and bridges in Louisiana. Among the people he knew and used as a pilot, was Roger

Smith, who some years before had known fellow pilots David Ferrie and his friend James Lewallen. Accordingly, Frances Anderson had taken an interest in Garrison's investigation of Ferrie, Ferrie's death, and Shaw's subsequent arrest. Frances Anderson first wrote to Shaw on March 19, advising Shaw to keep his "chin up!" and saying that, "Most people don't care about guilt or innocence...they like excitement—Roman arena style." She said that she hoped Shaw was feeling better after his recent hospitalization shortly after being indicted by a grand jury, and that he was "encouraged and strengthened" for the battle ahead. She mused about "how important every choice in life is," and that "the imperatives of destiny are so strange." She urged Shaw not to be discouraged by his predicament.[1963]

During the first few months after his arrest, Shaw avoided direct phone calls from old friends, asking that they communicate either through his attorney, Edward Wegmann, or his long-time friend Jeff Biddison. A few people found an irritated Shaw when they tried to call him directly. One was John Leonard, the first Public Relations Director of the Mart back in 1948 and 1949. Another was Shaw's old friend Cecil E. Foster, who lived in Muskegon, Michigan, but spent his spring breaks in Florida. In mid-March 1967, Foster wrote, saying that he was "sorry if I upset you with my call," saying that he "just wanted to help" and "make the situation better." He closed with, "I realize your problems" were more than he could imagine.[1964]

The writer Oliver Evans wrote on March 20, 1967, from Bangkok, Thailand, where he was lecturing at Chulalongkorn University. Evans said that he was "sickened" by the judges' decision to bring Shaw to trial, and that "you must not fail to keep your courage." Evans indicated that he would be passing through New Orleans in early June, and hoped to see Shaw at that time.[1965]

Theater designer Edith Bel Geddes, who had known Shaw since his own New York days, wrote from New York City, saying that she believed in Shaw's innocence and that she was "shocked that you should have been so treated."[1966] Bel Geddes and her husband, Norman Bel Geddes, were both still active in theater circles; Norman Bel Geddes was the father of actress Barbara Bel Geddes.

The third week of March, Goldie Moore reported to Lloyd Cobb that seven membership applications for the Plimsoll Club were missing from the Mart's files. Also missing was a book used by Moore to record attendance at the Executive Committee and Board of Directors meetings. The book had Clay Shaw's name written in gold leaf letters, and Moore attributed the theft to malicious vandalism related to the events currently taking place.[1967]

Owen M. Wright II had been arrested the same night as Shaw, for allegedly interfering with a news photographer at Shaw's residence who was trying to take his photograph; Shaw later had seen Wright being booked on assault charges. On March 21, 1967, Wright was interviewed by investigator William Gurvich on behalf of Garrison's office. Wright said he was currently unemployed, but had been a pilot with Southern Airlines from June 1960 to June 1963. He acknowledged that he had been arrested in June of 1962 for soliciting homosexual acts in a public restroom, although he said he didn't know Michael Moreno, the man supposedly arrested along with him. He also admitted that he had been arrested for driving while intoxicated in Baton Rouge, Louisiana in October 1957, for drunkenness in Tucson, Arizona in August 1958, and in June of 1962 for making false statements to United States Marshals.[1968]

On March 22, Shaw's Chicago friend, Patrick O'Rourke, wrote to Jeff Biddison, saying that he had spoken to Shaw that same day and that he sounded more like himself than when he had spoken to him shortly after the arrest. O'Rourke enclosed a $350 check for the defense fund, although he indicated that he was still in between jobs. He noted that the letter contained no jokes, that he was "following your instructions explicitly."[1969] Edward Wegmann had advised all of those around Shaw to watch their telephone conversations and written correspondence in the aftermath of Shaw's arrest, to prevent something being said or written that might be misinterpreted.

An Englishman, Thomas Gunn, who had met Shaw once through his friend Don Doody, contacted him, offering 3,500 British pounds for Shaw's defense. There is no evidence Shaw ever received the money, however; of all those who knew him and thought well of him, very few individuals actually contributed to Shaw's defense.

In addition to interviewing friends and acquaintances of Shaw, Garrison's office also continued to keep tabs on Shaw's personal activities. A memo dated March 22, 1967, noted that Shaw had left the residence of Marilyn Tate that day, and had walked and wandered aimlessly through the French Quarter without stopping or speaking to anyone.[1970]

For the most part, Shaw continued to live his life as he had before his arrest, but with several important changes. First, he stopped his real estate activity with the Marilyn Tate agency, as he was absorbed in his case, and his association with her business might have impacted it negatively. Second, he had to cut back on his living expenses, because of the large legal and investigative expenses he was incurring. His attorneys went relatively easy on him with regard to their own legal fees, but investigative expenses eventually would exceed $50,000 in hard 1960s-era dollars. Accordingly, although he continued to purchase somewhat freely and eat out, he had to be much more careful with his finances than before his arrest. He also had to be much more conservative in his private life, ceasing contact with many young men in the gay community until things blew over. And he had to seek court permission to travel beyond the borders of Orleans Parish, even within Louisiana.

Virginia Johnson was interviewed by a representative from Garrison's office. Johnson had worked as Shaw's maid for eight years, from 1957 until leaving in September 1965, shortly after Hurricane Betsy hit New Orleans, and shortly before Shaw retired from the Mart. She said that she had never seen David Ferrie, Lee Harvey Oswald, or attorney Dean Andrews with Shaw. She also said that she had never seen any letters sent to "Clay Bertrand," although, curiously, she said that Shaw's friend William Formyduval, had used the word "Bertrand." Formyduval often came to town and did patio work and other types of remodeling or renovation for Shaw, staying with Shaw during his visit. She was sure she had heard the word "Bertrand" from Formyduval, but she was unable to say with certainty that he had referred to Shaw as "Bertrand." Johnson also said that she had made a black hood for Shaw to wear as part of a Mardi Gras costume, and that his friends appeared to be, as the memo describing the interview put it, "effeminate" and "gay."[1971] The use of the word "gay" was somewhat unusual at that time among the general population.

Cecil Foster wrote from Muskegon, Michigan on March 23, giving his "heartfelt sympathies" at Shaw's predicament. He said that if he could help in some small way he would do so, calling Shaw the "most sincere friend I ever had." Foster indicated that, with asthma, hospitalization and other difficulties, life had been a struggle not conducive to writing in recent years.[1972]

Foster, who included the additional difficult detail that he had not worked since the previous November, wrote again the next day, saying that he had lost fifteen pounds worrying about Shaw. He said that, "Knowing that you hold an optimistic point of view is a relief to me," and that he had "wanted to get down to see you for many years." Foster said that, "You befriended me when I was going through a terrible time," and "I treasure the memories." Foster said that his wife, Marj, was still teaching. He indicated that he could go to New Orleans on his way back from Florida to Michigan if Shaw allowed, and asked him to "never forget there is something far greater than mortal man."[1973]

Shaw received a letter from Cynthia Koenig, daughter of Mary Moore Sanford, who had worked in Le Petit Theatre in the late 1920s and 1930s. Koenig wrote thanking Shaw for his kindness and friendship to her mother, to herself, and her children, and said she believed in his "ultimate vindication."[1974]

Henri Gomez wrote Shaw from Caracas, Venezuela on March 25, addressing the letter to Shaw in care of Marilyn Tate's real estate agency, where Shaw now was discreetly receiving his mail. Gomez, who had known Shaw since he was a young man, and was a friend of Mario Bermúdez, alluded to Shaw's homosexuality as a possible cause of his arrest. He said that he would have written sooner, but was "feeling inarticulate related to the demands of the situation." He said it (Shaw's arrest) "could have happened to any of us," and "gives me much to digest." Gomez wrote that he now had self-assurance and self-confidence in how he chose to live his life, and that he had just read *The Mask of Apollo* by Mary Renault, a favorite of gay male readers. After reading the novel, Gomez said that he felt that he was writing to Plato—during Dionysius's quest in Ortygia. Gomez wrote that he was proud of himself now in every respect, and most assuredly in response to sex. He indicated that he had always admired Shaw for that pride, and said that, "I've become more like you," and that "your reserve of this quantity has allowed you to take the attacks in stride." Gomez lamented that, "our taste" was so discriminated against in the United States, although he pointed out that "in Venezuela our taste is not classified as a legal sin," and that "few countries can boast that their last three or four presidents have more often been than not been." He concluded the letter by saying that, "I, unlike Mario [Bermúdez], cannot build you statues; however, if you come to Caracas, I promise to present you in quality and quantity enough models for building a new autinopolis."[1975]

A letter on March 26 came from Stan Picher and Wally Goodman, who were on a trip to the Middle East; the letter was sent from the American Colony Hotel in Jerusalem, which was part of Jordan at that time, prior to the Six-Day War. They wrote that they hoped the "mess will pass and you can clear out of Louisiana and live where a person can live his life in peace," adding that the "whole thing is filthy and frightening." They mentioned that they were "terribly saddened" by their friend (and Shaw's) Chuck Walton's death around the time Shaw was arrested, after they had left on their trip, but they had known they would not see him again. Picher and Goodman ended by wishing Shaw "the expedient and most complete clearance possible."[1976]

Another person who had known Shaw before, and who apparently had a crush of sorts on him, was Helen Marges from Albany, New York. During the 1930s, she and her husband, immigrants from Lithuania, had lived in New York City, where he had operated a restaurant. In her first letter, she wrote, "You handsome Mr. Clay…Have a Happy Easter up here with ME." She signed the letter, "Your little Peter Pan who's waiting breathlessly, all my love to you."[1977] Marges wrote again on March 26, 1967 and, in a separate plain envelope, enclosed a greeting card on which she had written the words of a song (possibly written by her) as follows:

> "Someone is playing the song I love
> It fills and thrills me through and through
> It speaks of moonlight and stars above
> And of the night when I met you you you
> There in the moonlight we strayed
> And all the plans that we made
> That night the orchestra played
> The song I love.
> Our passion burst into flame
> You said the song was to blame
> And that's just how it became
> The song I love.
> Is our flame of love, dear?
> Just an ember
> Have you forgotten all that I remember
> Or do you wish I were near
> And do you cry for me dear?
> The way I cry when I hear
> The song I love."

At the end of the card, after the words to the song, she wrote, "You handsome Mr. Clay—with love and best wishes always—your little Peter Pan—Helen Marges."[1978]

Another old New York friend, George Freedley, wrote saying that he had "thought of you often," and remembered "with pleasure our meetings in New York just prior to your military service" in 1942. Freedley, a longtime employee of the New York Public Library and historian of theater, had met Shaw in New York theater circles. He said that the accusations were "just not in character for you," and they "must be mere political opportunism." Freedley mentioned that Edith Bel Geddes had given him Shaw's address, and noted that Bel Geddes had said that she had seen Shaw when he was last in New York City. Freedley indicated that he remembered the Audubon house that Shaw had lived in "with pleasure."[1979] Hinting at the possibility of Shaw's mail being monitored by Garrison's office, Bel Geddes, in giving Freedley the address, had written "Please do not write on library paper or envelope—it could hurt you and your pension."[1980]

William Taliaferro, who had run a maintenance service clearinghouse in New Orleans during the early 1960s, but now lived in Thousand Oaks, California and worked for a real estate agency, wrote on March 27, 1967, saying that he was "shocked beyond belief." Taliaferro said that he hoped that Shaw would "bear up and not be bitter," and that he would "sue the bastard" when it was all over. Taliaferro wrote that, "When I left my wife...you were a friend," and "you were the best customer when I had" his maintenance business, adding, "You taught me the right way to make martinis." Taliaferro said that he was remarried now and very happy, and had custody of his eight-year-old child.[1981]

Meanwhile, an informant reported to the FBI that, in Mobile, Alabama, Richard Murphy and Charles Liner had become visibly upset upon hearing the news of Shaw's arrest while visiting the Mobile Public Library.[1982] Liner, who had long been associated with the arts community in Mobile, had known Shaw for some time, and had sometimes introduced young men who were visiting New Orleans from Mobile to Shaw.

Some of those who contacted Shaw took unusual actions that have never been fully explained. Andre Shaw, who at the time of Shaw's arrest lived in El Paso, Texas, telephoned the FBI office in El Paso the night of Shaw's arrest, and told the agent on duty that if they wanted more information about Shaw, they should contact Mario Bermúdez in New Orleans. Andre Shaw, who telephoned the FBI again the following day to say that he was not related to Clay Shaw, sent a telegram to Shaw on March 30, 1967 saying simply, "Call me," and giving his telephone number.[1983] [1984] Two years later, Andre Shaw would write Shaw again, after his trial.

Many more letters and telegrams poured in, mainly during the first few weeks of March. Some of the writers kept track of daily developments in New Orleans, and occasionally followed up with lengthier letters. None of the individuals who knew, or had known, Shaw expressed anything less than complete support for him, and often used the words "indignity," "outrage," and "despicable" to describe Garrison's actions against him.

A character named Bertrand appeared in some of the tales of the Marquis de Sade and his writings, and rumors of such stories floated around New Orleans at the time, and soon worked their way into conversations about the case. A local attorney, Sherman Farnum Conrad, told the FBI that in 1961, he had been approached by local homosexuals for legal help in forming a Clay Bertrand Society. He said the name had been lifted from French literature.[1985]

A series of letters during 1967, some lengthy, and written in a somewhat rambling style and erratic voice, came from Frances Thrasher, the daughter of General Charles O. Thrasher, on whose staff Shaw had served, during World War II, from early 1944 to late 1945. The first letter Frances Thrasher sent to Shaw after his arrest was on March 29, 1967; it was mailed from Fort Riley, Kansas, where she worked as a stenographer. She reminded

Shaw of who she was—Frances Loraine Thrasher—and mentioned other members of General Thrasher's family who she said were all concerned about Shaw.[1986] Frances Thrasher apparently had been very disturbed by Shaw's arrest, and her letters convey an over-the-top concern, although she often seems distracted from Shaw's predicament. Thrasher wrote numerous letters to Shaw, but she also wrote a lengthy letter to Jim Garrison, before Shaw requested that she refrain from communicating with Garrison. The letter to Garrison was seven single-spaced typed pages, and told some of the history of her family, and specifically General Thrasher.

According to her letters, after the war General Thrasher was employed by Spiegel's of Chicago, then was made manager at the Kansas City Stone Company, and moved to Kansas City, Missouri. The store went out of business, so he became Director of Civil Defense in Kansas City, died on September 2, 1960, and was buried in Arlington National Cemetery. Shaw had visited Thrasher in Kansas City during the summer of 1956 while on a trip for the Mart; he had gone to Thrasher's home, and had met Frances during that visit. Later, Thrasher and his wife visited Shaw in New Orleans, without Frances. Frances indicated that she worked for the JAG Corps as a court reporter, and that her mother, General Thrasher's wife, had died in May of 1966 in Junction City, Kansas, and was buried at Arlington National Cemetery, along with her father. She said that Shaw's arrest had shocked her, partly because photographs of him showed that he had become an "old man, not vigorous as in 1956."

It is difficult to know how much of the information Frances Thrasher put in the letters to Shaw and Garrison was accurate. She mentioned that she had called the FBI at midnight one night, and asked them to reopen the case of the Kennedy assassination, but the agency had refused to do so. She mentioned that Perry Russo, during his preliminary hearing testimony, had testified that Oswald, at the conspiracy party which Shaw supposedly attended, had been playing with an old general's hat, and she wondered if that might have been a hat owned by her father. The FBI reviewed Russo's testimony and found nothing to indicate that Russo had made such a claim. Frances Thrasher also recalled being the stenographer at a military trial given to Lee Harvey Oswald in Japan during 1956, well before Oswald was in Japan with the Marine Corps. The FBI interviewed Thrasher's boss, who explained that since Shaw's arrest, Thrasher had been consumed with the case and its rapid and bewildering developments, and had been tremendously upset over Shaw's predicament.

Frances Thrasher apparently visited Shaw around April 19 to April 22, 1967, as she was traveling around the country. After her visit, she sent a letter to Shaw mentioning that she had noticed his chess set at his home at 1313 Dauphine Street. She commented that the game required patience, and perhaps he could use that to outwit Garrison in his prosecutorial efforts.

At one point in her correspondence, Thrasher commented that Shaw had said that initially her father had not liked him, but that Shaw had saved General Thrasher's career after he had lost his confidence due to signing a bad procurement order.[1987]

After visiting Shaw, Frances Thrasher also wrote to a Mr. Hall in Kansas City, a man who was seemingly the head of the Hallmark Card Company. She told Hall she had visited Shaw recently, that she was convinced of his innocence, and asked for help from a Charles Stevenson of the Hallmark Company. She said that she had retired as a civilian employee working as a court reporter at Fort Riley, Kansas. She maintained that she had seen Oswald on a flight to Japan from Travis Air Force Base in California in 1954, and had also seen him in the waiting room at Atsugi Marine Base in Japan in 1956, where he was tried for subversive activities, and for the murder of another Marine.[1988]

In another letter to Shaw, Frances Thrasher wrote that her "Oswald memory panel has been opened," and that she could "relate the series of events like a Technicolor movie." She noted Shaw's lack of response to her other mailings, and said that it was useless for her to drive down to New Orleans if she was not wanted there, but that she could fill the car with recording equipment, and enough clothes to last the rest of the summer, if she could be of help.[1989]

Thrasher shared in another letter that Oswald had been one of the passengers on a MATS flight to Tokyo, and that he had appeared in the courtroom at Tokyo International Airport as part of the 1503rd Air Transport Wing, after being involved in a barroom fight, that he was later court marshaled for subversive activities and murder in 1959-60 under General Edwin Walker in Augsburg, Germany; Thrasher said she used to see him around her office..[1990]

In yet another letter, Thrasher was slightly more low-key, but still with a wild edge to her statements. She mentioned that she knew a Colonel Thomas Weed, who resembled Jack Ruby, and wondered if he might have been in New Orleans during relevant times related to the assassination. She advised Shaw to "take it all stoically," and that "it will make a terrific book."[1991]

Shaw began to read the twenty-six volumes of the Warren Commission Report, and related exhibits, after his arrest. It is not known that he actually made it through the entire set of material, although he indicated to interviewer Gordon Donaldson of Canadian Broadcasting Company in October 1967 that he had been through the Warren Commission Report "in some detail."

Shaw and his attorneys speculated on Garrison's motives in charging him. Based upon his initial questioning in December 1966, Shaw thought that Garrison's investigation must have begun with the theory that Cuban exiles living in New Orleans had been unhappy with President Kennedy over the failure of the Bay of Pigs Invasion in 1961. Oswald was known to have had some association with those Cuban exiles, although Oswald's exact motives in that regard have been the subject of much debate since 1963. Shaw and his attorneys also felt there was a possibility that Garrison could be out for the sheer publicity related to the entire investigation, and that Shaw, being a well-known local personality, would be a good suspect to fuel that publicity. Because of Shaw's homosexuality, there has been much speculation over the years that Garrison had some type of prejudice against gays. However, Shaw never attributed that motive to Garrison, at least not overtly, in any of the written accounts he produced related to his situation, or in private correspondence that has surfaced, nor did he talk publicly about that possibility.

Another attempt to raise funds for the defense came about in the form of a proposal to film the trial for a public television station in New Orleans. Ben Toledano, a local attorney, represented the station, and a documentary filmmaking team of Britisher Richard Leacock and former New Orleans area native Noel Parmentel would be responsible for the filming. Richard Leacock was a friend of Shaw's New York friend Edith Bel Geddes. Shaw hoped his attorneys could work out a deal with Leacock and Parmentel, something that would allow him to preserve all of his legal safeguards, but would also help him to pay legal and investigative expenses. Apparently, Jim Garrison approved of the proposal to film the trial, as did Irvin Dymond, but the proposal ran into a roadblock with Edward Wegmann, who was coordinating and directing Shaw's defense. Wegmann wanted monetary compensation in return for agreeing to allow the filming; he saw that as the only valid reason for going along with the idea. Neither the public television station nor the documentary filmmakers had any substantial financial assets that could be expended toward the project, and by late summer the idea was essentially dead. After that point, Wegmann officially opposed any effort to film the trial.

Shaw and his attorneys were also continuing to work with local agents Peter Dassinger and Wilma Francis to market Shaw's diary for a possible book or movie sale. As of mid-April 1967, the initial word was that long-time film director Mervyn LeRoy was interested in the project. If it panned out, selling the movie rights would be an excellent way to get money quickly for the defense, helping to prevent Shaw from rapidly draining his bank account to pay for attorney fees and investigative expenses. However, the prospective film deal never came through.

Beginning in late 1966, Jim Garrison's office had worked quietly with Richard Billings, the *LIFE* magazine reporter who had been interested in the Kennedy assassination and Cuban exile activities for years; Billings had entrée to the goings-on within Garrison's investigation for at least two months prior to Shaw's arrest. When Shaw was arrested, there was a hum of activity at *LIFE*. Not only was Billings involved, but also photographer Lawrence Schiller, who later became an author of accounts of the O.J. Simpson murder trial and the Jon Benet Ramsey murder case. Among the stable of writers for *LIFE* was Holland McCombs, who had covered aspects of the Kennedy assassination in 1963 and after, but who also had covered the opening of the International Trade Mart in 1948 as a correspondent for *Fortune* magazine. McCombs knew Shaw rather well, and had corresponded with him throughout the 1950s and 1960s. McCombs also knew Charles Nutter, Richard Swenson, and numerous others involved in the international trade community in New Orleans. McCombs had traveled throughout the world, particularly in Latin America, and knew many people in many different venues.

McCombs was skeptical from the start about any involvement by Shaw in the Kennedy assassination. First, he knew Shaw somewhat well and simply did not think it was likely that Shaw had any connection to such a gruesome act. Secondly, McCombs had been active in Dallas, covering various angles related to the assassination almost from the time it happened.

Accordingly, a behind-the-scenes battle went on within *LIFE* related to whether the magazine would become more actively involved in Garrison's investigation, and how the magazine would cover the rapidly developing story. Garrison had hoped that he could reach an exclusive agreement with *LIFE* magazine, whereby he would allow the magazine a scoop on developments in the investigation, in exchange for publicity for his efforts. Billings pushed in favor of that arrangement, while McCombs fought against it. McCombs gathered detailed statements from Charles Nutter, Richard Swenson, and William McFadden Duffy in support of Shaw, and also generated his own written statement of support. All of the men acknowledged Shaw's homosexuality, and to some degree his mysterious nature, but nevertheless vouched for his character. How the internal debate at *LIFE* played out over the next year has not been totally revealed, but it is obvious that McCombs succeeded in convincing the magazine to back off, not to give Garrison undiluted favorable publicity, and over time to distance itself completely from the investigation. A year or so later, Shaw would write to McCombs, recalling the important part McCombs had played in keeping the publicity from *LIFE* to a minimum following Shaw's arrest. *LIFE* did not even cover Shaw's trial in 1969, although McCombs prompted them to do so.

There was plenty of publicity, however, from just about every other media source. *LIFE*'s sister publication, *TIME*, covered the events after they first became public, as did *Newsweek*, *The New York Times*, *The Washington Post*, the *Los Angeles Times*, the major television networks, and almost every other major national and international media outlet. The bubble that had formed after the initial announcement of Garrison's investigation, and then re-formed after Ferrie's death, re-ballooned to even new heights after Shaw's arrest.

Holland McCombs, Charles Nutter, and Richard Swenson all passed through New Orleans to visit with Shaw during the initial period after his arrest. Friends from across the U.S. also were calling Shaw, and his family in outlying areas within two hundred miles of New Orleans, trying to figure out what the arrest was all about, and how it could have happened. Various members of the Formyduval extended family in and around Whiteville, North Carolina, called, wired or wrote. Most of those people were related, either directly or by marriage, to Shaw's long-time intimate friend, William Henry Formyduval; Shaw had met and visited with them over the fifteen-year period prior to his arrest. On an odd note, the grand matriarch of the clan, Mae Hobson, told family friend Jesse Fisher that there just might be something to the charges. "Where there's smoke, there's fire," she told Fisher.[1992]

Among the individuals Shaw socialized with on a regular basis during the first few months after his arrest were Marilyn Tate, owner of the real estate agency where Shaw and Jeff Biddison worked, Jill Young, daughter of John Wray Young and Margaret Mary Young with the Shreveport Little Theater, Patricia Chandler, French-born wife of David Chandler, the former reporter for the *States-Item*, and now a stringer with *LIFE* magazine, and Claire Evangelista, a Philadelphia transplant and sculptor who had been married briefly to Edward S. Morrison, a cousin of former mayor Chep Morrison. Generally, Shaw associated with friends and neighbors in the immediate French Quarter area, as he continued to dine out frequently, and see plays performed at small theaters in the area.

Marilyn Tate, sixty-two years old in 1967, was a widow who had been in New Orleans for a number of years.[1993] She had been married three times, and had given Shaw the impression that she had always been a "rebel."[1994] Tate contributed an interesting anecdote in an interview with author James Kirkwood in May 1968. After Shaw's arrest, he began to stay at her home rather than his own, to avoid the media and the curious public. Sometime before the preliminary hearing began, Shaw, apparently afraid that gritty details of his personal life would be revealed at the hearing, told Tate that she probably would not want him to stay at her place anymore after hearing the evidence to be presented against him. Tate told Kirkwood she had immediately dismissed Shaw's suggestion, asking what could possibly sway her long-held opinion of his overall good character.

Tate helped Shaw greatly during the period from March 1 into the summer, allowing him to spend time at her place, where he could be out of the spotlight to a limited extent. Staying with Tate during the first two months after his arrest, Shaw met some of her friends from years past. Near the end of April, Liz Mattes, who had known Tate in New York State years before but had not seen her for seventeen years, stopped in New Orleans while driving from her current residence in Menlo Park, California on her way to Pensacola, Florida, where her son Peter was stationed in the Navy.

Shaw paid attorneys Irvin Dymond, Edward Wegmann, and William "Billy" Wegmann $2,500 each as a retainer for their services. Over the next few years, but particularly during the two years immediately following his arrest, this sum would be dwarfed by the amount of his assets that Shaw would need to spend on assorted investigative expenses. Garrison seemed always to be spinning new tangents; Shaw's attorneys needed to determine if there was any credibility to such items, and also to determine if any evidence developed that could be used against Shaw. In the spring of 1969, after Shaw had been acquitted, Dymond told author James Kirkwood that the $7,500 in initial retainer fees was the total of legal fees paid by Shaw to that date, whereas the amount of investigative expenses had far exceeded that amount.[1995] Dymond and Wegmann fronted most of the expenditures through their respective offices, and occasionally Dymond raised objections with Wegmann about the slowness with which Shaw provided money to meet those expenses. At the time of his arrest, Shaw had a fair amount of cash set aside in certificates of deposit that he was able to use to finance the initial phases of the defense. The attorneys, Dymond told Kirkwood, had also taken out a second mortgage on Shaw's main residence, and had an interest in a book that Shaw might write about his experiences, although that book never materialized.[1996]

Later in March, after the preliminary hearing had been completed and Shaw had been bound over for trial by the three-judge panel, he was indicted by a grand jury. Jim Garrison had taken another step in placing an official stamp of approval upon his initially single-handed action in charging Shaw. Although Garrison's office could have relied upon the initial charge ordered by Garrison to prosecute Shaw, Garrison chose to add the more official imprint of the preliminary hearing and, separately, the grand jury indictment. Some speculated that he wanted that more official approval in order to be able to withstand any future legal action by Shaw for wrongful arrest. Others speculated that the additional actions by seemingly independent bodies, such as the three-judge panel and the grand jury, gained Garrison additional publicity that effectively lasted throughout the month of March. In any case, by the end of March, Shaw had been charged for the same offense by three different methods.

Shaw, who had suffered from bad back problems since his Army days, was hospitalized for back pains shortly after the grand jury's action. His entry into the hospital added somewhat to the mystery surrounding the entire affair, and gave a public impression that perhaps the pressure was getting to him, and that there might be another development similar to Ferrie's untimely death in February. However, Shaw was released within a few days, and the furor over that mini-episode subsided.

Shaw, who to this point in his life had not been a religious person in any formal sense, began to explore Catholicism to some degree. At Margaret Mary Young's suggestion, he had met with a priest, prior to the preliminary hearing, and frankly discussed the strengths and weaknesses of his life to that point. His friend Jill Young invited him to visit a Catholic retreat, Xavier Hall, located in Pass Christian, Mississippi, on the Gulf Coast. Until 1949, it had been the Hotel Graycastle, before being taken over by the Catholic Church.[1997] After the grand jury indictment, Shaw spent the following weekend there.[1998] On March 25, during that retreat, Shaw declared in his diary that, although he had been close to conversion at other times in his life, he thought that he would now become a Catholic.[1999] The next day, Shaw attended Mass for the first time since his childhood, when he had attended Mass with Catholic friends.[2000] Shaw would take several trips to Xavier Hall during the first six months after his arrest, mingling with a group of priests, and resurrecting long-forgotten rituals, such as regular prayer, in an attempt to gain some peace of mind.

At the end of March, Garrison's office interviewed local French Quarter resident Betty Parent (sometimes spelled Betty Parrott). Parent said that New Orleans FBI agent Regis Kennedy, who had been involved in investigating the Kennedy assassination in November 1963, had told her that Clay Shaw was a former CIA agent who had worked for the agency in Italy over a five-year span.[2001] The anecdote is a good example of how information from law enforcement informants, and even well-meaning respectable citizens, contained in official-looking memos, must be analyzed for truthfulness and accuracy. Perhaps Regis Kennedy had actually told Betty Parent such a story, but there is no truth to the assertion that Shaw was a former "CIA agent," or that he had spent five years in Italy at any time of his life.

In late March, Assistant District Attorney John Volz, who essentially had been removed from major parts of the investigation, returned to duty, making an extensive examination of Shaw's files, particularly for the crucial period of September 1963, summarizing his meetings and letters in preparation for Shaw's testimony at the upcoming trial. Goldie Moore, Shaw's long-time secretary, told Volz that Shaw never traveled by plane unless it was absolutely necessary.[2002]

Approximately three weeks after Shaw's arrest, his defense attorneys retained at least two private investigative firms to interview various characters and potential witnesses involved in the case. The two firms, Southern Research and Wackenhut, used former FBI agents in the New Orleans area to conduct investigations, along with some other individuals with private investigative experience. The purpose of the investigation by the defense seemed to be two-fold: to investigate potential witnesses against Shaw and determine their story and background, and to investigate friends and acquaintances of Shaw, probably to determine if Shaw was telling the defense attorneys everything about himself that they needed to know. Accordingly, people who knew Perry Russo and Vernon Bundy were interviewed, as were members of the French Quarter gay community, including some young friends of Shaw, to nail down their precise connection with Shaw. The two main investigators were Robert Wilson and Charles Carson.

In a letter dated March 22, 1967, Edward Wegmann wrote to Charles Carson with Southern Research Company, setting out an initial list of people for the company to interview. One was Layton Martens, who had been a roommate and friend of Ferrie, and who also knew Shaw. Another was Kenneth France, who had called Wegmann, anonymously at first, then later identified himself and said that he had gone to a party attended by Russo in 1963. Wegmann also asked the investigator to check out Sandra Moffett, Niles "Lefty" Peterson, Dr. Esmond Fatter, and most of all Perry Russo himself.[2003]

In another letter dated March 27, Wegmann advised Carson to check out Todd Payne, the owner of The Steak Pit restaurant in the French Quarter, whom Wegmann referred to as a leader of homosexuals in the French Quarter. Wegmann also suggested that Carson check out Clayton R. Bertrand, a crane operator for Southern Scrap Company, for obvious reasons.[2004] Carson responded to Wegmann that he also planned to interview Eugene Davis, whom he referred to as a "homosexual informant" to the police, and others mentioned in Wegmann's letter.[2005]

Very early on, reporters such as Hugh Aynesworth, of *Newsweek* magazine, and Richard Townley, of WDSU-TV Channel 6, were conferring with the defense attorneys, running errands for them that coincided with their own investigative work, and generally cooperating fully. On March 27, Wegmann wrote to Townley, returning the notes of Townley's recent interview with Layton Martens, and asking Townley to locate an interview, or paper, by Dr. Esmond Fatter on hypnosis, which had recently been mentioned on WDSU-TV.[2006] The same day, Wegmann wrote a letter to Phillip Carter, an associate of Hugh Aynesworth, enclosing a biographical sketch of Shaw, and indicating that it had been nice recently to meet Carter and Aynesworth. Wegmann wrote that he had had some difficulty transcribing Aynesworth's recent taped phone conversation with Julian Buznedo, a former associate of David Ferrie.[2007]

Wegmann wrote again to Charles Carson on March 31, asking him to check out Sandra Anderson, who once had worked for attorney G. Wray Gill; Gill had employed Ferrie as a private investigator in 1963. Wegmann requested that Carson not share the information on Sandra Anderson with Richard Townley of WDSU-TV; Townley was separately checking on stories that Anderson claimed to have seen Shaw and Ferrie photographed together in G. Wray Gill's office. Wegmann advised Carson to check on telephone calls received by attorney Dean Andrews at the hospital during the days immediately after the Kennedy assassination, and asked Carson to get a photograph of Clayton Blackshear, who was employed by previously mentioned "homosexual leader" Todd Payne at The Steak Pit.[2008] In a letter dated April 3, 1967, Wegmann asked Carson to check on Elmer Renfroe, whom he described as a friend of Gordon Novel who had recently been questioned by Garrison's office.[2009]

Wegmann and Dymond also began to solicit the advice of various attorneys and medical doctors regarding the use of hypnosis, and drugs such as sodium pentothal. They learned that both methods could elicit false stories under certain conditions, and so gave strong consideration to using experts on such subjects at Shaw's trial. One such expert was Dr. Fredrick Redlich, Dean of the School of Medicine at Yale University.[2010] Wegmann wrote to Redlich, the plan being to have Redlich testify for the defense as an expert witness about hypnosis, and/or narcoanalysis, the use of drugs to influence witnesses or elicit testimony.[2011]

Dymond, already generally familiar with the Warren Commission Report, began to explore some of the conspiracy theory thinking on the assassination. He wrote to author Harold Weisberg, one of the main critics of the Warren Commission's conclusions, ordering a copy of Weisberg's recently released book, *Whitewash II*; Dymond already had purchased a copy of Weisberg's original *Whitewash*.[2012]

The American Civil Liberties Union (ACLU) soon became involved, to the extent of objecting to various public pronouncements by Jim Garrison; the organization believed Shaw was being tried, to a certain degree, in the media. However, because Shaw's attorneys never sought ACLU help directly, the organization had little or no direct involvement in Shaw's defense.

Edward Wegmann wrote to Shaw's friend Muriel Bultman Francis, reporting on general conditions related to Shaw's defense. Wegmann indicated that he had not had much success with raising money through a defense fund, and he related how he was using Southern Research Company to investigate the principals of the case. Wegmann reported that so far the defense had received a contribution from Shaw's friend Patrick O'Rourke of Chicago, and $10 from a Joe M. Clements. Wegmann said that he had spent three hours the previous week with Nicholas Gordon of Atlantic and Gulf Steamship Company, and with Lloyd Cobb, Shaw's former boss and still President of the Mart, but had received no monetary contributions from them, just "a lot of legal advice." Wegmann suggested that if six or eight prominent members of society in New Orleans could be pulled together, and the fund publicized somewhat, "it will take care of itself." Wegmann said that the local and national press was generally sympathetic to Shaw, but that the district attorney's office was receiving monetary contributions from the general public, in addition to those provided by the Truth and Consequences organization composed of key Garrison supporters. Wegmann suggested several names for the committee to raise money for Shaw's defense, including Lloyd Cobb, Harold Roberts of Texas Transport Terminal, Edith Stern, Mrs. Azel Cooper, Lawrence Merrigan, John Oulliber, Robert E. Elliott, Dr. Alton Ochsner, Mario Bermúdez, architect Edward Durell Stone, and Ella Brennan Martin of Brennan's restaurant. Wegmann inquired if Muriel Francis had heard anything on her inquiries for financial support sent to Tennessee Williams and Truman Capote.[2013]

Wegmann received information about the main witness against Shaw almost immediately, including an anonymous letter that indicated Perry Russo was a gay hustler who had had relations with Ferrie, and with the letter writer, for money. The letter said that Russo might be a male prostitute, and that he used to "roll drunks and queers." Wegmann also had heard that a friend of Russo, Glenn Latino, had witnessed Russo trying to jump out of a window in a suicide attempt, and that Jim Clark, another Russo friend, had said that Russo was into hypnosis and gay pornography.

Wegmann had also been clued in by Sheriff's Office employee Nina Sulzer that an inmate at the parish prison, John Cancler, could tell the investigators about the other witness against Shaw, Vernon Bundy; Sulzer said that she would arrange for defense investigators to have a confidential interview with Cancler. Others to be interviewed, according to Wegmann's directions, were Goldie Moore, Josephine "Jo" Hug, a former Mart employee who had testified recently before the grand jury, and Jean Heid of the Gallery Circle Theater, who Wegmann understood had been saying that Shaw was known as the "Queen of the homosexuals," and that he was the person who had used the name "Clay Bertrand." Wegmann also had been drawn to the article in the *Omaha World Herald* about Sandra Moffett, because of the mention about Moffett's past connection with Russo, and because of Moffett's contention that she had not met David Ferrie until 1965, almost two years after the assassination.

Another person Wegmann wanted to investigate and interview was a "Negro" male named either "Johnny" or "Frank," who had spent Saturday, February 25, 1967 at Shaw's home, keeping the defendant company. Shaw apparently had not given Wegmann much of a description, only that the young man was six feet or taller in height.[2014]

Several of the long-time Mart employees were interviewed by defense investigators. J.B. Dauenhauer indicated that he had been employed at the Mart on April 18, 1946, as assistant to Shaw, and had continued in that position until Shaw's retirement in October 1965. He said that he never heard the name "Clay Bertrand," and rarely saw Shaw socially. He said that he never heard of Ferrie or Oswald in any capacity, except in newspapers related to the various investigations into Kennedy's assassination. He indicated that Josephine Hug, formerly Lefevre, had resigned from the Mart some years back because she did not get along with Jesse Core, the public relations director who served from 1955 to 1963. Dauenhauer indicated that Lloyd Cobb had at one point decided to get rid of Core, but that Shaw had wanted to keep him on. He said that Shaw's main friends were Jeff Biddison, Marilyn Tate, Ruth Sullivan, a former *States-Item* reporter now living in Dallas, Texas, and Muriel Bultman Francis, now Bogner.

Goldie Moore also was interviewed. She indicated that she had been employed by Shaw in February 1946, and also had worked for him until his retirement. She said that prior to the departure of Mary [Catanese] Craft, she had worked for J.B. Dauenhauer and John Leonard, but from 1950 forward, she had worked mainly for Shaw. She said she had never heard the name "Clay Bertrand." She named some of the other employees over the years as being Josephine Hug, Yvonne Menuet, Carmen Martinez, and Darlyn Mercadal. She indicated that Shaw's main friends included Jeff Biddison, Robert Morgan, Ella Brennan, and Edith Stern. Like Dauenhauer, she said she had never heard of Oswald or Ferrie, except as they related to the assassination investigations. She also gave the names of some events that Shaw had attended around the period of mid-to-late September 1963, including a French celebration for the president and members of the French Commission of the French National Assembly, a reception in honor of the anniversary of Mexican independence, and two Japanese-related receptions.

Reporter David Chandler was interviewed as well. Chandler was cooperative but wanted to be subpoenaed, because of his connection with *LIFE* magazine. Chandler had interviewed Oswald, when he had been a reporter at the *States-Item*, in the newspaper's office in August or September of 1963, after Oswald made the news of being arrested because of his scuffle with anti-Castro Cubans. Chandler said he thought the Mafia might be responsible for the assassination, mentioning that Layton Martens had had a card from Jack Wasserman, the Washington, D.C. attorney for New Orleans Mafia chieftain Carlos Marcello in his deportation hearings, in his pocket when he had been interrogated at Ferrie's home after the assassination. Chandler mentioned that Tom Bethell, a young Britisher working as a researcher in Garrison's office, had called him before accepting employment with Garrison's investigation; Chandler had given a positive recommendation on Garrison to Bethell. Chandler said that Garrison had told him in December 1966 that he was conducting the investigation, and there had been a meeting in Garrison's office with an editor from *LIFE* magazine. Garrison said he thought that Dean Andrews had lied when he said there was no such person as "Clay Bertrand," that Andrews was protecting the mysterious "client." Shaw was identified by Garrison's office because he was homosexual, spoke Spanish, and his parents lived in Hammond, Louisiana, which was somewhat near an anti-Castro Cuban training camp across Lake Ponchartrain. Garrison had explained to Chandler that Oswald really had been anti-Castro, but had posed as being pro-Castro. Chandler understood that Garrison had wanted to arrest Ferrie in January, but that his staff had talked him out of it. Chandler said he lost interest in the probe when none of the Mafia leads were pursued. He said he had no knowledge of Shaw's involvement, and did not know anything about Russo or his circle of friends.[2015]

Charles Earl Daniels, who had been arrested the previous fall for indecent exposure while driving a car that was still listed as being owned by Shaw, was interviewed by defense investigators on March 29; his lawyer, Walter Moehle of Belleville, Illinois, where Daniels was now living, was also present. Daniels, a black man, was born in 1942 in Magnolia, Mississippi, and grew up in New Orleans. He said that, in 1959, he and three friends had found Shaw's keys outside of his residence, and had brought them to him. Shaw invited them in, gave them drinks and money, and showed them his dwelling on Burgundy Street. Over the next few years, Daniels did various types of work for Shaw three to five times per week, including bartending at parties and painting at some of Shaw's homes. Daniels remembered that William "Bill" Formyduval from North Carolina would visit frequently and stay with Shaw. Shaw acknowledged to Daniels that he was a homosexual, but Daniels said he never made advances to him. Daniels remembered several other visitors to Shaw, including Muriel Bultman Francis. Daniels remembered in particular two types of friends who visited Shaw: those who were prominent citizens around New Orleans, and those Daniels referred to as "gay artist types."

Daniels felt that he knew more about Shaw than anyone else, based upon their detailed discussions over the years. He said that Shaw drank quite a bit, on a regular basis. He said that Shaw was kindhearted, that he was not a rich man but made a good income, and that Shaw had been very generous money-wise with Daniels prior to 1961, when Daniels went into the Army for four years. After he had been released from the Army, Shaw was still friendly, but less giving on a monetary basis. Daniels recalled Shaw being a "great chess player," with no firm political agenda. However, he recalled Shaw saying that Communist China should be admitted into the United Nations, and that Japan and China would be at war with the United States and Russia one day. Shaw indicated to Daniels that some people in New Orleans thought he was a Communist, because of his liberal views, and that Shaw thought the war in Vietnam was not feasible and not in the US interest. He also thought the Bay of Pigs Invasion had been a flop, and after the assassination of President Kennedy, Shaw had commented to Daniels that Kennedy had been killed because "he happened to be the President, not because he was President Kennedy." Shaw always said that Oswald had acted alone, and Daniels said he had never known Ferrie, Oswald or any character named "Bertrand" to associate with Shaw. Daniels did, however, know Vernon Bundy, the witness against Shaw at the preliminary hearing, and termed him very "unreliable."[2016]

Various friends of Perry Russo, including Nelson Wayne Thomas, Niles "Lefty" Peterson, and Milton Fontenot, were interviewed by defense investigators in late March. Some indicated that they had been to parties with Russo, possibly at Ferrie's, but said they had never seen Shaw or Oswald. Some discussed Russo allowing friends to have sex with Sandra Moffett for five dollars per person; Lefty Peterson had supposedly "hustled" to get the customers for Russo. According to one story, seventeen males, in less than two hours, had sex with Moffett, although it was not known if she charged them all. One of Russo's friends said that he had stolen money from the Goldwater for President campaign, and had used it to buy baseball equipment. The friends acknowledged that Russo was a homosexual, or at least had committed homosexual acts.[2017]

Other friends of Perry Russo were soon interviewed, including Michael Fitzpatrick on April 4. Fitzpatrick said that, on one occasion, he had found Russo passed out with his arm cut, and he had wondered if Russo had tried to commit suicide.[2018] Glenn Latino was interviewed; he said he had heard that Russo had jumped out of a window once, in a fit of anxiety, although he had not witnessed the incident.[2019]

Adele Maquar was interviewed on March 30, 1967; she had met Russo in 1957, and had ended her association with him in 1961, when she had married. She said that sometime in 1961, she and Russo, and a friend named Al Landry, had gone to Ferrie's mother's house in Kenner, Louisiana, so that Ferrie could hypnotize Landry. Shaw had not been there, but a large man wearing a suit came by and talked to Ferrie. Russo had first told the district attorney that Maquar had been present at the conspiracy party attended by Ferrie, Shaw and Oswald, but had later switched the identity to Sandra Moffett.[2020]

A number of the interviews had to do with sexual activities of Russo, Ferrie, or even Shaw. Don Merrill Jordan, an acquaintance of Russo, confirmed to investigators how Russo used to talk his girlfriend, Sandra Moffett, into having sex with multiple men, one after the other.[2021] Eric Crouchet, interviewed on April 21, had been the underage boy with whom

Ferrie had been accused of having sexual relations in 1961; the charges were eventually dropped. Crouchet would not talk about homosexual relations with Ferrie, and said that he would take the Fifth Amendment if asked about it in court; he said that he did not know Clay Shaw. [2022]

Other aspects of interviews had to do with offbeat behavior on Russo's part. Some of the people interviewed described Russo as performing hypnosis, much the way that Russo had described to Garrison's investigators how Ferrie had done the same thing to individuals. Don Merrill Jordan told Shaw's investigator that Russo had once cut his own wrists with a razor blade. He also said that Russo had once hypnotized him, and that he had sex with Sandra Moffett while under this state of hypnosis. [2023]

In the midst of the interviews, Shaw's defense attorneys hired a man named Chandler Josey to inspect Shaw's home telephone to determine if it had been tapped. Josey reported back that there was no tap on the line. [2024] Jim Garrison also worried about wiretappers and eavesdroppers, especially anyone connected with the Federal government, such as the FBI or CIA. It was part of the culture of New Orleans; you were either part of this team, or you were part of the opposing team.

Defense investigators pursued a variety of leads in the attempt by Shaw's counsel to clear their client's name. One effort involved trying to obtain a copy of Jim Garrison's medical discharge from the Army in the early 1950s, which had floated around limited circles in New Orleans for at least two years. The issue had arisen during Garrison's 1965 re-election campaign, when his opponent, Malcolm O'Hara, had been quoted in the *Times-Picayune* about Garrison's discharge for psychiatric reasons. However, Charles Carson reported to Edward Wegmann that the *Times-Picayune* did not have a copy of Garrison's discharge papers. [2025]

Among the anti-Castro Cubans in New Orleans who were interviewed by Garrison's men were Carlos Bringuier and Carlos Quiroga. Bringuier had been involved in the street scuffle with Oswald in 1963, when Oswald was passing out pro-Castro leaflets. Bringuier told Shaw's investigators that he had first heard of Garrison's investigation into the Kennedy assassination in late 1966. David Ferrie had told him of being interviewed in mid-December, and Bringuier said Ferrie felt he was being framed so that Garrison could run for higher office. Newsman Sam DePino had also mentioned Garrison's investigation to him around the same time, Bringuier said. Bringuier had taken a lie detector test for Garrison in January, and said that he had challenged the examiner to ask him about the "ridiculousness" of the investigation. During the test, he was asked about Shaw, "Bertrand," and secret meetings with Oswald. Garrison told him that William B. Reily, who owned the Reily Coffee Company where Oswald has worked briefly in 1963, had brought Oswald to New Orleans. Bringuier added that on February 18, 1967, he had written a letter directly to J. Edgar Hoover, head of the FBI, informing him about Garrison's investigation, and the false nature of it. Bringuier said that Garrison had personally apologized for troubling him, and had said that he had found no Cuban involvement yet in the probe. Bringuier had met with Ferrie around February 20, two days before his death, and the two had discussed their concerns about Garrison's investigation. On February 21, Bringuier had contact with an investigator for Garrison's office, who had told him he had his own doubts about the truthfulness of the investigation. Bringuier said that Garrison was sharing information with *LIFE* magazine, and with reporter David Chandler. [2026]

Carlos Quiroga was questioned about Ferrie, Shaw, and the other alleged participants, in much the same manner as Bringuier. He said that Garrison had related the anti-Castro plot to him, and it was Quiroga's opinion that it was Jack Martin who was telling Garrison the various stories upon which the probe was based. [2027]

Elmer Renfroe was interviewed by defense investigators on March 31, 1967, along with a friend of his, Francis Bordelon; Bordelon told the interviewers that he "takes care" of

Renfroe. Bordelon said he did not know Shaw, Ferrie, or Russo, but acknowledged he was a homosexual. He said he had been framed on an arrest charge in 1965, and he thought that Eugene Davis, a local bar owner, fit the description of the mysterious "Clay Bertrand," in that Davis was the type of person who helped homosexuals in trouble. Bordelon said that Dean Andrews had done work for Eugene Davis, and Renfroe said that Davis had once wanted him to use Dean Andrews when he got in trouble. He said that Davis used to work at the Court of Two Sisters restaurant, and also at the Greyhound bus station.[2028] Renfroe, who had also been a former bartender at the Greyhound bus station, was interviewed a second time, where he related that Ferrie used to go to the bus station looking for "homosexual Negroes." Someone had told the investigators that Renfroe knew of a "wedding" that had taken place between Perry Russo and David Ferrie, but Renfroe denied that in the interview.

The Metropolitan Crime Commission under Aaron Kohn used confidential informants, much as the FBI did and does. As Kohn was an ex-FBI employee, the Commission used some of the FBI's techniques. Not all of the Metropolitan Crime Commission's informants told the truth, however; reports based upon their input must be compared with other available information to determine their veracity. In April 1967, not long after Shaw's arrest, confidential informant number 15 told Kohn of a meeting at the Tall Oaks Lounge on Airline Highway with Elmer Renfroe and Robert Grant, two local homosexuals. The informant said that Renfroe had told him that Ferrie and Russo had been "married" to each other some time back, in an unofficial "gay wedding" ceremony—Russo had played the "female part," and Shaw had "officiated" the wedding.[2029] Garrison's office, and the defense investigators, had heard the same rumor, but Renfroe firmly denied it, and no other evidence of such an event has surfaced.

Layton Martens told defense investigators that he had met Ferrie in 1958, when he had been a member of the Civil Air Patrol, which he described as an aviation group that matched experienced pilots with young men who wanted to learn to fly. Martens reiterated that he had severed his connection with Ferrie sometime after the Kennedy assassination, and that he had never known Shaw and Ferrie to know each other.[2030]

Shaw's friend, Don Doody, was interviewed by Shaw's investigators on April 5. Doody was an interesting figure; he had known Shaw since the 1950s, often accompanying him to events, although the two were never sexually involved.[2031] Doody had moved to San Francisco, but was back in New Orleans in 1967, after Shaw's arrest, in preparation for going to Montreal to report on the 1967 Expo, a world's fair. Doody had been in a low-level intelligence position while in the Air Force in the 1950s, had visited Cuba in 1959 after Castro's revolution, and had been in Mexico during the summer of 1963, several months before Oswald. Doody also spoke some Russian, having been trained at Syracuse University prior to entering the Air Force. Doody was a friend of Jim Dondson, the San Francisco resident who had spent the night before Kennedy's assassination with Shaw. Doody also knew Layton Martens; either Martens or Martens's mother had been treated by Dr. Thomas Rafferty, a gay psychiatrist known to Doody who had introduced Martens to Shaw. Doody did not know either Martin Palmer, Shaw's doctor, or Mary Sherman, the orthopedic surgeon who had been murdered in 1964. He thought he might have met Mario Bermúdez, but did not know Perry Russo, Dick Randolph, a friend of Dondson and Shaw, or Oswald, Ferrie, or James Lewallen. Doody said that when he had first met Shaw back in 1957, Shaw had been writing his play about Antonio de Ulloa, the first Spanish governor of Louisiana, who had been expelled by a Creole uprising in 1768; Shaw was still working on this play at the time of his arrest. Doody said that Garrison had flown Jim Dondson and his friend, Jere Franzway, to Las Vegas to interview them shortly after Shaw's arrest, as they had knowledge of Shaw's activities in San Francisco in 1963.

Doody also had been called in by the district attorney for questioning, and had talked informally to him and his assistants, but told them he really required a subpoena in order to talk. He said the district attorney had asked him about Shaw's possible CIA connection, and had hinted that he had possession of a letter Oswald had written to Shaw seeking financial help for his Fair Play for Cuba group. Doody also had been asked about Gordon Novel; he was familiar with Gordon Novel, whom he said insurance companies regarded as a "storm trooper," someone who would destroy property for a fee so that the owner could collect on insurance.[2032]

Newsman Sam DePino was interviewed on April 7. He said that in November 1966, he had begun looking into whether the Warren Commission had thoroughly covered the New Orleans aspects of the assassination. Someone had told Garrison about DePino's investigation, and Garrison had gotten in touch with him. DePino said that he knew nothing linking Shaw to the assassination except Perry Russo's testimony, and that he had interviewed David Ferrie, but that Ferrie had never mentioned Shaw or Russo to him.[2033]

Louis Fischer, the French Quarter woman who for decades had gathered around her individuals of varied background, sexual orientation, and occupation, and who had designed Mardi Gras costumes and floats, was also interviewed by Shaw's investigators. She indicated that Assistant District Attorney Andrew Sciambra had asked her about whether she had had an affair with Shaw; Sciambra said that the rumor was that she called him "Bertie," and that he called her "Sissy." Fischer, who was interviewed with her husband, Lawrence Fischer, asked Sciambra if he really thought she would admit to an affair with Shaw in the presence of her husband. [2034]

John Cancler, a career criminal who often cooperated with law enforcement, had a long history as a burglar. He told Shaw's defense investigators on April 13 that, at a time he estimated to have been late January or early February, district attorney's investigator Lynn Loisel had asked him to burglarize Shaw's residence at 1313 Dauphine Street, and plant something in the residence. Cancler said he did not know what the item was to have been, and when he learned the plan had something to do with the Kennedy assassination, he refused to proceed. [2035] Cancler would later appear on the NBC News telecast about Garrison's investigation in June telling the same story. He also would attempt to discredit Vernon Bundy, the black heroin addict who had testified against Shaw at the preliminary hearing in March. Cancler said that Bundy had made up the story while the two were in the Parish prison, and had even discussed it with him while he was inventing it. However, Cancler would eventually refuse to repeat that story before a grand jury, and his own lengthy criminal background worked to discredit him in the eyes of Garrison's supporters.

Morris Brownlee was interviewed on April 14. Brownlee said that there was no photo of him, Ferrie and Shaw together, as Sandra Anderson, who worked with Richard Townley's wife and may have once worked at attorney G. Wray Gill's office, had supposedly said. Brownlee said that he attended a party given by French Quarter personality Barbara Reid in 1966, and that Shaw might have been at the party, but told investigators nothing to incriminate Shaw. [2036] Brownlee, who had been a close friend of Ferrie, was one of the individuals who tried to work both sides of the case, communicating with both prosecution and defense. He contacted investigator Robert Wilson on May 3, saying he wanted to clear Ferrie's name. He said that he could be forced to testify against Shaw because he was vulnerable to pressure from Garrison's investigators, who had been pushing him to come up with something about Shaw. Brownlee offered to work for the defense as an investigator for $100 per week, saying that he would make false statements to the district attorney's men. The defense rejected that offer, and had little contact with Brownlee after that point. [2037]

One of the most colorful characters around the case, Gordon Novel, was interviewed on April 16 and 17. He told defense investigators that Garrison had wanted him to shoot a dart into Ferrie, and get him to confess to his involvement in the Kennedy assassination; Novel had suggested hitting Ferrie in the base of the neck with a rubber mallet, so that no mark would be left. Novel said that, presumably due to knowledge of Ferrie, he was to be the main witness in the case up until February 21, 1967, the day before Ferrie died. Novel also said that he and Dean Andrews, his attorney, had been at the New Orleans Athletic Club some years before, when Shaw had come in to talk to Novel about opening a concession at the new International Trade Mart building. Novel said that Andrews had been asleep at the time Shaw entered, did not see Shaw, and did not know him. Novel said that he had met Shaw at an Autorama racing event he had put on in 1959, and had seen him several times through the years.[2038]

Eleanor Bares was interviewed on April 19; she was represented by attorney Ed Baldwin.[2039] Ed Baldwin had been an assistant district attorney during the 1950s, and was the brother of David Baldwin, who had worked under Clay Shaw as Public Relations Director for the Mart from 1953 to 1955, and with the Louisiana Purchase Sesquicentennial celebration during 1953. Ed Baldwin would represent several individuals investigated by Jim Garrison's office during 1967. Eleanor Bares, whose name is misidentified in some documents as either "Eleanor Bauers" or "Eleanor Barros," was a school teacher who lived in an apartment behind Clay Shaw's residence at 1313 Dauphine Street. She said that she had also been interviewed by Garrison investigator Lynn Loisel on March 17. According to Baldwin, Loisel had tried to get her to say that Ferrie had come by Shaw's residence. Bares told defense investigators that the detectives had put no direct pressure on her, but that her apartment had been entered and ransacked after the interview. Bares's name later would pop up during witness Charles Spiesel's testimony at Shaw's trial in February 1969, when Shaw's attorney, Irvin Dymond, at Shaw's suggestion, would ask Spiesel if he knew "Eleanor Barros."

On April 20, television reporter Richard Townley was interviewed; he was interviewed again on June 7, while he was preparing for the upcoming NBC News television special critical of Garrison's investigation.[2040] Townley said that Sandra Anderson, the woman who worked with Townley's wife, had told him that she was in a photo between Shaw and David Ferrie. She said that she no longer had the photo, because the FBI had taken it from her in March. She indicated that Morris Brownlee, a friend of Ferrie, had taken the photo of her at the Criminal Court building some years before, when she had worked for attorney G. Wray Gill, who in 1963 had employed Ferrie as a private investigator assisting in the defense of New Orleans mobster Carlos Marcello. According to Townley, Anderson also said that she had made reservations for Ferrie and "Clay Bertrand" to go to Dallas at the time of the assassination.

Townley also related that Betty Parent (often spelled Parrott) was a French Quarter character who used to take photographs of "gay weddings"; Townley indicated that she was the "mother hen" to all homosexuals in New Orleans. He also indicated that William Martin, an attorney now working for Garrison, had once worked for the Southern Research Company, and for the International Trade Mart (Martin had actually worked for International House).[2041]

The issue of Shaw's homosexuality was becoming an issue to be dealt with by the defense, even aside from Garrison's potential accusations about it. Edward Wegmann consulted with Dr. C.D. Dwyer, a psychiatrist in Houston, Texas, who told Wegmann that, under the law, homosexuals were considered psychotic, and their testimony was considered unreliable without independent corroboration.[2042]

Although he had not been subjected directly to any harassing behavior since his arrest, Shaw's attorneys had some protective barriers installed to his residence. On March 28, the glass from approximately 120 broken liquor and wine bottles was used to line the top of the wall at his home.[2043] Shaw's neighbor, Howard Eager, immediately objected to the glass being placed on his portion of the front wall.[2044]

The attorney and author Mark Lane, who had written the bestselling book *Rush to Judgment*, which had appeared in 1966 and was one of the most popular and heavily publicized criticisms of the Warren Report, was becoming more involved in Garrison's investigation, and was prominent in the New Orleans area during the weeks and months after Shaw's arrest. Lane, who had "represented" Oswald before the Warren Commission, appeared on local radio, saying that there was no doubt that Shaw was the mysterious "Clay Bertrand" who had called Dean Andrews the day after the assassination. On the broadcast, and in interviews, Lane routinely referred to Shaw as "Clay Shaw, alias Clay Bertrand."

During the spring of 1967, former district attorney's investigator Freddie Williams assisted Irvin Dymond with information from inside the office. Although he was not directly involved in the Kennedy assassination investigation, he heard things around the office and passed them on to Dymond; Williams had been disappointed at being removed from the district attorney's investigative staff shortly before the investigation picked up steam. Williams also provided information based upon his own knowledge of events. Among other things, he said that Shaw had called the First District Police Station, on behalf of recently arrested homosexuals, in 1959 and 1960, when Williams had been a police officer there.[2045]

At the end of March 1967, Layton Martens was indicted by a local grand jury, not because he had insisted Ferrie and Shaw did not know each other, but because he had, under oath before the Grand Jury, denied knowing Gordon Novel, denied knowing the purpose of the 1961 trip to burglarize a bunker allegedly containing explosives in Houma, Louisiana, and because he said that he did not remember local anti-Cuban activist Sergio Arcacha Smith being along on the trip to burglarize the Houma bunker.[2046] It was an example of how Garrison sometimes held an alleged offense of a totally different purpose over someone in order to elicit their cooperation in testifying against Shaw. In Martens's case, the effort would ultimately fail.

In early April, William Gurvich, who in some memos referred to himself as "Special Aide" to Garrison, wrote a memo about going to Freemason Island in extreme southeastern Louisiana to explore rumors that David Ferrie had flown Shaw there on a fishing trip in July 1965. The island was remote enough that Gurvich needed a seaplane to get there. Gurvich found that the logs for the flights from that era had been destroyed when Hurricane Betsy hit the area in the fall of 1965. The owners said that Ferrie had made several trips there, but they could not identify Shaw for certain, although the seaplane pilot said that a man he flew back on one occasion could have been Shaw.[2047]

On the night of April 3, 1967, while seated between Wegmann and Dymond at a reception for news reporters at Wegmann's home, Shaw held a general press conference; the purpose was primarily for national media to learn something personal about him, since his name had never been publicly raised in connection with Kennedy's assassination prior to his arrest. Shaw was asked why he had left the Mart; he said it was time to let someone else carry forward with those duties. He said that he had declared his intention to resign more than a year before he actually left, and that he had ideas for several plays that he wanted to write. Asked about why he preferred New Orleans, he said he liked the "ambiente" there, the "culture and flavor" of the city, which he compared to San Francisco, saying that if he lived anywhere else besides New Orleans, it would be there.[2048]

Asked whether he labeled himself a liberal or conservative, Shaw said that he did not like to be labeled at all, but if he had to, he would prefer the liberal label; he said that he believed generally in the social legislation that Franklin Roosevelt, Woodrow Wilson, and Kennedy had supported. Asked about Cuba, Shaw said that he had visited the island twice during his duties with the Mart, and that initially he had liked the changes he thought would come with Castro, but that soon a "tyranny of the left" had taken over. He said that General Charles Thrasher, his boss during World War II, had been a strong influence on his postwar life, and that books he had read had also influenced him. He also said that he considered China the main threat to world peace, and indicated that he had never been involved with the Cuban refugee struggle, and implied that any connections he had with anti-Castro Cubans had been incidental.[2049]

Two new people with whom Shaw socialized somewhat regularly during the spring and summer of 1967, and continuing for the remainder of his life, were Nina and Jeff Sulzer. Nina Sulzer was an employee of the Orleans Parish Sheriff's Office, in charge of making arrangements for the housing of prisoners in the Parish jail, and assisting with seating of participants and spectators at trials and other court hearings. She had met Shaw at the time of the preliminary hearing, as a part of her duties with the sheriff's office, and the two had begun a lasting friendship. She and her husband, Jeff, had met in Puerto Vallarta, Mexico in the 1950s, when Jeff, then an artist, was attempting to attend an art institute in central Mexico. After moving to New Orleans, Jeff Sulzer had achieved a doctorate in psychology at Tulane University, and now taught there. Both feisty, interesting personalities, they warmed to Shaw quickly, as he did to them. Nina Sulzer was the great niece of soprano Emma Eames.

Shaw also socialized occasionally with David Chandler, reporter for the *States-Item*, and his wife Patricia, who lived at the Spanish Stables, Shaw's old building of apartments on Governor Nicholls Street in the French Quarter. Chandler had been a friend of Jim Garrison, and Garrison had served as the best man at his and Patricia's wedding. However, Chandler had angered Garrison in late 1966, by reporting on organized crime in New Orleans, and suggesting that there might be a coverup of sorts among law enforcement related to it. Chandler was also a stringer for *LIFE* magazine, and had been present at some of the early meetings among Garrison's office staff related to the Kennedy assassination investigation. It was Chandler who alerted *LIFE* magazine to the investigation, and put Garrison in touch with Richard Billings, the magazine reporter who had long been interested in the Kennedy assassination. Chandler had very quickly become skeptical of Garrison's investigation into the assassination.

Shaw's longtime friend, Don Doody, had come into contact with Layton Martens, who was at the center of his own storm following his indictment. Doody was concerned about Martens freely giving interviews to reporters, and about his personality in general, fearing that he might glibly say something that might get Shaw into serious trouble. Shaw requested that Doody puts his thoughts into writing and send them to Edward Wegmann. Doody's letter to Wegmann detailed his recent discussions with Martens, and expressed his concerns about Martens's lack of discretion and his seeming intoxication with the media attention surrounding his involvement in the case; Wegmann acknowledged Doody's letter, indicating he would monitor the situation.[2050]

Meanwhile, the idea of filming the progress of the case was still alive. On April 4, 1967, Noel E. Parmentel, Jr. wrote to Wegmann suggesting ground rules for the proposed film documentary that he and Richard Leacock would make concerning the case, and the trial. Parmentel suggested allowing a camera and sound into everything dealing with the case from that point forward; the producers would then turn over the film and tape that had been produced to the defense team until after the trial had taken place. Parmentel said that, "Two hulking specimens such as us" eventually "become part of the wallpaper;" he said the camera was practically silent, the recording equipment was silent, and there would be no lights or tripods. Parmentel thought it important to show Shaw's reactions to various information and developments. He said that he was also presenting the idea to the prosecution, and noted that he and Leacock had already done a documentary about the Ku Klux Klan. Parmentel, a personal friend of Garrison, and Leacock were staying at the Ponchartrain Hotel at the time.[2051]

In early April, Shaw began to venture out to see some plays with his friends Jill Young, Claire Evangelista, and others. On April 5, he went to see *Rivals*, where he was greeted with warm support from individuals he encountered at the play, along with much curiosity about his situation.

One of the oddest portions of the evidence which was eventually presented at trial against Clay Shaw first started to take form in early 1967. At trial in February 1969, various witnesses were presented from the area around Clinton and Jackson, Louisiana, two towns that are approximately one hundred miles northwest of New Orleans. An odd mixture of individuals, some African-American and some white, collectively testified that Lee Harvey Oswald had appeared in the area in the summer of 1963, seeking a job at a nearby mental hospital, and that a short time later, a long black limousine carrying Shaw, David Ferrie, and Oswald had appeared during a voter registration drive sponsored by the Congress of Racial Equality (CORE). It has never been fully explained how the story originated, or how Jim Garrison's office became aware of it, but apparently there had been a rumor around Clinton, Louisiana, which had begun sometime after the assassination, to the effect that Oswald had been in the town, perhaps even seeking a job somewhere. According to the FBI, no one had ever reported the observation, and it lay dormant until Garrison's office began checking on it in the spring of 1967.

One of the earliest records of a possible investigation by Garrison's office of incidents related to Oswald's activities in Louisiana, but well outside of the New Orleans area, is a memo dated April 6, 1967, from investigator Frank Meloche to Garrison, which includes a transcript of a telephone conversation with Lieutenant Francis Fruge with the Louisiana State Police. In the conversation, Meloche asked Fruge to investigate Oswald's possible activities in Lafayette, Louisiana, and some stories related to some "degenerates" at a school there. Fruge said that Oswald supposedly had stayed at a Holiday Inn, where he had gotten into a fight with a homosexual, and had left the motel owing money. It was noted in the conversation that Layton Martens, who attended college in Lafayette, was also involved with "degenerates" there; Meloche ended by saying that Garrison wanted to press for any details related to Martens. Nothing is mentioned about Clinton or Jackson, Louisiana in that transcript.[2052]

William Wood soon joined Jim Garrison's office as an investigator, using the alias "Bill Boxley." Wood had worked for the Central Intelligence Agency during the early 1950s, before being dismissed due to problems with alcoholism. He had worked at various jobs over the years, including managing the *Houston Tribute*, a minor newspaper there. Wood somehow knew Lieutenant Francis Fruge of the Louisiana State Police, who was assisting Garrison's office in investigating witnesses in Clinton and Jackson, as well as re-investigating the Rose Cheramie episode that occurred the weekend of Kennedy's assassination (some maintained that Cheramie, a mental patient at the Jackson state mental hospital, had predicted Kennedy would be assassinated shortly before it happened). Fruge put Wood in touch with Garrison's office through investigator Frank Meloche in the spring of 1967.[2053]

While still with the CIA, William Wood had suffered a nervous breakdown in March of 1952, due at least partly to problems from alcohol use. Under sodium pentothal in the early 1950s, he had expressed extreme antagonism towards the agency. In a bizarre turn of events, Wood, some time after leaving the CIA, knowing he was going to be under anesthesia during surgery, had written to the agency, inviting them to be in the room. The CIA, while not acknowledging Wood's invitation, secretly reached agreement with the operating physician allowing Agency employees to be present during Wood's surgery, so that any comments he made while under anesthesia could be taken down. The Domestic Contact Service of the agency had requested using Wood in February 1967, years after his departure, but had dropped the idea after the FBI told the agency Wood was drinking again.[2054]

In addition to Lieutenant Fruge, Garrison's office utilized Anne Dischler, a Louisiana State Revenue Department employee, to assist in investigating, or at least locating, some of the Clinton/Jackson witnesses. Some of the expense sheets Dischler and Fruge submitted, from May 31, 1967, to October 6, 1967, indicated that the purpose of their work was for a "special investigation," or in a limited number of instances, "Re: C.S. info for trial preparation." While some accounts of the Clinton/Jackson witnesses episode have Dischler and Fruge performing the main work up to a certain point, it is clear that a number of individuals in Garrison's office worked from the beginning at locating and interviewing witnesses in the area. Virtually none of the surviving memos from Garrison's office's files were written by either Dischler or Fruge.[2055] Dischler and Fruge would make the Louisiana newspapers approximately a year after working for Garrison, when it was revealed that the two had worked on Garrison's probe while they were employed with other State departments.[2056]

An undated letter from Garrison investigator Lynn Loisel to Fruge, obviously written early in the Clinton/Jackson episode investigation, enclosed photographs of Shaw, Guy Banister, Oswald, and Ferrie. Loisel asked Fruge to determine if news media had been present at the 1963 CORE voter drive, and if so, which media. Loisel also wrote that Garrison's office had been unable to immediately determine the license number of any Cadillac owned by the International Trade Mart.[2057]

Another memo, undated but obviously around the same time period, written by an unknown author, listed people connected with the Clinton voter registration episode, and mentioned that one of the city councilmen in Clinton was married to Clay Shaw's cousin. It also mentioned that a Dr. Frank Silva worked at the hospital in Jackson, Louisiana, and that, in 1963, Oswald supposedly had told one of the future witnesses at Shaw's trial, Henry Earl Palmer, the registrar of voters in Clinton, that he was living with a doctor at the hospital. The memo mentioned various CORE activities related to voter registration of African Americans, and indicated that John Manchester, the town marshal there who would also be a witness at Shaw's trial, might be able to identify Shaw if he saw him in person. The memo concluded by saying that the information contained within had been given to Lieutenant Francis Fruge and Anne Dischler.[2058]

William Wegmann, Edward's brother and one of Shaw's four attorneys, wrote to his brother and Dymond regarding a recent meeting he had had with Lou Gurvich, brother of William Gurvich, who was an investigator inside Garrison's investigation. Lou Gurvich had told Wegmann that Perry Russo apparently believed everything to which he had testified during the preliminary hearing, and that the district attorney's staff, not William Gurvich, actually had made the arrest of Shaw (William Gurvich had read an announcement of Shaw's arrest to reporters the evening of the arrest.). Lou Gurvich told Wegmann that there seemed to be two investigations going on—one dealing with the anti-Castro Cuban element (William Gurvich had mainly been involved in that aspect), and another related to Clay Shaw.[2059]

Meanwhile, the new Mart tower was nearing its grand opening. At an Executive Committee meeting of the Mart on April 13, Lloyd Cobb announced that the building was now 95% rented, and would be at 100% by summer. He said it was currently 85-95% occupied, and that many tourists had been coming in, wanting to go to the top of the building, even though there had been virtually no publicity yet about the building's informal opening.[2060]

By this time, rumors were in the air about arrests that Garrison's office might make of prominent individuals. Edward Wegmann wrote to Mario Bermúdez, who was staying in Bogota, Colombia at the time, and discussed Garrison's recent actions and the theories he was propounding. Wegmann warned Bermúdez that he might be arrested immediately upon his return to New Orleans. Wegmann advised him to be careful about what he said and with whom he talked, and asked him to contact Wegmann upon his return.[2061]

Wegmann also wrote Robert Wilson, the investigator with Southern Research Company, advising him of the need to interview Miguel Torres, whom Wegmann said could be sprung on the defense as "another Russo." The defense had gotten word that Torres, an inmate in the state penitentiary in Angola, Louisiana, was being pressured by Garrison's office to connect Shaw with either Ferrie or Oswald. Additionally, Wegmann told Wilson that Shaw had said that Mario Bermúdez had once brought anti-Castro Cuban activist Sergio Arcacha Smith into the Mart, when Shaw still managed it, and had asked Shaw to provide Arcacha Smith with an office free of charge for a period of time; at the time, Arcacha Smith was looking for jobs for newly arrived Cuban refugees in the New Orleans area. Wegmann suggested that Wilson check with Alicia Will, one of Bermúdez's former secretaries, who might know more about the connection.[2062] Clearly, the defense was checking Shaw's story independently of what he told them, to ensure there were no surprises in the case down the road.

Irvin Dymond's assistant, William Crull, III, had been sent to Orleans Parish Prison to interview inmate Vernon Bundy, who had testified at the preliminary hearing that he had seen Shaw meeting Oswald near the seawall on Lake Ponchartrain during 1963. Crull had uncovered three other inmates, Carl Alexis, Albert Franklin, and Edward Mitchell, all of whom said that Bundy had told them he would get favored treatment for testifying against Shaw.[2063]

An interesting legal issue arose early on with regard to Shaw's case; he was being accused of conspiring in Louisiana with Oswald and Ferrie to carry out a crime, the assassination of President Kennedy, which occurred in Texas. Robert L. "Buck" Kleinpeter, a prominent attorney in Baton Rouge, wrote to Dymond, advising that the Louisiana conspiracy statute might not cover a crime committed in Texas.[2064]

By mid-April, a rumor had developed around New Orleans that Shaw's 1948 full-length play, *Memorial*, was a story about a returning soldier assassinating a president. As a result of the evolving rumor, Shaw's attorneys asked him to track down the play, a copy of which Shaw had not even retained. He eventually was able to locate someone in local theater circles who had kept a copy, and the rumor soon died away.

Shaw heard from Nina Brown in Tucson, Arizona; she was one of the daughters of Elena Lyons. Shaw replied that her mother and two sisters had been "a Godsend," that they had visited him during his recent stay in the hospital with gifts, including a painting by Nonie, and a bottle of bourbon. In closing, Shaw used a line that he often used in letters he wrote during that period of time, which was that one day he would tell her "the whole story of what lies behind" his arrest. He closed by saying that he was glad to have Irvin Dymond, who knew the Lyons family well, in his corner.[2065]

Jim Garrison's investigators were still busy as well. They interviewed Eve Springer, attorney Dean Andrews's secretary during 1963, including at the time of the Kennedy assassination. She indicated that Andrews had been in the hospital approximately three to four weeks around the time of the assassination, and was out of the office for a week following the assassination. She said that Andrews had tried to get her to remember Oswald and his wife coming into the office prior to the assassination, but she could not recall them doing so. Springer said that she never heard of the name "Clay Bertrand," and that she knew Clay Shaw only from the International Trade Mart, not from Andrews's office. She said that mostly women came to see Andrews to have him represent them, not Latinos as Andrews had said. She said she did not remember a break-in at Dean Andrews's office while she was working there (Andrews had said that might account for missing files), and that she never heard of David Ferrie prior to him appearing in the news in 1967. She also said she did not remember the name of "Clay" being used for a "voice on the phone," as Andrews had put it in one of his varied descriptions of the situation surrounding "Clay Bertrand." She mentioned that Sergeant Prentiss Davis had worked for Andrews in 1963 as well.[2066]

On April 9, Prentiss Davis had visited Shaw, offering his help. Having worked in Dean Andrews's office in 1963, Davis had some inside knowledge as to whether Oswald or the mysterious "Clay Bertrand" had ever been clients of Andrews. Shaw told Davis to call Edward Wegmann and coordinate with him. Shaw's attorneys soon met with Davis, who then apparently wavered in whatever story he was claiming as the truth. Edward Wegmann considered Prentiss Davis's information totally without value to the defense.[2067]

This question about whether or not Oswald had ever actually been a client of Andrews had been lingering for a while. Andrews had kept no records of it, and no one else in the office remembered Oswald. In addition to possibly solving that mystery, Shaw's attorneys had hoped that Prentiss Davis would be the one finally to identify the real "Clay Bertrand," as they were sure it was not Shaw. The entry in Shaw's diary for April 10, 1967 indicates that Prentiss Davis was unable to identify a picture of "TD,"[2068] presumably someone who fit the type of person Andrews had described—a person who helped out gays who had gotten into trouble with the law. The mysterious "TD" has never been identified, although Shaw had a friend named Tom Dawson, an architect who, in 1967, was living in California. Dawson had responded quickly with a telegram of support after Shaw's arrest, and he would later connect Shaw with writer James Leo Herlihy, who would in turn introduce Shaw to writer James Kirkwood, who would write the definitive book about Shaw's 1969 trial.

By mid-April 1967, a story had begun to circulate about how the name "Clay Bertrand" had first entered Dean Andrews's mind. By mid-summer, before the grand jury, and then later at trial in 1969, Andrews would "come clean" with the story that the name "Clay Bertrand" had been jokingly applied to a friend of his, gay bar owner Eugene Davis, some years before, when the two were attending a "fag wedding reception" at a gay bar in the French Quarter. Andrews said that a lesbian prostitute named Helen Girt, also known as "Big Joe," had referred to Davis by that name, purely as a joke. On April 12, Shaw recorded in his diary that he had heard the story of a "special wedding reception" from his friend Louis Fischer.[2069]

Shaw and his attorneys were continuing to attempt to raise funds for the defense through the sale of Shaw's story, either to a book publisher, a documentary filmmaker, or the movie industry. On April 14, 1967, local New Orleans agent Peter Dassinger, Edward Wegmann, Irvin Dymond, and Shaw talked with film director Mervyn LeRoy regarding the possible sale of movie rights.[2070] LeRoy had directed numerous movies over the years, including *I'm a Fugitive from a Chain Gang* in the 1930s, and *Mister Roberts* in the 1950s.

Shaw finally was able to answer his old World War II friend Alison Marks on April 16, 1967. "How very nice to hear from you again after all these years! I am only sorry that such a vicious and idiotic situation arose to bring us together again. I have thought of you so many times since the war and wondered how you were doing. I do hope that life has treated you kindly and well; you deserve it if anyone ever did." Turning to his own situation, Shaw added, "One day let's have a drink and I'll tell you the real story behind the story." [2071] Shaw's repeated use of that phrase in letters to friends during the first few months after his arrest could give the impression that there was an ulterior motive to Garrison's prosecution, beyond simply a misguided effort to investigate aspects of the Kennedy assassination that had originated in New Orleans. Such language dovetails with theories that there might have been other motives on Garrison's part, perhaps a personal measure of revenge for some slight that Shaw had, knowingly or unknowingly, inflicted on Garrison, or some other unknown motive buried deep with the recesses of Garrison's mind.

Ken Williams wrote from his agency in New York City. Williams, who had been to Mardi Gras several times over the years, mentioned that his sister Sylvia, her husband Robert Jackson, and he were restoring a townhouse in Old San Juan, Puerto Rico, overlooking the ocean, and invited Shaw to stay there and rest up in preparation for the ordeal that lay ahead of him.[2072]

An old friend from the Mart days, shipping executive Harold Roberts, dropped by to visit in mid-April. Roberts mentioned the rumor around New Orleans that he and several other prominent businessmen, associated with either the International Trade Mart or International House, might be indicted soon. Those included Lloyd Cobb and Dr. Alton Ochsner. Others frequently mentioned in the same rumor was William B. Reily of the Reily Coffee Company, where Oswald had worked briefly during the summer of 1963, and William Monteleone, of the Monteleone hotel family.

The defense, striking out in all directions, began to investigate the various conspiracy theorists who were flocking to New Orleans to assist Garrison, both publicly and behind the scenes. It developed that Mark Lane, who had been retained by Lee Harvey Oswald's mother to "represent" Oswald during the Warren Commission inquiry in 1964, had been in the New York legislature some years before, but had chosen not to run for re-election, possibly for mysterious reasons. In a letter to Irvin Dymond, Chauncey Guidry of Los Angeles wrote to Dymond mentioning a book called *The Truth About the Assassination*, by Charles Roberts, which Guidry said told the story of Lane, and why he had been discouraged from running for re-election.[2073] Guidry had earlier written to Dymond, mentioning that Garrison would appear on a radio show in Los Angeles hosted by Mort Sahl, the political satirist who was a friend of Mark Lane.[2074] Guidry made a tape of Garrison's appearance on the show, at Dymond's request.[2075]

Mark Lane had succeeded in getting an invitation before the Louisiana State Bar Association meeting being held in Biloxi, Mississippi. Dymond and the Wegmann brothers jointly sent a telegram to the Association protesting Lane's speech, suggesting that it violated trial judge Edward A. Haggerty, Jr.'s guidelines restricting public comment about the case, and the canons of ethics of the legal profession.[2076]

On April 16, Shaw wrote to Edith Bel Geddes in New York City. He mentioned her friend Richard Leacock, who along with Noel Parmentel was interested in filming a documentary about the case; Shaw said that legal reasons had kept the defense team from agreeing to it. He mentioned that he hoped to see Bel Geddes and their mutual friends Carl and Marion Seidenbach, soon, "and tell you the whole story of what lies behind this incredible business."[2077]

On April 18, Shaw had lunch with Edith Stern, his wealthy friend and Sears Roebuck heiress. Shaw had been advised, not long after his arrest, that Stern and their mutual friend, Muriel Bultman Francis, had met to discuss his plight. According to Stern, it had been decided at that meeting that neither would contribute directly to his financial situation, but rather would organize an informal committee to raise money on Shaw's behalf. However, the Bultman family business did make a contribution to Shaw's defense, according to court filings in Shaw's later civil suit against Jim Garrison. At the luncheon, Stern told Shaw that she would join a citizen's group organized to support Shaw, but that she would not take on Jim Garrison directly by herself. In his diary, Shaw remarked about Stern's "healthy fear" of Garrison, even with her wealth and power.[2078]

As part of his efforts to generate financial support, Shaw also had decided to approach Lloyd Cobb directly for contributions to his defense. He expected Cobb to decline such support, but Shaw was determined to make Cobb say "no" directly to him. Cobb would provide no financial support, but ultimately testified at the trial on Shaw's behalf, regarding Shaw's activities during a crucial block of time.

The same day, Shaw hired Dottie D'Amico, a sister of Marge Odair, to do part-time secretarial work, including typing his fragmentary notes from March 1 through mid-April, and typing his thoughts from dictation from mid-April forward. D'Amico was engaged to work twelve hours per week: three hours each night on Tuesday, Wednesday and Friday nights, and three additional hours on Saturday. Beryl Donnath, Mario Bermúdez's secretary, had helped to type some of the recordings Shaw had made, prior to his hiring D'Amico.

In a memo dated April 18, Irvin Dymond, relying on information from Freddie Williams, made a note to ask Shaw if he had ever been arrested on a morals charge between 1950 and 1953, under the name of either Clem or Claude Bertrand. Williams also reported to Dymond that Dave Bartran, one of the people under consideration by the defense attorneys as possibly being the mysterious "Clay Bertrand," was also known as "Clay Bartrand." Bartran, who had been killed in an automobile accident a year or so before, had been a Major in the United States Army, and had then worked for a Texas company.[2079]

Richard Swenson, who had been Public Relations Director for the Port of New Orleans in the late 1940s and early 1950s, and who had worked closely with Shaw in the international trade arena, wrote in mid-April, saying that he and his wife, Gwen, would be in town the following Saturday; he asked Shaw to join them for dinner at Antoine's restaurant with Charles and Eleanor Nutter.[2080]

An undated letter in Spanish, but translated into English through Mario Bermúdez's office, began with "Querido Clay" and opened with, "Would like to say many things but words hurt me." The letter, probably from Mario Bermúdez, said that he had "talked with Jose Nieto at Turkish Baths at Hotel Tequendama [in Bogota, Colombia] who believed that a book with your name could be a great success." The letter writer indicated that, "Jose would like to write the Spanish version and would like to hear from you with your emotional impressions."[2081]

Marty Cocita, the cab driver who had befriended Shaw after his arrest, and who regularly transported him to various places, failed to show up on the night of April 19, 1967. Shaw called Cocita's wife, who told him that Cocita had told her he had gone to transport Shaw. Shaw worried that a recent disagreement about the civil rights movement, then at its peak of volatility in Louisiana and the country, with Shaw taking a favorable position and Cocita an opposing one, might have affected their relationship. However, Shaw saw Marty Cocita within a week of their discussion of the issue, and broached the issue directly with Cocita. Cocita indicated that he did not have any hard feelings about the discussion, and respected Shaw's position, and the issue was closed from that point forward.

An analysis of checks written by Shaw during this period show that many of his expenditures were for typing services, mostly related to his journal, laundry, purchases of cigarettes and alcoholic beverages, meals at restaurants, maid services, and taxi fares. Marty Cocita did not normally charge Shaw for individual trips around town. Instead, Shaw wrote him checks for lump sum amounts, based upon whatever understanding they had reached; the checks to Cocita were for $50 or $100, or sometimes more, at irregular intervals.[2082]

Shaw retained his regular maid, Willie Mae Guidry, an African-American woman, throughout the remainder of his life, until he became extremely ill toward the end. A review of expenditures shows regular payments to Guidry of $25 to $35 on each occasion.[2083]

Kenneth France, an entertainer who also went by the name Joe Kenny, had contacted Edward Wegmann, anonymously, by telephone, shortly after Shaw's arrest. In-mid April, France told Irvin Dymond that he had come to New Orleans during mid-September 1963 with a friend of his named Philip Vernon Holt. The two had met someone else, and had then gone on to a gay party at Louisiana Avenue Parkway, possibly at Ferrie's residence. France said that Russo was at the party, as was Ferrie's roommate, whom he described as "a good looking blonde" male.[2084]

Philip Vernon Holt, interviewed by defense investigators on May 2 in Atlanta, told of going to the party in New Orleans, and said another friend named Joe Smallwood may have attended as well. Holt said that France's mother and brother lived in New Orleans, and that France palled around with someone named William Price Wynn of Atlanta.[2085] Holt was interviewed again by defense investigators in Atlanta on May 20; he said that NBC News correspondent Frank Grimsley had heard of the story, and had contacted him requesting his help on the upcoming NBC program dealing with Garrison's investigation, which would air in mid-June.[2086]

On April 17, 1967, Shaw had a buzzer and intercom system installed at the door of his home, on the instruction of Edward Wegmann.[2087] That, along with the broken glass that had been placed on top of the wall separating his residence from the street, now presumably isolated Shaw in his home from certain unwanted elements. By mid-April, he had begun to move more freely about the French Quarter, and experienced no trouble from curiosity-seekers or cranks.

Shaw's visits to Xavier Hall and association with some of the Catholic rituals, along with, possibly, the mere passage of time since his arrest, and the growing confidence that his defense was in capable hands, soon seemed to have positive effects. He spent the night at his old friend Louis Fischer's home, and wrote in his diary that at one point he had awakened, fearful, in the middle of the night, but with prayer had been able to get back to sleep.

In one of the most curious entries of Shaw's diary, he discussed a mid-April crisis of sorts, which made him inclined to discuss his general problems of temptation with Father Sheridan, the priest who had secretly met with him the previous month, just prior to the preliminary hearing. Shaw indicated that, after his arrest, and as a result of it, he had resolved "to change my life completely and to let die certain aspects of my personality which should have been disposed of years ago." However, he indicated that on this day, April 17, 1967, "for the first time, the trap door lifted slightly, and I was troubled with memories, reflections, and desires—vivid, intense, and disturbing." Although the meaning of that passage has never been made clear, it is quite possible that Shaw was discussing his past involvement in sadism and masochism role-playing. Shaw went on to say that he recalled a passage in *Religion and Personality*, by Adrian Van Kaam, which discussed how, when one part of a person's personality dies, there was a period of mourning for it, and sometimes also a period of regression back to it. Shaw vowed to himself that that regression would not happen, and he wrote that he said the Lord's Prayer over and over, concentrating on "Thy will be done." His sense of humor never too far away even in those trying times, Shaw added that later, when his lawyers were done with him, he would concentrate on the passage from the Lord's Prayer of "Give us this day our daily bread." He closed the entry by indicating that, by afternoon, the temptation had disappeared.

On April 19, 1967, Shaw received a $500 commission from the Marilyn Tate Agency for the sale of a property owned by Virginia Kirk; Kirk was the sister of Artelle Trelford, who had purchased the 505 Dauphine Street residence from Shaw during the 1950s. While Shaw welcomed the proceeds, he commented that it was merely a "drop in the bucket" compared to the amount he really needed to finance his defense.[2088]

Dean Andrews, meanwhile, was out talking to people, and telling different stories in the wake of Shaw's arrest. On April 19, Andrews and reporter Richard Townley spoke together to defense investigators. Andrews said that the defense should try to see if Shaw knew Walter Jenkins, a former close aide to President Lyndon Johnson, who had been fired several years before because of a homosexual solicitation of an undercover cop in a bathroom in Washington, D.C.; rumors about Shaw and Jenkins made it into FBI memos during 1967, possibly as a result, at least partially, of Andrews's stories. Andrews said that Garrison's current theory was that Robert Kennedy had tried to assassinate Castro, and that the CIA had turned on John F. Kennedy due to a lack of support by the Kennedy brothers. Andrews mentioned Shaw's 1940s play *Memorial* as dealing with a returning soldier who assassinates the president in order to change history; Shaw's attorneys already had begun to check out the story. Andrews further stated that he understood that three prominent individuals would testify that Shaw was involved in the plot to kill Kennedy, including Lord Beaverbrook, the very prominent English publisher, and a bank vice president in New Orleans who had a Latin wife. Andrews said that "Clay Bertrand" was not Shaw, and that he was also not "Clayton Blackshear" or "Dave Bartran," two individuals whom the defense lawyers suspected might be the mysterious person. Andrews went on to say that he probably never would identify "Bertrand," as it would destroy not only him, but the person to whom he revealed the identity. He finished off the colorful interview by saying that Garrison had told him that if he was successful in prosecuting Shaw, Andrews would be made ambassador to England.[2089]

Old friends continued to drop by to visit with Shaw. On April 20, the New Orleans writer Harnett Kane called on him. While not especially close to Shaw in recent years, Kane had kept in touch. Kane, a New Orleans writer of some renown, was known for asking individuals at a gathering if they would like a copy of one of his books. If the person agreed, Kane would send them a copy of the book, along with an invoice.[2090]

At a meeting of the Executive Committee of the Mart, Lloyd Cobb brought up the fact that J.B. Dauenhauer, Carmen Martinez, and Goldie Moore had incurred legal bills related to being questioned by the district attorney's office. He proposed that the Mart should pay the fees, as it had been because of their association with the Mart that they had been questioned in the first place; the Executive Committee approved Cobb's recommendation.[2091]

Shaw's mother, Alice, wrote letters regularly during the spring of 1967, and on into 1968, directly to Jeff Biddison. Biddison effectively had been Shaw's business manager for some years, handling routine income and expense items. Shaw's mother submitted expenses to Biddison, who then paid for them out of Shaw's bank accounts. Apparently not wanting to bother Shaw directly, Alice Shaw wrote Biddison intelligent, heartfelt letters giving her input on current events, but rarely directly mentioning Shaw's predicament. She acknowledged Biddison's current friend, Jack Sawyer, and sometimes asked about Biddison's mother as well.[2092]

Letters were still arriving from friends spread far and wide. Tom Oliphant, who lived in northern California, wrote, "That damned Louisiana corruption is bad enough to read about, let alone live with."[2093]

Richard Townley reported on the recent lunch he had had with Dean Andrews, as he continued to try to learn the identity of "Clay Bertrand." Townley said that Andrews refused to name Clayton Blackshear, Clint Bolton, Eddie Morrison, or David Bartran as being the mysterious "Clay Bertrand;" all four men were under consideration by the defense attorneys as possibly being the unknown "client" of Andrews. Townley said that Andrews now maintained that "Bertrand" was married with children. [2094]

Alison Marks wrote again to Shaw, a longer letter this time. She indicated that she was still a social worker, and that she "says it without pride." She said that she was becoming a passionate gardener, and that she was going to England soon to look up old friends in Bishop's Lydeard. Marks, who had a crush on Shaw for many years, remarked that she would never fail to recognize him, and that many recent pictures of Shaw were "reassuringly attractive and vital." She said that she now "wears glasses, dammit," and that they did "dilute the personality." She commented that the case against Shaw seemed to go "from insanity to insanity," but that she had "little hope for the world anyway."[2095]

On April 22, in the midst of answering as many well-wishers as he could, Shaw wrote to James Formyduval, brother of his friend William Formyduval, and James's wife, Judy. Shaw said, "I'm sorry I've been so long in answering [your letter] but I am sure you can realize what pressure I've been operating under these past seven weeks...The charge, of course, is nonsense, as anyone who knows me realizes; but it's going to take three to six months to clear the matter up, the American judicial system being what it is...I talked to the newlyweds last week and apparently all is going well there. I do hope this is the solution...When this is all over I look forward to visiting you in Charlotte and telling you the full story behind the story..."[2096]

Shaw's comment about the newlyweds meant William Formyduval and his friend, Louise Claremont, who had either married or entered into an "arrangement" around the time of Shaw's arrest; the two had known each other for years. It is unclear exactly what led Formyduval away from Shaw and to Louise Claremont, but it is generally suspected that his drinking became so out of control that he needed a stabilizing force in his life. Unfortunately, Claremont was also an alcoholic.

On April 24, Shaw's old employer, L.S. McClaren, wrote from his law office in McComb, Mississippi, saying that the whole "mess" sounded like a "witchhunt for publicity." McClaren said that he and his friend Jess Walls had "hashed this out, and had come to the conclusion that people believe "where there's smoke there is fire." McClaren said a district attorney had the "power to persecute," and "cost a person much expense without being accountable for error." McClaren, who had been the district attorney in McComb in the 1940s and 1950s, indicated that he was "behind you all the way."[2097]

W. Robert Morgan, who had been around Shaw during the days following his arrest, wrote on April 21, 1967. Not having seen Shaw for a while, he said, "Let's get together for a drink," or "spend the weekend in the country." Morgan said that Pleasant Hill, Louisiana (population 600), the place where Morgan's wife was practicing as a doctor, would be the ideal place. He asked Shaw to call when he had a chance, and thanked Shaw for his recent letter.[2098] Morgan had pretty much disappeared from sight after the first week following Shaw's arrest. Shaw's close friends did not like him very much, and he had gone out on a limb about helping Shaw finance his defense, but had failed to come through with any funds.

James Phelan's article about Perry Russo's contradictory stories appeared in the *Saturday Evening Post* at the end of April 1967. Phelan continued to stay in touch with Russo, even after the article appeared, and during one visit he asked Russo if he would be willing to meet with Shaw in order to further verify his identification. The idea was that he would sit and talk with Shaw in order to determine if he really had ever known him or seen him in the past. Shaw was agreeable to the idea, but his lawyers were suspicious, fearing a trap by the prosecution. However, the defense team finally agreed that under carefully controlled conditions, Russo and Shaw could meet. By that time, though, Russo, perhaps fearing a backlash from the district attorney's office, declined to meet with Shaw.

Phelan also would stay in touch with Shaw's defense team. The attorneys had contacted Phelan about testifying on Shaw's behalf; Phelan had guardedly agreed to help, subject to his employer's permission. In a letter dated April 26, 1967, Edward Wegmann thanked Phelan for his cooperation.[2099] The *Saturday Evening Post* would soon cease publication, partly as a result of monetary damages awarded against it for libelous articles unrelated to the Garrison/Shaw case, and Phelan eventually would testify for the defense at Shaw's trial in February 1969.

At the time of the publication of James Phelan's article, the *States-Item* ran a story by reporters Hoke May and Ross Yockey indicating that there was "mounting evidence" of CIA involvement in Kennedy's assassination. Some have maintained that reporters May and Yockey worked too closely with Garrison's office, and blindly accepted some of the statements that came from within it, primarily from Garrison himself. There was a division of opinion among news media personnel on this matter—locally, nationwide and worldwide. Some immediately thought that Garrison's investigation was flawed, perhaps even a hoax. Others thought he was on to something, and wanted to cooperate more closely with his office than was normally accepted in media circles, in order to gain early access to breaking news. Some suspected Garrison's office, aware that Phelan's potentially damaging article was about to appear, leaked the story of CIA involvement to divert attention, as a form of damage control.

On April 26, Dean Andrews gave an interview to WDSU Radio correspondent Bill Slater. Andrews said that his first conversation with Garrison about the identity of "Clay Bertrand" had been on October 29, 1966. Andrews said he did not, at present, know where "Bertrand" was, or if he was even alive.[2100] James Phelan, now publicly a part of the debate over Garrison's case against Shaw, and Garrison's entire investigation, called into the show while Andrews was on the air.

Around this time, Shaw was reading, at a friend's recommendation, the book *Report to Greco*, a non-fiction work by Nikos Kazantzakis, author of *Zorba the Greek*, *The Last Temptation of Christ*, and many other works. Additionally, he welcomed his old friends Charles and Eleanor Nutter, and Richard and Gwen Swenson, to town. Swenson was in New Orleans to attend the Mississippi Valley World Trade Conference, of which Shaw had been Secretary for a number of years. Both Nutter and Swenson had recently assisted *LIFE* magazine writer Holland McCombs in developing background material on Shaw, which McCombs had used to caution the magazine's executives against continuing its cooperation with Jim Garrison in his investigation.

During this period, Jill Young occasionally socialized with Shaw until the late hours of the night. In his diary entry of April 24, he mentioned that it had been several days since he had seen her, and noted that he missed her presence.

Aaron Kohn, who was beginning to step up efforts to coordinate with Shaw's attorneys in efforts against Garrison, reported that on April 25, patrolman John Taylor, with the Juvenile Division of the New Orleans Police Department, had called him and related that Perry Russo was a "sexual pervert." Taylor said that Russo showed pornography to teenagers, and set them up for encounters with homosexuals, and that the police had planned to raid his residence, but had called off the raid when Russo became identified with Garrison's probe into the assassination.[2101]

A controversy of sorts had arisen over Shaw's military record. Ever since his arrest, there had been rumors about Shaw's background, and possible connections, and how they might relate to the assassination, if at all. The district attorney's office wanted to subpoena the military record, but Judge Haggarty denied the request. Because the district attorney's office made a public issue of it, however, Shaw's attorneys, with Shaw's permission, requested that it be released. In a letter written on Edward Wegmann's stationery and sent to C.C. Bass, Jr., chief attorney of the Veterans Administration regional office in New Orleans, Shaw authorized release of any information concerning him to the district attorney's office.[2102] The file was released in late April; Shaw's attorneys then released the complete file to the public. That gesture angered Garrison's office, which then sought through court action to keep the file private. However, Shaw's lawyers succeeded in releasing it to the media. The file, which is now stored at the National Archives, is the most complete file of Shaw's Army career. The official records kept by the National Personnel Records Center in St. Louis, Missouri were destroyed in an infamous fire in 1973, which similarly destroyed many other World War II military personnel records. The fire itself has, over the years, become the target of conspiracy theories among veterans who need their military records in order to claim certain benefits.

Other revelations soon began to dog Garrison's investigation, especially the prosecution of Shaw. It developed that a young man named Alvin Beauboeuf, a long-time friend of Ferrie, had been pressured by the district attorney's investigators to link Ferrie and Shaw. Beauboeuf had refused to do so, at least under oath, and Garrison's men had seemingly offered him a job with an airline, a position in which Beauboeuf was very interested, in exchange for Beauboeuf's favorable testimony. During a meeting in March with Lynn Loisel, one of Garrison's investigators, Hugh Exnocios, Beauboeuf's attorney, taped a conversation that soon became important in the playing out of the Garrison investigation over the next few months. In the transcript from the tape, it appears that Loisel offers Beauboeuf a possibility of a job in exchange for favorable testimony, but only if the testimony is the truth. When Exnocios asked what would happen if whatever Beauboeuf knew turned out to be unhelpful to the prosecution, Loisel said that he believed that Beauboeuf did know something of use to the investigation. Therefore, the offer of a bribe was somewhat murky, and the investigator was later cleared by an in-house police department investigation. However, the revelation of this episode caused much negative publicity for Garrison's office. Among others in the media, reporter Hugh Aynesworth of *Newsweek* magazine quickly got wind of the story, and reported it in a May 1967 issue. Alvin Beauboeuf would be arrested in early May 1968 for the theft of $4,000 worth of gasoline. He would never be called to testify at Shaw's trial.

On March 24, 1967, James Louviere, an African American who used to work for David Ferrie and Alvin Beauboeuf at the service station they jointly owned, had been interviewed by Garrison's men. Louviere said that he never saw Shaw at the service station.[2103] Interesting in relation to Alvin Beauboeuf's charge that Garrison's investigators had tried to bribe him was the fact that Louviere later said that Beauboeuf had promised him five to ten percent of any money he got from the district attorney's office, although Beauboeuf denied the accusation. Louviere would not testify at Shaw's trial, as he had said initially he had never seen Shaw. However, he is sometimes listed as a possible witness for Shaw's later scheduled perjury trial, which never occurred, indicating that he would be called to testify that Shaw knew Ferrie.

For a while, the defense concentrated on the alleged bribery attempt of Beauboeuf. After making the allegations of bribery against one of the district attorney's investigators, though, Beauboeuf had publicly withdrawn them. In a letter to Louis C. LaCour, United States Attorney in New Orleans, Irvin Dymond, referring to their telephone conversation that morning, said that investigators Louis Ivon and Loisel had visited Beauboeuf at his home, in the presence of his wife, had threatened him physically, and had shown him embarrassing photographs that had been taken of him some years before, which had found their way into the district attorney's files. Beauboeuf's former lawyer, Hugh Exnicios, had dropped Beauboeuf as a client because he would not press the bribery case against Garrison's investigators. Dymond told LaCour that the bribery constituted a Federal violation.[2104]

Shaw's attorneys also were in contact with the producers of the upcoming NBC News special report concerning Garrison's investigation, which would eventually air in mid-June. In a letter to Fred Freed, the producer of the show, Dymond referred to Beauboeuf's situation in some detail. According to Dymond, Beauboeuf had been pressured by the district attorney's investigators to say that Ferrie and Shaw had known each other; in early March, he had been offered help finding a job if he would give the right testimony. Beauboeuf later said that investigator Lynn Loisel had told him that he would put "hot lead up his ass" if he accused Loisel of bribery. The investigators had also let Beauboeuf know they had the aforementioned photos, and that they could be used against him, if he did not cooperate with them.[2105] The photos, at least some of which today are in the National Archives, do not show sexual activity with Ferrie, but rather are nude photos similar to modeling photos.

Reporter Richard Townley had obtained a transcript of the recording that Beauboeuf's attorney had made of investigator Lynn Loisel. On May 8, Dymond wrote to Wegmann, indicating that Townley would deliver the transcript to Wegmann the next morning.[2106] "Guard it with your life," Dymond said, also mentioning that Beauboeuf's new attorney, Burt Klein, would be in Washington the next day. Klein was in Washington meeting with officials with the NBC network, who were working to put together the news special critical of Garrison's investigation.

The broadcast, which aired on June 19, 1967, was a coordinated effort. NBC reporter Walter Sheridan, the former FBI agent, National Security Administration (NSA) employee, and investigator for Attorney General Robert Kennedy at the Department of Justice, who had interviewed Shaw shortly before his arrest, was working with local NBC affiliate reporters Richard Townley and Jim Michie to develop the contents of the program. *Saturday Evening Post* reporter James Phelan also conducted some interviews in preparation for the broadcast.

Sheridan was not on good terms with the FBI, but through his attorney, Herbert "Jack" Miller of Washintgon, D.C., he communicated with the CIA, which, like the FBI, had monitored Garrison's investigation from the beginning. In early May, Miller told Richard Landsdale, Assistant General Counsel for the CIA, that Sheridan had told him that the forthcoming special on Garrison's investigation would "bury" Garrison.[2107] Sheridan was willing to brief the CIA, through Miller, on the contents of the NBC program before it was broadcast, in order to, in effect, swap information about Garrison's probe with the CIA. The CIA considered the offer, but was uncertain whether to accept it; Miller, at the time, represented, individually, a CIA employee being sued for invasion of privacy in a matter not related to the Kennedy assassination.[2108]

Sheridan and Townley worked behind the scenes, and Jim Michie, another WDSU-TV reporter, shared developments on the air, leading up to the NBC special. Their efforts have been criticized by some over the years for undermining Garrison's investigation before it could proceed to court. In fact, it is the Sheridan-Townley combination in particular, along with the efforts of James Phelan and Hugh Aynesworth, that often gives supporters of the Garrison investigation somewhat legitimate grounds for saying that there was a media conspiracy of sorts against Garrison. Townley and Sheridan interviewed witnesses who had testified, or would testify, against Shaw. Perry Russo, in particular, was the target of Walter Sheridan's efforts. Russo would later accuse Sheridan and Townley of offering him financial rewards if he would change his testimony. Garrison's office even went so far as to tape conversations between Russo and Townley, as well as between Russo and Phelan.

In an interview in June 2007, Townley told the author that he had been "a better reporter" than Sheridan, but that Sheridan was "a better investigator." Townley was familiar with the accusations that Sheridan had attempted to bribe Russo, or at least offer him a comfortable situation of sorts, if Russo would change his testimony against Shaw. Townley indicated that, although he had no first-hand knowledge of such an offer being made, after working with Sheridan, he could believe that such a scenario might have happened.[2109]

Stories about Sheridan's and Townley's efforts to develop critical information about Garrison's probe soon made it back to the district attorney's office. John Emrold, who used to co-own Ali Baba Turkish Baths with Fred Leemans, another potential witness against Shaw, told Garrison's men that Sheridan had contacted him to find out whether Shaw had ever come into the baths, and under what circumstances, and that Sheridan had told Emrold that there would be no trial, because Russo would not be in the state to testify.[2110]

Once Garrison's investigation had been made public back in February, information came in from sources across the United States. With Ferrie's subsequent death and the arrest of Shaw, the publicity reached new heights, and new leads arrived in an even larger volume. It seemed as if anyone who had ever known Shaw or Ferrie, or claimed to have known them, contacted the district attorney's office. Many also made a connection between Shaw and Ferrie, after the issue of whether the two had known each other had reached the media. Over the course of the next year, several convicts in prisons around the country contacted Garrison's office, trying to place Shaw with Ferrie, or Shaw with Oswald, or Ferrie with Oswald, or some connection involving Dean Andrews or anti-Castro Cubans. Whatever Garrison's office seemed to need, someone was willing to supply it. Most such potential witnesses were weeded out by Garrison's staff, and almost none made it to Shaw's trial, although occasionally such unverified information was used as the basis for court filings.

Among such potential witnesses who emerged early was Clyde Johnson, a sometime preacher who had run as an arch-segregationist during the 1963 gubernatorial race; he had served prison time in Mississippi for burglary. Shaw's friend, Dr. Thomas Rafferty, a psychiatrist who had worked at the state mental institution at Mandeville, Louisiana, confidentially told Shaw of Johnson's confinement there in 1959.[2111] Johnson, also known as "Slidin' Clyde," lived north of New Orleans in the countryside, near where Shaw was born. He initially had been interviewed at the district attorney's office on March 30, by James Alcock and Lou Ivon.[2112] He indicated that he had been present at a meeting at a hotel in Baton Rouge in 1963, along with Shaw, Jack Ruby, and Oswald. Some of the district attorney's office's motions regarding the case actually incorporated Johnson's expected testimony for the trial, then set for September 1967.

Soon, however, cracks began to appear in Johnson's story. Shaw's cousin by marriage, Archie Wall, lived across the street from an Ed McMillin, south of Kentwood, Louisiana. McMillin told Wall that one night, he and Clyde Johnson had been drinking heavily, and Johnson had concocted the story that he would tell Garrison regarding seeing Ruby, Oswald and Shaw in a hotel in Baton Rouge during 1963.[2113] Ed McMillin eventually contacted Wegmann confirming the story.[2114]

However, while Johnson's erratic behavior caused him to eventually fade from the public scene, and by the fall he was no longer considered a credible witness, like other possible witnesses, he worked both sides of the fence, periodically contacting Irvin Dymond to offer information that would help the defense. Dymond told author James Kirkwood, after the trial, that Johnson would frequently call him up in the dead of night, always heavily intoxicated, offering to provide sensational information for use by the defense.[2115]

Another potential witness, Connie T. Kaye, was a singer at Pat O'Brien's bar. She had told Garrison's investigators that Oswald had come into the bar in September 1963 with two days' growth of beard on his face. Perry Russo also had described Oswald as having a short growth of beard, whereas most reports of Oswald described him as being clean-shaven all the time. Kaye never implicated Shaw or Ferrie, and was never a witness at any court proceeding.

Two more potential witnesses who had come forward against Shaw were Cedric Von Rolleston, of Emporia, Kansas, and his wife. Von Rolleston had spoken with the FBI in 1963, shortly after the assassination, with a story that did not mention either Shaw or Ferrie. Now, in 1967, he and his wife were saying that they had seen Shaw and Oswald together at the Bentley Hotel in Alexandria, a medium-sized city in north central Louisiana; their names were identified in some court filings by the prosecution. Edward Wegmann asked reporter Hugh Aynesworth to check them out, in a letter in which Wegmann also advised Aynesworth that *LIFE* magazine was no longer working with Garrison.[2116] Aynesworth reported back ten days later that he had checked out Von Rolleston, and opined that the defense attorneys should be able to "destroy him" if he appeared in court.[2117] The Von Rollestons eventually would meet with Shaw, and decide that he was not the person they had seen at the hotel. Accordingly, they never appeared as witnesses at Shaw's trial. A decade later, when the House Select Committee on Assassinations (HSCA) of the U.S. House of Representatives was re-investigating the Kennedy assassination, Von Rolleston wrote a bizarre letter to the committee wanting to get involved again, with yet another story about the assassination.

A strange series of telegrams following Shaw's arrest, and continuing throughout 1967, came from Jack Sellers (sometimes spelled Sellars) in Florence, South Carolina. Sellers, who addressed Shaw in all correspondence as "Major," Shaw's ending rank in World War II, indicated that he was following developments in the case as they occurred, and that either he or his son might show up in court in support of Shaw. The first telegram from Sellers arrived on March 2, 1967. It indicated that, "We appreciate your fight—my family and myself are behind you."[2118] Later the same day, Sellers sent a second telegram to Shaw that said, "We appreciate your fight—my wife and myself are behind you."[2119]

Another telegram from Sellers arrived on March 21, 1967, and stated simply, "Please never lose faith."[2120] Another arrived on March 24, 1967 with the words, "Happy Easter – May the joy and gladness of this day be with you through all the days that lie ahead." It was signed, "Jack Sellers and Family."[2121] On April 1, 1967, Sellers wrote, saying, "You are a winner—Everruso."[2122]

A telegram from Sellers dated April 22, 1967, shared that, "At time of your exoneration I will be there."[2123] On May 20, 1967, another telegram noted, "My family and I are still with you."[2124] Sellers wrote again on June 23, 1967, following the NBC special, with, "Dear Major—that man's face is red—as I told you before you are a winner. God Bless You, Major."[2125] He followed up the next day, June 24, with, "Dear Major—that man's face is red now—you are very innocent—my family and I are with you—A man [sic] must want to become President of the United States."[2126]

There followed a long gap, then in a telegram in mid-October 1967, at a time when Shaw's trial appeared as if it might go forward soon, Sellers indicated that, "My son is in Louisiana—will be at your trial in the event I am not there."[2127] The telegrams seem to have stopped at that point.

Shaw sent out form letters to many of the individuals who wrote him after his arrest. The volume of mail was so heavy that he did not have time to write individual letters to everyone, and he either did not know many of the individuals, or had not seen or heard from them in many years. Regarding Jack Sellers, it appears that Shaw did not know the man; Shaw's form letter to him with no street address was returned because the address was insufficient. Sellers's telegrams had only Florence, South Carolina as the address.

Perry Russo, the prosecution's star witness, was meeting quietly with skeptical reporters during March, April, and May 1967, discussing his reservations about his own testimony, and at the same time recording conversations with those reporters to give the prosecutors and their investigators information about what the reporters knew, and what the defense team was planning. Among the reporters approached in this manner were Richard Townley, Walter Sheridan, and James Phelan.

Jack Martin, who had originated the story of Ferrie knowing Oswald back in 1963, was publicly feuding with Garrison, even filing a lawsuit against him, but also was recording conversations with defense attorneys and newsmen who were critical of Garrison's investigation. Among others, Martin recorded conversations with reporter Richard Townley, Aaron Kohn, and attorney Steven Plotkin, who represented Gordon Novel.

In his diary, Shaw continued to record both serious developments and ordinary, day-to-day goings-on. On May 1, 1967, he recorded that the pattern of his life was the same—a general loneliness at night.[2128] On May 15, 1967, he noted that his friend Claire Evangelista, who had lived in New Orleans for some years after attending college there, had visited for dinner and announced her intention of moving to the New York City area. Evangelista had been married to Edward S. "Eddie" Morrison, a cousin of deceased former mayor Chep Morrison, and one of the individuals suspected by Shaw and his attorneys as possibly being the real "Clay Bertrand," if indeed such a person existed.

Aaron Kohn encountered Pershing Gervais, who had been one of Garrison's chief investigators until shortly after the Kennedy assassination probe began. Gervais told Kohn that he was only interested in "making money," and that he was not involved in Garrison's investigation in any way. He said that he was only good for "kicking down doors and roughing up people," and that, in his opinion, Oswald had been a "nut."[2129]

Another letter to Shaw from Mario Bermúdez, written on May 5, and signed only "B," asked, "What is G up to?"..."These questions keep me awake." Bermúdez went on to say, "Wish I were in your position," adding, "I am trickier a little bit than you" and "in making the others unhappy I would have some fun." He went on to say that, "If we share ideas we can figure out what's behind this cruel and unnecessary mystery." Invoking the name of Marcel Gomez, who had worked with Shaw and Bermúdez in the 1950s and early 1960s as a translator and errand boy in Bermúdez's office, Bermúdez said that he had gone to Cartagena, Colombia the week before and had "found Marcel over hot sand and feeling sorry for himself—like twenty years ago."[2130]

Lloyd Cobb was interviewed by defense investigators on May 6. He said that he had never heard the name "Clay Bertrand," and commented on aspects of the Mart's history. Cobb voiced his opinion that former Public Relations Director Jesse Core might be responsible for some of Shaw's troubles. Cobb said that Core hated the Mart, Shaw, and Cobb, and that Cobb had fired him, calling him a "square peg in a round hole," but that Shaw had kept him on. One reason Cobb had fired Core was that Core had become the campaign manager for Jim Garrison's first campaign for district attorney while still on the Mart payroll, without permission; Cobb speculated that Core may be working with Garrison as revenge against Shaw. Cobb said he knew that Garrison had been paid $25,000 for a recent article in *Quick*, a German publication, and that Garrison was violating ethical rules by receiving money for the article. Cobb further said that the Truth and Consequences organization funding Garrison was possibly illegal, and that Judge Benjamin Bagert, who had presided at the preliminary hearing and participated in the indictment of Shaw, had agreed with Cobb that no overt criminal act had been shown. Cobb ended by stating he might be able to obtain a psychiatric record on Jack Martin, Garrison's informant who had initiated the allegations against David Ferrie in 1963.[2131]

It is interesting to note that, while Lloyd Cobb believed that Jesse Core felt negatively toward Shaw, in interviews in later years Core always spoke highly of Shaw. When the author interviewed Core in 1995, he did the same, but spoke somewhat harshly of Cobb.

Letters and telegrams continued to trickle in from people Shaw had known over a period of many years. The actress Margalo Gillmore wrote from New York City on May 5, expressing "my sympathy and my faith in you."[2132]

Another letter came from Cecil E. Foster, Shaw's old friend from years before, now living in Muskegon, Michigan. The letter, written on stationery from the Regional Council of the Michigan Education Association and dated May 11, 1967, indicated that Foster had spoken with Shaw the week before. He said that he "had a few nips before we talked," and rued his "small life" about which "nothing can be done." Foster said that he had "written many pages," but "never sent them." He indicated that, "It is difficult writing around" the subject, but "will have a long talk when you come up." Foster added that, "Seeing you (my best pal) will give me a morale lift I have needed for a long time." Foster indicated that he was back into painting and decorating work, and that his wife, Marj, now wanted a swimming pool in the back of their home.[2133]

Another interesting development occurred in mid-May when Roy Jacobs, the polygraph examiner who had attempted to conduct an examination on Perry Russo on March 8, contacted Irvin Dymond about the test results. Apparently, Russo had shown deception during the early stages of the test, and Assistant District Attorney James Alcock had then ordered that the test be stopped. Jacobs was willing to cooperate with the defense, and Dymond indicated that he would defend Jacobs if Garrison tried to make trouble for him.[2134]

Around the same time, it developed that another polygraph examiner, Lieutenant Edward O'Donnell, had given a polygraph test to the other major witness at the preliminary hearing, Vernon Bundy, which O'Donnell said had indicated deception on Bundy's part.[2135] Despite the results of those tests on their only two eyewitnesses against Shaw, Garrison's office decided to present both men as credible witnesses at the preliminary hearing. As a result of their testimony, Shaw had been bound over for trial.

Interestingly, in his initial interview with Garrison's investigators, Bundy had said that he would be willing to take a polygraph test. He also had indicated that Shaw had called Oswald "Pete" during their rendezvous on the lakefront.[2136]

John Leonard, who had worked for the Mart as its first Public Relations Director from 1948 to 1949, was in town in mid-May, staying at the Monteleone hotel. He wrote Shaw, indicating that he and his wife's "affections" were with him, and that everything was going to be "coming up roses."[2137]

Shaw's attorneys became aware that a set of photographs from the late 1940s had been published in a segregationist, generally right-wing, newspaper called the *Councilor*, published several hundred miles away in Shreveport. The articles that accompanied the photograph indicated that they showed Shaw along with David Ferrie. There were several photographs; one group showed Shaw and several other men wearing white wigs, almost as if they were English barristers, and the others showed the men in business suits.

Shaw (second from right) at costume party, late 1940s. Some thought the man at far left looked like David Ferrie, because of his striking eyebrows (National Archives: photo taken by Myles DeRussy)

Indeed, one of the men in the photographs did bear a similarity to David Ferrie, although his real identity turned out to be Bob Brannon, a man who had been active in the Gallery Circle Theater in New Orleans at the time the photographs were taken. Another young man in some of the photos, who in years to come some writers would try to pass off as Lee Harvey Oswald, bore much less of a resemblance. As the photographs were taken in the late 1940s, Oswald would have been approximately ten years old at the time.

Shaw, standing at far right, at 1940s party. Some thought the man standing second from left was David Ferrie. The man seated on far right is Jeff Biddison. The man kneeling in front is the party's host, Wynn Pearce (National Archives: photo taken by Myles DeRussy)

It is unclear if all of the photographs were taken at the same get-together, but as the details of the story unfolded, it became known that at least some of them had been taken around 1948 at a party thrown by a wealthy Tulane University student named Wynn Pearce, a Texan who later became a television actor and playwright. According to Shaw's friend, Jeff Biddison, Pearce held many parties during the late 1940s and early 1950s, some with as many as 150 people in attendance. Biddison said that, as of 1967, he had not seen Pearce in at least fifteen years.

Lloyd Cobb advised the defense attorneys on May 12 that the *Councilor* newspaper had the photos. Jeff Biddison contacted Shaw's friend, Louis Fischer, who produced fourteen photos supposedly taken at the party. Several people, including Fischer and WYES-TV employee Robert Cahlman, identified Bob Brannon, who had more recently lived in Dallas, Texas, as the man resembling Ferrie. Some of the other known figures in the photographs were Fritz Paul, Wynn Pearce, Shaw, and Jeff Biddison. Another photograph had a local dentist, J. Mofield Roberts, and Archie Bland, a local interior decorator, and Shaw and Biddison as well.

Shaw told his attorneys that his recollection was that the party had been held to celebrate a performance of Tennessee Williams's play, *A Streetcar Named Desire*, which was touring in New Orleans at the time. Jeff Biddison said that the party with him and Shaw in white mop-hair wigs was an "Adventure" party, with most guests in costume. It is possible that the photos were taken at two separate parties, although the details of that are unclear.

Chauncey Guidry wrote to Irvin Dymond from California again in mid-May, reporting on *LIFE* magazine photographer Lawrence Schiller. Guidry indicated that Schiller did very good work, but could not be trusted; Guidry said that Schiller would do anything in order to obtain a photograph or a tape of someone involved in a controversial matter.[2138]

Defense investigator Robert Wilson wrote to Dymond, indicating that he would not interview three inmates—Carl Alexis, Albert Franklin, and Edward Mitchell—housed at the Louisiana State Penitentiary in Angola, Louisiana; the three were ready to say that Garrison's office had pressured them to give false testimony. NBC News personnel, with whom the defense team was eagerly cooperating, would conduct the interviews instead. Wilson asked Dymond for input on whether to interview Josephine Hug, a former employee under Shaw who had testified before the grand jury, after stating in public that Shaw and Ferrie had known each other. Wilson also reported that a Herb O'Neil of Thibodaux, Louisiana, had information on Jim Garrison being photographed with a woman in Houston, Texas; John Wilbur Beason supposedly had knowledge about the photograph as well.[2139]

A memo by FBI Agent Regis Kennedy at this time summarized his recent testimony before a grand jury; the questioning had been under Garrison's direction. Kennedy said that whenever he had been asked about the FBI investigating Clay Shaw, either as Shaw or "Bertrand," he had invoked his Federal privilege against testifying.[2140] FBI agents testifying in state court were subject to the control of the United States attorney general as to the areas and content of their testimony. Accordingly, Regis Kennedy could only answer certain questions before the grand jury, and in February 1969 at Shaw's trial, because of those directions from above. At Shaw's trial, future District Attorney Harry Connick, who would ultimately lose a race to Jim Garrison in 1969, then defeat Garrison in 1973, stood by and advised Kennedy if it was permissible to answer each question.

In the early days of the investigation, up to the point of Shaw's arrest and shortly thereafter, Garrison had discussed privately with individual reporters the possibility that Kennedy's assassination had been a homosexual-related "thrill killing." Because both Ferrie and Shaw, and many of their friends, were rumored to be homosexuals, and because attorney Dean Andrews had indicated that "Clay Bertrand" had associated with homosexuals, there was speculation among the public and in the media that there might be some connection between that inclination and Kennedy's assassination. However, by mid-May, Garrison was telling media representatives that homosexuality had no bearing on the case.

The story of Texan Lee Odom broke around mid-May. Odom had come to New Orleans in the fall of 1966, seeking to bring a "bloodless bullfight" to New Orleans. He had encountered Shaw at Pat O'Brien's club in the French Quarter, and they had exchanged addresses. Shaw had then recorded Odom's address, which was a post office box in Dallas Texas, in his address book, which was seized by authorities during the execution of the search warrant on Shaw's residence the night of his arrest. Garrison had made a public issue that the post office box number, 19106, was the same number that had appeared in Oswald's address book, although the number in Oswald's book did not reference a Lee Odom, and was not a post office box. Garrison went public with the similarity, and maintained that it signified a complicated code related to Jack Ruby's telephone number. Senator Russell Long, who had been publicly supporting Garrison's probe, soon appeared on a Sunday morning national news program and attempted to explain the code to skeptical panelists.

The issue of that coincidence, and its significance to Shaw's arrest, was to pass relatively quickly, although it was necessary for Shaw's attorneys to contact Odom and fly him to New Orleans for a court hearing. It turned out that the post office box in question had come into existence some time after Kennedy had been assassinated, and the number in Oswald's book referred to a telephone number in Russia. Odom told Edward Wegmann that he had met Shaw at Pat O'Brien's bar, and for lunch at the bar at the Roosevelt hotel, during his stay in New Orleans the previous November, and had not seen Shaw again until he returned to New Orleans for the court hearing on June 12, 1967.[2141]

Dr. Harold Lief was a medical professor at Tulane University, specializing in sexual matters. At one time, he had rented a space on Dauphine Street from Shaw. Lief was even considered by Shaw's defense attorneys for a role in analyzing Perry Russo's preliminary hearing testimony. In May 1967, Lief told Aaron Kohn that Garrison was a "paranoid schizophrenic," with an extraordinary sexual life, and a fear of latent or active homosexuality.[2142] Although some accounts have quoted Lief as possibly believing in Shaw's guilt, there is no doubt that he never took Garrison's investigation seriously, or that he always believed in Shaw's innocence.

Jim Garrison wrote directly to Irvin Dymond, Shaw's chief defense counsel, objecting to the defense lawyers making statements to the press proclaiming Shaw's innocence. Garrison slyly mentioned that he had not said anything publicly about the "five whips" that he said had been found under Shaw's bed. Garrison had toyed with the idea of the conspiracy behind Kennedy's assassination having an origin in the homosexual world, but had supposedly backed away from that thought. However, his mention of that in the letter to Dymond seemed to indicate that he thought it was still a pressure point to be touched every now and then. Dymond replied to Garrison two days later, indicating that Shaw, while generally abiding by the court-ordered restriction on public comments, had every right to proclaim his innocence, even publicly. Dymond also mentioned that Shaw's military record would be made public soon, and he offered to meet with Garrison to discuss any disputed issues about procedure.

Shaw's attorneys were still theorizing that Shaw's arrest could have been related to his homosexuality. Irma Fasnacht was interviewed by defense investigators on May 23. Fasnacht and her sister, "Dixie," operated Dixie's Bar of Music on Bourbon Street; the well-known gay bar also attracted straight customers, and had been in operation for many years. Irma Fasnacht indicated that she had known Shaw for a long time, but that she had no knowledge of persecution of homosexuals by Jim Garrison's office related specifically to the Shaw case.[2143]

The routines of Shaw's family, beginning with his mother and spreading out among his aunts, uncles, and cousins out in the countryside, had been disrupted as a result of his arrest. Shaw received a letter from Hazel Shaw, a relative in Clinton, Louisiana. At Shaw's trial, the town of Clinton would become important, as he was accused of visiting there, in 1963, with Oswald and Ferrie. At trial, Shaw denied ever going to Clinton, although he acknowledged that he had some relatives there. In the letter, Hazel Shaw wrote that, "Mr. Garrison" had "caused many family phone calls" and "family gettogethers," and that she had heard from certain members of the family for the first time in years.[2144]

Jack Martin, the quirky, alcoholic private investigator, who had originated one strand of the story that eventually ensnared Shaw in Garrison's grasp, was, during the spring of 1967 recording conversations with various individuals in an attempt to help Garrison's office. While Martin sometimes publicly disassociated himself from Garrison, criticizing him severely and even filing a lawsuit against him, he was recording, among others, Irvin Dymond, Aaron Kohn of the Metropolitan Crime Commission, attorney Steven Plotkin (who was representing Gordon Novel), and reporter Richard Townley. According to a narrative Martin wrote at the time, the tapes were intended to gain information about the motives of those individuals who were then investigating Garrison's probe into the assassination.[2145] Specifically, Martin tried to find out information about the ongoing NBC News investigation into Garrison's case. He wanted to learn from attorney Steven Plotkin whether Gordon Novel was receiving help from the CIA (Novel constantly claimed to have CIA connections) or otherwise; Plotkin denied it.[2146] He spoke with attorney Irvin Dymond, and told him that David Ferrie had known Oswald, but that was the extent of the associations. Dymond told him to stop playing games, and to stop telling bits of the truth, and that he would support him if he would tell the complete truth; Martin seemed to hint at wanting money.[2147]

In a conversation with Richard Townley, Martin said that he could blow Garrison's case up by cooperating with NBC; he mentioned his recent home renovations, and how much it had cost him. Townley said that there was no way NBC would pay him, and Martin protested that he did not want to stand out "like a pimple on a whore's tit,"[2148] a phrase Martin seemed to use quite often. In a conversation with Aaron Kohn, Martin said that the prosecution had offered to pay him $1,000, and he asked Kohn to ask Walter Sheridan for some type of monetary compensation; Kohn declined to ask Sheridan for it.[2149]

On May 27, Martin spoke with Plotkin again, and Plotkin told him that NBC News would not pay Martin any money for his story. Plotkin advised Martin to stay out of the entire thing, saying that he would look very bad if he chose to get involved. Plotkin also advised Martin to tell Garrison if he knew anything of relevance.[2150]

In a further conversation with Richard Townley, Townley told Martin that NBC only needed Martin to tell his story. He said that NBC News had its own proof that Garrison's investigation was a hoax.[2151] In yet another talk, Jack Martin asked Richard Townley not to use his photograph on the air in the NBC special, saying that it could get him killed.[2152]

Meanwhile, Perry Russo was working to record journalist James Phelan and others, in an attempt to discredit their work. In their first interview on May 24, Phelan discussed the concept of hypnotism, which Russo had undergone at least three times, and talked about his conversations with Dr. Esmond Fatter about the subject. Phelan said that Dr. Fatter had told him he would hate to be the judge or jury who decided the case based solely upon Fatter's testimony about the results of Russo under hypnosis. Fatter also had told Phelan, "What we really know about hypnosis right now is about as much as a bear cub knows about taking a sliver out of a gnat's ass while wearing boxing gloves."[2153] Russo had suggested to Phelan that perhaps he meet with Shaw personally in order to determine if Shaw was the man he had seen along with Oswald at Ferrie's apartment in 1963. In their second recorded conversation on May 25, Phelan told Russo that Shaw was somewhat reluctant to meet him, fearing a trap. Phelan also said he did not know whether Shaw would testify at the upcoming trial.[2154]

Two other informants for Garrison, George Wyatt (using the name of John George or John Jorge) and Morris Brownlee, also would get involved with Walter Sheridan later that summer in an attempt to interfere with his ongoing involvement in the prosecution of former Teamsters president Jimmy Hoffa, a case not directly related to the Garrison investigation into the assassination. In mid-May, however, they still were talking mainly with Richard Townley as a gateway to Sheridan in an attempt to discover what NBC was up to with its documentary, in an effort to gain Garrison's favor and show their worth. In fact, Morris Brownlee had stopped by Garrison's office some time earlier and spoken with James Alcock and Lou Ivon, offering to work for them on the Shaw case.[2155] Simultaneously, however, Brownlee also was offering to work for Shaw's attorneys to obtain information from Garrison.

In a conversation with Townley on May 21, 1967, Wyatt and Brownlee discussed the information they had, and the types of guarantees Townley could give them in exchange for that information. Townley told them that Walter Sheridan could not speak as freely as he could, and went on to say that NBC News was interested in specific acts by Garrison's office, or specific things about Garrison, that would discredit him. Townley said that he had helped Alvin Beaubouef find the right people to assist him with his civil rights complaint against Garrison for attempting to influence his testimony; Beaubouef had met with Sheridan in Washington, D.C., and was satisfied with the help he had received. Townley said that he had wanted exclusive rights to Beaubouef's information, and had made a deal to help him get his story out. Townley went on to say that both NBC and WDSU-TV could bring pressure to bear on parties to obtain information about Garrison's investigation. In the conversation, Townley discussed his concerns that Wyatt (George) and Brownlee might be working for Garrison, and indicated that Garrison would love to "hang a rap" on him.[2156]

On May 22, Townley and Brownlee spoke again. Townley referred to Garrison's statements in the newspapers that the CIA was paying attorney Burt Klein, Alvin Beaubouef's current attorney, to represent Beaubouef, and Townley indicated that he thought Garrison suspected he was the intermediary transferring the funds from the CIA to Klein. Townley told George Wyatt that he had known of the investigation two months before it broke, and that he had searched the French Quarter, but could find nothing to tie Shaw to the mysterious "Clay Bertrand." Then, he said, he had heard of the tactics being used by Garrison's investigators to coerce witnesses into testifying a certain way, and that he now believed that Garrison was not competent to conduct the investigation. Townley mentioned that Russo had failed a polygraph test, even though it was never completed, and that that would be the detail that would sink Russo.[2157]

George Wyatt (John George) spoke with Townley again on May 24. In a discussion about Garrison trying to obtain information to discredit NBC's investigation, Townley acknowledged that NBC was looking at all angles, including income tax evasion on Garrison's part, in an attempt to discredit Garrison, and by extension, his own investigation.[2158]

Edward Wegmann had early on attempted to contact U. S. Attorney General Ramsey Clark for his assistance in refuting Garrison's allegations about Shaw. The thinking was that, as the chief law enforcement officer of the United States, Clark would back the FBI's investigation following the Kennedy assassination in 1963 and 1964, which had formed the basis of the Warren Report's conclusions that there had been no conspiracy, and that Oswald had acted alone. However, Clark had sent word that he could not intervene in Shaw's prosecution, since the charge against Shaw was a state law, not a Federal one. Wegmann reached out to Clark again, this time on May 24, 1967, to ask for clarification of the statement Clark had made the day after Shaw's arrest. Clark had stated on March 2 that the FBI had investigated Shaw during the aftermath of the assassination, but had found no connection between Shaw and the assassination, and that he had been cleared of any involvement. Shaw and his attorneys always had been puzzled that he had even been investigated, as he had not been aware of it at the time. Officials under Clark in the Justice Department, without being identified, had "confirmed," shortly after Shaw's arrest, that Shaw was indeed the "Clay Bertrand" character who had called attorney Dean Andrews the day after the assassination; that supposed phone call was what had started Garrison's probe into Shaw's possible involvement.

Shortly after news articles appeared in the New Orleans newspapers with screaming headlines linking the CIA to the Kennedy assassination, Lloyd Ray, chief of the local CIA office in New Orleans, wrote a letter to his boss at Agency headquarters, lamenting the turn of events. Ray noted that Garrison was attempting to promote this link, and concluded that he was succeeding. Ray said the CIA might need to explain publicly to people its role in the aftermath of the assassination in some fashion, a development that Ray said would have been unthinkable only a few years before. He noted, however, that the CIA had had bad publicity during the 1960s, and that now such an explanation might be necessary. Ray further added that Jacob Morrison, half-brother of the late mayor Chep Morrison, had told him that many of his friends thought that Garrison "has something," and that the CIA was hampering Garrison's investigation.[2159] Ray was well aware of the run of negative publicity the CIA had suffered in recent years, starting with the Bay of Pigs Invasion, and including its activities in Vietnam in the early phase of the buildup of the war. A disclosure around the time of Shaw's arrest that the CIA had been secretly funding the National Student Association (NSA), an important college group, added to the agency's declining image.

The CIA, like the FBI, had monitored Garrison's investigation closely, both from its New Orleans office and from Washington. Immediately upon hearing of Shaw's arrest, local officials Hunter Leake and Lloyd Ray, Leake's boss, recalled vividly that Shaw had been a source for them for approximately eight years from the late 1940s through the mid-1950s. Lloyd Ray queried his boss in Washington as to what action he should take if Garrison should call him in and ask him about Shaw. The answer soon came down from headquarters: if asked, Ray should tell Garrison about Shaw's connection to the agency. However, Garrison would never make an official inquiry of any kind in that regard.

In a memo on May 24, Garrison assistant William R. Martin summarized for Garrison various CIA connections in the New Orleans area. Martin, who was born in the Dominican Republic and spoke fluent Spanish, had worked as Director of International Relations under Paul Fabry at International House during the mid-1960s, then had become an attorney and joined Garrison's staff as an investigator related to the Kennedy assassination and the Shaw prosecution. During his time as Public Relations Director at International House, Martin had been a contact for the Central Intelligence Agency, although it is not clear that he ever related that fact to Garrison.[2160]

In the memo, Martin indicated that he had recently had lunch with a friend who was a former employee of the CIA and resident of New Orleans. The friend said that William Burke had been in charge of the local office at one time, and that attorney Monte Lemann, of the law firm Monroe and Lemann, had originally approved Burke for the job during the late 1940s. Martin wrote that Stephen B. Lemann of the same firm handled the payroll, and would advance funds to attorneys Steven Plotkin and Burt Klein, who were currently representing persons of interest in Garrison's probe. Martin said that David Baldwin, who had worked as Public Relations Director at the Mart from late 1953 to early 1955, and who prior to that had worked with Clay Shaw during 1953 as part of the Louisiana Purchase Sesquicentennial celebration, had been a CIA employee in India, and that Baldwin had either recruited Shaw, or Shaw had already been recruited by the time Baldwin arrived at the Mart. Martin also shared that the CIA had sponsored Baldwin's employment at the Mart, and that Baldwin had used a cover identity in India, representing himself as being with various newspapers, including the *Louisville Courier Journal*, *The New Orleans Item*, and the North American Newspaper Alliance. Martin closed by recommending that Garrison use another staff member to check out those various bits of information, as Martin knew most of the parties involved. However, he considered the information to be accurate.[2161]

The above memo shows the danger of total reliance on even contemporaneous memos related to Garrison's probe into the Kennedy assassination, and his prosecution of Shaw. Presumably, Martin believed what he was saying in the memo. However, it is only partially accurate. For example, William Burke was indeed in charge of the local CIA office in New Orleans from its inception into the 1960s, and the firm of Monroe and Lemann, or at least one or more individual attorneys there, may have had some importance in recommending initial personnel for the office, and for handling legal affairs in New Orleans for the CIA. However, no one has credibly produced information that attorneys Steven Plotkin and Burt

Klein received attorney fees from the CIA to represent persons of interest in Garrison's probe. It also has not been shown that the CIA sponsored David Baldwin's employment at the Mart. On the contrary, Baldwin had been terminated from his CIA job in India in 1952, as a result of his romantic involvement with a woman, Lillian Baxter, and the subsequent leaking of secret information during that relationship. Baldwin came back to New Orleans, and had worked briefly for the Bauerlein Advertising Agency, which was handling the Louisiana Purchase Sesquicentennial celebration account. Baldwin joined the association shortly after Shaw took over as Managing Director, and Shaw brought Baldwin back to the Mart as Public Relations Director following the departure of Glenn Weekley, who had been the Public Relations Director since 1949. It was true, however, that Baldwin used a newspaper job as cover during his time in India with the CIA, and that the *Louisville Courier-Journal* was, if not the only newspaper cover he used, at least one of them.

As a related note to his investigative efforts, William Martin also was assigned by Garrison to read *Submerged*, the early play that Shaw had co-authored with Herman Stuart Cottman. Martin reported that he found nothing of importance in the manuscript that would help the case against Shaw.[2162]

Juan M. Valdes was interviewed by defense investigators on May 26. Valdes is notable because he is sometimes considered a suspicious character in the death of orthopedic surgeon Mary Sherman in the summer of 1964. According to some accounts, Jim Garrison would quietly try to connect the Mary Sherman murder with Clay Shaw, following Shaw's arrest. Valdes is described in the memo of his interview as a "troublemaker" who "associated with homosexuals." He was employed by a firm, All Transport, Inc., that was located in the Mart. Valdes, of Cuban background, but with no noticeable accent, told the investigators that he knew Shaw only from seeing him in the Mart building.[2163]

Meanwhile, Garrison's office began to step up efforts to find potential witnesses in the Jackson and Clinton, Louisiana area. A memo dated May 22, 1967, from Frank Meloche to Lou Ivon, dealt with other instructions given to Lieutenant Francis Fruge. It does not mention anyone related to Clinton, Louisiana, but mentions nurses at the Jackson, Louisiana mental hospital who had been present at a situation in 1963 when Rose Cheramie had been confined there.[2164] Lieutenant Fruge had been involved in that Rose Cheramie incident at the time, having initially taken her to the hospital for commitment.

A memo dated May 25, by an unidentified author, deals with Oswald supposedly attempting to register to vote in East Feliciana Parish, home to both Jackson and Clinton, Louisiana. The memo notes that Parish Clerk of Court Henry Earl Palmer was interviewed on May 23, and said that Oswald had identified himself using a military identification card. Palmer said that a local resident, Estes Morgan, also had been standing in line to register to vote, and that a large black Cadillac, with two men in it, had been parked in front of Corcoran's Drug Store on Main Street in Clinton; Oswald eventually got into the limosine. Palmer identified Shaw as the driver of the car, but was unable to identify Ferrie as a passenger. He said that Town Marshal John Manchester, who supposedly had gone up to the car and questioned the occupants, had run a check on the vehicle; the name of the International Trade Mart had come back. Manchester was unable to positively identify either photograph shown him, although photos of Shaw and Ferrie were "highly familiar" to him. Essie Watson, a local law enforcement clerk, had supposedly told Palmer that she remembered running a check on the vehicle, but she denied that to the district attorney's investigators. The memo also goes on to mention that former state legislator Reeves Morgan had told a story of Oswald coming to his home seeking a job;[2165] Morgan would repeat that story at Shaw's trial almost two years later.

Town Marshall John Manchester would be one of the main Clinton/Jackson witnesses to testify at Shaw's trial. He, like several others, testified that he had stopped the black limousine and questioned the occupants, who turned out to be Shaw, Ferrie, and Oswald.

However, in a 1967 statement to Garrison's office, he said that he had only seen Shaw in newspaper photos, and that he did not remember much about the passengers. According to his statement, he recalled that the black limousine was a Cadillac, that it was registered to the International Trade Mart, and that the occupants had told Parish Clerk of Court Henry Earl Palmer that they were selling bananas.[2166]

Shaw testified at trial that the International Trade Mart had never owned any vehicles. A review of balance sheets and other financial records for the Mart, from its inception through the 1960s, also shows no evidence of vehicle ownership or leasing by the Mart.

Some of the internal memos related to the Clinton/Jackson witnesses are contradictory in summarizing what the witnesses first said. Henry Earl Palmer would testify at the trial that Oswald had attempted to register to vote in the voter line sponsored by CORE, and that he also noticed a black limousine that day, with Shaw and Ferrie in it. However, in a statement dated May 28, 1967, one of the first generated by Garrison's office dealing with a statement by one of the Clinton/Jackson witnesses, Palmer told Garrison's investigators that he could not identify Shaw from a photo, although he also said that the photograph looked like one of the men who had come into town that day. He said that Oswald would not have needed to be a registered voter in order to get a job at East Louisiana State Hospital, the state mental hospital in nearby Jackson, as another witness, Reeves Morgan, would testify at trial. Palmer also identified another man, Estes Morgan, as someone who was going to work at the mental institution. Palmer said that he had spoken with John Manchester about the incident after Garrison's investigation had appeared into the newspapers, and that Manchester had told him he could not identify the men in the car. Palmer also noted that Doris Shaw, a first cousin of Shaw, worked at a bank in Clinton, Louisiana.[2167]

Reeves Morgan, a former member of the Louisiana House of Representatives, was interviewed on May 29, 1967. He said that Oswald had come to see him, and that he had told him that he needed to be a registered voter in order to get a job at the mental hospital. He said that Aline Woodside, who worked at the hospital, had seen Oswald's application, but did not know what had happened to it in the intervening years.[2168] Woodside would not testify at Shaw's trial.

Mary Morgan, Reeves Morgan's daughter, was interviewed on June 3, 1967, although the memo was not written until January 29, 1968. The memo seemed to indicate that she identified Oswald, but it is not explicitly clear.[2169] She supposedly had been present when Oswald had come by Reeves Morgan's home to ask about a job in 1963. Mary Morgan would not testify at Shaw's trial, although her father would.

Shaw had sustained severe "shock" by the arrest and accusations, but by late May he was settling into his new reality. Edward Wegmann wrote to Holland McCombs that, "Although this situation insofar as Clay is concerned is but 83 days old, it seems as though it has been going on for years. He has now recovered from the shock and has his feet on the ground once again. To whatever extent it may be possible, he has adjusted to the situation, returned to his home and attempts to live a normal life."[2170]

David Baldwin wrote Shaw on May 31, enclosing a recent column by former New Orleanian Clayton Fritchey regarding Garrison's prosecution of Shaw; Fritchey was now writing a nationally syndicated column. Baldwin was living in Evanston, Illinois, still serving in a public relations capacity with a division of the American Medical Association. Baldwin indicated that, "With my own CIA connections, I may be seeing you sooner than you think," alluding jokingly to a possible prosecution by Garrison's office. Baldwin added that, "I would be delighted to tell Garrison what an idiot I think he is."[2171]

By the end of May, the idea was still alive among the defense team that, in addition to presenting an official criminal defense in court against the charges against Shaw, perhaps a publicity campaign of some sort should be mounted against Garrison, to expose his own numerous contradictory statements and seemingly wild theories. Since the case had first emerged publicly on February 17, Garrison had made a number of sensational statements that had kept the publicity about his investigation escalating. For example, shortly after the case broke, but before Garrison was aware of Perry Russo and before Shaw was arrested, he indicated that he and his staff had solved the assassination. In an interesting contradiction, he had made that statement just as a Baton Rouge newsman, Bill Bankston, was interviewing Russo, who had just emerged publicly. David Ferrie, seemingly Garrison's main target in the probe to that point, had died, but Russo had not yet identified Shaw, and had not yet even spoken to representatives of the district attorney's office. Accordingly, the question arose in many minds how Garrison could have solved the case without knowledge of Russo, who ultimately became the main witness at Shaw's trial.

Such sweeping statements by Garrison, which would go on throughout 1967 and into the following year, almost never mentioned Shaw directly, which enabled Garrison to work around the court restriction on public statements about the prosecution. Instead, Garrison spoke about the Kennedy assassination in a larger sense, as a conspiracy involving a large number of individuals, and perhaps some government agencies as well. In a striking contradiction, Garrison often said that "Lee Harvey Oswald never fired a shot" the day of the assassination, even though the charge against Shaw was that he had conspired with Oswald and Ferrie to assassinate Kennedy, with the implication that Oswald's later actions represented the actual carrying-out of the conspiracy. Researcher Tom Bethell, the young Englishman working inside Garrison's office, recalls James Alcock, the assistant district attorney who would eventually prosecute the case against Shaw, objecting to the inconsistency in a talk with Garrison, saying that such statements might hurt the prosecution's case; Garrison calmly replied that Alcock should simply argue that Garrison's public statements had nothing to do with the case in court.

Garrison's investigation had begun with the twin threads of David Ferrie and his alleged acquaintanceship with Lee Harvey Oswald, and attorney Dean Andrews's story about the mysterious "Clay Bertrand" calling him to represent Oswald the day after the assassination. From there, the investigation had quickly widened to include the anti-Castro Cubans who lived in New Orleans, who might have been antagonistic toward Kennedy because of the failed Bay of Pigs Invasion in 1961. With the *Paesa Sera* article alleging Shaw's CIA involvement, which appeared immediately after Shaw's arrest, Garrison began to include the CIA more and more in his public accusations. He also would include right-wing elements, including oil millionaires in Texas, as part of the conspiracy, and would ultimately, on an appearance on NBC's *Tonight Show with Johnny Carson* at the end of January 1968, accuse President Lyndon Johnson of being actively involved in the coverup related to the assassination, although not the actual assassination. The ever-expanding nature of Garrison's accusations had been widely criticized in the national media outside of New Orleans, and Shaw and his attorneys hoped to in some way turn the growing negative publicity toward Garrison into some use in Shaw's criminal case.

William Gurvich, who along with his brothers ran an investigative and security agency, had joined Garrison's investigation in early 1967. He was paid some for his services, although not as much as he could have made at an outside job. On May 31, 1967, as he was quickly growing more and more disenchanted with Garrison's investigation and the prosecution of Shaw, Gurvich wrote Garrison a letter saying that he had only received $1,000 as of that date, and that he had incurred out-of-pocket expenses totaling at least $3,500. Gurvich noted that his income and earning power had been affected by his full-time duties with Garrison's office.[2172] Although some have characterized Gurvich as Garrison's "chief investigator," almost as if he was in charge of the entire investigation, it is clear that Gurvich only handled specific tasks, and had no knowledge of certain key aspects of the investigation that were going on, even while he was present on the investigative team. For example, when he gave a detailed interview with Shaw's defense attorneys in August 1967, he made no mention of Charles Spiesel, who would become one of the sensational witnesses at Shaw's trial. Similarly, he made no mention of the Clinton, Louisiana area witnesses who would testify that they had seen Shaw, Ferrie, and Oswald together in the small town in 1963. Gurvich had a clear understanding of where he ranked in the operation. In a memo to Garrison dated March 23, 1967, Gurvich gave his title as "Investigative Aide."[2173] In a memo dated April 4, 1967, Gurvich used the title "Special Aide."[2174]

Gurvich would defect from the investigation toward the end of June, while in New York City. He then gave television and newspaper interviews criticizing Garrison's investigation, and met secretly with Senator (and former Attorney General) Robert Kennedy, President Kennedy's brother. In late August, Gurvich sat down with Shaw's defense attorneys and discussed his knowledge of the inside of the Jim Garrison investigation. Gurvich would work with them until Shaw's death on tasks related both to Shaw's criminal defense, and to the civil suit Shaw filed in February 1970, which was ongoing even after Shaw's death.

At the end of May 1967, Aaron Kohn wrote a lengthy report commenting on several aspects of Garrison's investigation. It mentioned Kohn's ongoing cooperation with Richard Townley and Walter Sheridan. Kohn and Sheridan already knew each other, through an association with Robert Kennedy in his efforts to combat organized crime beginning in the late 1950s as part of the McClellan Committee of the U.S. Senate, which had investigated racketeering and other illegal activities; Sheridan had been a key investigator working for Kennedy for many years. Kohn had detailed Garrison's past history for Sheridan, going back to the era of District Attorney Leon Hubert. Among the things Kohn reported to Sheridan was that, according to Garrison's friend Pershing Gervais, Garrison had on one occasion had intercourse with a stripper in front of forty people. Kohn also had recently spoken with Brigadier General Raymond Hufft, head of the Louisiana National Guard, and ironically, the person Shaw had succeeded as Managing Director of the Louisiana Purchase Sesquicentennial celebration in early 1953. Hufft told Kohn that "Washington" had been telephoning him daily for news of Garrison's investigation. Hufft commented to Kohn that Garrison's ascension to the office of district attorney had been due to the fact that, when the wife of *Times-Picayune* publisher John F. Tims had killed someone while driving while intoxicated during the late 1950s, Garrison, as Assistant District Attorney, had let the charges drop. Meanwhile, he had prosecuted the man who had killed the wife of Leander Perez, Jr., son of the powerful, popular, but also corrupt and racist, leader of nearby Plaquemines Parish, under similar conditions. Hufft also mentioned that Garrison had recently resigned from the National Guard, after a long series of absences from Guard functions for which he had improperly claimed attendance. Kohn also commented in his report that John Pat Little, President of the Louisiana Bar Association, had recently told him that nothing could be done on a statewide level to check the power of a district attorney. Little said that at one time, a Louisiana attorney general could remove a district attorney from a case, but that Governor Huey Long had abused that power in removing a New Orleans district attorney during his reign in the 1930s, and that the rules had since been changed.[2175]

Kohn's comments about a higher official, in effect, taking over an investigation from a district attorney, or rather the lack of any such official ability to do so, was a common topic of discussion in the aftermath of Shaw's arrest, and for the duration of the criminal cases against him. Many wished that there had been a procedure whereby someone at a higher level, such as the state attorney general, could have stepped in and reviewed the case to determine if it was a valid one; there was no such procedure. Years later, in 2007, the author asked Harry Connick, who succeeded Jim Garrison as district attorney in 1974 and served for approximately three decades, if there was any such safeguard in place today in Louisiana against an unscrupulous prosecutor (short of a vigorous defense at trial). Connick said that the situation had not changed much since Garrison's days in office.[2176]

On June 2, Edward Wegmann received a call from a prominent employee of the Department of Justice in Washington, D.C.[2177] The call apparently was to inform Wegmann that Attorney General Ramsay Clark was about to acknowledge that Shaw had, in fact, never been investigated by the FBI in 1963, and that Clark had made a mistake in saying so on March 2, the day after Shaw's arrest. What he had meant to say, supposedly, was that the FBI had searched for the "Clay Bertrand" character named by Dean Andrews, rather than that Shaw had ever been investigated in any way. The three-month period between Clark's initial statement after Shaw's arrest and his retraction in early June followed a series of efforts by Clark to quietly put the blame on the FBI for misinforming him about the nature of the 1963 investigation. However, the FBI officials who had briefed Clark stood firm by their version that they had made a clear distinction between the "Clay Bertrand" character and Shaw, and that they had never maintained that the FBI had investigated Shaw in 1963. Clark finally gave in and issued the public retraction in early June.

In order to combat Garrison publicly, Shaw and Edward Wegmann had several meetings with a public relations man, Paul Martin, who had been married for some years to Shaw's old friend, Ella Brennan, the owner of Brennan's restaurant. The meetings with Martin, which began as early as June 1967 and continued at least through the time that Shaw ended his diary in mid-October 1967, were for the purpose of effectively "belling the cat," meaning to expose Garrison in areas that might not be otherwise noted by the public. It is unclear exactly what the group had in mind, and the idea went nowhere. Irvin Dymond, for one, was skeptical of the idea of appearing to "try Garrison" in public. He felt that such an effort would be frowned upon by the legal establishment, and might rebound to the defense's ultimate detriment. Edward Wegmann tended to agree with Dymond on the caution that needed to be exercised in working within the legal system, and both men believed that Shaw's defense should proceed as much as possible through the tedious but necessary legal process. In an entry for October 17, 1967, Shaw mentioned arguing with his lawyers about whether to do anything to force an investigation of Garrison's office by some outside entity. Shaw lamented the combination of his lawyers' lack of imagination and his own lack of legal training, believing that such a combination made for an ineffective counterforce to Garrison's own efforts.

Reminders of more frivolous times were addressed in a letter to Shaw, in early June, from George Haverstick, now living in San Diego, California and attending law school. Haverstick wrote that he admired Shaw's courage and resolve in the face of the charges against him, and that it frightened him to think of the financial aspect of defending against them. Haverstick indicated that he had recently bought a home to refurbish, and was putting in a pool just like Shaw had done at his residence in the mid-1950s. Haverstick said the home had five large bedrooms, and a bath large enough "to hold a ball in," like one or two homes that Shaw had owned.[2178]

Jack Rogers, a Baton Rouge attorney, was counsel to the Louisiana Joint Legislative Committee on Un-American Activities. He was close to both Jim Garrison and to the CIA personnel in New Orleans, and was one of the individuals who had access, to some degree, to both sides of those opposing forces. In early June 1967, Rogers told Lloyd Ray, the local CIA chief, that Garrison had been receiving contributions for the investigation from Edith Stern.[2179] That would have been somewhat of a bombshell, as Stern was a friend and ardent supporter of Shaw during his ordeal. One of her sons was a major owner of WDSU-TV Channel 6 in New Orleans, whose investigative reporters were highly critical of Garrison's investigation.

Internal CIA memos indicate that many of the individuals around the entire Kennedy assassination case in New Orleans, from 1963 forward, had at some point been of interest for one reason or another to the CIA. For example, the William B. Reily Company, the coffee company where Oswald worked for a brief time, had been of interest back in 1949.[2180] An internal memo from November 1975, in response to an inquiry by the U.S. Senate Select

Committee on Intelligence Activities (the Church Committee) indicated that the William B. Reily Company's only connection to the CIA had been in 1949, for any information useful to the CIA's Domestic Collection Division.[2181]

Hoke S. May, the New Orleans reporter who some thought had gotten too friendly with Garrison and his investigation, was discussed in a July 1967 memo. It indicated that May's grandfather had been a former governor and senator from Georgia, and that May himself had been employed by *The New York Times* from 1948 to 1949. It also stated that May had been issued a Covert Security Approval for unwitting use in April 1958, when he had worked for a business firm that had been involved in the CIA's Project FJINDULGE.[2182]

The CIA was very concerned about being dragged into Garrison's investigation. As an important hearing approached on June 5, 1967, the CIA's assistant general counsel, John Greaney, advised William Gause, a CIA recruiter in New Orleans, to remain outside of Louisiana until after the hearing date, to avoid being called into court.[2183]

After his arrest, Shaw had begun to read more about the Kennedy assassination, and the blooming literature that questioned the official conclusions. He purchased a copy of *Accessories After the Fact* by Sylvia Meagher, generally considered to be one of the more levelheaded criticisms of the Warren Commission. Shaw remained convinced that the official explanation of the assassination, by the Warren Commission, was correct, if imperfect. He exchanged letters with Meagher, politely disagreeing with her own conclusions, although the two were in agreement about Shaw's own non-involvement in the crime.

Defense investigators continued to interview individuals who might shed light on various angles of the case. One of the persons interviewed, on June 7, was Bill McKenzie, co-owner, along with Steve DiVincenti, of the Finale Bar. Dealing candidly with aspects of the case that touched on homosexuality, McKenzie related that Shaw had been in the bar the night of November 13, 1966, when police had raided it and arrested juveniles in attendance. He also brought up an episode where approximately one hundred gays had been arrested at a party in suburban Metairie in 1962.[2184] Leo LeVeque, Jr., a Jefferson Parish bail bondsman, told defense investigators that Al Dargis, another bail bondsman who had bonded Ferrie out twice when he had been in trouble in the early 1960s, also had bonded forty-five of the ninety-six men arrested at the February 1962 gathering, a gay costume ball on Edenborn Street.[2185] According to an account in the *Times-Picayune* thirty years after the bust, the event had taken place at the Ramblers' Club; ninety-four of the men arrested were from Jefferson Parish, and the other two were from Orleans Parish.[2186] Jim Garrison eventually would procure a list of the individuals arrested in the somewhat notorious incident, and attempt, without success, to match the names up with Shaw, Oswald, Ferrie, and others impacted by his investigation.

Attorney Ben Toledano, who was representing those parties still interested in filming a documentary about the Shaw case, to be made by filmmakers Richard Leacock and Noel Parmentel, wrote to Wegmann on June 8. Referencing his letter of May 24, regarding the filming of certain aspects of the case, Toledano said that Garrison was willing to allow the documentary filmmakers to film the prosecution's preparation of the case, and that they also wanted to film the defense conferences and meetings as the case progressed. The filmmakers hoped to film the trial, but Toledano understood Wegmann was not ready to agree to that yet. Wegmann had mentioned that Shaw was writing a book about his involvement, and was concerned about the documentary film affecting the profitability of Shaw's effort; Toledano indicated that he believed the film would help the sales of Shaw's subsequent book.[2187] Wegmann replied on June 13 that the defense team would not be interested in allowing any aspect of their meetings and conferences, or the trial itself, to be filmed, unless "substantial compensation" was paid.[2188]

Indeed, defense costs, particularly investigative expenses, were continuing to mount up, and by mid-June, the problem over finances was paramount, at least from a cash-flow standpoint. Wegmann reported to *LIFE* magazine writer Holland McCombs that money was "tight," and that Shaw's finances were "quite limited."[2189] Wegmann added, "Clay is in reasonably good spirits, however all of us are most concerned about finances. We are confident of victory in the end, however the time when this will come is apparently in the somewhat distant future and in the meantime we must continue to investigate and to work. All of this costs money and as you well know, Clay's finances are quite limited and are not what the public believes and is led to believe by various media."[2190]

Edwin Lea McGehee, a barber in Jackson, Louisiana, was interviewed by Garrison's investigators on June 17. At the trial in early 1969, he would testify that Oswald had come into his barber shop in 1963, looking for a job at the nearby mental hospital. He had suggested Oswald would have better luck if he was a registered voter, and referred Oswald to Reeves Morgan, a state legislator at the time, for information on how to get a job in the area. However, in this June 1967 interview for Garrison's office, McGehee said that his wife worked at the hospital, and that no one there ever mentioned Oswald showing up in search of a job.[2191]

On June 20, Wegmann wrote to Wilma Francis, the agent who was helping to market Shaw's diary to the movie industry, care of Mrs. Sylvia McGraw in North Hollywood, California. Wegmann questioned Francis's statements in her earlier note that the material was "too hot, too controversial," to produce a sale, suggesting that its interesting nature should provoke interest. Wegmann predicted there would be a trial, saying that Garrison was too far along in his efforts to stop the proceedings. Wegmann sent along Shaw's entire updated journal through March 31, the first month after his arrest.[2192]

As stories about Jack Martin and his 1963 attempt to implicate David Ferrie made the rounds, it also emerged that Martin had been questioned by Secret Service agents shortly after the assassination, and basically had admitted to making wild telephone calls while intoxicated, discrediting his own story that Ferrie was involved in the assassination. On June 8, 1967, Martin called former Secret Service agent Anthony Garrich and accused him of lying in the 1963 report, about Martin essentially recanting his story about Ferrie. Garrich ended the conversation by hanging up on Martin.[2193]

In mid-June, as court filings in his case were heating up again, Shaw found time to send Edith Stern some yellow roses. Stern thanked him with a card from the Cosmopolitan Club in New York City, saying that roses only came her way "via Phil Stern [her son] or Clay Shaw."[2194] Stern's family owned WDSU-TV, the NBC affiliate in New Orleans, which would, three days later, broadcast NBC's harsh critique of Garrison's investigation.

Garrison had been collaborating with noted conspiracy theorists and other critics of the Warren Commission report, and had sometimes promised individuals separately that he or she could write the official history of his investigation. In a letter dated June 19, 1967, Mark Lane wrote to Garrison, discussing the case against Shaw. Lane wrote that people should not place too much emphasis on the actual court case, because Shaw could simply state in court that the CIA had ordered him to engage Oswald, and win an acquittal in that manner. Lane said that if Shaw was acquitted for those reasons, it would not change the theories behind the case. Lane also indicated that local reporter June Rolfe had recently called Lane's publisher and said that she was writing a book about the case, with Garrison's authorization. Lane said he was under the impression that he would write the inside account of the investigation, and that if not, he did not know if he could continue with the project.[2195] As with Lane, Garrison had earlier promised both CBS News and *LIFE* magazine the exclusive story behind the investigation in exchange for prominent treatment. June Rolfe, who bore an old grudge against Shaw over a rent dispute, would, after Shaw's acquittal in March 1969, sign an affidavit allowing Garrison to charge Shaw with perjury, and thereby continue the prosecution efforts for another two years.

The investigation by Walter Sheridan and Richard Townley led up to a one-hour special report on NBC television, broadcast on June 19. The program was devoted to analyzing, and to a large degree criticizing, the Jim Garrison investigation, particularly the arrest and continuing prosecution of Shaw. James Phelan helped with some of the interviewing that was done for the program. Several individuals, including Alvin Beauboeuf, appeared on the program and discussed efforts by Garrison's assistants to shape their potential testimony, or to get them to say more than they could truthfully admit about Shaw's participation in a conspiracy, or about his connections with either Oswald or Ferrie. Shaw was interviewed in May, and appeared briefly on the program to deny that he was "Clay Bertrand." The interviews were mostly conducted in the offices of the Metropolitan Crime Commission; Aaron Kohn had actively helped with the special report. Years later, when the U.S. House of Representatives Select Commission on Assassinations (HSCA) was conducting its re-investigation of the Kennedy assassination from 1976 to 1979, Kohn provided the committee with rough transcripts totaling 429 pages of interviews done for the documentary.[2196] Not all of the people interviewed made it onto the air, and only a portion of any individual interview was aired.

The NBC program was produced by Fred Freed, a prominent NBC News producer, and Walter Sheridan was the lead investigator and on-air interviewer; the program was hosted by veteran newsman Frank McGee. Freed and Sheridan had produced a three-hour documentary about organized crime during 1966, much of which dealt with Mafia activity in Louisiana; Garrison had been interviewed for that program. All during April and May the two had worked, interviewing witnesses and piecing the documentation together, with help not only from Kohn, but also from Shaw's attorneys and other critics of Garrison. At a Metropolitan Crime Commission awards luncheon held on May 22, Freed and Sheridan had both been seated at the head table for the event.

Information about Garrison and the investigation had been openly shared by the parties. Fred Freed told Kohn that a Garrison trip to Las Vegas during October 1966 had been paid for by Carlos Marcello, and that a line of credit for $5,000 had been established for Garrison at one of the casinos, with Marcello's help. However, reporter James Phelan, who had connections at the Sands Hotel in Las Vegas, said that on a later trip by Garrison in March 1967, shortly after Shaw's arrest, there had been no line of credit established for Garrison.[2197]

John Cancler, a serial burglar who had come forward to dispute Vernon Bundy's preliminary hearing testimony, said in his interview on the NBC program that on January 23, 1967, or thereabouts, he went with investigator Lynn Loisel to Shaw's home, where he was asked to plant some type of "evidence." When he found out that it was related to the Kennedy assassination, he had refused to do so, although he had never learned what the "evidence" was.[2198] Cancler indicated that he had discussed Bundy's testimony with him, and that Bundy had obviously concocted his testimony in order to receive an early release from jail, where he was being held at the time of the preliminary hearing.

Miguel Torres told a story of being visited at the Louisiana State Penitentiary at Angola, Louisiana, where he was serving time for a felony conviction. Torres indicated the district attorney's office had wanted him to testify against Shaw, but that he had refused to do so.

Layton Martens said in his interview that he had first met Shaw at Mardi Gras of 1965. Shaw had been dressed in a black cloak and hood with a rope tied around him, and that he carried chains, and a whip that he had purchased in Mexico. Martens said that there was an order of monks who supposedly wore that type of dress, and that Shaw had worn that costume for many years during Mardi Gras festivities.[2199]

Eleanor Bares, the schoolteacher who lived a few doors down from Shaw, was interviewed as well. She said she had lived next to Shaw for two or three years, but did not know him, although she could see into his patio from her porch. She said that she had seen Ferrie one time, although not with Shaw, and that she had never talked to him. Investigator Lynn Loisel had come to see her in mid-April 1967, requesting that she take a polygraph, be hypnotized, or take sodium pentothal, but she had refused to do so. She said Loisel told her that those types of tests had worked with one person in discovering information that became his testimony, but she told them she was not interested in joining "the varied group of witnesses" in the case.[2200]

Bill Bankston, a reporter for a Baton Rouge newspaper who had interviewed Perry Russo when Russo had first spoken publicly, but before Garrison's assistant Andrew Sciambra had interviewed Russo, also was interviewed in preparation for the program. Bankston said that Russo did not mention much of what he testified to several weeks later at the preliminary hearing, aside from saying that he had known David Ferrie. Bankston recalled that, immediately after interviewing Russo on February 24, 1967, he saw a news item where Garrison said that he had solved the assassination. Knowing that Russo had not yet talked to Garrison, he was quite surprised when, several weeks later, Russo seemed to be the main witness against Shaw at the preliminary hearing. He said that had Russo told him the full story to which he testified at the preliminary hearing, his article about Russo would have gotten much better play in the Baton Rouge newspaper.[2201]

Polygraph examiner Roy Jacobs was interviewed. He said that he had administered a polygraph test to Russo on March 8, 1967, and that Russo had shown deception when he had identified photographs of Shaw and of Oswald. He said he had then been instructed by the district attorney's representatives, James Alcock and William Gurvich, not to continue to interrogate Russo.[2202] Jacobs, who had done polygraph examinations on various individuals for Garrison's investigation, at Gurvich's request, wanted to speak out about the results of the those tests, but was reluctant to do so, as he only had one more year of employment with the Jefferson Parish Sheriff's Office before retirement. Jacobs taped an interview with NBC, but the Sheriff's Office told him not to get involved with the case.[2203]

Another man who appeared on the NBC program was Fred Leemans, an ex-boxer who, in the years before 1963, had owned a half-interest in a Turkish bath and massage parlor on Canal Street in New Orleans. As Leemans described the operation, during the daytime the clientele was mainly heterosexual men looking for a massage, even a sexual release, and at nighttime the "gay crowd" took over. Leemans had given a statement to Garrison's office on May 5 saying that a man had come into his massage parlor using the name "Clay Bertrand;" he identified the man as Shaw. He also said the same man had come in at times with someone named "Lee," and with some Latinos.[2204]

By the time NBC began to conduct filmed interviews for its special report, Leemans had changed his mind, and decided to come clean about his false prospective testimony. Leemans called Irvin Dymond on May 22 to tell his story. He told Dymond that he had been contacted by Assistant District Attorney Robert E. Lee approximately one month earlier. When Leemans asked if the district attorney's office could help him financially, Lee referred him to Garrison, saying, "Garrison helps those who help him." Some years earlier, Leemans and John Emrald had owned the Canal Street Baths; Clay Shaw had been a patron of the baths during that time. Leemans said that he had told the district attorney's office that Shaw had come in using the name "Clay Bertrand," sometimes with Cubans, and sometimes with a guy named Lee, who had looked like Oswald. However, Leemans told Dymond that was actually the story the district attorney's office wanted him to tell, and that he had gone along with it in exchange for a promise of financial support. Leemans now told Dymond that although Shaw had come into the baths, he had used his own name, and that if he had ever come in with anyone else, Leemans was unaware of it.[2205]

At the end of May, Leemans, in a letter probably written by Dymond, informed Garrison that he was retracting parts of his earlier statement to Garrison's office related to Clay Shaw. Leemans now said that Shaw had only come into the Canal Street Baths by himself, and only using his own name.[2206] He then appeared on the NBC program, telling the story of how Garrison's office had attempted to elicit false testimony from him.

Almost two years later, in January 1969, just before Shaw's trial began, Leemans would reverse his position again, this time talking to local newspapers rather than in official testimony, and maintain that the reason he had changed his story back in 1967 to help Shaw was that he had been visited by some type of Federal agent who had pressured him into doing so. In this final version, he stood by his original story, as told to Garrison's office, that Shaw had visited the baths using the name "Clay Bertrand," and also had visited in the company of someone who looked like Oswald.

In an interview with author James Kirkwood in the spring of 1969, after Shaw's trial, Irvin Dymond said that Leemans had come to his attention in May 1967, approximately a month before the NBC special aired. Dymond had, some years before, represented Leemans's daughter, Colleen Leemans, on a narcotics charge. Because Dymond was representing Shaw, and had done a good job of representing her, Colleen Leemans had prevailed upon her father to visit Dymond and reveal the efforts of the district attorney's office to get him to testify falsely against Shaw. Accordingly, Dymond put Leemans in touch with the people involved with the NBC News special report, and Leemans had appeared on the program. However, during the next year and a half, Dymond told Kirkwood, Leemans would call him occasionally, hinting that he was in bad financial condition, and that he needed help. Dymond indicated that he tried to ignore the requests, but that Leemans continued to call, and eventually his pleas became more urgent. Among other things, his wife was ill and had large medical bills, and he needed help paying the home mortgage. Dymond continued to ignore Leemans's pleas for monetary assistance, so apparently Leemans decided to revert to his original story in order to help Garrison's office with its prosecution of Shaw. However, because Leemans never actually testified at trial, none of those conflicting motives that triggered such changes in his story were ever revealed or explored under oath.[2207]

The stories told to NBC News by such a strange mix of potential witnesses were not automatically believed, at least partly because of the checkered pasts of the various men. Several of them were convicted criminals, while others told contradictory accounts throughout Garrison's investigation. Indeed, other potential witnesses besides the ones who appeared on the NBC program worked both sides of the aisle, in effect offering to help both the prosecution and the defense for some type of compensation, often monetary compensation.

Dean Andrews also appeared on the broadcast, to deny that Clay Shaw was "Clay Bertrand." Andrews seemed to enjoy frustrating (and perhaps bewildering) interviewer Walter Sheridan, who was trying to get the denial from Andrews. Andrews gave it to him, but in a hedging manner, clearly not the forthright, no-reservations denial for which Sheridan had hoped.

NBC had a dramatic announcement of its own during the program: that it had identified the man known as "Clay Bertrand," that he was a homosexual living in New Orleans, and that he was not Clay Shaw. NBC did not name the man or its source, but the information had come once again from attorney Dean Andrews. This time, Andrews had identified an old client and friend, gay bar owner Eugene Davis, as "Clay Bertrand." In spite of NBC's on-air secrecy about the name, Eugene Davis was soon identified publicly, setting off a new media scramble to learn more about him.

Eugene Davis had abandoned his wife and five children in Pennsylvania in the early 1950s, and had assumed a gay lifestyle. He made his way to New Orleans, where he worked for gay bars and restaurants before eventually owning his own gay bar in the 1960s. He was no stranger to authorities over the years. Soon after he had arrived in New Orleans, Eugene Davis witnessed an incident while a bartender at Le Rendezvous Bar. Two New Orleans police officers had entered the bar while intoxicated, and had verbally and physically abused the two patrons present, a male and a female, calling them "you fruity bunch of bastards" and "Queers."[2208] Davis was mysteriously bludgeoned to death in 1984, a crime that has never been solved.

The FBI interviewed Eugene Davis a few days after the NBC report. He denied being "Clay Bertrand," and told them that Phil Schatz, who had died in 1965, may have used the name "Clay Bertrand" or "Clem Bertrand." Davis acknowledged to the FBI that he was a homosexual, and voiced concerns about the possibility of being harassed by Garrison related to the Shaw case.[2209] The FBI tracked down Phil Schatz's sister in Wisconsin, who confirmed that Schatz was deceased, and said that she did not know anything about Eugene Davis, Dean Andrews, or the name "Clay Bertrand."

In mid-July, Captain Roy Allemand of the New Orleans Harbor Police told the FBI of a conversation he had recently had with former Garrison investigator William Gurvich. Gurvich told Allemand his version of how the investigation had begun, and he also volunteered that Dean Andrews and Eugene Davis had planned together how to handle the "Clay Bertrand" issue. Gurvich told Allemand that Andrews would identify Davis as "Clay Bertrand," Davis would deny it, and mention the name of Schatz as being "Bertrand," knowing that Schatz had been deceased for some years.[2210] To the end of his life, Eugene Davis would always deny that he had used the name "Clay Bertrand," or that he had called Dean Andrews after the assassination seeking representation for Oswald, or for any other reason.

Many of Shaw's supporters tuned in to the program. Following the broadcast, Shaw received a telegram from Charles Bushong, with the National Foreign Policy Association in New York, whom he had known during the 1950s. Bushong congratulated Shaw on his "complete exoneration by NBC."[2211]

The day following the program, Aaron Kohn sent a telegram to NBC producer Fred Freed, congratulating him, Walter Sheridan, and the NBC staff on the program. Kohn said that the Metropolitan Crime Commission would now demand a probe of Garrison.[2212]

Gordon Novel, the somewhat mysterious entrepreneur and "electronics expert," by this time living in Columbus, Ohio, where he had fled to avoid appearing before the grand jury in New Orleans, called Kohn the same day. Novel told Kohn a mixture of truth and fiction, in quintessential Novel fashion. He said that he had initially been totally taken in by Garrison's probe, and that he was not involved in any way with the Federal government in monitoring or disrupting the probe, as Garrison had inferred. He said that Garrison had caused Ferrie's death by trying to force a confession out of Ferrie, and attempting to frame him, putting him under extreme pressure. Novel also said that he had seen investigator William Gurvich and Garrison and others coming out of Ferrie's apartment early on the morning of Ferrie's death.[2213]

Even after the NBC documentary appeared, Perry Russo still was talking openly with newsmen, seemingly without concern about being quoted. In an interview with George Lardner of *The Washington Post* that appeared on June 22, 1967, three days after the broadcast, Russo talked in general terms about the weaknesses of Garrison's case against Shaw. Russo even said that he would disclose those weaknesses for a price, but told Lardner he would deny saying that.[2214] Apparently, Russo had not sworn Lardner to secrecy, as Lardner reported Russo's offer, and related comments, in the article.

On June 29, Shaw's old Army buddy Gordon Berger sent a letter, commenting on the unfolding status of Shaw's case, and how NBC News had recently debunked Jim Garrison's case against Shaw. Berger jokingly stated that he had a certain "status for your niche" until Shaw's innocence had been revealed.[2215] Berger's ironic point, somewhat indirectly, was that everyone had known an innocent man, but very few had known someone who had participated in the assassination of a president.

William Taliaferro, who formerly had run a maintenance clearing service that Shaw had used for his properties in New Orleans, now worked in Thousand Oaks, California for a realty agency. In a letter to Shaw, he indicated that he was sorry that Shaw's savings were being depleted by having to defend himself, but that it seemed as if Garrison was "being worn down," and that reason was prevailing. Taliaferro mentioned that he knew it took money to live well in New Orleans, and that Shaw would be hurt financially.[2216]

In late June, beginning approximately one week after NBC had aired its investigative special, CBS News ran a four-part special dealing with the Warren Commission investigation and its aftermath. Garrison was interviewed on one part of the program by correspondent Mike Wallace. In the interview, Garrison said that he had other witnesses against Shaw besides Russo, and that Russo was even not the main witness in the case.[2217]

At the end of June, Garrison and Aaron Kohn met in Garrison's office, with several assistant district attorneys present. A transcript of the session has survived, and shows that Garrison and Kohn traded very direct and often heated comments about Kohn's criticism of Garrison's investigation. Kohn admitted that he had no information, independent of what he had heard in news reports, that would cause him to be critical of Garrison's investigation. Garrison at one point called Kohn a "professional liar," and Assistant District Attorneys James Alcock and Richard Burnes pressed Kohn for solid evidence as well.[2218] After his meeting with Garrison, Alcock, and Burnes, Kohn commented that only time would tell whether Garrison had been misguiding the course of criminal justice.[2219]

Kohn would later take credit for two Federal investigations into Garrison's activities. Kohn contended that the Federal government had initiated a probe in 1968, related to tax evasion by Garrison, based upon a request by Kohn to the Internal Revenue Service. Although that investigation did not quickly result in an arrest of Garrison, it was well known in Shaw's defense circles that the investigation was ongoing. Shaw occasionally mentioned in letters during 1968 that Garrison was being investigated, and that he might not even be in office to prosecute him. Kohn also took credit for the 1971 investigation that did result in Garrison's arrest on racketeering charges, and in two trials, including one related to income tax evasion; Kohn said that he had written a letter to U.S. Attorney Gerald Gallinghouse that initiated the investigation. Years later, at the time of Garrison's second trial in 1973, Kohn would summarize his efforts in an internal Metropolitan Crime Commission report, and wryly note that when reporter Rosemary James asked Garrison how it felt to be on trial, Garrison had responded that, "It's considerably below an orgasm and considerably above a cremation."[2220] Kohn also told select individuals, correctly or not, that shortly before Garrison launched his Kennedy assassination investigation, which resulted in the arrest and trial of Shaw, that the Federal government was already investigating Garrison, the implication being that Garrison might have launched the assassination investigation in the hopes that the attendant publicity, combined with Garrison's attacks on the Federal government, would ward off that pending investigation.[2221]

Paul Fabry, Managing Director at International House, and his wife, Luly, visited Shaw off and on during the spring and summer of 1967; they lived nearby in the French Quarter. On one occasion, Fabry mentioned how William Martin had become an attorney, and was now working for Garrison's office. Fabry said that Martin had been questioning International House staff about Shaw, and aspects of his life and background.

Shaw's mother, Alice Shaw, came to visit Shaw during the summer, along with Tulip Atkins; both of the women lived in Hammond, Louisiana. Atkins had been married at one time to Clay Atkins, a cousin of Shaw. Like many women, she had been romantically interested in Shaw, and he had maintained a friendly detachment. Shaw would later leave Tulip Atkins a cash bequest in his will.

When Shaw's mother, whom he referred to as "Al," visited him, Shaw turned his bedroom over to her. In his diary, he made a note to expand more fully in the future on his thoughts of the difficulties of sharing living quarters with his mother, on several levels, although he did not directly address those concerns.

Garrison's investigation occasionally affected CIA activities in New Orleans during this period. In 1967, the CIA was attempting to grant a covert security approval (CSA) to William George Helis, Jr., a member of a prominent family in New Orleans, and a person who had been associated with the international trade community over the years. During the investigation, the CIA came upon a very indirect rumor concerning Shaw, Helis's sister Virginia, and Isabel Monteleone, the daughter of hotel magnate William Monteleone. FBI Special Agent James J. McCabe's wife had heard the rumor from a friend or neighbor, who had in turn heard it from a socially prominent woman at her hairdresser's shop. The rumor had to do with Shaw, Virginia Helis, and Isabel Monteleone being members of a sexual "cult whose immorality was known and tacitly accepted" in New Orleans.[2222] The CIA later would point to this rumor as a reason for not using Lloyd Cobb, President of the Mart since 1962, as an outside counsel for the Agency. Cobb was considered as an outside counsel during 1968 because of some successful cases he had handled in the past, one being where he had represented a shipping line attempting to collect a debt from the government of Cuba, which had defaulted after Castro had taken over power. Cobb had prevailed in the case (the Cuban government, ironically, had been represented at the time by Irvin Dymond, now Shaw's chief criminal defense attorney). Because Cobb was associated with Shaw, and might have to participate in Shaw's upcoming trial, the CIA decided not to use him as an outside counsel, referring specifically to the rumor of Shaw being involved in the clandestine sex "cult" of unspecified activity.

On July 7, Wegmann wrote to Wynn Pearce regarding a 1948 party at Pearce's home at 1000 Royal Street, where Shaw and Biddison had been photographed with individuals who some said resembled David Ferrie and Lee Harvey Oswald. Wegmann indicated that he understood that the party had been given for the cast of *A Streetcar Named Desire*, the touring production of the Tennessee Williams smash play, then playing in New Orleans. Wegmann identified the six people in one photograph as an unknown person, Bob Brannon, Fritz Paul, Clay Shaw, Jeff Biddison, and Wynn Pearce, who was kneeling in the photo. Wegmann's letter referenced that he had talked with Pearce on May 29, and that Pearce had said that Brannon, the man said to resemble David Ferrie, had committed suicide some years before.[2223]

Garrison's office continued to investigate many leads about Shaw that poured in regularly. One such lead was that Elliott Hay, a 27-year-old homosexual, supposedly had said that an insurance executive had told him that Shaw had introduced himself as "Bertrand" around 1959 or 1960. On July 10, 1967, investigator Cliency Navarre interviewed Elliott Collins Hay, who gave his age as forty-four. Hay said that he did not know Shaw, that he knew no such insurance executive, and that no one had ever told him that Shaw was "Bertrand." He said he suspected that Llona George, the manager of the apartment complex where he lived, might have said that about him, because he was in a dispute with her over rental payments. He said that she had once met Shaw at a real estate party in the French Quarter.[2224]

As already mentioned, a number of convicts contacted Garrison's office during the course of Shaw's case. One was William A. Morris, who was serving time in prison on a homosexuality-related charge; he had been in prison for seven years. Morris, originally from Tennessee, said that he had met Shaw under the name of "Bertrand" in 1958. He said that "Bertrand" did not wear a hat when he first met him, but later took to wearing one. Morris said that "Bertrand" lived with his mother, and worked for General Electric. Morris's description of "Bertrand," including the height he gave to Garrison's interviewer, conflicted with Shaw's physical description. Morris also said that he had been with Shaw and gay bar owner Eugene Davis on a trip aboard a yacht owned by a man named Bill Boone, former owner of the Masquerade Bar, a gay bar in New Orleans.[2225] Boone later was interviewed by William Martin of Garrison's office, and told Martin that neither William Morris nor Shaw nor Eugene Davis had ever been on board his yacht.[2226] Eugene Davis was also interviewed by William Martin, and denied ever being on Boone's yacht.[2227] Morris was not used at trial.

The NBC News report that aired on June 19 could have been devastating to Garrison's prosecution of Shaw. However, by that time, Garrison had become somewhat seasoned to sensational headlines, contradictory charges back and forth, and the general circus atmosphere that prevailed around New Orleans, which had reached new heights after the arrest of Shaw. Accordingly, Garrison was able to deflect the main charges that appeared in the NBC report, because the public had become used to the idea that there were at least two sides to the entire investigation, and most were willing to wait until it played out in court.

In reaction to the broadcast, however, Garrison had complained to the Federal Communications Commission, requesting equal time to rebut the documentary. The FCC ordered NBC to grant him thirty minutes of rebuttal time, which was to air on July 15. Irvin Dymond wrote to NBC, requesting that the network cancel Garrison's rebuttal in the interest of Shaw's rights to a fair trial. However, on July 7, NBC responded by telegram to Dymond, indicating that they were refusing to cancel Garrison's rebuttal.[2228] As the rebuttal date neared, Willard Robertson, one of Garrison's earliest and staunchest supporters, urged him to prepare carefully for his talk.[2229]

In that presentation, a relaxed Jim Garrison seized on the perception held by a majority of the public—that there had been some type of coverup in the original Kennedy assassination investigation. Garrison responded, in a very general way, that establishment forces were trying to head off his investigation. He asked the public not to be fooled, and to reserve judgment on his efforts. He did not directly address the specific charges related to his investigation of Shaw, including possible manipulation of witnesses. In fact, after arresting Shaw, Garrison had generally avoided making any direct comment about Shaw, and confined himself to criticizing the past efforts to investigate the Kennedy assassination, including going off on many tangents that would never be explored at Shaw's trial.

On July 16, 1967, the day after Garrison gave his rebuttal speech to NBC's report from June 19, 1967, a young woman from California, Patricia Lambert, wrote a telegram to President Lyndon Johnson. It read as follows: "Garrison has turned the knob on the door of truth—it is up to you whether that door will swing open wide or close irrevocably—the people are watching. History will be your judge."[2230] More than thirty years later, Lambert would author a book giving one of the most unequivocal debunkings of Garrison's entire investigation, and his case against Shaw in particular.

In mid-July, attorney Ross Scaccia, representing gay bar owner Eugene Davis, attempted to hold a meeting between Shaw and Davis, apparently in an attempt for the two men to meet and discuss the "Clay Bertrand" issue. For secrecy reasons, the meeting was to be held in the office of another attorney, Lee Leonard. However, according to the FBI's informant about the matter, Louis Francis Giusti, Shaw arrived for the meeting, but Davis did not appear.[2231]

Concern over costs of the litigation continued to mount. Edward Wegmann wrote to Holland McCombs that, "There is no doubt that the harm which has been suffered by Clay is immeasurable. Costs and expenses continue to increase and he will suffer a very substantial loss as a result of this situation."[2232]

Meanwhile, Shaw received a letter from his friend William Mehrten of Chicago; Mehrten worked for McGraw Hill and Company, but was getting ready to move to California. Mehrten indicated that he had met a person named Bernie, who would not give his last name. Bernie had told Mehrten that he understood that, one day at lunch at Brennan's restaurant, Shaw had insulted Garrison's wife, and that Garrison had sworn to "hang Shaw by the balls." Bernie also had said that Garrison had a Section 8 discharge from the Army for anxiety, unrelated to homosexuality on his part.[2233] Mehrten hit on two rumors that had buzzed around New Orleans since Shaw's arrest—that Garrison had gone after Shaw for personal reasons, and that Garrison was struggling with issues of homosexuality.

In mid-July, Shaw received the first letter since his arrest from Princess Jacqueline de Chimay, whom he had met at Rheims, France, while he was serving under General Charles Thrasher after the D-Day invasion. Chimay was a member of one of the prominent champagne families in the area, and an author of various books. She indicated that, "You would not recognize the place since we sat in the kitchen roasting potatoes and all was a wreck." She wrote that she still asked God to bless "our liberators" of 1944, and all of the friends she had made as a result of the U.S. Army's presence there, "and especially yourself." She ended by asking Shaw to visit her as soon as he got a chance.[2234]

Charles I. Spiesel, who would become one of the most memorable witnesses at Clay Shaw's trial, now emerged in the case. At trial, Spiesel's appearance would generate great interest, both because of his testimony on direct examination about a meeting where Shaw and Ferrie discussed killing Kennedy, and also because of the brutal cross-examination he underwent from Irvin Dymond, where Dymond exposed Spiesel's bizarre past activities related to wild accusations he had made against individuals, frivolous lawsuits he had filed, and his accounts of numerous attempts by mysterious individuals to hypnotize him.

Spiesel originally had approached a CBS News producer in New York, who was working on what would become the four-part television show aired in late June 1967 dealing with the Kennedy assassination, the Warren Commission, and the growing body of conspiracy theories related to the assassination. James Alcock soon went to New York City, and found Spiesel working at Slattery Construction Company, doing auditing work. Spiesel and Alcock met in the lobby of the New York Hilton, and ate at a restaurant in Greenwich Village. Spiesel told Alcock that he had been doing per diem accounting work in New Orleans in June 1963, and had gone to Lafitte's Blacksmith Shop, a famous nightclub in the French Quarter. While there, he had seen Ferrie, whom Spiesel thought he had known during World War II. They struck up a conversation, and then went to an apartment in the French Quarter, although Spiesel did not recall the address of the place. The two men went two flights up, and found themselves in a kitchen-dining area that had an orange and yellow brick wall, with a grill built into the wall. There were other individuals there. One man had a month's growth of beard on his face, and a splint with adhesive tape on the middle finger of his left hand. Spiesel estimated that man's height at 5'9", and his weight at 160 to 170 pounds. There were several airline stewardesses at the gathering, although Spiesel could not recall the name of the airline. A discussion of killing President Kennedy began, and the use of a high-powered rifle with a telescopic sight from one-half mile to a mile away was mentioned. According to Spiesel, Shaw, who also was present, laughed at all of this, and asked Ferrie if the shooter could be flown to safety. Spiesel said that Ferrie was initially taken aback by the question, but then said that could be done. The man with the beard said he would kill the president. Spiesel became alarmed at the man's demeanor, and the look in his eyes, and left the party. He later saw Ferrie two more times at Lafitte's Blacksmith Shop, where Ferrie advised him that Shaw could help him get accounting work. Spiesel tried to reach Shaw, and left word for him, but never heard back. He said that Ferrie later told him that he had spoken to Shaw, and that Shaw said he was unable to help Spiesel in his search for work. Spiesel said that was the last time he had seen Ferrie. He said that he was willing to testify, and requested that Alcock assist him in getting more per diem accounting work.[2235]

Charles Spiesel had been referred to Garrison's office originally by Robert Richter, the producer for CBS-TV to whom Spiesel initially had taken the story. During the winter and spring of 1967, Richter helped to prepare the CBS-TV special program about the Kennedy assassination, which aired in late June 1967, a week or so after the NBC News investigative report. Originally, Richter said, that program had begun as a program to highlight criticism of the Warren Commission report, but soon morphed into a program more supportive of the report.

Richter had deduced that Garrison was investigating something to do with the assassination after he encountered Garrison's researcher Tom Bethell at the National Archives in Washington, D.C. in February 1967. Bethell was researching Warren Commission and FBI records for Garrison's office, and Richter was doing the same thing for the upcoming CBS documentary.[2236]

Richter then met with Garrison in mid-February 1967, shortly before news of the investigation broke, and Garrison had offered CBS cooperation with his office in exchange for coverage of the investigation when developments allowed. Richter offered to run the idea by his bosses at CBS, but before he could do so, news of Garrison's investigation broke in the local newspapers. Along the way, Richter met many individuals with information to offer about the Kennedy assassination. He was at a party one evening when an attorney present said that he had a client who had some information Richter might find interesting, and wondered if Richter would see her. Richter said he would, and Ruth Jacobs soon came to his office, bringing along Charles Spiesel. Jacobs's information did not have to do with the New Orleans investigation, and therefore was not useful to Garrison, but Spiesel told Richter a story of going to Louisiana to visit his daughter at college, and having met Ferrie at Lafitte's Blacksmith's Shop, a French Quarter bar, and thinking he knew Ferrie from the war, went to an apartment where a party was going on, and a plot to kill Kennedy was discussed. Spiesel said that Shaw was present at the party and participated in the discussion. Both Jacobs and Spiesel wanted monetary compensation for their stories, but Richter declined to pay them, referring Spiesel instead to Jim Garrison to report the information he had about the New Orleans party. Richter labeled Jacobs a "mental case," and had doubts about Spiesel's sanity as well. More than a year and a half later, on the eve of trial, a reporter called Richter to confirm that Spiesel had first contacted him, and that Spiesel had wanted to be paid. Richter confirmed the information, then read in the paper shortly thereafter how Shaw's attorneys were cross-examining Spiesel about that information.[2237]

Charles Spiesel had a history of bizarre contact with New Orleans public officials. He had contacted Aaron Kohn of the Metropolitan Crime Commission back in 1965. Although Kohn had never heard of Spiesel, he received a subpoena out of the blue, asking him to produce everything he had in the way of documents relating to the man. Jim Garrison and New Orleans Superintendent of Police Joseph Giarusso also received subpoenas, even though they had not heard of Spiesel, either. Spiesel eventually accepted a letter from Kohn, stating that he did not have any information regarding him in his files.[2238]

Spiesel's unusual encounters were not limited to politicians. In October 1962, he had written to then-CIA Director John McCone, saying that unless the pattern of harassing activities against him, including hypnosis and being followed around, were halted, he would turn over a report about his father's services with the FBI in 1946-47 to the Soviet government.[2239] Spiesel maintained that his father, Boris Spiesel, had been a furrier in New York City, and had occasionally been used as an informant by the FBI for information about Communist activities in New York City during that era.

FBI files on Spiesel indicate that, going back at least to the early 1950s, he had contacted the FBI with offbeat, inaccurate information. The FBI had checked with Spiesel's father, who had confirmed that his son had mental problems. The FBI quickly learned to tolerate Spiesel without taking his revelations seriously.

By February 1969, Spiesel would be, in effect, the backup witness to Perry Russo at Shaw's trial, as far as testimony concerning Shaw discussing the prospective assassination was concerned. Unlike many of the questionable witnesses at Shaw's trial, including Perry Russo and others, who had essentially been groomed by Andrew Sciambra in preparation for their testimony, Spiesel's testimony lay at the feet of James Alcock, the man who would be the main prosecutor at Shaw's trial.

As the case progressed gradually over the summer of 1967, Shaw's attorneys made various motions before the court, including one for the return of property seized during the search on Shaw's residence. The items that Shaw requested be returned included; three pieces of rope, five whips, one piece of chain, two pieces of leather, one black hood and cape, one black net-type hat, one black gown, and various other possessions, including personal papers.[2240]

A number of individuals who were informants to the FBI during the time of Garrison's investigation also provided details to Garrison's office. Among them was Joseph Oster, an employee with Southern Research Company, the private investigative agency staffed mainly by former FBI agents. Oster was identified by the FBI as informant number 1309-C. Another informant was Betty Parent, the French Quarter resident supposedly well-informed about gay activities in the French Quarter; her FBI informant number was 949-C. Eugene Davis, the gay bar owner whom Dean Andrews ultimately maintained was the real "Clay Bertrand," was FBI informant number 1189-C.

By mid-summer, Garrison's office had indicted television reporters Richard Townley and Walter Sheridan. Townley would be forced to leave New Orleans as a result of the indictment and seek work elsewhere. Sheridan, who was only in New Orleans to cover the Garrison investigation anyway, simply avoided the jurisdiction. The charges had to do with witness tampering, primarily with Perry Russo, in what was alleged to be Townley's and Sheridan's attempt to get Russo to change his testimony from the preliminary hearing to say that he did not recognize Shaw as the man he had seen with Oswald and Ferrie. Sheridan, with close ties to former Attorney General and now Senator Robert F. Kennedy, President Kennedy's brother, seemingly dropped away from the Garrison investigation after the summer of 1967.

However, in late summer 1967, a story broke that recalled one of Sheridan's major successes—the prosecution several years before of former Teamsters Union president Jimmy Hoffa. Sheridan had been the lead investigator for then-Attorney General Robert Kennedy during the prosecution efforts related to Hoffa, which had spread over several trials and several years; the appeals were ongoing in 1967. One of Hoffa's co-defendants had been a New Orleans-area contractor named Zachary "Red" Strate. Strate was a building promoter who had been convicted in Federal court for unauthorized use of $5 million in Teamster's Union Health and Welfare Funds to finance part of the Fontainebleau motel in New Orleans in the early 1960s.[2241] Strate maintained that Sheridan had approached him in the early summer of 1967 offering to, in effect, go easy on Strate in his criminal appeals related to the Hoffa case, if he would provide information that, effectively, would wreck Garrison's investigation. The NBC News special that aired on June 19 was about to air when the two men met, and Sheridan was seeking any information that would discredit Garrison's investigation. Strate and several New Orleans attorneys who were involved in arranging the meeting between Strate and Sheridan testified before an Orleans Parish grand jury, whereas Sheridan ignored a subpoena to appear before the same panel. Sheridan maintained that the story was exactly the reverse, that Strate had approached him offering information that would discredit Jim Garrison's investigation into the Kennedy Assassination if Sheridan would acknowledge during his criminal appeals that the investigation years before involving Hoffa had involved illegal wiretaps, enabling Strate to go free.

Another important development happened during late June, shortly after NBC News had broadcast its harsh critique of Garrison's investigation: William Gurvich, the outside private investigator who had joined Garrison's investigation around the beginning of the year, quit the prosecution team; he soon contacted the defense attorneys. Gurvich had become disillusioned with the investigation, believing that Shaw was innocent and never should have been arrested in the first place. Gurvich had witnessed the heated argument between journalist James Phelan and Andrew Sciambra at Garrison's home, related to whether Perry Russo had contradicted himself under oath compared with what he had told Sciambra on February 25, 1967, and had been quite disturbed by the episode.

As Gurvich was defecting from Garrison's team, he was interviewed on June 27 by Ford Rowan of WDSU-TV. Gurvich said that he believed there was a real "Clay Bertrand," but would not comment on his identity. Gurvich mentioned, by occupation, several prominent people whom Garrison had planned to have arrested, including a doctor, a hotel owner, and a coffee company owner. Gurvich said that Shaw had some superficial similarities with descriptions of "Clay Bertrand" mentioned in the Warren Report.[2242] Regarding "Clay Bertrand," Gurvich probably had in mind gay bar owner Eugene Davis, who had recently been identified by Dean Andrews, accurately or not, as the person who had called him on November 23, 1963, asking him to represent Oswald. The doctor mentioned by Gurvich was supposedly Dr. Alton Ochsner, the hotel owner was William Monteleone of the Monteleone hotel, and the coffee company owner was William B. Reilly, whose company had employed Oswald for a brief time during 1963.

In late August 1967, Gurvich met with the defense attorneys, who recorded a lengthy interview with him about things that had gone on within Garrison's investigation through the time of Gurvich's defection. Gurvich also turned over copies of any internal memos he had written or acquired to the defense attorneys.

Gurvich indicated that Josephine Hug, who had worked at the Mart for a number of years under Shaw, had, shortly after Shaw's arrest, said to a group of people at a restaurant that Shaw had known Ferrie very well. Hug had been subpoenaed to testify before the grand jury, and testified twice, subsequently backing off of her assertion that Shaw had known Ferrie.

Gurvich also claimed that Marlene Mancuso, former wife of the colorful and eccentric Gordon Novel, had developed an intimate relationship with Assistant District Attorney Andrew Sciambra, and might even be living with him. Additionally, Gurvich said that Lynn Loisel, one of Garrison's main investigators, had told Gurvich in January that Garrison wanted to plant some type of evidence in Shaw's residence, and had requested that Gurvich help with that assignment; Gurvich indicated he had refused to do so.

Gurvich discussed the homosexual angle, saying that Garrison had described Kennedy's handsome looks and viral nature, and Shaw's possible jealousy of Kennedy. He indicated that Assistant District Attorney John Volz had gotten out of the case in January 1967, wanting nothing to do with it, and that Charles Ward, the second in command in the office under Jim Garrison, had refused to work on the case at all (although Ward did make some trips and interview some potential witnesses).

In response to a question by Wegmann, Gurvich said that he had never seen any evidence in Garrison's office that Shaw had any real CIA connections. Was Wegmann asking because he didn't know if Shaw had such a connection, but had seen speculation in the media, or was he asking to see how much Garrison knew? The question of whether Shaw ever told his own attorneys of his limited CIA connections from more than a decade before is an intriguing one, which has never been fully answered.

Gurvich was asked about two incidents that were rumored to have occurred at Brennan's restaurant that might have impacted Garrison's decision to arrest Shaw. One supposedly occurred not long before Shaw was arrested, when Garrison, his wife and another couple were dining at Brennan's, and Shaw was seated with another group at a nearby table. An argument began between Garrison and his wife, and Garrison threw his glass of wine into his wife's face. The incident, which is still discussed in New Orleans circles to this day, has several variations; some versions have Shaw merely witnessing the event without doing anything, while others have Shaw going over to Garrison's table and chastising Garrison in front of his friends.

The other incident at Brennan's was said to involve someone overhearing Garrison saying, "I'm going to get that son of a bitch," supposedly meaning Shaw. Some versions combine both stories, with Shaw intervening first, and Garrison then threatening to "get" him. Gurvich told the defense attorneys that he had heard no discussion of either incident at Brennan's during his tenure in the office.

An FBI memo discussing the first incident at Brennan's restaurant said that Shaw was present and intervened in the matter, which, according to the memo, occurred about two weeks before Shaw's arrest.[2243] Other witnesses have disputed that Shaw intervened in the incident, or that there was any interaction between anyone at Shaw's table and Garrison's table. The timing is also subject to question, as there is no other independent report of exactly when the incident supposedly occurred. Shaw later told writer James Kirkwood that, although some thought that the incident might have been part of Garrison's motive in pursuing him, Shaw thought that was stretching a connection too far. Shaw never mentioned actually intervening in the dispute between Garrison and his wife.

Gurvich noted Garrison's interest in city directories, books that gave a person's name and physical address in the city. He said that Garrison would study the directories all day long, trying to find connections between two or more people based upon their residential address. As an example, Gurvich noted that Miguel Torres had initially become involved in the case only because he at one time had lived in the 5000 block of Magazine Street, while Oswald had lived at 4907 Magazine Street when he lived in New Orleans in 1963. Gurvich also recalled that Garrison had frequently said that he was going to solve the assassination with "an Esso roadmap and a city directory."[2244]

According to Gurvich, one of the individuals Garrison intended to use as a witness against Clay Shaw in the trial, then scheduled for September, was an ex-convict named Darrell "Dago" Garner, who is at least once referred to as "Jack Armstrong" in a memo of that period. The trial, initially scheduled for the fall of 1967, eventually was postponed, but Garrison still considered Garner as a possible witness for a number of months. In an interview with Garrison himself on November 12, 1967, Garner said that he had seen Shaw at Jack Ruby's Carousel Club in Dallas.[2245] Garner, who had a long rap sheet, disappeared soon thereafter, and was never called at Shaw's trial.

Garrison's office continued to seek potential witnesses in the Clinton/Jackson area. Andrew Dunn, another resident of the area, gave a statement dated July 13, 1967. He said that four men had come into Clinton in a black limousine in the summer of 1963, and that Shaw had been one of them. He also indicated that local resident Estes Morgan had been in the line at the time, waiting to register to vote.[2246]

In a memo dated July 17, Andrew Sciambra summarized what Andrew Dunn supposedly had said in a recent interview, presumably at the time of his statement described above. Dunn said that he had seen four men with the black car; Shaw was driving, and New Orleans private investigator Guy Banister had been in the back seat.[2247] Apparently, Dunn did not identify either Oswald or Ferrie as having been present during the interview. Andrew Dunn did not testify at Shaw's trial, although a man named William Dunn did. Later, Andrew Dunn was sometimes listed as a possible witness at Shaw's perjury trial, which never happened. He died shortly before that trial was to have taken place in January 1971. His recollections as reflected in that July 1967 memo, however, contradict the testimony of the Clinton/Jackson witnesses at the trial, in that none of them remembered Guy Banister being there.

In view of evidence that has surfaced over the years about the tactics used by Garrison's office, and by Andrew Sciambra in particular, in eliciting and shaping witness testimony, it is reasonable to wonder if the Clinton/Jackson witnesses actually said some of the things attributed to them in the various statements and memos. Perhaps the desired information was agreed to before these documents were generated, on the basis of nothing more than that the prosecution desired it in order to help make its case against Shaw, and the witnesses were willing, if not always eager, to provide it, for motives which remain undiscovered. Even so, the testimony at trial, for those individuals ultimately used as witnesses. was often different than the details in the internal case memos.

The defense team regularly sought information from the media in order to bolster its case, or to undermine Garrison's case. The defense had helped behind the scenes with the NBC News report that had aired on June 19, helping to schedule interviews with key participants, and sharing information with Richard Townley and Walter Sheridan. The team also sought various types of information from other media sources. For example, on July 14, 1967, Edward Wegmann wrote to Irvin Dymond, enclosing transcripts of WWL-TV Channel 4's interviews with Layton Martens and William Gurvich.[2248] Hugh Aynesworth of *Newsweek* magazine, another member of the media friendly to the defense, had interviewed inmate John Cancler, the long-time burglar who had appeared on the NBC documentary raising questions about witness Vernon Bundy's motives in testifying against Shaw. Wegmann wrote to Aynesworth regarding material Cancler had in his possession, such as a log of his meetings with Garrison investigators Lou Ivon and Lynn Loisel. Wegmann asked Aynesworth's advice on how to get copies of the material in Cancler's possession.[2249]

The author Harold Robbins, famous for such novels as *The Carpetbaggers* and other pulpy bestsellers, wrote to Attorney General Ramsey Clark in mid-July, comparing Garrison's investigation to the Dreyfus case in France in the 1890s. Dreyfus supposedly had been wrongfully convicted because he was a Jew, and although usually unstated, some thought Shaw was being prosecuted because he was a homosexual. It was an idea that circulated during the time of Shaw's case, given the enormity of the alleged crime, and Shaw even referred to himself as "Dreyfus" in signing a letter to James Kirkwood after his trial; he would allude to the famous case in a January 1971 television interview shortly before a crucial Federal court hearing that ultimately led to the halting of further prosecution of him. Robbins went on to say that he had concluded that the motive of Garrison's investigation was to link a Jew to the assassination, apparently because Garrison had charged that Ruby was in on the actual assassination of President Kennedy, in addition to the murder of Oswald. Curiously, Robbins mentioned nothing explicitly about homosexuality in his letter, although he was bisexual himself, and clearly was hinting at it in his critique of Garrison's activities.[2250]

Perry Russo evidently had begun to enjoy his celebrity status during the spring and summer of 1967, after being the main witness at the preliminary hearing. He was filmed often by the news media, although portrayed in a critical light by some elements of it, and by the summer he was speaking publicly about his role, at least outside of the New Orleans area. On the occasion when he addressed the East Baton Rouge Parish Lions Club, Shaw, who had often spoken to such civic groups, noted in his diary that Russo had joined the "broiled chicken and green pea circuit," referring to the type of fare usually served at such meetings. Russo was asked by a member of the audience how Garrison could have solved the case, as he claimed to have done on February 24, 1967, when Russo had not talked to Garrison's staff until the next day. Russo indicated that he did not know all of the evidence behind Garrison's case against Shaw and, therefore, did not know upon what information Garrison had based his comment.

Another letter arrived from Mrs. Edwin S. "Frances" Anderson, saying that she had "met the nervous Jim Lewallen," Ferrie's close friend, who some thought might have been the person Perry Russo had mistaken for Oswald. Mrs. Anderson said that her friend Roger Smith and his mother were looking for some "circa 1950" photographs that showed Ferrie, perhaps with "Mrs. Knotts" (probably Jean Naatz), a friend of Ferrie in Cleveland. Anderson also noted that Ferrie was known for using an awful lot of profanities, and mentioned that Stan, her husband, knew some of Shaw's family members in the Amite, Louisiana area.[2251]

The defense team had debated the issue of whether to take the deposition of Sandra Moffett, now known as Lillie McMaines, and had made no decision as of yet. Moffett had moved from Omaha, Nebraska, across the border to Iowa, which had no extradition relationship with Louisiana. Lex Hawkins, Moffett's attorney in Iowa, said that Moffett was willing to have her deposition taken in Des Moines, Iowa, but that she would not return to New Orleans.[2252]

In early August, Shaw commented on Nina and Jeff Sulzer in his diary. He referred to Nina as "flamelike," like Miranda in *The Collector*. He said that Nina and Jeff were both alike in their strong temperaments, and he wondered how they made it work, referring to it as "steel meeting steel." Shaw had seen the couple often during the months since his arrest, and had sometimes hosted Nina alone at his place.

After his arrest, Shaw had begun taking a nightly sleeping pill. He continued to drink during this period, as he always had, although some thought his drinking became heavier after his arrest, especially during the first month or two. By early August, he noted that he was sleeping well without pills, and that he no longer needed the crutch, that alcohol worked by itself; a couple of shots of bourbon had the same effect as the sleeping pill.

Shaw often visited with Artelle Trelford and her sister, Virginia Kirk. Artelle Trelford had purchased a home from Shaw some years before at a handsome price, and he still held a note and received regular payments from her. In his diary, he commented on the wealthy Trelford's excessive use of alcohol, and the problems she was having with her sister, who burdened her in every way possible, using what Shaw called "the tyranny of the weak."

Jules Ricco Kimble, another potential witness for the prosecution, claimed he could put Shaw and either Ferrie and/or Oswald together. Like many of the potential witnesses for Garrison, Kimble had a criminal background, and tried to work more than one side of the case. In a memo dated August 4, 1967, Lloyd Ray of the New Orleans CIA office wrote to his superior at Agency headquarters, advising that Kimble had called the New Orleans office the same day and told Ray that Garrison was interested in Kimble as a potential suspect in the case. Kimble said that Garrison had accused him of taking some papers from David Ferrie's residence the day after Ferrie's death.[2253] Kimble, like other Louisiana characters who entered and exited the case during the two years between Shaw's arrest and trial, had somewhat of a history of inserting himself into public situations. He eventually would disappear from the case, vanish into semi-obscurity, and re-emerge more than a decade later in the Jim Leslie murder case, a sensational Baton Rouge murder which occurred at the height of an effort to pass a right-to-work law in Louisiana; Kimble and his brother were convicted of being involved in the murder of the man who had been hired to murder Leslie, and both were sentenced to years in Federal prison.

Reporters Hoke May and Ross Yockey, who worked for New Orleans newspapers, had written a number of stories, if not favorable to Garrison's investigation, at least putting forth Garrison's theories of the assassination somewhat uncritically. The two also had written articles about the investigation, using pen names, for *New Orleans* magazine. During the summer of 1967, former Garrison investigator William Gurvich, and Ed Baldwin, a lawyer and former assistant district attorney who represented some of the principals accused by Garrison of events related to obstructing the prosecution of Shaw, met with George Healy, the editor of the two major local newspapers, and made him aware of the situation. May and Yockey were soon removed from coverage of Garrison's Kennedy assassination investigation.[2254]

In early August, Edward Wegmann wrote to Dymond and William Wegmann, discussing information he had heard, directly or indirectly, from friends of Shaw, to the effect that Garrison had some personal animosity towards Shaw. Wegmann mentioned the incident that supposedly had occurred in Brennan's restaurant, when Shaw had witnessed Garrison and his wife get into a physical altercation involving the throwing of their drinks, as well as the other alleged occasion at Brennan's, where Garrison supposedly had been heard to say, "I'm going to destroy that bastard."[2255]

Bobbie Dedon was interviewed by Garrison's investigators on August 4, although the memo of her interview is dated January 29, 1968. She worked at East Louisiana State Hospital, the mental institution in Jackson, Louisiana, and she said that Oswald had stopped by the front office and asked her for directions to the personnel office. She associated him with Estes Morgan, although she did not specify exactly how.[2256] She would testify in a similar matter at Shaw's trial, although the name Estes Morgan did not come up in her testimony.

Members and staff of the Warren Commission mostly distanced themselves from Garrison's investigation. In early August, when Assistant District Attorney James Alcock tried to convince commission staffer Wesley Liebeler, who had conducted a lengthy interview with Dean Andrews about the "Clay Bertrand" episode in 1964, to come down to testify at Andrews's upcoming perjury trial, Liebeler was hesitant; he said that he did not want to cooperate because of his general attitude toward Garrison's investigation of the Kennedy assassination. However, Garrison's office had actually indicted Andrews for perjury not directly related to the Clay Shaw/"Clay Bertrand" issue, so Alcock tried to convince Liebeler that the case was actually about Andrews lying about paroling an individual as a favor for David Ferrie, rather than directly involving Garrison's investigation. He suggested that if Liebeler would come to New Orleans, the district attorney's office could issue him an official subpoena. Liebeler responded that he was concerned that the whole Andrews matter had to do with Clay Shaw's case, and asked Alcock to subpoena him officially through a court in Vermont, where Liebeler lived at the time.[2257]

Meanwhile, Shaw was interested in mounting an offensive against Garrison, based upon his lack of good faith in the prosecution, and because of Garrison's constant pronouncements in the media. Wegmann indicated to Dymond and William Wegmann that Shaw wanted Garrison off the case because he had supposedly said, "I am going to destroy that bastard," meaning Shaw, and because of the deal Garrison had supposedly cut with *LIFE* magazine, whereby Garrison's office stood to gain extraordinary publicity in exchange for sharing behind-the-scenes information with the magazine.[2258] At that point, the defense team still employed Southern Research Company investigators Charles Carson and Robert Wilson, but were slowly growing disenchanted with them, even before questions had arisen concerning whether details of their work had been shared with members of the prosecution team. At the time, Wegmann wrote to Dymond that he regarded them both as honest individuals, but thought that Wilson in particular could use more "ingenuity and aggressiveness."[2259]

Following up with Wynn Pearce, Wegmann told him that he might need to testify in court as to the identities of the individuals in the controversial photos taken at the party on Royal Street in the 1940s.[2260] Regarding the photographs, Wegmann wrote to the Department of Vital Statistics in Big Sur, California, seeking a death certificate on Robert Brannon, the man in the photographs who resembled David Ferrie; Wegmann understood he had died in California.[2261] Wegmann also wrote to Jim Loring of KLIF Radio in Dallas, Texas, to inquire about Brannon, as Wegmann had learned that Brannon used to be a disc jockey at the station, and had committed suicide several years earlier.[2262]

Dr. John Nichols, a medical doctor, and Associate Professor of Pathology at the University of Kansas Medical Center in Kansas City, emerged as a possible witness for the prosecution. He would testify at Shaw's trial regarding his criticisms of the official autopsy of President Kennedy. Nichols originally contacted Garrison's office in the summer of 1967. In a letter dated August 10, which refers to an earlier letter in July, Nichols mentioned his experiments concerning shooting a gun into recently amputated arms and legs; he said that he was waiting on a recently dead, intact body on which he could try similar experiments. Nichols related that he amputated many legs during the normal course of his work on corpses, but got few arms on which to experiment, and that he received very few bodies that were "recently dead," intact and "unembalmed."[2263]

On August 15, Layton Martens ran into Perry Russo by chance. Both had been in the news over the previous five months or more, appearing both in print and on television, and Russo sought a conversation with Martens. Russo told Martens that he had met Ferrie initially through Al Landry's mother; she was worried about Landry becoming physically involved with Ferrie. Discussing the Shaw case, Martens said that Russo told him, "I'm not really sure if they were plotting against Castro or Kennedy."[2264] Milton Brener, Martens's attorney, summarized the results of the meeting between Martens and Russo in a memo, which he then sent to Irvin Dymond; Dymond forwarded a copy on to Edward and William Wegmann for their review.[2265] Martens then met with Edward Wegmann and related the contents of the conversation.[2266]

Dean Andrews, the roly-poly, jive-talking attorney who had originated the "Clay Bertrand" story, was coming to trial for perjury because of his contradictory stories about the incident, although Garrison's office had structured the indictment as being related to a peripheral matter. He had been represented initially by an attorney named Sam Monk Zelden, then by the Burglass brothers, a trio who backed out of the case as it was going to trial because of disagreements with Andrews about strategy. Cecil Burglass, the most prominent of the trio, had met recently with Garrison and his chief prosecutor, James Alcock, and the Shaw case had come up in conversation. Attorney Ed Baldwin had encountered Burglass, who told him the results of that conversation. Baldwin, who had been an assistant district attorney in the past, and who coincidentally was the brother of David Baldwin, who had worked for Shaw during the 1950s, said that Garrison had stated he would convict Shaw with utmost certainty. James Alcock had told Burglass that he did not know whether or not Shaw was guilty of the conspiracy charge, but he could not understand why Shaw had lied about knowing certain people, presumably Ferrie at least, and possibly Oswald. Wegmann wrote to Dymond, relaying the information, and saying that Shaw denied lying to or misleading investigators during his questioning; Wegmann said the defense should request copies of all tapes, notes and any other record of interviews with Shaw in the possession of the district attorney's office, including any tapes made from "bugs or wiretaps."[2267]

Interestingly, Sam Monk Zelden, Andrews's first attorney, maintained that he had received an important call of his own the weekend after the assassination. Zelden said that Marguerite Oswald, Oswald's mother, had called him directly, asking him to represent Oswald, but that he had wanted time to think it over, having admired Kennedy, and that Oswald had been shot and killed by Jack Ruby before he could decide; he said that Marguerite Oswald never called him again. If true, could Andrews have picked up on Zelden's story in order to generate publicity for himself, inventing the story of "Clay Bertrand" knowing that no one could contradict him, and knowing that, with Oswald dead, the issue of defending him was moot. Zelden would tell author James Kirkwood, after Shaw's trial, that Dean Andrews had never "come clean" with him about the whole story.[2268] Zelden never reported his own story to the FBI or the Warren Commission after the assassination, and Marguerite Oswald denied ever calling him.

Dean Andrews initially was charged with perjury, at least indirectly, because he had refused to identify Clay Shaw as "Clay Bertrand." In early testimony before a grand jury, Andrews refused to say either that Shaw was or was not "Clay Bertrand." Later, he appeared before the grand jury and said that Shaw definitely was not "Clay Bertrand," saying instead that the person who had called him at the hospital the day after the assassination was Eugene Davis, the gay bar owner. Andrews would ultimately be charged with at least three sets of perjury charges related to his various appearances before grand juries and at trials. He would be convicted of perjury at his first trial, and would battle the other sets of charges for years before eventually getting out from under all of them.

During Andrews's August 1967 trial, several newsmen from the New Orleans area testified as to their knowledge of Garrison's investigation. Newsman Sam DePino said that he had talked with Garrison in November 1966 about the investigation. David Chandler of *LIFE* magazine testified that he had been assigned to the Garrison investigation around the end of November 1966, and that in December he talked with Garrison, who told him he had the assassination solved. According to Chandler, on December 8, 1966, Garrison went into details in his office, but did not mention Dean Andrews. Later in December 1966, Garrison mentioned Andrews in the context of Clay Shaw, and said that Andrews was lying about the identity of "Clay Bertrand" when he refused to say that Shaw was "Bertrand." Chandler said that Garrison thought Shaw was "Bertrand" because he was gay, because he had a home in Hammond near where an anti-Castro Cuban guerilla-warfare style camp was positioned, and because Shaw spoke Spanish; Chandler placed the latter meeting before December 20, 1966, which would make it before Shaw was initially brought in for questioning.[2269]

Newsman Ross Yockey said he first began covering the story when David Ferrie died, and could not recall any discussions about Dean Andrews with either Garrison or his staff. Reporter Jack Dempsey, one of the three who had broken the story to the public in a news article on February 17, 1967, testified that he first inquired into the investigation in mid-December 1966, when he had spoken with Assistant District Attorney Charles Ward.[2270]

William Gurvich, who identified himself as a "special aide" for Garrison from late December 1966 until late June 1967, testified that he had heard Andrews's name mentioned in relation to the identity of "Clay Bertrand." He said that from mid-May forward, Garrison characterized Dean Andrews's credibility as suspect, and said that Andrews was sometimes discussed as having been an attorney for Gordon Novel during his attempted dealings with Clay Shaw prior to the opening of the new International Trade Mart tower, as if Shaw might have met Andrews during that representation. Even Jim Garrison testified, saying that he had lunch with Andrews early on in the investigation to discuss Andrews's testimony before the Warren Commission. Andrews's Warren Commission testimony, of course, had given some detail, if conflicting within itself, about the identity and description of "Clay Bertrand."[2271]

Shaw's old friend, Tom Dawson, who now lived in Los Angeles, dropped into New Orleans in mid-August. Dawson, a colorful, opinionated character who had been one of the first to respond by telegram after Shaw was arrested, calling his arrest the result of a "bizarre witch hunt," spent the night at Jeff Biddison's residence. Shaw met him at Marilyn Tate's place during his visit, and told Dawson the complete story of his ordeal from beginning through the present. Dawson, who had worked for the William Morris Agency before opening his own business as an interior decorator and architect, listened to the story, and he and Shaw discussed whether a jury would believe Garrison's theories. Dawson happened to be a longtime friend of writer James Leo Herlihy, author of *Midnight Cowboy*, *All Fall Down*, and *Blue Denim*. Dawson put Shaw in touch with Herlihy, and while Shaw was in New York City in October of 1967, Herlihy introduced Shaw to Herlihy's friend and fellow author James Kirkwood, perhaps ultimately best known for his 1970s play, *A Chorus Line*. As a result of their meeting, and hearing Shaw's story, Kirkwood decided to become involved in the case, first writing a profile of Shaw when he was halfway between arrest and trial in May 1968; the article appeared in *Esquire* magazine near the end of 1968. By the time of publication, Kirkwood had decided to cover the entire trial as well, and would go on to produce a major book about the case, *American Grotesque*.

On August 22, 1967, Wynn Pearce came through New Orleans and met with Shaw and his attorneys. He identified the people in the party photographs from the late 1940s, confirming that the character who had been identified as David Ferrie was, in fact, Bob Brannon. Pearce was very cooperative, and told Shaw of his activities over the years. He was a playwright now, after years of being a bit actor, and had recently been awarded the Schubert Award of $2,500 for his first play. The next day, Shaw met Pearce for cocktails at the Royal Orleans hotel before Pearce departed town.

Garrison's office continued to interview individuals in the Clinton and Jackson area about the incident with the black limousine, sometimes referred to as a black Cadillac. Some remembered hearing talk about the incident, including that a black Cadillac had come into town, and that a "smart-aleck white boy" had been standing in a voter registration line, but most of the people interviewed either never saw the incident, or could not identify photos of individuals shown to them by Garrison's investigators. At one time, Garrison's investigators showed up at a well-attended meeting of Congress of Racial Equality (CORE) members in

Clinton and showed them photographs of various individuals on a projector. For the most part, the African Americans present were noncommittal about identifying any of the individuals whose photographs were shown.[2272]

Another interesting development occurred during the summer of 1967, when an article appeared in a Vancouver, British Columbia newspaper, the *Vancouver Sun*, reporting that a Donald P. Norton, who claimed he had been with the CIA, also said that Shaw was with the CIA. Assistant District Attorney Charles Ward, who had disassociated himself from the investigation, came back into service to interview Norton in July 1967. Norton was thirty-five years old, a native of Griffin, Georgia; he still lived with his parents in Columbus, Georgia. Ward indicated that he thought Norton was a homosexual; Norton shared that he had been hired by the CIA to root out homosexuals in the military, and told Ward he had seen Shaw on two occasions: once in Albany, Georgia, and once at the Domino Lounge in Atlanta. He also maintained that Shaw and Ferrie had known each other. Ward's memo indicates that *LIFE* reporter Richard Billings also had interviewed Norton, and had found his entire story "dubious."[2273] Norton's story, once it hit the papers, would spark interest from the Central Intelligence Agency, since Norton claimed to be an employee there. Lloyd Ray, who managed the New Orleans CIA office and was a longtime friend of Shaw's defense attorney Irvin Dymond, would quietly, if unsuccessfully, seek the CIA's cooperation in helping Dymond to discredit Norton. Ultimately, Norton, like many others, would disappear from the news, and would not testify at Shaw's trial.

As a result of the story, however, Irvin Dymond asked Lloyd Ray to ask if the CIA would provide information about Norton, and whether he had ever been with the CIA. Presumably, Dymond also had made inquiries as to whether Shaw was with the CIA, but Ray was not yet in a position to pass that information on to Dymond.

Additionally, Shaw's attorneys followed up with the newspaper that had printed the story. In a letter dated October 17, 1967 to John Taylor, the reporter in Vancouver who had written the piece, Edward Wegmann said that Shaw was not then, and never had at any time in the past, been directly or indirectly associated or connected with the CIA in any capacity.[2274] That type of blanket denial, also engaged in by Shaw himself in at least one media appearance around the same time, accounts for a great deal of the continuing curiosity about Shaw's possible involvement in the assassination, and skepticism about his denials of such involvement. It also raises the question of whether he ever told his attorneys the full story of his contacts with the CIA from the late 1940s through the mid-1950s.

In early September, Edward Wegmann wrote to Dymond concerning the story about Donald Norton and Shaw being involved with the CIA. The letter also referenced the upcoming visit of Dymond and Wegmann to meet with officials of the U.S. Department of Justice in Washington, in approximately ten days. Wegmann said that he had spoken recently with Ed Bostick, and had determined that Ramsey Clark was a "poor" and "weak" attorney general who could offer them little help, and that it would also be a waste of time to try to see Bobby Kennedy or Hale Boggs. Wegmann sought to have Garrison, Andrew Sciambra, Russo, and Dr. Esmond Fatter, the hypnotist, criminally indicted, or to file a civil suit for civil rights violations against them. His letter also referenced that Dymond was talking with a local CIA man, undoubtedly Lloyd Ray, to get an appointment with CIA officials in Washington, D.C.[2275]

Dymond had written to Lloyd Ray on September 5 about Donald Norton, referencing their conversation that same day about the subject.[2276] Lloyd Ray contacted CIA officials in Washington and reported on Dymond's conversation, saying it was the first time Dymond had ever spoken to him on any subject related to the Clay Shaw case, even though the two had seen each other often, and had played golf together, since Shaw's arrest some six months earlier. Ray sought permission from the CIA to tell Dymond that Norton had no connection with the agency; it is unclear if he ever received explicit permission to pass along that information to Dymond. The same day, Dymond wrote to Edward Wegmann listing things to do in relation to the case. The last item on the list was to see someone in authority at the CIA in Washington to get their cooperation, possibly in determining the exact nature of Shaw's connections.[2277] Dymond also sought the cooperation of friendly reporters to debunk the Donald Norton story; he wrote to Richard Townley[2278] and Hugh Aynesworth[2279] seeking their assistance.

As late as September 1, 1967, Charles Ward, Garrison's top assistant who had asked to remain uninvolved in the Shaw case, was in fact still involved, at least around the edges. A memo dated that day from Assistant District Attorney Richard Burnes to Tom Bethell asked Bethell to get addresses from the list of witnesses who had appeared in the Warren Commission report, so the district attorney's office could subpoena those whom Charles Ward decided were necessary for Shaw's trial, still scheduled for later that month.[2280]

What became known as the Eastern Airlines VIP Room incident began around late August 1967, when Garrison's office was notified that the visitor register in the room at the New Orleans International Airport contained the signatures of some Latin men, and the signature "Clay Bertrand." The VIP Room was a place where Eastern Airlines customers could relax, have a drink, and eat something, before or in between flights. Someone apparently had gone into the room and signed the name "Clay Bertrand" on the register entry for December 14, 1966, approximately two and a half months before Shaw was arrested, and well before Garrison's investigation was announced to the public.

The person who reported the signature in the guest register at the VIP Room to Garrison's office was Ronald R. Raymond, of LaPlace, Louisiana, a town just outside New Orleans. According to his affidavit, Raymond said that a friend of his, Deuce Parent, a Sergeant on the Kenner, Louisiana police force, had told him that an employee of Eastern Airlines had shown him the guest register, and that it had been signed by at least six people on December 14, 1966, including four Latins, "Clay Bertrand," and Arthur Davis.[2281] Parent apparently chose not to become directly involved with Garrison's investigation, and so did not report the information himself.

Investigators C.J. Navarre and Fenner Sedgebeer (The name of "Fenner Sedgebeer" appears on a number of memos during Jim Garrison's Kennedy assassination investigation. Some have maintained that "Fenner Sedgebeer" was an alias used by Jim Garrison during the investigation for memos authored by him.) went to the Eastern Airlines VIP Room on September 1, 1967 to take photographs of the guest register that contained the signature of "Clay Bertrand." The name "Clay Bertrand" was indeed there, along with the names of several men who seemed to be of Latino descent, for the date of December 14, 1966.

Garrison's investigators began to interview employees who were present on that day. This portion of the investigation quickly centered on Jessie Parker, an African-American woman who on December 14, 1966 was a hostess in the VIP Room. She was employed by Gulf Janitorial Service, which contracted its services for hosting and janitorial duties; she had only begun with that company a month before. In an affidavit dated September 12, 1967, Jessie Parker set forth her initial version of what she remembered about that day and the signature in the register. Andrew Sciambra had interviewed her and shown her approximately forty photos of people, from which she selected three who looked familiar. She said that Shaw frequently came to the VIP Room, always bringing others with him. She said that he usually brought two or three people in at a time, that she would make him a Bloody Mary each visit, and that he spoke a foreign language at times. She said that on December 14, 1966, he had come in with four people from Caracas, Venezuela, with a person dressed in "London-type clothes," who she thought was possibly an interpreter, and with a woman. The group was waiting for someone to come in on a flight, and she asked them to sign the register. Shaw had signed in as "Clay Bertrand," and had introduced her to the people from Venezuela. She said that "Bertrand" wanted his regular drink, and that she mixed him a

Bloody Mary. Of the other two people whose photos she thought looked familiar, she could not place where or when she had seen them. Parker also said that, when she left duty at 2:00 p.m., Cecilia Fagan had replaced her, and that "Bertrand" and his group had still been there. Andrew Sciambra and Lorraine Schuler, Jim Garrison's secretary, witnessed her affidavit. Interestingly, Charles Ward served as the Notary Public.[2282]

On September 13, 1967, Andrew Sciambra interviewed Cecilia Fagan, who worked with Jessie Parker at the VIP Room. She said that her memory was hazy about December 14, 1966, but Fagan recalled the four individuals from Caracas, Venezuela. However, she said that she never saw Clay Shaw in the room, and that she did not know the name "Clay Bertrand" had been written into the guest register. Fagan thought that the Venezuelans had signed the guest register while she was there, and that they had been present in the room for a long period of time.[2283][2284]

The discovery of the signature in the guest register, coming just before Shaw's trial, then scheduled to begin in just a few weeks, could have produced an explosive result. However, the trial would be delayed, not once but several times until January 1969, and much would happen with this part of the story in the meantime.

Sometime along the way, Garrison's men thought it might be prudent to track down the other men listed on the guest register for that day. Accordingly, in early 1968, Andrew Sciambra began to locate and find those whose names appeared on December 14, 1966. It was soon revealed that the Latino men were a group of visitors from Venezuela, who were being accompanied by U.S. Department of State employees and a military escort. A memo dated April 2, 1968 from Sciambra to Garrison indicated that he had interviewed Captain John Warren, the military escort for State Department employee Theodore Herrera and the visiting Venezuelans. Warren remembered one man being in the room at the time the group was in the VIP room, but he did not remember what the man looked like, and did not recognize any of the photos shown to him by Sciambra, including that of Shaw.[2285] Another memo dated April 2, 1968 referenced Sciambra's interview with State Department employee Theodore Herrera in Washington, D.C. Herrera said that he recognized the photo of Shaw, because he had dealt with Shaw in the past in his duties with the State Department when Shaw had been an employee with the International Trade Mart prior to his retirement. However, Herrera said that he had not seen Shaw at the airport on December 14, 1966.[2286]

Another memo dated April 2, 1968 has Sciambra reporting to Garrison that Sciambra and prominent Kennedy assassination conspiracy theorist Harold Weisberg had interviewed Mr. and Mrs. Ross P. Pope in Washington, D.C.. Pope was also a State Department employee who had been involved with escorting the visiting Venezuelans through New Orleans. Pope remembered a man in the VIP room when the group entered, and picked a photo of Gordon Novel as possibly being that person. Pope recognized Shaw from various newspaper photos that had appeared throughout 1967, but did not identify him as having been in the VIP room on December 14, 1966. Sciambra noted in the memo that Pope's version could not "help us or hurt us."[2287]

Shaw's attorneys would not know about the discovery of the signature in the guest register until shortly before the trial finally began in January 1969. That discovery, probably triggered by Garrison office researcher Tom Bethell's defection to the defense side of the case, set in motion a frantic effort by Edward Wegmann to locate the same State Department officials in order to learn the context of their visit, and that of the Venezuelans, to the room, and to determine if they had seen Shaw there.

Jessie Parker's testimony at Shaw's trial was probably the most quietly sensational of all witnesses against Shaw. It was a mystery, and remains so to this day, why Shaw would have entered a room at the airport and signed an alias that had been tied to the Kennedy assassination three years earlier, for no apparent purpose. What has not been revealed before is that records regarding what Parker supposedly saw that day changed from her original statement in September 1967 to a new one generated shortly before Shaw's trial in January 1969. The two statements conflict greatly, and there is a specific reason that they do.

As mentioned above, in her original statement of September 12, 1967, Jessie Parker supposedly said (subject to the condition mentioned earlier regarding memos generated by some Garrison investigators, especially Assistant District Attorney Andrew Sciambra, and whether the individuals concerned actually said what is in the memos) that the man she identified as "Clay Bertrand" had been in before, with two or three other people each time, and had always ordered Bloody Marys to drink. This time, he had come in with a group of Venezuelans. Parker also originally had said that, when she left duty at 2:00 p.m., Cecilia Fagan had replaced her, and that "Bertrand" and his group had still been there.[2288]

However, Cecilia Fagan, the employee who took over for Parker at 2:00 p.m. on the afternoon in question, told Garrison's investigators she did not remember Shaw being there, and did not know the name "Bertrand" had been written in the guest register. Also, as it emerged that the group of Venezuelans had been accompanied by State Department employees, at least one of whom had known Shaw, and none of whom recalled him being there, it slowly became apparent that Jessie Parker's story, as originally told, had serious problems.

What to do, then? One solution simply would be to change what Parker would testify that she had seen. Accordingly, shortly before Shaw's trial, someone, presumably someone in Garrison's office, underlined portions of Jessie Parker's original September 12, 1967 affidavit that were to be removed; the altered version does not contain the statements about Shaw coming in with the Venezuelans, and ordering the Bloody Mary drinks, or about his having been in the room before. A new affidavit was generated to become the affidavit of January 1969, about which Parker would then testify in court. In her court testimony, Parker would say that Shaw had simply come into the room with another man, whom she could not identify, at a time when there were no other visitors in the room. Parker stuck with that simplified testimony under cross-examination, although she would concede that she could not pick any other day for a reasonable period around December 14, 1966 and offer the same level of certainty concerning who came into the room, or who signed the guest register.

Jessie Parker's testimony remains somewhat of a mystery. However, with the discovery of the conflicting versions of her recollection, the mystery has shifted from why Shaw would sign such a notorious alias in the guest register for no obvious logical reason, to how the prosecution was able to convince, or perhaps pressure, Jessie Parker to say the contradictory things she supposedly said, including her final trial testimony.

At Shaw's trial, since Shaw contested that he had ever been in the Eastern Airlines VIP Room, Garrison's office would attempt to link him to the "Clay Bertrand" signature in the book by use of a handwriting expert. Although Elizabeth McCarthy Bailey, who had participated in some of the appeals related to the Alger Hiss case for Hiss's defense team, eventually would testify as Garrison's handwriting expert witness, Garrison's office first had sought the services of local handwriting expert Gilbert Fortier. Checks signed by Shaw were sent to Fortier on August 31, 1967, obviously in preparation for the trial then scheduled for September 1967. Fortier, though, was not used at trial by either the prosecution or the defense, which also had its own handwriting expert.

The defense attorneys had the cooperation of officials within the district attorney's office in Dallas, Texas, who were skeptical of the entire New Orleans angle related to the Kennedy assassination. On September 1, Edward Wegmann wrote to Assistant District Attorney Bill Alexander, who had been involved in the investigations of Ruby and Oswald in the immediate aftermath of the Kennedy assassination, thanking him for his "past and ongoing help."[2289]

The same day, Wegmann wrote to attorney Lex Hawkins in Iowa regarding the Sandra Moffett deposition. Wegmann said that Judge Edward Haggerty, who would be presiding over Shaw's trial, would not allow the taking of a deposition that could then be used in court, but that Wegmann wanted to take a sworn statement from Moffett before a stenographer, anyway.[2290]

In its continuing efforts to interview potentially helpful witnesses among the nation's prison population, Garrison's office spoke with Valentine Ashworth, a man who claimed to have CIA connections (a relationship denied by the CIA) and who was housed at a jail in Lake Charles, Louisiana. Ashworth maintained that he had seen Oswald and Shaw (with Shaw using the name "Bertrand") together in Ohio and New Orleans. He also said that he had seen Ferrie and Russo together in conversations with Shaw.[2291] Ashworth was never used at Shaw's trial. Obviously; having a person testify that he had seen Russo, Ferrie, and Shaw having conversations would have conflicted with Perry Russo's own testimony, which never mentioned a Valentine Ashworth.

Another inmate who initiated contact with Garrison's office was Edward James Whalen, a 43-year-old who had been in trouble with the law all of his life, and who had spent most of his adult life in prison. James Alcock traveled to Federal prison and interviewed Whalen in September 1967. Whalen said that he had met David Ferrie in 1965, and that Ferrie had then introduced him to Shaw at the Absinthe House on Bourbon Street. Ferrie, Whalen said, had referred to Shaw as "Clay Bertrand." Shaw allegedly said that he was willing to pay $10,000 up front to have Jim Garrison killed, and that Shaw would give Whelan $15,000 more after the job was completed, for a total of $25,000. Whelan said that he was reluctant to do the job, but that he later went to Shaw's residence, where attorney Dean Andrews had come by. Shaw told Whelan that Whelan's daughter, who had polio, could get the best medical treatment with the money Shaw would pay him. Whelan also mentioned a meeting in Baton Rouge with Ruby, Shaw, and Oswald that had been talked about by either Ferrie or Shaw. However, Whelan could not remember the striking red color of the door at Shaw's residence, or much about the interior, although he remembered a patio when asked about it. Whelan said that after he left New Orleans, he had been caught and convicted of armed robbery.[2292]

At the same time, the defense team was communicating with Jack Ruby's sister, Eva Grant; Wegmann wrote to her concerning Ruby's whereabouts during September 1963.[2293] He was concerned about the story by Clyde Johnson, the former minor gubernatorial candidate in Louisiana, which had arisen during the summer. Johnson claimed that he had been in a meeting with Clay Shaw, Jack Ruby and Oswald in a hotel in Baton Rouge in September 1963.

Attorney Jack Mulverhill (the correct spelling may be Mulvihill) reported to the FBI in September 1967 that he recently had sat with Garrison in a steam room at the New Orleans Athletic Club. Mulverhill, who thought that Garrison seemed almost incoherent during the conversation, said that Garrison had told him that the CIA would kill Shaw in order to prevent a trial.[2294] Years later, former New Orleans mayor Moon Landrieu, who replaced Garrison as a judge after Garrison retired from the court, told the author that Garrison, as late as the 1990s, had been afraid to sit near a window in his office because he still feared an assassination attempt by the CIA.[2295]

Henry Burnell Clark, another of the potential Clinton/Jackson witnesses, gave a statement on September 12 to Garrison's investigators, saying that he had seen Shaw there in the summer of 1963, but with no hat on (some Clinton/Jackson witnesses were recalling that the older, gray-haired man in the limousine had worn a hat), walking toward him. Clark, who was then twenty-nine years old, said he saw Shaw get into the black car, make a U-turn, and drive away He said that he also recognized a man with "unusual" hair during the same general period, but did not specifically identify him in the memo as David Ferrie.[2296] The affidavit is somewhat unclear, in that Clark seems to say he saw the two men on separate days.[2297] Although Clark was expected by Shaw's attorneys to be a prosecution witness at the trial, he did not testify.[2298]

In September 1967, Shaw's attorneys, Edward Wegmann and Irvin Dymond, went to Washington, D.C., to meet with officials in the Department of Justice, in order to explore making an official civil rights complaint about Garrison's treatment of Shaw. After the meeting, Justice Department officials commented to CIA officials that Shaw's attorneys did not seem to be aware of Shaw's past connections with the CIA. The Justice Department attorneys, which included Nathaniel Kossack, sent those impressions along to Lawrence Houston, the CIA's general counsel. CIA officials thought that Shaw surely must have told his own attorneys about such a connection. When it appeared that his lawyers perhaps really were in the dark on this matter, CIA officials considered how to get information to Irvin Dymond directly, as it seemed that Shaw was not being forthright with his counsel. However, Houston advised that the CIA should only talk with Shaw's attorneys if they could be trusted absolutely.[2299]

The CIA's concern, of course, was the if Shaw's attorneys were totally unaware of Shaw's earlier connection with the agency, they could be ambushed by Garrison's men at the upcoming trial. Garrison had made sweeping public accusations about the CIA's involvement in the assassination, and a conviction of Shaw would seriously stain the agency if accusations that he had agency connections were not put in proper perspective. However, the agency did not want to go public with an explanation of Shaw's connections, thereby seemingly involving itself in Garrison's case.

The CIA forwarded the Department of Justice's comments to its New Orleans office, trying to further clarify Shaw's relationship with them many years before.[2300] The New Orleans office responded that they had assumed, much like their D.C. counterparts, that Shaw must have discussed his history with their office with Irvin Dymond. It indicated that there was no record or recollection on the part of any employee of Shaw ever signing a secrecy agreement, but that it would have been stressed to Shaw at the beginning of the relationship that secrecy, and the classified nature of what he was doing, was of the utmost importance.[2301]

On September 27, following the visit with Department of Justice officials, Edward Wegmann wrote to John Doar with the Civil Rights Division of the Justice Department, following up on the potential complaint defense attorneys would soon file.[2302] Shaw's attorneys also approached Herbert "Jack" Miller, Walter Sheridan's well-connected Washington attorney, around the same time, hoping he could help them determine if Shaw was leveling with them about his background with governmental agencies.

Also on September 27, an anonymous caller called Irvin Dymond's office and spoke to his employee, Ronnie Wicker. Wicker, then Dymond's paralegal, but later a lawyer and Federal judge, reported to Dymond in a handwritten note that the man who called said that in 1949 a CIA employee, whom he identified only as J. Burtham, had approached the caller and Shaw to do work for the Central Intelligence Agency. The caller said that J. Burtham worked for International House, but that J. Burtham had not been his real name. The caller said that he and Shaw had gone to school to speak, write, and read Spanish during the 1940s, before they began their work for the Central Intelligence Agency.[2303]

Wegmann received some discouraging news toward the end of September. James Eddy of the public relations firm McFadden, Strauss, Eddy, and Irwin said that he had watched Jim Garrison appear on the *Page One* show in New York City, and felt that Garrison had come off very well in discrediting the Warren Report. Eddy said that he could not tell what evidence Garrison had against Shaw from his appearance, but suggested that the defense should have "moneyed" New Orleans people hire a public relations firm to take on Garrison.[2304]

In early October, Frances Anderson wrote to Shaw that there were some photos of David Ferrie and Lewallen, among others, taken "around 1950" in the Washington, D.C. area, which her friend Roger Smith should be able to send to Shaw; Anderson asked that Shaw's use of the photos not be detrimental to James Lewallen. She also mentioned a letter that David Ferrie had written to Roger Smith in 1963, asking him to obtain medical information from David Ripton, whom she understood was the son of Ferrie's late physician, in an effort by Ferrie to prove that he had never been in a mental institution, in jail, or had any psychiatric problems. Anderson further wondered to Shaw if her young friend at the Pyewacket Antique Shop could possibly discredit Perry Russo. Anderson's friend was actually Tommy Compton, who had been Anderson's lab partner during her student years at Southeastern Louisiana College in Hammond, Louisiana; Compton was also the person whom Ferrie had gone to visit in Hammond after returning to New Orleans from his trip to Texas shortly after Kennedy's assassination. Anderson said that Compton believed that Sandra Moffett had told the truth when she had denied attending the alleged conspiracy party in 1963 involving Shaw, Ferrie, Oswald, and Russo. Compton apparently had stayed for a time with Ferrie, and was familiar with his acquaintances during that time. Anderson told Shaw that Compton lived from "crisis to crisis," and that his very conservative parents had disowned him because of his lifestyle.[2305]

Also in early October, now seven months after Shaw's arrest, a local television station took a poll among viewers, hosted by prominent local newscaster Alec Gifford. The poll used a call-in method, whereby viewers had the opportunity to express whether or not they had confidence in District Attorney Jim Garrison; Shaw, Marilyn Tate, and approximately ten other friends called the number repeatedly to vote "No." Shaw indicated in his diary that shortly thereafter, all of them had developed calluses on their fingers, proving, he noted ironically, how fair the poll had been. The final results were that 56% said that they had confidence in Jim Garrison, while 44% said they did not.

On October 5, Shaw sat for an interview with Gordon Donaldson of the Canadian Broadcasting System. It was one of the rare television or radio interviews his lawyers allowed him to do during the two-year period between his arrest and trial, possibly because it would not be shown in the United States; Jim Garrison had been interviewed the day before. A 22-minute clip of the entire broadcast shown on Canadian TV can be found on the Internet today, one of the few surviving examples of Shaw speaking for any length on film.

In his approximately four-minute interview with Donaldson, Shaw proclaimed his innocence, and denied any involvement in President Kennedy's assassination, although he said that he was constrained by court order not to discuss the specifics of the case. Shaw indicated that he had never known Oswald or Ferrie at any time. In the most interesting part of the interview, Shaw maintained that he never had any connection with the Central Intelligence Agency. At that point, Donaldson followed up with a question intended to clarify that Shaw meant absolutely no contact with the Agency in any form whatsoever, and Shaw reconfirmed that he had never had anything to do with the Agency in any capacity. As it turned out, that answer was untruthful, a glaring contradiction to Shaw's normally sterling reputation for truthfulness. It is a prime example of why suspicions linger to this day about Shaw's possible involvement with the assassination. One could argue that it also calls into question his unqualified denial about ever knowing Oswald or Ferrie in the same interview.

Shaw's involvement with the Central Intelligence Agency, as a source of information related mainly to his travels in foreign countries, from December 1948 to 1956, was not revealed publicly until December 1973, less than a year before his death. The first mention of it was by a small independent (some would say left-wing) news organization, Zodiac News Service, and few, if any, major media outlets picked up the story. The actual account of his involvement was somewhat inaccurate, but did seem to originate with a former employee of the agency. Shaw avoided being questioned directly about it for the remaining eight months of his life, so it has never been clear why he felt it necessary to give the flat-out denials of his earlier connection while he was being interviewed in 1967.

By October, Shaw had quit using the Dictaphone and an outside typist, finding it easier to type his daily notes himself. He asked his old friend Muriel Bultman Francis (now Bogner) to talk to Senator Jacob Javits and Congressman Ben Kupperman, whom she had known from her days of living in New York, about having a Congressional investigation of the Warren Commission's findings. It was interesting for Shaw, who always publicly maintained his belief in the Warren Commission's conclusions, to recommend such an investigation, a version of which did indeed take place in the late 1970s with the House Select Committee on Assassinations (HSCA).

On October 4, Shaw met Father Ed Sheridan in Edward Wegmann's office. Shaw told Sheridan of an "apocalyptic" moment he had recently while walking down Baronne Street in the French Quarter, where he realized that "God is," and "God is not mocked."

On October 6, Shaw noted that, upon waking in the morning, "all is well" with his spirits. Then, depression began to set in for half an hour to an hour. He used prayer to help himself out of it, and then his defenses were "re-erected" for the rest of the day.

Shaw continued to press his attorneys to challenge Garrison more, and to develop a timetable for doing so. It was Shaw's theory that Garrison drew back when he was challenged, and he hoped to convince his attorneys of that strategy. Shaw now was thinking of the whole case somewhat in political terms, as many do even today. He began to hope that David Chandler, the former *States-Item* reporter and now *LIFE* magazine stringer, who had recently been investigating the Mafia's influence in New Orleans and Louisiana, would be indicted by Garrison's office. Chandler had been subpoenaed before a grand jury to try to persuade him to give up his sources, and there was a serious possibility that he would be forced to reveal his hand, or be indicted. It was Shaw's hope that if Chandler was indicted, it would cause *LIFE* magazine to launch a full-fledged attack upon Garrison. If it had happened, it would have represented quite a turnaround from *LIFE*'s cooperation with Garrison during the early stages of his investigation.

Jim Garrison received a huge publicity boost by granting a lengthy interview to *Playboy* magazine, which appeared in the October 1967 issue; the issue began to appear around the country at the end of August. Although *Playboy* mentioned the Clay Shaw case in its introduction to the interview, Garrison, as he usually did, mostly steered clear of direct mention of the Shaw case, and concentrated on what he saw as wider aspects of a conspiracy to kill Kennedy. Garrison later would tell contradictory stories about how some of his statements in the interview had come to be. He told researcher Tom Bethell that he had written both the questions and the answers for at least major parts of the interview, while he told author James Kirkwood, after Shaw's trial, that Eric Norden, the interviewer, had "dropped" certain things into the interview aside from what Garrison had actually said. Still later, in answers to interrogatories resulting from Shaw's civil suit against him, Garrison would back away from some of the most controversial statements in the interview, acknowledging problems with their accuracy; one of those, as an example, had to do with CIA financing of Shaw's legal defense.

As a result of statements Garrison was quoted as making about Gordon Novel in the interview, Novel filed a large civil suit against Garrison and *Playboy*. *Playboy*, then perhaps at the height of its popularity and influence, financed the main defense costs of the case, which would stretch out over several years, and would generate an approximately 1,600-page deposition of Gordon Novel, giving a detailed account of his colorful life up to 1969. Novel was represented in the lawsuit by famed Chicago attorney Elmer Gertz, known for his representations of Nathan Leopold, one of the Loeb-Leopold "thrill-killing" defendants, and Jack Ruby, on appeal of his conviction for killing Oswald. Gertz would share information he gained about Garrison and the case against Shaw with Shaw's attorneys, who reciprocated with information that came into their hands.

Shaw's attorneys were concerned that Garrison might have been paid for the *Playboy* interview, and requested that Shaw's friend Patrick O'Rourke in Chicago check into the matter. O'Rourke met with Richard Rosenschweig, Executive Assistant to Hugh Hefner,

*Playboy*'s publisher; Rosenschweig "was quite frank when he said they did not pay for interviews."[2306] Rosenschweig, O'Rourke said, had added, "We never pay for interviews; hell, they should pay us ."[2307]

Shaw, rarely a follower of sporting events, commented in his diary on October 8 that he did not even know who was playing in the World Series. That same evening, he went to a black tie gathering at Edith Stern's house just over the line in neighboring Jefferson Parish; approximately 250 guests were there to help inaugurate Stern's newly designed garden. Shaw's visit to Stern's home was noted in a CIA memo at the time, and signaled Edith Stern's quiet but public support of Shaw during his time of crisis.

Jules Ricco Kimble already had inserted himself into the case by contacting the CIA. He now gave a statement to Garrison's office, saying that he had been at the Golden Lantern, a gay bar in the French Quarter, along with Shaw and Ferrie, in late 1960, and that he had flown to Montreal in late 1961 or early 1962, with Ferrie and Shaw, and that Shaw had brought a Latino back to New Orleans with him.[2308] Kimble, who would only have been seventeen years old in 1960, was another potential "witness" developed by Andrew Sciambra.

Shaw's trial, initially set for September, had been postponed; the defense team had asked for a six-month continuance to further prepare its case, in view of the rapidly breaking developments that had occurred continuously since Shaw's arrest. Meanwhile, rumors continued to spread about various possible scenarios. Jones Harris, a conspiracy theorist at one time associated with writer Edward J. Epstein, who had written *Inquest*, one of the more credible critiques of the Warren Commission's findings, advised Garrison researcher Tom Bethell that an "unimpeachable source" had advised Harris that Shaw's lawyers, believing that he would be convicted at trial, would allow Shaw to appear on television, risking a contempt-of-court citation, to make statements of an "unknown content" about the case.[2309] No such televised appearance by Shaw, or anything remotely resembling what Harris had described, ever occurred.

The case was scheduled for a major court hearing in mid-October. Shaw decided to take a trip to Chicago and then on to New York City following the hearing; it was his first trip out of state since his arrest, other than excursions to the Catholic retreat on the Gulf Coast. On October 11, David Chandler met with Shaw, and suggested that Shaw see *LIFE* magazine writer Richard Billings in New York during his trip. That same evening, *Item* reporter Rosemary James, one of three who had broken the original story of Garrison's investigation, and her husband, Judson James, were at a party attended by Shaw. Shaw commented humorously in his diary that Rosemary James was worried about the amount of drinking her husband was doing, but eventually gave up the battle and slowly became intoxicated herself. James, along with co-author and fellow reporter Jack Wardlaw, was the author of a new book, *Plot or Politics*, which summed up the Garrison investigation from the beginning through the late summer, and would get much attention upon its publication; it would be used as a primer on the case by out-of-town reporters through the end of Shaw's trial.

On October 12, Shaw noted his plans to stay at Claire Evangelista's home in Mount Kisco, New York during his trip. He also indicated that Nina and Jeff Sulzer were keeping an "uncensored" journal, much as Shaw was, which would give the readers of those journals a "*Rashonon*" experience, as they showed Shaw's predicament from various angles.

The next day, Shaw commented that two long-time acquaintances of his had told Jeff Biddison the day of the arrest that they would mortgage their home to help Shaw pay for his defense costs. On that same front, the poet Thom Gunn had earlier given Shaw's friend, Don Doody, a blank check for use up to 3,500 English pounds to put toward Shaw's defense. However, it is unclear that either of those prospective sources of defense funds was ever tapped, or even requested by Shaw.

On October 14, Shaw noted that, according to a newspaper report, Attorney General Ramsey Clark, speaking at the University of Virginia in Charlottesville, had commented to the audience that he might have to prosecute Garrison for his treatment of Shaw. Clark later said that he had never made the comment, but the reporter in the audience stuck by the story. During the talk, Clark also had referred to Shaw as a "fine man;" Shaw attributed that view to Congressman Hale Boggs, who he speculated had passed it on to Clark. That same day, Shaw commented that his life had not been ruined by the experience thus far, as he now believed it could not be ruined without his consent.

Charles Nutter, Shaw's long-time counterpart as Managing Director at International House from 1946 to 1961, wrote to Attorney General Ramsey Clark in October. Nutter gave Clark his background with the Associated Press during the 1920s and 1930s, as well as his employment with International House, and mentioned that he was now the owner of the Picayune, Mississippi *Item* newspaper. Nutter vigorously defended Shaw in the letter, and commended Clark on his recent speech at the University of Virginia. Nutter said that Garrison would never prove a case against Shaw, because the entire case was a "fabrication." He said the silence of New Orleans businessmen concerning Shaw's innocence was "inexcusable," and was due to a fear of Garrison's reprisals. Nutter concluded that there was no other purpose to the investigation, and the charges against Shaw, than for Garrison to "reap a sheaf of headlines" and "personal glory."[2310]

An unsigned letter to the Department of Justice shortly after Clark's appearance at the University of Virginia mentioned that Garrison had been running a "homosexual setup business" related to entrapment of Northern visitors.[2311] In the climate of the times, however, any complaints about Shaw's predicament that brought up the issue of homosexuality in his defense generally fell on deaf ears. Homosexuals, at the time, had no protections under Federal civil rights laws, and crimes related to homosexuality and their enforcement were a local issue into which the Federal government generally did not intrude.

On October 15, Shaw noted his mother's 79th birthday. She had stayed away for much of the time since his arrest, at Shaw's request. Two days later, Louis Fischer called with news that his long-time friend and companion, William Formyduval, and his "wife," Louise, were "looking for asylum," apparently meaning a place to stay other than Shaw's home, which was now off-limits to any controversial visitors. On the same day, focusing on legal instead of personal matters, Shaw argued with his lawyers about his timetable for pressuring Garrison. The lawyers said that it was dangerous to force an investigation of Garrison's office, as it might be viewed by the courts as interfering with the prosecution's case.

Local character Gordon Novel had fled in the spring to Ohio, to avoid having to appear before the Orleans Parish grand jury hearing evidence from Garrison's investigation, and was still wanted for questioning by Garrison's office. However, in October, a grand jury in East Baton Rouge Parish convened to hear a criminal case regarding organized labor troubles, and Novel was subpoenaed to testify. Jim Garrison, showing his own flexibility, signed a letter granting Novel immunity from prosecution during his visit to testify before the panel in Baton Rouge.

The following day was October 18, 1967, and Shaw made no entry in his diary. He then left on his trip to Chicago and New York City. If he continued the daily diary after that point, no record of it has surfaced, although he generated some narrative accounts that cover events beyond that date.

In Chicago, Shaw saw his friends Patrick and Edna O'Rourke; he had spent Thanksgiving Day with the couple following the Kennedy assassination in 1963. Patrick O'Rourke was assisting the defense in minor ways, including communicating with *Playboy* magazine, headquartered in Chicago, about the circumstances dealing with its interview with Jim Garrison. In New York, Shaw stayed part of the time with his friend, sculptress Claire Evangelista, who had moved from New Orleans back in June, and was now living just outside of New York City. Shaw then moved to the Plaza Hotel in the city, where he stayed for the remainder of his visit. It was on this trip that Shaw, at the initiative of writer James Leo Herlihy's mutual friend Tom Dawson, met Herlihy and fellow writer James Kirkwood.

Kirkwood, a former actor and comedian with long roots in the entertainment industry, was immediately captivated by Shaw's story, and quickly became interested in doing a project related to the case. Kirkwood would wind up writing a magazine article for *Esquire*, prior to the trial, and a lengthy book about the trial itself, perhaps the most definitive book about the Shaw case during that era, although one that is not without controversy in conspiracy theory circles.

Some accounts say that Shaw, on the visit to New York, was searching for an out-of-town attorney to assist with, or even take over, his defense. He had grown somewhat wary of his legal team's conservatism in fighting Garrison's charges, and was perhaps open to a change by the fall of 1967. Years later, the author found, on the back of Shaw's copy of his New York hotel folio, a handwritten note with a telephone number and the words "from Sheridan." It is not known whether this referred to Walter Sheridan, and whether Shaw had some type of communication or meeting with Sheridan in New York City during the trip. Sheridan had worked with the defense team, and he had an active involvement in the goings-on of the Garrison investigation, even before Shaw was arrested. Sheridan worked as an NBC News employee, and had participated in the documentary critical of Garrison that had appeared in June, and he also had very close ties to then U.S. Senator Robert Kennedy, the former Attorney General and brother of President John F. Kennedy. Some sources indicate that Sheridan was communicating with Robert Kennedy during his investigative work involving the Garrison probe into the Kennedy assassination, although Sheridan denied that under oath in a deposition in Gordon Novel's lawsuit against *Playboy*.[2312] Others said that, through Sheridan, Garrison's office's files given to him by William Gurvich made their way to John Seigenthaler, Editor of the Nashville *Tennessean* newspaper, and a former aide to Robert Kennedy.

During the trip to New York, Shaw apparently attempted to find representation for a book he might eventually write about his troubles. He met with author's representative James McCormack, who set up a meeting with representatives of Fawcett Publishing Company. In late November, McCormack wrote Shaw, indicating that he was "proud to be with you" at the meeting with the Fawcett representatives. He added he was still trying to arrange a more formal meeting with representatives of the company to discuss a possible book deal, and he commented that not all of his authors were as impressive as Shaw.[2313]

By October 1967, J.B. Dauenhauer had retired from the Mart, which was now in the new tower building. Mario Bermúdez still had an office there, and Channel 26, the UHF television station, was on the air broadcasting from the Mart tower building.[2314]

Garrison's investigation of the Kennedy assassination in general, and his prosecution of Shaw in particular, had been plagued by opposing newsmen since it had first become public. Richard Townley, Hugh Aynesworth, James Phelan, and Walter Sheridan were among the most diligent in trying to unearth information that would undermine Garrison's case. In general terms, reporters from outside of New Orleans were more skeptical of the case, and of Garrison's motives, at least openly, than those who worked for the two main New Orleans newspapers, the *States-Item* and the *Times-Picayune*. However, in the fall of 1967, Rosemary James paired with writer Jack Wardlaw to write a book called *Plot or Politics?* The book was published by Pelican Publishing House, a New Orleans area publisher, and delved into the history of the case through the date of publication, with a large gallery of photographs of all of the main characters, of which there were many by that time. The book is still in print today, and serves as a good introduction to the case. Rosemary James has never been shy about expressing her condemnation of Garrison's prosecution of Shaw; she apparently formed her conclusions relatively early. In an interview with the *Dallas Morning News* on October 30, 1967, Rosemary James discussed the book and the case, commenting that Shaw was innocent of the charges.[2315]

Garrison's men continued to investigate the Eastern Airlines VIP Room signature incident. One of the names signed that day on the same page with "Clay Bertrand" was Arthur Q. Davis; Davis was called in for questioning on November 3. He said that he knew Shaw and another name that appeared in the book, Alfred Moran, but that he had not seen either one of the men there that day.[2316] Davis later would testify, related to the incident, as a defense witness at Shaw's trial.

On November 14, Layton Martens met with Shaw, back from New York, and Jeff Biddison at Marilyn Tate's residence, where he relayed to them things that Perry Russo had told him. Russo had said that he had not mentioned Shaw as being present at a party gathering at Ferrie's apartment, along with Oswald, to Andrew Sciambra in their initial meeting in Baton Rouge on February 25, 1967. Russo also had told Martens that, "My main interest is to make some money" out of his involvement in the case.[2317]

On November 17, James Alcock and Sergeant Tom Duffy interviewed Alfred Moran. Moran, a prominent citizen in New Orleans, had worked with Shaw during the 1950s on printing and publication assignments for the Mart. Moran, who had signed the guest register at the Eastern Airlines VIP Room on December 14, 1966, said that Shaw had not been in the room on that date, or he would have remembered him.[2318]

Alfred Moran was a friend of Hunter Leake, the CIA employee in New Orleans who had been Shaw's contact during the 1950s. Moran's connection with the agency was more involved than Shaw's; he actually let the agency use one or more of his businesses as fronts for agency activities, running payroll and other expenses through them, whereas Shaw simply had been an informal information source. After meeting with Garrison's men, Moran reported the encounter to Hunter Leake. Some of the memos from the New Orleans CIA office say that Moran had seen Clay Shaw in the VIP Room on December 14, 1966, and the CIA feared such testimony could seriously hurt Shaw's chances at trial.

In a memo dated November 30, CIA General Counsel Lawrence Houston wrote to the New Orleans CIA office, asking Hunter Leake to follow up with Alfred Moran about Moran's conversations with Garrison's staff regarding the "Clay Bertrand" signature in the guest register. As there was still a question about whether Shaw had been completely candid with his defense attorneys about his life, Houston stressed that the CIA had a way of getting information to Shaw's attorney Irvin Dymond without involving either Hunter Leake or the CIA directly.[2319] However, Leake soon reported back the correct version—that Alfred Moran had *not* seen Shaw in the VIP Room on the day in question.

On December 1, Edward Wegmann wrote to John Doar, with the Civil Rights Division of the Department of Justice in Washington, setting out a civil rights complaint against Garrison and others for their treatment of Shaw. He sought the indictments of Garrison, Dr. Esmond Fatter, investigator Lynn Loisel, investigator Louis Ivon, Assistant District Attorney Andrew Sciambra, and the main witness against Shaw, Perry Russo. The letter listed a lengthy series of questionable tactics used by Garrison and his men.[2320] John Doar later would serve as the counsel to the House of Representatives Judiciary Committee that heard evidence in the impeachment hearings against President Richard Nixon in 1974.

Among other things, Wegmann mentioned problems with Perry Russo, including his failure to tell a consistent story, with Vernon Bundy and his efforts to get out of jail by cooperating with Garrison's office, the attempted bribery of Al Beauboeuf, the arrest of Walter Sheridan and Richard Townley, and the attempted bribery of Fred Leemans, all as examples of the attempt by Garrison's office to persecute Shaw.[2321]

On December 6, Garrison's office obtained a statement from Herbert R. Wagner, Jr. Wagner is significant because, although he did not testify at Shaw's trial in February 1969, he was mentioned as a possible witness to be presented at Shaw's perjury trial in 1971, which ultimately never happened because of Federal court intervention. Even today, some books indicate that Wagner could have testified that Shaw and Ferrie knew each other. However, Wagner's statement of December 6, 1967 contradicts this. He said that he met Ferrie around

1952, and had gotten to know him well; Wagner owned planes at the New Orleans Lakefront Airport, where Ferrie often flew. He knew Sergio Arcacha Smith, and knew of his involvement in anti-Castro activities. He also had been a character witness for Ferrie during some of Ferrie's legal troubles prior to Garrison's Kennedy assassination investigation. He said, however, that he did not know Shaw, although he recalled that, when Ferrie had owned his service station on Veterans Highway, he had seen a large man with a limp who sometimes hung around the station. However, he did not identify that man as Shaw.[2322]

Another prison inmate interviewed by James Alcock was Edward Julius Girnus, who resided in Federal prison in Atlanta, Georgia in December 1967. Girnus told Alcock that he owed the State of Virginia twenty-eight years related to previous crimes, and told a meandering story about meeting Jack Ruby, meeting Shaw at the Alpine restaurant on a trip to New Orleans, and driving Oswald to Texas in September 1963. Girnus told Alcock that he had attended several parties with Shaw, one in Hammond, Louisiana.[2323] Girnus was not used at the trial.

A letter from Shaw's friend Princess Jacqueline de Chimay arrived from Paris, France. She indicated she had received Shaw's recent letter, and shared there had been nothing more in the local newspapers about his troubles. She criticized the powers given to policemen, and the methods used by police, and characterized the investigation of Shaw as a "witch hunt."[2324]

In mid-December 1967, Shaw received a letter from a Paul (last name unknown), whom Shaw had also known during World War II in Rheims, France. A friend of Princess Chimay, he commented that twenty-two years had passed since "the dark hours of Rheims," and that he would like to see Shaw again "and talk and talk" about the "bright hours" of Franco-American relations, which he said had been "shadowed temporarily and superficially by disagreements" about the conduct of world policy. He commented on his amazement at what had appeared in the newspapers about Shaw's case, and speculated that there was some kind of a "coup" behind it. He offered to testify to Shaw's devotion, patriotism, and discipline.[2325]

Garrison's medical records from his Army days, which had been used by opponents in his 1965 re-election race in an attempt to discredit him, were released again, this time to a Chicago newspaper, which ran a story about their contents. After the publication of the records, which included the details of his psychiatric treatment and his resignation from the service, the records were freely passed around by Shaw's defense attorneys, by sympathetic newsmen, and by Aaron Kohn as well, to other parties who were interested in them. As late as late 1968, Aaron Kohn, writing Dr. Joseph G. Pasternak related to a discussion about a recent article on the autopsy of President Kennedy's body, enclosed a copy of the 1951 medical report on Garrison.[2326]

In the fall, *LIFE* magazine had run articles describing a heavy Mafia influence in Louisiana. The articles linked Garrison, among others, to such influence. While Garrison denied it, he seemed to take an ambivalent attitude toward the articles, although by now Richard Billings had fallen away from his investigation, and *LIFE* no longer seemed interested in cooperating with Garrison.

In a telephone conversation in mid-December, Garrison's investigator, former CIA employee William Wood, using his alias Bill Boxley, spoke with Billings about the *LIFE* articles, about local *LIFE* stringer reporter David Chandler, and about Garrison's investigation into the Kennedy assassination. Billings indicated that he wanted to get back into the investigation, but did not want to be subpoenaed before a grand jury about what he knew regarding the *LIFE* articles about Mafia influence in Louisiana. Wood mentioned viewing a recent presentation by Dr. John Nichols, although he did not give Nichols's name, that Wood said proved one of the assassination shots came from the front, and had hit Kennedy in the throat. Wood indicated the presentation was compelling and convincing, and he seemed very supportive of Garrison's investigation thus far.[2327]

On December 15, William Wegmann wrote to Dymond and Edward Wegmann, suggesting that they put together a chronological list of statements made to the press, either verbally or through press releases, by Garrison, and by Warren Commission skeptics Harold Weisberg and Mark Lane. Weisberg and Lane had assisted Garrison's investigation almost from the time it had been publicly reported, and had spoken frequently about it on television and in the newspapers. Wegmann suggested using the list of their statements to seek a court injunction to the prosecution of Shaw until the atmosphere in New Orleans had settled down.[2328] Others would soon use such a list of Garrison's statements to attack the credibility of Garrison's character, and by extension, the investigation. Perhaps the most notable example of such usage would be by Johnny Carson of *The Tonight Show*, when Garrison appeared on the program at the end of January 1968. Carson opened the questioning by reading a lengthy list of Garrison's prior public statements about who was behind the assassination—the suspects ranged from anti-Castro Cubans to right-wing "oil millionaires," and the conspiracy to cover it up reached into the highest circles of the White House. "Isn't that terribly confusing, and don't you seem to be riding off in all directions?" Carson asked Garrison, opening an hour-long cat-and-mouse exchange between the two.

The following day, William Wegmann wrote to Dymond and Edward Wegmann again, suggesting that a conspiracy to commit murder in Texas would not be a crime in Louisiana.[2329] That suggestion had been made to Dymond and Wegmann by other attorneys early in the case. However, as the case progressed, the defense could not find a court that agreed with that argument.

Even in the midst of his troubles, Shaw remained friendly with many members of the news media in New Orleans. Hal Lidin, News Director with WVUE-TV Channel 12 in New Orleans, and his wife Carmen sent Shaw a Christmas card, along with an invitation to an open house at their residence on New Year's Day.[2330]

After Shaw's indictment, much of the publicity surrounding Garrison's investigation centered on Shaw's prosecution. However, Garrison also indicted other individuals along the way. Attorney Dean Andrews was indicted for perjury, and convicted in August 1967. Kerry Thornley, who had known Oswald very briefly in the Marines, and had written a novel partly based upon him, was indicted for perjury as well. However, the only other man Garrison indicted for conspiracy in the actual assassination was Edgar Eugene Bradley, indicted at the end of 1967. Bradley, an associate of 1960s conservative radio evangelist Carl McIntyre, had come to Garrison's office's attention not long after Shaw's arrest, when individuals who knew Bradley in California passed on derogatory information about him.[2331] Bradley was charged in one draft with conspiring with Shaw, Ferrie, Jack Ruby, Lawrence Howard, Jack Lawrence, and Loren Hall to kill Kennedy. One draft indicated that the conspiracy took place between March 30, 1963 and November 22, 1963; another draft said the conspiracy took place between August 1, 1963 and November 22, 1963.[2332] Loren Hall, Jack Lawrence, and Lawrence Howard were other individuals investigated by Garrison in late 1967 or early 1968, although they were never indicted.

David F. Lewis, an associate of Jack Martin who had given Garrison's investigation information in late 1966 and early 1967, said that he had seen Bradley and David Ferrie in New Orleans, having dinner with an unknown person, in May or June of 1964. Lewis also said that Bradley had been in a religious field, possibly Presbyterian, in New Orleans in 1954 or 1955.[2333]

As part of his accusations against Bradley, Garrison accused him of being at the Lakefront Airport in New Orleans, where David Ferrie had worked, in the fall of 1963, but that story was debunked very early on by none other than Andrew Sciambra. In a memo dated December 26, 1967, just days after Bradley was indicted, Sciambra wrote to Garrison that he had been checking out reports that Bradley had been at the airport, but that he had found the name of a Lesley P. Bradley instead, and said that the situation might have resulted from a mix-up in identification.[2334] In a follow-up memo on December 28, Sciambra wrote to Garrison that the Bradley who had been at the Lakefront Airport in 1958, and again in 1963, was either Lesley P. Bradley or Lesley James Bradley.[2335]

Others who had already become potential witnesses to Garrison's case against Shaw got involved in the Edgar Eugene Bradley situation as well. Roger Craig, a former sheriff's deputy from Dallas County, Texas, had come to the attention of the Warren Commission and the FBI in 1963 by telling a story of a Rambler station wagon he had seen around Dealey Plaza at the time of the assassination. His story generally had been dismissed by investigating authorities, but Garrison had gotten wind of it, and was planning to use him in the Shaw case. On December 22, 1967, Craig told Garrison's aide Numa V. Bertel, Jr. that he had not only seen the Rambler station wagon in Dealey Plaza on November 22, 1963, but that he also had seen the recently indicted Californian Edgar Eugene Bradley there, pretending to be a Secret Service agent. Craig said that Bradley had shown no interest at the time in the information Craig possessed about the Rambler station wagon.[2336] In February 1968, Roger Craig gave an official affidavit to Garrison's office, also saying that he had encountered Bradley in Dallas at the scene of the assassination, posing as a Secret Service agent.[2337] At Shaw's trial in February 1969, Craig would testify about the Rambler station wagon, but not about seeing Edgar Eugene Bradley at the scene of the assassination; the case against Bradley had been weak from the start, even more so than the case against Shaw, and California Governor Ronald Reagan had refused to allow Bradley to be extradited to Louisiana.

Roger Craig had been communicating with Garrison's office even before Bradley's arrest, but it was not until Bradley's indictment that Craig mentioned the story of seeing Bradley at the scene of the assassination posing as a Secret Service agent. On December 7, 1967, Craig wrote a memo to Garrison, saying that he was interviewing people in Dallas, and would be reporting them to Garrison. A mention of some homosexual doctors in Dallas prompted a handwritten note by Garrison about "doctors" whose names had popped up in the case, especially Dr. Tom Rafferty, who had introduced Layton Martens to Shaw, Dr. Martin Palmer, who had been Shaw's personal physician, and Dr. Mary Sherman, the prominent orthopedic surgeon who was brutally murdered in 1964, and who had known some of the individuals later investigated by Garrison.[2338]

To help Roger Craig financially, Garrison got him a job working at the Volkswagen dealership owned by financial supporter Willard Robertson. By early January 1968, after only a month, Craig had resigned from the dealership, because he said Robertson had made it clear that he had no work for Craig, and that he had only employed Craig as a favor to Garrison, a charitable gesture for someone who needed money.[2339] Craig's salary was $9,600 per year, more than he had made in the Dallas County Sheriff's office. Before departing New Orleans, Craig wrote Garrison a letter relating those details, indicating that he was broke and had to leave for Dallas while he could afford to buy gasoline for the trip.[2340] Garrison wrote Roger Craig a letter of recommendation for Craig's use in finding another job, commenting that he would add him to his staff if expenses permitted.[2341]

Ultimately, Garrison was unsuccessful in getting Edgar Eugene Bradley extradited from California. By the spring of 1969, not long after Shaw's trial had ended in his acquittal, Edgar Eugene Bradley and Garrison were back on somewhat good terms. Responding to a letter Garrison had written to him on April 24, 1969, Bradley wrote that he believed Garrison had been "set up" to indict Bradley in order to discredit Garrison, and to keep him from solving the Kennedy assassination. Bradley asked Garrison to meet with him at his convenience.[2342]

It was not quite over, however. In mid-September 1969, Bradley wrote to Garrison saying that Roger Craig had called him twice, wanting money. Bradley said that Craig had been totally untruthful about the matter, and that he had never seen or talked to anyone in

Dallas. Bradley mentioned that people would not let up on the subject until Garrison met with Bradley and publicly cleared him.[2343]

Although Garrison's investigation has often been criticized over the years for ignoring the possible involvement of organized crime in Kennedy's assassination, the idea was at least explored by someone in Garrison's office. A memo from December 24, 1967, by an unknown author, analyzed the possibility. The memo listed Ruby, Oswald, and Ferrie as individuals having connections to the underworld, and acknowledged the possibility of organized crime involvement.[2344] However, there is no evidence that Garrison's office actively pursued any living Mafia figures, and Ruby, Oswald, and Ferrie were all dead at the time the memo was written.

In addition to Tom Bethell, the young Englishman who had joined Garrison's forces in late 1966 as an archivist and researcher, by the end of 1967 Garrison also had very young, student-age investigators, Gary Sanders and Jody Duek, on his staff in New Orleans, both of whom reported to Lou Ivon. Sanders would be drafted into the military in the midst of the Garrison investigation, which took place at the height of the Vietnam War. Sanders and Duek worked their way up and down the French Quarter and other parts of New Orleans, and even across to the north side of Lake Ponchartrain, where they interviewed individuals who might have information about the case. They sometimes found themselves in conflict with Tom Bethell, who was in charge of keeping all the records together, and Bethell sometimes had to enlist Lou Ivon's help in smoothing over the conflict. Although the two had no previous law enforcement experience, they were issued limited credentials showing their connection with the district attorney's office.

The young investigators went to work right away, following leads and interviewing potential witnesses. In December 1967, Gary Sanders wrote a memo to Lou Ivon, saying that he was checking on convict Edward Julius Girnus's story. Sanders said that he had reviewed receipts at the Royal Orleans Hotel for the period from April through July 1963, and had found no evidence of Girnus's supposed stay there.[2345]

Steven Burton, now a law professor, along with his college associate Steve Jaffe, helped Garrison's office run down leads on the West Coast. The two, who also were issued official credentials of a sort, had been active as skeptics of the official conclusions of the Warren Commission even before Garrison had begun his investigation. Burton, in particular, would become thoroughly disenchanted with Garrison's investigation by the time of Shaw's trial, and would rapidly fall away from any involvement with the conspiracy theory view of the assassination.

# 26 · Appeals and Delays on the Way to Trial

As 1968 began, Shaw still was receiving supportive letters from friends around the country. Phillip Carey Jones, an actor friend in Los Angeles, wrote that he had "never known a cooler, more level-headed scrupulous, unprejudiced man" than Shaw, a man, he said, who was "always on the liberal side of things." Jones acknowledged that Garrison "may be right" about certain actions of the FBI and CIA related to the assassination, but dismissed Shaw's involvement. He added that, "Ever since I've known you, you've been one of my very favorite people."[2346]

Shaw's old friend William Formyduval had reunited with a female friend of his, Louise Claremont. The two may have been married once, and it is unclear if they ever divorced, but by early 1968 they were back together, both suffering from problems related to heavy alcohol consumption.[2347]

Shaw wrote to James and Judy Formyduval, brother and sister-in-law of William Formyduval. He asked them to write more often, thinking that their letters would "cheer me up. Not that I am depressed, really. But to live under arrest for almost a year charged with the worst crime of the century, about which you know nothing, is a rather unusual experience... The DA now says he wants to go to trial in mid-February. Well and good. Let's get on with it, say I. He is, of course, absolutely mad. But I know of no way of ever making this clear except by a trial. And I am rather looking forward to it now since I can prove what a paranoid son of a bitch he really is...Had a note from Wimmery [William Henry Formyduval] saying he was still in the hospital...I had hoped this remarriage would be a solution for him, and did not know that Louise had a similar problem. Well, maybe they can help each other, or, at least, work out what the psychologists call a folie a deux! Let us hope so. What a waste of a really nice human being."[2348]

After the release of Garrison's Army medical records from the early 1950s, *Newsweek* reporter Hugh Aynesworth sent a telegram to Garrison, saying that he was "very shocked at *Chicago Tribune* implying your sanity in question—as an old friend once said, 'Let the truth be known though the heavens fall'—Please send me a letter authorizing me to examine your service records—in this way all those people whom you claim have a right to know all will know all." Someone in Garrison's office handwrote on the telegram, "To: NUTFILE—No answer needed."[2349] The quotation Aynesworth mentioned was one by Garrison, related to his opinion that the public had a right to see all governmental records related to the Kennedy assassination.

Aynesworth shared some of the information he learned about Garrison's probe directly with the FBI, as did several other newsmen of the day. Aynesworth was well known to prominent Federal government agencies. A memo by Ernest Bische of the CIA's Houston field office in February 1968 discussed Aynesworth, and his personal history. It indicated that Aynesworth had expressed an interest in employment with the CIA in October 1963. He was considered a good reporter, although with a tendency to sometimes interpose his own views, and he was sometimes lacking in objectivity. The CIA considered him a supporter of the Warren Commission regarding the assassination.[2350]

On January 2, 1968, Andrew Sciambra wrote a memo to Garrison, listing possible dates during the last two weeks of August 1963, and the first three weeks of September 1963, when the incident in Clinton, Louisiana with the black limousine could have occurred;

Sciambra's memo listed only Thursdays and Fridays of each week, and mentioned that the last week in August and the first two weeks of September created the most likely time frame. It is somewhat significant, however, that Corrie Collins, one of the potential witnesses from that area, had said that the event could have occurred only on Wednesday or Thursday, his days off. Interestingly, a list of people who registered to vote between August 22, 1963 and September 20, 1963 showed no familiar names, either as potential witnesses, or as the names of suspects, such as Lee Harvey Oswald. Sciambra mentioned in the memo that state employees Francis Fruge and Anne Dischler, who were assisting the investigation, had a separate list of those who had applied for voter registration but did not actually register. They also had a list of CORE workers, and a list of business owners, in the nearby area.[2351]

Edward S. Butler of Information Counsel of the Americas (INCA), a right-wing organization dealing with U.S. policy in Latin America that had once been a tenant at the Mart, had spoken out critically of Garrison and conspiracy theorist author Mark Lane. Edward Wegmann wrote to Butler on January 4, 1968, seeking information on Lane, and on former FBI agent William Turner, who recently had written a laudatory article about Garrison's investigation in *Ramparts*, a left-wing magazine published during the 1960s.[2352] Wegmann also wrote to Louisiana Congressman F. Edward Hebert, seeking information on these same men.[2353] He also reached out to Nathanial Kossack, an employee of the U.S. Department of Justice whom Wegmann had met on his trip to Washington, seeking information on Turner's past service with the FBI.[2354]

Aaron Kohn, with the Metropolitan Crime Commission, prepared a memo explaining how John Oswald, a reporter for the *Chicago Tribune*, had come to New Orleans during December and advised Kohn that the *Tribune* would be running an article about Garrison's release from the Army in the early 1950s for psychiatric reasons. Oswald permitted Kohn to copy the relevant documents, and told Kohn that a military physician had told him that Garrison's family and medical background was "typical for homosexuals."[2355]

Among those to whom Kohn passed Garrison's Army medical records was Dr. Alton Ochsner. In a letter to Kohn thanking him for sending the material, Ochsner said that Garrison was a "sick man" and needed help, but "probably won't get it."[2356]

Shortly after the first of the year, a letter arrived from Robert Jackson, son of Shaw's old employer, J. C. Jackson of Western Union. Robert Jackson lived in New York with his wife, Sylvia, and visited New Orleans from time to time. In the letter, Jackson mentioned that he had received Shaw's recent Christmas card, and also that he had seen Garrison at the New Orleans Athletic Club. Jackson commented that Garrison was in "terrible condition" physically, and Jackson generally found him "unsavory." He complimented Shaw by saying that he combined "good food, good talk and a pleasant environment," and that "miserable people" could not tolerate Shaw. However, he also added that Shaw's recent Christmas card had indicated that he was resisting the idea that he had "determined his own fate."[2357]

Years later, Gordon Jackson would interpret his uncle Robert Jackson's last remark. It had to do with Robert Jackson's years-earlier immersion in the Christian Science philosophy, where one is taught that he determines his own reality, but that there are sometimes unwelcome circumstances invited in by one's own mind. Robert Jackson also had analyzed Shaw from a Freudian sense, and concluded that some of Shaw's career moves and lifestyle choices were partly a reaction to his overly stern, introverted father, and in this sense Robert Jackson seemed to be combining the two philosophies: Jim Garrison was the "inevitable and unwelcome re-emergence into Shaw's life" representing Shaw's father, "the irrational authority figure, mindlessly exacting 'justice.'"[2358]

The name of Estes Morgan often popped up to Garrison's investigators in interviews with various people in Clinton or Jackson. For example, Bobbie Dedon, a receptionist at the mental institution in Jackson, said that she had directed Oswald to the personnel office, and that she associated Oswald in her mind with Estes Morgan, whom her family knew.[2359]

Others placed Estes Morgan in the voter registration line along with Oswald. However, Andrew Sciambra interviewed Estes Morgan's wife on January 8, 1968. She said that although Morgan had tried to register to vote several times during the summer of 1963, he had never mentioned anything to her about the assassination, or knowing Oswald.[2360]

On January 9, Sciambra interviewed Melvie Morgan, a sister of Estes Morgan. Melvie Morgan said that her brother had never mentioned anything about a black Cadillac, even through his multiple attempts to register in 1963 (and which he finally succeeded in doing in 1964). She said that he had exchanged words with a "smart-aleck" young white man in the voter registration line; the young man had told Morgan it was useless to try to register, because only "coloreds" could, and that black people would eventually take over society.[2361] Others remembered Estes Morgan mentioning a black Cadillac, with four people in it, which had almost hit him as it drove away. Others also recalled Morgan mentioning the smart-aleck white boy in line who appeared to be a "nigger lover," a disparaging remark of that era used to describe a white person sympathetic to civil rights causes.[2362]

On January 10, Andrew Dunn was interviewed. He said he remembered the black car during the voter registration drive, and recalled that he had seen Shaw in the front seat, Guy Banister in the rear seat, and Jack Ruby driving the car.[2363] At Shaw's trial, none of the witnesses would say that they had seen either Banister or Ruby in Clinton. In fact, Henry Earl Palmer, who testified at the trial, told Andrew Sciambra that he and Guy Banister had been in the Army together in Orlando, Florida in 1944. He said that Banister was doing intelligence work at the time, and that he had never seen Banister after that year, in Clinton or anywhere else.[2364] At the trial, Palmer would testify that he had known Banister, and did not recognize him in the group of people that came through Clinton in 1963.

The investigation by Garrison's office into the rumors about a mysterious appearance of Oswald and others in Clinton and/or Jackson, Louisiana, was carried on mostly behind the scenes. However, on January 13, 1968, a clipping appeared in one of the New Orleans newspapers about the probe into the Clinton story. It quoted a Clinton merchant as saying that rumors had persisted over the years that Oswald had been seen in a voter registration line before or around the time of the assassination.

Writer James Leo Herlihy, fresh from meeting Shaw in October 1967, acknowledged Shaw's recent Christmas card to him, and added he would be down in New Orleans for Mardi Gras the following month.[2365] Meanwhile, Herlihy's friend, James Kirkwood, had taken steps to try to interest a major publication in running an article, to be written by Kirkwood, about Shaw's life since the arrest, and how the whole ordeal had affected him.

William Turner, the former FBI agent turned conspiracy theorist and left-wing commentator, had written, in his *Ramparts* article, that a library card had been issued by the New Orleans Public Library to a "Clem Bertrand." However, Edward Wegmann wrote to Dymond and William Wegmann on January 16, indicating that he had checked with City Librarian Gene Wright, who had said that the card could not have been issued before 1966; Wright thought it was a prank.[2366]

Garrison investigators Jody Duek and Gary Sanders interviewed Richard and June Rolfe in January 1968, which is captured in a lengthy memo. The Rolfes were supporters of Jim Garrison generally, and of his investigation; June Rolfe was one of the few media personalities who openly voiced her belief in Shaw's guilt through the trial and beyond. Although Richard Rolfe talked about his dealings with Cuban activist Sergio Arcacha Smith, Clay Shaw is not mentioned at all in the memo. The Rolfes do mention a person named "Deema," a lesbian whom they termed the "Clem Bertrand" of the girls."[2367]

On January 15, 1968, Layton Martens met with Edward Wegmann again about conversations he had with Perry Russo. He said that Russo had admitted that he could have been hypnotized and misled into the entire story that he had told at the preliminary hearing. Russo told Martens that he never been shown any photos of Guy Banister, who had known Ferrie well; many believed that people who thought they had seen Shaw somewhere might actually have seen Guy Banister. Russo also said that Jim Garrison had told him he would give him $25,000 for his part in the case, but that he had only received $300-$400 to date; Russo later told Martens his talk about receiving money for his testimony had been a joke. Russo said that he had never seen Guy Banister or James Lewallen; some thought that Lewallen could have been the person Russo thought was Oswald. Russo also indicated that he thought that Shaw had been present at the meeting, but that it could have been the hypnosis that had convinced him of that. Russo also said that he hated Walter Sheridan and Richard Townley for the things they had said about him on the NBC news special criticizing Garrison's investigation.[2368] Martens said that Russo told him he had never made statements to Sheridan and Townley that he wanted out of the case, or that he regretted ever speaking to Garrison's office. However, Martens said that Russo was now saying that very thing, as of January 1968.[2369]

Russo said that Clay Shaw's defense team should have elected to go to trial back in September 1967, when the trial was first scheduled, because there were many more witnesses against Shaw as of early 1968. Russo mentioned that the prosecution had Shaw's signature as "Clay Bertrand" on an airline room guest register, and that it had evidence of other conspiracy conversations besides the one attributed to Russo. Russo said that the prosecutors wanted the date of the meeting at Ferrie's apartment, which he said he had witnessed, left open for a week or so, so that it could not be pinned down to a particular day; Martens said that, for the same reason, Russo had been vague about who had been at the party.[2370] Significantly, Russo indicated to Martens that he had actually known Ferrie, but not very well.[2371]

Russo shared that Garrison had scheduled the preliminary hearing to protect himself against future lawsuits by Shaw. Russo also said that if he testified that other witnesses had been present during the conspiracy discussion at Ferrie's, it would have contradicted his version that only he, Oswald, Ferrie, and Shaw were there. Martens said that he had initially met with Russo on August 15, 1967, and had seen him approximately once a week since that time, at either basketball games or parties. He said that Russo still had a job selling insurance.

Edward Wegmann wrote to Dymond and William Wegmann, indicating that he had met recently with Martens and his attorney, Milton Brener, and had discussed Martens's series of meetings with Russo. Wegmann enclosed a transcript of their conversation of January 15, and Martens's own memo of his meeting with Russo on August 15, 1967.[2372]

The defense continued to consult with experts on hypnosis, including Herbert Spiegel. Spiegel had been referred to them by Walter Sheridan and Fred Freed of NBC, when the two had been preparing the critical report about Garrison's investigation that aired the summer before. Wegmann wrote to Spiegel in mid-January, seeking his input on the issues of the case.[2373]

Some inside Garrison's office who were not involved with the investigation remained highly skeptical of it. Captain Roy Allemand, with the New Orleans Harbor Police Department, reported to the FBI in January 1968 that Leonard Gurvich, brother of former Garrison investigator William Gurvich, had told him that Charles Ward, Garrison's main assistant district attorney, while drinking heavily, had told him that Garrison was "going down" because of the Shaw case, and would take "all of us" with him.[2374]

William Dunn was interviewed on January 17 by investigators Frank Ruiz and Kent Simms. Dunn said that he tried to register to vote nine or ten times in Clinton before October 1963, and that the black car, a Cadillac, had always been parked near a downtown drug store. Dunn identified Shaw as being seated in the rear of the car, and Thomas Edward Beckham, another man Garrison was investigating, as being seated in the front. Dunn said that a total of three or four males had been in the car.[2375] At trial, no one would testify to seeing Thomas Edward Beckham in the Clinton or Jackson area.

The difficulty that Dunn, Estes Morgan, and others encountered in registering to vote can be at least partially, perhaps totally, explained by the atmosphere of the civil rights situation of the era, and the pervasive discrimination that had existed for centuries. African Americans, in particular, were systematically denied the right to vote based upon legal obstacles, such as literacy tests or stringent identification requirements. Poor whites sometimes were affected by such laws as well, although to a much lesser extent. In the 1960s, such laws collided with the civil rights movement, one of whose goals was to register African Americans voters in large numbers throughout the South, even in the most race-hardened rural areas.

Detectives Kent Simms and Frank Ruiz interviewed fifty-three individuals in the Clinton/Jackson area from January 10 to January 18, 1968, and summarized their findings in a memo to Lou Ivon. They reported that most of the potential witnesses did not remember the large black car, although some of them recalled white strangers in town trying to register to vote several years before.[2376]

Regarding the issue of Oswald applying for a job at East Louisiana State Hospital, the mental institution in Jackson, Louisiana, Andrew Sciambra interviewed Guy Broyles, the personnel manager at the hospital. Broyles said that two employees, Maxine Kemp and Aline Woodside, had seen the job application filled out by Oswald around the time he applied, but that that application could not be found as of 1967.[2377]

On January 22, Andrew Sciambra wrote to Elmer Litchfield, an FBI agent in Baton Rouge, indicating that former State Representative Reeves Morgan had told Garrison's office that he had called the FBI in 1963, after the assassination, to report that Oswald had visited with him in Jackson, Louisiana, seeking a job in the local area.[2378] Sciambra also wrote to J. Edgar Hoover on February 19, 1968, inquiring about Oswald's presence in Jackson and Clinton.[2379]

The story broke in some Louisiana newspapers that Reeves Morgan now maintained that Oswald had come to see him in 1963, seeking a job, and that he had contacted the FBI after the assassination with that information, but that the FBI had informed him it already knew of Oswald's presence in Clinton and Jackson. Morgan would testify to substantially the same story at Shaw's trial a year later. However, Special Agent Elmer D. Litchfield and other agents in the Baton Rouge area, who would have handled inquiries regarding the Clinton/Jackson area, denied receiving any call from Morgan that Oswald had been in that area, or of hearing information to that effect from any other source. Special Agents Michael Baron and Earl R. Peterson gave statements to the same effect.[2380] Special Agent Richard Smallwood said that Morgan had indeed contacted him on August 13, 1963, more than three months before the assassination, not about Oswald (whose name would have meant nothing to someone in the area at the time), but regarding a civil rights investigation taking place in that area.[2381] Ironically, that date was around the time of the alleged incident involving Oswald, Ferrie, and Shaw making their appearance in Clinton in a black limousine. The Department of Justice also reported, in a memo dated February 14, 1968, that Morgan had contacted the FBI in August 1963, but on a matter unrelated to Oswald or the Kennedy assassination.[2382]

Edward Wegmann continued his inquiries about Mark Lane's background, and whether he was a member in good standing with the New York Bar. On January 22, 1968, attorney Theodore Geffner, with the firm of Wasserman, Chinitz, and Geffner, wrote Wegmann that he had checked with the New York Appellate Division of the Supreme Court, and found that Lane had been admitted to practice in June of 1951, and that insofar as could be determined he was still a member in good standing.[2383] On January 25, Wegmann wrote directly to the New York Supreme Court, seeking further information on whether Lane was in good standing, or had been disbarred.[2384]

On January 24, Vernon Bundy was released after being booked for robbery. As with many of the individuals questioned by Garrison's office in its hunt for potential witnesses against Shaw, Bundy had difficulty staying out of trouble with the law.

*Newsweek* reporter Hugh Aynesworth continued his efforts on behalf of the defense; by this time, Aynesworth was not even pretending to be even-handed about the case. On January 25, 1968, Wegmann wrote to Aynesworth, indicating that he would be meeting him in Houston the following Sunday, when Wegmann was on his way to Dallas.[2385]

Wegmann was by now also communicating directly with Chicago attorney Elmer Gertz, who was representing Gordon Novel in his libel suit against Garrison and *Playboy* magazine, related to Garrison's lengthy interview in the magazine in the fall of 1967. Novel had alleged that Garrison had made libelous statements about him, and had sued for ten million dollars. Wegmann wrote to Gertz on January 26, discussing Garrison's *Playboy* interview, and indicating that he understood that it had originally contained information about Garrison's case against Shaw, but that the information had been deleted from the final version.[2386]

During January, an employee for the wealthy Hunt family in Texas produced a memo to members of the family, discussing Garrison and his investigation. At the time, Garrison was openly talking about "oil millionaires" in Texas having something to do with the assassination. The memo said that Garrison was a heavy drinker, and that he intended to implicate the Hunt family in the assassination. It said that Garrison's efforts were backed by the Stern family, obviously meaning Edith Stern's family, who opposed the Hunt family's efforts in the political arena.[2387]

It was not at all uncommon, during the two-year period between Shaw's arrest and trial, for sensational revelations to be reported as fact to governmental agencies monitoring Garrison's case. In late January, as Shaw's scheduled trial was again approaching, former Garrison investigator William Gurvich told a Dallas FBI agent that Shaw would take the stand and admit that he was a "sex pervert," but would deny all allegations of being involved in the Kennedy assassination.[2388]

A story in one of the New Orleans papers on January 31 indicated that bar owner Eugene Davis, whom Dean Andrews had named finally as being the "Clay Bertrand" who had called him the day after the assassination, had been arrested on an obscenity charge involving a sixteen-year-old boy. The longer the case against Shaw lingered, it became less and less unusual for those cooperating with one side or another in the case to have some type of charge hanging over their heads.

In an update to his original recollections, Henry Earl Palmer told Andrew Sciambra that he had in fact witnessed the incident with the black limousine in Clinton while he had been walking with John Rarick, at the time a judge in that area and later a congressman.[2389] The author interviewed John Rarick by e-mail in April 2007. Rarick recalled the incident, remembering that there had been a large, limousine-type black car, and he recalled Town Marshal John Manchester asking the men to step out of the car and making them stand spread-eagled across the hood while he patted them down. Rarick soon forgot about the incident until it arose later, after Garrison's investigation into the Kennedy assassination hit the news in 1967. Rarick said he never heard the names of Lee Harvey Oswald, David Ferrie, or Clay Shaw mentioned in relation to the incident until after Garrison's investigation began to be publicly discussed in 1967.[2390]

Interestingly, Henry Earl Palmer also would tell Garrison's office that Town Marshal John Manchester had told him that he had seen someone who looked like Oswald coming out of a meeting of CORE workers around the time of the incident with the black limousine.[2391] However, Manchester would not testify about that separate incident with Oswald at Shaw's trial.

On January 29, Andrew Sciambra interviewed Mary Morgan, daughter of former state legislator Reeves Morgan, who would testify at Shaw's trial that Oswald had come to his home seeking a job at the local mental institution. Morgan's daughter said that she remembered the event, and had seen a woman in the car along with the man; she said the car was a 1950s model. However, it is unclear from the memo that she actually identified Oswald as the person who spoke with her father.[2392]

Corrie Collins was interviewed on January 31, 1968, although the memo spells his name as "Corey" Collins; he was one of the African-American witnesses who eventually would appear at the trial in February 1969. He did not identify any specific individuals as being in town that day, but he did remember that the driver of the car had worn a hat.[2393] However, at Shaw's trial, Collins would identify Shaw, Ferrie, and Oswald as the individuals who came into town in a black Cadillac that day.

Corrie Collins gave a written statement the same day, mentioning the black car, and indicating that Town Marshal John Manchester had spoken with the occupants of the vehicle. Collins identified a photograph of Oswald and said that the driver looked somewhat like Shaw, but he did not positively identify Shaw. He also said that the driver was wearing a light-colored hat. Collins said that a woman named Verla Bell had been with him at the time, and that she thought the car might have been connected to the FBI.[2394]

In what may be a separate account of the same interview, Collins said that he, and either Verna Lee or Laura Davis (he couldn't recall which), had seen the black car in Clinton, parked in front of a drug store. Collins said that someone had gotten out of the car and stood in the voter registration line. John Manchester, the Town Marshal, had gone up to the car and spoken with an individual within it. Collins said that he thought the men in the car were "Federal people" and that they might be "trading with the enemy," meaning Manchester, who in his official role allegedly had tried to suppress African-American voter registration at that time. Collins said there had been two people in the front of the car, and that the driver had on a light-colored hat; the other person was younger and casually dressed. Collins identified Oswald and Ferrie (although the memo is not clear he said directly that Ferrie was there on that day), and he said that Shaw was large enough to have been the driver, that his face looked familiar, but that he was not certain. Collins also said that local citizens Huey Richardson and Estes Morgan had registered to vote around that time.[2395]

William Dunn, one of the Clinton/Jackson witnesses who would testify at Shaw's trial, was interviewed on January 31 by Garrison's investigators. He said that he had seen Shaw in the rear seat of the black Cadillac, and that Thomas Beckham, an individual whom Garrison tried to link to Shaw and the assassination, had been sitting in the front of the car.[2396] A year later, at Shaw's trial, Dunn would say that he had seen Shaw behind the wheel of the Cadillac, rather than in the back seat, and would not mention Beckham at all.

Various other individuals, both black and white, were interviewed by Garrison's investigators. Several of them remembered the incident with a black car, and several "white men" parked near the drugstore, or elsewhere, in the center of town, but could make no specific identifications. One woman initially said that a photo of Shaw resembled a man she had seen in the voter registration office, then later, when shown a picture of Shaw again, she said, "Why, yes, that's Mr. Garrison, isn't it?"[2397] Others tentatively identified photographs of various individuals shown to them by Garrison's investigators, then acknowledged they were not really sure of anything they were saying.

After Shaw's trial, initially scheduled for September 1967, had been delayed, it had been reset for February 1968. A number of the memos summarizing things supposedly said by the Clinton/Jackson witnesses were dated in late January 1968, although many of the interviews had been conducted during the spring and summer of 1967. It is likely that Garrison's assistants were turning the raw information into specific testimony that would then be presented at trial. After the trial was further delayed until January 1969, the mix of testimony appeared to have changed again.

Meanwhile, comedian Mort Sahl, a friend of author Mark Lane, had appeared on *The*

*Tonight Show*, hosted by Johnny Carson, in mid-January 1968. During a discussion of the Kennedy assassination, Sahl had challenged Carson to invite Jim Garrison to appear on the show. At that time, Shaw's trial still was set for the following month. Carson rose to the bait, and after being prompted by a telegram from Garrison, invited him on the show of January 31, 1968. Irvin Dymond and Edward Wegmann, upon hearing the news, sent a telegram to NBC, protesting Garrison's upcoming appearance, on the grounds that letting Garrison air his opinions before a mass audience would violate Shaw's rights to a fair trial. However, Thomas Ervin, Vice President and legal counsel at NBC, sent a telegram to Dymond the day of Garrison's appearance, refusing to cancel it.[2398]

After the show had aired, Thomas Ervin sent Wegmann a transcript of Garrison's appearance. Wegmann wrote to thank Ervin, and indicated that the public in New Orleans had reacted favorably to Garrison, thinking that host Johnny Carson had been rude in his interruptions of him.[2399] During the program, a combative Carson seemed to have Garrison cornered several times with contradictory or absurd statements, but Garrison was able to turn the tables on Carson each time, and seemed to win over the audience. The case against Shaw was not discussed on the program except peripherally, at Garrison's insistence. However, Garrison was able to capitalize upon the general public's skepticism about the official explanation of the Kennedy assassination. Garrison's biggest moment came when Carson asked him, just before a commercial break, why it was taking so long to prosecute people. Garrison responded after the break that, "We've already convicted one man [Dean Andrews, of perjury], we're trying to get the second man [Shaw] to trial…and the third man [Edgar Eugene Bradley] is fighting extradition. We're moving as fast as we can, John, with five men. Remember it took 6,000 men [the FBI and other investigators after the assassination] to do nothing. We're moving with five. If it's a little slow, I apologize." After Garrison delivered the remarks with perfect timing and intonation, the studio audience broke into their loudest applause of the night.

Toward the end of Garrison's appearance on the show, Carson, somewhat frustrated by Garrison's ability to bring up seemingly brand-new accounts of witnesses coming forward, hit on a highly important aspect of objectively investigating any complex case. Garrison had just finished telling Carson about how a man had recently told conspiracy author Mark Lane, who Garrison announced was an investigator for his office, a somewhat sensational story about the FBI's supposed involvement in the coverup of the assassination; Lane had sworn out an affidavit to that effect. When Carson asked, "Is that a fact?", Garrison hesitated noticeably, no doubt thinking Lane's affidavit should be convincing enough. Carson, obviously irritated, then said, "You said that Mark Lane said a man told him this. But did it actually happen?" It was a valid point, especially considering the number of individuals who have come forward since the day of the assassination, up to the present day, with bizarre, often unprovable and unbelievable stories.

Shaw wrote again to James and Judy Formyduval, indicating that his defense lawyers' motion for a change of venue for the upcoming trial had been denied, that they were now trying to move the case into Federal court, and that the trial, if it did occur, would now not begin until fall. Shaw commented that he had seen Garrison's appearance on *The Tonight Show*. "I thought Carson took him thoroughly. But the reaction among many New Orleanians was surprising…and so southern…'Well, I thought Mr. Carson was downright RUDE to Mr. Garrison!' There is no telling how people will react. People keep asking me about Garrison's actions and reactions. Why did he do this? How dare he do that? The only answer, of course, is that he is now well gone in an advanced stage of paranoia and the reasons for his actions are the same reasons the tubercular patient spits up blood. Symptoms of the disease. Which, while explanatory, is not terribly helpful to me, the victim…Hope William and Louise have managed to stay with AA. It seems about the only solution left."[2400]

While appearing on *The Tonight Show*, Garrison mentioned a story about an FBI clerk named William S. Walter, who had reportedly said that, before the assassination, he had seen a Telex message come through the New Orleans FBI office asking the FBI to "stand down" and not interfere with the actual assassination, which was essentially predicted in the Telex message. Walter, a security patrol clerk in November 1963, basically sent and received telegrams for the office personnel, so he offered some legitimacy to the charge. However, no one else in the office remembered the incident when it was investigated after Walter's statements were made public, and when the FBI interviewed Walter in early February 1968, he denied the entire story, saying that author Mark Lane had been pestering him about it.[2401] He later would resurrect the story at his convenience, whenever he found a willing listener, and as long as he didn't have to set his story down in official form under oath, as was the practice of a number of individuals who generated sensational stories related to the assassination.

Shaw continued to receive many letters and cards during the long interval between arrest and trial. The Welsh dramatist and actor Emlyn Williams, known for his work on various plays, screenplays, and his acting, and in the 1960s for his readings of famous works in public performances, had visited Shaw early in 1968 in the company of his current companion, Robert Crawley. Williams engaged in homosexual relationships all throughout his marriage and after his wife's death in 1970. He wrote Shaw in early February 1968, thanking him for his hospitality the week before, and saying, "Bob was delighted to see you, too." Williams indicated that Shaw was "fighting fit" in the face of the challenges before him. He had left his glasses at Shaw's place, and asked him to forward them to Beverly Hills, California, in care of the film director Joshua Logan.[2402]

Gaines Kincaid wrote Shaw from Austin, Texas. Kincaid, a West Texan, had lived in New Orleans around 1950, and had then lived in New York for several years. Kincaid, who had a journalism degree, had come across a publication entitled *An Almanac of Jim Garrison's Investigation Into The Assassination of John F. Kennedy–The Crime of Silence*, a thirty-page book more or less pieced together from newspaper articles. Shaw asked him to check into the individuals behind the publication, and to pass the information on to Shaw and his attorneys. Kincaid commented that, "Austin has lots of nuts," and that he "should have moved here twenty years ago," saying that he loved it, and would not move away for any reason.[2403]

By early 1968, the Ford Foundation had proposed to film the trial, whenever it occurred. Shaw's defense team, though, was again opposed to such a proposal, as were major news organizations.[2404] However, the notion of filming certainly was still on the table, and an organization called the Public Broadcast Laboratory was behind another proposal to televise the trial. Edward Wegmann had emerged as the main person opposing any televising of any aspect of the case or the trial, unless monetary compensation to help defray Shaw's defense costs could be obtained. On February 2, 1968, Wegmann wrote to Judge Edward A. Haggerty, opposing the televising of the trial, even though Garrison supported doing so. Wegmann said that Shaw would "be deprived of his right to judicial serenity and calm."[2405]

Writer James Kirkwood was still exploring, with his agent, the possibility of writing a profile on Shaw as a magazine article. Kirkwood shopped the article, which eventually appeared in *Esquire*, to the *Saturday Evening Post* and *Playboy*, both of whom turned it down.

As early as February 1968, a story was developing that a postal carrier who delivered mail to 1414 Chartres Street, the residence of Shaw's friend Jeff Biddison, was telling people that he had delivered letters to that address that had been addressed to "Clay Bertrand," including very recently. In a memo to Garrison, Andrew Sciambra wrote that a Lillian Bisso had said that another woman, Evelyn Jahncke, had said her postal carrier had told her he had delivered such mail shortly before Shaw's preliminary hearing back in March 1967.[2406]

Wegmann's meeting with Department of Justice attorneys in September was bearing fruit. Fred Vinson, one of the attorneys with whom Wegmann and Dymond had met, sent Wegmann information regarding William Turner, and his dismissal from the FBI in 1961.[2407] Wegmann wrote to Vinson approximately a week later, thanking him for the information, and indicating he was also seeking feedback from the Civil Service Commission.[2408]

On February 19, after the trial had been delayed again, Wegmann wrote to Stephen Pollack of the Civil Rights Division of the Department of Justice, following up on his earlier civil rights complaint. Wegmann wrote that Shaw had been subjected to mental anguish, humiliation, and indignities, such as Garrison's public comments about Shaw committing suicide before the case would ever come to trial, or being assassinated, or being found guilty.[2409]

Wegmann also wrote to a Washington, D.C. attorney named Peyton Ford, who was chairman of the Section Committee on Abuse of Process of the American Bar Association, complaining about the treatment Shaw had received, and asking the committee to investigate.[2410] The purpose of the committee was to seek out examples of abuse of authority and legal process in the criminal law field, and to evolve remedies for those situations. Ford responded that he had discussed it with the other committee members, who had decided that since Shaw's criminal case was now pending before the courts, the committee could not get involved in Shaw's situation at that time.

Former CIA Director Allen Dulles, who served from the early 1950s until 1961, and who also had been a member of the Warren Commission, was subpoenaed by Garrison's office during February 1968. Federal Marshals, however, refused to serve the subpoena on Dulles, as present and former Federal officials in certain capacities did not have to respond to state court subpoenas. On March 1, Edward Wegmann wrote to Dulles, commenting on the subpoena and mentioning that he and Dymond would be in Washington on March 22; Wegmann asked if Dulles would meet with him.[2411] The proposed meeting with Dulles, who died shortly after jury selection began for Shaw's trial in January 1969, apparently never took place.

Wegmann continued to press his case with officials in the Civil Rights Division of the Department of Justice.[2412] He also wrote to Representative Hale Boggs, from whom the defense had not gotten much help since Shaw's arrest, mentioning the ongoing civil rights complaint, and how the defense attorneys had requested a meeting with the attorney general.[2413]

Wegmann copied some of his correspondence to Department of Justice officials to Herbert "Jack" Miller, the prominent Washington attorney who represented investigative reporter Walter Sheridan in his ongoing legal dealings with Garrison's office. A number of attorneys in New Orleans, and around the country, who represented parties at odds with Garrison in the Kennedy assassination case, shared information with each other and with writers skeptical of Garrison's efforts. That joint communication lasted from 1967 throughout the period of Shaw's involvement with criminal charges.

In the midst of his troubles, Shaw never forgot those who had helped him, and were continuing to help him. He sent Edith Stern roses in early March,[2414] and around the same time he sent a silver porringer and baby cup to Hugh Aynesworth and his wife, Paula.[2415]

A letter arrived in early March from Holland McCombs, offering encouragement to Shaw. McCombs said he was "enraged and amazed" by "the length of time this has gone on." McCombs also mentioned that he had tried to visit recently with Charles and Eleanor Nutter, and Richard and Gwen Swenson.[2416]

In mid-March, Aaron Kohn sent information to the Internal Revenue Service, indicating that Garrison's expenditures far exceeded his income, and enclosed information about Garrison's two homes; Kohn suggested the IRS investigate Garrison for tax evasion.[2417] Kohn had been involved in a continuing effort since at least 1966 to jump-start a Federal investigation into Garrison's activities. However, the Federal government appeared reluctant to get involved as long as Garrison's investigation into President Kennedy's assassination was ongoing.

By far, the most unusual communication Shaw received during the long interval between his arrest and trial was a greeting card, now contained in his collection of letters at the National Archives. Printed on the card was the phrase, "A friendly note to say—Hello—hoping this little message will brighten your day—and show you're being thought about in the warmest, friendliest way!" On the inside of the card had been glued a newspaper photograph of a head shot of Jim Garrison. Below the photograph was the handwritten note, "Je pense a toi – toujours a toi."[2418] No envelope was associated with the letter, so it was impossible to tell when it had been sent, or from where it had been mailed, but in view of the rumors, which have survived to this day, of a possible relationship between Shaw and Garrison that pre-dated Garrison's investigation into the Kennedy assassination, the greeting card and its message contained within are very interesting indeed.

Meanwhile, the defense was continuing to monitor the activities of main witness Perry Russo. On March 13, Irvin Dymond wrote to former Garrison investigator William Gurvich, who now was helping the defense, regarding Doris Washofsky, who supposedly was "shacking up" with Russo. Dymond called her a "tramp in spades," and indicated he would discuss the matter with Gurvich in person.[2419]

In early 1968, Garrison appeared on a local Miami television talk show on WTVJ-TV, hosted by Larry King, the same Larry King who would later host nationwide radio and television talk shows. During the program, Garrison attacked the Central Intelligence Agency, saying that rogue employees of the Agency, employing anti-Castro Cubans, had killed President Kennedy; Garrison discussed the concept of "Executive Action," a program within the agency related to possible assassinations of heads of states of foreign countries, in his general attack on the agency. The vice-president at WTVJ-TV, William R. Brazzil, immediately reported the contents of Garrison's appearance directly to Richard Helms, then Director of the CIA.[2420]

The Department of Justice chose not to pursue Shaw's initial civil rights complaint. In a memo dated March 22, 1968, John J. Kirby, Jr. discussed a conversation he and Stephen Pollack of the Justice Department had with Edward Wegmann, in a meeting held shortly before in Washington, D.C. Pollack had told Wegmann that there was no basis on which to proceed with Shaw's complaint. He said that Wegmann was in the best position to protect his client, by defending him at trial, or in pre-trial hearings and motions. In the meeting, Wegmann said that he already had told them about everyone related to persecution of Shaw, except for Mr. and Mrs. Cedric von Rolleston. Wegmann also had said that he expected Shaw to be convicted at trial, but that it might be possible to win on appeal. Wegmann shared that he might go to the U.S. Attorney in New Orleans and publicize his request for an investigation, or try to remove the criminal case to Federal Court. Pollack told Wegmann that the normal procedure was to allow for state prosecution to proceed before the Federal government would take action, unless circumstances dictated otherwise.[2421]

Wegmann also was corresponding with attorney George Jensen, who represented Edgar Eugene Bradley, the California man who had been indicted by Garrison in December.[2422] The indictment of Bradley had raised even more eyebrows than the indictment of Shaw, because with Shaw there at least were surface reasons possibly connecting him to a conspiracy in New Orleans, while nothing seemed to connect Bradley as directly.

Writer Edward Jay Epstein was another person who was in Wegmann's field of interest. Epstein had written *Inquest*, one of the early, and more low-key, critiques of the Warren Commission. When Garrison's case had broken in the news in 1967, Epstein had traveled to New Orleans, met with Garrison and his staff, and watched as the investigation unfolded. Relatively quickly, he became skeptical of the investigation, and eventually wrote a critical article about it for *The New Yorker* that would appear in mid-1968. Epstein kept the defense team advised of the article as it progressed, and Wegmann requested a copy from Epstein in advance of publication.[2423]

In a letter to Stephen Pollack dated March 28, 1968, Wegmann said he regretted that the Department of Justice would not get involved in the civil rights complaint. He enclosed the von Rollestons' retraction of their earlier statement that they had seen Shaw and Oswald at the Bentley Hotel in Alexandria, Louisiana. The retraction, done on March 15, 1968, applied to their earlier statement of July 17, 1967, and followed their first actual meeting with Clay Shaw; the von Rollestons stuck with the rest of their story they had told earlier, but removed Shaw from the equation.[2424]

By late March 1968, Shaw had adjusted somewhat to the fact that the case was not going away anytime soon. He wrote to his friend Holland McCombs, thanking him for his ongoing support. In the letter, Shaw commented that, "It is outrageous and shocking that a thing like this can occur in the latter half of the 20th century in these United States of America...and yet there it is. When confronted with madness there seems no solution except to stand as rock-firm as one can until the waves of paranoia break over you and exhaust themselves. And this is what I have tried to do these past 13 months. I ran across a line in Nietzsche the other day which seems applicable...'What doesn't kill me, strengthens me.' Let's hope he's right!"[2425]

The international trade community, of which Shaw had played such an important part for so long, kept a healthy distance from the investigation, probably for good reason. The 1967 Annual Report of the President of International House, issued in early 1968, made no mention of Shaw's predicament related to the Garrison investigation.

Wegmann wrote again to Peyton Ford with the Section Committee on Abuse of Process of the American Bar Association, responding to Ford's refusal to get involved in the Shaw case. Wegmann said that Shaw's only avenue of vindication would be an appeal if he was convicted, and requested that Ford reconsider the matter; he copied the letter to attorney Herbert Miller in Washington, D.C.[2426]

By April 5, Wegmann had a copy of Edward Jay Epstein's upcoming article for *The New Yorker*. He discussed it with attorney Elmer Gertz in Chicago,[2427] and attorney George Jensen in California.[2428] Wegmann complained to Gertz about the coast-to-coast publicity tour for Garrison that had been financed by *Playboy*, to promote the issue in which the interview with Garrison had appeared the previous fall.

David Logan was interviewed by Assistant District Attorney James Alcock, by telephone, on April 13, 1968, and a transcript of that interview survives. David Logan had mentioned possibly knowing important information that might be helpful to Garrison's case to an acquaintance of his in Chicago, Henry Lesnick, a faculty member at Northwestern University. When Alcock spoke with Logan, Logan said that he had met Shaw at Dixie's Bar around 1961, and also at The Galley House. He said that he went to Shaw's residence, where he recalled a nine-foot dinner table, where Shaw would sit at one end and Logan at the other end while the two had dinner together. He said that he engaged in various types of sadism and masochism with Shaw, including whippings, defecation, and urination. He said that such behavior had shocked him, as it was the first time he had ever encountered it. Logan also recalled Shaw only having one nipple, which other individuals over the years have recalled as well.

Logan also mentioned several of Shaw's friends, such as John Dodt, Carroll Glynn, and Joe St. Cyr; he remembered that Glynn and St. Cyr had owned an antique store called The London Shop. Logan recalled several prominent gay bars in New Orleans, including Tony Becino's, Dixie's, and Lafitte's in Exile. He also remembered Shaw's friend from North Carolina, William Formyduval, although not by name, recalling that he struggled with alcohol problems, and had a lot of female clothing in his wardrobe. Of interest to conspiracy writers is whether Logan ever saw Shaw and Ferrie together. Some books have mentioned that Logan definitely put the two together, and he is mentioned by name in the Oliver Stone movie, *JFK*. However, in the transcript of the telephone interview, Logan said he attended a party hosted by the two owners of The London Shop where Shaw was present, and that Logan had met another man there who was later identified to Logan as David Ferrie. However, he never says directly in the transcript that Shaw and Ferrie knew each other, or interacted in any way at the party. Rather, Alcock and Logan leave the subject open for a future telephone call.[2429] If that call was ever made, no record of it has survived. Logan was not called to testify in the trial. Even today, however, Logan is sometimes cited by conspiracy theorists as providing reliable evidence that Shaw knew Ferrie, without any further investigation of his background or motives for getting involved in the case.

Many researchers know the Office of Naval Intelligence (ONI) as one of the more difficult agencies from which to gain access to documents, even those more than forty years old. The office has always maintained that it guards the United States from perils arising on the world's oceans. However, in 1968, it interrupted that important task for another one of perhaps lesser importance. It had come to the Navy's attention that one of its Marines, George Woodcock, Jr., might have known David Ferrie, and the Navy had apparently become aware of newspaper reports about Ferrie's behavior during his lifetime. Accordingly, in April 1968, the Office of Naval Intelligence interviewed Woodcock at Gulfport, Mississippi. Specifically, the agency wanted to know whether Woodcock had known David Ferrie, whether he used narcotics, and whether he had ever engaged in homosexual relations with Ferrie, who had been dead for more than a year at that point. Woodcock, who had been in the Army and was now in the Marines, had served in Vietnam and was now married. His cousin was Andrew Blackmon, who had been involved with Ferrie, Sergio Arcacha Smith, and others in the Cuban Revolutionary Council in the early 1960s. Woodcock told the ONI that Ferrie had offered for him and Blackman to go to South America for training, eventually to be used in a Cuban invasion, but the two decided against it. Woodcock denied any knowledge of the use of narcotics, or of participating in homosexual acts, although he said that he had been told of Ferrie's homosexuality and earlier troubles with Eastern Airlines. He said that Ferrie had once given him and Blackmon a package to destroy that supposedly contained pornographic photos of Mexicans, after the Sheriff's Office had searched Ferrie's place. He said that Ferrie was always dirty and smelled bad, and that he liked to attempt to impress people. Ferrie never talked about women or associated with them, Woodcock said.[2430]

After being involved with Garrison's investigation from the very beginning, months before it broke in the newspapers until sometime later in the spring of 1967, Richard Billings and *LIFE* magazine had fallen away from Garrison's investigation. The reasons were never made perfectly clear, although there was definitely an internal battle within *LIFE* magazine once Garrison arrested Shaw. Shaw's old acquaintance, Holland McCombs, who had worked for *LIFE* and *Fortune* magazines, and had written extensively about the International Trade Mart and the Kennedy assassination, presented the point of view that Shaw could have had nothing to do with it, and he must have at least partially persuaded *LIFE* to back away. Also, Billings had begun to be concerned about Garrison demonizing the Federal government in his public accusations. In a letter to Garrison dated April 22, 1968, Billings wrote that he still wanted "to be friends," but criticized Garrison's attacks on the Federal government establishment. He acknowledged that Garrison was on to something interesting, and wondered if Garrison had not stumbled onto a conspiracy that had nothing to do with the Kennedy assassination.[2431]

Richard Billings also said that he would cover the trials of any persons accused as a result of Garrison's investigation. The letter came after a series of articles he had written, somewhat critical of Garrison's investigation, which had appeared in *Newsday*, the Long Island, New York newspaper. Garrison sent Billings's letter to James Alcock, Andrew Sciambra, and Lou Ivon, asking for their comments. In a note attached to the letter, Garrison said that if Billings could not see the case more clearly after a year of being associated with their office, he should be "covering baseball games."2432

Long after defense investigators had wrapped up their work from the spring of 1967, one of the invoices for those services, for $1,933.40 with Charles R. Carson of Wackenhut, would remain unpaid for a very long time. On April 10, 1968, Edward Wegmann wrote to Carson saying that he had a problem with the invoice, but would discuss it either in another letter, or by appointment.2433 In a letter to Carson dated August 12, 1968, Wegmann said that he was refusing to pay the invoice, because information gathered in the investigations had been shared by Carson or his employees with others besides Shaw and his attorneys.2434 Wegmann noted that all other invoices had been paid, but that the defense might request a refund of those amounts. Wegmann had learned from William Gurvich, who had defected from Garrison's probe, that friends of Carson, such as Joe Oster, an investigator who had once been an associate of Guy Banister, had gained access to the information that was supposedly proprietary to Shaw's defense team.2435

In the spring of 1968, Garrison's office inquired of the U.S. Passport Office about Clay Shaw's historical activity with that office. Robert D. Johnson, Acting Director of the office, supplied information to Garrison that more or less confirmed the official record. Shaw's initial passport had been issued on May 16, 1947, after Shaw presented an affidavit from his father that he was born on March 17, 1913, at Kentwood, Louisiana. The passport was renewed on June 15, 1949, and again on November 5, 1951. Those initial passports were so that Shaw could travel to various South American countries. The passport was renewed on March 31, 1954, for Shaw's intention to travel to Western Europe. On February 19, 1958, another one was issued so that Shaw could visit the Caribbean. Shaw's last passport up to 1968 had been issued on September 21, 1965, for Shaw's intentions to go to the West Indies and Mexico.2436

In early 1968, information began coming in from the discovery process of the lawsuit by Gordon Novel against *Playboy* magazine and Jim Garrison. In its answers to interrogatories propounded to it, HMH Publishing, which owned *Playboy*, responded that it knew the names of no CIA personnel involved in the assassination, and that Garrison had not given it any names in relation to the interview. It also indicated that Garrison was the source for saying that attorney Steven Plotkin was receiving CIA funds for his legal services representing Gordon Novel. HMH Publishing also shared that it had relied on Jim Garrison in saying that right-wing extremists were involved in the assassination.2437

Jim Garrison also was answering interrogatories related to Novel's lawsuit. In January 1968, he responded that Kennedy assassination conspiracy theorists Mark Lane and Harold Weisberg were associated with the investigation only as friends, not in an official capacity.2438 In May 1968, Garrison said that *Playboy* had not arranged a speaking tour around the country for him along with the interview, as some had suspected.2439

Novel's lawsuit originally was filed in New Orleans, but then dropped and re-filed in Chicago. Novel was represented there by attorney Elmer Gertz. Shaw's attorney Edward Wegmann began communicating with Gertz soon thereafter about developments in Shaw's case, a communication that would extend for at least the next six or seven years. Gertz, in turn, kept Wegmann informed on developments in the libel suit against Garrison and *Playboy*. In a letter dated January 26, 1968 from Wegmann to Gertz, Wegmann referred to Gertz's previous letter wherein Gertz had mentioned that *Playboy* magazine's materials related to the Garrison interview had been "fascinating."2440 A letter dated March 22, 1968 from Wegmann to Gertz referred to a recent court hearing at which Shaw's attorneys attempted to obtain a change of venue in the criminal case. During that hearing, the attorneys had been able to question Garrison, but only to a limited extent.2441 On May 14, 1968, Wegmann wrote to Gertz, indicating that the Louisiana Supreme Court had turned down all appeals related to preventing Shaw from being prosecuted, and that the matter now would move to the Federal U.S. District Court in an attempt to show that the prosecution was fraudulent, and that Garrison was using the case against Shaw mainly as a pretext to attack the Warren Commission report.[2442]

On May 6, 1968, Wegmann wrote to Gertz again, offering to put the "master file" from Garrison's office that he had received from William Gurvich the previous summer at Gertz's disposal. Wegmann mentioned, however, that he had seen a recent series of articles in the *Chicago Daily News* by Richard Billings (the same as had appeared in *Newsday*, the Long Island publication), who had access to many of the same documents Gurvich had turned over to Wegmann. Wegmann noted the lack of depth in the articles by Billings, which indicated the lack of value of the master file to the defense in any meaningful sense.[2443]

It is clear that Gurvich had been excluded from key portions of the investigation. For instance, in his lengthy interview with the defense attorneys back in August 1967, after his defection, he had said nothing about witness Charles Spiesel, or about the Clinton/Jackson witnesses. Most internal memos suggest that Gurvich had been used primarily related to investigation of David Ferrie and the anti-Castro Cubans, and that, while he had made the announcement of Shaw's arrest the evening it happened, he had very little to do with building the case against Shaw.

Shaw's friend, Jill Young, and Brian Latell wed in May of 1968. An article in the *Shreveport Times* listed the out-of-town visitors; they included Father Edward Sheridan, to whom Shaw had made his "confession" following his arrest, at Margaret Mary Young's suggestion, but Shaw was not listed among the guests at the wedding.[2444]

Latell had spent the year 1966 to 1967 in Shreveport, stationed at Barksdale Air Force Base. A newspaper article in September 1967 indicated that he had served with the Department of Defense while in Shreveport, but was now permanently assigned to Air Force headquarters at Bowling Air Force Base in Washington, as an intelligence officer.

Latell actually had joined the CIA during the 1960s. In 1977, writing to his in-laws, John Wray and Margaret Mary Young, he commented that it was a tumultuous time to be working for the CIA, following the various investigations of the agency by committees of both the U.S. Senate and U.S. House of Representatives. He suggested that, as John Wray Young knew from "the Clay Shaw experience," many sides were on the conspiracy bandwagon, including conservatives, liberals, [Jimmy] Carter's people, various congressmen, and *The Washington Post*. Latell added that being an historian and an existentialist helped him get through "the daily mazes and crazes."[2445] In 1978, Latell would begin teaching a course on "Revolutions in Latin America" at Georgetown University. His appointment there was somewhat controversial, in that a portion of his salary was paid by Georgetown, and a portion by the CIA.

On May 30, 1968, Wegmann wrote to Edward Jay Epstein about the series of articles by Richard Billings that had appeared in *Newsday*, and in the *Chicago Daily News*. Wegmann thought it interesting that Billings apparently had left out the story of a crucial meeting that Billings had with Andrew Sciambra, Perry Russo, and Garrison at Broussard's restaurant on the evening of February 27, 1967.[2446] At that meeting, Russo supposedly expressed surprise when told that, during his sodium pentothal session that same day, he had identified a tall white-haired man named "Bertrand" as someone to whom he had once been introduced at David Ferrie's residence. Billings later would acknowledge, in a letter to Wegmann, that such a conversation had indeed occurred.

The same day, Wegmann wrote to Attorney General Ramsey Clark, asking Clark to intervene in the Shaw prosecution on behalf of the Federal government. Wegmann asked for a meeting with Clark to discuss that rather dramatic proposal.[2447]

By this time, Wegmann had asked for a civil hearing in Federal court to press a civil rights complaint against Garrison's office for violating Shaw's rights. In a letter on May 31 to Elmer Gertz, Wegmann indicated that he wanted to depose Garrison's assistant district attorneys and investigators about the origins of the case; Wegmann expressed confidence that the case "may be over" after the Federal hearing was held.[2448]

Wegmann also wrote to U.S. Attorney Louis Lacour regarding the civil rights complaint, asking Lacour, in his role as a Federal attorney, to investigate certain aspects of the Shaw prosecution. In particular, Wegmann mentioned Cedric Von Rolleston and his wife.[2449]

The von Rollestons, like many who connected themselves with the Kennedy assassination during the years following it, told various stories at different times. They had told one story back in 1963, shortly after the assassination, and told conflicting stories related to the Clay Shaw case. Later, in the 1970s, Cedric von Rolleston would write to the House Select Committee on Assassinations (HSCA), which was officially re-investigating Kennedy's assassination, dramatically asking to be given the most powerful polygraph test available in order to determine the truthfulness of his account and involvement.

The White House received many telegrams over the years, particularly under the reign of President Johnson, urging it to open the archives related to the Kennedy assassination. The Kennedy assassination always attracted an unusual mix of individuals with varying political viewpoints, left and right. One telegram to the White House in 1968 from Sophia, Illinois, told the president to "open those archives or there will be a white peoples' march that you will never forget."[2450]

Jim Garrison drew a mixture of support as well. He generally treated black defendants with more respect than they had ever been used to, and therefore attracted a heavy black majority vote whenever he ran for election. Many on the left supported Garrison because of his critiques of government institutions such as the military and the CIA. However, there were plenty of that same ideological leaning who did not support Garrison, as he targeted some of their favorite politicians and judges who, no matter how far to the left they positioned themselves, were still part of the mainstream of American politics and government. On the other hand, many on the right side of the spectrum, who normally would not have supported the Kennedys, were nevertheless drawn to Garrison precisely because he criticized the Federal government and defended his own powers as a state governmental official, an argument that resonated well with those who had opposed the Federal government's initiatives in the civil rights area.

By the summer of 1968, Shaw's attorneys had succeeded in getting a Federal District Court hearing to deal with their complaint that Shaw's civil rights were being violated, and that he should not have to stand trial. Prior to the Federal court hearings, Shaw's attorneys were given authorization to take the depositions of key individuals involved in Garrison's investigation into the Kennedy assassination. Accordingly, in early June, Shaw's attorneys took depositions of Assistant District Attorneys Andrew Sciambra and James Alcock, and investigators Lou Ivon and Lynn Loisel. However, all of the men had been instructed by Garrison not to answer any questions, other than perhaps minor ones acknowledging their identity, so Shaw's attorneys failed in their effort to obtain inside information about the investigation.

Department of Justice attorneys continued to monitor the progress of Shaw's case from afar. In a memo dated June 11, 1968, from Edward L. Weisl, Jr. of the Civil Rights Division to Fred M. Vinson, Jr., in the Criminal Division of the Justice Department, Weisl commented on Wegmann's attempt to remove the case to Federal court, which was then ongoing in New Orleans. Weisl said that he saw no need for the department to intervene in the case; he commented that Federal jurisdiction was at best "dubious" related to Shaw's plight, and said that Shaw had an opportunity to defend himself in state court proceedings before alleging any type of civil rights violation.[2451]

In June, in preparation for the somewhat involved hearing to be held in Federal District Court, Shaw's attorney William Wegmann traveled to Des Moines, Iowa to take the deposition of Lillie Mae McMaines, the former Sandra Moffett. At the preliminary hearing held in mid-March 1967, Perry Russo, the main witness against Shaw, had testified that Moffett had been present at the party in September 1963, where Shaw, Ferrie, and Oswald allegedly conspired to kill President Kennedy. Moffett, then living in Omaha, Nebraska, had quickly denied, in stories printed in various newspapers, that she had been at such a party, saying that she had only met Ferrie in 1965.

In the deposition, McMaines, now living in Iowa, testified that she had been known as Sandra Moffett for the period of 1963 to 1965. She said that she had met Russo in 1962, and had given birth to his child in August of 1963. She testified that she had not attended the party described by Russo in September 1963; she had been in New Orleans only until September 20, 1963, at which time she and an acquaintance, James Robert Ervin, had gone with her baby to Mobile, Alabama, then to California, then back to New Orleans in June of 1964. She said that she did not see Russo from September 3, 1963 until either August or September of 1964. When she saw him again, Russo had a cast on his leg, and had marks where he had slashed his wrists. McMaines testified that she met Ferrie in early 1965, and that Ferrie had come into a bar where she worked a week or so later. She said that in 1965, Russo had asked her to marry him, but she refused. She testified that she left New Orleans in the fall of 1965 to go to Philadelphia, had returned to New Orleans and stayed until late January 1966, and had not been back since. She said that she had never seen Shaw in person, but that she may have heard Russo mention "Leon," the name he had given to Lee Harvey Oswald. McMaines said that she never heard Russo mention the Kennedy assassination, or talk of assassination at all. She said that Russo had hypnotized her at one time, and that she had never heard of Ferrie until she met him in 1965. The district attorney's office had contacted her on March 8, 1967, when two detectives knocked on her door at 11:00 at night and asked her to come to New Orleans with them immediately. She and her husband had refused, and had eventually moved to Iowa.[2452] After reviewing the transcript of McMaines's deposition, Edward Wegmann congratulated his brother for obtaining what Shaw's defense needed from such a key witness.[2453]

In mid-1968, Edward Jay Epstein published his lengthy piece in *The New Yorker*, criticizing Garrison's case against Shaw. The article went into perhaps more detail than any other critique of Garrison to date about the flaws in the case, and received a lot of attention nationwide. Emlyn Williams, the Welsh dramatist, wrote Shaw referencing the article, and thanking him for the good things Shaw had written to Williams's about his new true-crime book, *Beyond Belief*. Williams said that William Friedkin, who years later would direct *The French Connection* and *The Exorcist*, was set to direct a film of *Beyond Belief*, and added that the book's subject, the Moors murders in Great Britain, would "always haunt" him. He also said he had good memories of his recent visit with Shaw, in the company of his friend Bob Crawley.[2454]

In late July, a story broke in the New Orleans newspapers that Officer Aloysius Habighorst, who had booked and fingerprinted Shaw the night of his arrest, was now maintaining that Shaw had freely given him the name "Clay Bertrand" as an alias that he had used in the past. An arrest form was released to the newspapers showing the name "Clay Bertrand" on the form, and Shaw's signature on the form as well, presumably agreeing to its contents. The next day, William Wegmann wrote to Edward Wegmann, referring to the need to suppress any such evidence that had been gathered while Shaw was under arrest, before he had advice of legal counsel.[2455] The disclosures by Officer Habighorst would become a major point of contention at Shaw's trial some six and a half months later, at which Habighorst ultimately would not be allowed to testify about his version of events in front of the jury.

Seven years earlier, Habighorst's brother, also a policeman, had made an unauthorized stop of a carload of prominent citizens while off-duty and out of uniform. When he approached the group in the car with a gun drawn, a scuffle had occurred and one of the passengers, a prominent city official, had been killed. The incident was somewhat scandalous, even by New Orleans police standards, and Habighorst's brother and his accomplice had been convicted and sentenced to a few years in prison. Irvin Dymond had represented Habighorst's brother in his criminal case. Some speculated at the time of the Clay Shaw case that Habighorst still held a grudge against Irvin Dymond for failing to get his brother off scot-free for the killing, providing a possible motive for inserting himself into Shaw's case.

*Newsweek* reporter Hugh Aynesworth wrote to Shaw in early August, referencing the dinner he and his wife Paula had with Shaw the week before. Aynesworth said he had suggested to Edward Wegmann that Shaw hire a new defense attorney, and said that he would speak with the noted Texas attorney Percy Foreman.[2456] It had been recommended to Shaw by others besides Aynesworth that he hire a more prominent national defense attorney, that Irvin Dymond was too interlocked with local New Orleans politics to be effective against Garrison's machine. Shaw apparently considered the idea of hiring another attorney until his final trial date neared; he was at least somewhat dissatisfied with his attorneys' lack of progress in fighting Garrison outside of the courtroom. However, in the end he decided to stick with his team of local attorneys.

Other national media continued to report on the case occasionally, but to some degree the general fascination had blown over. A *Time* magazine article about Jim Garrison in the August 2, 1968, issue mentioned that Shaw was well known at several levels of New Orleans society, "high and low."[2457]

A letter to Shaw in early August 1968 from Holland McCombs mentioned that McCombs recently had made a speech about the assassination to an audience in San Antonio. McCombs also mentioned another lively discussion that he had had with his *LIFE* magazine colleagues about the Garrison investigation.[2458]

In August, an old issue flared up, one that had been simmering for well over a decade, and which brought Shaw back into the affairs of the International Trade Mart. Rachlin and Company, the broker for the sale of the original Mart building to the trio of New York owners in 1955, was owed the second half of its commission from those owners as soon as the Mart no longer leased space in the building. At the time of the original sale, it had been expected that the Mart would be vacating the premises within two years, and that the commission would be paid in a prompt fashion. However, due to the lengthy delay in finding a location for a new building, finding the financing for that building, and other aspects that delayed completion of what ultimately became the Mart tower in 1966-67, the commission payment was delayed many years longer than originally expected.

In April 1964, Albert D. Meltz, who had been the representative of Rachlin and Company who handled the sale, wrote to Shaw asking about the Mart's status, and raising the issue of the long-delayed payment. Shaw advised Meltz that the Mart still held the note that secured the commission. Meltz and Shaw had been corresponding back and forth since approximately 1956 regarding the commission issue, and Meltz always had reminded Shaw to retain the note that protected Rachlin's interest.[2459]

After Shaw's retirement, Meltz continued to write with his concerns. In early November 1965, however, Goldie Moore had written to Howard Soloman, another representative of Rachlin, indicating that Lloyd Cobb was now handling the issue on behalf of the Mart, but that he had not been well.[2460]

In early August 1968, John C. Lankenau, the attorney for Rachlin and Company, wrote Cobb, seeking the information needed to collect the commission from the buyers of the original Mart building sale in 1955. Apparently, after the Mart had vacated the building in 1967, the owners of the original building had failed to pay the second half of the commission, as they were obligated to do. Lankenau was seeking the whereabouts of Shaw, Rudolf Hecht, former Mart attorney Kenneth Barranger, and others associated with the sale of the building.[2461] Cobb made Edward Wegmann, Shaw's attorney, aware of the situation, and Wegmann wrote to Cobb in late December, requesting the documents sought by Lankenau.[2462]

During the summer of 1969, after Shaw's trial had been completed, he would journey to New York City to testify in the litigation that revolved around payment of the commission.

In the fall of 1968, Shaw purchased a combination of properties on St. Peter Street from architect Arthur Davis. The group of buildings included a four-family dwelling at 1020-22-24 St. Peter Street, with another four-family dwelling in the rear. It also included a set of twelve apartments at 1028 St. Peter Street, and a parking garage at 1027 Toulouse Street. The mortgage on the property was held by Edith Stern, Shaw's wealthy friend, who helped Shaw purchase the property at a time when he could not obtain bank financing, and he would continue paying on that mortgage for the rest of his life. The original loan by Stern was for $185,000, and Stern loaned Shaw an additional $40,000, in more than one installment, later in 1968 and in early 1969. Accordingly, by 1970 the loan balance had reached $228,347.50.[2463] At the time of his death, that set of properties would be the major holding of Shaw's estate, and the complete settlement of his estate would be delayed for a year and a half until the property sold at what the executor of the estate thought was a reasonable price, one that would pay all outstanding obligations of the estate.

As of Fall 1968, Shaw was still collecting monthly payments on the home at 505 Dauphine Street that he had sold in the 1950s, as well as on the properties at 908 Esplanade Avenue and on the Spanish Stables at 716 Governor Nicholls Street, both of which he had sold in the mid-1960s. Along the way, with his various restorations, Shaw started a new business called C.L. Shaw d/b/a Vieux Carré Restorations.

Garrison's investigators were, to a lesser extent, still pursuing additional leads in the case, albeit very quirky ones. Andrew Sciambra wrote to Garrison, outlining a charge made by James J. Plaine of Houston, Texas. Plaine said that a Dick White (sometimes spelled Wight) of the Freeport Sulphur Company had once contacted him about assassinating Fidel Castro. Plaine also mentioned a story that Shaw had been the part owner of a nickel mine in Cuba that would be used in manufacturing.[2464] Plaine had been sentenced to two years in the Oklahoma State Penitentiary in the late 1940s, for passing a bogus check.[2465]

The Freeport Sulphur story, which has been freely circulated over the years by conspiracy theorists, has an element of truth in it, as there had been plans for such a manufacturing facility back in the 1950s, as discussed earlier. However, Shaw had no part in it, and the actual facility was never built, probably because of the takeover in Cuba by Fidel Castro's forces. An examination of Shaw's income tax returns and other business records show no such ownership; Shaw's investments were almost exclusively in local real estate. The anecdote by Plaine, whose credibility has never been established, is usually pyramided into larger stories based upon alleged past foreign shenanigans supposedly engaged in over many decades by Freeport Sulphur, which, whether true or not, have nothing at all to do with Shaw.

By October 1968, Shaw's cash flow situation, always somewhat precarious since his arrest, continued its downward trend, and now he was receiving late notices from businesses. One, dated October 31, 1968, was from the writer Christopher Blake, who owned a restaurant patronized by Shaw.[2466] By September 1969, the accounting firm Alexander Grant sent Shaw an understanding letter, noting his predicament but indicating that it needed payment for its preparation of the past two years of income tax returns.[2467] Shaw paid the bill on October 14, 1969.

However, in spite of his legal and investigative expenses, which ultimately amounted to a large sum, Shaw had enough cash flow to maintain himself during his long legal ordeal, although perhaps not at the level for which had so long planned. He had occasional shortages, and periods when he had to live less lavishly, but there was never a period when he had to borrow money for day-to-day living expenses.

Long-time television newscaster Alec Gifford, who spent approximately fifty years on the air in New Orleans, had, ironically, been working in New York City for NBC when the entire Garrison investigation of the Kennedy assassination had broken in February 1967, and Shaw had been arrested in March. By late 1968, however, Gifford was back in New Orleans with WVUE-TV Channel 12, an ABC affiliate. On November 6, he wrote Shaw from New Orleans, saying that he had read the recent article in *Esquire* magazine by James Kirkwood, and commented that it was "interesting and helpful" to Shaw. Gifford indicated that he had returned from New York, and would like to meet and talk with Shaw about the case, off the record if Shaw preferred.[2468] Shaw telephoned Gifford, and said that he would speak with him after the trial. Gifford would conduct separate televised interviews with Garrison and Shaw during the two weeks following the trial.

After gay bar owner Eugene Davis had been named by attorney Dean Andrews as "Clay Bertrand," there was much curiosity about Davis. Some came forward to Garrison's office and said that they had seen Davis with Shaw in the presence of Lee Harvey Oswald at the Court of Two Sisters restaurant in the French Quarter in the early 1960s. In a memo to Garrison in December 1968, Andrew Sciambra reported that Davis said that he had never seen Oswald, although it was possible Oswald had come in the restaurant at some time; Davis gave Sciambra the names of two other restaurant employees with whom to confer. Sciambra also questioned Davis about why Dean Andrews had named him as "Clay Bertrand." Davis said he had no idea, but that before any of the news of "Clay Bertrand" had been made public, Andrews had asked Davis if he would like to become famous by Andrews naming him as "Bertrand." Davis said that he had not taken Andrews seriously, and had declined the offer.[2469]

During the summer, Shaw's attorneys had failed to convince the Federal district court to intervene in his case; the court took the position that Shaw's attorneys could protect Shaw's rights most effectively by defending him at trial. The attorneys then appealed to higher Federal courts. In late 1968, the U.S. Supreme Court turned down Shaw's request for an injunction against prosecution; the Court refused to hear appeals from an earlier U.S. Fifth Circuit Court of Appeals ruling.

In mid-December 1968, Shaw's attorneys held a conference to discuss the trial, the witnesses to be used, and the issues ahead. Richard Townley was listed as a witness, although he never testified. Writer James Phelan had promised to make himself available. The defense had decided that reporter Hugh Aynesworth, who was helping them investigate witnesses as they materialized, would be more valuable in the courtroom as an observer than as a witness. Walter Sheridan maintained that he had no first-hand knowledge of events in the case, but merely had reported on them, and therefore would not make a good witness. Sheridan had told the defense he had learned that Russo would not be a witness for the prosecution, so the defense subpoenaed Russo to testify. Russo, though, wound up being the major prosecution witness as to the conspiracy charge against Shaw, and spent two full days on the witness stand. The defense had been advised by Layton Martens's attorney that Martens would be unreliable as a witness, so the desire for his testimony was eliminated. James Lewallen, however, was still regarded as important at that late date, as he had been one of Ferrie's closest friends in 1963. The defense team indicated that it was seeking the most intelligent jury possible, regardless of "race, creed, or color."[2470]

The names of several character witnesses suggested by Shaw were discussed during the month preceding the opening of the trial. Among the names considered were Lloyd Cobb, Robert Elliott, Harold Roberts, all businessmen Shaw had known for many years, as well as Edith Stern and architect Edward Durell Stone. William Wegmann, however, expressed some concern that those individuals would all be considered as "members of the Establishment," and that they might not play well with a jury of more modest circumstances.[2471] Eventually, no character witnesses would appear for Shaw, although Lloyd Cobb, his former boss at the Mart, would appear as a fact witness in support of Shaw, providing detail of Shaw's activities during late summer 1963, the period during which the alleged conspiracy party had supposedly taken place at Ferrie's residence, and the visit to Clinton, Louisiana was said to have occurred.

Investigator William Gurvich, who had worked for Garrison during the first six months of the investigation but had dropped out to great publicity, was prepared to testify for the defense. In a memo summarizing Gurvich's potential testimony prepared in mid-January 1969, the lawyers noted that Gurvich could testify that Assistant District Attorney Charles Ward had told him that Garrison had ordered Shaw's arrest on "sheer political power." Gurvich also indicated that after Shaw initially had been interrogated in December 1966, Garrison had told some newsmen that Shaw had absolutely nothing to do with the assassination.[2472]

The defense team also speculated on potential witnesses that the district attorney's office would call at trial. In addition to Russo and Vernon Bundy, they also knew about Clyde Johnson, who was still considered a witness at least as late as the end of June 1968. The defense team had obtained a list of witnesses as of mid-1968 from Tom Bethell, the young British researcher working for Garrison who had defected behind the scenes in approximately August 1968 and begun giving information to the defense team. The witness list as of June 27, 1968, mentioned Charles Spiesel, Clyde Johnson, Vernon Bundy, Perry Russo, Connie T. Kaye, a vocalist at Pat O'Brien's bar, and the bulk of the eventual Clinton/Jackson witnesses.[2473] Witnesses to Oswald's distribution of pro-Castro leaflets on the streets of New Orleans were also included in the prosecution list drawn up shortly before the trial began.

Another potential prosecution witness was Ray R. Hiatt, an African-American man who had purchased Jeff Biddison's black Cadillac about a year before the trial.[2474] The black Cadillac tied in with the story told by the Clinton/Jackson witnesses of a similar car having been used by the men who arrived in Clinton during a CORE voter registration drive in 1963. Hiatt ultimately would not testify at trial.

The defense team scrambled frantically as the trial approached, running down leads and digesting new information provided to it. The attorneys and their investigators were still investigating witnesses up to the time of the trial, and even after the trial began, as they focused on discrediting the testimony of each potential prosecution witness.

# 27 · A Verdict, and Another Arrest

Shortly before Shaw's trial, Jeff Biddison had lunch with Harry Connick, Sr., father of the famous singer. Connick was then a Federal attorney in New Orleans who soon would play a part in the upcoming trial, advising testifying FBI agents of the answers they could give to various prosecution questions during their sworn testimony. Connick was apparently already planning to run for district attorney against Jim Garrison; the election would take place in November 1969. In a letter to Biddison dated January 11, 1969, Connick acknowledged their recent lunch, and thanked him for his support.[2475]

On January 13, with Shaw's trial set to begin in approximately one week, Garrison's archivist and researcher for the Kennedy assassination investigation files, Tom Bethell, called investigator Lou Ivon, wanting to meet immediately. When Ivon arrived, Bethell confessed that he had met with Shaw defense attorney Sal Panzeca in August 1968, had made an extra copy of the file he kept within the office that included a list of trial witnesses, and given it to Panzeca. Panzeca and Bethell had met again, in December 1968, after the U.S. Supreme Court had refused to hear the case for dismissing charges against Shaw. At that meeting, Panzeca asked Bethell if there were any new witnesses. He also told Bethell that chief defense attorney Irvin Dymond might not directly see any of the material that Bethell had given to him. According to Ivon, Bethell reacted emotionally during their meeting, saying that he was sorry about what he had done, and that he knew he would go to jail. Ivon and Bethell then went to prosecutor James Alcock's home and discussed the issue with him. After a while, Andrew Sciambra joined them for coffee.[2476]

At Ivon's request, Bethell wrote a memo on January 16, 1969, setting out the details of his involvement with Panzeca.[2477] Bethell now no longer had access to inside information, and he played no role in Shaw's trial, either for the prosecution or the defense, after his confession to Ivon. After the trial was over, Garrison would have Bethell indicted, and requested that Ivon write up a formal memo of his account of Bethell's confession.

The memo of witnesses that Bethell gave to Panzeca was probably the memo prepared on June 27, 1968, giving a list of witnesses and the description of their testimony as of that date. The witnesses included Charles Spiesel, Clyde Johnson, postman James Hardiman, Jessie Parker, Connie Kaye, Jules Ricco Kimble, Thomas C. Breitner, Peggy Landry, and various witnesses from the Clinton/Jackson area.[2478]

The list of witnesses is interesting in that it includes several who were not used at trial. Those included Clyde Johnson and Jules Ricco Kimble, generally considered to have been two of the most disreputable witnesses Garrison's office had considered during the two years between Shaw's arrest and trial. It also included Thomas C. Breitner, who was generally considered to be the possible surprise witness, who eventually turned out to be Charles Spiesel—someone who could bolster Perry Russo's testimony about Shaw having an interest in Kennedy's assassination.

Another potential witness, Peggy Landry, who also would not appear at Shaw's trial, said that she had met a man named "Bertrand" at John Campbell's home in 1961 or 1962. However, she said she was not sure if the man was Shaw.[2479]

Journalist Hugh Aynesworth was active in locating potential witnesses and interviewing them on the defense's behalf. Aynesworth also recommended at least two private investigators to assist the defense in locating witnesses and developing their backgrounds.

Aynesworth had started out interested in the assassination, and willing to help Garrison. On March 10, 1967, he sent photos of various people to Lou Ivon, and was clearly communicating with Garrison's investigators.[2480] However, the alleged bribery attempt of potential witness Alvin Beauboeuf in mid-March 1967 had quickly turned Aynesworth into a critic of the entire investigation. On the eve of trial, Aynesworth published a five-part series of articles in the *Pittsburgh Free Press*. He gave some of Shaw's background, saying that Shaw had made a "killing" buying and selling homes, and that Shaw had been an early and enthusiastic supporter of President Kennedy. Aynesworth said that Shaw had become a chain smoker, and had developed a twitch and a peculiar nervous laugh, as a result of his ordeal at Garrison's hands. Aynesworth reported that shortly after Shaw's arrest, Garrison had predicted Shaw would kill himself, and had followed up by saying, "I hope the SOB does kill himself." Aynesworth considered the Louisiana conspiracy law under which Shaw was charged and tried "spectacularly vague," and wrote that the case definitely would be reversed on appeal. Interestingly, Aynesworth casually identified Ferrie as a homosexual, but not Shaw.[2481]

As the trial approached, Walter Holloway, a private detective from Houston, Texas who had been recommended by Aynesworth, began to check on newly discovered witnesses from the information provided by Tom Bethell. Those included Jessie Parker, who had worked in the Eastern Airlines VIP Room at the New Orleans Airport in December 1966, when someone had supposedly signed the guest register using the name "Clay Bertrand." Investigators contacted her ex-husband, Joseph Parker, from whom she had been divorced for ten years. Investigators also contacted Barbara Spiesel Turner, the daughter of witness Charles Spiesel, and her husband, Dr. Bruce Turner, who worked at Charity Hospital in the Urology Section; they lived in Metairie, Louisiana, just outside of New Orleans.[2482]

One of the most important witnesses for the defense would have been Richard Billings, the *LIFE* magazine reporter, who in late 1966 and the first few months of 1967 had an inside track on Garrison's investigation. On January 3, 1969, Edward Wegmann wrote to Billings, indicating the need for his testimony, particularly on a key point: Billings was in a position to testify that Andrew Sciambra had not told Garrison that Russo had mentioned a third encounter with Shaw in his initial interview, that encounter being the party where David Ferrie and Oswald had been present and the assassination discussed. The first time the story of the assassination party had been mentioned was after Russo had undergone a sodium pentothal test, when Sciambra had informed Russo that he had told the story of such a party, although Russo did not remember doing so.[2483]

However, Billings's testimony was not to be. Billings answered Wegmann's letter later in the month, opening the letter by saying, "How can I make the point more precisely? I am in no way inclined to come to New Orleans to testify in defense of Clay Shaw or for any other reason."[2484]

Billings maintained that he was a professional journalist, and that in late 1966 he had come to New Orleans to investigate the assassination of President Kennedy on an assignment for *LIFE*. In the process he encountered Jim Garrison, who claimed to have a case against certain conspirators, primarily David Ferrie. While Billings did not deny that he did, in fact, know the information that Wegmann indicated would help Shaw's defense, Billings said that, "Even if I were inclined to become involved in the trial I would not do so as a partisan for either the defense or the prosecution...and you should realize that my role as a witness could backfire. I was unable to make a final determination on Russo's credibility, but Garrison and Alcock both know I believe elements of his story...This is not to say I believe your client guilty of the assassination, for I don't. I am not so certain however about an acquaintance with Ferrie or an affiliation with the intelligence agency." Billings closed the letter by indicating that he had a new job with *Congressional Quarterly*, and that he was going to concentrate fully on his new duties.[2485]

As Shaw's trial was finally set to begin, a local newspaper published an article about

Louisiana's conspiracy law, which was actually not that different from conspiracy laws in most other states, or in the Federal legal system. The law required that two or more persons work in combination to develop a conspiracy to commit a crime. Once the agreement has been reached, each person who wants to back away from it must inform each other person in the conspiracy that he or she was backing out of it. A person could be prosecuted both for conspiracy, and for the underlying crime itself—in Shaw's case the actual Kennedy assassination—if the evidence permitted. In Louisiana, the law required a jury verdict by twelve individuals, nine of whom must agree on the verdict of either guilty or not guilty. A person could be convicted if any member of the conspiracy, after the conspiracy had been formulated, committed any act that furthered the conspiracy, even if the actual underlying crime was never committed, or if someone who was not part of the conspiracy committed it.[2486]

Therefore, in Shaw's case, if a jury believed that he, Oswald and Ferrie, by their conversation, had engaged in an actual conspiracy to assassinate President Kennedy, then any act in furtherance of that conspiracy, such as Oswald going to Dallas, or bringing the rifle he had purchased into the building where he worked, and of course the actual assassination, would be enough to convict Shaw, even if Shaw, once having agreed to the conspiracy, then had changed his mind, but failed to inform Ferrie and Oswald. This likely was a heavy burden for Shaw's attorneys as their courtroom appearance drew closer.

Throughout 1968, there had been rumors of a possible investigation of Garrison by the Federal government related to income tax evasion, and Shaw and his attorneys hoped that Garrison might even be removed from office before Shaw's trial came to pass. Garrison was also having trouble with the State of Louisiana, which had sent him a notice indicating that he was five years behind on filing his state income tax returns. In a letter to the Louisiana Department of Revenue on February 13, 1969, in the very midst of Shaw's trial, Garrison explained his tardiness in filing, saying, "It has been a habit of mine to wait several years and file my state tax returns in groups" of several years at a time.[2487]

As writer James Kirkwood had begun to cover Shaw's case, he became well aware of rumors that Garrison also engaged in homosexual activities. For one thing, investigator William Gurvich had told Kirkwood, during Kirkwood's May 1968 trip to New Orleans to research what became the *Esquire* article, that Garrison was a "known homosexual."[2488] On the eve of trial, Kirkwood attended a gathering with some of Shaw's friends. Among those present was Edith Stern, who told a story that circulated around New Orleans, to the effect that sometime in the early 1960s, Garrison's wife Liz had filed for divorce and made allegations of homosexual activity against Garrison. The pair reconciled, and according to Ms. Stern, the rumors were that the records containing such allegations had disappeared from the courthouse files.[2489] Part of the expense for Kirkwood's eventual book about the trial, *American Grotesque*, was financed by the Stern Family Fund, a nonprofit organization founded by Edith Stern's family.

In late January, after jury selection had begun but before the first testimony had been heard, Hugh Aynesworth wrote to Edward Wegmann, discussing the trial. Aynesworth said he still expected "Slidin Clyde" Johnson to testify, and mentioned that Charles Spiesel might testify as well. Aynesworth said that Garrison knew that the defense team had tried to contact Spiesel, and that he expected some testimony about a June 1963 plot discussion.[2490]

On January 29, 1969, Jessie Parker submitted her revised affidavit about what she had witnessed in the Eastern Airlines VIP room on December 14, 1966. In the memo, consistent with her testimony at trial a few weeks later, Parker did not mention, as she had in her first affidavit, the group of Venezuelans she had said came in with Shaw, nor did she mention Shaw's preference for Bloody Marys, as she had earlier. This time, she said he came in with only one other man, signed the register, and then left, at a time when no one else had been in the room.[2491]

As Shaw's attorneys had learned of the possible use of Charles Spiesel, they also became aware of the possible use of another witness, Thomas Breitner, a lab technician in the molecular biology lab at the University of California at Berkeley. William Turner, a former FBI agent turned conspiracy buff who had cooperated to some degree with Garrison's probe, apparently located Breitner and interviewed him in late March 1967, approximately a month after Shaw's arrest. Turner reported that Breitner was a Jewish refugee from Nazi concentration camps. Turner said that Breitner had seen Shaw a few days before Kennedy's assassination in a stockroom at the lab in Berkeley, California, visiting with one of the "anti-Semites" working there. Breitner also told Turner that David Hackett, a professor there, had been murdered, and that the murder had never been solved. Also, a person named "Johnny" who worked at the lab had left with plane tickets on November 22, 1963, and had come back in the late afternoon. Turner considered Breitner an "objective and careful witness."[2492] In a memo from Turner to Garrison dated September 23, 1967, Turner said that Thomas Breitner remembered Shaw introducing himself as "Clay Bertram." Breitner said that Shaw had at first introduced himself using the first name of "Clem," which he had then quickly corrected to "Clay."[2493]

After Shaw's trial had begun, Walter Holloway, the private investigator, checked Breitner out and reported on his assertions. Holloway said that Breitner had reported to the police on April 2, 1965, that his wife had put poisonous powder in his soup in an attempt to kill him.[2494] Breitner ultimately was not called to testify; he died in October 1989.

On December 10, 1968, William Wood, also known as "Bill Boxley," had been fired by Garrison. William Wood soon called Stephen Aldrich, his old boss with the CIA; he told Aldrich that he had some information to tell the Agency, and asked the FBI to contact him.[2495] Wood then visited with Paul Rothermel, Jr., an employee of the Hunt family in Dallas, Texas; Wood had known Rothermel for some years. In a letter dated January 29, 1969, which would up in CIA files, Rothermel summarized Wood's visit to him, saying that Wood had been nervous during his visit, and had told Rothermel that he had written a 28,000-word manuscript about Garrison's investigation. Wood predicted that Shaw's trial would end in the "middle," and said that Garrison had a contact with the clerk in the Louisiana Supreme Court, so that he received advance notice of the Court's decisions.[2496]

Kennedy assassination researcher George Rennar interviewed Wood in Dallas in late summer of 1971. Wood told Rennar that he had had a meeting in mid-1968 with Garrison, Charles Ward, James Alcock, Lou Ivon, and Andrew Sciambra, where he learned that there was no real case against Shaw. However, he would not specify what was discussed in the meeting.[2497]

The jury selection process for Shaw's trial took approximately two weeks; more than 1,600 potential jurors were questioned before twelve jurors, and two alternate jurors, all male, eventually were selected. The CIA ran name searches in its records on all of the jurors picked to serve in the trial.[2498]

Gail Baumgartner was an acquaintance of Shaw's from the French Quarter social scene. She and her husband and another couple, the Reids, had sometimes socialized during the 1960s. When Gail Baumgartner and her husband Warren separated sometime after Shaw's arrest, she began to spend more time with Shaw, sometimes on a one-on-one basis, as he maintained a certain surface appearance during the period between his arrest and trial. Once the trial began, she was one of the most devoted attendees of all of his friends. Many of his friends stayed away, perhaps not wanting to draw the spotlight of Garrison's office, or the media, or due to time constraints or a sense of frustration at Shaw's predicament. These concerns did not seem to apply to Baumgartner; she often would pick Shaw up in her car after the day's trial was over and take him to her residence, where she would make dinner for him.[2499]

Author James Kirkwood commented that Gail Baumgartner laughed a lot, but that the trial was very tough on her. He also noted how very few friends of Shaw showed up at the trial, which he found puzzling. When he asked Marilyn Tate, the realtor, why she did not attend the trial, she said that she would be a "nervous wreck," and that she felt there was nothing she could do about Shaw's situation.[2500]

Some thought that Gail Baumgartner had misinterpreted Shaw's attention towards her, and concluded that he was interested in a real romantic relationship with her. If so, it was a common mistake. Shaw's well-groomed looks, gentlemanly manner, and more than adequate financial means combined to attract a number of eligible women over the years, even if most of them realized, deep down, that due to his sexual leanings, he was "unhaveable," to quote the daughter of one such admiring woman.

Jim Garrison made a lengthy opening statement to the jury, detailing all of the charges against Shaw, laying out the specific nature of meetings Shaw supposedly held in conspiring to assassinate Kennedy, and details that Garrison said linked Shaw to Oswald, Ferrie, and to the name "Clay Bertrand." Garrison's opening statement was very low key, and "fact"-oriented, in contrast to his somewhat abstract closing statement at the end of the trial, which would be designed to appeal purely to the jury's emotions.

During this opening effort, Garrison mentioned Shaw's name a number of times, another tactic from which he would depart in his closing. On June 30, 1970, the *States-Item* newspaper reported on a hearing related to Shaw's fight against perjury charges that had been leveled against him after the end of the conspiracy trial. At that hearing, a year and several months after Shaw had been acquitted of conspiracy charges, Assistant District Attorney James Alcock testified that he had written most of the statement that Garrison had used at the opening of the conspiracy trial.[2501]

After the jury had been picked, and opening statements given, testimony at Shaw's trial began in early February 1969. After a few minor witnesses, the Clinton/Jackson witnesses took the stand. Essentially, their story, spread out among the witnesses, was that Oswald had come to town looking for a job at the mental institution in Jackson, and had been told that he would stand a better chance of getting such a job if he was a registered voter. Later, the story of the black limousine entered the picture, supposedly with Oswald, Ferrie, and Shaw driving into Clinton during a voter registration drive that included a large number of African Americans. Town Marshal John Manchester was perhaps the most important witness, in that he maintained he had clearly seen the men, including Shaw, who had told Manchester he was from the International Trade Mart in New Orleans. While the Clinton/Jackson witnesses' testimony alone did not touch directly on conspiracy to assassinate Kennedy, it presented a number of witnesses who placed Shaw, Ferrie, and Oswald together. Therefore, Garrison quickly set up a dynamic which has followed Shaw and his reputation to this day, even among some who do not believe he was involved with the actual planning of the assassination—that Shaw had known Ferrie and/or Oswald. Since Shaw maintained he had never known either man, it allowed Garrison to introduce additional witnesses indicating that he did know one or both of them, even though only Perry Russo testified that he had witnessed the makings of an actual conspiracy.

Irvin Dymond limited his cross-examination of the Clinton/Jackson witnesses mainly to the length of time they had waited before coming forward, the fact that they had never told their stories to anyone else during the period immediately following the assassination, and the unlikelihood of anyone positively identifying individuals they had never seen before or since from a short encounter more than five years before. Not all courtroom observers were impressed with Dymond's cross-examination of those witnesses, and some began to wonder if Shaw had indeed made a mistake in not getting a more prominent attorney.

Witness Charles Spiesel soon took the stand, and testified that he had been at a party where he had overheard Ferrie and Shaw, but without Oswald being present, discussing the possibility of an assassination. What Spiesel testified to sounded even more like idle comments, rather than a real plan to kill the president, than Russo's testimony, but it was dramatic, nevertheless. Spiesel, a calm, short, balding man from New York, apparently made a good impression on direct examination. However, the defense team had been at work uncovering Spiesel's background, which included the bizarre accusations he had made about various individuals, and the sweeping lawsuits he had filed against individuals, businesses, and governmental bodies who allegedly had participated in hypnotizing him, and driving him out of his income tax preparation business. Spiesel did not deny any of his background, freely admitted that people had tried to hypnotize him, and explained it as if it had been the most logical development in the world.

Spiesel had placed the home where the meeting took place near the corner of Dauphine Street and Esplanade Avenue, at the back side of the French Quarter. On cross-examination, Irvin Dymond had Spiesel describe both the outside of the building and the inside of the actual unit, in as great a detail as he could muster; Dymond had to press him for such details throughout parts of his testimony. After what seemed to be the end of his testimony, as Spiesel had left the witness stand and was exiting the witness area, Dymond asked the court for permission to take the witness and the jury to the location at Dauphine and Esplanade to see if Spiesel could identify the actual building, and the unit within the building. Accordingly, court adjourned and the entire gathering made its way to that location, where Spiesel, after hesitating for a short period, entered the building at 906 Esplanade, a building that had been owned by Shaw in the early 1950s, and sold by him a couple of years later. With Spiesel back on the stand a short time later, Dymond made the point that the interior of that particular building had differed quite a bit from the description Spiesel had given earlier of the inside of the residence. Spiesel never positively identified the building, but said of all the buildings in the area that one was the closest to what he remembered. He soon left the witness stand; the effective cross-examination of him perhaps marked the turning point in the trial.

Perry Russo then took the stand and testified for two entire days. He testified that, at the party where Oswald, Ferrie, and Shaw had supposedly discussed the assassination, Ferrie had done most of the talking, indicating how a "triangulation of crossfire" could be used against Kennedy's motorcade, and that the chaos at the scene would allow the actual assassins to escape. Shaw's participation was limited mainly to objecting to the possibility of carrying it off, because of the inability to quickly escape from the scene, with Ferrie answering that the assailants could be flown to safety to Mexico, Brazil, or Cuba. Russo also said that Shaw had indicated that he could go to "the coast" on business as an alibi during the assassination.

After approximately half a day of direct testimony, Dymond took over on cross-examination, and succeeded in getting some rather dramatic admissions out of Russo. One was to the effect that although Ferrie had talked about killing the president many times, neither Oswald nor Shaw as "Clem Bertrand" had formally agreed to the assassination. In another exchange, Dymond got Russo to admit that the conversation at Ferrie's residence had not sounded like a legitimate plot to assassinate Kennedy, that it sounded more like "shooting the bull."

Russo testified that his loyalty to Ferrie was not such that he would not have reported the discussion to authorities, if he had taken it seriously. He also said that after the assassination had occurred, at no time had Ferrie ever approached him and asked him to forget about what he had heard at Ferrie's residence the night of the discussion with Shaw and Oswald.

In other areas, Dymond got Russo to discuss a long list of inaccuracies in the memo that Andrew Sciambra had prepared regarding his initial meeting with Russo in February 1967, just days before Shaw's arrest, wherein the meeting at Ferrie's place had never even been mentioned. Russo also discussed various things he had told individuals between the time of the preliminary hearing and the actual trial, including conversations he had with

Layton Martens and reporter James Phelan that indicated he was not certain about major portions of his testimony. Dymond also had an exchange with Russo about a second polygraph test, during which he had asked that it be stopped, and then discussed his misgivings about ever becoming involved in the case with the polygraph examiner, Lieutenant Edward O'Donnell of the New Orleans Police Department.

Dymond questioned Russo about inconsistencies with his testimony at the preliminary hearing. The most notable was that Russo had testified at that hearing that Sandra Moffett had been present at the party with Shaw, Ferrie, and Oswald. Moffett had, of course, immediately denied that, and said that she had not even met Ferrie until 1965. Accordingly, at trial, Russo changed his testimony and essentially indicated that he could not recall anyone identifiable who had been present, other than Shaw, Ferrie, Oswald, and Russo.

In the preliminary hearing in March 1967, when Dymond had known little about Russo and was concentrating on undermining his testimony in order to prevent Shaw from even being bound over for trial, Dymond had treated Russo in a thoroughly disrespectful, surly manner, calling him by his last name, asking him if he believed in God, and in general treating him in a somewhat rude and minimizing way. At the trial, however, Dymond treated Russo with more respect, generally questioning him in a much softer tone of voice with little or no sarcasm, trying to gain admissions from Russo that would weaken his testimony to where it fell below what was necessary to convict Shaw of conspiracy. The difference paid off. After the trial, Dymond told author James Kirkwood that very soon into the testimony, "I could see that it was going to work."[2502]

By the time Russo left the witness stand, it was generally considered that his testimony against Shaw had been considerably weakened, compared to the way it had been received two years before. The defense team had had those two years to explore inconsistencies in his story, and Russo had contributed to that effect by discussing his reservations about his own testimony openly with others outside of the courtroom. Additionally, while Russo generally stuck with his prior testimony, he had volunteered comments that gave the impression no real plot had been agreed to by the participants in the discussion.

A number of witnesses from Dallas, Texas, testified to things they had seen or heard the day of the assassination, or thought that they had. These tended to be details that contradicted the stories that the overwhelming number of witnesses there, taken as a whole, had offered to authorities. While not directly related to the charges against Shaw, presenting their testimony was a way for the prosecution to strengthen the idea to the jury that there had indeed been a conspiracy.

Dr. John Nichols testified at length to what he considered to be problems with the original autopsy conducted on Kennedy, particularly with regard to the interpretation of the direction of the rifle shots that had killed him. The CIA generated a memo discussing Dr. John Nichols at the time of his testimony. It indicated that Dr. Nichols had been born in 1921 in Charleston, West Virginia, had gone to medical school at the Medical College of Virginia, and that he had been approved for contact by the CIA's Office of Security in 1957, after he had visited Czechoslovakia.[2503]

Abraham Zapruder, a Dallas bystander who had filmed the most famous sequence of the Kennedy assassination, which remained unseen by the general public for a number of years until its showing at Shaw's trial, testified for the prosecution. During his testimony, the "Zapruder film" would be shown several times, producing a noticeably downbeat mood in the courtroom as all the spectators watched the dramatic repetition of Kennedy's assassination. Zapruder had originally been interviewed by Assistant District Attorney Alvin Oser and archivist Tom Bethell in early August 1968. Their memo of the meeting indicated that Zapruder was cold and arrogant at the first meeting, and they concluded that he would be a very reluctant witness. The next day, they met with Zapruder again, this time with his attorney, Samuel Passman, present. They described Zapruder as being less belligerent at this meeting, but still very difficult. However, he indicated he would be willing to testify to what he had seen and done at the scene of the assassination.[2504]

During the period of testimony from the Dallas witnesses and from Dr. Nichols, Shaw's name was not mentioned for several days at his own trial, a turn of events that, while unusual, is not unique. It is this phase of the prosecution's testimony, which the defense team fought unsuccessfully to prevent the jury from hearing, due primarily to its inflammatory nature, that has generally led to accusations that Garrison was merely using Shaw's trial as a pretext to present general evidence of a conspiracy in the Dallas shooting of Kennedy—a conspiracy that, the accusation goes, may not have even involved Shaw.

James A. Hardiman, Jr., a postal carrier, testified that he had delivered mail to 1414 Chartres, the address of the home of Shaw's longtime friend Jeff Biddison, which carried the name of "Clem Bertrand." Hardiman had given a statement to Garrison's office back on May 7, 1968, also indicating that he had delivered letters to Biddison's home which were addressed to Clay Shaw, although those letters had been forwarded from another location.[2505] After the trial, it developed that Hardiman's nephew had charges pending against him from 1968 that had not been acted upon by the district attorney's office as of the time of Shaw's trial. Hardiman also would stumble during his testimony on cross examination when Irvin Dymond invented at least two names, and Hardiman testified that he had also delivered mail addressed with those names to Biddison's home.

Jessie Parker testified to her simplified story of Shaw appearing with another man at the Eastern Airlines VIP Room, signing the guest register using the name "Clay Bertrand," then leaving, an event witnessed by no one else but her. She could not identify the other man, nor could she identify or remember any specific person on any day surrounding the date that incident had supposedly occurred, December 14, 1966. The defense, not knowing of her contradictory statements, concerned itself with trying to leave an impression of the absurdity of such an event, that Shaw would go into a room for no other purpose than to leave behind an alias that had already been linked to the assassination, particularly an alias that he supposedly had used himself.

The defense team's most important witness was Shaw himself. He took the stand, and what many thought would be a lengthy day or two on the witness stand turned into a simple hour and a half of testimony. Dymond questioned him for about thirty minutes, asking him a few simple questions about his early background, then venturing into a long series of denials in which Shaw asserted that he had never known or seen Oswald or Ferrie, that he had never been in Clinton, Louisiana, that he had never been in the Eastern Airlines VIP Room, that he had never used the name "Clay Bertrand" or "Clem Bertrand," and that he had never known attorney Dean Andrews and had never sent any clients to him under any circumstances. Dymond also asked Shaw whether he had ever "worked" for the CIA; Shaw denied ever having done so. During the slightly longer cross examination, prosecutor James Alcock asked Shaw several series of indirect inquiries designed to raise doubt as to the truthfulness of Shaw's denials, but without going back over the same ground covered by Shaw's attorneys. Many thought it strange that Alcock never asked Shaw directly about the conspiracy party supposedly attended by Shaw, Ferrie, Oswald, and Russo. Alcock also asked no questions related to any type of connection Shaw may have ever had with the CIA.

Dr. Pierre Finck, one of the military officers who had participated in the original autopsy of President Kennedy's body at Bethesda Naval Hospital, testified for the defense in an effort to refute the earlier testimony of Dr. John Nichols. Dr. Finck came across well enough on direct examination, but became confused and defensive, even defiant, on cross examination, as the prosecution succeeded in at least partially nullifying his testimony.

Dean Andrews testified for the defense that the name "Clay Bertrand" had originated while he was attending a "fag wedding reception" at the Rendezvous bar in the late 1950s. Andrews said that a lesbian patron there, Helen Girt, whom he characterized as a "butch" known to locals as "Big Joe," had jokingly referred to Eugene Davis as "Clay Bertrand" in a moment of total frivolity. Although no one ever officially followed up on that angle, even though Andrews had given the same testimony before the grand jury in 1967, the FBI, at the time of Shaw's trial, quickly identified Helen Girt as Helen J. Watson, who had been involved in the mid-1950s in a lengthy prostitution investigation in the Quad Cities area of Illinois and Iowa; Watson was identified in the FBI memos as an admitted lesbian. She had lived in New Orleans in the 1950s, as well as in Illinois.

Marina Oswald Porter, Lee Harvey Oswald's widow, testified on Shaw's behalf to the effect that she had never heard of Shaw, David Ferrie, or Perry Russo. However, she also left the impression that she hadn't really known that much about her husband's activities while they lived in New Orleans.

On redirect examination, the prosecution would present a man and wife, Nicholas and Matilda Tadin, who maintained they had seen Shaw and Ferrie together at the New Orleans Lakefront Airport some years before. Shaw's attorney, Irvin Dymond always attributed the testimony by the Tadins to an incident that had occurred a year or so before trial. Dymond had been in a nightclub owned by a woman friend of his, listening to music, when one of the musicians began arguing heatedly with the woman. Dymond, who was "a little loaded," spoke up in her defense and asked the man to step outside to settle the matter. Nicholas Tadin was the business agent for the local musicians' union, and supposedly had gone around, after the incident, saying things that indicated he was seeking revenge against Dymond.[2506] After the trial, Dymond would report the episode to the FBI as part of a new civil rights complaint filed by Shaw. Ironically, Nicholas Tadin later would serve with Shaw on the French Market Board, a group that looked after certain interests in the French Quarter, after all criminal charges against Shaw had been dropped.

The prosecution also presented, on redirect, gay bar owner Eugene Davis, who maintained he had not called Dean Andrews the day after the assassination seeking representation for Oswald, and had never used the name "Clay Bertrand." Davis did acknowledge that he "might have" sent Andrews some clients in the past. In an ironic twist, after the prosecution had avoided going into Shaw's homosexuality, Dymond went after Davis on that very subject, drawing an admission from Davis that his bar was "predominantly frequented by homosexuals."

In his closing statement to the jury, Irvin Dymond commented that it would have been much safer if Shaw had been able to say he had known David Ferrie. The trial presented a number of witnesses whose testimony attempted to establish nothing more than that Shaw had known Ferrie and/or Oswald, and it might have been easier and simpler if Shaw had been able to simply admit he knew Ferrie, but deny ever having participated in any discussion about killing Kennedy.

During the course of the trial, author James Kirkwood and various members of the press would gather in the evenings for dinner and drinking bouts. As the festivities grew merrier, one or more of the assembled journalists would offer up an Irish-style limerick, and Kirkwood captured a number of them in *American Grotesque*, his book about the trial. However, two that he left out, but which remained in his personal papers, captured the spirit of the overtones of homosexuality that hung over the entire case:

"The jury got horny as hell
Their cocks were beginning to swell
They questioned the judge about sodomy
He said sure, if it relieves the monotony
But Don't tell the press
And Don't make a mess
Or I'll order a frontal lobotomy."

AND

"There was a young witness named Perry
Who persuaded a fairy named Ferrie
With his medical skill
To concoct a pink pill
That made any young man yield his cherrie."[2507]

The jury received the case shortly before midnight on February 28, 1969, and returned a verdict of not guilty in less than an hour. Many have pointed to the limited amount of jury deliberations as evidence of the weakness of the prosecution's case, and it is difficult to argue with that sentiment. However, one could point out other cases decided quickly that yielded questionable results, such as the O.J. Simpson murder case, where jurors deliberated for approximately four hours after an eight and a half month trial before finding Simpson not guilty, a decision many have questioned, including some who thought the Shaw jury reached the right decision. It also ignores cases in the South where all-white juries quickly acquitted white defendants for alleged crimes against black citizens, or convicted black defendants for alleged crimes against whites, during the Jim Crow era.

As the jurors drove away from the courthouse after the verdict, several of them were interviewed by reporters. One of the African-American jurors said that the jurors did not believe that the prosecution had proved a "meeting of the minds" on the issue of conspiracy in the meeting described by Perry Russo, nor did they believe it had proven that Shaw knew either Ferrie or Oswald.[2508]

The night of the verdict, after Shaw had gone home to rest quietly, the buzzer on the outside door leading into his patio rang. It was Layton Martens, wanting to talk to Shaw after the long silence between them; they had not spoken since December 1966, when both of them had ridden with Detective Lester Otillio for their initial questioning by the district attorney's office, two months before the probe was made public. Shaw looked through his viewer that let him know who was outside the door, saw that it was Martens, then went back inside, took a sleeping pill and fell asleep.[2509]

During the days after the verdict, jurors were again interviewed by the local newspapers. In general, they said there had been little discussion of the case during deliberations, and that no actual conspiracy had been proven. One juror said that Perry Russo "wouldn't know the truth if it slapped him in the face." Most jurors thought the defense did a good job, and that the prosecution simply did not prove its contention that Shaw was part of a conspiracy. All the prosecution had, the jurors seemed to say, was "Perry Russo," which was "not much." However, some of the jurors said that they would vote for Jim Garrison again when he came up for re-election in the fall of that year.

Judge Edward A. Haggarty, who presided over the trial, said in press interviews that the biggest problem he had was not to commit reversible error, with both sides fighting the case so tenaciously. He commented that the State had tried the Warren Report, but had not proved a meeting of the minds related to the conspiracy allegation against Shaw. He also said that the prosecutors had not proven that Shaw knew Ferrie or Oswald, and that there had been too many flaws and contradictions in Russo's testimony. Judge Haggarty said that neither Irvin Dymond's hard-hitting closing argument, nor Garrison's closing statement invoking the patriotic duty of the jury, had much influence on the outcome.

The transcript of the trial, like those of the preliminary hearing two years earlier, and the Federal court hearing held before Judge Herbert Christenberry two years later to determine whether Shaw would have to stand trial for perjury charges, would become important historical documents related to the Kennedy assassination. However, the testimony of some of the key witnesses was never transcribed, including that of Charles Spiesel, Vernon Bundy, Eugene Davis, and Jessie Parker. According to Helen Dietrich, the main court reporter, Charles Neyrey, one of the other court reporters, never bothered to transcribe the testimony he took, unless one of the parties to the trial paid for that work to be done, whereas Dietrich transcribed all of the testimony under her direct responsibility. However, Dietrich seemed to contradict that version when interviewed by documentary filmmaker Stephen Tyler for his film *He Must Have Something* in the early 1990s, where she describes taking Charles Spiesel's testimony herself.

Dietrich found herself at the center of a controversy in 1977 when the House Select Committee on Assassinations (HSCA) went searching for a transcript of the trial. Dietrich took the position that the partial trial transcript in her possession was an historical document, and wanted to charge the committee at least $10,000 for it. She became somewhat angry when the committee representatives tried to lean on her either to give up the transcript for nothing, or for a nominal amount, accusing them of bullying her. The committee prevailed upon Jim Garrison to negotiate with her about the importance of the transcript, and eventually obtained a copy. During the 1980s, Dietrich was a literary agent with Southern Writers Agency, and worked with Garrison on trying to secure a publishing contract for his version of the Shaw investigation and trial.

After all concerned had a good night's sleep, a press conference was held by Shaw and his attorneys on Saturday afternoon, March 1, at Edward Wegmann's home at 350 Broadway in New Orleans. An upbeat Shaw refused to criticize Garrison or speculate about his motives for instigating the prosecution, although he opined that Garrison had used the trial to get criticism of the Warren Commission findings into a court record. In answer to an indirect question about whether Garrison might be the real "villain" in the case, Shaw said that this particular chapter of his life "has not ended here." Most interpreted the remark to mean that Shaw was at least considering filing a civil suit related to his arrest and prosecution.

On March 3, 1969, Jim Garrison personally charged Shaw with perjury, resulting from Shaw's denials during the conspiracy trial that he had known either Ferrie or Oswald. None of Shaw's assistant prosecutors would sign the arrest warrant, so Garrison did it himself.[2510] While extremely disappointed, Shaw soon resigned himself to the fact that the episode could go on for several more years.

On March 6, possibly to buttress the new charges, Garrison obtained a statement from June A. Rolfe, who was a reporter for Channel 26 in New Orleans, and who had covered Shaw's trial. Rolfe and her husband, Richard Rolfe, were supporters of Garrison, and close to him socially. Some years before, June Rolfe had had a dispute with Shaw over a rental payment owed to him, and his reporting that she had never made the payment had caused her some credit problems later. In the statement, she said that in the early 1960s she had seen Shaw in the front seat of a light-colored Ford Thunderbird with the top down along with two young men, an arm around each one; David Ferrie had been riding in the back seat.[2511]

Immediately after Shaw's trial, Dean Andrews was charged again with perjury related to testimony he shared at the trial, in which he had reiterated his claim that Shaw was not "Clay Bertrand."[2512] Like Shaw, Andrews knew the battle could go on for years. Unlike Shaw, however, there was little doubt that Andrews had told different versions of the same story, even while under oath.

In a meeting with the New Orleans FBI office, Shaw and his attorneys soon filed another civil rights complaint against Garrison's office. That complaint expanded upon the earlier one filed in December 1967, but pointed also to the witnesses used at the trial itself, and to the perjury charges which immediately followed his acquittal. In the complaint, Shaw alleged that he had originally been arrested by Garrison "solely and only for the illegal purpose of providing him [Garrison] and other critics of the Warren Report with a judicial forum for their attacks upon the Report of the Warren Commission." The complaint also said that Garrison had told New Orleans reporter Hoke May in January 1969 that, "The whole thing is a personal vendetta. The case is not being tried with any intent of conviction—but the SOB will have to live with it the rest of his life."[2513]

Shaw's place of birth has been mentioned in various books and articles over the years as either Kentwood, Louisiana, or New Orleans. It is pretty clear that Kentwood was his actual birthplace, as Shaw gave that information in many official documents. Another reference is an FBI memo dated March 4, 1969, regarding the visit by Shaw and his attorneys to the New Orleans office in order to file this latest civil rights complaint against Garrison. The information recorded by the FBI in that meeting lists Kentwood as Shaw's birthplace.[2514]

In a memo dated April 3, 1969, David Bonderman, with the Civil Rights Division of the Justice Department, commented that he had examined Shaw's complaint, and noted that false testimony, as mentioned throughout Shaw's complaint, was not within the umbrella of civil rights laws that would require involvement by the Justice Department. He observed that the attempts to bribe Alvin Beauboeuf and Fred Leemans might fall under conspiracy to deprive Shaw of his civil rights, under the doctrine of "color of law." However, a decision already had been made, related to the complaint filed in December 1967, not to investigate based on those alleged bribery attempts, and he pointed out that neither Beauboeuf nor Leemans had actually testified at Shaw's trial, or in any other judicial forum under oath.[2515] In a letter to Edward Wegmann on April 16, 1969, D. Robert Owen of the Justice Department relayed the points in Bonderman's memo.[2516] Dean Andrews also made a civil rights complaint after Shaw's trial, but the Justice Department decided not to investigate his complaint as well.

On March 17, 1969, the Consul General of El Salvador invited Shaw to a reception for Louisiana Governor John McKeithen and New Orleans Mayor Victor Schiro that was to be held at the Plimsoll Club at the new Mart tower.[2517] It was a black tie affair; the invitation showed that Shaw had not lost the respect of many of his old colleagues in the international trade community, or perhaps had regained it somewhat as a result of the trial.

After Shaw's acquittal, he received numerous letters and telegrams from friends and admirers around the country, and some from overseas, many of them the same people who had written him after his arrest. Many of the correspondents sent along newspaper clippings or editorials from the newspapers in their area, almost all of which were in support of the verdict. In an interesting column dated February 28, 1969, before the verdict, New York columnist James Wechsler said that Bobby Kennedy had told him, after Walter Sheridan's initial investigation, that he could "forget about Garrison" having anything legitimate.[2518] There had long been a suspicion that Walter Sheridan had communicated directly with Bobby Kennedy during his investigation into Garrison's probe, when Sheridan was employed by NBC News. Ed Planer, News Director at WDSU-TV Channel 6 at the time, commented to the author his own belief that Sheridan was directly communicating with Kennedy,[2519] although Sheridan denied it under oath in a deposition taken in 1969 related to Gordon Novel's civil suit against *Playboy* magazine and Garrison.

Carlos Quiroga, the anti-Castro Cuban activist who had been interviewed by Garrison's office before the story broke in the press in February 1967, wrote Shaw shortly after the verdict. Quiroga had had a bad experience with representatives of Garrison's office, and was still angry about the probe. He suggested to Shaw that a television show exposing Garrison was needed, to make the public fully aware of what had happened.[2520]

Dr. Martin Palmer, Shaw's former personal physician, wrote on March 1 from Anchorage, Alaska, where he had moved during the heat of the Garrison investigation. He told Shaw he had sent a telegram to Garrison that said, "Your wicked lies and persecution of the innocent has gotten exactly what it deserved." Palmer indicated that he liked Alaska—that he was skiing, ice skating and fly fishing, and had a sense of freedom after being in a large city for so many years.[2521]

Shaw's long-time assistant at the Mart, J.B. Dauenhauer, responded immediately, the day of the verdict, with a letter saying that Shaw had been brilliant on television at the press conference held at the home of Edward Wegmann on the afternoon of March 1. Dauenhauer indicated that Shaw should make the cover of *TIME* magazine, and that he should let "Little Willard R[obertson] have it with both barrels," referring to one of the founders of the Truth and Consequences organization who had financed part of the investigation against Shaw. Dauenhauer indicated that he had gone "to St. Louis Cathedral today" to pray, adding "a sinner's prayers are best."[2522]

A letter dated March 2 from Clint Bolton, who had worked with Shaw during the Louisiana Purchase Sesquicentennial celebration in 1953, said that, "In 40 years of news work," he had never seen a district attorney misuse his power so much. Bolton enclosed an editorial published in the *Vieux Carré Courier*, a local French Quarter newspaper, written on February 27, 1969, before the verdict, predicting Shaw's acquittal. Bolton also said that his wife sent good wishes and that he would be glad to "take a shot" at the Truth and Consequences organization.[2523]

The editorial Bolton referred to appeared in the *Vieux Carré Courier* on February 28, 1969, the last day of the trial but before the verdict was announced late that night, and was entitled "His Friends." The small editorial indicated the paper's support for Shaw before the verdict, saying, "We feel sure Clay Shaw will come away from the trial the same honorable man who went in, head erect, carriage military, with the respect and affection of his friends and neighbors."[2524]

Many who wrote Shaw had known him during his years with the Mart. Dr. Ettore Scampicchio, who had managed the Italian Tourist Commission office in the Mart, wrote from Italy congratulating him, and suggesting he come to Rome and relax.[2525] William G. Zetzmann, Jr., son of the man who had served as President of the Mart from 1953 until 1962, wrote that his brother Robert and he congratulated Shaw on the verdict, and added that his father had always held Shaw in high esteem.[2526] Holland McCombs, the long-time *LIFE* and *Fortune* magazine writer, who had covered the opening of the Mart in 1948 and who had also covered various aspects of the Kennedy assassination, including coming to Shaw's defense behind the scenes at *LIFE* magazine during the early days after Shaw's arrest, praised Shaw's dignity in a telegram on March 2; McCombs offered to help Shaw recover in any way possible.[2527] Charles and Eleanor Nutter wired from Singapore on March 2 with their congratulations over Shaw's acquittal.[2528]

On March 3, as new charges for perjury were being pressed against Shaw directly by Garrison, Knox Burger and Walter Fultz with Fawcett Publications sent Shaw a telegram congratulating him on the "expected verdict," and expressing their "continuing interest" in a book project they had discussed the year before with Shaw and literary agent Jim McCormick.[2529] At that point, at least, a book that Shaw might have written was apparently still a possibility; Irvin Dymond and the other attorneys on Shaw's criminal defense team had a stake in any such book Shaw might have written. But it was not to be; the perjury charges effectively nullified such Shaw efforts that might have earned him extra income following the acquittal.

Dr. Alton Ochsner wrote to congratulate Shaw, indicating that he was the victim of a person wanting publicity, although Ochsner did not identify Garrison by name in the letter.[2530] Ochsner supposedly had been one of the prominent individuals in New Orleans whom Garrison had considered arresting during the early months of his probe.

Shaw's old friend Cecil E. Foster, who lived in Muskegon, Michigan, but wintered in Lakeland, Florida, wrote Shaw in mid-March, indicating that hard times had fallen upon him, but that he hoped to regain solvency soon. He indicated that writing letters regarding Shaw and his situation had been difficult, and that he had lived through the past few years with Shaw, as he had watched Shaw's troubles unfold.[2531]

One interesting telegram came from John W. Campbell, President of the Cleveland, Ohio Mattachine Society. Campbell congratulated Shaw on the verdict, and indicated that he would like Shaw to address his group, at Shaw's convenience.[2532] The Mattachine Society was one of the early groups that promoted gay rights in the United States, often working quietly and behind the scenes, but with a more public face than might have been expected for such a group in the 1950s and 1960s. There was no record that Shaw ever responded to the invitation or addressed the group, and it was uncharacteristic of Shaw to take a publicly active role in gay rights issues, although perhaps toward the very end of his life he became more open to the idea.

Wynn Pearce, who had thrown the late-1940s party where photographs of Shaw, Biddison and others would later be given a sinister interpretation by conspiracy theorists, sent a telegram from Los Angeles congratulating Shaw. Pearce commented that "Kafka can't always be right," and indicated he wished he could have been of more help to Shaw.[2533]

Pancho Rodriguez, Tennessee Williams's long-time lover in New Orleans, wrote saying, "Dear Clay, You extended your hand Friday out of the car," and indicating that it was a "pleasure to have known you" and telling Shaw to "walk majestically as you always have."[2534]

Shaw's old employee, John Leonard, who had been the first Public Relations Director at the Mart during 1948-49, sent a telegram from Lake Forest, Illinois, indicating that the verdict was what he "knew it would be," and adding that he hoped to see Shaw again sometime.[2535]

A telegram from Henri Gomez in Caracas, Venezuela congratulated Shaw for "holding up magnificently throughout" the ordeal. Gomez predicted that one day Shaw would "recall it with humor."[2536]

A telegram from Sally Galjour and her husband Warren arrived from Brooklyn, New York. Galjour, sister of Marge O'Dair, wrote, "So you're not guilty—what else is new?"[2537] Gaines Kincaid, Shaw's old friend from the early 1950s in New Orleans, sent a telegram from Austin, Texas saying, "The photo of grinning man in tonight's paper looks more like my old white chested, barrel-headed friend," jokingly mixing two of Shaw's most noted characteristics. Kincaid's telegram concluded, "God bless you—I am delighted."[2538]

From London came a wire from Emlyn Williams that simply said, "Thrilled—Fondest love."[2539] From Bayport, New York, came a telegram from soap opera and western actor, Val Dufour, saying, "Congrats—let me know if you need anything—I love you."[2540]

Another telegram arrived from Chicago attorney Elmer Gertz, who represented Gordon Novel in his libel suit against *Playboy* magazine and Jim Garrison. Gertz said, "I rejoice with you on this great day of your vindication—I hope to complete the Garrison debacle—May you live happily hereafter."[2541]

Another letter, written the day of the verdict, came from Sylvia Meagher in New York City. Meagher was a Warren Commission critic who had, over several books, placed the Warren Commission information in a more understandable order. One of the books, *Accessories After the Fact*, was widely read by students of the assassination. She had corresponded with Shaw during the period between his arrest and trial, and they had respectfully disagreed about the conclusions of the Warren Commission, with Shaw generally supporting the Commission findings and Meagher differing with them. However, she extended her congratulations to Shaw on the verdict, saying that anything else would have been an "intolerable miscarriage of justice."[2542]

Shaw's old employer from International Harvester in the early 1930s, L.S. "Mac" McClaren in McComb, Mississippi, wired his congratulations the first day, saying that the big mystery was "how Garrison got so many unmitigated liars lined up." McClaren said that he would have offered his services to Shaw, but he knew Shaw had good attorneys in Dymond and Wegmann.[2543]

Many of the congratulatory records and telegrams that were written to Shaw after the trial ended, but more than a few days after the verdict, were tempered by news of the perjury charges that had been filed by Garrison against Shaw on March 3, 1969. Dr. Thomas Rafferty wrote Shaw that he was "sorry that your trials are not yet over," but that he hoped "that moment is not far off." Rafferty also indicated that, "I hope you do not hold me responsible for the enclosed outrage."[2544] It was unclear what Rafferty enclosed in the letter to Shaw, but he could have attributed the perjury charges to Shaw's acquaintanceship with Layton Martens, to whom Rafferty had introduced Shaw several years earlier.

Writer James Leo Herlihy wrote a letter immediately after the perjury charges had been filed against Shaw saying, "So now you're a perjurer—can't you learn to behave?"[2545] Herlihy would remain friends with Shaw the rest of Shaw's life.

John R. Stiles, a long-time friend of Gerald Ford, the Michigan congressman, and later vice president and president, who had been a member of the Warren Commission, wrote to Shaw offering his congratulations, saying that no one had doubted Shaw's innocence. Stiles, who had co-authored a book called *Portrait of the Assassin*, which backed the Warren Commission conclusions, suggested that Shaw could sue the "Jolly Green Giant,"[2546] the nickname given to Jim Garrison, supposedly by Dean Andrews, for his height.

Albert Lemón sent a card on March 7. Lemón had taught Shaw Spanish during 1948, prior to Shaw's initial trip to Central and South America. Lemón said that his whole family had prayed and hoped that everything would turn out in Shaw's favor, calling the whole affair a "nightmare," and saying that it was impossible to believe it had happened to someone like Shaw.[2547]

Many of the correspondents suggested that Shaw could sue Garrison, and the idea clearly had been in the air almost from the time Shaw had been arrested. Any plans Shaw might have had for immediately filling a lawsuit, however, were derailed due to the perjury charges filed immediately after his acquittal. Some have speculated that the reason Garrison charged Shaw with perjury was to keep any civil action Shaw might file at bay, in addition to stretching out the publicity of the case for Garrison's benefit.

On March 7, Jim Garrison wrote to Ralph Schoenman, an assistant to British philosopher Bertrand Russell, discussing the case and its aftermath. Garrison said that, "We will win" the perjury case against Shaw "if I survive in office and get him to trial." Garrison maintained that the prosecution's case at the recently concluded trial had "destroyed" the Warren Commission report, but complained that the press presented the viewpoint that the verdict acquitting Shaw had essentially upheld the report.[2548]

A letter to Shaw written on March 9 came from Caroline Christenberry, the wife of Federal District Judge Herbert Christenberry.[2549] Ms. Christenberry congratulated Shaw on the verdict and recalled a time, years before, when she had worked at Maison de Ville Hotel in the French Quarter, handling reservations for, among others, guests referred there by the International Trade Mart. In an ironic twist, she added that, "Should your case have eventually found its way to Federal Court and been allotted to my husband you most certainly would have had a fair trial." In January 1971, the new perjury case against Shaw would indeed find its way into Herbert Christenberry's court, with dramatic consequences for Shaw, and for Garrison's office.

On March 11, 1969 Shaw was interviewed on WVUE-TV, by noted local broadcaster Alec Gifford. Shaw said that his ordeal could have happened to anyone, and pointed critically to the private financing of the district attorney's investigation by local wealthy individuals; he proposed legislation to ban that practice. He indicated that after the verdict, "for the first time in two years I can draw a really deep breath." He added that, "We have reached the end of the beginning, and I hope very shortly we can begin the beginning of the end," possibly hinting at a future lawsuit against Garrison and others. Gifford, who was sometimes direct and borderline combative with Shaw, asked about the items seized from Shaw's residence the night of his arrest, such as whips, chains, and black costumes. Shaw said the black costume was a monk's costume that he had worn approximately a dozen times at Mardi Gras during the past fifteen years, and that all of the seemingly strange paraphernalia seized was related somehow to Mardi Gras costumes. Shaw talked of trying to avoid hatred of any individual over his ordeal, saying that hatred was a damaging emotion, very corrosive, and a psychological luxury that he could not afford. He indicated that bills were still coming in, saying that, "All precincts haven't been heard from." He said that he would be seeking work in the international trade arena, because he was a frustrated playwright who had never had a major success. Shaw spoke of the play he was writing about former governor Ulloa, the first Spanish governor of Louisiana, who had been expelled from Louisiana after a revolution by the French against the Spanish; Ulloa had turned down the local Indians' offer to help annihilate the French, choosing to be expelled from the colony rather than extend the violence.

Shaw said the experience he had undergone had deepened his life, and that he was now very much aware of spiritual values he had neglected before. He said that he appreciated the value of friends more, adding that no friends had deserted him, only some casual acquaintances. He said he did not know how history would view the event, but he predicted that interest in it would be there for many years afterwards, although he called it "a minor footnote in history." [2550]

Gifford asked Shaw directly why Garrison would go after him if he was not involved. Shaw indicated that he had learned a great deal about the law since he had been arrested, and that when one wanted to know a fact, the best thing to do was to look at the "best evidence." In his particular case, Shaw said, the "best evidence would be Perry Russo. Did you ask him?" Gifford acknowledged that he had not. Gifford also asked Shaw about his statement at the post-verdict press conference on Saturday, March 1, held at Edward Wegmann's home, where Shaw had said the matter was "not over yet." Gifford tied the comment to the new perjury charges against Shaw filed on Monday, March 3, 1969, and Shaw replied that that was "not what he had had in mind" when he had made the statement on the previous Saturday. [2551]

In a somewhat humorous footnote to the interview itself, author James Kirkwood, in New Orleans at the time, working on what would become *American Grotesque*, recorded the interview with Shaw by Gifford. Apparently objecting to Gifford's direct questioning, particularly about the items seized in Shaw's residence the night of his arrest, with the hint of sadism, masochism, and homosexuality involved, Kirkwood can be heard on the recording saying, "Asshole," as the program was ending. [2552]

On March 12, 1969, Edward Wegmann wrote to attorney Elmer Gertz in Chicago, who, as mentioned earlier, represented Gordon Novel. Gertz had written Wegmann on March 1, 1969, the day of the verdict, offering his congratulations. Wegmann offered his assistance to Gertz in the suit against Garrison and said that, "The mind of Garrison" "can only be" described as "perverted, distorted, paranoid." Wegmann also indicated that had the defense not found out about witness Charles Spiesel in advance, Shaw could easily have been convicted.[2553]

In fact, the defense team had been fortunate in many ways, beginning even before Shaw's arrest. Important news reporters had heard of Garrison's investigation before it had broken publicly, and had begun to examine it critically, even before Shaw emerged as a suspect. Through newsman James Phelan, the defense team had gotten hold of Andrew Sciambra's memo describing his interview with Perry Russo on February 25, 1967, which contained many inaccuracies and omissions, the most important of which were that Russo had apparently not even mentioned a conspiracy meeting with Shaw, Ferrie, and Oswald in attendance, had not indicated that Shaw even knew Oswald at all, and had not linked Shaw with the name "Bertrand," whether "Clay" or "Clem."

Additionally, the defections from the prosecution team of both William Gurvich and Tom Bethell, separately but at key junctures, had provided the defense attorneys with the names of almost all prosecution witnesses, whom they then proceeded to investigate. Potential prosecution witnesses, such as Fred Leemans, Clyde Johnson, Miguel Torres, and

Alvin Beauboeuf, had boomeranged on the prosecution, out of court but in such a public way as to give Shaw an even chance with the public (and therefore the jury pool) at trial. And at trial, the testimony of Charles Spiesel had backfired for the prosecution in a spectacular fashion, because of the investigation conducted by the defense.

At trial, in a key decision, the testimony of Officer Aloysius Habighorst, to the effect that, during his booking, Shaw had admitted to him that he had used the alias "Clay Bertrand," was not allowed to be heard by the jury; since Shaw did not have a lawyer present, the supposed admission violated the U.S. Supreme Court's "Escobido" decision, which ruled that a suspect must have a lawyer present at all key phases of questioning—and other officers seriously contradicted that Habighorst would even have collected such information from a suspect.

Perhaps most importantly, the defense had two years to concentrate on the character of Perry Russo, and the truthfulness, or lack thereof, of his testimony from the preliminary hearing in March 1967. Russo had spoken freely with news reporters, and with various characters around the case, and by the time of the trial, the defense had collected an assortment of his various doubts about his own testimony.

Alec Gifford interviewed Jim Garrison on television on March 13, 1969, two nights after he had spoken with Shaw. Gifford, perhaps unintentionally, tripped Garrison up on such an easy question as how he had stumbled onto Clay Shaw as being a participant in the assassination, leading to a lengthy, rambling response by Garrison that never actually answered the question. Gifford also critically questioned Garrison about re-charging Shaw with perjury, and about the negative public perceptions of the case, including the quick jury decision and the quality, or lack thereof, of the witnesses.[2554]

Shortly after the verdict, in mid-March 1969, Shaw gave an interview to William Greider, which appeared in the *Tulsa Sunday World* newspaper. The article quoted Shaw as saying that he would have to return to work as a result of the legal and investigative expenses associated with his defense. Shaw said, "The French have a proverb, 'The wounds that come from money are not fatal.' I hope that's true."[2555]

The issue of how Shaw would make up the money he had spent on his defense, with more to come because of the perjury charges, was very much on his mind. *The New York Times* reporter Martin Waldron, who had covered the trial on a daily basis for the newspaper, sent Shaw, shortly after the trial, an astrological prediction for the Pisces sign that had appeared in a horoscope column in *Harper's Bazaar* magazine for April 1969. The prediction said, "No more restrictions in earnings or assets—you exercise control of your affairs."[2556]

By mid-March, things had settled down somewhat. Two friends from Houston sent Shaw a telegram on March 17, Shaw's 56th birthday, saying, "Deleting the Giant, we'd like to say, 'Have a jolly green St. Patrick's Day.'"[2557] Others who wrote included Mrs. Hodding Carter, wife of the prominent Southern journalist, and mother of William Hodding Carter, III, also a journalist, and Assistant Secretary of the State Department under President Jimmy Carter.[2558]

After the not guilty verdict, both New Orleans newspapers, the *Times-Picayune* and the *States-Item*, owned by the same publishing company, ran editorials calling for Garrison's resignation. When Garrison followed up by charging Shaw with perjury on March 3, he ignited a whole new controversy about the case. On March 18, 1969, a full page ad was taken out on Jim Garrison's behalf by approximately 250 individuals, many of them attorneys. The most familiar name in relation to the Shaw case was Eberhard Deutsch, head of the firm Deutsch, Kerrigan, and Stiles, which had handled most of the appellate work related to the Clay Shaw case for Garrison's office. The only other name with any direct connection to the case was attorney Sam Monk Zelden, who had represented Dean Andrews in 1967 for a time, related to the perjury charges against him. It was an election year for

Garrison, so the advertisement, coming so soon after the unfavorable newspaper editorials, probably carried a great deal of weight with the general public.[2559]

In an undated letter from the spring of 1969, Garrison wrote to Eberhard Deutsch, giving an analysis of the case. Among other things, Garrison said that the prosecution could have used Shaw's personal life against him, but had not done so.[2560] Many on both sides of the case felt that to use Shaw's homosexuality, and his participation in sadism and masochism, would have backfired on the prosecution, but there has always been a bit of mystery surrounding its almost complete omission from the trial in direct relation to Shaw (although aspects of homosexuality were discussed in relation to David Ferrie and others).

On April 3, 1969, Shaw appeared on the nationally syndicated Mike Douglas talk show. He told Douglas that Garrison had tried to connect him to anti-Castro Cubans, because Oswald had passed out Cuba-related leaflets in front of the Mart in 1963, and that Garrison had linked Shaw into the investigation because of the "Clay Bertrand" story that had floated around New Orleans since the assassination. Shaw described the Mart as a non-profit corporation that basically used a building to house tenants in an effort to promote trade through the Port of New Orleans. When Douglas asked how Shaw had retired so early, Shaw said that it was not a matter of him being a man of "many means," but rather that he was a man of "not too many wants." Shaw said that Garrison had used him to promote an attack on the Warren Commission report, a charge his attorney, Irvin Dymond, had made to the jury in his closing argument. Shaw emphasized that his situation could happen anywhere, but that perhaps it was more likely to happen in New Orleans, because of specific characteristics of the city and its population. Shaw acknowledged that many people believed in a conspiracy related to President Kennedy's assassination, and indicated that all of his friends in Europe believed in one. While Shaw generally acquitted himself well in his appearance on the show, his fallback on somewhat clichéd phrasing that he had used throughout his ordeal caused Douglas to treat him with a polite skepticism.[2561]

After the verdict, Shaw received a few requests by mail for his autograph, usually from individuals who collected autographs from characters involved in various aspects of the Kennedy assassination. It is not always clear whether, or how, Shaw responded to any such requests. In at least one instance, a young man from Trenton, New Jersey, sent Shaw a newspaper clipping, and asked that he autograph the clipping. Since the clipping was still in the letter in Shaw's personal papers some forty years later, it is apparent that Shaw did not grant the young man's request.[2562]

James Kirkwood had covered the trial in hopes of having an article about it published in *Playboy*; he had press credentials from the magazine, and sat in the press section of the court during proceedings. However, *Playboy*, which generally had a pro-conspiracy theory bent to its editorial position (and was to some degree dependent on Jim Garrison's cooperation in the lawsuit by Gordon Novel against the magazine), ultimately rejected Kirkwood's article, after cautioning him not to be too critical of Garrison, and Kirkwood soon embarked on an expanded project that would become the detailed book *American Grotesque*, the most complete account of the trial.

After the trial, defense attorney Irvin Dymond sat down with Kirkwood for a lengthy interview about the case. Kirkwood quoted isolated bits of the conversation in *American Grotesque* to make it seem as if it had occurred before or during the trial, but he did not publish most of the comments from Dymond in the book. Dymond discussed various potential witnesses who had come and gone between arrest and trial, such as Reverend Clyde Johnson, who had concocted a story about seeing Shaw, Jack Ruby, and Oswald at a hotel in Baton Rouge in 1963. Dymond said that Johnson called him numerous times before and during the trial, offering to testify; Johnson was always intoxicated, and the call always came in the "wee hours of the morning."[2563]

Sal Panzeca had obtained the prosecution's witness list in August, but he and Edward

Wegmann had withheld it from Dymond until approximately ten days before the trial.[2564] Dymond said that some witnesses had to be hurriedly investigated, including Charles Spiesel; information related to Spiesel's lawsuits and mental problems had arrived from the investigator shortly before Dymond began questioning Spiesel on cross-examination.[2565]

Dymond said that, as of the end of the trial, he had only received $2,500 in fees, and each of the Wegmann brothers had received $2,500 as well. He said that Shaw also had given each of them a second mortgage note of $5,000 on his residence on Dauphine Street, and an interest in any book he might write about his ordeal. Dymond said he had been afraid to charge Shaw more in legal fees, because investigative expenses had eaten up so much of Shaw's cash assets that the defense would be unable to pay for investigations it might need in the future. He added that it was fortunate that Shaw at least had cash resources that could be used to pay for such investigations, something that was not possible for most clients. Dymond acknowledged that the case might be beneficial to him in the long run, because of the publicity, but said that as of the end of the trial, it had put him in "a hell of a financial hole," which was only starting fully to hit as he and Kirkwood spoke. Dymond indicated that Shaw had used up all of the cash at his disposal in paying attorney fees and investigative expenses, and that after the trial he could not pay the second mortgages on his home that he had given to the defense attorneys.[2566] Shaw eventually would sell his residence at 1313 Dauphine Street in August 1969, some six months after the trial.

Dymond related that Shaw had not been able to help the defense much with information, because he honestly did not know any of the witnesses who testified against him, and had no idea what they would say, or why, until they took the stand. He theorized that Garrison had gone after Shaw because of Shaw's vulnerability related to his personal life, because Clay was his first name, and because of Shaw's prominence in the community, leading to greater publicity for Garrison.[2567]

When Kirkwood asked why the prosecution had not gone more into Shaw's personal life, particularly the issue of homosexuality, Dymond said that he had a "little secret weapon" that kept the prosecution at bay. However, when Kirkwood asked what it was, Dymond asked him to turn off the tape recorder, and explained it without being recorded.[2568]

One of the things Dymond may have had in mind in using against the prosecution, if they brought up Shaw's homosexuality, was the district attorney's employees' involvements with actual or potential witnesses. An FBI memo in June 1967 reported that Assistant District Attorney Andrew Sciambra, on a trip to Lafayette, Louisiana, had stayed in the same hotel with Marlene Mancuso, former beauty contest and former wife of Gordon Novel.[2569] Or it could have been Perry Russo's own homosexuality, which remained submerged at the trial, even as other embarrassing things, such as his alleged attempts to commit suicide, were openly discussed in court.

Dymond discussed other potential defense witnesses who did not testify. He said that James Lewallen would not "tell the truth" about the situation, meaning that he would not candidly discuss the full extent of his friendship with Ferrie, including whether Ferrie had known Oswald. Alvin Beauboeuf had "chickened out" for reasons Dymond refused to specify, but which probably related to nude photographs of him that had been seized from Ferrie's residence in 1963. Richard Billings, the *LIFE* magazine reporter who had partnered with Garrison at the beginning of his probe, but had broken with Garrison along the way, had refused to testify as well. The defense had prepared an interstate subpoena for Billings, requiring him to come to Louisiana and testify, but Billings had maintained that he would be out of the country at the time, and avoided the subpoena.[2570]

Dymond discussed his relationship with Garrison, saying that since Garrison had taken over as district attorney in 1962, he had been good financially for defense attorneys, in the sense that he required defendants to work more officially through their attorneys, which increased defense attorney fees. Dymond said that he and Garrison had seen each other since the trial ended, and that he did not expect the bitterly-fought case to change their cordiality towards each other "on either side" of the relationship. Dymond also discussed trial Judge Edward Haggerty, acknowledging Haggerty's drinking habits by saying that, "You can't drink that much whiskey and not have it affect you."[2571]

On a more humorous note, when Kirkwood asked about how long it had taken Dymond to compose his closing argument, Dymond openly laughed. When Kirkwood questioned his response, Dymond volunteered that he "had a broad up there" while he was working on what he would way. Both men immediately realized the tape-recorder was still running, before someone said, "Jesus!" and hurriedly turned it off.[2572]

In a more somber portion of the interview, Dymond discussed the new perjury charges against Shaw. He acknowledged they would be difficult to fight, because Shaw was "somewhat unforgettable" once someone had met him, and any witness who would say that he saw Shaw together with Ferrie or Oswald would potentially be very difficult to refute. When the subject turned to prosecutor James Alcock, who seemed to have put all of his considerable energies and talent into a case that some felt he did not believe in, Dymond said, "The power to rationalize is a very potent thing." Discussing that Alcock would proceed with the new perjury case simply because it was beneficial to him career-wise within the prosecutor's office, even though Alcock must have serious questions in his own mind about Shaw's guilt, Dymond added that, "If you want to convince yourself of something, it's usually not too hard to do so."[2573]

Dymond commented on the fact that more than 1,600 potential jurors had been questioned before a jury could be seated for the trial, and he said that there had been an epidemic of "loving husbands and fathers" who could not do without seeing their spouses for the duration of the trial, a situation Dymond said New Orleans had never seen before.[2574]

Dymond commented on the irony that he could not introduce the Warren Report at the preliminary hearing, to refute charges that anyone besides Oswald had been involved in the assassination, because the judges had ruled that it was not material to the case, whereas during the trial evidence had been freely admitted that criticized the Warren Report.[2575] In a sense, the prosecution had been able to pile on evidence of a possible conspiracy that had had no connection to Shaw, hoping that the jury first would decide that there had been a conspiracy, and then decide that since Shaw was the one on trial, he must have been involved in it.

Miguel Torres, who in 1967 had been a prisoner at Louisiana State Penitentiary in Angola, Louisiana, had said that Garrison's men had come to the penitentiary and interviewed him, wanting him to say that he had been to Shaw's residence and engaged in sadomasochistic sex with Shaw. Torres told James Kirkwood he had never met Shaw, although he had lived near him.[2576] Irvin Dymond told Kirkwood that he was reluctant to use Torres on the stand, because all of the witnesses on Shaw's side had generally impeccable reputations, whereas most of the witnesses on the prosecution side had very checkered pasts, and he wanted to preserve that distinction. He also said that it was difficult to tell how a man like Torres would react under a strong cross-examination.[2577]

Dymond said that one of his big challenges had been whether to treat Perry Russo as "crazy" or as "a liar." If he had chosen to treat Russo as "crazy," he would have gone into Russo's background of wild sexual activity, pornographic movies, and other episodes that cast doubt upon his mental character. In order to do that, he might have needed to subpoena a psychiatrist to testify, and he said that jurors were sometimes skeptical of expert medical testimony, wanting simply to know whether what a witness said was true or false. Accordingly, Dymond decided the best way to treat Russo was to expose the falsity of his statements, by approaching him in a gentle, relatively non-combative manner.[2578]

Dymond said that another problem to solve was whether to delve into the issue of the prosecution's misdeeds related to gathering evidence and eliciting testimony from witnesses. He decided the best way was simply to expose contradictions in the witness testimony, as if he was attacking the witnesses and not the prosecution. He said that a jury would sometimes become frustrated if the defense attempted to put the prosecution on trial, leaving it to wonder if the defense simply was trying to divert attention away from the actual defendant who was on trial.[2579]

After the trial, Shaw contracted with a company called American Program Bureau to make speeches around the country, primarily on college campuses. The general topic of his speeches was the ordeal he had gone through during the days since March 1, 1967. Shaw obviously hoped to recoup much, if not all, of the money he had spent on legal fees and expenses, and put himself back into a relatively sound financial position, at least as far as cash flow was involved. However, Garrison's re-indictment of Shaw on perjury charges blunted the impact of the idea of Shaw as a totally innocent victim who had been acquitted. The cloud of suspicion still hung over him, and would not be removed for several more years, by which time, in the rapidly moving world of the early 1970s, Shaw had long since moved out of the headlines, and onto the very back pages of newspapers around the country.

With Shaw under the new indictment for perjury, Garrison's staff continued to investigate leads related to him. W. Robert Morgan, who had been a fairly close acquaintance around the time of his arrest, was interviewed on April 21, 1969, with Edna Sakir, his attorney, present. Edna Sakir had also joined Morgan in several get-togethers with Shaw after his arrest. Morgan later would divorce his wife, Dr. Jacqueline Gribble Morgan, and marry Sakir. In 1981, Sakir would be murdered when a masked gunman entered her home office during broad daylight and shot her; one of her former clients, upset that she had netted his civil suit damages against an outstanding criminal defense fee, was convicted of the crime. Morgan said that he met Shaw at International House in 1961, and that he went to Shaw's place sometimes to play chess. He recalled meeting Jill Young, Mario Bermúdez, Marilyn Tate, and Jeff Biddison. Morgan said that he never knew or met David Ferrie. He did not volunteer his closeness to Shaw at the time of his arrest, or report his offer, never carried out, to help finance Shaw's defense.[2580]

A letter arrived from Kay Lucas Leake Dart, written on May 4, 1969, wherein she wondered if Shaw might "renew a once fairly intensive correspondence with someone you haven't seen since the early 1940s." She recounted Shaw's influence on her, including "chess games, shared troubles, concerts, honest affection," and, she mentioned again, "727 St. Ann" Street. She commented that she had "cared since 1933."[2581]

On May 27, Garrison gave an interview with an unnamed interviewer, a transcript of which can be found in records that have survived, wherein he discussed his theory of the assassination. According to Garrison, Kennedy would have ended the Cold War, and the military-industrial complex wanted him out of office. Garrison said his investigation had stumbled across evidence that CIA employees (presumably including Shaw in that mix, but without naming him directly) in New Orleans had helped to set up Oswald as a "lone nut." Garrison lamented that he could not convict Shaw because, he said, it was impossible to try a clandestine organization, such as the CIA, in an American courtroom, due to the protection of the defendant's rights afforded by the American legal system. However, Garrison said he would not change that aspect of America's legal system. He said that Shaw's political beliefs and personal support of Kennedy had not been important in relation to his "mission" of helping the operation along, although he did not directly answer a question about Shaw's involvement with the intelligence community. Garrison insisted that the International Trade Mart was not an ordinary office building, intimating that because it contained offices such as foreign consuls and import-export agencies, it had a more sinister purpose. Garrison indicated that most people in New Orleans were unaware of the purpose of the organization, and he stressed the unusual nature of the building. He also added that because its director, Shaw, had had meetings with Oswald, it took on an even greater significance.

Garrison ended by saying that the conspiracy was much larger than the people in New Orleans who were involved, that there had been many others involved outside of the city.[2582]

On May 29, June Rolfe gave a more detailed affidavit to Lou Ivon related to Shaw and Ferrie. She repeated her story that, around 1960 or 1961, she had seen Shaw in a light-colored Ford Thunderbird driving around the French Quarter. Shaw had been sitting in the front seat, with his arm around two boys; David Ferrie had been in the back seat. Rolfe further indicated that she had seen Ferrie at the Lakefront Airport, and that she had been told Ferrie was a Civil Air Patrol instructor. She recalled that she had been in Shaw's office at the International Trade Mart many times, and had interviewed him on occasion in her role as a reporter.[2583]

In June, Garrison's chief assistant district attorney, Charles Ward, who mostly had refused to participate in the Shaw prosecution or the entire Kennedy assassination investigation, resigned, and shortly thereafter announced that he was running against Garrison for district attorney in the November election. In an article in *The Christian Science Monitor* in August, Ward is reported as saying that he had listened to Perry Russo's story shortly after Russo came forward, and that he had told Garrison he did not consider Russo credible; Ward also had told Garrison he wanted no part in the assassination probe. Garrison had responded that he could "convict Shaw against twelve of his relatives." However, Garrison agreed that Ward did not have to take part in the probe. After that, Garrison had continued forcefully to assert that the case was solidly supported by evidence, to the extent that Ward was surprised at how "flimsy the case actually was when it was presented in court."[2584]

Tom Bethell, the former researcher and archivist in Garrison's office during the investigation, had secretly passed information on to the defense attorneys, beginning during the last half of 1968. He had finally acknowledged that activity to Lou Ivon, one of Garrison's investigators with whom he was close, and after Shaw's trial ended Garrison's office charged Bethell with theft. In order to defend him, Bethell's lawyers wanted Shaw's attorneys to testify in Bethell's defense. However, Shaw, in a court hearing on June 27, 1969, indicated that he did not want his lawyers testifying in the Bethell case, as it would violate his own lawyer-client privilege at a time when he still had the newly-filed perjury charges hanging over his head.[2585]

During the months after Shaw's trial, he was still in the news, mainly attending hearings related to the perjury charges, or giving interviews about his future intentions. A television film clip caught him being questioned by reporters Jim Michie and Rosemary James as he walked along a sidewalk. Shaw recently had signed up for a speaking tour, and was asked by Michie how many speeches he would be giving; he replied that he would speak as often as the speaking bureau could schedule him. Rosemary James then asked if Shaw was planning to write a book about his experiences, noting that she knew he had been keeping a journal of some sort during the period between arrest and trial. Without missing a beat, Shaw quipped, "I was keeping a journal in the hope that it would one day keep me."[2586]

After Garrison charged Shaw with perjury, a long wait began as Garrison became ill, and the case sat for well over a year without any significant activity. Shaw and his attorneys, meanwhile, continued to explore the possibility that Garrison might have had some sinister motive in both prosecuting Shaw in the first place, and in continuing to pursue him after his acquittal. A memo from Shaw to Edward Wegmann, written sometime after his trial ended and sometime after author James Kirkwood had interviewed Perry Russo at length, mentioned that, according to unnamed sources, Russo and Garrison had known each other before the case began, and that they were involved sexually. Another story was that Garrison had told Russo what to do in relation to his testimony in the case, and that Russo had been paid for his cooperation.[2587]

During the summer of 1969, an incident took place at the New Orleans Athletic Club, whereby Jim Garrison supposedly molested a 13-year-old boy. Aaron Kohn quickly got wind of the story, and in the fall of 1969 wrote to William J. Krummel, Sr., who was then foreman of the Orleans Parish Grand Jury. The letter reported the incident of alleged child molestation by Garrison, and indicated that the father of the supposed victim had made the allegation to *Newsweek* reporter Hugh Aynesworth, reporter John McMillan of WDSU-TV, and investigator William Gurvich.[2588] The incident was not reported at all in any of the New Orleans newspapers, and only appeared in print anywhere in a column by muckraking columnist Jack Anderson during the spring of 1970, a column that the New Orleans papers failed to carry, although Anderson's column ordinarily appeared there. No charges were ever filed against Garrison, but reports of the incident have lingered to this day.

In the original manuscript for *American Grotesque*, his full-length work about the trial, James Kirkwood handled Garrison's molestation charge by saying that the charge against Garrison was not true. When his editor asked if the accusation against Garrison was indeed false, Kirkwood said, "No but we had probably better say that it is," to which his editor responded, "How can we?"[2589] Kirkwood eventually would explain the gradual unfolding of the accusation against Garrison, but without commenting one way or the other on its truthfulness.

*Newsweek* reporter Hugh Aynesworth initially had provided Kirkwood with information about the Garrison molestation charge, in a letter in October 1969. Aynesworth said that Charles Ward, who was then running against Garrison for district attorney, was thinking of breaking the story publicly. Aynesworth also informed Kirkwood that the alleged victim of Garrison's molestation was the son of a member of the Belgian consulate, which had its office in the Mart. In the same letter, Aynesworth also advised that Terry Hardiman, a relative of postal carrier James Hardiman, who had testified at Shaw's trial that he had delivered mail directed to "Clem Bertrand" to Jeff Biddison's residence, had been charged with an offense in 1968, but that nothing had been done about it. Aynesworth intimated that James Hardiman's testimony at Shaw's trial was linked to the lack of activity on the charges against Terry Hardiman.[2590]

In the summer of 1969, Shaw traveled to New York City to testify in the old legal case involving Tra-Mar, Inc., the company that had purchased the Mart building at 124 Camp Street during the mid-1950s. One of the brokers on the sale was still owed fees, which would have been due whenever the Mart operations vacated the premises of the building. That had been expected to take place within two or three years of the sale, but did not actually occur until 1967. Shaw testified in favor of the broker, garnering some attention in the New York City press.[2591]

Shaw sold his property at 1313 Dauphine Street in the late summer of 1969, months after the trial ended, in order to pay his attorneys more legal fees. Until that time, Shaw had only paid a total of $7,500 in legal fees; $2,500 each to Irvin Dymond, Edward Wegmann, and William Wegmann. Sal Panzeca, a junior partner in William Wegmann's firm, received no specific fees for his rather significant services. After the sale of the Dauphine Street property, Shaw paid Dymond and the two Wegmann brothers each an additional $5,000, a total of $15,000. Combined with the earlier payment totaling $7,500, Shaw's payment for legal fees (as opposed to outside expenses, which were much greater) totaled $22,500; that amount was all he would pay in actual legal fees for his defense from March 1, 1967, through his death, related to his various cases. After the sale, Shaw lived at 427 Burgundy, Apartment 3, in the French Quarter.

In August, more than five months after Shaw's trial had ended, *LOOK* magazine published a lengthy article about Shaw's situation by reporter Warren Rogers. The article detailed Shaw's story since his arrest on March 1, 1967, and discussed the perjury charges against him, which the article indicated were a form of continuing persecution of Shaw. The article openly identified Shaw as a homosexual, an unusual step in that era. During Shaw's civil suit against Garrison and others, some of the preliminary answers his attorneys prepared in answer to interrogatories indicated that either Shaw or his attorneys, or both, had entered into some form of financial arrangement with *LOOK* magazine as early as April 1967, and other answers indicated that either Shaw or his attorneys may have received payment of several thousand dollars for the *LOOK* article that appeared in August 1969.

In a speech before the Young Men's Business Club on August 7, Charles Ward told his version of the history of Garrison's office, and the origins of Garrison's Kennedy assassination probe. Among other things, Ward said that Garrison had attended the International Association of Petroleum Operators in New York City in the fall of 1966, and had flown back to New Orleans with Senator Russell Long of Louisiana. After their discussion concerning the Warren Commission report and its flaws, Garrison read the report, and also read some of the books promoting conspiracy theories that had appeared since the Warren Report had been issued. Ward said that Garrison developed his general theory before interviewing anyone in the case. After listening to Perry Russo's story, Ward argued that Russo was not telling the truth, and that Shaw should not be arrested. Ward said that U. S. Attorney General Ramsey Clark had made a statement, shortly after Garrison's probe became public, that there would be no arrests as a result of Garrison's probe, which prompted Garrison to action. On March 1, 1967, a meeting of approximately twenty people, consisting of twelve employees of the district attorney's office and eight volunteer investigators, had been held in Garrison's office. A vote was taken, and the result was 18-2 against arresting Shaw. Ward also said that, at the end of 1967, the arrest of Edgar Eugene Bradley, the California man, had been done after pressure from newsmen on Garrison as to why no further arrests had been made.[2592]

Charles Ward, in another speech on the campaign trail, emphasized his differences with both Garrison and Aaron Kohn in relation to running the district attorney's office. Appearing at a candidates' forum at which Garrison and Kohn were both present, Ward charged that Garrison saw conspiracy in everything, and Kohn saw a Mafia influence in everything, hinting that accounted for their hostility towards each other. Ward suggested that a district attorney should focus on real violent crime that affected the average person.[2593]

In the fall of 1969, there was also a mayoral race in New Orleans. Democrat Moon Landrieu was the heavy favorite, but due to a backlash against the various civil rights developments of the past decade, Republican Ben C. Toledano, who had indirectly represented filmmakers Richard Leacock and Noel Parmentel in their effort to film the Shaw case back in the spring of 1967, stood a better than normal chance of winning, and was garnering a lot of publicity. In a speech Toledano gave at a meeting of the Junior League of New Orleans at Ursuline Academy, he addressed the prosecution of Shaw. "The persecution of Clay Shaw will go down in the history of New Orleans as one of our darkest hours," Toledano said. "Every candidate should do what he can to see that Jim Garrison is defeated."[2594]

In early November, just before the election for district attorney was held, fifty local criminal attorneys purchased an ad endorsing Garrison for re-election. None of Shaw's defense attorneys participated in the ad, although Guy Johnson, who had initially represented Shaw during the first few days after his arrest, before Irvin Dymond became his main criminal defense attorney, signed the ad. Also signing was G. Wray Gill, for whom David Ferrie had worked as a private investigator during 1963, and Sam Monk Zelden, who had initially represented Dean Andrews on the perjury charges filed by Garrison in 1967.[2595]

Jim Garrison was easily re-elected against a group of challengers, including the most competitive of them, Harry Connick, Sr. Garrison did very well in majority-black precincts, and won a majority of the overall vote, avoiding a runoff election. He promised to continue the prosecution of Shaw.

Nina Sulzer, Shaw's friend from the time of his arrest, was fired from her job with the Sheriff's Office in November, shortly after the elections. Although James Kirkwood indicated in *American Grotesque* that no reason was given for the firing, Sulzer's husband told the author that the firing was related to a changing of the guard; a new Sheriff was taking over after the elections, and wanted his own staff in place.[2596]

Shaw developed a somewhat close relationship with James Kirkwood as a result of the favorable coverage Kirkwood provided in the original *Esquire* article, and in the full-length book, *American Grotesque*. Until his death, Shaw would sometimes send Kirkwood playful messages involving news of characters involved in his case. He noted in December 1969 that Judge Edward A. Haggerty had been arrested at a stag party being held in a local motel, attended by several prostitutes. The judge was wrestled to the floor by arresting officers, and the entire incident was caught by local television cameras who had been alerted to the raid. Shaw sent Kirkwood a card and a clipping related to the event. He addressed the card to "Norma Schwackheimer;" he would continue using the practice of addressing Kirkwood under catchy names with feminine undertones from then on.[2597] Later, in 1970, Shaw would pass along to Kirkwood a letter that reporter James Phelan had written to Garrison, taking jabs at Garrison's own recently-published book, *A Heritage of Stone*, which appeared the same year as Kirkwood's book and was sometimes reviewed along with it. Shaw addressed the letter to Kirkwood as "Zana" or "Lana," and signed it "Dreyfus."[2598]

Judge Haggerty was quickly acquitted by a local New Orleans court, but almost a year later he was removed from office by the Louisiana Bar. Many saw his arrest as a reprisal for some of his rulings against the prosecution during the trial, particularly the ruling that Officer Aloysius Habighorst's testimony about Shaw admitting he had used the name "Clay Bertrand" as an alias could not be presented to the jury. James Alcock, who had fervently prosecuted the main body of the Shaw trial, was appointed to Haggerty's former position in late 1970; Alcock would lose a bid for re-election a year later.

# PART IV

# 28 · Turning the Tables: A Lawsuit is Filed

Newsman Hugh Aynesworth was still actively involved in Shaw's legal proceedings. On February 18, 1970, Edward Wegmann wrote to Aynesworth, saying that he had not been invited to a recent dinner held in Jim Garrison's honor, and that New Orleans Mayor Moon Landrieu had been forced to speak at the event against his wishes.[2599]

On February 27, 1970, just short of a year after his acquittal on conspiracy charges, and three years after his arrest, Shaw filed a civil suit against Jim Garrison, Perry Russo, the hypnotist Dr. Esmond Fatter, and the three wealthy backers of the Truth and Consequences organization: Cecil Shilstone, Joseph M. Rault, Jr., and Willard Robertson. The suit asked for $5 million in damages. Before the suit could proceed very far, Garrison sought to block it through the doctrine of "official immunity" granted to law enforcement officers and district attorneys; the principle was designed to prevent all persons who had been investigated and later exonerated, or who had been tried and acquitted, from filing suit against officials simply doing their job.

It had often been speculated that Garrison had taken his case against Shaw to both a grand jury and a preliminary hearing, in addition simply to ordering Shaw charged with conspiracy, in order to protect himself against future civil litigation by Shaw. It has similarly been speculated that Garrison, after Shaw was acquitted of conspiracy charges on March 1, 1969, immediately had charged Shaw with perjury in order to delay and/or negate the effects of any civil suit Shaw might file. Indeed, Shaw had waited a year after his acquittal in order to file the civil suit, even though it is clear that Shaw had considered the possibility of filing a civil action for damages almost from the time he was arrested.

Shaw chose a course of action that did not have strong legal precedent on his side. It is difficult to sue a prosecutor, or even a police officer, acting in the line of duty. In fact, a month after Shaw's original arrest in 1967, *Time* magazine had run a short article related to the liability of prosecutors after false arrest, or rigging of evidence. The article concluded that it was very rare that prosecutors were punished for unethical conduct.[2600]

After some initial discovery, the civil suit essentially would languish for years as Shaw's lawyers dealt with the ongoing perjury charges, which would not be concluded until late Spring 1971. In the initial discovery that was done for the civil suit during 1970, however, Shaw's attorneys obtained certain materials which later helped them in successfully obtaining a permanent injunction against further prosecution of Shaw. Most of those materials had to do with the inner financial workings of Garrison's investigation, as supported by contributions from the Truth and Consequences organization, and with how Garrison's case against Shaw had initially developed, and how the witnesses had been discovered as the case progressed. The civil lawsuit for damages effectively overlapped with the later civil lawsuit for an injunction from further prosecution for the purposes of gathering critical information.

Edward Wegmann sent a copy of the lawsuit complaint to attorney Herbert "Jack" Miller, Walter Sheridan's attorney in Washington. Miller then passed the suit on to John Greaney, a CIA attorney; Miller said that Wegmann had told him that because of his long criminal defense, financial problems Shaw was having at the time mandated that a civil suit would not be "vigorously pressed." Miller added that Wegmann had a theory that, because

Garrison had conspired with outside third parties in planning the investigation and prosecution, he was not immune to civil liability simply because of his role as a prosecutor.[2601]

In March 1970, Dean Andrews was awarded a preliminary injunction against the new perjury charges against him that stemmed from later grand jury appearances during 1967, and from the 1969 trial of Clay Shaw. Later, he would win a permanent injunction, although the conviction related to older perjury charges from his testimony before the grand jury earlier in 1967 still stood; he had that conviction under appeal.

A two-part article in the *National Insider*, a tabloid newspaper similar to the *National Enquirer*, appeared in mid-April 1970. It covered Garrison's case against Shaw in a general sense, but added other aspects as well. Specifically, it covered the recent accusation against Garrison, which alleged that he had molested a 13-year-old boy in the "Slumber Room" at the New Orleans Athletic Club. Columnist Jack Anderson had broken the story in early 1970, but the case had never been officially investigated by authorities in New Orleans, for obvious reasons. The *National Insider* article actually gave the name of the family involved in the case, the head of which turned out to be none other than James L. Bezou, who had been the former Chancellor at the Belgian consulate in New Orleans, and was in 1970 Executive Director of the Louisiana Council for Music and Performing Arts. James Bezou had known Shaw well during the Mart days. His brother, the boy's uncle, was Monsignor Henry C. Bezou, Superintendent of Catholic Schools in New Orleans.[2602]

The *National Insider* article also dealt with a rumor that would pop up for years after the Garrison prosecution of Shaw, to the effect that Garrison and Shaw had gotten crosswise over a young man in the gay community, resulting in a vendetta by Garrison against Shaw. In this particular version, Shaw had "stolen the friendship" of a "handsome young Latin man" from Garrison. The article did label the story merely a rumor, saying that the reporter had researched it and found no evidence of it. The article also indicated that Shaw was just a "shell of his former self" and that he had been called "the unlikeliest villain since Oscar Wilde.[2603]

The story of Garrison and Shaw possibly having some relationship in the gay community, either with each other, or with a third, younger male, a relationship that turned sour at some point, has been mentioned to the author as a possible motive for Garrison's prosecution of Shaw on numerous occasions during the research for this book. However, the author was unsuccessful in finding anyone who had first-hand knowledge of such a relationship or incident, someone who could give specific names, dates, or places. Much like the story related to Garrison and his wife getting into a physical argument involving the tossing of alcoholic drinks at Brennan's restaurant, an encounter which Shaw apparently witnessed in the mid-1960s, it is difficult to credibly link the rumor to Garrison's later investigation into the Kennedy assassination, and his prosecution of Shaw. Both theories are much discussed even today, however, and remain as intriguing possibilities.

At least one of Shaw's attorneys seemed inclined not to believe that Garrison had homosexual tendencies. When the author asked him years later why such rumors of possible homosexual activity on the former district attorney's part had endured over the years, the attorney attributed the phenomenon to an element of the gay community that insists certain public or historical figures are gay, even when the evidence is less than conclusive; "Queers want people to believe that other people are queers," he said.

Sometime during the years from 1966 to 1970, someone produced a translation of Alejandro Casona's play, *The Trees Die Standing*. Although some have credited the translation to Shaw, it is doubtful that he handled the entire translation alone; it is more likely that he had the assistance of Mario Bermúdez, or some other member of the Latino community associated with the Mart or International House. On June 23, 1970, Shaw received a letter from literary agent Elizabeth Marton, indicating that she had Shaw's translation of the play, and that she had written about it to a Spanish representative who knew the widow of the playwright.[2604] Apparently, Shaw had never received official permission to produce a translated version of the play several years before, during or immediately after his trip to Spain in 1966. On July 7, 1970, Marton wrote to Shaw again, declining to represent him, but indicating she was still checking with the widow about securing the rights.[2605]

An article in the *Times-Picayune* on June 26, 1970 indicated that Garrison's office had dropped charges against Edgar Eugene Bradley, due to the death of a major witness. Assistant District Attorney John Volz handled the dropping of the charge, but indicated he could not comment on the case.[2606] Many scratched their heads, wondering who the major witness against Bradley was who had died, as the arrest of Bradley seemed to have been based on murky information anyway, without a clear indication of the evolution of the charges.

By mid-1970, the perjury case against Shaw was in a long period of dormancy, and the earlier conspiracy case against him had almost been forgotten. An article by Nicholas Chriss in the *Los Angeles Times* said that Garrison's investigation of the Kennedy assassination was now dead. Chriss interviewed Shaw, and discussed the issue of whether he was really as bad off financially as others had claimed. When asked whether he was "getting by," Shaw indicated that it depended on what one meant by the phrase. The article noted that he now lived in a small apartment in the French Quarter (he had never lived in a very large residence, although he had owned some apartment buildings), and was renovating a building several blocks away.

The conversation was not limited to Shaw's financial status, however. When discussing his reaction to the arrest, Shaw recalled the first sentence in Kafka's *The Trial*, saying "Here I am." The article also commented that Irvin Dymond, Shaw's main defense attorney during the criminal trial, was then serving as campaign chairman for Alvin Oser, one of Garrison's assistant district attorneys now running for judge.[2607] Oser had helped to prosecute Shaw by handling that aspect of the trial that dealt with witnesses from Dallas, Texas, who had been at Dealey Plaza the day of the assassination and thought they had heard or seen something different than the official version of what took place that day. Dymond's advocacy of Oser, who was running for judge, is a striking indicator of the closeness of the legal community in New Orleans, a closeness that was echoed in the general business community, and to some degree in the French Quarter community as well.

In July 1970, Edith Stern went as far as writing to former Attorney General Ramsey Clark, asking for his input related to Shaw's perjury charges. She asked if Clark would meet with Shaw, saying that no one could explain the reason why all of the events since March 1, 1967 had happened to him, and that he was a "good and rare man."[2608] There is no indication that Clark responded to the letter.

Mrs. Stern had, in fact, contacted several legal scholars related to Shaw's predicament shortly after perjury charges were filed. In March 1969, she discussed the case with Jefferson Fordham, Dean of the Law School at the University of Pennsylvania. Fordham shared Stern's view about Shaw's dilemma, but could offer no helpful advice.[2609] Stern also reached out to Adolf Berle, Jr.,[2610] a noted attorney who had been a prominent member of President Franklin Roosevelt's administration, and to Dean Paul Hebert with Louisiana State University's law school in Baton Rouge,[2611] asking for assistance. Hebert was the longest-serving Dean of LSU Law School, serving in that role almost continuously for forty years. However, no one could help.

Shaw's arrangement with the speakers' bureau in Massachusetts allowed him to tell his side of the story in more detail, and to collect badly needed income at a time when the full impact of his legal bills was being realized. Among other places, he spoke on December 8, 1969, at the University of Wyoming, and collected a fee of $1,050. On May 9, 1970, he spoke at Memphis State University and collected $525. On May 14, 1970, he spoke at Genesea State College, collecting $830, and on May 25, 1970, he spoke at Thomas Jefferson Institute in Philadelphia for a fee of $525. On October 27, 1970, he spoke at American University, and was paid $700. On November 15, 1970, he spoke at Moore Park College in southern California, and again was paid $700.

A recording of Shaw's presentation at Moore Park College survives, and can be listened to online. In it, Shaw details some of the more bizarre aspects of the case, including some of the offbeat individuals who came forward as the months rolled by. The audience listened politely, but it is difficult to tell whether Shaw was successful in winning anyone over, as clearly there were a number of conspiracy-theory believers (although perhaps not all supporters of the Jim Garrison investigation) in attendance. In one particular exchange, Shaw was asked why, if Garrison was so far off on his theory, he had been re-elected so easily in November 1969, after the trial. Shaw attributed Garrison's re-election mostly to local political issues, such as the improved manner in which his office had treated African Americans, showing them more respect and allowing them a certain amount of dignity compared with the terrible situation they had faced over the years; Shaw commented that Garrison deserved credit for that aspect of his tenure.

In August 1970, Perry Russo was arrested for receiving stolen property and, in what seems to be an unfortunate coincidence, he also applied for a position with the New Orleans Police Department. A pre-employment screening of Russo contained the results of a polygraph examination he took on August 10. During interviews related to possible employment, Russo admitted that he had engaged in gay acts approximately 100 times in the past, from the age of thirteen until "six months ago." The information indicated that Russo liked group sex, had a large collection of pornographic movies, had been in a mental institution before, had smoked marijuana, and had received stolen goods. Russo listed Assistant District Attorney Andrew Sciambra as a reference in his application for employment. The Department noted Russo's 1-Y classification on the military draft (an indicator that he should only be inducted in case of a national emergency or a declared war; the status was usually the result of a physical ailment), and said that it should be investigated by police.[2612] He was not hired for the force.

On September 22, Edward Wegmann wrote to Hugh Aynesworth, indicating that the defendants to Shaw's civil suit had attempted to have it dismissed on the grounds of prosecutorial immunity. Wegmann also reported that the Louisiana State Supreme Court was set to rule on Judge Edward Haggarty's conduct related to being in the company of several prostitutes at a party held at a local motel; Wegmann indicated that the "good Judge has had it."[2613] In a letter to Aynesworth dated October 2, Wegmann enclosed recent pleadings by Shaw's attorneys in the civil suit, and interrogatories propounded to defendant Willard Robertson.[2614]

James Kirkwood's book, *American Grotesque*, the most detailed account of the trial to date, appeared in print in November 1970, a relatively quick turnaround at the time, considering the length and scope of the book. Edith Stern, whose private foundation had helped to finance Kirkwood's work on the book, hosted a party for the author at her home on November 20. Many local media personalities were invited to the event, as were friends of Shaw, including Mrs. Paul Martin, formerly known as Ella Brennan, owner of Brennan's restaurant.[2615]

The book generated a fair amount of attention, and was sometimes paired in book reviews with Jim Garrison's book, *A Heritage of Stone*, which appeared around the same time and for which Garrison received an advance of $2,250. Kirkwood's book was much more detailed and specific related to Shaw's trial, whereas Garrison's book contained hardly any information about the trial, or Shaw's case, concentrating instead on the theory of an overall conspiracy theory related to the Kennedy assassination.

Kirkwood's book attracted a review from Benjy Morrison in the *Times-Picayune* newspaper, and additional reviews by columnist Rex Reed, author James Leo Herlihy, who had introduced Kirkwood to Shaw, and playwright Tennessee Williams. However, the book, lengthy at 650 pages, with numerous unedited excerpts from relevant documents, did not sell well with the general public. It was generally looked upon as merely another Kennedy assassination-related book, and the mainstream press was already jaded to such literature.

Shortly after the appearance of *American Grotesque*, Kirkwood appeared on the Barry Gray radio show in New York City. He said that Shaw had been in New York City in October 1967 to investigate the possibility of hiring a new lawyer for his defense team; Kirkwood had wound up in a small group who had listened to Shaw tell his story at dinner. Kirkwood had then called his agent to get an assignment to do a story on Shaw, which became the article in *Esquire* magazine, and that eventually led to him getting a contract to write the book. Kirkwood said that he did not believe that Shaw knew Oswald, although he said that he was now no longer certain that Oswald acted totally alone. Kirkwood sometimes referred to David Ferrie as a "homosexual," preserving the distinction that many in the press had originated, whereby Ferrie was often labeled a homosexual, but Shaw was not. Kirkwood said that Shaw was "fairly wealthy," but not a millionaire, and that his defense had cost him $400,000 or $500,000 thus far.[2616] Kirkwood's estimated amount of Shaw's spending is greatly in excess of the numbers submitted in court filings several years later during Shaw's civil suit against Garrison, which indicated that Shaw's outlays for his defense were just under $75,000, including legal fees and expenses. It is particularly curious that Kirkwood would have thrown around such large amounts, given that he and Irvin Dymond had explicitly discussed the amounts Shaw had incurred through the spring of 1969, after Shaw's trial had ended.

In November 1970, all charges related to Layton Martens' involvement in the Kennedy assassination probe were dropped by the district attorney's office.[2617] Martens had been charged with perjury, related to his refusal to confirm that Shaw and David Ferrie had known each other. Martens had known both men, but had insisted he had known them at different times, and that, to his knowledge, they had not known each other.

The civil lawsuit filed by Shaw against Garrison and others was entitled *Clay L. Shaw vs. Jim Garrison, Joseph M. Rault, Jr., Cecil M. Shilstone, Willard E. Robertson, Perry Raymond Russo, and Dr. Esmond A. Fatter*. Interrogatories were propounded during the fall of 1970 to Garrison, Rault, Shilstone, and Robertson. Most of the questions dealt with the origins of Garrison's investigation into President Kennedy's assassination. Garrison's answers to the initial set of interrogatories were filed on December 21, 1970, shortly before Shaw's upcoming perjury trial was set to begin. Before the trial could begin, however, a lengthy Federal court hearing was held, in January 1971, before Judge Herbert Christenberry to determine whether the perjury prosecution should even go forward. At that hearing, Garrison and many of the prosecutors, investigators, and financial backers of the investigation were questioned under oath by Shaw's attorneys. Garrison's and the other defendants' answers to the initial interrogatories were utilized by Shaw's attorneys to question Garrison and others about the financing of Garrison's investigation.[2618]

Shaw sent out copies of *American Grotesque* to various friends. To Patrick and Edna O'Rourke in Chicago, he wrote, "I love the book but then I can hardly be objective about it since it practically canonizes me. Do you suppose I shall become St. Clay, patron saint of conspirators and that the bones of my inner ear shall be a holy relic to be exposed on the altar for the veneration of the faithful on my birthday? Bizarre notion? Yes quite. But hardly more bizarre than what has ALREADY happened to me!!"[2619]

# 29 · A Key Court Decision, and a Job Offer

Reporter Rosemary James wrote an article about Shaw's continuing legal troubles, which appeared in *New Orleans* magazine in early 1971. The article was entitled, "The Dark Side of Not Guilty," and Shaw was given a rough draft prior to publication. In the draft, Shaw said that Garrison must have disliked him for some reason, but that Shaw did not know it at the time. He mentioned the incident at which he had witnessed Garrison throwing a glass of wine onto his wife at Brennan's restaurant as the only possible motivation; he had, two years earlier, told author James Kirkwood that he doubted that incident was Garrison's motive. The issue of homosexuality was discussed in the article in relation to David Ferrie, the "Clay Bertrand" character, and Garrison's crackdowns on gay bars in the past. However, Shaw did not acknowledge his own preferences, and therefore did not speculate on whether Garrison went after him because of them. Shaw indicated that he would have to go back to work within a year or so, but that it was difficult to do so as long as he was under the aura of the continuing perjury charges.[2620]

Shaw was set to go on trial for the perjury charges in mid-January 1971. A list of supposed new prosecution witnesses for trial included Betty Rubio, who was going to testify that she had seen Shaw and Ferrie together at the Lakefront airport, Herbert Wagner, who claimed (at least in later years) to have seen them together at Ferrie's service station, James Louviere, who also would say he saw Shaw and Ferrie together at Ferrie's service station and at Ferrie's home, and James Laurent, who would offer a similar testimony. It is noteworthy that Wagner told Garrison's office in 1967 that he could not identify Shaw, and Louviere also never identified Shaw to Garrison's office with any certainty in 1967. Another witness was Andrew Dunn, a Clinton/Jackson witness not used at Shaw's earlier trial, and not to be confused with William Dunn, who had testified at Shaw's trial as part of the Clinton/Jackson witnesses.[2621]

Shaw's lawyers, who had been seeking to have the charges thrown out and/or to have the trial delayed, had filed a Federal civil rights suit asking for a permanent injunction on further prosecution of Shaw, which would effectively prevent Shaw from being tried again related to the Kennedy assassination. The motion came before U.S. District Judge Judge Herbert Christenberry in January 1971. Christenberry denied the motion for an injunction, and Shaw's attorneys appealed it to the United States Court of Appeals for the Fifth Circuit, which was located in New Orleans. That appellate court ordered Christenberry to hold a hearing for the purposes of determining whether Shaw should receive a temporary injunction that would immediately postpone the trial, and beyond that a permanent injunction against further prosecution. In accordance with the appellate court's instructions, Christenberry ordered the hearing, which would take place over several days in late January. That hearing became a very important part of the entire Jim Garrison investigation, particularly with regard to the charges against Shaw. Many of the members of the prosecution team, including Jim Garrison, the trial prosecutor James Alcock, Andrew Sciambra, and investigator Louis Ivon took the stand. Shaw testified as well, along with reporter Hugh Aynesworth, William Gurvich, and the three men behind the Truth and Consequences organization—Cecil Shilstone, Joseph Rault, Jr., and Willard Robertson.

Garrison and his associates feared the worst when Christenberry announced the hearing. Shaw and his attorneys also must have had some reason to believe that Christenberry would lean in their favor. As the hearing was underway, James Kirkwood wrote to Patrick O'Rourke, "Latest word from the City of Perpetual Manipulation is that there is at last a judge who is making sense out of the whole business."[2622]

Just before the hearing began, CBS broadcast a segment about Shaw and his ongoing case on its evening news; reporter Foster Davis interviewed Shaw in New Orleans. Shaw indicated that he was the "forgotten man" to the public, which he attributed to the impact of television, where something new was always demanded by the public to hold its interest. He mentioned the Dreyfus case in France, saying that had it happened after television had come along, he doubted that the public's interest could have been sustained long enough to win support for Dreyfus's predicament. Regarding his financial situation, Shaw told Davis that was not "starving to death," but compared with "what I had," he was suffering. Shaw acknowledged that he might have to continue fighting the cloud over him for the rest of his life, smiling wanly as he asked, "What choice do I have?"[2623]

Perry Russo also appeared before the Federal hearing, but he exercised his Fifth Amendment right against self-incrimination for almost all questions put to him. Behind the scenes, another development was happening with Russo. On the night of January 26, 1971, he had appeared at Irvin Dymond's office, and spoken with Dymond about his intention to "plead the Fifth" during his appearance before the hearing. He indicated that he no longer knew if Shaw was the person he had seen at the gathering at Ferrie's apartment in September 1963, and he put the blame squarely on Andrew Sciambra, for effectively implanting the idea in his mind. He indicated that after the sodium pentothal test, and after the hypnosis sessions, Sciambra forcefully told him that under the influence of those methods, Russo had identified Shaw as being at the gathering, and that from then on, he must stick with that testimony, or face the consequences of possible prosecution himself. [2624]

Russo told Dymond that he never had been sure Shaw was the person he had seen. He said that he had not mentioned Shaw to Andrew Sciambra during the Baton Rouge meeting on February 25, 1967, and that he had told the district attorney's men that he had grave doubts about his identification of Shaw, but that they had told him that Shaw was the man he had seen. When Shaw was arrested, Russo said that he had expressed his hope that the decision to arrest Shaw had not been based on what he had said about Shaw. He said that Sciambra had told him he was only one of many witnesses the prosecution had, and that he might not even be used at trial. He said that Lieutenant Edward O'Donnell, the police officer who had attempted to give him a second lie detector test in June 1967, had told the complete truth at Shaw's trial, and that O'Donnell had had a terrible scene with the district attorney's aides after he and Russo had a conversation during which Russo expressed doubts about his identification, and anxiety about becoming involved in the Shaw prosecution in the first place. [2625]

Russo told Dymond that the district attorney's men seemed to know what Judge Edward Haggarty's decisions would be in advance during the buildup to the trial, and that they also had known how the three-judge panel would rule at the preliminary hearing in March 1967. However, he said the district attorney's office had been shocked by Haggarty's ruling to exclude Officer Aloysius Habighorst from testifying that Clay Shaw, the night he was arrested, had admitted using the name "Clay Bertrand" as an alias. Russo had discussed his own unorthodox sex life with the district attorney's men, who had told him that the court would not let the defense use it against him. Russo also confirmed something that William Gurvich had said almost three and a half years before, when he had first talked to the defense attorneys—that Jim Garrison had attempted to connect the infamous murder of Dr. Mary Sherman, the orthopedic surgeon murdered in 1964 in her apartment, with Shaw, along with another murder, that of teenager Jimmy Rupp, who had been mutilated in the early 1960s. [2626]

Russo discussed his financial arrangements with Garrison's office, saying that approximately $15,000 had been spent for him on meals and lodging, and that he had been told he would be paid a per diem of about $22 per day for every day that he was in New Orleans, once the entire case was over, including Shaw's civil suit against Garrison. He ended by saying that he was willing to testify to what he was now telling Dymond at Shaw's perjury trial, if the Federal court ruling by Judge Herbert Christenberry did not go in Shaw's favor, and the prosecution continued.[2627]

Russo then took the stand before Judge Christenberry in the ongoing Federal hearing, and invoked his privilege against self-incrimination. Because he had testified in Shaw's trial two years earlier, it is likely that his current attorney advised him not to testify at the hearing, to avoid contradicting his past testimony under oath.

A few nights later, on January 29, 1971, after the Federal hearing before Judge Christenberry was over, Russo sat down for an interview with William Gurvich at Gurvich's office. Irvin Dymond also was present, as was, for at least part of the meeting, William Gurvich's brother, Leonard. A transcript was made of the interview, which covered many topics, but was left open for an additional interview, which did not take place until late March 1971.[2628]

In the January 29th interview, Russo said that his initial letter to Garrison's office had been written on February 20 or 21, 1967, shortly before Ferrie's death, and had only mentioned David Ferrie, not Lee Harvey Oswald or Shaw. Russo said that Sciambra had gone to Baton Rouge to meet him following Russo's appearance on television, after Russo had contacted several members of the news media. [2629]

Russo said that he thought he knew Oswald, but was not sure, as of January 1971. He said that he knew Shaw right away, however, because he had seen him at President Kennedy's speech in May 1962, at the dedication of the Nashville Avenue Wharf in New Orleans. Russo said there was no question that he had seen Shaw on that occasion. [2630]

Russo shared that he was given the sodium pentothal test on February 27, 1967, that no tape recording had been made, and no stenographer had been present. He indicated that he had first been given one bottle of clear liquid, which had no immediate effect, then was given another bottle of liquid, which had an instant effect on him. He said that he was strapped down to a table, and had violent reactions to the drugs, and that he did not remember any of the questions or answers that occurred during the session. He said, however, that later that night he became clear in his mind about seeing Shaw and Oswald somewhere. However, he repeated that he was not sure, as of January 1971, that he had ever known Oswald, although he continued to maintain that he had seen Shaw on at least the one occasion at the Nashville Avenue Wharf. He said that he had been hypnotized, at Andrew Sciambra's suggestion, on February 28, 1967, again on March 2, 1967, and again on either March 12 or March 13, 1967, just before the preliminary hearing began. Russo said that prosecutor James Alcock had been present at the second hypnosis session, as had investigator Lynn Loisel. He said that in preparing for his testimony at the preliminary hearing in mid-March 1967, Sciambra had drilled him, working from the hypnosis transcripts, so that he could recall his testimony in great detail. Russo said that he thought that he had spoken of a party-type gathering at Ferrie's before any of the hypnosis sessions.[2631]

Russo said that he had been unaware of the controversial memorandum that Andrew Sciambra had written summarizing his initial interview on February 25, 1967, until *Saturday Evening Post* writer James Phelan made an issue of it after the preliminary hearing. Russo said that Sciambra showed him the memo prior to Phelan traveling to Baton Rouge to confront Russo about the contradictions between it and his testimony at the preliminary hearing. Reinforcing the shakiness of his own testimony, Russo said that he had told Sciambra and Alcock, "I sure hope you haven't arrested that man based upon what I said," at least ten to fifteen times over the six-month period after Shaw was arrested. [2632]

Sciambra told him at the time of his identification of Shaw, Russo maintained, that he probably would not be a witness at the trial, that the prosecutors were just using him to identify Shaw, and that the case would "be a cinch." Sciambra also had told Russo that he should only talk to certain newsmen, and not to any of the defense attorneys. Russo explained that he had been wired for sound with reporters James Phelan and Richard Townley, in order to capture any type of bribes they may have offered him to change his testimony.[2633]

Russo equivocated on the issue of how it had come about that he had identified Shaw. He was asked if he had said that he had seen Shaw at Ferrie's apartment initially, or whether Sciambra had told him that he had said it under either sodium pentothal or hypnosis. Russo, at one point during the transcript, indicated that, at that stage in early 1971, he was not sure what exactly he knew or remembered about knowing Shaw.[2634]

Interestingly, when Russo was asked why he invoked the Fifth Amendment during the just-completed Federal hearing before Judge Christenberry, he asked for the tape to be turned off so that he could explain his reasons. Once this request was granted, he asked that the attorneys and Gurvich not repeat the information or discuss it once the tape was rolling again. Russo acknowledged smoking marijuana in the past, but he did not want to discuss whether or not he was a homosexual. When asked why he had not wanted to meet Shaw back in May of 1967, he indicated that it might have been because he had realized that he could have been mistaken in his identification of Shaw.[2635]

Russo discussed several less than favorable incidents in his past. He said that he had taken a test for a friend, Steve Derby, and that Derby had been kicked out of Louisiana State University for it. However, Jim Garrison had called Governor John McKeithen, and Derby was eventually reinstated. Steve Derby and C.G. Mitchell, two friends of Russo, had been involved in theft of money from parking meters, but they were never prosecuted, as a favor to Russo. John Sydney Seruntine, another friend of Russo, had avoided the military draft during the height of the Vietnam War, through a false charge filed against him by the Orleans Parish district attorney's office. The charge hung over him until he was free of the draft obligation, then the charge was dropped; the entire episode was a favor to Russo during his status as an important witness against Shaw. After talking about those personal incidents from the past, Russo requested that the interview be adjourned for the day, agreeing that he would resume it at a later, unspecified date.[2636]

The Federal court hearing before Judge Herbert Christenberry contained some interesting testimony. The three men behind the Truth and Consequences organization, which had partially funded Garrison's investigation, all testified that they had left the investigation entirely to Garrison, and had been surprised by Shaw's arrest; all three men had known Shaw from his days at the Mart. Jim Garrison testified, but refused to answer questions put to him about the origins and internal workings of the case against Shaw. Clay Shaw testified as to the effect of the prosecution upon him, explaining that he had been shunned by some in the business community, and was no longer invited to certain events he used to attend in the past. The details of the financing of the investigation were presented to the court. Shaw's attorneys also zeroed in on determining if there had ever been an instance in New Orleans, particularly during Garrison's time in office, in which a man had taken the stand in his own defense, been acquitted, then been re-indicted for perjury; Garrison's office could not provide such an example. The hearing ended with the judge taking the matter under advisement for a ruling in due time.

In spite of Edith Stern's loans to him for the purchase of the properties on St. Peter Street in 1968, Shaw occasionally needed additional help. In early February 1971, with the cloud of Judge Christenberry's decision on his fate hanging over his head, Shaw asked Edith Stern if he could pay interest only on his loan of $228,000 for the next six months, subject to review at that time.[2637] [2638] Toward the end of the six-month period, in mid-July, Shaw asked if he could draw $3,000 from Mrs. Stern's loan account. When Mrs. Stern's business manager, Joseph Falgout, queried her about that amount, Mrs. Stern said that although Shaw considered it a loan, she considered it a gift, noting that either would be tax-exempt for Shaw.[2639]

In March 1971, Shaw visited Key West, Florida for the first time, at the invitation of James Kirkwood. The *Key West Citizen* published an article about Shaw, wherein he discussed the architecture of Key West in contrast to New Orleans, the wooden structures versus stone ones. Asked why he had very little of the typical Southern accent, Shaw attributed the relative absence of one to having lived in Colorado with his parents when he was a child, and also to having worked in New York City during the 1930s and 1940s. Shaw also discussed how his grandfather had been Marshal in Tangipahoa Parish in Louisiana around the turn of the century, supposedly had been shot twice, and had killed a couple of men in the line of duty. Shaw indicated that he might have to go back to work, and that he would make a decision on the issue after Judge Christenberry handed down his Federal court decision related to enjoining Shaw's prosecution.[2640]

Meanwhile, Shaw was somewhat forgotten at the Mart, even as his ordeal plodded towards an end. At a meeting of the Board of Directors toward the end of March 1971, it was announced that the Plimsoll Club at the Mart had operated at a profit for the first time since it opened several years before. It was also noted that the Mart was coming into criticism that it was simply an office building and nothing else, an opinion that had been whispered about even during Shaw's tenure there.[2641]

The next interview with Perry Russo by the defense attorneys did not occur until March 26, 1971, during Shaw's trip to Key West. Russo was interviewed again by William Gurvich, as well as by Shaw attorneys Irvin Dymond, Sal Panzeca, and Edward Wegmann. At the beginning of the transcript, Russo indicated that he was getting ready to leave for California for a while.[2642]

Russo said that he initially was paid $200 by Garrison's office, and that his bills while staying at the Fontainebleau Hotel, during his trips to New Orleans from Baton Rouge, also had been paid. Russo indicated that he and his friends had held parties at the hotel while he was in New Orleans during the buildup to the preliminary hearing. He said that investigator Louis Ivon originally told him that he eventually would be paid for each of the days he had helped the investigation, and that the case would all be over within six months, by the fall of 1967. However, Russo said that Garrison delayed paying him, even after the case had been tried at a much later date, because of inquiries about possible payments to Russo in a civil lawsuit filed by Shaw; Russo said he was ultimately paid $30 per day for 107 days.[2643]

Russo indicated that, after the perjury charges had been filed against Shaw, following Shaw's acquittal on conspiracy charges, Andrew Sciambra and Louis Ivon had told him that a perjury conviction would be the same in the public mind as a conviction on the original conspiracy charges.[2644] If true, it might explain Garrison's motive in keeping the case going against Shaw, as a vindication of his original efforts, in a neater, simpler manner than would the alternative explanation of a dark, hidden personal vendetta against Shaw based upon some isolated incident.

Russo said that he had initially told *Saturday Evening Post* reporter James Phelan that it had only been in New Orleans that he had first mentioned the party-type gathering at Ferrie's where a conspiracy to kill Kennedy had been discussed by Shaw, Ferrie, and Oswald, not in Baton Rouge during the initial interview with Sciambra. However, he then received pressure from Garrison's assistants, and stuck with the official version that he had told Sciambra about the gathering in their first meeting in Baton Rouge. Interestingly, Russo also said that one of his other identifications of Shaw—that of seeing him at David Ferrie's service station in 1964—might not be accurate. He said that he might have seen Shaw there, but he could not be sure at this point.[2645]

Russo said that he always could figure out what information Sciambra wanted to know from his questions, and could tailor his answers toward those questions. He said there had been very little discussion of Oswald during the interview in Baton Rouge. Russo said the prosecutors had later shown him the signature book from the Eastern Airlines VIP Room, and told him that they had witnesses who would say that it was Shaw's signature in the book using the name "Clay Bertrand."[2646]

Russo had been told, either by Garrison or his assistants, that Shaw liked to be beaten, that he was into various types of sexual practices. He was told that Kennedy represented youth to Shaw, and at one point was informed that Shaw felt that if Kennedy would not whip him, Shaw would kill him. Sciambra also indicated that the district attorney's office had either photographs or film of two large "Negros" nude with Shaw on his patio.[2647]

Russo said that Sciambra had told him that Shaw used the alias "Bertrand." Russo said that during the day of February 27, 1967, the discussion centered mostly on Oswald, not Shaw. However, during the sodium pentothal test later in the day, the main emphasis became to ask Russo about whether he had been introduced to Shaw while he was using the name "Bertrand."[2648]

As the attorneys tried to pin Russo down on the crucial issue of whether he had seen Shaw at the gathering at David Ferrie's apartment, Russo wavered between whether he had actually seen him, or had simply been told he said that he had seen him while under sodium pentothal or hypnosis. At one point, Edward Wegmann said, "You're equivocating again, Perry," and Russo then stated more firmly that he had not been introduced to Shaw under any name, including Shaw or "Bertrand."[2649]

He did reiterate, however, that he had seen Shaw at the Nashville Avenue Wharf during Kennedy's speech, and that he might have seen him at Ferrie's service station after the assassination.[2650]

Russo reiterated that he had been hypnotized on three separate occasions, once without any transcript being made. The first time had been on Tuesday, February 28, 1967, the day before Shaw's arrest; Russo had asked the physician who conducted the hypnosis sessions, Esmond Fatter, not to go into Russo's sexual habits during the sessions. Russo said that after the hypnosis, he was clear in his mind about what had happened during the supposed conspiracy meeting at Ferrie's, but that those certainties began to fade after the questions posed to him by James Phelan, and by other factors that developed during the first few months after Shaw's arrest. However, he said that Andrew Sciambra kept telling him that he had identified Shaw, and that Sciambra and James Alcock rehearsed Russo's testimony for the preliminary hearing directly from the two hypnosis transcripts.[2651]

To anyone who followed the case, and Russo's testimony under oath at both the preliminary hearing and the trial, one of the curiosities was that, aside from Shaw, Ferrie, and Oswald, and aside from friends of his who later denied ever being at such a party, Russo had been unable to identify any other individuals by name at the party gathering. Now, he told Shaw's defense team that both Alcock and Sciambra had told him not to give any names of other people at the conspiracy meeting, besides Shaw, Ferrie, and Oswald.[2652]

Russo said that he was not under hypnosis during the preliminary hearing, but that Dr. Nicholas Chetta, the Parish Coroner, had given him a tranquilizer to take before cross-examination began. Russo also said that Dr. Fatter had told him that he would be his "friend in the courtroom" during Russo's testimony.[2653]

The prosecution team also had tried to hypnotize Russo's friend, Niles "Lefty" Peterson, but the hypnosis did not work on Peterson. Russo said that the prosecutors wanted Russo to work with Peterson to come up with stories that would support the case, although Peterson never wound up testifying at trial.[2654]

Russo said that he had no doubt at this stage that the story about Shaw being at the party gathering had been implanted in his mind by sodium pentothal, hypnosis, and badgering by Andrew Sciambra. He also said that it had been made clear to him that Ferrie and Shaw needed to be connected in as many ways as possible, so the incident of seeing Shaw at Ferrie's service station connected them in a sighting separate from the party gathering.[2655]

Andrew Sciambra told Russo that if he talked with either the defense attorneys or with

Southern Research personnel, who were assisting the defense attorneys, the verdict would be thrown out of court. Astoundingly, Russo said that only in January 1969, on the eve of the long-delayed trial, did he finally become fully aware that he was the key witness, although he said that he had guessed that somewhat earlier from the various news reports about the case.[2656]

Russo said he had feared that his sex life would come out on cross-examination at the preliminary hearing, but that Garrison's men had told him in advance that Judge Benjamin Bagert, who was presiding over the preliminary hearing, would not allow questions on that subject.[2657]

Russo again discussed taking a college test for his friend, Steve Derby, and how Derby had been reinstated at LSU with Garrison's help. He also again mentioned the deal he had made with the district attorney's office to help his friend, John Sidney Seruntine. Seruntine had wanted to avoid the military draft at the height of the Vietnam war, so he had been arrested on a trumped-up theft charge. A woman named Kathy Wilkerson Walden had given the district attorney's office a statement about Seruntine stealing either her projector or camera; the military draft was delayed pending the charges. Lou Ivon, who dealt with Russo directly, checked with Garrison about making the deal. Seruntine was arraigned in mid-March 1969, and the case was dropped in mid-April 1970. In order that the charges could be dropped, Kathy Wilkerson Walden gave a subsequent statement indicating that she had recovered the camera or projector.[2658]

Russo said that the Kennedy assassination investigation by Garrison's office was the first case in which Andrew Sciambra had a significant participation after he began with the district attorney's office. Sciambra liked the limelight and the headlines, and had told Russo that one day he would be district attorney.[2659]

At one point in the transcript, Russo referred to the case against Shaw as a "fraud." Considering that the entire idea of a party gathering where Shaw, Ferrie, and Oswald discussed assassinating Kennedy, the central allegation of the case against Shaw, had supposedly originated with Russo, the statement was significant indeed.[2660]

Russo said that the theory in Garrison's office was that the "big fish" related to the assassination were in Washington, D.C. That included President Lyndon Johnson on down, although the thinking was that Johnson had hidden the facts about the case from the American people, not that he had planned the actual assassination. Russo agreed with the suggestion by Shaw's attorneys that Shaw merely had been a "patsy" for Garrison, a way for Garrison to get publicity for his own activities investigating the Kennedy assassination without actually having to pursue the higher-ups in other jurisdictions.[2661]

Willard Robertson, one of the three principals behind the Truth and Consequences organization that provided private financial support to Garrison for the investigation, at one point had helped Russo get a $400 loan to aid him through some tough financial times. Russo said that Robertson could walk into Garrison's office without knocking, which was rare for anyone to be able to do. Russo also said that at one point, Robertson told him that Garrison was so powerful that he could murder anyone in the city and get away with it.[2662]

Russo said that he had always had doubts about his testimony, and agreed that the story that he told at the preliminary hearing had been full of half-truths combined with complete truths.[2663] Russo had acknowledged during the trial that he had become angry at chief defense counsel Irvin Dymond's first series of questions on cross-examination at the hearing, whereby Dymond questioned whether Russo believed in God, and that Russo had stretched certain points of his testimony because of his anger at Dymond.

Garrison and Sciambra told Russo that Shaw knew he was guilty, and that they expected him to commit suicide before trial. Accordingly, they said, they needed to keep Shaw alive in order for him to stand trial. As the end of the second lengthy interview neared, Russo reiterated again how Sciambra had rehearsed him before the trial using the hypnosis transcript. And, to strengthen the sentiment that his own testimony was not to be trusted, Russo admitted that James Alcock had been extremely nervous about putting him on the stand.[2664]

Russo said that the prosecution's attempt to delay the trial immediately before it finally began, a move which the prosecution reversed very quickly, had been merely a ploy on Garrison's part to "sucker" the defense into not asking for its own delay of the trial. Russo reiterated that the prosecution seemed to know how Judge Edward Haggarty would rule on individual motions before it actually happened.[2665]

Russo had been told to "stick with his story" or he would be charged with perjury. He said that he now feared what would happen if Garrison found out he had talked to Shaw's defense attorneys. He even told the attorneys that he had been instructed, two years earlier, to lure various newsmen, such as Walter Sheridan, Richard Townley, and James Phelan into bribing him, so that they could be arrested. Eventually, Russo had sought out Irvin Dymond's son for advice on how to approach the defense attorneys, and thereby extricate himself from the "mess" in which he had been involved for almost four years.[2666]

Taken together, Russo's initial statement to Dymond before he was to take the stand in the Federal court hearing before Judge Christenberry, and the two subsequent lengthy recorded interviews, added up to a damning indictment of the prosecution's entire case against Shaw. Russo's testimony had been central to the case, the only testimony of conspiracy involving Oswald and Shaw, and aside from the thoroughly discredited witness Charles Spiesel, the only direct testimony regarding a discussion by Shaw involving assassinating Kennedy. Although Russo's new accounts never made it into any of the official filings related to the criminal cases against Shaw, they would be used in certain pleadings related to Shaw's civil case against Garrison, the Truth and Consequence founders, Dr. Esmond Fatter, and Russo. Even if Russo's "recantations" must be viewed with caution, both because of his propensity for stretching the truth or outright lying, and because of his desire to end his own ordeal of being seemingly permanently involved in the cases against Shaw, the contradictions alone seem to be enough to sink any criminal case against Shaw.

It should be noted that, while record of Russo's new version of events sat locked away in defense files over the years, Russo periodically resurrected his story of seeing Shaw at the conspiracy party for anyone willing to hear it. Therefore, around the time of the filming and release of Oliver Stone's movie *JFK*, and here and there to conspiracy theorists writing accounts of the Garrison case, Russo was drawn, like a moth to a flame, to retell the earlier version, seemingly oblivious to what had put down on paper two decades earlier. It was not a habit unique to Russo among Garrison investigation participants.

Judge Herbert Christenberry handed down his decision on May 27, 1971, issuing a permanent injunction against further prosecution of Shaw related to Garrison's Kennedy assassination investigation. The judge had reviewed the evidence from the hearing in January, both witness testimony and exhibits, all of which had been presented by Shaw's team; Garrison's office had not called any witnesses, but had limited itself to cross-examining those called by Shaw. Judge Christenberry found problems with Garrison's investigation from the very beginning, continuing all the way through the perjury charges. He found that Garrison never had any legitimate basis for launching an investigation in the first place, as he had no specific evidence that should have led him to believe a re-opening of the original investigation was warranted. Christenberry also pointed to the many contradictions in Perry Russo's testimony from the very beginning, and the way in which Russo's testimony had been elicited and solidified by the use of sodium pentothal and hypnosis. He also noted the crises of confidence Russo had in his own testimony, which Russo had experienced several times during the two years between Shaw's arrest and trial. Christenberry drew an inference from Russo's refusal to testify at the hearing in January, concluding that Russo had substantial doubts as to the truthfulness of his own testimony that he had given at the trial in February 1969.

Judge Christenberry also found faults with the financing of Garrison's investigation. He found that most of the expenses of Garrison's office related to the Kennedy assassination investigation had been spent in pursuit of the prosecution of Shaw on conspiracy charges. He also found that much of that financing had come from the private organization Truth and Consequences, and that Garrison's office had kept much of the money spent on the investigation segregated in a separate account that was not subject to an independent audit. Christenberry also concluded that Garrison's office had failed to pass on to the defense certain exculpatory evidence to which it was entitled, and that Garrison had a financial interest in continuing the Kennedy assassination investigation, in order to help sales of his book, *A Heritage of Stone*. Judge Christenberry summed up his decision by saying that "the court finds that the pending [perjury] prosecution was brought in bad faith and that such bad faith constitutes irreparable injury which is great and immediate."

Garrison had testified at the Federal hearing before Judge Christenberry that his investigation was essentially over. Following Christenberry's decision, Garrison sarcastically lashed out against Christenberry in public, and his office promptly appealed Christenberry's decision to the U.S. Fifth Circuit Court of Appeals.

Shortly after the permanent injunction was handed down by Christenberry, Ivor Trapolin, a local attorney, expressed the sentiments of many by calling for Garrison's resignation. In the late 1940s, Trapolin had sparred with Mart officials, including Shaw, over the presence of the Czechoslovakian trade exhibit in the Mart building.

Shaw's attorneys filed an amended civil complaint against Garrison and the other defendants on June 11, 1971, based upon new information gained from the Federal court hearing the previous January, and from the recorded interviews with Perry Russo. With the criminal charges now out of the way, subject to the outcome of the appeal by Garrison's office, the civil suit could proceed on its own timetable.

With Shaw's seeming new freedom, the tables were then turned on Jim Garrison. In late June 1971, Garrison was arrested at his home, shortly after daybreak, on Federal racketeering charges related to bribes from businessmen who sold and operated illegal pinball machines. The Federal investigation had been going on for some time, and involved Garrison's former, and controversial, investigator, Pershing Gervais, whom the government had squeezed and turned on Garrison. A number of others, including businessmen and police officials, were arrested in the same sweep.

The local newspapers ran a series of articles which reprinted affidavits against the defendants, along with transcripts of taped conversations between the defendants and informants whom the government had relied upon in making the charges. Some of the taped recordings were of Garrison speaking with Pershing Gervais, who had turned informant after working out a deal on his own pending charges with the Federal government. Interestingly, one of the defendants filed a lawsuit to stop the newspapers from running the articles with the transcripts and affidavits; Irvin Dymond presented the lawsuit, although he was not the attorney specifically representing Jim Garrison.

In July, Federal District Judge R. Blake West issued a permanent injunction against the prosecution of the second set of perjury charges against Dean Andrews. Andrews had been convicted of perjury charges in August 1967, and had been charged two more times with perjury based on testimony either before a grand jury, or at his own trial, or at Shaw's trial. Executive Assistant District Attorney Frank Klein, now back with Garrison's office after Garrison's arrest on racketeering charges, did not oppose the motion. Therefore, the charges were permanently dismissed.[2667]

Other old cases peripherally connected to Shaw's case, were being discontinued as well. Charges against Walter Sheridan and Richard Townley, which had been initiated in the summer of 1967, were dropped in late July 1971, after Garrison's office received an unfavorable higher court decision in the matter.[2668]

On July 19, New Orleans Mayor Moon Landrieu unilaterally appointed Shaw to an unpaid position with the French Market Board; the group looked after various aspects of the French Quarter. Landrieu later said he appointed Shaw to the position as his attempt to "make it up to Clay Shaw" for his four-and-a-half year ordeal. Landrieu said he was not prompted by anyone to do so, but rather felt that he had an obligation to do it because of Shaw's long service to the city.[2669]

On September 2, 1971, Shaw sat for an interview with Canadian Broadcasting Company, for which he was paid $800. On November 1, 1971, he spoke at Stonehill College in Massachusetts, and was paid $700.

In October 1971, Shaw was to speak to a group of law students at Case Western Reserve University in Cleveland, Ohio; he would visit his friend Patrick O'Rourke while there. However, the speech was canceled due to an unusual occurrence. A law student and member of the Student Bar Association felt that certain of his rights had been denied, and enjoined the Association from meeting while he awaited his right to trial. As a result, the Association could not allocate funds for Shaw's speech.[2670] Shaw passed the letter on to O'Rourke with a note indicating the student's claim of denial of his rights, saying "Talk of being hoist on one's own petard!" In the same letter, Shaw enclosed to O'Rourke a notice he had discovered of someone selling separate autographed photographs of him and Jim Garrison at an auction. Shaw commented that the "item is...interesting, not to say downright bizarre. It makes me feel so posthumous, quite like Button Gwinnet or John Hancock. It should, however, clear up for you the minor mystery of why I write you so seldom. It's not that I'm lazy (heaven forfend) or that I don't love you, (which I do); but simply entrepreneurial greed whereby limiting supply increases the demand and the price. So, now you know." He signed it, "Clay," and added in parentheses, "Shaw, that is, should you decide to sell this."[2671]

Jim Garrison's lawyers had asked the United States Supreme Court to order the U.S. Fifth Circuit Court of Appeals to consider his argument that judicial immunity prevented Shaw's civil suit from proceeding to trial. The Fifth Circuit had directed that the local Federal district judge rule on the matter. On November 5, 1971, Federal district judge Frederick Heebe said that Shaw's civil suit could proceed.

On November 24, 1971, Jim Garrison and HMH Publishing Company, owners of *Playboy* magazine, won a summary judgment on the libel suit filed against them by Gordon Novel as a result of Garrison's 1967 *Playboy* interview. The defendants were awarded costs of $4,484.34 in a further judgment on December 28, 1971. The court found that Garrison, at *Playboy's* initiation, had granted the interview to interviewer Eric Norden on an unpaid basis. Garrison and Eric Norden had checked the galleys of the interview, and Garrison approved the interview prior to its publication. *Playboy* verified some of Garrison's statements through other media, but did not contact individuals mentioned in the interview, including Novel, for their version of the story. The court found that Novel was involved in an event of public or general interest, and that the plaintiff's counsel had provided no reference in briefs for summary judgment that any actual malice had been committed against Novel, a condition he would have to prove, since the court essentially ruled that Novel had become a public figure through his own efforts related to Garrison's Kennedy assassination investigation. Accordingly, the judge found no convincing evidence of malice in the record, and ruled that *Playboy* had merely presented what Garrison said about a case that was of international significance. A number of statements that were alleged to be libelous against Novel had, in fact, originated with him, the court found, such as his voluntary revelation to Garrison about a burglary he had committed at the bunker in Houma, Louisiana. Novel had voluntarily described his relationship with David Ferrie to Garrison, and also his supposed connections with the CIA. The court found that there was nothing to show that Garrison knew the statements by Novel were false. Garrison's interview in *Playboy* had not described Novel as a conspirator in the Kennedy assassination, but rather as a key witness in the case.[2672]

The court's decision was based to a major degree upon numerous depositions taken by *Playboy's* attorney, David Krupp, including those of Novel himself, and of various newsmen in Columbus, Ohio, the Washington, D.C. area, and New Orleans. Those included Walter Sheridan, local New Orleans television and print newsmen, and NBC News employees. Krupp also had deposed Novel's long-time friend Rancier Blaise Ehlinger, Novel's former employer (and Garrison supporter) Willard E. Robertson, and attorneys Dean Andrews and Steven Plotkin.

Krupp deposed Novel over approximately a week's time, spread over a two-month period in the spring of 1969, not long after Shaw's trial, producing an approximately 1600-page deposition. Krupp's persistent questioning, based upon investigation of Novel's background, covered Novel's entire life up to that point, including various businesses he had operated and then closed, his friends and business associates, his marriages, and various publicity Novel had received over the years. Krupp also obtained from the CIA, through civil procedure rules, a Certificate of Lack of Official Record, the agency's official assertion that it had never employed Novel, who had claimed association or employment with the agency many times, even going so far as refusing to answer deposition questions based upon the National Security Act of 1947, which established the CIA.

Dean Andrews was no less colorful, in his deposition taken March 12, 1970, than he was at any other appearance, public or private. Andrews said that he kept three files—past, present, and future rumors—and that Novel appeared in all three files. In discussing the mysterious "Clay Bertrand," Andrews said if you wanted to "clean a joint out," say "There is Clay Bertrand," and everyone would scatter (alluding to the idea that everyone seemed to deny being "Clay Bertrand"). He said that Novel had shown up at his place one night, saying something about Andrews and Shaw once meeting at the New Orleans Athletic Club (both men had denied ever meeting), a detail that Novel had dangled in front of both Garrison and Shaw's attorneys at one time. Andrews said that he had responded to Novel by saying, "See that chair? I'm about to comb your hair with it."[2673]

The deposition of Walter Sheridan was taken on March 30, 1970 in Washington, D.C. Sheridan was represented by Herbert "Jack" Miller, who would become one of the most powerful Washington attorneys in the second half of the 20th century. Miller, well aware that Sheridan was still under indictment by Garrison's office in New Orleans, cautioned *Playboy's* attorney, David Krupp, that he did not want Sheridan's deposition to be used as part of discovery related to the indictment against him. Krupp assured Miller that he represented *Playboy* magazine and HMH Publishing Company, and that none of the information from the deposition would go directly to Garrison.[2674]

Sheridan said that he still worked as an investigative reporter with NBC, as he had since 1965. He said that on February 22, 1967, the day Ferrie died, the NBC News division told him to go to New Orleans and find out what was going on. He was in New Orleans much of the time from February to June 1967. He had met Novel on March 1, 1967, the evening of Shaw's arrest, in the office of Dean Andrews; he had heard Andrews's name when Shaw was arrested, and had gone to meet him. Sheridan said he had met with Shaw when he first got to New Orleans to ask him about the "Clay Bertrand" alias, and Shaw had denied being "Clay Bertrand." He had gone to Shaw's residence again the night of Shaw's arrest, and had found it very crowded, so he had then gone to Dean Andrews's office. Novel came into Andrews's office approximately a half hour later; it was the first time Sheridan had ever seen or heard of Novel. He said Novel began talking about a photograph of a truck that Garrison had shown him, taken from a fleet of laundry trucks in New Orleans; Garrison suspected it might have been used in the assassination. Andrews and Novel then had begun talking to each other at a rapid pace, mentioning numerous characters, and that Sheridan very quickly became both fascinated and confused by the personalities and the banter of the two men.[2675]

Sheridan testified that he had never said that Robert Kennedy had thought that Garrison's investigation was a fraud, and that he had not spoken to Kennedy about it, nor had he ever said that he represented the Kennedy family. He acknowledged that he may have, on another occasion, said that since Kennedy had been attorney general at the time of the assassination, he must have known that Garrison's case was fraudulent.[2676]

Sheridan said that he had agreed to pay Gordon Novel $500 for two weeks of work as a consultant to the NBC News report on Garrison's investigation broadcast in June 1967, since Novel knew so many people in the area. Novel knew Sergio Arcacha Smith, Layton Martens, and others, and was helpful in locating them; he also had taken Sheridan to David Ferrie's house to look it over. Sheridan said that he did not check Novel out at first, but learned things about him later on. He said that he did not recall if he made notes of Novel's conversations.[2677]

Later, Sheridan attended a polygraph examination for Novel arranged by journalist Les Whitten, an associate of newspaper columnist Jack Anderson, and that NBC News had interviewed Novel on camera in McLean, Virginia, where the polygraph examination was held; some of the footage had been shown that evening on the *Huntley-Brinkley Report*. NBC also had paid for some telephone calls Novel made, and had considered using Novel in the special report on Garrison's investigation, but ultimately decided not to. Sheridan said he had seen Novel in New York City on certain occasions since March 1967, and had received some litigation documents related to Novel's suit against *Playboy*.[2678]

Walter Sheridan denied in his deposition that he had kept any notes related to the Garrison investigation However, years later, when the Assassination Records Review Board (ARRB) was gathering and declassifying records, an interesting situation developed. On October 14, 1976, the Kennedy Library in Boston had received thirty-three boxes of personal records from Sheridan. In October 1993, after Sheridan had learned that the newly created ARRB would be collecting information, even from private collections, related to the Garrison investigation, Sheridan contacted the Kennedy Library and asked that thirteen folders of material related to his work on the Garrison investigation be returned to him. Officials at the Kennedy Library requested that Sheridan allow his material to be turned into part of the archives related to the Kennedy assassination, but he had refused to do so.[2679] The ARRB, learning of this turn of events after Sheridan's death in 1995, issued a subpoena for the records to Sheridan's wife, Nancy. Nancy Sheridan enlisted the services of Herbert "Jack" Miller once again, and NBC News became involved in the dispute as well, maintaining that the records were its work product for the 1967 documentary. At the present time, the papers are still in the possession of NBC, and are not available to researchers. However, a summary list of Sheridan's "Garrison" materials can be found in the ARRB files. It includes sections identified as "handwritten" notes, among other materials.[2680]

In December 1971, Shaw was appointed as Managing Director of the French Market Corporation, which was responsible for renovating and developing the old French Market at the edge of the French Quarter. It was a paid position, and Shaw was paid a salary of $24,000, somewhat comparable to his salary with the Mart, during 1972 and 1973, and for a portion of 1974, although due to health problems, and ultimately his death, he was generally inactive that entire year. Shaw had been informed of the appointment in early November. He wrote to his friend Patrick O'Rourke in Chicago that "it will be delightful to have a substantial income again. Of course, the job has many fringe benefits…economic and psychological…not the least of the latter being Jim Garrison's reaction to the news!"[2681]

Among the congratulations Shaw received was one from Richard "Dick" Rolfe, who wrote that, "June joins me in our delight that the French market is in such capable hands. We are also delighted that you have found an outlet for your talents which will benefit the entire city."[2682] Shaw passed the telegram on to Patrick O'Rourke with a note saying, "They never give up."

Toward the end of 1971, Jim Garrison attempted an unusual move related to the criminal charges for which he had been arrested by the Federal government in late June. He tried to obtain an indictment by the State of Louisiana on identical charges, in order to avoid the Federal prosecution. He alleged that, due to a delay in the filing of Federal charges after his arrest, the State of Louisiana had the right to prosecute him. Many saw it as a ruse on Garrison's part to secure a prosecution within the more favorable (to him) state legal system, rather than risking a more independent Federal prosecution. Garrison's tactic ultimately did not work, and he was tried twice within the Federal system. In an ironic twist, Judge Herbert Christenberry would preside over at least one of Garrison's criminal trials. Garrison tried to get Christenberry to recuse himself due to a conflict of interest, but Christenberry refused. Garrison was found not guilty in both trials.

Meanwhile, the appeal by Garrison's office of Christenberry's ruling in the Shaw criminal case was approaching a hearing. Garrison's appellate lawyers, with the firm of Deutsch, Kerrigan, and Stiles, alleged that Judge Christenberry had been biased in the manner in which he had conducted the entire hearing. The appeal asserted that Christenberry had repeatedly taken over the questioning from Shaw's attorneys, and had tried to assist Shaw with his proof of the case. Years later, one of the prosecutors who represented Garrison at the Christenberry hearing in 1971 told the author that the prosecutors had heard rumors well before the hearing took place that Christenberry was strongly inclined to rule in Shaw's favor, even before any evidence had been heard. The American Civil Liberties Union filed a brief in support of Shaw's position on appeal; it maintained that "bad faith" on the part of the prosecution was the only real issue.

## 30 · Free at Last? A Cruise on the Mediterranean

A column by syndicated gossip columnist Robin Adams Sloan, dealing with Shaw's ordeal at Garrison's hands, appeared in the *Washington Star* edition of January 6, 1972; the same column appeared in other newspapers throughout the nation around the same time. Responding to a question by a writer with the initials G.H. in Shreveport, Louisiana, which asked the real reason behind Garrison's accusations against Shaw, Sloan replied that "aristocratic insiders" in New Orleans believed that jealousy was the motive, because Shaw had been allowed into the homes of the most socially prominent families in New Orleans, and Garrison never had been invited into that "social set."[2683] That rumor about Garrison's motives, like many other rumors speculating about his real intentions and goals, has survived to this day, without any concrete evidence having been provided.

Shaw apparently enjoyed Sloan's column so much that he decided to pass it along to others. On January 13, 1972, he sent a letter to the playwright and chef, Chris Blake, and enclosed the column, which he said that Blake and his friend, Roc, would find "amusing."[2684]

In early 1972, Shaw communicated with his interior designer friend, Tom Dawson in California, about possibly going to Veracruz, Mexico for Carnival. Shaw indicated he was pleased that Dawson was sending his "friend" from Florida, who turned out to be Casey Jones, and not another young man Dawson had sent him before, to visit Shaw in New Orleans. Shaw mentioned that the Veracruz trip was still on, indicating that he could go from New Orleans to Veracruz for a reasonable price. In checking on the matter, he found out that the dates for Carnival in Veracruz were often moved around to suit the weather. Shaw mentioned an upcoming interview he would do for CBS-TV in Houston, Texas on March 1, the fifth anniversary of his arrest and the third anniversary of his acquittal. He also noted the recent column by Robin Sloan. Shaw closed by saying it was good to be "gainfully employed again" and to have a "charming secretary" for dictation.[2685] It is uncertain that Shaw and Dawson ever made the trip to Veracruz, Mexico, as there was no further correspondence that indicated the trip had taken place.

Shaw's new secretary was Nita Putnam, who would work for him until he eventually had to leave the project due to illness during 1974. Putnam recalled later that Shaw:

"...was my mentor, my father, my brother, my teacher, my occasional companion—enjoyed many wonderful meals together. He was the most eloquent speaker/writer I've ever known...He showed me by example his intolerance of bigotry and that, if one must judge another, to judge them by what's in their heart and head, not by what your eyes are seeing. Look deeper...if you're open, you'll be pleasantly surprised more often than not. I was blessed to have met and known Clay; having known him has made me a better person. He left an indelible and wonderful mark on my psyche for which I'll forever be grateful. How many people can say they've known such an amazing person...I am truly blessed with my memories.[2686]...I recall something Clay said that has stayed with me these years. I commented to him that he must hate Garrison. His answer was: 'Hate requires too much energy that can be put to a better use.' He truly lived that philosophy. That I could be so generous; not so sure. But I've never forgotten that simple stated philosophy and knew he really lived it."[2687]

Edith Stern usually left New Orleans for the Mardi Gras season, because Jewish people, no matter how wealthy or prominent, were generally not invited to take part in many of the official Mardi Gras programs. Shaw, who had been an enthusiastic participant in Mardi Gras for decades, putting on full costume and frolicking in the streets, maintained an ambivalent attitude with Stern over the issue of the famous celebration. On January 26, 1972, even as he was planning a Mardi Gras celebration with an out-of-town companion, Shaw wrote Stern about an article he had seen recently, which indicated that Mardi Gras only generated $6.1 million from outside visitors, out of $200 million of annual tourist revenue for the city. Shaw indicated, however, that, "No politician will tax Mardi Gras to fund" more worthwhile civic projects, as it would be "like shooting Santa Claus."[2688]

In early February, Shaw heard from journalist Holland McCombs. The letter discussed Shaw's legal situation generally, but McCombs also commented on *TIME* magazine and its "latest gullibility" regarding the fraudulent Howard Hughes autobiography that had been exposed within the past month.[2689] The Hughes autobiography, supposedly done with his cooperation, had been exposed as a fraud. Author Clifford Irving actually was working at least partly, without authorization, from an older manuscript by another author (ironically, by journalist James Phelan, who had played an active role in Shaw's defense). Hughes himself had come forward by telephonic press conference to denounce Irving's work as a fraud.

As mentioned earlier, Tom Dawson sent Casey Jones from Florida to spend the Mardi Gras week with Shaw. Jones worked for a Hollywood, Florida radio station, WGMA, and had met Shaw some time before. In a letter on December 27, 1971, Jones said he was looking forward to continuing the "unfinished business" with "baited 'breath.'" In the same letter, Jones enclosed some clippings related to a criminal case against Miami, Florida radio and television personality Larry King, the same Larry King who later became a nationwide radio and television talk show host. King had been indicted after charges were pressed by millionaire Louis Wolfson. Wolfson supposedly had entrusted King, several years before, with $5,000 to be passed on to Jim Garrison to help with the financing of Garrison's investigation into the Kennedy assassination, and by extension, the prosecution of Shaw. King had apparently kept the money, never delivered it to Garrison, and never repaid Wolfson. However, King was able to get off of the charges on a technicality; the statute of limitations had expired. Jones commented to Shaw that King was the "most disliked broadcast personality in town," meaning the Miami, Florida area, that King was reportedly "a kleptomaniac caught several years ago by a station manager with several thousand dollars worth of station equipment," and that King still owed the owners of the station $750 that he had "borrowed" from them.[2690] Shaw replied on February 7, thanking Jones for the clippings and indicating that while it was unfortunate that King had gotten off on a technicality, at least Shaw could take some pleasure in the fact that King had stolen the money rather than passed it on to Garrison. He closed by indicating that he was looking forward to Jones's arrival for Mardi Gras the following weekend.[2691]

Millionaire Louis Wolfson had been somewhat enthusiastic about Garrison's investigation. An article in the *Miami Herald* for January 16, 1972, had reported on a telephone conversation that Wolfson and Jim Garrison had two years before, in mid-February 1970. Wolfson had attempted to transmit $25,000 to Garrison's investigation by giving a portion of it to Richard Gerstein, Florida State's Attorney for metropolitan Miami, Florida, and a portion to Larry King.[2692] Although the theft charge against King had been dropped because the statute of limitations had passed, King was fired from his broadcasting jobs, and became more or less unemployable in the Miami area for several years.

In that same *Miami Herald* article, Garrison discussed that he was minimizing travel at that time, because the Federal government was trying to set him up [on some type of illicit sex charge] in airports. Garrison also commented on the case he had presented in court during Shaw's trial, saying, "You cannot unfold a coup d'état [meaning the assassination of

Kennedy] in a courtroom. This I learned. It's too complex. It's like opening a box of octopuses in a closet."[2693]

On February 9, 1972, Shaw wrote to Grace Herlihy, mother of author and playwright James Leo Herlihy. Shaw indicated that, "Jamie was coming to New Orleans" for Mardi Gras, and that Shaw wished she could come along with him.[2694] Shaw must have planned a quiet stay for his Florida friend Casey Jones, with little outdoor activity. He turned down an invitation from Roland Dobson for an invitation to a Mardi Gras party that included cocktails and a viewing of the Endymion parade.[2695]

In mid-February, Monk Simons, with the D.H. Holmes department store, sent Shaw a clipping related to Shaw's activities in his new position with the French Market. It was an old tradition that Simons had begun years before, and now he was continuing it with Shaw's new job. Shaw wrote thanking him for the clipping, and "your continuing interest in my career."[2696]

Garrison's office had appealed the ruling by Judge Herbert Christenberry that Garrison's prosecution against Shaw for perjury could not proceed. The hearing by the Fifth U.S. Circuit Court of Appeals was held on February 24, 1972. In a letter to William Gurvich, Edward Wegmann commented that Garrison's attorney, Eberhard Deutsch, had argued the case better during a recent television appearance than he had in the courtroom.[2697]

By 1972, Shaw was back on a full speaking schedule in his role with the French Market complex. A letter on February 24, 1972, to Commander R. Russell of the United States Coast Guard, confirmed Shaw's speech at the Coast Guard Officers' Luncheon Meeting on April 4, 1972, at the Coast Guard base on Industrial Canal in New Orleans. The subject was, "French Market Development."[2698] On March 8, 1972, Shaw wrote to Duffy Wall confirming his speech to the Press Club at the Newsmaker Luncheon on March 27, 1972.[2699] Duffy Wall was an executive with the Freeport Sulphur Company, sometimes linked in conspiracy literature with the CIA and the Garrison investigation. On March 14, 1972, he wrote to Vincent Arena regarding a speech on March 23, 1972 to the Young Men's Business Club of Jefferson; the letter confirmed that Arena and Shaw would have dinner together, then go to the meeting.[2700] Shaw spoke to the Chamber of Commerce on March 16, 1972, and received a Certificate of Appreciation at the ceremony at the Roosevelt hotel. Shaw spoke at the Men's Club on April 6, 1972.[2701]

Casey Jones, the young man who had spent Mardi Gras with Shaw, wrote on March 11 saying that he had enjoyed the day, summing his visit up as, "A loaf of bread, a jug of wine, and thou."[2702] Shaw responded on March 17, reiterating, no doubt with mixed emotions, that it was a pity that broadcaster Larry King would get off on a technicality for his theft of monies intended for Garrison's investigation.[2703]

Around his birthday in 1972, Shaw received a card from Sally Galjour and her husband, Warren, in Brooklyn, New York. Sally Galjour was the former Sally O'Dair, and the sister of Marge O'Dair, who worked in Marilyn Tate's real estate agency and was good friends with both Shaw and Jeff Biddison. The Galjours indicated that they were happy for Shaw in his "new life" as a free man, managing the French Market project.[2704] Shaw eventually replied on April 27, 1972, saying that he was busy at "gainful employment," which "consumes more time" than he had remembered.[2705]

Edith Stern invited Shaw to accompany her on an ocean cruise in the fall, one that would stop at various European cities and islands where the two would hear musical concerts. In a letter to his old friend Princess Jacqueline de Chimay in Paris, Shaw mentioned the trip, and said that the ship would be docking at Nice, France on September 15, 1972, that he would spend September 16 and 17 in Paris, and that he hoped to see her there. Shaw, who addressed her as "Madame La Princesse Du Caraman Chimay," asked her opinion of *American Grotesque*, by James Kirkwood, which gave a full account of Shaw's trial, and also asked her opinion of the "whole bizarre paranoid affair."[2706] Chimay answered, quoting

Shaw's own words that, "Garrison is mad. I mean literally mad!" She had noted that Garrison was in trouble now because of his own legal problems related to his arrest in June 1971 on bribery charges, and should be indicted for slander for the charges he had made against Shaw in public. She referred Shaw to a novel by Voltaire for a similar type of situation, and ended the letter with, "Good luck to you, My Dear Clay."[2707]

In mid-April, Shaw wrote to Emlyn Williams, the Welch actor and dramatist, mentioning that his friend Tom Dawson would be visiting England for several weeks, and suggesting that Williams get together with him. Referring to Williams's earlier companion, Shaw asked, "What happened to that charming Bob Crawley?" and mentioned that twice a year he drove to South Carolina from New Orleans, passing through Social Circle, Georgia, Crawley's hometown; Williams and Crawley had stayed with Shaw several years before.[2708]

In late April 1972, Shaw wrote to Mary Brandon and J. Lawrence Smith in Charlotte, North Carolina. The couple was part of the large group of people associated with the Formyduvals of Whiteville, North Carolina; J. Lawrence Smith had managed a store there, part of a regional chain. Shaw mentioned his job with the French Market, and said that he was "enjoying himself immensely," and was "happy to be gainfully employed" again. He mentioned that he had talked to William Henry Formyduval recently, and found that Formyduval's aunt, Mae Hobson, was doing well in spite of her various ailments.[2709]

In mid-May, Shaw received a letter from Lelah Halton in California. Halton had been married, until his death in the late 1950s, to the character actor Charles Halton, best known for playing the ultra-serious bank examiner in *It's a Wonderful Life*. She indicated that Judson O'Donnell, Shaw's old friend from the New York days, had "absented himself" from her. She said that he had done this once before for an alleged (but unspecified in her letter) reason.[2710] Shaw did not reply until mid-July, where he indicated that he now often saw Tennessee Williams, who had settled into the French Quarter recently. Shaw mentioned that Judson O'Donnell was back from a visit to England, but that he did not hear from him as often as he used to.[2711]

On May 19, 1972, Shaw was issued a passport for use on his European cruise with Edith Stern in September. It was the last passport he would obtain, and the cruise would be the last time he would use a passport. Shaw's initial passport had issued on May 16, 1947, and he used it on the 1949, 1950, and 1951 Latin American and Caribbean trips. On November 5, 1951, he was issued another passport, which he used on European trips in 1952 and 1954. He was issued another passport on February 19, 1958, but it was not stamped by any country, although he did make a lengthy trip to Puerto Rico in 1958. He received another passport on September 21, 1965, just a little more than a week before his retirement from the Mart. He used that passport when visiting Mexico in the fall of 1965 (it showed him leaving through the port of Veracruz), and then in Spain, France and England during the summer of 1966. While Shaw developed a reputation for continuous international travel, he really only had a few selected long trips, mostly in the late 1940s and during the first half of the 1950s, usually not making more than one international trip per year. After the 1955 trip to Mexico, he visited Cuba, and made his 1958 visit to Puerto Rico for business reasons; the remaining trips were after retirement, for personal reasons.[2712]

On May 31, 1972, Shaw wrote to John Henry Bogle confirming his appearance for a speech in Mrs. Donald George's courtyard at 521 St. Louis Street on July 5. The speech also was regarding the ongoing revamping of the French Market complex.[2713] On May 31, 1972, Shaw wrote to Mrs. Richard Bosse, confirming his speech before the Newcomers Club on June 27, 1972, at the Jung Hotel.[2714] On June 1, 1972, Shaw agreed to address the Mayor's Ladies group regarding the French Market restoration.[2715]

Shaw prepared financial information in early June 1972 showing a personal net worth of $228,817, after netting all of his assets against all of his existing liabilities.[2716] While the value of real properties owned by Shaw was always subject to fluctuations, the statement is further proof that Shaw's net worth had substantially survived the multi-year prosecutorial effort by Garrison's office.

In mid-1972, Shaw purchased a property at 1034 Dauphine Street from Joan Nish, a doctor from Houston, Texas. In a letter to Shaw in early April, Nish had written that there was "no one I would rather see living in the cottage and enjoying it," and that she was "glad you heard we were selling." She asked that Shaw send her the floor plans for his improvements after he began work on the residence, "for I am interested in what your good taste, experience, and imagination can do with the cottage."[2717] Shaw purchased the property with a loan for $24,000, and resold the property in mid-January 1973 for $35,000, showing his real estate market instincts had not deserted him.

Shaw attended, at the invitation of Mario Bermúdez, a cocktail party for the Colombian delegation, which was celebrating the inaugural flight by Braniff Airlines from Colombia to New Orleans. He also helped with a tour of wives attending the U.S. Conference of Mayors.[2718]

In his post-defendant status after 1971, Shaw often found himself in contact with individuals who had played parts, major and minor, in his prosecution. While appearing on the Annual Program of the Institute of Internal Auditors Convention, Shaw found himself in proximity to Albert Labiche, who had been the foreman of the grand jury that indicted many, if not most, of the individuals indicted during Garrison's investigation of President Kennedy's assassination.

In late July 1972, Shaw wrote to Alison Marks, informing her of the music cruise aboard the *Renaissance* that he and Edith Stern were taking. The voyage would go from Lisbon to Turkey, Shaw wrote, stopping at various islands, where the passengers would disembark for symphony concerts.[2719]

On July 31, 1972, the U.S. Fifth Circuit Court of Appeals affirmed Judge Herbert Christenberry's decision enjoining further prosecution of Shaw. While the news was welcome, and had the promise of finality to it, Jim Garrison's office promptly appealed to the U.S. Supreme Court.

Emlyn Williams wrote during the summer of 1972 that he would be conducting a tour where he read from the works of Charles Dickens throughout South America, and a later Dylan Thomas-related reading tour in the United States, although not in New Orleans. Shaw replied to Williams in early August that he was moving to a larger place in October, and invited Williams to come stay with him on his next visit. Shaw mentioned that the civil suit against Garrison and others continued to "drag on," but Shaw commented that, "While I won't get $5,000,000 [the requested amount in the suit], I do think I will get something."[2720]

Another old friend with whom Shaw reconnected in the summer of 1972 was Valerian Rybar, a Yugoslavian immigrant who had started as a clerk in a department store and risen to become "the world's most expensive decorator," according to his 1990 obituary in *The New York Times*, a person known for creating opulent rooms and extravagant parties. Shaw indicated that it was nice to have seen Rybar after such a long time, implying that Shaw may have known him during his New York days of the 1930s and early 1940s.[2721]

A review of Shaw's 1972 daily planner shows visits with Tennessee Williams on January 2, a visit with attorney Cecil Burglass, who had represented Dean Andrews on one of his perjury charges for a time, the visit by Miami friend Casey Jones in late February and early March, and another visit with Tennessee Williams on May 18, 1972. The calendar also shows the 10:30 a.m. hearing of the Fifth U.S. Circuit Court of Appeals on February 24, 1972, at which the Court heard Jim Garrison's office's appeal of Judge Herbert Christenberry's injunction against further prosecution of Shaw. Beginning in mid-1972, Shaw received a number of visits from Victor Campbell, who was known at the time as a companion of Tennessee Williams. Campbell visited on several occasions throughout the last seven months of 1972.[2722]

The planner also gives the general itinerary of the cruise Shaw took with Edith Stern. He left for New York City on August 25, stayed a couple of days, then left at 10:00 p.m. on August 27 on a flight to London. He spent a few days in London before beginning the cruise on September 1, 1972. On September 15, 1972, the ship docked at Cannes, France, and he took the overnight train to Paris. On September 20, 1972, he returned to New Orleans.[2723]

While in London on August 31, he granted an interview to British author Roy S. Simmonds, who was planning to write a biography of William March, the mid-century writer whom Shaw had known in New York City, and later in New Orleans. March wrote a number of novels and short stories; his most famous was *The Bad Seed*, later made into a play and a motion picture. Simmonds's biography of the writer, *The Two Worlds of William March*, appeared in the 1980s.

The interview with Shaw is noteworthy not only because it gives Shaw's impressions and recollections of March in some detail, but also because Simmonds thereafter mentioned Shaw's name whenever he wrote to any person who might know of Shaw, such as Tennessee Williams or Alistair Cooke, perhaps in the hope that Shaw's prominence would persuade them to share their own thoughts about March. That technique, after Shaw's death, brought forth a response from Robert Clark (real name: J.L. Clay), a French Quarter artist who had been March's companion in his last days, a response that was so unusually negative it is worth quoting:

> "Clay Shaw, I regret to announce, had a low opinion of everything and everyone not known as Clay Shaw. Brilliant and witty, urbane and sophisticated—yes. A warm, loving, trusted friend—no. I find there is a certain type of terribly fearful person who surrounds himself with books and material things, higher education beyond his needs and a superciliousness which transcends the possibility of sharing. His name is Clay Shaw."[2724]

The agenda for the cruise included the cities of London, Le Havre, Lisbon, Gibraltar, Rhodes, Confu, Syracuse, Cannes, and Nice. At the recommendation of Mr. and Mrs. John Weinstock of New Orleans, Shaw stayed at the Hotel Monte Lambert in Paris after the cruise ended.[2725]

As Shaw prepared for the Mediterranean cruise, he wrote to his friend Jack Davis in London, indicating that he would be there soon, and would tell him "everything that has happened" during the last five years. Shaw promised that, "You won't believe it, but it's all true."[2726]

In late September, after the cruise was over, Shaw wrote Edith Stern, indicating that he recently had attended a reception for Pierre Salinger, President Kennedy's former press secretary, who was appearing in New Orleans on behalf of Senator George McGovern's campaign for president that year. Shaw commented that the promotion of the event had not mentioned McGovern at all, and that not that many people had turned out, besides a few standard New Orleans liberals. Shaw commented on their trip together, indicating that Paris was now "filled with too many Parisians," and that "too many skyscrapers" were being built there. He said that the cruise was "exhilarating, charming and enchanting, but then so has been every other aspect of my knowing you."[2727]

Shaw wrote Princess Jacqueline de Chimay after the trip, saying that the "hand of time has dealt very lightly with you." Shaw commented that Paris had improved over the years since he had seen it during the war and shortly thereafter. He mentioned that Jim Garrison's office was appealing the decision by the U.S. Fifth Circuit Court of Appeals upholding the injunction against his further prosecution, but that, in a bit of hopeful news, his lawyers had advised that the odds were 5,000 to one against the Supreme Court agreeing to hear the appeal.[2728]

Shaw also wrote to Olwen Janson and her husband, Hugh, at their residence on the Isle of Wight, after he had visited with them as a side trip from the cruise. Shaw had befriended Olwen Janson when she was Olwen Harriss during the 1950s in New Orleans; she had married and moved back to England at the end of the decade. He thanked them for a recent gift of ashtrays they had sent to him, and said that it had been "good to see you in London," adding that he had "been to London many times," but had never "penetrated so deeply." He added that he had sent one of the ashtrays they had sent to him to "sweet William," meaning William Formyduval, whom Janson had known during her time in New Orleans. He ended by saying that he hoped to see them on a future trip, which never materialized.[2729]

Shaw still took a pride in the city of New Orleans. He had considered moving to another location after his legal troubles were over, but apparently had never seriously pursued the idea. In October 1972, he wrote to an acquaintance who was visiting the city for the first time with some friends that, "New Orleans is a lovely city and I enjoy showing it off."[2730]

However, a few years before, after his arrest, Shaw must have gone through a thorough reevaluation of his feelings about the city. In one of the writings he generated during the period between arrest and trial, he committed some strongly negative feelings about the city and its culture to paper (errors in original):

> "Among the delusions that affect the city:
>
> "That it is the capital of cuisine. Not true. There is some fairly good food in the city but its excellence really depends on the fact that there is no competition in the South. There is probably no region in the world in which home cooking is so good and restaurant food so bad as in the Southern United States. And, in this culinary desert, New Orleans beams as a bright oasis. But stacked up against any really (sic) center of cuisine, it couldn't compete.
>
> "That we are a citadel of culture. Quite untrue. The symphony is not one of the best and lives precariously from year to year from the neglect of all but handful of people in the city. No theater...no good bookstores, no ballet. The six operas given a year are pitiful. Again we look better than we are because of the surrounding Sahara of the beaux artes.
>
> "That we are a great port and distributing center. A port we are and will always be so long as the Mississippi drains the west central plain past our door. But the Dock Board finds itself in financial trouble, the wharves are not being maintained, traffic is moving to more vigorous and more realistic gulf ports. As for a distributing center... sheer nonsense. Twenty years ago Atlanta set out to be the distributing center for the Southeast and Dallas for the Southwest. And they have succeeded beyond their wildest dreams, leaving New Orleans a very tiny area to serve. New Orleans' leadership or lack of it in the past twenty years has promoted it from the first city of the south to about the tenth...using any realistic index, construction, bank deposits, power consumption...you name it...we are well down the list.
>
> "That the city's future is bright and rosy. Again, quite untrue. It is extremely shaky. The city's economy is a three legged stool...the port, the petro chemical industry which has grown up along the river from New Orleans to Baton Rouge, and the NASA space center which is dedicated to developing the vehicle which will hopefully put a man on the moon in this decade. The port as noted is declining, the petro chemical industry is owned and controlled from Eastern financial centers which drain off its profits from the area, and NASA suffers from periodic tremors which run through the whole economy when there is a threatened cutback in space activity. And such a cutback could happen any year.
>
> "And yet the average New Orleans, and indeed the most prominent citizens of the city, accept all these undocumented delusions as gospel truth.

"But of all the delusions held by New Orleans, Mardi Gras is the most fantastic. I doubt that anywhere in the world can one find such a vast number of people whose lives are ordered and regulated by a fervent dedication to unreality.

"The tourist sees only Mardi Gras day...But the Mardi Gras day that the visitor sees, is only the final climax, to a vast and complex year round delusion which has grown to the proportions of an important industry...The day one Mardi Gras is over, preparations begin for the next year. Floats and set designers, costume makers, painters and workmen get busily to work to see that next year surpasses this. After all they have only 365 days in which to work....

"Originally there were some twenty organizations which gave carnival balls during this period. These were relatively exclusive. It was only after world war two that people who could not get into any of these organizations began to form their own. And now there are some seventy five of them all trying to give balls more elaborate and expensive than the others.

"The real importance of the balls and the carvival (sic) organizations that stage them is they constitute the real pecking order of New Orleans. It is by your membership in what organizations that business men judge each other's importance. And the savage in-f9ghting (sic) among business tycoons to see who will be the kings and dukes of their organization for the annual ball has to be seen to be believed....

"All of which might be taken as more or less amusing social history...Except for the fact that some several thousand of the city's leaders are preo ccupied (sic) on almost a full time basis with this fantasy.

"They really forget that they are not REALLY dukes and kings and that their daughters are not REALLY queens. So that the unreality of the social order inevitably slops over into the business life and indeed all of the life of the city....

"The Boston Club is the citadel of power in New Orleans and their Carnival organization, called COMUS, is the most prestigious of all. To be king or queen of Comus is the ultimate honor the city has to offer....

"To give one an idea of the importance they attach to COMUS their carnival club, let me tell you a story.

"Some eight or ten years ago, the Duke and Dutchess of Windsor came to New Orleans forthe (sic) carnival. There was anguished debate within the club as to whether or not the Dutchess would be asked to curtsy to the queen of Comus. The medieval arguments as to how many angels could dance on the head of a pin was as nothing to it. Of course, she was a REAL duchess...But on the other had (sic) the Queen of Comus was a QUEEN. Finally a committee was formed to approach her grace, who, being a woman of good sense, said of course she would follow the local custom, and indeed did drop a deep curtsy when she was presented at court.

"In the meantime, a local official of the club had approached the city's rpotocal (sic) chief who was making arrangements for the visit and said the club would like to give a stag dinner for Windson (sic) on the night before Mardi Gras. This was agreed and the official gave the protocol chief a list of the twlve (sic) men who were to be invited. Since they seemed a not very homogenous group, the protocol chief asked politely why these particular twelve were to be invited. The official drew himself up and said that these were the only living ex-kings of Comus and they were theonly (sic) people suitable to dine with the ex king of England.

"So there it is...New Orleans...city of unreality of fantasy of paranoia. It is the only city in which the coutry (sic) where the incredible Garrison probe of the assassination could have happened. How Big Jim must have loved this city when he first arrived some 15 years ago from the somewhat less flamboyant lands of Iowa and Illinois. What a sense of homecoming he must have felt. How like a bacterium placed in his favorite culture.

"It remained only for him to set to work to warp this mad city to his own mad plans. And in fifteen years he has done a very good job of it."[2731]

Shaw ultimately chose to stay in New Orleans; he may have had no comparable alternative. Perhaps his acquittal, the halting of further prosecution by the Federal courts, and the job offer from the French Market Corporation all combined to weaken his negativity, although it is likely that a significant residue of those feelings remained with him.

**Shaw in a pensive mood in late life, probably early 1970s (Courtesy: National Archives)**

Meanwhile, the question of whether Shaw's civil suit could proceed against Garrison and others had stalled in a round of appeals. Garrison's office had appealed on the grounds of prosecutorial immunity, which was almost absolute in most cases. Courts had taken a dim view of efforts by acquitted defendants to sue the prosecutors who had tried them, fearing that it might open the door to multiple lawsuits, and make district attorneys hesitant to act in prosecuting crimes of any sort. However, in the fall of 1972, the U.S. Supreme Court cleared the way for Shaw's lawsuit to proceed, although it left the door open for the issue of prosecutorial immunity to be taken into account in various aspects of the case.

On September 27, International House librarian Mina Crais wrote Shaw, confirming his upcoming speech there on October 24, as part of the "Paul Fabry Speaks" series.[2732] A letter to Shaw on October 2, from Donald M. Soignet, thanked Shaw for his recent presentation on the development of the French Market Arena before the Louisiana Section of the American Chemical Society.[2733]

Lloyd Cobb passed away in the fall of 1972, and Captain J.W. Clark took his place as President of the International Trade Mart. At a meeting of the Executive Committee in mid-October 1973, a year following Cobb's death, his widow was given $1,000 per month for three years, with a recommendation that that monthly allowance continue after the three-year period if the Mart was financially sound.[2734]

Before Shaw's retirement in October 1965, the Mart had considered offering a salary of between $50,000 and $75,000 for a new Managing Director to replace him. However, as of the time of Lloyd Cobb's death in the fall of 1972, no Managing Director had been hired. Cobb held down the job of President of the organization, and also performed the Managing Director's duties, for a salary of $36,000 per year.[2735] Cobb had taken substantial time away from his law practice to actively manage the Mart over that period.

Some of the original plans for the plaza around the grounds of the new Mart tower were beginning to be realized at long last. Shaw received an invitation to a ceremony on October 25, where the ambassador of France and his wife dedicated the Place du France, and the unveiling of a statue of Joan of Arc.[2736] The installation and dedication of the long-awaited Spanish Plaza, which Shaw, Lloyd Cobb, Mario Bermúdez and others had worked so hard to secure, would not take place until after Shaw's death.

In early November 1972, Leonard Haertter, the St. Louis travel agency owner who had planned the Mediterranean cruise for Shaw and Edith Stern, wrote that he was arranging a trip for the St. Louis Symphony to New Orleans, and wanted Shaw's advice about seeing the city. Shaw mentioned taking a boat on the Mississippi River, having cocktails and dinner at the Plimsoll Club at the top of the new Mart, and seeing the Oak Alley Plantation, located just outside of New Orleans.[2737]

On November 13, 1972, Shaw spoke to the alumni chapter of Phi Mu fraternity at Newcomb College regarding the French Market project.[2738] Also in mid-November, he was invited to be interviewed, as one of a number of people, by twenty-two New Orleans broadcasters as part of the license renewal process of the Greater New Orleans Broadcasters Association, held at the Howard Johnson hotel. Shaw was asked to discuss the question, "What, in your opinion, are the problems, needs and interests of this community?"[2739]

Shaw's attorneys had advised him that there was only a very slim chance that the U.S. Supreme Court would even hear Garrison's office's appeal from the decision by the U.S. Fifth Circuit Court of Appeals upholding the enjoinment of further prosecution. On November 21, 1972, the Supreme Court declined to hear the appeal. The decision effectively ended the possibility of any further criminal prosecution against Shaw related to the Kennedy assassination. A newspaper article in the *Times-Picayune* quoted Shaw as saying that he had been confident of the decision by the Court, but that it was still a "load off his back" to have it in official form. Shaw was critical of the wealthy financial contributors to Garrison's prosecution, whom he now was suing, and of the grand jury system that had investigated him, although he acknowledged that he did not know how to appropriately change the legal system. Shaw said, "They say that ages 54 to 59 are the golden years; they weren't for me." Jim Garrison called the Supreme Court decision "the final nail in John Kennedy's coffin," saying that it completed a "circle of deception" by the Federal government, and brought "to an end the only honest official inquiry" into the assassination.[2740]

Over the years, various published comments have estimated the amount Shaw had spent on his defense, usually very inexactly; author James Kirkwood's estimate has been discussed earlier. The figures, which reached legendary status in their retelling, were freely circulated as if assumed to be accurate. An article in the *States-Item* on March 17, 1972 mentioned a recent paper by Tulane University professor Bennett H. Wall. Wall said that Shaw's lawyers took no fee at all, and that his investigative expenses had totaled approximately $250,000.[2741] As can be seen from court filings related to Shaw's civil suit, expenses totaled far less than that amount, and his lawyers did in fact collect total legal fees of $22,500, split among three of the four attorneys who defended him.

Ralph L. Kaskell, Jr., a member of the firm of Deutsch, Kerrigan and Stiles, wrote a letter of congratulations to Edward Wegmann about the U.S. Supreme Court decision, and Wegmann's work on the case; Wegmann copied the letter on to Shaw.[2742] It was somewhat ironic that a member of the firm that had so ably defended the legal positions of Garrison's office against Shaw over a five-and-a-half year period had so directly shown a measure of approval for the actions of the opposing attorney. It could have been an indication that some members of the legal profession who found themselves in the position of opposing Shaw over the years felt that the law might have been on their side, but their sympathies were with him, nevertheless.

Lois Kirkpatrick wrote Shaw on November 24, 1972, confirming her recent call about his upcoming speech on December 4 to the Vieux Carré Action Association. In the letter, Kirkpatrick apologized for calling Shaw on "such an important day." In view of the proximity to the Supreme Court decision refusing to hear the prosecution's appeal in Shaw's criminal case, it is probable Kirkpatrick was referring to that date.[2743]

Holland McCombs wrote regarding the recent Supreme Court decision. Shaw responded that Garrison was "mad," but that "no one has put the net over him yet," quoting George Bernard Shaw, and commenting that he had had a recent letter from Charles Nutter regarding his lawsuit against Garrison. Shaw ended by saying that he did not know how much he would get, "if anything," from the civil action.[2744]

George Gaston Johnston wrote from his new residence in Rio de Janeiro, Brazil, also commenting on the Supreme Court decision. Shaw indicated that he might get an offer on his lawsuit, but he did not know how much, "if anything," he would get. Johnston noted how favorably Rio was acting on his physical ailments, and added, mysteriously, that the next time he was in New Orleans he would take Shaw to Brennan's restaurant, "which has always been the post at which the plot thickened."[2745] The latter sentence was undoubtedly a reference to Shaw's encounter with Garrison and his wife, Liz, during which Garrison and his wife had become involved in a physical altercation. It may also have been a reference to the other rumors about happenings at Brennan's, with varying degrees of confrontation between Shaw and Garrison, that have circulated for some years.

Shaw's optimism about the civil suit varied over the months and years. At times during 1972, he told friends that he might get as much as $1,000,000 in a settlement of the suit. At other times, he was less certain of getting anything. He must have known it was a tough pursuit, even as he must have known that he had little choice but to pursue it; it was too much a part of his psyche by now to consider dropping it altogether.

Mrs. Edwin S. "Frances" Anderson wrote from Amite, Louisiana, following the Supreme Court decision. She wished him a happy "Alleluia Day," and apparently shipped some type of amusing wastebasket as a gift for Shaw.[2746] Shaw replied on December 27, thanking her for the gift, saying that it reminded him of the "final conclusion" of his case. Shaw indicated that his mother had been delighted by Frances Anderson's recent visit, and Shaw said that he hoped to meet her soon, but was heading to the West Coast for business later in the week.[2747]

In late November 1972, the poet and songwriter Rod McKuen played a concert in New Orleans, and invited Shaw to it. However, Shaw was otherwise occupied that evening, and notified McKuen that he could not make it.[2748]

Long after Shaw's legal troubles were over, and continuing until today, many believed that if Shaw was not guilty of any type of conspiracy in the Kennedy assassination, that he definitely knew Oswald and/or Ferrie, and therefore was guilty of perjury for his trial testimony denying those associations. Even the writer Gore Vidal once commented to the author, "I talked a good deal about him [Shaw] with Jimmy Kirkwood who told me that Clay had seen Oswald, hustling, he thought, in a fag bar but there was no further contact."[2749] The author wrote to Vidal several years later to clarify those remarks, and Vidal responded that, "Clay, speaking in retrospect, never said he knew or spoke to Oswald but, 'I think I may have seen this ex-Marine hustling in a gay bar'."[2750] The author reviewed James Kirkwood's papers at Boston University in some detail, but found no reference in which Shaw told Kirkwood he had seen Oswald in any capacity.

In mid-December 1972, Shaw wrote to Princess Jacqueline de Chimay, saying that he had read her sketch of *The Widow Cliquot*. Shaw commented that she had taken her husband's death very hard, and that she thought that somehow it had ended her life, too. He said that, "Your tribute to him is a beautiful thing, a spiritual garland of love and devotion." Shaw commented "how extraordinary that he should arouse such devotion from people from such varied walks of life."[2751]

An indication of the fluid nature of New Orleans political and legal activities took place when, in December, Jim Garrison wrote a letter to the Louisiana State Bar Association in support of the re-instatement of Dean Andrews's license to practice law. In the letter, Garrison downplayed Andrews's role in the entire Kennedy assassination case as "minor,"[2752] even though his office had vigorously pursued Andrews through three sets of perjury charges, convicting him once. With the Shaw criminal case seemingly behind him for good after the Supreme Court decision in November, and Shaw's civil suit still in front of him, Garrison had decided to let bygones be bygones regarding Dean Andrews.

With Shaw's highly unusual criminal case now permanently behind him, the local chapter of the American Civil Liberties Union (ACLU) invited him to speak at its annual meeting. On December 27, 1972, Shaw wrote to Paulette Rittenberg of the New Orleans chapter, confirming his upcoming speech on February 18, 1973. Shaw, who was offered his choice of topic for his talk, chose "The Law's Delay–The Insolence of Office."[2753]

At the end of the year, Shaw received from architect August Perez III a book called *The Last Line*, a history of the St. Charles Avenue streetcar. Shaw noted that he had grown up on Banks Street in the Third Ward of New Orleans, and that the streetcar had been "part and parcel" of his childhood and adolescence.[2754]

Shaw's 1972 Federal income tax return showed salaried income of $23,000 from the French Market Corporation. That salary approximated the salary he had earned at the Mart in the early 1960s, up until his last year or so of tenure there, when construction of the new Mart tower was progressing, although some years of notable inflation had intervened. For the 1972 return, Shaw showed no income from his activities as a playwright, or as a lecturer, indicating that his speaking activities of 1969-71 had dried up.[2755] As he had commented in his January 1971 interview with CBS newsman Foster Davis, he was the "forgotten man."

# 31 · The Beginning of the End

During 1973, Shaw continued his schedule of speeches from 1972. However, the number decreased somewhat, as he took time off for health reasons. Almost all of the speeches dealt with the progress at the French Market Complex. A letter to Shaw on January 5 from George Connoly, Jr. confirmed Shaw's upcoming speech on February 2, before the Civic Council of New Orleans.[2756] On January 10, Keith A. Bordelon, Vice-President of Delta Sigma Pi fraternity, wrote Shaw confirming his speech before the Chapter on February 7, at Louisiana State University of New Orleans (now University of New Orleans).[2757] On February 6, Shaw wrote to Max Barnett, confirming his speech before the Kiwanis Club of New Orleans; the subject of his speech was the "New French Market Complex."[2758] On February 19, Shaw wrote to George E. Kollasch, of the Gentilly Insurance Agency, confirming his speech before the Gentilly Rotary Club at Vista Shores Club.[2759]

Some of the individuals and organizations that swirled around Jim Garrison's investigation into the Kennedy assassination later crossed paths with the Mart. Although Ed Butler with the conservative, anti-Communist Information Council of the Americas (INCA) organization had no major interaction with Shaw during his tenure at the Mart, it was later discussed that the Mart should perhaps support INCA. At a meeting of the Executive Committee in mid-January 1973, Captain J.W. Clark, the current President of the Mart, indicated that the Mart and INCA had common goals.[2760] A week earlier, at another Executive Committee meeting, it was mentioned that Louis Gurvich, brother of former Garrison investigator, and later Shaw supporter, William Gurvich, had been hired by the Mart to evaluate security for the organization.[2761]

On February 18, Shaw spoke to the New Orleans chapter of the American Civil Liberties Union. The ACLU had provided Shaw with very little help during his case. However, Shaw's chief criminal defense attorney, Irvin Dymond, had resisted having the ACLU become involved, probably because he feared the negative publicity attached to the ACLU at the time in New Orleans and much of the South, and possibly because he felt his own talents would be enough to carry Shaw's defense, if he was allowed to work properly.

Meanwhile, the defendants in the civil lawsuits filed by Shaw had propounded interrogatories to Shaw and his attorneys. In February, Edward Wegmann wrote to Malcolm Monroe of the Deutsch, Kerrigan and Stiles firm, asking for an extension of time to file answers to the initial set of interrogatories. In the letter, Wegmann mentioned settlement talks with one of the defendants.[2762] Monroe responded that he had no knowledge of any such talks related to settlement, and that he understood that any such talks that had been held had broken down. He did not agree to an extension, and reminded Wegmann that the answers were due on March 3.[2763]

Shaw's answers to the initial interrogatories in the civil suit were filed in early March 1973. His attorneys objected to many of the questions, and eventually an amended and supplemental set of answers was filed on July 17, 1974, approximately a month before Shaw's death. The judge in the case had ruled that some of the questions had to be answered, including ones about whether dried blood had been on the whips seized in Shaw's apartment, and the purpose of the hooks in the ceiling beams in Shaw's bedroom.[2764]

Shaw received the usual round of birthday greetings for his sixtieth birthday on March 17, 1973. Sally and Warren Galjour wrote from Brooklyn, New York. Carmen and Elena

Martinez, old friends from the International Trade Mart/International House days, wrote as well. Patrick Vaughn, a young man from Birmingham, Alabama, wrote that, "Fate brought us together again" recently, and that he "enjoyed the hour or so together." Vaughn closed by saying, "Please plan to use your key whenever. Love, Pat." Fred O'Bryan, whom Shaw had known since speaking at a small Catholic college in Mobile, Alabama during the 1960s, wrote that he could not make it to Carnival that year, but that he hoped to get down to New Orleans soon.[2765] Shaw generally replied to all birthday greetings that year that the "kindest thing" or "best thing" to do was to "overlook birthdays at my age."

In mid-March, Edward Wegmann wrote to Gordon Novel, asking if he would testify for Shaw in his civil suit against Garrison and others; the letter was returned.[2766] The elusive Novel would eventually make his way back to New Orleans by the mid-1970s, where he would become involved in serious criminal charges related to a supposed plot to commit arson on a downtown building. Ironically, Novel would be represented at trial by none other than Jim Garrison, who had pursued Novel so relentlessly, and faced off with him in a large civil suit, only a few years before.

Cash flow continued to be an issue for Shaw, and he was still dependent upon receiving rental payments from his tenants. Virginia Kirk had inherited properties owned by her sister, Artelle Trelford, along with the two notes Mrs. Trelford owed to Shaw, the former owner of the properties. Years before, Shaw had commented, in the diary that he kept after his arrest, how Virginia Kirk had constantly intruded in her sister's life, a phenomenon he had dubbed "tyranny of the weak." On May 17, 1973, Shaw wrote to Kirk, indicating that he was going into the hospital soon, and that he needed her payments on the mortgage, of which four payments were currently due, as soon as possible.[2767] Kirk replied to Shaw the next day, saying that she was selling the house, and that everything in it except the pictures would go with the sale.[2768]

Shaw's combination of health issues began to form the deadly force that accelerated rapidly beginning at the end of 1973. Shaw's calendar for 1973 showed that in mid-May of that year, he had a scan of his liver and spleen, and X-rays of his colon.[2769] A statement to Shaw from Ochsner Foundation, covering the period of May 21 to June 9, 1973, showed several pages of charges for various medicines and tests, including a brain scan, a lung test and stomach tests.[2770] The statement for June 7, 1973 indicates charges for field supervolt radiation, used for cancer treatment.[2771]

In a letter in June 1973 to some friends who had taken him out for a recent boating expedition on Lake Ponchartrain, Shaw indicated that it had been a perfect day, and thanked them for the photos of the occasion. Shaw informed them that he had since become ill with two bleeding ulcers. Doctors, he said, had advised him not to have any alcohol, which he said "annoys me greatly," and they had placed him on a "dull diet."[2772]

In another letter to Virginia Kirk, Shaw mentioned his illness, his abstention from alcohol, and indicated that he had to "drink a toast with Grade A Milk." He thanked Kirk for her response in paying rent, indicating that his "medical bills add up."[2773]

By late 1972, Shaw had purchased a property at 1027 Toulouse Street. Around that same time, he had attended a zoning hearing to appeal a covenant that any new construction on the property had to be the same as the type that already existed. Shaw had been unable to attend an earlier meeting of the Vieux Carré Commission that occurred in mid-September 1972, because he was on the cruise with Edith Stern. Shaw was interested in demolishing one of the buildings on the property, and rebuilding in some fashion. In mid-February 1973, Shaw wrote to the fire department, saying that he would demolish a portion of the slave quarters building, then seal and replace the deteriorated balconies on the roof as required.[2774] Shaw's 1973 desk calendar shows a note on April 24, 1973 that the property at 1000 Toulouse "must be torn down immediately."[2775] In late April 1973, Wayne Collier of the Vieux Carré Commission, a division of the City of New Orleans, wrote to Shaw, indicating that the building on the property was to be demolished to the first floor, and the wall on the property was to be reduced to the height of the wall on the adjacent property.[2776] The demolition of the slave quarters and wall took place from April 25 to April 29, 1973.[2777] By mid-June 1973, the Vieux Carré Commission had ordered the wall on the North Rampart Street side of the property to be repaired.[2778]

Peter Panno, who owned an adjacent property at 610 North Rampart Street, wrote Shaw on June 28 requesting that the wall be brought down to eight feet, saying that otherwise it could fall on his property.[2779] Shaw obtained an estimate for demolishing the wall from Ricco Demolishing Corporation, which he turned into his insurance company.[2780] The insurance company denied coverage for the demolition, saying that the wall had already sunk by eighteen inches. When the demolition actually was carried out later in the summer, damage was done to a large brick wall on the adjacent property owned by Panno. As a result of that, Panno claimed $1,162 of damages against Shaw and others.[2781] The dispute over the cost claimed by Panno would be unresolved at the time of Shaw's death.

In the meantime, the Gervais Favrot Company had rented 2,400 square feet of the extreme rear right-hand corner of Shaw's property to use for the storage of masonry materials, adjacent to the Vieux Carré Hotel. Gervais Favrot rented the property until the end of February 1974, at which time it canceled the rental agreement, which had increased from $240 per month to $500 per month over the lifespan as more space was needed.[2782]

Shaw continued to hear from people who had participated in one aspect or another of his criminal case. William Gurvich sent Shaw a greeting card that showed a man holding a green ball in each hand. The caption read, "Know what you'd have if you had a big green ball in each hand?" If one turned the page of the card, the inside revealed a very angry Jolly Green Giant with the caption, "You'd have the Jolly Green Giant madder than hell." The allusion, of course, was to Jim Garrison, the 6'6" district attorney who was popularly referred to by that nickname.

After starting with the French Market project, Shaw had resumed his participation in numerous civic events, as he had in the old days with the Mart. On July 14, 1973, he attended a reception for the Consul General of France at the Plimsoll Club at the top of the new Mart building.

Shaw had become somewhat friendly with the famous playwright Tennessee Williams during the early 1970s, when Williams took a place near Shaw in the French Quarter. It is unclear if Shaw knew Williams earlier, when Williams had been in New Orleans during the 1940s, and if so, how well. Probably not well at all, as writer James Leo Herlihy had encouraged Shaw to associate with Williams when Williams moved back to New Orleans in the early 1970s, indicating to Shaw how interesting a person Williams could be to hang around with. Shaw's datebook indicates several meetings for cocktails with Williams during the early 1970s, and Williams's various papers demonstrate knowing Shaw during that period as well. The two men had something in common, as they were both aging gay men whose youth had gradually, and almost imperceptibly, slipped away, and whose careers had passed their peaks. Williams's best days of playwriting, or at least his days of best reviews, had slipped by him as of the mid-1960s, around the same time that Shaw retired from the Mart and entered the long, dark period of his life. In addition, love and sexual activity no longer came so easily to either man. In a letter to his agent, Bill Barnes, in July 1973, Williams commented that, "A homosexual at my age had to put love back in his pocket like a key to a house whose address he has forgotten.[2783]

Even as Shaw was dealing with health issues in the summer of 1973, Jeff Biddison was beginning to struggle with his own. Biddison developed heart problems early, and eventually became one of the early recipients of a heart transplant. In response to a Mississippi friend, Thomas Jefferson Young, who had written to see if Biddison had retained some pictures of him taken in Dallas years before, Shaw replied that Biddison no longer had the pictures, that they had been "swallowed by the maw of time." Shaw indicated that Biddison had recently bought Marilyn Tate's real estate company, but that his health was not good. Young had expressed concern about whether he had the correct mailing address for Shaw, as Shaw had moved around so much in recent years; Shaw assured him that after the last five years, mail reached him "at any address."[2784]

Shaw took a trip to North Carolina in late July to visit the Formyduvals in Whiteville, North Carolina.[2785] Even though William Henry Formyduval was no longer a regular visitor to New Orleans, and not as close to Shaw as he once had been, Shaw remained on excellent terms with the larger family.

Shaw's 1973 calendar shows visits with Carl Cramer, the local sculptor who had created a posthumous bust of Theodore Brent in 1953, and Layton Martens, who had played such an important role in the Garrison investigation, having known both Shaw and Ferrie. Shaw also met with Marty Shambra, the restaurateur known for owning establishments that allowed gay couples to dine in a friendly environment.[2786]

On August 6, Leonard J. Salathe of the Institute of Internal Auditors wrote Shaw, confirming his speech at their upcoming meeting at International House.[2787] On August 10, Shaw met with actor Val Dufour, formerly of New Orleans, and now somewhat prominent in soap operas.[2788]

During this period, Shaw continued to work on his long-delayed project about Antonio de Ulloa, the first Spanish governor of Louisiana. Shaw's friend Chuck Deville, residing in Princeton, New Jersey, sent Shaw an article about Spanish Louisiana history for Shaw's use on the project.[2789]

On August 29, Shaw entertained Gordon Novel, who had been actively involved in Shaw's case in his own peculiar way, and in other events surrounding Garrison's investigation in 1967.[2790] Novel now had known Shaw for well over a decade, and had communicated with him at odd intervals while Shaw had been under indictment, and Novel had been on the run from Garrison.

Pancho Rodriguez, Tennessee Williams's one-time companion from the 1940s, who remained a friend and correspondent with Williams for the next four decades, kept a journal wherein he recorded some associations of Shaw and Williams. On September 22, 1973, he and Williams and Victor Campbell, Williams's current lover, went to Shaw's apartment at 1024 St. Peter Street. Rodriguez commented, "How charming and gracious is Clay Shaw. And what an expensive, luxurious apartment he has. It's done in impeccable taste." The four of them went out to dinner that night and "Clay and Tennessee talked and we listened." Rodriguez said that Shaw suggested that "Tennessee re-read *The Tempest* by Shakespeare" and that Williams talked about "The Red Devil Battery Sign," his new play set in Texas, which began on the day Ruby shot Oswald. Williams also commented that night about the memoirs he was planning to write, which he said would be about his love life, and "must be the truth." Shaw indicated that he supported the idea of "publish it and be damned!" even if a prominent name had to be mentioned; Williams agreed with that assessment.[2791]

A review of Shaw's medical bills in October 1973 showed that he had X-rays taken during the month, as well as radiation therapy.[2792] He met with famous jazz musician Al Hirt on October 4 and with Layton Martens on October 8.[2793]

Shaw had kept in touch with Marty Cocita, the cab driver who had befriended him in 1967 during the worst of his post-arrest days. He had attended the wedding of at least one of Cocita's children, and in October 1973 he enclosed a small check for newborn Anthony Cocita, son of Lori and Louis Cocita, and Marty's grandson.[2794]

On November 12, Shaw wrote to Cynthia Wegmann, daughter of his attorney Edward Wegmann, saying that he would not be able to attend a celebration being held soon in her honor, because his mother had recently had eye surgery, and he had to spend every weekend with her.[2795] His mother would be deceased before the end of 1973.

In mid-November, author James Kirkwood's mother, the silent film actress Lila Lee, passed away. Shaw had met her in Key West, Florida in the spring of 1971, after Kirkwood's book about the trial had appeared. Shaw wrote Kirkwood expressing his sympathies, saying that his mother was "an individual."[2796] Kirkwood answered shortly with a letter thanking Shaw for his sentiments, and commenting, "Still, what a wrench it is when death comes. Oh, the wonder and the finality of it."[2797]

On November 26, Shaw wrote to Edward Wegmann, urging him to proceed more quickly with the civil suit, and referencing the Supreme Court decision more than a year before that had allowed the suit to proceed. Shaw gently took Wegmann to task for not pushing the lawsuit faster, and compared Wegmann's excuse that he had several other cases going on at the same time to a doctor who let one patient die while attending to an interesting, but much more minor, medical situation with another patient. Shaw mentioned the possibility of having a meeting with Wegmann, his brother William Wegmann, and Sal Panzeca, to discuss the suit, and to determine if they were still interested in handling the case.[2798] Shaw must have known at the time that his health was a major issue, and perhaps he even knew that his time was limited, even if he did not know the severity of what was ahead. For that reason, the civil suit must have taken on an additional urgency to him at that time, even beyond the fact that it had been more than three and a half years since it initially had been filed.

Shaw had tried to prompt Wegmann regarding the civil suit earlier during 1973. On August 14, he had written Wegmann, enclosing a clipping from a rural newspaper of a column written by Nicholas R. Murray. The article had appeared on July 18, 1973, but was a reprint of a column originally published on March 14, 1969, not long after Shaw's conspiracy trial had ended. Murray, who knew Shaw and many members of his family, opined that Shaw had been set up to an unknowing Garrison by the real conspirators in the Kennedy assassination, but that Shaw was innocent nevertheless. The column also indicated that many thought Shaw was guilty, and that Garrison had been right about him all along, which was the point Shaw was making to Wegmann—his reputation had been severely damaged by the ordeal.[2799]

In late November, Shaw's old employee Jesse Core sent him a book about Vermont folk medicine. Core had kept in touch with Shaw to some degree over the years since Shaw had retired from the Mart, even as Core had assisted Jim Garrison with public relations work. Shaw replied that 1973 had been a bad year for him healthwise, recounting a savage attack of London flu that he had in January, and his two bleeding ulcers in spring and summer.[2800]

In mid-August, Shaw had attended a dinner for Harry Connick, Sr, who was running again for district attorney against Jim Garrison. Shaw, understandably, was one of the financial contributors to Connick's campaign. Shaw had coffee with Connick on September 9, at the patio at 1025 Chartres Street. In December, Connick would defeat Jim Garrison, in the closest election for district attorney in New Orleans history.[2801] Connick had lost badly to Garrison in November 1969, even though Shaw's trial had ended poorly for Garrison. This time around, Garrison's own criminal troubles had sacked his popularity, even though he, too, had been acquitted. Apparently, the electorate could forgive him for a losing effort in trying to solve the assassination, but not for the appearance of corruption. Garrison had served twelve years as district attorney.

As of early December, Shaw again was planning a trip to Mexico for Carnival week, this time with his friend Patrick O'Rourke from Chicago. The idea was to fly to Merida, in the Yucatan Peninsula, then take the train to Veracruz in time for Carnival.[2802] However, it was not to be.

In mid-December, Shaw had a brain scan and further X-rays at Ochsner Clinic.[2803] He also accompanied Tennessee Williams to his own doctor. Williams wrote to his agent Bill Barnes that he recently had "got myself out to Ochsner Clinic, escorted by the eminent Clay

Shaw, for a checkup by a very nice old gay doctor there who even examined my balls."[2804]

Shaw's mother then passed away, and he was occupied over the Christmas holidays of 1973 with going to Hammond, Louisiana, and settling her estate. Shaw already had reflected that 1973 had not been a very good year for him, especially healthwise. His mother's death ended it on an even more tragic note.

As of the end of 1973, the ledger for Vieux Carré Restorations, the company Shaw had started as he picked up his real estate activities again, showed an equity balance of almost $90,000 in one account, and more than $20,500 in another account, indicating that the equity Shaw had in his properties had survived over the years, even as his cash had been substantially reduced.[2805]

At his trial, Shaw had testified that he had never worked for the Central Intelligence Agency, which could be regarded as technically correct, as he had never been an employee and had received no compensation. Prosecutor James Alcock had asked no questions on cross-examination about that subject, indicating that Garrison's office either did not know about Shaw's connection as an information contact for the CIA's Domestic Contact Division, or had no hard proof if Shaw's attorneys challenged them on that point. However, in at least one interview, conducted in October 1967 with Gordon Donaldson of Canadian Broadcasting Company, Shaw had denied ever having any connection at all with the CIA, which was clearly incorrect. On December 21, 1973, Zodiac News Service of California issued a news release, apparently based on information supplied by Victor Marchetti, a former CIA administrative employee who recently had co-authored a book about his time with the agency, saying that Shaw had been a paid CIA contact, and that Shaw and Ferrie had both worked in the Bay of Pigs operation[2806] (In a deposition before the Rockefeller Commission investigating the CIA approximately eighteen months later, Marchetti, hinting that he had been misquoted by the news service, would describe Shaw more accurately as a traveling businessman who had been interviewed by the CIA for informational purposes). Remarkably, no major news organization followed up on the press release, and there is no indication that Shaw was ever questioned about it. Perhaps his preoccupation with his mother's death and the resulting responsibilities kept him from offering his response. And as 1973 turned into 1974, he soon began having a series of health problems that would result in his death in August of that year. Therefore, his possible reaction to the news soon passed with him.

Others in the international trade field in New Orleans, including some in both the Mart building and International House, were sources for the CIA as well. One of those was William George Gaudet, who published the newsletter *Latin American Reports*, which had an office in the Mart from the very beginning of operations into the 1960s. Gaudet had provided information to the CIA based on his travels throughout Central America, South America, and the Caribbean, during the 1940s. In early 1950, Gaudet signed a Secrecy Agreement with the CIA and entered into a new arrangement through which he would supply reports on specified Latin American topics to the CIA, upon its request; his services were provided at cost to the Agency. The Secrecy Agreement that Gaudet signed indicated that he could not reveal his relationship with the Agency without prior permission, under penalty of law as designated by the Espionage Act; no exceptions to that requirement were mentioned in the agreement.[2807] The Secrecy Agreement had been recommended by CIA employee Sheffield Edwards, who would, in 1960, be one of the major CIA figures involved in the attempts to use members of organized crime to recruit an assassin to kill Cuban President Fidel Castro.

Another internal CIA memo said that William George Gaudet had been approved for contact by the agency in 1948, and that the CIA had later paid him for special reports compiled, again at the CIA's request, from 1950 to March of 1953. He then had been re-approved for contact up to the "Secret" level, but there was no record of how long the contact had been maintained, or if there had been any clandestine assignments.[2808] It appears, however, that Gaudet's only use was his knowledge of Latin American affairs.

In January 1976, Jackson R. Horton, Chief of the Domestic Collection Division within the CIA, told the Senate committee investigating the CIA, known as the Church Committee, that William Gaudet had been a source for the New Orleans Domestic Collection Division from 1948 to 1955, providing information about South American political and economic conditions. He had also, from 1955 to 1961, furnished fragmentary intelligence to the Agency about similar conditions. Horton said that Gaudet had tried to obtain loans from the CIA to support his publications dealing with Latin America, and the connection had ended in 1961.[2809] That same month in 1976, a time when the Church Committee's investigation had been in the news almost daily for the previous year, Gaudet gave an interview to a newspaper reporter where he insisted that he had "joined" the CIA in 1947 and served with them until 1969.[2810]

During the late 1970s, when the House Select Committee on Assassinations (HSCA) was reviewing CIA activity with regard to the Kennedy assassination, it requested from the CIA's Legislative Counsel a release from any prior secrecy obligations for, among others, William Gaudet, so that those individuals, including Gaudet, could answer any questions HSCA had for them. Lyle Miller, the CIA's Legislative Counsel, confirmed that Gaudet had been involved with the CIA only in a minor way, but Miller added that Gaudet had not executed a Secrecy Agreement with the CIA, contradicting the assertion in an earlier CIA internal memo that Gaudet had executed such an agreement. In any case, the CIA freed Gaudet to fully answer all questions put to him by HSCA. However, it also urged HSCA to respect the confidential nature of Gaudet's past relationship with the agency, unless Gaudet chose to make it public.[2811] Gaudet had chosen to make it public earlier, although in a somewhat exaggerated manner.

Many researchers into the Kennedy assassination had long awaited the flood of governmental documents that would eventually be released in the 1990s. Many of the documents concerned intelligence gathering organizations, such as the FBI or the CIA, and researchers poured through the documents, attempting to find ones that would connect Oswald, Ruby, Shaw, Ferrie, and others to one of the intelligence agencies. In some cases, they were successful, but only to a tantalizing extent, as in the case of Shaw. In the case of Ferrie, for instance, there was no definite connection to be found, and the CIA always has denied any connection with Ferrie.

In looking for a paper trail of CIA connections, it is important to remember that the details of one of the most secret CIA operations of all time were, initially, never put down on paper. In 1960, the CIA, using its Office of Security, which normally checked the backgrounds of job applicants, potential sources, and others, rather than its Department of Plans, which normally carried out covert operations, approached private investigator Robert Maheu, who had handled independent contracting assignments for the Office of Security, asking him to find individuals who could assassinate Cuban President Fidel Castro. Maheu knew John Roselli, a Las Vegas mobster, and approached him about the assignment. Roselli met with CIA employee James O'Connell and agreed to the job, although he was not told officially that he would be working on behalf of the CIA. Roselli introduced O'Connell to Chicago mobster Sam Giancana, who in turn introduced him to his Tampa counterpart Santos Trafficante. Giancana and Trafficante were supposed to find a Cuban who would be in a position to assassinate Castro. The effort lasted some months, without success, and eventually evolved into a more widespread program to overthrow Castro, and possibly assassinate him as well. The initial operation began under the Eisenhower administration, and was separate from the Bay of Pigs Invasion.

Apparently, Robert Maheu told Roselli that he was working for the CIA, and Roselli passed that information on to Giancana and Trafficante. Up to that point, no details of the operation had been put down on paper within the CIA. However, during the course of the operation, Giancana had become concerned that entertainer Dan Rowan, later of *Rowan and Martin's Laugh-In* fame, was carrying on with Giancana's girlfriend at the time, singer Phyllis McGuire, in Las Vegas, while Giancana was back in Chicago. Accordingly, Giancana asked Maheu for assistance in recording conversations that took place in Rowan's hotel room in Las Vegas. Maheu requested that the CIA cover the costs of the operation, since he was helping them with the Castro assassination plot, and apparently the CIA consented to that arrangement. While the bugs were being installed in Rowan's room, however, hotel security caught the individuals Maheu had subcontracted to perform the task, and they were arrested and indicted.

Several years later, when Sam Giancana was coming up for trial in Chicago on a matter, he threatened to expose the CIA's Castro assassination operation if the charges were not dropped. Accordingly, Sheffield Edwards, the CIA employee who had supervised O'Connell in the operation but had never met any of the Mafia figures, had to visit Attorney General Robert Kennedy along with CIA General Counsel Lawrence Houston. Together, the two explained the history of the operation to Kennedy, and why it would not be prudent to prosecute Giancana. Years later, in a deposition before the Church Committee, CIA counsel Lawrence Houston recalled the low-slung eyes and cold gaze of Bobby Kennedy as he instructed the CIA employees to always inform him in advance of any such operation in the future. As a result of the meeting with Kennedy, Edwards had to write a memo for Kennedy's benefit that spoke in veiled terms of the Castro assassination operation. This marked the first time anything had been put down on paper about the operation.

Several years later, mobster John Roselli was threatened with deportation by the U.S. government. He also attempted to use the Castro assassination operation as leverage to help his case. However, this time the CIA decided to ignore him, and Roselli, working through his Washington attorney Robert Morgan, leaked the information to newspaper columnist Drew Pearson, who then contacted Supreme Court Chief Justice Earl Warren about it. Warren, who had served as head of the Warren Commission investigating Kennedy's assassination, was intrigued by the story. Accordingly, Drew Pearson and his assistant, Jack Anderson, wrote a column explaining the CIA plots to kill Castro. The matter was buzzed about in the press in March of 1967, the very time Shaw's arrest was breaking in the news. President Johnson, alarmed by reports of the assassination operation that he had known nothing about, ordered the CIA's Inspector General's office to generate a detailed report of the CIA's activities regarding assassinations of heads of foreign states. That report was released in 1967; a copy was given to Johnson, and a copy was retained by the Agency. Now, the full details of the operation were down on paper, with some inaccuracies. For example, the report indicated that CIA employee James O'Connell, who had actually met with the mobsters, was unaware in advance of the effort to bug entertainer Dan Rowan's hotel room in Las Vegas. Years later, then-CIA Director William Colby would inform the Rockefeller Commission, another commission that in 1975 was looking into CIA activities, that O'Connell had known in advance of the bugging operation done as a favor to Sam Giancana.

Several years later, in 1970, John Roselli again threatened to reveal everything about the Castro assassination operation if no legal help was given to him in his deportation case. Roselli now was under indictment for an illegal gambling case in California, and had requested that charge be dropped as well. However, the CIA once again refused to go along with the pressure Roselli was applying to them, so Roselli released more details, which made their way to columnist Jack Anderson, who wrote columns about the subject that appeared in January and February 1971.

Among the other New Orleans citizens used by the CIA over the years was Guy Persac Johnson, who had served as Clay Shaw's initial chief defense lawyer during the week after Shaw's arrest, prior to Irvin Dymond taking over the job. Johnson had been used in Guam as a contract agent some years before.[2812] Dr. Alton Ochsner had also been of contact interest for the CIA in 1947 and 1948, and had been a cleared source for them from mid-1955 to early 1962.[2813]

David Baldwin, of course, had been a covert employee at one time. Irvin Dymond also had a connection with the agency that has never been explained. CIA files on Baldwin and Dymond are still unavailable for review. Baldwin, being a former employee, falls into a special category, as the agency rarely releases employee files.

The CIA had also conducted other activities in New Orleans, including a mail monitoring and opening program for a brief time during the mid-1950s. The size of the program, which was run through the U.S. Customs Service, was nowhere near the size of a similar operation in New York City, where 215,000 pieces of mail to and from Moscow had been photographed, along with 2,000,000 mail package exteriors (covers). Twenty-eight million pieces of mail had passed through the New York program, which was entitled HTLINGUAL.

Gordon Novel was another person involved around Garrison's investigation who claimed to have CIA connections. In 1967, Novel requested a job interview with the CIA. He was given an interview on December 22, 1967, but the CIA declined to employ him, or to continue the job application process.[2814] Later, Novel refused to answer certain questions during his deposition related to his civil suit against Garrison and *Playboy* magazine, citing the 1947 National Security Act as if he was a CIA employee. *Playboy's* attorney then filed a motion with the court, requesting the CIA to provide an official indication that Novel was not employed with the agency. Novel, perhaps sensing that he was being outflanked, requested the same thing from his side of the lawsuit, in what the CIA speculated was a clever effort on Novel's part to prove his "connection" with the Agency by getting it to deny such a connection.

Novel sometimes approached the New Orleans office with proposals, threatening to go to the Director of the CIA if he was refused. Peter Houck, who was in charge of the New Orleans office from the late 1960s forward, sometimes was contacted directly by Novel to verify or deny his association with the Agency. A 1975 memo on Novel's approach to the New Orleans office said that, "We would not recommend Novel for any operational undertaking."[2815]

In July 1975, while applying for a telephone connection with Southwestern Bell, under "Activities," Novel wrote that he could be appointed the next Director of Central Intelligence.[2816] The telephone company, perhaps merely in verifying Novel's claim, reported the matter to the CIA.

In one of the most surprising turnarounds in the entire episode of odd individuals that circulated around Garrison's investigation, in the mid-1970s Novel would be charged with conspiracy to commit arson for planning to burn a building in the New Orleans Central Business District. One of the attorneys who represented Novel was none other than Jim Garrison, then in private practice after his defeat for re-election in late 1973. Harry Connick, who had defeated Garrison, was the district attorney at the time, and his assistant, William Wessel, who was trying the case against Novel, jokingly wondered to a newspaper reporter if Garrison's fees were being paid by the Central Intelligence Agency, a charge Garrison frequently had made about Shaw's defense attorneys, and about other defense attorneys involved in Garrison's Kennedy assassination probe years earlier. The CIA, seeing Wessel's quotation in the newspaper, cautiously indicated that Wessel appeared to be joking when he made the remark.

In March 1975, Kennedy assassination researcher Paul Hoch sent a twenty-five-page essay to the Rockefeller Commission, which was investigating the CIA, discussing both the CIA itself and the Warren Commission. Hoch raised questions about whether David Ferrie and Guy Banister (and Banister's associates) had been involved with the CIA. In a memo in response to Hoch's essay, the CIA indicated that Ferrie had never been associated with the CIA, and neither had Banister or his associates, nor had Oswald. The CIA indicated that it had considered using Banister as a foreign intelligence source, and his investigative firm for cover purposes, but decided not to because of his "lack of professional conduct."[2817] The phrase no doubt referred, at least in part, to his firing from the New Orleans police force for the aforementioned incident in a bar in the late 1950s, when Banister had waved a gun at individuals.

As CIA documents began to be released in the 1980s and early 1990s, even before the creation of the Assassination Record Review Board (ARRB), which would release records on a much more comprehensive basis than ever before, researchers noticed a memo from 1967 in which Marguerite D. Stevens (M.D. Stevens), of the OS/Security Research Staff of the CIA, indicated that Shaw had been part of a CIA program designated as QKENCHANT. Marguerite D. Stevens had, over the years, reported internally on defectors and their activities, including Lee Harvey Oswald.[2818] The memo seemed oddly detached from Shaw's earlier activity from 1948 to 1956, which dealt with his travels overseas. It also mentioned that J. Monroe Sullivan, Managing Director of the San Francisco World Trade Center, with whom Shaw had visited on the day of the Kennedy assassination, was also part of the QKENCHANT program. The question then arose as to what exactly the program was, why Shaw and Sullivan had been part of it, and whether the two men were connected in some way other than their meeting on November 22, 1963. It was indeed an odd bit of information. During the mid-to-late 1990s, the ARRB attempted to answer that question by posing queries to the CIA, among the host of other issues with which the two agencies were grappling. Interestingly, the question of QKENCHANT was one of the very last to be answered by the CIA, literally as the ARRB was shutting its doors. ARRB had made several queries about the issue, and it seemed to have been dropped into a black hole of sorts before an answer was forthcoming, very late in the game, which added another bit of mystique to the whole issue.[2819]

QKENCHANT was listed as an issue still to be resolved as late as July 15, 1998, according to a letter from T. Jeremy Gunn, Executive Director and General Counsel of ARRB, to Robert McNamara, General Counsel of the Central Intelligence Agency.[2820] The CIA finally responded to ARRB concerning QKENCHANT in September 1998, providing a series of memos stretching over several years. Essentially, the conclusion was that QKENCHANT had been a project for obtaining clearances, including Provisional Covert Security Approvals (PCSA's) and Covert Security Approvals (CSA's), with the CIA's Office of Security, in connection with the acquisition of information from sources, or other use of individuals or entities. Generally, the CIA required that some sources be effectively "pre-cleared" before they could be used. In Shaw's case, he had received a "five agency" clearance on March 23, 1949; such pre-clearance was required for him to be used as a source prior to his first trip to South America. The program named QKENCHANT had not begun until 1952, so Shaw obviously had not initially been pre-cleared under it; the CIA speculated that he may have been approved under it at a later stage of his involvement, prior to his last contact with the Agency in the mid-1950s. A follow-up memo from the CIA to the ARRB said that QKENCHANT was the name of an Agency project used to provide security approvals on non-Agency personnel and facilities. It said that approvals were required so that Agency personnel then could meet with the individuals to discuss proposed projects, activities, and possible relationships. It reiterated that Shaw had not initially been pre-cleared under QKENCHANT because his approval pre-dated the program, but that he must have been approved under it at a later date. The same information applied to J. Monroe Sullivan, although he apparently had not been approved prior to the beginning of the QKENCHANT program.[2821]

Another person cleared under QKENCHANT was major Watergate burglary participant E. Howard Hunt, a person often mentioned in Kennedy assassination theories after (but never before) the Watergate burglary occurred. On June 3, 1970, a covert security approval under QKENCHANT was granted for Hunt, a former CIA employee who then was working for a private business. The approval was granted by the Deputy Director of Security of the CIA; it indicated that Hunt should not represent himself as an employee of the CIA. The approval became invalid after six months, meaning that if Hunt was not actually used by the Central Intelligence Agency for any purpose during that time, the approval expired. The memo also said that if Hunt's employment status changed prior to him being used by the Agency, his existing approval status would need to be reapproved by the Department of Security.[2822]

# 32 · The End? Not Just Yet

As 1974 began, Shaw found time to donate to favored organizations, even though he was in the midst of various family and personal health issues. He donated $100 to the Anti-Defamation League, the Jewish organization that fights anti-Semitism.[2823]

Events at the end of 1973, however, had combined to keep Shaw preoccupied, and unable to answer correspondence quickly. His continuing medical tests, his mother's death, and the handling of her estate and dispersal of her personal property, kept him busy continuously through the month of December. He received a card dated November 11, 1973 from his friend, Thomas Jefferson Young, in Monticello, Mississippi, who had complained that he did not like the one-way streets in the French Quarter.[2824] Shaw did not reply until January 17, 1974, wherein he indicated that he did not mind the one-way streets, but did not like the no-parking signs that limited his ability to park near where he lived.[2825]

Shaw's old friend, Virginia van Tienhoven, wrote to say that she was sorry to hear about Shaw's mother's death.[2826] Shaw replied on January 23, saying that there had been "no way to prepare" for his mother's death, and that she had died quickly at age 85, after a "long and happy life with no lingering or pain."[2827]

Alison Marks had written on December 8, 1973, asking Shaw to send her word of how things were with him, and in an allusion to the ongoing Watergate affair, said that Garrison had been ahead of his times in the "dirty tricks department," and that "others are catching up." She ended by saying that she wished Shaw was there in Massachusetts to help her celebrate the holidays.[2828] Shaw did not reply until January 17, 1974, when he told Marks that he had sent no Christmas cards at the end of 1973, for the first time in many years. He informed her that his mother had passed away, and also that Jim Garrison had lost his bid for re-election during December. Shaw commented that his job restoring the French Market was interesting, and kept him busy, and in an ironic comment, said that "1974 has to be better than 1973."[2829]

Shaw received a Christmas card from his British friends, Olwen and Hugh Janson on the Isle of Wight, inviting him to visit them again during 1974.[2830] Shaw replied on January 17, 1974, that 1973 "was a real bummer." The energy crisis set in motion by OPEC was sweeping the world by the end of 1973, and Shaw alluded to it, saying that "things sound grim in England," and that "you both should flee back to New Orleans."[2831]

The poet and songwriter Rod McKuen had sent Shaw a Christmas card at the end of 1973, which Shaw finally found time to answer on January 17, 1974. Shaw indicated that there had been no Christmas for him in 1973, due to the death of his mother, and that 1973 had been bad throughout the year. He indicated that he had had two bleeding ulcers, in addition to a lung cancer "now happily cured." He closed by saying that 1974 could "scarcely be worse than its predecessor."[2832]

In late 1973, Shaw received a card from his friend Kenneth Sheehan in Los Angeles. Sheehan indicated that he was trying to retire from his real estate business, that he had sold his last property in January of 1973. He had heard about Shaw's mother's death, and expressed his sympathy.[2833] Shaw replied on January 17, 1974, saying that he had spent Christmas weekend doing the "dreary task" of sorting out letters, clothes, papers, etc. that had belonged to his mother.[2834]

An interesting Christmas card came from Mr. and Mrs. Wyatt Cooper, who lived at the

United Nations Plaza in New York City. Mr. and Mrs. Wyatt Cooper were Gloria Vanderbilt and her husband. The Coopers enclosed an article about Dorothy Parker, and recent photographs of their young sons, Carter and Anderson Cooper, the same Anderson Cooper who became an anchorman for CNN.[2835] Shaw answered on January 8, 1974, saying that it was a "very handsome picture of the boys," and that he had enjoyed the article about Dorothy Parker. He added that, "Val was in town shortly after you were," and indicated that the last time he had seen Cooper, he and the boys had been going to the small town of Ponchatoula, Louisiana. Shaw said that he hoped they had made it, and "had strange and exciting adventures there."[2836]

On February 4, 1974, while driving a car, Shaw suffered a seizure that caused him to have an accident and be hospitalized. He crashed the car in a minor accident, and although he was unhurt from the impact itself, an ambulance had arrived and taken him from the corner of Jefferson Davis and Tulane Avenue to Ochsner Clinic.[2837] It was effectively the beginning of the end, as Shaw would spend several months recovering the use of one side of his body that was rendered useless by the seizure, only to find that he was diagnosed with cancer again in the spring of 1974. He attempted to return to work, but soon left the French Market Corporation, and spent the time from the end of May through mid-August 1974 slowly dying.

Just before Shaw's seizure happened, Alison Marks had written him a letter saying how horrified she was to hear how bad 1973 had been for him, including the death of his mother. She said she thought that at last he would be enjoying some success after his vindication in the criminal process, and she recommended he read Romain Gary's *Promise at Dawn*, about the death of a parent. Marks said that she was in "undeserved good health and spirits," and that Shaw "must" take care of himself. She indicated that she might take a trip to England in the spring.[2838] Shaw, unable to reply until March 6, wrote her about the seizure he had while driving, indicating that no one had been injured, and mentioning that the fluid between his cranium and the envelope that encased his brain had been removed. He said that the doctors had indicated that it could have been seepage from an old fall of his, that he had spent two weeks in the hospital, and had been home for a week. He said that he was reading Nicholson's *Portrait of a Marriage*, and Lillian Hellman's autobiography. Shaw advised her that perhaps she should retire and write about others whose lives had been fulfilling to her own.[2839]

A letter from Olwen and Hugh Janson, written on February 4, 1974, arrived after Shaw had his seizure. Olwen Janson commented on the death of Shaw's mother, saying that she knew he had always been close to her, and asked about the progress of the French Market project. Olwen, who could be somewhat racy in her letters, indicated that she was keeping her "fingers crossed, but not her legs (HA HA)" that Shaw would visit them in 1974. She said that it was "hellish here," with "endless strikes and endless shortages even of soap and toilet (lav) paper." She indicated that she and Hugh were just finishing fourteen years of marriage, and added that she hoped 1974 would be good for Shaw.[2840]

Shaw also received a number of letters written after news of his seizure had reached those who knew him; he answered them as soon as he was able. One such letter was written on February 5 by Thomas Greene, manager of the New Orleans Philharmonic Symphony Orchestra. Greene said he hoped that Shaw would get well soon, and mentioned one piece of contemporary music the orchestra was currently playing that sounded like a cross "between a stray barge grinding into a ferry boat, a water buffalo at Audubon Zoo giving birth to a porcupine, and a partridge in a pear tree."[2841] Shaw replied on March 6 that he was delighted he was still around to hear those recordings, and "others I like better."[2842]

Another letter came on February 14 from Ray Seale, an old friend of Shaw now living in Naples, Florida with his wife, Almeta. Seale had served with Shaw's father at the Department of the Treasury many years before; Almeta worked for the CIA in Washington from the 1950s until retirement. The letter mentioned Shaw's recent illness, and wished him well.[2843] Shaw replied March 6, saying that the doctors had removed a blood clot of 9-1/2 ounces. He stressed that there had been "no permanent damage," that he was "no crazier than he was before."[2844]

After the batch of letters Shaw answered on March 6, he apparently became occupied both with trying to get back into work mode, and with rapidly evolving health problems. He did relatively little work at the French Market Corporation after his seizure. Loans were beginning to become due on some of his properties, and he was finding it difficult to make the payments. He found it necessary to skip a payment to Edith Stern on her loan for the St. Peter Street property. From mid-March forward, he failed to answer many letters immediately after receiving them, and it was around the Easter holiday that he received word that he likely had terminal cancer.

One letter he answered was from Lewis Fulton Kempf II, with W.R. McCutchon Real Estate in Waveland, Mississippi, who wrote wishing Shaw well on April 11, 1974. He had been a nurse on duty during Shaw's recent hospital stay, and had since gone into the real estate business.[2845] Shaw replied on April 19, saying that his eyes were still weak, as was his left leg, and that he was spending half of his work day at home and the other half at the office.[2846]

John Wray Young, who, along with his wife Margaret Mary Young, managed the Shreveport, Louisiana Little Theater, had written on January 24, 1974 that Margaret was recovering from recent surgery with 100 stitches. Young noted that in forty-four seasons with the theater, the couple had, as director and designer, generated 332 productions, adding that he was trying to save the entertainment business from "Alice Cooper and *Deep Throat*." Young said that his daughter, Jill, who had been so close to Shaw during the immediate aftermath of his arrest in the spring of 1967, and her husband, Brian Latell, now with the Central Intelligence Agency, were back from spending three months in Buenos Aires, Argentina. Young mentioned that he now had seven books regarding the American theater scene in print, more than any other living writer.[2847] The letter must have arrived just before Shaw had his seizure in early February, because he did not respond to Young's letter until May 1, 1974. Shaw recounted the seizure incident, and how he had been rushed to the hospital, where doctors had operated in three spots where brain fluid had gathered between the cranium and the optic thalamus; the doctor had said he would recover from the event. Shaw indicated that he had not known how much John Wray Young had written, but that he wished "I could join you on old happy holidays on Huron St. as once we did." Shaw closed by saying that, "Margaret and I will compare notes on all the doctors did to us and said to us," which he said "should be amusing."[2848]

Alison Marks wrote Shaw again in late March 1974, saying, "I can't stand the things that have happened to you…It's not fair." She discussed different trips she was planning on taking, and said that she "would love to see you." She said that she had tried to write to him recently, but what she had written "came out like dry shredded wheat."[2849] Shaw finally replied on May 1, saying that he still had some troubles in his left leg, and that his eyes were "a little blurry." He said that his neurologist had told him that his vision should clear up, and that he was spending half his time at the office, and half at home nursing his illness. He ended by noting that he had enjoyed reading the Romain Gary book that Marks had sent him.[2850]

Shaw received a number of letters from distant relatives, including Fannie Mae Shaw in Paducah, Kentucky. She mentioned that she was sorry she had missed Shaw's mother's funeral, and hoped he was improving.[2851] Shaw replied March 6, indicating that he was returning to good health, was "in good shape and far too mean to kill." He added that his left leg needed exercise.[2852]

Shaw's old Public Relations Director from the Mart, Jesse Core, wrote on March 19 pushing certain ideas for the new French Market when it was completed. Core suggested making it an authentic crafts production place, using historical authenticity, as had been done at Williamsburg, Virginia. Core added that he was having to "run from a bill collector!" and that he was "trying to get back to solvency."[2853]

Marymor "Boo" Cravens, of Sewanee, Tennessee, home of University of the South, wrote on March 2, 1974. "Boo" Cravens was the daughter of Mary Moore Sanborn, who had been active with Shaw in Le Petit Theatre during the late 1920s and early 1930s. Her aunt, Cynthia Smith Koenig, had sent her a clipping about Shaw's recent illness, and she invited him to the "best porch in Sewanee," which overlooked the valleys around the beautiful college town.[2854] Shaw replied on March 6, indicating that it was "nice to hear from you after all these years." He indicated that he would try to visit her, but had to get back to work.[2855]

Gina Jackson, a New York City photographer who had taken photographs of Shaw for the article in the Key West newspaper that appeared after Shaw's visit there with author James Kirkwood in 1971, wrote to Shaw indicating that she had been in Europe and was putting a book together on her life with her husband, Ferdnand Legros, who had been involved in selling paintings by legendary art forger Elmyr de Hory. She mentioned that she had found a 1956 photo of a friend of Shaw, taken at Elmwood Plantation just outside of New Orleans.[2856] Shaw replied on May 1, indicating that he would like the photograph, and saying that the young man in the picture was William Henry Formyduval.[2857]

Shaw resigned from the French Market Board in mid-May 1974.[2858] He was still owed approximately $4,000 in salary, but the French Market Corporation was short on funds, and would delay paying him.[2859] By mid-summer, with Shaw mentally incapacitated, Edward Wegmann wrote to French Market Board President A.J. Duplantier, asking that the $4,000 in salary be sent directly to him.[2860]

In late May, Shaw went to North Carolina to, in effect, say final goodbyes to members of the Formyduval family. He then settled in, with close friends Don Doody and Gail Baumgartner, and later with medical student Wayne Julian, as sitters, as his life slowly came to a close.

Some conspiracy writers have found it unusual that Don Doody, with his varied background, would be a sitter with Shaw during the last few months of his life. It has been alleged that Doody, with his intelligence background, served as someone to watch over Shaw, to make certain he didn't blurt out something sensitive in his final days. The truth was much less sinister. Shaw had found out that Doody, who had been away from New Orleans for much of the past decade, was coming back for a while, and asked if he would stay with him during the period of his decline. He had always liked Doody; he respected his level of education and his opinions on various topics. Doody, who came from a family of means and often had no regular job, had the time and flexibility to spend the months at Shaw's side.[2861]

Shaw's former properties on Dauphine Street, which had been purchased by Artelle Trelford and had been used by her sister, Virginia Kirk, were facing potential default. Virginia Kirk wrote asking for a delay in payment on the loan for those properties, but Edward Wegmann replied that he could not make such an extension, saying that Shaw was in need of all sources of income at that point.[2862]

As Shaw began to wind down his affairs, completing an update of his will and paying his maid of more than seven years, Willie Mae Guidry, through May 1974, the civil action was preparing to move into a more active phase. Early on, each side had propounded a list of interrogatories to be answered, but beyond the answers to those initial questions, not much happened until the late spring of 1974. On May 31, Edward Wegmann wrote, mentioning the need to file amended answers to the original sets of interrogatories. He asked for Shaw's 1972 Federal income tax return, and for a list and description of all speaking engagements Shaw had from 1967 to 1972, including any radio and television appearances. Wegmann indicated there was no use filing for a summary judgment in Shaw's favor on the lawsuit at that point.[2863]

Shaw's attorneys began to gather answers to the revised first set of interrogatories, which had been filed by the defendants sometime before. In a set of notes dated May 31, 1974 regarding those answers, Wegmann mentioned prosecutor James Alcock, who had left Garrison's office in December 1970 to become a judge, had been defeated in his bid for re-election to judge in late 1971, and had since entered private practice. In reference to the inner workings of Garrison's prosecution of Shaw over more than four years, Wegmann wrote, "GIVE CONSIDERATION AS TO WHETHER OR NOT WE SHOULD NOW SEEK ALCOCK'S AID AND ASSISTANCE, SINCE OSTENSIBLY HE HAS BEEN GIVEN THE BOOT BY GARRISON, OR IN THE ALTERNATIVE, HAS BECOME HONEST."[2864]

On June 27, a status conference was held and the presiding judge ordered that the plaintiffs were to answer all outstanding interrogatories by July 17, that discovery would be complete by August 28, and that the deadline for motions would be September 10. A pre-trial conference was set for October 23, with the actual trial by jury to begin on November 4, 1974. The presiding judge was U.S. District Judge Frederick Heebe, who had been one of several Federal judges who had heard Shaw's civil rights case during the summer of 1968, when Shaw's attorneys had sought to prevent the initial prosecution from occurring. Wegmann advised Shaw, who now was rapidly approaching a point where he could not understand such communications, of the developments.[2865]

As Shaw's attorneys geared up for the civil trial, they attempted to piece together all of the investigative expenses, other than legal fees, for which Shaw had spent his money over the years since his arrest. A preliminary total through 1969 was $55,024.96, although some entries were crossed out in the documents contained in Shaw's attorneys' files. There were entries that seemed to indicate that $4,000 may have been received for the August 1969 article in *LOOK* magazine by Warren Rogers, with one-third of that amount going to each of attorneys Irvin Dymond, William Wegmann, and Edward Wegmann.[2866]

The defendants to the civil litigation filed by Shaw were represented by several firms, and there were several changes in the attorney lineup for the civil suit during 1974. Most notably, Jim Garrison and Joseph Rault, Jr. were now represented by the firm of Deutsch, Kerrigan and Stiles, in the person of Malcolm W. Monroe. John Volz, an assistant district attorney, had served as counsel for Garrison until Garrison left office as district attorney on April 1, 1974. Monroe came on board as Volz's replacement, though it should be noted that Monroe was no stranger to the details involved. He had represented Garrison's office in various appeals related to the Shaw's prosecution, including the fight against efforts to obtain an injunction against prosecution prior to the original conspiracy-related trial, and those related to overturning the permanent injunction against further prosecution issued by Judge Christenberry in 1971. Years later, some of those who knew Monroe well would note the irony that Monroe, a gay man, had worked so diligently to thwart Shaw's best interests in all aspects of his prosecution at Garrison's hands.

Additional changes to counsel included Richard C. Baldwin of the firm of Adams and Reese becoming counsel for defendant Dr. Esmond Fatter on July 8, 1974. Irvin Dymond, who had been consulting on the civil suit behind the scenes, but had not been too actively involved in it, was designated an official counsel of record for the plaintiffs in the summer of 1974 as well.

By the summer of 1974, relations between William Formyduval and Jeff Biddison had become strained, as a result of remarks Formyduval had made that had angered and upset Shaw during his illness; Shaw's friend, Don Doody, characterized the remarks as "woman's talk."[2867] In a letter to Shaw during the summer of 1974, Formyduval, then living in Boynton Beach, Florida, said that he was going to Machu Picchu in Peru. Formyduval commented that, "Mr. Alexander G. Bill" was "an apostle for the devil himself." The name probably referred to Jeff Biddison, whose full name was Arthur Jefferson Biddison.[2868]

In late June, attorney Thomas Lemann, of the firm of Monroe and Lemann, wrote to Edith Stern, indicating that a codicil to Shaw's loan would give her his real property if she assumed responsibility for the mortgage payments related to the existing debt at the time of his death.[2869] Shortly after, on July 2, Joseph J. Falgout of Starwood Corporation, Edith Stern's business manager, summarized her loans to Shaw related to the properties on St. Peter and Toulouse streets. Stern had loaned Shaw $30,000 in October 1968, and another $10,000 in July 1969. In March 1969, Shaw had exercised an option to buy the properties from architect Arthur Q. Davis, and had borrowed $228,347.50 from Stern at that time. Over the years since then, Shaw had repaid approximately $40,000, plus $3,347.50 of interest (interest of six percent had been paid monthly through May 31, 1974), leaving a balance as of July 2, 1974 of $223,292.19. An appraisal of the property was to be done, but Falgout noted that Elmer Miester of the Leo Fellman and Company estimated that the ground value alone was $300,000.[2870]

On July 8, as Shaw was beginning to fade away from consciousness, Edith Stern wrote to him. She said that she had spoken to Dr. Batson, Shaw's personal physician, who had spoken to a Dr. Sample, and both agreed it was worth a try to start chemotherapy. Stern noted that some patients had unpleasant side effects from the procedure, and that it required a signed release, but that a relation of hers had had great improvements with it. Stern copied Shaw's friend Gail Baumgartner on the letter.[2871]

As of July 1974, Shaw's attorneys were still keeping tabs on Perry Russo; William Gurvich was assisting them. On July 8, Gurvich reported to Wegmann that Russo was now driving a taxi cab, and had been arrested recently at the Carib Motel, to which he had invited three "subjects" to join him. The police had found sex toys, lubricants, and pornography, and had charged the group with possession of amphetamines.[2872]

Around this time, there were efforts to settle the case, as well as efforts to push the case forward in case it never settled. On July 17, Wegmann wrote to Malcolm Monroe, enclosing amended answers to interrogatories. The original set of interrogatories had contained a list of somewhat controversial questions, including some about Shaw's personal life. Shaw's attorneys had refused to answer some of them, and the defendants had taken the issue to the judge, who had ordered that most of the questions had to be answered. Wegmann noted in his letter to Monroe that he was still searching for invoices for two private investigators, one in Houston and one in New York City, whom he had used to investigate witness Charles Spiesel and others at the time of the trial.[2873] Earlier in the month, Wegmann had written to Dymond and William Wegmann, saying that it was necessary to get the interrogatories answered quickly, and motions prepared. Wegmann indicated that the work "must be divided" amongst them, as he could not possibly do it all by himself by the deadline.[2874]

Also on July 17, Dr. Fatter's lawyers made a motion for a partial summary judgment to remove certain "loose language" in the complaint, to the extent the complaint had alleged that Dr. Fatter had engaged in professional negligence. Dr. Fatter's lawyer maintained that removing that language would not affect the civil rights action by Shaw, the actual purpose of the lawsuit; his contention was that only Perry Russo, as the one who had undergone hypnosis under Dr. Fatter, could assert a claim of negligence.[2875]

In the amended and supplemental answers to interrogatories, Shaw's attorneys answered a number of key questions posed by the defendants. For instance, they said that attorney fees for the trial in the criminal conspiracy case had totaled $22,500, and that those legal fees had been the only ones paid to date. They itemized investigative expenses exceeding $51,000. Therefore, through July 17, 1974, Shaw had paid slightly less than $75,000 of total expenses, legal and investigative. That amount greatly conflicts with reports of much higher numbers that have appeared in print over the years, some of which estimated that Shaw spent as much as half a million dollars on his defense. However, it should be noted that Shaw's attorneys indicated that Shaw owed them at least $50,000 for representation at the lengthy hearing before Judge Herbert Christenberry, and for all other matters, including the defense of the perjury charges, as well as their efforts to date in the civil lawsuit. It is obvious that Shaw's attorneys were essentially representing him in an arrangement whereby he would not pay them up front, but rather would generously share with them any award or settlement he received from the civil lawsuit. However, there was no written agreement for that arrangement.

The amended and supplemental answers also broke out the five million dollar figure that originally had been sought when the suit was filed. It indicated that one million dollars was being sought for loss of reputation, two million dollars for mental anguish and continuous harassment, and two million dollars for pain and suffering and irreparable damage to health. The answers charged that most of the defendants had sought to improve their political influence in New Orleans in some way. Garrison hoped to springboard to higher office, and Shilstone, Robertson and Rault received business either from the government or government-controlled agencies, and it was important for them to be on friendly terms with local elected officials. The attorneys cited the search of Shaw's residence, restrictions on his travel, fear of conviction and prison, his inability to obtain employment, and the surveillance on his home as factors that had contributed directly to his injury. They said he was the victim of selective prosecution, with chilling effects on his personal life and his relations with friends. The lawyers charged that the prosecutions had been effectively a conspiracy between Garrison and the other defendants, and they imputed knowledge of all acts against Shaw to all defendants, whether each party had individually known about each aspect or not.

The meager contributions made by others to the defense over the years were broken out as follows: Bultman Mortuary, the business run by Murial Bultman Francis's family, had contributed $1,000; a C. Greenway had contributed $1; Shaw's friend Patrick O'Rourke had contributed $350 and $100; Joe M. Clements had contributed $10; A.C. Cook had contributed $25; and S.B. "Shirley" Braselman had contributed $100. The answers indicated that no compensation had been paid to William Gurvich, Tom Bethell, or anyone else for copies of the district attorney's files received from them, such as memos (including the infamous Andrew Sciambra memo of his initial interview with Perry Russo), or transcripts of the sodium pentothal session or hypnosis sessions. Lieutenant Edward O'Donnell, who had conducted the second polygraph examination of Perry Russo in the summer of 1967, had approached the defense attorneys voluntarily at the time of trial; no compensation for him had ever been discussed or given. The defense attorneys had used Wackenhut Corporation out of Florida, and Southern Research Company, in its initial investigations, the purpose of which was to investigate various witnesses; they later used two investigators in Houston and New York to investigate Charles Spiesel.

The attorneys indicated that Shaw had told them he did not know either Ferrie or Oswald. The answers further indicated that Shaw alone controlled the right to settle or dismiss the lawsuit; there was no fee contract relative to the suit, and all compensation arrangements were to be decided later. Shaw indicated in the answers that he had not been advised of his rights, including right to counsel, during his initial questioning in December 1966, or during his interrogation on March 1, 1967, until he had indicated he wanted to call an attorney.[2876]

One of the interrogatories propounded to Shaw asked about his income based upon his tax returns during the 1960s and into the 1970s. The answers show that Shaw's income generally exceeded $20,000 every year through 1963 and then jumped to $29,250 in 1964, before dropping to $22,500 in 1965, when he only worked three-fourths of the year. In 1966, he showed income of $6,928; in 1967, $17,779; in 1968, $8,506; in 1969, $8,108; in 1970, $7,618; in 1971, $5,681. Most of his income after his retirement in 1965, through his return to paid work in December 1971, was either from sales of property, or interest income from certificates of deposit.

In his answers, Shaw indicated that his life savings had been depleted, and that he had suffered depression, pain, mental anguish, humiliation, embarrassment, and suffering. Shaw said that he had tried to find employment with one or more management consulting firms in New York City, the names of which he did not recall, all to no avail. He said that no employment had been offered to him until he joined the French Market Corporation, at a salary of $24,000 per year, on December 15, 1971.[2877] Shaw said that he had a verbal contract with his attorneys to handle the civil case on a contingent fee basis, with Shaw paying out-of-pocket expenses and court costs. To his knowledge, his attorneys had not been paid by any other source. Shaw estimated that his attorney fees and expenses to date totaled approximately $75,000, but he did not go into details of those costs. He said that he had not been billed anything yet for the hearing in January 1971, related to enjoining his criminal prosecution for perjury.[2878]

The court had ruled that Shaw did not need to answer two very personal questions that had been originally propounded to him. One of those questions had asked the purpose of the large hooks found screwed into the beam in the ceiling of his bedroom; the other asked if there had been dried blood on the whips seized from his bedroom. Although the answers were never filed in court, informal answers can be found in Shaw's attorneys' files. Regarding the whips, Shaw indicated he knew of no blood on them. Regarding the hooks screwed into the beam of his bedroom ceiling, Shaw indicated that they had been used for hanging plants.[2879]

Earlier, Jim Garrison had also given some interesting answers in response to interrogatories propounded by Shaw's attorneys. Garrison asserted that Kennedy had been killed by a military-oriented intelligence apparatus of the U.S. government, as amplified in his book, *A Heritage of Stone*, published in November 1970. Interestingly, Garrison contended that he had never said that Shaw's attorneys had been paid by the CIA, never said that Shaw was "Clay Bertrand," and never said that he had "solved the assassination weeks ago" shortly after the investigation became public in February 1967. Garrison also stated that no one had ever suggested to him that he conduct the probe, but that after a conversation with U.S. Senator Russell Long, he had ordered all volumes of the Warren Commission Report and exhibits, and commenced the investigation. He said that he knew there were questions about the accuracy of many of the statements in his interview in *Playboy* magazine in the October 1967 issue, but contended that he was not responsible for such inaccuracies.[2880]

In answer to a question about whether Oswald had been with the CIA, Garrison said that issue had also been covered in his book, *A Heritage of Stone*. He said that no documentation remained of that connection to Oswald, however, because the documents had been burned while being copied by the CIA on a Thermofax machine on November 23, 1963.[2881]

Shortly after Shaw's attorneys submitted answers to the amended and supplemental set of initial interrogatories during the summer of 1974, the defendants propounded a second set of interrogatories, consisting of twenty-three questions, some of which had multiple parts. The new interrogatories requested detailed information about Shaw's health going back to 1941, including the names of physicians used for each illness, the nature of each illness and how it had affected Shaw's health, and questions about Shaw's income and net worth, and how they had been impacted by his prosecution. The defendants also asked a number of questions about how the Truth and Consequences defendants, Shilstone, Rault, and Robertson, had gained because of their association with Garrison, and their funding of his case. The questions also asked how those three individuals had concurred in each of Garrison's actions involving the manufacture of evidence, the procuring of witnesses, the importing of witnesses from out of state, and the retaining of the handwriting expert from Boston who had been used at Shaw's trial.[2882] Answers to the second set of interrogatories were never filed with the court before Shaw died.

In mid-July 1974, Biddison received a letter from Father Ed Sheridan, expressing sympathy for Shaw's illness. Sheridan mentioned Gail Baumgartner, and John Wray Young and Margaret Mary Young, through whom he had initially met Shaw, shortly after his arrest in 1967.[2883] While Shaw evidently had reconsidered his inclination, shortly after his arrest, to become a Catholic, he had stayed in touch with Father Sheridan over the years.

On July 26, 1974, a legal motion was made to associate attorneys Peter J. Butler and Clem Sehrt as co-counsel with original attorney A.E. Papale, Jr., representing defendant Cecil Shilstone.[2884] As has been mentioned, back in 1963, Oswald's mother had supposedly attempted to contact Clem Sehrt to represent her son. The day before officially being associated as counsel, Peter J. Butler wrote to all attorneys involved in the case, indicating that he wanted to take Shaw's deposition on August 6, 1974, at the offices of Deutsch, Kerrigan, and Stiles. Butler requested that Shaw bring all documents and records that he would use at trial, and all income records and Federal income tax returns.[2885]

On July 30, 1974, Wegmann wrote to Irvin Dymond and William Wegmann regarding Shaw's upcoming deposition. Wegmann said that he had visited with Shaw "a week or ten days ago" to have him sign an affidavit annexed to the amended answers to interrogatories. Wegmann said that Shaw had recognized him, but was very confused, and was hallucinating during the visit. Wegmann indicated that the situation had not improved since then, and recommended that the other two attorneys visit with Shaw, and then the three of them could determine the appropriate action that should be taken moving forward.[2886]

The same day, Dr. Hugh Batson visited with Shaw. Two days later, he wrote to Wegmann, indicating that Shaw would not be able to give testimony.[2887] Wegmann then wrote again to his brother and Dymond to discuss the upcoming status conference with the judge on August 6, 1974. He indicated that he had discussed the matter the day before with Dr. Batson, who had told him that it was unlikely Shaw would ever be able to give a deposition. Wegmann said that, with the trial set to begin November 4, the defense should make it known that Shaw would be unable to face questioning, and let the case move forward from that point. Wegmann recommended that the attorneys "get the law with respect to heritability" of the situation.[2888]

On August 1, Dr. Batson provided a letter to Wegmann indicating the present state of Shaw's health, and reiterating his conclusion that Shaw was unable to give testimony in his civil suit.[2889] Wegmann answered, telling Batson that he now needed a detailed account of Shaw's mental and physical health over the years, preferably within thirty days. Wegmann also indicated the defense needed an official diagnosis, and prognosis, for Shaw's condition.[2890][2891]

Up to the day of Shaw's death, his attorneys were gathering information about expenses incurred during Shaw's criminal ordeal, and answering interrogatories propounded to them. On August 14, 1974 (Shaw would die that night), Edward Wegmann wrote to Malcolm Monroe enclosing an invoice of $4,428.14 from Walter C. Holloway, the private investigator from Texas who, on the recommendation of newsman Hugh Aynesworth, had investigated important witnesses such as Charles Spiesel and Jessie Parker shortly before, and even after, the trial had begun in 1969. Wegmann indicated that he had yet another invoice from a different investigator to submit, as soon as he found it in his records.[2892]

That night, shortly after midnight, Clay Shaw died. Soon thereafter, someone reported to authorities that a body had been taken into Shaw's residence on St. Peter Street, and then a body (presumably Shaw's) had been taken out again not long afterward. As a result, the Orleans Parish coroner, Dr. Frank Minyard, opened an unofficial investigation into Shaw's death, and requested that police detectives get involved in its circumstances. On August 19, 1974, Edward Wegmann wrote to Dymond and William Wegmann regarding Minyard's actions. Wegmann said that he had requested that Chief of Detectives Henry Morris make it a formal investigation, and Morris had agreed to that.[2893] On August 23, Wegmann wrote again to share that he was off to The Cloister resort at Sea Island, Georgia; he asked the two attorneys to let him know immediately if Dr. Minyard attempted "to stir up anything" Wegmann noted that the attorneys could successfully prevent Minyard from exhuming the body, but he questioned whether they wanted to do so, or if it would be more advantageous simply to let the investigation proceed to its conclusion, in view of the fact that, in Wegmann's view, there were no mysterious circumstances surrounding Shaw's death. Wegmann attached a statement he was releasing to the press requesting the official investigation.[2894]

Police detectives, led by John Dillmann, would soon interview Don Doody, Gail Baumgartner, and medical student Wayne Julian, all sitters of Shaw in his declining months, and Dr. Hugh Batson, about Shaw's death. Following the interviews, the police detectives concluded that Shaw had died of natural causes at the St. Peter Street residence, shortly after midnight on August 15, 1974. Their report, which is now in the National Archives, details Shaw's increasingly worsening condition over the summer of 1974, and his rebellion against taking needed medication, including throwing his medicine on the floor in frustration, during the last days of his ordeal. The matter of Shaw's "mysterious death" died soon thereafter in local police circles, although it has been resurrected periodically in conspiracy theory accounts.

An article in the *States-Item* dated August 15, 1974 indicated that Shaw had died shortly after 1:00 a.m. that morning. It mentioned he had resigned from the French Market Corporation on May 31, 1974, and it contained a standard biography. The piece claims that Shaw had attended Columbia University in New York City in 1935 (Shaw only arrived in New York City in early 1936), although today Columbia has no record of any attendance by Shaw, even at audited classes, and Shaw testified at his trial that he had never attended college. The article quoted Shaw, saying about his arrest seven years before, "At first I was stunned. But man is endlessly adaptable. You can get used to almost anything."[2895]

The article also mentioned that yet another of several perjury cases against attorney Dean Andrews that had been filed by Garrison's office over the years had recently been thrown out by the judge in the case. Andrews had been convicted of one set of charges in August 1967, but had at least two more filed against him for contradictory testimony, either in court or before a grand jury. The office of the district attorney, now headed by Harry Connick, had opposed the quashing of the charges, but was unsuccessful in its efforts.

Clay Shaw's official death certificate shows his time and date of death as 12:40 a.m. on August 15, 1974. The place of death was 1022 St. Peter Street. The cause of death was metastatic lung malignancy, into the brain and liver, due to adenocarcinoma of lung. The death certificate was signed by Shaw's personal physician of the time, Dr. Hugh Batson.[2896]

The list of invitees for Shaw's funeral was an unusual mix of gay friends and companions over the years, family members in rural areas around south Louisiana, members of the Latino community who had worked for, or were otherwise associated with, either the Mart or International House, and members of the general business community. The poet Rod McKuen was on the list, as was playwright Tennessee Williams. Shaw's old friend at Western Union, Bruce Mitchell of New York City, and his friend Val Dufour, were invited, as were restaurateur and art dealer John Iacometti of San Francisco and architect Tom Dawson of Los Angeles. His former companions Judson O'Donnell and William Formyduval, were on the list, as was Patrick O'Rourke of Chicago. Also invited was Brian Latell, the CIA employee who was married to Jill Young, daughter of John Ray Young and Margaret Mary Young.[2897]

Shaw's funeral was held on August 16, 1974 and was a relatively low-key affair, considering Shaw's former standing in the community over two decades. Mayor Moon Landrieu was the only major political figure on hand. Two priests—Father Edward Sheridan, now of Greenville, Mississippi, and Father M.V. Garreau, of Loyola University—conducted the ceremony. There was no music and no formal eulogy. The priests read a funeral rite and prayed. A tribute to Shaw written by Rod McKuen was read. McKuen's tribute, which was also printed in *Variety* magazine in California, went as follows:

"The country didn't kill him—but it did little to help him live...Clay deserved something better—because he was better. He deserves to remain in our hearts and minds as someone very special. Special to each of us in a different way—yes—but most of all special because he was one—of how many others we do not know—one man totally incorruptible, uncompromising, and unable to cheat any man for any price...In his passing he is not the victim. Those of us remaining are. For it will be some time, if ever, that a man of his integrity comes into our lives again."

McKuen's tribute was the only mention, however indirect, of Shaw's ordeal at the hands of Jim Garrison.[2898] Shaw was buried in the local cemetery at Kentwood, Louisiana.

Shaw's cousin Peggy Day sent a sympathy card to Jeff Biddison after Shaw's death, indicating that at least some members of Shaw's outlying family knew of their longtime relationship. With no siblings, children, living parents, or spouse, Shaw left behind no immediate family.

Shaw's many friends felt his death right away. A friend of Muriel Bultman Francis wrote to her the next day, saying how sorry he was to hear about Shaw's death. He said that it was expected, but realized that it had to be a blow to her nonetheless. "At least it came quick and you were there to help," he said.[2899]

Shaw's last will, dated March 7, 1974, left a number of individual gifts of cash. His cousins Peggy Herrington Day, Mary Alice Herrington Broussard, and Suzanne Day Bassett each received $2,000. His cousin Winston Gene Wall received $5,000. Shaw's maid, Willie Mae Guidry, received $1,500. Shaw's friend since the 1950s, William Henry Formyduval, received $7,500 in cash, and all of the furniture, fixtures and contents Shaw owned at his 1024 St. Peter Street residence. Friend Tommy Cox received all of the real property and improvements at 511 South Walnut Street, Hammond, Louisiana, where Shaw's father and mother had lived until their deaths, in 1966 and 1973, respectively; Cox also received the furniture and fixtures present in the house.[2900]

Judson O'Donnell of Hollywood, California, Shaw's companion from the 1930s, received the income from the Tri-E note that had financed the purchase of the Spanish Stables at 716 Governor Nicholls in 1964. Arthur Jefferson "Jeff" Biddison received everything else Shaw owned, including the remaining real estate properties and contents. The will stipulated that property taxes on the estate should not be prorated against anyone receiving a specific bequest from the estate.[2901]

A partial list of current expenses outstanding at the time of Shaw's death, according to his estate documents, show that he owed a little over $13,000 to the Tate Company, Marilyn Tate's old real estate agency, now owned by Jeff Biddison. That amount related primarily to expenses fronted by the company, related to management of his properties, that Shaw was expected to reimburse. He also owed almost $2,600 to Ochsner Clinic, almost $1,300 to Ochsner Hospital, and nearly $1,000 to Paps Cleaners and Laundry. All in all, the total current debts listed were close to $18,000.[2902] Edward Wegmann was owed a relatively small amount for expenses, although the attorneys clearly expected to share in proceeds, if any, from the settlement of Shaw's ongoing civil lawsuit against Garrison and others.

The succession of Clay Shaw broke out his assets and liabilities into major categories. Three real estate properties in New Orleans, and one in Hammond, Louisiana, were left behind. The New Orleans properties were located at 1020-22 St. Peter Street, 1028 St. Peter Street and 1027 Toulouse Street, all part of the group of properties bought from architect Arthur Davis some years before. The properties consisted of three brick buildings with fifteen unfurnished apartments, a swimming pool, cabana, laundry, and parking lot. Those three real estate properties were appraised on September 16, 1974, for $300,000.[2903] However, the appraisal was conducted purely for estate purposes, and such appraisals sometimes do not reflect fair market value. The lot in Hammond, Louisiana, with the home in which

Shaw's father and mother had lived from 1953 until their deaths, appraised at $18,600.

There were three promissory notes receivables related to previous sales of real estate property. The largest of those, with a balance of $47,990, was for the Tri-E Corporation, which had defaulted on the note. However, that note had been picked up by salon owner Roland Chiara, who now owned the Spanish Stables. The notes receivable for properties purchased from Shaw in October 1956 by Mrs. Artelle Kirk Trelford had principal balances of $3,562, and $8,671.[2904]

Shaw also held two whole life insurance policies with his mother, now deceased, as beneficiary on both of them. One had a balance of $2,534, and another had a balance of $7,647. Shaw also had certificates of deposit, other bank accounts, and stocks totaling approximately $33,000.[2905]

Miscellaneous property included a 1970 Chevy Caprice appraised at $300, salary owed by the French Market Corporation of $4,000, and an unvalued claim for damages on the civil suit against Jim Garrison, Joseph Rault, Cecil Shilstone, Willard Robertson, Perry Russo, Esmond Fatter, et al.[2906]

The contents of Shaw's residence were broken out. The most notable items were a marble bust estimated at $150, a portrait of Shaw by Noni (Sonia) Lyons, a red and white ivory chess set appraised at $250, a pair of wooden polychrome Japanese antique statues from the Tam-a-Kura Dynasty, estimated at $1,500, and three garden statues with four pedestals estimated at $450, which had been a gift from Edith Stern. Along with many other items, including lamps, chairs, and tables, the total contents was valued at $9,076. Another estimated $500 in contents at Hammond, Louisiana brought the total to $9,576.[2907]

The total assets were estimated at $419,163, of which $318,600 was real estate and $48,226 was promissory notes.[2908]

On the liability side, the largest single liability was a note payable to Bearer, and held by Edith Stern, for $223,999. It was secured by a mortgage on the real estate at St. Peter and Toulouse streets in New Orleans.

Other liabilities included funeral expenses at the House of Bultman funeral home of $1,648, medical expenses at Ochsner Clinic and Ochsner Foundation Hospital totaling more than $3,200, a promissory note to Central Savings and Loan for $5,445, another promissory note to the First National Bank of Commerce totaling $5,612, and expenses owed to The Tate Company, the real estate company formerly owned by Marilyn Tate, and now owned by Jeff Biddison, totaling $7,418. The amount due Edward Wegmann for expenses was $2,261, and miscellaneous open accounts were estimated at $10,000.[2909]

The relatively low amount due to Edward Wegmann, and the absence of amounts owed to attorneys Irvin Dymond, William Wegmann, and Salvatore Panzeca, confirm, indirectly, that Shaw's attorneys had essentially counted on winning a settlement of Shaw's civil suit against Garrison and others to pay for their time through the years 1967 through 1974 that had not been satisfied by the $22,500 in total payments for legal fees made by Shaw during that time. As Wegmann wrote to Jeff Biddison at the very end of the civil case in 1978, his arrangement with Shaw had been for Shaw to pay only expenses, with the implication that Wegmann would be compensated for his time through the settlement or favorable verdict in the civil case.

Total liabilities were estimated at $259,620, leaving a net estate value of $159,543.[2910]

The plaintiffs had not had time to answer the second set of interrogatories before Shaw died. On August 26, Edward Wegmann wrote to William Wegmann, discussing how to handle the document, and sharing his conviction that the lawsuit was still a viable one. Wegmann added that he would like for it to proceed to a trial, and had asked Dr. Batson for a full and complete report of the medical treatment Shaw had undergone. Wegmann asked if the plaintiffs should obtain a copy of Shaw's complete records at Ochsner Hospital, as Shaw had been there a number of times in recent years.[2911] Wegmann also wrote to Malcolm Monroe on August 26, assuring him that the second set of interrogatories would be answered by the plaintiffs, but that they needed to obtain the medical information requested in those interrogatories.[2912]

Shaw's attorneys then made a list of relevant issues that could affect the civil suit. They included: 1) whether Edward Wegmann could be substituted as the plaintiff in the civil suit; 2) whether the civil action could survive Shaw's death; 3) whether plaintiffs could overcome the doctrine of judicial immunity for a prosecutor such as Garrison; 4) the merits of the case itself, in proving that Shaw had been damaged and to what extent; 5) whether the lawsuit was a personal injury lawsuit or a property damage case; and 6) whether the Civil Rights Act of 1964 applied to the particulars of the case.[2913]

The opposing attorneys, however, must have regrouped almost immediately following Shaw's death to discuss the application of Louisiana law to the civil lawsuit. Very soon after Shaw's death, all of the defendants filed a suggestion of death, a notice to dismiss for extinguishment of claim with the court to indicate the death of a party to a lawsuit. Under Louisiana law at the time, it was generally thought that a personal injury action could not survive the death of the plaintiff, if the plaintiff had no living parents, no spouse, no children, and no siblings, as was the situation with Shaw. The motions to dismiss the lawsuit also pointed out that the suit had failed to allege racial or class-based discrimination, which would be necessary to keep such a lawsuit alive under the circumstances.

Jim Garrison also filed a separate motion to dismiss the claim, based upon prosecutorial immunity. The doctrine made it almost impossible to recover from a prosecutor performing his duties, although Shaw's attorney believed that, since Garrison's office had initiated and carried out the investigation (as opposed to receiving the case after a normal police investigation), the court might allow an exception to the standard immunity.

A crucial issue was whether Shaw's claim was a personal injury claim or a property damage claim, as property damage claims survived the death of the plaintiff, even under the circumstances which Shaw had died, whereas personal injury claims did not. Shaw's attorneys would make an effort to fit Shaw's civil suit into the property damage category, but even the Federal district judge who initially allowed the suit to proceed after Shaw's death refused to go along with that contention, ruling it was a personal injury claim.

As a result of the filings by the defense, Wegmann hired attorney Miriam Cooney Abbott to assist him with the pleadings for the specialized legal aspects of the case. Abbott had performed legal research for a number of judges over the years. On September 11, 1974, Abbott wrote to Wegmann asking for all the pleadings in the civil suit, and opined that there was a tendency in courts to let "every man have his day;" she was optimistic that Shaw's estate would succeed in getting the case heard by a Federal court.[2914]

Wegmann informed Abbott that Jeff Biddison was the residuary legatee, whereas Wegmann was the executor of the estate, and also a creditor among other substantial creditors. Wegmann asked if either he or Biddison should be substituted as the plaintiff in the case. Wegmann told Abbott that the estate was probably solvent, even without consideration of the value of the claim in the lawsuit, but the solvency depended primarily on the market value of the St. Peter Street property, and finding a buyer in a timely fashion. He asked Abbott to prepare necessary pleadings in response to the motions made by the defendants, as well as memoranda in support thereof. He also indicated that he needed to know her fee, as it had to be approved by the legatee (Biddison), and perhaps by the court.[2915]

In a letter dated September 13, Abbott indicated to Wegmann that she would not charge "an exorbitant fee," but that she must first determine the amount of work involved before knowing what her fee would be.[2916] Wegmann said he would have the will probated and get himself named testamentary executor. He said there was no Louisiana case with identical facts as Shaw's civil suit, that the Civil Rights Act of 1964 must be thoroughly researched, and that the damage done to Shaw and to the estate must be itemized.

Jim Garrison was continuing to seek to have the suit dismissed both on the grounds that the suit could not survive Shaw's death, and on the grounds of judicial immunity. In a letter dated September 27, Edward Wegmann wrote William Wegmann, discussing the original motions to dismiss based upon judicial immunity. Edward reminded his brother that those motions had been denied after a lengthy Federal court hearing, that the Fifth U.S. Circuit Court of Appeals had affirmed the initial ruling, and that the United States Supreme Court had declined to hear the case. Edward Wegmann said Garrison was now seeking dismissal on the same ground, as well as on the survival issue.[2917]

On September 28, attorney Thomas Lemann wrote to Edith Stern, informing her that the succession of Shaw's estate was now open. Lemann promised Stern that he would "keep an eye" on the proceedings, and would advise when an inventory of the estate appeared.[2918]

As previously discussed, Garrison had left office unwillingly in the spring of 1974, and was now partnered in private practice with an attorney named Russell Schonekas. Shortly after Shaw's death, Judge Frederick Heebe, the U.S. District Judge then presiding over the civil lawsuit, who also had presided over Shaw's attempt to get his criminal conspiracy case halted by a Federal court in the summer of 1968, had been arrested for driving while intoxicated, and he retained Schonekas as his defense attorney. In a letter dated November 15, 1974, Edward Wegmann wrote to Dymond and William Wegmann, recommending leaving the civil lawsuit in Heebe's court, even with the recent developments.

Although Wegmann initially must have been somewhat pessimistic about the continuation of Shaw's suit following his death, his mood apparently shifted as the fall proceeded, after engaging Abbott to work on the case. In a letter to Jeff Biddison on December 13, 1974, Wegmann discussed the issue of Shaw having no surviving spouse, children, parents, or siblings, and said that the court was "bending over backward" to maintain the viability of the litigation, and that it was trying to apply common law rather than Louisiana law in deciding the issues of the case.[2919]

# 33 · A Plaque on a Building

Attorneys Peter Butler, Antonio Papale, Jr., and Clem Sehrt represented defendant Cecil Shilstone, one of the Truth and Consequences founders. Attorneys Richard Baldwin and Lawrence Wiedermann represented Dr. Esmond Fatter, the physician who had hypnotized Perry Russo, and had helped to draw out of Russo the story that he eventually told in court. Attorneys Michael Goldblatt and Malcolm Monroe of Deutsch, Kerrigan and Stiles represented defendants Willard Robertson and Joseph Rault, Jr., the other two Truth and Consequences founders. Jim Garrison had also been represented at one time by the firm of Deutsch, Kerrigan and Stiles, but he eventually represented himself in the civil suit. The firm also would eventually cease to represent Joseph Rault, Jr. before the case was over, in his instance due to non-payment of legal fees, and the firm would wind up using Jim Garrison as a witness in a court proceeding against Rault in an attempt to collect the fees.

On January 27, 1975, Edward Wegmann wrote to his brother, with a copy to Dymond and Jeff Biddison, regarding his substitution as the plaintiff in place of the deceased Shaw. Wegmann mentioned again that the original motion to dismiss the lawsuit on the basis of judicial immunity for Garrison had been denied by the district court, and upheld by the U.S. Circuit Court of Appeals.[2920]

On March 13, 1975, the Federal District Court in New Orleans denied the defendants' motion to dismiss the suit.[2921] Jeff Biddison was the residuary legatee, the only person who had an interest in the damages, since he inherited most of the estate. However, the district court allowed the executor of the estate, Edward Wegmann, Shaw's long-time civil attorney, to be substituted as the plaintiff on the case. Wegmann had tried to convert the claim from a personal injury claim to a property damage claim, because property damage claims more clearly survived under Louisiana law in the case of a deceased plaintiff in Shaw's situation. However, the judge ruled that the suit was properly a civil rights claim, not a property damage claim.

After Shaw's death, sale of the properties on St. Peter and Toulouse streets held up the closing out of the succession for Shaw's estate until 1976, approximately a year and a half later. Edith Stern held a lien on the properties, and after Shaw's death she agreed to accept interest only on the mortgage she held, until the sale of the property. It was necessary to find a buyer at an appropriate market price in order that the estate could realize its full potential. In the atmosphere of 1974-75, no buyers approached with a reasonable offer, and it was not until the end of 1975 that a purchaser was found.

In mid-March 1975, Edward Wegmann reported to Edith Stern on the progress of settling the estate, and the efforts to sell the real property and pay off the debts the estate owed to her. Wegmann advised that Jeff Biddison was still maintaining the property, and showing it to prospective buyers. Wegmann returned a check found in Shaw's wallet that had been written to him by Stern;[2922] Stern replied that Shaw had informed her many months ago that he thought he had lost the check.

The defendants immediately appealed the local Federal court decision allowing Shaw's civil suit to continue to the U.S. Fifth Circuit Court of Appeals. On April 7, 1975, Miriam Cooney Abbott wrote to Wegmann, saying she had read the appellate brief by the defendants. She said she believed that the Fifth U.S. Circuit Court of Appeals would decide in Wegmann's favor, but if not, he could always appeal to the U.S. Supreme Court.[2923]

Chicago attorney Alan S. Adelson, who had represented Jack Ruby's family over the years, had cooperated with Wegmann during the period since Shaw had been arrested with information about Ruby and Dallas aspects of the Kennedy assassination. On April 7, Wegmann wrote to Adelson, who had asked about Garrison's two criminal trials. Wegmann reported that Garrison had been tried separately for bribery and for income tax fraud, and had been acquitted both times, after defending himself. Adelson raised the question of whether Garrison had received any monies for his Kennedy assassination investigation from individuals in Dallas, Texas, but Wegmann said he knew nothing about that. Wegmann also mentioned that in the answers Garrison had given in Shaw's civil lawsuit, Garrison had never mentioned the funds that had been transmitted from Louis Wolfson in Miami through Florida State's Attorney Richard Gerstein, and through radio and television personality Larry King.[2924]

Jim Garrison, in addition to being a defendant in Shaw's civil suit, was very much in the news after leaving office. He had lost a race for the Louisiana Supreme Court during the summer of 1974, around the time of Shaw's death; some attributed his loss to the news of Shaw's death awakening negative memories about him among the electorate, but it was more likely the continuing effect of his own criminal trials.

In 1975, even with no political race ongoing, Garrison was in the news again. A *Times-Picayune* article on May 1 related how, back in November 1974, Garrison had been awarded $109,400 by a jury in a lawsuit against Hotel Dieu Hospital, after one hour of deliberation. Garrison had claimed that he suffered an infection during a stay there in December 1969. The judgment was reversed in April 1975.[2925] Garrison indeed had been ill during much of 1969 and 1970, following the verdict in Shaw's conspiracy trial. He had been unable to campaign much for re-election that fall, instead relying instead on television ads that made effective use of the medium. The hospital stay during which he supposedly suffered the infection at issue occurred shortly after the election.

Miriam Cooney Abbott continued to be more upbeat than Wegmann about the final outcome of the civil suit. She wrote to Wegmann in late May, enclosing her own appellate brief responding to the defendants, and asking for $1,000 in fees for the work she had done. Cooney said that she expected the U.S. Fifth Circuit Court of Appeals to uphold the Federal district court decision, and for the U.S. Supreme Court then to refuse a *writ of certiorari*, effectively allowing the suit to proceed notwithstanding Shaw's death.[2926]

Although Edward Wegmann, as Shaw's civil attorney of twenty-five years, was the main engine behind the continuing civil suit, he persuaded the other criminal attorneys to remain involved in the case, on an unpaid basis. As of June 1975, Irvin Dymond, William Wegmann, and Sal Panzeca were all still listed as attorneys of record for the case.

The properties owned by Shaw had fallen into disrepair in the last year or so of Shaw's life, and continued to decline after his death. Apparently, the class of tenants the property attracted was less than desirable as well. In a letter to Edith Stern in late May 1975, Edward Wegmann referred to an insurance claim the property had to file related to the "horrible shooting incident" of February 28 that had occurred at or near the property.[2927]

In mid-June 1975, Stern's attorney Thomas Lemann again reported to Stern on various court filings related to Shaw's estate. He said that since Shaw's death, most of the filings had been related to payment of debt, including those owed to Ochsner Hospital, the Bultman funeral home, First National Bank of Commerce, Edward Wegmann, and the Tate Company.[2928]

Although he had tried to maintain his optimism, and despite encouragement from Abbott, Edward Wegmann actually had been very surprised when the Federal district court allowed Shaw's suit to continue. Judge Heebe had recognized there were differing opinions about the law in the case, so he allowed an immediate appeal of the issues on which he had ruled. In a letter to Jeff Biddison in mid-June, Wegmann wrote, "In my humble opinion, the Trial Judge erred when he denied the motion to dismiss and failed and refused to apply Louisiana law. I anticipate that the Appellate Court will reverse the Trial Court and grant the motion to dismiss by application of Louisiana law." Wegmann sent the letter in an envelope that also contained a copy of the brief filed by the defendants appealing the decision.[2929]

In a letter to Biddison in mid-July, Edward Wegmann advised of the brief he was filing in the case in answer to the defendants' appeal. He reiterated that the trial judge in the case had refused to apply Louisiana law, yielding a temporary outcome in favor of Shaw's estate. However, Wegmann predicted to Biddison that the appellate court would reverse the trial court, and dismiss the suit.[2930]

One of the defendant appellant briefs pointed out the irony that if Shaw had died without a will, his property would have reverted to the State of Louisiana, which then would sue itself for damages under Shaw's lawsuit claims. Shaw's suit specifically was "for damages for injuries sustained by plaintiff as a result of his having been deprived of the rights, privileges and immunities secured to him by the Constitution and laws of the United States," and claimed these damages based on Section 1983 of the Civil Rights Act.

In mid-August, Joseph Falgout wrote to Edith Stern, indicating that revenues from the St. Peter and Toulouse Street property, owned by Shaw's estate and on which Stern held a lien, was sufficient to pay Tate Company for its management services, and to pay the interest to Stern, but not to maintain the property. He indicated that the estate was still looking for a buyer.[2931]

On August 26, 1975, Edith Stern wrote to Wegmann, saying that some years ago she had loaned four small marble statues to Shaw for his courtyard at the St. Peter and Toulouse Street properties; she wondered if she might claim them back now.[2932] Wegmann replied that he would find out about the statues.[2933] Several months later, Wegmann wrote that he was returning three of the marble statues, and four pedestals that went with them, to Stern. He noted that one statue had been stolen sometime in the past, and that the neck had been broken on another.[2934]

Some months after Shaw's death, a group of his friends, primarily female friends, had discussed the idea of placing a plaque in Shaw's honor on the Spanish Stables building on Governor Nicholls Street in the French Quarter. Shaw had owned the building in the early 1960s, and had refurbished it and sold it a few years later at what was then the highest price a French Quarter residential property had ever fetched.

Shaw's friend Gail Baumgartner was among those involved in planning the plaque. She wrote to Edith Stern in early April 1975, recounting her involvement with Shaw. She said that she had met Shaw at the beginning stages of his troubles with Garrison. Both were avid readers and read from each other's libraries of books. She said that in the beginning of their relationship, both had found a great deal of comfort in the "exhilaration" of a new relationship. She said that around Easter the year before, in 1974, they both had gone through a painful period when Shaw had acknowledged the possibility of "brain involvement" related to his cancer. She said that at the time, there seemed to be "no distant future" to him. She said she realized, perhaps for the first time, Shaw's loneliness as he felt strongly "the absence of descendants," at one part remarking to her, "Who will say Kaddish" for him? How, she asked Stern, does one go about "the memories of seven years?" She said that Shaw had lived, and "our lives are infinitely richer for this," as "he had a way of humanizing people."[2935]

Reading her letter, it is interesting to speculate on the nature of the relationship between Shaw and Baumgartner. Some maintain that Baumgartner and Shaw knew each other well before the period marking the beginning of Shaw's troubles with Garrison, that the two had known each other earlier in the 1960s from the French Quarter social scene. Others have doubted that the two had any kind of serious romantic relationship, although perhaps Baumgartner desired this, as she was a lonely person following her divorce from her husband, around the time of Shaw's arrest. The closeness of friendship came about at a time after Shaw's arrest when issues of homosexuality were swirling around him, when arguably he needed female friends, and at least temporarily had to abandon some of his ties with younger males.

In early May, Edith Stern wrote to Edward Wegmann, asking if he was agreeable to having checks related to financing the plaque in Shaw's honor sent to his office;[2936] Wegmann accepted the offer of collecting and coordinating the payments.Various drafts of the wording to be placed on the plaque were generated during the course of the campaign; some of the early drafts were by local journalist David Chandler and Edith Stern. Some of the early accounts of his life had him born in Livingston Parish, Louisiana, rather than Tangipahoa Parish.

Among those to whom Edith Stern reached out for funding of the plaque in Shaw's memory was Judson O'Donnell, Shaw's friend from his New York days, who had lived in southern California since at least the 1940s. O'Donnell wrote to Stern that he was "Clay Shaw's oldest friend," and said that the two had shared several apartments together in Manhattan during the 1930s. He said the two had first met through Muriel [Bultman] Francis, who had also lived in New York City during those days. Interestingly, O'Donnell went on to say that, "I am the principal beneficiary of Clay's will." He discussed the Mediterranean cruise that Shaw and Stern had taken three years before, saying that Shaw had spoken in particular about the Isaac Stern concert in North Africa, and about the impression the entire trip had made on him. He said that Shaw had often discussed his fondness for Edith Stern while visiting O'Donnell on trips to Los Angeles. He told Stern that on Shaw's trip to California at the time of the Kennedy assassination (he mistakenly placed their visit as the night before the assassination, whereas Shaw had been in San Francisco on that night), he and Shaw had seen the movie *Tom Jones*, before Shaw had gone on to San Francisco. O'Donnell said that he spoke to Gail Baumgartner occasionally, and that he had wanted to write Stern many times, to thank her for all that she had done for Shaw.[2937]

Stern passed O'Donnell's letter on to Gail Baumgartner for her perusal, indicating that it was such a "nice surprise" that "I had to share it with you." She went on to note that she "must say that is news" that O'Donnell was the principal beneficiary of Shaw's will, indicating that she hoped "there is something to inherit" after all debts were paid. She reported that there was "not a nibble on the 'Whore House,'" meaning the property on which she held the mortgage, no doubt referring to the quality of tenants it had attracted in recent times.[2938]

Stern sent Judson O'Donnell the proposed wording for the plaque, which spoke generally about Shaw's effort in restoring properties throughout the French Quarter, but said nothing about his ordeal at the hands of Jim Garrison. O'Donnell replied in early October, saying that he was glad about the plaque, but believed the language on it was "restrained." O'Donnell said that, "Clay Shaw was killed by outrageous accusations," such that his "central nervous system" was seriously affected by the tremendous tension and anxiety that he endured. He noted that all through his life every decision and action of Shaw's had been determined by "high principle," and that the years of agony he had endured were unfair. Ultimately, though, O'Donnell agreed that the more moderate language on the plaque was appropriate, and suggested that Stern see that photographs were taken of the ceremony.[2939]

Mayor Moon Landrieu and his wife, Verna, also were asked to participate in the project. Verna Landrieu wrote to Edith Stern in October 1975, saying that, "Moon and I are grateful to be included among friends of this remarkable man." She added that, "I have felt a touch of admiration and affection for him."[2940] Indeed, Edith Stern, with her customary care for such occasions, attempted to include anyone who might be interested, and wished to show respect for Shaw. One note indicates she wanted to locate the taxi driver, Marty Cocita, who had regularly helped Shaw with transportation after his arrest, and whose entire immediate family had become friends with Shaw.[2941]

French Quarter artist Lin Emery designed the plaque in Shaw's honor. Among the contributors were former *States-Item* reporter David Chandler, Roland Chiara, current owner of the Spanish Stables, and owner of a hair and nail spa that Shaw had patronized for many years, reporter Iris Kelso, former Garrison investigator turned Shaw supporter William Gurvich, Judson O'Donnell, author James Kirkwood, Mrs. Herbert Christenberry, wife of the Federal judge whose ruling had finally freed Shaw from all prosecution in 1971, and a number of others, including the playwright and restaurateur Chris Blake.[2942]

The plaque, made at the Ed Smith Stencil company,[2943] listed the various properties that Shaw had restored during his life in the French Quarter. Those included nine restorations, among them 909 St. Louis Street, 505, 507, 509, and 511 Dauphine Street, 921 and 927 Burgundy Street, 1313 Dauphine Street, and 716-24 Governor Nicholls Street, the Spanish Stables itself. Jeff Biddison provided a list of the restorations Shaw had done.[2944] Curiously, the plaque does not list Shaw's original French Quarter home on Barracks Street, nor does it list the complex at 906 Esplanade, or the one at 908 Esplanade, although 1313 Dauphine Street was the original carriage house to the property at 906 Esplanade.

Jeff Biddison, who started having heart problems years before, became a patient at Stanford Medical Center in Palo Alto, California during the long period when the plaque was being planned, although he assisted whenever information was needed. Biddison would not outlive Shaw by many years, passing in 1981, not long after Shaw's other longtime romantic interest, William Henry Formyduval, who died in 1980.

Attorney James J. Gleason, III had been retained originally to represent Perry Russo as one of the defendants Shaw was suing in the civil case against Jim Garrison and others. On December 2, 1975, Gleason filed a motion to withdraw from the case, indicating that he had taken a job in St. Tammany Parish, across Lake Ponchartrain from New Orleans. In an interview with the author in 2002, Gleason said that when he had been hired, he was told that the bulk of the defense of the lawsuit would be handled by Malcolm Monroe, and that Gleason would not have to be heavily involved. He said that he never liked Russo, whom he took as someone who tried to impress younger, more innocent people around him. He remembered Russo calling him out of the blue once, demanding to know when he was going to receive his money from the lawsuit; Gleason had to inform Russo that he was being sued by Shaw, and the question was whether he would owe anything at the end of the lawsuit, not whether he would collect anything.[2945]

On December 11, 1975, Edward Wegmann advised Edith Stern that a purchaser had finally been found for the St. Peter and Toulouse Street property, enabling him to close the succession, and pay the mortgage debt to Stern in full. He indicated that the sale would take place on January 15, 1976, seventeen months after Shaw's death.[2946]

At the end of January 1976, Edith Stern's business manager, Joseph Falgout of Starwood Corporation, wrote her, indicating that the property on St. Peter Street had sold two weeks before to a Dr. Stanfield, for $345,000. Falgout analyzed the history of the loan for Mrs. Stern, and indicated that she had collected $78,442.19 in interest income over the life of the loan. The original full loan amount had been $228,347.50 as of March 26, 1970, and the payoff amount was $224,557.51 on January 30, 1976.[2947]

The property had been valued at $300,000 as part of Shaw's estate. With the sale bringing a significantly higher value, the actual net value of Shaw's estate would have been closer to $200,000, a tidy sum in 1974 dollars.

The plaque in Shaw's honor was finally dedicated and installed on the Spanish Stables building on September 28, 1976. Among the attendees was William Formyduval, Shaw's long-time companion, who had drifted away from Shaw in the mid-1960s, and had been informally prohibited by Jeff Biddison from contacting Shaw during the last months of his life. Edward Wegmann was unable to attend the plaque dedication, because he had to be in Federal district court in Houston, Texas at the time.[2948]

On January 24, 1977, the U.S. Fifth Circuit Court of Appeals in New Orleans upheld the decision by the Federal district court in New Orleans, ruling that Shaw's lawsuit could proceed. The decision surprised Shaw's attorneys, who were obviously happy about it. However, the defendants appealed quickly to the United States Supreme Court.

On June 22, 1977, Edward Wegmann wrote to Malcolm Monroe, the defendants' chief counsel, saying that his client, presumably meaning Jeff Biddison, had asked him to inquire about the possibility of settlement of the claim; Wegmann asked Monroe to discuss it with his clients.[2949] Monroe responded the next day, saying that his firm now only represented defendant Willard Robertson. Monroe said that progress toward a settlement could be made by Wegmann's client putting forth a "realistic figure" to pass on to all parties for their individual consideration. Monroe said that Willard Robertson was preparing a petition to the U.S. Supreme Court, and that he did not know if the case could be settled, but if so, it would have to be done promptly, to avoid further costs and expenses.[2950]

On July 27, Jim Garrison filed a motion to dismiss the lawsuit against him, based upon a new Supreme Court ruling that dealt with judicial immunity. The case, *Imbler v. Pachtman, District Attorney*, handed down in 1976, held that a prosecuting attorney was absolutely immune from a civil suit for damages for alleged deprivation of the constitutional rights of an accused. The decision strengthened the already almost absolute immunity of a prosecutor. The case was being used, a dozen years later, to block civil rights lawsuits against prosecutors in Dallas, Texas, one of the most notorious jurisdictions in the country for wrongful prosecutions.

As the summer of 1977 progressed, Edward Wegmann wrote to his brother, advising of Malcolm Monroe's petition of a *writ of certiorari* to the United Supreme Court. Wegmann said the chances were slim to none that the Supreme Court would accept the petition, but he still recognized that anything was possible in an individual court decision.[2951]

On December 5, 1977, the U.S. Supreme Court served notice that it had indeed granted the writ, agreeing to hear the case.

Edward Wegmann argued the case before the Supreme Court for the Estate of Clay Shaw, qualifying for admission to the bar of the court only a few months before.[2952] Malcolm Monroe argued the case for the various defendants to the original civil suit.[2953] The case was styled as *Willard E. Robertson vs. Edward F. Wegmann, Executor of the Estate of Clay Shaw*, as the original defendants to the civil suit were appealing an adverse verdict from the Fifth U.S. Circuit Court of Appeals.

A group called the Lawyers' Committee for Civil Rights Under Law wished to submit an *amicus curiae* brief on behalf of Shaw's estate. Edward Wegmann did not wish their help, and rejected the group's efforts, as did, obviously for different reasons, Malcolm Monroe representing the defendants. However, the Supreme Court allowed the brief. The group had been organized in 1963, at the request of President Kennedy, to involve private attorneys in assisting with cases involving civil rights violations. The group was interested in remedies for those affected by police or other official misconduct. In putting forward its brief, the Committee said that the parties on both sides of the suit had discussed only the narrow interests of Clay Shaw's death under Louisiana law, and that neither party was represented by counsel who frequently litigated civil rights actions.

On May 31, 1978, approximately eleven years and three months after Shaw had first been arrested, the U.S. Supreme Court reversed the judgment of the Fifth U.S. Circuit Court of Appeals, deciding that Louisiana law would apply, and that Shaw's lawsuit could not continue, due to his death and the lack of legally interested parties. Additionally, the Supreme Court ruled that the defendants could recover costs of $309.89 from Edward Wegmann, acting as executor of the estate.

Wegmann wrote to Jeff Biddison that he had done his best for Shaw for more than eleven years, but that nothing further could be done. He enclosed a final invoice for expenses incurred, indicating that his agreement with Shaw had been to invoice him for expenses only, not his actual time.[2954] Notably, Wegmann also cautioned Biddison that, had the lawsuit been allowed to proceed, there was no guarantee of it being successful, as Garrison was challenging it based upon the relatively recent ruling by the U.S. Supreme Court concerning prosecutorial immunity. It was an important point, as a number of authors have assumed that Shaw would have won the lawsuit, had he only lived to see it through.

The firm of Deutsch, Kerrigan and Stiles earned significant fees representing Garrison, his office as district attorney, and other clients related to the Clay Shaw case over the years, beginning in 1967. The firm represented Garrison in various appeals related to Shaw's criminal conspiracy case, appeals related to the permanent injunction granted by Judge Herbert Christenberry in Shaw's perjury case, defended Garrison and others in Shaw's civil suit against them, defended Garrison related to the libel suit filed by Gordon Novel, and was involved in aspects of the Edgar Eugene Bradley case. An invoice from the firm covering the period from February 28, 1970 through December 31, 1971, related to the civil suit alone, totaled $46,350, of which Garrison was to pay half, with Willard Robertson and Joseph Rault splitting the remainder.[2955]

# Aftermath

The case against Clay Shaw had all but been discredited following his acquittal on March 1, 1969. The speed with which the jury had returned its verdict, combined with the general shakiness of most or all of the important witnesses against him, combined to turn most independent-minded people against the case, although not necessarily against Jim Garrison personally, as reflected by Garrison's overwhelming re-election the following November. While Garrison was able to hold the potential perjury prosecution over Shaw's head for another three and a half years, to most individuals that was merely proof of a vendetta that Garrison had against Shaw, not of any actual guilt on Shaw's part.

Even in the Kennedy assassination conspiracy community, the Jim Garrison investigation was discredited. Some researchers applauded Garrison for unearthing new leads about previously undiscovered characters, such as David Ferrie, the anti-Castro Cubans and others who may have played a role in the assassination, or who could at least be fit into alternative conspiracy theories, ones that did not involve Shaw. Some also applauded Garrison for generating the first public showing of the Zapruder film, which captured the actual assassination, and which the general public had never seen.

After the perjury prosecution of Shaw was permanently stopped, what little support remained for Garrison's investigation more or less collapsed completely. Jim Garrison, however, resurrected himself in New Orleans legal circles, published a novel, and generally shied away from discussions of the Shaw case, although he assisted the House Select Committee on Assassinations in the late 1970s with input on his theories about the assassination, and with leads developed during his investigation.

The death of Garrison's case against Shaw merely reinforced, to a greater degree than ever, feelings about Shaw among those who had long known him. If one set out to examine any individual's life, it would be difficult to find a greater degree of unanimity of good feeling than that expressed toward Clay Shaw by those who had known him. The feeling cut across the grain; individuals in the business world, whether conservative or liberal, members of the gay community, males and females, young and old, black and white, all liked him immensely and found him to be a courteous, intelligent, generous, polished, and kind individual. With a tiny number of exceptions, including those somehow aligned with Garrison, or those who might have had a business dispute with Shaw in the past, everyone liked him and remembered him fondly. There were some who were uncomfortable with Shaw's homosexuality, but as Shaw had never played the issue up, even those individuals tended to downplay it and concentrate their comments on the wrong he had suffered.

The genuinely high regard in which most people held Shaw was shared even by some whose only contact with him was as a sexual partner. One such man, who had participated in some of the same circles as Shaw, said after several discussions with the author, "I wish I could help you more, but the only thing that really connected us was sex." Nonetheless, he spoke admiringly of Shaw as a person, and recalled an instance when he passed Shaw on the street after his arrest. Thinking that, because of the way they had known each other, Shaw might not want to acknowledge him, he pretended he did not recognize Shaw; he later learned that his well-meaning action had hurt Shaw's feelings during that critical time.

Even within the New Orleans-based anti-Communist Information Council of the Americas (INCA), Shaw's homosexuality had not been much of an issue, having been overridden by the organization's opposition to Garrison's investigation based upon the leftist influence around it. In a 1978 letter to Elizabeth Finnell of Freedom's Foundation in New Orleans, Ed Butler of INCA discussed Garrison's investigation, although he did not name Garrison in the letter. Butler said that "anti-American vultures" had "moved to exploit the investigation," adding that, "The scavengers had the full power of arrest and prosecution of the DA behind them," and that it was "a preview of what a police state in America would look like." Butler recalled how the "balloon-like investigation began to collapse as soon as it was challenged."[2956]

On November 20, 1983, the *Times-Picayune* ran an article entitled "The Case That Never Was," an account of Garrison's prosecution of Shaw, which appeared as part of the newspaper's coverage of the twentieth anniversary of Kennedy's assassination. Written by reporter Dean Baquet, the article featured comments from Garrison, several of his assistant district attorneys who had participated in either prosecuting or investigating the case, and from Shaw's chief defense attorney Irvin Dymond.[2957] Their perspectives are interesting, coming at a time when the case was completely dead, having been, in the eyes of most, thoroughly discredited for well over a decade.

Several of Garrison's aides said that, before the Kennedy assassination investigation began, Garrison had become bored and restless in the job, that he worked just a few hours a day, coming into work around midday, and leaving in the late afternoon. Once the investigation began, however, he seemed energized by it, and began working an increased number of hours.

Charles Ward, who at the time was Garrison's chief assistant, was the first man to ask to be removed from the investigation. He said that Garrison altered the case to fit the facts, and marshaled the facts to support his theory rather than letting the evidence lead to a logical conclusion.[2958]

John Volz, another assistant, was dismissed from the case by Garrison after he failed to, in Garrison's eyes, follow up adequately on certain leads. Although Volz would later re-enter the case during the attempted perjury prosecution of Shaw, following James Alcock's departure from the district attorney's office, Volz partly attributed his later being appointed as a Federal attorney in New Orleans to his not being too closely identified with Garrison's Kennedy assassination investigation[2959]

After the death of David Ferrie, some of Garrison's aides begged him to drop the entire investigation, saying that Ferrie's death gave them a logical way out of the hole into which the office had dug itself. Garrison acknowledged that his aides had asked him to stop the investigation, and said that he regretted that he had not done so after Ferrie's death.[2960]

Regarding the actual prosecution of Shaw, three of the assistants directly involved with the prosecution commented on the case. Andrew Sciambra recalled a potential witness volunteering to help the investigation; it was discovered that he was calling from a mental institution. However, Sciambra apparently was not asked about, and did not volunteer information about, what appeared to be questionable techniques used by him to procure testimony from many of the more questionable witnesses at Shaw's trial.[2961]

Alvin Oser, who during the trial handled the portions related to Dallas witnesses, and the events that unfolded during the actual assassination, said that he did not know if Shaw was innocent or guilty, and had only argued a portion of the case because Garrison asked him to do so. Oser said that he believed in a conspiracy related to the assassination, and that more than one gunman had been involved.[2962]

Prosecutor James Alcock, who had prosecuted the bulk of the case against Shaw, maintained that there had been enough evidence to bring the case to trial, although he acknowledged that there had been trouble with some individual witnesses, and with some of the evidence coming together so that a jury would see the prosecution's point. He said that the Federal government had not provided some of the information related to Kennedy's death that might have helped the prosecution.[2963]

When asked whether he actually believed Shaw was guilty, Alcock replied that it was not a matter of whether he believed it or not; it was a matter of his believing whether the case should be presented to a jury. In his opinion, it was up to the jury to decide Shaw's guilt or innocence. Alcock said that he had advised Garrison that a jury might have trouble believing certain witnesses, such as Vernon Bundy or Charles Spiesel (an ironic comment, since Spiesel, of all the controversial witnesses, had been "discovered" by James Alcock rather than by Andrew Sciambra). He also said that he had never been fully convinced of Garrison's claim that Clay Shaw had worked for the Central Intelligence Agency (although the prosecution never made that point in the actual trial).[2964]

Shaw's chief criminal attorney, Irvin Dymond, said he had theorized that Shaw had been picked because he had been a homosexual, and was therefore vulnerable to such a prosecution.[2965] Although Dymond didn't elaborate on the comment, many have wondered over the years whether Shaw had been arrested simply because he was a homosexual. It is probably true that Shaw's homosexuality played a part in suspicion falling upon him in the first place, simply because David Ferrie's alleged homosexuality, and the comments of Dean Andrews, had already introduced the subject into the main body of possible suspects that had come to the attention of the investigators. As to whether Garrison had any particular prejudice against homosexuals more than the norm of that time, the evidence is somewhat lacking. Some point to raids made against gay bars during the era, but such bars in those days were often owned and run by organized crime, which needed to make payoffs to local authorities in order to stay open and operating. Some have maintained that even the famous Stonewall gay bar riots in New York City in 1969 were triggered by a police raid that came after a failure of organized crime payments to reach the police in time. Many gays in New Orleans knew and interacted with Garrison, and although many viewed him suspiciously after the Shaw case began, it is doubtful that there is any type of overriding evidence that Garrison systematically persecuted gays during his terms of office. It is possible, however, that he looked upon gays as a vulnerable community, much like African Americans, who could be milked for information, and possibly favorable testimony, in a close case.

If one accepts the jury's verdict that Shaw was not guilty, a question arises, unlike in many wrongful prosecutions, whether any crime was committed at all—by anyone. The nature of the conspiracy laws makes such a scenario possible, and differentiates it from other miscarriages of justice, where a real crime occurred but the wrong person was prosecuted because of mistaken identity, planted evidence, or perjured testimony. Shaw's case seemingly had such elements as well, but in the end it was a question of whether a conversation occurred, and if so, whether it rose to the level of a real conspiracy.

Garrison's unwillingness to cooperate with other authorities, specifically Federal authorities, may have prevented some questions that arose during his investigation from ever being successfully answered. As an example, Dean Andrews testified, finally, that a Helen Girt had been the person he heard call gay bar owner Eugene Davis "Clay Bertrand." The FBI seemed to know of her, and possibly where she was as well, but never followed up on the question. Similarly, when Hammond, Louisiana, funeral home director Carroll Thomas told an FBI agent that Shaw had introduced him to David Ferrie, seemingly one of the most credible assertions of the two having known each other, the FBI chose not to follow up, because it was avoiding involvement in Garrison's investigation.

Jim Garrison apparently never forgot about the case. He would continue to accumulate information about Shaw and other aspects of the case over the years until his death in 1992. He was interviewed by the House Select Committee on Assassinations (HSCA) in 1977, related to the Federal government's congressionally authorized reinvestigation of the Kennedy assassination. The same year, possibly to assist HSCA in its inquiry, or to assist him in gathering information he gave to it, Garrison had someone investigate various buildings owned by Shaw in the French Quarter as to the dates of purchase and sale of each, including 1313 Dauphine Street, where Shaw lived for some years, and 906 Esplanade, where he also had lived, and where witness Charles Spiesel, at Shaw's trial, had indicated he might have attended a party along with Shaw and Ferrie in 1963.

In 1988, Garrison published *On the Trail of the Assassins*, his most direct account of the Shaw case and trial. Garrison made some questionable assertions in the book, one of the most notable of which was that he was present for much of the trial and, in particular, present during Shaw's testimony, which the overwhelming majority of observers deny.

Former WDSU-TV reporter Richard Townley got quite a surprise when he read the book. Although Garrison had indicted Townley for allegedly interfering with his investigation, forcing Townley to leave New Orleans, in November 1973 Garrison had agreed to give Townley, then a reporter for a television station in another city, a filmed interview on the occasion of the tenth anniversary of the assassination. When Townley arrived at Garrison's office to conduct the interview, Garrison had given him a copy of his relatively recent book, *A Heritage of Stone*, with the handwritten inscription, "For Rick Townley. With warmest regards and appreciation and admiration—Jim Garrison."

Townley, who had therefore long assumed that Garrison had agreed to let bygones be bygones, was stunned to open Garrison's 1988 book about the case to discover that he had once again emerged as a chief villain in the case. Perhaps he shouldn't have been so surprised; many had noted Garrison's quality of compartmentalizing people, ideas, and situations, placing them aside when he no longer needed them, and resurrecting them when he needed them once more. Charging attorney Dean Andrews with perjury several times, then later supporting Andrews's bid to regain his license to practice law after the Shaw criminal case was over and done, is a case in point.

Garrison generated a memo in 1990 in which he recounted a phone call from a supposed friend of Clay Shaw to Ellen Ray, the publisher of Garrison's book. The call was said to have come from New Orleans, and the caller told Ray that Garrison's book was true in its charges that Shaw and Ferrie had known each other. The caller also said that one lover of Shaw's had had a sex change, and that Shaw had then rejected him. The memo also mentioned that another friend of Shaw, a Jim Belsome, had agreed with the caller about the truthfulness of Garrison's book. None of the statements in the memo, of course, are verifiable in that form to any independent researcher.[2966]

In 1991, partially using Garrison's book as source material, film director Oliver Stone released *JFK*, a movie dealing primarily with the Kennedy assassination, resurrecting the case against Shaw as the centerpiece of the story. As with any fictionalized film version of history, names, places, and situations were shifted around to create a history that never quite existed. While some of the dialogue in the movie commented on the doubtful nature of the case against Shaw, the overwhelming impact of the film left an impression upon most viewers unfamiliar with the history of Garrison's case that Shaw could very well have been guilty of the charges against him. A backlash began against the film six months before it was even released, while it was still being shot, primarily from reporters and researchers who were thoroughly familiar with Garrison's case against Shaw, and the reasons why it had failed so completely. Some elements of the gay community, to whom Shaw had become a sort of heroic victim over the years, protested as well. However, the overwhelming nature of the movie's presentation succeeded in bringing Garrison's case, and his theories, back to prominence.

As a result of the movie, a new surge of interest was generated in Kennedy's assassination, and in requiring the government to release records of the investigation that had long been withheld. Accordingly, in the 1990s, a Federal board, the Assassination Records Review Board (ARRB), began the process of declassifying and releasing governmental agency records, including those from the CIA and the FBI. At last, researchers had access to information directly concerning Shaw's long-rumored CIA connections. However, the release of the information, while it created a decade-long interest, and new speculation about Shaw's past, over time did little to satisfy many skeptics as to the exact nature of Shaw's relationship with the agency. By the turn of the century, the tide had turned against Garrison again, and belief in his case and theories receded once more.

Meanwhile, the institution that Clay Shaw managed for the first twenty years has fallen on hard times. After finally joining with International House in the 1980s, the International Trade Mart became the World Trade Center, still occupying the 33-story building the Mart had opened in the mid-1960s. A long, serious decline began; by the mid-1990s, the building was approximately half-occupied. Proposals to put a five-star hotel in the building fell through for one reason or another. By 2012, New Orleans Mayor Mitch Landrieu, whose father had appointed Shaw to the French Market Board in 1971, effectively fully restoring Shaw's reputation in the city in a publicly official way, was proposing to tear the building down.

# Acknowledgments

One of the great pleasures of working on this project over an 18-year period was being able to meet and deal with a large number of very nice people. Those included friends and acquaintances of Clay Shaw, of course, but also people who helped me move the project along in many different ways: researchers, personnel at libraries, family members, transcriptionists, database managers, and others who volunteered suggestions about the manuscript or particular pieces of information along the way.

The following is, I hope, a comprehensive listing of those who either granted me interviews or communicated via e-mail related to various aspects of the project. Many directly had knowledge of Shaw; others had knowledge of a person whom Shaw knew, or some other indirect aspect of his life or the Jim Garrison investigation.

Leith Adams
Rick Adams
William Alford
Andy Anderson
Frances Anderson
Michael Arnold
William Aylward
Hugh Aynesworth
Dahleen Bache
James Bacque
Virginia Baldwin
Dean Baquet
Steven Baril
Robert Barkerding
G. K. Barranger
Carolyn Barrois
Denis Barry
William Barry
Roberts Batson
James Beazor-Williams
Arthur Beckenstein
Pieter Van Bennekom
Gordon Berger
Rafael Bermúdez
Tom Bethell

Kent Biffle
Chris Blake
Mary Cobb Block
Hermann Bockelmann
Eric Bogner
Gary Bolding
Gretchen Bomboy
Lyle Bongé
Bruce Bonnecarrere
Fred Bookhardt
Gene Bourg
William Brazzil
Helen Breckinridge
Milton Brener
Dottie Brennan
Ella Brennan
Alice Brin
Tito Brin
Jack Brooking
James Brugger
Johann Bultman
Steven Burton
Charles Cabibi, Jr.
Allen Campbell
Marisol Canedo

Arthur Carpenter
Bob Carr
Jan Carr
Jeffrey Caulfield
Kevin Cessna
Patricia Chandler
Grace Charbonnet
Bonnie Chiara
Edmund Christy, Jr.
S. Michael Clark
Sandra Clark
Peter Cocita
Harry Connick, Sr.
Jesse Core
Clayton Cote
Walter Cowan
Arlen Coyle
Miller Cragon
Mina Crais
Marymor Cravens
Andy Crocchiolo
Tina Dart
Alicia Davis
Arthur Q. Davis
Millie Davis
Gerard de Ayala
Chester Delacruz
Manuel Delgado
Sam DePino
Donna Dezube
Jeffrey Dobson
Jim Dondson
Don Doody
Richard Doskey
Patrick Duffy
William Duffy
Carlton Dufrechou
David Duggins
George Dureau

F. Irvin Dymond
Jim Dymond
Robert Eckardt
Patrick Eddings
Bruce Eggler
Lloyd Eisinger
Scott Ellis
Lin Emery
Claire Evangelista
Paul Fabry
John Faust
Otis Fennell
Jane Fischer
Jesse Fisher
C. Stocker Fontelieu
James Formyduval
Mike Formy-Duval
Alberto Fowler
Remy Fransen
Ria Fransway
Mildred Cardenas Freudiger
Anthony Frewin
Marguerite Furr
Alec Gifford
Ruth Glass
Trudy Glass
Polly Goldberg
Henri Gomez
Dale Goudeau
Bob Greene
William Griffin
Odette Reising Grosz
William Grundmeyer
James Guedry
Christopher Guidroz
Betty Guillaud
James Gulotta
Charlene Harper
Marjorie Harwood

Maurice Hattier
Charles Haver
Clarke Hawley
Susan Faller Hayes
Jean Heid
Martha Hess
Edward Heymann
Richard Hicks
Paul Hoch
Faye Hogan
Kenneth Holditch
Jack Holman
Christopher Hopkins
Joe Horton
Ann Meadors Huey
John Iacometti
Eugene Ingram
Louis Ivon
Gordon Jackson
Wes Jackson
Olwen Janson
Erik Johnsen
Ann Jones
Wayne Julian
Irene Karlton
Sheldon Karon
Rosemarie Kaskell
Ernest Kelly
John Kelly
Gaines Kincaid
Burton Klein
William Klein
Richard Kluger
John Korbell
Michael Korda
Omer Kuebel
Michael Kurtz
Patricia Lambert
Moon Landrieu

Howard Leach
Richard Leacock
Hunter Leake III
Judy Ledner
Robert E. Lee
Anne Legett
Arthur Lemann
Nicholas Lemann
Thomas Lemann
Albert LeMón III
James Lesar
Henry Lesnick
Jane Lewis
Julius Lewis
Caleb Lief
David Lifton
Winston Lill
Sharon Litwin
William Livesay
Bobby Lodrigues
Alecia Long
J. Robert Lunney
Brobson Lutz
Sonia Lyons
Paolo Maffei
Thomas Mallon
Katherine Margas
Alison Marks
Mary Ellen Martens
Alvaro Martinez
Elena Martinez
Jean Masson
Peter Mattes
Thomas McBride
Leroy McClaren
Paul McClaren
Len McCormick
Floyd McLamb
Robert Mellon

Charles Menard
Wilbur Meneray
Henry Messer
Donald Meyer
James Michie
Frank Mike
Wallace Milam
Leon Miller
Mrs. Harry Miller
John Mitzel
Andrew Given Tobias Moore II
Alfred Jay Moran
Malcolm Moran
Christopher Morgan
Judy Morgan
Nicholas Morgan
Irene Morris
Benjamin Morrison
Christian Morrison
Herrise Morrison
Roger Moseley
Teresa Neaves
Linda Newton
Charles W. Nutter
Fred O'Bryan
John Ochsner, Sr.
Donald Organ
Tom Ostendorff
Joseph Oster
William Ousley
Kenneth Owen
Manuel Paez
Martin Palmer
Salvatore Panzeca
Michael Parks
Noel Parmentel
Carl Pelleck
Jerry Perkins
Dave Perry

Clyde Peterson
Karla Peterson
Henry Piarrot
Peter Pizzo
Ed Planer
Steven Plotkin
Julia Polk
Gerald Posner
Ross Pritchard
Nita Putnam
Carlos Quiroga
John Rarick
Kay Ravenel
Marcus Leslie Reed
George Rennar
Kenneth Reynolds
Evan Rhodes
Julie Rice
Robert Richter
Bill Rittenberg
Terry Flettrich Rohe
Robert Rolfe
George Roth
Ford Rowan
Gus Russo
Clyde Sakir
Edward Sakir
Albert Salzer
Thomas Samoluk
Kari Borg Samuels
Ross Scaccia
Darrah Schaefer
Gary Schoener
Sherman Schroeder
Don Schueler
Leonard Schwartzman
Jean-Pierre Schweitzer
Leslie Seale
Jean Seidenberg

Sarah Sell
W. L. Sellers
Henry Sender
Elton Shaw
Kendall Shaw
Al Shea
Laura Sitges
David Snyder
Michael Snyder
David Sogge
Chesley Soileau
Charles Spiesel
Edward Sporl III
Carl Sprick
Shelby Spuhler
James Squires
Bob Stuart
Jeff Sulzer
Victoria Hawes Sulzer
Wink Dameron Blair Sutz
William Taliaferro
Rowena Thompson
Fred W. Todd
Ben Toledano
Richard Townley
Laveau Truth
John Tunheim
James G. Tuthill

Steve Tyler
John Uhl
Pieter Van Bennekom
Louis Vargas
Bob Vernon
Gore Vidal
John Volz
Dave Wagenvoord
Jack Wardlaw
Judy Weekley
Cynthia Wegmann
William Wegmann
Joel Weinstock
Hanaba Munn Welch
Fred Westenberger
Wallace Westfeldt
Elena Rudeke White
Jeff Whiting
Thomas Wicker
Carolyn Wildenthal
David Wilk
Gary Williams
Dwight Wilson
Robert Wilson
Mack Wood
Ross Yockey
Mike Zelden
Tom Zung

The following is a listing of the major libraries that assisted me in one way or the other. It is probably not a complete listing, as there were numerous state, county, and city libraries that furnished information about individuals around the fringes of the project. A special thanks goes to the personnel at Tulane University Special Collections, Historic New Orleans Collection, and the National Archives at College Park, Maryland, where I spent the most time in active research.

Columbia University

Eisenhower Presidential Library

Historic New Orleans Collection

Johnson Presidential Library

Kennedy Presidential Library

Library of Congress

Long Vue (Edith Stern Papers)

Louisiana State University

Louisiana State University—Shreveport

Louisiana State University—New Orleans

Louisiana Archives

Louisiana Tech

Louisiana State Television Archives

Margaret Herrick Library

McMaster University Library

National Archives

New York Public Library

New Orleans Public Library

Newcomb University

Northwestern State University of Louisiana

Pearl River County Library

Princeton University

Southeastern Louisiana University Library

Tulane University

University of Alabama

University of Southern California

University of Tennessee

University of Tennessee—Martin

Warner Brothers

Warren Easton High School

Among independent researchers who assisted me, I would mention in particular Mary Ann DiNapoli for her work related to Shaw's time in New York City during the 1930s. Thanks to Sarah Moore for editing the manuscript, and to Scott Ellis for reading it through after the initial editing and making valuable suggestions. Thanks to Charles Hooper for his striking cover design.

Others had special roles as well. Donna Dariano and Sherry Jolly gave great assistance over many years in organizing the numerous names and notes that eventually made their way into the complete manuscript. Neana Saylor Clark, working over a three and a half year period, lent invaluable assistance in helping to turn the many years of research and note-taking into the manuscript.

Others who shared insight or information over the years included Professor John McAdams, who also read the manuscript, Steve Roy, Jerry Shinley, Steve Tyler, and Dave Reitzes.

Among the many people who knew Clay Shaw and cooperated in this project, it would be unfair to single out any names in particular, as each person did his or her best to help fill in gaps and share knowledge of him. But I would like to offer a collective thanks to a great group of people. Clay Shaw generally chose a high quality of person to be his friend, and perhaps that type of person naturally gravitated toward him as well.

# Endnotes

1. Record of Funeral for Glaris Lenora Shaw, Author's Private Collection.
2. Bureau of Internal Revenue, Employee Statement of Federal and Military Service, Department of the Treasury Employee File for Glaris Lenora Shaw, Author's Private Collection.
3. Personal History Statement, U.S. Prohibition Service, Department of the Treasury Employee File for Glaris Lenora Shaw, Author's Private Collection.
4. See New Orleans City Directories for 1922, 1923, 1924, and 1925, Tulane University, New Orleans, Louisiana.
5. See New Orleans City Directory for 1926, Tulane University, New Orleans, Louisiana.
6. See New Orleans City Directories for 1927 and 1928, Tulane University, New Orleans, Louisiana.
7. Department of the Treasury Employee File for Glaris Lenora Shaw, Author's Private Collection.
8. See New Orleans City Directory for 1929, Tulane University, New Orleans, Louisiana.
9. 1927 Edition of Warren Easton High School Annual, the *Eastonite*.
10. 1928 Edition of *The Eagle*, a publication of the graduating class of Warren Easton High School, contained in the high school annual, the *Eastonite*.
11. 1928 Edition of Warren Easton High School Annual, the *Eastonite*.
12. 1928 Edition of Warren Easton High School Annual, the *Eastonite*.
13. The *Turkey Buzzard*, a satirical "future newspaper" as part of the 1928 Annual for Warren Easton High School.
14. 1928 Edition of Warren Easton High School Annual, the *Eastonite*.
15. Le Petit Theatre Collection, Historic New Orleans Collection, New Orleans, Louisiana.
16. Le Petit Theatre Collection, Historic New Orleans Collection, New Orleans, Louisiana.
17. Le Petit Theatre Collection, Historic New Orleans Collection, New Orleans, Louisiana.
18. Le Petit Theatre du Vieux Carré–Programs, November-June 1920-29, Tulane University, New Orleans, Louisiana.
19. Le Petit Theatre Collection, Historic New Orleans Collection, New Orleans, Louisiana.
20. Le Petit Theatre Collection, Historic New Orleans Collection, New Orleans, Louisiana.
21. Le Petit Theatre Collection, Historic New Orleans Collection, New Orleans, Louisiana.
22. Interview with Marymor Cravens by author, July 11, 2007.
23. Letter, Fall 1928, Mary Moore Sanborn to Cynthia Sanborn, Letters from Mary Moore Sanborn to Cynthia Sanborn, Private Collection owned by Mrs. Duval Cravens, Sewanee, Tennessee.
24. Le Petit Theatre Collection, Historic New Orleans Collection, New Orleans, Louisiana.

25. Le Petit Theatre Collection, Historic New Orleans Collection, New Orleans, Louisiana.
26. See newspaper article about *Submerged*, date and newspaper unknown, Donated Papers of Clay Shaw, National Archives, College Park, Maryland.
27. Interview with Grace Charbonnet by author, January 30, 2009.
28. Le Petit Theatre Collection, Historic New Orleans Collection, New Orleans, Louisiana.
29. See New Orleans City Directory for 1929, Tulane University, New Orleans, Louisiana.
30. See New Orleans City Directory for 1930, Tulane University, New Orleans, Louisiana.
31. E-mail dated March 31, 2010, Gordon S. Jackson to Author.
32. E-mail dated March 31, 2010, Gordon S. Jackson to Author.
33. Le Petit Theatre Collection, Historic New Orleans Collection, New Orleans, Louisiana.
34. Le Petit Theatre Collection, Historic New Orleans Collection, New Orleans, Louisiana.
35. Claude M. Wise Papers, Louisiana State University, Baton Rouge, Louisiana.
36. Claude M. Wise Papers, Louisiana State University, Baton Rouge, Louisiana.
37. Claude M. Wise Papers, Louisiana State University, Baton Rouge, Louisiana.
38. Claude M. Wise Papers, Louisiana State University, Baton Rouge, Louisiana.
39. Le Petit Theatre Collection, Historic New Orleans Collection, New Orleans, Louisiana.
40. See New Orleans City Directory for 1931, Tulane University, New Orleans, Louisiana.
41. Interview with Leroy S. McClaren by Author, March 21, 2009.
42. See New Orleans City Directory for 1932, Tulane University, New Orleans, Louisiana.
43. Le Petit Theatre du Vieux Carré–Programs, October-May 1929-39, Tulane University, New Orleans, Louisiana.
44. Le Petit Theatre du Vieux Carré–Programs, October-May 1929-39, Tulane University, New Orleans, Louisiana.
45. Letter dated April 24, 1967, Kay Lucas Leake Dart to Shaw, Author's Personal Collection.
46. Letter dated March 4, 1969, Kay Lucas Leake Dart to Shaw, Author's Personal Collection.
47. See New Orleans City Directory for 1935, Tulane University, New Orleans, Louisiana.
48. Department of the Treasury Employee File for Glaris Lenora Shaw, Author's Private Collection.
49. Letter dated April 30, 1953, J.H. Newman to Glaris L. Shaw, Author's Private Collection.
50. Letter dated March 9, 1936, Shaw to Lyle Saxon, Lyle Saxon Collection, Tulane University, New Orleans, Louisiana.
51. Letter dated March 9, 1936, Shaw to Lyle Saxon, Lyle Saxon Collection, Tulane University, New Orleans, Louisiana.
52. Letter dated March 9, 1936, Shaw to Lyle Saxon, Lyle Saxon Collection, Tulane University, New Orleans, Louisiana.
53. Interview with Clay Shaw by Roy S. Simmonds, August 31, 1972, Roy S. Simmonds Collection, The W.S. Hoole Special Collections Library, The University of Alabama, Tuscaloosa, Alabama.
54. Letter dated August 24, 1936, Mary Moore Sanborn to Cynthia Sanborn, Letters from Mary Moore Sanborn to Cynthia Sanborn, Private Collection owned by Mrs. Duval Cravens, Sewanee, Tennessee.

55 Interview with Marymor Cravens by author, July 11, 2007.

56 E-mail dated July 22, 2010, Gordon S. Jackson to Author.

57 See contract between H. Stuart Cottman and Le Vergne Shaw and The Dramatic Publishing Company, March 21, 1938, Donated Papers of Clay Shaw, National Archives, College Park, Maryland.

58 Snyder, Michael. "'I Feel Like a Spring Lamb': What Clay Shaw's Literary Life Reveals." *JFK: History, Memory, Legacy*. Eds. John Delane Williams, Robert G. Waite and Gregory S. Gordon. 2007. Web.

59 Snyder, Michael. "'I Feel Like a Spring Lamb': What Clay Shaw's Literary Life Reveals." *JFK: History, Memory, Legacy*. Eds. John Delane Williams, Robert G. Waite and Gregory S. Gordon. 2007. Web.

60 E-mail from Bill Santin to author, April 4, 2007.

61 Article dated January 25, 1939, *The New Orleans Item*, by Harnett Kane, Donated Papers of Clay Shaw, National Archives, College Park, Maryland.

62 Article dated January 25, 1939, *The New Orleans Item*, by Harnett Kane, Donated Papers of Clay Shaw, National Archives, College Park, Maryland.

63 Article dated January 25, 1939, *The New Orleans Item*, by Harnett Kane, Donated Papers of Clay Shaw, National Archives, College Park, Maryland.

64 Article dated January 25, 1939, *The New Orleans Item*, by Harnett Kane, Donated Papers of Clay Shaw, National Archives, College Park, Maryland.

65 Letter, no date, but probably 1938 or 1939, Judson O'Donnell to Muriel Francis, Bultman Family Papers, Historic New Orleans Collection, New Orleans, Louisiana.

66 Obituary for Lee Keedick, *The New York Times*, August 18, 1959.

67 Notification of Personnel Action dated July 1, 1953, Department of the Treasury Employee File for Glaris Lenora Shaw, Author's Private Collection shows Shaw's father's highest annual salary was $5,370 at the end of his service with the Department of the Treasury in 1953.

68 See newspaper article about Shaw becoming Aide-de-Camp to General Charles Thrasher, unknown newspaper, around 1945, Donated Papers of Clay Shaw, National Archives, College Park, Maryland.

69 Letter dated March 27, 1942, Shaw to Norman Cousins, Author's Collection.

70 Letter dated March 27, 1942, Shaw to Norman Cousins, Author's Collection.

71 Letter dated March 27, 1942, Shaw to Norman Cousins, Author's Collection.

72 Letter dated October 28, 1942, Norman Cousins to Shaw, Author's Collection.

73 Report of Physical Exam and Induction, October 16, 1942, Donated Papers of Edward Wegmann, National Archives, College Park, Maryland.

74 See Report of Physical Examination for Officer Candidate School, Donated Papers of Edward Wegmann, National Archives, College Park, Maryland.

75 Shaw military records, Donated Papers of Edward Wegmann, National Archives, College Park, Maryland.

76 See Chief Complaint Report related to back injury at Camp Barkley, Texas, Donated Papers of Edward Wegmann, National Archives, College Park, Maryland.

77 Report dated May 4, 1943 regarding Shaw's back injury, Donated Papers of Edward Wegmann, National Archives, College Park, Maryland.

78  See Certificate of Service for serial number 0-2047-494, Shaw's record as officer, Donated Papers of Edward Wegmann, National Archives, College Park, Maryland.

79  Folder: MDGH 127-0 (48839), History, 127th General Hospital, 15 Jan 43–13 Oct 45, Record Group 94, The Adjutant General's Office, World War II Operations Reports 1940-48, Medical, MDGH 127-0 to MDGH 127-1.13, Box number 21612, National Archives, College Park, Maryland.

80  Folder: MDGH 127-0 (48839), History, 127th General Hospital, 15 Jan 43–13 Oct 45, Record Group 94, The Adjutant General's Office, World War II Operations Reports 1940-48, Medical, MDGH 127-0 to MDGH 127-1.13, Box number 21612, National Archives, College Park, Maryland.

81  Folder: MDGH, 127-0.7 (26700), Diary, 127th General Hospital, 1 Jan 43-31 Jan 44, Record Group 94, Records of the Office of the Surgeon General, World War II Administrative Reports, 1940-1949, Unit Annual Reports, National Archives, College Park, Maryland.

82  Folder: MDGH 127-0 (48839), History, 127th General Hospital, 15 Jan 43–13 Oct 45, Record Group 94, The Adjutant General's Office, World War II Operations Reports 1940-48, Medical, MDGH 127-0 to MDGH 127-1.13, Box number 21612, National Archives, College Park, Maryland.

83  Folder: 127th General Hospital ETO, Final Report, 127th General Hospital, Record Group 112, Records of the Office of the Surgeon General, World War II Administrative Reports, 1940-1949, Unit Annual Reports, National Archives, College Park, Maryland.

84  Folder: MDGH, 127-0.7 (26700), Diary, 127th General Hospital, 1 Jan 43-31 Jan 44, Record Group 94, Records of the Office of the Surgeon General, World War II Administrative Reports, 1940-1949, Unit Annual Reports, National Archives, College Park, Maryland.

85  Folder: 127th General Hospital ETO, Final Report, 127th General Hospital, Record Group 112, Records of the Office of the Surgeon General, World War II Administrative Reports, 1940-1949, Unit Annual Reports, National Archives, College Park, Maryland.

86  Folder: MDGH, 127-0.7 (26700), Diary, 127th General Hospital, 1 Jan 43-31 Jan 44, Record Group 94, Records of the Office of the Surgeon General, World War II Administrative Reports, 1940-1949, Unit Annual Reports, National Archives, College Park, Maryland.

87  Folder: MDGH 127-0 (48839), History, 127th General Hospital, 15 Jan 43–13 Oct 45, Record Group 94, The Adjutant General's Office, World War II Operations Reports 1940-48, Medical, MDGH 127-0 to MDGH 127-1.13, Box number 21612, National Archives, College Park, Maryland.

88  Folder: MDGH 127-0 (48839), History, 127th General Hospital, 15 Jan 43–13 Oct 45, Record Group 94, The Adjutant General's Office, World War II Operations Reports 1940-48, Medical, MDGH 127-0 to MDGH 127-1.13, Box number 21612, National Archives, College Park, Maryland.

89  Folder: MDGH 127-0.1 (17952), History, 127th General Hospital, 18 Oct–31 Dec 43, Record Group 94, The Adjutant General's Office, World War II Operations Reports 1940-48, Medical, MDGH 127-0 to MDGH 127-1.13, Box number 21612, National Archives, College Park, Maryland.

90  Folder: MDGH 127-0 (48839), History, 127th General Hospital, 15 Jan 43–13 Oct 45, Record Group 94, The Adjutant General's Office, World War II Operations Reports 1940-48, Medical, MDGH 127-0 to MDGH 127-1.13, Box number 21612, National Archives, College Park, Maryland.

91  Interview with Alison Marks by Author, August 22, 1999.

92  *Some of my Army Experiences during WWII*, an unpublished account by Father Jack Holman, excerpt in author's possession.

[93] Folder: MDGH, 127-0.7 (26700), Diary, 127th General Hospital, 1 Jan 43-31 Jan 44, Record Group 94, Records of the Office of the Surgeon General, World War II Administrative Reports, 1940-1949, Unit Annual Reports, National Archives, College Park, Maryland.

[94] Folder: MDGH 127-0 (48839), History, 127th General Hospital, 15 Jan 43–13 Oct 45, Record Group 94, The Adjutant General's Office, World War II Operations Reports 1940-48, Medical, MDGH 127-0 to MDGH 127-1.13, Box number 21612, National Archives, College Park, Maryland.

[95] Folder: MDGH 127-0 (48839), History, 127th General Hospital, 15 Jan 43–13 Oct 45, Record Group 94, The Adjutant General's Office, World War II Operations Reports 1940-48, Medical, MDGH 127-0 to MDGH 127-1.13, Box number 21612, National Archives, College Park, Maryland.

[96] Folder: 127th General Hospital ETO, History, 1 Jan 1944-31 Mar 1944, Record Group 112, Records of the Office of the Surgeon General, World War II Administrative Reports, 1940-1949, Unit Annual Reports, National Archives, College Park, Maryland.

[97] Folder: 601, History Southern Base Section, SOS, ETOUSA, from 4 Aug 1942 to 31 Dec 1943, Record Group 498, Records of Headquarters, European Theater of Operations, United States Army (World War II), European Theater of Operations, Historical Division, Administrative File, 1942-Jan 1946, National Archives, College Park, Maryland.

[98] Letter, undated, probably late February or early March 1944, Shaw to Alison Marks, Author's collection.

[99] Folder: MDGH 127-0 (48839), History, 127th General Hospital, 15 Jan 43–13 Oct 45, Record Group 94, The Adjutant General's Office, World War II Operations Reports 1940-48, Medical, MDGH 127-0 to MDGH 127-1.13, Box number 21612, National Archives, College Park, Maryland.

[100] Letter dated April 2, 1944, Shaw to Alison Marks, Author's Collection.

[101] Letter dated April 2, 1944, Shaw to Alison Marks, Author's Collection.

[102] Letter dated April 2, 1944, Shaw to Alison Marks, Author's Collection.

[103] Folder: Organization History, HQ and HQ Co., Southern Base Section, July 20, 1942-December 31, 1942, 97-BS9-HQ-0.2, Record Group 407, Records of the Adjutant General's Office, WWII Operations Reports, 1940-48, European Theater, National Archives, College Park, Maryland.

[104] Folder: 601, History Southern Base Section, SOS, ETOUSA, from 4 Aug 1942 to 31 Dec 1943, Record Group 498, Records of Headquarters, European Theater of Operations, United States Army (World War II), European Theater of Operations, Historical Division, Administrative File, 1942-Jan 1946, National Archives, College Park, Maryland.

[105] Letter dated November 13, 1943, Colonel Charles Thrasher to Commanding Officers, all SOS Units in SBS, Folder: Southern Base Section, General, 315, Administrative History Collection, ETOUSA, Record Group 498, Records of Headquarters, European Theater of Operations, United States Army (World War II), Historical Division, Administrative File 1942-Jan 1946, National Archives, College Park, Maryland.

[106] Roster of Officers, January 31, 1944, Headquarters Command, Headquarters, Southern Base Section, Folder: Southern Base Section, General, 315, Administrative History Collection, SOS ETOUSA, Record Group 498, Records of Headquarters, European Theater of Operations, United States Army (World War II), Historical Division, Administrative File 1942-Jan 1946, National Archives, College Park, Maryland.

[107] Gordon Berger, *Daddy—What Did You Do in the War?* (Compromise Press, approximately late 1990s.)

[108] Gordon Berger, *Daddy—What Did You Do in the War?* (Compromise Press, approximately late 1990s.)

[109] Gordon Berger, *Daddy—What Did You Do in the War?* (Compromise Press, approximately late 1990s.)

[110] Transcript of radio broadcast, March 7, 1944, on Mutual Broadcasting System, by reporter John Thompson, Folder: Southern Base Section, General, 315, Administrative History Collection, SOS ETOUSA, Record Group 498, Records of Headquarters, European Theater of Operations, United States Army (World War II), Historical Division, Administrative File 1942-Jan 1946, National Archives, College Park, Maryland.

[111] Order dated April 5, 1944, Folder: Southern Base Section, General, 315, Administrative History Collection, SOS ETOUSA, Record Group 498, Records of Headquarters, European Theater of Operations, United States Army (World War II), Historical Division, Administrative File 1942-Jan 1946, National Archives, College Park, Maryland.

[112] Roster of Officers dated March 27, 1944, Headquarters Command, Headquarters, Southern Base Section, Folder: Southern Base Section, General, 315, Administrative History Collection, SOS ETOUSA, Record Group 498, Records of Headquarters, European Theater of Operations, United States Army (World War II), Historical Division, Administrative File 1942-Jan 1946, National Archives, College Park, Maryland.

[113] General Order number 52 dated April 18, 1944, Folder: Southern Base Section, General, 315, Administrative History Collection, SOS ETOUSA, Record Group 498, Records of Headquarters, European Theater of Operations, United States Army (World War II), Historical Division, Administrative File 1942-Jan 1946, National Archives, College Park, Maryland.

[114] Administrative Order #7, Folder: Administrative Orders #6 and #7, HQ Southern Base Section, 1944, Record Group 407, Records of the Adjutant General's Office, WWII Operations Reports, 1940-48, European Theater, National Archives, College Park, Maryland.

[115] Letter dated May 29, 1944, Shaw to Alison Marks, Author's Collection.

[116] Letter dated June 13, 1944, Shaw to Alison Marks, Author's Collection.

[117] Letter dated June 13, 1944, Shaw to Alison Marks, Author's Collection.

[118] Letter dated June 13, 1944, Shaw to Alison Marks, Author's Collection.

[119] Letter dated June 13, 1944, Shaw to Alison Marks, Author's Collection.

[120] Notes on Command and Staff Conference dated August 2, 1944 by General Charles Thrasher, Folder: Southern Base Section, General, 315, Administrative History Collection, SOS ETOUSA, Record Group 498, Records of Headquarters, European Theater of Operations, United States Army (World War II), Historical Division, Administrative File 1942-Jan 1946, National Archives, College Park, Maryland.

[121] Folder: Oise Intermediate Section, History 15 Sep 1944-V-E Day, Historical Section, ETOUSA, Record Group 498, Records of Headquarters, European Theater of Operations, United States Army (World War II), Historical Division, Administrative File 1942-Jan 1946, National Archives, College Park, Maryland.

[122] Folder: 594, Oise Intermediate Section History, 15 Sep 1944 to V-E Day, Record Group 498, Records of Headquarters, European Theater of Operations, United States Army (World War II), European Theater of Operations, Historical Division, Administrative File, 1942-Jan 1946, National Archives, College Park, Maryland.

[123] Folder: Oise Intermediate Section, History 15 Sep 1944-V-E Day, Historical Section, ETOUSA, Record Group 498, Records of Headquarters, European Theater of Operations, United States Army (World War II), Historical Division, Administrative File 1942-Jan 1946, National Archives, College Park, Maryland.

[124] Folder: Oise Intermediate Section, History 15 Sep 1944-V-E Day, Historical Section, ETOUSA, Record Group 498, Records of Headquarters, European Theater of Operations, United States Army (World War II), Historical Division, Administrative File 1942-Jan 1946, National Archives, College Park, Maryland.

[125] Folder: Oise Intermediate Section, History 15 Sep 1944-V-E Day, Historical Section, ETOUSA, Record Group 498, Records of Headquarters, European Theater of Operations, United States Army (World War II), Historical Division, Administrative File 1942-Jan 1946, National Archives, College Park, Maryland.

[126] Folder: Oise Intermediate Section, History 15 Sep 1944-V-E Day, Historical Section, ETOUSA, Record Group 498, Records of Headquarters, European Theater of Operations, United States Army (World War II), Historical Division, Administrative File 1942-Jan 1946, National Archives, College Park, Maryland.

[127] Thick binder; Oise Historical Program Files, 8 May 45-14 Jan 46, preface by Roger A. Clarke, First Lieutenant, AC, Historian, Oise Intermediate Section, Folder: Letters, 21 Dec-22 Dec 44, Record Group 498, Records of the Headquarters, European Theater of Operations, United States Army (World War II), ETO Historical Division Program Files, Oise Intermediate Section, 1944-46, National Archives, College Park, Maryland.

[128] Folder: 594, Oise Intermediate Section History, 15 Sep 1944 to V-E Day, Record Group 498, Records of Headquarters, European Theater of Operations, United States Army (World War II), European Theater of Operations, Historical Division, Administrative File, 1942-Jan 1946, National Archives, College Park, Maryland.

[129] Folder: Oise Intermediate Section, History 15 Sep 1944-V-E Day, Historical Section, ETOUSA, Record Group 498, Records of Headquarters, European Theater of Operations, United States Army (World War II), Historical Division, Administrative File 1942-Jan 1946, National Archives, College Park, Maryland.

[130] Folder: Oise Intermediate Section, History 15 Sep 1944-V-E Day, Historical Section, ETOUSA, Record Group 498, Records of Headquarters, European Theater of Operations, United States Army (World War II), Historical Division, Administrative File 1942-Jan 1946, National Archives, College Park, Maryland.

[131] Folder: Oise Intermediate Section, History 15 Sep 1944-V-E Day, Historical Section, ETOUSA, Record Group 498, Records of Headquarters, European Theater of Operations, United States Army (World War II), Historical Division, Administrative File 1942-Jan 1946, National Archives, College Park, Maryland.

[132] Folder: Oise Intermediate Section, History 15 Sep 1944-V-E Day, Historical Section, ETOUSA, Record Group 498, Records of Headquarters, European Theater of Operations, United States Army (World War II), Historical Division, Administrative File 1942-Jan 1946, National Archives, College Park, Maryland.

[133] Folder: Oise Intermediate Section, History 15 Sep 1944-V-E Day, Historical Section, ETOUSA, Record Group 498, Records of Headquarters, European Theater of Operations, United States Army (World War II), Historical Division, Administrative File 1942-Jan 1946, National Archives, College Park, Maryland.

[134] Folder: Oise Intermediate Section, History 15 Sep 1944-V-E Day, Historical Section, ETOUSA, Record Group 498, Records of Headquarters, European Theater of Operations, United States Army (World War II), Historical Division, Administrative File 1942-Jan 1946, National Archives, College Park, Maryland.

[135] Folder: SOP, Military Labor Service, Oise Intermediate Section, May 1945, Record Group 407, Records of the Adjutant General's Office, WWII Operations Reports, 1940-48, European Theater, National Archives, College Park, Maryland.

136. Folder: Oise Intermediate Section, History 15 Sep 1944-V-E Day, Historical Section, ETOUSA, Record Group 498, Records of Headquarters, European Theater of Operations, United States Army (World War II), Historical Division, Administrative File 1942-Jan 1946, National Archives, College Park, Maryland.

137. Folder: Oise Intermediate Section, History 15 Sep 1944-V-E Day, Historical Section, ETOUSA, Record Group 498, Records of Headquarters, European Theater of Operations, United States Army (World War II), Historical Division, Administrative File 1942-Jan 1946, National Archives, College Park, Maryland.

138. Folder: Oise Intermediate Section, History 15 Sep 1944-V-E Day, Historical Section, ETOUSA, Record Group 498, Records of Headquarters, European Theater of Operations, United States Army (World War II), Historical Division, Administrative File 1942-Jan 1946, National Archives, College Park, Maryland.

139. Letter dated December 28, 1944, Representative Overton Brooks to Glaris and Alice Shaw, Donated Papers of Clay Shaw, National Archives, College Park, Maryland.

140. Folder: Oise Intermediate Section, History 15 Sep 1944-V-E Day, Historical Section, ETOUSA, Record Group 498, Records of Headquarters, European Theater of Operations, United States Army (World War II), Historical Division, Administrative File 1942-Jan 1946, National Archives, College Park, Maryland.

141. Letter dated December 22, 1944 from F.W. Brown, Lieutenant Colonel, Adjutant General, by command of Brigadier General Thrasher, Folder: Letters, 21 Dec-22 Dec 44, Record Group 498, Records of the Headquarters, European Theater of Operations, United States Army (World War II), ETO Historical Division Program Files, Oise Intermediate Section, 1944-46, National Archives, College Park, Maryland.

142. Folder: Oise Intermediate Section, History 15 Sep 1944-V-E Day, Historical Section, ETOUSA, Record Group 498, Records of Headquarters, European Theater of Operations, United States Army (World War II), Historical Division, Administrative File 1942-Jan 1946, National Archives, College Park, Maryland.

143. Folder: Oise Intermediate Section, History 15 Sep 1944-V-E Day, Historical Section, ETOUSA, Record Group 498, Records of Headquarters, European Theater of Operations, United States Army (World War II), Historical Division, Administrative File 1942-Jan 1946, National Archives, College Park, Maryland.

144. Gordon Berger, *Daddy—What Did You Do in the War?* (Compromise Press, approximately late 1990s.)

145. Letter dated May 8, 1945, General John C.H. Lee to General Charles Thrasher, Record Group 498, Records of Headquarters, European Theater of Operations, United States Army (World War II), G-1 Section, Administrative Branch, Copies of Letters sent by John C. Lee, March-June 1945, Organizational and Tactical Unit Records March-December 1945, Correspondence Re: Labor Negotiations with Switzerland 1945, National Archives, College Park, Maryland.

146. Letter dated May 27, 2011, James Brugger to Author.

147. Letter dated May 27, 2011, James Brugger to Author.

148. Letter dated May 27, 2011, James Brugger to Author.

149. Letter dated May 27, 2011, James Brugger to Author.

150. Letter dated May 27, 2011, James Brugger to Author.

151. E-mail dated June 29, 2011, James Brugger to Author.

[152] Folder: Oise Intermediate Section, History 15 Sep 1944-V-E Day, Historical Section, ETOUSA, Record Group 498, Records of Headquarters, European Theater of Operations, United States Army (World War II), Historical Division, Administrative File 1942-Jan 1946, National Archives, College Park, Maryland.

[153] Folder: Oise Intermediate Section, History 15 Sep 1944-V-E Day, Historical Section, ETOUSA, Record Group 498, Records of Headquarters, European Theater of Operations, United States Army (World War II), Historical Division, Administrative File 1942-Jan 1946, National Archives, College Park, Maryland.

[154] Thick binder; Oise Historical Program Files, 8 May 45-14 Jan 46, preface by Roger A. Clarke, First Lieutenant, AC, Historian, Oise Intermediate Section, Folder: Letters, 21 Dec-22 Dec 44, Record Group 498, Records of the Headquarters, European Theater of Operations, United States Army (World War II), ETO Historical Division Program Files, Oise Intermediate Section, 1944-46, National Archives, College Park, Maryland.

[155] Thick binder; Oise Historical Program Files, 8 May 45-14 Jan 46, preface by Roger A. Clarke, First Lieutenant, AC, Historian, Oise Intermediate Section, Folder: Letters, 21 Dec-22 Dec 44, Record Group 498, Records of the Headquarters, European Theater of Operations, United States Army (World War II), ETO Historical Division Program Files, Oise Intermediate Section, 1944-46, National Archives, College Park, Maryland.

[156] Thick binder; Oise Historical Program Files, 8 May 45-14 Jan 46, preface by Roger A. Clarke, First Lieutenant, AC, Historian, Oise Intermediate Section, Folder: Letters, 21 Dec-22 Dec 44, Record Group 498, Records of the Headquarters, European Theater of Operations, United States Army (World War II), ETO Historical Division Program Files, Oise Intermediate Section, 1944-46, National Archives, College Park, Maryland.

[157] Secret Register, HQ Base, Section #1, COM Z, ETOUSA, Office of the Engineer, APO 350, Folder: Correspondence Registers, HQ, Base Section #1, COM Z, ETOUSA, 1944-45, Record Group 407, Records of the Adjutant General's Office, WWII Operations Reports, 1940-48, European Theater, National Archives, College Park, Maryland.

[158] Letter dated July 1, 1945, Lieutenant General John C.H. Lee to General Dwight D. Eisenhower, Record Group 498, Records of Headquarters, European Theater of Operations, United States Army (World War II), ETO Secretary General Staff, Correspondence Re: Promotions of General Officers 1944-45, National Archives, College Park, Maryland.

[159] Promotion Recommendation from Lieutenant General John C.H. Lee for Brigadier General Charles Thrasher, May 1945, Record Group 498, Records of Headquarters, European Theater of Operations, United States Army (World War II), ETO Secretary General Staff, Correspondence Re: Promotions of General Officers 1944-45, National Archives, College Park, Maryland.

[160] Memo dated August 16, 1945, General John C.H. Lee to Commanding General, Oise Intermediate Section, Record Group 498, Records of Headquarters, European Theater of Operations, United States Army (World War II), G-1 Section, Administrative Branch, Copies of Letters sent by John C. Lee, March-June 1945, Organizational and Tactical Unit Records March-December 1945, Correspondence Re: Labor Negotiations with Switzerland 1945, National Archives, College Park, Maryland.

[161] Roster of Officers, Oise Intermediate Section, undated, probably Fall, 1945, author's private collection.

[162] Sworn statement dated October 22, 1945, by Major William H. Haight, Folder: 383.6/1, Employment of POWs by the French, 1945, Record Group 498, Records of Headquarters, European Theater of Operations, United States Army (World War II), Records of the Secretary, General Staff, Classified General Correspondence, 1944-45, 381.-383.6, National Archives, College Park, Maryland.

163 Memo dated November 5, 1945, General W.B. Smith to General Lee, Folder: 383.6/1, Employment of POWs by the French, 1945, Record Group 498, Records of Headquarters, European Theater of Operations, United States Army (World War II), Records of the Secretary, General Staff, Classified General Correspondence, 1944-45, 381.-383.6, National Archives, College Park, Maryland.

164 Memo dated November 12, 1945, Major General Carter B. Magruder to General W.B. Smith, Folder: 383.6/1, Employment of POWs by the French, 1945, Record Group 498, Records of Headquarters, European Theater of Operations, United States Army (World War II), Records of the Secretary, General Staff, Classified General Correspondence, 1944-45, 381.-383.6, National Archives, College Park, Maryland.

165 Memo dated December 23, 1945, Colonel Thomas M. McGrail to Major General Carter B. Magruder, Folder: 383.6/1, Employment of POWs by the French, 1945, Record Group 498, Records of Headquarters, European Theater of Operations, United States Army (World War II), Records of the Secretary, General Staff, Classified General Correspondence, 1944-45, 381.-383.6, National Archives, College Park, Maryland.

166 Application for Authority to Construct, International Trade Mart Records, Tulane University, New Orleans, Louisiana.

167 Minutes of meeting of August 15, 1940 related to planned Pan-American Fiesta, International Trade Mart Records, Tulane University, New Orleans, Louisiana.

168 Letter dated February 26, 1945, J. Stanton Robbins to Alger Hiss, International Trade Mart Records, Tulane University, New Orleans, Louisiana.

169 Letter dated May 19, 1945, Alger Hiss to J. Stanton Robbins, International Trade Mart Records, Tulane University, New Orleans, Louisiana.

170 Letter dated June 30, 1945, J. Stanton Robbins to Alger Hiss, International Trade Mart Records, Tulane University, New Orleans, Louisiana.

171 Memo dated July 2, 1945, Mario Bermúdez to J. Stanton Robbins, International Trade Mart Records, Tulane University, New Orleans, Louisiana.

172 Typed history (10 pages) of International Trade Mart and International House, approximately 1977, International Trade Mart Records, Tulane University, New Orleans, Louisiana.

173 General materials related to Staubitz, International Trade Mart Records, Tulane University, New Orleans, Louisiana.

174 Preliminary memorandum on proposed International Trade Mart, International Trade Mart Records, Tulane University, New Orleans, Louisiana.

175 Confidential Preliminary Memo of proposed ITM by unnamed author, International Trade Mart Records, Tulane University, New Orleans, Louisiana.

176 Minutes, meeting of Board of Directors, March 3, 1948, International Trade Mart Records, Tulane University, New Orleans, Louisiana.

177 Mart Realty Company Charter, International Trade Mart Records, Tulane University, New Orleans, Louisiana.

178 Press release dated November 14, 1945, altered to reflect Shaw taking over as Managing Director, International Trade Mart Records, Tulane University, New Orleans, Louisiana.

179 Mart Realty Company, Mortgage and Act of Sale and Dissolution, International Trade Mart Records, Tulane University, New Orleans, Louisiana.

180 From preliminary report on proposed construction by Rathbone DeBuys, Godat and Heft, Architects – Engineers, International Trade Mart Records, Tulane University, New Orleans, Louisiana.

[181] Preliminary report on International Trade Mart, December 14, 1945, International Trade Mart Records, Tulane University, New Orleans, Louisiana.

[182] Preliminary report on International Trade Mart, December 14, 1945, International Trade Mart Records, Tulane University, New Orleans, Louisiana.

[183] Letter dated October 20, 1947 from J.B. Dauenhauer to stockholders of Mart Realty Company, International Trade Mart Records, Tulane University, New Orleans, Louisiana.

[184] Letter dated October 30, 1946 from Shaw to Mrs. James Gibbons of Du-Vernay-Hart, Inc., International Trade Mart Records, Tulane University, New Orleans, Louisiana.

[185] Letter dated January 19, 1946 from Theodore Brent to the Executive Committee of the International Trade Mart, International Trade Mart Records, Tulane University, New Orleans, Louisiana.

[186] Payroll records, International Trade Mart Records, Tulane University, New Orleans, Louisiana.

[187] See New Orleans City Directory for 1945-46, Tulane University, New Orleans, Louisiana.

[188] The proposal attached to Brent's letter of January 19, 1946, International Trade Mart Records, Tulane University, New Orleans, Louisiana.

[189] Memo dated February 11, 1946, Shaw to Kenneth Barranger, International Trade Mart Records, Tulane University, New Orleans, Louisiana.

[190] E-mail from Andrew Moore to Author, January 28, 2010.

[191] Memo dated May 14, 1946, J.B. Dauenhauer to Shaw, International Trade Mart Records, Tulane University, New Orleans, Louisiana.

[192] E-mail from Andrew Moore to Author, January 28, 2010.

[193] E-mail from Andrew Moore to Author, January 28, 2010.

[194] E-mail dated January 28, 2010, Richard Doskey to Author.

[195] Letter dated March 20, 1948, from Rae Ordorica to David F. Howe, Manager, Foreign Trade Division, Milwaukee Chamber of Commerce, International Trade Mart Records, Tulane University, New Orleans, Louisiana.

[196] Memo dated March 28, 1946, Shaw to Theodore Brent, International Trade Mart Records, Tulane University, New Orleans, Louisiana.

[197] Undated letter, probably around 1946, Shaw to J.B. Dauenhauer, International Trade Mart Records, Tulane University, New Orleans, Louisiana.

[198] Letter dated April 5, 1946, Shaw to Allen Ellender, International Trade Mart Records, Tulane University, New Orleans, Louisiana.

[199] Letter dated May 1, 1946, Shaw to Loring Hammond, International Trade Mart Records, Tulane University, New Orleans, Louisiana.

[200] Letter dated May 3, 1946, Shaw to George Markley, National Federation of Sales Executives, International Trade Mart Records, Tulane University, New Orleans, Louisiana.

[201] Memo dated August 31, 1946, Brent to Shaw, International Trade Mart Records, Tulane University, New Orleans, Louisiana.

[202] Letter dated April 26, 1946, Shaw to William Parker of Chicago and Southern Air Lines, International Trade Mart Records, Tulane University, New Orleans, Louisiana.

[203] Letter dated June 17, 1946, Shaw to American Airlines, International Trade Mart Records, Tulane University, New Orleans, Louisiana.

204 Letter dated September 16, 1946, Shaw to Jerry Curtis, International Trade Mart Records, Tulane University, New Orleans, Louisiana.

205 Memo dated October 25, 1946, Shaw to Theodore Brent, International Trade Mart Records, Tulane University, New Orleans, Louisiana.

206 Letter dated November 4, 1946, Shaw to Rudolf Hecht, International Trade Mart Records, Tulane University, New Orleans, Louisiana.

207 Letter dated November 30, 1946, Shaw to Jerry Curtis, International Trade Mart Records, Tulane University, New Orleans, Louisiana.

208 Report dated December 10, 1946, by Mark J. Trazivuk, International Trade Mart Records, Tulane University, New Orleans, Louisiana.

209 Letter dated November 5, 1945, Rudolf Hecht to C.G. Staubitz, International Trade Mart Records, Tulane University, New Orleans, Louisiana.

210 Letter November 19, 1946, Shaw to *Architectural Forum*, International Trade Mart Records, Tulane University, New Orleans, Louisiana.

211 Memo dated November 20, 1946, Shaw to Theodore Brent, International Trade Mart Records, Tulane University, New Orleans, Louisiana.

212 Letter dated December 20, 1946, Muriel Bultman Francis to her parents, Bultman Family Papers, Historic New Orleans Collection, New Orleans, Louisiana.

213 Letters dated December 24, 1946 and December 30, 1946, Shaw to Jerry Curtis, International Trade Mart Records, Tulane University, New Orleans, Louisiana.

214 See New Orleans City Directory for 1947, Tulane University, New Orleans, Louisiana.

215 See Application dated January 14, 1947 by Shaw, possibly for insurance, Papers Donated by Lyon Garrison, National Archives, College Park, Maryland.

216 Claim made by Shaw with U.S. Army for compensation, January 1947, Donated Papers of Edward Wegmann, National Archives, College Park, Maryland.

217 Letter dated February 27, 1947, Shaw to Cecil Shilstone, International Trade Mart Records, Tulane University, New Orleans, Louisiana.

218 Letter dated February 28, 1947, Shaw to Herman Deutsch, International Trade Mart Records, Tulane University, New Orleans, Louisiana.

219 Letter dated March 3, 1947, C.E. Becker to Shaw, International Trade Mart Records, Tulane University, New Orleans, Louisiana.

220 Letter dated May 20, 1947, Shaw to Jason Elsas, International Trade Mart Records, Tulane University, New Orleans, Louisiana.

221 Letter, no date, Monte Lemann to Bertha Elsas, International Trade Mart Records, Tulane University, New Orleans, Louisiana.

222 Letter dated May 7, 1947, Shaw to J.F. Odenheimer, International Trade Mart Records, Tulane University, New Orleans, Louisiana.

223 Letter dated August 27, 1947, Caye A. Nelson to Shaw, International Trade Mart Records, Tulane University, New Orleans, Louisiana.

224 Letter dated December 30, 1947, Shaw to Godat and Heft, International Trade Mart Records, Tulane University, New Orleans, Louisiana.

225 Letter dated August 29, 1947, Shaw to Godat and Heft, International Trade Mart Records, Tulane University, New Orleans, Louisiana.

226 Letter dated July 9, 1947, Rathbone DeBuys to Shaw International Trade Mart Records, Tulane University, New Orleans, Louisiana.

227 Letter dated June 2, 1947, Shaw to Godat and Heft, International Trade Mart Records, Tulane University, New Orleans, Louisiana.

228 Letter dated September 19, 1947, Shaw to Consul General of Argentina, International Trade Mart Records, Tulane University, New Orleans, Louisiana.

229 Memo dated October 6, 1947, Shaw to Theodore Brent, International Trade Mart Records, Tulane University, New Orleans, Louisiana.

230 Letter dated March 20, 1948, from Rae Ordorica to David F. Howe, Manager, Foreign Trade Division, Milwaukee Chamber of Commerce, International Trade Mart Records, Tulane University, New Orleans, Louisiana.

231 Letter dated March 20, 1948, from Rae Ordorica to David F. Howe, Manager, Foreign Trade Division, Milwaukee Chamber of Commerce, International Trade Mart Records, Tulane University, New Orleans, Louisiana.

232 Letter dated July 15, 1947, setting out the terms of his contract, International Trade Mart Records, Tulane University, New Orleans, Louisiana.

233 Letter dated March 17, 1947, from Shaw to Roland Neff, Public Relations Director for Chicago and Southern Airlines, International Trade Mart Records, Tulane University, New Orleans, Louisiana.

234 Letter dated December 18, 1947, Shaw to Rudolf Hecht, International Trade Mart Records, Tulane University, New Orleans, Louisiana.

235 Letter dated February 27, 1948, Hecht to Arthur Kleeman, International Trade Mart Records, Tulane University, New Orleans, Louisiana.

236 Letter dated January 8, 1948, James G. Aldige, Mr. to Shaw, International Trade Mart Records, Tulane University, New Orleans, Louisiana.

237 John Erskine's employment agreement dated March 5, 1948, International Trade Mart Records, Tulane University, New Orleans, Louisiana.

238 Letter dated May 14, 1948, Shaw to John Erskine, International Trade Mart Records, Tulane University, New Orleans, Louisiana.

239 Letter dated May 7, 1948, Shaw to John Erskine, International Trade Mart Records, Tulane University, New Orleans, Louisiana.

240 Letter dated June 15, 1948, Shaw to John Erskine, International Trade Mart Records, Tulane University, New Orleans, Louisiana.

241 Letter dated April 1, 1949, John Erskine to Shaw, International Trade Mart Records, Tulane University, New Orleans, Louisiana.

242 Memo dated March 31, 1948, Shaw to Theodore Brent, International Trade Mart Records, Tulane University, New Orleans, Louisiana.

243 Wall Street Journal article dated April 28, 1948, International Trade Mart Records, Tulane University, New Orleans, Louisiana.

244 Letter dated May 3, 1948, Roy Bartlett to Shaw, International Trade Mart Records, Tulane University, New Orleans, Louisiana.

245 Letter dated December 15, 1948, Charles T. Taylor to Shaw, International Trade Mart Records, Tulane University, New Orleans, Louisiana.

246 Letter dated May 26, 1948, Shaw to Roy Alciatore, International Trade Mart Records, Tulane University, New Orleans, Louisiana.

247 Letter dated June 11, 1948, Shaw to Rathbone DeBuys, International Trade Mart Records, Tulane University, New Orleans, Louisiana.

248 Transcript of broadcast by John Cameron Swayze about opening of International Trade Mart, June 30, 1948, International Trade Mart Records, Tulane University, New Orleans, Louisiana.

249 Letter dated June 5, 1948, to Shaw regarding building of two record cabinets, International Trade Mart Records, Tulane University, New Orleans, Louisiana.

250 Invitation dated June 14, 1948, International Trade Mart Records, Tulane University, New Orleans, Louisiana.

251 Letter dated August 25, 1948, Mario Bermúdez to Shaw, International Trade Mart Records, Tulane University, New Orleans, Louisiana.

252 Letter dated July 26, 1948, Louis Boasberg to Shaw, International Trade Mart Records, Tulane University, New Orleans, Louisiana.

253 Letter dated August 23, 1948, Helen Dietrich to Shaw, International Trade Mart Records, Tulane University, New Orleans, Louisiana.

254 Minutes from Board of Directors' Meeting, September 3, 1948, International Trade Mart Records, Tulane University, New Orleans, Louisiana.

255 Letter dated October 13, 1948, A.E. Hegewisch, President, International House, International Trade Mart Records, Tulane University, New Orleans, Louisiana.

256 Letter dated September 14, 1948, from Jennings Randolf to Shaw, International Trade Mart Records, Tulane University, New Orleans, Louisiana.

257 Letter dated September 10, 1948, Shaw to Towel & Linen Rental Company, International Trade Mart Records, Tulane University, New Orleans, Louisiana.

258 Letter dated November 12, 1948, W. (Bill) Edgar, Jr. to Shaw, International Trade Mart Records, Tulane University, New Orleans, Louisiana.

259 Invitation dated October 19, 1948, International Trade Mart Records, Tulane University, New Orleans, Louisiana.

260 Letter dated November 12, 1948, Jose Moreno, consul of the Philippines, to Shaw, International Trade Mart Records, Tulane University, New Orleans, Louisiana.

261 Letter dated August 3, 1948, Shaw to Mrs. Charlotte Zetzmann Schmitt, International Trade Mart Records, Tulane University, New Orleans, Louisiana.

262 Telegram Shaw to K.B. Mitchell, November 1, 1948, International Trade Mart Records, Tulane University, New Orleans, Louisiana.

263 Letter dated November 29, 1948, Stanton P. Nickerson to Shaw, International Trade Mart Records, Tulane University, New Orleans, Louisiana.

264 Letter dated February 14, 1949, Stanton P. Nickerson to Shaw, International Trade Mart Records, Tulane University, New Orleans, Louisiana.

265 Letter dated November 16, 1948, Dave McGuire, City of New Orleans Public Relations Director, to Shaw, International Trade Mart Records, Tulane University, New Orleans, Louisiana.

266 Letter dated December 15, 1948, Shaw to all employees, International Trade Mart Records, Tulane University, New Orleans, Louisiana.

267 Copy of Le Petit Theatre Program for *Memorial*, Author's Possession.

268 Summary of *Memorial*, by May Ross, New York Office of Warner Brothers Studios, March 11, 1949, Author's Possession.

[269] Article, date unknown, probably late 1948, *The New Orleans Item*, Donated Papers of Clay Shaw, National Archives, College Park, Maryland.

[270] Comment on *Memorial*, May Ross to Jacob Wilk, March 11, 1949.

[271] E-mail dated June 3, 2011, Michael Snyder to Author.

[272] E-mail dated June 3, 2011, Michael Snyder to Author.

[273] E-mail dated June 3, 2011, Michael Snyder to Author.

[274] See file on Clay Shaw, CIA Miscellaneous Files, JFK Assassination Collection, National Archives, College Park, Maryland.

[275] E-mail dated January 28, 2010, Richard Doskey to Author.

[276] Letter dated January 25, 1949, Shaw to Armour Research Foundation, International Trade Mart Records, Tulane University, New Orleans, Louisiana.

[277] See New Orleans City Directory for 1949, Tulane University, New Orleans, Louisiana.

[278] Memo dated January 6 1949, Charles Nutter to Hecht, International Trade Mart Records, Tulane University, New Orleans, Louisiana.

[279] Tenant's newsletter dated January 12, 1949, International Trade Mart, International Trade Mart Records, Tulane University, New Orleans, Louisiana.

[280] Memo dated March 7, 1949, John Leonard to tenants, International Trade Mart Records, Tulane University, New Orleans, Louisiana.

[281] Letter dated July 29, 1949, Shaw to Charles Leonard, Consul General of Belgium in New Orleans, International Trade Mart Records, Tulane University, New Orleans, Louisiana.

[282] Interview with Albert LeMon III by author, July 14, 2009.

[283] Invitation dated April 18, 1947, Charles Leonard to Shaw, International Trade Mart Records, Tulane University, New Orleans, Louisiana.

[284] Minutes from Board of Directors' Meeting, May 26, 1949, International Trade Mart Records, Tulane University, New Orleans, Louisiana.

[285] Letter dated June 22, 1949, Shaw to M. Pepe, International Trade Mart Records, Tulane University, New Orleans, Louisiana.

[286] Letter dated February 14, 1949, Shaw to Aguiar Mendenca, International Trade Mart Records, Tulane University, New Orleans, Louisiana.

[287] Memo dated March 10, 1949, Shaw to J.B. Dauenhauer, International Trade Mart Records, Tulane University, New Orleans, Louisiana.

[288] Letter dated January 6, 1949, G.E. Roper, Jr. to Shaw, International Trade Mart Records, Tulane University, New Orleans, Louisiana.

[289] Letter dated March 2, 1949, Mary Catanese to Clarence Hyams of Long Beach, New York, International Trade Mart Records, Tulane University, New Orleans, Louisiana.

[290] Letter dated March 11, 1949, John Leonard to Thomas R. Curran, International Trade Mart Records, Tulane University, New Orleans, Louisiana.

[291] Memo dated February 18, 1949 by Lyman B. Kirkpatrick, CIA Miscellaneous Files, JFK Assassination Collection, National Archives, College Park, Maryland.

[292] Letter dated March 22, 1949, Shaw to J.B. Dauenhauer from Dominican Republic, International Trade Mart Records, Tulane University, New Orleans, Louisiana.

293 Letter dated March 19, 1949, Shaw to Mary Catanese, International Trade Mart Records, Tulane University, New Orleans, Louisiana.

294 Telegram dated April 20, 1949, J.B. Dauenhauer to Theodore Brent, International Trade Mart Records, Tulane University, New Orleans, Louisiana.

295 Letter of Introduction dated November 25, 1949, Shaw to M.V. O'Connell, International Trade Mart Records, Tulane University, New Orleans, Louisiana.

296 Postcard dated December 1, 1949, Alma Rawlinson to International Trade Mart.

297 Letter dated July 21, 1949, Shaw to A. Terkuhle, International Trade Mart Records, Tulane University, New Orleans, Louisiana.

298 Letter dated April 7, 1949, J.B. Dauenhauer to Herbert Schwartz, Rudolf Hecht, and Kenneth Barranger, International Trade Mart Records, Tulane University, New Orleans, Louisiana.

299 Letter dated April 8, 1949, Shaw to J.B. Dauenhauer, International Trade Mart Records, Tulane University, New Orleans, Louisiana.

300 Letter dated April 13, 1949, Shaw to J.B. Dauenhauer, International Trade Mart Records, Tulane University, New Orleans, Louisiana.

301 Telegram dated April 19, 1949, Rudolf Hecht to Shaw, International Trade Mart Records, Tulane University, New Orleans, Louisiana.

302 Letter dated April 21, 1949, Shaw to Rudolf Hecht from Quito, Ecuador, International Trade Mart Records, Tulane University, New Orleans, Louisiana.

303 Letter dated May 9, 1949, Shaw to J.B. Dauenhauer, International Trade Mart Records, Tulane University, New Orleans, Louisiana.

304 Letter dated May 13, 1949, J.B. Dauenhauer to Shaw, International Trade Mart Records, Tulane University, New Orleans, Louisiana.

305 Letter dated May 2, 1949, J.B. Dauenhauer to Shaw, International Trade Mart Records, Tulane University, New Orleans, Louisiana.

306 Memo dated March 23, 1950, Shaw to Rudolf Hecht, International Trade Mart Records, Tulane University, New Orleans, Louisiana.

307 Memo dated March 17, 1950, Shaw to Theodore Brent, International Trade Mart Records, Tulane University, New Orleans, Louisiana.

308 Letter dated May 3, 1949, John Leonard to Shaw, International Trade Mart Records, Tulane University, New Orleans, Louisiana.

309 Letter dated May 9, 1949, J.B. Dauenhauer to Shaw, International Trade Mart Records, Tulane University, New Orleans, Louisiana.

310 Letter dated May 13, 1949, J.B. Dauenhauer to Shaw, International Trade Mart Records, Tulane University, New Orleans, Louisiana.

311 Letter dated May 13, 1949, J.B. Dauenhauer to Shaw, International Trade Mart Records, Tulane University, New Orleans, Louisiana.

312 Letter dated April 5, 1949, Mary Catanese to Shaw, International Trade Mart Records, Tulane University, New Orleans, Louisiana.

313 Letter dated May 24, 1949, Shaw to U.S. Passport Office, International Trade Mart Records, Tulane University, New Orleans, Louisiana.

314 Letter dated June 6, 1949, Shaw to U.S. Passport Office, International Trade Mart Records, Tulane University, New Orleans, Louisiana.

[315] Letter dated May 23, 1949, Shaw to Rene Grau D, International Trade Mart Records, Tulane University, New Orleans, Louisiana.

[316] Letter dated August 9, 1949, Rene Grau D to Shaw, International Trade Mart Records, Tulane University, New Orleans, Louisiana.

[317] Letter dated August 19, 1949, Shaw to Rene Grau D, International Trade Mart Records, Tulane University, New Orleans, Louisiana.

[318] Telegram dated November 10, 1949, Shaw to President Ulate, International Trade Mart Records, Tulane University, New Orleans, Louisiana.

[319] Letter dated May 27, 1949, Brent to Board of Directors, International Trade Mart Records, Tulane University, New Orleans, Louisiana.

[320] Form letter dated July 22, 1949, Shaw to prospective tenants, International Trade Mart Records, Tulane University, New Orleans, Louisiana.

[321] Letter dated October 19, 1949, Shaw to Harry J. Williams with Peat, Marwick, CPA's, International Trade Mart Records, Tulane University, New Orleans, Louisiana.

[322] Letter dated July 21, 1949, Shaw to Assistant Commercial Attaché, Embassy of Yugoslavia, International Trade Mart Records, Tulane University, New Orleans, Louisiana.

[323] Letter dated August 5, 1949, Shaw to Carlo Mario Camusso in Lima, Peru, International Trade Mart Records, Tulane University, New Orleans, Louisiana.

[324] Letter dated September 17, 1949, John Leonard to Shaw, International Trade Mart Records, Tulane University, New Orleans, Louisiana.

[325] Letter dated July 27, 1949, Louisiana Department of Labor to International Trade Mart, International Trade Mart Records, Tulane University, New Orleans, Louisiana.

[326] Letter dated August 2, 1949, J.B. Dauenhauer to Louisiana Department of Labor, International Trade Mart Records, Tulane University, New Orleans, Louisiana.

[327] Letter dated September 22, 1949, Shaw to John Leonard, International Trade Mart Records, Tulane University, New Orleans, Louisiana.

[328] Letter dated August 7, 1949, Glenn Weekley to Shaw, International Trade Mart Records, Tulane University, New Orleans, Louisiana.

[329] Letter dated September 6, 1949, Shaw to Glenn E. Weekley, International Trade Mart Records, Tulane University, New Orleans, Louisiana.

[330] Letter dated September 13, 1949, Glenn E. Weekley to Shaw, International Trade Mart Records, Tulane University, New Orleans, Louisiana.

[331] Memo dated December 22, 1949, Glenn E. Weekely to tenants, International Trade Mart Records, Tulane University, New Orleans, Louisiana.

[332] Letter dated August 11, 1949, Mario Bermúdez to Shaw, International Trade Mart Records, Tulane University, New Orleans, Louisiana.

[333] Letter dated June 20, 1949, Shaw to Eunice Laird, International Trade Mart Records, Tulane University, New Orleans, Louisiana.

[334] Letter dated September 12, 1949, Shaw to J.P. Morris, Jr., International Trade Mart Records, Tulane University, New Orleans, Louisiana.

[335] Letter dated December 9, 1948, Shaw to John B. Ferran, Louisiana Forestry Association, International Trade Mart Records, Tulane University, New Orleans, Louisiana.

[336] Letter dated August 25, 1949, Shaw to Richard Swensen, International Trade Mart Records, Tulane University, New Orleans, Louisiana.

337 Letter dated September 19, 1949, Rudolf Hecht to Shaw, International Trade Mart Records, Tulane University, New Orleans, Louisiana.

338 Letter dated September 26, 1949, Rudolf Hecht to Shaw, International Trade Mart Records, Tulane University, New Orleans, Louisiana.

339 Letter dated November 2, 1949, J.B. Dauenhauer to Fred Greschner, Building Superintendent, International Trade Mart Records, Tulane University, New Orleans, Louisiana.

340 Letter dated September 16, 1949, Shaw to Mrs. Park B. Pedrick, International Trade Mart Records, Tulane University, New Orleans, Louisiana.

341 Letter dated September 27, 1949, Shaw to Max Finlay, International Trade Mart Records, Tulane University, New Orleans, Louisiana.

342 Letter dated October 1, 1949, Shaw to Nicholas Murray, publisher of the independent newspaper, *Independence Louisiana*, International Trade Mart Records, Tulane University, New Orleans, Louisiana.

343 Tenant's newsletter dated October 12, 1949, International Trade Mart, International Trade Mart Records, Tulane University, New Orleans, Louisiana.

344 Tenant's newsletter dated October 26, 1949, International Trade Mart, International Trade Mart Records, Tulane University, New Orleans, Louisiana.

345 Crippled Children's Hospital Folder, International Trade Mart Records, Tulane University, New Orleans, Louisiana.

346 Memo dated November 28, 1949, Shaw to tenants, International Trade Mart Records, Tulane University, New Orleans, Louisiana.

347 Letter dated December 8, 1949, Shaw to Charles Taylor, International Trade Mart Records, Tulane University, New Orleans, Louisiana.

348 Letter dated December 21, 1949, Student Edward Jonson at Purdue University to Shaw, International Trade Mart Records, Tulane University, New Orleans, Louisiana.

349 Letter dated October 24, 1949, Shaw to William B. Tate, Jr., Georgia Marble Company, International Trade Mart Records, Tulane University, New Orleans, Louisiana.

350 Letter dated July 26, 1949, Shaw to J.G. Kunz, The Kinnear Manufacturing Company, International Trade Mart Records, Tulane University, New Orleans, Louisiana.

351 Letter dated December 2, 1949, Shaw to Lieutenant Colonel Alfredo Tejada, International Trade Mart Records, Tulane University, New Orleans, Louisiana.

352 Letter dated December 21, 1949, William Gaudet to Shaw, International Trade Mart Records, Tulane University, New Orleans, Louisiana.

353 Report, Holland McCombs to Will Lang, undated but most likely early March 1967, Holland McCombs Collection, University of Tennessee-Martin, Martin, Tennessee.

354 Report, Holland McCombs to Will Lang, undated but most likely early March 1967, Holland McCombs Collection, University of Tennessee-Martin, Martin, Tennessee.

355 Report, Holland McCombs to Will Lang, undated but most likely early March 1967, Holland McCombs Collection, University of Tennessee-Martin, Martin, Tennessee.

356 Report, Holland McCombs to Will Lang, undated but most likely early March 1967, Holland McCombs Collection, University of Tennessee-Martin, Martin, Tennessee.

357 Report, Holland McCombs to Will Lang, undated but most likely early March 1967, Holland McCombs Collection, University of Tennessee-Martin, Martin, Tennessee.

358 Report, Holland McCombs to Will Lang, undated but most likely early March 1967, Holland McCombs Collection, University of Tennessee-Martin, Martin, Tennessee.

359 Report, Holland McCombs to Will Lang, undated but most likely early March 1967, Holland McCombs Collection, University of Tennessee-Martin, Martin, Tennessee.

360 Letter dated April 11, 1950, Shaw to Acme Electric Heating Company, International Trade Mart Records, Tulane University, New Orleans, Louisiana.

361 Letter dated January 13, 1950, WMRY Radio to Shaw, International Trade Mart Records, Tulane University, New Orleans, Louisiana.

362 Invitation to Shaw by WDSU TV, International Trade Mart Records, Tulane University, New Orleans, Louisiana.

363 Memo dated January 3, 1950, Shaw to Rudolf Hecht, International Trade Mart Records, Tulane University, New Orleans, Louisiana.

364 Memo dated January 30, 1950, Shaw to Rudolf Hecht, International Trade Mart Records, Tulane University, New Orleans, Louisiana.

365 Letter dated January 4, 1950, Chep Morrison to Shaw, International Trade Mart Records, Tulane University, New Orleans, Louisiana.

366 Letter dated April 24, 1950, Chep Morrison to Shaw, International Trade Mart Records, Tulane University, New Orleans, Louisiana.

367 Letter dated March 20, 1950, Bernard J. McCloskey to Shaw, International Trade Mart Records, Tulane University, New Orleans, Louisiana.

368 Newspaper article, *New Orleans States*, January 3, 1950, International Trade Mart Records, Tulane University, New Orleans, Louisiana.

369 Buyers' newsletters for 1950, International Trade Mart Records, Tulane University, New Orleans, Louisiana.

370 Transcript of WWL Radio program broadcast from lobby of International Trade Mart, February 14, 1950, International Trade Mart Records, Tulane University, New Orleans, Louisiana.

371 Letter dated February 9, 1950, Shaw to Cecil London, International Trade Mart Records, Tulane University, New Orleans, Louisiana.

372 Memo dated February 24, 1950, Shaw to Theodore Brent, International Trade Mart Records, Tulane University, New Orleans, Louisiana.

373 Tenants' newsletter dated February 22, 1950, International Trade Mart, International Trade Mart Records, Tulane University, New Orleans, Louisiana.

374 Letter dated March 7, 1950, Clem Bernard to Shaw, International Trade Mart Records, Tulane University, New Orleans, Louisiana.

375 Memo dated March 23, 1950, Shaw to Rudolf Hecht, International Trade Mart Records, Tulane University, New Orleans, Louisiana.

376 *Rotaripost* for Rotary Club of Shreveport, March 3, 1950.

377 Interview with Richard Townley by author, June 25, 2007.

378 Letter dated February 23, 1950, Allen Knolle to Shaw, International Trade Mart Records, Tulane University, New Orleans, Louisiana.

379 Letter dated April 20, 1950, Allen Knolle to Shaw, International Trade Mart Records, Tulane University, New Orleans, Louisiana.

380 Letter dated April 24, 1950, Shaw to Allen Knolle, International Trade Mart Records, Tulane University, New Orleans, Louisiana.

381 Letter dated March 3, 1950, from Ted Lala to Shaw, International Trade Mart Records, Tulane University, New Orleans, Louisiana.

382 Letter dated October 18, 1950, Shaw to Irma Lagan, Assistant to Seymour Weiss, International Trade Mart Records, Tulane University, New Orleans, Louisiana.

383 Letter dated November 7, 1950, Shaw to Victor W. Bennett, International Trade Mart Records, Tulane University, New Orleans, Louisiana.

384 Letter dated July 28, 1950, Arthur W. Brooks, Secretary of Miami Sales Executive Club, to Shaw, International Trade Mart Records, Tulane University, New Orleans, Louisiana.

385 Letter dated March 15, 1950, Shaw to Bernard McCloskey, acting Mayor of New Orleans, International Trade Mart Records, Tulane University, New Orleans, Louisiana.

386 Letter dated January 31, 1949, Shaw to Hale Boggs, International Trade Mart Records, Tulane University, New Orleans, Louisiana.

387 Report to Board of Directors by Rudolf Hecht dated April 19, 1950, International Trade Mart Records, Tulane University, New Orleans, Louisiana.

388 Letter dated April 11, 1950, J.B. Dauenhauer to Shaw, International Trade Mart Records, Tulane University, New Orleans, Louisiana.

389 Letter dated May 18, 1950, from Goldie Moore to Citizen's Committee to Honor Prime Minister of Pakistan, and attached memo, International Trade Mart Records, Tulane University, New Orleans, Louisiana.

390 Letter dated April 5, 1950, Shaw to Torsten Lehtanen, International Trade Mart Records, Tulane University, New Orleans, Louisiana.

391 Letter dated June 3, 1949, Shaw to Torsten Lehtanen, International Trade Mart Records, Tulane University, New Orleans, Louisiana.

392 Letter dated September 12, 1950, Shaw to H. Fujita, Acting Chief, Promotions Section, Ministry of International Trade and Industry-Government of Japan, International Trade Mart Records, Tulane University, New Orleans, Louisiana.

393 Letter dated May 4, 1950, Shaw to Japanese Ministry International Trade and Industry, International Trade Mart Records, Tulane University, New Orleans, Louisiana.

394 Letter dated February 13, 1950, Theodore Brent to General Douglas MacArthur, International Trade Mart Records, Tulane University, New Orleans, Louisiana.

395 Letter dated May 15, 1950, Chep Morrison to Shaw, International Trade Mart Records, Tulane University, New Orleans, Louisiana.

396 Letter dated January 25, 1950, Shaw to James Fitzmorris, General Chairman, Industry-Army Conference 1950, International Trade Mart Records, Tulane University, New Orleans, Louisiana.

397 Letter to Shaw dated March 10, 1950, International Trade Mart Records, Tulane University, New Orleans, Louisiana.

398 Letter dated May 15, 1950, Geneva Palmer to Shaw, International Trade Mart Records, Tulane University, New Orleans, Louisiana.

399 Letter dated May 8, 1950, Shaw to Propeller Club, International Trade Mart Records, Tulane University, New Orleans, Louisiana.

400 Letter dated May 17, 1950, Glenn Weekley in response to inquiry, International Trade Mart Records, Tulane University, New Orleans, Louisiana.

401 Letter dated June 1, 1950, Tana Losada to Shaw, International Trade Mart Records, Tulane University, New Orleans, Louisiana.

[402] Letter dated July 24, 1951, from American Machine and Foundry Company to Shaw, International Trade Mart Records, Tulane University, New Orleans, Louisiana.

[403] Letter dated June 28, 1950, Shaw in response to inquiry, International Trade Mart Records, Tulane University, New Orleans, Louisiana.

[404] Letter dated October 13, 1950, J.M. Guillory to Shaw, International Trade Mart Records, Tulane University, New Orleans, Louisiana.

[405] Letter dated July 14, 1950, J.B. Dauenhauer to Maxwell Fisher, International Trade Mart Records, Tulane University, New Orleans, Louisiana.

[406] Tenants' newsletter dated August 9, 1950, International Trade Mart, International Trade Mart Records, Tulane University, New Orleans, Louisiana.

[407] Letter dated September 7, 1950, Shaw to Colonel John Hartigan, Economic Cooperation Administration of Washington, D.C., International Trade Mart Records, Tulane University, New Orleans, Louisiana.

[408] Letter dated March 17, 1950, W. Ray Scheuring to Shaw, International Trade Mart Records, Tulane University, New Orleans, Louisiana.

[409] Letter dated March 8, 1950, Jesuit House of Studies Building Fund to Shaw, International Trade Mart Records, Tulane University, New Orleans, Louisiana.

[410] Letter dated March 14, 1950, Shaw to Jesuit House of Studies Building Fund, International Trade Mart Records, Tulane University, New Orleans, Louisiana.

[411] Letter dated March 7, 1950, Shaw to John Leonard, International Trade Mart Records, Tulane University, New Orleans, Louisiana.

[412] Letter dated May 9, 1950, Shaw to Clayton Fritchey, International Trade Mart Records, Tulane University, New Orleans, Louisiana.

[413] Letter dated May 11, 1950, Theodore Brent to Shaw, International Trade Mart Records, Tulane University, New Orleans, Louisiana.

[414] Interview with Robert Stuart, January 13, 2008.

[415] Letter dated May 3, 1950, Hibernia Bank to Shaw, International Trade Mart Records, Tulane University, New Orleans, Louisiana.

[416] Letter dated August 27, 1950, Edward Wegmann to Office of Housing Expeditors, International Trade Mart Records, Tulane University, New Orleans, Louisiana.

[417] Letter dated May 26, 1950, Edward Wegmann to Herman L. Midlo, International Trade Mart Records, Tulane University, New Orleans, Louisiana.

[418] Letter dated January 23, 1950, Edward Wegmann to Shaw, International Trade Mart Records, Tulane University, New Orleans, Louisiana.

[419] Letter dated November 13, 1950, Shaw to Mario Bermúdez, International Trade Mart Records, Tulane University, New Orleans, Louisiana.

[420] Letter dated February 16, 1950, Shaw to Epsilon Sigma Fraternity, International Trade Mart Records, Tulane University, New Orleans, Louisiana.

[421] Letter dated October 17, 1950, Shaw to Delta Kappa Gamma, International Trade Mart Records, Tulane University, New Orleans, Louisiana.

[422] Letter dated September 18, 1950, Shaw to J. Gibson Kerr, International Trade Mart Records, Tulane University, New Orleans, Louisiana.

[423] Letter dated October 2, 1950, Peggy Day to Shaw, International Trade Mart Records, Tulane University, New Orleans, Louisiana.

424 Correspondence, November 1950, between Shaw and Ken Williams, International Trade Mart Records, Tulane University, New Orleans, Louisiana.

425 Letter dated December 18, 1950, Shaw to George Kein, International Trade Mart Records, Tulane University, New Orleans, Louisiana.

426 New Orleans Association of Building Owners and Managers Folder, International Trade Mart Records, Tulane University, New Orleans, Louisiana.

427 Telegram dated December 4, 1950, Shaw to Judson O'Donnell, International Trade Mart Records, Tulane University, New Orleans, Louisiana.

428 Telegram dated December 6, 1950, Shaw to Marion Seidenbach, International Trade Mart Records, Tulane University, New Orleans, Louisiana.

429 Letter dated December 28, 1950, Shaw to Leland Cutler, International Trade Mart Records, Tulane University, New Orleans, Louisiana.

430 Tenants' newsletter dated December 20, 1050, International Trade Mart, International Trade Mart Records, Tulane University, New Orleans, Louisiana.

431 Letter dated September 29, 1950, Shaw to Maria Imelda Paprotna, International Trade Mart Records, Tulane University, New Orleans, Louisiana.

432 Letter dated November 10, 1950, Shaw to Maria Paprotna, International Trade Mart Records, Tulane University, New Orleans, Louisiana.

433 Memo dated December 15, 1950, Shaw to employees, International Trade Mart Records, Tulane University, New Orleans, Louisiana.

434 Annual Report for 1950, International Trade Mart, International Trade Mart Records, Tulane University, New Orleans, Louisiana.

435 Notes from March 30, 1951, meeting of Contributors and Debenture Holders, International Trade Mart, International Trade Mart Records, Tulane University, New Orleans, Louisiana.

436 Telegram dated January 8, 1951, Maria Paprotna to International Trade Mart, International Trade Mart Records, Tulane University, New Orleans, Louisiana.

437 Letter dated January 17, 1951, W.J. Sheridan to Shaw, International Trade Mart Records, Tulane University, New Orleans, Louisiana.

438 Letter dated July 18, 1951, Shaw in response to inquiry, International Trade Mart Records, Tulane University, New Orleans, Louisiana.

439 Tenants' Bulletin dated January 4, 1951, International Trade Mart, International Trade Mart Records, Tulane University, New Orleans, Louisiana.

440 Letter dated January 31, 1951, Shaw to Theodore Brent and Rudolf Hecht, International Trade Mart Records, Tulane University, New Orleans, Louisiana.

441 Letter dated April 6, 1951, Shaw to Vicente Manzorro, International Trade Mart Records, Tulane University, New Orleans, Louisiana.

442 Letter dated April 23, 1951, Shaw to jeweler in Rio de Janeiro, Brazil, International Trade Mart Records, Tulane University, New Orleans, Louisiana.

443 Tenants' newsletter dated February 14, 1951, International Trade Mart, International Trade Mart Records, Tulane University, New Orleans, Louisiana.

444 Telegram dated January 1951, J.B. Dauenhauer to Stan Picher, International Trade Mart Records, Tulane University, New Orleans, Louisiana.

445 Telegram dated January 19, 1951, J.B. Dauenhauer to Ken Williams, International Trade Mart Records, Tulane University, New Orleans, Louisiana.

446 Letter dated February 16, 1951, Shaw to Brazil Ministry of Exterior Relations, International Trade Mart Records, Tulane University, New Orleans, Louisiana.

447 Letter dated February 13, 1951, J.L. Barnicle to Theodore Brent, International Trade Mart Records, Tulane University, New Orleans, Louisiana.

448 Letter dated February 16, 1951, Theodore Brent to A.B. Paterson, International Trade Mart Records, Tulane University, New Orleans, Louisiana.

449 Letter dated March 14, 1951, Theodore Brent to Senator Allen Ellender, International Trade Mart Records, Tulane University, New Orleans, Louisiana.

450 Letter dated August 21, 1951, Theodore Brent to Representative Henry D. Larcade, Jr., International Trade Mart Records, Tulane University, New Orleans, Louisiana.

451 Memo dated February 7, 1951, Foreign Service of Department of State, Montevideo, Uruguay, Record Group 59, General Records of the Department of State, JFK Assassination Collection, National Archives, College Park, Maryland.

452 Letter dated March 17, 1951, Edward W. Barrett, Assistant Secretary of State, to Shaw, International Trade Mart Records, Tulane University, New Orleans, Louisiana.

453 Letter dated July 16, 1951, Charles Nutter to Rudolf Hecht, International Trade Mart Records, Tulane University, New Orleans, Louisiana.

454 Memo dated July 18, 1951, Department of State, Record Group 59, General Records of the Department of State, JFK Assassination Collection, National Archives, College Park, Maryland.

455 Letter dated March 30, 1951, Theodore Brent to Rudolf Hecht, International Trade Mart Records, Tulane University, New Orleans, Louisiana.

456 Tenants' newsletter dated April 11, 1951, International Trade Mart, International Trade Mart Records, Tulane University, New Orleans, Louisiana.

457 Letter dated May 4, 1951, Richard de Ayala to Shaw, International Trade Mart Records, Tulane University, New Orleans, Louisiana.

458 Letter dated May 18, 1951, Shaw to Richard de Ayala, International Trade Mart Records, Tulane University, New Orleans, Louisiana.

459 Letter dated May 11, 1951, Shaw to Sir Harold Boulton, International Trade Mart Records, Tulane University, New Orleans, Louisiana.

460 Letter dated May 9, 1951, Richard A. Fiessler to J.B. Dauenhauer, International Trade Mart Records, Tulane University, New Orleans, Louisiana.

461 Letter dated May 8, 1951, Shaw to Antonio Cirera, International Trade Mart Records, Tulane University, New Orleans, Louisiana.

462 Letter dated June 22, 1951, Shaw to Frank Runyan, International Trade Mart Records, Tulane University, New Orleans, Louisiana.

463 Interview with Mrs. Harry Miller, April 7, 2008.

464 Memo dated February 10, 1951, Glenn Weekely to Shaw, International Trade Mart Records, Tulane University, New Orleans, Louisiana.

465 Letter dated June 13, 1951, Shaw to unidentified inquirer, International Trade Mart Records, Tulane University, New Orleans, Louisiana.

466 Letter dated May 9, 1951, Shaw to Isaac J. Osario Padron of Caracas, Venezuela, International Trade Mart Records, Tulane University, New Orleans, Louisiana.

467 Letter dated June 27, 1951, Shaw to Rudolf Hecht, International Trade Mart Records, Tulane University, New Orleans, Louisiana.

468 Letter dated July 9, 1951, Rudolf Hecht to Shaw, International Trade Mart Records, Tulane University, New Orleans, Louisiana.

469 Letter dated July 16, 1951, Hale Boggs to Shaw, International Trade Mart Records, Tulane University, New Orleans, Louisiana.

470 Letter dated August 15, 1951, Harold C. Jackson and Paul L. Vogel to Shaw, International Trade Mart Records, Tulane University, New Orleans, Louisiana.

471 Letter dated September 11, 1951, Shaw to Ruth Carrétte Turner, International Trade Mart Records, Tulane University, New Orleans, Louisiana.

472 Letter dated November 8, 1951, from New Orleans Business and Professional Women's Club to Shaw, International Trade Mart Records, Tulane University, New Orleans, Louisiana.

473 Letter dated August 31, 1951, Rafael Escallón Villa to Shaw, International Trade Mart Records, Tulane University, New Orleans, Louisiana.

474 Cable dated October 30, 1951, from Colombia Contest Secretary General to International Jury members for contest, International Trade Mart Records, Tulane University, New Orleans, Louisiana.

475 Letter dated November 28, 1951, Shaw to Rafael Escallón Villa, International Trade Mart Records, Tulane University, New Orleans, Louisiana.

476 Letter dated December 17, 1951, Bonifacio Velez to Shaw, International Trade Mart Records, Tulane University, New Orleans, Louisiana.

477 Letter dated November 27, 1951, Shaw to Bonifacio Velez, International Trade Mart Records, Tulane University, New Orleans, Louisiana.

478 Letter dated October 19, 1951, Shaw to customer, and letter dated November 19, 1951, Shaw to Diplomatic Mission, Federal Republic of Germany, International Trade Mart Records, Tulane University, New Orleans, Louisiana.

479 Letter dated December 10, 1951, Henry Kaiser to Shaw, International Trade Mart Records, Tulane University, New Orleans, Louisiana.

480 Letter dated December 5, 1941, Shaw to Charles E. White, International Trade Mart Records, Tulane University, New Orleans, Louisiana.

481 Annual Report 1951, International Trade Mart, International Trade Mart Records, Tulane University, New Orleans, Louisiana.

482 Report on New Orleans economy, 1951, International Trade Mart Records, Tulane University, New Orleans, Louisiana.

483 See New Orleans City Directory for 1952-53, Tulane University, New Orleans, Louisiana.

484 Interview with Martin Palmer by author, November 7, 2005.

485 Letter dated February 28, 1952, Hale Boggs to Shaw, International Trade Mart Records, Tulane University, New Orleans, Louisiana.

486 Memo dated January 17, 1952, Richard B. Swensen to various parties, International Trade Mart Records, Tulane University, New Orleans, Louisiana.

487 Telegram dated January 11, 1952, Shaw to Henry Grady Hotel, International Trade Mart Records, Tulane University, New Orleans, Louisiana.

488 Letter dated January 29, 1952, Shaw to Mario Bermúdez, International Trade Mart Records, Tulane University, New Orleans, Louisiana.

489 Letter dated February 18, 1952, Billy Murphy to Shaw, International Trade Mart Records, Tulane University, New Orleans, Louisiana.

[490] Letter dated February 4, 1952, J.B. Dauenhauer to unspecified inquirer, International Trade Mart Records, Tulane University, New Orleans, Louisiana.

[491] Letter dated February 6, 1952, Dr. Jutta Schaller to Glenn Weekley, International Trade Mart Records, Tulane University, New Orleans, Louisiana.

[492] Letter dated February 20, 1952, Glenn E. Weekley to Dr. Jutta Schaller, International Trade Mart Records, Tulane University, New Orleans, Louisiana.

[493] Letter dated February 20, 1952, Shaw to Hunter Leake II, International Trade Mart Records, Tulane University, New Orleans, Louisiana.

[494] Letter dated February 28, 1952, unknown author to Daniel Rudsten, International Trade Mart Records, Tulane University, New Orleans, Louisiana.

[495] Note from Goldie Moore dated September 19, 1952, International Trade Mart Records, Tulane University, New Orleans, Louisiana.

[496] Folder, Italian Flood Relief Committee, International Trade Mart Records, Tulane University, New Orleans, Louisiana.

[497] Letter dated March 7, 1952, Seymour Weiss to Theodore Brent, International Trade Mart Records, Tulane University, New Orleans, Louisiana.

[498] Minutes from Board of Directors meeting, International Trade Mart, March 27, 1952, International Trade Mart Records, Tulane University, New Orleans, Louisiana.

[499] Letter dated February 14, 1952, Major C.J. George to Shaw, International Trade Mart Records, Tulane University, New Orleans, Louisiana.

[500] Letter dated April 18, 1952, Shaw to J.B. Dauenhauer, International Trade Mart Records, Tulane University, New Orleans, Louisiana.

[501] Letter dated April 25, 1952, J.B. Dauenhauer to Shaw, International Trade Mart Records, Tulane University, New Orleans, Louisiana.

[502] April 1952 issue of *The Breeze*, International Trade Mart Records, Tulane University, New Orleans, Louisiana.

[503] Letter dated June 6, 1952, Shaw to Charles Empson, International Trade Mart Records, Tulane University, New Orleans, Louisiana.

[504] Letter dated June 18, 1952, Letter of Introduction regarding John Kelleher by Shaw, International Trade Mart Records, Tulane University, New Orleans, Louisiana.

[505] Letter dated July 1, 1952, Shaw to Robert H. Johnson, International Trade Mart Records, Tulane University, New Orleans, Louisiana.

[506] Minutes of meeting of Board of Directors, July 11, 1952, International Trade Mart, International Trade Mart Records, Tulane University, New Orleans, Louisiana.

[507] Memo dated June 10, 1952, Shaw to Rudolf Hecht, International Trade Mart Records, Tulane University, New Orleans, Louisiana.

[508] Letter dated July 17, 1952, Shaw to Mrs. J.F. Vreden-Van Den Brine, International Trade Mart Records, Tulane University, New Orleans, Louisiana.

[509] Letter dated August 5, 1952, Shaw to Richard Swensen, International Trade Mart Records, Tulane University, New Orleans, Louisiana.

[510] Letter dated August 6, 1952, Shaw to Lewis Bourgeois, International Trade Mart Records, Tulane University, New Orleans, Louisiana.

[511] Letter dated December 8, 1952, Shaw to Lewis Bourgeois, International Trade Mart Records, Tulane University, New Orleans, Louisiana.

512  Letter dated June 24, 1952, J.B. Dauenhauer to May H. Weidmanns, of Weidmanns' Restaurant, Meridian, Mississippi, International Trade Mart Records, Tulane University, New Orleans, Louisiana.

513  Letter dated August 29, 1952, Kenneth Barranger to Peat, Marwick, International Trade Mart Records, Tulane University, New Orleans, Louisiana.

514  Memo dated June 19, 1952, Rudolf Hecht to Shaw, International Trade Mart Records, Tulane University, New Orleans, Louisiana.

515  Letter dated June 24, 1952, Rudolf Hecht to Shaw, International Trade Mart Records, Tulane University, New Orleans, Louisiana.

516  Memo dated August 7, 1952, Shaw to Glenn Weekley, International Trade Mart Records, Tulane University, New Orleans, Louisiana.

517  Memo dated March 28, 1951, Glenn Weekley to Shaw, International Trade Mart Records, Tulane University, New Orleans, Louisiana.

518  Letter dated August 1, 1952, Theodore Brent to Shaw, with Shaw reply to Brent, International Trade Mart Records, Tulane University, New Orleans, Louisiana.

519  Letter dated August 1, 1952, Theodore Brent to Rudolf Hecht, International Trade Mart Records, Tulane University, New Orleans, Louisiana.

520  Letter dated August 12, 1952, Rudolf Hecht to Theodore Brent, International Trade Mart Records, Tulane University, New Orleans, Louisiana.

521  Letter dated September 19, 1952, Theodore Brent to Richard Jones, International Trade Mart Records, Tulane University, New Orleans, Louisiana.

522  Letter dated August 29, 1952, Helen Brett to Shaw, International Trade Mart Records, Tulane University, New Orleans, Louisiana.

523  Letter dated October 15, 1952, M.F. Rice to Shaw, International Trade Mart Records, Tulane University, New Orleans, Louisiana.

524  Letter dated October 16, 1951, Frank Runyon to Shaw, International Trade Mart Records, Tulane University, New Orleans, Louisiana.

525  Letter dated October 21, 1952, Rudolf Hecht to Karl Haller, International Trade Mart Records, Tulane University, New Orleans, Louisiana.

526  Memo dated October 7, 1952, Shaw to Theodore Brent and Rudolf Hecht, International Trade Mart Records, Tulane University, New Orleans, Louisiana.

527  Letter dated October 13, 1952, Shaw to Lawrence Fischer, International Trade Mart Records, Tulane University, New Orleans, Louisiana.

528  Telegram dated November 10, 1952, Shaw to Waldorf Astoria, with reply, International Trade Mart Records, Tulane University, New Orleans, Louisiana.

529  See invitation dated June 6, 1952 to dedication of Mary Buck Soraparu Park Health Center, signed by Chep Morrison and Thomas H. Brahney, Jr., Commissioner of Institutions, Public Health, International Trade Mart Records, Tulane University, New Orleans, Louisiana.

530  Letter dated November 5, 1952, Michael Buzon, Jr., Department of State, to Shaw, International Trade Mart Records, Tulane University, New Orleans, Louisiana.

531  Letter dated November 6, 1952, Shaw to Michael Buzon, Jr., Department of State, International Trade Mart Records, Tulane University, New Orleans, Louisiana.

532  Letter dated December 15, 1952, Shaw to Joseph Montgomery, International Trade Mart Records, Tulane University, New Orleans, Louisiana.

533 Letter dated September 30, 1952, Shaw to International House, International Trade Mart Records, Tulane University, New Orleans, Louisiana.

534 Letter dated November 13, 1952, Shaw to Governor Robert F. Kennon, International Trade Mart Records, Tulane University, New Orleans, Louisiana.

535 Letter dated August 17, 1951, J.B. Dauenhauer to an employee, International Trade Mart Records, Tulane University, New Orleans, Louisiana.

536 December 12, 1952, Memo from J.B. Dauenhauer to James B. Mitchell, International Trade Mart Records, Tulane University, New Orleans, Louisiana.

537 Letter dated December 11, 1952, Harold C. Jackson and Paul L. Vogel to Shaw, International Trade Mart Records, Tulane University, New Orleans, Louisiana.

538 Letters to and from Worldwide Broadcasting System during December 1952, International Trade Mart Records, Tulane University, New Orleans, Louisiana.

539 Letter dated January 7, 1953, Gerhard Voss to Shaw, International Trade Mart Records, Tulane University, New Orleans, Louisiana.

540 Letter dated December 17, 1952, Commercial Attaché of Honduras to Shaw, International Trade Mart Records, Tulane University, New Orleans, Louisiana.

541 Letter dated December 9, 1952, Shaw to Commercial Counselor, Embassy of Nicaragua, International Trade Mart Records, Tulane University, New Orleans, Louisiana.

542 Letter dated December 26, 1952, Shaw to Leland W. Cutler, International Trade Mart Records, Tulane University, New Orleans, Louisiana.

543 Income statement for full year 1952, International Trade Mart, International Trade Mart Records, Tulane University, New Orleans, Louisiana.

544 Interview with Don Schueler by Author, March 20, 2007.

545 Annual Report, 1952, International Trade Mart, International Trade Mart Records, Tulane University, New Orleans, Louisiana.

546 Memo dated January 13, 1953, Shaw to Audrey Copping, International Trade Mart Records, Tulane University, New Orleans, Louisiana.

547 Letter dated February 9, 1953, Shaw to Mississippi Shipping Company, International Trade Mart Records, Tulane University, New Orleans, Louisiana.

548 Letter dated February 9, 1953, Marcel Gomez to Travel Agency requesting refund for Shaw's airfare, International Trade Mart Records, Tulane University, New Orleans, Louisiana.

549 Letter dated February 5, 1953, Shaw to Mrs. Richard Swenson, International Trade Mart Records, Tulane University, New Orleans, Louisiana.

550 Minutes of Board of Directors meeting, February 4, 1953, International Trade Mart, International Trade Mart Records, Tulane University, New Orleans, Louisiana.

551 Memo entitled, "Only Ten More Days," by Clay Shaw, International Trade Mart Records, Tulane University, New Orleans, Louisiana.

552 Letters dated February and April 1953, Dr. Jutta Schaller to the Mart, International Trade Mart Records, Tulane University, New Orleans, Louisiana.

553 Minutes to Contributors and Debenture Holders meeting, March 17, 1953, International Trade Mart Records, Tulane University, New Orleans, Louisiana.

554 Letter dated March 12, 1953, Chep Morrison to speakers before Louisiana Municipal Association Convention, International Trade Mart Records, Tulane University, New Orleans, Louisiana.

555 Undated handwritten note, Shaw to Dave McGuire, International Trade Mart Records, Tulane University, New Orleans, Louisiana.

556 Letter dated April 27, 1953, Joseph M. O'Meallie to Shaw, International Trade Mart Records, Tulane University, New Orleans, Louisiana.

557 Letter dated April 20, 1953, Chep Morrison to Shaw, International Trade Mart Records, Tulane University, New Orleans, Louisiana.

558 Letter dated April 24, 1953, Shaw to David O. Mansfield, International Trade Mart Records, Tulane University, New Orleans, Louisiana.

559 Memo dated April 21, 1953, Shaw to Rudolf Hecht, International Trade Mart Records, Tulane University, New Orleans, Louisiana.

560 Letter dated April 30, 1953, Rudolf Hecht to Karl Haller, International Trade Mart Records, Tulane University, New Orleans, Louisiana.

561 Letter dated May 14, 1953, Ella Brennan to Shaw, International Trade Mart Records, Tulane University, New Orleans, Louisiana.

562 Letter dated April 13, 1953, Edgar B. Stern, Jr. to Shaw, International Trade Mart Records, Tulane University, New Orleans, Louisiana.

563 Letter dated May 11, 1953, J.B. Dauenhauer in answer to inquiry, International Trade Mart Records, Tulane University, New Orleans, Louisiana.

564 Letter dated December 1, 1953, J.B. Dauenhauer in response to inquiry, International Trade Mart Records, Tulane University, New Orleans, Louisiana.

565 Letter dated June 1, 1953, Glenn Weekley to Shaw, International Trade Mart Records, Tulane University, New Orleans, Louisiana.

566 Memo dated July 7, 1953, from J.B. Dauenhauer, International Trade Mart Records, Tulane University, New Orleans, Louisiana.

567 Letter dated April 10, 1953, J.B. Dauenhauer to Dr. Homer J. Dupuy, International Trade Mart Records, Tulane University, New Orleans, Louisiana.

568 News article dated June 13, 1953, newspaper unknown, Hines/Ochsner Collection, 1930-1985, Historic New Orleans Collection, New Orleans, Louisiana.

569 See biographical information in J. Blanc Monroe Collection, Historic New Orleans Collection, New Orleans, Louisiana.

570 See information contained in Hines/Ochsner Collection, 1930-1985, Historic New Orleans Collection, New Orleans, Louisiana.

571 See information contained in Hines/Ochsner Collection, 1930-1985, Historic New Orleans Collection, New Orleans, Louisiana.

572 Minutes, Board of Directors meeting of July 7, 1953, International Trade Mart, International Trade Mart Records, Tulane University, New Orleans, Louisiana.

573 Memo dated June 9, 1953, J.B. Dauenhauer to tenants, International Trade Mart Records, Tulane University, New Orleans, Louisiana.

574 Memo dated June 17, 1953, J.B. Dauenhauer to tenants, International Trade Mart Records, Tulane University, New Orleans, Louisiana.

575 Letter dated December 1, 1953, J.B. Dauenhauer to W.R. Parker, International Trade Mart Records, Tulane University, New Orleans, Louisiana.

576 Memo dated August 20, 1953, from M.O. Delgado, Jr., International Trade Mart Records, Tulane University, New Orleans, Louisiana.

577 Letter dated December 8, 1953, Shaw to William Zetzmann, International Trade Mart Records, Tulane University, New Orleans, Louisiana.

578 July 20, 1953 edition of *The New Orleans Item Industrial Weekly*, International Trade Mart Records, Tulane University, New Orleans, Louisiana.

579 Letter dated August 3, 1953, Loyal Phillips to Charles Nutter, International Trade Mart Records, Tulane University, New Orleans, Louisiana.

580 Letter dated September 1, 1953, Shaw to Captain Neville Levy, Equitable Equipment Company, International Trade Mart Records, Tulane University, New Orleans, Louisiana.

581 Memo dated November 25, 1953, Shaw to Rudolf Hecht, International Trade Mart Records, Tulane University, New Orleans, Louisiana.

582 Letter dated September 9, 1953, Mario Bermúdez to J.B. Dauenhauer, International Trade Mart Records.

583 Letter dated September 14, 1953, J.B. Dauenhauer in response to inquiry, International Trade Mart Records, Tulane University, New Orleans, Louisiana.

584 Letter dated September 29, 1953, J.B. Dauenhauer in response to inquiry, International Trade Mart Records, Tulane University, New Orleans, Louisiana.

585 Letter dated October 1, 1953, Frances Parkinson Keyes to Shaw, International Trade Mart Records, Tulane University, New Orleans, Louisiana.

586 Letter dated October 28, 1953, Shaw to Frances Parkinson Keyes, International Trade Mart Records, Tulane University, New Orleans, Louisiana.

587 Letter dated October 27, 1953, Shaw to Chamber of Commerce of Augusta, Georgia, International Trade Mart Records, Tulane University, New Orleans, Louisiana.

588 *Saturday Evening Post*, October 10, 1953 edition, International Trade Mart Records, Tulane University, New Orleans, Louisiana.

589 See *Trade Winds* issue dated November 18, 1953, International Trade Mart Records, Tulane University, New Orleans, Louisiana.

590 Letter dated November 9, 1953, N.A. Russell to Shaw, International Trade Mart Records, Tulane University, New Orleans, Louisiana.

591 Series of telegrams to and from Bruce Mitchell and Shaw, International Trade Mart Records, Tulane University, New Orleans, Louisiana.

592 Telegram dated November 13, 1953, Shaw to K. Bruce Mitchell, International Trade Mart Records, Tulane University, New Orleans, Louisiana.

593 Telegram dated November 6, 1953, Shaw to Beverly Hotel, International Trade Mart Records, Tulane University, New Orleans, Louisiana.

594 Letter dated November 25, 1953, Shaw to Irving S. Preston, International Trade Mart Records, Tulane University, New Orleans, Louisiana.

595 Letter dated December 29, 1953, Gwen Randolph to Shaw, International Trade Mart Records, Tulane University, New Orleans, Louisiana.

596 Minutes of Executive Committee meeting, December 8, 1953, International Trade Mart Records, Tulane University, New Orleans, Louisiana.

597 Letter dated December 15, 1953, Shaw to Betty Morris, International Trade Mart Records, Tulane University, New Orleans, Louisiana.

598 Letter dated June 22, 1953, Robert H. Macy to J.B. Dauenhauer, International Trade Mart Records, Tulane University, New Orleans, Louisiana.

599 Letter dated December 10, 1953, Charles Nutter to International House members, International Trade Mart Records, Tulane University, New Orleans, Louisiana.

600 E-mail from Mike Formy-Duval to author, September 8, 2000.

601 Interview of Gaines Kincaid by Author, October 13, 2006.

602 Telegram dated October 12, 1953, Tom Dutton and Louie Clay to Shaw, International Trade Mart Records, Tulane University, New Orleans, Louisiana.

603 Memo dated March 27, 1952, by William Zetzmann, Clay Shaw Louisiana Purchase Sesquicentennial Papers, Historic New Orleans Collection, New Orleans, Louisiana.

604 Letter dated July 3, 1952, Charles Nutter to Rudolf Hecht, Clay Shaw Louisiana Purchase Sesquicentennial Papers, Historic New Orleans Collection, New Orleans, Louisiana.

605 Memorandum dated September 1952, by Clarke Salmon, Sr. of Bauerlein's, Inc., Clay Shaw Louisiana Purchase Sesquicentennial Papers, Historic New Orleans Collection, New Orleans, Louisiana.

606 Budget dated September 20, 1952, Clay Shaw Louisiana Purchase Sesquicentennial Papers, Historic New Orleans Collection, New Orleans, Louisiana.

607 Letter dated January 30, 1953, Raymond Hufft to E.V. Richards, Jr., International Trade Mart Records, Tulane University, New Orleans, Louisiana.

608 Letter dated October 10, 1952, Raymond Hufft to Colonel Edwin A. Walker, Clay Shaw Louisiana Purchase Sesquicentennial Papers, Historic New Orleans Collection, New Orleans, Louisiana.

609 Minutes to Board of Directors meeting, February 2, 1953, Louisiana Purchase 150th Anniversary Association, Clay Shaw Louisiana Purchase Sesquicentennial Papers, Historic New Orleans Collection, New Orleans, Louisiana.

610 Letter dated February 10, 1953, Shaw to Monk Simons, Clay Shaw Louisiana Purchase Sesquicentennial Papers, Historic New Orleans Collection, New Orleans, Louisiana.

611 Letter dated September 14, 1952, Monk Simons to E.V. Richards, Clay Shaw Louisiana Purchase Sesquicentennial Papers, Historic New Orleans Collection, New Orleans, Louisiana.

612 Letter dated October 22, 1952, Mrs. James Bond, Secretary to Mrs. Edgar B. Stern, to Raymond F. Hufft, Clay Shaw Louisiana Purchase Sesquicentennial Papers, Historic New Orleans Collection, New Orleans, Louisiana.

613 Memo dated September 30, 1952, David Baldwin to Raymond Hufft, Clay Shaw Louisiana Purchase Sesquicentennial Papers, Historic New Orleans Collection, New Orleans, Louisiana.

614 Letter dated February 25, 1953, Shaw to Scott Wilson, Clay Shaw Louisiana Purchase Sesquicentennial Papers, Historic New Orleans Collection, New Orleans, Louisiana.

615 Letter dated November 10, 1952, E.V. Richards, Jr. to Chep Morrison, Clay Shaw Louisiana Purchase Sesquicentennial Papers, Historic New Orleans Collection, New Orleans, Louisiana.

616 Letter dated December 5, 1952, John A. Reilly to Raymond Hufft, Clay Shaw Louisiana Purchase Sesquicentennial Papers, Historic New Orleans Collection, New Orleans, Louisiana.

617 Letter dated January 14, 1953, Raymond Hufft to John A. Reilly, Clay Shaw Louisiana Purchase Sesquicentennial Papers, Historic New Orleans Collection, New Orleans, Louisiana.

618 Letter dated February 5, 1953, James Aldige, Jr. to Louisiana Purchase 150th Anniversary Celebration, Clay Shaw Louisiana Purchase Sesquicentennial Papers, Historic New Orleans Collection, New Orleans, Louisiana.

619 Letter dated February 16, 1953, Shaw to James Aldige, Jr., Clay Shaw Louisiana Purchase Sesquicentennial Papers, Historic New Orleans Collection, New Orleans, Louisiana.

620 Letter dated February 20, 1953, Stanley J. Reyes to Shaw, Clay Shaw Louisiana Purchase Sesquicentennial Papers, Historic New Orleans Collection, New Orleans, Louisiana.

621 Letter dated February 24, 1953, Shaw to Stanley J. Reyes, Clay Shaw Louisiana Purchase Sesquicentennial Papers, Historic New Orleans Collection, New Orleans, Louisiana.

622 Letter dated February 12, 1953, Elmo Avet to Shaw, Clay Shaw Clay Shaw Louisiana Purchase Sesquicentennial Papers, Historic New Orleans Collection, New Orleans, Louisiana.

623 Letter dated February 16, 1953, Shaw to Elmo Avet, Clay Shaw Clay Shaw Louisiana Purchase Sesquicentennial Papers, Historic New Orleans Collection, New Orleans, Louisiana.

624 Letter dated February 23, 1953, Shaw to Harnett T. Kane, Clay Shaw Louisiana Purchase Sesquicentennial Papers, Historic New Orleans Collection, New Orleans, Louisiana.

625 Letter dated February 13, 1953, Shaw to Norman Cousins, Clay Shaw Louisiana Purchase Sesquicentennial Papers, Historic New Orleans Collection, New Orleans, Louisiana.

626 Minutes to Board of Directors Meeting, March 9, 1953, Louisiana Purchase 150th Anniversary Association, Clay Shaw Louisiana Purchase Sesquicentennial Papers, Historic New Orleans Collection, New Orleans, Louisiana.

627 Budget dated December 16, 1952, Clay Shaw Louisiana Purchase Sesquicentennial Papers, Historic New Orleans Collection, New Orleans, Louisiana.

628 Letter dated April 21, 1953, Shaw to E.V. Richards, Jr., Clay Shaw Louisiana Purchase Sesquicentennial Papers, Historic New Orleans Collection, New Orleans, Louisiana.

629 Letter dated March 17, 1953, Shaw to Carmen C. Brezeale, Chairman of Chamber of Commerce of Natchitoches Parish, Clay Shaw Louisiana Purchase Sesquicentennial Papers, Historic New Orleans Collection, New Orleans, Louisiana.

630 Letter dated July 5, 1953, Shaw to B. Bennett Singer, The Amsterdam Company, Clay Shaw Louisiana Purchase Sesquicentennial Papers, Historic New Orleans Collection, New Orleans, Louisiana.

631 Letter dated May 14, 1953, Shaw to H. LeFevre, Clay Shaw Clay Shaw Louisiana Purchase Sesquicentennial Papers, Historic New Orleans Collection, New Orleans, Louisiana.

632 Letter dated May 8, 1953, Shaw to Owen Brennan, Clay Shaw Louisiana Purchase Sesquicentennial Papers, Historic New Orleans Collection, New Orleans, Louisiana.

633 Letter dated April 21, 1953, Shaw to Victor Schiro, Clay Shaw Louisiana Purchase Sesquicentennial Papers, Historic New Orleans Collection, New Orleans, Louisiana.

634 Letter dated April 22, 1953, Shaw to Victor Schiro, Clay Shaw Louisiana Purchase Sesquicentennial Papers, Historic New Orleans Collection, New Orleans, Louisiana.

635 Letter dated December 19, 1952, Raymond Hufft to Clarke Salmon, Sr., Clay Shaw Louisiana Purchase Sesquicentennial Papers, Historic New Orleans Collection, New Orleans, Louisiana.

636 Undated Letter, Clint Bolton to Raymond Hufft, Clay Shaw Louisiana Purchase Sesquicentennial Papers, Historic New Orleans Collection, New Orleans, Louisiana.

637 Letter dated April 24, 1953, Shaw to David O. Mansfield, Clay Shaw Louisiana Purchase Sesquicentennial Papers, Historic New Orleans Collection, New Orleans, Louisiana.

638 Letter dated April 28, 1953, Shaw to Margaret L. Marks, Clay Shaw Louisiana Purchase Sesquicentennial Papers, Historic New Orleans Collection, New Orleans, Louisiana.

639 Letter dated May 21, 1953, E.P. Devron to David Baldwin, Clay Shaw Louisiana Purchase Sesquicentennial Papers, Historic New Orleans Collection, New Orleans, Louisiana.

640 Letter dated July 3, 1953, Shaw to A.J. Jacquot, Jr., Clay Shaw Louisiana Purchase Sesquicentennial Papers, Historic New Orleans Collection, New Orleans, Louisiana.

641. Letter dated September 18, 1953, David Baldwin to A.J. Jacquot, Jr., Clay Shaw Louisiana Purchase Sesquicentennial Papers, Historic New Orleans Collection, New Orleans, Louisiana.

642. Letter dated July 7, 1953, David Baldwin to A.J. Jacquot, Jr., Clay Shaw Louisiana Purchase Sesquicentennial Papers, Historic New Orleans Collection, New Orleans, Louisiana.

643. Sesquicentennial Daily Report dated October 2, 1952, Bauerlein, Inc. to Raymond Hufft, Clay Shaw Louisiana Purchase Sesquicentennial Papers, Historic New Orleans Collection, New Orleans, Louisiana.

644. Letter dated October 13, 1952, Clarke Salmon, Sr. to David Baldwin and Clint Bolton, Clay Shaw Louisiana Purchase Sesquicentennial Papers, Historic New Orleans Collection, New Orleans, Louisiana.

645. Letter dated October 23, 1952, David Baldwin to Clarke Salmon, Sr., Clay Shaw Louisiana Purchase Sesquicentennial Papers, Historic New Orleans Collection, New Orleans, Louisiana.

646. Letter dated November 10, 1952, David Baldwin to Clarke Salmon, Clay Shaw Louisiana Purchase Sesquicentennial Papers, Historic New Orleans Collection, New Orleans, Louisiana.

647. Letter dated January 26, 1953, Robert Tallant to E.V. Richards, Clay Shaw Louisiana Purchase Sesquicentennial Papers, Historic New Orleans Collection, New Orleans, Louisiana.

648. Letter dated February 20, 1953, E.V. Richards to Robert Tallant, Clay Shaw Louisiana Purchase Sesquicentennial Papers, Historic New Orleans Collection, New Orleans, Louisiana.

649. Letter dated May 3, 1953, George H. Gardiner to Shaw, Clay Shaw Louisiana Purchase Sesquicentennial Papers, Historic New Orleans Collection, New Orleans, Louisiana.

650. Letter dated May 8, 1953, Shaw to George H. Gardiner, Clay Shaw Louisiana Purchase Sesquicentennial Papers, Historic New Orleans Collection, New Orleans, Louisiana.

651. Letter dated July 8, 1953, Shaw to Streuby Drumm, Clay Shaw Louisiana Purchase Sesquicentennial Papers, Historic New Orleans Collection, New Orleans, Louisiana.

652. Letter dated March 18, 1953, Arthur J. Chapital, Sr. to E.V. Richards, Jr., Clay Shaw Louisiana Purchase Sesquicentennial Papers, Historic New Orleans Collection, New Orleans, Louisiana.

653. Undated letter, David Baldwin to Dr. G.A. Ackal, Clay Shaw Louisiana Purchase Sesquicentennial Papers, Historic New Orleans Collection, New Orleans, Louisiana.

654. Letter dated September 10, 1953, Shaw to Dr. G.A. Ackal, Clay Shaw Louisiana Purchase Sesquicentennial Papers, Historic New Orleans Collection, New Orleans, Louisiana.

655. Letter dated October 3, 1953, Shaw to Dr. G.A. Ackal, Clay Shaw Louisiana Purchase Sesquicentennial Papers, Historic New Orleans Collection, New Orleans, Louisiana.

656. Letter dated March 1953, Mrs. George M. Bezou to Editor, *New Orleans States* with copy to Shaw, Clay Shaw Louisiana Purchase Sesquicentennial Papers, Historic New Orleans Collection, New Orleans, Louisiana.

657. Letter dated March 6, 1953, Shaw to Mrs. George M. Bezou, Clay Shaw Louisiana Purchase Sesquicentennial Papers, Historic New Orleans Collection, New Orleans, Louisiana.

658. Letter dated August 25, 1953, Shaw to Major D.H. Clark, American Legion, Clay Shaw Louisiana Purchase Sesquicentennial Papers, Historic New Orleans Collection, New Orleans, Louisiana.

659. Letter dated September 3, 1953, Shaw to James F. Bezou, Clay Shaw Louisiana Purchase Sesquicentennial Papers, Historic New Orleans Collection, New Orleans, Louisiana.

660. Letter dated May 11, 1953, David Baldwin to R.T. Andrews, Clay Shaw Louisiana Purchase Sesquicentennial Papers, Historic New Orleans Collection, New Orleans, Louisiana.

661 Memo dated November 3, 1952, David Baldwin to Streuby Drumm, E.V. Richards, Jr., and General Raymond F. Hufft, Clay Shaw Louisiana Purchase Sesquicentennial Papers, Historic New Orleans Collection, New Orleans, Louisiana.

662 Memo dated November 4, 1952, Clint Bolton to E.V. Richards, Streuby Drumm, and General Raymond F. Hufft, Clay Shaw Louisiana Purchase Sesquicentennial Papers, Historic New Orleans Collection, New Orleans, Louisiana.

663 Letter dated October 13, 1953, Theodore Lafair to Shaw, Clay Shaw Louisiana Purchase Sesquicentennial Papers, Historic New Orleans Collection, New Orleans, Louisiana.

664 Letter dated October 27, 1953, Shaw to Theodore Lafair, Clay Shaw Louisiana Purchase Sesquicentennial Papers, Historic New Orleans Collection, New Orleans, Louisiana.

665 Letter dated November 24, 1953, Mrs. W.H. Dawson to Shaw, Clay Shaw Louisiana Purchase Sesquicentennial Papers, Historic New Orleans Collection, New Orleans, Louisiana.

666 Letter dated December 2, 1953, Shaw to Mrs. W.H. Dawson, Clay Shaw Louisiana Purchase Sesquicentennial Papers, Historic New Orleans Collection, New Orleans, Louisiana.

667 Memorandum dated October 6, 1952, from Bauerlein, Inc., Clay Shaw Louisiana Purchase Sesquicentennial Papers, Historic New Orleans Collection, New Orleans, Louisiana.

668 Letter dated October 1, 1952, David Baldwin to Clayton Fritchey, Clay Shaw Louisiana Purchase Sesquicentennial Papers, Historic New Orleans Collection, New Orleans, Louisiana.

669 Letter dated December 19, 1952, David Baldwin to Raymond Hufft, Clay Shaw Louisiana Purchase Sesquicentennial Papers, Historic New Orleans Collection, New Orleans, Louisiana.

670 Minutes of Board of Directors Meeting, April 23, 1953, Louisiana Purchase 150th Anniversary Celebration, Clay Shaw Louisiana Purchase Sesquicentennial Papers, Historic New Orleans Collection, New Orleans, Louisiana.

671 Letter dated June 29, 1953, Shaw to Joseph Montgomery, Clay Shaw Louisiana Purchase Sesquicentennial Papers, Historic New Orleans Collection, New Orleans, Louisiana.

672 Letter dated January 27, 1953, Charles H. Blake to Isidore Newman II, Clay Shaw Louisiana Purchase Sesquicentennial Papers, Historic New Orleans Collection, New Orleans, Louisiana.

673 Letter dated February 13, 1953, Shaw to Charles H. Blake, Clay Shaw Louisiana Purchase Sesquicentennial Papers, Historic New Orleans Collection, New Orleans, Louisiana.

674 Letter dated March 19, 1953, Mortimer Frankel to Governor Robert F. Kennon, Clay Shaw Louisiana Purchase Sesquicentennial Papers, Historic New Orleans Collection, New Orleans, Louisiana.

675 Letter dated March 25, 1953, Mortimer Frankel to Shaw, Clay Shaw Louisiana Purchase Sesquicentennial Papers, Historic New Orleans Collection, New Orleans, Louisiana.

676 Letter dated April 15, 1953, Shaw to Mortimer Frankel, Clay Shaw Louisiana Purchase Sesquicentennial Papers, Historic New Orleans Collection, New Orleans, Louisiana.

677 Letter dated May 11, 1953, Shaw to Mortimer Frankel, Clay Shaw Louisiana Purchase Sesquicentennial Papers, Historic New Orleans Collection, New Orleans, Louisiana.

678 Letter dated April 1953, Shaw to Nathan E. Jacobs, Clay Shaw Louisiana Purchase Sesquicentennial Papers, Historic New Orleans Collection, New Orleans, Louisiana.

679 Letter dated February 20, 1953, Beverly Brown to Shaw, Clay Shaw Louisiana Purchase Sesquicentennial Papers, Historic New Orleans Collection, New Orleans, Louisiana.

680 Memo dated July 17, 1953, Clay Shaw to E.V. Richards, Clay Shaw Louisiana Purchase Sesquicentennial Papers, Historic New Orleans Collection, New Orleans, Louisiana.

681. Letter dated July 14, 1953, David Baldwin to Florence Britton, Clay Shaw Louisiana Purchase Sesquicentennial Papers, Historic New Orleans Collection, New Orleans, Louisiana.

682. Letter dated August 25, 1953, Russ McFarland to Shaw, Clay Shaw Louisiana Purchase Sesquicentennial Papers, Historic New Orleans Collection, New Orleans, Louisiana.

683. Letter dated August 31, 1953, Shaw to Russ McFarland, Clay Shaw Louisiana Purchase Sesquicentennial Papers, Historic New Orleans Collection, New Orleans, Louisiana.

684. Unsigned Memorandum dated August 31, 1953 to Clay Shaw, Clay Shaw Louisiana Purchase Sesquicentennial Papers, Historic New Orleans Collection, New Orleans, Louisiana.

685. Unsigned Memorandum to Clay Shaw dated August 31, 1953, Clay Shaw Louisiana Purchase Sesquicentennial Papers, Historic New Orleans Collection, New Orleans, Louisiana.

686. Letter dated March 20, 1953, P.J. Rinderle to David Baldwin, Clay Shaw Louisiana Purchase Sesquicentennial Papers, Historic New Orleans Collection, New Orleans, Louisiana.

687. Letter dated May 26, 1953, Shaw to J.M. Engster, Clay Shaw Louisiana Purchase Sesquicentennial Papers, Historic New Orleans Collection, New Orleans, Louisiana.

688. Letter dated May 14, 1953, F.H. Collins to Streuby Drumm, Clay Shaw Louisiana Purchase Sesquicentennial Papers, Historic New Orleans Collection, New Orleans, Louisiana.

689. Letter dated February 24, 1953, David Baldwin to Earle Newton, Clay Shaw Louisiana Purchase Sesquicentennial Papers, Historic New Orleans Collection, New Orleans, Louisiana.

690. Letter dated April 27, 1953, Shaw to Carl Carmer, Clay Shaw Louisiana Purchase Sesquicentennial Papers, Historic New Orleans Collection, New Orleans, Louisiana.

691. Letter dated June 4, 1953, Carl Carmer to Shaw, Clay Shaw Louisiana Purchase Sesquicentennial Papers, Historic New Orleans Collection, New Orleans, Louisiana.

692. Letter dated June 9, 1953, Shaw to Carl Carmer, Clay Shaw Louisiana Purchase Sesquicentennial Papers, Historic New Orleans Collection, New Orleans, Louisiana.

693. Letter dated March 21, 1953, Shaw to Edward L. Bernays, Clay Shaw Louisiana Purchase Sesquicentennial Papers, Historic New Orleans Collection, New Orleans, Louisiana.

694. Letter dated March 26, 1953, Edward L. Bernays to Shaw, Clay Shaw Louisiana Purchase Sesquicentennial Papers, Historic New Orleans Collection, New Orleans, Louisiana.

695. Letter dated March 25, 1953, Monita Goldsby to E.V. Richards, Clay Shaw Louisiana Purchase Sesquicentennial Papers, Historic New Orleans Collection, New Orleans, Louisiana.

696. Letter dated September 22, 1953, Shaw to Mrs. Camille Cazdussus, Clay Shaw Louisiana Purchase Sesquicentennial Papers, Historic New Orleans Collection, New Orleans, Louisiana.

697. Telegram dated June 10, 1953, David L. Pearce to Shaw, Clay Shaw Louisiana Purchase Sesquicentennial Papers, Historic New Orleans Collection, New Orleans, Louisiana.

698. Letter dated August 19, 1953, E.V. Richards, Jr. to Shaw, Clay Shaw Louisiana Purchase Sesquicentennial Papers, Historic New Orleans Collection, New Orleans, Louisiana.

699. Letter dated April 9, 1953, Shaw to Charles Burnham, Clay Shaw Louisiana Purchase Sesquicentennial Papers, Historic New Orleans Collection, New Orleans, Louisiana.

700. Letter dated April 20, 1953, Phyllis Wellford to Linda Bohnenstiehl, Clay Shaw Louisiana Purchase Sesquicentennial Papers, Historic New Orleans Collection, New Orleans, Louisiana.

701. Letter dated June 4, 1953, David Baldwin to Helen Budd, Clay Shaw Louisiana Purchase Sesquicentennial Papers, Historic New Orleans Collection, New Orleans, Louisiana.

702. Contact Report dated October 14, 1952, Clay Shaw Louisiana Purchase Sesquicentennial Papers, Historic New Orleans Collection, New Orleans, Louisiana.

703 Letter dated June 15, 1953, David Baldwin to Ellis P. Laborde, Clay Shaw Louisiana Purchase Sesquicentennial Papers, Historic New Orleans Collection, New Orleans, Louisiana.

704 Letter dated June 24, 1953, Ellis P. Laborde to David Baldwin, Clay Shaw Louisiana Purchase Sesquicentennial Papers, Historic New Orleans Collection, New Orleans, Louisiana.

705 Memo dated February 24, 1953, David Baldwin to Shaw, Clay Shaw Louisiana Purchase Sesquicentennial Papers, Historic New Orleans Collection, New Orleans, Louisiana.

706 Letter dated September 24, 1953, Shaw to James Louis Randolph Kean, Clay Shaw Louisiana Purchase Sesquicentennial Papers, Historic New Orleans Collection, New Orleans, Louisiana.

707 Letter dated September 10, 1953, Shaw to Mario Bermúdez, Clay Shaw Louisiana Purchase Sesquicentennial Papers, Historic New Orleans Collection, New Orleans, Louisiana.

708 Letter dated February 25, 1953, Shaw to E.C. Messner, Clay Shaw Louisiana Purchase Sesquicentennial Papers, Historic New Orleans Collection, New Orleans, Louisiana.

709 Letter dated April 21, 1953, Francis Parkinson Keyes to Shaw, Clay Shaw Louisiana Purchase Sesquicentennial Papers, Historic New Orleans Collection, New Orleans, Louisiana.

710 Letter dated May 4, 1953, Shaw to Francis Parkinson Keyes, Clay Shaw Louisiana Purchase Sesquicentennial Papers, Historic New Orleans Collection, New Orleans, Louisiana.

711 Letter dated September 1, 1953, Francis Parkinson Keyes to Shaw, Clay Shaw Louisiana Purchase Sesquicentennial Papers, Historic New Orleans Collection, New Orleans, Louisiana.

712 Letter dated September 10, 1953, Shaw to Francis Parkinson Keyes, Clay Shaw Louisiana Purchase Sesquicentennial Papers, Historic New Orleans Collection, New Orleans, Louisiana.

713 Letter dated September 22, 1953, Shaw to T.L. Riggin, Clay Shaw Louisiana Purchase Sesquicentennial Papers, Historic New Orleans Collection, New Orleans, Louisiana.

714 Letter dated September 28, 1953, Harold Brayman to Shaw, Clay Shaw Louisiana Purchase Sesquicentennial Papers, Historic New Orleans Collection, New Orleans, Louisiana.

715 Letter dated April 7, 1953, Shaw to Ray Cantrell, Clay Shaw Louisiana Purchase Sesquicentennial Papers, Historic New Orleans Collection, New Orleans, Louisiana.

716 Letter dated June 15, 1953, Shaw to Major C.E. Corley, Jr., USMC, Clay Shaw Louisiana Purchase Sesquicentennial Papers, Historic New Orleans Collection, New Orleans, Louisiana.

717 Letter dated April 24, 1953, Shaw to Louis Clay, Clay Shaw Louisiana Purchase Sesquicentennial Papers, Historic New Orleans Collection, New Orleans, Louisiana.

718 Letter dated May 28, 1953, Shaw to Tom Dutton, Clay Shaw Louisiana Purchase Sesquicentennial Papers, Historic New Orleans Collection, New Orleans, Louisiana.

719 Letter dated July 16, 1953, Shaw to Chris Cross, Clay Shaw Louisiana Purchase Sesquicentennial Papers, Historic New Orleans Collection, New Orleans, Louisiana.

720 Letter dated July 15, 1953, David Baldwin to Henry Bertch, Clay Shaw Louisiana Purchase Sesquicentennial Papers, Historic New Orleans Collection, New Orleans, Louisiana.

721 Letter dated August 20, 1953, David Baldwin to L. Curvier, Clay Shaw Louisiana Purchase Sesquicentennial Papers, Historic New Orleans Collection, New Orleans, Louisiana.

722 Letter dated August 26, 1953, Shaw to W.F. Cotton, Clay Shaw Louisiana Purchase Sesquicentennial Papers, Historic New Orleans Collection, New Orleans, Louisiana.

723 Letter dated September 23, 1953, Shaw to Mrs. C. Vernon Cloutier, Clay Shaw Louisiana Purchase Sesquicentennial Papers, Historic New Orleans Collection, New Orleans, Louisiana.

724 Letter dated May 1, 1953, Shaw to John Derr of CBS Radio, Clay Shaw Louisiana Purchase Sesquicentennial Papers, Historic New Orleans Collection, New Orleans, Louisiana.

725  Letter dated September 8, 1953, Shaw to Charles R. Newman, Clay Shaw Louisiana Purchase Sesquicentennial Papers, Historic New Orleans Collection, New Orleans, Louisiana.

726  Letter dated October 8, 1953, Carl Cramer to E.V. Richards, Clay Shaw Louisiana Purchase Sesquicentennial Papers, Historic New Orleans Collection, New Orleans, Louisiana.

727  Letter dated April 7, 1953, Harlean James to Shaw, Clay Shaw Louisiana Purchase Sesquicentennial Papers, Historic New Orleans Collection, New Orleans, Louisiana.

728  Letter dated May 4, 1953, Shaw to Harlean James, Clay Shaw Louisiana Purchase Sesquicentennial Papers, Historic New Orleans Collection, New Orleans, Louisiana.

729  Letter dated March 26, 1953, Shaw to Lillian Meyer, Clay Shaw Louisiana Purchase Sesquicentennial Papers, Historic New Orleans Collection, New Orleans, Louisiana.

730  Letter dated May 7, 1953, Shaw to John J. Morrissey, Clay Shaw Louisiana Purchase Sesquicentennial Papers, Historic New Orleans Collection, New Orleans, Louisiana.

731  Letter dated May 25, 1953, Shaw to John J. Morrissey, Clay Shaw Louisiana Purchase Sesquicentennial Papers, Historic New Orleans Collection, New Orleans, Louisiana.

732  1953 Memo by Horace Renegar, Clay Shaw Louisiana Purchase Sesquicentennial Papers, Historic New Orleans Collection, New Orleans, Louisiana.

733  Undated letter, Shaw to Lutheran Layman's League, Clay Shaw Louisiana Purchase Sesquicentennial Papers, Historic New Orleans Collection, New Orleans, Louisiana.

734  Letter dated August 3, 1953, David Baldwin to Glen Douthit, Clay Shaw Louisiana Purchase Sesquicentennial Papers, Historic New Orleans Collection, New Orleans, Louisiana.

735  Letter dated March 18, 1953, John E. Rousseau to E.V. Richards, and Letter dated March 21, 1953, Shaw to John E. Rousseau, Clay Shaw Louisiana Purchase Sesquicentennial Papers, Historic New Orleans Collection, New Orleans, Louisiana.

736  Letter dated February 13, 1953, Shaw to Stanley J. Guerin, Clay Shaw Louisiana Purchase Sesquicentennial Papers, Historic New Orleans Collection, New Orleans, Louisiana.

737  Letter dated March 26, 1953, Shaw to B. Grenrood, Illinois Central Railway, Clay Shaw Louisiana Purchase Sesquicentennial Papers, Historic New Orleans Collection, New Orleans, Louisiana.

738  Letter dated October 23, 1953, David Baldwin to Georgia C. Rawson, Clay Shaw Louisiana Purchase Sesquicentennial Papers, Historic New Orleans Collection, New Orleans, Louisiana.

739  Letters dated December 2 through December 4, 1953, Shaw to various teachers' magazines, Clay Shaw Louisiana Purchase Sesquicentennial Papers, Historic New Orleans Collection, New Orleans, Louisiana.

740  Memo dated April 9, 1953, Shaw to E.V. Richards, Jr., Clay Shaw Louisiana Purchase Sesquicentennial Papers, Historic New Orleans Collection, New Orleans, Louisiana.

741  Letter dated August 6, 1953, Cecil B. DeMille to E.V. Richards, Jr., Clay Shaw Louisiana Purchase Sesquicentennial Papers, Historic New Orleans Collection, New Orleans, Louisiana.

742  Letter dated September 16, 1953, Shaw to the assistant to Cecil B. DeMille, Clay Shaw Louisiana Purchase Sesquicentennial Papers, Historic New Orleans Collection, New Orleans, Louisiana.

743  Letter dated November 28, 1953, Miss Amy Boudreau to Shaw, Clay Shaw Louisiana Purchase Sesquicentennial Papers, Historic New Orleans Collection, New Orleans, Louisiana.

744  Letter dated June 25, 1953, Lester Lautenschlaeger to Shaw, Clay Shaw Louisiana Purchase Sesquicentennial Papers, Historic New Orleans Collection, New Orleans, Louisiana.

745 Letter dated August 8, 1953, J.C. Jackson to Louisiana Purchase 150th Anniversary Association, Clay Shaw Louisiana Purchase Sesquicentennial Papers, Historic New Orleans Collection, New Orleans, Louisiana.

746 Letter dated August 3, 1953, J.C. Jackson to K.M. Partridge, Clay Shaw Louisiana Purchase Sesquicentennial Papers, Historic New Orleans Collection, New Orleans, Louisiana.

747 Letter dated August 6, 1953, Shaw to J.C, Jackson, Clay Shaw Louisiana Purchase Sesquicentennial Papers, Historic New Orleans Collection, New Orleans, Louisiana.

748 Undated telegram, Shaw to W.J. Gosen, Clay Shaw Louisiana Purchase Sesquicentennial Papers, Historic New Orleans Collection, New Orleans, Louisiana.

749 Letter dated October 13, 1953, Charles Genella to Shaw, Clay Shaw Louisiana Purchase Sesquicentennial Papers, Historic New Orleans Collection, New Orleans, Louisiana.

750 Correspondence Shaw to Mr. and Mrs. Antony Geyelin, International Trade Mart Records, Tulane University, New Orleans, Louisiana.

751 Letter dated October 19, 1953, Nicholas J. Chetta to Shaw, Clay Shaw Louisiana Purchase Sesquicentennial Papers, Historic New Orleans Collection, New Orleans, Louisiana.

752 Letter dated October 26, 1953, Shaw to Nicholas J. Chetta, Clay Shaw Louisiana Purchase Sesquicentennial Papers, Historic New Orleans Collection, New Orleans, Louisiana.

753 The President's Appointments Saturday, October 17, 1953, Material provided by Dwight D. Eisenhower Library.

754 Letter dated October 23, 1953, Rathbone DeBuys to Shaw, Clay Shaw Louisiana Purchase Sesquicentennial Papers, Historic New Orleans Collection, New Orleans, Louisiana.

755 Letter dated October 27, 1953, Shaw to Rathbone DeBuys, Clay Shaw Louisiana Purchase Sesquicentennial Papers, Historic New Orleans Collection, New Orleans, Louisiana.

756 Letter dated October 29, 1953, Shaw to Marcella Billups, Theone Marr, and Phyllis Wellford, Clay Shaw Louisiana Purchase Sesquicentennial Papers, Historic New Orleans Collection, New Orleans, Louisiana.

757 Undated letter, E.V. Richards and Clay Shaw to David Baldwin, Theone B. Maher, Phyllis B. Wellford, and Marcella Billups, Clay Shaw Louisiana Purchase Sesquicentennial Papers, Historic New Orleans Collection, New Orleans, Louisiana.

758 Letter dated November 6, 1953, E.V. Richards, Jr. to Shaw, Clay Shaw Louisiana Purchase Sesquicentennial Papers, Historic New Orleans Collection, New Orleans, Louisiana.

759 Telegram dated February 3, 1954, Senator Russell Long to E.V. Richards, Clay Shaw Louisiana Purchase Sesquicentennial Papers, Historic New Orleans Collection, New Orleans, Louisiana.

760 Letters dated December 1953, E.V. Richards, Jr. and Shaw to employees of the Louisiana Purchase 150th Anniversary Celebration, Clay Shaw Louisiana Purchase Sesquicentennial Papers, Historic New Orleans Collection, New Orleans, Louisiana.

761 Memo dated April 25, 1955, E.B. Keane to Shaw, Clay Shaw Louisiana Purchase Sesquicentennial Papers, Historic New Orleans Collection, New Orleans, Louisiana.

762 Letter dated April 26, 1955, H.K. Oliphant to Shaw, International Trade Mart Records, Tulane University, New Orleans, Louisiana.

763 Annual Report for 1953, International Trade Mart Records, Tulane University, New Orleans, Louisiana.

764 See New Orleans City Directory for 1954-55, Tulane University, New Orleans, Louisiana.

765 Letter dated February 16, 1954, Shaw to Otis Elevator Company, International Trade Mart Records, Tulane University, New Orleans, Louisiana.

766  Letter dated July 21, 1954, Shaw in response to inquiry, International Trade Mart Records, Tulane University, New Orleans, Louisiana.

767  Letter dated February 16, 1954, Shaw to Fidelity and Casualty Company, International Trade Mart Records, Tulane University, New Orleans, Louisiana.

768  Notes, meeting of Contributors and Debenture Holders, April 8, 1954, International Trade Mart, International Trade Mart Records, Tulane University, New Orleans, Louisiana.

769  Memo dated March 24, 1954, David Baldwin to Shaw, International Trade Mart Records, Tulane University, New Orleans, Louisiana.

770  Undated memo, Spring 1954, William McFadden Duffy to Charles Nutter, International Trade Mart Records, Tulane University, New Orleans, Louisiana.

771  Memo dated June 7, 1954, David Baldwin to William McFadden Duffy, International Trade Mart Records, Tulane University, New Orleans, Louisiana.

772  Letter dated May 29, 1961, David Baldwin to Jesse Core, International Trade Mart Records, Tulane University, New Orleans, Louisiana.

773  Minutes for Executive Committee meeting dated June 21, 1954, International Trade Mart, International Trade Mart Records, Tulane University, New Orleans, Louisiana.

774  Letter dated May 15, 1954, S.V. Massimini to William Zetzmann, International Trade Mart Records, Tulane University, New Orleans, Louisiana.

775  Letter dated December 5, 1954, Pendleton E. Lehde, Chairman of the Board of Foreign Policy Association of New Orleans, International Trade Mart Records, Tulane University, New Orleans, Louisiana.

776  Letter dated February 11, 1954, Rear Admiral K.D. Ringall, U.S. Navy, retired to Shaw, International Trade Mart Records, Tulane University, New Orleans, Louisiana.

777  Letter dated March 10, 1954, Shaw to William T. Walshe, International Trade Mart Records, Tulane University, New Orleans, Louisiana.

778  Letter dated September 3, 1954, Shaw to Perle Mesta, International Trade Mart Records, Tulane University, New Orleans, Louisiana.

779  Letter dated October 15, 1954, Shaw to Glen Douthit, International Trade Mart Records, Tulane University, New Orleans, Louisiana.

780  Memo dated November 2, 1954, written by Shaw, International Trade Mart Records, Tulane University, New Orleans, Louisiana.

781  Letter dated November 18, 1954, Robert Keedick to Shaw, International Trade Mart Records, Tulane University, New Orleans, Louisiana.

782  Letter dated December 9, 1954, Shaw to Robert Keedick, International Trade Mart Records, Tulane University, New Orleans, Louisiana.

783  Letter dated September 15, 1954, Tom Richards to Shaw, International Trade Mart Records, Tulane University, New Orleans, Louisiana.

784  Letter dated November 18, 1954, Tom Richards to Shaw, International Trade Mart Records, Tulane University, New Orleans, Louisiana.

785  Telegram dated December 13, 1954, Shaw to Charles Bushong, International Trade Mart Records, Tulane University, New Orleans, Louisiana.

786  Note dated December 6, 1954, Shaw to Rudolf Hecht, International Trade Mart Records, Tulane University, New Orleans, Louisiana.

787 Letter dated September 22, 1954, Representative of the Shah of Iran to Shaw, International Trade Mart Records, Tulane University, New Orleans, Louisiana.

788 Letter dated December 11, 1954, Shaw to the Shah of Iran, International Trade Mart Records, Tulane University, New Orleans, Louisiana.

789 Letter dated December 6, 1954, Shaw to Mrs. L. Kemper Williams, International Trade Mart Records

790 Letter dated January 11, 1955, Shaw to Rudolf Hecht, International Trade Mart Records, Tulane University, New Orleans, Louisiana.

791 Handwritten 1954 letter, Shaw to William Zetzmann, from Brussels, Belgium, International Trade Mart Records, Tulane University, New Orleans, Louisiana.

792 Letter dated December 11, 1954, Shaw to Foreign Policy Association of New Orleans members, International Trade Mart Records, Tulane University, New Orleans, Louisiana.

793 Letter, Shaw to unknown person in Rheims, France, undated, International Trade Mart Records, Tulane University, New Orleans, Louisiana.

794 Letter, Shaw to Marion Seidenbach, undated, probably spring 1954, International Trade Mart Records, Tulane University, New Orleans, Louisiana.

795 Handwritten 1954 letter, Shaw to William Zetzmann, from Brussels, Belgium, International Trade Mart Records, Tulane University, New Orleans, Louisiana.

796 Letter dated May 28, 1954, President of International House to William Zetzmann, International Trade Mart Records, Tulane University, New Orleans, Louisiana.

797 Letter dated July 1, 1954, Clem Bernard to Shaw, International Trade Mart Records, Tulane University, New Orleans, Louisiana.

798 Letter dated April 12, 1954, James Barr to Shaw, International Trade Mart Records, Tulane University, New Orleans, Louisiana.

799 Letter dated 1954, Shaw to James Barr, International Trade Mart Records, Tulane University, New Orleans, Louisiana.

800 Letter dated January 7, 1954, William Zetzmann to New Orleans Better Business Bureau, International Trade Mart Records, Tulane University, New Orleans, Louisiana.

801 Letter dated September 11, 1953, Carl Cramer to William Zetzmann, International Trade Mart Records, Tulane University, New Orleans, Louisiana.

802 Letter dated October 7, 1954, E. Allen Davis, Ochsner Medical Foundation to International Trade Mart, International Trade Mart Records, Tulane University, New Orleans, Louisiana.

803 Letter dated November 2, 1953, Albert W. Sherer to Charles I. Denechaud, International Trade Mart Records, Tulane University, New Orleans, Louisiana.

804 Letter dated December 8, 1954, Shaw in response to inquiry, International Trade Mart Records, Tulane University, New Orleans, Louisiana.

805 Letter dated June 1, 1954, Shaw to Rudolf Hecht, International Trade Mart Records, Tulane University, New Orleans, Louisiana.

806 Memo dated July 12, 1954, Shaw to Rudolf Hecht, International Trade Mart Records, Tulane University, New Orleans, Louisiana.

807 Memo dated July 16, 1954, Shaw to Rudolf Hecht, International Trade Mart Records, Tulane University, New Orleans, Louisiana.

808 Letter dated August 18, 1954, Rudolf Hecht to Shaw, International Trade Mart Records, Tulane University, New Orleans, Louisiana.

809 Letter dated June 9, 1954, Shaw to United States Immigration Service, International Trade Mart Records, Tulane University, New Orleans, Louisiana.

810 Letter dated November 23, 1954, Wallace M. Davis to Shaw, International Trade Mart Records, Tulane University, New Orleans, Louisiana.

811 Letter dated July 9, 1954, Shaw to C.C. Walther, International Trade Mart Records, Tulane University, New Orleans, Louisiana.

812 Letter dated June 3, 1954, Shaw to E.T. Colton, President, The Lighthouse for the Blind, International Trade Mart Records, Tulane University, New Orleans, Louisiana.

813 Letter dated November 2, 1954, Irwin Poche to Shaw, International Trade Mart Records, Tulane University, New Orleans, Louisiana.

814 Letter dated January 13, 1954, Shaw to John Kobler, International Trade Mart Records, Tulane University, New Orleans, Louisiana.

815 Letter dated November 4, 1954, National Research Bureau, Inc. to Shaw, International Trade Mart Records, Tulane University, New Orleans, Louisiana.

816 Letter dated November 10, 1954, Shaw to National Research Bureau, Inc., International Trade Mart Records, Tulane University, New Orleans, Louisiana.

817 Minutes of 1954 Annual Meeting, New Orleans Association of Building Owners and Managers, International Trade Mart Records, Tulane University, New Orleans, Louisiana.

818 Letter dated November 16, 1954, Shaw to George F. Johnson, International Trade Mart Records, Tulane University, New Orleans, Louisiana.

819 Letter dated June 16, 1954, Shaw to reception committee of International House, International Trade Mart Records, Tulane University, New Orleans, Louisiana.

820 Letter dated July 21, 1954, Shaw to Mississippi Shipping Company, International Trade Mart Records, Tulane University, New Orleans, Louisiana.

821 Letter dated June 17, 1954, Shaw to representative of the Phillipines, International Trade Mart Records, Tulane University, New Orleans, Louisiana.

822 Memo dated November 1, 1954, Shaw to David Baldwin, International Trade Mart Records, Tulane University, New Orleans, Louisiana.

823 Letter, Shaw to Seymour Weiss, International Trade Mart Records, Tulane University, New Orleans, Louisiana.

824 Letter dated January 14, 1954, George G. Herz to Shaw, International Trade Mart Records, Tulane University, New Orleans, Louisiana.

825 Letter dated September 20, 1954, Shaw to W. Marion, International Trade Mart Records, Tulane University, New Orleans, Louisiana.

826 Letter dated July 12, 1954, Shaw in response to inquiry, International Trade Mart Records, Tulane University, New Orleans, Louisiana.

827 Letter dated November 12, 1954, Lew Barnum to Shaw, International Trade Mart Records, Tulane University, New Orleans, Louisiana.

828 Letter dated March 4, 1954, Shaw to Chep Morrison, International Trade Mart Records, Tulane University, New Orleans, Louisiana.

829 Letter dated August 23, 1954, Shaw to Senator Russell Long, International Trade Mart Records, Tulane University, New Orleans, Louisiana.

830 Letter dated March 22, 1954, Congressman Overton Brooks to Shaw, International Trade Mart Records, Tulane University, New Orleans, Louisiana.

831 Letter dated August 7, 1954, Charles L. Luedtke to Shaw, International Trade Mart Records, Tulane University, New Orleans, Louisiana.

832 Letter dated February 3, 1954, Shaw to Sarah Gertrude Knott, International Trade Mart Records, Tulane University, New Orleans, Louisiana.

833 Letter dated June 23, 1954, Shaw in response to inquiry, International Trade Mart Records, Tulane University, New Orleans, Louisiana.

834 Letter dated June 3, 1954, Shaw to *Esquire* magazine, International Trade Mart Records, Tulane University, New Orleans, Louisiana.

835 Memo dated November 13, 1954, Anne O. Busby to Shaw, International Trade Mart Records, Tulane University, New Orleans, Louisiana.

836 Letter dated February 16, 1954, Eikichi Araki to Shaw, International Trade Mart Records, Tulane University, New Orleans, Louisiana.

837 Letter dated April 7, 1954, Raymond A. Nix to Shaw, International Trade Mart Records, Tulane University, New Orleans, Louisiana.

838 Letter dated January 6, 1954, David Baldwin to Thomas B. Lemann, International Trade Mart Records, Tulane University, New Orleans, Louisiana.

839 Telegram dated February 19, 1954, David Baldwin to Jesse Core, International Trade Mart Records, Tulane University, New Orleans, Louisiana.

840 Memo dated September 20, 1954, Shaw to David Baldwin, International Trade Mart Records, Tulane University, New Orleans, Louisiana.

841 Letter dated November 8, 1954, Charles Nutter to Chep Morrison, International Trade Mart Records, Tulane University, New Orleans, Louisiana.

842 Letter dated October 5, 1954, Shaw to Miss Tamar Woolf, International Trade Mart Records, Tulane University, New Orleans, Louisiana.

843 Letter dated March 25, 1954, Shaw to K.C. Barranger, International Trade Mart Records, Tulane University, New Orleans, Louisiana.

844 Letter dated November 23, 1954, Ed Paramore, New Orleans Division, Halliburton Oil Well Cementing Company to Shaw, International Trade Mart Records, Tulane University, New Orleans, Louisiana.

845 Letter dated November 9, 1954, Henri Gomez to Shaw, International Trade Mart Records, Tulane University, New Orleans, Louisiana.

846 Letter dated December 1, 1954, Shaw to John Wray Young, John Wray and Margaret Mary Young Collection, LSU-Shreveport, Shreveport, Louisiana.

847 Minutes of Board of Directors meeting of December 28, 1954, International Trade Mart, International Trade Mart Records, Tulane University, New Orleans, Louisiana.

848 Letter dated December 1, 1954, Shaw to E.S. Binnings, International Trade Mart Records, Tulane University, New Orleans, Louisiana.

849 Newspaper article dated December 15, 1954, newspaper unknown but probably in New Orleans, Donated Papers of Clay Shaw, National Archives, College Park, Maryland.

850 Income statement for year ended December 31, 1954, International Trade Mart, International Trade Mart Records, Tulane University, New Orleans, Louisiana.

851 Letter dated January 26, 1955, Val C. Mogensen, Executive Director, Bureau of Governmental Research, to Shaw, International Trade Mart Records, Tulane University, New Orleans, Louisiana.

852 Minutes to Board of Directors meeting, January 5, 1955, International Trade Mart, International Trade Mart Records, Tulane University, New Orleans, Louisiana.

853 Memo dated January 28, 1955, Shaw to Rudolf Hecht, International Trade Mart Records, Tulane University, New Orleans, Louisiana.

854 Memo dated February 7, 1955, Shaw to Rudolf Hecht, International Trade Mart Records, Tulane University, New Orleans, Louisiana.

855 Handwritten letter dated March 26, 1955, M. Ayub to Shaw, International Trade Mart Records, Tulane University, New Orleans, Louisiana.

856 Letter dated February 18, 1955, Shaw to Mario Bermúdez, International Trade Mart Records, Tulane University, New Orleans, Louisiana.

857 Letter dated February 18, 1955, Shaw to Rudolf Hecht, International Trade Mart Records, Tulane University, New Orleans, Louisiana.

858 Letter dated March 17, 1955, William Zetzmann to Leon Irwin, International Trade Mart Records, Tulane University, New Orleans, Louisiana.

859 Memo dated February 1, 1955, Shaw to Rudolf Hecht, International Trade Mart Records, Tulane University, New Orleans, Louisiana.

860 Memo dated February 17, 1955, David Baldwin to Shaw, International Trade Mart Records, Tulane University, New Orleans, Louisiana.

861 Letter dated March 8, 1955, Group in Alabama to David Baldwin, International Trade Mart Records, Tulane University, New Orleans, Louisiana.

862 Memo dated January 10, 1955, David Baldwin to Shaw, International Trade Mart Records, Tulane University, New Orleans, Louisiana.

863 1954 Annual Report, International Trade Mart, International Trade Mart Records, Tulane University, New Orleans, Louisiana.

864 Minutes to Executive Committee meeting of the Board of Directors, International Trade Mart, International Trade Mart Records, Tulane University, New Orleans, Louisiana.

865 Minutes to meeting of Contributors and Debenture Holders, March 31, 1955, International Trade Mart, International Trade Mart Records, Tulane University, New Orleans, Louisiana.

866 Telegram dated April 11, 1955, R.G. Jones, President, International House, and William Zetzmann to Isadore Newman, International Trade Mart Records, Tulane University, New Orleans, Louisiana.

867 Minutes to Board of Directors meeting, April 19, 1955, International Trade Mart, International Trade Mart Records, Tulane University, New Orleans, Louisiana.

868 Telegram dated April 25, 1955, Shaw to Mr. and Mrs. John Wray Young, John Wray and Margaret Mary Young Collection, LSU-Shreveport, Shreveport, Louisiana.

869 Minutes to Executive Committee meeting of Board of Directors, April 19, 1955, International Trade Mart, International Trade Mart Records, Tulane University, New Orleans, Louisiana.

870 Newspaper article dated May 12, 1955, newspaper unknown but probably in New Orleans, Donated Papers of Clay Shaw, National Archives, College Park, Maryland.

871 Letter dated May 27, 1955, Chep Morrison to Shaw, International Trade Mart Records, Tulane University, New Orleans, Louisiana.

872 Letter dated January 13, 1955, Richard Jones to Shaw, International Trade Mart Records, Tulane University, New Orleans, Louisiana.

873 Letter dated May 18, 1955, Richard Jones to Shaw, International Trade Mart Records, Tulane University, New Orleans, Louisiana.

874 Letter dated April 27, 1955, William McFadden Duffy to Shaw, International Trade Mart Records, Tulane University, New Orleans, Louisiana.

875 Rudolf Hecht statement dated January 31, 1955, International Trade Mart Records, Tulane University, New Orleans, Louisiana.

876 Letter dated March 8, 1955, Shaw to Wright McKenzie, International Trade Mart Records, Tulane University, New Orleans, Louisiana.

877 Letter dated April 29, 1955, Shaw to Henry Hurt Keith, International Trade Mart Records, Tulane University, New Orleans, Louisiana.

878 Letter dated April 13, 1955, Shaw to Dr. Werner Seldis, International Trade Mart Records, Tulane University, New Orleans, Louisiana.

879 Letter dated April 2, 1955, Warren Hampton to Shaw, International Trade Mart Records, Tulane University, New Orleans, Louisiana.

880 Letter dated January 20, 1955, Logan Perkins to International Trade Mart, International Trade Mart Records, Tulane University, New Orleans, Louisiana.

881 Letter dated March 5, 1955, Jesse Core to Shaw, International Trade Mart Records, Tulane University, New Orleans, Louisiana.

882 Letter dated March 16, 1955, Shaw to Jesse Core, International Trade Mart Records, Tulane University, New Orleans, Louisiana.

883 Letter in Spanish dated March 28, 1955, Jesse Core to Shaw, International Trade Mart Records, Tulane University, New Orleans, Louisiana.

884 Letter dated May 18, 1955, Shaw to Jesse Core, International Trade Mart Records, Tulane University, New Orleans, Louisiana.

885 Special Report, mid-year 1955, International Trade Mart, International Trade Mart Records, Tulane University, New Orleans, Louisiana.

886 Letter dated March 16, 1955, Richard B. Swenson to Shaw, International Trade Mart Records, Tulane University, New Orleans, Louisiana.

887 Letter dated May 3, 1955, Clem I. Bernard to Shaw, International Trade Mart Records, Tulane University, New Orleans, Louisiana.

888 Letter dated March 7, 1955, Shaw to Charles Nutter, International Trade Mart Records, Tulane University, New Orleans, Louisiana.

889 Letter dated December 29, 1955, Shaw to Grace Sims Peat, International Trade Mart Records, Tulane University, New Orleans, Louisiana.

890 Letter dated March 7, 1955, Shaw to Robert Keedick, International Trade Mart Records, Tulane University, New Orleans, Louisiana.

891 Letter dated February 11, 1955, Shaw to John Minor Wisdom, International Trade Mart Records, Tulane University, New Orleans, Louisiana.

892 Letter dated February 10, 1955, Shaw to Harold Stassen, International Trade Mart Records, Tulane University, New Orleans, Louisiana.

893 Letter dated December 5, 1955, Shaw to Clayton Fritchey, International Trade Mart Records, Tulane University, New Orleans, Louisiana.

894 Letter from Walter W. Schroeder of First Republic Bank, Dallas, Texas to Shaw, International Trade Mart Records, Tulane University, New Orleans, Louisiana.

895 Letter dated April 5, 1955, Shaw to Mena, Arkansas Chamber of Commerce, International Trade Mart Records, Tulane University, New Orleans, Louisiana.

896 Letter dated May 26, 1955, Shaw to Charles Arning, International Trade Mart Records, Tulane University, New Orleans, Louisiana.

897 Letter dated September 12, 1955, Shaw to Dr. G.A. Ackal, International Trade Mart Records, Tulane University, New Orleans, Louisiana.

898 Letter dated January 5, 1955, Shaw in response to inquiry, International Trade Mart Records, Tulane University, New Orleans, Louisiana.

899 Letter dated June 1, 1955, Shaw in response to inquiry, International Trade Mart Records, Tulane University, New Orleans, Louisiana.

900 Letter dated April 13, 1955, Shaw to Federico Sanchez Fogarty, International Trade Mart Records, Tulane University, New Orleans, Louisiana.

901 Letter dated June 30, 1955, Shaw to Fernando Gonzalez de la Roza, International Trade Mart Records, Tulane University, New Orleans, Louisiana.

902 Folder-Mexico trip, 7/1/55-7/10/55, International Trade Mart Records, Tulane University, New Orleans, Louisiana.

903 Letter dated July 23, 1955, Natalie Scott to Herman Deutsch, Herman B. Deutsch Papers, Tulane University, New Orleans, Louisiana.

904 Letter dated July 13, 1955, Shaw to William Spratling, International Trade Mart Records, Tulane University, New Orleans, Louisiana.

905 Letter dated July 13, 1955, Shaw to Natalie Scott, International Trade Mart Records, Tulane University, New Orleans, Louisiana.

906 Letter dated November 18, 1955, J.B. Dauenhauer to Jorge Alayeto, International Trade Mart Records, Tulane University, New Orleans, Louisiana.

907 Letter dated October 12, 1955, Shaw to St. Louis Convention and Publicity Bureau, International Trade Mart Records, Tulane University, New Orleans, Louisiana.

908 Letter dated August 5, 1955, Shaw to Allen G. Brookes, International Trade Mart Records, Tulane University, New Orleans, Louisiana.

909 Letter dated May 12, 1955, Shaw to Rudolf Hecht, International Trade Mart Records, Tulane University, New Orleans, Louisiana.

910 Letter dated August 25, 1955, Andres Horcasitas to Shaw, International Trade Mart Records, Tulane University, New Orleans, Louisiana.

911 Letter dated November 10, 1955, Charles W. Lerch to J.B. Dauenhauer, International Trade Mart Records, Tulane University, New Orleans, Louisiana.

912 Letter dated January 4, 1955, Shaw to New Orleans Hotel Association, International Trade Mart Records, Tulane University, New Orleans, Louisiana.

913 Letter dated February 18, 1955, John F. Crawford to Shaw, International Trade Mart Records, Tulane University, New Orleans, Louisiana.

914 Memo dated February 21, 1955, J.B. Dauenhauer to tenants, International Trade Mart Records, Tulane University, New Orleans, Louisiana.

915 Letter dated January 4, 1955, Leland W. Cutler to Shaw, International Trade Mart Records, Tulane University, New Orleans, Louisiana.

916 Letter dated May 15, 1955, William Zetzmann to Nisal Sato, International Trade Mart Records, Tulane University, New Orleans, Louisiana.

917 Letter dated July 20, 1955, David Baldwin to Prince Youssuf Mirza, International Trade Mart Records, Tulane University, New Orleans, Louisiana.

918 Letter dated August 17, 1955, Shaw in response to inquiry, International Trade Mart Records, Tulane University, New Orleans, Louisiana.

919 See memo related to Shaw attendance at 1955 Czechoslovak Engineering Exhibition, CIA Miscellaneous Files, JFK Assassination Collection, National Archives, College Park, Maryland.

920 Letter dated August 24, 1955, William Gaudet to Shaw, International Trade Mart Records, Tulane University, New Orleans, Louisiana.

921 Press release dated October 2, 1955, by William Gaudet, International Trade Mart Records, Tulane University, New Orleans, Louisiana.

922 Letter dated December 21, 1955, William Gaudet to Shaw, International Trade Mart Records, Tulane University, New Orleans, Louisiana.

923 Letter dated August 4, 1955, John Lynn to Shaw, International Trade Mart Records.

924 Letter dated August 19, 1955, Shaw to John Lynn, International Trade Mart Records.

925 Letter dated October 5, 1955, Jesse Core to Dallas press members, International Trade Mart Records, Tulane University, New Orleans, Louisiana.

926 Letter dated October 7, 1955, Jesse Core to Dechard Turner, International Trade Mart Records, Tulane University, New Orleans, Louisiana.

927 Letter dated October 14, 1955, Shaw to Rudolf Hecht, International Trade Mart Records, Tulane University, New Orleans, Louisiana.

928 Letter dated October 26, 1955, Chep Morrison to Shaw, International Trade Mart Records, Tulane University, New Orleans, Louisiana.

929 Letter dated November 21, 1955, May L. Fleury to Shaw, International Trade Mart Records, Tulane University, New Orleans, Louisiana.

930 Letter dated November 14, 1955, Gordon E. Brown to Shaw, International Trade Mart Records, Tulane University, New Orleans, Louisiana.

931 Letter dated November 7, 1955, Shaw to Mr. and Mrs. Charles Leonard, International Trade Mart Records, Tulane University, New Orleans, Louisiana.

932 Letter dated January 11, 1956, Hale Boggs to Shaw, International Trade Mart Records, Tulane University, New Orleans, Louisiana.

933 Letter dated November 23, 1955, Bess C. Noble to Shaw, International Trade Mart Records, Tulane University, New Orleans, Louisiana.

934 Letter dated November 15, 1955, Muriel Bultman Francis to A. Fred Bultman, Bultman Family Papers, Historic New Orleans Collection, New Orleans, Louisiana.

935 Letter dated December 26, 1955, Monk Simons to Shaw, International Trade Mart Records.

936 Letter dated June 1, 1955, Shaw to Monk Simons, International Trade Mart Records, Tulane University, New Orleans, Louisiana.

937 Minutes to Board of Directors meeting, December 19, 1955, International Trade Mart, International Trade Mart Records, Tulane University, New Orleans, Louisiana.

938 Report to Board of Directors, December 19, 1955, by William Zetzmann, International Trade Mart, International Trade Mart Records, Tulane University, New Orleans, Louisiana.

939 Minutes of Policy Committee meeting, January 5, 1956, International House, International Trade Mart Records, Tulane University, New Orleans, Louisiana.

940 Letter dated January 10, 1956, Rudolf Hecht to Richard Jones, International Trade Mart Records, Tulane University, New Orleans, Louisiana.

941 Letter dated January 17, 1956, Jesse Core to Dr. Wirt Williams, International Trade Mart Records, Tulane University, New Orleans, Louisiana.

942 Note dated February 16, 1956, Jesse Core to Shaw, International Trade Mart Records, Tulane University, New Orleans, Louisiana.

943 See New Orleans City Directory for 1956, Tulane University, New Orleans, Louisiana.

944 Letter dated January 20, 1956, William Zetzmann to George Dinwiddie, International Trade Mart Records, Tulane University, New Orleans, Louisiana.

945 Letter dated January 19, 1956, Carl Cramer to William Zetzmann, International Trade Mart Records, Tulane University, New Orleans, Louisiana.

946 Memo dated April 11, 1955, Shaw to Rudolf Hecht, International Trade Mart Records, Tulane University, New Orleans, Louisiana.

947 Memo dated January 6, 1956, Rudolf Hecht to Shaw, International Trade Mart Records, Tulane University, New Orleans, Louisiana.

948 Letter dated February 24, 1956, Shaw to Charles Logan, International Trade Mart Records, Tulane University, New Orleans, Louisiana.

949 Letter dated December 28, 1954, U.S. Department of Labor to Shaw, International Trade Mart Records, Tulane University, New Orleans, Louisiana.

950 Letter dated February 9, 1956, Bess Noble to Shaw, International Trade Mart Records, Tulane University, New Orleans, Louisiana.

951 Letter dated December 18, 1956, Shaw to Paul Klemens, International Trade Mart Records, Tulane University, New Orleans, Louisiana.

952 Letter dated March 12, 1956, Jesse Core to Decherd Turner, International Trade Mart Records, Tulane University, New Orleans, Louisiana.

953 Memo dated March 23, 1956, Jesse Core to Howard, International Trade Mart Records, Tulane University, New Orleans, Louisiana.

954 Letter dated April 6, 1956, Jesse Core to David Baldwin, International Trade Mart Records, Tulane University, New Orleans, Louisiana.

955 Letter dated June 25, 1956, Jesse Core to Shaw, International Trade Mart Records, Tulane University, New Orleans, Louisiana.

956 Letter dated July 2, 1956, Shaw to Jesse Core, International Trade Mart Records, Tulane University, New Orleans, Louisiana.

957 Letter dated April 17, 1956, Shaw to Harry X. Kelly, International Trade Mart Records, Tulane University, New Orleans, Louisiana.

958 Minutes to meeting of Executive Committee of Board of Directors, May 29, 1956, International Trade Mart, International Trade Mart Records, Tulane University, New Orleans, Louisiana.

959 Letter dated June 15, 1956, E.D. Wingfield to Shaw, International Trade Mart Records, Tulane University, New Orleans, Louisiana.

960 Letter of Recommendation dated January 27, 1956, by Shaw regarding Leopoldo Herrera, International Trade Mart Records, Tulane University, New Orleans, Louisiana.

961 Letter dated July 18, 1956, Jesse Core in response to inquiry, International Trade Mart Records, Tulane University, New Orleans, Louisiana.

[962] Letter dated February 20, 1956, Shaw in response to inquiry, International Trade Mart Records, Tulane University, New Orleans, Louisiana.

[963] Letter dated December 4, 1956, Shaw in response to inquiry, International Trade Mart Records, Tulane University, New Orleans, Louisiana.

[964] Letter dated June 27, 1956, Oliver P. Schulingkamp to William Zetzmann, International Trade Mart Records, Tulane University, New Orleans, Louisiana.

[965] Letter dated September 10, 1956, Shaw to Robert J. Miranda, International Trade Mart Records, Tulane University, New Orleans, Louisiana.

[966] Letter dated November 16, 1956, Chep Morrison to Shaw, International Trade Mart Records, Tulane University, New Orleans, Louisiana.

[967] Letter dated May 29, 1956, Ambassador to the United States from Denmark to Shaw, International Trade Mart Records, Tulane University, New Orleans, Louisiana.

[968] Letter dated June 25, 1956, Shaw to WTPS Radio, International Trade Mart Records, Tulane University, New Orleans, Louisiana.

[969] Minutes to meeting of Board of Directors, July 6, 1956, International Trade Mart, International Trade Mart Records, Tulane University, New Orleans, Louisiana.

[970] Minutes of Executive Committee meeting of Board of Directors, September 5, 1956, International Trade Mart, International Trade Mart Records, Tulane University, New Orleans, Louisiana.

[971] Minutes to joint meeting of Executive Committees of International House and International Trade Mart, September 11, 1956, International Trade Mart Records, Tulane University, New Orleans, Louisiana.

[972] Letter dated December 7, 1956, Leonard Huber to Shaw, International Trade Mart Records, Tulane University, New Orleans, Louisiana.

[973] Joint meeting of Executive Committees of International House and International Trade Mart, September 18, 1956, International Trade Mart Records, Tulane University, New Orleans, Louisiana.

[974] Letter dated July 20, 1956, Charles Nutter to Richard G. Jones, International Trade Mart Records, Tulane University, New Orleans, Louisiana.

[975] Letter from Enrique A. Mantello to J.B. Dauenhauer, International Trade Mart Records, Tulane University, New Orleans, Louisiana.

[976] Letter dated July 12, 1956, Shaw to Enrique A. Mantello, International Trade Mart Records, Tulane University, New Orleans, Louisiana.

[977] Letter dated June 6, 1956, Shaw letter of recommendation regarding Manuel O. Delgado, International Trade Mart Records, Tulane University, New Orleans, Louisiana.

[978] Letter dated February 11, 1955, Shaw letter of recommendation regarding Marcel Gomez, International Trade Mart Records, Tulane University, New Orleans, Louisiana.

[979] Letter dated September 13, 1956, Shaw to E. Stewart Skidmore, International Trade Mart Records, Tulane University, New Orleans, Louisiana.

[980] Letter dated February 6, 1956, Shaw to Ted Sexton, International Trade Mart Records, Tulane University, New Orleans, Louisiana.

[981] Letter dated April 26, 1956, Shaw to Franklin Lane, International Trade Mart Records, Tulane University, New Orleans, Louisiana.

[982] Letter dated January 3, 1956, Lee S. Thomas to Shaw, International Trade Mart Records, Tulane University, New Orleans, Louisiana.

983 Letter dated May 30, 1956, Shaw in response to inquiry, International Trade Mart Records, Tulane University, New Orleans, Louisiana.

984 Letter dated October 11, 1956, Shaw in response to inquiry, International Trade Mart Records, Tulane University, New Orleans, Louisiana.

985 Letter dated June 27, 1956, Shaw in response to inquiry, International Trade Mart Records, Tulane University, New Orleans, Louisiana.

986 Letter dated December 17, 1956, Shaw in response to inquiry, International Trade Mart Records, Tulane University, New Orleans, Louisiana.

987 Altrusa Club Bulletin dated October 21, 1956, International Trade Mart Records, Tulane University, New Orleans, Louisiana.

988 Letter dated June 22, 1956, Goldie Moore to Mrs. Joey McCulloch, International Trade Mart Records, Tulane University, New Orleans, Louisiana.

989 Letter dated March 8, 1956, Robert S. Smith to Thomas Griffin, International Trade Mart Records, Tulane University, New Orleans, Louisiana.

990 Letter dated April 26, 1956, Robert S. Smith to Jill Jackson, International Trade Mart Records, Tulane University, New Orleans, Louisiana.

991 Letter dated April 30, 1956, Shaw to Robert S. Smith, International Trade Mart Records, Tulane University, New Orleans, Louisiana.

992 Letter dated May 13, 1956, Shaw to Robert S. Smith, International Trade Mart Records, Tulane University, New Orleans, Louisiana.

993 Letter dated May 17, 1956, Shaw to Robert S. Smith, International Trade Mart Records, Tulane University, New Orleans, Louisiana.

994 Letter dated May 30, 1956, Shaw to Robert S. Smith, International Trade Mart Records, Tulane University, New Orleans, Louisiana.

995 Letter dated June 19, 1956, Robert S. Smith to Shaw, International Trade Mart Records, Tulane University, New Orleans, Louisiana.

996 Letter dated September 24, 1956, Robert S. Smith to Shaw, International Trade Mart Records, Tulane University, New Orleans, Louisiana.

997 Letter dated October 10, 1956, Robert Stuart Smith to Shaw, International Trade Mart Records, Tulane University, New Orleans, Louisiana.

998 Letter dated December 16, 1955, Richard B. Swenson to Rudolf Hecht, International Trade Mart Records, Tulane University, New Orleans, Louisiana.

999 Letter dated March 2, 1956, Richard B. Swenson to Richard Jones, International Trade Mart Records, Tulane University, New Orleans, Louisiana.

1000 Letter dated April 23, 1956, Richard B. Swenson to William Zetzmann, International Trade Mart Records, Tulane University, New Orleans, Louisiana.

1001 Letter dated May 30, 1956, Shaw to Al Alice, International Trade Mart Records, Tulane University, New Orleans, Louisiana.

1002 Letter dated June 18, 1956, Shaw to Rudolph Frigerio, International Trade Mart Records, Tulane University, New Orleans, Louisiana.

1003 Letter dated August 17, 1956, Lloyd Cobb to Shaw, International Trade Mart Records, Tulane University, New Orleans, Louisiana.

1004 Letter dated January 9, 1956, Albert D. Meltz to Shaw, International Trade Mart Records, Tulane University, New Orleans, Louisiana.

[1005] Letter dated January 20, 1956, Shaw to Albert D. Meltz, International Trade Mart Records, Tulane University, New Orleans, Louisiana.

[1006] Letter dated October 12, 1956, Scott Wilson to William Zetzmann, International Trade Mart Records, Tulane University, New Orleans, Louisiana.

[1007] "Lagniappe" column dated June 29, 1956, written by Shaw for *The New Orleans Item*, International Trade Mart Records, Tulane University, New Orleans, Louisiana.

[1008] Letter dated October 31, 1956, Bill Monroe to Shaw, International Trade Mart Records, Tulane University, New Orleans, Louisiana.

[1009] Articles of Incorporation, Mississippi Valley World Trade Council, International Trade Mart Records, Tulane University, New Orleans, Louisiana.

[1010] Letter dated April 16, 1956, Charles Nutter to Michael Buzon, Jr., International Trade Mart Records, Tulane University, New Orleans, Louisiana.

[1011] Memo dated September 25, 1970, Basil Rusovich to Mart employees, International Trade Mart Records, Tulane University, New Orleans, Louisiana.

[1012] Letter dated December 20, 1956, Paul M. White, Jr. to George Chaplin, International Trade Mart Records, Tulane University, New Orleans, Louisiana.

[1013] Letter dated September 25, 1956, Robert R. Barkerding to Shaw, International Trade Mart Records, Tulane University, New Orleans, Louisiana.

[1014] Letter dated October 1, 1956, Hale Boggs to Shaw, International Trade Mart Records, Tulane University, New Orleans, Louisiana.

[1015] Letter dated October 25, 1956, Bess C. Noble to Shaw, International Trade Mart Records, Tulane University, New Orleans, Louisiana.

[1016] Letter dated November 2, 1956, E.O. Jewell to Shaw, International Trade Mart Records, Tulane University, New Orleans, Louisiana.

[1017] Will of Judson O'Donnell dated October 12, 1956, Donated Papers of Clay Shaw, National Archives, College Park, Maryland.

[1018] Joint meeting of Board of Directors of International House and International Trade Mart, October 31, 1956, International Trade Mart Records, Tulane University, New Orleans, Louisiana.

[1019] Letter dated May 25, 1956, William P. Burke to Somerville, CIA Miscellaneous Files, JFK Assassination Collection, National Archives, College Park, Maryland.

[1020] Letter dated December 12, 1956, Shaw to Alexander Bruce Ray, Customer Relations Manager, Southern Bell, International Trade Mart Records, Tulane University, New Orleans, Louisiana.

[1021] Letter dated July 6, 1956, Shaw to Vic Malandro, International Trade Mart Records, Tulane University, New Orleans, Louisiana.

[1022] Undated memo, around 1957, Jesse Core to Shaw, International Trade Mart Records, Tulane University, New Orleans, Louisiana.

[1023] Letter dated November 1, 1956, Shaw to William Gaudet, International Trade Mart Records, Tulane University, New Orleans, Louisiana.

[1024] Letter dated March 15, 1956, Jesse Core to George Seale, International Trade Mart Records, Tulane University, New Orleans, Louisiana.

[1025] Letter dated December 18, 1956, Jesse Core to Shaw, International Trade Mart Records, Tulane University, New Orleans, Louisiana.

[1026] Letter dated November 20, 1956, Richard de Ayala to Shaw, International Trade Mart Records, Tulane University, New Orleans, Louisiana.

[1027] Letter dated January 4, 1957, Shaw to Richard de Ayala, International Trade Mart Records, Tulane University, New Orleans, Louisiana.

[1028] Letter dated May 22, 1956, Tom Maupin to Shaw, International Trade Mart Records, Tulane University, New Orleans, Louisiana.

[1029] Letter dated December 3, 1956, H. Neil Mecasky, Jr. to Shaw, International Trade Mart Records, Tulane University, New Orleans, Louisiana.

[1030] Letter, January 2000, Gore Vidal to Author.

[1031] Letter, November 1995, Gore Vidal to Author.

[1032] Interview with Don Schueler by Author, March 20, 2007.

[1033] Letter dated January 16, 1957, Shaw to John G. Burton, International Trade Mart Records, Tulane University, New Orleans, Louisiana.

[1034] Minutes to meeting of Executive Committee of International House, January 8, 1957, International Trade Mart Records, Tulane University, New Orleans, Louisiana.

[1035] Minutes of Executive Committee meeting, January 22, 1957, International House, International Trade Mart Records, Tulane University, New Orleans, Louisiana.

[1036] Minutes to meeting of Executive Committee of International House, January 29, 1957, International Trade Mart Records, Tulane University, New Orleans, Louisiana.

[1037] Minutes to joint meeting of Board of Directors of International House and International Trade Mart, February 27, 1957, International Trade Mart Records, Tulane University, New Orleans, Louisiana.

[1038] Minutes to meeting of Contributors and Debenture Holders, March 14, 1957, International Trade Mart Records, Tulane University, New Orleans, Louisiana.

[1039] Letter dated August 6, 1957, Dr. Frederick Wolfe to William Zetzmann, International Trade Mart Records, Tulane University, New Orleans, Louisiana.

[1040] Annual Report by William Zetzmann, March 14, 1957, International Trade Mart Records, Tulane University, New Orleans, Louisiana.

[1041] Letter dated February 7, 1957, Jimmie Fitzpatrick to Shaw, International Trade Mart Records, Tulane University, New Orleans, Louisiana.

[1042] Minutes to meeting of Board of Directors, March 22, 1957, International Trade Mart, International Trade Mart Records, Tulane University, New Orleans, Louisiana.

[1043] Memo dated March 12, 1957, Shaw to William Zetzmann, International Trade Mart Records, Tulane University, New Orleans, Louisiana.

[1044] Report to Board of Directors by William Zetzmann, July 23, 1957, International Trade Mart Records, Tulane University, New Orleans, Louisiana.

[1045] Minutes to meeting of Executive Committee, July 16, 1957, International Trade Mart, International Trade Mart Records, Tulane University, New Orleans, Louisiana.

[1046] Minutes to meeting of Board of Directors, July 23, 1957, International Trade Mart Records, Tulane University, New Orleans, Louisiana.

[1047] Letter dated May 24, 1957, George Healy, Vice-President of *Times-Picayune*, to William Zetzmann, International Trade Mart Records, Tulane University, New Orleans, Louisiana.

[1048] Letter dated June 20, 1957, Shaw to George Healy, International Trade Mart Records, Tulane University, New Orleans, Louisiana.

[1049] Letter dated April 3, 1957, Charles Nutter to E.D. Wingfield, International Trade Mart Records, Tulane University, New Orleans, Louisiana.

[1050] *Times-Picayune* clipping dated April 15, 1957, with handwritten note by Shaw, International Trade Mart Records, Tulane University, New Orleans, Louisiana.

[1051] Letter dated April 18, 1957, Joseph M. Rault to William Zetzmann, International Trade Mart Records, Tulane University, New Orleans, Louisiana.

[1052] Minutes to Executive Committee meeting, June 14, 1957, International Trade Mart, International Trade Mart Records, Tulane University, New Orleans, Louisiana.

[1053] Minutes to Executive Committee meeting, June 18, 1957, International Trade Mart, International Trade Mart Records, Tulane University, New Orleans, Louisiana.

[1054] Letter dated October 2, 1957, Shaw to Pierre Clemenceau, International Trade Mart Records, Tulane University, New Orleans, Louisiana.

[1055] Letter dated June 24, 1957, Peter Simpson Stovall to Shaw, International Trade Mart Records, Tulane University, New Orleans, Louisiana.

[1056] Letter dated July 3, 1957, Shaw to Dr. Ralph C. Howe, International Trade Mart Records, Tulane University, New Orleans, Louisiana.

[1057] Letter dated April 9, 1957, Shaw in response to inquiry, International Trade Mart Records, Tulane University, New Orleans, Louisiana.

[1058] Letter dated May 28, 1957, Shaw in response to inquiry, International Trade Mart Records, Tulane University, New Orleans, Louisiana.

[1059] Letter dated March 13, 1957, Shaw in response to inquiry, International Trade Mart Records, Tulane University, New Orleans, Louisiana.

[1060] Letter dated August 28, 1957, Shaw to Richard R. Daniels, International Trade Mart Records, Tulane University, New Orleans, Louisiana.

[1061] See correspondence and check dated July 5, 1957, Shaw to Texan Publishing Company, Donated Papers of Clay Shaw, National Archives, College Park, Maryland.

[1062] Letter dated June 6, 1957, Shaw to Robert D. Hess, International Trade Mart Records, Tulane University, New Orleans, Louisiana.

[1063] Letter dated September 3, 1957, Mrs. Hamilton Polk Jones to Shaw, International Trade Mart Records, Tulane University, New Orleans, Louisiana.

[1064] Letter dated February 5, 1957, Robert Keedick to Shaw, International Trade Mart Records, Tulane University, New Orleans, Louisiana.

[1065] Letter dated February 11, 1957, Shaw to Robert Keedick, International Trade Mart Records, Tulane University, New Orleans, Louisiana.

[1066] Letter dated March 19, 1957, John F. Crawford to Shaw, International Trade Mart Records, Tulane University, New Orleans, Louisiana.

[1067] Letter dated April 4, 1957, Shaw to John F. Crawford, International Trade Mart Records, Tulane University, New Orleans, Louisiana.

[1068] Telegram dated June 11, 1957, Shaw to Miller Cragon, International Trade Mart Records, Tulane University, New Orleans, Louisiana.

[1069] Letter dated July 7, 1957, Norwood Jatho, Sr. to Shaw, International Trade Mart Records, Tulane University, New Orleans, Louisiana.

[1070] Letter dated September 13, 1957, Lloyd Cobb to Shaw, International Trade Mart Records, Tulane University, New Orleans, Louisiana.

[1071] Letter dated January 16, 1957, Shaw to Century Club of Coral Gables, Florida, International Trade Mart Records, Tulane University, New Orleans, Louisiana.

1072 Letter dated September 12, 1957, Shaw to Reginald C. Reindorp, International Trade Mart Records, Tulane University, New Orleans, Louisiana.

1073 Letter dated November 9, 1957, H.J. Williams to William Zetzmann, International Trade Mart Records, Tulane University, New Orleans, Louisiana.

1074 Letter dated November 18, 1957, Alvin H. Jennings to Shaw, International Trade Mart Records, Tulane University, New Orleans, Louisiana.

1075 Letter dated December 17, 1957, Merle S. Wick to Shaw, International Trade Mart Records, Tulane University, New Orleans, Louisiana.

1076 Letter dated November 18, 1957, J. Frank Jarman to Shaw, International Trade Mart Records, Tulane University, New Orleans, Louisiana.

1077 Letter dated November 29, 1957, Shaw to J. Frank Jarman, International Trade Mart Records, Tulane University, New Orleans, Louisiana.

1078 Letter dated April 4, 1957, Shaw to E. Newton Wray, International Trade Mart Records, Tulane University, New Orleans, Louisiana.

1079 Letter dated July 27, 1957, Shaw to Paul Martin, enclosing Letter of Introduction, International Trade Mart Records, Tulane University, New Orleans, Louisiana.

1080 Letter dated February 4, 1957, Monte Lemann to Shaw, International Trade Mart Records, Tulane University, New Orleans, Louisiana.

1081 Letter dated February 15, 1957, Shaw to Monte Lemann, International Trade Mart Records, Tulane University, New Orleans, Louisiana.

1082 Letter dated September 16, 1957, William N. Owen, Jr. to Shaw, International Trade Mart Records, Tulane University, New Orleans, Louisiana.

1083 Postcard dated October 23, 1957, George Boggs to J.B. Dauenhauer, International Trade Mart Records, Tulane University, New Orleans, Louisiana.

1084 Letter dated July 23, 1957, Shaw to H.R.P. Katzenberg, International Trade Mart Records, Tulane University, New Orleans, Louisiana.

1085 Letter dated October 12, 1957, Acme Carriers, Inc. to George Haverstick, with handwritten note from Haverstick to Shaw, International Trade Mart Records, Tulane University, New Orleans, Louisiana.

1086 Letter dated December 5, 1957, Peggy Smith to Shaw, International Trade Mart Records, Tulane University, New Orleans, Louisiana.

1087 Memo dated August 5, 1957, J.B. Dauenhauer to Hollis Bridges, International Trade Mart Records, Tulane University, New Orleans, Louisiana.

1088 Minutes to Executive Committee meeting, December 13, 1957, International Trade Mart Records, Tulane University, New Orleans, Louisiana.

1089 Invitation to reception preview of "Contemporary Japan," International Trade Mart Records, Tulane University, New Orleans, Louisiana.

1090 Letter dated June 17, 1957, Robert Brown to Shaw, International Trade Mart Records, Tulane University, New Orleans, Louisiana.

1091 Letter dated November 13, 1956, William G. Helis, Jr. to Shaw, International Trade Mart Records, Tulane University, New Orleans, Louisiana.

1092 Letter dated July 18, 19567, Chep Morrison to Shaw, International Trade Mart Records, Tulane University, New Orleans, Louisiana.

[1093] Letter dated April 16, 1957, Shaw in response to inquiry from LaGrange Texas, International Trade Mart Records, Tulane University, New Orleans, Louisiana.

[1094] Letter dated January 2, 1957, Ross J. Prichard to Shaw, International Trade Mart Records, Tulane University, New Orleans, Louisiana.

[1095] *The New Orleans Item* for July 22, 1957, International Trade Mart Records, Tulane University, New Orleans, Louisiana.

[1096] Minutes to meeting of Executive Committee of International House, November 26, 1957, International Trade Mart Records, Tulane University, New Orleans, Louisiana.

[1097] Minutes to Board of Directors meeting, July 23, 1957, International Trade Mart Records, Tulane University, New Orleans, Louisiana.

[1098] Letter dated July 17, 1957, William Zetzmann to Joseph Rault, International Trade Mart Records, Tulane University, New Orleans, Louisiana.

[1099] Letter dated September 6, 1957, William Zetzmann to Board of Directors, International Trade Mart Records, Tulane University, New Orleans, Louisiana.

[1100] Letter dated August 6, 1957, Rathbone DeBuys to Shaw, International Trade Mart Records, Tulane University, New Orleans, Louisiana.

[1101] Letter dated July 17, 1957, Roland von Kurnatowski, International Trade Mart Records, Tulane University, New Orleans, Louisiana.

[1102] Memo dated September 23, 1957, International Trade Mart Records, Tulane University, New Orleans, Louisiana.

[1103] Press Release about Shaw, undated, probably 1956-57, International Trade Mart Records, Tulane University, New Orleans, Louisiana.

[1104] Letter dated November 29, 1957, Shaw to Aurelie Alost, International Trade Mart Records, Tulane University, New Orleans, Louisiana.

[1105] Letter dated September 13, 1957, Chep Morrison to Shaw, International Trade Mart Records, Tulane University, New Orleans, Louisiana.

[1106] Letter dated October 16, 1957, Samuel L. Gandy to Shaw, International Trade Mart Records, Tulane University, New Orleans, Louisiana.

[1107] Letter dated October 29, 1957, Shaw to E. Davis McCutcheon, International Trade Mart Records, Tulane University, New Orleans, Louisiana.

[1108] Letter dated October 29, 1957, Jesse Core to Dinty Warmington-Whiting, International Trade Mart Records, Tulane University, New Orleans, Louisiana.

[1109] Letter dated November 18, 1957, Jesse Core to Richard Cross, International Trade Mart Records, Tulane University, New Orleans, Louisiana.

[1110] Memo dated November 8, 1957, Jesse Core to Shaw, International Trade Mart Records, Tulane University, New Orleans, Louisiana.

[1111] Letter dated December 16, 1957, Jill Jackson to Jesse Core, International Trade Mart Records, Tulane University, New Orleans, Louisiana.

[1112] Minutes to meeting of Executive Committee of International House, December 19, 1957, International Trade Mart Records, Tulane University, New Orleans, Louisiana.

[1113] Letter dated December 13, 1957, William Zetzmann to employees, International Trade Mart Records, Tulane University, New Orleans, Louisiana.

[1114] Letter dated May 9, 1957, J.B. Dauenhauer to Hospital Services Association, International Trade Mart Records, Tulane University, New Orleans, Louisiana.

1115 Letter dated November 8, 1957, Senator Albert Gore to C.C. Walther, International Trade Mart Records, Tulane University, New Orleans, Louisiana.

1116 Minutes to meeting of Executive Committee of Board of Directors, February 14, 1958, International Trade Mart, International Trade Mart Records, Tulane University, New Orleans, Louisiana.

1117 Minutes to meeting of Executive Committee of Board of Directors, March 17, 1958, International Trade Mart, International Trade Mart Records, Tulane University, New Orleans, Louisiana.

1118 Letter dated February 7, 1958, Shaw to Hale Boggs, International Trade Mart Records, Tulane University, New Orleans, Louisiana.

1119 Letter dated February 19, 1958, Shaw to William Gaudet, International Trade Mart Records, Tulane University, New Orleans, Louisiana.

1120 Letter dated May 6, 1958, Shaw to William Gaudet, International Trade Mart Records, Tulane University, New Orleans, Louisiana.

1121 Letter dated February 7, 1958, Shaw to Puerto Rican representatives, International Trade Mart Records, Tulane University, New Orleans, Louisiana.

1122 Letter dated February 28, 1958, Goldie Moore to Shaw, International Trade Mart Records, Tulane University, New Orleans, Louisiana.

1123 Letter dated March 4, 1958, J.B. Dauenhauer to Shaw, International Trade Mart Records, Tulane University, New Orleans, Louisiana.

1124 Letter dated March 13, 1958, J.B. Dauenhauer to Shaw, International Trade Mart Records, Tulane University, New Orleans, Louisiana.

1125 Letter dated March 18, 1958, Leon S. Felde to Shaw, International Trade Mart Records, Tulane University, New Orleans, Louisiana.

1126 Letter dated April 21, 1958, Shaw to Leandro Rivera, International Trade Mart Records, Tulane University, New Orleans, Louisiana.

1127 Letter dated June 9, 1958, Shaw to Leandro A. Rivera, International Trade Mart Records, Tulane University, New Orleans, Louisiana.

1128 Letter dated April 7, 1958, Shaw to Doña Felicia Rincon de Gauthier, International Trade Mart Records, Tulane University, New Orleans, Louisiana.

1129 Minutes to Board of Directors meeting, March 27, 1958, International Trade Mart, International Trade Mart Records, Tulane University, New Orleans, Louisiana.

1130 Report by William Zetzmann to Board of Directors, March 27, 1958, International Trade Mart, International Trade Mart Records, Tulane University, New Orleans, Louisiana.

1131 Letter dated April 9, 1958, George J. Young to Shaw, International Trade Mart Records, Tulane University, New Orleans, Louisiana.

1132 Letter dated April 23, 1958, William Zetzmann to Benson and Riehl, Architects, International Trade Mart Records, Tulane University, New Orleans, Louisiana.

1133 Letter dated April 9, 1958, Shaw to Chep Morrison, International Trade Mart Records, Tulane University, New Orleans, Louisiana.

1134 Letter dated May 27, 1958, Mrs. Robert D. Holmes to Shaw, International Trade Mart Records, Tulane University, New Orleans, Louisiana.

1135 Letter dated April 18, 1958, Manfred H. Askowitz to Shaw, International Trade Mart Records, Tulane University, New Orleans, Louisiana.

[1136] Telegram dated April 25, 1958, Shaw to Señor Alberto Lleras Camargo, International Trade Mart Records, Tulane University, New Orleans, Louisiana.

[1137] Letter by Jesse Core, published in *Times-Picayune* edition of May 9, 1986, International Trade Mart Records, Tulane University, New Orleans, Louisiana.

[1138] Letter dated June 6, 1958, William Zetzmann to Paul Hoots, International Trade Mart Records, Tulane University, New Orleans, Louisiana.

[1139] Minutes to combined meeting of Executive Committee and Building Committee of Board of Directors, June 25, 1958, International Trade Mart, International Trade Mart Records, Tulane University, New Orleans, Louisiana.

[1140] Minutes to combined meeting of Executive Committee and Building Committee of Board of Directors, June 25, 1958, International Trade Mart, International Trade Mart Records, Tulane University, New Orleans, Louisiana.

[1141] Letter dated April 14, 1958, Shaw to Asher B. Shaw, International Trade Mart Records, Tulane University, New Orleans, Louisiana.

[1142] Letter dated January 31, 1958, Curt Siegelin to Shaw, International Trade Mart Records, Tulane University, New Orleans, Louisiana.

[1143] Minutes to Executive Committee meeting, November 11, 1958, International House, International Trade Mart Records, Tulane University, New Orleans, Louisiana.

[1144] Minutes to Executive Committee meeting, November 4, 1958, International House, International Trade Mart Records, Tulane University, New Orleans, Louisiana.

[1145] Minutes to Executive Committee meeting, August 12, 1958, International House, International Trade Mart Records, Tulane University, New Orleans, Louisiana.

[1146] Minutes to meeting of World Trade Development Council, July 10, 1958, International Trade Mart Records, Tulane University, New Orleans, Louisiana.

[1147] *Trade Winds* issue dated November 24, 1958, International Trade Mart Records, Tulane University, New Orleans, Louisiana.

[1148] Letter dated September 11, 1958, Robert D. Swezey to Shaw, International Trade Mart Records, Tulane University, New Orleans, Louisiana.

[1149] Letter dated September 15, 1958, Shaw to Robert D. Swezey, International Trade Mart Records, Tulane University, New Orleans, Louisiana.

[1150] Letter dated July 23, 1958, Shaw to Charles Lessing Company, International Trade Mart Records, Tulane University, New Orleans, Louisiana.

[1151] Letter dated August 1, 1958, United States Mercantile Company, Inc. to Shaw, International Trade Mart Records, Tulane University, New Orleans, Louisiana.

[1152] Telegram dated December 5, 1958, Shaw to Mrs. Carl Seidenbach, International Trade Mart Records, Tulane University, New Orleans, Louisiana.

[1153] Letter dated September 12, 1958, Holland McCombs to Shaw, International Trade Mart Records, Tulane University, New Orleans, Louisiana.

[1154] Letter dated June 13, 1958, Antonio de Grassi to Shaw, International Trade Mart Records, Tulane University, New Orleans, Louisiana.

[1155] Letter dated March 31, 1958, Shaw to Leon Godchaux II, International Trade Mart Records, Tulane University, New Orleans, Louisiana.

[1156] Letters dated September 4, 1958 and October 2, 1958, Consul General of Italy in New Orleans to Shaw, International Trade Mart Records, Tulane University, New Orleans, Louisiana.

[1157] Telegram dated October 7, 1958, William Spratling to Shaw, International Trade Mart Records, Tulane University, New Orleans, Louisiana.

[1158] Letter dated July 30, 1958, Arthur Q. Davis to Shaw, International Trade Mart Records, Tulane University, New Orleans, Louisiana.

[1159] Telegram dated June 9, 1958, Shaw to Michael Kirk, International Trade Mart Records, Tulane University, New Orleans, Louisiana.

[1160] Letter dated June 18, 1958, Chep Morrison to Shaw, International Trade Mart Records, Tulane University, New Orleans, Louisiana.

[1161] Telegram dated June 11, 1958, Shaw to Hale Boggs, International Trade Mart Records, Tulane University, New Orleans, Louisiana.

[1162] Letter dated December 4, 1958, Shaw to George Moses, International Trade Mart Records, Tulane University, New Orleans, Louisiana.

[1163] Letter dated August 18, 1958, Shaw to John Crawford, International Trade Mart Records, Tulane University, New Orleans, Louisiana.

[1164] Letter dated November 7, 1958, Shaw in response to inquiry, International Trade Mart Records, Tulane University, New Orleans, Louisiana.

[1165] Letter dated October 15, 1958, Clarence K. Streit to Shaw, International Trade Mart Records, Tulane University, New Orleans, Louisiana.

[1166] Letter dated June 9, 1958, Clarence K. Streit to Monte Lemann, International Trade Mart Records, Tulane University, New Orleans, Louisiana.

[1167] Letters dated January 13, 1958 and January 27, 1958, Jesse Core in response to inquiries, International Trade Mart Records, Tulane University, New Orleans, Louisiana.

[1168] Letter dated July 16, 1958, Shaw to M. Kimoto, International Trade Mart Records, Tulane University, New Orleans, Louisiana.

[1169] Letter dated April 24, 1958, Shaw to Carloss A. San Roman, International Trade Mart Records, Tulane University, New Orleans, Louisiana.

[1170] Letter dated January 9, 1958, Shaw in response to inquiry, International Trade Mart Records, Tulane University, New Orleans, Louisiana.

[1171] Letter dated December 23, 1958, J.B. Dauenhauer in response to inquiry, International Trade Mart Records, Tulane University, New Orleans, Louisiana.

[1172] Letter dated May 22, 1958, Shaw to Dorothy F. Bauman, International Trade Mart Records, Tulane University, New Orleans, Louisiana.

[1173] Letter dated May 27, 1958, Shaw to Hungarian Embassy, International Trade Mart Records, Tulane University, New Orleans, Louisiana.

[1174] Letter dated July 1, 1958, William Zetzmann to Harold Roberts, International Trade Mart Records, Tulane University, New Orleans, Louisiana.

[1175] Minutes to meeting of Building and Executive Committees, July 28, 1958, International Trade Mart, International Trade Mart Records, Tulane University, New Orleans, Louisiana.

[1176] Minutes to Meeting of Building and Executive Committees, August 4, 1958, International Trade Mart, International Trade Mart Records, Tulane University, New Orleans, Louisiana.

[1177] Draft Programs for New International Trade Mart Building, International Trade Mart Records, Tulane University, New Orleans, Louisiana.

[1178] Promotional folder entitled "Trends in the Office," Volume Two, Number One, International Trade Mart Records, Tulane University, New Orleans, Louisiana.

[1179] Letter dated July 26, 1958, Enrico Mantello to Shaw, Donated Papers of Clay Shaw, National Archives, College Park, Maryland.

[1180] Preliminary Report dated August 7, 1958, Ettore Scampiccio to Shaw, Donated Papers of Clay Shaw, National Archives, College Park, Maryland.

[1181] Telegram dated August 7, 1958, Shaw to Permindex, Donated Papers of Clay Shaw, National Archives, College Park, Maryland.

[1182] Telegram dated August 7, 1958, Shaw to Enrico Mantello, International Trade Mart Records, Tulane University, New Orleans, Louisiana.

[1183] Letter dated September 18, 1958, Shaw to Sue Cardozo, International Trade Mart Records, Tulane University, New Orleans, Louisiana.

[1184] Letter dated April 14, 1959, Ann Wolf Carnahan to Shaw, Donated Papers of Clay Shaw, National Archives, College Park, Maryland.

[1185] Letter dated May 5, 1959, Shaw to Ann Wolf Carnahan, Donated Papers of Clay Shaw, National Archives, College Park, Maryland.

[1186] Correspondence between Shaw and Fred McDermott, September and October 1960, Donated Papers of Clay Shaw, National Archives, College Park, Maryland.

[1187] Letters, Shaw to Permindex, declining to attend board meetings of July 5, 1960 and March 16, 1961, Donated Papers of Clay Shaw, National Archives, College Park, Maryland.

[1188] Letter dated August 15, 1958, Chep Morrison to Shaw, International Trade Mart Records, Tulane University, New Orleans, Louisiana.

[1189] Letter dated October 6, 1958, Shaw to Chep Morrison, International Trade Mart Records, Tulane University, New Orleans, Louisiana.

[1190] Letter dated December 13, 1958, Shaw to Ruth Anne (Mrs. Stephen) Lichtblaw, International Trade Mart Records, Tulane University, New Orleans, Louisiana.

[1191] Letter dated December 18, 1958, Shaw to Gilbert M. Mellin, International Trade Mart Records, Tulane University, New Orleans, Louisiana.

[1192] Memo dated October 23, 1958, Shaw to William Zetzmann, International Trade Mart Records, Tulane University, New Orleans, Louisiana.

[1193] Letter dated June 19, 1958, Alice Hunt to J. Edgar Hoover, copy in author's possession.

[1194] Letter dated August 22, 1958, Gilbert Mellin to Shaw, International Trade Mart Records, Tulane University, New Orleans, Louisiana.

[1195] Letter dated September 18, 1958, George Haverstick to Shaw, International Trade Mart Records, Tulane University, New Orleans, Louisiana.

[1196] Letter dated September 17, 1958, Shaw letter announcing George Sawicki as representative of International Trade Mart in London, England, International Trade Mart Records, Tulane University, New Orleans, Louisiana.

[1197] Memo dated September 10, 1958, Shaw memo of reference for Alberto LeMoń, International Trade Mart Records, Tulane University, New Orleans, Louisiana.

[1198] Herman Deutsch column, October 22, 1958, *States-Item*, International Trade Mart Records, Tulane University, New Orleans, Louisiana.

[1199] Memo dated July 15, 1958, Mario Bermúdez to Shaw, International Trade Mart Records, Tulane University, New Orleans, Louisiana.

[1200] Letter dated October 3, 1958, William Zetzmann to Richard Freeman, International Trade Mart Records, Tulane University, New Orleans, Louisiana.

[1201] Minutes to Meeting of Building and Executive Committees, October 9, 1958, International Trade Mart, International Trade Mart Records, Tulane University, New Orleans, Louisiana.

[1202] Letter dated October 21, 1958, Jesse Core to William Faulkner, International Trade Mart Records, Tulane University, New Orleans, Louisiana.

[1203] Letter dated October 30, 1958, Jesse Core to William Spratling, International Trade Mart Records, Tulane University, New Orleans, Louisiana.

[1204] Letter dated October 6, 1958, Shaw to Representative Hale Boggs, International Trade Mart Records, Tulane University, New Orleans, Louisiana.

[1205] Letter dated November 14, 1958, Shaw to Arab Information Center, International Trade Mart Records, Tulane University, New Orleans, Louisiana.

[1206] Letter dated November 26, 1958, Vernon F. Cook, Program Director, WYES-TV, to Shaw, International Trade Mart Records, Tulane University, New Orleans, Louisiana.

[1207] Letter dated May 26, 1958, Roswell J. Weil to Shaw, International Trade Mart Records, Tulane University, New Orleans, Louisiana.

[1208] Letter dated November 24, 1958, Shaw to Charles Nutter, International Trade Mart Records, Tulane University, New Orleans, Louisiana.

[1209] Letter dated December 17, 1958, Shaw to Richard Freeman, International Trade Mart Records, Tulane University, New Orleans, Louisiana.

[1210] Minutes to meeting of Building and Executive Committees, November 28, 1958, International Trade Mart, International Trade Mart Records, Tulane University, New Orleans, Louisiana.

[1211] Letter dated December 10, 1958, Muriel Francis to Shaw, International Trade Mart Records, Tulane University, New Orleans, Louisiana.

[1212] Letter dated November 24, 1958, Chep Morrison to Shaw, International Trade Mart Records, Tulane University, New Orleans, Louisiana.

[1213] Letter dated January 21, 1959, Shaw to Chep Morrison, International Trade Mart Records, Tulane University, New Orleans, Louisiana.

[1214] Letter dated January 7, 1959, Shaw to Jack Crawford, International Trade Mart Records, Tulane University, New Orleans, Louisiana.

[1215] *VISION* issue dated January 16, 1959, International Trade Mart Records, Tulane University, New Orleans, Louisiana.

[1216] *Wall Street Journal* article, January 8, 1959, International Trade Mart Records, Tulane University, New Orleans, Louisiana.

[1217] Letter dated January 23, 1959, Shaw to Southern Bell, International Trade Mart Records, Tulane University, New Orleans, Louisiana.

[1218] Letter dated November 5, 1958, Irvin M. Orner to William Zetzmann, International Trade Mart Records, Tulane University, New Orleans, Louisiana.

[1219] Letter dated November 13, 1958, William Zetzmann to Irvin M. Orner, International Trade Mart Records, Tulane University, New Orleans, Louisiana.

[1220] Letter dated March 3, 1959, Irvin M. Orner to William Zetzmann, International Trade Mart Records, Tulane University, New Orleans, Louisiana.

[1221] Minutes of Executive Committee meeting, February 3, 1959, International House, International Trade Mart Records, Tulane University, New Orleans, Louisiana.

[1222] Telegram dated January 12, 1959, Shaw to Val Dufour, International Trade Mart Records, Tulane University, New Orleans, Louisiana.

[1223] Undated Memo from J.B. Dauenhauer to tenants, International Trade Mart Records, Tulane University, New Orleans, Louisiana.

[1224] Memo dated February 20, 1959, J.B. Dauenhauer to tenants, International Trade Mart Records, Tulane University, New Orleans, Louisiana.

[1225] Telegram dated March 16, 1959, Shaw to J.C. Jackson, International Trade Mart Records, Tulane University, New Orleans, Louisiana.

[1226] Report dated March 12, 1959, William Zetzmann to Board of Directors, International Trade Mart, International Trade Mart Records, Tulane University, New Orleans, Louisiana.

[1227] *States-Item* dated March 20, 1959, International Trade Mart Records, Tulane University, New Orleans, Louisiana.

[1228] Minutes to meeting of Contributors and Debenture Holders, March 12, 1959, International Trade Mart, International Trade Mart Records, Tulane University, New Orleans, Louisiana.

[1229] Minutes to meeting of Board of Directors, March 20, 1959, International Trade Mart, International Trade Mart Records, Tulane University, New Orleans, Louisiana.

[1230] Letter dated April 6, 1959, Mrs. Edward (Maria) Durell Stone to Shaw, International Trade Mart Records, Tulane University, New Orleans, Louisiana.

[1231] Letter dated March 25, 1959, Muriel Francis to Shaw and Jesse Core, International Trade Mart Records, Tulane University, New Orleans, Louisiana.

[1232] Letter dated April 27, 1959, Muriel Francis to Shaw, International Trade Mart Records, Tulane University, New Orleans, Louisiana.

[1233] Letter dated May 5, 1959, Shaw to Muriel Francis, International Trade Mart Records, Tulane University, New Orleans, Louisiana.

[1234] Minutes to meeting of Building and Executive Committees, April 3, 1959, International Trade Mart, International Trade Mart Records, Tulane University, New Orleans, Louisiana.

[1235] See exchange of letters in April 1959 between William Zetzmann and George Dinwiddie, International Trade Mart Records, Tulane University, New Orleans, Louisiana.

[1236] Letter dated December 19, 1958, Emile Comar, President, Press Club of New Orleans, to Shaw, International Trade Mart Records, Tulane University, New Orleans, Louisiana.

[1237] Letter dated May 5, 1959, Albert Terkuhle to Nils Lundberg, with copy to Shaw, International Trade Mart Records, Tulane University, New Orleans, Louisiana.

[1238] Letter dated May 7, 1959, Jesse Core to Shaw, International Trade Mart Records, Tulane University, New Orleans, Louisiana.

[1239] Letter dated May 29, 1959, John R. Campbell to Shaw, International Trade Mart Records, Tulane University, New Orleans, Louisiana.

[1240] Letter dated June 24, 1959, Shaw to all current tenants of the Mart, International Trade Mart Records, Tulane University, New Orleans, Louisiana.

[1241] Letter dated July 23, 1959, Shaw to Victor H. Baker, International Trade Mart Records, Tulane University, New Orleans, Louisiana.

[1242] Letter dated June 8, 1959, Shaw in response to prospective tenant, International Trade Mart Records, Tulane University, New Orleans, Louisiana.

[1243] Letter dated September 9, 1959, Shaw to Guy L. Smith, International Trade Mart Records, Tulane University, New Orleans, Louisiana.

[1244] Letter dated May 29, 1959, George S. Dinwiddie to International House members, International Trade Mart Records, Tulane University, New Orleans, Louisiana.

1245 Minutes to meeting of Board of Directors, October 21, 1959, International House, International Trade Mart Records, Tulane University, New Orleans, Louisiana.

1246 Letter dated February 19, 1959, Michael Buzan, Jr. to Shaw, International Trade Mart Records, Tulane University, New Orleans, Louisiana.

1247 Undated postcard from Luis (Louis) Vargas to Shaw, International Trade Mart Records, Tulane University, New Orleans, Louisiana.

1248 Letter dated December 9, 1959, Frank E. Stanton to Shaw, International Trade Mart Records, Tulane University, New Orleans, Louisiana.

1249 Card dated November 28, 1959, Sid and Eleni Epstein to Shaw, International Trade Mart Records, Tulane University, New Orleans, Louisiana.

1250 Letter dated October 22, 1959, Warren T. Lindquist to Shaw, International Trade Mart Records, Tulane University, New Orleans, Louisiana.

1251 Letter dated July 1, 1959, Holland McCombs to Shaw, International Trade Mart Records, Tulane University, New Orleans, Louisiana.

1252 Letter dated March 11, 1959, Shaw to Robert M. Tuttle, International Trade Mart Records, Tulane University, New Orleans, Louisiana.

1253 Letter dated March 26, 1959, Mario Bermúdez to Shaw, International Trade Mart Records, Tulane University, New Orleans, Louisiana.

1254 Letter dated May 7, 1959, Pepsi-Cola Bottling Company to Shaw, International Trade Mart Records, Tulane University, New Orleans, Louisiana.

1255 Note dated May 8, 1959, indicating that Goldie Moore called to express regrets, International Trade Mart Records, Tulane University, New Orleans, Louisiana.

1256 Letter dated January 16, 1959, Shaw to Spanish Office of Exterior Economy, International Trade Mart Records, Tulane University, New Orleans, Louisiana.

1257 Letter dated November 17, 1959, Shaw to Stanislaw Zawadski, International Trade Mart Records, Tulane University, New Orleans, Louisiana.

1258 Letter dated August 14, 1959, from S.L. Richardson to Shaw, International Trade Mart Records, Tulane University, New Orleans, Louisiana.

1259 Telegram dated November 3, 1959, Shaw to Horace Ainsworth, International Trade Mart Records, Tulane University, New Orleans, Louisiana.

1260 Letter dated March 26, 1959, Shaw in response to inquiry, International Trade Mart Records, Tulane University, New Orleans, Louisiana.

1261 Letter dated April 27, 1959, Shaw in response to inquiry of March 25, 1959, International Trade Mart Records, Tulane University, New Orleans, Louisiana.

1262 Letter dated October 20, 1959, Shaw to Barbara Makanowitzky, International Trade Mart Records, Tulane University, New Orleans, Louisiana.

1263 Letter dated November 11, 1959, Shaw to Cal Cagno of National Bank of Commerce, International Trade Mart Records, Tulane University, New Orleans, Louisiana.

1264 Letter dated October 20, 1959, Shaw to Jerry E. Ryan, International Trade Mart Records, Tulane University, New Orleans, Louisiana.

1265 Letter dated August 5, 1959, Jesse Core to Tommy Griffin, International Trade Mart Records, Tulane University, New Orleans, Louisiana.

1266 Letter dated July 22, 1959, Ruth Barnett to Jesse Core, International Trade Mart Records, Tulane University, New Orleans, Louisiana.

[1267] Letter dated June 25, 1959, Jesse Core to Tommy Griffin, International Trade Mart Records, Tulane University, New Orleans, Louisiana.

[1268] Letter dated June 1, 1959, Shaw to Senator J. William Fulbright, International Trade Mart Records, Tulane University, New Orleans, Louisiana.

[1269] 1960 Federal Income Tax Return for Shaw, Donated Papers of Clay Shaw, National Archives, College Park, Maryland.

[1270] Minutes to meeting of Board of Directors, August 25, 1959, International Trade Mart Records, International Trade Mart Records, Tulane University, New Orleans, Louisiana.

[1271] Minutes to Building Committee meeting, September 14, 1959, International Trade Mart, International Trade Mart Records, Tulane University, New Orleans, Louisiana.

[1272] Letter dated August 7, 1959, J.B. Dauenhauer in response to inquiry, International Trade Mart Records, Tulane University, New Orleans, Louisiana.

[1273] Letter dated August 31, 1959, Monk Simons to Shaw, International Trade Mart Records, Tulane University, New Orleans, Louisiana.

[1274] See photo taken August 21, 1959, Shaw and Ernest Theiler, Donated Papers of Clay Shaw, National Archives, College Park, Maryland.

[1275] Minutes to meeting of Executive, Finance, and Building Committees, September 9, 1959, International Trade Mart, International Trade Mart Records, Tulane University, New Orleans, Louisiana.

[1276] Interview with Hermann O. Bockelmann, approximately August 23, 1967, by William Wood/Bill Boxley, Wood/Boxley Files, JFK Assassination Collection, National Archives, College Park, Maryland.

[1277] Interview with Hermann O. Bockelmann by author, February 11, 2010.

[1278] Letter dated September 18, 1959, Rear Admiral W.G. Schindler, U.S. Navy, to Shaw, International Trade Mart Records, Tulane University, New Orleans, Louisiana.

[1279] Letter dated September 23, 1959, Shaw to William Zetzmann, International Trade Mart Records, Tulane University, New Orleans, Louisiana.

[1280] Memo dated November 5, 1959, Shaw to Harold Roberts, International Trade Mart Records, Tulane University, New Orleans, Louisiana.

[1281] Bulletin from Shaw to tenants, October 1, 1959, International Trade Mart Records, Tulane University, New Orleans, Louisiana.

[1282] Minutes to meeting of Executive Committee, October 13, 1959, International House, International Trade Mart Records, Tulane University, New Orleans, Louisiana.

[1283] Minutes to meeting of Building and Executive Committees, October 16, 1959, International Trade Mart, International Trade Mart Records, Tulane University, New Orleans, Louisiana.

[1284] Letter dated October 19, 1959, William Zetzmann to Edmund Christy, International Trade Mart Records, Tulane University, New Orleans, Louisiana.

[1285] Letter dated October 30, 1959, George Dinwiddie to International House members, International Trade Mart Records, Tulane University, New Orleans, Louisiana.

[1286] Letter dated September 15, 1959, J. Mason Guillory to Vernon Cook, International Trade Mart Records, Tulane University, New Orleans, Louisiana.

[1287] *Off-Camera* issue dated November 18, 1959, International Trade Mart Records, Tulane University, New Orleans, Louisiana.

[1288] Letter dated November 19, 1959, William Phillips to Shaw, International Trade Mart Records, Tulane University, New Orleans, Louisiana.

[1289] E-mail dated February 3, 2009, Evan Rhodes to author.

[1290] Letter dated November 30, 1959, Shaw to Kit Mueller, International Trade Mart Records, Tulane University, New Orleans, Louisiana.

[1291] Letter dated December 18, 1959, Shaw to Clinton W. Murchison, International Trade Mart Records, Tulane University, New Orleans, Louisiana.

[1292] Minutes to meeting of Board of Directors, December 10, 1959, International Trade Mart, International Trade Mart Records, Tulane University, New Orleans, Louisiana.

[1293] Letter dated January 5, 1960, Shaw to Albert D. Meltz, International Trade Mart Records, Tulane University, New Orleans, Louisiana.

[1294] Minutes to meeting of Building and Executive Committees, January 25, 1960, International Trade Mart, International Trade Mart Records, Tulane University, New Orleans, Louisiana.

[1295] Letter dated December 14, 1959, R.E. Stackpole and Edwin A. Leland, Jr. to Shaw, International Trade Mart Records, Tulane University, New Orleans, Louisiana.

[1296] Letter dated January 22, 1960, Shaw to Consul General of Japan, International Trade Mart Records, Tulane University, New Orleans, Louisiana.

[1297] *Trade Winds* bulletin, January 13, 1960, International Trade Mart Records, Tulane University, New Orleans, Louisiana.

[1298] Letter dated February 8, 1960, Chep Morrison to T.H. Lyons, International Trade Mart Records, Tulane University, New Orleans, Louisiana.

[1299] Letter dated February 8, 1960, Charles Nutter to T.H. Lyons, International Trade Mart Records, Tulane University, New Orleans, Louisiana.

[1300] Letter dated February 8, 1960, Mario Bermúdez to Colonel Provosty Dayries, International Trade Mart Records, Tulane University, New Orleans, Louisiana.

[1301] Minutes to meeting of World Trade Development Committee, February 18, 1960, International House, International Trade Mart Records, Tulane University, New Orleans, Louisiana.

[1302] Minutes to meeting of Contributors and Debenture Holders, March 10, 1960, International Trade Mart, International Trade Mart Records, Tulane University, New Orleans, Louisiana.

[1303] Letter dated March 23, 1960, Jesse Core to Paul Green, International Trade Mart Records, Tulane University, New Orleans, Louisiana.

[1304] Letter dated March 15, 1960, Robert D. Hess to Shaw, International Trade Mart Records, Tulane University, New Orleans, Louisiana.

[1305] Letter dated March 28, 1960, Robert E. Wall to Shaw, International Trade Mart Records, Tulane University, New Orleans, Louisiana.

[1306] Newspaper clipping dated March 16, 1960, *States-Item*, International Trade Mart Records, Tulane University, New Orleans, Louisiana.

[1307] *Trade Winds* bulletin, April 1, 1960, International Trade Mart Records, Tulane University, New Orleans, Louisiana.

[1308] Letter dated March 28, 1960, Shaw to Dr. Dov Biegen, International Trade Mart Records, Tulane University, New Orleans, Louisiana.

[1309] Letter dated March 22, 1960, Shaw to Ken Lott, International Trade Mart Records, Tulane University, New Orleans, Louisiana.

[1310] Minutes to Executive Committee meeting, March 29, 1960, International House, International Trade Mart Records, Tulane University, New Orleans, Louisiana.

[1311] Minutes to Board of Directors meeting, March 25, 1960, International Trade Mart, International Trade Mart Records, Tulane University, New Orleans, Louisiana.

[1312] Minutes to meeting of Building and Executive Committees, April 22, 1960, International Trade Mart, International Trade Mart Records, Tulane University, New Orleans, Louisiana.

[1313] Letter of recommendation dated April 6, 1960, for Richard Doskey by Shaw, International Trade Mart Records, Tulane University, New Orleans, Louisiana.

[1314] Form letter dated April 1, 1960, Cecil M. Shilstone to Shaw, International Trade Mart Records, Tulane University, New Orleans, Louisiana.

[1315] Minutes to meeting of Board of Directors, April 20, 1960, International House, International Trade Mart Records, Tulane University, New Orleans, Louisiana.

[1316] Letter dated April 11, 1960, Jesse Core to Buckingham O. Marryat, International Trade Mart Records, Tulane University, New Orleans, Louisiana.

[1317] Letter dated April 18, 1960, Shaw to Consul General of Japan, International Trade Mart Records, Tulane University, New Orleans, Louisiana.

[1318] Letter dated April 5, 1960, Robert D. Hess to Shaw, International Trade Mart Records, Tulane University, New Orleans, Louisiana.

[1319] Letter dated April 7, 1960, James M.E. O'Grady to Shaw, International Trade Mart Records, Tulane University, New Orleans, Louisiana.

[1320] Minutes to meeting of Building and Executive Committees, May 18, 1960, International Trade Mart, International Trade Mart Records, Tulane University, New Orleans, Louisiana.

[1321] Letter dated May 13, 1960, Shaw to Saab Motors, Inc. in Jacksonville, Florida, International Trade Mart Records, Tulane University, New Orleans, Louisiana.

[1322] Letter dated May 10, 1960, Shaw to Brazilian Government Trade Bureau, International Trade Mart Records, Tulane University, New Orleans, Louisiana.

[1323] Letter dated July 25, 1960, Shaw to Dorothy E. Ausfahl, International Trade Mart Records, Tulane University, New Orleans, Louisiana.

[1324] Letter dated May 20, 1960, Seymour Weiss to William Zetzmann, International Trade Mart Records, Tulane University, New Orleans, Louisiana.

[1325] Minutes to meeting of Board of Directors, May 25, 1960, International Trade Mart, International Trade Mart Records, Tulane University, New Orleans, Louisiana.

[1326] Letter dated June 1, 1960, Shaw to Young Republican Federation of Louisiana, International Trade Mart Records, Tulane University, New Orleans, Louisiana.

[1327] Letter dated September 8, 1960, Shaw to insurance company related to theft claim, Donated Papers of Clay Shaw, National Archives, College Park, Maryland.

[1328] Minutes to meeting of Board of Directors, June 15, 1960, International House, International Trade Mart Records, Tulane University, New Orleans, Louisiana.

[1329] *Trade Winds* bulletin, July 18, 1960, International Trade Mart Records, Tulane University, New Orleans, Louisiana.

[1330] Minutes to meeting of Building Committee, July 1, 1960, International Trade Mart, International Trade Mart Records, Tulane University, New Orleans, Louisiana.

[1331] Letter dated September 23, 1960, Shaw to Olaf C. Lambert, International Trade Mart Records, Tulane University, New Orleans, Louisiana.

[1332] Letter dated September 30, 1960, James J. Coleman to Shaw, International Trade Mart Records, Tulane University, New Orleans, Louisiana.

[1333] Telegram dated October 10, 1960, Chep Morrison to Shaw, International Trade Mart Records, Tulane University, New Orleans, Louisiana.

[1334] Letter dated October 31, 1960, Mr. and Mrs. Eberhard P. Deutsch to Shaw, International Trade Mart Records, Tulane University, New Orleans, Louisiana.

[1335] Telegram dated November 17, 1960, Chep Morrison to Shaw, International Trade Mart Records, Tulane University, New Orleans, Louisiana.

[1336] Letter dated November 15, 1960, Aurelie Alost to Shaw, International Trade Mart Records, Tulane University, New Orleans, Louisiana.

[1337] Memo dated October 20, 1960, Marcel Gomez to Shaw, International Trade Mart Records, Tulane University, New Orleans, Louisiana.

[1338] Letter dated October 17, 1960, Shaw to William Spratling, International Trade Mart Records, Tulane University, New Orleans, Louisiana.

[1339] Letter dated June 13, 1960, Shaw in response to inquiry, International Trade Mart Records, Tulane University, New Orleans, Louisiana.

[1340] Letter dated June 26, 1959, Shaw to George Sawicki, International Trade Mart Records, Tulane University, New Orleans, Louisiana.

[1341] Letter dated June 29, 1959, George Sawicki to Shaw, International Trade Mart Records, Tulane University, New Orleans, Louisiana.

[1342] Letter dated July 16, 1959, George Sawicki to Shaw, International Trade Mart Records, Tulane University, New Orleans, Louisiana.

[1343] Letter dated February 15, 1960, Shaw to Sam Shaw, International Trade Mart Records, Tulane University, New Orleans, Louisiana.

[1344] Letter dated February 13, 1960, Mary Rich to William Zetzmann, International Trade Mart Records, Tulane University, New Orleans, Louisiana.

[1345] Letter dated May 3, 1960, Shaw to Bess C. Noble, International Trade Mart Records, Tulane University, New Orleans, Louisiana.

[1346] Letter dated May 20, 1960, Shaw to member of Jacksonville International Trade Mart, International Trade Mart Records, Tulane University, New Orleans, Louisiana.

[1347] Letter dated July 14, 1960, Shaw to Jacksonville International Trade Mart, International Trade Mart Records, Tulane University, New Orleans, Louisiana.

[1348] Article, "5 Pittsburgh Priests Went to Prison," in *Pittsburgh Post-Gazette* of February 28, 2004.

[1349] Minutes to meeting of Executive Committee of Foreign Policy Association of New Orleans, August 4, 1960, International Trade Mart Records, Tulane University, New Orleans, Louisiana.

[1350] Minutes to meeting of Executive Committee of Foreign Policy Association of New Orleans, July 8, 1960, International Trade Mart Records, Tulane University, New Orleans, Louisiana.

[1351] Letter dated July 21, 1960, Monk Simons to Shaw, International Trade Mart Records, Tulane University, New Orleans, Louisiana.

[1352] Letter dated November 17, 1960, George Chaplin to Shaw, International Trade Mart Records, Tulane University, New Orleans, Louisiana.

[1353] Minutes to Executive Committee meeting, July 19, 1960, International House, International Trade Mart Records, Tulane University, New Orleans, Louisiana.

[1354] Letter dated June 17, 1960, L.S. McClaren to Shaw, International Trade Mart Records, Tulane University, New Orleans, Louisiana.

[1355] Telegram dated July 26, 1960, William Spratling to Shaw, International Trade Mart Records, Tulane University, New Orleans, Louisiana.

[1356] Letter dated March 23, 1960, Leopoldo Herrera to Shaw, International Trade Mart Records, Tulane University, New Orleans, Louisiana.

[1357] Letter dated May 5, 1960, Shaw to Commercial Attaché at Embassy of Portugal, International Trade Mart Records, Tulane University, New Orleans, Louisiana.

[1358] Letter dated July 13, 1960, Tim Pasma to Shaw, International Trade Mart Records, Tulane University, New Orleans, Louisiana.

[1359] Letter dated August 26, 1960, Vaughn Bryant to Shaw, International Trade Mart Records, Tulane University, New Orleans, Louisiana.

[1360] Letter dated November 23, 1960, Shaw to Joan S. Pokross, International Trade Mart Records, Tulane University, New Orleans, Louisiana.

[1361] Letter dated October 19, 1960, Shaw to Whitaker F. Riggs, Jr., International Trade Mart Records, Tulane University, New Orleans, Louisiana.

[1362] Letter dated December 16, 1960, Robert D. Hess to Shaw, International Trade Mart Records, Tulane University, New Orleans, Louisiana.

[1363] Letter dated November 16, 1960, Shaw to Jack Crawford, International Trade Mart Records, Tulane University, New Orleans, Louisiana.

[1364] Letter dated November 29, 1960, J.B. Dauenhauer in response to inquiry, International Trade Mart Records, Tulane University, New Orleans, Louisiana.

[1365] Letter dated November 4, 1960, J.B. Dauenhauer in response to inquiry, International Trade Mart Records, Tulane University, New Orleans, Louisiana.

[1366] Letter dated July 1, 1960, Morey L. Sear to Chep Morrison, with handwritten note from Morrison to Shaw, International Trade Mart Records, Tulane University, New Orleans, Louisiana.

[1367] Letter dated February 12, 1960, Shaw to Trammel Crow, International Trade Mart Records, Tulane University, New Orleans, Louisiana.

[1368] Articles dated April 1960 and July 1960, *House and Home*, Donated Papers of Clay Shaw, National Archives, College Park, Maryland.

[1369] Article in *House and Home*, July 1960, Donated Papers of Clay Shaw, National Archives, College Park, Maryland.

[1370] Letter dated August 16, 1960, Jesse Core to Lt. General C.P. Cabell, International Trade Mart Records, Tulane University, New Orleans, Louisiana.

[1371] Letter dated August 22, 1960, Shaw to Lt. General C.P. Cabell, U.S.A.F., International Trade Mart Records, Tulane University, New Orleans, Louisiana.

[1372] *Foreign Trader* bulletin of Export Managers Club, September 1960, International Trade Mart Records, Tulane University, New Orleans, Louisiana.

[1373] Letter dated September 2, 1960, Shaw to Edward J. Steimel, International Trade Mart Records, Tulane University, New Orleans, Louisiana.

[1374] Letter dated September 19, 1960, Shaw to Wylie F.L. Tuttle, International Trade Mart Records, Tulane University, New Orleans, Louisiana.

[1375] Letter dated September 26, 1960, Frances E. Goetz to Shaw, International Trade Mart Records, Tulane University, New Orleans, Louisiana.

[1376] Letter dated September 14, 1960, Neville Levy to International House members, International Trade Mart Records, Tulane University, New Orleans, Louisiana.

[1377] Letter dated October 12, 1960, Joseph Merrick Jones to Neville Levy, International Trade Mart Records, Tulane University, New Orleans, Louisiana.

[1378] Letter dated October 19, 1960, Shaw to Chep Morrison, International Trade Mart Records, Tulane University, New Orleans, Louisiana.

[1379] Letter dated October 20, 1960, from Centro Mondiale Commerciale, Publicity Department, to International Trade Mart, International Trade Mart Records, Tulane University, New Orleans, Louisiana.

[1380] Letter dated October 28, 1960, Chep Morrison to William Zetzmann, with note by Shaw, International Trade Mart Records, Tulane University, New Orleans, Louisiana.

[1381] Letter dated October 17, 1960, I.W. "Pat" Patterson to Shaw, International Trade Mart Records, Tulane University, New Orleans, Louisiana.

[1382] Report dated October 28, 1960, by William Zetzmann to Board of Directors, International Trade Mart, International Trade Mart Records, Tulane University, New Orleans, Louisiana.

[1383] Minutes to meeting of Board of Directors, October 28, 1960, International Trade Mart, International Trade Mart Records, Tulane University, New Orleans, Louisiana.

[1384] Letter dated November 22, 1960, William Zetzmann to Shaw, International Trade Mart Records, Tulane University, New Orleans, Louisiana.

[1385] Letter dated December 6, 1960, Don Driscoll to Shaw, International Trade Mart Records, Tulane University, New Orleans, Louisiana.

[1386] Letter dated December 27, 1960, Charles Leonard to Shaw, International Trade Mart Records, Tulane University, New Orleans, Louisiana.

[1387] Typed note from Charles Leonard to "Clay" on small Foreign Policy Association of New Orleans notepaper, International Trade Mart Records, Tulane University, New Orleans, Louisiana.

[1388] Telegram dated December 26, 1960, Chep Morrison to Shaw, International Trade Mart Records, Tulane University, New Orleans, Louisiana.

[1389] Year-End Report to Citizens of New Orleans by Chep Morrison, International Trade Mart Records, Tulane University, New Orleans, Louisiana.

[1390] Minutes to Executive Committee meeting, December 13, 1960, International House, International Trade Mart Records, Tulane University, New Orleans, Louisiana.

[1391] Statement dated December 14, 1960, "Frosty" Blackshear, International Trade Mart Records, Tulane University, New Orleans, Louisiana.

[1392] Letter dated December 8, 1960, Shaw to Mario Bermúdez, International Trade Mart Records, Tulane University, New Orleans, Louisiana.

[1393] Letter dated March 24, 1951, Leonard Huber to Jacob Morrison, Papers of Mary and Jacob Morrison, Historic New Orleans Collection, New Orleans, Louisiana.

[1394] Letter dated July 24, 1958, Colonel Provosty A. Dayries to Mayor's Special Citizens' Committee, Papers of Mary and Jacob Morrison, Historic New Orleans Collection, New Orleans, Louisiana.

[1395] Letter, undated, Natalie Scott to Mrs. R.G. Robinson, Natalie Scott Papers, Tulane University, New Orleans, Louisiana.

[1396] Letter to the editor, *Times-Picayune* edition of March 15, 1954, Special Citizens Investigating Committee Collection, Tulane University, New Orleans, Louisiana.

[1397] Letter dated June 5, 1951, Richard R. Foster to Joseph L. Scheurering, Richard R. Foster Civic and Community Papers, Historic New Orleans Collection, New Orleans, Louisiana.

[1398] Booklet issued by Joint Legislative Committee on Un-American Activities, Louisiana State Legislature, *Activities of the Ku Klux Klan and Certain Other Organizations in Louisiana*, Legislative Research Library Collection 1955-1981, Louisiana State Archives, Baton Rouge, Louisiana.

[1399] *The Washington Post* article, February 19, 1965, and accompanying note by Ed Butler to Alton Ochsner, John Wilds Alton Ochsner Working Papers, Historic New Orleans Collection, New Orleans, Louisiana.

[1400] Letter postmarked August 14, 1945, Muriel Bultman Francis to her parents, Bultman Family Papers, Historic New Orleans Collection, New Orleans, Louisiana.

[1401] Notes to meeting of Board of Directors, January 24, 1961, International Trade Mart, International Trade Mart Records, Tulane University, New Orleans, Louisiana.

[1402] Letter dated January 13, 1961, Jack Harris to Shaw, International Trade Mart Records, Tulane University, New Orleans, Louisiana.

[1403] Article in *Wall Street Journal*, February 6, 1961, Donated Papers of Clay Shaw, National Archives, College Park, Maryland.

[1404] Letters of recommendation dated February 8, 1961, for Shelby Spuhler by Shaw and J.B. Dauenhauer, International Trade Mart Records, Tulane University, New Orleans, Louisiana.

[1405] Notes to Executive Committee meeting, February 10, 1961, International Trade Mart, International Trade Mart Records, Tulane University, New Orleans, Louisiana.

[1406] Minutes to meeting of Executive Committee, February 7, 1961, International House, International Trade Mart Records, Tulane University, New Orleans, Louisiana.

[1407] Biography of Captain Neville Levy, International Trade Mart Records, Tulane University, New Orleans, Louisiana.

[1408] Minutes to meeting of Bondholders, March 9, 1961, International Trade Mart, International Trade Mart Records, Tulane University, New Orleans, Louisiana.

[1409] Minutes to Annual Meeting, March 9, 1961, International Trade Mart, International Trade Mart Records, Tulane University, New Orleans, Louisiana.

[1410] Minutes to meeting of Board of Directors, March 20, 1961, International Trade Mart, International Trade Mart Records, Tulane University, New Orleans, Louisiana.

[1411] Letter dated March 23, 1961, Shaw to Paul Spargnapani, International Trade Mart Records, Tulane University, New Orleans, Louisiana.

[1412] Telegram dated January 26, 1961, William Zetzmann to Shaw, International Trade Mart Records, Tulane University, New Orleans, Louisiana.

[1413] Letter dated March 29, 1961, Senator Jacob K. Javits to Shaw, International Trade Mart Records, Tulane University, New Orleans, Louisiana.

[1414] Letter dated April 4, 1961, Shaw to L.S. McClaren, International Trade Mart Records, Tulane University, New Orleans, Louisiana.

[1415] Letter of recommendation dated April 24, 1961, for Josephine Pennestri by J.B. Dauenhauer, International Trade Mart Records, Tulane University, New Orleans, Louisiana.

[1416] Letter dated May 8, 1961, Shaw to Wylie Tuttle, International Trade Mart Records, Tulane University, New Orleans, Louisiana.

[1417] Letter dated January 4, 1961, Jesse Core to Charles Cabell, International Trade Mart Records, Tulane University, New Orleans, Louisiana.

[1418] Letter dated February 23, 1961, Walter Elder to Charles Leonard, International Trade Mart Records, Tulane University, New Orleans, Louisiana.

[1419] Letter dated March 28, 1961, Jesse Core to Walter Elder, International Trade Mart Records, Tulane University, New Orleans, Louisiana.

[1420] Biographical sketch of General Charles Cabell, U.S.A.F., dated February 1, 1961, International Trade Mart Records, Tulane University, New Orleans, Louisiana.

[1421] Press release related to General Charles Cabell's speech, International Trade Mart Records, Tulane University, New Orleans, Louisiana.

[1422] Letter dated May 12, 1961, C.C. Walther to Shaw, International Trade Mart Records, Tulane University, New Orleans, Louisiana.

[1423] Correspondence related to Charles Cabell's speech to Foreign Policy Association of New Orleans on May 9, 1961, Record Group 233, Records of the U.S. House of Representatives, Select Committee on Assassinations, Segregated CIA Collection, JFK Assassination Collection, National Archives, College Park, Maryland.

[1424] *States-Item*, May 10, 1961, International Trade Mart Records, Tulane University, New Orleans, Louisiana.

[1425] "Lagniappe" column in *States-Item*, May 13, 1961, International Trade Mart Records, Tulane University, New Orleans, Louisiana.

[1426] Letter, no date, never mailed, Jesse Core to Charles Cabell, International Trade Mart Records, Tulane University, New Orleans, Louisiana.

[1427] Report of International Relations Office to the Board of Directors, March 1, 1961, International House, International Trade Mart Records, Tulane University, New Orleans, Louisiana.

[1428] Minutes to Executive Committee meeting, May 16, 1961, International House, International Trade Mart Records, Tulane University, New Orleans, Louisiana.

[1429] Minutes to Executive Committee meeting, May 30, 1961, International House, International Trade Mart Records, Tulane University, New Orleans, Louisiana.

[1430] Press release dated June 13, 1961, International House, International Trade Mart Records, Tulane University, New Orleans, Louisiana.

[1431] Memo dated January 22, 1962, Shaw to International House Finance Committee, International Trade Mart Records, Tulane University, New Orleans, Louisiana.

[1432] Letter dated August 18, 1961, Charles Nutter to Kenneth Barranger, International Trade Mart Records, Tulane University, New Orleans, Louisiana.

[1433] Memo dated July 26, 1961, Maurice Barr to Richard G. Jones, International Trade Mart Records, Tulane University, New Orleans, Louisiana.

[1434] Undated Memo about Charles Nutter pension issue, International Trade Mart Records, Tulane University, New Orleans, Louisiana.

[1435] Letter dated November 15, 1961, Richard B. Swenson to Lawrence Molony, International Trade Mart Records, Tulane University, New Orleans, Louisiana.

[1436] Letter dated November 17, 1961, Lawrence Molony to Richard B. Swenson, International Trade Mart Records, Tulane University, New Orleans, Louisiana.

[1437] Letter dated June 28, 1961, Shaw to Representative Hale Boggs, International Trade Mart Records, Tulane University, New Orleans, Louisiana.

[1438] Letter dated June 14, 1961, Harnett Kane to Shaw, International Trade Mart Records, Tulane University, New Orleans, Louisiana.

[1439] Letter dated June 21, 1961, Shaw to Harnett Kane, International Trade Mart Records, Tulane University, New Orleans, Louisiana.

[1440] Letter dated May 2, 1961, Shaw in response to inquiry, International Trade Mart Records, Tulane University, New Orleans, Louisiana.

[1441] Letter dated May 19, 1961, Arnold H. Lubasch to Shaw, International Trade Mart Records, Tulane University, New Orleans, Louisiana.

[1442] Letter dated June 8, 1961, Shaw to Arnold H. Lubasch, International Trade Mart Records, Tulane University, New Orleans, Louisiana.

[1443] Letter dated May 17, 1961, Shaw to Robert R. Eckardt, International Trade Mart Records, Tulane University, New Orleans, Louisiana.

[1444] Letter dated February 24, 1961, Chep Morrison to Shaw, International Trade Mart Records, Tulane University, New Orleans, Louisiana.

[1445] Letter dated May 22, 1961, Goldie Moore in response to inquiry, International Trade Mart Records, Tulane University, New Orleans, Louisiana.

[1446] Letter dated January 27, 1961, William R. Klein to Shaw, International Trade Mart Records, Tulane University, New Orleans, Louisiana.

[1447] Letter dated January 5, 1961, Ed Butler to Shaw, International Trade Mart Records, Tulane University, New Orleans, Louisiana.

[1448] Letter dated August 15, 1961, Walter B. Hoover to Shaw, International Trade Mart Records, Tulane University, New Orleans, Louisiana.

[1449] Letter dated August 31, 1961, B. Pederson to Shaw, International Trade Mart Records, Tulane University, New Orleans, Louisiana.

[1450] Letter dated September 26, 1961, Shaw to B. Pederson, International Trade Mart Records, Tulane University, New Orleans, Louisiana.

[1451] Memo dated January 24, 1961, Marcel Gomez to Shaw, International Trade Mart Records, Tulane University, New Orleans, Louisiana.

[1452] Telegram dated January 30, 1961, Harry M. England to Shaw, International Trade Mart Records, Tulane University, New Orleans, Louisiana.

[1453] Letter dated April 18, 1961, Edwin A. Leland, Jr. to Shaw, International Trade Mart Records, Tulane University, New Orleans, Louisiana.

[1454] Letter dated July 7, 1961, Neville Levy to Shaw, International Trade Mart Records, Tulane University, New Orleans, Louisiana.

[1455] Telegram dated July 11, 1961, Chep Morrison to William Zetzmann, International Trade Mart Records, Tulane University, New Orleans, Louisiana.

[1456] Telegram dated July 15, 1961, Jesse Core to various newsmen, International Trade Mart Records, Tulane University, New Orleans, Louisiana.

[1457] Letter dated September 9, 1961, Cecil M. Shilstone to Shaw, International Trade Mart Records, Tulane University, New Orleans, Louisiana.

[1458] Telegram dated September 19, 1961, Victor Schiro to Shaw, International Trade Mart Records, Tulane University, New Orleans, Louisiana.

[1459] Letter dated October 16, 1961, Basement Book Shop to Shaw, International Trade Mart Records, Tulane University, New Orleans, Louisiana.

[1460] Letter dated December 12, 1961, Alton Ochsner to Shaw, International Trade Mart Records, Tulane University, New Orleans, Louisiana.

[1461] Letter dated December 17, 1961, Horace Renegar to Shaw, International Trade Mart Records, Tulane University, New Orleans, Louisiana.

[1462] Telegram dated November 2, 1961, Shaw to William Spratling, International Trade Mart Records, Tulane University, New Orleans, Louisiana.

[1463] Letter dated February 14, 1961, Bess C. Noble to Shaw, International Trade Mart Records, Tulane University, New Orleans, Louisiana.

[1464] Letter dated October 3, 1961, Dorothy Garnier to Shaw, International Trade Mart Records, Tulane University, New Orleans, Louisiana.

[1465] Letter dated October 6, 1961, Bess C. Noble to Shaw, International Trade Mart Records, Tulane University, New Orleans, Louisiana.

[1466] Letter dated September 27, 1961, Harnett Kane to Shaw, International Trade Mart Records, Tulane University, New Orleans, Louisiana.

[1467] Letter dated August 17, 1961, Shaw in response to prospective tenant, International Trade Mart Records, Tulane University, New Orleans, Louisiana.

[1468] Letter dated August 21, 1961, Shaw to Robert Holmes, Governor of Oregon, International Trade Mart Records, Tulane University, New Orleans, Louisiana.

[1469] Letter dated October 9, 1961, Ray Curtis to Shaw, International Trade Mart Records, Tulane University, New Orleans, Louisiana.

[1470] Letter dated October 13, 1961, Victor H. Schiro to Shaw, International Trade Mart Records, Tulane University, New Orleans, Louisiana.

[1471] Note from Shaw to Bob Best, undated, International Trade Mart Records, Tulane University, New Orleans, Louisiana.

[1472] Minutes to Executive Committee meeting, August 14, 1961, International Trade Mart, International Trade Mart Records, Tulane University, New Orleans, Louisiana.

[1473] Promotional letter from WWL Radio dated August 9, 1961, International Trade Mart Records, Tulane University, New Orleans, Louisiana.

[1474] Letter dated September 26, 1961, Bess C. Noble to Shaw, International Trade Mart Records, Tulane University, New Orleans, Louisiana.

[1475] Memo dated October 18, 1961, Maurice Barr to Shaw, International Trade Mart Records, Tulane University, New Orleans, Louisiana.

[1476] Letter dated October 7, 1961, Jimmy Fitzmorris to Shaw, International Trade Mart Records, Tulane University, New Orleans, Louisiana.

[1477] Letter dated October 17, 1961, Charles G. Holle to Shaw, International Trade Mart Records, Tulane University, New Orleans, Louisiana.

[1478] Minutes to Executive Committee meeting, October 26, 1961, International Trade Mart, International Trade Mart Records, Tulane University, New Orleans, Louisiana.

[1479] Letter dated November 5, 1961, Glenn D. Stotz to J.B. Dauenhauer, International Trade Mart Records, Tulane University, New Orleans, Louisiana.

[1480] Letter dated November 15, 1961, John W. Goemans to Shaw, International Trade Mart Records, Tulane University, New Orleans, Louisiana.

[1481] Minutes to Executive Committee meeting, December 15, 1961, International Trade Mart, International Trade Mart Records, Tulane University, New Orleans, Louisiana.

[1482] Clay Shaw testimony of December 11, 1961, before Joint Economic Subcommittee of Congress, International Trade Mart Records, Tulane University, New Orleans, Louisiana.

[1483] 1961 Federal Income Tax Return for Shaw, Donated Papers of Clay Shaw, National Archives, College Park, Maryland.

[1484] 1962 Federal Income Tax Return for Shaw, Donated Papers of Clay Shaw, National Archives, College Park, Maryland.

[1485] 1963 Federal Income Tax Return for Shaw, Donated Papers of Clay Shaw, National Archives, College Park, Maryland.

[1486] Letter dated January 19, 1962, Shaw in response to inquiry, International Trade Mart Records, Tulane University, New Orleans, Louisiana.

[1487] Letter dated May 7, 1962, Frank M. Patty to Shaw, International Trade Mart Records, Tulane University, New Orleans, Louisiana.

[1488] Letter dated January 10, 1962, Shaw to William Zetzmann and Pendleton Lehde, International Trade Mart Records, Tulane University, New Orleans, Louisiana.

[1489] Memo dated February 16, 1962, Mario Bermúdez to Shaw, International Trade Mart Records, Tulane University, New Orleans, Louisiana.

[1490] Letter dated February 8, 1962, Thank you card to International Trade Mart from Jeff and Jo Hug, International Trade Mart Records, Tulane University, New Orleans, Louisiana.

[1491] Letter dated March 28, 1962, Paul A. Fabry to Shaw, International Trade Mart Records, Tulane University, New Orleans, Louisiana.

[1492] Letter dated March 28, 1962, Rodolphe Huart to Shaw, International Trade Mart Records, Tulane University, New Orleans, Louisiana.

[1493] Letter dated April 2, 1962, Shaw to Rodolphe Huart, International Trade Mart Records, Tulane University, New Orleans, Louisiana.

[1494] Report of William Zetzmann to Annual Meeting of International Trade Mart, March 8, 1962, International Trade Mart Records, Tulane University, New Orleans, Louisiana.

[1495] Minutes to Executive Committee meeting, March 19, 1962, International Trade Mart, International Trade Mart Records, Tulane University, New Orleans, Louisiana.

[1496] Press Release dated April 20, 1962, announcing death of William Zetzmann, International Trade Mart Records, Tulane University, New Orleans, Louisiana.

[1497] Letter dated April 2, 1962, Shaw to New Orleans Traffic and Transportation Board, International Trade Mart Records, Tulane University, New Orleans, Louisiana.

[1498] Letter dated April 10, 1962, Vernon Cook to Shaw, International Trade Mart Records, Tulane University, New Orleans, Louisiana.

[1499] Letter dated April 30, 1962, Victor Schiro to Shaw, International Trade Mart Records, Tulane University, New Orleans, Louisiana.

[1500] Minutes to meeting of Board of Directors, April 30, 1962, International Trade Mart, International Trade Mart Records, Tulane University, New Orleans, Louisiana.

[1501] Letter dated April 30, 1962, Congressman Hale Boggs to Shaw, Donated Papers of Clay Shaw, National Archives, College Park, Maryland.

[1502] Letter dated April 30, 1962, Label A. Katz to Shaw, Donated Papers of Clay Shaw, National Archives, College Park, Maryland.

[1503] Letter dated April 25, 1962, Lawrence H. Stevens to Shaw, Donated Papers of Clay Shaw, National Archives, College Park, Maryland.

[1504] Letter dated December 12, 1961, Bess Noble to Shaw, International Trade Mart Records, Tulane University, New Orleans, Louisiana.

[1505] Letter dated January 2, 1962, Shaw to Bess Noble, International Trade Mart Records, Tulane University, New Orleans, Louisiana.

[1506] Letter dated May 8, 1962, Congressman Hale Boggs to Shaw, International Trade Mart Records, Tulane University, New Orleans, Louisiana.

[1507] Interview with Denis Barry by author, February 26, 2008.

[1508] Interview with Denis Barry by author, February 26, 2008.

[1509] Letter dated May 8, 1962, Shaw to Alton Ochsner, International Trade Mart Records, Tulane University, New Orleans, Louisiana.

[1510] Letter dated May 27, 1962, Shaw in response to prospective tenant, International Trade Mart Records, Tulane University, New Orleans, Louisiana.

[1511] Letter dated May 25, 1962, Neville Levy to Shaw, International Trade Mart Records, Tulane University, New Orleans, Louisiana.

[1512] Minutes to meeting of Board of Directors, June 21, 1962, Foreign Relations Association of New Orleans, International Trade Mart Records, Tulane University, New Orleans, Louisiana.

[1513] Letter dated June 8, 1962, Shaw to Chep Morrison, International Trade Mart Records, Tulane University, New Orleans, Louisiana.

[1514] Letter dated June 19, 1962, Shaw to Winston Lill, International Trade Mart Records, Tulane University, New Orleans, Louisiana.

[1515] Minutes to Executive Committee meeting, June 15, 1962, International Trade Mart, International Trade Mart Records, Tulane University, New Orleans, Louisiana.

[1516] Letter dated June 28, 1962, consul of Mexico in New Orleans to Shaw, International Trade Mart Records, Tulane University, New Orleans, Louisiana.

[1517] Letter dated July 2, 1962, Shaw to consul of Mexico in New Orleans, International Trade Mart Records, Tulane University, New Orleans, Louisiana.

[1518] Letter dated August 2, 1962, Shaw to Dr. J.A. Diaz, International Trade Mart Records, Tulane University, New Orleans, Louisiana.

[1519] Minutes to meeting of Board of Directors, August 1, 1962, International Trade Mart, International Trade Mart Records, Tulane University, New Orleans, Louisiana.

[1520] Letter dated September 14, 1962, Richard M. Boesen to Shaw, International Trade Mart Records, Tulane University, New Orleans, Louisiana.

[1521] Letter dated October 31, 1962, Paul Fabry to Shaw, International Trade Mart Records, Tulane University, New Orleans, Louisiana.

[1522] Letter dated October 18, 1962, Guy Banister nee D. Roberts to Shaw, International Trade Mart Records, Tulane University, New Orleans, Louisiana.

[1523] Letter dated October 19, 1962, Shaw to Guy Banister Associates, Inc., International Trade Mart Records, Tulane University, New Orleans, Louisiana.

[1524] Letter dated October 9, 1962, Clarence Streit to Shaw, International Trade Mart Records, Tulane University, New Orleans, Louisiana.

[1525] Letter dated November 23, 1962, George Chaplin to Shaw, International Trade Mart Records, Tulane University, New Orleans, Louisiana.

[1526] Letter dated December 13, 1962, Shaw to Chep Morrison, International Trade Mart Records, Tulane University, New Orleans, Louisiana.

[1527] Letter dated January 2, 1963, Chep Morrison to Shaw, International Trade Mart Records, Tulane University, New Orleans, Louisiana.

[1528] Postcard dated March 20, 1963, Chep Morrison to Shaw, Donated Papers of Clay Shaw, National Archives, College Park, Maryland.

[1529] Letter dated February 8, 1963, William G. Zetzmann, Jr. to Shaw, International Trade Mart Records, Tulane University, New Orleans, Louisiana.

[1530] Letter dated April 12, 1962, Jesse Core to Lloyd Cobb, International Trade Mart Records, Tulane University, New Orleans, Louisiana.

[1531] Letter dated January 12, 1963, Lloyd Cobb to Lawrence A. Molony, International Trade Mart Records, Tulane University, New Orleans, Louisiana.

[1532] Letter dated January 24, 1963, Lawrence A. Molony to Lloyd Cobb, International Trade Mart Records, Tulane University, New Orleans, Louisiana.

[1533] Letter dated January 31, 1963, Lloyd Cobb to Lawrence A. Molony, International Trade Mart Records, Tulane University, New Orleans, Louisiana.

[1534] Letter dated January 24, 1963, Shaw to Lawrence A. Molony, International Trade Mart Records, Tulane University, New Orleans, Louisiana.

[1535] Letter dated January 28, 1963, Joseph Murphy, Regional Director, National Association of Christians and Jews, to Shaw, International Trade Mart Records, Tulane University, New Orleans, Louisiana.

[1536] Letter dated February 19, 1963, Francis Doyle to Shaw, Donated Papers of Clay Shaw, National Archives, College Park, Maryland.

[1537] Letter dated April 4, 1963, Shaw to Bruce Mitchell, Donated Papers of Clay Shaw, National Archives, College Park, Maryland.

[1538] Letter dated April 1963, Southern Baptist Hospital to Shaw, Donated Papers of Clay Shaw, National Archives, College Park, Maryland.

[1539] Letter dated April 18, 1963, Mrs. Brett Howard to Shaw, Donated Papers of Clay Shaw, National Archives, College Park, Maryland.

[1540] Letter dated March 28, 1963, George Healy to Lawrence Molony, International Trade Mart Records, Tulane University, New Orleans, Louisiana.

[1541] Letter dated April 9, 1963, Lawrence Molony to Lloyd Cobb, International Trade Mart Records, Tulane University, New Orleans, Louisiana.

[1542] Letter dated March 6, 1963, George Healy to Lawrence Molony, International Trade Mart Records, Tulane University, New Orleans, Louisiana.

[1543] Letter dated April 4, 1963, Marge Henderson to Shaw, International Trade Mart Records, Tulane University, New Orleans, Louisiana.

[1544] Letter dated April 18, 1963, Shaw to Marge Henderson, International Trade Mart Records, Tulane University, New Orleans, Louisiana.

[1545] Letter dated April 12, 1963, E. Davis McCutchon to Shaw, International Trade Mart Records, Tulane University, New Orleans, Louisiana.

[1546] Letter dated September 26, 1963, E. Davis McCutchon to Shaw, International Trade Mart Records, Tulane University, New Orleans, Louisiana.

[1547] Letter dated May 7, 1963, Shaw to John Cieutat, International Trade Mart Records, Tulane University, New Orleans, Louisiana.

[1548] Letter dated May 28, 1963, Shaw to a German industrial publication, International Trade Mart Records, Tulane University, New Orleans, Louisiana.

[1549] Letter dated May 9, 1963, Mrs. Edwin Blum to Shaw, Donated Papers of Clay Shaw, National Archives, College Park, Maryland.

[1550] Minutes to Executive Committee meeting, May 16, 1963, International Trade Mart, International Trade Mart Records, Tulane University, New Orleans, Louisiana.

[1551] New clipping regarding Mario Bermúdez's resignation as Director of International Relations for International House, International Trade Mart Records, Tulane University, New Orleans, Louisiana.

[1552] Letter dated May 31, 1963, Lawrence Molony to Dr. Alton Ochsner, International Trade Mart Records, Tulane University, New Orleans, Louisiana.

[1553] Report dated July 19, 1961 concerning International House's Department of International Relations, Shaw to Maurice F. Barr, International Trade Mart Records, Tulane University, New Orleans, Louisiana.

[1554] Telegram dated May 17, 1963, Paul Fabry to Alberto Fowler, International Trade Mart Records, Tulane University, New Orleans, Louisiana.

[1555] Minutes to Executive Committee meeting, June 7, 1963, International Trade Mart, International Trade Mart Records, Tulane University, New Orleans, Louisiana.

[1556] Letter dated June 10, 1963, William Hague to Shaw, Donated Papers of Clay Shaw, National Archives, College Park, Maryland.

[1557] Letter dated July 3, 1963, Shaw to Vincent Furno, International Trade Mart Records, Tulane University, New Orleans, Louisiana.

[1558] Letter dated September 6, 1963, Edward Durell Stone to Shaw, International Trade Mart Records, Tulane University, New Orleans, Louisiana.

[1559] Telegram dated March 7, 1963, Shaw to George Chaplin, International Trade Mart Records, Tulane University, New Orleans, Louisiana.

[1560] Spring Hill College website.

[1561] Letter dated September 20, 1963, Shaw to Daughters of American Revolution in Amite, Louisiana, International Trade Mart Records, Tulane University, New Orleans, Louisiana.

[1562] Letter dated February 14, 1963, Richard Swenson to Shaw, International Trade Mart Records, Tulane University, New Orleans, Louisiana.

[1563] Postcard dated August 26, 1963, John Kamas to Shaw, International Trade Mart Records, Tulane University, New Orleans, Louisiana.

[1564] Letter dated July 30, 1963, Shaw to WWL-TV, International Trade Mart Records, Tulane University, New Orleans, Louisiana.

[1565] Letter dated October 17, 1963, Shaw to Mrs. Edgar B. Stern, International Trade Mart Records, Tulane University, New Orleans, Louisiana.

[1566] Minutes to meeting of Board of Directors, August 2, 1963, International Trade Mart, International Trade Mart Records, Tulane University, New Orleans, Louisiana.

[1567] Letter dated August 8, 1963, Shaw to William Spratling, Donated Papers of Clay Shaw, National Archives, College Park, Maryland.

[1568] Letter dated August 12, 1963, Frank Hemenway to Shaw, Donated Papers of Clay Shaw, National Archives, College Park, Maryland.

[1569] Minutes to Executive Committee meeting, August 20, 1963, International Trade Mart, International Trade Mart Records, Tulane University, New Orleans, Louisiana.

[1570] Letter dated August 19, 1963, John Wray Young to Shaw, Donated Papers of Clay Shaw, National Archives, College Park, Maryland.

[1571] Letter dated August 23, 1963, Hal Ross Yockey to Shaw, International Trade Mart Records, Tulane University, New Orleans, Louisiana.

[1572] Letter dated September 9, 1963, Shaw to Mr. and Mrs. Alfred Moran, Donated Papers of Clay Shaw, National Archives, College Park, Maryland.

[1573] Letter dated September 3, 1963, Shaw to Ruben M. Gaxiola, Donated Papers of Clay Shaw, National Archives, College Park, Maryland.

[1574] Letter dated September 26, 1963, Shaw letter of recommendation for Andrew Given Tobias Moore, II for admission to bar in Delaware, International Trade Mart Records, Tulane University, New Orleans, Louisiana.

[1575] Letter dated May 10, 1963, William Wells to Shaw, International Trade Mart Records, Tulane University, New Orleans, Louisiana.

[1576] Letter dated September 11, 1963, William R. Wells to Shaw, International Trade Mart Records, Tulane University, New Orleans, Louisiana.

[1577] Letter dated September 18, 1963, Goldie Moore to Portland, Oregon Chamber of Commerce, International Trade Mart Records, Tulane University, New Orleans, Louisiana.

[1578] *Harbor News*, October 1963, International Trade Mart Records, Tulane University, New Orleans, Louisiana.

[1579] Brochure for Fifth Annual Columbia Basin Export-Import Conference, International Trade Mart Records, Tulane University, New Orleans, Louisiana.

[1580] Letter dated November 20, 1963, David B. Porter to Goldie Moore, International Trade Mart Records, Tulane University, New Orleans, Louisiana.

[1581] Letter dated November 13, 1963, Shaw to William R. Wells, International Trade Mart Records, Tulane University, New Orleans, Louisiana.

[1582] Letter dated July 18, 1963, Fred Vanderhurst to Shaw, International Trade Mart Records, Tulane University, New Orleans, Louisiana.

[1583] Letter dated July 26, 1963, Shaw to Fred B. Vanderhurst, International Trade Mart Records, Tulane University, New Orleans, Louisiana.

[1584] Letter dated November 4, 1963, Shaw to Theodore Bruinsma, International Trade Mart Records, Tulane University, New Orleans, Louisiana.

[1585] Telegram dated October 14, 1963, Lloyd Cobb to numerous individuals, International Trade Mart Records, Tulane University, New Orleans, Louisiana.

[1586] Telegram dated October 15, 1963, J. Ronald Hanover to Shaw, International Trade Mart Records, Tulane University, New Orleans, Louisiana.

[1587] Letter dated October 19, 1963, W.J. Ford, Jr. to Shaw, International Trade Mart Records, Tulane University, New Orleans, Louisiana.

[1588] Letter dated October 24, 1963, Shaw to W.J. Ford, Jr., International Trade Mart Records, Tulane University, New Orleans, Louisiana.

[1589] "Proposed Organizational and Operational Plan for The New International Trade Mart," undated, no author indicated, but probably early 1960s, International Trade Mart Records, Tulane University, New Orleans, Louisiana.

[1590] Letter dated October 24, 1963, Shaw to John Oulliber, International Trade Mart Records, Tulane University, New Orleans, Louisiana.

[1591] Letter dated October 24, 1963, Shaw to Edward Durell Stone, International Trade Mart Records, Tulane University, New Orleans, Louisiana.

[1592] Letter dated October 28, 1963, Shaw to Martha Ann Samuel, Donated Papers of Clay Shaw, National Archives, College Park, Maryland.

[1593] Letter dated November 13, 1963, Shaw to Monroe Sullivan, International Trade Mart Records, Tulane University, New Orleans, Louisiana.

[1594] Telegram dated November 13, 1963, Monroe Sullivan to Shaw, International Trade Mart Records, Tulane University, New Orleans, Louisiana.

[1595] Interview with James Dondson by author, May 25, 2006.

[1596] Interview with James Dondson by author, May 25, 2006.

[1597] Portion of copy of FBI record on Edward Stewart Suggs, Donated Papers of Edward Wegmann, National Archives, College Park, Maryland.

[1598] Letter dated April 19, 1967, Jack Martin to Representative Hale Boggs, Donated Papers of Edward Wegmann, National Archives, College Park, Maryland.

[1599] Letter dated April 19, 1967, Jack Martin to Senator Russell Long, Donated Papers of Edward Wegmann, National Archives, College Park, Maryland.

[1600] Memo dated August 17, 1967, Andrew Sciambra to Jim Garrison, Papers Donated by Lyon Garrison, National Archives, College Park, Maryland.

[1601] Police report dated November 25, 1963 related to Guy Banister beating of Jack Martin, Donated Papers of Edward Wegmann, National Archives, College Park, Maryland.

[1602] Memo dated October 28, 1968, Andrew Sciambra to Jim Garrison, Files Received from Harry Connick, National Archives, College Park, Maryland.

[1603] Internal Metropolitan Crime Commission report dated May 3, 1962 by Aaron Kohn, Records of the New Orleans Metropolitan Crime Commission, National Archives, College Park, Maryland.

[1604] Memo dated February 15, 1967, William Gurvich to Jim Garrison, Papers Donated by Lyon Garrison, National Archives, College Park, Maryland.

[1605] Internal Metropolitan Crime Commission report dated July 11, 1960 by Aaron Kohn, Records of the New Orleans Metropolitan Crime Commission, National Archives, College Park, Maryland.

[1606] Memo dated March 6, 1967, Record Group 65, FBI Files, JFK Assassination Collection, National Archives, College Park, Maryland.

[1607] Internal Metropolitan Crime Commission report dated November 25, 1963 by Aaron Kohn, Records of the New Orleans Metropolitan Crime Commission, National Archives, College Park, Maryland.

[1608] FBI memo dated November 30, 1963, Record Group 263, Records of the Central Intelligence Agency, Personality File on Lee Harvey Oswald, JFK Assassination Collection, National Archives, College Park, Maryland.

[1609] Memo dated October 14, 1968, Andrew Sciambra to Jim Garrison, Files Received from Harry Connick, National Archives, College Park, Maryland.

[1610] FBI memo dated December 9, 1963, Record Group 65, FBI Files, JFK Assassination Collection, National Archives, College Park, Maryland.

[1611] Analysis of Castro speech to Havana University, November 27, 1963, CIA Miscellaneous Files, JFK Assassination Collection, National Archives, College Park, Maryland.

[1612] Letter dated November 26, 1963, Ruben M. Gaxiola to Shaw, International Trade Mart Records, Tulane University, New Orleans, Louisiana.

[1613] Letter dated December 12, 1963, Shaw to Ruben M. Gaxiola, International Trade Mart Records, Tulane University, New Orleans, Louisiana.

[1614] Letter dated December 4, 1963, Shaw to William R. Wells, International Trade Mart Records, Tulane University, New Orleans, Louisiana.

[1615] Letter dated December 2, 1963, Marion C. Kretsinger to Shaw, International Trade Mart Records, Tulane University, New Orleans, Louisiana.

[1616] Letter dated December 3, 1963, Joseph W. Simon, Jr. to Shaw, International Trade Mart Records, Tulane University, New Orleans, Louisiana.

[1617] Letter dated December 12, 1963, Shaw to Fred B. Vanderhurst, International Trade Mart Records, Tulane University, New Orleans, Louisiana.

[1618] Letter dated December 12, 1963, Shaw to J. Monroe Sullivan, International Trade Mart Records, Tulane University, New Orleans, Louisiana.

[1619] Letter dated November 26, 1963, J.B. Dauenhauer to M.J. Gruber, International Trade Mart Records, Tulane University, New Orleans, Louisiana.

[1620] Letter dated December 28, 1963, Eberhard P. Deutsch to Shaw, Donated Papers of Clay Shaw, National Archives, College Park, Maryland.

[1621] Letter dated December 30, 1963, Seymour Weiss to Shaw, Donated Papers of Clay Shaw, National Archives, College Park, Maryland.

[1622] E-mail dated January 29, 2011, Faye Hogan to author.

[1623] Letter dated January 29, 1964, Don Nay to Shaw, Donated Papers of Clay Shaw, National Archives, College Park, Maryland.

[1624] Letter dated February 18, 1964, Shaw to Don Nay, Donated Papers of Clay Shaw, National Archives, College Park, Maryland.

[1625] See New Orleans City Directory for 1964, Tulane University, New Orleans, Louisiana.

[1626] Letter dated January 16, 1964, Pension and Group Consultants to Shaw, International Trade Mart Records, Tulane University, New Orleans, Louisiana.

[1627] Letter dated January 15, 1964, Paul Fabry to Shaw, International Trade Mart Records, Tulane University, New Orleans, Louisiana.

[1628] Letter dated February 19, 1964, Shaw in response to inquiry, International Trade Mart Records, Tulane University, New Orleans, Louisiana.

[1629] Letter dated February 24, 1964, J.B. Dauenhauer in response to inquiry, International Trade Mart Records, Tulane University, New Orleans, Louisiana.

[1630] Minutes to Executive Committee meeting, January 8, 1964, International Trade Mart, International Trade Mart Records, Tulane University, New Orleans, Louisiana.

[1631] Letter dated February 5, 1964, Willard E. Robertson to Lloyd Cobb, International Trade Mart Records, Tulane University, New Orleans, Louisiana.

[1632] Minutes to Executive Committee meeting, February 13, 1964, International Trade Mart, International Trade Mart Records, Tulane University, New Orleans, Louisiana.

[1633] Minutes to Executive Committee meeting, February 26, 1964, International Trade Mart, International Trade Mart Records, Tulane University, New Orleans, Louisiana.

[1634] Telegram dated March 6, 1964, Lloyd Cobb to 82 individuals, International Trade Mart Records, Tulane University, New Orleans, Louisiana.

[1635] Letter dated March 20, 1964, Lloyd Cobb to Harry Bloomfield, International Trade Mart Records, Tulane University, New Orleans, Louisiana.

[1636] Minutes to meeting of Board of Directors, March 25, 1964, International Trade Mart, International Trade Mart Records, Tulane University, New Orleans, Louisiana.

[1637] Letter dated April 8, 1964, Joseph P. Murphy to Leo Willette of WWL-TV, International Trade Mart Records, Tulane University, New Orleans, Louisiana.

[1638] Minutes to Executive Committee meeting, April 29, 1964, International Trade Mart, International Trade Mart Records, Tulane University, New Orleans, Louisiana.

[1639] Letter dated April 29, 1964, Charles H. Liner, Jr. to Shaw, International Trade Mart Records, Tulane University, New Orleans, Louisiana.

[1640] Letter dated May 5, 1964, Siegfried B. Christensen to Shaw, International Trade Mart Records, Tulane University, New Orleans, Louisiana.

[1641] Letter dated May 14, 1964, Isador Lazarus to Lloyd Cobb, International Trade Mart Records, Tulane University, New Orleans, Louisiana.

[1642] Letter dated May 22, 1964, Edward Wegmann to Shaw and Marilyn Tate, Donated Papers of Clay Shaw, National Archives, College Park, Maryland.

[1643] Letter dated September 21, 1964, Edward Wegmann to Ray Liuzza, Donated Papers of Clay Shaw, National Archives, College Park, Maryland.

[1644] Minutes to Executive Committee meeting, May 21, 1964, International Trade Mart, International Trade Mart Records, Tulane University, New Orleans, Louisiana.

[1645] Memo dated May 21, 1964, Shaw to Executive Committee, with handwritten note, International Trade Mart Records, Tulane University, New Orleans, Louisiana.

[1646] Letter dated May 31, 1964, Barbara D. Corbin to Shaw, International Trade Mart Records, Tulane University, New Orleans, Louisiana.

[1647] Minutes to Executive Committee meeting, May 27, 1964, International Trade Mart, International Trade Mart Records, Tulane University, New Orleans, Louisiana.

[1648] Memo dated June 2, 1964, Shaw to J.B. Dauenhauer, International Trade Mart Records, Tulane University, New Orleans, Louisiana.

[1649] Letter dated June 4, 1964, Shaw to Edward Durell Stone, International Trade Mart Records, Tulane University, New Orleans, Louisiana.

[1650] Minutes to Executive Committee meeting, June 3, 1964, International Trade Mart, International Trade Mart Records, Tulane University, New Orleans, Louisiana.

[1651] Letter dated June 18, 1964, Sales and Marketing Executives-International to Shaw, International Trade Mart Records, Tulane University, New Orleans, Louisiana.

[1652] Minutes to Executive Committee meeting, June 24, 1964, International Trade Mart, International Trade Mart Records, Tulane University, New Orleans, Louisiana.

[1653] Letter dated July 22, 1964, Shaw to Charles Nutter, International Trade Mart Records, Tulane University, New Orleans, Louisiana.

[1654] Notice of luncheon seminar dated November 20, 1964, Foreign Relations Association, International Trade Mart Records, Tulane University, New Orleans, Louisiana.

[1655] Letter dated September 15, 1964, Charles H. Liner, Jr. to Shaw, International Trade Mart Records, Tulane University, New Orleans, Louisiana.

[1656] Minutes to Executive Committee meeting, July 8, 1964, International Trade Mart, International Trade Mart Records, Tulane University, New Orleans, Louisiana.

[1657] Letter dated July 6, 1964, Paul Fabry to Shaw, International Trade Mart Records, Tulane University, New Orleans, Louisiana.

[1658] Letter dated July 20, 1964, Camilla Mays Frank to Shaw, International Trade Mart Records, Tulane University, New Orleans, Louisiana.

[1659] Letter dated July 31, 1964, C. Dewey Crowder, Jr. to Shaw, International Trade Mart Records, Tulane University, New Orleans, Louisiana.

[1660] Letter dated August 6, 1964, Glenn Weekley to Shaw, International Trade Mart Records, Tulane University, New Orleans, Louisiana.

[1661] Letter dated August 10, 1964, Willard E. Robertson to Shaw, International Trade Mart Records, Tulane University, New Orleans, Louisiana.

[1662] Announcement of dedication of Volkswagen Distributor executive offices, with note of Shaw acceptance, International Trade Mart Records, Tulane University, New Orleans, Louisiana.

[1663] Minutes to Executive Committee meeting, August 12, 1964, International Trade Mart, International Trade Mart Records, Tulane University, New Orleans, Louisiana.

[1664] Minutes to Executive Committee meeting, August 27, 1964, International Trade Mart, International Trade Mart Records, Tulane University, New Orleans, Louisiana.

[1665] Interview with George Dureau by author, March 29, 2007.

[1666] Memo dated May 27, 1964, George E. Maddocks to Robert D. Johnson, Record Group 59, General Records of the Department of State, JFK Assassination Collection, National Archives, College Park, Maryland.

[1667] Minutes to Executive Committee meeting, September 21, 1964, International Trade Mart, International Trade Mart Records, Tulane University, New Orleans, Louisiana.

[1668] Minutes to Executive Committee meeting, October 2, 1964, International Trade Mart, International Trade Mart Records, Tulane University, New Orleans, Louisiana.

[1669] Letter dated October 30, 1964, David M. Kleck to Shaw, International Trade Mart Records, Tulane University, New Orleans, Louisiana.

[1670] Minutes to Executive Committee meeting, October 28, 1964, International Trade Mart, International Trade Mart Records, Tulane University, New Orleans, Louisiana.

[1671] Telegram dated November 17, 1964, Nathaniel Jacobs to Shaw, International Trade Mart Records, Tulane University, New Orleans, Louisiana.

[1672] Letter dated November 11, 1964, Paul Fabry to Shaw, International Trade Mart Records, Tulane University, New Orleans, Louisiana.

[1673] Letter dated August 15, 1964, Flora Field to Sydney Field, Flora Field Collection, Newcomb College, New Orleans, Louisiana.

[1674] Letter dated November 28, 1964, Flora Field to Sydney Field, Flora Field Collection, Newcomb College, New Orleans, Louisiana.

[1675] Letter dated approximately February 6, 1965, Flora Field to Sydney Field, Flora Field Collection, Newcomb College, New Orleans, Louisiana.

[1676] Letter dated December 10, 1964, William Bailey Smith to Shaw, International Trade Mart Records, Tulane University, New Orleans, Louisiana.

[1677] Minutes to Executive Committee meeting, December 8, 1964, International Trade Mart, International Trade Mart Records, Tulane University, New Orleans, Louisiana.

[1678] Letter dated May 11, 1964, Shaw to consul of Mexico in New Orleans, International Trade Mart Records, Tulane University, New Orleans, Louisiana.

[1679] Letter dated December 14, 1964, Shaw to consul of Japan in New Orleans, International Trade Mart Records, Tulane University, New Orleans, Louisiana.

[1680] Income Statement for year ended December 31, 1964, International Trade Mart Records, Tulane University, New Orleans, Louisiana.

[1681] Minutes to Executive Committee meeting, January 7, 1965, International Trade Mart, International Trade Mart Records, Tulane University, New Orleans, Louisiana.

[1682] E-mail dated July 14, 2006, Paul Fabry to Author.

[1683] "History of the International Trade Mart," a report prepared prior to projected opening date of October 1, 1965, International Trade Mart Records, Tulane University, New Orleans, Louisiana.

[1684] Letter dated February 11, 1965, Shaw to Gary A. Bolding, International Trade Mart Records, Tulane University, New Orleans, Louisiana.

[1685] E-mail dated January 19, 2010, Gary Bolding to Author.

[1686] E-mail dated January 21, 2010, Gary Bolding to Author.

[1687] Minutes of Executive Committee meeting, February 25, 1965, International Trade Mart, International Trade Mart Records, Tulane University, New Orleans, Louisiana.

[1688] Letter dated May 11, 1965, Alton Ochsner to Shaw, Alton Ochsner Papers, Historic New Orleans Collection, New Orleans, Louisiana.

[1689] Letter dated February 8, 1965, Nicholas Katzenbach to Chief Postal Inspector Henry B. Montague, Records of the Post Office Department, JFK Assassination Collection, National Archives, College Park, Maryland.

[1690] Minutes to Executive Committee meeting, February 25, 1965, International Trade Mart, International Trade Mart Records, Tulane University, New Orleans, Louisiana.

[1691] Minutes to Executive Committee meeting, March 10, 1965, International Trade Mart, International Trade Mart Records, Tulane University, New Orleans, Louisiana.

[1692] Minutes to Annual Meeting of Contributors and Debenture Members, International Trade Mart, International Trade Mart Records, Tulane University, New Orleans, Louisiana.

[1693] Letter dated March 17, 1965, Willard E. Robertson to Lloyd Cobb, International Trade Mart Records, Tulane University, New Orleans, Louisiana.

[1694] Letter dated March 15, 1965, Shaw to Willard E. Robertson, International Trade Mart Records, Tulane University, New Orleans, Louisiana.

[1695] Letter dated March 18, 1965, Shaw to Roland Dabson, International Trade Mart Records, Tulane University, New Orleans, Louisiana.

[1696] Letter dated April 1, 1965, Shaw to Lloyd Cobb, International Trade Mart Records, Tulane University, New Orleans, Louisiana.

[1697] Minutes to Executive Committee meeting, April 1, 1965, International Trade Mart, International Trade Mart Records, Tulane University, New Orleans, Louisiana.

[1698] Minutes to Executive Committee meeting, May 20, 1965, International Trade Mart, International Trade Mart Records, Tulane University, New Orleans, Louisiana.

[1699] Ledger covering the years 1951 to 1965 concerning properties owned by Shaw, Donated Papers of Clay Shaw, National Archives, College Park, Maryland.

[1700] Letter dated April 27, 1965, Shaw to Frances Parkinson Keyes, International Trade Mart Records, Tulane University, New Orleans, Louisiana.

[1701] Minutes to Executive Committee meeting, April 30, 1965, International Trade Mart, International Trade Mart Records, Tulane University, New Orleans, Louisiana.

[1702] Minutes to Executive Committee meeting, June 3, 1965, International Trade Mart, International Trade Mart Records, Tulane University, New Orleans, Louisiana.

[1703] Minutes to Executive Committee meeting, June 10, 1965, International Trade Mart, International Trade Mart Records, Tulane University, New Orleans, Louisiana.

[1704] Letter dated June 1, 1965, Shaw in response to inquiry, International Trade Mart Records, Tulane University, New Orleans, Louisiana.

[1705] Minutes to Executive Committee meeting, June 17, 1965, International Trade Mart, International Trade Mart Records, Tulane University, New Orleans, Louisiana.

[1706] Minutes to Board of Directors meeting, June 24, 1965, International Trade Mart, International Trade Mart Records, Tulane University, New Orleans, Louisiana.

[1707] Letter dated May 5, 1965, J. Taylor Rooks to Shaw, International Trade Mart Records, Tulane University, New Orleans, Louisiana.

[1708] Letter dated May 12, 1965, Shaw to Dorothy Garnier, International Trade Mart Records, Tulane University, New Orleans, Louisiana.

[1709] Letter dated May 10, 1965, Mrs. Connor Sanders Davis to Shaw, International Trade Mart Records, Tulane University, New Orleans, Louisiana.

[1710] Letter dated May 13, 1965, Shaw to Mrs. Connor Sanders Davis, International Trade Mart Records, Tulane University, New Orleans, Louisiana.

[1711] Letter dated August 13, 1965, Lloyd Cobb to T. Sterling Dunn, International Trade Mart Records, Tulane University, New Orleans, Louisiana.

[1712] Letter dated August 6, 1965, VISION magazine to Shaw, International Trade Mart Records, Tulane University, New Orleans, Louisiana.

[1713] Letter dated September 9, 1965, Shaw to members of Executive Committee of International Trade Mart, International Trade Mart Records, Tulane University, New Orleans, Louisiana.

[1714] Letter dated August 6, 1965, Shaw to Tom Zung, International Trade Mart Records, Tulane University, New Orleans, Louisiana.

[1715] Letter dated August 4, 1965, Shaw to Michael Mora, International Trade Mart Records, Tulane University, New Orleans, Louisiana.

[1716] Letter dated August 6, 1965, Shaw to Jack Sawyer, International Trade Mart Records, Tulane University, New Orleans, Louisiana.

[1717] Minutes to Executive Committee meeting, September 9, 1965, International Trade Mart, International Trade Mart Records, Tulane University, New Orleans, Louisiana.

[1718] Letter dated September 14, 1965, Shaw to Argyll Campbell, International Trade Mart Records, Tulane University, New Orleans, Louisiana.

[1719] Letter of Recommendation for Hollis Bridges dated October 4, 1965 by Shaw, International Trade Mart Records, Tulane University, New Orleans, Louisiana.

[1720] Letter of Recommendation for Darlyn Mercadal dated September 30, 1965 by Shaw, International Trade Mart Records, Tulane University, New Orleans, Louisiana.

[1721] Letter dated September 15, 1965, Bess Noble to Shaw, International Trade Mart Records, Tulane University, New Orleans, Louisiana.

[1722] Letter dated September 16, 1965, Shaw to Bess Noble, International Trade Mart Records, Tulane University, New Orleans, Louisiana.

[1723] Minutes to Executive Committee meeting, September 23, 1965, International Trade Mart, International Trade Mart Records, Tulane University, New Orleans, Louisiana.

1724 Letter dated September 17, 1965, Governor John McKeithen to Officers and Directors of the International Trade Mart, International Trade Mart Records, Tulane University, New Orleans, Louisiana.

1725 Letter dated October 5, 1965, Jack Gremillion to Shaw, International Trade Mart Records, Tulane University, New Orleans, Louisiana.

1726 Letter dated September 17, 1965, Seymour Weiss to Shaw, International Trade Mart Records, Tulane University, New Orleans, Louisiana.

1727 Letter dated July 13, 1965, Seymour Weiss to Shaw, International Trade Mart Records, Tulane University, New Orleans, Louisiana.

1728 Memo dated September 29, 1965, Beryl Donnath to Lloyd Cobb, International Trade Mart Records, Tulane University, New Orleans, Louisiana.

1729 Memo dated September 29, 1965, Beryl Donnath to Lloyd Cobb, International Trade Mart Records, Tulane University, New Orleans, Louisiana.

1730 Copy of Lloyd Cobb's remarks upon Shaw's retirement, in rough form, International Trade Mart Records, Tulane University, New Orleans, Louisiana.

1731 Article dated September 30, 1965, *Times-Picayune*, Donated Papers of Clay Shaw, National Archives, College Park, Maryland.

1732 Article in *ITM News*, June 1978, International Trade Mart Records, Tulane University, New Orleans, Louisiana.

1733 Letter dated October 4, 1965, Shaw to Dr. Ettore Scampicchio, International Trade Mart Records, Tulane University, New Orleans, Louisiana.

1734 Letter dated October 4, 1965, Shaw to Odette Reising, International Trade Mart Records, Tulane University, New Orleans, Louisiana.

1735 Letter dated October 4, 1965, Shaw to Larry Barry, International Trade Mart Records, Tulane University, New Orleans, Louisiana.

1736 Letter dated October 4, 1965, Shaw to James Coleman, International Trade Mart Records, Tulane University, New Orleans, Louisiana.

1737 Letter dated October 4, 1965, Shaw to New Orleans Athletic Club, Donated Papers of Clay Shaw, National Archives, College Park, Maryland.

1738 Letter dated October 4, 1965, Shaw to Hotel Majestic, Donated Papers of Clay Shaw, National Archives, College Park, Maryland.

1739 Letter dated October 10, 1965, Shaw to Dr. B.N. Addis, Donated Papers of Clay Shaw, National Archives, College Park, Maryland.

1740 Letter dated October 27, 1965, J.B. Dauenhauer to Young Men's Business Club of Greater New Orleans, International Trade Mart Records, Tulane University, New Orleans, Louisiana.

1741 Letter dated November 26, 1965, J.B. Dauenhauer in response to inquiry, International Trade Mart Records, Tulane University, New Orleans, Louisiana.

1742 Telegram dated November 25, 1965, Shaw to Jeff Biddison, Donated Papers of Clay Shaw, National Archives, College Park, Maryland.

1743 New Orleans police report dated December 3, 1965, regarding Charles Earl Daniels arrest, Donated Papers of Edward Wegmann, National Archives, College Park, Maryland.

1744 Minutes to Executive Committee meeting, December 9, 1965, International Trade Mart, International Trade Mart Records, Tulane University, New Orleans, Louisiana.

[1745] Christmas card, no year, but probably 1965, Shaw to Muriel Francis, Bultman Family Papers, Historic New Orleans Collection, New Orleans, Louisiana.

[1746] 1965 Federal Income Tax Return for Shaw, Donated Papers of Clay Shaw, National Archives, College Park, Maryland.

[1747] Letter dated June 5, 1978, Herbert E. Longenecker to Alberto Fowler, International Trade Mart Records, Tulane University, New Orleans, Louisiana.

[1748] Article in *New Orleans Business*, August 18-24, 1986, International Trade Mart Records, Tulane University, New Orleans, Louisiana.

[1749] Interview with Jesse Core by author, July 28, 1995.

[1750] Letter dated January 10, 1966, Shaw to Clara Huge, International Trade Mart Records, Tulane University, New Orleans, Louisiana.

[1751] Letter dated February 3, 1966, Erik Nielsen to Shaw, International Trade Mart Records, Tulane University, New Orleans, Louisiana.

[1752] Letter dated March 10, 1966, Lloyd Cobb to tenant, International Trade Mart Records, Tulane University, New Orleans, Louisiana.

[1753] Minutes of Executive Committee meeting, March 3, 1966, International Trade Mart, International Trade Mart Records, Tulane University, New Orleans, Louisiana.

[1754] Letter dated March 21, 1966, Goldie Moore to Carmen Anguis, International Trade Mart Records, Tulane University, New Orleans, Louisiana.

[1755] See New Orleans City Directory for 1966, Tulane University, New Orleans, Louisiana.

[1756] See purchase records for the airline ticket, Donated Papers of Clay Shaw, National Archives, College Park, Maryland.

[1757] Postcard in Donated Papers of Clay Shaw, National Archives, College Park, Maryland.

[1758] Letter dated March 24, 1966, Edward Wegmann to Shaw, Donated Papers of Clay Shaw, National Archives, College Park, Maryland.

[1759] Letter dated March 24, 1966, Edward Wegmann to Shaw, Donated Papers of Clay Shaw, National Archives, College Park, Maryland.

[1760] Minutes of Executive Committee meeting, March 31, 1966, International Trade Mart, International Trade Mart Records, Tulane University, New Orleans, Louisiana.

[1761] Minutes of Executive Committee meeting, May 26, 1966, International Trade Mart, International Trade Mart Records, Tulane University, New Orleans, Louisiana.

[1762] Letter dated June 16, 1966, Goldie Moore to National Bank of Commerce, International Trade Mart Records, Tulane University, New Orleans, Louisiana.

[1763] Note from Goldie Moore regarding purchase of steamship ticket, Donated Papers of Clay Shaw, National Archives, College Park, Maryland.

[1764] Letter dated March 7, 1966, Mario Bermúdez to widow of Alejandro Casona, Donated Papers of Clay Shaw, National Archives, College Park, Maryland.

[1765] Letter dated October 24, 1966, Beryl Donnath to Shaw, Donated Papers of Clay Shaw, National Archives, College Park, Maryland.

[1766] E-mail date June 3, 2011, Michael Snyder to author.

[1767] Article in unnamed Spanish newspaper, March 7, 1967, about Shaw's visit to Spain during summer 1966, Donated Papers of Edward Wegmann, National Archives, College Park, Maryland.

[1768] E-mail dated April 8, 2009, David Sogge to Author.

[1769] E-mail dated April 23, 2009, David Sogge to Author.

[1770] E-mail dated April 8, 2009, David Sogge to Author.

[1771] Letter dated August 12, 1966, Jeff Biddison to Shaw, Papers Donated by Lyon Garrison, National Archives, College Park, Maryland.

[1772] Letter dated October 13, 1966, Lloyd Cobb to Louis Wall, Jr., International Trade Mart Records, Tulane University, New Orleans, Louisiana.

[1773] Letter dated October 19, 1966, George V. Talbott to Lloyd Cobb, International Trade Mart Records, Tulane University, New Orleans, Louisiana.

[1774] Letter dated November 28, 1966, Delores to Shaw, Donated Papers of Clay Shaw, National Archives, College Park, Maryland.

[1775] Internal Metropolitan Crime Commission report dated December 9, 1971 by Aaron Kohn, Records of the New Orleans Metropolitan Crime Commission, National Archives, College Park, Maryland.

[1776] See undated Metropolitan Crime Commission report dealing with meeting between Jim Garrison, Chep Morrison, and Marc Antony, Records of the New Orleans Metropolitan Crime Commission, National Archives, College Park, Maryland.

[1777] Memo dated March 29, 1967 by Aaron Kohn, Records of the New Orleans Metropolitan Crime Commission, National Archives, College Park, Maryland.

[1778] Memo dated March 16, 1959, Aaron Kohn to Robert F. Kennedy, Records of the New Orleans Metropolitan Crime Commission, National Archives, College Park, Maryland.

[1779] Memo dated March 19, 1959, Aaron Kohn to Robert F. Kennedy, Records of the New Orleans Metropolitan Crime Commission, National Archives, College Park, Maryland.

[1780] Internal Metropolitan Crime Commission report dated March 10, 1958 by Aaron Kohn, Records of the New Orleans Metropolitan Crime Commission, National Archives, College Park, Maryland.

[1781] Congratulatory note dated April 12, 1962, Aaron Kohn to Jim Garrison, Records of the New Orleans Metropolitan Crime Commission, National Archives, College Park, Maryland.

[1782] Letter dated March 22, 1963, Aaron Kohn to Jim Garrison, Records of the New Orleans Metropolitan Crime Commission, National Archives, College Park, Maryland.

[1783] See report regarding first year of Garrison's tenure, Records of the New Orleans Metropolitan Crime Commission, National Archives, College Park, Maryland.

[1784] Letter dated July 2, 1962, Jim Garrison to Aaron Kohn, Records of the New Orleans Metropolitan Crime Commission, National Archives, College Park, Maryland.

[1785] Internal Metropolitan Crime Commission report dated May 31, 1962 by Aaron Kohn, Records of the New Orleans Metropolitan Crime Commission, National Archives, College Park, Maryland.

[1786] Internal Metropolitan Crime Commission report dated March 14, 1963 by Aaron Kohn, Records of the New Orleans Metropolitan Crime Commission, National Archives, College Park, Maryland.

[1787] Letter dated February 1, 1964, Jim Garrison to Aaron Kohn, Records of the New Orleans Metropolitan Crime Commission, National Archives, College Park, Maryland.

[1788] Letter dated February 4, 1964, Aaron Kohn to Jim Garrison, Records of the New Orleans Metropolitan Crime Commission, National Archives, College Park, Maryland.

[1789] Letter dated February 28, 1964, Jim Garrison to Aaron Kohn, Records of the New Orleans Metropolitan Crime Commission, National Archives, College Park, Maryland.

[1790] Letter dated June 7, 1963, Jim Garrison to Aaron Kohn, enclosing *Civic Review*, Records of the New Orleans Metropolitan Crime Commission, National Archives, College Park, Maryland.

[1791] Internal Metropolitan Crime Commission report dated September 3, 1964 by Aaron Kohn, Records of the New Orleans Metropolitan Crime Commission, National Archives, College Park, Maryland.

[1792] Transcript of interview of Raymond Comstock by Aaron Kohn, September 19, 1964, Records of the New Orleans Metropolitan Crime Commission, National Archives, College Park, Maryland.

[1793] Internal Metropolitan Crime Commission report dated November 9, 1965 by Aaron Kohn, Records of the New Orleans Metropolitan Crime Commission, National Archives, College Park, Maryland.

[1794] Letter dated August 26, 1966, Jim Garrison to Aaron Kohn, JFK Assassination Collection, New Orleans Public Library, New Orleans, Louisiana.

[1795] Memo dated November 27, 1966, Jim Garrison to Staff, JFK Assassination Collection, New Orleans Public Library, New Orleans, Louisiana.

[1796] Letter dated December 21, 1966, Jim Garrison to E.C. Upton, Records of the New Orleans Metropolitan Crime Commission, National Archives, College Park, Maryland.

[1797] Internal Metropolitan Crime Commission report dated November 23, 1966 by Aaron Kohn, Records of the New Orleans Metropolitan Crime Commission, National Archives, College Park, Maryland.

[1798] Internal Metropolitan Crime Commission report dated November 28, 1966 by Aaron Kohn, Records of the New Orleans Metropolitan Crime Commission, National Archives, College Park, Maryland.

[1799] See Garrison military record, Files Received from Harry Connick, National Archives, College Park, Maryland.

[1800] Letter dated July 23, 1952, Jim Garrison to A.L. Fierst Literary Agent, Papers Donated by Lyon Garrison, National Archives, College Park, Maryland.

[1801] Interview with David Chandler by James Kirkwood, spring 1969, James Kirkwood Collection, Boston University, Boston, Massachusetts.

[1802] Sworn statement by David Chandler, August 16, 1967, Files Received from Harry Connick, National Archives, College Park, Maryland.

[1803] Memo dated January 11, 1967, Lynn Loisell to Louis Ivon, Donated Papers of Edward Wegmann, National Archives, College Park, Maryland.

[1804] Memo dated January 18, 1967 by George Eckert, interview with Sam Newman, Donated Papers of Edward Wegmann, National Archives, College Park, Maryland.

[1805] Letter dated December 6, 1966, Lorraine G. Le Bouef to U.S. Government Printing Office, JFK Assassination Collection, New Orleans Public Library, New Orleans, Louisiana.

[1806] Letter dated January 3, 1966 (should be January 3, 1967), Jim Garrison to U.S. Government Printing Office, JFK Assassination Collection, New Orleans Public Library, New Orleans, Louisiana.

[1807] Memo dated January 16, 1967, Jim Garrison to James Alcock, John Volz, Andrew Sciambra, Alvin Oser and Lou Ivon, Donated Papers of Edward Wegmann, National Archives, College Park, Maryland.

[1808] Memo about interview with David Ferrie by John Volz, December 15, 1966, Donated Papers of Edward Wegmann, National Archives, College Park, Maryland.

[1809] Memo dated December 16, 1966, Record Group 65, FBI Files, JFK Assassination Collection, National Archives, College Park, Maryland.

[1810] Memo dated December 23, 1966, Record Group 65, FBI Files, JFK Assassination Collection, National Archives, College Park, Maryland.

[1811] FBI Memo dated February 21, 1967, Record Group 60, General Records of the Department of Justice, Classified Subject Files, 129-11, JFK Assassination Collection, National Archives, College Park, Maryland.

[1812] Donated Papers of Clay Shaw, National Archives, College Park, Maryland.

[1813] Notice dated December 20, 1966, The National Bank of Commerce to Shaw, Donated Papers of Clay Shaw, National Archives, College Park, Maryland.

[1814] Interview with Clay Shaw by Andrew Sciambra and Jim Garrison, December 23, 1966, Memo dated February 9, 1967, Legal Files of F. Irvin Dymond—Clay Shaw Case, Historic New Orleans Collection, New Orleans, Louisiana.

[1815] Statement of Layton Martens dated December 23, 1966, Legal Files of F. Irvin Dymond—Clay Shaw Case, Historic New Orleans Collection, New Orleans, Louisiana.

[1816] Memo dated December 24, 1966, Record Group 65, FBI Files, JFK Assassination Collection, National Archives, College Park, Maryland.

[1817] Memo dated February 20, 1967, Record Group 65, FBI Files, JFK Assassination Collection, National Archives, College Park, Maryland.

[1818] Financial letters related to Shaw properties, Donated Papers of Clay Shaw, National Archives, College Park, Maryland.

[1819] "Smith" Case memo dated January 7, 1967, author unknown, Donated Papers of Edward Wegmann, National Archives, College Park, Maryland.

[1820] Memo dated June 12, 1967 by Aaron Kohn, Records of the New Orleans Metropolitan Crime Commission, National Archives, College Park, Maryland.

[1821] Memo dated January 4, 1967, Record Group 65, FBI Files, JFK Assassination Collection, National Archives, College Park, Maryland.

[1822] Memo dated January 20, 1967, Lloyd Cobb to Executive Committee, International Trade Mart, International Trade Mart Records, Tulane University, New Orleans, Louisiana.

[1823] Letter dated July 14, 1967, Lisa B. Matkin to Lloyd Cobb, International Trade Mart Records, Tulane University, New Orleans, Louisiana.

[1824] Letter dated January 16, 1967, Shaw to Tom Korman, Donated Papers of Clay Shaw, National Archives, College Park, Maryland.

[1825] FBI memo dated January 19, 1967, Record Group 65, FBI Files, JFK Assassination Collection, National Archives, College Park, Maryland.

[1826] Memo dated January 6, 1967, Andrew Sciambra to Jim Garrison, Donated Papers of Edward Wegmann, National Archives, College Park, Maryland.

[1827] Memo dated February 8, 1967, Lynn Loisel and Charles Jonau to Jim Garrison, Donated Papers of Edward Wegmann, National Archives, College Park, Maryland.

[1828] Memo dated January 17, 1967, Record Group 65, FBI Files, JFK Assassination Collection, National Archives, College Park, Maryland.

[1829] Memo dated February 3, 1967, Record Group 65, FBI Files, JFK Assassination Collection, National Archives, College Park, Maryland.

[1830] Five-page memo to file on "Smith Case" by Jim Garrison, dated February 10, 1967, Legal Files of F. Irvin Dymond—Clay Shaw Case, Historic New Orleans Collection, New Orleans, Louisiana.

[1831] Memo dated February 9, 1967, Lou Ivon to Garrison, Donated Papers of Edward Wegmann, National Archives, College Park, Maryland.

[1832] Memo dated February 18, 1967, Interview with Melvin Coffey by John Volz and James Alcock, Donated Papers of Edward Wegmann, National Archives, College Park, Maryland.

[1833] Memo dated February 10, 1967, Interview of J.B. Dauenhauer by Andrew Sciambra, Donated Papers of Edward Wegmann, National Archives, College Park, Maryland.

[1834] Memo dated June 12, 1967 by Aaron Kohn, Records of the New Orleans Metropolitan Crime Commission, National Archives, College Park, Maryland.

[1835] Memo dated February 10, 1967, Agent #1 (Jimmy Johnson) to Jim Garrison, Donated Papers of Edward Wegmann, National Archives, College Park, Maryland.

[1836] Unpublished *Narrative Report on Garrison Probe* by Richard Townley, Author's Possession.

[1837] Unpublished *Narrative Report on Garrison Probe* by Richard Townley, Author's Possession.

[1838] Internal Metropolitan Crime Commission report dated May 10, 1973 by Aaron Kohn, Records of the New Orleans Metropolitan Crime Commission, National Archives, College Park, Maryland.

[1839] Memo dated February 28, 1967 of interview with David Ferrie, February 18, 1967, by Andrew Sciambra and Lou Ivon, Donated Papers of Edward Wegmann, National Archives, College Park, Maryland.

[1840] Memo dated March 6, 1967, Interview with Dante Marochini, March 3 1967, by James Alcock and Lou Ivon, Donated Papers of Edward Wegmann, National Archives, College Park, Maryland.

[1841] Memo dated February 20, 1967, Interview with James Lewallen on February 16, 1967, by James Alcock and Lou Ivon, Donated Papers of Edward Wegmann, National Archives, College Park, Maryland.

[1842] Interview with F. Irvin Dymond by James Kirkwood, approximately spring 1969, James Kirkwood papers, Boston University.

[1843] Transcript of Garrison news conference, February 20, 1967, Records of the New Orleans Metropolitan Crime Commission, National Archives, College Park, Maryland.

[1844] Memo dated February 20, 1967 regarding interview with Ampala Rocha by James Alcock, Papers Donated by Lyon Garrison, National Archives, College Park, Maryland.

[1845] Record Group 457, Records of the National Security Agency, Office of Policy, JFK Assassination Collection, National Archives, College Park, Maryland.

[1846] Memo dated February 23, 1967, Record Group 65, FBI Files, JFK Assassination Collection, National Archives, College Park, Maryland.

[1847] Memo dated February 23, 1967, Record Group 65, FBI Files, JFK Assassination Collection, National Archives, College Park, Maryland.

[1848] Shaw Diary entry dated March 20, 1967, Donated Papers of Clay Shaw, National Archives, College Park, Maryland.

[1849] Statement by U.S. Senator Russell Long, February 23, 1967, Russell B. Long Collection, Louisiana State University, Baton Rouge, Louisiana.

[1850] Statement by U.S. Senator Russell Long, February 23, 1967, Russell B. Long Collection, Louisiana State University, Baton Rouge, Louisiana.

[1851] Statement by U.S. Senator Russell Long, February 23, 1967, Russell B. Long Collection, Louisiana State University, Baton Rouge, Louisiana.

1852 Transcript of interview with Jim Garrison by Murphy Martin of ABC News, February 24, 1967, Records of the New Orleans Metropolitan Crime Commission, National Archives, College Park, Maryland.

1853 Transcript of interview with Perry Russo by James Kemp on February 24, 1967, Donated Papers of Edward Wegmann, National Archives, College Park, Maryland.

1854 Memo dated February 25, 1967, Lou Ivon to Jim Garrison, Legal Files of F. Irvin Dymond—Clay Shaw Case, Historic New Orleans Collection, New Orleans, Louisiana.

1855 Interview with Louis Ivon by author, June 15, 2007.

1856 Memo dated March 7, 1967, Record Group 65, FBI Files, JFK Assassination Collection, National Archives, College Park, Maryland.

1857 Memo dated March 23, 1967 by Aaron Kohn regarding meeting with Frank Klein and D'Alton Williams on February 27, 1967, Records of the New Orleans Metropolitan Crime Commission, National Archives, College Park, Maryland.

1858 Memo dated February 28 1967, Record Group 65, FBI Files, JFK Assassination Collection, National Archives, College Park, Maryland.

1859 Letter dated February 28, 1967, George Healy to International Trade Mart, International Trade Mart Records, Tulane University, New Orleans, Louisiana.

1860 Letter, Asahel W. Cooper, Jr. to George Healy, International Trade Mart Records, Tulane University, New Orleans, Louisiana.

1861 Letter dated October 14, 1966, Captain J.W. Clark to Lloyd Cobb, International Trade Mart Records, Tulane University, New Orleans, Louisiana.

1862 Article in *The New York Times*, December 17, 1963.

1863 Merle Miller, *On Being Different: What it Means to be a Homosexual* (Random House, 1971).

1864 Article in *Harper's* magazine, September 1970, quoted in Merle Miller, *On Being Different: What it Means to be a Homosexual* (Random House, 1971)...

1865 Article in *Harper's* magazine, September 1970, quoted in Merle Miller, *On Being Different: What it Means to be a Homosexual* (Random House, 1971)...

1866 Interview with Mike Nichols, *Playboy*, June 1966.

1867 Interview with Bob Carr by author, February 14, 2008.

1868 Some of the diaries and narratives can be found in the Sharon Litwin collection at the Historic New Orleans Collection in New Orleans, Louisiana. Other versions can be found in the Donated Papers of Clay Shaw at the National Archives in College Park, Maryland.

1869 Interview with Shaw by James Kirkwood, May 1968, James Kirkwood Collection, Boston University, Boston, Massachusetts.

1870 Some of the diaries and narratives can be found in the Sharon Litwin collection at the Historic New Orleans Collection in New Orleans, Louisiana. Other versions can be found in the Donated Papers of Clay Shaw at the National Archives in College Park, Maryland.

1871 Interview with Shaw by James Kirkwood, May 1968, James Kirkwood Collection, Boston University, Boston, Massachusetts.

1872 Some of the diaries and narratives can be found in the Sharon Litwin collection at the Historic New Orleans Collection in New Orleans, Louisiana. Other versions can be found in the Donated Papers of Clay Shaw at the National Archives in College Park, Maryland.

1873 Interview with Shaw by James Kirkwood, May 1968, James Kirkwood Collection, Boston University, Boston, Massachusetts.

[1874] Memo dated March 1, 1967, Lester Otillio to Louis Ivon, Donated Papers of Edward Wegmann, National Archives, College Park, Maryland.

[1875] Interview with Shaw by James Kirkwood, May 1968, James Kirkwood Collection, Boston University, Boston, Massachusetts.

[1876] Interview with Shaw by James Kirkwood, May 1968, James Kirkwood Collection, Boston University, Boston, Massachusetts.

[1877] References taken from results of polygraph examination of James Lewallen dated March 4, 1967 by examiner Roy Jacobs, Legal Files of F. Irvin Dymond—Clay Shaw Case, Historic New Orleans Collection, New Orleans, Louisiana.

[1878] Interview with F. Irvin Dymond by James Kirkwood, approximately spring 1969, James Kirkwood papers, Boston University.

[1879] Memo dated March 3, 1967, Record Group 65, FBI Files, JFK Assassination Collection, National Archives, College Park, Maryland.

[1880] Memo dated March 4, 1967, Record Group 65, FBI Files, JFK Assassination Collection, National Archives, College Park, Maryland.

[1881] Memo dated March 2, 1967, Record Group 65, FBI Files, JFK Assassination Collection, National Archives, College Park, Maryland.

[1882] Page 10 of Shaw Post-Arrest Narrative, Donated Papers of Clay Shaw, National Archives, College Park, Maryland.

[1883] Memo dated March 3, 1967, Record Group 65, FBI Files, JFK Assassination Collection, National Archives, College Park, Maryland.

[1884] Interview with Dean Andrews, March 2, 1967, Files Received from Harry Connick, National Archives, College Park, Maryland.

[1885] Telegram dated March 1, 1967, W. Robert Morgan to Shaw, Donated Papers of Clay Shaw, National Archives, College Park, Maryland.

[1886] Page 10 of Shaw Post-Arrest Narrative, Donated Papers of Clay Shaw, National Archives, College Park, Maryland.

[1887] FBI memo dated March 21, 1968, Record Group 60, General Records of the Department of Justice, Classified Subject Files, 129-11, JFK Assassination Collection, National Archives, College Park, Maryland.

[1888] Page 6 of Shaw Post-Arrest Narrative, Donated Papers of Clay Shaw, National Archives, College Park, Maryland.

[1889] Page 10 of Shaw Post-Arrest Narrative, Donated Papers of Clay Shaw, National Archives, College Park, Maryland.

[1890] Page 6 of Shaw Post-Arrest Narrative, Donated Papers of Clay Shaw, National Archives, College Park, Maryland.

[1891] Page 6 of Shaw Post-Arrest Narrative, Donated Papers of Clay Shaw, National Archives, College Park, Maryland.

[1892] Shaw Diary entry dated March 11, 1967, Donated Papers of Clay Shaw, National Archives, College Park, Maryland.

[1893] Police report dated August 22, 1961 regarding break-in at bunker in Houma, Louisiana owned by Schlumberger Corporation, Donated Papers of Edward Wegmann, National Archives, College Park, Maryland.

[1894] Memo dated August 9, 1967, Lorraine LeBouef to Jim Garrison, Donated Papers of Edward Wegmann, National Archives, College Park, Maryland.

[1895] Undated report dealing with 1953 matters, Records of the New Orleans Metropolitan Crime Commission, National Archives, College Park, Maryland.

[1896] Shaw Diary entry dated March 9, 1967, Donated Papers of Clay Shaw, National Archives, College Park, Maryland.

[1897] Shaw Diary entry dated March 9, 1967, Donated Papers of Clay Shaw, National Archives, College Park, Maryland.

[1898] Interview with F. Irvin Dymond by author, June 29, 1995.

[1899] Minutes of Executive Committee meeting, March 9, 1967, International Trade Mart, International Trade Mart Records, Tulane University, New Orleans, Louisiana.

[1900] Letter dated March 10, 1967, Irvin Dymond to Ralph Sneed, Legal Files of F. Irvin Dymond—Clay Shaw Case, Historic New Orleans Collection, New Orleans, Louisiana.

[1901] Letter dated March 10, 1967, John James Overstreet, Jr. to Jim Garrison, JFK Assassination Collection, New Orleans Public Library, New Orleans, Louisiana.

[1902] Memo dated March 2, 1967, Record Group 65, FBI Files, JFK Assassination Collection, National Archives, College Park, Maryland.

[1903] FBI note dated March 2, 1967, Record Group 65, FBI Files, JFK Assassination Collection, National Archives, College Park, Maryland.

[1904] Memo dated February 27, 1967, Record Group 65, FBI Files, JFK Assassination Collection, National Archives, College Park, Maryland.

[1905] See copies of *Newsweek* articles about arrest of Walter Jenkins, October 1964, Files Received from Harry Connick, National Archives, College Park, Maryland.

[1906] Letter dated March 2, 1967, L.S. McClaren to Shaw, Donated Papers of Clay Shaw, National Archives, College Park, Maryland.

[1907] Letter dated March 2, 1967, Thomas H. Weil to Shaw, Donated Papers of Clay Shaw, National Archives, College Park, Maryland.

[1908] Letter dated March 2, 1967, David Baldwin to Shaw, Donated Papers of Clay Shaw, National Archives, College Park, Maryland.

[1909] Telegram dated March 2, 1967, Don Schueler to Shaw, Donated Papers of Clay Shaw, National Archives, College Park, Maryland.

[1910] Letter dated March 3, 1967, George Haverstick to Shaw, Donated Papers of Clay Shaw, National Archives, College Park, Maryland.

[1911] Letter dated March 2, 1967, Marcel Gomez to Shaw, Donated Papers of Clay Shaw, National Archives, College Park, Maryland.

[1912] Telegram dated March 3, 1967, Tom Dawson to Shaw, Donated Papers of Clay Shaw, National Archives, College Park, Maryland.

[1913] Card dated March 3, 1967, Pat O'Brien to Shaw, Donated Papers of Clay Shaw, National Archives, College Park, Maryland.

[1914] Letter dated March 3, 1967, Martin Palmer to Shaw, Donated Papers of Clay Shaw, National Archives, College Park, Maryland.

[1915] Interview with Martin Palmer by author, November 7, 2005.

[1916] Letter dated March 3, 1967, Don Doody to Shaw, Donated Papers of Clay Shaw, National Archives, College Park, Maryland.

[1917] Telegram dated March 2, 1967, "Frosty" Blackshear to Shaw, Donated Papers of Clay Shaw, National Archives, College Park, Maryland.

[1918] Letter dated March 3, 1967, Claire Evangelista Morrison to Shaw, Donated Papers of Clay Shaw, National Archives, College Park, Maryland.

[1919] Letter dated March 3, 1967, Gordon Berger to Shaw, Donated Papers of Clay Shaw, National Archives, College Park, Maryland.

[1920] Telegram dated March 3, 1967, Charles Bushong to Shaw, Donated Papers of Clay Shaw, National Archives, College Park, Maryland.

[1921] Card dated March 3, 1967, Reverend Miller M. Cragon to Shaw, Donated Papers of Clay Shaw, National Archives, College Park, Maryland.

[1922] Telegram dated March 3, 1967, Joseph W. Faulkner to President Lyndon Johnson, Senator Robert Kennedy, Attorney General Ramsey Clark, Chief Justice Earl Warren, Donated Papers of Clay Shaw, National Archives, College Park, Maryland.

[1923] Letter dated March 4, 1967, Alison Marks to Shaw, Donated Papers of Clay Shaw, National Archives, College Park, Maryland.

[1924] Letter dated March 3, 1967, Phillip Carey Jones to Shaw, Donated Papers of Clay Shaw, National Archives, College Park, Maryland.

[1925] Letter dated March 3, 1967, David Sogge to Shaw, Donated Papers of Clay Shaw, National Archives, College Park, Maryland.

[1926] Telegram dated March 3, 1967, Cecil E. Foster to Shaw, Donated Papers of Clay Shaw, National Archives, College Park, Maryland.

[1927] Card dated March 5, 1967, Bess Noble to Shaw, Donated Papers of Clay Shaw, National Archives, College Park, Maryland.

[1928] Undated letter with no surviving envelope from "Bill," probably Frank William Mehrten, to Shaw, Donated Papers of Clay Shaw, National Archives, College Park, Maryland.

[1929] See two telegrams dated March 7, 1967, Kay Lucas Leake Dart to Shaw, Donated Papers of Clay Shaw, National Archives, College Park, Maryland.

[1930] Letter dated April 24, 1967, Kay Lucas Leake Dart to Shaw, Donated Papers of Clay Shaw, National Archives, College Park, Maryland.

[1931] Letter dated March 8, 1967, James M. Cain to Shaw, Donated Papers of Clay Shaw, National Archives, College Park, Maryland.

[1932] Undated card, probably March 1967, Marion Seidenbach to Shaw, Donated Papers of Clay Shaw, National Archives, College Park, Maryland.

[1933] Letter dated March 6, 1967, Sarah Hill Moore to Shaw, Donated Papers of Clay Shaw, National Archives, College Park, Maryland.

[1934] Letter dated March 3, 1967, Mary Lou Baxter Hunter to Shaw, Donated Papers of Clay Shaw, National Archives, College Park, Maryland.

[1935] FBI Memo dated March 6, 1967, Record Group 60, General Records of the Department of Justice, Classified Subject Files, 129-11, JFK Assassination Collection, National Archives, College Park, Maryland.

[1936] FBI Memo dated March 16, 1967, Record Group 60, General Records of the Department of Justice, Classified Subject Files, 129-11, JFK Assassination Collection, National Archives, College Park, Maryland.

[1937] Letter dated March 6, 1967, Merriman Smith to Cartha D. Deloach, Record Group 60, General Records of the Department of Justice, Classified Subject Files, 129-11, JFK Assassination Collection, National Archives, College Park, Maryland.

[1938] Memo dated March 7, 1967, Record Group 65, FBI Files, JFK Assassination Collection, National Archives, College Park, Maryland.

[1939] Memo dated March 10, 1967, regarding March 9, 1967 interview with Thomas Compton by Tom Duffy and Cliency Navarre, Donated Papers of Edward Wegmann, National Archives, College Park, Maryland.

[1940] Memo dated March 17, 1967, Cliency Navarre to Louis Ivon, Donated Papers of Edward Wegmann, National Archives, College Park, Maryland.

[1941] Undated memo, probably Winter 1967, Bob Greene to Charles Ward, Donated Papers of Edward Wegmann, National Archives, College Park, Maryland.

[1942] Memo with March 13, 1967, by Edward Wegmann, Legal Files of F. Irvin Dymond—Clay Shaw Case, Historic New Orleans Collection, New Orleans, Louisiana.

[1943] Memo dated March 14, 1967, Record Group 65, FBI Files, JFK Assassination Collection, National Archives, College Park, Maryland.

[1944] Memo dated March 16, 1967, Record Group 65, FBI Files, JFK Assassination Collection, National Archives, College Park, Maryland.

[1945] Memo dated March 13, 1967, by Edward Wegmann, Legal Files of F. Irvin Dymond—Clay Shaw Case, Historic New Orleans Collection, New Orleans, Louisiana.

[1946] Memo dated March 13, 1967, by Edward Wegmann, Legal Files of F. Irvin Dymond—Clay Shaw Case, Historic New Orleans Collection, New Orleans, Louisiana.

[1947] Memo dated May 31, 1968 related to James Phelan, Legal Files of F. Irvin Dymond—Clay Shaw Case, Historic New Orleans Collection, New Orleans, Louisiana.

[1948] Transcript of recorded conversation between Perry Russo and James Phelan, May 24, 1967, Files Received from Harry Connick, National Archives, College Park, Maryland.

[1949] Shaw Diary entry dated March 14, 1967, Donated Papers of Clay Shaw, National Archives, College Park, Maryland.

[1950] Letter dated March 17, 1967, Frances Bryson Moore to Shaw, Donated Papers of Clay Shaw, National Archives, College Park, Maryland.

[1951] Birthday card, Marilyn Tate to Shaw, sent shortly before March 17, 1967, Donated Papers of Clay Shaw, National Archives, College Park, Maryland.

[1952] Shaw Diary entry dated March 17, 1967, Donated Papers of Clay Shaw, National Archives, College Park, Maryland.

[1953] Telegram dated March 16, 1967, Sol Dann to Irvin Dymond, Legal Files of F. Irvin Dymond—Clay Shaw Case, Historic New Orleans Collection, New Orleans, Louisiana.

[1954] Letter dated March 20, 1967, Arthur Locke King to Irvin Dymond, Legal Files of F. Irvin Dymond—Clay Shaw Case, Historic New Orleans Collection, New Orleans, Louisiana.

[1955] Memo dated March 12, 1967, Kent Simms and Charles Jonau to Louis Ivon, Legal Files of F. Irvin Dymond—Clay Shaw Case, Historic New Orleans Collection, New Orleans, Louisiana.

[1956] Article in *Omaha World-Herald*, March 24, 1967, Legal Files of F. Irvin Dymond—Clay Shaw Case, Historic New Orleans Collection, New Orleans, Louisiana.

[1957] Memo dated March 29, 1967, Kent Simms to Louis Ivon, Legal Files of F. Irvin Dymond—Clay Shaw Case, Historic New Orleans Collection, New Orleans, Louisiana.

[1958] Memo dated March 22, 1967, Lynn Loisel to Jim Garrison, Donated Papers of Edward Wegmann, National Archives, College Park, Maryland.

[1959] Letter dated March 16, 1967, George Gaston Johnston to Jeff Biddison, Donated Papers of Clay Shaw, National Archives, College Park, Maryland.

[1960] Letter dated March 18, 1967, Chris Blake to Shaw, Donated Papers of Clay Shaw, National Archives, College Park, Maryland.

[1961] Memo dated March 23, 1967, summarizing interview with Mrs. Vizaid by Kent Simms and Cliency Navarre, Legal Files of F. Irvin Dymond—Clay Shaw Case, Historic New Orleans Collection, New Orleans, Louisiana.

[1962] Letter dated March 18, 1967, Alison Marks to Shaw, Donated Papers of Clay Shaw, National Archives, College Park, Maryland.

[1963] Letter dated March 19, 1967, Frances Anderson to Shaw, Donated Papers of Clay Shaw, National Archives, College Park, Maryland.

[1964] Letter dated March 1967, C.E. Foster to Shaw, Donated Papers of Clay Shaw, National Archives, College Park, Maryland.

[1965] Letter dated March 20, 1967, Oliver Evans to Shaw, Donated Papers of Clay Shaw, National Archives, College Park, Maryland.

[1966] Letter dated March 20, 1967, Mrs. Norman Bel Geddes to Shaw, Donated Papers of Clay Shaw, National Archives, College Park, Maryland.

[1967] Memo dated March 21, 1967, Goldie Moore to Lloyd J. Cobb, International Trade Mart Records, Tulane University, New Orleans, Louisiana.

[1968] Memo dated March 21, 1967, regarding interview with Owen Wright II, William Gurvich to Jim Garrison, Donated Papers of Edward Wegmann, National Archives, College Park, Maryland.

[1969] Letter dated March 27, 1967, Patrick O'Rourke to Jeff Biddison, Donated Papers of Clay Shaw, National Archives, College Park, Maryland.

[1970] Memo dated March 22, 1967, regarding Shaw's activities that day, Legal Files of F. Irvin Dymond—Clay Shaw Case, Historic New Orleans Collection, New Orleans, Louisiana.

[1971] Memo dated March 22, 1967, regarding interview with Virginia Johnson, C.J. Navarre to Lou Ivon, Donated Papers of Edward Wegmann, National Archives, College Park, Maryland.

[1972] Letter dated March 23, 1967, Cecil E. Foster to Shaw, Donated Papers of Clay Shaw, National Archives, College Park, Maryland.

[1973] Letter dated March 24, 1967, Cecil E. Foster to Shaw, Donated Papers of Clay Shaw, National Archives, College Park, Maryland.

[1974] Letter dated March 1967, Cynthia Koenig to Shaw, Donated Papers of Clay Shaw, National Archives, College Park, Maryland.

[1975] Letter dated March 25, 1967, Henri Gomez to Shaw, Donated Papers of Clay Shaw, National Archives, College Park, Maryland.

[1976] Letter dated March 26, 1967, Stan Picher and Wally Goodman to Shaw, Donated Papers of Clay Shaw, National Archives, College Park, Maryland.

[1977] Card dated March 18, 1967, Helen Marges to Shaw, Donated Papers of Clay Shaw, National Archives, College Park, Maryland.

[1978] Letter and greeting card dated March 26, 1967, Helen Marges to Shaw, Donated Papers of Clay Shaw, National Archives, College Park, Maryland.

[1979] Letter dated March 27, 1967, George Freedley to Shaw, Donated Papers of Clay Shaw, National Archives, College Park, Maryland.

[1980] Letter dated March 24, 1967, Edith Bel Geddes to George Freedley, George Freedley Papers, New York Public Library, New York, New York.

[1981] Letter dated March 27, 1967, William Taliaferro to Shaw, Donated Papers of Clay Shaw, National Archives, College Park, Maryland.

[1982] Letter dated February 27, 1967 (Perhaps should be March 27, 1967) by James E. Pryor, Record Group 60, General Records of the Department of Justice, Classified Subject Files, 129-11, JFK Assassination Collection, National Archives, College Park, Maryland.

[1983] Memo dated March 2, 1967, Record Group 65, FBI Files, JFK Assassination Collection, National Archives, College Park, Maryland.

[1984] Telegram dated March 30, 1967, Andre Shaw to Shaw, Donated Papers of Clay Shaw, National Archives, College Park, Maryland.

[1985] Memo dated March 21, 1967, Record Group 65, FBI Files, JFK Assassination Collection, National Archives, College Park, Maryland.

[1986] Letter dated March 29, 1967, Frances Thrasher to Shaw, Donated Papers of Clay Shaw, National Archives, College Park, Maryland.

[1987] See Frances Thrasher's numerous letters to Shaw during 1967, Donated Papers of Clay Shaw, National Archives, College Park, Maryland.

[1988] Undated letter, probably 1967, Frances Thrasher to Mr. Hall of Hallmark Card Company, Donated Papers of Clay Shaw, National Archives, College Park, Maryland.

[1989] Undated letter, probably 1967, Frances Thrasher to Shaw, Donated Papers of Clay Shaw, National Archives, College Park, Maryland.

[1990] Undated letter, probably 1967, Frances Thrasher to Shaw, Donated Papers of Clay Shaw, National Archives, College Park, Maryland.

[1991] Undated letter, Frances Thrasher to Shaw, Donated Papers of Clay Shaw, National Archives, College Park, Maryland.

[1992] Interview with Jesse Fisher, June 11, 2007.

[1993] Page 10 of Shaw Post-Arrest Narrative, Donated Papers of Clay Shaw, National Archives, College Park, Maryland.

[1994] Page 6 of Shaw Post-Arrest Narrative, Donated Papers of Clay Shaw, National Archives, College Park, Maryland.

[1995] Interview with F. Irvin Dymond by James Kirkwood, approximately Spring, 1969, James Kirkwood Papers, Boston University

[1996] Interview with F. Irvin Dymond by James Kirkwood, approximately Spring, 1969, James Kirkwood Papers, Boston University

[1997] Shaw Diary entry dated March 21, 1967, Donated Papers of Clay Shaw, National Archives, College Park, Maryland.

[1998] Shaw Diary entry dated March 22-March 25, 1967, Donated Papers of Clay Shaw, National Archives, College Park, Maryland.

[1999] Shaw Diary entry dated March 25, 1967, Donated Papers of Clay Shaw, National Archives, College Park, Maryland.

[2000] Shaw Diary entry dated March 26, 1967, Donated Papers of Clay Shaw, National Archives, College Park, Maryland.

[2001] Memo dated March 31, 1967, regarding interview with Betty Parent (Parrott), Andrew Sciambra to Jim Garrison, Legal Files of F. Irvin Dymond—Clay Shaw Case, Historic New Orleans Collection, New Orleans, Louisiana.

[2002] Memo dated March 27, 1967, John Volz to Jim Garrison, Donated Papers of Edward Wegmann, National Archives, College Park, Maryland.

[2003] Letter dated March 22, 1967, Edward Wegmann to Charles Carson, Legal Files of F. Irvin Dymond—Clay Shaw Case, Historic New Orleans Collection, New Orleans, Louisiana.

[2004] Letter dated March 27, 1967, Edward Wegmann to Charles Carson, Legal Files of F. Irvin Dymond—Clay Shaw Case, Historic New Orleans Collection, New Orleans, Louisiana.

[2005] Letter dated March 27, 1967, Charles R. Carson to Edward Wegmann, Legal Files of F. Irvin Dymond—Clay Shaw Case, Historic New Orleans Collection, New Orleans, Louisiana.

[2006] Letter dated March 27, 1967, Edward Wegmann to Richard Townley, Legal Files of F. Irvin Dymond—Clay Shaw Case, Historic New Orleans Collection, New Orleans, Louisiana.

[2007] Letter dated March 27, 1967, Edward Wegmann to Phillip Carter, Legal Files of F. Irvin Dymond—Clay Shaw Case, Historic New Orleans Collection, New Orleans, Louisiana.

[2008] Letter dated March 31, 1967, Edward Wegmann to Charles Carson, Legal Files of F. Irvin Dymond—Clay Shaw Case, Historic New Orleans Collection, New Orleans, Louisiana.

[2009] Letter dated April 3, 1967, Edward Wegmann to Charles Carson, Legal Files of F. Irvin Dymond—Clay Shaw Case, Historic New Orleans Collection, New Orleans, Louisiana.

[2010] Letter dated April 4, 1967, Edward Wegmann to Dr. Fredrick Redlich, Legal Files of F. Irvin Dymond—Clay Shaw Case, Historic New Orleans Collection, New Orleans, Louisiana.

[2011] Letter dated April 25, 1967, Edward Wegmann to Dr. Fredrick Redlich, Legal Files of F. Irvin Dymond—Clay Shaw Case, Historic New Orleans Collection, New Orleans, Louisiana.

[2012] Letter dated April 6, 1967, Irvin Dymond to Harold Weisberg, Legal Files of F. Irvin Dymond—Clay Shaw Case, Historic New Orleans Collection, New Orleans, Louisiana.

[2013] Letter dated April 7, 1967, Edward Wegmann to Muriel Bultman Francis, Legal Files of F. Irvin Dymond—Clay Shaw Case, Historic New Orleans Collection, New Orleans, Louisiana.

[2014] Memo dated March 13, 1967, by Edward Wegmann, Legal Files of F. Irvin Dymond—Clay Shaw Case, Historic New Orleans Collection, New Orleans, Louisiana.

[2015] Interview with David Chandler, March 24, 1967, Legal Files of F. Irvin Dymond—Clay Shaw Case, Historic New Orleans Collection, New Orleans, Louisiana.

[2016] Interview with Charles Earl Daniels, March 29, 1967, Legal Files of F. Irvin Dymond—Clay Shaw Case, Historic New Orleans Collection, New Orleans, Louisiana.

[2017] Interviews with Nelson Wayne Thomas, Milton Fontenot, and Niles Peterson, March 29, 1967, Legal Files of F. Irvin Dymond—Clay Shaw Case, Historic New Orleans Collection, New Orleans, Louisiana.

[2018] Interview with Michael Fitzpatrick, April 4, 1967, Legal Files of F. Irvin Dymond—Clay Shaw Case, Historic New Orleans Collection, New Orleans, Louisiana.

[2019] Interview with Glen Latino, March 27, 1967, Legal Files of F. Irvin Dymond—Clay Shaw Case, Historic New Orleans Collection, New Orleans, Louisiana.

[2020] Interview with Adele Maquar, March 30, 1967, Legal Files of F. Irvin Dymond—Clay Shaw Case, Historic New Orleans Collection, New Orleans, Louisiana.

[2021] Interview with Don Merrill Jordan, April 14, 1967, Legal Files of F. Irvin Dymond—Clay Shaw Case, Historic New Orleans Collection, New Orleans, Louisiana.

2022 Interview with Eric Crouchet, April 21, 1967, Legal Files of F. Irvin Dymond—Clay Shaw Case, Historic New Orleans Collection, New Orleans, Louisiana.

2023 Statement of Don Merrill Jordan dated April 14, 1967 to Robert Wilson, Donated Papers of Edward Wegmann, National Archives, College Park, Maryland.

2024 Memo dated April 20, 1967, regarding Chandler Josey's inspection of Shaw's telephone, Legal Files of F. Irvin Dymond—Clay Shaw Case, Historic New Orleans Collection, New Orleans, Louisiana.

2025 Letter dated May 11, 1967, Charles R. Carson to Edward Wegmann, Legal Files of F. Irvin Dymond—Clay Shaw Case, Historic New Orleans Collection, New Orleans, Louisiana.

2026 Interview with Carlos Bringuier,, March 31, 1967, Legal Files of F. Irvin Dymond—Clay Shaw Case, Historic New Orleans Collection, New Orleans, Louisiana.

2027 Interview with Carlos Quiroga, March 29, 1967, Legal Files of F. Irvin Dymond—Clay Shaw Case, Historic New Orleans Collection, New Orleans, Louisiana.

2028 Interview with Elmer Renfroe and Francis Bordelon, March 31, 1967, Legal Files of F. Irvin Dymond—Clay Shaw Case, Historic New Orleans Collection, New Orleans, Louisiana.

2029 Memo dated April 21, 1967 by Aaron Kohn, Records of the New Orleans Metropolitan Crime Commission, National Archives, College Park, Maryland.

2030 Interview with Layton Martens, April 1967, Legal Files of F. Irvin Dymond—Clay Shaw Case, Historic New Orleans Collection, New Orleans, Louisiana.

2031 Interview with Don Doody by author, January 11, 2006.

2032 Interview with Donald Doody, April 5, 1967, Legal Files of F. Irvin Dymond—Clay Shaw Case, Historic New Orleans Collection, New Orleans, Louisiana.

2033 Interview with Sam DePino, April 7, 1967, Legal Files of F. Irvin Dymond—Clay Shaw Case, Historic New Orleans Collection, New Orleans, Louisiana.

2034 Interview with Louis Fischer by Shaw's attorneys' investigators, Legal Files of F. Irvin Dymond—Clay Shaw Case, Historic New Orleans Collection, New Orleans, Louisiana.

2035 Interview with John Cancler, April 13, 1967, Legal Files of F. Irvin Dymond—Clay Shaw Case, Historic New Orleans Collection, New Orleans, Louisiana.

2036 Interview with Morris Brownlee, April 14, 1967, Legal Files of F. Irvin Dymond—Clay Shaw Case, Historic New Orleans Collection, New Orleans, Louisiana.

2037 Summary of interview with Morris Brownlee, May 3, 1967, Legal Files of F. Irvin Dymond—Clay Shaw Case, Historic New Orleans Collection, New Orleans, Louisiana.

2038 Interview with Gordon Novel, April 16 and 17, 1967, Legal Files of F. Irvin Dymond—Clay Shaw Case, Historic New Orleans Collection, New Orleans, Louisiana.

2039 Interview with Eleanor Bares, April 19, 1967, Legal Files of F. Irvin Dymond—Clay Shaw Case, Historic New Orleans Collection, New Orleans, Louisiana.

2040 Interviews with Richard Townley, April 20, 1967 and June 7, 1967, Legal Files of F. Irvin Dymond—Clay Shaw Case, Historic New Orleans Collection, New Orleans, Louisiana.

2041 Interviews with Richard Townley, April 20, 1967 and June 7, 1967, Legal Files of F. Irvin Dymond—Clay Shaw Case, Historic New Orleans Collection, New Orleans, Louisiana.

2042 Notes from conversation with Dr. C.D. Dwyer by Edward Wegmann, Legal Files of F. Irvin Dymond—Clay Shaw Case, Historic New Orleans Collection, New Orleans, Louisiana.

2043 Shaw Diary entry dated March 28, 1967, Donated Papers of Clay Shaw, National Archives, College Park, Maryland.

[2044] Shaw Diary entry dated March 29, 1967, Donated Papers of Clay Shaw, National Archives, College Park, Maryland.

[2045] Memo regarding information from Freddie Williams, March 28, 1967, Legal Files of F. Irvin Dymond—Clay Shaw Case, Historic New Orleans Collection, New Orleans, Louisiana.

[2046] Grand Jury indictment of Layton Martens, March 29, 1969, Files Received from Harry Connick, National Archives, College Park, Maryland.

[2047] Memo dated April 5, 1967, regarding trip to Freeman Island, William Gurvich to Jim Garrison, Legal Files of F. Irvin Dymond—Clay Shaw Case, Historic New Orleans Collection, New Orleans, Louisiana.

[2048] Video archives of WWL-TV Channel 4 in New Orleans, Louisiana State Archives, Baton Rouge, Louisiana.

[2049] Video archives of WWL-TV Channel 4 in New Orleans, Louisiana State Archives, Baton Rouge, Louisiana.

[2050] Letter dated April 25, 1967, Edward Wegmann to Donald Doody, Legal Files of F. Irvin Dymond—Clay Shaw Case, Historic New Orleans Collection, New Orleans, Louisiana.

[2051] Letter dated April 4, 1967, Noel E. Parmentel, Jr. to Edward Wegmann, Legal Files of F. Irvin Dymond—Clay Shaw Case, Historic New Orleans Collection, New Orleans, Louisiana.

[2052] See sub-folder marked "Info assigned to investigators," April 6, 1967, Memo from Frank Meloche to Jim Garrison, including transcript of telephone conversation with Lieutenant Francis Fruge, Files Received from Harry Connick, National Archives, College Park, Maryland.

[2053] Memo dated January 14, 1969, Frank Meloche to Lou Ivon, Files Received from Harry Connick, National Archives, College Park, Maryland.

[2054] See memo entitled Garrison and the Kennedy Assassination, June 5, 1968, CIA Miscellaneous Files, JFK Assassination Collection, National Archives, College Park, Maryland.

[2055] See expense sheets submitted by Anne Dischler and Francis Fruge, May 31-October 6, 1967, Files Received from Harry Connick, National Archives, College Park, Maryland.

[2056] See newspaper clippings about Anne Dischler and Francis L. Fruge working for Garrison's office, Files Received from Harry Connick, National Archives, College Park, Maryland.

[2057] Undated letter, probably May 1967, Lynn Loisel to Francis Fruge, Files Received from Harry Connick, National Archives, College Park, Maryland.

[2058] Undated memo, by unknown author, related to early development of Clinton, Louisiana voter registration attempt by Lee Harvey Oswald, Files Received from Harry Connick, National Archives, College Park, Maryland.

[2059] Letter dated April 7, 1967, William Wegmann to Edward Wegmann and Irvin Dymond, Legal Files of F. Irvin Dymond—Clay Shaw Case, Historic New Orleans Collection, New Orleans, Louisiana.

[2060] Minutes of Executive Committee meeting, April 13, 1967, International Trade Mart, International Trade Mart Records, Tulane University, New Orleans, Louisiana.

[2061] Letter dated April 10, 1967, Edward Wegmann to Mario Bermúdez, Legal Files of F. Irvin Dymond—Clay Shaw Case, Historic New Orleans Collection, New Orleans, Louisiana.

[2062] Letter dated April 11, 1967, Edward Wegmann to Robert Wilson, Legal Files of F. Irvin Dymond—Clay Shaw Case, Historic New Orleans Collection, New Orleans, Louisiana.

[2063] Letter dated April 12, 1967, Irvin Dymond to Robert Wilson, Legal Files of F. Irvin Dymond—Clay Shaw Case, Historic New Orleans Collection, New Orleans, Louisiana.

[2064] Letter dated April 13, 1967, Robert L. Kleinpeter to Irvin Dymond, Legal Files of F. Irvin Dymond—Clay Shaw Case, Historic New Orleans Collection, New Orleans, Louisiana.

[2065] Letter dated April 12, 1967, Shaw to Mrs. Richard "Nina" Brown, Donated Papers of Clay Shaw, National Archives, College Park, Maryland.

[2066] Transcript of interview with Eve Springer, April 13, 1967, by Tom Duffy, Fenner Sedgebeer, and Cliency Navarre, Papers Donated by Lyon Garrison, National Archives, College Park, Maryland.

[2067] Shaw Diary entry dated April 9, 1967, Donated Papers of Clay Shaw, National Archives, College Park, Maryland.

[2068] Shaw Diary entry dated April 9, 1967, Donated Papers of Clay Shaw, National Archives, College Park, Maryland.

[2069] Shaw Diary entry dated April 12, 1967, Donated Papers of Clay Shaw, National Archives, College Park, Maryland.

[2070] Shaw Diary entry dated April 14, 1967, Donated Papers of Clay Shaw, National Archives, College Park, Maryland.

[2071] Letter dated April 16, 1967, Shaw to Alison Marks, Author's Collection.

[2072] Letter dated April 14, 1967, Ken R. Williams to Shaw, Donated Papers of Clay Shaw, National Archives, College Park, Maryland.

[2073] Letter dated April 24, 1967, Chauncey Guidry to Irvin Dymond, Legal Files of F. Irvin Dymond—Clay Shaw Case, Historic New Orleans Collection, New Orleans, Louisiana.

[2074] Letter dated April 12, 1967, Chauncey Guidry to Irvin Dymond, Legal Files of F. Irvin Dymond—Clay Shaw Case, Historic New Orleans Collection, New Orleans, Louisiana.

[2075] Letter dated April 14, 1967, Irvin Dymond to Chauncey Guidry, Legal Files of F. Irvin Dymond—Clay Shaw Case, Historic New Orleans Collection, New Orleans, Louisiana.

[2076] Telegram dated April 26, 1967, Irvin Dymond, Edward Wegmann and William Wegmann to Louisiana State Bar Association, Legal Files of F. Irvin Dymond—Clay Shaw Case, Historic New Orleans Collection, New Orleans, Louisiana.

[2077] Letter dated April 16, 1967, Shaw to Mrs. Norman (Edith) Bel Geddes, Donated Papers of Clay Shaw, National Archives, College Park, Maryland.

[2078] Shaw Diary entry dated April 18, 1967, Donated Papers of Clay Shaw, National Archives, College Park, Maryland.

[2079] Memo dated April 18, 1967, Irvin Dymond regarding information from Freddie Williams, Legal Files of F. Irvin Dymond—Clay Shaw Case, Historic New Orleans Collection, New Orleans, Louisiana.

[2080] Letter dated April 18, 1967, Richard B. Swenson to Shaw, Donated Papers of Clay Shaw, National Archives, College Park, Maryland.

[2081] Letter in Spanish, translated into English with the name scratched out, to Shaw, Donated Papers of Clay Shaw, National Archives, College Park, Maryland.

[2082] Checks and deposit slips for Shaw's accounts for various periods can be found in Donated Papers of Clay Shaw, National Archives, College Park, Maryland.

[2083] See checks to Willie Mae Guidry, Donated Papers of Clay Shaw, National Archives, College Park, Maryland.

[2084] Memo dated April 17, 1967, by Irvin Dymond regarding interview with Ken France, Legal Files of F. Irvin Dymond—Clay Shaw Case, Historic New Orleans Collection, New Orleans, Louisiana.

[2085] Interview with Philip Vernon Holt, May 2, 1967, Legal Files of F. Irvin Dymond—Clay Shaw Case, Historic New Orleans Collection, New Orleans, Louisiana.

[2086] Interview with Philip Vernon Holt, May 20, 1967, Legal Files of F. Irvin Dymond—Clay Shaw Case, Historic New Orleans Collection, New Orleans, Louisiana.

[2087] Shaw Diary entry dated April 17 1967, Donated Papers of Clay Shaw, National Archives, College Park, Maryland.

[2088] Shaw Diary entry dated April 19, 1967, Donated Papers of Clay Shaw, National Archives, College Park, Maryland.

[2089] Interview with Dean Andrews and Rick Townley, April 19, 1967, Legal Files of F. Irvin Dymond—Clay Shaw Case, Historic New Orleans Collection, New Orleans, Louisiana.

[2090] Interview with Dr. Martin Palmer by author, November 7, 2005.

[2091] Minutes of Executive Committee meeting, April 20, 1967, International Trade Mart, International Trade Mart Records, Tulane University, New Orleans, Louisiana.

[2092] See letters from Alice Shaw to Jeff Biddison, 1967 and 1968, Donated Papers of Clay Shaw, National Archives, College Park, Maryland.

[2093] Letter dated April 20, 1967, Tom Oliphant to Shaw, Donated Papers of Clay Shaw, National Archives, College Park, Maryland.

[2094] Memo dated April 20, 1967, Richard Townley regarding lunch with Dean Andrews, Legal Files of F. Irvin Dymond—Clay Shaw Case, Historic New Orleans Collection, New Orleans, Louisiana.

[2095] Letter dated April 21, 1967, Alison P. Marks to Shaw, Donated Papers of Clay Shaw, National Archives, College Park, Maryland.

[2096] Letter dated April 22, 1967, Shaw to James and Judy Formyduval, Author's Collection.

[2097] Letter dated April 24, 1967, L.S. McClaren to Shaw, Donated Papers of Clay Shaw, National Archives, College Park, Maryland.

[2098] Letter dated April 21, 1967, W. Robert Morgan to Shaw, Donated Papers of Clay Shaw, National Archives, College Park, Maryland.

[2099] Letter dated April 26, 1967, Edward Wegmann to James Phelan, Legal Files of F. Irvin Dymond—Clay Shaw Case, Historic New Orleans Collection, New Orleans, Louisiana.

[2100] Summary of interview of Dean Andrews on WDSU Radio by Bill Slater, April 26, 1967, Legal Files of F. Irvin Dymond—Clay Shaw Case, Historic New Orleans Collection, New Orleans, Louisiana.

[2101] Memo dated June 9, 1967 by Aaron Kohn regarding April 25, 1967 telephone call from patrolman John Taylor, Records of the New Orleans Metropolitan Crime Commission, National Archives, College Park, Maryland.

[2102] Letter dated April 18, 1967, Shaw to C.C. Bass, Jr., Legal Files of F. Irvin Dymond—Clay Shaw Case, Historic New Orleans Collection, New Orleans, Louisiana.

[2103] Interview with James Louviere, March 24, 1967, Files Received from Harry Connick, National Archives, College Park, Maryland.

[2104] Letter dated April 20, 1967, Irvin Dymond to Louis C. LaCour, Legal Files of F. Irvin Dymond—Clay Shaw Case, Historic New Orleans Collection, New Orleans, Louisiana.

[2105] Letter dated May 10, 1967, Irvin Dymond to Fred Freed, Legal Files of F. Irvin Dymond—Clay Shaw Case, Historic New Orleans Collection, New Orleans, Louisiana.

2106 Letter dated May 8, 1967, Irvin Dymond to Edward Wegmann, Legal Files of F. Irvin Dymond—Clay Shaw Case, Historic New Orleans Collection, New Orleans, Louisiana.

2107 Memo dated May 8, 1967 by Richard Landsdale, CIA Miscellaneous Files, JFK Assassination Collection, National Archives, College Park, Maryland.

2108 Memo dated May 11, 1967 by Richard H. Lansdale, CIA Miscellaneous Files, JFK Assassination Collection, National Archives, College Park, Maryland.

2109 Interview with Richard Townley, June 25, 2007.

2110 Statement by John Emrold, July 5, 1967, Papers Donated by Lyon Garrison, National Archives, College Park, Maryland.

2111 Shaw Diary entry dated June 17, 1967, Donated Papers of Clay Shaw, National Archives, College Park, Maryland.

2112 Statement of Clyde Johnson, dated April 5, 1967, following interview on March 30, 1967, by James Alcock and Lou Ivon, Legal Files of F. Irvin Dymond—Clay Shaw Case, Historic New Orleans Collection, New Orleans, Louisiana.

2113 Memo, undated, Clay Shaw to Edward Wegmann, Donated Papers of Edward Wegmann, National Archives, College Park, Maryland.

2114 Letter dated October 6, 1967, Edward Wegmann to William J. McNamara, Legal Files of F. Irvin Dymond—Clay Shaw Case, Historic New Orleans Collection, New Orleans, Louisiana.

2115 Interview with F. Irvin Dymond by James Kirkwood, approximately spring 1969, James Kirkwood papers, BostonUniversity.

2116 Letter dated October 6, 1967, Edward Wegmann to Hugh Aynesworth, Legal Files of F. Irvin Dymond—Clay Shaw Case, Historic New Orleans Collection, New Orleans, Louisiana.

2117 Letter dated October 16, 1967, Hugh Aynesworth to Edward Wegmann, Legal Files of F. Irvin Dymond—Clay Shaw Case, Historic New Orleans Collection, New Orleans, Louisiana.

2118 Telegram dated March 2, 1967, Jack Sellers to Shaw, Donated Papers of Clay Shaw, National Archives, College Park, Maryland.

2119 Telegram dated March 2, 1967, Jack Sellers to Shaw, Donated Papers of Clay Shaw, National Archives, College Park, Maryland.

2120 Telegram dated March 21, 1967, Jack Sellers to Shaw, Donated Papers of Clay Shaw, National Archives, College Park, Maryland.

2121 Telegram dated March 24, 1967, Jack Sellers to Shaw, Donated Papers of Clay Shaw, National Archives, College Park, Maryland.

2122 Telegram dated April 1, 1967, Jack Sellers to Shaw, Donated Papers of Clay Shaw, National Archives, College Park, Maryland.

2123 Telegram dated April 22, 1967, Jack Sellers to Shaw, Donated Papers of Clay Shaw, National Archives, College Park, Maryland.

2124 Telegram dated May 20, 1967, Jack Sellars to Shaw, Donated Papers of Clay Shaw, National Archives, College Park, Maryland.

2125 Telegram dated June 23, 1967, Jack Sellers to Shaw, Donated Papers of Clay Shaw, National Archives, College Park, Maryland.

2126 Telegram dated June 24, 1967, Jack Sellers to Shaw, Donated Papers of Clay Shaw, National Archives, College Park, Maryland.

2127 Telegram dated October 21, 1967, Jack Sellars to Shaw, Donated Papers of Clay Shaw, National Archives, College Park, Maryland.

[2128] Shaw Diary entry dated May 1, 1967, Donated Papers of Clay Shaw, National Archives, College Park, Maryland.

[2129] Memo dated June 13, 1967 by Aaron Kohn regarding May 9, 1967 encounter with Pershing Gervais, Records of the New Orleans Metropolitan Crime Commission, National Archives, College Park, Maryland.

[2130] Letter dated May 5, 1967, signed "B.", probably from Mario Bermúdez to Shaw, Donated Papers of Clay Shaw, National Archives, College Park, Maryland.

[2131] Interview with Lloyd Cobb, April 6, 1967, Legal Files of F. Irvin Dymond—Clay Shaw Case, Historic New Orleans Collection, New Orleans, Louisiana.

[2132] Letter dated March 5, 1967, Margalo Gillmore to Shaw, Donated Papers of Clay Shaw, National Archives, College Park, Maryland.

[2133] Letter dated May 11, 1967, no name, but obviously written by Cecil E. Foster to Shaw, Donated Papers of Clay Shaw, National Archives, College Park, Maryland.

[2134] Letter dated May 15, 1967, Irvin Dymond to Roy Jacobs, Legal Files of F. Irvin Dymond—Clay Shaw Case, Historic New Orleans Collection, New Orleans, Louisiana.

[2135] Memo dated June 15, 1967 by Aaron Kohn, Records of the New Orleans Metropolitan Crime Commission, National Archives, College Park, Maryland.

[2136] Transcript of initial interview with Vernon Bundy, Files Received from Harry Connick, National Archives, College Park, Maryland.

[2137] Letter dated May 10, 1967, John B. Leonard to Shaw, Donated Papers of Clay Shaw, National Archives, College Park, Maryland.

[2138] Letter dated May 18, 1967, Chauncey Guidry to Irvin Dymond, Legal Files of F. Irvin Dymond—Clay Shaw Case, Historic New Orleans Collection, New Orleans, Louisiana.

[2139] Letter dated May 18, 1967, Robert A. Wilson to Irvin Dymond, Legal Files of F. Irvin Dymond—Clay Shaw Case, Historic New Orleans Collection, New Orleans, Louisiana.

[2140] FBI memo dated May 18, 1967 by Regis Kennedy, Record Group 60, General Records of the Department of Justice, Classified Subject Files, 129-11, JFK Assassination Collection, National Archives, College Park, Maryland.

[2141] Memo dated June 13, 1967, by Edward Wegmann regarding Lee Odom, Legal Files of F. Irvin Dymond—Clay Shaw Case, Historic New Orleans Collection, New Orleans, Louisiana.

[2142] Memo dated July 28, 1967 regarding May 1967 encounter with Dr. Harold Lief by Aaron Kohn, Records of the New Orleans Metropolitan Crime Commission, National Archives, College Park, Maryland.

[2143] Interview with Irma Fasnacht, May 23, 1967, Legal Files of F. Irvin Dymond—Clay Shaw Case, Historic New Orleans Collection, New Orleans, Louisiana.

[2144] Letter dated May 29, 1967, Hazel to Shaw, Donated Papers of Clay Shaw, National Archives, College Park, Maryland.

[2145] See Jack Martin narrative discussing his tape-recordings of May 1967, Files Received from Harry Connick, National Archives, College Park, Maryland.

[2146] Transcript of telephone conversation between Jack Martin and Steven Plotkin, May 25, 1967, Files Received from Harry Connick, National Archives, College Park, Maryland.

[2147] Transcript of conversation between Jack Martin and Irvin Dymond, transcribed May 29, 1967, Files Received from Harry Connick, National Archives, College Park, Maryland.

[2148] Transcript of telephone conversation between Jack Martin and Richard Townley, May 25, 1967, Files Received from Harry Connick, National Archives, College Park, Maryland.

[2149] Transcript of telephone conversation between Jack Martin and Aaron Kohn, May 29, 1967, Files Received from Harry Connick, National Archives, College Park, Maryland.

[2150] Transcript of telephone conversation between Jack Martin and Steven Plotkin, May 27, 1967, Files Received from Harry Connick, National Archives, College Park, Maryland.

[2151] Transcript of telephone conversation between Jack Martin and Richard Townley, May 28, 1967, Files Received from Harry Connick, National Archives, College Park, Maryland.

[2152] Transcript of telephone conversation between Jack Martin and Richard Townley, June 1, 1967, Files Received from Harry Connick, National Archives, College Park, Maryland.

[2153] Transcript of first interview between Perry Russo and James Phelan, May 24, 1967, Files Received from Harry Connick, National Archives, College Park, Maryland.

[2154] Transcript of second interview between Perry Russo and James Phelan, May 25, 1967, Files Received from Harry Connick, National Archives, College Park, Maryland.

[2155] Note dated May 4, 1967 regarding Morris Brownlee offering to work for Garrison's office, Files Received from Harry Connick, National Archives, College Park, Maryland.

[2156] Transcript of telephone conversation between Richard Townley and John George and Morris Brownlee, May 21, 1967, Files Received from Harry Connick, National Archives, College Park, Maryland.

[2157] Transcript of telephone conversation between Richard Townley and Morris Brownlee, May 22, 1967, Files Received from Harry Connick, National Archives, College Park, Maryland.

[2158] Transcript of telephone conversation between Richard Townley and John George, May 24, 1967, Files Received from Harry Connick, National Archives, College Park, Maryland.

[2159] Memo dated May 23, 1967, Lloyd Ray to Director, Domestic Contact Service, Record Group 233, Records of the U.S. House of Representatives, Select Committee on Assassinations, Segregated CIA Collection, Printed Microfilm, JFK Assassination Collection, National Archives, College Park, Maryland.

[2160] Memo dated January 3, 1968, Lloyd Ray to Director, Domestic Contact Service, Record Group 233, Records of the U.S. House of Representatives, Select Committee on Assassinations, Segregated CIA Collection, JFK Assassination Collection, National Archives, College Park, Maryland.

[2161] Memo dated May 24, 1967 regarding CIA connections in New Orleans, William R. Martin to Jim Garrison, Donated Papers of Edward Wegmann, National Archives, College Park, Maryland.

[2162] Memo dated June 5, 1967, William R. Martin to Jim Garrison, Papers Donated by Lyon Garrison, National Archives, College Park, Maryland.

[2163] Interview with Juan M. Valdez, May 26, 1967, Legal Files of F. Irvin Dymond—Clay Shaw Case, Historic New Orleans Collection, New Orleans, Louisiana.

[2164] Memo dated May 22, 1967, Frank Meloche to Lou Ivon, Files Received from Harry Connick, National Archives, College Park, Maryland.

[2165] Memo dated May 25, 1967, author unknown, Files Received from Harry Connick, National Archives, College Park, Maryland.

[2166] Statement by John Manchester, 1967, Papers Donated by Lyon Garrison, National Archives, College Park, Maryland.

[2167] Statement of Henry Earl Palmer, May 28, 1967, Papers Donated by Lyon Garrison, National Archives, College Park, Maryland.

[2168] Interview with Reeves Morgan, May 29, 1967, Papers Donated by Lyon Garrison, National Archives, College Park, Maryland.

[2169] Statement of Mary Morgan, June 3, 1967, Papers Donated by Lyon Garrison, National Archives, College Park, Maryland.

[2170] Letter dated May 24, 1967, Edward Wegmann to Holland McCombs, Holland McCombs Collection, University of Tennessee-Martin, Martin, Tennessee.

[2171] Letter dated May 31, 1967, David Baldwin to Shaw, Donated Papers of Clay Shaw, National Archives, College Park, Maryland.

[2172] Letter dated May 31, 1967, William Gurvich to Jim Garrison, Donated Papers of Edward Wegmann, National Archives, College Park, Maryland.

[2173] Memo dated March 23, 1967 regarding Charles Earl Daniels, William Gurvich to Jim Garrison, Donated Papers of Edward Wegmann, National Archives, College Park, Maryland.

[2174] Memo dated April 4, 1967, regarding attempt to interview Sergio Arcacha Smith, William Gurvich to Jim Garrison, Donated Papers of Edward Wegmann, National Archives, College Park, Maryland.

[2175] Internal Metropolitan Crime Commission report dated May 31, 1967 by Aaron Kohn, Records of the New Orleans Metropolitan Crime Commission, National Archives, College Park, Maryland.

[2176] Interview with Harry Connick by author, July 11, 2007.

[2177] Shaw Diary entry dated June 2, 1967, Donated Papers of Clay Shaw, National Archives, College Park, Maryland.

[2178] Letter dated June 5, 1967, George Haverstick to Shaw, Donated Papers of Clay Shaw, National Archives, College Park, Maryland.

[2179] Memo dated June 5, 1967 by Lloyd Ray, Record Group 233, Records of the U.S. House of Representatives, Select Committee on Assassinations, Segregated CIA Collection, JFK Assassination Collection, National Archives, College Park, Maryland.

[2180] Memo dated January 31, 1964 by M.D. Stevens, Record Group 263, Records of the Central Intelligence Agency, Office of Security, File on Lee Harvey Oswald, JFK Assassination Collection, National Archives, College Park, Maryland.

[2181] Memo dated November 17, 1975 to The Review Staff, Record Group 263, Records of the Central Intelligence Agency-LA Division Work Files, JFK Assassination Collection, National Archives, College Park, Maryland.

[2182] Memo dated July 5, 1967 by M.D. Stevens, Record Group 263, Records of the Central Intelligence Agency, Office of Security, File on Lee Harvey Oswald, JFK Assassination Collection, National Archives, College Park, Maryland.

[2183] Memo dated May 18, 1967 by John K. Greaney, Record Group 233, Records of the U.S. House of Representatives, Select Committee on Assassinations, Segregated CIA Collection, JFK Assassination Collection, National Archives, College Park, Maryland.

[2184] Interview with Bill McKenzie, June 7, 1967, Legal Files of F. Irvin Dymond—Clay Shaw Case, Historic New Orleans Collection, New Orleans, Louisiana.

[2185] Interview with Leo Le Veque, Jr. by Shaw's attorneys' investigators, Legal Files of F. Irvin Dymond—Clay Shaw Case, Historic New Orleans Collection, New Orleans, Louisiana.

[2186] *Times-Picayune* article dated February 26, 1992, Legal Files of F. Irvin Dymond—Clay Shaw Case, Historic New Orleans Collection, New Orleans, Louisiana.

[2187] Letter dated June 8, 1967, Ben Toledano to Edward Wegmann, Legal Files of F. Irvin Dymond—Clay Shaw Case, Historic New Orleans Collection, New Orleans, Louisiana.

[2188] Letter dated June 14, 1967, Edward Wegmann to Holland McCombs, Legal Files of F. Irvin Dymond—Clay Shaw Case, Historic New Orleans Collection, New Orleans, Louisiana.

[2189] Letter dated May 18, 1967, Robert A. Wilson to Irvin Dymond, Legal Files of F. Irvin Dymond—Clay Shaw Case, Historic New Orleans Collection, New Orleans, Louisiana.

[2190] Letter dated June 14, 1967, Edward Wegmann to Holland McCombs, Holland McCombs Collection, University of Tennessee-Martin, Martin, Tennessee.

[2191] Interview with Edwin Lea McGehee, June 17, 1967, Papers Donated by Lyon Garrison, National Archives, College Park, Maryland.

[2192] Letter dated June 20, 1967, Edward Wegmann to Wilma Francis, Legal Files of F. Irvin Dymond—Clay Shaw Case, Historic New Orleans Collection, New Orleans, Louisiana.

[2193] Transcript of telephone conversation between Jack Martin and Anthony Garrich, June 8, 1967, Files Received from Harry Connick, National Archives, College Park, Maryland.

[2194] Card dated June 19, 1967, Edith Stern to Shaw, Donated Papers of Clay Shaw, National Archives, College Park, Maryland.

[2195] Letter dated June 19, 1967, Mark Lane to Jim Garrison, Files Received from Harry Connick, National Archives, College Park, Maryland.

[2196] Letter dated January 12, 1978, Aaron Kohn to G. Robert Blakey, Records of the New Orleans Metropolitan Crime Commission, National Archives, College Park, Maryland.

[2197] Memo dated June 15, 1967 by Aaron Kohn, Records of the New Orleans Metropolitan Crime Commission, National Archives, College Park, Maryland.

[2198] Unedited interview with John Cancler, Records of the New Orleans Metropolitan Crime Commission, National Archives, College Park, Maryland.

[2199] Unedited interview with Layton Martens, Records of the New Orleans Metropolitan Crime Commission, National Archives, College Park, Maryland.

[2200] Unedited interview with Eleanor Bares, Records of the New Orleans Metropolitan Crime Commission, National Archives, College Park, Maryland.

[2201] Unedited interview with Bill Bankston, Records of the New Orleans Metropolitan Crime Commission, National Archives, College Park, Maryland.

[2202] Unedited interview with Roy Jacobs, Records of the New Orleans Metropolitan Crime Commission, National Archives, College Park, Maryland.

[2203] Memo dated June 15, 1967 by Aaron Kohn, Records of the New Orleans Metropolitan Crime Commission, National Archives, College Park, Maryland.

[2204] Statement of Fred Hendrick Leemans, Jr., May 5, 1967, Papers Donated by Lyon Garrison, National Archives, College Park, Maryland.

[2205] Memo dated May 24, 1967, by Irvin Dymond regarding Fred Leemans, Legal Files of F. Irvin Dymond—Clay Shaw Case, Historic New Orleans Collection, New Orleans, Louisiana.

[2206] Letter dated May 30, 1967, Fred Leemans, Jr. to Jim Garrison, Legal Files of F. Irvin Dymond—Clay Shaw Case, Historic New Orleans Collection, New Orleans, Louisiana.

[2207] Interview with F. Irvin Dymond by James Kirkwood, approximately spring 1969, James Kirkwood papers, Boston University.

[2208] See report dated February 2, 1952 regarding incident that occurred December 14, 1952, Records of the New Orleans Metropolitan Crime Commission, National Archives, College Park, Maryland.

[2209] FBI Memo dated June 27, 1967, Record Group 60, General Records of the Department of Justice, Classified Subject Files, 129-11, JFK Assassination Collection, National Archives, College Park, Maryland.

[2210] Memo dated July 28, 1967, Record Group 65, FBI Files, JFK Assassination Collection, National Archives, College Park, Maryland.

[2211] Telegram dated June 20, 1967, Charles Bushong to Shaw, Donated Papers of Clay Shaw, National Archives, College Park, Maryland.

[2212] Telegram dated June 20, 1967, Aaron Kohn to Fred Freed, Records of the New Orleans Metropolitan Crime Commission, National Archives, College Park, Maryland.

[2213] Transcript of June 20, 1967 telephone call between Gordon Novel and Aaron Kohn, dated June 30, 1967, Records of the New Orleans Metropolitan Crime Commission, National Archives, College Park, Maryland.

[2214] Article in *The Washington Post*, June 22, 1967 by George Lardner, Record Group 263, Records of the Central Intelligence Agency, Personality File on Lee Harvey Oswald, JFK Assassination Collection, National Archives, College Park, Maryland.

[2215] Letter dated June 29, 1967, Gordon Berger to Shaw, Donated Papers of Clay Shaw, National Archives, College Park, Maryland.

[2216] Letter dated June 30, 1967, William Taliaferro to Shaw, Donated Papers of Clay Shaw, National Archives, College Park, Maryland.

[2217] Transcript of June 1967 CBS News television special regarding the Warren Commission, Records of the New Orleans Metropolitan Crime Commission, National Archives, College Park, Maryland.

[2218] Transcript of discussion with Aaron Kohn by Jim Garrison, James Alcock, and Richard Burnes, June 29, 1967, Files Received from Harry Connick, National Archives, College Park, Maryland.

[2219] Letter dated August 25, 1967, Aaron Kohn to Albert Labiche, Records of the New Orleans Metropolitan Crime Commission, National Archives, College Park, Maryland.

[2220] Internal Metropolitan Crime Commission report dated August 23, 1973 by Aaron Kohn, Records of the New Orleans Metropolitan Crime Commission, National Archives, College Park, Maryland.

[2221] Interview of Martin Palmer by author, November 7, 2005.

[2222] FBI memo dated July 25, 1967 by Special Agent James J. McCabe, Record Group 233, Records of the U.S. House of Representatives, Select Committee on Assassinations, Segregated CIA Collection, JFK Assassination Collection, National Archives, College Park, Maryland.

[2223] Letter dated July 7, 1967, Edward Wegmann to Wynn Pearce, Legal Files of F. Irvin Dymond—Clay Shaw Case, Historic New Orleans Collection, New Orleans, Louisiana.

[2224] Memo dated July 10, 1967 regarding interview with Elliott Collins Hay, Cliency Navarre to Lou Ivon, Donated Papers of Edward Wegmann, National Archives, College Park, Maryland.

[2225] Interview with William A. Morris, July 12, 1967, Papers Donated by Lyon Garrison, National Archives, College Park, Maryland.

[2226] Memo dated August 14, 1967 regarding interview with Bill Boone by William R. Martin, Papers Donated by Lyon Garrison, National Archives, College Park, Maryland.

[2227] Memo dated August 3, 1967 regarding interview with Eugene Davis by William R. Martin, Papers Donated by Lyon Garrison, National Archives, College Park, Maryland.

[2228] Telegram dated July 7, 1967, NBC News to Irvin Dymond, Legal Files of F. Irvin Dymond—Clay Shaw Case, Historic New Orleans Collection, New Orleans, Louisiana.

[2229] Letter dated July 11, 1967, Willard Robertson to Jim Garrison, JFK Assassination Collection, New Orleans Public Library, New Orleans, Louisiana.

[2230] Telegram dated July 16, 1967, Patricia Lambert to President Lyndon B. Johnson, Record Group 60, General Records of the Department of Justice, Classified Subject Files, 129-11, JFK Assassination Collection, National Archives, College Park, Maryland.

[2231] Memo dated August 24, 1967, Record Group 65, FBI Files, JFK Assassination Collection, National Archives, College Park, Maryland.

[2232] Letter dated July 14, 1967, Edward Wegmann to Holland McCombs, Holland McCombs Collection, University of Tennessee-Martin, Martin, Tennessee.

[2233] Letter dated July 18, 1967, Bill Mehrten to Shaw, Donated Papers of Clay Shaw, National Archives, College Park, Maryland.

[2234] Letter dated July 19, 1967, Jacqueline de Chimay to Shaw, Donated Papers of Clay Shaw, National Archives, College Park, Maryland.

[2235] Memo dated July 17, 1967 regarding Charles K. Spiesel, James Alcock to Jim Garrison, Donated Papers of Edward Wegmann, National Archives, College Park, Maryland.

[2236] E-mail exchange between Robert Richter and author, July 2007. Also see memo dated February 21, 1967, from Tom Bethell at National Archives, Files Received from Harry Connick, National Archives, College Park, Maryland.

[2237] E-mail exchange between Robert Richter and author, July 2007. Also see memo dated August 14, 1967, Tom Bethell to Jim Garrison, Files Received from Harry Connick, National Archives, College Park, Maryland.

[2238] Notes of Aaron Kohn related to his conversations with Charles Spiesel, November 3, November 4, and November 5, 1965, Records of the New Orleans Metropolitan Crime Commission, National Archives, College Park, Maryland.

[2239] CIA memo dated February 12, 1969, Record Group 233, Records of the U.S. House of Representatives, Select Committee on Assassinations, Segregated CIA Collection, JFK Assassination Collection, National Archives, College Park, Maryland.

[2240] Motion for Return of Seized Property by Shaw's defense attorneys, Files Received from Harry Connick, National Archives, College Park, Maryland.

[2241] Memo dated July 5, 1967 by Aaron Kohn, Records of the New Orleans Metropolitan Crime Commission, National Archives, College Park, Maryland.

[2242] Transcript of June 27, 1967 interview of William Gurvich by Ford Rowan of WDSU-TV, Records of the New Orleans Metropolitan Crime Commission, National Archives, College Park, Maryland.

[2243] FBI Memo dated June 21, 1967, Record Group 60, General Records of the Department of Justice, Classified Subject Files, 129-11, JFK Assassination Collection, National Archives, College Park, Maryland.

[2244] Interview of William Gurvich by defense attorneys, August 29, 1967, Legal Files of F. Irvin Dymond—Clay Shaw Case, Historic New Orleans Collection, New Orleans, Louisiana.

[2245] Transcript of interview with Darrell Garner by Jim Garrison, November 12, 1967, Files Received from Harry Connick, National Archives, College Park, Maryland.

[2246] Statement of Andrew Dunn, July 13, 1967, Papers Donated by Lyon Garrison, National Archives, College Park, Maryland.

[2247] Memo dated July 17, 1967, by Andrew Sciambra, Files Received from Harry Connick, National Archives, College Park, Maryland.

[2248] Letter dated July 14, 1967, Edward Wegmann to Irvin Dymond, Legal Files of F. Irvin Dymond—Clay Shaw Case, Historic New Orleans Collection, New Orleans, Louisiana.

[2249] Letter dated August 2, 1967, Edward Wegmann to Hugh Aynesworth, Legal Files of F. Irvin Dymond—Clay Shaw Case, Historic New Orleans Collection, New Orleans, Louisiana.

[2250] Letter dated July 15, 1967, Harold Robbins to Ramsey Clark, Record Group 60, General Records of the Department of Justice, Classified Subject Files, 129-11, JFK Assassination Collection, National Archives, College Park, Maryland.

[2251] Undated letter, sometime in mid-1967, Mrs. Edwin S. Anderson to Shaw, Donated Papers of Clay Shaw, National Archives, College Park, Maryland.

[2252] Letter dated August 4, 1967, Lex Hawkins to Jim Garrison, Edward Wegmann, and Irvin Dymond, Legal Files of F. Irvin Dymond—Clay Shaw Case, Historic New Orleans Collection, New Orleans, Louisiana.

[2253] Memo dated August 4, 1967, Lloyd Ray to Director, Domestic Contact Office, Record Group 233, Records of the U.S. House of Representatives, Select Committee on Assassinations, Segregated CIA Collection, JFK Assassination Collection, National Archives, College Park, Maryland.

[2254] Internal Metropolitan Crime Commission report dated August 10, 1967 by Aaron Kohn, Records of the New Orleans Metropolitan Crime Commission, National Archives, College Park, Maryland.

[2255] Letter dated August 2, 1967, Edward Wegmann to Irvin Dymond and William Wegmann, Legal Files of F. Irvin Dymond—Clay Shaw Case, Historic New Orleans Collection, New Orleans, Louisiana.

[2256] Memo dated January 29, 1968, interview August 4,1967 with Bobbie Dedon, Papers Donated by Lyon Garrison, National Archives, College Park, Maryland.

[2257] Notes regarding telephone conversation between Wesley Liebeler and James Alcock, by S. Scalia, August 2, 1967, Files Received from Harry Connick, National Archives, College Park, Maryland.

[2258] Letter dated August 2, 1967, Edward Wegmann to Irvin Dymond and William Wegmann, Legal Files of F. Irvin Dymond—Clay Shaw Case, Historic New Orleans Collection, New Orleans, Louisiana.

[2259] Letter dated August 2, 1967, Edward Wegmann to Irvin Dymond and William Wegmann, Legal Files of F. Irvin Dymond—Clay Shaw Case, Historic New Orleans Collection, New Orleans, Louisiana.

[2260] Letter dated August 4, 1967, Edward Wegmann to Wynn Pearce, Legal Files of F. Irvin Dymond—Clay Shaw Case, Historic New Orleans Collection, New Orleans, Louisiana.

[2261] Letter dated August 4, 1967, Edward Wegmann to Department of Vital Statistics, State of California, Legal Files of F. Irvin Dymond—Clay Shaw Case, Historic New Orleans Collection, New Orleans, Louisiana.

[2262] Letter dated August 4, 1967, Edward Wegmann to Jim Loring, Legal Files of F. Irvin Dymond—Clay Shaw Case, Historic New Orleans Collection, New Orleans, Louisiana.

[2263] Letter dated August 10, 1967, John Nichols, M.D. to Jim Garrison, Files Received from Harry Connick, National Archives, College Park, Maryland.

[2264] Handwritten Memo by Layton Martens of meeting with Perry Russo, August 15, 1967, Legal Files of F. Irvin Dymond—Clay Shaw Case, Historic New Orleans Collection, New Orleans, Louisiana.

[2265] Letter dated August 21, 1967, Irvin Dymond to Edward and William Wegmann, Legal Files of F. Irvin Dymond—Clay Shaw Case, Historic New Orleans Collection, New Orleans, Louisiana.

[2266] Memo of conversation with Layton Martens by Edward Wegmann, August 18, 1967, Legal Files of F. Irvin Dymond—Clay Shaw Case, Historic New Orleans Collection, New Orleans, Louisiana.

[2267] Letter dated August 17, 1967, Edward Wegmann to Irvin Dymond and William Wegmann, Legal Files of F. Irvin Dymond—Clay Shaw Case, Historic New Orleans Collection, New Orleans, Louisiana.

[2268] Interview with Sam Monk Zelden by James Kirkwood, Spring 1969, James Kirkwood Papers, Boston University, Boston, Massachusetts.

[2269] Transcript of Dean Andrews trial hearing, August 1967, Record Group 60, Department of Justice, Civil Rights Division, 1967-69, JFK Assassination Collection, National Archives, College Park, Maryland.

[2270] Transcript of Dean Andrews trial hearing, August 1967, Record Group 60, Department of Justice, Civil Rights Division, 1967-69, JFK Assassination Collection, National Archives, College Park, Maryland.

[2271] Transcript of Dean Andrews trial hearing, August 1967, Record Group 60, Department of Justice, Civil Rights Division, 1967-69, JFK Assassination Collection, National Archives, College Park, Maryland.

[2272] Memo dated August 23, 1967, by Andrew Sciambra, Files Received from Harry Connick, National Archives, College Park, Maryland.

[2273] Interview with Donald P. Norton by Charles Ward, July 1967, Papers Donated by Lyon Garrison, National Archives, College Park, Maryland.

[2274] Letter dated October 17, 1967, Edward Wegmann to John Taylor, Legal Files of F. Irvin Dymond—Clay Shaw Case, Historic New Orleans Collection, New Orleans, Louisiana.

[2275] Letter dated September 11, 1967, Edward Wegmann to Irvin Dymond, Legal Files of F. Irvin Dymond—Clay Shaw Case, Historic New Orleans Collection, New Orleans, Louisiana.

[2276] Letter dated September 5, 1967, Irvin Dymond to Lloyd Ray, Legal Files of F. Irvin Dymond—Clay Shaw Case, Historic New Orleans Collection, New Orleans, Louisiana.

[2277] Letter dated September 5, 1967, Irvin Dymond to Edward Wegmann, Legal Files of F. Irvin Dymond—Clay Shaw Case, Historic New Orleans Collection, New Orleans, Louisiana.

[2278] Letter dated September 7, 1967, Irvin Dymond to Richard Townley, Legal Files of F. Irvin Dymond—Clay Shaw Case, Historic New Orleans Collection, New Orleans, Louisiana.

[2279] Letter dated September 7, 1967, Irvin Dymond to Hugh Aynesworth, Legal Files of F. Irvin Dymond—Clay Shaw Case, Historic New Orleans Collection, New Orleans, Louisiana.

[2280] Memo dated September 1, 1967, Richard Burnes to Tom Bethell, Files Received from Harry Connick, National Archives, College Park, Maryland.

[2281] Affidavit by Ronald R. Raymond, Files Received from Harry Connick, National Archives, College Park, Maryland.

[2282] Affidavit of Jessie Parker, September 12, 1967, related to Eastern Airlines VIP Room incident, Donated Papers of Edward Wegmann, National Archives, College Park, Maryland.

[2283] Memo dated September 13, 1967, Andrew Sciambra to Jim Garrison, Files Received from Harry Connick, National Archives, College Park, Maryland.

[2284] Interview with Cecilia Fagan, September 13, 1967, Files Received from Harry Connick, National Archives, College Park, Maryland.

[2285] Memo dated April 2, 1968, Andrew Sciambra to Jim Garrison regarding interview with Captain John Warren, Legal Files of F. Irvin Dymond—Clay Shaw Case, Historic New Orleans Collection, New Orleans, Louisiana.

[2286] Memo dated April 2, 1968, Andrew Sciambra to Jim Garrison and Harold Weisberg regarding interview with Theodore Herrera, Legal Files of F. Irvin Dymond—Clay Shaw Case, Historic New Orleans Collection, New Orleans, Louisiana.

[2287] Memo dated April 2, 1968, Andrew Sciambra to Jim Garrison regarding interview with Mr. and Mrs. Ross P. Pope, Legal Files of F. Irvin Dymond—Clay Shaw Case, Historic New Orleans Collection, New Orleans, Louisiana.

[2288] Affidavit of Jessie Parker, September 12, 1967, related to Eastern Airlines VIP Room incident, Files Received from Harry Connick, National Archives, College Park, Maryland.

[2289] Letter dated September 1, 1967, Edward Wegmann to Bill Alexander, Legal Files of F. Irvin Dymond—Clay Shaw Case, Historic New Orleans Collection, New Orleans, Louisiana.

[2290] Letter dated September 1, 1967, Edward Wegmann to Lex Hawkins, Legal Files of F. Irvin Dymond—Clay Shaw Case, Historic New Orleans Collection, New Orleans, Louisiana.

[2291] Memo dated September 8, 1967 regarding interview with Valentine Ashworth by Richard Burnes, Papers Donated by Lyon Garrison, National Archives, College Park, Maryland.

[2292] Memo dated September 18, 1967 regarding Edward James Whalen, James Alcock to Jim Garrison, Donated Papers of Edward Wegmann, National Archives, College Park, Maryland.

[2293] Letter dated September 19, 1967, Edward Wegmann to Eva Grant, Legal Files of F. Irvin Dymond—Clay Shaw Case, Historic New Orleans Collection, New Orleans, Louisiana.

[2294] Memo dated September 25, 1967, Record Group 65, FBI Files, JFK Assassination Collection, National Archives, College Park, Maryland.

[2295] Interview of Moon Landrieu by author, February 22, 2007.

[2296] Statement of Henry Clark, September 12, 1967, Papers Donated by Lyon Garrison, National Archives, College Park, Maryland.

[2297] Affidavit of Henry Burnell Clark, September 12, 1967, Files Received from Harry Connick, National Archives, College Park, Maryland.

[2298] Statement of Henry Burnell Clark, September 12, 1967, Files Received from Harry Connick, National Archives, College Park, Maryland.

[2299] Memo dated September 18, 1967 by Lawrence Houston, CIA Miscellaneous Files, JFK Assassination Collection, National Archives, College Park, Maryland.

[2300] Memo dated September 29, 1967 from Office of General Counsel, Headquarters, Record Group 233, Records of the U.S. House of Representatives, Select Committee on Assassinations, Segregated CIA Collection, Printed Microfilm, JFK Assassination Collection, National Archives, College Park, Maryland.

[2301] Memo dated September 29, 1967, New Orleans CIA Office to Office of General Counsel, CIA Headquarters, Record Group 233, Records of the U.S. House of Representatives, Select Committee on Assassinations, Segregated CIA Collection, Printed Microfilm, JFK Assassination Collection, National Archives, College Park, Maryland.

[2302] Letter dated September 27, 1967, Edward Wegmann to John Doar, Legal Files of F. Irvin Dymond—Clay Shaw Case, Historic New Orleans Collection, New Orleans, Louisiana.

[2303] Handwritten note dated September 27, 1967, Ronnie Wicker to Irvin Dymond, Legal Files of F. Irvin Dymond—Clay Shaw Case, Historic New Orleans Collection, New Orleans, Louisiana.

[2304] Letter dated September 25, 1967, James Eddy to Edward Wegmann, Legal Files of F. Irvin Dymond—Clay Shaw Case, Historic New Orleans Collection, New Orleans, Louisiana.

[2305] Letter dated October 2, 1967, Mrs. Edwin S. Anderson to Shaw, Donated Papers of Clay Shaw, National Archives, College Park, Maryland.

[2306] Letter dated September 27, 1967, Patrick O'Rourke to Edward Wegmann, Author's Collection.

[2307] Letter dated September 27, 1967, Patrick O'Rourke to Shaw, Author's Collection.

[2308] Statement of Jules Ricco Kimble, October 10, 1967, Papers Donated by Lyon Garrison, National Archives, College Park, Maryland.

[2309] Memo dated October 10, 1967, Tom Bethell to Jim Garrison, Files Received from Harry Connick, National Archives, College Park, Maryland.

[2310] Letter dated October 16, 1967, Charles Nutter to Ramsey Clark, Record Group 60, General Records of the Department of Justice, Classified Subject Files, 129-11, JFK Assassination Collection, National Archives, College Park, Maryland.

[2311] Unsigned handwritten letter dated October 14, 1967 to Department of Justice, Record Group 60, General Records of the Department of Justice, Classified Subject Files, 129-11, JFK Assassination Collection, National Archives, College Park, Maryland.

[2312] The deposition of Walter Sheridan was taken in the case of *Novel v. Garrison*, and can be found in the records from that case at the National Archives in College Park, Maryland.

[2313] Letter dated November 27, 1967, James McCormack to Shaw, Donated Papers of Clay Shaw, National Archives, College Park, Maryland.

[2314] Minutes of Executive Committee meeting, October 26, 1967, International Trade Mart, International Trade Mart Records, Tulane University, New Orleans, Louisiana.

[2315] Newspaper article in *Dallas Morning News*, October 30, 1967, Donated Papers of Edward Wegmann, National Archives, College Park, Maryland.

[2316] Memo dated November 6, 1967 regarding interview with Arthur Q. Davis, James Alcock to Jim Garrison, Donated Papers of Edward Wegmann, National Archives, College Park, Maryland.

[2317] Memo dated January 11, 1968, summarizing things Perry Russo told Layton Martens, Legal Files of F. Irvin Dymond—Clay Shaw Case, Historic New Orleans Collection, New Orleans, Louisiana.

[2318] Interview with Alfred Moran by James Alcock and Sergeant Tom Duffy, November 17, 1967, Files Received from Harry Connick, National Archives, College Park, Maryland.

[2319] Memo dated November 30, 1967, Lawrence Houston to CIA New Orleans Office, Record Group 233, Records of the U.S. House of Representatives, Select Committee on Assassinations, Segregated CIA Collection, Printed Microfilm, JFK Assassination Collection, National Archives, College Park, Maryland.

[2320] Letter dated December 1, 1967, Edward Wegmann to John Doar, Legal Files of F. Irvin Dymond—Clay Shaw Case, Historic New Orleans Collection, New Orleans, Louisiana.

[2321] Letter dated December 1, 1967, Edward Wegmann to John Doar, Record Group 60, Department of Justice, Civil Rights Division, 1967-69, JFK Assassination Collection, National Archives, College Park, Maryland.

[2322] Statement of Herbert R. Wagner, Jr., December 6, 1967, Papers Donated by Lyon Garrison, National Archives, College Park, Maryland.

[2323] Memo dated December 7, 1967 regarding interview with Edward Julius Girnus, James Alcock to Jim Garrison, Donated Papers of Edward Wegmann, National Archives, College Park, Maryland.

[2324] Letter dated December 2, 1967, Princess Jacqueline de Chimay to Shaw, Donated Papers of Clay Shaw, National Archives, College Park, Maryland.

[2325] Letter dated December 10, 1967, Paul (last name unknown) to Shaw, Donated Papers of Clay Shaw, National Archives, College Park, Maryland.

[2326] Letter dated December 18, 1968, Aaron Kohn to Dr. Joseph Pasternak, Records of the New Orleans Metropolitan Crime Commission, National Archives, College Park, Maryland.

[2327] Transcript of telephone conversation between William Wood (alias Bill Boxley) and Richard Billings, December 11, 1967, Files Received from Harry Connick, National Archives, College Park, Maryland.

[2328] Letter dated December 15, 1967, William Wegmann to Irvin Dymond and Edward Wegmann, Legal Files of F. Irvin Dymond—Clay Shaw Case, Historic New Orleans Collection, New Orleans, Louisiana.

[2329] Letter dated December 16, 1967, William Wegmann to Irvin Dymond and Edward Wegmann, Legal Files of F. Irvin Dymond—Clay Shaw Case, Historic New Orleans Collection, New Orleans, Louisiana.

[2330] Christmas card dated December 24, 1967, Carmen and Hal Lidin to Shaw, Donated Papers of Clay Shaw, National Archives, College Park, Maryland.

[2331] See letter dated April 10, 1967, Thomas L. Thornhill to Mike Karmazin, Files Received from Harry Connick, National Archives, College Park, Maryland.

[2332] See drafts of criminal charge against Edgar Eugene Bradley, Files Received from Harry Connick, National Archives, College Park, Maryland.

[2333] Statement of David F. Lewis, December 28, 1967, Files Received from Harry Connick, National Archives, College Park, Maryland.

[2334] Memo dated December 26, 1967, Andrew Sciambra to Jim Garrison, Files Received from Harry Connick, National Archives, College Park, Maryland.

[2335] Memo dated December 28, 1967, Andrew Sciambra to Jim Garrison, Files Received from Harry Connick, National Archives, College Park, Maryland.

[2336] Memo dated December 26, 1967 regarding interview of Roger Craig by Numa V. Bertel, Jr. on December 22, 1967, Files Received from Harry Connick, National Archives, College Park, Maryland.

[2337] Affidavit of Roger Craig, February 1968, Files Received from Harry Connick, National Archives, College Park, Maryland.

[2338] Memo dated December 7, 1967, Roger Craig to Jim Garrison, Files Received from Harry Connick, National Archives, College Park, Maryland.

[2339] Letter dated January 5, 1968, Roger Craig to Willard Robertson, Files Received from Harry Connick, National Archives, College Park, Maryland.

[2340] Letter dated January 5, 1968, Roger Craig to Jim Garrison, Files Received from Harry Connick, National Archives, College Park, Maryland.

[2341] Letter of recommendation dated January 17, 1968, Jim Garrison for Roger Craig, JFK Assassination Collection, New Orleans Public Library, New Orleans, Louisiana.

[2342] Letter dated May 22, 1969, Edgar Eugene Bradley to Jim Garrison, Files Received from Harry Connick, National Archives, College Park, Maryland.

[2343] Letter dated September 17, 1969, Edgar Eugene Bradley to Jim Garrison, Files Received from Harry Connick, National Archives, College Park, Maryland.

[2344] Garrison office memo dated December 24, 1967, author unknown, Wood/Boxley Files, JFK Assassination Collection, National Archives, College Park, Maryland.

[2345] Memo, undated but after December 7, 1967, Gary Sanders to Lou Ivon, Files Received from Harry Connick, National Archives, College Park, Maryland.

[2346] Letter dated January 2, 1968, Phillip Carey Jones to Shaw, Donated Papers of Clay Shaw, National Archives, College Park, Maryland.

2347 Undated letter, early 1968, Mrs. James Dixon Formyduval to Shaw, Donated Papers of Clay Shaw, National Archives, College Park, Maryland.

2348 Letter, undated but probably early 1968, Shaw to James and Judy Formyduval, Author's Collection.

2349 Telegram dated January 2, 1968, Hugh Aynesworth to Jim Garrison, Wood/Boxley Files, JFK Assassination Collection, National Archives, College Park, Maryland.

2350 Memo dated February 25, 1968, Ernest Bische to Director, Domestic Contact Service, Record Group 233, Records of the U.S. House of Representatives, Select Committee on Assassinations, Segregated CIA Collection, Printed Microfilm, JFK Assassination Collection, National Archives, College Park, Maryland.

2351 Memo dated January 2, 1968, Andrew Sciambra to Jim Garrison, Files Received from Harry Connick, National Archives, College Park, Maryland.

2352 Letter dated January 4, 1968, Edward Wegmann to Edward S. Butler, Legal Files of F. Irvin Dymond—Clay Shaw Case, Historic New Orleans Collection, New Orleans, Louisiana.

2353 Letter dated January 4, 1968, Edward Wegmann to Representative F. Edward Hebert, Legal Files of F. Irvin Dymond—Clay Shaw Case, Historic New Orleans Collection, New Orleans, Louisiana.

2354 Letter dated January 4, 1968, Edward Wegmann to Nathanial Cossack, Legal Files of F. Irvin Dymond—Clay Shaw Case, Historic New Orleans Collection, New Orleans, Louisiana.

2355 Memo dated January 4, 1968 by Aaron Kohn Records of the New Orleans Metropolitan Crime Commission, National Archives, College Park, Maryland.

2356 Letter dated January 8, 1968, Alton Ochsner to Aaron Kohn, Records of the New Orleans Metropolitan Crime Commission, National Archives, College Park, Maryland.

2357 Letter dated January 5, 1968, Robert Jackson to Shaw, Donated Papers of Clay Shaw, National Archives, College Park, Maryland.

2358 E-mail dated April 2, 2010, Gordon S. Jackson to Author.

2359 Memo dated January 29, 1968, Andrew Sciambra to Jim Garrison, Files Received from Harry Connick, National Archives, College Park, Maryland.

2360 Memo dated January 8, 1968, Andrew Sciambra to Jim Garrison, Files Received from Harry Connick, National Archives, College Park, Maryland.

2361 Memo dated January 17, 1968 regarding interview with Melvie Morgan Ellis and John Ellis by Andrew Sciambra on January 9, 1968, Files Received from Harry Connick, National Archives, College Park, Maryland.

2362 Memo dated January 23, 1968, Andrew Sciambra to Jim Garrison, regarding interviews with people in Jackson and Clinton, Files Received from Harry Connick, National Archives, College Park, Maryland.

2363 Memo dated January 30, 1968 regarding interview with Andrew Dunn by Frank Ruiz and Kent Simms on January 10, 1968, Files Received from Harry Connick, National Archives, College Park, Maryland.

2364 Memo dated October 9, 1968, Andrew Sciambra to Jim Garrison, Files Received from Harry Connick, National Archives, College Park, Maryland.

2365 Letter dated January 17, 1968, James Leo Herlihy to Shaw, Donated Papers of Clay Shaw, National Archives, College Park, Maryland.

2366 Letter dated January 16, 1968, Edward Wegmann to Irvin Dymond and William Wegmann, Legal Files of F. Irvin Dymond—Clay Shaw Case, Historic New Orleans Collection, New Orleans, Louisiana.

[2367] Memo dated January 13, 1968, Wood/Boxley Files, JFK Assassination Collection, National Archives, College Park, Maryland.

[2368] Transcript of interview with Layton Martens by Edward Wegmann, January 15, 1968, Legal Files of F. Irvin Dymond—Clay Shaw Case, Historic New Orleans Collection, New Orleans, Louisiana.

[2369] Transcript of interview with Layton Martens by Edward Wegmann, January 15, 1968, Legal Files of F. Irvin Dymond—Clay Shaw Case, Historic New Orleans Collection, New Orleans, Louisiana.

[2370] Transcript of interview with Layton Martens by Edward Wegmann, January 15, 1968, Legal Files of F. Irvin Dymond—Clay Shaw Case, Historic New Orleans Collection, New Orleans, Louisiana.

[2371] Transcript of interview with Layton Martens by Edward Wegmann, January 15, 1968, Legal Files of F. Irvin Dymond—Clay Shaw Case, Historic New Orleans Collection, New Orleans, Louisiana.

[2372] Letter dated January 25, 1968, Edward Wegmann to Irvin Dymond and William Wegmann, Legal Files of F. Irvin Dymond—Clay Shaw Case, Historic New Orleans Collection, New Orleans, Louisiana.

[2373] Letter dated January 18, 1968, Edward Wegmann to Herbert Spiegel, Legal Files of F. Irvin Dymond—Clay Shaw Case, Historic New Orleans Collection, New Orleans, Louisiana.

[2374] FBI Memo dated January 18, 1968, Record Group 60, General Records of the Department of Justice, Classified Subject Files, 129-11, JFK Assassination Collection, National Archives, College Park, Maryland.

[2375] Memo dated January 31, 1968 regarding interview with William Dunn by Frank Ruiz and Kent Simms on January 17, 1968, Files Received from Harry Connick, National Archives, College Park, Maryland.

[2376] Memo dated January 29, 1968 regarding interviews with 53 individuals from January 10 through January 18, 1968 by Kent Simms and Frank Ruiz, Files Received from Harry Connick, National Archives, College Park, Maryland.

[2377] Memo dated January 23, 1968, Andrew Sciambra to Jim Garrison, regarding interview with Guy Broyles, Files Received from Harry Connick, National Archives, College Park, Maryland.

[2378] Letter dated January 22, 1968, Andrew Sciambra to Elmer Litchfield, Record Group 60, General Records of the Department of Justice, Classified Subject Files, 129-11, JFK Assassination Collection, National Archives, College Park, Maryland.

[2379] Letter dated February 19, 1968, Andrew Sciambra to J. Edgar Hoover, Record Group 60, General Records of the Department of Justice, Classified Subject Files, 129-11, JFK Assassination Collection, National Archives, College Park, Maryland.

[2380] Memo dated January 25, 1968, Statements by Elmer D. Litchfield, Michael Baron, and Earl R. Peterson, Record Group 65, FBI Files, JFK Assassination Collection, National Archives, College Park, Maryland.

[2381] Memo dated January 25, 1968 regarding ASAC Sylvester and SA Richard Smallwood, Record Group 65, FBI Files, JFK Assassination Collection, National Archives, College Park, Maryland.

[2382] Department of Justice Reply dated February 14, 1968, Record Group 60, General Records of the Department of Justice, Classified Subject Files, 129-11, JFK Assassination Collection, National Archives, College Park, Maryland.

[2383] Letter dated January 22, 1968, Theodore Geffner to Edward Wegmann, Legal Files of F. Irvin Dymond—Clay Shaw Case, Historic New Orleans Collection, New Orleans, Louisiana.

[2384] Letter dated January 25, 1968, Edward Wegmann to New York Supreme Court, Legal Files of F. Irvin Dymond—Clay Shaw Case, Historic New Orleans Collection, New Orleans, Louisiana.

[2385] Letter dated January 25, 1968, Edward Wegmann to Hugh Aynesworth, Legal Files of F. Irvin Dymond—Clay Shaw Case, Historic New Orleans Collection, New Orleans, Louisiana.

[2386] Letter dated January 26, 1968, Edward Wegmann to Elmer Gertz, Legal Files of F. Irvin Dymond—Clay Shaw Case, Historic New Orleans Collection, New Orleans, Louisiana.

[2387] Memo dated January 26, 1968 to members of the Hunt family, Record Group 233, Records of the U.S. House of Representatives, Select Committee on Assassinations, Segregated CIA Collection, Printed Microfilm, JFK Assassination Collection, National Archives, College Park, Maryland.

[2388] Memo dated January 30, 1968, Record Group 65, FBI Files, JFK Assassination Collection, National Archives, College Park, Maryland.

[2389] Memo dated January 29, 1968, by Andrew Sciambra, Files Received from Harry Connick, National Archives, College Park, Maryland.

[2390] E-mail exchange between author and John Rarick, April 2007.

[2391] Memo dated January 22, 1968, Andrew Sciambra to Jim Garrison, Files Received from Harry Connick, National Archives, College Park, Maryland.

[2392] Memo dated January 29, 1968, Andrew Sciambra to Jim Garrison, Files Received from Harry Connick, National Archives, College Park, Maryland.

[2393] Interview with Corrie Collins, January 31, 1968, Papers Donated by Lyon Garrison, National Archives, College Park, Maryland.

[2394] Statement of Corey Collins, January 31, 1968, Files Received from Harry Connick, National Archives, College Park, Maryland.

[2395] Memo dated January 31, 1968, regarding interview with Corey Collins by Andrew Sciambra and James Alcock Files Received from Harry Connick, National Archives, College Park, Maryland.

[2396] Interview with William Dunn by Frank Ruiz and Kent Simms, January 31, 1968, Files Received from Harry Connick, National Archives, College Park, Maryland.

[2397] Memo dated January 31, 1968 regarding interview with Janie Daniels by Frank Ruiz and Kent Simms on January 16, 1968, Files Received from Harry Connick, National Archives, College Park, Maryland.

[2398] Telegram dated January 31, 1968, Thomas E. Ervin to Irvin Dymond, Legal Files of F. Irvin Dymond—Clay Shaw Case, Historic New Orleans Collection, New Orleans, Louisiana.

[2399] Letter dated February 12, 1968, Edward Wegmann to Thomas E. Ervin, Legal Files of F. Irvin Dymond—Clay Shaw Case, Historic New Orleans Collection, New Orleans, Louisiana.

[2400] Letter, undated but probably February 1968, Shaw to James and Judy Formyduval, Author's Collection.

[2401] FBI memo dated February 5, 1968, Record Group 59, General Records of the Department of State, JFK Assassination Collection, National Archives, College Park, Maryland.

[2402] Letter dated February 8, 1968, Emlyn Williams to Shaw, Donated Papers of Clay Shaw, National Archives, College Park, Maryland.

[2403] Undated letter, probably late 1967 or 1968, Gaines Kincaid to Shaw, Donated Papers of Clay Shaw, National Archives, College Park, Maryland.

[2404] Article in Baton Rouge *Morning Advocate*, February 21, 1968, Records of the New Orleans Metropolitan Crime Commission, National Archives, College Park, Maryland.

[2405] Letter dated February 2, 1968, Edward Wegmann to Judge Edward A. Haggarty, Legal Files of F. Irvin Dymond—Clay Shaw Case, Historic New Orleans Collection, New Orleans, Louisiana.

[2406] Memo dated February 19, 1968, Andrew Sciambra to Jim Garrison, Files Received from Harry Connick, National Archives, College Park, Maryland.

[2407] Letter dated January 31, 1968, Fred Vinson to Edward Wegmann, Legal Files of F. Irvin Dymond—Clay Shaw Case, Historic New Orleans Collection, New Orleans, Louisiana.

[2408] Letter dated February 9, 1968, Edward Wegmann to Fred Vinson, Legal Files of F. Irvin Dymond—Clay Shaw Case, Historic New Orleans Collection, New Orleans, Louisiana.

[2409] Letter dated February 19, 1968, Edward Wegmann to Stephen Pollack, Legal Files of F. Irvin Dymond—Clay Shaw Case, Historic New Orleans Collection, New Orleans, Louisiana.

[2410] Letter dated February 20, 1968, Edward Wegmann to Peyton Ford, Legal Files of F. Irvin Dymond—Clay Shaw Case, Historic New Orleans Collection, New Orleans, Louisiana.

[2411] Letter dated March 1, 1968, Edward Wegmann to Allen Dulles, Legal Files of F. Irvin Dymond—Clay Shaw Case, Historic New Orleans Collection, New Orleans, Louisiana.

[2412] Letter dated March 8, 1968, Edward Wegmann to Stephen Pollack and Robert Owens, Legal Files of F. Irvin Dymond—Clay Shaw Case, Historic New Orleans Collection, New Orleans, Louisiana.

[2413] Letter dated March 8, 1968, Edward Wegmann to Hale Boggs, Legal Files of F. Irvin Dymond—Clay Shaw Case, Historic New Orleans Collection, New Orleans, Louisiana.

[2414] Card dated March 5, 1968, Edith Stern to Shaw, Donated Papers of Clay Shaw, National Archives, College Park, Maryland.

[2415] Card dated March 8, 1968, Paula and Hugh Aynesworth to Shaw, Donated Papers of Clay Shaw, National Archives, College Park, Maryland.

[2416] Letter dated March 9, 1968, Holland McCombs to Shaw, Donated Papers of Clay Shaw, National Archives, College Park, Maryland.

[2417] Letter dated August 13, 1969, Aaron Kohn to Warren Rogers, Records of the New Orleans Metropolitan Crime Commission, National Archives, College Park, Maryland.

[2418] Greeting card with newspaper photograph of Garrison inside, no envelope, sent to Shaw possibly in 1968, Donated Papers of Clay Shaw, National Archives, College Park, Maryland.

[2419] Letter dated March 13, 1968, Irvin Dymond to William Gurvich, Legal Files of F. Irvin Dymond—Clay Shaw Case, Historic New Orleans Collection, New Orleans, Louisiana.

[2420] Letter dated March 21, 1968, William R. Brazzil to Richard Helms, CIA Miscellaneous Files, JFK Assassination Collection, National Archives, College Park, Maryland.

[2421] Memo dated March 22, 1968 by John J. Kirby, Jr., Record Group 60, Department of Justice, Civil Rights Division, 1967-69, JFK Assassination Collection, National Archives, College Park, Maryland.

[2422] Letter dated March 27, 1968, Edward Wegmann to George Jensen, Legal Files of F. Irvin Dymond—Clay Shaw Case, Historic New Orleans Collection, New Orleans, Louisiana.

[2423] Letter dated March 27, 1968, Edward Wegmann to Edward Jay Epstein, Legal Files of F. Irvin Dymond—Clay Shaw Case, Historic New Orleans Collection, New Orleans, Louisiana.

[2424] Letter dated March 28, 1968, Edward Wegmann to Stephen Pollack, Record Group 60, Department of Justice, Civil Rights Division, 1967-69, JFK Assassination Collection, National Archives, College Park, Maryland.

[2425] Letter dated March 22, 1968, Shaw to Holland McCombs, Holland McCombs Collection, University of Tennessee-Martin, Martin, Tennessee.

[2426] Letter dated April 1, 1968, Edward Wegmann to Peyton Ford, Legal Files of F. Irvin Dymond—Clay Shaw Case, Historic New Orleans Collection, New Orleans, Louisiana.

[2427] Letter dated April 5, 1968, Edward Wegmann to Elmer Gertz, Legal Files of F. Irvin Dymond—Clay Shaw Case, Historic New Orleans Collection, New Orleans, Louisiana.

[2428] Letter dated April 5, 1968, Edward Wegmann to George Jensen, Legal Files of F. Irvin Dymond—Clay Shaw Case, Historic New Orleans Collection, New Orleans, Louisiana.

[2429] Transcript of interview with David Logan by James Alcock, April 13, 1968, Papers Donated by Lyon Garrison, National Archives, College Park, Maryland.

[2430] Report dated April 17, 1968 by Office of Naval Intelligence, Record Group 526, Records of the Office of the Chief of Naval Operations-Naval Criminal Investigative Service, JFK Assassination Collection, National Archives, College Park, Maryland.

[2431] Letter dated April 22, 1968, Richard Billings to Jim Garrison, Files Received from Harry Connick, National Archives, College Park, Maryland.

[2432] Letter dated April 22, 1968, Richard Billings to Jim Garrison, with Garrison's comments attached, Files Received from Harry Connick, National Archives, College Park, Maryland.

[2433] Letter dated April 10, 1968, Edward Wegmann to Charles R. Carson, Legal Files of F. Irvin Dymond—Clay Shaw Case, Historic New Orleans Collection, New Orleans, Louisiana.

[2434] Letter dated August 12, 1968, Edward Wegmann to Charles R. Carson, Legal Files of F. Irvin Dymond—Clay Shaw Case, Historic New Orleans Collection, New Orleans, Louisiana.

[2435] Interview of William Gurvich by defense attorneys, August 29, 1967, Legal Files of F. Irvin Dymond—Clay Shaw Case, Historic New Orleans Collection, New Orleans, Louisiana.

[2436] Letter dated April 26, 1968, Robert D. Johnson to Jim Garrison, Record Group 60, General Records of the Department of Justice, Classified Subject Files, 129-11, JFK Assassination Collection, National Archives, College Park, Maryland.

[2437] Answers to Interrogatories by HMH Publishing, February 12, 1968, related to lawsuit by Gordon Novel against *Playboy* and Jim Garrison, Donated Papers of Edward Wegmann, National Archives, College Park, Maryland.

[2438] Answers to Interrogatories by Jim Garrison, January 23, 1968, related to lawsuit by Gordon Novel against *Playboy* and Jim Garrison, Donated Papers of Edward Wegmann, National Archives, College Park, Maryland.

[2439] Answers to Interrogatories by Jim Garrison, May 3, 1968, related to lawsuit by Gordon Novel against *Playboy* and Jim Garrison, Donated Papers of Edward Wegmann, National Archives, College Park, Maryland.

[2440] Letter dated January 26, 1968, Edward Wegmann to Elmer Gertz, Donated Papers of Edward Wegmann, National Archives, College Park, Maryland.

[2441] Letter dated March 22, 1968, Edward Wegmann to Elmer Gertz, Donated Papers of Edward Wegmann, National Archives, College Park, Maryland.

[2442] Letter dated May 14, 1968, Edward Wegmann to Elmer Gertz, Donated Papers of Edward Wegmann, National Archives, College Park, Maryland.

[2443] Letter dated April 6, 1968, Edward Wegmann to Elmer Gertz, Legal Files of F. Irvin Dymond—Clay Shaw Case, Historic New Orleans Collection, New Orleans, Louisiana.

[2444] Article in *Shreveport Times*, May 26, 1968, John Wray and Margaret Mary Young Collection, LSU-Shreveport, Shreveport, Louisiana.

[2445] Letter dated July 13, 1977, Brian Latell to John Wray and Margaret Mary Young, John Wray and Margaret Mary Young Collection, LSU-Shreveport, Shreveport, Louisiana.

[2446] Letter dated May 30, 1968, Edward Wegmann to Edward Jay Epstein, Legal Files of F. Irvin Dymond—Clay Shaw Case, Historic New Orleans Collection, New Orleans, Louisiana.

[2447] Letter dated May 30, 1968, Edward Wegmann to Ramsey Clark, Legal Files of F. Irvin Dymond—Clay Shaw Case, Historic New Orleans Collection, New Orleans, Louisiana.

[2448] Letter dated May 31, 1968, Edward Wegmann to Elmer Gertz, Legal Files of F. Irvin Dymond—Clay Shaw Case, Historic New Orleans Collection, New Orleans, Louisiana.

[2449] Letter dated May 31, 1968, Edward Wegmann to Louis Lacour, Legal Files of F. Irvin Dymond—Clay Shaw Case, Historic New Orleans Collection, New Orleans, Louisiana.

[2450] Telegram to White House approximately May-June, 1968, Record Group 60, General Records of the Department of Justice, Classified Subject Files, 129-11, JFK Assassination Collection, National Archives, College Park, Maryland.

[2451] Memo dated June 11, 1968, Edwin L. Weisl, Jr. to Fred M. Vinson, Jr.., Record Group 60, Department of Justice, Civil Rights Division, 1967-69, JFK Assassination Collection, National Archives, College Park, Maryland.

[2452] Deposition of Lillie Mae McMaines taken June 24, 1968 by William Wegmann, Donated Papers of Edward Wegmann, National Archives, College Park, Maryland.

[2453] Letter dated July 8, 1968, Edward Wegmann to William Wegmann, Legal Files of F. Irvin Dymond—Clay Shaw Case, Historic New Orleans Collection, New Orleans, Louisiana.

[2454] Undated letter, probably mid-1968, Emlyn Williams to Shaw, Donated Papers of Clay Shaw, National Archives, College Park, Maryland.

[2455] Letter dated August 1, 1968, William Wegmann to Edward Wegmann, Legal Files of F. Irvin Dymond—Clay Shaw Case, Historic New Orleans Collection, New Orleans, Louisiana.

[2456] Letter dated August 2, 1968, Hugh Aynesworth to Shaw, Donated Papers of Clay Shaw, National Archives, College Park, Maryland.

[2457] Article dated August 2, 1968, *Time* magazine, Donated Papers of Clay Shaw, National Archives, College Park, Maryland.

[2458] Letter dated August 8, 1968, Holland McCombs to Shaw, Donated Papers of Clay Shaw, National Archives, College Park, Maryland.

[2459] Letter dated April 29, 1964, Shaw to Albert D. Meltz, and related correspondence between Shaw and Meltz, International Trade Mart Records, Tulane University, New Orleans, Louisiana.

[2460] Letter dated November 2, 1965, Goldie Moore to Howard Soloman, International Trade Mart Records, Tulane University, New Orleans, Louisiana.

[2461] Letter dated August 7, 1968, John C. Lankenau to Lloyd Cobb, International Trade Mart Records, Tulane University, New Orleans, Louisiana.

[2462] Letter dated December 23, 1968, Edward Wegmann to Lloyd Cobb, International Trade Mart Records, Tulane University, New Orleans, Louisiana.

[2463] Records related to these loans are located in Donated Papers of Clay Shaw, National Archives, College Park, Maryland.

[2464] Memo dated October 9, 1968, Andrew Sciambra to Jim Garrison, Papers Donated by Lyon Garrison, National Archives, College Park, Maryland.

[2465] Plaine v. Burford, Warden, 180 F.2d 724 (1950).

[2466] See past due restaurant bill dated October 31, 1968, Christopher Blake to Shaw, Donated Papers of Clay Shaw, National Archives, College Park, Maryland.

[2467] Letter dated September 29, 1969, Alexander Grant (firm) to Shaw, Donated Papers of Clay Shaw, National Archives, College Park, Maryland.

[2468] Letter dated November 6, 1968, Alec Gifford to Shaw, Donated Papers of Clay Shaw, National Archives, College Park, Maryland.

[2469] Memo dated December 16, 1968, Andrew Sciambra to Jim Garrison, Files Received from Harry Connick, National Archives, College Park, Maryland.

[2470] Trial Memorandum, Conference of December 18, 1968, defense attorneys, Legal Files of F. Irvin Dymond—Clay Shaw Case, Historic New Orleans Collection, New Orleans, Louisiana.

[2471] Trial Memorandum, Conference of December 18, 1968, defense attorneys, Legal Files of F. Irvin Dymond—Clay Shaw Case, Historic New Orleans Collection, New Orleans, Louisiana.

[2472] Memo dated January 15, 1968, summarizing William Gurvich's potential testimony at trial, Legal Files of F. Irvin Dymond—Clay Shaw Case, Historic New Orleans Collection, New Orleans, Louisiana.

[2473] Memo dated June 27, 1968, list of prosecution witnesses, Legal Files of F. Irvin Dymond—Clay Shaw Case, Historic New Orleans Collection, New Orleans, Louisiana.

[2474] Memo dated January 13, 1968, list of prosecution witnesses, Legal Files of F. Irvin Dymond—Clay Shaw Case, Historic New Orleans Collection, New Orleans, Louisiana.

[2475] Letter dated January 11, 1969, Harry Connick to Jeff Biddison, Donated Papers of Clay Shaw, National Archives, College Park, Maryland.

[2476] Memo dated May 6, 1969, Lou Ivon to Jim Garrison, JFK Assassination Collection, New Orleans Public Library, New Orleans, Louisiana.

[2477] Memo dated January 16, 1969 by Tom Bethell, witnessed by Lou Ivon, JFK Assassination Collection, New Orleans Public Library, New Orleans, Louisiana.

[2478] Memo dated June 27, 1968 containing list of witnesses for Shaw's trial and description of each witness's testimony, JFK Assassination Collection, New Orleans Public Library, New Orleans, Louisiana.

[2479] Memo dated June 27, 1968 containing list of witnesses for Shaw's trial and description of each witness's testimony, JFK Assassination Collection, New Orleans Public Library, New Orleans, Louisiana.

[2480] See photos of various people sent to Lou Ivon by Hugh Aynesworth in large brown envelope, Files Received from Harry Connick, National Archives, College Park, Maryland.

[2481] See five-part series of articles in *Pittsburgh Free Press* by Hugh Aynesworth, early 1969, Files Received from Harry Connick, National Archives, College Park, Maryland.

[2482] Undated memo, possibly from either Hugh Aynesworth or Walter Holloway, probably February 1969, Donated Papers of Edward Wegmann, National Archives, College Park, Maryland.

[2483] Letter dated January 3, 1969, Edward Wegmann to Richard Billings, Holland McCombs Collection, University of Tennessee-Martin, Martin, Tennessee.

[2484] Letter, undated, probably January 1969, Richard Billings to Edward Wegmann, Holland McCombs Collection, University of Tennessee-Martin, Martin, Tennessee.

[2485] Letter, undated, probably January 1969, Richard Billings to Edward Wegmann, Holland McCombs Collection, University of Tennessee-Martin, Martin, Tennessee.

[2486] Newspaper article dated January 22, 1969 about Louisiana Conspiracy Law, Records of the New Orleans Metropolitan Crime Commission, National Archives, College Park, Maryland.

[2487] Letter dated February 13, 1969, Jim Garrison to Louisiana Department of Revenue, Files Received from Harry Connick, National Archives, College Park, Maryland.

[2488] May 1968 interview with William Gurvich by James Kirkwood, James Kirkwood Collection, Boston University, Boston, Massachusetts.

[2489] Note dated January 26, 1969 regarding party attended by Edith Stern and her remarks related to Garrison's wife filing for divorce and making allegations of homosexuality James Kirkwood Collection, Boston University, Boston, Massachusetts.

[2490] Letter dated January 30, 1969, Hugh Aynesworth to Edward Wegmann, Donated Papers of Edward Wegmann, National Archives, College Park, Maryland.

[2491] Affidavit of Jessie Parker, January 29, 1969, Papers Donated by Lyon Garrison, National Archives, College Park, Maryland.

[2492] Report of interview of Thomas Breitner, March 29, 1967, William W. Turner to New Orleans district attorney's office, Donated Papers of Edward Wegmann, National Archives, College Park, Maryland.

[2493] Memo dated September 23, 1967, William Turner to Jim Garrison, Donated Papers of Edward Wegmann, National Archives, College Park, Maryland.

[2494] Report dated February 5, 1969 by Walter Holloway, Donated Papers of Edward Wegmann, National Archives, College Park, Maryland.

[2495] Memo dated January 3, 1969 by Donovan Pratt, CIA Miscellaneous Files, JFK Assassination Collection, National Archives, College Park, Maryland.

[2496] Letter dated January 29, 1969 by Paul Rothermel, Record Group 233, Records of the U.S. House of Representatives, Select Committee on Assassinations, Segregated CIA Collection, Printed Microfilm, JFK Assassination Collection, National Archives, College Park, Maryland.

[2497] Interview with William Wood by George E. Rennar, in August/September 1971, Wood/Boxley Files, JFK Assassination Collection, National Archives, College Park, Maryland.

[2498] See name search records regarding jurors in Shaw trial, Record Group 233, Records of the U.S. House of Representatives, Select Committee on Assassinations, Segregated CIA Collection, JFK Assassination Collection, National Archives, College Park, Maryland.

[2499] Uncut manuscript of *American Grotesque*, James Kirkwood Collection, Boston University, Boston, Massachusetts.

[2500] Uncut manuscript of *American Grotesque*, James Kirkwood Collection, Boston University, Boston, Massachusetts.

[2501] *States-Item* article dated June 30, 1970, Donated Papers of Clay Shaw, National Archives, College Park, Maryland.

[2502] Interview with F. Irvin Dymond by James Kirkwood, approximately spring 1969, James Kirkwood Collection, Boston University, Boston, Massachusetts.

[2503] Memo dated February 27, 1969, Record Group 233, Records of the U.S. House of Representatives, Select Committee on Assassinations, Segregated CIA Collection, Printed Microfilm, JFK Assassination Collection, National Archives, College Park, Maryland.

[2504] Memo dated August 7 and August 8, 1968, interview with Abraham Zapruder by Alvin Oser and Tom Bethell, Files Received from Harry Connick, National Archives, College Park, Maryland.

[2505] Statement of James A. Hardiman, Jr., May 7, 1968, Papers Donated by Lyon Garrison, National Archives, College Park, Maryland.

[2506] Interview with F. Irvin Dymond by author, June 29, 1995.

[2507] James Kirkwood papers, Boston University.

[2508] Video archives of WWL-TV Channel 4 in New Orleans, Louisiana State Archives, Baton Rouge, Louisiana.

[2509] Uncut manuscript of *American Grotesque*, James Kirkwood Collection, Boston University, Boston, Massachusetts.

[2510] Author's interview with William Alford, October 4, 2002, Donated Papers of Edward Wegmann, National Archives, College Park, Maryland.

[2511] Statement of June A. Rolfe, March 6, 1969, Donated Papers of Edward Wegmann, National Archives, College Park, Maryland.

[2512] Article in *Times-Picayune*, March 6, 1969, Records of the New Orleans Metropolitan Crime Commission, National Archives, College Park, Maryland.

[2513] Affidavit by Shaw, March 13, 1969, Record Group 60, Department of Justice, Civil Rights Division, 1967-69, JFK Assassination Collection, National Archives, College Park, Maryland.

[2514] FBI memo dated March 4, 1969, Record Group 60, General Records of the Department of Justice, Classified Subject Files, 129-11, JFK Assassination Collection, National Archives, College Park, Maryland.

[2515] Memo dated April 3, 1969, David Bonderman to D. Robert Owen., Record Group 60, Department of Justice, Civil Rights Division, 1967-69, JFK Assassination Collection, National Archives, College Park, Maryland.

[2516] Letter dated April 16, 1969, D. Robert Owen to Edward Wegmann., Record Group 60, Department of Justice, Civil Rights Division, 1967-69, JFK Assassination Collection, National Archives, College Park, Maryland.

[2517] Invitation dated March 17, 1969, Consul General of El Salvador to Shaw, Donated Papers of Clay Shaw, National Archives, College Park, Maryland.

[2518] Column dated February 28, 1969 by James A. Wechsler, Donated Papers of Clay Shaw, National Archives, College Park, Maryland.

[2519] Interview with Ed Planer by author, June 24, 2010.

[2520] Letter written shortly after trial verdict on March 1, 1969, Carlos Quiroga to Shaw, Donated Papers of Clay Shaw, National Archives, College Park, Maryland.

[2521] Letter dated March 1, 1969, Martin Palmer to Shaw, Donated Papers of Clay Shaw, National Archives, College Park, Maryland.

[2522] Letter dated March 1, 1969, J.B. Dauenhauer to Shaw, Donated Papers of Clay Shaw, National Archives, College Park, Maryland.

[2523] Letter dated March 2, 1969, Clint Bolton to Shaw, Donated Papers of Clay Shaw, National Archives, College Park, Maryland.

[2524] Editorial dated February 28, 1969, *Vieux Carré Courier*, Donated Papers of Clay Shaw, National Archives, College Park, Maryland.

[2525] Undated card written shortly after March 1, 1969, Ettore Scampicchio to Shaw, Donated Papers of Clay Shaw, National Archives, College Park, Maryland.

[2526] Letter dated March 12, 1969, William G. Zetzmann, Jr. to Shaw, Donated Papers of Clay Shaw, National Archives, College Park, Maryland.

[2527] Telegram dated March 2, 1969, Holland McCombs to Shaw, Donated Papers of Clay Shaw, National Archives, College Park, Maryland.

[2528] Telegram dated March 2, 1969, Charles and Eleanor Nutter to Shaw, Donated Papers of Clay Shaw, National Archives, College Park, Maryland.

[2529] Telegram dated March 3, 1969, Knox Burger and Walter Fultz to Shaw, Donated Papers of Clay Shaw, National Archives, College Park, Maryland.

[2530] Letter dated March 5, 1969, Alton Ochsner to Shaw, Donated Papers of Clay Shaw, National Archives, College Park, Maryland.

[2531] Letter dated March 14, 1969, C.E. Foster to Shaw, Donated Papers of Clay Shaw, National Archives, College Park, Maryland.

[2532] Telegram dated March 1, 1969, John W. Campbell to Shaw, Donated Papers of Clay Shaw, National Archives, College Park, Maryland.

[2533] Telegram dated March 1, 1969, Wynn Pearce to Shaw, Donated Papers of Clay Shaw, National Archives, College Park, Maryland.

[2534] Letter dated March 2, 1969, Pancho Rodriguez to Shaw, Donated Papers of Clay Shaw, National Archives, College Park, Maryland.

[2535] Telegram dated March 1, 1969, John Leonard to Shaw, Donated Papers of Clay Shaw, National Archives, College Park, Maryland.

[2536] Undated telegram, Henri Gomez to Shaw, Donated Papers of Clay Shaw, National Archives, College Park, Maryland.

[2537] Telegram dated March 1, 1969, Sally and Warren Galjour to Shaw, Donated Papers of Clay Shaw, National Archives, College Park, Maryland.

[2538] Telegram dated March 1,1969, Gaines Kincaid to Shaw, Donated Papers of Clay Shaw, National Archives, College Park, Maryland.

[2539] Telegram dated March 2, 1969, Emlyn Williams to Shaw, Donated Papers of Clay Shaw, National Archives, College Park, Maryland.

[2540] Telegram dated March 1, 1969, Val Dufour to Shaw, Donated Papers of Clay Shaw, National Archives, College Park, Maryland.

[2541] Telegram dated March 1, 1969, Elmer Gertz to Shaw, Donated Papers of Clay Shaw, National Archives, College Park, Maryland.

[2542] Letter dated March 1, 1969, Sylvia Meagher to Shaw, Donated Papers of Clay Shaw, National Archives, College Park, Maryland.

[2543] Letter dated March 1, 1969, L.S. McClaren to Shaw, Donated Papers of Clay Shaw, National Archives, College Park, Maryland.

[2544] Letter dated March 5, 1969, Tom Rafferty to Shaw, Donated Papers of Clay Shaw, National Archives, College Park, Maryland.

[2545] Undated letter written shortly after March 1, 1969, James Leo Herlihy to Shaw, Donated Papers of Clay Shaw, National Archives, College Park, Maryland.

[2546] Telegram dated March 1, 1969, John R. Stiles to Shaw, Donated Papers of Clay Shaw, National Archives, College Park, Maryland.

[2547] Card dated March 7, 1969, Albert Lemón to Shaw, Donated Papers of Clay Shaw, National Archives, College Park, Maryland.

[2548] Letter dated March 7, 1969, Jim Garrison to Ralph Schoenman, JFK Assassination Collection, New Orleans Public Library, New Orleans, Louisiana.

[2549] Letter dated March 9, 1969, Caroline Christenberry to Shaw, Donated Papers of Clay Shaw, National Archives, College Park, Maryland.

[2550] Interview with Shaw by Alec Gifford, March 11, 1969, on WVUE-TV, James Kirkwood Collection, Boston University, Boston, Massachusetts.

[2551] Interview with Shaw by Alec Gifford, March 11, 1969, on WVUE-TV, James Kirkwood Collection, Boston University, Boston, Massachusetts.

[2552] Interview with Shaw by Alec Gifford, March 11, 1969, on WVUE-TV, James Kirkwood Collection, Boston University, Boston, Massachusetts.

[2553] Letter dated March 12, 1969, Edward Wegmann to Elmer Gertz, Donated Papers of Edward Wegmann, National Archives, College Park, Maryland.

[2554] Transcript of interview with Jim Garrison by Alec Gifford, March 13, 1969, on WVUE-TV, Records of the New Orleans Metropolitan Crime Commission, National Archives, College Park, Maryland.

[2555] Article dated March 16, 1969, by William Greider, *Tulsa Sunday World*, Donated Papers of Clay Shaw, National Archives, College Park, Maryland.

[2556] Letter from Martin Waldron, probably March or April 1969, enclosing *Harper's Bazaar* horoscope column, Donated Papers of Clay Shaw, National Archives, College Park, Maryland.

[2557] Telegram dated March 17, 1969, Kent and Hugh to Shaw, Donated Papers of Clay Shaw, National Archives, College Park, Maryland.

[2558] Card dated March 3, 1969, Ms. Hodding Carter to Shaw, Donated Papers of Clay Shaw, National Archives, College Park, Maryland.

[2559] See full page advertisement, *Times-Picayune*, dated March 18, 1969 in support of Jim Garrison, Donated Papers of Clay Shaw, National Archives, College Park, Maryland.

[2560] Undated letter, probably March or April 1969, Jim Garrison to Eberhard Deutsch, JFK Assassination Collection, New Orleans Public Library, New Orleans, Louisiana.

[2561] Tape of Shaw appearance on Mike Douglas show, April 3, 1969, James Kirkwood Collection, Boston University, Boston, Massachusetts.

[2562] Letter dated March 3, 1969, Curt Dalaba to Shaw, Donated Papers of Clay Shaw, National Archives, College Park, Maryland.

[2563] Interview with F. Irvin Dymond by James Kirkwood, approximately Spring 1969, James Kirkwood Collection, Boston University, Boston, Massachusetts.

[2564] Interview with F. Irvin Dymond by James Kirkwood, approximately Spring 1969, James Kirkwood Collection, Boston University, Boston, Massachusetts.

[2565] Interview with F. Irvin Dymond by James Kirkwood, approximately Spring 1969, James Kirkwood Collection, Boston University, Boston, Massachusetts.

[2566] Interview with F. Irvin Dymond by James Kirkwood, approximately Spring 1969, James Kirkwood Collection, Boston University, Boston, Massachusetts.

[2567] Interview with F. Irvin Dymond by James Kirkwood, approximately Spring 1969, James Kirkwood Collection, Boston University, Boston, Massachusetts.

[2568] Interview with F. Irvin Dymond by James Kirkwood, approximately Spring 1969, James Kirkwood Collection, Boston University, Boston, Massachusetts.

[2569] FBI Memo dated June 23, 1967, Record Group 60, General Records of the Department of Justice, Classified Subject Files, 129-11, JFK Assassination Collection, National Archives, College Park, Maryland.

[2570] Interview with F. Irvin Dymond by James Kirkwood, approximately Spring 1969, James Kirkwood Collection, Boston University, Boston, Massachusetts.

[2571] Interview with F. Irvin Dymond by James Kirkwood, approximately Spring 1969, James Kirkwood Collection, Boston University, Boston, Massachusetts.

[2572] Interview with F. Irvin Dymond by James Kirkwood, approximately Spring 1969, James Kirkwood Collection, Boston University, Boston, Massachusetts.

2573 Interview with F. Irvin Dymond by James Kirkwood, approximately Spring 1969, James Kirkwood Collection, Boston University, Boston, Massachusetts.

2574 Interview with F. Irvin Dymond by James Kirkwood, approximately Spring 1969, James Kirkwood Collection, Boston University, Boston, Massachusetts.

2575 Interview with F. Irvin Dymond by James Kirkwood, approximately Spring 1969, James Kirkwood Collection, Boston University, Boston, Massachusetts.

2576 Interview with Miguel Torres by James Kirkwood, approximately Spring 1969, James Kirkwood Collection, Boston University, Boston, Massachusetts.

2577 Interview with F. Irvin Dymond by James Kirkwood, approximately Spring 1969, James Kirkwood Collection, Boston University, Boston, Massachusetts.

2578 Interview with F. Irvin Dymond by James Kirkwood, approximately Spring 1969, James Kirkwood Collection, Boston University, Boston, Massachusetts.

2579 Interview with F. Irvin Dymond by James Kirkwood, approximately Spring 1969, James Kirkwood Collection, Boston University, Boston, Massachusetts.

2580 Memo dated May 20, 1969 regarding interview of W. Robert Morgan by William Alford, April 21, 1969, Papers Donated by Lyon Garrison, National Archives, College Park, Maryland.

2581 Letter dated May 4, 1969, Kay Lucas Leake Dart to Shaw, Donated Papers of Clay Shaw, National Archives, College Park, Maryland.

2582 Interview with Jim Garrison, unknown interviewer, May 27, 1969, Files Received from Harry Connick, National Archives, College Park, Maryland.

2583 Affidavit of June A. Rolfe to Lou Ivon, May 29, 1969, Files Received from Harry Connick, National Archives, College Park, Maryland.

2584 Article dated August 11, 1969 in *Christian Science Monitor*, Donated Papers of Clay Shaw, National Archives, College Park, Maryland.

2585 Article dated July 3, 1969, *Times-Picayune*, Donated Papers of Clay Shaw, National Archives, College Park, Maryland.

2586 Video archives of WWL-TV Channel 4 in New Orleans, Louisiana State Archives, Baton Rouge, Louisiana.

2587 Undated memo, Shaw to Edward Wegmann regarding Garrison and Russo involvement, Donated Papers of Edward Wegmann, National Archives, College Park, Maryland.

2588 Letter dated November 5, 1969, Aaron Kohn to William J. Krummel, Sr., Records of the New Orleans Metropolitan Crime Commission, National Archives, College Park, Maryland.

2589 Uncut manuscript of *American Grotesque*, James Kirkwood Collection, Boston University, Boston, Massachusetts.

2590 Letter dated October 10, 1969, Hugh Aynesworth to James Kirkwood, James Kirkwood Collection, Boston University, Boston, Massachusetts.

2591 News clipping regarding Shaw testimony in Tra-Mar, Inc. lawsuit, James Kirkwood Collection, Boston University, Boston, Massachusetts.

2592 Internal Metropolitan Crime Commission report dated August 21, 1969 by Aaron Kohn, Records of the New Orleans Metropolitan Crime Commission, National Archives, College Park, Maryland.

2593 Article in *Times-Picayune*, July 25, 1969, Files Received from Harry Connick, National Archives, College Park, Maryland.

2594 Newspaper article in *Times-Picayune*, March 1, 1971, Records of the New Orleans Metropolitan Crime Commission, National Archives, College Park, Maryland.

2595 Newspaper article in *States-Item*, November 7, 1969, Records of the New Orleans Metropolitan Crime Commission, National Archives, College Park, Maryland.

2596 Author interview with Jeff Sulzer, October 4, 2002.

2597 Card, December 1969, Shaw to James Kirkwood regarding arrest of Judge Edward A. Haggerty, James Kirkwood Collection, Boston University, Boston, Massachusetts.

2598 Letter, undated, Shaw to James Kirkwood, enclosing letter of November 15, 1970 from James Phelan to Jim Garrison, James Kirkwood Collection, Boston University, Boston, Massachusetts.

2599 Letter dated February 18, 1970, Edward Wegmann to Hugh Aynesworth, Donated Papers of Edward Wegmann, National Archives, College Park, Maryland.

2600 *Time* magazine article dated March 31, 1967, Donated Papers of Clay Shaw, National Archives, College Park, Maryland.

2601 Letter dated March 4, 1970, Herbert Miller to John Greaney, 3 Series General Counsel, Records of the Assassination Records Review Board, National Archives, College Park, Maryland.

2602 *National Insider* articles dated April 12, 1970 and April 19, 1970, Donated Papers of Clay Shaw, National Archives, College Park, Maryland.

2603 *National Insider* articles dated April 12, 1970 and April 19, 1970, Donated Papers of Clay Shaw, National Archives, College Park, Maryland.

2604 Letter dated June 23, 1970, Elizabeth Marton to Shaw, Donated Papers of Clay Shaw, National Archives, College Park, Maryland.

2605 Letter dated July 7, 1970, Elizabeth Marton to Shaw, Donated Papers of Clay Shaw, National Archives, College Park, Maryland.

2606 *Times-Picayune* article dated June 26, 1970, Donated Papers of Clay Shaw, National Archives, College Park, Maryland.

2607 *Los Angeles Times* article by Nicholas Chriss, as it appeared in the *Greeneville, Mississippi Delta-Democrat-Times*, Donated Papers of Clay Shaw, National Archives, College Park, Maryland.

2608 Letter dated July 1, 1970, Edith Stern to Ramsey Clark, Private Collection of Edith Stern related to Clay Shaw, Longue Vue, New Orleans, Louisiana.

2609 Letter dated March 23, 1969, Edith Stern to Jefferson Fordham, Private Collection of Edith Stern related to Clay Shaw, Longue Vue, New Orleans, Louisiana.

2610 Letter dated April 2, 1969, Edith Stern to A.A. Berle, Jr., Private Collection of Edith Stern related to Clay Shaw, Longue Vue, New Orleans, Louisiana.

2611 Letter dated April 2, 1969, Edith Stern to Dean Paul Hebert, Private Collection of Edith Stern related to Clay Shaw, Longue Vue, New Orleans, Louisiana.

2612 Pre-employment screening on Perry Russo by New Orleans Police Department, August 1970, Donated Papers of Edward Wegmann, National Archives, College Park, Maryland.

2613 Letter dated September 22, 1970, Edward Wegmann to Hugh Aynesworth, Donated Papers of Edward Wegmann, National Archives, College Park, Maryland.

2614 Letter dated October 2, 1970, Edward Wegmann to Hugh Aynesworth, Donated Papers of Edward Wegmann, National Archives, College Park, Maryland.

[2615] Correspondence from Margie Ann Ramagos, Secretary to Edith Stern, to Shaw, enclosing list of invitees to November 20, 1970 party for James Kirkwood, Donated Papers of Clay Shaw, National Archives, College Park, Maryland.

[2616] Transcript of James Kirkwood appearance on Barry Gray show, December 3, 1970, Record Group 233, Records of the U.S. House of Representatives, Select Committee on Assassinations, Segregated CIA Collection, JFK Assassination Collection, National Archives, College Park, Maryland.

[2617] Article dated November 21, 1970 in *Times-Picayune*, Donated Papers of Clay Shaw, National Archives, College Park, Maryland.

[2618] Record Group 21, Records of U.S. District Courts, Records from the District Court of Louisiana, New Orleans Division, Case #70-466, Clay L. Shaw vs. Jim Garrison, Joseph M. Rault, Jr., Cecil M. Shilstone, Willard E. Robertson, Perry Raymond Russo, and Dr. Esmond A. Fatter, JFK Assassination Collection, National Archives, College Park, Maryland.

[2619] Holiday Greeting Card, December 1970, Shaw to Patrick and Edna O'Rourke, Author's Collection.

[2620] Rough draft of article by Rosemary James, "The Dark Side of Not Guilty," approximately January 1971, Donated Papers of Clay Shaw, National Archives, College Park, Maryland.

[2621] List of new witnesses for 1971 perjury trial, Papers Donated by Lyon Garrison, National Archives, College Park, Maryland.

[2622] Letter dated January 29, 1971, James Kirkwood to Patrick O'Rourke, Author's Collection.

[2623] *CBS Evening News* segment about Clay Shaw and his case, by reporter Foster Davis, January 23, 1971.

[2624] Memo dated January 27, 1971 regarding conversation with Perry Russo by Irvin Dymond, Donated Papers of Edward Wegmann, National Archives, College Park, Maryland.

[2625] Memo dated January 27, 1971 regarding conversation with Perry Russo by Irvin Dymond, Donated Papers of Edward Wegmann, National Archives, College Park, Maryland.

[2626] Memo dated January 27, 1971 regarding conversation with Perry Russo by Irvin Dymond, Donated Papers of Edward Wegmann, National Archives, College Park, Maryland.

[2627] Memo dated January 27, 1971 regarding conversation with Perry Russo by Irvin Dymond, Donated Papers of Edward Wegmann, National Archives, College Park, Maryland.

[2628] The transcripts of the January 29, 1971 and March 26, 1971 interviews with Russo may be found in the Sharon Litwin Collection at Historic New Orleans Collection in New Orleans, Louisiana, and in the Donated Papers of the Metropolitan Crime Commssion in the JFK Assassination Collection at the National Archives in College Park, Maryland A summary of Irvin Dymond's conversation with Russo on the evening of January 26, 1971 may be found in the Donated Papers of Edward Wegmann at the National Archives in College Park, Maryland.

[2629] The transcripts of the January 29, 1971 and March 26, 1971 interviews with Russo may be found in the Sharon Litwin Collection at Historic New Orleans Collection in New Orleans, Louisiana, and in the Donated Papers of the Metropolitan Crime Commssion in the JFK Assassination Collection at the National Archives in College Park, Maryland A summary of Irvin Dymond's conversation with Russo on the evening of January 26, 1971 may be found in the Donated Papers of Edward Wegmann at the National Archives in College Park, Maryland.

[2630] The transcripts of the January 29, 1971 and March 26, 1971 interviews with Russo may be found in the Sharon Litwin Collection at Historic New Orleans Collection in New Orleans, Louisiana, and in the Donated Papers of the Metropolitan Crime Commssion in the JFK Assassination Collection at the National Archives in College Park, Maryland A summary of Irvin Dymond's conversation with Russo on the evening of January 26, 1971 may be found in the Donated Papers of Edward Wegmann at the National Archives in College Park, Maryland.

2631 The transcripts of the January 29, 1971 and March 26, 1971 interviews with Russo may be found in the Sharon Litwin Collection at Historic New Orleans Collection in New Orleans, Louisiana, and in the Donated Papers of the Metropolitan Crime Commssion in the JFK Assassination Collection at the National Archives in College Park, Maryland A summary of Irvin Dymond's conversation with Russo on the evening of January 26, 1971 may be found in the Donated Papers of Edward Wegmann at the National Archives in College Park, Maryland.

2632 The transcripts of the January 29, 1971 and March 26, 1971 interviews with Russo may be found in the Sharon Litwin Collection at Historic New Orleans Collection in New Orleans, Louisiana, and in the Donated Papers of the Metropolitan Crime Commssion in the JFK Assassination Collection at the National Archives in College Park, Maryland A summary of Irvin Dymond's conversation with Russo on the evening of January 26, 1971 may be found in the Donated Papers of Edward Wegmann at the National Archives in College Park, Maryland.

2633 The transcripts of the January 29, 1971 and March 26, 1971 interviews with Russo may be found in the Sharon Litwin Collection at Historic New Orleans Collection in New Orleans, Louisiana, and in the Donated Papers of the Metropolitan Crime Commssion in the JFK Assassination Collection at the National Archives in College Park, Maryland A summary of Irvin Dymond's conversation with Russo on the evening of January 26, 1971 may be found in the Donated Papers of Edward Wegmann at the National Archives in College Park, Maryland.

2634 The transcripts of the January 29, 1971 and March 26, 1971 interviews with Russo may be found in the Sharon Litwin Collection at Historic New Orleans Collection in New Orleans, Louisiana, and in the Donated Papers of the Metropolitan Crime Commssion in the JFK Assassination Collection at the National Archives in College Park, Maryland A summary of Irvin Dymond's conversation with Russo on the evening of January 26, 1971 may be found in the Donated Papers of Edward Wegmann at the National Archives in College Park, Maryland.

2635 The transcripts of the January 29, 1971 and March 26, 1971 interviews with Russo may be found in the Sharon Litwin Collection at Historic New Orleans Collection in New Orleans, Louisiana, and in the Donated Papers of the Metropolitan Crime Commssion in the JFK Assassination Collection at the National Archives in College Park, Maryland A summary of Irvin Dymond's conversation with Russo on the evening of January 26, 1971 may be found in the Donated Papers of Edward Wegmann at the National Archives in College Park, Maryland.

2636 The transcripts of the January 29, 1971 and March 26, 1971 interviews with Russo may be found in the Sharon Litwin Collection at Historic New Orleans Collection in New Orleans, Louisiana, and in the Donated Papers of the Metropolitan Crime Commssion in the JFK Assassination Collection at the National Archives in College Park, Maryland A summary of Irvin Dymond's conversation with Russo on the evening of January 26, 1971 may be found in the Donated Papers of Edward Wegmann at the National Archives in College Park, Maryland.

2637 Memo dated February 8, 1971, Edith Stern to Joseph Falgout, Private Collection of Edith Stern related to Clay Shaw, Longue Vue, New Orleans, Louisiana.

2638 Correspondence dated February 1971 between Edith Stern and Shaw, Donated Papers of Clay Shaw, National Archives, College Park, Maryland.

2639 Memo dated July 9, 1971, Joseph Falgout to Edith Stern, Private Collection of Edith Stern related to Clay Shaw, Longue Vue, New Orleans, Louisiana.

2640 Article dated March 28, 1971 in *Key West Citizen*, Donated Papers of Clay Shaw, National Archives, College Park, Maryland.

2641 Minutes of Board of Directors meeting, March 26, 1971, International Trade Mart, International Trade Mart Records, Tulane University, New Orleans, Louisiana.

2642 The transcripts of the January 29, 1971 and March 26, 1971 interviews with Russo may be found in the Sharon Litwin Collection at Historic New Orleans Collection in New Orleans, Louisiana, and in the Donated Papers of the Metropolitan Crime Commssion in the JFK Assassination Collection at the National Archives in College Park, Maryland A summary of Irvin Dymond's conversation with Russo on the evening of January 26, 1971 may be found in the Donated Papers of Edward Wegmann at the National Archives in College Park, Maryland.

[2643] The transcripts of the January 29, 1971 and March 26, 1971 interviews with Russo may be found in the Sharon Litwin Collection at Historic New Orleans Collection in New Orleans, Louisiana, and in the Donated Papers of the Metropolitan Crime Commssion in the JFK Assassination Collection at the National Archives in College Park, Maryland A summary of Irvin Dymond's conversation with Russo on the evening of January 26, 1971 may be found in the Donated Papers of Edward Wegmann at the National Archives in College Park, Maryland.

[2644] The transcripts of the January 29, 1971 and March 26, 1971 interviews with Russo may be found in the Sharon Litwin Collection at Historic New Orleans Collection in New Orleans, Louisiana, and in the Donated Papers of the Metropolitan Crime Commssion in the JFK Assassination Collection at the National Archives in College Park, Maryland A summary of Irvin Dymond's conversation with Russo on the evening of January 26, 1971 may be found in the Donated Papers of Edward Wegmann at the National Archives in College Park, Maryland.

[2645] The transcripts of the January 29, 1971 and March 26, 1971 interviews with Russo may be found in the Sharon Litwin Collection at Historic New Orleans Collection in New Orleans, Louisiana, and in the Donated Papers of the Metropolitan Crime Commssion in the JFK Assassination Collection at the National Archives in College Park, Maryland A summary of Irvin Dymond's conversation with Russo on the evening of January 26, 1971 may be found in the Donated Papers of Edward Wegmann at the National Archives in College Park, Maryland.

[2646] The transcripts of the January 29, 1971 and March 26, 1971 interviews with Russo may be found in the Sharon Litwin Collection at Historic New Orleans Collection in New Orleans, Louisiana, and in the Donated Papers of the Metropolitan Crime Commssion in the JFK Assassination Collection at the National Archives in College Park, Maryland A summary of Irvin Dymond's conversation with Russo on the evening of January 26, 1971 may be found in the Donated Papers of Edward Wegmann at the National Archives in College Park, Maryland.

[2647] The transcripts of the January 29, 1971 and March 26, 1971 interviews with Russo may be found in the Sharon Litwin Collection at Historic New Orleans Collection in New Orleans, Louisiana, and in the Donated Papers of the Metropolitan Crime Commssion in the JFK Assassination Collection at the National Archives in College Park, Maryland A summary of Irvin Dymond's conversation with Russo on the evening of January 26, 1971 may be found in the Donated Papers of Edward Wegmann at the National Archives in College Park, Maryland.

[2648] The transcripts of the January 29, 1971 and March 26, 1971 interviews with Russo may be found in the Sharon Litwin Collection at Historic New Orleans Collection in New Orleans, Louisiana, and in the Donated Papers of the Metropolitan Crime Commssion in the JFK Assassination Collection at the National Archives in College Park, Maryland A summary of Irvin Dymond's conversation with Russo on the evening of January 26, 1971 may be found in the Donated Papers of Edward Wegmann at the National Archives in College Park, Maryland.

[2649] The transcripts of the January 29, 1971 and March 26, 1971 interviews with Russo may be found in the Sharon Litwin Collection at Historic New Orleans Collection in New Orleans, Louisiana, and in the Donated Papers of the Metropolitan Crime Commssion in the JFK Assassination Collection at the National Archives in College Park, Maryland A summary of Irvin Dymond's conversation with Russo on the evening of January 26, 1971 may be found in the Donated Papers of Edward Wegmann at the National Archives in College Park, Maryland.

[2650] The transcripts of the January 29, 1971 and March 26, 1971 interviews with Russo may be found in the Sharon Litwin Collection at Historic New Orleans Collection in New Orleans, Louisiana, and in the Donated Papers of the Metropolitan Crime Commssion in the JFK Assassination Collection at the National Archives in College Park, Maryland A summary of Irvin Dymond's conversation with Russo on the evening of January 26, 1971 may be found in the Donated Papers of Edward Wegmann at the National Archives in College Park, Maryland.

[2651] The transcripts of the January 29, 1971 and March 26, 1971 interviews with Russo may be found in the Sharon Litwin Collection at Historic New Orleans Collection in New Orleans, Louisiana, and in the Donated Papers of the Metropolitan Crime Commssion in the JFK Assassination Collection at the National Archives in College Park, Maryland A summary of Irvin Dymond's conversation with Russo on the evening of January 26, 1971 may be found in the Donated Papers of Edward Wegmann at the National Archives in College Park, Maryland.

[2652] The transcripts of the January 29, 1971 and March 26, 1971 interviews with Russo may be found in the Sharon Litwin Collection at Historic New Orleans Collection in New Orleans, Louisiana, and in the Donated Papers of the Metropolitan Crime Commssion in the JFK Assassination Collection at the National Archives in College Park, Maryland A summary of Irvin Dymond's conversation with Russo on the evening of January 26, 1971 may be found in the Donated Papers of Edward Wegmann at the National Archives in College Park, Maryland.

[2653] The transcripts of the January 29, 1971 and March 26, 1971 interviews with Russo may be found in the Sharon Litwin Collection at Historic New Orleans Collection in New Orleans, Louisiana, and in the Donated Papers of the Metropolitan Crime Commssion in the JFK Assassination Collection at the National Archives in College Park, Maryland A summary of Irvin Dymond's conversation with Russo on the evening of January 26, 1971 may be found in the Donated Papers of Edward Wegmann at the National Archives in College Park, Maryland.

[2654] The transcripts of the January 29, 1971 and March 26, 1971 interviews with Russo may be found in the Sharon Litwin Collection at Historic New Orleans Collection in New Orleans, Louisiana, and in the Donated Papers of the Metropolitan Crime Commssion in the JFK Assassination Collection at the National Archives in College Park, Maryland A summary of Irvin Dymond's conversation with Russo on the evening of January 26, 1971 may be found in the Donated Papers of Edward Wegmann at the National Archives in College Park, Maryland.

[2655] The transcripts of the January 29, 1971 and March 26, 1971 interviews with Russo may be found in the Sharon Litwin Collection at Historic New Orleans Collection in New Orleans, Louisiana, and in the Donated Papers of the Metropolitan Crime Commssion in the JFK Assassination Collection at the National Archives in College Park, Maryland A summary of Irvin Dymond's conversation with Russo on the evening of January 26, 1971 may be found in the Donated Papers of Edward Wegmann at the National Archives in College Park, Maryland.

[2656] The transcripts of the January 29, 1971 and March 26, 1971 interviews with Russo may be found in the Sharon Litwin Collection at Historic New Orleans Collection in New Orleans, Louisiana, and in the Donated Papers of the Metropolitan Crime Commssion in the JFK Assassination Collection at the National Archives in College Park, Maryland A summary of Irvin Dymond's conversation with Russo on the evening of January 26, 1971 may be found in the Donated Papers of Edward Wegmann at the National Archives in College Park, Maryland.

[2657] The transcripts of the January 29, 1971 and March 26, 1971 interviews with Russo may be found in the Sharon Litwin Collection at Historic New Orleans Collection in New Orleans, Louisiana, and in the Donated Papers of the Metropolitan Crime Commssion in the JFK Assassination Collection at the National Archives in College Park, Maryland A summary of Irvin Dymond's conversation with Russo on the evening of January 26, 1971 may be found in the Donated Papers of Edward Wegmann at the National Archives in College Park, Maryland.

[2658] The transcripts of the January 29, 1971 and March 26, 1971 interviews with Russo may be found in the Sharon Litwin Collection at Historic New Orleans Collection in New Orleans, Louisiana, and in the Donated Papers of the Metropolitan Crime Commssion in the JFK Assassination Collection at the National Archives in College Park, Maryland A summary of Irvin Dymond's conversation with Russo on the evening of January 26, 1971 may be found in the Donated Papers of Edward Wegmann at the National Archives in College Park, Maryland.

[2659] The transcripts of the January 29, 1971 and March 26, 1971 interviews with Russo may be found in the Sharon Litwin Collection at Historic New Orleans Collection in New Orleans, Louisiana, and in the Donated Papers of the Metropolitan Crime Commssion in the JFK Assassination Collection at the National Archives in College Park, Maryland A summary of Irvin Dymond's conversation with Russo on the evening of January 26, 1971 may be found in the Donated Papers of Edward Wegmann at the National Archives in College Park, Maryland.

2660 The transcripts of the January 29, 1971 and March 26, 1971 interviews with Russo may be found in the Sharon Litwin Collection at Historic New Orleans Collection in New Orleans, Louisiana, and in the Donated Papers of the Metropolitan Crime Commssion in the JFK Assassination Collection at the National Archives in College Park, Maryland A summary of Irvin Dymond's conversation with Russo on the evening of January 26, 1971 may be found in the Donated Papers of Edward Wegmann at the National Archives in College Park, Maryland.

2661 The transcripts of the January 29, 1971 and March 26, 1971 interviews with Russo may be found in the Sharon Litwin Collection at Historic New Orleans Collection in New Orleans, Louisiana, and in the Donated Papers of the Metropolitan Crime Commssion in the JFK Assassination Collection at the National Archives in College Park, Maryland A summary of Irvin Dymond's conversation with Russo on the evening of January 26, 1971 may be found in the Donated Papers of Edward Wegmann at the National Archives in College Park, Maryland.

2662 The transcripts of the January 29, 1971 and March 26, 1971 interviews with Russo may be found in the Sharon Litwin Collection at Historic New Orleans Collection in New Orleans, Louisiana, and in the Donated Papers of the Metropolitan Crime Commssion in the JFK Assassination Collection at the National Archives in College Park, Maryland A summary of Irvin Dymond's conversation with Russo on the evening of January 26, 1971 may be found in the Donated Papers of Edward Wegmann at the National Archives in College Park, Maryland.

2663 The transcripts of the January 29, 1971 and March 26, 1971 interviews with Russo may be found in the Sharon Litwin Collection at Historic New Orleans Collection in New Orleans, Louisiana, and in the Donated Papers of the Metropolitan Crime Commssion in the JFK Assassination Collection at the National Archives in College Park, Maryland A summary of Irvin Dymond's conversation with Russo on the evening of January 26, 1971 may be found in the Donated Papers of Edward Wegmann at the National Archives in College Park, Maryland.

2664 The transcripts of the January 29, 1971 and March 26, 1971 interviews with Russo may be found in the Sharon Litwin Collection at Historic New Orleans Collection in New Orleans, Louisiana, and in the Donated Papers of the Metropolitan Crime Commssion in the JFK Assassination Collection at the National Archives in College Park, Maryland A summary of Irvin Dymond's conversation with Russo on the evening of January 26, 1971 may be found in the Donated Papers of Edward Wegmann at the National Archives in College Park, Maryland.

2665 The transcripts of the January 29, 1971 and March 26, 1971 interviews with Russo may be found in the Sharon Litwin Collection at Historic New Orleans Collection in New Orleans, Louisiana, and in the Donated Papers of the Metropolitan Crime Commssion in the JFK Assassination Collection at the National Archives in College Park, Maryland A summary of Irvin Dymond's conversation with Russo on the evening of January 26, 1971 may be found in the Donated Papers of Edward Wegmann at the National Archives in College Park, Maryland.

2666 The transcripts of the January 29, 1971 and March 26, 1971 interviews with Russo may be found in the Sharon Litwin Collection at Historic New Orleans Collection in New Orleans, Louisiana, and in the Donated Papers of the Metropolitan Crime Commssion in the JFK Assassination Collection at the National Archives in College Park, Maryland A summary of Irvin Dymond's conversation with Russo on the evening of January 26, 1971 may be found in the Donated Papers of Edward Wegmann at the National Archives in College Park, Maryland.

2667 News clipping dated July 21, 1971 related to permanent injunction against second perjury prosecution of Dean Andrews, Records of the New Orleans Metropolitan Crime Commission, National Archives, College Park, Maryland.

2668 Newspaper article in *States-Item*, July 28, 1971, Records of the New Orleans Metropolitan Crime Commission, National Archives, College Park, Maryland.

2669 Interview with Moon Landrieu that appears in documentary *He Must Have Something*, 1992.

2670 Letter dated October 20, 1971, A. Marcy Newman to Shaw, Author's Collection.

2671 Letter dated November 3, 1971, Shaw to Patrick O'Rourke, Author's Collection.

[2672] Court decision on summary judgment dated November 24, 1971 and order regarding bill of costs dated December 28, 1971, Record Group 21, Administrative Office of the U.S. Courts, Gordon Novel vs. Jim Garrison and HMH Publishing Company, JFK Assassination Collection, National Archives, College Park, Maryland.

[2673] Deposition of Dean Andrews, March 12, 1970, Record Group 21, Administrative Office of the U.S. Courts, Gordon Novel vs. Jim Garrison and HMH Publishing Company, JFK Assassination Collection, National Archives, College Park, Maryland.

[2674] Deposition of Walter J. Sheridan, March 30, 1970, Record Group 21, Administrative Office of the U.S. Courts, Gordon Novel vs. Jim Garrison and HMH Publishing Company, JFK Assassination Collection, National Archives, College Park, Maryland.

[2675] Deposition of Walter J. Sheridan, March 30, 1970, Record Group 21, Administrative Office of the U.S. Courts, Gordon Novel vs. Jim Garrison and HMH Publishing Company, JFK Assassination Collection, National Archives, College Park, Maryland.

[2676] Deposition of Walter J. Sheridan, March 30, 1970, Record Group 21, Administrative Office of the U.S. Courts, Gordon Novel vs. Jim Garrison and HMH Publishing Company, JFK Assassination Collection, National Archives, College Park, Maryland.

[2677] Deposition of Walter J. Sheridan, March 30, 1970, Record Group 21, Administrative Office of the U.S. Courts, Gordon Novel vs. Jim Garrison and HMH Publishing Company, JFK Assassination Collection, National Archives, College Park, Maryland.

[2678] Deposition of Walter J. Sheridan, March 30, 1970, Record Group 21, Administrative Office of the U.S. Courts, Gordon Novel vs. Jim Garrison and HMH Publishing Company, JFK Assassination Collection, National Archives, College Park, Maryland.

[2679] 3 Series General Counsel, Records of the Assassination Records Review Board, National Archives, College Park, Maryland.

[2680] 3 Series General Counsel, Records of the Assassination Records Review Board, National Archives, College Park, Maryland.

[2681] Letter dated November 3, 1971, Shaw to Patrick O'Rourke, Author's Collection.

[2682] Telegram dated December 15, 1971, Dick Rolfe to Shaw, Author's Collection.

[2683] Column by Robin Adams Sloan appearing in January 6, 1972 edition of *Washington Star*, Record Group 233, Records of the U.S. House of Representatives, Select Committee on Assassinations, Segregated CIA Collection, JFK Assassination Collection, National Archives, College Park, Maryland.

[2684] Letter dated January 13, 1972, Shaw to Chris Blake, Donated Papers of Clay Shaw, National Archives, College Park, Maryland.

[2685] Letter dated January 13, 1972, Shaw to Tom Dawson, Donated Papers of Clay Shaw, National Archives, College Park, Maryland.

[2686] E-mail dated December 20, 2012, Nita Putnam to author.

[2687] E-mail dated December 21, 2012, Nita Putnam to author.

[2688] Letter dated January 26, 1972, Shaw to Edith Stern, Donated Papers of Clay Shaw, National Archives, College Park, Maryland.

[2689] Letter dated February 7, 1972, Holland McCombs to Shaw, Donated Papers of Clay Shaw, National Archives, College Park, Maryland.

[2690] Letter dated December 27, 1971, Casey Jones to Shaw, Donated Papers of Clay Shaw, National Archives, College Park, Maryland.

[2691] Letter dated February 7, 1972, Shaw to Casey Jones, Donated Papers of Clay Shaw, National Archives, College Park, Maryland.

[2692] News article in *Miami Herald*, January 16, 1972, Donated Papers of Edward Wegmann, National Archives, College Park, Maryland.

[2693] News article in *Miami Herald*, January 16, 1972, Donated Papers of Edward Wegmann, National Archives, College Park, Maryland.

[2694] Letter dated February 9, 1972, Shaw to Grace Herlihy, Donated Papers of Clay Shaw, National Archives, College Park, Maryland.

[2695] Letter dated February 8, 1972, Shaw to Roland Dobson, Donated Papers of Clay Shaw, National Archives, College Park, Maryland.

[2696] Letter dated February 17, 1972, Shaw to Monk Simons, Donated Papers of Clay Shaw, National Archives, College Park, Maryland.

[2697] Letter dated March 15, 1972, Edward Wegmann to William Gurvich, Donated Papers of Edward Wegmann, National Archives, College Park, Maryland.

[2698] Letter dated February 24, 1972, Shaw to Commander R. Russell, Donated Papers of Clay Shaw, National Archives, College Park, Maryland.

[2699] Letter dated March 8, 1972, Shaw to Duffy Wall, Donated Papers of Clay Shaw, National Archives, College Park, Maryland.

[2700] Letter dated March 14, 1972, Shaw to Vincent Arena, Donated Papers of Clay Shaw, National Archives, College Park, Maryland.

[2701] Letter dated April 25, 1972, W.T. "Bill" Berniard to Shaw, thanking him for appearance, Donated Papers of Clay Shaw, National Archives, College Park, Maryland.

[2702] Letter dated March 11, 1972, Casey Jones to Shaw, Donated Papers of Clay Shaw, National Archives, College Park, Maryland.

[2703] Letter dated March 17, 1972, Shaw to Casey Jones, Donated Papers of Clay Shaw, National Archives, College Park, Maryland.

[2704] Card, undated, probably around March 17, 1972, Sally and Warren Galjour to Shaw, Donated Papers of Clay Shaw, National Archives, College Park, Maryland.

[2705] Letter dated April 27, 1972, Shaw to Sally and Warren Galjour, Donated Papers of Clay Shaw, National Archives, College Park, Maryland.

[2706] Letter dated April 9, 1972, Shaw to Jacqueline de Chimay, Donated Papers of Clay Shaw, National Archives, College Park, Maryland.

[2707] Undated letter, probably late April or early May 1972, Jacquelin de Chimay to Shaw, Donated Papers of Clay Shaw, National Archives, College Park, Maryland.

[2708] Letter dated April 20, 1972, Shaw to Emlyn Williams, Donated Papers of Clay Shaw, National Archives, College Park, Maryland.

[2709] Letter dated April 27, 1972, Shaw to Mary and J. Lawrence Smith, Donated Papers of Clay Shaw, National Archives, College Park, Maryland.

[2710] Letter dated May 22, 1972, Lelah Halton to Shaw, Donated Papers of Clay Shaw, National Archives, College Park, Maryland.

[2711] Letter dated July 25, 1972, Shaw to Lelah Halton, Donated Papers of Clay Shaw, National Archives, College Park, Maryland.

[2712] See Shaw's passports, Donated Papers of Clay Shaw, National Archives, College Park, Maryland.

[2713] Letter dated May 31, 1972, Shaw to John Henry Bogle, Donated Papers of Clay Shaw, National Archives, College Park, Maryland.

2714 Letter dated May 31, 1972, Shaw to Mrs. Richard Bosse, Donated Papers of Clay Shaw, National Archives, College Park, Maryland.

2715 Letter dated June 1, 1972, Shaw to Mrs. John Holihan, Donated Papers of Clay Shaw, National Archives, College Park, Maryland.

2716 Personal financial information as of June 4, 1972, Donated Papers of Clay Shaw, National Archives, College Park, Maryland.

2717 Letter dated April 5, 1972, Joan Nish to Shaw, Donated Papers of Clay Shaw, National Archives, College Park, Maryland.

2718 Letter dated June 8, 1972, Mayor Moon Landrieu to Shaw, Donated Papers of Clay Shaw, National Archives, College Park, Maryland.

2719 Letter dated July 25, 1972, Shaw to Alison P. Marks, Donated Papers of Clay Shaw, National Archives, College Park, Maryland.

2720 Letter dated August 3, 1972, Shaw to Emlyn Williams, Donated Papers of Clay Shaw, National Archives, College Park, Maryland.

2721 Letter dated August 1, 1972, Shaw to Valerian Rybar, Donated Papers of Clay Shaw, National Archives, College Park, Maryland.

2722 See Shaw's daily planner for 1972, Donated Papers of Clay Shaw, National Archives, College Park, Maryland.

2723 See Shaw's daily planner for 1972, Donated Papers of Clay Shaw, National Archives, College Park, Maryland.

2724 Letter dated May 28, 1976, Bob Clark to Roy S. Simmonds, Roy S. Simmonds Collection, The W.S. Hoole Special Collections Library, The University of Alabama, Tuscaloosa, Alabama.

2725 Letter dated August 24, 1972, Shaw to Hotel Monte Lambert, Donated Papers of Clay Shaw, National Archives, College Park, Maryland.

2726 Letter dated August 16, 1972, Shaw to Jack Davis, Donated Papers of Clay Shaw, National Archives, College Park, Maryland.

2727 Letter dated September 26, 1972, Shaw to Edith Stern, Donated Papers of Clay Shaw, National Archives, College Park, Maryland.

2728 Letter dated October 9, 1972, Shaw to Jacqueline de Chimay, Donated Papers of Clay Shaw, National Archives, College Park, Maryland.

2729 Letter dated November 7, 1972, Shaw to Olwen and Hugh Janson, Donated Papers of Clay Shaw, National Archives, College Park, Maryland.

2730 Letter dated October 17, 1972, Shaw to Gloria Safier, Donated Papers of Clay Shaw, National Archives, College Park, Maryland.

2731 Narrative dealing with negative aspects of New Orleans, Donated Papers of Clay Shaw, National Archives, Washington, D.C.

2732 Letter dated September 27, 1972, Shaw to Mrs. Mina L. Crais, Donated Papers of Clay Shaw, National Archives, College Park, Maryland.

2733 Letter dated October 2, 1972, Donald M. Soignet to Shaw, Donated Papers of Clay Shaw, National Archives, College Park, Maryland.

2734 Minutes of Executive Committee meeting, October 11, 1973, International Trade Mart, International Trade Mart Records, Tulane University, New Orleans, Louisiana.

2735 Minutes of Contributors and Debenture Holders, April 19, 1972, International Trade Mart, International Trade Mart Records, Tulane University, New Orleans, Louisiana.

[2736] Invitation related to dedication ceremony of Place du France, Donated Papers of Clay Shaw, National Archives, College Park, Maryland.

[2737] Letter dated November 7, 1972, Shaw to Leonard H. Haertter, Donated Papers of Clay Shaw, National Archives, College Park, Maryland.

[2738] Letter dated August 3, 1972, Shaw to Phi Mu Fraternity, Donated Papers of Clay Shaw, National Archives, College Park, Maryland.

[2739] Letter dated November 13, 1972, inviting Shaw to be interviewed, Donated Papers of Clay Shaw, National Archives, College Park, Maryland.

[2740] Newspaper article in *Times-Picayune*, November 22, 1972, Donated Papers of Clay Shaw, National Archives, College Park, Maryland.

[2741] Newspaper article in *States-Item*, March 17, 1972, Donated Papers of Clay Shaw, National Archives, College Park, Maryland.

[2742] Letter dated November 22, 1972, Ralph L. Kaskell, Jr. to Edward Wegmann, Donated Papers of Clay Shaw, National Archives, College Park, Maryland.

[2743] Letter dated November 24, 1972, Lois Kirkpatrick, Donated Papers of Clay Shaw, National Archives, College Park, Maryland.

[2744] Letter dated November 29, 1972, Shaw to Holland McCombs, Donated Papers of Clay Shaw, National Archives, College Park, Maryland.

[2745] Letter, no date, George Gaston Johnston to Shaw, with reply letter dated November 29, 1972, Shaw to George Gaston Johnston, Donated Papers of Clay Shaw, National Archives, College Park, Maryland.

[2746] Letter dated November 20, 1972, Mrs. Edwin S. Anderson to Shaw, Donated Papers of Clay Shaw, National Archives, College Park, Maryland.

[2747] Letter dated December 27, 1972, Shaw to Mrs. Edwin S. Anderson, Donated Papers of Clay Shaw, National Archives, College Park, Maryland.

[2748] Letter dated November 29, 1972, Shaw to Rod McKuen, Donated Papers of Clay Shaw, National Archives, College Park, Maryland.

[2749] Letter, November 1995, Gore Vidal to Author.

[2750] Letter, January 2000, Gore Vidal to Author.

[2751] Letter dated December 13, 1972, Shaw to Princess Jacqueline de Chimay, Donated Papers of Clay Shaw, National Archives, College Park, Maryland.

[2752] Letter dated December 14, 1972, Jim Garrison to Louisiana State Bar Association, JFK Assassination Collection, New Orleans Public Library, New Orleans, Louisiana.

[2753] Letter dated December 27, 1972, Shaw to Paulette Rittenberg, Donated Papers of Clay Shaw, National Archives, College Park, Maryland.

[2754] Letter dated December 27, 1972, Shaw to August Perez III, Donated Papers of Clay Shaw, National Archives, College Park, Maryland.

[2755] Shaw's 1972 Federal Income Tax Return, Donated Papers of Clay Shaw, National Archives, College Park, Maryland.

[2756] Letter dated January 5, 1973, George Connoly, Jr. to Shaw, Donated Papers of Clay Shaw, National Archives, College Park, Maryland.

[2757] Letter dated January 10, 1973, Keith A. Bordelon to Shaw, Donated Papers of Clay Shaw, National Archives, College Park, Maryland.

2758 Letter dated February 6, 1973, Shaw to Max Barnett, Donated Papers of Clay Shaw, National Archives, College Park, Maryland.

2759 Letter dated February 18, 1973, Shaw to George E. Kollasch, Donated Papers of Clay Shaw, National Archives, College Park, Maryland.

2760 Minutes to Executive Committee meeting, January 18, 1973, International Trade Mart, International Trade Mart Records, Tulane University, New Orleans, Louisiana.

2761 Minutes of Executive Committee meeting, January 11, 1973, International Trade Mart, International Trade Mart Records, Tulane University, New Orleans, Louisiana.

2762 Letter dated February 21, 1973, Edward Wegmann to Malcolm Monroe, JFK Assassination Collection, New Orleans Public Library, New Orleans, Louisiana.

2763 Letter dated February 21, 1973, Malcolm Monroe to Edward Wegmann, JFK Assassination Collection, New Orleans Public Library, New Orleans, Louisiana.

2764 Record Group 21, Records of U.S. District Courts, Records from the District Court of Louisiana, New Orleans Division, Case #70-466, Clay L. Shaw vs. Jim Garrison, Joseph M. Rault, Jr., Cecil M. Shilstone, Willard E. Robertson, Perry Raymond Russo, and Dr. Esmond A. Fatter, JFK Assassination Collection, National Archives, College Park, Maryland.

2765 See 1973 Birthday Cards to Shaw, Donated Papers of Clay Shaw, National Archives, College Park, Maryland.

2766 Letter dated March 19, 1973, Edward Wegmann to Gordon Novel, Donated Papers of Edward Wegmann, National Archives, College Park, Maryland.

2767 Letter dated May 17, 1973, Shaw to Virginia Kirk, Donated Papers of Clay Shaw, National Archives, College Park, Maryland.

2768 Letter dated May 18, 1973, Virginia Kirk to Shaw, Donated Papers of Clay Shaw, National Archives, College Park, Maryland.

2769 See Shaw's personal daily calendar for 1973, Donated Papers of Clay Shaw, National Archives, College Park, Maryland.

2770 See statement from Ochsner Foundation to Shaw, May 21 to June 9, 1973, Donated Papers of Clay Shaw, National Archives, College Park, Maryland.

2771 Ochsner Foundation statement dated June 7, 1973, Donated Papers of Clay Shaw, National Archives, College Park, Maryland.

2772 Letter dated June 28, 1973, Shaw to John and Ginnie (no last name), Donated Papers of Clay Shaw, National Archives, College Park, Maryland.

2773 Letter dated June 5, 1973, Shaw to Mrs. Virginia Kirk, Donated Papers of Clay Shaw, National Archives, College Park, Maryland.

2774 Letter dated February 13, 1973, Shaw to New Orleans Fire Department, Donated Papers of Clay Shaw, National Archives, College Park, Maryland.

2775 See Shaw's desk calendar for 1973, Donated Papers of Clay Shaw, National Archives, College Park, Maryland.

2776 Letter dated April 15, 1973, Wayne Collier to Shaw, Donated Papers of Clay Shaw, National Archives, College Park, Maryland.

2777 Letter dated July 5, 1973, Gervais Favrot Company to Shaw, Donated Papers of Clay Shaw, National Archives, College Park, Maryland.

2778 Letter dated June 22, 1973, Wayne A. Collier to Shaw, Donated Papers of Clay Shaw, National Archives, College Park, Maryland.

[2779] Letter dated June 28, 1973, Peter Panno to Shaw, Donated Papers of Clay Shaw, National Archives, College Park, Maryland.

[2780] Letter dated July 20, 1973, Shaw to his insurance company, Donated Papers of Clay Shaw, National Archives, College Park, Maryland.

[2781] Letter dated December 10, 1973, Arthur C. Reuter to Shaw, Donated Papers of Clay Shaw, National Archives, College Park, Maryland.

[2782] Letter dated February 25, 1974, Gervais Favrot Company to Shaw, Donated Papers of Clay Shaw, National Archives, College Park, Maryland.

[2783] Letter dated July 19, 1973, Tennessee Williams to Bill Barnes, Fred W. Todd Collection—Tennessee Williams, Historic New Orleans Collection, New Orleans, Louisiana.

[2784] Letter dated August 6, 1973, Shaw to Thomas J. Young, Donated Papers of Clay Shaw, National Archives, College Park, Maryland.

[2785] See Shaw's desk calendar for 1973, Donated Papers of Clay Shaw, National Archives, College Park, Maryland.

[2786] See Shaw's personal daily calendar for 1973, Donated Papers of Clay Shaw, National Archives, College Park, Maryland.

[2787] Letter dated August 6, 1973, Leonard J. Salathe to Shaw, Donated Papers of Clay Shaw, National Archives, College Park, Maryland.

[2788] See Shaw's desk calendar for 1973, Donated Papers of Clay Shaw, National Archives, College Park, Maryland.

[2789] Undated letter, probably late summer 1973, Chuck Deville to Shaw, Donated Papers of Clay Shaw, National Archives, College Park, Maryland.

[2790] See Shaw's desk calendar for 1973, Donated Papers of Clay Shaw, National Archives, College Park, Maryland.

[2791] Entry from Pancho Rodriguez's diary, September 22, 1973, Fred W. Todd Collection—Tennessee Williams, Historic New Orleans Collection, New Orleans, Louisiana.

[2792] See Shaw's medical bills, Donated Papers of Clay Shaw, National Archives, College Park, Maryland.

[2793] See Shaw's desk calendar for 1973, Donated Papers of Clay Shaw, National Archives, College Park, Maryland.

[2794] Letter dated October 18, 1973, Shaw to Lori and Louis Cocita, Donated Papers of Clay Shaw, National Archives, College Park, Maryland.

[2795] Letter dated November 12, 1973, Shaw to Cindy Wegmann, Donated Papers of Clay Shaw, National Archives, College Park, Maryland.

[2796] Letter dated November 15, 1973, Shaw to James Kirkwood, Donated Papers of Clay Shaw, National Archives, College Park, Maryland.

[2797] Undated letter, probably late November, 1973, James Kirkwood to Shaw, Donated Papers of Clay Shaw, National Archives, College Park, Maryland.

[2798] Letter dated November 26, 1973, Shaw to Edward Wegmann, Donated Papers of Clay Shaw, National Archives, College Park, Maryland.

[2799] Letter dated August 14, 1973, Shaw to Edward Wegmann, enclosing column by Nicholas R. Murray, Donated Papers of Clay Shaw, National Archives, College Park, Maryland.

[2800] Letter dated December 3, 1973, Shaw to Jesse Core, Donated Papers of Clay Shaw, National Archives, College Park, Maryland.

[2801] See Shaw's desk calendar for 1973, Donated Papers of Clay Shaw, National Archives, College Park, Maryland.

[2802] Letter dated December 2, 1973, Patrick O'Rourke to Shaw, Author's Collection.

[2803] See Shaw's personal daily calendar for 1973, Donated Papers of Clay Shaw, National Archives, College Park, Maryland.

[2804] Letter dated December 19, 1973, Tennessee Williams to Bill Barnes, Fred W. Todd Collection—TennesseeWilliams, Historic New Orleans Collection, New Orleans, Louisiana.

[2805] Ledgers related to Shaw properties, Donated Papers of Clay Shaw, National Archives, College Park, Maryland.

[2806] News release, Zodiac News Service, December 21, 1973, Papers Donated by Lyon Garrison, National Archives, College Park, Maryland.

[2807] Secrecy Agreement of William G. Gaudet and accompanying paperwork, Record Group 233, Records of the U.S. House of Representatives, Select Committee on Assassinations, Segregated CIA Collection, JFK Assassination Collection, National Archives, College Park, Maryland.

[2808] Memo by R.M. Reardon to Chief, Security Analysis Group, Record Group 263, Records of the Central Intelligence Agency, Office of Security, File on Lee Harvey Oswald, JFK Assassination Collection, National Archives, College Park, Maryland.

[2809] Letter dated January 23, 1976 by Jackson R. Horton, CIA Miscellaneous Files, JFK Assassination Collection, National Archives, College Park, Maryland.

[2810] See newspaper article dated January 15, 1976 about William Gaudet, CIA Miscellaneous Files, JFK Assassination Collection, National Archives, College Park, Maryland.

[2811] Letter from Lyle Miller to House Select Committee on Assassinations, CIA Miscellaneous Files, JFK Assassination Collection, National Archives, College Park, Maryland.

[2812] See memo entitled Garrison and the Kennedy Assassination, June 5, 1968, CIA Miscellaneous Files, JFK Assassination Collection, National Archives, College Park, Maryland.

[2813] See memo entitled Garrison and the Kennedy Assassination, June 5, 1968, CIA Miscellaneous Files, JFK Assassination Collection, National Archives, College Park, Maryland.

[2814] Memo dated February 24, 1983, CIA Miscellaneous Files, JFK Assassination Collection, National Archives, College Park, Maryland.

[2815] Memo dated October 31, 1975, CIA Miscellaneous Files, JFK Assassination Collection, National Archives, College Park, Maryland.

[2816] See letter to AT&T-Southwestern Bell by Gordon Novel, July 1975, CIA Miscellaneous Files, JFK Assassination Collection, National Archives, College Park, Maryland.

[2817] Memo from CIA discussing Paul Hoch's March 24, 1975 essay sent to Rockefeller Commission, CIA Miscellaneous Files, JFK Assassination Collection, National Archives, College Park, Maryland.

[2818] Memo dated December 22, 1997, CIA Miscellaneous Files, JFK Assassination Collection, National Archives, College Park, Maryland.

[2819] See letter regarding unresolved issues including QKENCHANT, Laura Denk to J. Barry Harrelson, July 27, 1998, CIA Miscellaneous Files, JFK Assassination Collection, National Archives, College Park, Maryland.

[2820] Letter dated July 15, 1998, T. Jeremy Gunn to Robert McNamara, CIA Miscellaneous Files, JFK Assassination Collection, National Archives, College Park, Maryland.

[2821] Memo dated February 27, 1998, Frederick C. Wickham, Jr. to Chief, JFK Declassification Project and Memo dated September 18, 1998, J. Barry Harrelson to Laura Denk, CIA Miscellaneous Files, JFK Assassination Collection, National Archives, College Park, Maryland.

[2822] Files of T. Jeremy Gunn, Records of the Assassination Records Review Board, National Archives, College Park, Maryland.

[2823] Letter dated February 25, 1974, Bernard Green to Shaw, Donated Papers of Clay Shaw, National Archives, College Park, Maryland.

[2824] Card dated November 11, 1973, Thomas Jefferson Young to Shaw, Donated Papers of Clay Shaw, National Archives, College Park, Maryland.

[2825] Letter dated January 17, 1974, Shaw to Thomas Jefferson Young, Donated Papers of Clay Shaw, National Archives, College Park, Maryland.

[2826] Undated card, Virginia van Tienhoven to Shaw, Donated Papers of Clay Shaw, National Archives, College Park, Maryland.

[2827] Letter dated January 23, 1974, Shaw to Virginia van Tienhoven, Donated Papers of Clay Shaw, National Archives, College Park, Maryland.

[2828] Card dated December 8, 1973, Alison Marks to Shaw, Donated Papers of Clay Shaw, National Archives, College Park, Maryland.

[2829] Letter dated January 17, 1974, Shaw to Alison Marks, Donated Papers of Clay Shaw, National Archives, College Park, Maryland.

[2830] Christmas card, December 1973, Olwen and Hugh Janson to Shaw, Donated Papers of Clay Shaw, National Archives, College Park, Maryland.

[2831] Letter dated January 17, 1974, Shaw to Olwen and Hugh Janson, Donated Papers of Clay Shaw, National Archives, College Park, Maryland.

[2832] Letter dated January 17, 1974, Shaw to Rod McKuen, Donated Papers of Clay Shaw, National Archives, College Park, Maryland.

[2833] Card, undated, probably Christmas 1973, Kenneth Sheehan to Shaw, Donated Papers of Clay Shaw, National Archives, College Park, Maryland.

[2834] Letter dated January 17, 1974, Shaw to Kenneth Sheehan, Donated Papers of Clay Shaw, National Archives, College Park, Maryland.

[2835] Card, undated, probably Christmas 1973, with enclosures, Mr. and Mrs. Wyatt Cooper to Shaw, Donated Papers of Clay Shaw, National Archives, College Park, Maryland.

[2836] Letter dated January 8, 1974, Shaw to Wyatt Cooper, Donated Papers of Clay Shaw, National Archives, College Park, Maryland.

[2837] See invoice from Mid-South Ambulance Service, Donated Papers of Clay Shaw, National Archives, College Park, Maryland.

[2838] Letter dated January 30, 1974, Alison Marks to Shaw, Donated Papers of Clay Shaw, National Archives, College Park, Maryland.

[2839] Letter dated March 6, 1974, Shaw to Alison Marks, Donated Papers of Clay Shaw, National Archives, College Park, Maryland.

[2840] Letter dated February 6, 1974, Olwen and Hugh Janson to Shaw, Donated Papers of Clay Shaw, National Archives, College Park, Maryland.

[2841] Letter dated February 5, 1974, Thomas A. Greene to Shaw, Donated Papers of Clay Shaw, National Archives, College Park, Maryland.

2842 Letter dated March 6, 1974, Shaw to Thomas A. Greene, Donated Papers of Clay Shaw, National Archives, College Park, Maryland.

2843 Letter dated February 14, 1974, Ray Seale to Shaw, Donated Papers of Clay Shaw, National Archives, College Park, Maryland.

2844 Letter dated March 6, 1974, Shaw to Ray Seale, Donated Papers of Clay Shaw, National Archives, College Park, Maryland.

2845 Letter dated April 11, 1974, Lewis Fulton Kempf II to Shaw, Donated Papers of Clay Shaw, National Archives, College Park, Maryland.

2846 Letter dated April 19, 1974, Shaw to Lewis Fulton Kempf II, Donated Papers of Clay Shaw, National Archives, College Park, Maryland.

2847 Letter dated January 24, 1974, John Wray Young to Shaw, Donated Papers of Clay Shaw, National Archives, College Park, Maryland.

2848 Letter dated May 1, 1974, Shaw to John Wray Young, Donated Papers of Clay Shaw, National Archives, College Park, Maryland.

2849 Letter dated March 23, 1974, Alison Marks to Shaw, Donated Papers of Clay Shaw, National Archives, College Park, Maryland.

2850 Letter dated May 1, 1974, Shaw to Alison Marks, Donated Papers of Clay Shaw, National Archives, College Park, Maryland.

2851 Undated letter, probably February 1974. Fannie Mae Shaw to Shaw, Donated Papers of Clay Shaw, National Archives, College Park, Maryland.

2852 Letter dated March 6, 1974, Shaw to Fannie Mae Shaw, Donated Papers of Clay Shaw, National Archives, College Park, Maryland.

2853 Letter dated March 19, 1974, Jessie Core to Shaw, Donated Papers of Clay Shaw, National Archives, College Park, Maryland.

2854 Card dated March 2, 1974, Mrs. Duval G. Cravens, Jr. to Shaw, Donated Papers of Clay Shaw, National Archives, College Park, Maryland.

2855 Letter dated March 6, 1974, Shaw to Mrs. Duval G. Cravens, Jr., Donated Papers of Clay Shaw, National Archives, College Park, Maryland.

2856 Letter dated March 12, 1974, Gina Jackson to Shaw, Donated Papers of Clay Shaw, National Archives, College Park, Maryland.

2857 Letter dated May 1, 1974, Shaw to Gina Jackson, Donated Papers of Clay Shaw, National Archives, College Park, Maryland.

2858 Letter dated May 23, 1974, A.J. Duplantier, Jr. to Shaw, Donated Papers of Clay Shaw, National Archives, College Park, Maryland.

2859 Letter dated June 18, 1974, French Market Board to Shaw, Donated Papers of Clay Shaw, National Archives, College Park, Maryland.

2860 Letter dated July 25, 1974, Edward Wegmann to A.J. Duplantier, Donated Papers of Clay Shaw, National Archives, College Park, Maryland.

2861 Interview with Donald Doody by author, January 11, 2006.

2862 Letter dated June 28, 1974, Virginia Kirk to Shaw with reply by Edward Wegmann, Donated Papers of Clay Shaw, National Archives, College Park, Maryland.

2863 Letter dated May 31, 1974, Edward Wegmann to Shaw, Donated Papers of Edward Wegmann, National Archives, College Park, Maryland.

[2864] Memo dated May 31, 1974, Notes regarding Amended Answers to Interrogatories, Legal Files of F. Irvin Dymond—Clay Shaw Case, Historic New Orleans Collection, New Orleans, Louisiana.

[2865] Letter dated July 2, 1974, Edward Wegmann to Shaw, Donated Papers of Edward Wegmann, National Archives, College Park, Maryland.

[2866] See preliminary list of expenses through 1969 in Shaw's defense attorneys' file, Donated Papers of Edward Wegmann, National Archives, College Park, Maryland.

[2867] Interview with Donald Doody by author, January 11, 2006.

[2868] Letter dated June 28, 1974, William Formyduval to Shaw, Donated Papers of Clay Shaw, National Archives, College Park, Maryland.

[2869] Letter dated June 29, 1974, Thomas Lemann to Edith Stern, Private Collection of Edith Stern related to Clay Shaw, Longue Vue, New Orleans, Louisiana.

[2870] Memo dated July 2, 1974, Joseph J. Falgout to Edith Stern, Private Collection of Edith Stern related to Clay Shaw, Longue Vue, New Orleans, Louisiana.

[2871] Letter dated July 8, 1974, Edith Stern to Shaw, Private Collection of Edith Stern related to Clay Shaw, Longue Vue, New Orleans, Louisiana.

[2872] Report dated July 8, 1974, William Gurvich to Edward Wegmann Donated Papers of Edward Wegmann, National Archives, College Park, Maryland.

[2873] Letter dated July 17, 1974, Edward Wegmann to Malcolm W. Monroe, Legal Files of F. Irvin Dymond—Clay Shaw Case, Historic New Orleans Collection, New Orleans, Louisiana.

[2874] Letter dated July 2, 1974, Edward Wegmann to Irvin Dymond and William Wegmann, Legal Files of F. Irvin Dymond—Clay Shaw Case, Historic New Orleans Collection, New Orleans, Louisiana.

[2875] Motion for Partial Summary Judgment by Dr. Fatter, July 17, 1974, Legal Files of F. Irvin Dymond—Clay Shaw Case, Historic New Orleans Collection, New Orleans, Louisiana.

[2876] Amended and Supplemental Answers to Interrogatories, July 17, 1974, Legal Files of F. Irvin Dymond—Clay Shaw Case, Historic New Orleans Collection, New Orleans, Louisiana.

[2877] Record Group 21, Records of U.S. District Courts, Records from the District Court of Louisiana, New Orleans Division, Case #70-466, Clay L. Shaw vs. Jim Garrison, Joseph M. Rault, Jr., Cecil M. Shilstone, Willard E. Robertson, Perry Raymond Russo, and Dr. Esmond A. Fatter, JFK Assassination Collection, National Archives, College Park, Maryland.

[2878] Record Group 21, Records of U.S. District Courts, Records from the District Court of Louisiana, New Orleans Division, Case #70-466, Clay L. Shaw vs. Jim Garrison, Joseph M. Rault, Jr., Cecil M. Shilstone, Willard E. Robertson, Perry Raymond Russo, and Dr. Esmond A. Fatter, JFK Assassination Collection, National Archives, College Park, Maryland.

[2879] Donated files of Edward Wegmann, National Archives, College Park, Maryland.

[2880] Record Group 21, Records of U.S. District Courts, Records from the District Court of Louisiana, New Orleans Division, Case #70-466, Clay L. Shaw vs. Jim Garrison, Joseph M. Rault, Jr., Cecil M. Shilstone, Willard E. Robertson, Perry Raymond Russo, and Dr. Esmond A. Fatter, JFK Assassination Collection, National Archives, College Park, Maryland.

[2881] Record Group 21, Records of U.S. District Courts, Records from the District Court of Louisiana, New Orleans Division, Case #70-466, Clay L. Shaw vs. Jim Garrison, Joseph M. Rault, Jr., Cecil M. Shilstone, Willard E. Robertson, Perry Raymond Russo, and Dr. Esmond A. Fatter, JFK Assassination Collection, National Archives, College Park, Maryland.

[2882] Second set of Interrogatories propounded to plaintiff, August 13, 1974, Legal Files of F. Irvin Dymond—Clay Shaw Case, Historic New Orleans Collection, New Orleans, Louisiana.

[2883] Letter dated July 17, 1974, Father Edward Sheridan to Jeff Biddison, Donated Papers of Clay Shaw, National Archives, College Park, Maryland.

[2884] Motion to Associate Counsel, July 26, 1974, Legal Files of F. Irvin Dymond—Clay Shaw Case, Historic New Orleans Collection, New Orleans, Louisiana.

[2885] Letter dated July 25, 1974, Peter J. Butler to all attorneys, Legal Files of F. Irvin Dymond—Clay Shaw Case, Historic New Orleans Collection, New Orleans, Louisiana.

[2886] Letter dated July 30, 1974, Edward Wegmann to Irvin Dymond and William Wegmann, Legal Files of F. Irvin Dymond—Clay Shaw Case, Historic New Orleans Collection, New Orleans, Louisiana.

[2887] Letter dated August 1, 1974, Dr. Hugh Batson to Edward Wegmann, Legal Files of F. Irvin Dymond—Clay Shaw Case, Historic New Orleans Collection, New Orleans, Louisiana.

[2888] Letter dated August 2, 1974, Edward Wegmann to Irvin Dymond and William Wegmann, Legal Files of F. Irvin Dymond—Clay Shaw Case, Historic New Orleans Collection, New Orleans, Louisiana.

[2889] Letter dated August 1, 1974, Dr. Hugh M. Batson, Jr. to Edward Wegmann, Donated Papers of Edward Wegmann, National Archives, College Park, Maryland.

[2890] Letter dated August 8, 1974, Edward Wegmann to Dr. Hugh Batson, Legal Files of F. Irvin Dymond—Clay Shaw Case, Historic New Orleans Collection, New Orleans, Louisiana.

[2891] Letter dated August 8, 1974, Edward Wegmann to Dr. Hugh M. Batson, Jr., Donated Papers of Edward Wegmann, National Archives, College Park, Maryland.

[2892] Letter dated August 14, 1974, Edward Wegmann to Malcolm Monroe, Donated Papers of Edward Wegmann, National Archives, College Park, Maryland.

[2893] Letter dated August 19, 1974, Edward Wegmann to Irvin Dymond and William Wegmann, Legal Files of F. Irvin Dymond—Clay Shaw Case, Historic New Orleans Collection, New Orleans, Louisiana.

[2894] Letter dated August 23, 1974, Edward Wegmann to Irvin Dymond and William Wegmann, Legal Files of F. Irvin Dymond—Clay Shaw Case, Historic New Orleans Collection, New Orleans, Louisiana.

[2895] Newspaper article in *States-Item*, August 15, 1974, Donated Papers of Clay Shaw, National Archives, College Park, Maryland.

[2896] Shaw death certificate, Papers Donated by Lyon Garrison, National Archives, College Park, Maryland.

[2897] Funeral lists can be found in Donated Papers of Clay Shaw, National Archives, College Park, Maryland.

[2898] See Rod McKuen's tribute to Shaw, Donated Papers of Clay Shaw, National Archives, College Park, Maryland.

[2899] Letter dated August 16, 1974, John (no last name) to Muriel Francis, Bultman Family Papers, Historic New Orleans Collection, New Orleans, Louisiana.

[2900] Shaw's will dated March 7, 1974, Donated Papers of Clay Shaw, National Archives, College Park, Maryland.

[2901] Shaw's will dated March 7, 1974, Donated Papers of Clay Shaw, National Archives, College Park, Maryland.

[2902] List of expenses outstanding by Shaw Estate, Donated Papers of Clay Shaw, National Archives, College Park, Maryland.

[2903] Appraisal dated September 16, 1974 of Shaw's St. Peter Street properties, Private Collection of Edith Stern related to Clay Shaw, Longue Vue, New Orleans, Louisiana.

[2904] Succession details of Clay Shaw's estate, Donated Papers of Clay Shaw, National Archives, College Park, Maryland.

[2905] Succession details of Clay Shaw's estate, Donated Papers of Clay Shaw, National Archives, College Park, Maryland.

[2906] Succession details of Clay Shaw's estate, Donated Papers of Clay Shaw, National Archives, College Park, Maryland.

[2907] Succession details of Clay Shaw's estate, Donated Papers of Clay Shaw, National Archives, College Park, Maryland.

[2908] Succession details of Clay Shaw's estate, Donated Papers of Clay Shaw, National Archives, College Park, Maryland.

[2909] Succession details of Clay Shaw's estate, Donated Papers of Clay Shaw, National Archives, College Park, Maryland.

[2910] Succession details of Clay Shaw's estate, Donated Papers of Clay Shaw, National Archives, College Park, Maryland.

[2911] Letter dated August 26, 1974, Edward Wegmann to William Wegmann, Legal Files of F. Irvin Dymond—Clay Shaw Case, Historic New Orleans Collection, New Orleans, Louisiana.

[2912] Letter dated August 26, 1974, Edward Wegmann to Malcolm Monroe, Legal Files of F. Irvin Dymond—Clay Shaw Case, Historic New Orleans Collection, New Orleans, Louisiana.

[2913] See list of issues regarding civil suit after death of Shaw, Donated Papers of Edward Wegmann, National Archives, College Park, Maryland.

[2914] Letter dated September 11, 1974, Miriam Cooney Abbott to Edward Wegmann, Donated Papers of Edward Wegmann, National Archives, College Park, Maryland.

[2915] Letter dated September 12, 1974, Edward Wegmann to Miriam Cooney Abbott, Legal Files of F. Irvin Dymond—Clay Shaw Case, Historic New Orleans Collection, New Orleans, Louisiana.

[2916] Letter dated September 13, 1974, Miriam Cooney Abbott to Edward Wegmann, Donated Papers of Edward Wegmann, National Archives, College Park, Maryland.

[2917] Letter dated September 27, 1974, Edward Wegmann to William Wegmann, Donated Papers of Edward Wegmann, National Archives, College Park, Maryland.

[2918] Letter dated September 28, 1974, Thomas Lemann to Edith Stern, Private Collection of Edith Stern related to Clay Shaw, Longue Vue, New Orleans, Louisiana.

[2919] Letter dated December 13, 1974, Edward Wegmann to Jeff Biddison, Donated Papers of Edward Wegmann, National Archives, College Park, Maryland.

[2920] Letter dated January 27, 1975, Edward Wegmann to William Wegmann, Legal Files of F. Irvin Dymond—Clay Shaw Case, Historic New Orleans Collection, New Orleans, Louisiana.

[2921] Article dated June 19, 1975, *Times-Picayune*, Donated Papers of Clay Shaw, National Archives, College Park, Maryland.

[2922] Letter dated March 18, 1975, Edward Wegmann to Edith Stern, Private Collection of Edith Stern related to Clay Shaw, Longue Vue, New Orleans, Louisiana.

[2923] Letter dated April 7, 1975, Miriam Cooney Abbott to Edward Wegmann, Donated Papers of Edward Wegmann, National Archives, College Park, Maryland.

[2924] Letter dated April 7, 1975, Edward Wegmann to Alan S. Adelson, Donated Papers of Edward Wegmann, National Archives, College Park, Maryland.

[2925] Article dated May 1, 1975, *Times-Picayune*, Donated Papers of Clay Shaw, National Archives, College Park, Maryland.

[2926] Letter dated May 23, 1975, Miriam Cooney Abbott to Edward Wegmann, Donated Papers of Edward Wegmann, National Archives, College Park, Maryland.

[2927] Letter dated May 27, 1975, Edward Wegmann to Edith Stern, Private Collection of Edith Stern related to Clay Shaw, Longue Vue, New Orleans, Louisiana.

[2928] Memo dated June 13, 1975, Thomas Lemann to Edith Stern, Private Collection of Edith Stern related to Clay Shaw, Longue Vue, New Orleans, Louisiana.

[2929] Letter dated June 12, 1975, Edward Wegmann to Jeff Biddison, Donated Papers of Edward Wegmann, National Archives, College Park, Maryland.

[2930] Letter dated July 12, 1975, Edward Wegmann to Jeff Biddison, Donated Papers of Clay Shaw, National Archives, College Park, Maryland.

[2931] Memo dated August 23, 1975, Joseph Falgout to Edith Stern, Private Collection of Edith Stern related to Clay Shaw, Longue Vue, New Orleans, Louisiana.

[2932] Memo dated August 26, 1975, Edith Stern to Edward Wegmann, Private Collection of Edith Stern related to Clay Shaw, Longue Vue, New Orleans, Louisiana.

[2933] Letter dated August 28, 1975 ,Edward Wegmann to Edith Stern, Private Collection of Edith Stern related to Clay Shaw, Longue Vue, New Orleans, Louisiana.

[2934] Letter dated December 2, 1975, Edward Wegmann to Edith Stern, Private Collection of Edith Stern related to Clay Shaw, Longue Vue, New Orleans, Louisiana.

[2935] Letter dated April 5, 1975, Gail Baumgartner to Edith Stern, Private Collection of Edith Stern related to Clay Shaw, Longue Vue, New Orleans, Louisiana.

[2936] Letter dated May 6, 1975, Edith Stern to Edward Wegmann, Private Collection of Edith Stern related to Clay Shaw, Longue Vue, New Orleans, Louisiana.

[2937] Letter dated September 9, 1975, Judson O'Donnell to Edith Stern, Private Collection of Edith Stern related to Clay Shaw, Longue Vue, New Orleans, Louisiana.

[2938] Letter dated September 15, 1975, Edith Stern to Gail Baumgartner, Private Collection of Edith Stern related to Clay Shaw, Longue Vue, New Orleans, Louisiana.

[2939] Letter dated October 9, 1975, Judson O'Donnell to Edith Stern, Private Collection of Edith Stern related to Clay Shaw, Longue Vue, New Orleans, Louisiana.

[2940] Note dated October 1975, Verna Landrieu to Edith Stern, Private Collection of Edith Stern related to Clay Shaw, Longue Vue, New Orleans, Louisiana.

[2941] Note by Edith Stern related to the taxi driver who helped Shaw, Private Collection of Edith Stern related to Clay Shaw, Longue Vue, New Orleans, Louisiana.

[2942] List of contributors to Clay Shaw Memorial Fund, Private Collection of Edith Stern related to Clay Shaw, Longue Vue, New Orleans, Louisiana.

[2943] Properties listed on Spanish Stables Plaque, Private Collection of Edith Stern related to Clay Shaw, Longue Vue, New Orleans, Louisiana.

[2944] Letter dated December 8, 1975, Lin Emery to John Eagan, Private Collection of Edith Stern related to Clay Shaw, Longue Vue, New Orleans, Louisiana.

[2945] Interview with James J. Gleason, III, by author, September 2002, Legal Files of F. Irvin Dymond—Clay Shaw Case, Historic New Orleans Collection, New Orleans, Louisiana.

[2946] Letter dated December 11, 1975, Edward Wegmann to Edith Stern, Private Collection of Edith Stern related to Clay Shaw, Longue Vue, New Orleans, Louisiana.

[2947] Memo dated January 30, 1976, Joseph Falgout to Edith Stern, Private Collection of Edith Stern related to Clay Shaw, Longue Vue, New Orleans, Louisiana.

[2948] Letter dated October 8, 1976, Edward Wegmann to Edith Stern, Private Collection of Edith Stern related to Clay Shaw, Longue Vue, New Orleans, Louisiana.

[2949] Letter dated June 22, 1977, Edward Wegmann to Malcolm Monroe, Donated Papers of Edward Wegmann, National Archives, College Park, Maryland.

[2950] Letter dated June 23, 1977, Malcolm Monroe to Edward Wegmann, Donated Papers of Edward Wegmann, National Archives, College Park, Maryland.

[2951] Letter dated August 2, 1977, Edward Wegmann to William Wegmann, Donated Papers of Edward Wegmann, National Archives, College Park, Maryland.

[2952] Letter dated December 12, 1977, Edward Wegmann to Michael Rodak, Record Group 267, Records of the U.S. Supreme Court, JFK Assassination Collection, National Archives, College Park, Maryland.

[2953] Letter dated March 3, 1978, Malcolm Monroe to Michael Rodak, Record Group 267, Records of the U.S. Supreme Court, JFK Assassination Collection, National Archives, College Park, Maryland.

[2954] Letter dated June 6, 1978, Edward Wegmann to Jeff Biddison, Donated Papers of Clay Shaw, National Archives, College Park, Maryland.

[2955] Deutsch, Kerrigan and Stiles invoice from February 28, 1970 through December 31, 1971 related to Shaw civil suit, JFK Assassination Collection, New Orleans Public Library, New Orleans, Louisiana.

[2956] Letter dated September 28, 1978, Ed Butler to Elizabeth Finnell, John Wilds Alton Ochsner Working Papers, Historic New Orleans Collection, New Orleans, Louisiana.

[2957] Article entitled "The Case That Never Was," *Times-Picayune*, November 20, 1983, by Dean Baquet.

[2958] Article entitled "The Case That Never Was," *Times-Picayune*, November 20, 1983, by Dean Baquet.

[2959] Article entitled "The Case That Never Was," *Times-Picayune*, November 20, 1983, by Dean Baquet.

[2960] Article entitled "The Case That Never Was," *Times-Picayune*, November 20, 1983, by Dean Baquet.

[2961] Article entitled "The Case That Never Was," *Times-Picayune*, November 20, 1983, by Dean Baquet.

[2962] Article entitled "The Case That Never Was," *Times-Picayune*, November 20, 1983, by Dean Baquet.

[2963] Article entitled "The Case That Never Was," *Times-Picayune*, November 20, 1983, by Dean Baquet.

[2964] Article entitled "The Case That Never Was," *Times-Picayune*, November 20, 1983, by Dean Baquet.

[2965] Article entitled "The Case That Never Was," *Times-Picayune*, November 20, 1983, by Dean Baquet.

[2966] Memo by Jim Garrison to Ellen Ray regarding 1990 phone call from friend of Clay Shaw, Papers Donated by Lyon Garrison, National Archives, College Park, Maryland.

Printed in Great Britain
by Amazon